COASTAL
CALIFORNIA

STUART THORNTON

Contents

DISCOVER

Coastal California

California exists on the edge of the continent, where land and sea collide. This primal collision is the source of stunning beauty and singular geological phenomena like the volcanic dome of Morro Rock, the honeycombs of sea caves along the La Jolla headlands, and the sheer walls of rock falling to the ocean at Big Sur. Waterfalls decorate cliff faces like ribbons and spring wildflowers paint the hillsides above the blue-green ocean.

This land- and seascape can push you to your physical limits. Catch your first wave in the surf at Santa Cruz. Dive into a Monterey kelp forest. Explore deep into a Channel Islands sea cave by kayak. Trek the wild Lost Coast Trail. You might spot condors swirling in the night sky like embers, elk appearing out of the fog on secluded beaches, or migrating gray whales sounding offshore. You'll never get closer to the natural world than you can here.

Along the more placid sections of the coastline, the crashing surf smooths out into gentle waves lapping soft sands. This is the California coast that people all over the world know through popular culture, where sun worshippers share the shoreline with movie stars. Warm sunshine, colorful boardwalks, and easy access attract visitors seeking pleasure and relaxation.

Clockwise from top left: Golden Gate Bridge from Baker Beach; view from the Pacific Coast Highway; California brown pelican; San Francisco street; organic wine grapes in Sonoma; vineyard in Mendocino.

California is also on the cutting edge of art, entertainment, and cuisine. Trends are born here before spreading to the rest of the country and the world. It's where we first heard the music of The Doors, the Grateful Dead, Dr. Dre, and Beck. You can still catch performances by up-and-coming bands of all stripes at venues like The Fillmore in San Francisco, The Echo in Los Angeles, or The Casbah in San Diego. Or see the art of the avant-garde at world-class museums and galleries. California gave the United States its first taste of sushi and its first native-born wines, and it still offers one-of-a-kind culinary experiences. Enjoy authentic dim sum in San Francisco, or sample Mexican street tacos topped with kimchi in Los Angeles. Head to Napa, Sonoma, Carmel Valley, or Paso Robles to discover your new favorite wine. Or visit one of the North Coast's many microbreweries for your first sip of oatmeal stout or tangerine wheat ale.

Drink it all in. You'll return from your adventures on the edge of the continent with stories at the tip of your tongue.

Clockwise from top left: Big Sur coastline at sunset; Laguna Beach's scenic Main Beach; common warning sign along California's coast; Santa Cruz Beach Boardwalk.

Planning Your Trip

Where to Go

San Francisco and the Bay Area

The politics, the culture, the food—these are what make San Francisco world famous. Dine on cutting-edge **cuisine** at high-end restaurants and offbeat food-trucks, tour classical and avant-garde **museums,** and bike through **Golden Gate Park** or stroll along **Fisherman's Wharf.** The surrounding region is as diverse as the city itself. To the north, **Marin** offers wilderness seekers a quick respite from the city, while ethnic diversity and intellectual curiosity give the **East Bay** a hip urban edge. Meanwhile, the beaches of **Coastside** are a short drive away.

Wine Country

Wine Country is famous for a reason. This is the place to pamper yourself with excellent wines, fantastic food, and luxurious spas. **Napa** offers all of the above in spades, while **Sonoma** boasts a bit of history and a mellower atmosphere. The **Russian River** adds redwoods and river rafting to the mix.

North Coast

For deserted beaches, towering redwoods, and scenic coastal towns, cruise north along the **Redwood Coast.** Explore Russian history at Fort Ross on the grassy bluffs of the **Sonoma Coast,** and fall in love with **Mendocino's** small-town charm and nearby wineries. Detour west to **the Lost Coast** to experience coastline barely touched by human development.

Monterey Bay

Go surfing in **Santa Cruz.** Witness gray whales

the Monterey Bay Aquarium

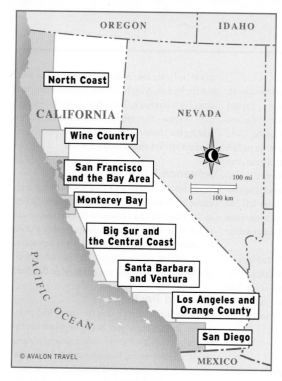

OREGON

IDAHO

North Coast

CALIFORNIA

NEVADA

Wine Country

San Francisco
and the Bay Area

0   100 mi

0   100 km

Monterey Bay

Big Sur and
the Central Coast

PACIFIC OCEAN

Santa Barbara
and Ventura

Los Angeles and
Orange County

San Diego

© AVALON TRAVEL

MEXICO

Santa Barbara and Ventura

Take in the picturesque **Santa Barbara Mission** and then stroll down the city's **State Street,** which is lined with shops, restaurants, and bars. Enjoy the lonely coastline of **Jalama Beach County Park** or, to truly get away from it all, take a boat ride out to **Channel Islands National Park.** Bask in Santa Barbara's abundant sunshine at nearby **Refugio State Beach** on the **Gaviota Coast** or visit the wine-tasting rooms of downtown Santa Barbara and the nearby **Santa Maria Valley.** Farther south, Ventura offers visitors a historic mission, a vibrant downtown, and a reliable surf break.

Los Angeles and Orange Country

For a taste of the iconic California dream, you can't beat Los Angeles. From the glitz and glamour of **Hollywood** and **Beverly Hills** to the camp and kitsch of **Santa Monica Pier,** L.A. is all California culture, all the time. Kids of all ages come to visit Walt's original **Disneyland,** while sun and surf worshippers ride the waves or relax on the sugar-sand **beaches.**

San Diego

For the sun-drenched, soft-sand California beach experience portrayed in endless films and TV shows, come to San Diego. Maritime museums ring the **downtown harbor,** while across the bay in **Coronado,** vibrant and historic Hotel del Coronado creates a centerpiece for visitors to the city. Gorgeous beaches stretch from **Point Loma** north to **La Jolla** and the **North County** coast, begging surfers, swimmers, strollers, and sunbathers to ply their sands.

and sea lions off rugged **Monterey Bay,** and then explore their environment at the world-class **Monterey Bay Aquarium.** Wander around in the art galleries of **Carmel-by-the-Sea** and then take a stroll on the light sands of **Carmel Beach.** If you are a wine lover, be sure to head out to **Carmel Valley** to taste some of the region's best varietals.

Big Sur and the Central Coast

Some of the most beautiful and most adventurous coastline in the world is along this section of the **Pacific Coast Highway.** Camp and hike the unspoiled wilderness of Big Sur, and then tour grandiose **Hearst Castle** in San Simeon. For a relaxing getaway, head to one of the region's beach towns: **Cambria, Cayucos, Morro Bay,** or **Pismo Beach.**

Before You Go

When to Go

California's best feature is its **all-season** appeal. **Summer** is the coast's travel season; expect crowds at popular attractions, wineries, beaches, and campgrounds. (Although the quote, "The coldest winter I ever spent was a summer in San Francisco," falsely attributed to Mark Twain, still holds true as the wind and fog that blows through the city June-August surprises unsuspecting visitors.) In **fall,** the summer crowds have left but the weather is still warm. It is also the time when some of the best waves occur along the coast for surfers.

Winter is the rainy season, with lots more precipitation falling on the northern section of the coastline than in the south. **Spring** is the best time of year for spotting wildflowers and waterfalls. It's less crowded than summer (except for spring break).

Transportation

The easiest airports to **fly** into are **San Francisco (SFO)** and **Los Angeles (LAX).** If you're flying into San Francisco, you can avoid some of the hassle by flying into nearby Oakland or San Jose. Similarly, Los Angeles offers several suburban airports—Burbank, Long Beach, Ontario, and John Wayne—that are less congested. If you are visiting the United States from abroad, you'll need your **passport** and possibly a **visa.**

Advance Reservations

Book **hotels** early and buy **tickets** for big-name attractions in advance. Purchase tickets to **Alcatraz** in San Francisco at least two weeks in advance. Save money buying advance tickets for **Disneyland** online. Make early reservations for big-name restaurants. Lodging and **campground reservations** are essential in **Big Sur.**

What to Pack

Summer **fog** is likely along the coast, and guaranteed in San Francisco. Bring **layered clothing,** especially a wind-resistant coat and a warm sweater. Expect warm temperatures and even desert heat in Los Angeles and San Diego in the summer. Bring **sunscreen;** that coastal fog doesn't stop UV rays.

Pacific Coast Road Trip

The ideal way to experience the California coast is to hit the road. Following this legendary road trip will take you through California's bustling cosmopolitan cities, small beach towns, redwood forests, and sandy beaches.

For the most part, you'll cover this stunning **850 miles** by following the legendary **Pacific Coast Highway** (Highway 1) and U.S. 101. You can switch back and forth between the two routes depending on your pace and your interests. **Highway 1** is generally more scenic; **U.S. 101** is usually faster. A few diversions onto other routes are necessary to cover the entire coast (for example, you'll be driving I-5 between San Diego and Los Angeles).

The day-by-day routes below begin in **Southern California,** but you can just as easily start in **Central** or **Northern California,** or reverse the route (from driving north to driving south) if that works better for you. Combine all three itineraries to make a 16-day tour of the coast. If you're pressed for time, choose just one or two of the itineraries.

Five Days in Southern California

San Diego
DAY 1
Easygoing San Diego is a great place to start any vacation. Upon arrival, orient yourself by driving to the top of **Mt. Soledad Veterans Memorial,** a small mountain that has views of the entire city. After that, head down to **La Jolla Cove** to go kayaking or snorkeling; or just lie on the beach.

In the afternoon, visit **Balboa Park,** where you'll spend most of your time at the **San Diego Zoo.** End your day with a craft beer at one of San Diego's many breweries, like the giant **Stone Brewing Co.,** followed by a meal in the **Gaslamp Quarter.** Try the historic **Grant Grill** or the nearby **Café Chloe.**

DAY 2
The fastest way to reach the **North County** beach towns of **Encinitas, Carlsbad,** and **Oceanside** is to take I-5 north out of San Diego. Or, to cruise along the coast, opt for North Coast Highway 101 (also called Camino del Mar, San Elijo Boulevard, and Carlsbad Boulevard as it travels from Torrey Pines State Beach to Oceanside). Make sure to stop for a surf or a swim since the ocean temperatures cool as you head up the coast.

Continue north on I-5 to visit **Huntington Beach** before turning off towards **Long Beach** for a nighttime ghost tour on **The Queen Mary,** an ocean liner that is now home to restaurants, a hotel, shops, and a museum. If you are daring enough, book a room for the night in the haunted ship.

Los Angeles
DAY 3
Jump on I-405 to save some time and drive about 30 miles north, exiting towards **Venice Beach.** Park your vehicle and take a stroll along the **Venice Boardwalk** to take in the local wildlife that includes bodybuilders, street performers, and alternative-culture types. Without getting back on the highway, take the local roads paralleling the beach 10 minutes north to **Santa Monica.** Enjoy the amusement park rides of the **Santa Monica Pier** or just take a break on **Santa Monica Beach.** For dinner, get a taste of the Caribbean at Santa Monica's casual but popular **Cha Cha Chicken** or backtrack to Venice for a hearty Italian meal at **C&O Trattoria.**

DAY 4
Consider heading inland for a day of culture (and pop culture). For aesthetic stimulation,

14

beach houses, Southern California

visit the world-famous **Getty Center** or the **Los Angeles County Museum of Art.** Less rigorous on the mind is a walk down the star-studded **Hollywood Walk of Fame** and a stop at the historic **TCL Chinese Theatre,** where you can find the handprints of your favorite movie stars. End the day with a cocktail at Sunset Boulevard's **Rainbow Bar & Grill.** There might even be a grizzled, past-his-prime rocker sitting in the booth next to you.

DAY 5
Take the Pacific Coast Highway (Highway 1) out of Santa Monica as it heads away from sprawling Los Angeles and into **Malibu.** Stop at Malibu's **Surfrider Beach** to watch the surfers compete for its famously peeling waves (or catch one yourself). After a morning outdoors, feed your mind with ancient art at **The Getty Villa** in Malibu. (Admission is free, but you'll need to reserve a ticket in advance.) Finish the day by watching the sun slide into the Pacific from the outdoor deck of **Neptune's Net** while enjoying fresh seafood.

If you want to spend more time in the Los Angeles area, you can easily fill a couple of days enjoying **Disneyland Resort.**

Call of the Wild

California's ecosystems host a wide range of wildlife. Here are some spots where you can view wild animals in their natural surroundings.

SAN FRANCISCO AND THE BAY AREA

- **San Francisco's Pier 39** has shops, restaurants, an aquarium...and its own colony of **California sea lions.**

- **Point Reyes National Seashore** is rich in wildlife from giant **elephant seals** to tiny, endangered **Myrtle's silverspot butterflies.**

- The **Farallon Islands** off San Francisco are home to a quarter-million **seabirds** and one of the world's largest **great white shark** populations.

- South of San Francisco, in the Coastside region, **Año Nuevo State Park** is home to one of the world's largest mainland breeding colonies of northern **elephant seals.** Secure a permit to walk out and see up to 10,000 of the giant creatures on the beach and in the surrounding waters.

NORTH COAST

- **Elk Prairie** and **Elk Meadow,** in Prairie Creek Redwoods State Park, are named after their inhabitants. A transplanted **herd of elk** also roams **Sinkyone Wilderness State Park.**

- **Bodega Head** offers views of migrating **gray whales** January-May.

MONTEREY BAY

- The eucalyptus grove at **Natural Bridges State Beach** hosts thousands of migrating **monarch butterflies** mid-October and mid-February. They also stop at Pacific Grove's **Monarch Grove Sanctuary.**

- Marshy reserve **Elkhorn Slough** hosts 340 **bird species,** including brown pelicans and snowy plovers. Here you can also paddle toward the bay to spot **sea lions, harbor seals,** and **sea otters,** as well as fish species like **bat rays** and **leopard sharks.**

- Walk out on **Monterey's Coast Guard Pier** to spot **sea lions** and **harbor seals** lounging on the breakwater.

monarch butterflies

BIG SUR AND THE CENTRAL COAST

- Keep your eyes peeled along **Big Sur's Highway 1** to spot **California condors,** North America's largest land birds.

- **Piedras Blancas Elephant Seal Rookery,** north of San Simeon, is a great place to see the beasts up close.

SANTA BARBARA AND VENTURA

- Unique native species like **island scrub jays** and **island foxes** are prevalent all over **Santa Cruz Island,** especially in the **Scorpion Ranch Campground.**

LOS ANGELES AND ORANGE COUNTY

- A **herd of bison** was introduced to **Catalina Island** in the 1920s for the filming of a movie, and has thrived in the years since.

- Take a snorkel or a scuba dive at the **Avalon Underwater Park** to view fish, including **garibaldi** and **gobies.**

- Even major cities like Los Angeles have their fair share of wildlife. **Coyotes, foxes, bobcats, mule deer,** and even **mountain lions** have been spotted in **Griffith Park.**

SAN DIEGO

- A little underwater park right off **La Jolla Cove** is home to **sardines, garibaldi,** and **leopard sharks.**

- Book a trip on one of San Diego's **whale- and dolphin-watching** cruises; you might also spot **sea lions** and **harbor seals.**

Six Days in Central California

Santa Barbara and Ventura
DAY 1
Wake up early and drive north on the scenic Pacific Coast Highway. Thirty-five miles from Malibu, at Oxnard, merge onto U.S. 101. Head north on U.S. 101 to Ventura and take the exit toward Ventura Harbor, where you can catch a boat out to **Channel Islands National Park** for a day of hiking, snorkeling, or kayaking on **Santa Cruz Island** or **Anacapa Island**. (Make boat reservations in advance.) Return to **Ventura** and eat dinner at one of its seafood restaurants, such as **Lure Fish House** or **Spencer Makenzie's Fish Company**. Or have an Italian meal and cocktail at hip **Café Fiore**.

DAY 2
Take U.S. 101 north a half hour (28 miles) to **Santa Barbara**. Get a history fix at the **Santa Barbara Mission**, which might be the most beautiful of the 21 Spanish missions in California.

Then taste some local wines on the **Urban Wine Trail,** comprising six tasting rooms on lower State Street, or head north for a day at palm-lined **Refugio State Beach,** 20 miles west of Santa Barbara on U.S. 101.

If your schedule is flexible, you might consider another full day in Santa Barbara, another day of wine-tasting in the nearby **Santa Maria Valley,** or a day on the **Gaviota Coast.** Whatever you do, stop at Santa Barbara's **State Street** for a fine meal or cocktail at a restaurant like the local favorite **Opal.** Or head off State Street for superb Mexican food at **La Super-Rica Taqueria.**

Big Sur and the Central Coast
DAY 3
Drive 1.75 hours (92 miles) north of Santa Barbara on U.S. 101 to **San Luis Obispo's Madonna Inn,** where you can take in its kitschy decor during a restroom-and-stretch-the-legs break.

Outdoor enthusiasts will want to head off the

Big Sur's Bixby Bridge

McWay Falls at Julia Pfeiffer Burns State Park

harbor seals in Monterey

highway and go west on Los Osos Valley Road just 20 minutes (12 miles) to **Montaña de Oro State Park,** one of the state's best coastal parks. Picnic at **Spooner's Cove** or hike to the top of 1,347-foot-high **Valencia Peak.** Then head back to U.S. 101 North, but be sure to turn onto Highway 1 north to take in sunset over **Morro Rock,** known as the "Gibraltar of the Pacific."

Another option is to drive an hour north (44 miles) to opulent **Hearst Castle.** Tours of this "ranch" built for newspaper magnate William Randolph Hearst offer insight into the lifestyle of the rich and infamous.

However you spend your day, end it with a meal in one of the Central Coast's unassuming beach towns: **Morro Bay, Cayucos,** or **Cambria.**

DAY 4

Head north on Highway 1 for what might be the most scenic day of driving on your whole trip. The two-lane highway here winds along the mountains of **Big Sur** with plentiful views of the ocean. From Cambria to the heart of Big Sur is 75 miles, but the scenery, winding roadway, and frequent road construction can make the drive last well over two hours. Be sure to make multiple stops to take in the scenery at places like **Salmon Creek Falls, Sand Dollar Beach,** and **Julia Pfeiffer Burns State Park.** Catch sunset at **Pfeiffer Beach** before spending the night camping in the redwoods of **Pfeiffer Big Sur State Park** or in the meadow at **Andrew Molera State Park.** Or splurge with a once-in-a-lifetime stay at the **Post Ranch Inn** or **Ventana Inn & Spa.**

Monterey Bay
DAY 5

Continue up Highway 1 for 45 minutes (less than 30 miles) through the northern section of Big Sur to the **Monterey Peninsula.** Take a walk in Carmel's **Point Lobos State Reserve** or head to scenic **Carmel Beach.** Then drive a few miles north into Monterey to spend the afternoon at the **Monterey Bay Aquarium.**

Dine on fresh seafood at Pacific Grove's **Passionfish, The Sandbar & Grill** in Monterey, or **Phil's Fish Market** up Highway 1 in Moss Landing.

If you want to spend another day in this area,

wander the galleries in **Carmel-by-the-Sea,** golf at **Pebble Beach,** or head inland to **Carmel Valley** for wine-tasting.

DAY 6
Getting to **Santa Cruz** is an easy 50-minute drive (44 miles) up Highway 1 from the Monterey Peninsula. The eclectic beach city is an ideal place for recreation whether you are surfing, stand-up paddleboarding, or hiking redwood-filled **Forest of Nisene Marks State Park** or the coastal bluffs of **Wilder Ranch State Park.** Refuel with a healthy snack at **The Picnic Basket** before ending the day with thrill rides at the **Santa Cruz Beach Boardwalk.**

If your adrenaline is still racing from the Boardwalk rides, calm down with a drink at **Red Restaurant & Bar** or **The Crepe Place.**

Five Days in Northern California

San Francisco
DAY 1
Wake up early for a drive on Highway 1 from Santa Cruz less than two hours (80 miles) to **San Francisco.** In the city, spend a few hours in the hands-on science museum **The Exploratorium.** As the sun goes down, make sure to head out for dinner, whether it's seafood at the **Tadich Grill,** modern Thai food at **Lers Ros,** or pizza at **Tony's Pizza Napoletana.** If you still have energy, make sure to check out some of San Francisco's vibrant nightlife or a concert at a venue like the **Great American Music Hall.**

DAY 2
Head out on San Francisco Bay to take a fascinating tour of the island prison **Alcatraz.** Or secure passage on a ferry to **Angel Island,** which has hiking trails that offer up some of the finest views of the city.

In the afternoon, shop the used clothing stores of **Haight-Ashbury** or the department stores of

Point Arena-Stornetta Unit of the California Coastal National Monument

Catch of the Day

Some of the state's best seafood can be found in unpretentious eateries just footsteps from the ocean.

SAN FRANCISCO AND THE BAY AREA

- Sit at the long marble bar at Swan Oyster Depot (page 93) to dine on seafood that was swimming in the ocean just hours earlier.

- Enjoy a decadent Dungeness crab roll or a superbly spicy salmon sandwich at Fish (page 104), right on the harbor in Sausalito.

- At Sam's Chowder House (page 144), enjoy both daily fresh catches and a great view of Half Moon Bay.

NORTH COAST

- The smoked wild salmon at tiny Katy's Smokehouse (page 284) in Trinidad may be the best you've ever eaten.

- Tomo Japanese Restaurant (page 281) in Arcata serves creative sushi rolls with local ingredients like smoked albacore.

- Eureka's Humboldt Bay Tourism Center (page 270) has a superb raw bar starring delicious Humboldt Bay oysters.

- Bodega Bay's Fishetarian Fish Market (page 218) is almost 600 miles from Baja, but their fresh rockfish tacos topped with two tasty sauces can hold their own with their southern counterparts.

MONTEREY BAY

- Monterey's Sandbar & Grill (page 334) serves up the seaside city's best calamari in a laid-back setting over the harbor.

- Get a taste of local Sicilian fishermen's recipes like squid pasta at Monterey's Fish House (page 334).

- Tucked between the harbor and the ocean in Moss Landing, Phil's Fish Market (page 321) serves up hearty and tasty cioppino and sea scallops.

BIG SUR AND THE CENTRAL COAST

- Just off Cayucos Beach, Rudell's Smokehouse (page 394) serves seafood tacos with big flavors, including smoked salmon, smoked albacore, and an unexpected topping: chopped apples.

- People line up at Splash Café (page 418) in Pismo Beach for a taste of rich, buttery clam chowder.

- Right on the Embarcadero in Morro Bay, Tognazzini's Dockside Restaurant (page 402) is the place for fresh barbecued oysters in garlic butter.

SANTA BARBARA AND VENTURA

- Ventura's Spencer Makenzie's Fish Company (page 454) is known for its fine tempura-battered fish tacos.

- Expect salmon, ahi, and swordfish at local favorite Brophy Brothers (page 443), with locations on both the Santa Barbara and Ventura harbors.

LOS ANGELES AND ORANGE COUNTY

- Enjoy crispy shrimp tacos topped with a pineapple salsa at local hangout Neptune's Net (page 514), overlooking a Malibu surf break.

- The Lobster Trap (page 543) on Catalina Island is all about tasty crustaceans, with options like lobster stuffed with bay shrimp.

SAN DIEGO

- Choose between 13 varieties of fish tacos, including ahi and shark, at San Diego's Blue Water Seafood Market & Grill (page 604).

- Point Loma Seafoods (page 608) is all about the freshest fish, which explains why the menu is full of seafood cocktail, sushi, and sashimi. Visit between October and March for locally caught lobster.

Union Square. Or browse the books at City Lights in North Beach.

You'll quickly fall in love with San Francisco; you can easily extend your romance to three or four days if you have the time.

The North Coast

DAY 3

Your journey north begins with a drive on U.S. 101 over San Francisco's iconic Golden Gate Bridge. After five miles, turn off U.S. 101 to Highway 1 at Mill Valley. On the slow, over-four-hour drive up the coast (around 160 miles), make time to stop at places like the tiny but unique Sea Ranch Chapel, which is just feet off Highway 1, and take a hike on the stunning cliffside trails in the Point Arena-Stornetta Unit of the California Coastal National Monument.

End the day in the community of Mendocino with a view of the sunset at Mendocino Headlands State Park or a pint at the lively Patterson's Pub or at the one-of-a-kind dive bar Dick's Place.

DAY 4

Drive Highway 1 north of Fort Bragg until the road turns inland to connect with U.S. 101 after about an hour of driving. Opt for the Avenue of the Giants, a drive through redwoods by the Eel River. Even though it's only 31 miles, the drive could take a few hours if you decide to get out of your car and ponder the trees.

Get back on U.S. 101 and head an hour north (60 miles) to Eureka. Stop to wander the city's Old Town and Waterfront. Taste some of the delicious oysters at the Humboldt Bay Tourism Center.

Continue on U.S. 101 another 10 minutes or so to charming Arcata. Wander through the redwoods of the Arcata Community Forest before sundown. Dine at one of the restaurants surrounding the lively Arcata Plaza.

DAY 5

Start your morning with a tasty crepe from Arcata's Renata's Creperie and Espresso before hitting U.S. 101 North on your final day. About 20 minutes (15 miles) north of Arcata, exit to the scenic coastal city of Trinidad. Have your camera handy for photos of Trinidad Memorial Lighthouse, Trinidad Head, and Trinidad State Beach.

Another half hour up U.S. 101 (26 miles), turn onto Newton B. Drury Scenic Drive to explore Prairie Creek Redwoods State Park. If you have the energy, drive out Davison Road to Gold Bluffs Beach, where Roosevelt elk roam the sands, and continue on the dirt drive to hike the one-mile round-trip Fern Canyon Trail, which passes through a steep canyon draped in bright green ferns.

Head back out to U.S. 101 to drive the 45 minutes (38 miles) to Crescent City, where you can get a hotel room and a full night's sleep.

Best Beaches

Wide golden beaches with abundant sunshine and legendary surf breaks. Lonely stretches of sand framed by coast redwoods and jagged cliffs. Boardwalks crowded with kids, cotton candy, and roller coasters. California has any kind of beach you could possibly want.

San Francisco and the Bay Area

The Bay Area is one of California's largest urban centers, but sand seekers can still find beaches within—or just outside of—city limits.

OCEAN BEACH
Best for Sunsets, Strolls

Ocean Beach runs for miles along the western edge of San Francisco, offering a break from busy streets and crowded tourist attractions (page 73).

BAKER BEACH
Best for Scenery, Photo Ops, Sunbathing

On the northern tip of San Francisco, this mile-long swath of sand is your best bet for

stunning views of the Golden Gate Bridge and San Francisco Bay. Its northernmost end is known for its nude sunbathers (page 74).

MUIR BEACH
Best for Scenery, Wildlife, Sunbathing

Wildlife enthusiasts flock to Muir Beach. It's a great place to spot migrating whales during the winter, while fall brings monarch butterflies. The stream that runs into the ocean at Muir Beach provides a habitat for shorebirds, salmon, trout, and amphibians. Meanwhile, the relatively secluded north side provides a habitat for nude sunbathers (page 110).

STINSON BEACH
Best for Families

In the summer, Stinson has lifeguards, a snack bar, picnic areas, and restrooms that are ideal for a family day at the beach. Surfers, kayakers, and paddleboarders test their skills in the surf (page 115).

Ocean Beach

AÑO NUEVO STATE PARK
Best for Wildlife

At Año Nuevo, gigantic elephant seals turn the beach into a battleground. You can also catch a glimpse of an eerie, abandoned light station buildings right offshore (page 147).

North Coast

These beaches showcase the wild, rugged beauty that happens when the land meets the sea with little or no human intervention. On these beaches there is frequently more wildlife than people. The coast up here is perfect for long contemplative walks—as long as you remember to bundle up. Opportunities for recreation include surfing, diving, kayaking, and stand-up paddleboarding, all without the crowds typical of beaches to the south.

MANCHESTER STATE PARK
Best for Beachcombing, Solitude

The long, debris-strewn beach at Manchester State Park is ideal for beachcombers and offers views of the Point Arena Lighthouse in the distance (page 226).

BIG RIVER
Best for Kayaking, Stand-Up Paddleboarding, Beginners' Surfing

Big River, just south of Mendocino Village, has a range of recreational opportunities. Surf the beach break, launch a kayak to explore the nearby headlands, or paddleboard the river before steering your board into the ocean (page 237).

EEL RIVER
Best for Swimming

Not all great beaches are on the ocean; beaches line the Eel River as it winds beside the popular Avenue of the Giants, offering motorists a cool dip and a place to bask in the sun (page 259).

BLACK SAND BEACH
Best for Scenery

An easier way to take in the rugged beauty of the Lost Coast is to marvel at Shelter Cove's Black Sand Beach, framed by the towering King Range (page 265).

the beautiful Trinidad coast

With great weather year-round, lots of ocean access, and a bounty of beaches, the California coast has a plethora of recreational opportunities.

SURFING

After Hawaiians introduced surfing to California, it became an essential part of the state's culture. California offers up waves for every level of surfer. Iconic surf breaks like San Diego's **Black's Beach,** San Onofre State Beach's **Trestles,** Santa Barbara's **Rincon,** and Santa Cruz's **Steamer Lane** make surfers from around the world drool with anticipation. Beginners can attempt their first waves at the gentle peeling waves of Santa Cruz's **Cowell's Beach** or Malibu's **Surfrider Beach.**

STAND-UP PADDLEBOARDING

California's many bays, inlets, and protected areas are the perfect places to get started in the coast's fastest-growing sport. Hit the water at Orange County's **Dana Point Harbor,** the Central Coast's **Cayucos Beach** or **Santa Cruz Harbor** or offshore along Monterey's **Cannery Row,** and at Mendocino's **Van Damme State Park** on the North Coast.

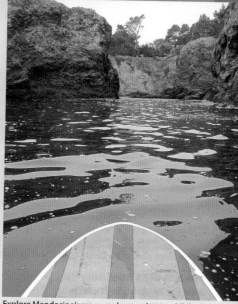
Explore Mendocino's sea caves by stand-up paddleboard.

SCUBA DIVING AND SNORKELING

The best way to see the multitude of sea life, kelp forests, and reefs off the California shoreline is to put on some snorkeling or scuba gear. The clear waters and swaying kelp forests of the **Monterey Peninsula** make it one of the biggest dive destinations in the state. **Santa Catalina Island** offers pristine underwater habitats for the adventurous, while San Diego's **La Jolla Cove** provides easy access to the undersea world.

BACKPACKING

To get away from the crowds, strap on a backpack and head to the state's more remote areas. The North Coast's **Lost Coast Trail** is a three-day backpacking trip along a 24-mile stretch of rugged coastline. Big Sur's **Ventana Wilderness** offers multiday excursions to hot springs and peaks with fabulous coast views. Or you can get away from it all at backcountry camps on Santa Cruz Island and Santa Rosa Island in **Channel Islands National Park.**

USAL BEACH
Best for Wildlife, Solitude

Follow the mountainous dirt road to Usal Beach, where you may spot Roosevelt elk. Even if you don't see these giant animals, you can bask in the solitude (page 268).

TRINIDAD STATE BEACH
Best for Scenery, Picnics

This scenic stretch of shore under the rounded knob of Trinidad Head is ideal for a family picnic—especially if you pick up some smoked salmon from nearby Katy's Smokehouse (page 282).

Venice Boardwalk

Santa Barbara and Ventura

The last strand of relatively undeveloped coast-line before Southern California is north of Santa Barbara. Ventura draws surfers from throughout the Southland.

ARROYO BURRO BEACH
Best for Dog Lovers

If you have a dog in tow, head to Santa Barbara's Arroyo Burro Beach. Past the slough, dogs are allowed off leash (page 434).

RINCON
Best for Surfing

Ranked 49th in a *Surfer Magazine* list of the 100 best waves in the world, Rincon can produce a long, peeling right with the right swell (page 435).

REFUGIO STATE BEACH
Best for Swimming, Families

The best beach on the Gaviota Coast is on this protected cove lined with palm trees. Its ocean waters are calm enough for wading children and beginning kayakers (page 446).

JALAMA BEACH COUNTY PARK
Best for Camping, Solitude

This beach park in the middle of nowhere is a refuge for surfers, anglers, beachcombers, and families who want to unplug from modern life (page 446).

CALIFORNIA STREET BEACH
Best for Surfing, Sightseeing

To catch some hot surfing action, head to Ventura's California Street Beach, known locally as "C Street" (page 452).

Los Angeles and Orange County

Los Angeles and neighboring Orange County share a wealth of superb beaches, known to the world from decades of movies and television shows: They're broad, sandy, and packed with people during the summer months. The best of the best have a little something that sets them apart.

VENICE BEACH
Best for People-Watching

Venice Beach is a people-watcher's paradise, with

a boardwalk filled with weightlifters, skateboarders, musicians, dancers, and vendors hawking their wares (page 482).

LEO CARRILLO STATE PARK
Best for Scenery, Camping, Dog Lovers
At the northern end of L.A. County, Leo Carrillo feels a world away from bustling Los Angeles. This 1.5-mile-long beach has tide pools, caves, and reefs. The northern section is also a perfect place to take your leashed pooch (page 494).

MALIBU SURFRIDER BEACH
Best for Surfing
Surfers flock to Malibu Surfrider Beach to catch one of California's greatest peeling waves or to soak up the vibe of the surf culture that was born here in the early 1960s (page 495).

SANTA MONICA STATE BEACH
Best for Families, Sunbathing
Take in the plentiful Southern California sunshine and the amusements available at the Santa Monica Pier (page 495).

HERMOSA BEACH
Best for Volleyball, Families
Hermosa Beach has the feel and attitude of a small beach town, even though it's surrounded by metropolitan Los Angeles. Volleyball nets are available for pickup games and "The Strand" is ideal for a jog or bike ride (page 531).

HUNTINGTON CITY BEACH
Best for Surfing, Sunbathing
Orange County's Huntington City Beach offers multiple recreation options, including surfing the waves that break on either side of the pier (page 545).

LAGUNA BEACH'S MAIN BEACH
Best for Tidepooling, Sunbathing
Main Beach is an ideal SoCal stretch of sand with palm trees and abundant sunshine. It gets even better at its north end, where some rocky tide pools are located (page 549).

San Diego
With warmer ocean temperatures and year-round sunshine, San Diego's beaches are the most welcoming in the state.

LA JOLLA COVE
Best for Sunbathing, Snorkeling, Kayaking
La Jolla Cove is a pocket beach between two cliffs. Sunbathers take up most of the real estate on crowded weekends. An underwater park with sea caves right offshore is perfect for snorkelers and kayakers (page 573).

OCEAN BEACH
Best for People-Watching, Dog Lovers
Lying at the end of an eclectic hippie community, this beach is popular with dogs—and their people (page 585).

BLACK'S BEACH
Best for Advanced Surfing, Sunbathing
Black's Beach is a legendary surf spot and also a nudist beach. Getting here involves an adventurous hiking path down 300-foot-high cliffs (page 586).

CORONADO MAIN BEACH
Best for Families, Sunsets
Spread out, catch some sun, and take in views of the nearby Hotel del Coronado (page 586).

Dog Days

Dog owners will have a lot more fun on the California coast with their furry friends along for the ride. Luckily, there are lots of options for people who want to bring their pets.

ACCOMMODATIONS

Kimpton Hotels, a luxury boutique hotel chain with 15 properties along the California coast, goes out of its way to welcome pets. It offers pet beds, food bowls, water bowls, and information about all the pet-friendly attractions and businesses in the area. Some of Kimpton's properties include San Diego's **Hotel Palomar,** Santa Barbara's **Canary Hotel,** and San Francisco's **Sir Francis Drake.**

In Del Mar, north of San Diego, **Les Artistes** has some pet-friendly rooms. Up the coast, the **Crowne Plaza Ventura Beach** has a whole floor of them.

Carmel-by-the-Sea is a superb place to vacation with your four-legged friend. Many hotels allow dogs including the **Tradewinds Carmel,** the **Coachman's Inn,** the **Lamp Lighter Inn,** and the **Cypress Inn,** which is co-owned by animal activist Doris Day.

In San Francisco's Pacific Heights neighborhood, rooms at the **Laurel Inn** are all pet friendly, with a two-dog limit.

Wine Country is surprisingly pro-pet with Napa's **Napa Inn,** Saint Helena's **El Bonita Motel,** and Guerneville's **Sonoma Orchid Inn** all catering to canines.

On the North Coast, Fort Bragg's **Beachcomber Motel** offers pet-friendly rooms, a dog park, and pet suites with doggie doors that open up to a fenced-in enclosure with a doghouse. In nearby Anderson Valley, both the **Anderson Valley Inn** and the **Boonville Hotel** reserve a couple of rooms for families with dogs.

BEACHES

A few California beaches permit and even encourage dog visitation. One of the best is **Carmel Beach** in Carmel-by-the-Sea. On any given day, more dogs roam this beach than people — and they can do so leash-free.

The north end of San Diego's **Ocean Beach** calls itself "The Original Dog Beach." It's also leash-free. **Del Mar City Beach** has a dog section that extends from 29th Street to Solana Beach.

There are lots of dog-friendly beaches on the California coast.

Known as "Surf City USA," Orange County's **Huntington Beach** might as well be called "Dog City USA." The north end between Seapoint Avenue and 21st Street allows pets.

Santa Barbara's **Arroyo Burro Beach** permits pets to be off leash past the slough, while **Montara State Beach** in the Bay Area's Coastside invites dogs as long as they're leashed.

PARKS

The second-largest park in San Francisco, **McLaren Park** has dog play areas. The **Coastside Trail** is a paved dog-friendly path that connects various Half Moon Bay beaches and the adjacent shoreline. One of the Monterey Peninsula's best places to hike with your dog is Carmel Valley's **Garland Ranch Regional Park.** The park has off-leash areas and water fountains designed to hydrate both you and your pet.

The **California State Parks** on the coast generally allow leashed dogs in the day-use areas but not on the trails. Contact the specific state park that you will be visiting to confirm where your pet is permitted.

French Laundry in Yountville, Napa Valley

Romantic Getaways

Crashing waves, breathtaking views, gourmet restaurants, and luxury hotels make the California coast perfect for romance.

San Francisco and the Bay Area

Have a wonderful meal together at a fine San Francisco restaurant like **State Bird Provisions** or **Michael Mina** and then take in an opera at the **War Memorial Opera House.** End the night by sipping a cocktail and looking at the lights of the city from **Harry Denton's Starlight Room.** If you can really splurge, check into a room at the high-rise **Mandarin Oriental San Francisco.**

Just north of San Francisco, the **Cavallo Point Lodge** feels a world away from the city but still has all the amenities for a romantic evening, including a fine restaurant, a spa, a pampering staff, and stunning views of the Golden Gate Bridge and the bay.

Down the coast, the Half Moon Bay area offers nice romantic retreats. Spend the night at the castle-like **Ritz-Carlton Half Moon Bay** or the bayside **Beach House at Half Moon Bay.**

Wine Country

Wineries, superb restaurants, and a multitude of spas all conspire to make Wine Country a romantic environment. Spend a few hours tasting sparkling wine at Sonoma's **Gloria Ferrer** or Rutherford's **Mumm** winery, then splurge for a couple's massage at **Spa Terra.** Treat your loved one to a meal at the revered **French Laundry** or **Auberge du Soleil,** with its wonderful views of Napa Valley.

North Coast

Pack up a bottle of wine and a blanket for a long walk on a secluded beach. Towards the upper end of the North Coast, **Trinidad State Beach** is a picturesque place to picnic. Farther south, **Manchester State Park**'s beach offers miles of uncrowded coastline and large beached logs perfect for watching the sunset.

Rent one of the four private Victorian cottages at Eureka's **Carter House Inns.** Or spend a night at the lovely **Elk Cove Inn,** where you can walk down to a beautiful cove. Another option is the **Sea Ranch Lodge,** where every room has a view of the serene Sonoma Coast. The village of Mendocino has a variety of romantic bed-and-breakfasts including the **Brewery Gulch Inn.**

Monterey Bay

Romance can blossom on a sunset walk on **Carmel Beach,** followed by a lovely French meal at **La Bicyclette.** Stay the night in one of Carmel's luxurious accommodations, like the opulent **La Playa Carmel** or the East-meets-West-themed **Tradewinds Carmel.** Or drive a few miles north to Pacific Grove to spend an evening at the **Green Gables Inn,** an ornate Victorian bed-and-breakfast with a view of the aptly named **Lover's Point** protruding into the bay.

Detour inland to Carmel Valley to visit one of the valley's many wine-tasting rooms at the luxurious **Bernardus Winery** or the unassuming **Heller Estate Organic Vineyards** with its outdoor sculpture garden. Then relax together at **Refuge Spa,** a collection of hot, warm, and cool water tubs nestled under the Santa Lucia Mountains.

Big Sur and the Central Coast

Big Sur is a great place for romantic walks, whether to **Pfeiffer Beach** or to see **McWay Falls** plunge into the Pacific at **Julia Pfeiffer Burns State Park.** Post hike, a posh night at the **Post Ranch Inn** or **Ventana Inn & Spa** will definitely impress your significant other. A less pricey but cozy alternative is **Deetjen's Big Sur Inn.**

South of Big Sur and inland, visit Paso Robles for wine-tasting and a growing foodie scene. Taste the excellent wines at **Eberle Winery** and then have a fine meal at **Artisan.** Spend a night at the boutique **Hotel Cheval** or the **Paso Robles Inn,** where you can snuggle in a private hot springs mineral pool on the deck of your room.

Back on the coast, a romantic evening will come easy with a night at Cambria's **Sand Pebbles Inn,** right across the street from Moonstone Beach. Another option is to reserve one of the rooms with a natural hot springs

the harbor at Catalina Island

the Scripps Pier in La Jolla, San Diego

water tub on the deck at the **Sycamore Mineral Springs Resort.**

Santa Barbara and Ventura

Filled with fragrant flowers and beautiful Spanish-influenced architecture, Santa Barbara is one of the coast's finest spots for romance. Take the **Urban Wine Trail** to wine-taste within the city and then have dinner at fancy French restaurant **Bouchon** or enjoy Middle Eastern food on the garden patio at **Zaytoon.**

The **Canary Hotel** is a luxury hotel with a rooftop deck and a fireplace for a romantic evening under the stars. Another option is the elegant **Cheshire Cat Inn,** a Victorian bed-and-breakfast; some rooms have soaking tubs.

Los Angeles and Orange County

Is there anything more romantic than heading out to an island together? Find out on a trip to **Catalina Island,** where you'll spend the night in the small harbor city of **Avalon.** Once there, enjoy a romantic dinner at **Avalon Grille** or **Ristorante Villa Portofino.** Then splurge for a night's stay at the **Pavilion Hotel** or **Villa Portofino.**

In Orange County, **The Inn at Laguna Beach** is perched right above the sand and sea. You can walk from there to **Watermarc** for small bites and wonderful cocktails.

San Diego

San Diego is a great place for relaxing, recharging, and romance. After enjoying the sun on one of the city's many fine beaches, head to the scenic coastal community of **La Jolla** for an afternoon of shopping. If you get hungry, enjoy a meal with ocean views inside **George's at the Cove.**

End the day with cocktails and seaside views at the historic **Hotel del Coronado.** Or opt for a drink at the **Grant Grill,** a restaurant and bar within the historic **US Grant Hotel,** located in the city's Gaslamp Quarter.

San Francisco and the Bay Area

Famed for its ethnic diversity, liberal politics, and chilly, dense fog, the San Francisco Bay Area manages to both embody and to defy the stereotypes heaped on it.

Street-corner protests and leather stores are certainly part of the landscape, but family farms and friendly communities also abound. English blends with languages from around the world in an occasionally frustrating, often joyful cacophony. Those who've chosen to live here often refuse to live anyplace else, despite the infamous cost of housing and the occasional violent earthquake.

San Francisco perches restlessly on an uneven spit of land overlooking the bay on one side and the Pacific Ocean on the other. Refer to the city as "San Fran," or worse, "Frisco," and you'll be pegged as a tourist immediately. To locals, the city is "the City," and that's that. Urban travelers can enjoy San Francisco's great art, world-class music, unique theater and comedy, and a laid-back club scene. Many visitors come to the city solely for the food; San Francisco functions as a culinary trendsetter that competes with the likes of Paris for innovation and prestige.

The Golden Gate Bridge leads into the North Bay, with its reputation for fertile farmland, intense material wealth, windswept coasts, and towering redwoods. An adventure here can be urban and touristy or rural and outdoorsy. The more locally used Bay Bridge leads to the East Bay and the city of Oakland. The one-time hardscrabble working-class town has entered a new phase of its evolution. Thanks to an influx of artists, creative chefs, and local entrepreneurs, the media has declared Oakland a hip destination. The East Bay is also home to erudite, progressive Berkeley—the birthplace of many liberal political movements from the 1960s to today. The original University of California sits in Berkeley, offering protest groups for liberals and top-flight technical educations to multitudinous engineers.

South of the city, Silicon Valley is all about the technology. With the likes of Hewlett-Packard, Apple, Google, and eBay headquartered here, it's no surprise that even the museums run to technology and the residents all seem to own the latest iPad.

For a more relaxed, outdoorsy experience,

Previous: Alcatraz; Golden Gate Bridge. **Above:** the historic Ferry Building in San Francisco.

Look for ★ to find recommended sights, activities, dining, and lodging.

Highlights

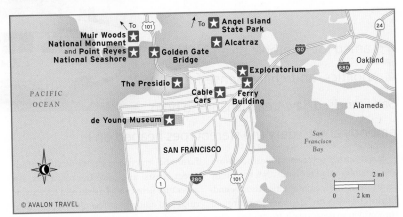

★ **Cable Cars:** Get a taste of free-spirited San Francisco—not to mention great views of Alcatraz and the bay—via open-air public transit (page 37).

★ **Ferry Building:** The 1898 Ferry Building has been renovated and reimagined as the foodie mecca of San Francisco. The Tuesday and Saturday Farmers Market is not to be missed (page 40).

★ **Alcatraz:** Spend the day in prison...at the famous former maximum-security penitentiary in the middle of the bay (page 44).

★ **Exploratorium:** Explore San Francisco's innovative and interactive science museum in its new bayside location. The exhibits here are meant to be touched, heard, and felt (page 46).

★ **The Presidio:** The original 1776 El Presidio de San Francisco is now a dormant military installation and national park (page 52).

★ **Golden Gate Bridge:** Nothing beats the view from one of the most famous and fascinating bridges in the country. Pick a fogless day for a stroll or bike ride across the 1.7-mile span (page 52).

★ **de Young Museum:** The showpiece of Golden Gate Park, the deYoung's mixed collection of media and regions is highlighted by the 360-degree view from the museum's tower (page 54).

★ **Angel Island State Park:** While it once served as a way station for immigrants, today this island offers hiking trails and amazing views of the city, Alcatraz, and the Golden Gate Bridge (page 105).

★ **Muir Woods National Monument:** Wander more than six miles of trails winding through redwoods—some of the most stunning and accessible of the big trees in the Bay Area (page 109).

★ **Point Reyes National Seashore:** At the tip of the Marin coast are acres of hiking, biking, and bird-watching (page 116).

San Francisco and the Bay Area

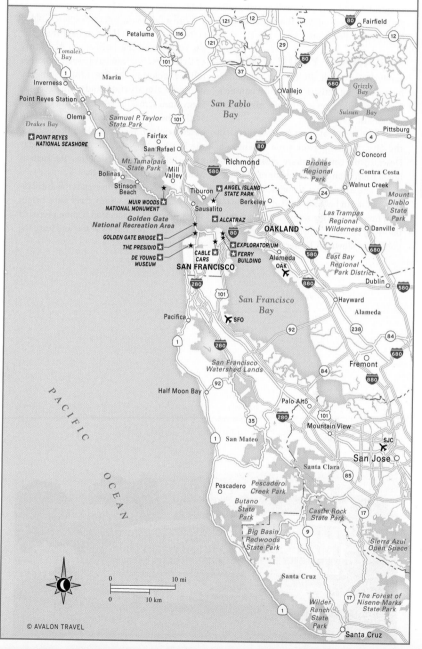

© AVALON TRAVEL

the coastal region has a small-town feel with big-time extreme ocean sports. Locals pack sweatshirts and parkas as well as swimsuits and sun hats for a day at the beach in Half Moon Bay or Pescadero.

PLANNING YOUR TIME

San Francisco's rich, diverse culture and immense range of activities and entertainment make it a destination worthy of a day, a week, or a month.

Try to spend at least one weekend in the city, focusing your time downtown. Downtown's Union Square makes a great home base, thanks to its plethora of hotels, shops, and easy access to public transportation, but it can be fairly dead at night. Spend your time grazing the sumptuous offerings at the **Ferry Building,** then hop onto a crowded **cable car** down to Fisherman's Wharf to catch the ferry to **Alcatraz.** At night, relax at one of San Francisco's many well-regarded restaurants.

With a full week, you can explore Golden Gate Park's excellent museums—the **de Young** and the **California Academy of Sciences.** You can easily spend another full day exploring **The Presidio,** visiting the nearby **Exploratorium,** and taking a scenic, foggy stroll across the **Golden Gate Bridge.** With a few more days, explore less tourist-focused neighborhoods like Haight-Ashbury, the Mission, or Noe Valley. Or spend a day exploring a region outside the city, such as Marin County or the East Bay.

San Francisco's weather tends toward blanket fog and chilly, windy days with bright spots of sun the exception. Come prepared with a warm coat and a sweater and leave the shorts at home.

Alcatraz

Sights

UNION SQUARE AND NOB HILL

Wealth and style mark these areas near the center of San Francisco. Known for their lavish shopping areas, cable cars, and mansions, Union Square and Nob Hill draw both local and visiting crowds all year long. Sadly, the stunning 19th-century mansions built by the robber barons on Nob Hill are almost all gone—shaken then burned in the 1906 earthquake and fire. But the area still exudes a certain elegance, and restaurants are particularly good on Nob Hill.

If you shop in only one part of San Francisco, make it Union Square. Even if you don't like chain stores, just climb up to the top of the square itself, grab a bench, and enjoy the views and the live entertainment on the small informal stage.

★ Cable Cars

Perhaps the most recognizable symbol of San Francisco is the **cable car** (www.sfcablecar. com), originally conceived by Andrew Smith Hallidie as a safe mode for traveling the steep, often slick hills of San Francisco. Cable cars ran as regular mass transit from 1873 into the 1940s, when buses and electric streetcars began to dominate the landscape.

Today, you can ride the cable cars from one tourist destination to another through the city for $5 per ride. A full-day "passport" ticket (which also grants access to streetcars and buses) costs $13 and is worth it if you want to run around the city all day. Cable car routes can take you up Nob Hill, through Union Square, down Powell Street, out to Fisherman's Wharf, and through Chinatown. Take a seat, or grab one of the exterior poles and hang on. The open-air car makes the ride chilly on foggy days.

The cable cars fill to capacity with tourists on weekends and with local commuters at rush hours. Expect to wait an hour or more for a ride from any of the turnaround points on a weekend or holiday. But a ride on a cable car from Union Square down to the wharf is more than worth the wait. The views from the hills down to the bay inspire wonder even in local residents.

For aficionados, a ride on the cars can take you to the **Cable Car Museum** (1201 Mason St., 415/474-1887, www.cablecarmuseum.org, Apr.-Sept. daily 10am-6pm, Oct.-Mar. daily 10am-5pm, free), which houses a few cable cars and overlooks the system that runs the active cars.

Grace Cathedral

Local icon **Grace Cathedral** (1100 California St., 415/749-6300, www.gracecathedral.org, Mon.-Fri. 7am-6pm, Sat. 8am-6pm, Sun. 8am-7pm) is many things to many people. The French Gothic-style edifice, completed in 1964, attracts architecture and beaux arts lovers by the thousands with its facade, stained glass, and furnishings. It has been photographed by Ansel Adams and was the site of a 1965 speech by Martin Luther King Jr. The labyrinths, replicas of the Chartres Cathedral labyrinth in France, appeal to meditative walkers seeking spiritual solace. Concerts featuring world music, sacred music, and modern classical ensembles draw audiences from around the bay and farther afield.

But most of all, Grace Cathedral opens its doors to the community as a vibrant, active Episcopal church. The doctrine of exploration and tolerance matches well with the San Francisco community, of which the church remains an important part.

To view some of the church's lesser-seen areas, sign up for the 1.5-hour **Grace Cathedral Grand Tour** (800/979-3370, $25).

San Francisco

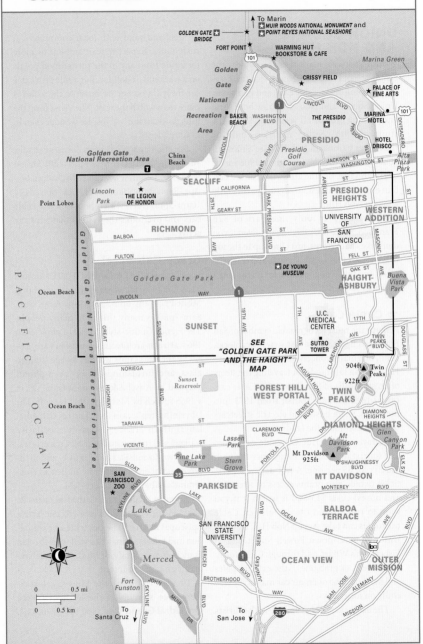

To Marin
★ MUIR WOODS NATIONAL MONUMENT and
★ POINT REYES NATIONAL SEASHORE

GOLDEN GATE
BRIDGE

FORT POINT

WARMING HUT
BOOKSTORE & CAFE

101

Marina Green

Golden
Gate

CRISSY FIELD

PALACE OF
FINE ARTS

National

101

Recreation

BAKER
BEACH

WASHINGTON
BLVD

THE PRESIDIO

MARINA
MOTEL

DIVISADERO

Area

LINCOLN BLVD

PRESIDIO

HOTEL
DRISCO

Golden Gate
National Recreation Area

China
Beach

Presidio
Golf
Course

PRESIDIO BLVD

JACKSON ST
WASHINGTON ST

Alta
Plaza
Park

PARK BLVD

PRESIDIO

SEACLIFF

ST

PRESIDIO
HEIGHTS

CALIFORNIA

Lincoln
Park

THE LEGION
OF HONOR

ST

WESTERN
ADDITION

Point Lobos

25TH

GEARY ST

ARGUELLO

PARK PRESIDIO BLVD

UNIVERSITY
OF
SAN
FRANCISCO

ST

MASONIC

ST

RICHMOND

AVE

BALBOA

AVE

FELL ST

FULTON

ST

OAK ST

AVE

Golden Gate National Recreation Area

DE YOUNG
MUSEUM

HAIGHT-
ASHBURY

Buena
Vista
Park

Ocean Beach

Golden Gate Park

LINCOLN

WAY

U.C.
MEDICAL
CENTER

7TH

17TH

PACIFIC

SUNSET

GREAT

SUNSET

19TH AVE

SEE
"GOLDEN GATE PARK
AND THE HAIGHT"
MAP

LAGUNA HONDA

CLARENDON

SUTRO
TOWER

AVE

TWIN
PEAKS
BLVD

DOUGLASS

ST

904ft ▲ Twin
Peaks

NORIEGA

ST

Sunset
Reservoir

FOREST HILL/
WEST PORTAL

DEWEY BLVD

922ft ▲

TWIN
PEAKS

O
C
E
A
N

Ocean Beach

TARAVAL

ST

DIAMOND
HEIGHTS

VICENTE

ST

CLAREMONT
BLVD

DIAMOND HEIGHTS

Mt
Davidson
Park

Glen
Canyon
Park

ELK ST

HIGHWAY

BLVD

Lassen
Park

PORTOLA DR

Mt Davidson ▲
925ft

O'SHAUGHNESSY
BLVD

SLOAT

Pine Lake
Park

Stern
Grove

BLVD

MT DAVIDSON

SAN
FRANCISCO
ZOO

35

SKYLINE BLVD

PARKSIDE

LAKE

MONTEREY

BLVD

BALBOA
TERRACE

AVE

BLVD

Lake

SAN FRANCISCO
STATE
UNIVERSITY

MERCED

FONT

SERRA

BLVD

OCEAN

AVE

OCEAN VIEW

AVE

BLVD

OUTER
MISSION

Merced

35

1

JUNIPERO

SAN JOSE

ALEMANY

Fort
Funston

JOHN

SKYLINE BLVD

MUIR DR

BROTHERHOOD

WAY

280

MISSION

0   0.5 mi
0   0.5 km

To
Santa Cruz ↓

To
San Jose ↓

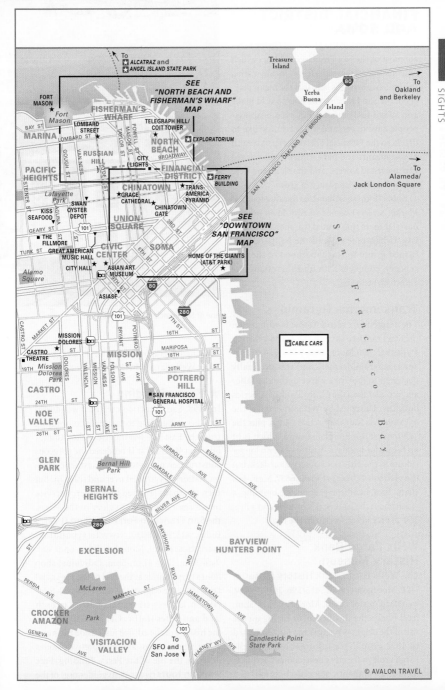

© AVALON TRAVEL

FINANCIAL DISTRICT AND SOMA

The skyscrapers of the Financial District create most of the San Francisco skyline, which extends out to the waterfront, locally called the Embarcadero. It's here that the major players of the San Francisco business world make and spend their money. But even businesspeople have to eat, and they certainly like to drink, so the Financial District offers a wealth of restaurants and bars. Hotels tend toward expensive tall towers, and the shopping here caters to folks with plenty of green.

SoMa (local shorthand for the area south of Market Street) was once a run-down postindustrial mess that rented warehouses to artists. Urban renewal and the ballpark have turned it into *the* neighborhood of the 21st century, complete with upscale restaurants and chichi wine bars.

one of San Francisco's cable cars

Transamerica Pyramid

The single most recognizable landmark on the San Francisco skyline, the **Transamerica Pyramid** (600 Montgomery St., www.transamericapyramidcenter.com) was originally designed to look like a tree and to be taller and prouder than the nearby Bank of America building. Designed by William Pereira, the pyramid has four distinctive wings, plus the 212-foot aluminum-plated spire, which is lit up for major holidays. Visitors can no longer ride up to the 27th-floor observation deck, but the **visitors center** (415/500-6637, Mon.-Fri. 10am-3pm) has displays about the building, a video about the landmark's history, and a live, 360-degree video feed from the top.

Wells Fargo Bank History Museum

The **Wells Fargo Bank History Museum** (420 Montgomery St., 415/396-2619, www.wellsfargohistory.com, Mon.-Fri. 9am-5pm, free) boasts the distinction of sitting on the site of the original Wells Fargo office, opened in 1852. You'll see information on Wells Fargo's role in the city's development. Exhibits include an authentic stagecoach as well as a working telegraph that can send messages to other Wells Fargo Museums.

★ Ferry Building

In 1898, San Francisco created a wonderful new Ferry Building to facilitate commuting from the East Bay. But the rise of the automobile after World War II rendered the gorgeous construction obsolete, and its aesthetic ornamentation was covered over and filled in. But then the roads jammed up and ferry service began again. Restored to glory in the 1990s, the **San Francisco Ferry Building** (1 Ferry Bldg., 415/983-8030, www.ferrybuildingmarketplace.com, Mon.-Fri. 10am-6pm, Sat. 9am-6pm, Sun. 11am-5pm, individual shop hours vary) stands at the end of the Financial District at the edge of the water. Its 230-foot-tall clock tower serves as a beacon to both land and water traffic. Get a brief lesson in the history of the edifice just inside the main lobby, where photos and interpretive plaques describe the life of the Ferry Building. Free **walking tours** (www.sfcityguides.org) of the building are offered on Saturday and Tuesday at noon.

Inside, it's all about the food. The permanent shops provide top-tier artisanal food and drink, from wine to cheese to high-end kitchenware, with local favorites like Cowgirl Creamery, Blue Bottle Café, and Acme Bread Company. The famous **Farmers Market** (415/291-3276, www.ferrybuildingmarketplace.com, Tues. and Thurs. 10am-2pm, Sat. 8am-2pm) draws crowds shopping for produce out front.

On the water side of the Ferry Building, ferries come and go from Sausalito, Tiburon, Larkspur, Vallejo, and Alameda each day. Check with the **Blue and Gold Fleet** (415/705-8200, www.blueandgoldfleet.com), **Golden Gate Ferry** (415/455-2000, www.goldengateferry.org), and **San Francisco Bay Ferry** (415/705-8291, http://sanfranciscobayferry.com) for information about service, times, and fares.

AT&T Park

AT&T Park (24 Willie Mays Plaza, 415/972-2000, http://sanfrancisco.giants.mlb.com) is home to the San Francisco Giants, endless special events, several great restaurants, and arguably California's best garlic fries. From the ballpark, you can look right out onto the bay. During baseball games, a motley collection of boats floats beside the stadium, hoping that an out-of-the-park fly ball will come sailing their way.

San Francisco Museum of Modern Art

In the spring of 2016, **SFMOMA** (151 3rd St., 415/357-4000, www.sfmoma.org, Thurs. 10am-9m, Fri.-Wed. 10am-5pm, adults $25, seniors $22, children free) reopened after an extensive renovation with a giant 235,000-square-foot annex and a major influx of new art into its permanent collection. The major museum expansion includes a vertical garden, an outdoor terrace, and lots of gallery space to showcase recently acquired works by Chuck Close, Roy Lichtenstein,

and Andy Warhol. Ongoing exhibits focus on American abstraction, pop art, and minimal art. SFMOMA's Pritzker Center for Photography is the largest space devoted entirely to the art of photography in the country.

CHINATOWN

The massive Chinese migration to California began almost as soon as the news of easy gold in the mountain streams made it to East Asia. Many never made it to the goldfields, preferring instead to remain in bustling San Francisco to open shops and begin the business of commerce in their new home. They were basically segregated to a small area beneath Nob Hill, where they built a motley collection of wooden shacks that served as homes, restaurants, and shops. This neighborhood quickly became known as Chinatown.

Today, small alleyways wend between the broad touristy avenues, entry points into the old Chinatown that remains. Beautiful Asian architecture mixes with more mundane city buildings.

Chinatown Gate

Visible from the streets leading into Union Square, the **Chinatown Gate** (Grant Ave. and Bush St.) perches at the southern "entrance" to the famous Chinatown neighborhood. The gate, built in 1970, is a relatively recent addition to this historic neighborhood. The design features Chinese dragons, pagodas, and other charming details. The inscription reads, "All under heaven is for the good of the people," a quote from Sun Yat-sen. Its gaudy, colorful splendor draws droves of visitors with cameras each day; on weekends it can be tough to find a quick moment to get your own picture taken at the gate.

Chinatown truly is a sight in itself. Visitors stroll the streets, exploring the tiny alleys and peeking into the temples, admiring the wonderful Asian architecture on occasionally unlikely buildings. Among the best known of these is the **Bank of America Building** (701 Grant Ave.), an impressive edifice with a Chinese tiled roof and 60 dragon medallions

Downtown San Francisco

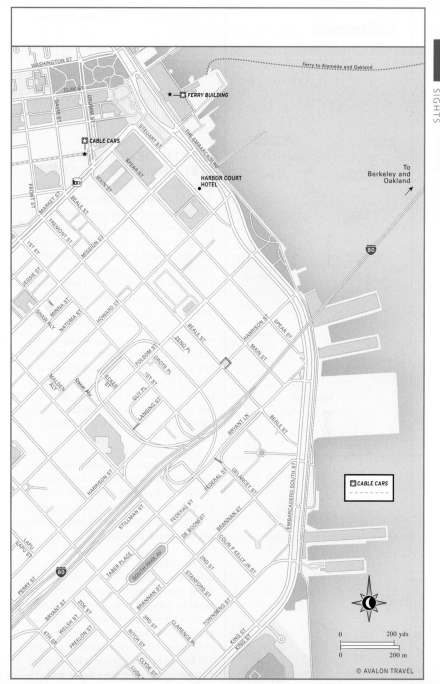

WASHINGTON ST

CLAY ST

★—☆ *FERRY BUILDING*

Ferry to Alameda and Oakland

DAVIS ST

DRUMM ST

★ ☆ *CABLE CARS*
★

STEUART ST

SPEAR ST

THE EMBARCADERO

To
Berkeley and
Oakland

FRONT ST

MARKET ST

BEALE ST

MAIN ST

HARBOR COURT
HOTEL

FREMONT ST

MISSION ST

80

1ST ST

JESSIE ST

HOWARD ST

SHAW ALY

MINNA ST

NATOMA ST

BEALE ST

ZENO PL

HARRISON ST

SPEAR ST

FOLSOM ST

GROTE PL

MAIN ST

MALDEN
ALY

Oscar Alv

JECKER
ST

1ST ST

GUY PL

LANSING ST

BRYANT LN

BEALE ST

HARRISON ST

FEDERAL ST

DELANCEY ST

EMBARCADERO SOUTH ST

STILLMAN ST

FEDERAL ST

DE BOOM ST

BRANNAN ST

☆ *CABLE CARS*
- - - - - - -

LAPU
LAPU ST

80

TABER PLACE

SOUTH PARK AV

2ND ST

COLIN P KELLY JR ST

PERRY ST

BRANNAN ST

STANFORD ST

TOWNSEND ST

BRYANT ST

ZOE ST

WELSH ST

FREELON ST

3RD ST

CLARENCE PL

KING ST

KING ST

4TH ST

RITCH ST

CLYDE ST

LUSK ST

0   200 yds

0   200 m

© AVALON TRAVEL

Chinatown

decorating the facade. The **Bank of Canton** (743 Washington St.) is even more traditional in its look. The small, beautiful building that acted as the Chinatown Telephone Exchange was constructed in this Chinese style just after the 1906 earthquake demolished the original structure. The **Sing Chong Building** (601 Grant Ave. at California St.) was another 1906 quick-rebuild.

NORTH BEACH AND FISHERMAN'S WHARF

Fisherman's Wharf and North Beach are an odd amalgam of old-school residential neighborhood and total tourist mecca. North Beach has long served as the Italian district of San Francisco, reflected in the restaurants in the area. Fisherman's Wharf was the spot where 19th-century Italians came to work; they were a big part of the fishing fleet that provided San Francisco with its legendary supply of fresh seafood.

In the 1950s, North Beach became one of the hubs of the Beat Generation, a group of groundbreaking writers that included Lawrence Ferlinghetti, Jack Kerouac, and Allen Ginsberg. Traces of the Beats remain in the area in The Beat Museum, down Jack Kerouac Alley, and in the famous City Lights bookstore, which was cofounded by Ferlinghetti in 1953.

Today, Fisherman's Wharf is where visitors come to snap photos. If you're not into crowds, avoid the area in the summer. For those who can cope with a ton of other people, some of the best views of the air show during Fleet Week and the fireworks on the Fourth of July can be found on the Wharf.

★ Alcatraz

Going to **Alcatraz** (www.nps.gov/alca), one of the most famous landmarks in the city, feels like going to purgatory: this military fortress turned maximum-security prison, nicknamed "The Rock," has little warmth or welcome on its craggy, forbidding shores. The fortress became a prison in the 19th century while it still belonged to the military, which used it to house Civil War prisoners. The isolation of the island in the bay, the frigid waters, and the nasty currents surrounding Alcatraz made it a perfect spot to keep prisoners contained; it offered little hope of escape and the prospect of near-certain death if the attempt was ever made. In 1934, after the military closed down their prison and handed the island over to the Department of Justice, construction began to turn Alcatraz into a new style of prison ready to house a new style of prisoner: Depression-era gangsters. A few of the honored guests of this maximum-security penitentiary were Al Capone, George "Machine Gun" Kelly, and Robert Stroud, "the Birdman of Alcatraz." The prison closed in 1963, and in 1964 and 1969 occupations were staged by Indians of All Tribes, an exercise that helped change federal policy toward North America's original inhabitants.

Today, **Alcatraz Cruises** (Pier 33, 415/981-7625, www.alcatrazcruises.com, daily 8:45am-6:30pm approx. every 30 min., adults $31-38, seniors $29-35, children $19-23) offers ferry rides out to Alcatraz and tours of the island and the prison. Tours depart from Pier 33. Once on the island, most visitors embark on the **Cellhouse Audio Tour,** a 45-minute walk through the imposing prison, narrated by the voices of former Alcatraz officers and prisoners. It's easy to get lost in the fascinating stories as you wander around. The 8:45am-departing **Early Bird Tour** is a way to experience the island with fewer people. Buy tickets at least a week in advance, especially for a summer weekend. Tours often sell out, particularly in the evening.

Fisherman's Wharf

Welcome to the tourist mecca of San Francisco! Just don't go looking for an actual wharf or single pier when you come to visit **Fisherman's Wharf** (Beach St. from Powell St. to Van Ness Ave., backs onto Bay St., 415/674-7503, www.fishermanswharf. org). In fact, the Fisherman's Wharf area, reachable by the Muni F line, sprawls along

the waterfront and inland several blocks, creating a large tourist neighborhood. The Wharf, as it's called by locals (who avoid the area at all costs), features all crowds, all the time. Be prepared to push through a sea of humanity to see sights, buy souvenirs, and eat seafood. Fisherman's Wharf includes many of the sights that people come to San Francisco to see: Pier 39, Ghirardelli Square, and, of course, the wax museum **Madame Tussauds San Francisco and the San Francisco Dungeon** (145 Jefferson St., 866/223-4240, www.madametussauds.com, Sun.-Thurs. 10am-9pm, Fri.-Sat. 10am-10pm, adults $18-38, children $16-36), the presence of which tells most serious travelers all they need to know about the Wharf. You can save money by purchasing tickets online.

One of the quirkier attractions in Fishermen's Wharf is the **Musée Mécanique** (Pier 45, 415/346-2000, www.museemecanique.org, Mon.-Fri. 10am-7pm, Sat.-Sun. 10am-8pm, free), a strange collection of over 300 working coin-operated machines from the 1800s to today. The most famous is "Laughing Sal," a machine that causes a giant redheaded woman to laugh maniacally for a couple of quarters. Other machines include a 3-D picture show of San Francisco after the catastrophic 1906 earthquake and fire, along with more modern games like Ms. Pac-Man.

Pier 39

One of the most-visited spots in San Francisco, **Pier 39** (Beach St. and The Embarcadero, www.pier39.com, individual shop hours vary) hosts a wealth of restaurants and shops. If you've come down to the pier to see the sealife, start with the unusual **Aquarium of the Bay** (415/623-5300, www.aquariumofthebay. org, Mar.-late May and early Sept.-Oct. daily 10am-7pm, June-early Sept. daily 9am-8pm, Nov.-Feb. daily 10am-6pm, adults $22, seniors and children $13). This 300-foot clear-walled tunnel lets visitors see thousands of species native to San Francisco Bay, including sharks, rays, and plenty of fish. For a special treat,

San Francisco Weekend

San Francisco may only be roughly seven miles long and seven miles wide, but it packs in historic neighborhoods, one of the West Coast's most iconic landmarks, and dozens of stomach-dropping inclines within its small area. Exploring all its hills and valleys takes some planning.

DAY 1

Start your day at the **Ferry Building** (page 40). Graze from the many vendors, including **Blue Bottle Café, Cowgirl Creamery,** and **Acme Bread Company.**

After touring the gourmet shops, catch the Muni F line (Steuart St. and Market St., $2) to Jefferson Street and take a stroll along **Fisherman's Wharf** (page 45). Stop into the **Musée Mécanique** to play a few coin-operated antique arcade games. Near Pier 39, buy tickets for the ferry to **Alcatraz** (page 44) or opt for a ride to **Angel Island** (page 105) at Pier 41. Alcatraz will fill your mind with amazing stories from the legendary island prison, while hiking around Angel Island will clear your mind and offer up scenic views of the bay.

After you escape from Alcatraz or return from Angel Island, make your way back to the foot of Beach and Hyde Streets and board the Powell-Hyde **cable car** ($6). Watch for gorgeous Bay views as the cable car crests Russian Hill around Filbert Street. Hop off at Sutter Street and walk three blocks east past **Union Square** to lunch at **Café Claude** (page 88), a classic French brasserie. After lunch, window-shop around Union Square, meandering down to the Powell Street Muni station at Market Street.

Take the N Judah line ($2) to 9th Avenue and Irving Street, then follow 9th Avenue north into **Golden Gate Park** (page 54). The fabulous **de Young Museum** (page 54) is directly across from the **California Academy of Sciences** (page 55). Art lovers and science geeks can part ways here—or squeeze in a trip to enjoy both! Stop in for a refreshing cup of tea at the adjacent **Japanese Tea Garden** (page 55).

Return by cab or Uber to the downtown Financial District for an upscale dinner at **Michael Mina** (page 88) or the **Tadich Grill** (page 89), where the tasty cocktails and extensive seafood menu will make for a perfect ending to your day. Consider starting the night with a martini at the swank **Top of the Mark** (page 58), with its view of the SF skyline.

---

take the Behind the Scenes Tour. The aquarium has extended hours the first two weeks of April and the last two weeks of December.

Farther down the pier is where visitors get close to the local colony of sea lions. These big, loud mammals tend to congregate at K-Dock in the West Marina. The best time to see the sea lions is winter, when the population grows into the hundreds.

A perennial family favorite, the **San Francisco Carousel** ($3 per ride) is painted with beautiful scenes of San Francisco. Kids also love the daily shows by local street performers. Depending on when you're on the pier, you might see jugglers, magicians, or stand-up comedians on the **Alpine Spring Water Center Stage** (showtimes vary, free).

★ Exploratorium

Kids around the Bay Area love the **Exploratorium** (Pier 15, Embarcadero at Green St., 415/528-4444, www.exploratorium.edu, Fri.-Wed. 10am-5pm, Thurs. 10am-5pm and 6pm-10pm for 18 years and older, adults $29, children 13 to 17 $24, children 12 and under $19). This innovative museum makes science the most fun thing ever for kids; adults are also welcome to enjoy the interactive exhibits. The Exploratorium seeks to be true to its name and encourages exploration into all aspects of science, and you can learn about everything from frogs to the physics of baseball. Expect lots of mirrors, coiled wires, blowing air, lights, magnets, and motors. Other exhibits include a bay observatory and a wind-activated installation com, Sun.-Thurs. 9am-11pm, Fri.-Sat. 9am-midnight) sits at the corner of the square. Browse the rambling shop and pick up truffles, wafers, candies, and sauces. Then get in line at the ice cream counter to order a hot-fudge sundae. Once you've finished gorging on chocolate, wander out into the square to enjoy more shopping (there's even a cupcake shop if your teeth haven't dissolved yet).

Lombard Street

You've no doubt seen it in movies, on TV, and on postcards: **Lombard Street,** otherwise known as "the crookedest street in the world." You can't beat the view from the top. With its 27 percent grade and eight hairpin curves, Lombard Street offers unobstructed vistas of San Francisco Bay, Alcatraz Island, Fisherman's Wharf, and Coit Tower.

The section that visitors flock to spans only a block, from Hyde Street at the top to Leavenworth Street at the bottom. Lombard was originally created to keep people from rolling uncontrolled down the treacherously steep grade. Brave pedestrians can walk up and down the sides of the brick-paved street, enjoying the hydrangeas and Victorian mansions that line the roadway. For convenience during the peak summer months, take a cable car directly to the top of Lombard Street and walk down the noncurvy stairs on either side.

Coit Tower

Since 1933, **Coit Tower** (1 Telegraph Hill Blvd., 415/249-0995, May-Oct. daily 10am-6pm, Nov.-Apr. daily 10am-5pm, elevator ride adults $8, seniors and ages 12-17 $5, under age 12 $2) has beautified the city just as benefactor Lillie Hitchcock Coit intended when she willed San Francisco one-third of her monumental estate. Inside, murals depicting city life and works of the 1930s cover the walls. From the top of the tower on a clear day, you can see the whole of the city and the bay. Part of what makes Coit Tower special is the walk up to it. Take public transit and walk up the Filbert Steps to the tower. It's steep, but there's no other way to see the lovely little cottages and gardens that mark the path up from the streets to the top of Telegraph Hill.

The Beat Museum

To some people, North Beach is still the old stomping grounds of the Beat Generation, a gang of 1950s writers that included Jack Kerouac, Allen Ginsberg, and Lawrence Ferlinghetti. Only a block or so from Ferlinghetti's famed City Lights bookstore,

DAY 2

Head to North Beach for brunch at **Mama's on Washington Square** (page 92), whose specialty "m'omelettes" have made this joint a local favorite for decades. Then explore the neighborhood. Stop in **City Lights** (page 70), the legendary Beat Generation bookstore, and then head across the street to check out **The Beat Museum** (page 50). Then further your tour of Beat haunts with a cappuccino at **Caffè Trieste** (page 91) or a cocktail at **Vesuvio** (page 60). You might also want to climb to the top of **Coit Tower** (page 50) to catch a great view of the city skyline—look west to find crooked **Lombard Street** (page 50).

Drive or take a cab to the Mission District for the afternoon. If you're hungry, enjoy an authentic Mission burrito at **Papalote Mexican Grill** (page 94). For something sweeter, try **Tartine Bakery** (page 94). History buffs will want to visit 18th-century **Mission Dolores** (page 53). Or check out the quirky Mission stores **826 Valencia** (page 72) and its neighbor **Paxton Gate** (page 72). Grab a cocktail and an empanada at the rooftop **El Techo de Lolinda** (page 61).

Then head out to catch some live music at one of San Francisco's great music venues like **The Fillmore** (page 64) or the **Great American Music Hall** (page 64). If you'd rather take in some other types of live entertainment, don't miss long-running, pop culture-skewering **Beach Blanket Babylon** (page 66) or a performance by the transgender entertainers at **AsiaSF** (page 59).

DAY 3

Start your day with a hearty New Orleans-style breakfast at **Brenda's French Soul Food** (page 87). Then head north out of the city to experience some of the Bay Area's impressive outdoors. Travel on U.S. 101 over the **Golden Gate Bridge** (page 52) to explore **Marin** (page 99), including **Muir Woods** (page 109), **Mount Tamalpais** (page 111), and **Muir Beach** (page 110). Stay the night at the English countryside-inspired **Pelican Inn** (page 111) or the luxurious **Cavallo Point Lodge** (page 102). Either way, grab a drink at Cavallo Point Lodge's **Farley Bar** (page 103) and a superb seafood sandwich at Sausalito's **Fish** (page 104).

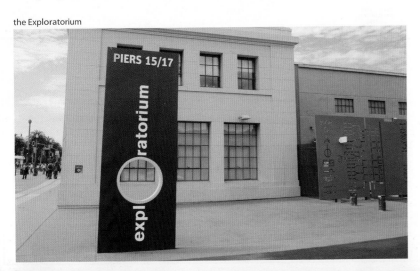

the Exploratorium

between Pier 15 and Pier 17 that records atmospheric measurements.

San Francisco Maritime Historical Park

The **San Francisco Maritime Historical Park** (900 Beach St., 415/561-7000, www.nps.gov/safr, daily 10am-4pm, adults $5, children free) comprises two parts: the visitors center museum on the bottom floor of the Argonaut Hotel and the ships at permanent dock across the street at the Hyde Street Pier. While the visitors center museum presents some of the long and amazing maritime history of San Francisco, the fun comes from climbing aboard the historic ships. The shiniest jewel of the museum's collection is the 1886 square-rigged *Balclutha,* a three-masted schooner. There are also several steamboats, including the workhorse ferry *Eureka* and a cool old steam paddle-wheel tugboat called the *Eppleton Hall.* Ranger-led tours and programs, included in the price of a ticket, make this inexpensive museum more than worthwhile. Check the website for details on the fall concert series.

Ghirardelli Square

Jammed in with Fisherman's Wharf and Pier 39, **Ghirardelli Square** (900 North Point St., 415/775-5500, www.ghirardellisq.com), pronounced "GEAR-ah-DEL-ee," has reinvented itself as an upscale shopping, dining, and living area. Its namesake, the famous **Ghirardelli Chocolate Factory** (900 North Point St., 415/474-3938, www.ghirardelli.

North Beach and Fisherman's Wharf

Lombard Street

The Beat Museum (540 Broadway, 800/537-6822, www.kerouac.com, daily 10am-7pm, adults $8, students and seniors $5) is rambling and occasionally fascinating. Displays explain how the term "Beatnik" was coined and go into detail about the obscenity trial that followed the publication of Beat poet Allen Ginsberg's *Howl and Other Poems*. Beat Generation fans can stare at Jack Kerouac's jacket and Neal Cassady's black-and-white-striped shirt that he wore while driving the bus trip chronicled in Tom Wolfe's *The Electric Kool-Aid Acid Test*. Displays illuminate the lives of lesser-known Beat characters like Gregory Corso and Lew Welch, a poet who disappeared in the mountains of California in 1971. An on-site bookstore sells iconic Beat works like Kerouac's *On the Road* and William S. Burroughs's *Naked Lunch*.

MARINA AND PACIFIC HEIGHTS

The Marina and Pacific Heights shelter some of the amazing amount of money that flows in

the city. The Marina is constructed on land-fill (sand dredged up from the bottom of the ocean and piled in what was once a marsh), a wealthy neighborhood with a couple of yacht harbors and lots of good museums, dining, and shopping.

Palace of Fine Arts

The Palace of Fine Arts (3301 Lyon St., 415/567-6642, www.palaceoffinearts.org) was originally meant to be nothing but a temporary structure built as a part of the Panama Pacific Exposition in 1915. But the lovely building won the hearts of San Franciscans, and a fund was started to preserve the Palace afterward. It houses the Palace of Fine Arts Theater, which hosts events nearly every day, from beauty pageants and national rock acts to conferences on the future of artificial intelligence.

Fort Mason Center

Once the Port of Embarkation from which the United States waged World War II in the Pacific, Fort Mason Center (Buchanan St. and Marina Blvd., 415/345-7500, www.fortmason.org, daily 9am-8pm, parking $2-14) now acts as home to numerous nonprofit, multicultural, and artistic organizations. Where soldiers and guns departed to fight the Japanese, visitors now find dance performances, independent theatrical productions, and art galleries. At any time of year, great shows are scheduled in the renovated historic white and red buildings of the complex; check the online calendar to see what is coming up during your visit.

Other fun features include installations of the Outdoor Exploratorium (www.exploratorium.edu/outdoor, daily dawn-dusk). Ranging all over Fort Mason, the Exploratorium exhibits appeal to all five senses (yes, even taste) and teach visitors about the world around them. You'll taste salt in local water supplies, hear a fog-horn, and see what causes the parking lot to crack and sink. It's free, and it's fascinating. Download a map from the website, or

SAN FRANCISCO BAY AREA

grab a guide from installation 5, Portable Observatories.

★ The Presidio

It seems strange to think of progressive, peace-loving San Francisco as a town with tremendous military history, yet the city's warlike past is nowhere more evident than at **The Presidio** (Montgomery St. and Lincoln Blvd., 415/561-4323, www.nps.gov/prsf, visitors center Thurs.-Sun. 10am-4pm, trails daily dawn-dusk, free). This sweeping stretch of land running along the San Francisco Headlands down to the Golden Gate has been a military installation since 1776, when the Spanish created their El Presidio del San Francisco fort on the site. In 1846 the U.S. Army took over the site (peacefully), and in 1848 the American Presidio military installation formally opened. It was abandoned by the military and became a national park in 1994. The Presidio had a role in every Pacific-related war from the Civil War through Desert Storm.

To orient yourself among the more than 800 buildings that make up the Presidio, start at the **Presidio Officers Club** (50 Moraga Ave., 415/561-4400, www.presidioofficersclub.com, Tues.-Sun. 10am-6pm), which re-opened as the Presidio's cultural and social center in the fall of 2014. The building's living room has a big fireplace and a view of the park, while the **Heritage Gallery** interprets seven eras of the Presidio to visitors. Fuel up at **Arguello** (415/561-3650, www.arguellosf.com, Wed.-Sat. 11am-9pm), a creative Mexican restaurant in the building. There's also **Warming Hut Bookstore & Café** (983 Marine Dr., 415/561-3040, daily 9am-5pm). As you explore the huge park, visit the pioneering aviation area **Crissy Field,** Civil War-era fortifications at **Fort Point,** and the **Walt Disney Family Museum** (104 Montgomery St., 415/345-6800, www.waltdisney.org, Wed.-Mon. 10am-6pm, adults $20, seniors and students $15, children 6-17 $12), which examines the cartoonist and animator's life. The Presidio is also home to art installations by Andy Goldsworthy, who works with natural materials. The most renowned is *Spire,* a sculpture that rises 90 feet into the air, utilizing 35 cypress tree trunks.

★ Golden Gate Bridge

People come from all over the world to see and walk the **Golden Gate Bridge** (U.S. 101/CA-1 at Lincoln Blvd., 415/921-5858, www.goldengatebridge.com, cars $6-7, pedestrians free). A marvel of human engineering constructed in 1936 and 1937, the suspension bridge spans the narrow "gate" from which the Pacific Ocean enters San Francisco Bay. On a clear day, pedestrians can see the whole Bay from the east sidewalk, then turn around to see the Pacific Ocean spreading out on the other side. Or take in the stunning bridge view from the Marin Headlands barracks, looking down from the northwest and in toward the city skyline.

The bridge itself is not golden, but a rich color called "international orange" that shines like gold when the sun sets behind it on a clear evening. Visitors beware: Not all days and precious few evenings at the bridge are clear. One of the most beautiful sights in San Francisco is the fog blowing in over the Golden Gate late in the afternoon. Unfortunately, once the fog stops blowing and settles in, the bridge is cold, damp, and viewless, so plan to come early in the morning, or pick spring or autumn for your best chance of a clear sight of this most famous and beautiful of structures.

The Golden Gate National Parks Conservancy has quit offering their Golden Gate Bridge Tours, but the nonprofit **City Guides** (415/557-4266, www.sfcityguides.org, donations welcome) leads bridge walks 2-3 times a week. Check their website for days and times.

CIVIC CENTER AND HAYES VALLEY

Some of the most interesting neighborhoods in the city cluster toward its center. The Civic Center functions as the heart of San Francisco and is actually the location of the mayor's office and much of San Francisco's government.

As the Civic Center melts toward Hayes Valley, the high culture of San Francisco appears. Near the border you'll find Davies Symphony Hall, home of the world-famous San Francisco Symphony, and the War Memorial Opera House. Catering to these notable establishments are some fabulous Hayes Valley hotels and restaurants.

City Hall

Look at San Francisco's **City Hall** (1 Dr. Carlton B. Goodlett Pl., 415/554-6139, www.sfgov.org, Mon.-Fri. 8am-8pm, free) and you'll think you've somehow been transported to Europe. The stately building with the gilded dome is the pride of the city and houses much of its government. (The dome is the world's fifth largest.) Complimentary 45-minute tours of City Hall are available weekdays at 10am, noon, and 2pm. You'll find a combination of historical grandeur and modern accessibility and convenience as you tour the Arthur Brown Jr.-designed edifice. The park-like square in front of City Hall is also enjoyable, although this area can get sketchy after dark.

Asian Art Museum

Across from City Hall is the **Asian Art Museum** (200 Larkin St., 415/581-3500, www.asianart.org, Tues.-Wed. and Fri.-Sun. 10am-5pm, Thurs. 10am-9pm, adults $15, seniors, students, and ages 13-17 $10, under age 12 free). Inside you'll have an amazing metaphorical window into the Asian cultures that have shaped and defined San Francisco and the Bay Area. The second and third floors of this intense museum are packed with great art from all across Asia, including a Chinese gilded Buddha dating from AD 338, the oldest known dated Chinese Buddha in the world. Sit down on a padded bench to admire paintings, sculpture, lacquered jade, textiles, jewels, and every type of art object imaginable. The breadth and diversity of Asian culture may stagger you; the museum's displays come from Japan, Vietnam, Tibet, and ancient China. Special exhibitions cost

extra—check the website to see what will be displayed on the ground-floor galleries when you're in town. The curators regularly rotate items from the permanent collection, so you'll probably encounter new beauty every time you visit.

Alamo Square

Possibly the most photographed neighborhood in San Francisco, **Alamo Square** (Hayes St. and Steiner St.) is home to the "painted ladies" on "postcard row." This is a row of stately Victorian mansions, all painted brilliant colors and immaculately maintained, that appear in many images of the city, including the opening sequence of the late 1980s-early 1990s sitcom *Full House*. Stroll in Alamo Square's green park and enjoy the serenity of this charming residential neighborhood.

MISSION AND CASTRO

Perhaps the most famous, or infamous, neighborhoods in the city are the Mission district and the Castro district. The Castro is the heart of gay San Francisco, with nightlife, festivals, and street-level activism centered on the LGBT community (not to mention leather bars and naughty shops).

With its mix of Latino immigrants, working artists, hipsters, and SUV-driving professionals, the Mission is a neighborhood bursting at the seams with idiosyncratic energy. Changing from block to block, the zone manages to be blue-collar, edgy, and gentrified all at once. The heart of the neighborhood is still very much Latin American, with delicious burritos and *pupusas* around every corner. It's a haven for international restaurants and real bargains in thrift shops, along with the hippest (and most self-conscious) clubs in the city.

Mission Dolores

Formally named Misión San Francisco de Asís, **Mission Dolores** (3321 16th St., 415/621-8203, www.missiondolores.org, May-Oct. daily 9am-4:30pm, Nov.-Apr. daily 9am-4pm, donation adults $5, seniors and students

$3) was founded in 1776. Today, the mission is the oldest intact building in the city, survivor of the 1906 earthquake and fire, the 1989 Loma Prieta quake, and more than 200 years of use. Visit the Old Mission Museum and the Basilica, which house artifacts from the Native Americans and the Spanish of the 18th century. The beauty and grandeur of the Mission recall the heyday of the Spanish empire in California, so important to the history of the state.

Precita Eyes Mural Arts and Visitors Center

The Mission is known for its wildly imaginative and colorful murals that decorate buildings and alleys. The brightly painted **Precita Eyes Mural Arts and Visitors Center** (2981 24th St., 415/285-2287, www. precitaeyes.org, Mon.-Fri. 10am-5pm, Sat. 10am-4pm, Sun. noon-4pm) provides mural tours, including the two-hour **Classic Mission Mural Walk** (Sat.-Sun. 1:30pm, adults $15-20, seniors and students $10, children 12-17 $6, children under 12 $3). The tour starts with a presentation at the center before striking out on a six-block walk to spot murals.

GOLDEN GATE PARK AND THE HAIGHT
Golden Gate Park

At 3.5 miles long and 0.5 miles wide, **Golden Gate Park** (main entrance at Stanyan St. at Fell St., McLaren Lodge Visitors Center, 501 Stanyan St., 415/831-2700, www.golden-gate-park.com, daily 5am-midnight, free) is a huge urban oasis even larger than New York's Central Park. Golden Gate is home to some of the city's finest attractions including the de Young Museum, the Japanese Tea Garden, and the California Academy of Sciences. There are also natural features including forests, formal gardens, and a buffalo pasture. In addition to its many sights, Golden Gate Park is also where San Francisco's Outside Lands and Hardly Strictly Bluegrass music festivals take place.

Haight-Ashbury

The neighborhood surrounding the intersection of **Haight and Ashbury Streets** (known locally as "the Haight") is best known for the wave of countercultural energy that broke out here in the 1960s. The area initially was a magnet for drifters, dropouts, and visionaries who preached and practiced a heady blend of peace, love, and psychedelic drugs. It reached a fever pitch during 1967's Summer of Love, with pioneering music acts like the Grateful Dead, Jefferson Airplane, and Janis Joplin.

Today, thousands of visitors stand at the iconic intersection, and what they see is Ben & Jerry's. The district is still home to plenty of independent businesses, including vintage stores, places to get pierced and tattooed, and, of course, head shops. Chain stores are interspersed with the indies, reminding visitors that the power of capitalism can intrude anywhere—even in a countercultural center.

A prettier aspect of local gentrification is the restored Victorian houses in the Haight. Stay in the bright, funky Red Victorian or check out the private homes on Page Street and throughout the neighborhood. To learn more about the history of the Haight and to walk past the famed homes of the Grateful Dead and Jefferson Airplane, take the **Flower Power Walking Tour** (starts at intersection of Stanyan St. and Waller St., 415/863-1621, www.hippygourmet.com, Tues. and Sat. 9:30am, Fri. 11am, $20).

★ de Young Museum

Take some time out to visit the **de Young Museum** (50 Hagiwara Tea Garden Dr., 415/750-3600, http://deyoung.famsf.org, Tues.-Thurs. and Sat.-Sun. 9:30am-5:15pm, Fri. 9:30am-8:45pm, adults $10, seniors $7, students and ages 13-17 $6, children under age 12 free) in Golden Gate Park. The collections at the de Young include works in various media: painting, sculpture, textiles, ceramics, modern graphic designs, and contemporary crafts. Some collections focus on artists from the United States, while many others contain art from around the world. Rotating exhibitions range from masterpieces to modernism. Head to the top of the tower for a 360-degree panoramic view of San Francisco. For a special treat, brave the lines and grab a meal at the museum's café.

California Academy of Sciences

A triumph of sustainable scientific principles, the **California Academy of Sciences** (55 Music Concourse Dr., 415/379-8000, www.calacademy.org, Mon.-Sat. 9:30am-5pm, Sun. 11am-5pm, adults $35, seniors, students, and ages 12-17 $30, ages 4-11 $25) drips with ecological perfection. From its grass-covered roof to its underground aquarium, visitors can explore every part of the universe. Wander through a steamy endangered rain forest contained inside a giant glass dome, or travel through outer space in the high-tech planetarium. More studious nature lovers can spend days examining every inch of the Kimball Natural History Museum, including the 87-foot-long blue whale skeleton. The Academy of Sciences takes pains to make itself kid-friendly, with interactive exhibits, thousands of live animals, and endless opportunities for learning. How could kids not love

a museum where the guards by the elevators have butterfly nets to catch the occasional "exhibit" that's trying to escape?

Japanese Tea Garden

The **Japanese Tea Garden** (75 Hagiwara Tea Garden Dr., 415/752-1171, http://japaneseteagardensf.com, Mar.-Oct. daily 9am-6pm, Nov.-Feb. daily 9am-4:45pm, adults $7, seniors and ages 12-17 $5, under age 12 $2) is a haven of peace and tranquility that's a local favorite within the park. The planting and design of the garden began in 1894 for the California Exposition. Today, the flourishing garden displays a wealth of beautiful flora, including stunning examples of rare Chinese and Japanese plants, some quite old. As you stroll along the paths, you'll come upon sculptures, bridges, ponds, a bronze Buddha, and even traditional *tsukubai* (a tea ceremony sink). Visit the teahouse, the brilliant pagoda and temple, and the gift shop as well.

San Francisco Botanical Gardens

Take a bucolic walk in the middle of Golden Gate Park by visiting the **San Francisco Botanical Gardens** (1199 9th Ave., at Lincoln Way, 415/661-1316, www.sfbotanicalgarden.

the stunning architecture of the de Young Museum

Golden Gate Park and the Haight

org, Apr.-Sept. daily 7:30am-6pm, Oct.-Nov. and Feb.-Mar. daily 7:30am-5pm, Nov.-Jan. daily 7:30am-4pm, adults $8, students and seniors $6, ages 5-11 $2, families $15, under age 4 and city residents with ID free). The 55-acre gardens are home to more than 8,000 species of plants from around the world, including a California Natives garden and a shady redwood forest. Fountains, ponds, meadows, and lawns are interwoven with the flowers and trees to create a peaceful, serene setting in the middle of the crowded city. The Botanical

Gardens are a great place to kick back with a book and a snack; the plants will keep you in quiet company as you rev up to tackle another round of touring.

Conservatory of Flowers

Lying at the northeastern entrance to Golden Gate Park, the **Conservatory of Flowers** (100 John F. Kennedy Dr., 415/831-2090, www.conservatoryofflowers.org, Tues.-Sun. 10am-4:30pm, adults $8, students and seniors $5, ages 5-11 $2) blooms year-round.

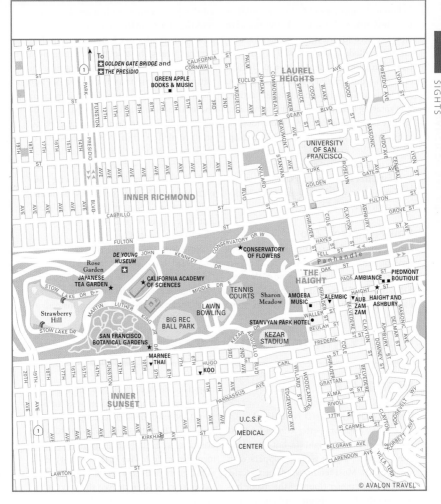

The exotic flowers grow in several "galleries" within the enormous, glassy-white Victorian-style greenhouse. Rare, slightly scary orchids twine around rainforest trees, eight-foot lily pads float serenely on still waters, and cheerful seasonal flowers spill out of containers in the potted plant gallery.

Public tours are available daily (11am, 12:30pm, and 2:30pm), as long as docents are available. Strollers are not permitted inside the conservatory; wheelchairs and power chairs are.

Legion of Honor

The full-size bronze cast of Rodin's *The Thinker* on the way into the **Legion of Honor** (100 34th Ave., at Clement St., 415/750-3600, http://legionofhonor.famsf.org, Tues.-Sun. 9:30am-5:15pm, adults $10, seniors $7, students and ages 13-17 $6, under age 13 free) is a sign that this ornate building sitting on its lonely promontory in Lincoln Park houses some serious art. A gift to the city from philanthropist Alma Spreckels in 1924, this French beaux arts-style building was built to honor the memory of California soldiers who died in World War I. Today, visitors can view the second-finest collection of sculptor August Rodin's works as well as gorgeous European paintings, decorative arts, ancient artifacts from around the Mediterranean, and thousands of drawings by great artists. The rotating temporary exhibits sometimes include fascinating looks into more modern artists like Man Ray and Marcel Duchamp. Visit the Florence Gould Theater or come to the museum on a Saturday or Sunday at 4pm for a free organ concert on the immense Skinner Organ, which is integral to the building's structure.

San Francisco Zoo

Lions, tigers, bears, penguins, and a host of other animals reside in the **San Francisco Zoo** (Sloat Blvd. at 47th Ave., 415/753-7080, www.sfzoo.org, summer daily 10am-5pm, winter daily 10am-4pm,

adults $17, seniors $14, ages 4-14 $11), making it a favorite excursion for locals and visitors all year long. Over the last several years the zoo has undergone a transformation, becoming an example for naturalized habitats and conservatory zoo practices. Today, animal lovers can enjoy the native plants and funny faces in the lemur habitat, the families of meerkats, and the bird sanctuary. Families come to check out the wealth of interactive children's exhibits as well as the various exotic animals. However, it's wise to bring your own picnic—the food offerings at the zoo have not improved as much as the habitats. But watch out for gulls—they fly low and love to steal snacks.

Note that the official address is 1 Zoo Boulevard, but if you put that address into a GPS system, it will take you to the zoo's service entrance. Go to the gate at the corner of Sloat Boulevard and 47th Avenue instead.

Entertainment and Events

NIGHTLIFE
Bars
UNION SQUARE AND NOB HILL

These ritzy areas are better known for their shopping than their nightlife, but a few bars hang in there, plying weary shoppers with good drinks. Most tend toward the upscale. Some inhabit upper floors of the major hotels, like the **Tonga Room and Hurricane Bar** (950 Mason St., 415/772-5278, www.fairmont.com, www.tongaroom.com, Wed.-Thurs. and Sun. 5pm-11:30pm, Fri.-Sat. 5pm-12:30am), where an over-the-top tiki theme adds a whimsical touch to the stately Fairmont Hotel on Nob Hill. Enjoy the tropical atmosphere with a fruity rum drink topped with a classic paper umbrella. Be prepared for the bar's virtual tropical storms that roll in every once and a while.

Part live-music venue, part elegant bar, **Top of the Mark** (InterContinental Mark

Hopkins, 999 California St., 415/392-3434, www.intercontinentalmarkhopkins.com, Sun. 5pm-11:30pm, Mon.-Thurs. 4:30pm-11:30pm, Fri.-Sat. 4:30pm-12:30am) has something for every discerning taste in nighttime entertainment. Since World War II, the views at the top of the InterContinental Mark Hopkins Hotel have drawn visitors to see the city lights. Tuesdays are movie nights, while bands play live music Wednesday-Sunday nights. The dress code is business casual or better and is enforced, so leave the jeans in your room. Have a top-shelf martini, and let your toes tap along.

Off Union Square, **Lefty O'Doul's Restaurant & Cocktail Lounge** (333 Geary St., 415/982-8900, www.leftyodouls.biz, daily 7am-2am) is named after the San Francisco native major-league baseball player. This informal sports bar with 12 TVs serves up hearty fare like hand-carved roast beef or roasted turkey dinners.

FINANCIAL DISTRICT AND SOMA

In urban-renewed SoMa (South of Market), upscale wine bars have become an evening institution. Among the trendiest is **District** (216 Townsend St., 415/896-2120, www.districtsf.com, Mon.-Fri. 4pm-close, Sat. 5pm-2am, Sun. 10am-2pm). It features bare brick walls, simple wooden furniture, and a big U-shaped bar at the center of the room with wineglasses hanging above it. While you can get a cocktail or a beer, the point of coming to District is to sip the finest wines from California, Europe, and beyond. With more than 40 wines available by the glass each night, it's easy to find a favorite, or enjoy a flight of three similar wines to compare. A lovely lounge menu offers small portions of delicacies to enhance your tasting experience.

Secret passwords, a hidden library, and an art deco vibe make **Bourbon and Branch** (505 Jones St., 415/346-1735, www.bourbonandbranch.com, daily 6pm-2am, reservations suggested) a must for lovers of the brown stuff. Tucked behind a nameless brown door, this resurrected 1920s speakeasy evokes its Prohibition-era past with passwords and secret passages. A business-class elite sips rare bourbon and scotch in dark secluded booths, while those without reservations step into the hidden library.

The **Rickhouse** (246 Kearney St., 415/398-2827, www.rickhousebar.com, Tues.-Fri. 3pm-2am, Sat. 6pm-2am, Mon. 5pm-2am) feels like a country shack plopped down in the midst of the Financial District. The artisanal cocktail bar draws in the city's plentiful young urban hipsters. It's dimly lit, the walls and floors are wood, and stacks of barrels and old bottles line the mantle. There's also live music on Saturday and Monday nights.

Take in one of the dinner shows at SOMA institution **AsiaSF** (201 9th St., 415/255-2742, www.asiasf.com, Fri. 7:15pm-2am, Sat. 5pm-2am, Wed.-Thurs. and Sun. 7:15pm-11pm, dinner and show $40-70). The transgender performers and servers, known as the Ladies of AsiaSF, strut across the top of the bar while lip-synching pop songs as diners feast on a three-course Asian fusion meal. It's rowdy, raunchy fun. The food is better than you might expect, especially the chicken satay appetizer, the miso-glazed salmon, and the banana beignets. Weekend reservations for dinner and a show include free admission to the dance floor downstairs.

Lefty O'Doul's Restaurant & Cocktail Lounge

CHINATOWN

Nightlife in Chinatown runs to dark, quiet dive bars filled with locals. Perhaps the perfect Chinatown dive, **Li Po Lounge** (916 Grant Ave., 415/982-0072, www.lipolounge. com, daily 2pm-2am, cash only) has an appropriately dark and slightly spooky atmosphere that recalls the opium dens of another century. Cheap drinks and Chinese dice games attract locals, and it's definitely helpful to speak Cantonese. But even an English-speaking out-of-town visitor can get a good, cheap (and strong!) mai tai or beer.

For dive bar aficionados, the **Buddha Lounge** (901 Grant Ave., 415/362-1792, daily 1pm-2am, cash only) is worth a stop. Expect a long bar, a humorous bartender, and a few regulars playing dice. One wall is decorated by a strange mural of a dragon and a peacock. To use the dungeon-like restroom, you need to have a gate buzzed open by the bartender. Expect to be messed with.

Chinatown entrance

NORTH BEACH AND FISHERMAN'S WHARF

Jack Kerouac loved **Vesuvio** (255 Columbus Ave., 415/362-3370, www.vesuvio.com, daily 6am-2am), which is why it's probably North Beach's most famous saloon. This cozy, eclectic bi-level hideout is an easy place to spend the afternoon with a pint of Anchor Steam. Its eclectic decor includes tables decorated with tarot cards.

Almost across the street from Vesuvio is one of the oldest and most celebrated bars in the city. **Tosca** (242 Columbus Ave., 415/986-9651, http://toscacafesf.com, daily 5pm-2am) has an unpretentious yet glam 1940s style. Hunter S. Thompson once tended bar here when the owner was out at the dentist. The jukebox plays grand opera to the patrons clustered in the big red booths. Locals love the lack of trendiness, the classic cocktails, and the occasional star sightings.

Known for its colorful clientele and cluttered decor, **Specs** (12 William Saroyan Pl., 415/421-4112, Mon.-Fri. 4:30pm-2am, Sat.-Sun. 5pm-2am, cash only) is a dive bar in a

North Beach alley. Its full name is the Specs' Twelve Adler Museum Café.

MARINA AND PACIFIC HEIGHTS

The Marina District's Chestnut Street is known for its high-end restaurants and swanky clientele. The **Horseshoe Tavern** (2024 Chestnut St., 415/346-1430, http://horseshoetavern-sf.com, Mon.-Thurs. noon-2am, Fri.-Sat. 10am-2am) is a place for people to let their hair down, shoot pool, and drink without pretension.

Get to really know your fellow beer drinkers at the tiny **Black Horse London Pub** (1514 Union St., 415/678-5697, www.blackhorselondon.com, Mon.-Thurs. 5pm-midnight, Fri. 2pm-midnight, Sat.-Sun. 11am-midnight, cash only), which can accommodate just nine people. Bottles of beer are served from a clawfoot bathtub behind the bar.

CIVIC CENTER AND HAYES VALLEY

Hayes Valley bleeds into Lower Haight (Haight St. between Divisadero St. and

Octavia Blvd.) and supplies most of the neighborhood bars. The independent spirit of the Haight lives on in spite of encroaching commercialism at the **Toronado** (547 Haight St., 415/863-2276, www.toronado.com, daily 11:30am-2am). This dimly lit haven maintains one of the finest beer selections in the nation, with a changing roster of several dozen microbrews on tap, including many hard-to-find Belgian ales. These are more potent than typical domestic beers and may have an alcohol content as high as 12 percent.

If you'd rather drink a cocktail, head over to **Smuggler's Cove** (650 Gough St., 415/869-1900, http://smugglerscovesf.com, daily 5pm-1:15am). The drink menu includes 70 cocktails and an impressive number of rare rums.

If what you really want is a dive bar, **Place Pigalle** (520 Hayes St., 415/552-2671, http://placepigallesf.com, Wed.-Sun. 2pm-2am, Mon.-Tues. 5pm-2am) is the place for you. This hidden gem in Hayes Valley offers over 20 craft beers on tap. It also has a pool table, lots of sofas for lounging, and an uncrowded, genuinely laid-back vibe on weeknights and even sometimes on weekends. The too-cool-for-school hipster vibe somehow missed this place, which manages to maintain its friendly neighborhood feel.

MISSION

These neighborhoods seem to hold a whole city's worth of bars. The Mission, despite a recent upswing in its economy, still has plenty of no-frills bars, many with a Latino theme. And, of course, men seeking men flock to the Castro's endless array of gay bars. For lesbians, the Mission might be a better bet.

Trick Dog (3010 20th St., 415/471-2999, www.trickdogbar.com, daily 3pm-2am) is shaking up the city's cocktail scene and was nominated for a 2015 James Beard Award for its outstanding bar program. Drinks use unexpected ingredients like dandelion, lychee, and horseradish (not all at the same time). The small food menu includes thrice-cooked fries, Scotch eggs, and a standout kale salad.

A red-lit bar and hipster hangout, **Amnesia** (853 Valencia St., 415/970-0012, www.amnesiathebar.com, daily 6pm-2am) has entertainment every night of the week. Among the most popular performances are the ongoing Monday bluegrass nights and Wednesday jazz nights.

Dalva (3121 16th St., 415/252-7740, http://dalvasf.com, daily 4pm-2am) is a small but sophisticated oasis in an ocean of overcrowded Mission hipster hangouts. You'll find dramatic high ceilings, modern paintings, and a jukebox stuffed with indie rock and electronica. Way back in the depths of the club, the Hideaway bar serves up a delectable array of cocktails poured by a rotating staff of local celebrity mixologists.

Excellent draft beers, tasty barbecue plates, and a motorcycle-inclined crowd give **Zeitgeist** (199 Valencia St., 415/255-7505, www.zeitgeistsf.com, daily 9am-2am) a punk-rock edge. This Mission favorite endears itself to all sorts, thanks to its spacious outdoor beer garden, 40 beers on tap, and popular Bloody Marys.

Get a sweeping view of the city with superb South American cocktails at **El Techo de Lolinda** (2518 Mission St., 415/550-6970, http://eltechosf.com, Mon.-Thurs. 4pm-11pm, Fri. 4pm-1am, Sat. 11pm-1am, Sun. 11am-11pm), a rooftop bar associated with the Argentinean steakhouse Lolinda. They serve margaritas by the pitcher, caipirinhas (a Brazilian cocktail resembling a mojito), and the best Cuba Libre in the city. The small food menu includes superb snacks like empanadas, ceviche, and a variety of skewers.

GOLDEN GATE PARK AND THE HAIGHT

Haight Street crowds head out in droves to the **Alembic** (1725 Haight St., 415/666-0822, www.alembicbar.com, Mon.-Fri. 4pm-2am, Sat.-Sun. noon-2am) for artisanal cocktails laced with American spirits. On par with the whiskey and bourbon menu is the cuisine including rich fare like jerk-spiced duck hearts and bone marrow.

Featured in an episode of Anthony Bourdain's travel show *No Reservations,* **Zam Zam** (1633 Haight St., 415/861-2545, http://zamzambar.com, Mon.-Fri. 3pm-2am, Sat.-Sun. 1pm-2am, cash only) is an old-school bar with an Arabian feel. Zam Zam doesn't take credit cards, but it does have an Arabian mural behind the U-shaped bar, where an interesting mix of locals and visitors congregate for the cheap drinks.

Clubs

Some folks are surprised at the smallish list of San Francisco clubs. The truth is, San Francisco just isn't a see-and-be-seen, hip-new-club-every-week kind of town. In the city, you'll find gay clubs, vintage dance clubs, Goth clubs, and the occasional underground Burner rave mixed in with the more standard dance floor-and-DJ fare.

If you're up for a full night of club hopping and don't want to deal with transit headaches, several bus services can ferry your party from club to club. Many of these offer VIP entrance to clubs and will stop wherever you want to go. **Think Escape** (800/823-7249, www.thinkescape.com) has buses and limos with drivers and guides to get you to the hottest spots with ease.

UNION SQUARE AND NOB HILL

Harry Denton's Starlight Room (450 Powell St., 21st Fl., 415/395-8595, www.starlightroomsf.com, Tues.-Thurs. 5pm-midnight, Fri.-Sat. 5pm-2am, cover up to $20) brings the flamboyant side of San Francisco downtown. Enjoy a cocktail in the early evening or a nightcap and dessert after the theater in this truly old-school nightclub. Dress in your best to match the glitzy red-and-gold decor and mirrors. Whoop it up at "Sunday's a Drag" shows (Sun. 11:30am and 1pm, $60). Reservations are recommended.

Defying San Francisco expectation, **Ruby Skye** (420 Mason St., 415/693-0777, www.rubyskye.com, Thurs. 9pm-2am, Fri.-Sat. 9pm-4am, cover charge, dress code enforced) books top DJs and occasional live acts into a big, crowded dance club. The building, dating from 1890, was originally the Stage Door Theatre, but it has been redone to create dance floors, bars, DJ booths, and VIP spaces. Crowds can get big on the weekend, and the patrons tend to be young and pretty and looking for action. The sound system rocks, so conversation isn't happening, and the drinks tend toward overpriced vodka and Red Bull.

FINANCIAL DISTRICT AND SOMA

It's dark, it's dank, and it's very Goth. The **Cat Club** (1190 Folsom St., 415/703-8965, www.sfcatclub.com, Tues.-Sat. 9pm-3am, cover charge) gets pretty energetic on 1980s dance nights, but it's still a great place to go on Goth-industrial-electronica nights. There's no dress code at the Cat Club, unlike many local nightspots. You'll find a friendly crowd, decent bartenders, strong drinks, and easy access to smoking areas. Each of the two rooms has its own DJ. Check the website to find the right party night for you, and expect the crowd to heat up after 11pm.

Monarch (101 6th St., 415/284-9774, www.monarchsf.com, bar hours Mon.-Fri. 5:30pm-2am, Sat.-Sun. 8pm-2am) is aiming to be a one-stop after-dark venue. Upstairs is a Victorian-inspired cocktail lounge, while the downstairs club hosts international and local DJs. You might also catch offbeat performers like acrobats twirling from the ceilings.

MARINA AND PACIFIC HEIGHTS

Clubs in the Marina are all about the trendy and the spendy. The **Hi-Fi Lounge** (2125 Lombard St., 415/345-8663, www.maximumproductions.com, Wed.-Sat. 8pm-2am, cover charge Fri.-Sat.) personifies the fun that can be had in smaller San Francisco venues. This one-floor wonder with a tiny dance floor gets incredibly crowded. Yet even the locals have a good time when they come out to the Hi-Fi. The decor is funky and fun, and the patrons are young and affluent. Most visitors find the staff friendly and the bartenders attentive. Because it's the Marina, come early to get decent parking and to avoid the cover charge. On Thursday and Friday, early birds get $1 draft beer.

CIVIC CENTER AND HAYES VALLEY

Not your typical slick, shiny nightclub, the **Rickshaw Stop** (155 Fell St., 415/861-2011, www.rickshawstop.com, Wed.-Thurs. 5pm-midnight, Fri.-Sat. 5pm-2am, cover $5-18) in the Hayes Valley neighborhood welcomes one and all with a cavernous lower bar, stage area, and dance floor, and a quirky balcony area complete with comfy old sofas. Up-and-coming live acts play here, DJs spin, and special events and parties add to the action almost every week. Have a drink, enjoy the music, and get comfortable—you'll feel almost as though you're in a friendly neighborhood coffee shop (albeit a really big one) than in some fancy nightspot. Check the website for events and club hours, as the schedule varies widely.

MISSION AND CASTRO

The Mission and the Castro are popular clubbing districts in San Francisco. Naturally the biggest concentration of gay clubs is in the Castro.

Mighty (119 Utah St., 415/626-7001, www.mighty119.com, Thurs.-Sat. 10pm-4am) brings big-name DJs including Mark Farina and Miguel Migs to the Mission. If you are not feeling the music in the big room, migrate to the smaller back area.

Part club and part art gallery, **Public Works** (161 Erie St., 415/496-6738, http://publicsf.com, Wed.-Thurs. 10pm-2am, Fri.-Sat. 10pm-4am) hosts everything from DJ sets by Basement Jaxx to *The Moth* StorySLAM. They have a cash-only bar.

Gay and Lesbian

San Francisco's gay nightlife has earned a worldwide rep for both the quantity and quality of options. In fact, the gay club scene totally outdoes the straight club scene for frolicsome, fabulous fun. While the city's queer nightlife caters more to gay men than to lesbians, there's plenty of space available for partiers of all persuasions. For a more comprehensive list of San Francisco's queer bars and clubs, visit http://sanfrancisco.gaycities.com/bars.

You'll have no trouble finding a gay bar in the Castro. One of the best is called simply **Q Bar** (456 Castro St., 415/864-2877, www.qbarsf.com, Mon.-Fri. 4pm-2am, Sat.-Sun. 2pm-2am). Just look for the red neon "Bar" sign set in steel out front. Inside, find the fabulous red decor known as "retro-glam," delicious top-shelf cocktails, and thrumming beats spun by popular DJs almost every night of the week. Unlike many Castro establishments, Q Bar caters to pretty much everybody: gay men, gay women, and gay-friendly straight folks. You'll find a coat check and adequate restroom facilities, and the strength of the drinks will make you want to stay awhile.

Unlike some of the harder-core Castro gay clubs, **Truck** (1900 Folsom St., 415/252-0306, www.trucksf.com, Tues.-Fri. 4pm-2am, Sat.-Sun. 2pm-2am) offers a friendly neighborhood vibe. Truck lures in patrons with cheap drinks, friendly bartenders, and theme nights every week. When it rains outside, they offer two-for-one cocktails.

The Lookout (3600 16th St., 415/431-0306, www.lookoutsf.com, Mon.-Fri. 3:30pm-2am, Sat.-Sun. 12:30pm-2am, cover charge) gets its name and much of its rep from its balcony overlooking the iconic Castro neighborhood. Get up there for some primo people-watching as you sip your industrial-strength alcoholic concoctions and nibble on surprisingly edible bar snacks and pizza. The Lookout hosts "events" that come with a cover charge.

Yes, there's a Western-themed gay bar in San Francisco. **The Cinch Saloon** (1723 Polk St., 415/776-4162, http://cinchsf.com, Mon.-Fri. 9am-2am, Sat.-Sun. 6am-2am) has a laid-back (no pun intended), friendly, male-oriented vibe that's all but lost in the once gay, now gentrified Polk Street hood. Expect fewer females and strong drinks to go with the unpretentious decor and atmosphere.

Live Music
ROCK AND POP

San Francisco is one of the best cities in the country to take in live music. Great Bay Area bands include Metallica, Santana, and newcomers like Mikal Cronin and The Fresh & Onlys. Almost any act touring the nation stops here.

With its marble columns and ornate balconies, the **Great American Music Hall** (859 O'Farrell St., 415/885-0750, www.slimspresents.com, prices vary) is one of the city's nicest places to see a nationally touring act. The venue has the bragging rights of hosting Arcade Fire and Patti Smith a few years back.

Opened in the late 1960s, **The Fillmore** (1805 Geary Blvd., 415/346-6000, www.thefillmore.com, prices vary) became legendary by hosting performances by rock acts like the Grateful Dead, Jefferson Airplane, and Carlos Santana. These days, all sorts of national touring acts stop by, sometimes for multiple nights. The Fillmore is also known for its distinctive poster art: Attendees to certain sold-out shows are given commemorative posters.

The **Warfield** (982 Market St., 415/345-0900, www.thewarfieldtheatre.com, prices vary) is one of the older rock venues in the city. Its configuration is that of a traditional theater, with a raised stage, an open orchestra section below it, and two balconies. There's limited table seating on the lowest level (mostly by reservation), reserved seats in the balconies, and open standing in the orchestra section. The Warfield books all sorts of big name acts, from John Prine to the Wu-Tang Clan. There's no parking here; you'll need to park in a public parking structure, and you'll pay for the privilege.

BLUES AND JAZZ

The neighborhood surrounding Union Square is one of the most fertile areas in San Francisco for live music. Whether you're into blues, rock, or even country, you'll find a spot to have a drink and listen to some wonderful live tunes.

The **Boom Boom Room** (1601 Fillmore St., 415/673-8000, www.boomboomblues.com, Tues.-Thurs. 4pm-2am, Fri. 4pm-2:30am, Sat. 3pm-2:30am, Sun. 3pm-1:30am) is where you'll find the latest in a legacy of live blues, boogie, groove, soul, and funk music. The Boom Boom Room is just across from The Fillmore, so stop in before or after the bigger shows across the road.

Biscuits and Blues (401 Mason St.,

legendary music venue Biscuits and Blues

415/292-2583, www.biscuitsandblues.com, Tues.-Thurs. 5:30pm-11pm, Fri.-Sat. 5:30pm-11:30pm, Sun. 5pm-10:30pm, prices vary) is a local musicians' favorite. Just around the corner from the big live drama theaters, this house dedicates itself to jazz and blues. Headliners have included Joe Louis Walker, Jimmy Thackery, and Jim "Kimo" West. One of the best things about this club is that you can, in fact, get biscuits as well as blues: Dinner is served nightly and features a surprisingly varied and upscale menu combining California cuisine with the mystical flavors of New Orleans. Show up early to enjoy a jam session and a meal, then stay on for the main acts and headliners (and, of course, cocktails).

Comedy

San Francisco's oldest comedy club, the **Punch Line** (444 Battery St., 415/397-7573, www.punchlinecomedyclub.com, hours and prices vary) is an elegant and intimate venue that earned its top-notch reputation with stellar headliners such as Ellen DeGeneres, Dave Chappelle, and the late Robin Williams. An on-site bar keeps the audience primed.

Cobb's Comedy Club (915 Columbus Ave., 415/928-4320, www.cobbscomedy.com, showtimes and cover vary, two-drink minimum) has played host to star comedians such as Jerry Seinfeld, Sarah Silverman, and Jim Norton since 1982. The 425-seat venue offers a full dinner menu and a bar to slake your thirst. Check your show's start time; some comics don't follow the usual Cobb's schedule.

THE ARTS
Theater

For a great way to grab last-minute theater tickets, walk right up to the **Union Square TIX** booth (350 Powell St., Union Square, 415/430-1140, www.tixbayarea.com, daily 10am-6pm). TIX sells same-day, half-price, no-refund tickets to all kinds of shows across the city. If you've got your heart set on a specific musical or play in a big theater, get to the booth early in the day and steel yourself for possible disappointment—especially on

weekends, when many top-shelf shows sell out. If you're flexible, you'll almost certainly find something available at a reasonable price. TIX also sells half-price tickets to same-day shows online—check the website at 11am daily for up-to-date deals.

If you really, really need to see a major musical while you're in San Francisco, check out **SHN** (www.shnsf.com). SHN operates the Orpheum, the Curran, and the Golden Gate Theater—the three venues where big Broadway productions land when they come to town.

UNION SQUARE AND NOB HILL

Just up from Union Square, on Geary Street, the traditional San Francisco theater district continues to entertain crowds almost every day of the week. The old Geary Theater is now the permanent home of **A.C.T.** (405 Geary St., 415/749-2228, www.act-sf.org, prices vary). A.C.T. puts on a season filled with big-name, big-budget productions. Each season sees an array of high-production-value musicals such as *Urinetown*, classics by the likes of Sam Shepard and Somerset Maugham, and intriguing new works; you might even get to see a world premiere. Don't expect to find street parking on Geary. Discount parking is available with a ticket stub from A.C.T. at the Mason-O'Farrell garage around the corner. Tickets can be reasonably priced, especially on weeknights. The high-altitude second balcony seats look straight down to the stage; take care if you're prone to vertigo.

The **Curran Theater** (445 Geary St., 888/746-1799, www.shnsf.com, prices vary), next door to A.C.T., has a state-of-the-art stage for high-budget productions. Audiences have watched *Les Misérables* and *War Horse* from the plush red-velvet seats. Expect to pay a premium for tickets to these shows, which can sometimes run at the Curran for months or even years. Children under age five aren't permitted.

At the **EXIT Theatre** (156 Eddy St., 415/931-1094, www.theexit.org), down in the Tenderloin, you'll see plenty of unusual experimental plays, many by local play-wrights. The EXIT also participates in the annual San Francisco Fringe Festival (415/931-1094, www.sffringe.org, Sept.).

NORTH BEACH AND FISHERMAN'S WHARF

There's one live show in the city that is al-ways different, yet it's been running con-tinuously for over four decades. This musical revue is crazy, wacky, and offbeat, and it pretty much defines live theater in San Francisco. It's Beach Blanket Babylon (678 Green St., 415/421-4222, www.beach-blanketbabylon.com, shows Wed.-Fri. 8pm, Sat. 6:30pm and 9:30pm, Sun. 2pm and 5pm, July only Tues. 8pm, $25-130). Because it mocks current pop culture, the show evolves almost continuously to take advantage of tabloid treasures and take aim at new celeb-rities and politicians. There are silly puns and the occasional dated joke, but the cast's exuberance and skills will win you over. And you'll never forget the hats! While minors are welcome at the Sunday matinees, eve-ning shows can get pretty racy, and liquor is served, so these are restricted to attendees 21 and over.

MARINA AND PACIFIC HEIGHTS

Beyond the bright lights of Geary and Market Streets lie tiny up-and-coming (or down-and-going, depending) theaters, many of which produce new plays by local playwrights. One of the best known of the "small" theaters, the Magic Theatre (Fort Mason Center, 2 Marina Blvd., Bldg. D, 3rd Fl., 415/441-8822, http://magictheatre.org, prices vary) produced Sam Shepard's new works back before he was anyone special. They're still committed to new works, so when you go to a show at the Magic, you're taking a chance or having an adventure, depending on how you look at it.

At the Palace of Fine Arts Theatre (3301 Lyon St., 415/567-6642, www.palaceof-finearts.org, cover varies) you'll find acces-sible avant-garde performing arts pieces, live musical performance, dance recitals, and the

Curran Theater

occasional children's musical recital or black-and-white film.

CIVIC CENTER AND HAYES VALLEY

Down on Market Street, the Orpheum Theater (1192 Market St., 888/746-1799, www.shnsf.com, prices vary) runs touring productions of popular Broadway musicals including *The Book of Mormon* and *Phantom of the Opera*.

MISSION AND CASTRO

Theatre Rhinoceros (800/838-3006, www.therhino.org, various venues, prices vary) puts on a wonderfully entertaining set of gay and lesbian plays and has branched out to explore the whole spectrum of human sexuality, es-pecially as it's expressed in anything-goes San Francisco. Some take place at the Eureka Theatre (215 Jackson St.).

Classical Music and Opera

Right around the Civic Center, music takes a turn for the upscale. This is the neighborhood where the ultra-rich and not-so-rich classics lovers come to enjoy a night out. Acoustically renovated in 1992, **Davies Symphony Hall** (201 Van Ness Ave., 415/864-6000, www.sfsymphony.org) is home to Michael Tilson Thomas's world-renowned San Francisco Symphony. Loyal patrons flock to performances that range from the classic to the avant-garde. Whether you love Mozart or Mahler, or you want to hear classic rock blended with a major symphony orchestra, the San Francisco Symphony does it.

The **War Memorial Opera House** (301 Van Ness Ave., 415/621-6600, www.sfwm-pac.org, performances Tues.-Sun.), a beaux arts-style building designed by Coit Tower and City Hall architect Arthur Brown Jr., houses the **San Francisco Opera** (415/864-3330, http://sfopera.com) and **San Francisco Ballet** (415/861-5600, www.sfballet.org). Tours (415/552-8338, Mon. 10am-2pm, adults $7, seniors and students $5) are available.

Cinema

A grand movie palace from the 1920s, the **Castro Theatre** (429 Castro St., 415/621-6120, www.castrotheatre.com, adults $11, children and seniors $8.50, matinees $8.50) and its lavish interior have enchanted San Francisco audiences for almost a century. The theater hosts everything from revival double features (from black-and-white through 1980s classics) to musical movie sing-alongs, live shows, and even the occasional book signing. It also screens current releases and documentaries about queer life. The theater doesn't have a dedicated parking lot.

FESTIVALS AND EVENTS

If you're in town for a big event, prepare to check your inhibitions at the airport. No town does a festival, holiday, or parade like San Francisco. Oddity abounds. Nudity and sex displays are possibilities, and even the "tame" festivals include things like fireworks and skeletons.

Gay Pride

Pride parades and events celebrating queer life have sprung up all over the country, spreading joy and love across the land. But the granddaddy of all Pride events still reigns in San Francisco. **San Francisco Pride Celebration** (Market St., 415/864-0831, www.sfpride.org, June) officially lasts for a weekend—the last weekend of June. But in truth, the fun and festivities surrounding Pride go on for weeks. The rainbow flags go up all over the city at the beginning of June, and the excitement slowly builds, culminating in the fabulous parade and festival. Everyone is welcome to join the wall-to-wall crowds out in the streets, to stroll the vendor booths, and pack in to see the Dykes on Bikes and cadres of magnificent drag queens.

Bay to Breakers

Are those naked people you see trotting through the fog? It must be **Bay to Breakers** (415/231-3130, www.baytobreakers.com, May). On the third Sunday of May every year since 1912, San Franciscans have gotten up early to get to the starting line of the legendary 12K race. But Bay to Breakers is like no other race in the world. Sure, there are plenty of serious runners who enter the race to win it or to challenge themselves and their abilities. But then there are the other racers—San Franciscans and visitors who turn out by the thousands wearing astonishing outfits, pulling carts and wagons, and stripping down to the buff as they make their way along the course without any concern about their pace. A huge audience packs the racecourse, eager to see costumes and conveyances that may well be recycled for Pride the following month.

Chinese New Year

When Chinese immigrants began pouring into San Francisco in the 19th century, they brought their culture with them. One of the most important (and most fun) traditions the Chinese brought is the **Southwest Chinese New Year Festival and Parade** (415/982-3000, www.

chineseparade.com, $30 parade bleacher seating, Jan. or Feb.). Here you can cast off the weariness and bad luck of the old year, and come party with the dragons to celebrate the new. Chinese New Year is a major cultural event in San Francisco: Schoolchildren of all races are taught the significance of the dancing dragons and the little red envelopes. The parade, with its costumed fan dancers and stunning handmade multicolored dragons' heads, is one of the most beautiful in the world. It's got more history than almost any other California celebration; the parades and festival events began in the 1860s, helping to bring a few days of joy to a Chinese population feeling the hardships of a life thousands of miles from home. Today, crowds in the tens of thousands join to help bring in the new year toward the end of January all the way to the end of February (on the Western calendar).

Dia de los Muertos

The Latino community turns out into the San Francisco streets each autumn to celebrate its ancestors. The **Dia de los Muertos Procession and Festival of Altars** (415/424-0826, www.dayofthedeadsf.org, Nov.) takes place as close as possible to All Saint's Day (also Halloween, Samhain, and other cultures' harvest festivals) in the Mission District. Walkers are encouraged to bring flowers, candles, and special items to create altars in honor of their deceased loved ones, and artists create beautiful murals and signs to celebrate those who have come and gone. You'll note a distinct theme to the artwork: skulls and bones, mostly, though roses also tend to twine through the scenes. This is not a funereal event, but a true celebration. Expect music, dancing, and a genuine sense of joy for the lives of the dead, rather than somber mourning.

Folsom Street Fair

Celebrating the uninhibited side of San Francisco each year, the **Folsom Street Fair** (Folsom St. between 8th and 13th Sts., www.folsomstreetfair.com, Sept.) brings sex out of the bedroom and into the streets. Literally. This fair pays homage to the fetishes of consenting adults. Watch a live BDSM show, shop for sex toys, get something pierced, or just listen to the top alternative bands rocking out on the main stage. The fair takes place at the end of September each year on Folsom Street between 8th and 13th Streets. It goes without saying that this major leather event is appropriate for adults only.

Outside Lands

San Francisco has a music festival to rival Chicago's Lollapalooza and Southern California's Coachella. In August, the world's biggest acts and lots of breakout Bay Area bands converge at the city's Golden Gate Park for three days of music during **Outside Lands** (www.sfoutsidelands.com, Aug.). The 2015 edition saw Elton John, Mumford & Sons, and The Black Keys performing on the fest's main stage. This being San Francisco, Outside Lands also has gourmet food vendors and top-notch wines to enjoy along with the music.

Hardly Strictly Bluegrass

A gift to the city from the late philanthropist Warren Hellman, **Hardly Strictly Bluegrass** (www.hardlystrictlybluegrass.com, Oct.) is a free three-day music festival in Golden Gate Park featuring the best roots music acts in the world. Regular performers at the early-October fest include Emmylou Harris, Steve Earle, and Gillian Welch. It has become one of the city's most beloved events.

Shopping

UNION SQUARE AND NOB HILL

For the biggest variety of chain and department stores, plus a few select designer boutiques, locals and visitors alike flock to Union Square (bounded by Geary St., Stockton St., Post St., and Powell St.). The shopping area includes more than just the square proper: More designer and brand-name stores cluster for several blocks in all directions.

Department Stores

Several big high-end department stores call Union Square home. **Macy's** (170 O'Farrell St., 415/397-3333, www.macys.com, Mon.-Sat. 10am-9pm, Sun. 11am-7pm) has two immense locations, one for women's clothing and another for the men's store and housewares. **Neiman Marcus** (150 Stockton St., 415/362-3900, www.neimanmarcus.com, Mon.-Wed. and Fri.-Sat. 10am-7pm, Thurs. 10am-8pm, Sun. noon-6pm) is a favorite among high-budget shoppers and PETA fur protesters, while **Saks Fifth Avenue** (384 Post St., 415/986-4758, www.saksfifthavenue.com, Mon.-Wed. 10am-7pm, Thurs.-Sat. 10am-8pm, Sun. noon-7pm) adds a touch of New York style to funky-but-wealthy San Francisco.

Clothing and Shoes

An elegant space on boutiquey Maiden Lane houses **Wolford** (115 Maiden Lane, 415/391-6727, www.wolford.com, Mon.-Sat. 10am-6pm, Sun. noon-5pm), the top name in hosiery. Stockings laced with elegant seams and zigzag patterns usually run $65, but sales can offer bargain prices. Upscale and inventive lingerie at **Agent Provocateur** (54 Geary St., 415/421-0229, www.agentprovocateur.com, Mon.-Sat. 11am-7pm, Sun. noon-5pm) promises a most unique and memorable souvenir to go with those Wolford stockings.

FINANCIAL DISTRICT AND SOMA

Is there any place in San Francisco where you *can't* shop? Even the Financial District has plenty of retail opportunities. Antiques, art, and design lovers come down to **Jackson Square** (Jackson St. and Montgomery St.) for the plethora of high-end shops and galleries. Don't expect to find much in the way of cheap tchotchkes—the objects d'art and interior accessories find places in the exquisite homes of the wealthy buyers who can afford such luxuries. But as always, it's free to look, to imagine, and to dream.

The Ferry Building Marketplace (1 Sausalito-San Francisco Ferry Bldg., 415/983-8030, www.ferrybuildingmarketplace.com, Mon.-Fri. 10am-6pm, Sat. 9am-6pm, Sun. 11am-5pm) has stalls selling kitchenware, meat, produce, and wine. It also houses Book Passage (415/835-1020, www.bookpassage.com, Mon.-Fri. 9am-7pm, Sat. 8am-6pm, Sun. 10am-6pm), an independent bookstore with fabulous views of the bay.

CHINATOWN

Shopping in Chinatown isn't about seeking out a specific store; instead, it's an experience of strolling from shop to endless shop. It can take hours just to get a few blocks up Grant Street, and a thorough perusal of all the side streets might take days. Narrow, cluttered T-shirt and tchotchke shops stand between jewelry stores offering genuine gems and antiques shops crammed with treasures. Clothing boutiques run to slippery silks, while home-decor stores offer table linens made out of real linen as well as statuary, art, and tea sets—everything a dedicated shopper could dream of and more.

Good gifts and souvenirs that cost less than $10 and fit easily in a carry-on bag include small China silk brocade items like wallets and jewelry pouches, colorful paper lanterns, small hand-painted china planters, chopsticks, and the good old Chinese waving cats. Be aware that in Chinatown shops you're not only allowed to ask for discounts, but haggling is expected and is part of the fun of shopping here. No matter what you're buying, ask for the special discount—you'll actually get it!

If you've only got a short time to shop, the epic **China Bazaar** (667 Grant Ave., 415/391-6369, daily 10am-9:30pm) has some of the best prices in the district for pottery items, Chinese and Buddhist-inspired statuary, chopsticks, tea sets, and much more.

Gourmet Goodies

For a sense (and a scent) of the more local side of Chinatown, head off the main drag to Stockton Street and seek out the local food markets. Or visit the **Red Blossom Tea Company** (831 Grant Ave., 415/395-0868, www.redblossomtea.com, Mon.-Sat. 10am-6:30pm, Sun. 10am-6pm). You'll find top-quality teas of every type you can think of and probably some you've never heard of. Red Blossom has been in business for more than 25 years importing the best teas available from all over Asia. For the tea-adventurous, the blossoming teas, specific varieties of oolong, and *pu-erh* teas make great souvenirs to bring home and share with friends. Red Blossom offers all their loose teas on the Internet.

The **Golden Gate Fortune Cookie Company** (56 Ross Alley, 415/781-3956, daily 9am-6pm) makes a great stop, especially if you've brought the kids along. Heck, even if you're alone, the delicious aromas wafting from the building as you pass the alley on Jackson Street may draw you inside. Expect to have a tray of sample cookies pressed on you as soon as you enter. Inside the factory, you'll see the cookies being folded into their traditional shapes by workers, but the best part is checking out all the different types of fortune cookies. There are lots of kinds you'll never see at a restaurant: chocolate and strawberry flavors, funky shapes, various sizes, and don't forget the cookies with the X-rated fortunes, perfect to bring home and share with friends.

Bags of cookies cost only $3-4, making them attractive souvenirs.

NORTH BEACH AND FISHERMAN'S WHARF

The best thing about the 40 zillion souvenir stores in the Fisherman's Wharf area is that they know what tourists to San Francisco really *need*: sweatshirts, hats, gloves, and fuzzy socks. For last-minute warm clothes on foggy days, you don't need a specific store. Just take a walk from the cable car turnaround down Hyde Street to Jefferson Street and then over to Mason Street. You'll find the heavy sweatshirt you need or cheap-and-cheesy gifts for friends—fridge magnets, snow globes, and pewter replicas of cable cars. For more unusual souvenirs, try Pier 39. Funky boutiques crowd both sides and both stories of the buildings that line the pier.

Books

The North Beach district is filled with fun, beauty, and great Italian restaurants and cafés. The Italian district also boasts some of the hippest shops in the city, so it's a great place for shoppers who eschew chains to seek out thrift shops and funky independents. One of the most famous independent bookshops in a city famous for its literary bent is **City Lights** (261 Columbus Ave., 415/362-8193, www.citylights.com, daily 10am-midnight). It was opened in 1953 by famous Beat poet Lawrence Ferlinghetti as an all-paperback bookstore with a decidedly Beat aesthetic, focused on selling modern literary fiction and progressive political tomes. As the Beats flocked to San Francisco and to City Lights, the shop put on another hat—that of publisher. Allen Ginsberg's *Howl* was published by the erstwhile independent. Today, they're still selling and publishing the best of cutting-edge fiction and nonfiction. Expect to find genre paperbacks along with the latest intriguing new works. The nonfiction selections can make you think about your world in a new way, which is just what the founders of City Lights wanted.

Clothing

For hip dressers who prefer classic style to the latest stuff fresh out of the sweatshops, **Old Vogue** (1412 Grant Ave., 415/392-1522, Mon.-Tues. and Thurs. 11am-6pm, Wed. 11am-8pm, Fri.-Sat. 11am-10pm, Sun. noon-6pm) is the perfect North Beach destination. Stop in at the funky little storefront and plan to spend a little while browsing through the racks of vintage apparel mostly for men: one floor dedicated to comfy old jeans and pants, the other to coats, blouses, dresses, and accessories. Old Vogue can provide you with just the perfect hat to top off your favorite clubbing outfit.

MARINA AND PACIFIC HEIGHTS

Pacific Heights and its neighbor Presidio Heights, two quiet residential areas, are connected by Sacramento Street, home to interior design and clothing boutiques that display high-end wares that appeal to the well-heeled residents of this area. With 12 blocks' worth of shops, galleries, salons, and eateries, the main trouble folks have is getting through all of it in one shopping session.

Gift and Home

It takes a ritzy San Francisco neighborhood to support a six-days-a-week orchid store. **Beautiful Orchids** (3319 Sacramento St., 415/567-2443, www.beautifulorchids.com, Mon.-Fri. 11am-5pm, Sat. 11am-4pm) specializes in rarified live orchid plants. Every color of the rainbow, amazing shapes, and waterfall figures spill from elegant planters. Expect to pay a premium for these rare hand-tended flowers, and to spend even more to ship them home. You can also find elegant home accessories here, most picked to complement the orchids rather than the other way around.

CIVIC CENTER AND HAYES VALLEY

In the Hayes Valley neighborhood adjacent to the Civic Center, shopping goes uptown, but the unique scent of counterculture creativity somehow makes it in. This is a fun neighborhood to get your stroll on, checking out the art galleries and peeking into the boutiques for clothing and upscale housewares, and then stopping at one of the lovely cafés for a restorative bite to eat.

Clothing and Shoes

Ver Unica (526 Hayes St., 415/621-6259, Mon.-Thurs. 11am-7pm, Fri.-Sat. 10am-8pm, Sun. noon-6pm) is a vintage boutique that attracts locals and celebrities with high-quality men's and women's clothing and accessories dating from the 1920s to the 1980s, along with a small selection of new apparel by up-and-coming designers.

The corset takes center stage at unique **Dark Garden** (321 Linden St., 415/431-7684, www.darkgarden.net, Sun.-Tues. 11am-5pm, Thurs. 11am-7pm, Fri.-Sat. 11am-8pm). Custom fitting and design doesn't come cheap, but you'll get quality. An assortment of lingerie is also sold here.

MISSION AND CASTRO

In the 21st century, the closest you can come to the old-school Haight Street shopping experience is in the Mission. The big shopping street with the coolest selections is definitely Valencia Street, which has all the best thrift shops and funky stuff.

On Castro Street, shopping is sexy. Whether you want leather or lace, or just a pair of fabulous spike-heeled boots, you can find it in one of the racy shops found in the notoriously "everything goes" district.

Books

There's a **Books Inc.** (2275 Market St., 415/864-6777, www.booksinc.net, Sun.-Thurs. 10am-9pm, Fri.-Sat. 10am-10pm) in the Castro. This small, independent Bay Area chain hosts numerous author events and stocks plenty of local authors. You can also find your favorite paperbacks. In keeping with the neighborhood of this location, the managers stock lots of great gay fiction and non-fiction. You're welcome to stay and browse as long as you like.

Clothing and Shoes

A local favorite vintage and secondhand clothing store in the Mission is **Schauplatz** (791 Valencia St., 415/864-5665, Mon. and Wed.-Sat. 1pm-7pm, Sun. 1pm-6pm). It might be a bit more expensive than your average Goodwill, but you'll be wowed by the fabulous and unusual apparel. Surf the racks for everything from 1940s dresses to vintage sunglasses.

Gift and Home

Author Dave Eggers's tongue-in-cheek storefront at **826 Valencia** (826 Valencia St., 415/642-5905, ext. 201, www.826valencia.org/store, daily noon-6pm) doubles as a youth literacy center and pirate supply shop. Underneath the hanging ropes and hooks, you'll find drawers that open to reveal shackles or fake mustaches for sale. You'll also find a good stock of literary journals and magazines, including *McSweeney's*, *The Believer*, and the DVD magazine *Wholphin*, all published by Eggers himself.

Therapy (545 Valencia St., 415/865-0981, www.shopattherapy.com, Mon.-Thurs. noon-9pm, Fri.-Sat. 11:30am-10:30pm, Sun. 11:30am-9pm) surpasses the nearby competition with its well-priced mix of clothing, accessories, and goofy gifts.

Need a bat skeleton or a freeze-dried frog carcass? Visit **Paxton Gate** (824 Valencia St., 415/824-1872, www.paxtongate.com, Sun.-Wed. 11am-7pm, Thurs.-Sat. 11am-8pm) next door to 826 Valencia. In addition to the fossilized creatures, this quirky spot sells garden supplies, books, and candles.

GOLDEN GATE PARK AND THE HAIGHT

In Golden Gate Park, the Museum Stores at the de Young and the Academy of Sciences sell high-priced but beautiful and unusual souvenirs—true remembrances of a visit to San Francisco. The Haight-Ashbury shopping district isn't what it used to be, but if you're willing to poke around a bit, you can still find a few bargains in the remaining thrift shops.

Books and Music

Music has always been a part of the Haight. To this day you'll find homeless folks pounding out rhythms on *doumbeks* and congas on the sidewalks. In an old bowling alley, **Amoeba Music** (1855 Haight St., 415/831-1200, www.amoeba.com, daily 11am-8pm) is a larger-than-life record store that promotes every type of music imaginable. Amoeba's staff, many of whom are musicians themselves, are among the most knowledgeable in the business. Amoeba also hosts free in-store performances. Check the website for upcoming shows.

Technically in the Richmond neighborhood, **Green Apple Books & Music** (506 Clement St., 415/387-2272, www.greenapplebooks.com, daily 10am-10:30pm) is worth the trek. Locals head to this fog belt location to get their fill of thousands of titles that include staff picks, new releases, and used nonfiction. Friendly sales staff are on hand to assist with navigating the myriad stacks.

Clothing

Originally a vaudeville theater, the capacious **Wasteland** (1660 Haight St., 415/863-3150, www.shopwasteland.com, Mon.-Sat. 11am-8pm, Sun. noon-7pm) has a traffic-stopping art nouveau facade, a distinctive assortment of vintage hippie and rock-star threads, and a glamour-punk staff.

Sports and Recreation

PARKS

Golden Gate Park

The largest park in San Francisco is **Golden Gate Park** (main entrance at Stanyan St. and Fell St., McLaren Lodge Visitors Center, 501 Stanyan St., at John F. Kennedy Dr., 415/831-2700, www.golden-gate-park.com, daily 5am-midnight). In addition to popular sights like the Academy of Sciences, the de Young, and the Japanese Tea Garden, Golden Gate Park is San Francisco's unofficial playground. There are three botanical gardens, a children's playground (Martin Luther King Jr. Dr. and Bowling Green Dr.), tennis courts, and a golf course. Stow Lake offers paddleboats for rent (50 Stow Lake Dr., 415/752-0347, daily 10am-4pm, $13-17 per hour), and the park even has its own bison paddock (off John F. Kennedy Dr.). On the weekend, you will find the park filled with locals roller-skating, biking, hiking, and even Lindy Hopping. Note that the main entrance at John F. Kennedy Drive off Fell Street is closed to motorists every Sunday for pedestrian-friendly fun.

Crissy Field

Crissy Field (1199 E. Beach, Presidio, 415/561-4323, www.parksconservancy.org, daily sunrise-sunset), in the Golden Gate National Recreation Area, is a park with a mission. In partnership with the National Park Service, ecology programs are the centerpiece. Check the website for a list of classes, seminars, and fun hands-on activities for all ages. Many of these include walks out into the marsh beyond the center and into the landscape of the Presidio and beyond.

Mission Dolores Park

Expect to see lots of locals when you visit **Mission Dolores Park** (Dolores St. and 19th St., 415/831-2700, http://sfrecpark.org, daily sunrise-sunset), usually called Dolores Park and a favorite of Mission district denizens.

Bring a beach blanket to sprawl on the lawn, enjoy the views, and do some serious people-watching; stroll on the paved pedestrian paths; or grab a game of tennis at one of the six courts. On weekends, music festivals and cultural events often spring up at Dolores Park.

McLaren Park

McLaren Park (Mansell St. between Excelsior District and Visitacion Valley, 415/831-2700, http://sfrecpark.org) is something of a hidden gem in the busy City—a crowd-free park with miles of hiking trails, dozens of picnic tables, athletic fields, an indoor pool, and even a nine-hole golf course. Enjoy a set of tennis, swim some laps, or play a quick round. But most of all, you can walk. Seven miles of trails are paved, and plenty of undeveloped trails wend off into the brush and trees all around. If you've got the stamina, you can circle the whole park by following its trails. Feel free to bring your canine companion with you to this dog-friendly park. Take care walking here if you're a woman alone; McLaren Park is generally quite safe in the daylight hours, but at night it becomes much less safe, so plan to finish up your hiking, picnicking, and playing by sunset.

BEACHES

Ocean Beach

San Francisco boasts of being a city that has everything, and it certainly comes close. This massive urban wonderland even claims several genuine sand beaches within its city limits. No doubt the biggest and most famous of these is **Ocean Beach** (Great Hwy., parking at Sloat Blvd., Golden Gate Park, and the Cliff House, 415/561-4323, www.parksconservancy.org). This 3.5-mile stretch of sand forms the breakwater for the Pacific Ocean along the whole west side of the city. Because it's so large, you're likely to find a spot to sit down and maybe even a parking spot along the beach, except perhaps on that rarest of occasions in San Francisco: a sunny, warm day. Don't go out for an ocean swim at Ocean Beach: Extremely dangerous rip currents kill at least one person every year.

Aquatic Park

The beach at **Aquatic Park** (Beach St. and Hyde St., 415/447-5000, www.nps.gov/safr) sits right in the middle of the Fisherman's Wharf tourist area. This makes Aquatic Park incredibly convenient for visitors who want to grab a picnic on the Wharf to enjoy down on the beach. The coolest part of Aquatic Park is its history rather than its current presence. It was built in the late 1930s as a bathhouse catering to wealthy San Franciscans, and swimming remains one of the park's main attractions. Triathletes and hard-core swimmers brave the frigid waters to swim for miles in the protected cove. More sedate visitors can find a seat and enjoy a cup of coffee, a newspaper, and some people-watching.

Baker Beach

Baker Beach (Golden Gate Point and the Presidio, 415/561-4323, www.parksconservancy.org) is best known for its scenery, and that doesn't just mean the lovely views of the Golden Gate Bridge from an unusual angle (from the west and below); Baker is San Francisco's own clothing-optional beach. But plenty of the denizens of Baker Beach wear clothes while flying kites, playing volleyball and Frisbee, and even just strolling on the beach. Because Baker is much smaller than Ocean Beach, it gets crowded in the summer. Whether you choose to sunbathe nude or not, don't swim here: The currents are strong and often dangerous this close to the Golden Gate.

SURFING

Some may find it hard to believe that you can even surf on a trip to San Francisco. **Ocean Beach** (Great Hwy., parking at Sloat Blvd., Golden Gate Park, and the Cliff House, www.parksconservancy.org) has a series of beach breaks that can get good in the fall and cause monstrous waves in the winter.

Ocean Beach is not for beginners; even accomplished surfers sometimes have difficulty paddling out. When it's windy or too big at Ocean Beach, surfers head 20 minutes south to the town of Pacifica's **Linda Mar Beach** (Cabrillo Hwy. and Linda Mar Blvd.).

Five blocks from Ocean Beach, **Aqua Surf Shop** (3847 Judah St., 415/242-9283, www.aquasurfshop.com, Sun.-Tues. 10am-5:30pm, Wed.-Sat. 10am-7pm, surfboards $25-35/day, wetsuits $15/day) is a good place to go for surf gear. They rent shortboards, longboards, and the ubiquitous 4/3 wetsuit.

BIKING

In other places, bicycling is a sport or a mode of transportation. In San Francisco, bicycling is a religion (the concept of mountain biking originated here). It may be wise to start off gently, perhaps with a guided tour that avoids areas with dangerous traffic. **Blazing Saddles** (various locations, 415/202-8888, www.blazingsaddles.com) rents bikes and offers guided bicycling tours all over the Bay Area. If you prefer the safety of a group, take the guided Urban Parks or Golden Gate Bridge tour (adults $55, children $35). The latter rides through San Francisco and across the Golden Gate Bridge into Marin County. You'll return to the city by ferry. Blazing Saddles can also supply intrepid cyclists with bike maps of the city and the greater Bay Area. For a sedate introductory ride, take the popular self-guided tour of the waterfront. With six locations in the Fisherman's Wharf area and one in Union Square, Blazing Saddles makes it easy to head out for a spin.

The easy and flat nine-mile ride across the **Golden Gate Bridge** and back is a great way to see the bridge and the bay for the first time, and it takes only an hour or two to complete. Another option is to ride across the bridge and into the town of Sausalito (8 miles) or Tiburon (16 miles), enjoy an afternoon and dinner, and then ride the ferry back into the city (bikes are allowed on board).

Twin Peaks

Twin Peaks rises up from the center of San Francisco, and is the second-highest point in the city. Twin Peaks divides the city between north and south, catching the fog bank that rolls in from the Golden Gate and providing a habitat for lots of wild birds and insects, including the endangered Mission blue butterfly.

While you barely need to get out of your car to enjoy the stunning 360-degree views of the city from the peaks, the best way to enjoy the vista is to take a hike. If you want to scale the less traveled South Peak, start at the pullout on the road below the parking lot. You'll climb a steep set of stairs up to the top of the South Peak in less than 0.2 miles. Stop and marvel at man's industry: the communications tower that's the massive eyesore just over the peak. Carefully cross the road to access the red-rock stairway up to the North Peak. It's only 0.25 mile, but as with the South Peak, those stairs seem to go straight up! It's worth it when you look out across the Golden Gate to Mount Tamalpais in the north and Mount Diablo in the east.

If it's the view you're seeking rather than the wildlife and exercise, head to Twin Peaks only on a sunny day. If the fog is in, as so often happens in the summertime, you'll have trouble seeing five feet in front of you. Oh, and don't expect a verdant paradise up there—the grass doesn't stay green long in the spring, so most visitors get to see the dried-out brush that characterizes much of the Bay Area in the summertime and fall.

To get there, drive west up Market Street (eventually turning into Portola Dr.), and turn right onto Twin Peaks Boulevard and past the parade of tour buses to the parking lot past the North Peak. Parking is free and Twin Peaks is open year-round.

If you've got more time, take a scenic ride on the paved paths of **Golden Gate Park** (main entrance at Stanyan St. and Fell St., McLaren Lodge Visitors Center at John F. Kennedy Dr., 415/831-2700, www.golden-gate-park.com) and the **Presidio** (Montgomery St. and Lincoln Blvd., 415/561-4323, www.nps.gov/prsf). A bike makes a perfect mode of transportation to explore the various museums and attractions of these two large parks.

Looking for some great urban mountain biking? Miles of unpaved roads and trails inside the city limits provide technically challenging rides for adventurous cyclists willing to take a risk or two. Check out the website for **San Francisco Mountain Biking** (www.sfmtb.com) for information about trails, roads, routes, and regulations.

GOLF

A number of golf courses hide in the parks of San Francisco. The premier golf course in the city, the **Presidio Golf Course** (300 Finley Rd. at Arguello St., 50 yards from Arguello Gate, 415/561-4661, www.presidiogolf.com, Mon.-Thurs. $125, Fri.-Sun. $145) was once reserved for the exclusive use of military officers, government officials, and visiting dignitaries. Since 1995 the 18-hole, par-72 course and its driving range, practice putting greens, and clubhouse have been available to the public. Reserve your tee time by phone or online.

Lincoln Park Golf Course (300 34th Ave., 415/221-9911, http://lincolnparkgolf-course.com, Mon.-Thurs. $38, Fri.-Sun. and holidays $42) is an 80-year-old public 18-hole, par-68 course in the Outer Richmond district. It hosts the annual San Francisco City Golf Championships. For tee times at any municipal course, call 415/750-4653.

HIKING

Yes, you can hike inside the city of San Francisco. Most of the parks in the city offer hiking trails to suit various tastes and ability levels. The City also boasts some longer and more interesting trails that present serious hikers with a real challenge.

For an easy nature walk in the Presidio, try the **Lobos Creek Trail** (0.8 miles round-trip, Lincoln St. at Bowley St., 415/561-5300, www.presidio.gov, daily dawn-dusk). Less than a mile long, this flat boardwalk trail is wheelchair-accessible and shows off the beginning successes of the ecological restoration of the Presidio. You'll get to see restored sand dunes and native vegetation; the flora has attracted butterflies and other insects, in turn bringing birds to the trail area. While it's still in the city, this trail gives walkers a glimpse of what the area might have been like 500 years ago. Another easy Presidio hike goes way back into the region's history. **Lover's Lane** (0.6 miles one-way, Funston Ave. and Presidio Blvd., 415/561-5300, www.presidio.gov) once served soldiers stationed at the Presidio who beat down the path into the city proper to visit their sweethearts. Today, you'll have a peaceful tree-shaded walk on a flat, semi-paved path that passes the former homes of the soldiers, crosses El Polin Creek, offers a view of Andy Goldsworthy's *Wood Lines* sculpture, and ends at the Presidio Gate.

Want to hike the entire **Bay Area Ridge Trail** (415/561-2595, www.ridgetrail.org)? Prepare to get serious—the whole trail runs more than 335 miles and grows longer annually. It crosses San Francisco from south to north. The easy Presidio section (Arguello Blvd. and Jackson St.) runs 2.7 miles from the Arguello Gate to the foot of the Golden Gate

Bridge. If you've been trudging the sidewalks and climbing the hills of the difficult seven-mile section from Stern Grove (Wawona St. and 21st Ave.) to the Arguello Gate, you'll be happy to find the gently sloping dirt footpaths through unpopulated forests and meadows of the Presidio. Another city section of the trail is a moderate 3.2 miles (one-way) from Fort Funston (off Fort Funston Rd.) to Stern Grove. If the weather is right, watch hang gliders fly at the fort before pointing your boots north to hike the paved trails through protected glens and residential neighborhoods that most visitors never see.

The **Land's End Trail** (2.9 miles round-trip) begins at the **Lands End Lookout Visitor Center** (680 Point Lobos Ave., 415/426-5240, www.parksconservancy.org, daily 9am-5pm) and then winds, drops, and rises from the ruins of the **Sutro Baths,** continues past the Legion of Honor, and moves on to the rugged cliffs and beaches where the North American continent ends. At low tide, you can see the leftover bits of three ships that all wrecked on the rocks of Point Lobos. Smaller side trails lead down to little beaches, and the views of the Golden Gate are the stuff of legend. The **El Camino Del Mar Trail** intersects Land's End, creating a big, mostly

ruins of the Sutro Baths at Land's End Trail

Go Wild on the Farallon Islands

On one of those rare clear San Francisco days, you might catch a glimpse of something far offshore in the distance. It's not a pirate ship or an ocean-based optical illusion: It's the **Farallon Islands,** a series of jagged islets and rocks 28 miles west of the Golden Gate Bridge.

At certain times, humans have attempted to make a living on these harsh rocky outcroppings. In the 1800s, Russians hunted the Farallons' marine mammals for their pelts and blubber. Following the Gold Rush, two rival companies harvested murre eggs on the Farallons to feed nearby San Francisco's growing population.

Now the islands have literally gone to the birds. The islands have been set aside as a National Wildlife Refuge, allowing the region's bird populations to flourish. The Farallons are home to the largest colony of Western gulls in the world and have half the world's Ashy storm petrels.

But this wild archipelago is also known for its robust population of great white sharks that circle the islands looking for seal and sea lion snacks. The exploits of a group of great white shark researchers on the island were detailed in Susan Carey's gripping 2005 book *The Devil's Teeth*.

Nature lovers who want to see the Farallons' wildlife up close can book an all-day boat trip through **San Francisco Whale Tours** (415/448-7570 or 888/235-6450, www.sanfranciscowhaletours.com, $79-99) or **SF Bay Whale Watching** (415/331-6267, www.sfbaywhalewatching.com, $79-99). Don't fall overboard.

paved loop for enthusiastic hikers who want to take on a three-plus-mile trek that hits most of the major landmarks of Land's End. Bring a camera on this hike. The views from this trail may be some of the most beautiful on Earth.

Probably the closest thing to a serene backwoods hike in San Francisco can be found at the easy trail at **Mount Davidson** (1 mile round-trip, Dalewood St., West Portal, http://sfrecpark.org, daily 6am-10pm), which is the highest point in the city at 938 feet. Park in the adjacent West Portal residential area and wander through the gate and into the woods. Take the main fire road straight up the gentle slope to the top of the mountain, then find the smaller track off to the left that leads to the famous "cross at the top of the mountain." To extend your stay in this pleasant place, either walk down the other side of the mountain or head back to find the smaller branch trails that lead off into the trees.

For a more vigorous and better-known walk, take the moderate trail at **Glen Canyon** (0.9 miles round-trip, Elk and Chenery Sts., http://sfrecpark.org). Feel free to bring your canine companion on this trail through a lovely little urban canyon. It only takes about half an hour to explore Islais Creek, the

nonnative eucalyptus and blackberries, and the attractive if unspectacular views. Take care to avoid the prolific poison oak that spreads throughout the canyon.

KAYAKING

For the adventurous, kayaking on San Francisco Bay is a great way to experience the famous waterway on a personal level. **City Kayak** (Pier 40, 415/294-1050, www.citykayak.com, kayaks $35-75/hour, $69-109/day, SUPs $35/hour, $69/day) rents stand-up paddleboards and different types of kayaks. Beginners can take guided paddles along the shoreline, getting a new view of familiar sights. More advanced kayakers can take trips out to the Golden Gate and around Alcatraz Island.

WHALE-WATCHING

With day-trip access to the marine sanctuary off the Farallon Islands, whale-watching is a year-round activity in San Francisco. **San Francisco Whale Tours** (Pier 39, Dock B, 415/706-7634 or 888/235-6456, www.sanfranciscowhaletours.com, daily, $79-89, advance purchase required) offers six-hour trips out to the Farallons almost every Saturday and Sunday, with almost-guaranteed whale sightings on each trip. Shorter whale-watching trips along the coastline run on weekdays, and 90-minute quickie trips out to see slightly smaller local wildlife, including elephant seals and sea lions, also go out daily. Children ages 3-15 are welcome on boat tours (for reduced rates), and kids often love the chance to spot whales, sea lions, and pelicans. Children under age three are not permitted for safety reasons.

YOGA

It's tough to walk two blocks in San Francisco without tripping over a yoga studio or finding people walking the streets with yoga mats tucked under their arms. To find a studio, check out listings in the *Yoga Journal* (www.yogajournal.com/directory). The magazine is based in San Francisco, and the editors not only recommend local studios, they practice in them.

The chain **Hiking Yoga** (1 Ferry Building Plaza, 888/589-2250, www.hikingyoga.com, $20 per hike, 3 hikes $50) has a facility in the Ferry Building. While it's not a traditional yoga class, Hiking Yoga gets you stretching, working out, and hiking around the city all in one 90-minute package. Bonus: Because it's outdoors, you don't need to lug a yoga mat along.

SPECTATOR SPORTS

Lovers of the big leagues will find fun in San Francisco and around the Bay Area. Major League Baseball's **San Francisco Giants** (http://sanfrancisco.giants.mlb.com), winners of the 2010, 2012, and 2014 World Series, play out the long summer baseball season at **AT&T Park** (24 Willie Mays Plaza, 3rd St. and King St., 415/972-2000). Come out to enjoy the game, the food, and the views. Giants games take place on weekdays and weekends, both day and night. It's not hard to snag last-minute tickets to a regular season game if you're willing to use third-party websites like StubHub.com. Check out the gourmet restaurants that ring the stadium; it wouldn't be San Francisco without top-tier cuisine.

The city is nominally home to the National Football League's **San Francisco 49ers** (www.49ers.com). After calling Candlestick Park home from 1971 to 2013, the team now plays at **Levi's Stadium** (4900 Marie P. DeBartolo Way, at Tasman Ave., 415/464-9377, www.levisstadium.com) in Santa Clara, 45 minutes south of the city. Check the website for current single-game ticket prices.

Accommodations

San Francisco has plenty of accommodations to suit every taste and most budgets. The most expensive places tend to be in Union Square, SoMa, and the Financial District. Cheaper digs can be had in the neighborhoods surrounding Fisherman's Wharf. You'll find the most character in the smaller boutique hotels, but a number of chain motels have moved into historic San Francisco buildings, creating a more unusual experience than you might expect from the likes of a Days Inn.

Many hotels in San Francisco are 100 percent nonsmoking—you can't even light up on your balcony. If you need a smoking room, you'll have to hunt hard. Be aware that many motels are cracking down on marijuana as well as on cigarettes.

Free parking with a hotel room is rare in the city, existing mostly in motor lodges and chain motels down by the wharf. Overnight garage parking downtown can be excruciatingly expensive. Check with your hotel to see if they have a "parking package" that includes this expense (and possibly offers valet service as well). If you don't plan to leave the city on your trip, consider saving a bundle by skipping the rental car altogether and using public transit. To explore outside the city limits, a car is a necessity.

UNION SQUARE AND NOB HILL

You'll find a plethora of hotels in and around Union Square and Nob Hill. As a rule, those closest to the top of the Hill or to Union Square proper are the most expensive. By staying 1-2 blocks away from the center, you get more personality and genuine San Francisco experience for less money. There are few inexpensive options in these areas; hostels appear in the direction of the Tenderloin, where safety becomes an issue after dark.

Under $150

Should you find the need for a full-service professional recording studio in your hotel, head straight for **The Mosser** (54 4th St., 800/227-3804, www.themosser.com, $129-289). The Mosser's inexpensive rooms have European-style shared baths in the hallway and spare, Asian-inspired interior decor. Pricier options include bigger rooms with private baths. Solo travelers can trim costs by getting a teensy room with a single twin bed. With a rep for cleanliness and pleasant amenities, including morning coffee and comfy bathrobes, this hotel provides visitors with a cheap crash space in a great location convenient to sights, shops, and public transportation.

$150-250

Just two blocks from Union Square, **The Marker San Francisco** (501 Geary St., 415/292-0100, http://themarkersanfrancisco. com, $200-500) features clean, modern rooms that make an ideal base to take in the hustle and bustle of the city. The welcoming, whimsically decorated lobby hosts a late-afternoon wine hour and offers complimentary morning coffee and tea. Guests get access to the downstairs fitness center and spa, which has a jetted tub, sauna, and steam room. All of the suites have a bedroom and a living room with a pullout sofa bed, while some also have their own jetted tub. The on-site **BDK Restaurant &**
Bar serves an American menu in a modern pub setting. These factors combine to make The Marker one of the best places to lay your head downtown.

While the best bargains aren't in these neighborhoods, you can still find one or two budget-conscious lodgings in the Union Square and Nob Hill area. One of the best deals in town can be had at the ★ **Golden Gate Hotel** (775 Bush St., 415/392-3702, www.goldengatehotel.com, $145-215). This narrow yellow building has 25 rooms decorated with antiques, giving it a bed-and-breakfast feel. The cheapest option is a room with a shared bath down the hall, though there are rooms with their own baths. Centrally located between Union Square and the top of Nob Hill, the Golden Gate serves a fine continental breakfast with fresh croissants.

★ **Hotel G** (386 Geary St., 877/828-4478, http://hotelgsanfrancisco.com, $229-369) impresses with understated style. The rooms in this boutique hotel are all simple, clean, and serene, with smart TVs, Nespresso coffeemakers, Tivoli clock radios, and comfy beds with denim headboards (a nod to the SF roots of Levi's). Colorful art provided by Creativity Explored, a nonprofit that showcases the work of artists with developmental disabilities, decorate the walls of the lobby and some guestrooms. Lower-level rooms have bathrooms with subway tile, while the upper-floor bathrooms feature marble. There are three drinking and dining establishments within the building: the **Klyde Café & Wine Bar,** the **398 Brasserie,** and the difficult-to-find speakeasy and oyster bar **Benjamin Cooper.** Your room will feel like a homey apartment even though the hotel is just a block from bustling Union Square.

A San Francisco legend, the **Clift** (495 Geary St., 415/775-4700, www.morganshotelgroup.com, $200-840) has a lobby worth walking into, whether you're a guest of the hotel or not. The high-ceilinged, gray industrial space is devoted to modern art, including a Salvador Dalí coffee table. By contrast, the big Philippe Starck-designed rooms are almost Spartan in their simplicity, with colors meant to mimic the city skyline. Stop in for a drink at the **Redwood Room,** done in brown leather and popular with a younger crowd. The **Velvet Room** serves breakfast and dinner. The Clift is perfectly located for theatergoers, and the square is an easy walk away.

Only half a block down from Union Square, the **Sir Francis Drake** (450 Powell St., 800/795-7129, www.sirfrancisdrake.com, $219-469) has its own history beginning in the late 1920s. Back then, it was the place to stay and play for vaudeville and silent-screen stars. Here at the Drake you'll find less opulence in the lobby and more in the rooms. The beefeater doorman (almost always available for a photo), the unique door overhang, and the red-and-gold interior all add to the character of this favorite. On the 21st floor, at **Harry Denton's Starlight Room,** you can take in views of the city skyline while enjoying a cocktail.

Despite its location in the seedy Tenderloin neighborhood—or perhaps because of it—the ★ **Phoenix Hotel** (601 Eddy St., 415/776-1380, www.jdvhospitality.com, $200-300) has serious rock-and-roll cred. The Phoenix has hosted a who's who of rock music, including the Red Hot Chili Peppers, Debbie Harry,

and Sublime. The main draw is the large deck with an inlaid heated pool. Palm trees rising overhead make the Phoenix feels like it's a beachside oasis rather than in a gritty urban neighborhood. At night, the sounds of the surrounding Tenderloin remind you of the hotel's true location, but most guests don't come here to catch up on their sleep.

Over $250

Just blocks from Union Square, **Hotel Rex** (562 Sutter St., 415/433-4434, www.jdvhotels.com/rex, $250-500) is an ideal writer's retreat. The spacious rooms all have wooden writing desks and are decorated with the work of local artists. The downstairs Library Bar is a fine place to sip a cocktail or glass of wine while browsing its shelves of hardback books. Old movies are screened on Monday night, and live jazz acts perform on Friday.

The opulence of the lobby at the **Westin St. Francis** (335 Powell St., 415/397-7000, www.westinstfrancis.com, $345-445) matches its elegant address. With more than a century of history as San Francisco's great gathering spot, the St. Francis still garners great prestige. Rooms are attractive but small. The cost of a stay pays mainly for the decadent fixtures of the common areas, the four eateries

Hotel G

(including Michael Mina's Bourbon Steak), the state-of-the-art gym, spa, top-quality meeting and banquet spaces, and the address on Union Square.

Certain names just mean luxury in the hotel world. The **Fairmont San Francisco** (950 Mason St., 415/772-5000, www.fairmont.com, $415-1,049) is among the best of these. With a rich history, above-and-beyond service, and spectacular views, the Fairmont makes any stay in the city memorable. Check online for package specials or to book a tee time or spa treatment. Head downstairs for a Mai Tai at the Tonga Room & Hurricane Bar.

The **Ritz-Carlton** (600 Stockton St., 415/296-7465, www.ritzcarlton.com, $429-800) provides patrons with ultimate pampering. From the high-thread-count sheets to the fine dining room and the full-service spa, guests at the Ritz all but drown in sumptuous amenities. Even the "standard" rooms are exceptional, but if you've got the bread, spring for the Club Floors, where they'll give you an iPod, a personal concierge, and possibly the kitchen sink if you ask for it.

FINANCIAL DISTRICT AND SOMA

Top business execs make it their, well, business to stay near the towering offices of the Financial District, whether down by the water on the Embarcadero or in SoMa. Thus, most of the lodgings in these areas cater to the expense account set. If you're paying your own way, look for smaller boutique and indie accommodations that won't tear your wallet to bits or laugh at your checking account.

$150-250

Upon entering the bright lobby exploding with color, you'll realize the ★ **Hotel Triton** (342 Grant Ave., 800/800-1299, www.hotel-triton.com, $160-500) is a different kind of hotel. The rooms are wallpapered with text from Jack Kerouac's *On the Road*, while copies of Allen Ginsberg's *Howl* take the place of the standard Gideon Bible. There are three specialty suites, including one designed by

musician Jerry Garcia and another designed by comedian Kathy Griffin. The third is a Häagen-Dazs "Sweet Suite" that comes with a fridge of the gourmet ice creams. You'll find the rooms small but comfortable and well stocked with ecofriendly amenities and bath products. The flat-panel TVs offer a 24-hour yoga channel, and complimentary yoga props are in each room.

★ **Hotel Zetta** (55 5th St., 415/543-8555, www.viceroryhotelgroup.com/en/zetta, $200-600) embraces San Francisco's reputation as a technology hub. The ultramodern rooms are equipped with a gaggle of gadgets, including a G-Link docking station for mobile devices and a device that streams content from your smartphone onto the large flat-screen TVs. There is also an espresso machine and a large butcher-block desk. The hotel's common rooms are more playful, with shuffleboard, a pool table, and an oversize game of Jenga. Recycled art throughout the building includes lobby chandeliers made of old eyeglasses. The upscale on-site restaurant **The Cavalier** features British-meets-California cuisine.

It may be part of a chain, but at the large **Park Central San Francisco** (50 3rd St., 415/974-6400, www.parkcentralsf.com, $189-335) you'll find plenty of charm at your doorstep. Guests stay in renovated rooms with pretty cityscapes. Amenities mimic the more expensive SoMa hotels, and seasonal special rates dip down into the genuinely affordable. The attached restaurant, **MaSo,** serves breakfast, lunch, and dinner on weekdays, and the lounge is open until midnight for nightcaps.

Over $250

With rooms on the 38th to 48th floors of San Francisco's third-tallest building, the **Loews Regency San Francisco** (222 Sansome St., 415/276-9888, www.loewshotels.com, $479-5,990) is all about the views. The rooms have muted colors so that more of your attention turns to the unparalleled vistas of the city, including the Bay Bridge and possibly the best view of the Transamerica Pyramid. Even the luxurious beds are raised for prime viewing.

You'll find elegant furnishings, a soaking tub, and incredible details, including complimentary hotel stationary personalized by request. The **Brasserie S&P** serves breakfast, lunch, and dinner, while the bar highlights its selection of gins and homemade tonics. With exceptional service, the Loews Regency makes everyone feel like a VIP.

Hotel Vitale (8 Mission St., 888/890-8688, www.hotelvitale.com, $309-899) professes to restore guests' vitality with its lovely rooms and exclusive spa, complete with rooftop hot soaking tubs and a yoga studio. Many of the good-size rooms also have private deep soaking tubs. The Vitale's **Americano Restaurant** serves Italian fare.

For something small but upscale, check out **Hotel Griffon** (155 Steuart St., 800/321-2201, www.hotelgriffon.com, $249-629), a boutique business hotel with a prime vacation locale on the Embarcadero, just feet from the Ferry Building. The Griffon offers business and leisure packages to suit any traveler's needs. Although they're pricy, the best rooms overlook the bay, with views of the Bay Bridge and Treasure Island.

Le Méridien San Francisco (333 Battery St., 415/296-2900, www.starwoodhotels.com, $265-470) stands tall in the Embarcadero Center, convenient to shopping, dining, and cable car lines. This expensive luxury hotel pampers guests with Frette sheets, down duvets, and stellar views. Amenities include 24-hour room service and an always-open fitness facility. A pedestrian bridge connects the hotel to the Federal Reserve Building.

For a true San Francisco hotel experience, book a room at the famous **Hotel Palomar** (12 4th St., 415/348-1111, www.hotelpalomar-sf.com, $268-549). You'll find every amenity imaginable, from extra-long beds for taller guests to in-room spa services and temporary pet goldfish. Get drinks and dinner at the on-site restaurant **Dirty Habit,** which names *Project Runway* finalist Melissa Fleis as a "muse and collaborator." Borrow one of the hotel's complimentary bikes to tool around town.

NORTH BEACH AND FISHERMAN'S WHARF

Perhaps it's odd, but the tourist mecca of San Francisco is not a district of a zillion hotels. Most of the major hostelries sit nearer to Union Square. Near the Wharf or in North Beach are plenty of chain motels, plus a few select boutique hotels in all price ranges.

Under $150

The **San Remo Hotel** (2237 Mason St., 800/352-7366, www.sanremohotel.com, $119-159) is one of the best bargains in the city. The blocky yellow building has been around since just after the 1906 earthquake, offering inexpensive rooms to budget-minded travelers. One of the reasons for the rock-bottom pricing is the baths: You don't get your own. Four shared baths with shower facilities in the hallways are available day and night. The rooms boast the simplest of furnishings and decorations as well as clean white walls and ceilings. Some rooms have their own sinks, all have either double beds or two twin beds, and none have telephones or TVs, so this might not be the best choice for large, media-addicted families. Couples on a romantic vacation can rent the Penthouse ($269), a lovely room for two with lots of windows and a rooftop terrace boasting views of North Beach and the bay.

$150-250

In a quieter section of the Embarcadero, the ★ **Harbor Court Hotel** (165 Steuart St., 415/882-1300, www.harborcourthotel.com, $150-500) is housed in an attractive brick building just a block from the Ferry Building. Spring for a harbor-view room to watch ships passing by during the day and the pulsing lights of the Bay Bridge after dark. Modern touches include iPod docks and flat-screen TVs. Guests get a day pass to the adjacent Embarcadero YMCA, which has a gym, a spa, and a swimming pool.

Hotel Bohème (444 Columbus Ave., 415/433-9111, www.hotelboheme.com, $194-384) offers comfort, history, and culture at a pleasantly low price for San Francisco. The

Bohème's long history has included a recent renovation to create an intriguing, comfortable lodging. Rooms are small but comfortable, Wi-Fi is free, and the spirit of the Beats lives on. The warmly colored and gently lit rooms are particularly welcoming to solo travelers and couples, with their retro wrought-iron beds covered by postmodern geometric spreads. All rooms have private baths, and the double-queen room can sleep up to four people for an additional charge.

The **Washington Square Inn** (1660 Stockton St., 800/388-0220, www.wsisf.com, $219-359) doesn't look like a typical California B&B. With its city-practical architecture and canopy out on the sidewalk, it's more like a small, elegant hotel. The inn offers 15 rooms with private baths, elegant appointments, and fine linens. Some rooms have spa bathtubs, and others have views of Coit Tower and Grace Cathedral. Only the larger rooms and junior suites are spacious. Amenities include a generous continental breakfast brought to your room daily, afternoon tea, a flat-screen TV in every room, and free Wi-Fi.

A great upscale hotel in the heart of San Francisco's visitors' district is the **Best Western Plus Tuscan Inn** (425 North Point St., 800/648-4626, www.tuscaninn.com, $209-479). This luxurious Italian-inspired hotel offers great amenities and prime access to Fisherman's Wharf, Pier 39, Alcatraz, shopping, and dining. The attractive, modern exterior gives way to earth tones and country-style charm in the common areas. Rooms boast bright colors and up-to-date furnishings, much fancier than you might be accustomed to from a Best Western. All rooms have private baths. They also have Internet access, cable TV, and limo service to the Financial District three times daily. Check online for discount rates if you're coming during the middle of the week or are booking more than two weeks in advance.

Over $250

For a luxurious stay in the city, save up for a room at **The Argonaut** (495 Jefferson St., 800/790-1415, www.argonauthotel.com, $249-849). With stunning Bay views from its prime Fisherman's Wharf location, in-room spa services, and a yoga channel, The Argonaut is pure San Francisco. The rooms feature exposed brick walls and nautical-inspired decor. Rooms range from cozy standards to upscale suites with separate bedrooms and whirlpool tubs. The SF Maritime National Historic Park's Visitors Center and Interactive Museum is in the same building as The Argonaut.

MARINA AND PACIFIC HEIGHTS

These areas are close enough to Fisherman's Wharf that guests can walk there for dinner, and the lodgings are far more affordable than downtown digs.

Under $150

For an unexpectedly bucolic hostel experience within walking and biking distance of frenetic downtown San Francisco, stop for a night at the **Fisherman's Wharf Hostel** (Fort Mason, Bldg. 240, 415/771-7277, www.sfhostels.com/fishermans-wharf, dorm $40-49, private room $90-120), which actually sits in Fort Mason. The best amenities (aside from the free parking, free continental breakfast, and no curfews or chores) are the views of the bay and Alcatraz, and the sweeping lawns and mature trees all around the hostel.

Few frills clutter the clean, comfortable rooms at the **Redwood Inn** (1530 Lombard St., 800/221-6621, www.sfredwoodinn.com, $179-229), but if you need a reasonably priced motel room in ever-expensive San Francisco, this is a great place to grab one. From the location on Lombard Street, you can get to points of interest throughout the city.

$150-250

Staying at the ★ **Marina Motel** (2576 Lombard St., 415/921-9406 or 800/346-6118, www.marinamotel.com, $189-349) feels like you have your own apartment in the Marina. This European-style motor lodge features rooms above little garages. More than half of the rooms have small kitchens with a stove, fridge, microwave, and dishes. Though the Marina Motel was built in the 1930s, the rooms are updated with modern amenities including Wi-Fi and TVs with cable. With major attractions like the Palace of Fine Arts within walking distance, this reasonably priced motel is a great place to hunker down for a few days. Reserve a room away from Lombard Street if you are a light sleeper.

The **Lombard Motor Inn** (1475 Lombard St., 415/441-6000, www.lombardmotorinn. com, $185-225) has the standard-issue amenities: reasonable-size rooms, flat-screen TVs, Internet, free parking, and location, location, location. Of course, the location means there's plenty of nighttime noise pouring in through the windows, especially on weekends.

Pack the car and bring the kids to the **Hotel del Sol** (3100 Webster St., 877/433-5765, www.thehoteldelsol.com, $209-449). This unique hotel-motel embraces its origins as a 1950s motor lodge, with the rooms decorated in bright, bold colors with whimsical accents, a heated courtyard pool, palm trees, hammocks, and parking that's just $10 a night. The Marina locale offers trendy cafés, restaurants, bars, and shopping within walking distance as well as access to major attractions.

Another Pacific Heights jewel, the **Jackson Court** (2198 Jackson St., 415/929-7670, www. jacksoncourt.com, $219-285) presents a lovely brick facade in the exclusive neighborhood. The 10-room inn offers comfortable, uniquely decorated queen rooms. They also do an afternoon tea and a luscious continental breakfast.

The stately **Queen Anne Hotel** (1590 Sutter St., 800/227-3970, www.queenanne. com, $175-665) brings the elegance of downtown San Francisco out to Pacific Heights. Sumptuous fabrics and rich colors in the rooms and common areas add to the feeling of decadence and luxury in this boutique hotel. Small, moderate rooms offer attractive accommodations on a budget, while superior rooms and suites are more upscale. Continental breakfast is included, as are high-end services such as courtesy car service and afternoon tea and sherry.

The exterior and interior amenities of the **Hotel Majestic** (1500 Sutter St., 415/441-1100, www.thehotelmajestic.org, $200-300) evoke the grandeur of early-20th-century San Francisco. It is said that one of the former hotel owner's daughters haunts the Edwardian-style 1902 building, which boasts antique furnishings and decorative items from England and France. Cozy rooms, junior suites, and one-bedroom suites are available. The on-site **Cafe Majestic** serves breakfast and dinner, with a focus on local, healthful ingredients.

Over $250

Tucked in among the money-laden mansions of Pacific Heights, **Hotel Drisco** (2901 Pacific Ave., 800/634-7277, www.hoteldrisco.com, $325-925) offers elegance to discerning visitors. Away from the frenzied pace and noise of downtown, at the Drisco you get quiet, comfy rooms with overstuffed furniture, breakfast with a latte, and a glass of wine in the evening. Families and larger groups can look into the hotel's suite with two bedrooms and two baths. They also have a morning car service to downtown on weekdays.

A small, cute inn only a short walk from the Presidio, the **Laurel Inn** (444 Presidio Ave., 800/552-8735, www.jdvhotels.com/laurel_inn, $339-439) is the perfect place for people with pets or extended-stay travelers. Many of the rooms have kitchenettes, and all are comfortable and modern. The **Swank Cocktail & Coffee Club** next door offers a nice place to stop and have a cocktail or a Blue Bottle coffee, and the exclusive boutiques of Pacific Heights beckon visitors looking for a way to part with their cash.

The aptly named **Inn at the Presidio** (42 Moraga Ave., 415/800-7356, www.innatthepresidio.com, $250-385) is just minutes from the heart of the city, but its location in the Presidio's green space makes it feel a world away. The inn offers immediate access to hiking trails and cultural attractions along with panoramic views of the bay and Alcatraz.

Most of the rooms are within a former housing unit for bachelor officers. While the inn is modernized, it nods to its past with military decorations on the lobby's walls. Continental breakfast is served in the former mess hall. Suites are spacious for the city, including a bedroom with an adjoining room, a pullout sofa, and a gas fireplace. The nearby four-bedroom **Funston House** is available for large groups.

CIVIC CENTER AND HAYES VALLEY

You'll find a few reasonably priced accommodations and classic inns in the Civic Center and Hayes Valley areas.

Under $150

San Francisco is an expensive place, so booking a bed or a private room in a hostel is one of the only economical options for those on a budget. One popular hostel is the **HI-San Francisco City Center Hostel** (685 Ellis St., 415/474-5721, www.sfhostels.org/city-center, dorm beds $44-46, private rooms $120-140) in the Tenderloin a few blocks from the Civic Center. The hostel is in what was once a 1920s-era hotel, and the dining room, where complimentary continental breakfasts are served, was once a speakeasy.

Take a step back into an older San Francisco at the **Chateau Tivoli** (1057 Steiner St., 800/228-1647, www.chateautivoli. com, $130-300). The over-the-top colorful exterior matches perfectly with the American Renaissance interior decor. Each unique room and suite showcases an exquisite style evocative of the Victorian era. Some furnishings come from the estates of the Vanderbilts and J. Paul Getty. Most rooms have private baths, although the two least expensive share a bath.

$150-250

It might seem strange to stay at an inn called **The Parsonage** (198 Haight St., 415/863-3699, www.theparsonage.com, from $240-280), but this classy Victorian bed-and-breakfast exemplifies the bygone elegance of

the city in one of its most colorful neighborhoods. Rooms are decorated with antiques, and baths have stunning marble showers. Enjoy pampering, multicourse breakfasts, and brandy and chocolates when you come "home" each night.

In Hayes Valley a few blocks from the Opera House, the **Inn at the Opera** (333 Fulton St., 888/298-7198, www.shellhospitality.com, $229-329) promises to have guests ready for a swanky night of San Francisco culture. Clothes-pressing services count among the inn's many amenities. French interior styling in the rooms and suites that once impressed visiting opera stars now welcomes guests from all over the world. The on-site restaurant **Plaj** serves Scandinavian fare.

MISSION AND CASTRO

Accommodations in these neighborhoods are few and tend to run toward modest B&Bs.

Under $150

For a romantic visit to the Castro with your partner, stay at the **Willows Inn Bed & Breakfast** (710 14th St., 800/431-0277, www.willowssf.com, $120-205). The Willows has shared baths and comfortable rooms with private sinks and bent-willow furnishings, and serves a yummy continental breakfast each morning. Catering to the queer community, the innkeepers at the Willows can help you with nightclubs, restaurants, and festivals in the city and locally in the Castro. One of the best amenities is the friendship and camaraderie you'll find with the other guests and staff at this great Edwardian B&B.

At the **Inn on Castro** (321 Castro St., 415/861-0321, www.innoncastro.com, $135-275), you've got all kinds of choices. Pick an economy room with a shared bath, an upscale private suite, or a self-service apartment. Once ensconced, chill out on the cute patio, or go out into the Castro to take in the nightlife. The self-catering apartments can sleep up to four and have fully furnished and appointed kitchens. Amenities include LCD TVs with cable, DVD players, and colorful modern art.

GOLDEN GATE PARK AND THE HAIGHT

Accommodations around Golden Gate Park are surprisingly reasonable. Leaning toward Victorian and Edwardian inns, most lodgings are in the middle price range for well-above-average rooms and services. However, getting downtown from the quiet residential spots can be a trek; ask at your inn about car services, cabs, and the nearest bus lines.

Out on the ocean side of the park, motor inns of varying quality cluster on the Great Highway. They've got the advantages of more space, low rates, and free parking, but they range from drab all the way down to seedy; choose carefully.

$150-250

The **Stanyan Park Hotel** (750 Stanyan St., 415/751-1000, www.stanyanpark.com, $179-349) graces the Upper Haight across the street from Golden Gate Park. This renovated 1904-1905 building, listed in the National Register of Historic Places, shows off its Victorian heritage both inside and out. Rooms can be small but are elegantly decorated. Multiple-room suites are available. Ask for a room overlooking the park. A stay includes a morning continental breakfast and a late-afternoon wine and cheese reception.

To say the **Seal Rock Inn** (545 Point Lobos Ave., 888/732-5762, www.sealrockinn.com, $144-182) is near Golden Gate Park pushes even the fluid San Francisco neighborhood boundaries. This pretty place perches near the tip of Land's End, only a short walk from the Pacific Ocean. All rooms have ocean views, private baths, free parking, free Wi-Fi, and a pleasantly modern ambience. The Seal Rock offers rooms with kitchenettes (two-day minimum stay to use the kitchen part of the room). Call and ask for a fireplace room that faces the Seal Rocks, so you can stay warm and toasty while training your binoculars on a popular spot for local sea lions. The restaurant serves breakfast and lunch; on Sunday you'll be competing with brunch-loving locals for a table.

Way over on the other side of the park, the **Great Highway Inn** (1234 Great Hwy., 800/624-6644, www.greathwy.com, $159-209) sits across the street from Ocean Beach. This old motor-lodge-style motel features big clean rooms, decent beds, road noise, and a short walk to the Pacific Ocean. Rooms have industrial carpets and private baths. A better option for travelers with cars, the Great Highway Inn has free parking in an adjacent lot. The motel offers discounted rates to families visiting patients at the nearby UCSF Medical Center.

SAN FRANCISCO AIRPORT

Because San Francisco Airport (SFO) is actually 13 miles south of the city on the peninsula, there are no airport hotels with a San Francisco zip code. If you're hunting for an urban-chic boutique hotel or a funky and unique hostel, the airport is *not* the place to motel-shop. SFO's hotel row has many mid-priced chain motels.

$150-250

A generous step up both in price and luxury is the **Bay Landing Hotel** (1550 Bayshore Hwy., Burlingame, 650/259-9000, www.baylandinghotel.com, $179-319). Updated rooms include pretty posted headboards, granite sinks in the baths, tub-shower combos, in-room safes, and free Wi-Fi. Free continental breakfast is served in the dining room, and you can enjoy your meal out on the terrace.

The **Villa Montes Hotel** (620 El Camino Real, San Bruno, 650/745-0111, http://villamonteshotel.com, $169-209) offers mid-tier accommodations and amenities on a fairly nice block. Both the exterior and the interior are attractive and modern, complete with an indoor hot soaking pool along with a dry sauna. Focusing on business travelers, the motel has free in-room Wi-Fi, multiline phones with voice mail, and copy and fax machines. There is also a free breakfast, and more importantly, a free airport taxi.

Millwood Inn & Suites (1375 El Camino Real, Millbrae, 650/583-3935, www.millwoodinn.com, $189-199) offers contemporary decor and big rooms designed for the comfort of both business and vacation travelers. Amenities include free Wi-Fi and satellite TV with an attached DVD player. Gorge on a bigger-than-average free buffet breakfast. The Millwood Inn offers a complimentary airport shuttle, which is something not all airport motels near SFO do.

Food

One of the main reasons people come to San Francisco from near and far is to eat. Some of the greatest culinary innovation in the world comes out of the city's kitchens. The only real problem is choosing which restaurant to eat dinner at tonight.

UNION SQUARE AND NOB HILL
Bakeries and Cafés
With a monopoly on the coffee available in the middle of Union Square, business is brisk at **Emporio Rulli** (350 Post St., Union Square, 415/433-1122, www.rulli.com, daily 7am-7pm, $10-20). This local chain offers frothy coffee, pastries, and upscale sandwiches, plus wine and beer. Expect everything to be overpriced at Rulli. In the summer, sitting at the outdoor tables feels comfortable. In the winter it's less pleasant, but it's fun to watch the skaters wobble around the tiny outdoor ice rink in the square.

Blue Bottle Café (66 Mint Plaza, 415/495-3394, www.bluebottlecoffee.net, daily 7am-7pm, $5-10), a popular local chain with multiple locations around the city, takes its equipment seriously. Get a good cup of joe and a small if somewhat pretentious meal at the Mint Plaza location, which is Blue Bottle's only café with a full food program. Other locations include the Ferry Building (1 Ferry Bldg., Suite 7), the Heath Ceramics Factory (2900 18th St.), and a Hayes Valley kiosk (315 Linden St.). Expect a line.

Breakfast
Even on a weekday morning there will be a line out the door of ★ **Brenda's French Soul Food** (652 Polk St., 415/345-8100, http://frenchsoulfood.com, Mon.-Tues. 8am-3pm, Wed.-Sat. 8am-10pm, Sun. 8am-8pm, $12-17). People come in droves to this Tenderloin eatery for its delectable and filling New Orleans-style breakfasts. Unique offerings include crawfish beignets, an Andouille sausage omelet, and beef cutlet and grits. Entrées like chicken étouffée and red beans and rice top the dinner menu.

California Cuisine
Make reservations in advance if you want to dine at San Francisco legend **Farallon** (450 Post St., 415/956-6969, www.farallonrestaurant.com, Mon. 5:30pm-9:30pm, Tues.-Thurs. 11:30am-3pm and 5:30pm-9:30pm, Fri.-Sat. 11:30am-3pm and 5:30pm-10pm, Sun. 5pm-9:30pm, $27-65). Dark, cave-like rooms are decorated in an under-the-sea theme completed by the unique Jellyfish Bar. The cuisine, on the other hand, is out of this world. Chef Mark Franz has made Farallon a 20-year fad that just keeps gaining momentum. The major culinary theme, seafood, dominates the pricey-but-worth-it menu.

Chinese
It may not be in Chinatown, but the dim sum at ★ **Yank Sing** (101 Spear St., 415/781-1111, www.yanksing.com, Mon.-Fri. 11am-3pm, Sat.-Sun. 10am-4pm, $4-11) is second to none. They even won a prestigious James Beard Award in 2009. The family owns and operates both this restaurant and its sister location (49 Stevenson St., 415/541-4949), and now the third generation is training to take over. Expect traditional steamed pork buns, shrimp dumplings, and egg custard tarts. Note that it's open for lunch only.

French

Tucked away in a tiny alley that looks like it might have been transported from Saint-Michel in Paris, **Café Claude** (7 Claude Ln., 415/392-3505, www.cafeclaude.com, Mon.-Sat. 11:30am-10:30pm, Sun. 5:30pm-10:30pm, $21-28) serves classic brasserie cuisine to French expatriates and Americans alike. Much French is spoken here, but the simple food tastes fantastic in any language. Café Claude is open for lunch through dinner, serving an attractive post-lunch menu. In the evening it can get crowded, but reservations aren't strictly necessary if you're willing to order a classic French cocktail or a glass of wine and enjoy live music (on weekends) for a few minutes. They also have a Marina location (2120 Greenwich St., 415/375-9550).

Thai

Just outside of the Union Square area, in the seedier Tenderloin, **Lers Ros Thai** (730 Larkin St., 415/931-6917, www.lesros.com, daily 11am-midnight, $9-18) is a great place to expand your knowledge of Thai cuisine. Daily specials might include stir-fried alligator or venison.

Vietnamese

It seemed unlikely that anything worthy could possibly replace Trader Vic's, the building's illustrious former tenant, but **Le Colonial** (20 Cosmo Pl., 415/931-3600, www.lecolonialsf.com, Sun.-Wed. 5:30pm-10pm, Thurs.-Sat. 5:30pm-11pm, $22-37) does it, while paying proper homage. This Vietnamese fusion hot spot takes pride in its tiki lounge, which features live musical acts and house DJs six nights a week. Cocktails are big and tropical, but don't skip the food; the lush French-Vietnamese fare blends flavors perfectly.

FINANCIAL DISTRICT AND SOMA
Bakeries and Cafés

One of the Ferry Building's mainstays, the **Acme Bread Company** (1 Ferry Plaza, Suite 15, 415/288-2978, http://acmebread.com, Mon.-Fri. 6:20am-7:30pm, Sat.-Sun. 8am-7pm) remains true to its name. You can buy bread here, but not sandwiches, croissants, or pastries. All the bread that Acme sells is made with fresh organic ingredients in traditional style; the baguettes are traditionally French, so they start to go stale after only 4-6 hours. Eat fast!

The motto of **Café Venue** (67 5th St., 415/546-1144, www.cafevenue.com, Mon.-Fri. 7am-3:30pm, Sat. 8am-2:30pm, $6-10) is "real food, fast and fresh." This simple strategy is clearly working: on weekdays, expect a long line of local workers grabbing a salad or a sandwich for lunch. The warm chicken pesto sandwich is a highlight.

California Cuisine

★ **Michael Mina** (252 California St., 415/397-9222, www.michaelmina.net, Mon.-Thurs. 11:30am-2pm and 5:30pm-10pm, Fri. 11:30am-2pm and 5:30pm-10:30pm, Sun. 5:30pm-10pm, $44-52) finds its namesake celebrity chef using Japanese ingredients and French influences to create bold California entrées. This sleek, upscale restaurant with attentive service is where Mina showcases his signature dishes, including his ahi tuna tartare and his Maine lobster potpie, an inventive take in which the lobster, lobster cream sauce, and vegetables are ladled over a flaky pastry crust. The nine-course chef's tasting menu is $99.

Farmers Markets

While farmers markets are found in just about every California town, the **Ferry Plaza Farmers Market** (1 Ferry Plaza, 415/291-3276, www.ferrybuildingmarketplace.com, Tues. and Thurs. 10am-2pm, Sat. 8am-2pm) is special. At the granddaddy of Bay Area farmers markets you'll find a wonderful array of produce, cooked foods, locally raised meats, and locally caught seafood. Expect to see the freshest fruits and veggies from local growers, grass-fed beef from Marin County, and seasonal seafood pulled from the Pacific beyond the Golden Gate. Granted, you'll pay for the privilege of purchasing from this market. Even locals flock downtown to the Ferry Building on Saturday mornings, especially in the summer when the variety of California's agricultural bounty becomes staggering.

Gastropub

★ **The Cavalier** (360 Jessie St., 415/321-6000, http://thecavaliersf.com, Sun.-Wed. 7am-10pm, Thurs.-Sat. 7am-11pm, $16-34) serves a California take on upscale British pub food. The restaurant is decorated like a British hunting lodge, with mounted game heads on the walls. A stuffed fox named Floyd reclines on a bookcase in the back. As for the food, it is inventive, tasty, sometimes rich, and surprisingly well priced. The farro (a grain) and roasted beet appetizer might be the healthiest pub dish around, while the golden-fried lamb riblets are worth the trip. Other entrées include classics like fish-and-chips and bangers-and-mash.

Italian

For fine Italian-influenced cuisine, make a reservation at **Quince** (470 Pacific Ave., 415/775-8500, www.quincerestaurant.com, Mon.-Sat. 5pm-10pm, $95-180). Chef-owner Michael Tusk blends culinary aesthetics to create his own unique style of cuisine. There are three tasting menus: a five-course seasonal menu, a nine-course garden menu featuring veggie dishes, and the nine-course Quince menu that employs both meat and vegetable dishes.

Japanese

In these neighborhoods you'll find plenty of sushi restaurants, from the most casual walk-up lunch places to the fanciest fusion joints. **Ame** (St. Regis Hotel, 689 Mission St., 415/284-4040, www.amerestaurant.com, Mon.-Thurs. 6pm-9:30pm, Fri.-Sat. 5:30pm-10pm, Sun. 5:30pm-9:30pm, $38-46) is one of the latter. This upscale eatery serves a California-Japanese seafood fusion. Start with the offerings from the sashimi bar or find a wealth of options in the appetizers and main

courses. The blocky, attractive dining room has a modern flair that's in keeping with the up-to-date cuisine coming out of the kitchen. Start out or round off your meal with a cocktail from the shiny black bar.

Forget your notions of the plain-Jane sushi bar; **Ozumo** (161 Steuart St., 415/882-1333, www.ozumosanfrancisco.com, Mon.-Thurs. 11:30am-2pm and 5:30pm-10:30pm, Fri. 11:30am-2pm and 5:30pm-11pm, Sat. 5:30pm-11pm, $28-46) takes Japanese cuisine upscale, San Francisco-style. Order some classic nigiri, tempura-battered dishes, or a big chunk of meat off the traditional *robata* grill. High-quality sake lines the shelves above the bar and along the walls. For non-imbibers, choose from a selection of premium teas. If you're a night owl, enjoy a late dinner on weekends and drinks in the lounge nightly.

Seafood

It's easy to see why the ★ **Tadich Grill** (240 California St., 415/391-1849, www.tadichgrill.com, Mon.-Fri. 11am-9:30pm, Sat. 11:30am-9:30pm, $15-38), claiming to be the oldest restaurant in the city, has been around since the mid-1800s. Sit at the long wooden bar, which stretches from the front door back to the kitchen, and enjoy the attentive service by the white-jacketed waitstaff. The food is classic and hearty, and the seafood-heavy menu has 75 entrées, including a dozen daily specials. One of the standouts is the restaurant's delectable seafood cioppino, which might just be the best version of this Italian-American stew out there.

Steak

Alexander's Steakhouse (448 Brannan St., 415/495-1111, www.alexanderssteakhouse.com, Mon.-Thurs. 5:30pm-9pm, Fri.-Sat. 5:30pm-10pm, Sun. 5:30pm-8:30pm, $32-355) describes itself as "where East meets beef." It's true: The presentation at Alexander's looks like something you'd see on *Iron Chef*, and the prices of the *wagyu* beef look like the monthly payment on a small Japanese car. This white-tablecloth steak house is the antithesis of a bargain, but the food, including the steaks, is more imaginative than most, and the elegant dining experience will make you feel special as your wallet quietly bleeds out.

How could you not love a steak house with a name like **Epic Roasthouse** (369 Embarcadero, 415/369-9955, www.epicroasthouse.com, Mon.-Thurs. 11:30am-2:30pm and 5:30pm-9:30pm, Fri. 11:30am-2:30pm and 5:30pm-10pm, Sat. 11am-2:30pm and 5:30pm-10pm, Sun. 11am-2:30pm and 5:30pm-9:30pm, $33-198)? Come for the wood-fired grass-fed beef; stay for the prime views over San Francisco Bay. Epic Roasthouse sits almost underneath the Bay Bridge, where the lights sparkle and flash over the deep-black water at night. The pricey steak menu even includes the name of the cut's butcher in some cases.

Vietnamese

Probably the single most famous Asian restaurant in a city filled with eateries of all types is **The Slanted Door** (1 Ferry Plaza, Suite 3, 415/861-8032, www.slanteddoor.com, Mon.-Sat. 11am-2:30pm and 5:30pm-10pm, Sun. 11:30am-3pm and 5:30pm-10pm, $11-45). Owner Charles Phan, along with more than 20 family members and the rest of his staff, pride themselves on their welcoming service and top-quality food. Organic local ingredients are used in both traditional and innovative Vietnamese cuisine, creating a unique dining experience. Even experienced foodies remark that they've never had green papaya salad, glass noodles, or shaking beef like this before. The light afternoon-tea menu (daily 2:30pm-4:30pm) can be the perfect pick-me-up, and Vietnamese coffee is the ultimate Southeast Asian caffeine experience.

CHINATOWN
Chinese Banquets

Banquet restaurants offer tasty meat, seafood, and veggie dishes along with rice, soups, and appetizers, all served family-style. Tables are often round, with a lazy Susan in the middle to facilitate the passing of communal serving bowls around the table. In the city, most banquet Chinese restaurants have at least a few dishes that will feel familiar to the American palate, and menus often have English translations.

Hunan Home's Restaurant (622 Jackson St., 415/982-2844, http://hunanhome.yp-guides.net, Sun.-Thurs. 11:30am-9:30pm, Fri.-Sat. 11:30am-10pm, $10-30) is more on the casual side. You'll find classic items such

Tadich Grill

as broccoli beef and kung pao chicken. Be cautious with menu items with a "spicy" notation on the menu: At Hunan Home's, and in fact at most Bay Area Chinese restaurants, they mean *really* spicy.

Dim Sum

The Chinese culinary tradition of dim sum is translated as "touch the heart," meaning "order to your heart's content" in Cantonese. In practical terms, it's a light meal composed of small bites of a wide range of dishes. Americans tend to eat dim sum at lunchtime, though it can just as easily be dinner or even Sunday brunch. In a proper dim sum restaurant, you do not order anything or see a menu. Instead, you sip your oolong and sit back as servers push loaded steam trays out of the kitchen one after the other. Servers and trays make their way around the tables; you pick out what you'd like to try as it passes, and enough of that dish for everyone at your table is placed before you.

One of the many great dim sum places in Chinatown is the **Great Eastern** (649 Jackson St., 415/986-2500, www.greateasternrestaurant.net, Mon.-Fri. 10am-11pm, Sat.-Sun. 9am-11pm, $15-25), which serves its dim sum menu 10am-3pm daily. It's not a standard dim sum place; instead of the steam carts, you'll get a menu and a list. You must write down everything you want on your list and hand it to your waiter, and your choices will be brought out to you, so family style is undoubtedly the way to go here. Make reservations or you may wait 30-60 minutes for a table. This restaurant jams up fast, right from the moment it opens, especially on weekends. Most of the folks crowding into Great Eastern are locals.

Ordering dim sum at **Delicious Dim Sum** (752 Jackson St., 415/781-0721, Mon.-Tues. and Thurs.-Sun. 7am-6pm, $3) may pose challenges. The signs are not in English, and they don't take credit cards. Also, there is only one table inside so you'll probably be getting your dim sum to go. The inexpensive dim sum, with options including the popular pork

buns and shrimp-and-cilantro dumplings, is worth rising to the challenge.

Tea Shops

Official or not, there's no doubt that the world believes that tea is the national drink of China. While black tea, often oolong, is the staple in California Chinese restaurants, you'll find an astonishing variety of teas if you step into one of Chinatown's small tea shops. Enjoy a hot cup of tea and buy a pound of loose tea to take home with you. Most tea shops also sell lovely imported teapots and other implements for proper tea making.

One option is **Blest Tea** (752 Grant Ave., 415/951-8516, http://blesttea.com, Sun.-Fri. 11am-7pm, Sat. 10am-8pm, tasting $3), which boasts of the healthful qualities of their many varieties of tea. You're welcome to taste what's available for a nominal fee. If you're lucky enough to visit when the owner is minding the store, she'll tell you everything you ever needed to know about tea.

NORTH BEACH AND FISHERMAN'S WHARF
Bakeries and Cafés

Widely recognized as the first espresso coffeehouse on the West Coast, family-owned **Caffé Trieste** (601 Vallejo St., 415/392-6739, http://coffee.caffetrieste.com, Sun.-Thurs. 6:30am-10pm, Fri.-Sat. 6:30am-11pm, cash only) first opened its doors in 1956. It became a hangout for Beat writers in the 1950s and 1960s and was where Francis Ford Coppola penned the screenplay for his classic film *The Godfather* in the 1970s. Sip a cappuccino, munch on Italian pastries, and enjoy frequent concerts at this treasured North Beach institution. There are now four locations across the greater Bay Area.

Serving some of the most famous sourdough in the city, the **Boudin Bakery & Café** (Pier 39, Space 5-Q, 415/421-0185, www.boudinbakery.com, Sun.-Thurs. 8am-8pm, Fri.-Sat. 8am-9pm, $6-8) is a Pier 39 institution. Grab a loaf of bread to take with you, or order in one of the Boudin classics. Nothing draws tourists like the fragrant clam chowder in a bread bowl, but you can try another soup, a signature sandwich, or even a fresh salad. For a more upscale dining experience with the same great breads, try **Bistro Boudin** (160 Jefferson St., 415/351-5561, Sun.-Thurs. 11:30am-10pm, Fri.-Sat. 11:30am-10:30pm, $13-38).

Breakfast

Smack-dab in the middle of North Beach, **Mama's on Washington Square** (1701 Stockton St., 415/362-6421, www.mamas-sf.com, Tues.-Sun. 8am-3pm, $8-10) is perched right across from the green lawn of Washington Square. This long-standing institution is the perfect place to fuel up on gourmet omelets, freshly baked breads that include a delectable cinnamon brioche, and daily specials like crab benedict before a day of sightseeing. Arrive early, or be prepared to wait . . . and wait.

California Cuisine

San Francisco culinary celebrity Gary Danko has a number of restaurants, but the finest is the one that bears his name. **Gary Danko** (800 North Point St., 415/749-2060, www.garydanko.com, daily 5:30pm-10pm, prix fixe $76-117) offers the best of Danko's California cuisine, from the signature horse-radish-crusted salmon medallions to the array of delectable fowl dishes. The herbs and veggies come from Danko's own farm in Napa. There's an a la carte menu and a five-course tasting menu ($117). Make reservations in advance to get a table, and dress up for your sojourn in the elegant white-tablecloth dining room.

Greek

In the Greek fishing village of Kokkari, wild game and seafood hold a special place in the local mythology. At **Kokkari Estiatorio** (200 Jackson St., 415/981-0983, www.kokkari.com, Mon.-Thurs. 11:30am-2:30pm and 5:30pm-10pm, Fri. 11:30am-2:30pm and 5:30pm-11pm, Sat. 5pm-11pm, Sun. 5pm-10pm, $22-49), patrons enjoy Mediterranean delicacies made with fresh California ingredients amid rustic elegance, feasting on such classic dishes as crispy zucchini cakes, moussaka, and grilled lamb chops.

Italian

North Beach is San Francisco's own version of Little Italy. Poke around and find one of the local favorite mom-and-pop pizza joints, or try a bigger, more upscale Italian eatery.

Want a genuine world-champion pizza while you're in town? Tony Gemignani, winner of 11 World Pizza Champion awards, can hook you up. ★ **Tony's Pizza Napoletana** (1570 Stockton St., 415/835-9888, www.tonyspizzanapoletana.com, Mon. noon-10pm, Wed.-Sun. noon-11pm, $15-30) has seven different pizza ovens that cook by wood, coal, gas, or electric power. Get a classic American pie loaded with pepperoni, a California-style pie with quail eggs and chorizo, or a Sicilian pizza smothered in meat and garlic. The special Neapolitan-style pizza margherita is perfection. The wood-fired atmosphere includes marble-topped tables, dark woods, and white linen napkins stuck into old tomato cans. The long bar dominates the front dining room, so grab a fancy bottle of wine or a cocktail to go with that champion pizza. For a slice to go, head next door to **Tony's Coal-Fired Pizza and Slice House** (1556 Stockton Ave., http://tonyscoalfired.com, Mon. 11:30am-10pm, Tues. 11:30am-8pm, Wed.-Sun. 11:30am-11pm, slices $4.50-5.50).

Trattoria Contadina (1800 Mason St., 415/982-5728, www.trattoriacontadina.com, Sun.-Thurs. 5pm-9pm, Fri.-Sat. 5pm-9:30pm, $18-35) presents mouthwatering Italian fare in a fun, eclectic dining room. Dozens of framed photos line the walls, and fresh ingredients stock the kitchen in this San Francisco take on the classic Italian trattoria. Menu items include ravioli, *frutti di mare*, and gnocchi. Kids are welcome, and vegetarians will find good meatless choices on the menu.

Steak

A New York stage actress wanted a classic steak house in San Francisco, and so **Harris' Restaurant** (2100 Van Ness Ave., 415/673-1888, www.harrisrestaurant.com, Mon.-Fri. 5:30pm-close, Sat.-Sun. 5pm-close, $32-195) came to be. The fare runs to traditional steaks and prime rib as well upscale features, with a Kobe-style *wagyu* beef and surf-and-turf featuring a whole Maine lobster. Music lovers can catch live jazz in the lounge most evenings.

MARINA AND PACIFIC HEIGHTS
Asian Fusion

The eclectic **Blackwood** (2150 Chestnut St., 415/931-9663, www.blackwoodsf.com, Mon.-Thurs. 9am-10pm, Fri.-Sun. 9am-10:30pm, $12-27) is best known for its "Millionaire bacon," a slightly sweet slab of pork as thick as a notebook; it's served on burgers and wrapped around scallops. Thai street food fills out the menu with pad thai and curries, and breakfast is served until 4pm.

Italian

For a southern Italian meal with a soft touch, **Capannina** (1809 Union St., 415/409-8001, www.capanninasf.com, Sun.-Thurs. 5pm-10pm, Fri.-Sat. 5pm-10:30pm, $16-32) is the place. Soft green walls with marble and glass accents provide a sense of peace. The menu features classic Italian with an emphasis on the fruits of the sea. Many of the ingredients are imported directly from Italy, enhancing the authenticity of each dish. A three-course prix fixe menu is offered daily 5pm-6pm for $25.

Japanese

If you're in Pacific Heights, give **Kiss Seafood** (1700 Laguna St., 415/474-2866, Wed.-Sat. 5:30pm-9:30pm, $30-60) a try. This tiny restaurant (12 seats in total) boasts some of the freshest fish in town, which is no mean feat in San Francisco. The lone chef prepares all the fish himself, possibly due to the tiny size

of the place. If you're up for sashimi, you'll be in raw-fish heaven. Round off your meal with a glass of chilled premium sake. Reservations are a good idea.

New American

The Brixton (2140 Union St., 415/409-1114, www.brixtonsf.com, daily 11am-midnight, entrées $14-24) might have rock posters on the wall and loud music blaring overheard, but that doesn't mean you shouldn't try their food. Their dinner menu goes late into the night and includes items like half a chicken, grilled pork chops, and a tasty burger. The appetizer menu, including a sashimi dish and a crab cake plate, is worth grazing, and the "Tacos of the Day" can sate smaller appetites.

Seafood

There will be a line out the door any time you come to the tiny ★ **Swan Oyster Depot** (1517 Polk St., 415/673-1101, www.sfswanoysterdepot.com, Mon.-Sat. 10:30am-5:30pm, $10-25, cash only). With limited stools at a long marble bar, Swan, which opened in 1912, is an old-school seafood place that serves fresh seafood salads, seafood cocktails, and clam chowder, the only hot item on the menu. The seafood is so fresh that you pass it resting on ice while waiting for your barstool.

CIVIC CENTER AND HAYES VALLEY
California Cuisine

Housed in a former bank, **Nopa** (560 Divisadero St., 415/864-8643, http://nopasf.com, Mon.-Fri. 5pm-1am, Sat.-Sun. 11am-1am, $16-31) brings together the neighborhood that the restaurant is named after with a whimsical mural by a local artist, a communal table, and a crowd as diverse as the surrounding area. A creative and inexpensive menu offers soul-satisfying dishes and keeps tables full into the wee hours. The cocktails are legendary. On weekends, Nopa also serves brunch.

State Bird Provisions (1529 Fillmore

St., 415/795-1272, http://statebirdsf.com, Sun.-Thurs. 5:30pm-10pm, Fri.-Sat. 5:30pm-11pm, $14-22) burst onto the city's dining scene in a big way: It won the James Beard Award for Best New Restaurant in 2013. Part of the unique menu is devoted to pancakes and toast, with items like a beef tongue-and-horseradish buckwheat pancake. Of course, they also serve the state bird (quail) with provisions.

French

Absinthe (398 Hayes St., 415/551-1590, www.absinthe.com, Tues.-Fri. 11:30am-midnight, Sat. 11am-midnight, Sun. 11am-10pm, $16-38) takes its name from the notorious drink made of liquor and wormwood. Absinthe indeed does serve absinthe, including locally made St. George Spirits Absinthe Verte. It also serves upscale French bistro fare, including what may be the best french fries in the city. The French theme carries into the decor as well, so expect the look of a Parisian brasserie or perhaps a café in Nice, with retro-modern furniture and classic prints on the walls. The bar is open until 2am Thursday-Saturday, so if you want drinks or dessert after a show at the Opera or Davies Hall, just walk around the corner.

German

Suppenküche (525 Laguna St., 415/252-9289, www.suppenkuche.com, Mon.-Sat. 5pm-10pm, Sun. 10am-2:30pm and 5pm-10pm, $12.50-20) brings a taste of Bavaria to the Bay Area. The beer list is a great place to start, since you can enjoy a wealth of classic German brews on tap and in bottles, plus a few Belgians thrown in for variety. For dinner, expect German classics with a focus on Bavarian cuisine. Spaetzle, pork, sausage—you name it, they've got it, and it will harden your arteries right up. They now serve a Sunday brunch that's almost as heavy as their dinners. Suppenküche also has a **Biergarten** (424 Octavia St., 415/252-9289, http://biergartensf.com, Wed.-Sat. 3pm-9pm, Sun. 1pm-7pm) two blocks away.

MISSION AND CASTRO
Bakeries and Cafés

A line snakes into the ★ **Tartine Bakery** (600 Guerrero St., 415/487-2600, Mon. 8am-7pm, Tues.-Wed. 7:30am-7pm, Thurs.-Fri. 7:30am-8pm, Sat. 8am-8pm, Sun. 9am-8pm, www.tartinebakery.com, $4-15) almost all day long, and the eatery's baked goods, breads, and sandwiches are the reasons why. A slab of the transcendent quiche made with crème fraîche, smoked ham, and organic produce is an inspired way to start the day. There is nothing quite like a piece of the Passion Fruit Lime Bavarian Rectangle, a cake that somehow manages to be both rich in flavor and light as air. Sister property **Bar Tartine** (561 Valencia St., www.bartartine.com, Mon.-Thurs. 5:30pm-10pm, Fri. 5:30pm-10:30pm, Sat. 11am-2:30pm and 5:30pm-10:30pm, Sun. 11am-2pm and 5:30pm-10pm, $21-27, prix fixe $76 pp) serves gourmet dinners.

Korean

Owned and operated by three brothers, **Namu Gaji** (499 Dolores St., 415/431-6268, www.namusf.com, Tues. 5pm-10pm, Wed.-Thurs. 11:30am-3pm and 5pm-10pm, Fri. 11:30am-3pm and 5pm-11pm, Sat. 10:30am-4pm and 5pm-11pm, Sun. 11:30am-3pm and 5pm-10pm, $14-22) presents a new take on Korean food. One standout dish is the *okonomiyaki*, a pan-fried entrée made with kimchee and oysters. The adventurous can try beef tongue, while the less courageous might opt for salmon or a burger.

Mexican

Much of the rich heritage of the Mission district is Latino, thus leading to the Mission being *the* place to find a good taco or burrito. For a famous iteration of the classic Mission burrito joint, join the crowd at **Papalote Mexican Grill** (3409 24th St., 415/970-8815, www.papalote-sf.com, Mon.-Sat. 11am-10pm, Sun. 11am-9pm, $5-12). Build your own plate of tacos or a burrito from a list of classic and specialty ingredients including carne asada, *chile verde,* grilled vegetables, and tofu. What will make you even happier is the price: It's possible to get a filling meal for less than $10.

Seafood

For great seafood in a lower-key atmosphere, locals eschew the tourist traps on the Wharf and head for the **Anchor Oyster Bar** (579 Castro St., 415/431-3990, www.anchoroysterbar.com, Mon.-Sat. 11:30am-10pm, Sun. 4pm-9:30pm, $14-39) in the Castro. The raw bar features different ways to have oysters, including an oyster *soju* shot. The dining room serves seafood, including local favorite Dungeness crab. Service is friendly, as befits a neighborhood spot, and it sees fewer large crowds. This doesn't diminish its quality, and it makes for a great spot to get a delicious meal before heading out to the local clubs for a late night out.

Sushi

Ichi Sushi & NI Bar (3282 Mission St., 415/525-4750, http://ichisushi.com, Mon.-Thurs. 5:30pm-10pm, Fri.-Sat. 5:30pm-11pm, $4.50-14.50) started out as a Bernal Heights food stall and evolved into a sleek restaurant. The emphasis is on sustainable sashimi. There are also rolls, a unique cold ramen with pesto, and some perfectly golden-brown chicken wings. Get good deals on appetizers and drinks at the bar's happy hour (Mon.-Fri. 5:30pm-7pm).

GOLDEN GATE PARK AND THE HAIGHT
Cafés

One of the prettiest spots in Golden Gate Park is the Japanese Tea Garden. Within the garden is the famous **Tea House** (75 Hagiwara Tea Garden Dr., 415/752-1171, http://japaneseteagardensf.com, Mar.-Oct. daily 9am-6pm, Nov.-Feb. daily 9am-4:45pm, $10-20), where you can purchase a cup of hot tea and a light Japanese meal within the beautiful and inspiring garden.

California Cuisine

One of the most famous restaurant locations on the San Francisco coast is the **Cliff House.** The high-end eatery inhabiting the famed facade is **Sutro's** (1090 Point Lobos Ave., 415/386-3330, www.cliffhouse.com, Sun. 11am-9:30pm, Mon.-Thurs. 11:30am-9:30pm, Fri.-Sat. 11:30am-10pm, $26-46). The appetizers and entrées are mainly seafood in somewhat snooty preparations. Although the cuisine is expensive and fancy, in all honesty it's not the best in the city. What *is* amazing are the views from the floor-to-ceiling windows out over the vast expanse of the Pacific Ocean. These views make Sutro's a perfect spot to enjoy a romantic dinner while watching the sun set over the sea.

The Cliff House also houses the more casual **Bistro** (1090 Point Lobos Ave., 415/386-3330, www.cliffhouse.com, Mon.-Sat. 9am-3:30pm and 4:15pm-9:30pm, Sun. 8:30am-3:30pm and 4:15pm-9:30pm, $15-30).

Japanese

Sushi restaurants are immensely popular in these residential neighborhoods. **Koo** (408 Irving St., 415/731-7077, www.sushikoo.com, Tues.-Thurs. 5:30pm-10pm, Fri.-Sat. 5:30pm-10:30pm, Sun. 5pm-9:30pm, $30-50) is a favorite. While sushi purists are happy with the selection of nigiri and sashimi, lovers of fusion and experimentation will enjoy the small plates and unusual rolls. Complementing the Japanese cuisine is a small but scrumptious list of premium sakes. Only the cheap stuff is served hot, as high-quality sake is always chilled.

Thai

Behind its nondescript storefront exterior, **Marnee Thai** (1243 9th Ave., 415/731-9999, www.marneethaisf.com, daily 11:30am-10pm, $10-20) cooks up some of the best Thai food in San Francisco, with a location convenient to Golden Gate Park. The corn-cake appetizer is a must.

Information and Services

VISITOR INFORMATION

The main San Francisco **Visitor Information Center** (900 Market St., 415/391-2000, www. sanfrancisco.travel, May-Oct. Mon.-Fri. 9am-5pm, Sat.-Sun. 9am-3pm, Nov.-Apr. Mon.-Fri. 9am-5pm, Sat. 9am-3pm) can help you even before you arrive. Check out its website for information about attractions and hotels, and to order a visitors' kit. Once you're in town, get a San Francisco book at the Market Street location as well as the usual brochures and a few useful coupons. Materials are available in 14 different languages; there's also a multilingual staff.

BANKS

ATMs abound, especially in well-traveled areas like Fisherman's Wharf and Union Square.

MEDICAL AND EMERGENCY SERVICES

The **San Francisco Police Department** (766 Vallejo St., 415/315-2400, www.sf-police.org) is headquartered in Chinatown, on Vallejo Street between Powell and Stockton Streets.

San Francisco boasts several full-service hospitals. The **UCSF Medical Center at Mount Zion** (1600 Divisadero St., 415/567-6600, www.ucsfhealth.org) is renowned for its research and advances in cancer treatments and other important medical breakthroughs. The main hospital is at the corner of Divisadero and Geary Streets. Right downtown, **St. Francis Memorial Hospital** (900 Hyde St., 415/353-6000, www.saintfrancismemorial.org), at the corner of Hyde and Bush Streets, has an emergency department.

Transportation

GETTING THERE
Air

San Francisco International Airport (SFO, 800/435-9736, www.flysfo.com) isn't within the city of San Francisco; it is actually about 13 miles south in the town of Millbrae, right on the bay. You can easily get a taxi ($35) or other ground transportation into the heart of the city from the airport. Both Caltrain and BART are accessible from SFO, and some San Francisco hotels offer complimentary shuttles from the airport as well. You can also rent a car here.

As one of the 30 busiest airports in the world, SFO has long check-in and security lines much of the time and dreadful overcrowding on major travel holidays. On an average day, plan to arrive at the airport about two hours before your domestic flight or three hours before an international flight.

Train and Bus

Amtrak does not run directly into San Francisco. You can ride into San Jose, Oakland, or Emeryville stations and then take a connecting bus into San Francisco.

Greyhound (200 Folsom St., 415/495-1569, www.greyhound.com, daily 5:30am-1am) offers bus service to San Francisco from all over the country.

GETTING AROUND
Car

The **Bay Bridge** (toll $4-6) links I-80 to San Francisco from the east, and the **Golden Gate Bridge** (toll $7) connects CA-1 from the north. From the south, US-101and I-280 snake up the peninsula and into the city. Get a detailed map and good directions because the freeway interchanges, especially those surrounding the east side of the Bay Bridge,

Walking Tours

The best way to see San Francisco is to get out and take a walk. Dozens of companies offer walking tours of different parts of the city. Here are a few of the best and most interesting.

San Francisco City Guides (415/557-4266, www.sfcityguides.org, free) is a team of enthusiastic San Francisco tour guides who want to show you more about their beloved city. Opt to learn about San Francisco sights like Fort Mason and Fisherman's Wharf or choose a walk where you'll hear about the locales used by famed director Alfred Hitchcock in his films including *Vertigo*. Visit the website for a complete schedule of the current month's offerings.

One of the most popular walking tour companies in the city is **Foot** (800/979-3370, www.foottours.com, $15-40/person). Foot was founded by stand-up comedian Robert Mac, and hires comics to act as guides for their many different tours around San Francisco. If you're a brand-new visitor to the city, pick the two-hour "San Francisco in a Nutshell" tour for a funny look at the basics of San Francisco landmarks and history, or the three-hour "Whole Shebang," a comprehensive if speedy look at Chinatown, Nob Hill, and North Beach. For visitors who are back for the second or third time, check out the more in-depth neighborhood tours that take in Chinatown, the Castro, or the Haight. You can even hit "Nude, Lewd, and Crude," a look at the rise of 18-and-up entertainment in North Beach. Tour departure points vary, so check the website for more information about your specific tour and about multitour packages.

For an inside look at the culinary delights of Chinatown, sign up for a spot on **I Can't Believe I Ate My Way Through Chinatown** (650/355-9657, www.wokwiz.com, $90/person). This three-hour bonanza will take you first for a classic Chinese breakfast, then out into the streets of Chinatown for a narrated tour around Chinatown's food markets, apothecaries, and tea shops. You'll finish up with lunch at one of tour guide Chef Shirley's favorite hole-in-the-wall dim sum places. For folks who just want the tour and lunch, or the tour alone, check out the standard Wok Wiz Daily Tour ($50/person with lunch, $35/person tour only).

To check out another side of Chinatown, take the **Chinatown Ghost Tour** (877/887-3373, www.sfchinatownghosttours.com, Fri.-Sat. 7:30pm-9:30pm, adults $48, children $24, tour lasts 2 hours). It's hard to find a neighborhood with a richer history rife with ghost stories than San Francisco's Chinatown. The whole thing burned down more than a century ago, and it was rebuilt in exactly the same spot, complete with countless narrow alleyways. This tour will take you into these alleys after the sun sets, when the spirits are said to appear on the streets. You'll start out at Four Seas Restaurant (731 Grant Ave.) and follow your loquacious guide along the avenues and side streets of Chinatown. As you stroll, your guide will tell you the stories of the neighborhood spirits, spooks, and ancestors. The curious get to learn about the deities worshipped by devout Chinese to this day, along with the folklore that permeates what was until recently a closed and secretive culture. Then you head into a former gambling den where a magician will attempt to conjure the soul of a long-dead gambler.

can be confusing, and the traffic congestion is legendary. For traffic updates and route planning, visit **511.org** (www.511.org).

CAR RENTAL

A car of your own is not necessarily beneficial in San Francisco. If you plan to spend a lot of time in the city, consider dispensing with a car and using cabs and public transit options. Rent a car when you're ready to leave San Francisco, or turn your rental in early if the city is your last stop. If you absolutely must have your car with you, try to get a room at a hotel with a parking lot and either free parking or a parking package for the length of your stay.

All the major car rental agencies have a presence at the **San Francisco Airport** (SFO, 800/435-9736, www.flysfo.com). In addition, most reputable hotels can offer or recommend a car rental. Rates tend to run $90-160 per day and $250-550 per week (including taxes and fees), with discounts for weekly and longer rentals. If you're flying into **Mineta San**

José Airport (SJC, www.flysanjose.com) or Oakland Airport (OAK, www.flyoakland. com), the cost can drop to $110-250 per week for budget agencies. Premium agencies like Hertz and Avis are much pricier: You'll pay $375-650 for the same car. Off-site locations may offer cheaper rates, in the range of about $375 per week.

DRIVING

Driving in San Francisco can be confusing. Like most major metropolitan centers, one-way streets, alleys, streetcars, taxis, bicycles, and pedestrians all provide impediments to navigation. Touring around the city to see the sights means traffic jams filled with workers on weekdays and travelers on weekends. It means negotiating the legendary steep hills without crashing into the cars behind and in front of you, and you must also watch out for pedestrians crossing the street when you have a green light.

PARKING

Parking a car in San Francisco can easily cost $50 per day or more. Most downtown and Union Square hotels do not include free parking with your room. Expect to pay $35-45 per night for parking, which may not include in-and-out privileges.

Street parking spots are rare and often require permits (which visitors cannot obtain). Parking lots and garages fill up quickly, especially during special events. You're more likely to find parking included at the motels along the edge of the city. Fisherman's Wharf, the Marina, and the Richmond and Sunset districts have the most motor inns with parking included.

Muni

The **Muni light rail system** (www.sfmta. com, adults $2, youths and seniors $0.75, cable car rides $6) has a reputation for delays, but it can get you where you want to go within San Francisco. A variety of lines snake through the city, including those that go down to Fisherman's Wharf using vintage streetcars

to heighten the fun for visitors. See the website for a route map, ticket information, and schedules.

To buy tickets, use one of the vending machines placed near some stops. Muni ticket machines are also outside the Caltrain station. See the website for more information about purchasing tickets.

Muni also runs the bus lines, which require the same fares; they can be slightly more reliable than the trains and go all over the city.

BART

Bay Area Rapid Transit (www.bart.gov, $3-10 one-way), or **BART,** is the Bay Area's late-coming answer to major metropolitan underground railways like Chicago's L trains and New York's subway system. Sadly, there's only one arterial line through the city. However, service directly from San Francisco Airport into the city runs daily, as does service to Oakland Airport, the cities of Oakland and Berkeley, and many other East Bay destinations. BART connects to the Caltrain system and San Francisco Airport in Millbrae. See the website for route maps, schedules (BART usually runs on time), and fare information.

To buy tickets, use the vending machines found in every BART station. If you plan to ride more than once, add money to a single ticket, and then keep that ticket and reuse it for each ride.

Caltrain

Commuter rail line **Caltrain** (www.caltrain. com, $3-13 one-way) runs along the peninsula into Silicon Valley, from San Francisco to San Jose, with limited continuing service to Gilroy. Baby Bullet trains can get you from San Jose to San Francisco in under an hour during commuting hours. Extra trains are often added for San Francisco Giants, San Francisco 49ers, and San Jose Sharks games.

You must purchase a ticket in advance at the vending machines found in all stations, or get your 10-ride card stamped before you board a train. The main Caltrain station in San Francisco is at the corner of 4th and King

Streets, within walking distance of AT&T Park and the Moscone Center.

Taxi

You'll find plenty of taxis in all the major tourist areas of the city. Feel free to wave one down or ask your hotel to call you a cab. If you need to call a cab yourself, try **City Wide Dispatch** (415/920-0700).

Marin County

Marin County, in the North Bay, is San Francisco's backyard. Beginning with the Marin Headlands at the terminus of the Golden Gate Bridge, there is a nearly unbroken expanse of wildlands from San Francisco Bay to Tomales Bay. Here you'll find rugged cliffs plunging into the Pacific, towering redwoods, the area's tallest mountain, and verdant pastures home to the Bay Area's celebrated grass-fed beef cattle and award-wining, cheese-producing dairy cows.

MARIN HEADLANDS

The Marin Headlands lie north of San Francisco at the north end of the Golden Gate Bridge. The land here encompasses a wide swath of virgin wilderness, former military structures, and a historic lighthouse.

Once over the bridge, the Alexander Avenue exit offers two options for exploring the headlands: Follow Alexander Avenue to Fort Baker and the Bay Area Discovery Museum, or turn left onto Bunker Road for the Marin Headlands Visitors Center and Nike Missile Site.

Vista Point

Aptly named **Vista Point,** at the north end of the Golden Gate Bridge, offers views from the Marin Headlands toward San Francisco. If you dream of walking across the **Golden Gate Bridge** (877/229-8655, http://golden-gate.org, gates Nov.-mid-Mar. daily 5am-6:30pm, mid-Mar.-Oct. daily 5am-9pm), bring a warm coat: The wind can really whip across the span. The bridge is 1.7 miles long, so a round-trip walk will turn into a 3.4-mile excursion. Bikes are allowed daily 24 hours, though after 9pm they must be buzzed through a gate.

To reach Vista Point, take U.S. 101 north across the Golden Gate Bridge. The first exit on the Marin County side is Vista Point; turn right into the parking lot. Note that this small parking lot often fills early.

Fort Baker

Standing at Crissy Field in San Francisco, you may wonder about those charming white buildings across the bay. They compose **Fort Baker** (435 Murray Circle, 415/331-1540, www.nps.gov/goga, daily sunrise-sunset, free), a 335-acre former army post established in 1905. Fort Baker is part of the Golden Gate National Recreation Area and is open to visitors. The location, just east of the Golden Gate Bridge but secluded in a shallow valley, makes it great for city views and a wind-free beach. The fort is the best example of military architecture from the Endicott Period. It includes many elegant homes with large sweeping porches arrayed around the oval parade grounds. Fort Baker houses a hotel, Cavallo Point Lodge, and a nonprofit called the Institute at the Golden Gate. The Bay Area Discovery Museum is also nearby, along with the tiny Presidio Yacht Club, where all are welcome to enjoy a drink by the water.

Bay Area Discovery Museum

The **Bay Area Discovery Museum** (557 McReynolds Rd., Sausalito, 415/339-3900, www.baykidsmuseum.org, Tues.-Fri. 9am-4pm, Sat.-Sun. 10am-5pm, $13-14) offers kids of all ages a chance to explore the world they live in. The focus is definitely on the younger

Marin Headlands

FORT CRONKHITE

Coastal Trail

HILL 88

Bird Island

Rodeo Beach

Lagoon Trail

MITCHELL RD

GATE

MARINE MAMMAL CENTER

Golden Gate National Recreation Area

POINT BONITA LIGHTHOUSE

Point Bonita

Point Bonita Trail

FIELD RD

NIKE MISSILE SITE

Rodeo Lagoon

BUNKER RD

CONZELMAN RD

SIMMONDS RD

MARIN HEADLANDS VISITORS CENTER

HEADLANDS CENTER FOR THE ARTS

MARIN HEADLANDS HOSTEL

Bonita Cove

BICENTENNIAL

FORT BARRY

Miwok Trail

Bobcat Trail

0   500 yds
0   500 m

Black Sands Beach

CONZELMAN RD

BUNKER RD

Rodeo Valley Trail

Coastal Trail

Point Diablo

ONE WAY ROAD

Hawk Hill

McCULLOUGH RD

MUIR WOODS NATIONAL MONUMENT, and POINT REYES NATIONAL SEASHORE

To Sausalito

GOLDEN

Kirby Cove

KIRBY COVE

CONZELMAN RD

Coastal Trail

BAKER-BARRY (BUNKER) RD

SCA Trail

ROBIN WILLIAMS TUNNEL

To Sausalito

GATE

GOLDEN GATE BRIDGE

Bicycle Path

Pedestrian Path

ALEXANDER AVE

FORT BAKER

MURRAY RD

EAST RD

To San Francisco

GOLDEN GATE BRIDGE

VISTA POINT

Horseshoe Cove

CAVALLO POINT LODGE/ FARLEY BAR/ MURRAY CIRCLE RESTAURANT

BAY AREA DISCOVERY MUSEUM

set; most of the permanent exhibits are geared toward small children, with lots of interactive components and places to play. Kids can check out easy-to-understand displays that describe the natural world, plus lots of Bay Area-specific exhibits. The Discovery Museum also boasts a theater and a café.

Marin Headlands Visitors Center

A great place to start your exploration is at the **Marin Headlands Visitors Center** (Field Rd. and Bunker Rd., 415/331-1540, www.nps.gov/goga, daily 9:30am-4:30pm), in the old chapel at Fort Barry. The park rangers can give you the current lowdown on the best trails, beaches, and campgrounds in the headlands.

Point Bonita Lighthouse

The **Point Bonita Lighthouse** (415/331-1540, www.nps.gov/goga, Sat.-Mon. 12:30pm-3:30pm, free) has been protecting the headlands for over 150 years and remains an active light station to this day. You need some dedication to visit Point Bonita, since it's only open a few days each week and there's no direct access by car. A 0.5-mile trail with steep sections leads from the trailhead on Field Road. Along the way, you'll pass through a hand-cut tunnel chiseled from the hard rock by the original builders of the lighthouse, and then you'll cross the dramatic suspension bridge that leads to the building. Point Bonita was the third lighthouse built on the West Coast and was the last staffed lighthouse in California. Today, the squat hexagonal building shelters automatic lights, horns, and signals. For a special treat, call the Marin Headlands Visitors Center (415/331-1540) to book a spot on a romantic 1.5-hour full-moon tour.

Marine Mammal Center

Inspired by the ocean's beauty and want to learn more about the animals that live in it? Visit the **Marine Mammal Center** (2000 Bunker Rd., 415/289-7325, www. marinemammalcenter.org, daily 10am-5pm, free) at Fort Cronkite in the Marin Headlands. The center is a hospital for sick and injured seals and sea lions. Wander around and look at the educational displays to learn more about what the center does. The one-hour docent-led **tours** (June-Aug. daily 11am, 1pm, 3pm; Sept.-May Fri. and Mon. 1pm and 3pm, Sat.-Sun. 11am, 1pm, 3pm; adults $7, seniors and ages 5-17 $5, under age 5 free) explain the program in greater depth. Visitors will also get an education on the impact of human activity on marine mammals, and maybe a chance for close encounters with some of the center's patients.

Nike Missile Site

Military history buffs jump at the chance to tour a restored Cold War-era Nike missile base, known in military speak as SF-88. The **Nike Missile Site** (Field Rd. past the Headlands Visitors Center, 415/331-1453, www.nps.gov/goga, Wed.-Fri. 12:30pm-3:30pm and first Sat. each month, free) is the only such restored Nike base in the United States. Volunteers continue the restoration and lead tours every hour at the base, which is overseen by the Golden Gate National Recreation Area. On the tour, you'll get to see the fueling area and the testing and assembly building, and even take a ride on the missile elevator down into the pits that once stored missiles built to defend the United States from the Soviet Union. Because restoration work is ongoing, the tour changes as new areas become available to visitors.

Hiking

Folks come from all over the world to hike the trails that thread through the Marin Headlands. The landscape is some of the most beautiful in the state, with unparalleled views of the Golden Gate Bridge and the Pacific Ocean.

From the Marin Headlands Visitors Center parking lot (Field Rd. and Bunker Rd.), the **Lagoon Trail** (1.75 miles round-trip, easy) encircles Rodeo Lagoon and gives bird-watchers an eagle's-eye view of the egrets, pelicans, and other seabirds that call the lagoon home. The lagoon is also home to the endangered tidewater goby, a small fish. The trailhead is near the restrooms.

An easy spot to get to, **Rodeo Beach** draws many visitors on summer weekends—do not expect solitude on the beach or the trails, or even in the water. Locals come out to surf when the break is going, while beachcombers look for the unique red and green pebbles on the shore. Note that the wind can really howl out here. The Lagoon Trail accesses the beach, but there is also a fairly large parking lot on Bunker Road that is much closer.

At Rodeo Beach is a trailhead for the **Coastal Trail.** To explore some of the battery ruins that pockmark these hills, follow the Coastal Trail (1.5 miles one-way, easy) north to its intersection with Old Bunker Road Trail and return to Bunker Road near the Marine Mammal Center. Or extend this hike by continuing 2.3 miles up the Coastal Trail to the summit of Hill 88 and stellar views. Loop this trail by linking it with Wolf Ridge Trail to Miwok Trail for a moderate 5.5-mile round-trip hike.

To reach the trailheads and parking lots, follow Bunker Road west to either Rodeo Beach or the Marin Headlands Visitors Center and their adjoining parking lots.

Cycling

If you prefer two wheels to two feet, you'll find the road and trail biking in the Marin Headlands both plentiful and spectacular. From the Tennessee Valley Trailhead, there are many multiuse trails designated for bikers as well as hikers. The **Valley Trail** (4 miles round-trip) takes you down the Tennessee Valley and all the way out to Tennessee Beach. A longer ride runs up the **Miwok Trail** (2 miles) northward. Turn southwest onto the **Coyote Ridge Trail** (0.9 miles), then catch the **Coastal Fire Road** (2 miles) the rest of the way west to Muir Beach. Another fun ride leads from just off U.S. 101 at the Rodeo Avenue exit. Park your car on the side of

Rodeo Avenue and then bike down the short **Rodeo Avenue Trail,** which ends in a T intersection after 0.7 miles at **Alta Trail.** Take a left, and access to **Bobcat Trail** is a few yards away. Continue on Bobcat Trail for 2.5 miles straight through the headlands to the **Miwok Trail** for just 0.5 miles, and you'll find yourself out at Rodeo Beach.

Need to rent a bicycle for your travels? In San Francisco, **Bike and Roll** (899 Columbus Ave., 415/229-2000, www.bikeandroll.com/ sanfrancisco, daily 8am-5pm, tours $60 for 5 hours) offers off-road biking tours of the Marin Headlands, plus bicycle rentals that let you go wherever the spirit moves you.

Accommodations

Lodging options are fairly limited in the Marin Headlands except for one luxurious lodge. Many other luxury-minded travelers choose to stay in Tiburon or Sausalito, while budget-motel seekers head for San Rafael.

Travelers who want budget accommodations indoors often choose the **Marin Headlands Hostel** (Bldg. 941, Fort Barry, 415/331-2777, www.norcalhostels.org/marin, dorm $28-35, private room $87-132). You'll find full kitchen facilities, Internet access, laundry rooms, and a rec room—all the amenities you'd expect from a high-end hotel. Surprisingly cozy and romantic, the hostel is sheltered in the turn-of-the-20th-century buildings of Fort Barry, creating a unique atmosphere. With the headlands right outside your door and 24-hour access for registered guests, there is no lack of activities or exploration opportunities.

The military personnel who stayed at Fort Baker would be floored by the ★ **Cavallo Point Lodge** (601 Murray Circle, Fort Baker, Sausalito, 415/339-4700, www.cavallopoint. com, $429-1,000) that is now on the old installation's grounds. Actually, anyone will be impressed with a stay in this luxurious lodge. Stay in beautiful historic homes, which were former officers' residences, featuring elegant early-20th-century woodwork, box-beam ceilings, and wraparound porches. Cavallo Point

Lodge also has rooms and suites in two-story, environmentally friendly buildings, which are situated on a hillside and offer floor-to-ceiling windows. All rooms have luxury amenities including gas fireplaces and large flat-screen TVs, while the contemporary rooms also include stone bathroom floors and deep soaking tubs. With the high-end restaurant Murray Circle and Farley Bar on site, and the Golden Gate Bridge within walking distance, you may not stray far from this rejuvenating oasis.

Camping

Camping here requires some planning; lots of other people have the same idea. Be forewarned about pitching a tent, as Marin can be foggy, cold, and windy at any time of year, even in July and August. Bring your warm camping gear if you plan to seek out one of the precious few campsites.

The most popular campground is **Kirby Cove** (877/444-6777, www.recreation.gov, reservations required, tent-only $25). Secluded and shaded campsites provide a beautiful respite. Make your reservations well in advance for summer weekends, as this popular campground fills up fast. To get there, follow the one-mile trail from Battery Spencer, the concrete military installation on Conzelman Road.

The **Bicentennial Campground** (Battery Wallace parking lot, 415/331-1540, free) boasts a whopping three campsites easily accessible from the parking lot. Each site can accommodate a maximum of three people, and there's no water available or fires allowed on-site. A nearby picnic area has barbecue grills that campers can use to cook a hot dinner.

Food

End a day of historic hiking with oysters and drinks at Cavallo Point Lodge's ★ **Farley Bar** (601 Murray Circle, Fort Baker, Sausalito, 415/339-4750, www.cavallopoint.com, Sun.-Thurs. 11am-11pm, Fri.-Sat. 11am-midnight, $10-38). Snag a blanket and a seat on the porch to watch the fog roll in over the Golden Gate Bridge. With only 12 drinks on the menu (all

$12), the bar boasts one of the most classic and contemporary cocktail menus around. After the sun goes down, mosey on inside, where lush leather chairs and sofas are arranged to maximize privacy and where a server is sure to hand you a bar menu with options including steamed mussels and a burger made from Marin-raised beef. There's also live music on Monday nights 7:30pm-9:30pm.

Also at Cavallo Point is the excellent **Murray Circle Restaurant** (Cavallo Point Lodge, 601 Murray Circle, Fort Baker, Sausalito, 415/339-4750, www.cavallopoint.com, Mon.-Thurs. 7am-11am, 11:30am-2pm, and 5:30pm-10pm; Fri. 7am-11am, 11:30am-2pm, and 5:30pm-11pm; Sat. 7am-11am, 11:30am-2:30pm, and 5:30pm-11pm; Sun. 7am-11am, 11:30am-2:30pm, and 5:30pm-10pm, $14-33). The long, slender dining room is draped in muted greens and golds, perfectly matching the simple, elegant style of the historic building. The menu is based on the best Marin produce, seafood, meat, and dairy. Simple dishes are executed with French technique. You'll find raw oysters, bouillabaisse, and alder grilled pork chops.

Information and Services

Aside from the visitors centers and museums, there isn't much in the way of services in the headlands. Likewise, cell-phone reception can be spotty. For a hospital or bank, you'll have to go to Sausalito or across the bridge to San Francisco.

Transportation

Fort Baker and the Marin Headlands are just north of the Golden Gate Bridge on Highway 1 and U.S. 101. To get to the headlands from San Francisco, take the Alexander Avenue exit, the second exit after you cross the bridge. From the north, Alexander Avenue is the last Sausalito exit. If the visitors center is the first stop on your itinerary, turn left onto Bunker Road and go through the one-way tunnel. If you want to hit Fort Barry and the Bonita Lighthouse first, follow Alexander Avenue right and travel under the highway to Conzelman Road, which leads up the hill along the edge of the headlands. Keep in mind that many of the roads are very narrow and become one-way in places.

Traffic in this area, particularly in the headlands, can be heavy on beautiful weekend days, so try and plan to get here early and spend the time that other people are stuck in their cars exploring the area on foot. Another option is to take bus route 76 of the **Muni** (415/701-2311, www.sfmta.com, Sun. 10am-7pm, $2.25 one-way). Making stops throughout downtown San Francisco and the north end of the city, this Sunday-only Muni line crosses the Golden Gate and ventures as far as Rodeo Cove in the headlands. It makes frequent trips, and you can even load bikes on the front.

SAUSALITO

The affluent town of Sausalito wraps around the north end of San Francisco Bay. The main drag runs along the shore, and the concrete boardwalk is perfect for strolling and biking. A former industrial fishing town, Sausalito still has a few old cannery buildings and plenty of docks, most now lined with pleasure boats. Sausalito has a community of people living on 400 houseboats along its northern end.

San Francisco Bay Model

One of the odder attractions you'll find in the North Bay is the **San Francisco Bay Model** (2100 Bridgeway, 415/332-3871, www.spn. usace.army.mil, summer Tues.-Fri. 9am-4pm, Sat.-Sun. 10am-5pm, winter Tues.-Sat. 9am-4pm, free), which is administered by the U.S. Army Corps of Engineers. It is a scale model of the way the bay works, complete with currents and tides. Scientists and engineering types love to see how the waters of the bay move and work.

Accommodations

The Gables Inn (62 Princess St., 415/289-1100, www.gablesinnsausalito.com, $225-500) opened in 1869 and is the oldest B&B in the area. Each of the nine rooms is appointed in tasteful earth tones, with white linens and several baths. Although this inn honors its long history, it has also kept up with the times, adding cable TV and Internet access. Genial innkeepers serve a continental breakfast, available for a few hours each morning, and host a wine and cheese soiree each evening.

With a checkered history dating back to 1915, the **Hotel Sausalito** (16 El Portal, 888/442-0700, www.hotelsausalito.com, $165-305) was a speakeasy, a bordello, and a home for the writers and artists of the Beat Generation. Today, this tiny boutique hotel, with its yellow walls and locally built furnishings, evokes the Mediterranean coast. Sink into your cozy room after a day spent walking or biking along the water and a scrumptious dinner out.

The **Casa Madrona Hotel and Spa** (801 Bridgeway, 800/288-0502, www.casamadrona.com, $300-1,000) is a sprawling collection of structures housing contemporary luxury hotel rooms and suites that satisfy even the pickiest celebrity guest. **Poggio,** the onsite restaurant, serves award-winning Italian food, and the full-service spa pampers guests with a full menu of body and salon treatments. If you're treating yourself to a room at Casa Madrona, ask for one with a view overlooking the bay or the harbor.

For a taste of the life of the richest residents of the area, stay at Sausalito's **Inn Above Tide** (30 El Portal, 800/893-8433, www.innabovetide.com, $360-1,600). The inn sits over the edge of the water looking out at the San Francisco skyline. Most rooms have private decks with sublime views (except when it's foggy). Inside, the appointments look like something you'd find in an upscale home rather than a hotel. From the hotel, walk downtown to enjoy the shops, spas, and restaurants of Sausalito. Take advantage of the morning continental breakfast and afternoon wine and cheese.

Food

Right on the water, ★ **Fish** (350 Harbor

Dr., 415/331-3474, www.331fish.com, daily 11:30am-8:30pm, $14-25) is known for serving sustainable seafood. Other reasons to visit are its rich Dungeness crab roll drenched in butter and its spicy Saigon salmon sandwich, an explosion of tastes with carrots, jalapeños, cilantro sprigs, and a house-made ginger-scallion sauce on a delectable roll.

For California-influenced Chinese food, go to **Tommy's Wok Chinese Cuisine** (3001 Bridgeway, 415/332-5818, http://tommyswok. com, Mon.-Thurs. 11:30am-3pm and 4pm-9pm, Fri.-Sat. 11:30am-3pm and 4pm-9:30pm, Sun. 4pm-9pm, $11-18.50). The menu includes organic free-range chicken, organic tofu, and a heavy emphasis on fresh vegetables—even in the meat dishes. Don't expect to find too many sweet, syrupy favorites; instead, take a chance on some tasty broccoli or asparagus. They even have lettuce wraps.

Information and Services

Get your visit started with a stop at the **Sausalito Visitors Center** (780 Bridgeway, 415/332-0505, www.sausalito.org, Tues.-Sun. 11:30am-4pm). Also known as the Ice House because it was used to store ice in the days before refrigeration technology, this tiny building has loads of Sausalito materials to browse and purchase. The helpful staff has free maps and tips and sells books, cards, and souvenirs.

Transportation

Sausalito is just over the Golden Gate Bridge from San Francisco and is easily accessible by bicycle on side roads or by car on U.S. 101. Once in town, navigating by car can be a challenge, as the narrow oceanfront main road gets very crowded on weekends. If you can, park and walk around town, both for your own comfort and to do your part to minimize traffic congestion. Street parking is mostly metered.

If you have the time, a great way to get to Sausalito from San Francisco is by ferry. Two companies make the trip daily, which takes roughly an hour or less. The scenery is beautiful, and it is a great chance to get out on the

bay a lot more cheaply than a tour. The **Blue and Gold Fleet** (415/705-8200, www.blue-andgoldfleet.com, check website for schedule, adults $10.75, children and seniors $6.25, under age 5 free) makes the trip from Pier 41. Largely serving commuters, the **Golden Gate Ferry** (415/455-2000, http://golden-gate.org, see website for schedule, adults $9.75, children and seniors $4.75, under age 5 free) leaves from the Ferry Building, closer to downtown San Francisco. The trip across the bay is cheaper and a bit faster than those that depart from Pier 41.

TIBURON

Once a simple fishing town, Tiburon now has some of the most expensive waterfront real estate in the world. The small downtown area that backs onto the marina is popular with the young and affluent crowd as well as longtime yacht owners. Aside from the views, one of the greatest draws to Tiburon is its proximity to Angel Island, the largest in the bay and a unique state park.

★ Angel Island State Park

The long history of **Angel Island** (415/435-5390, www.parks.ca.gov, daily 8am-sunset) begins with regular visits (though no permanent settlements) by the Coastal Miwok people. During the Civil War the U.S. Army created a fort on the island in anticipation of Confederate attacks from the Pacific. The attacks never came, but the army maintained a base here. Today, many of the 19th-century military buildings remain and can be seen on the **tram tour** (1 hour, $10-15), on foot, or on a docent-led Segway or Digger electric scooter tour (both 2 hours, $68 pp). If you'd rather get around by pedal power, rent bikes ($12.50/hour, $40/day) to explore the island. During the Cold War the army built a Nike missile base on the island to protect San Francisco from possible Soviet attacks. The missile base is not open to the public, but it can be seen from roads and trails.

Angel Island's history also has a shameful

side. It served as an immigration station for Chinese emigrants from 1910 to 1940, a holding center for prisoners of war during World War II, and a Japanese internment camp. During its time as an immigration checkpoint, Europeans were waved through with little more than a head-lice check, while the Chinese were herded into barracks while government officials scrutinized their papers. After months and sometimes years of waiting, many were shipped back to China. Today, poetry covers the walls of the barracks, expressing the despair of the immigrants who had hoped for a better life and found little more than prison. Docent-led **tours** (Wed.-Fri. 10am-3pm, Sat.-Sun. 10am-4pm, $5) show this poetry and the buildings of the camps.

Angel Island is a major destination for both casual and serious hikers. Trails of varying difficulty crisscross the island, creating fun for hikers and bikers alike. Adventurous trekkers can scale Mount Livermore via either the **North Ridge Trail** or the **Sunset Trail.** Each runs about 4.5 miles round-trip for a moderate, reasonably steep hike. Stop at the summit's picnic tables and wooden benches for a rest and to watch boats sketch white lines on the blue-green bay. This is also a great place to take in the expanse of the bay region including the skyscrapers of San Francisco, the lonely rock of Alcatraz, and the Golden Gate Bridge. For the best experience, make a loop by taking one trail up the mountain and the other back down. For a long paved-road hike, take the **Perimeter Road** (5 miles, moderate) all the way around the island.

While there is no store on the island for supplies, the **Cove Café** (415/435-3392, www. angelisland.com, Mar.-Oct. Mon.-Fri. 10am-3pm, Sat.-Sun. 10am-4pm, $11-30) serves hot sandwiches, wraps, salads, and even a gourmet cheese platter from Cowgirl Creamery. Craving oysters and a beer? Stroll next door to the **Cove Cantina Oyster Bar** (Memorial Day-Sept. Thurs.-Fri. 11am-3pm, Sat.-Sun. 11am-5pm).

CAMPING

Camping (800/444-7275, www.reserveamerica.com, $30) is available at nine primitive sites that fill up quickly (reserve six months in advance). The campsites themselves are characterized as "environmental sites"; each is equipped with food lockers, surprisingly nice outhouses, running water, and a barbecue. You must bring your own charcoal or camp stove, as wood fires are strictly prohibited. Three of the sites, the Ridge Sites, sit on the southwest side of the island, known to be fairly windy. The other six sites, the East Bay and Sunrise Sites, face the East Bay. Wherever you end up, plan on walking 0.5-1.75 miles from the ferry to your campsite. Despite the dramatic urban views, camping here is a little like backpacking.

TRANSPORTATION

Angel Island State Park is in the middle of San Francisco Bay. To get here, you must either boat in or take one of the ferries that serve the island. The harbor at Tiburon is the easiest place to access Angel Island. The private **Angel Island-Tiburon Ferry** (21 Main St., Tiburon, 415/435-2131, www.angelislandferry. com, adults $15, ages 6-12 $13, ages 3-5 $5, bicycles $1) can get you out to the island in about 10 minutes and runs several times a day. You can also take the **Blue and Gold Fleet** (415/705-8200, www.blueandgoldfleet.com, one-way $14.50-17) to Angel Island if you are departing from either Oakland-Alameda (2990 Main St., Alameda, summer-fall only) or San Francisco (Pier 41). Check website for current schedule, as the ferry might not run daily in the winter.

Ferries have plenty of room for you to bring your own bicycle, or you can rent one (Mar.-Nov. Sat.-Sun., Apr.-Oct. daily, $12.50 per hour, $40 per day) at the main visitors area near the ferry dock. Rentals must always be returned by 4pm. Grab a map from the gift shop. Not all trails are open to bikes, but those that are include the easy five-mile paved Perimeter Road around the island, perfect for newcomers.

Accommodations

It would be difficult to find a place to stay closer to the water than the ★ **Waters Edge Hotel** (25 Main St., 415/789-5999, www.marinhotels.com, $237-432). This boutique hotel is actually perched on a historic dock over the bay. Most rooms have views of the bay and sights like Angel Island and San Francisco in the distance. They also include luxurious beds and wood-burning fireplaces. The staff delivers a full continental breakfast to your room every morning.

Wonderfully close to the water and the attractions of downtown Tiburon, the **Lodge at Tiburon** (1651 Tiburon Blvd., 415/435-3133, www.thelodgeattiburon.com, $229-289) offers the comforts and conveniences of a larger hotel while providing the personal attention and atmosphere of a boutique inn. All the rooms are soothing and pretty, but for a special treat book the Spa Room, which has a huge raised whirlpool tub overlooking the water. Have dinner or a drink at the attached Tiburon Tavern in the evening.

Food

There are many visitor-friendly restaurants in downtown Tiburon. For a good Italian meal, head for **Servino** (9 Main St., 415/435-2676, www.bestservino.com, Mon.-Thurs. 11:30am-4pm and 5pm-10pm, Fri. 11:30am-4pm and 5pm-11pm, Sat. 11:30am-4pm and 5pm-11pm, Sun. 11:30am-3:30pm and 5pm-10pm, $11-30) on the waterfront. A huge outdoor patio offers stunning views of the bay, Angel Island, and the San Francisco cityscape. Service is as warm and friendly as the classic Italian cuisine. The menu runs to hearty, Americanized Italian dishes. The full bar makes a great place to sit should you need to wait for a table, and Servino hosts live music on Friday nights.

A Tiburon mainstay is **Sam's Anchor Café** (27 Main St., 415/435-4527, www.samscafe.com, Mon.-Thurs. 11am-9:30pm, Fri. 11am-10pm, Sat. 9:30am-10pm, Sun. 9:30am-9:30pm, $15-28). Sitting on the water and boasting a large glassed-in deck, Sam's specializes in seafood, liberally poured glasses of wine, and lounging in the sun on beautiful weekend afternoons. You'll find many locals and visitors catching some rays over oysters on the half shell, fish-and-chips, or a burger. At night, the fare becomes a bit fancier as dining moves indoors amid low lighting. You'll find more elegantly plated dishes, but seafood still reigns, as does the good-time vibe.

Information and Services

The **Tiburon Chamber of Commerce** (96 Main St., 415/435-5633, 9am-4pm Mon.-Fri.) is a small office, but the staff will be able to answer any questions you may have and will provide maps and recommendations. The town of Tiburon is small, so don't expect a whole lot in the way of services.

Transportation

Tiburon is on a peninsula about eight miles north of the Golden Gate Bridge. From San Francisco, take U.S. 101 north to the Tiburon Boulevard exit. Stay to the right and follow the road along the water for nearly six miles until you reach the small downtown area.

Like Sausalito, Tiburon is very walkable and is a great destination via the ferry from San Francisco. The **Blue and Gold Fleet** (415/705-8200, http://blueandgoldfleet.com, daily, 30-minute ride, check website for current schedule, adults $10.50, children and seniors $6.25, under age 5 free) runs daily trips to Tiburon from San Francisco's Pier 41.

MILL VALLEY

Situated in the shadow of 2,571-foot Mount Tamalpais, Mill Valley is a great base for an exploration of Marin County's many attractions. Named for a former mill that occupied the area in the 1800s, this upscale city has a walkable downtown with great restaurants, a state-of-the-art music venue, and a theater that hosts all sorts of events including the world-renowned Mill Valley Film Festival. There are also recreational opportunities, including the start of the Dipsea Trail, which climbs out of the valley and eventually ends at Muir Beach, and nearby Mount Tamalpais, where you can score some of the best views of the Bay Area.

Entertainment and Events

Mill Valley Beerworks (173 Throckmorton Ave., 415/888-8218, www.millvalleybeerworks.com, Mon. 5:30pm-9pm, Tues.-Thurs. 5:30pm-9:30pm, Fri. 5:30pm-10:30pm, Sat. 11:30am-3pm and 5:30pm-10:30pm, Sun. 11:30am-3pm and 5:30pm-9pm) is a great place to sip a beer after a hike up nearby Mount Tamalpais or following a day of climbing up and down the Dipsea Trail. Beerworks has a rotating menu of seasonally brewed beers made in-house as well as an extensive list of bottled beer from around the world. Sip your suds at the bar or at the long wooden tables.

In 2012, the Grateful Dead's Bob Weir helped to open the state-of-the-art **Sweetwater Music Hall** (19 Corte Madera Ave., 415/388-1100, www.sweetwatermusichall.com), which hosts rock, blues, funk, and New Orleans acts on a good-sized stage with pristine sound. The mostly middle-aged crowd goes wild on the wooden dance floor. A café serves up creative small bites like meatloaf sliders.

The **142 Throckmorton Theatre** (142 Throckmorton Ave., 415/383-9600, www.142throckmortontheatre.com) is the place to see all sorts of plays, musicals, and concerts. It's probably best known though for its Tuesday comedy nights, where locals like Dana Carvey frequently stop in to perform.

Founded in 1978 by the California Film Institute, the **Mill Valley Film Festival** (www.mvff.com) has expanded to an 11-day showcase of films from over 200 filmmakers that occurs every October. The films are shown in Mill Valley and the surrounding area. Heavy-hitting filmmakers and actors, including Sean Penn, Helen Mirren, and Forest Whitaker, have made appearances at the fest. Mill Valley's other big annual event happens the second Sunday of June: The **Dipsea Race** (www.dipsea.org) is the oldest footrace in the nation, with participants running up and down the steep Dipsea Trail.

Accommodations

The place to stay in Mill Valley is hands down the ★ **Mill Valley Inn** (165 Throckmorton Ave., 415/389-6608, www.marinhotels.com, $319-509). Situated in Mill Valley's downtown, the Mill Valley Inn has rooms in the modern main building and a historic creekside house. For more seclusion, opt for one of the two single-bedroom cottages shaded by towering redwoods. The rooms in the main building are decorated with repurposed wood furniture and have small balconies overlooking Throckmorton Street or the small redwood forest behind the inn. Other nice touches include a deluxe continental breakfast and free use of a fleet of mountain bikes for tooling around town or attempting to summit nearby Mount Tamalpais.

Situated on sparkling Richardson Bay, **Acqua Hotel** (555 Redwood Hwy., 415/380-0400, www.marinhotels.com, $210-270) has serene rooms and suites. A night's stay includes a hot breakfast buffet and complimentary use of the hotel's mountain bikes, which can be put to good use on the multiuse trail out front. Though Acqua is walking distance to a couple of restaurants, it is two miles from the downtown section of Mill Valley.

Food

For a small city, Mill Valley has a significant number of notable restaurants. The **Dipsea Café** (200 Shoreline Hwy., 415/381-0298, www.dipseacafe.com, Mon.-Fri. 7am-3pm, Sat.-Sun. 7am-4pm, $11-30) is a great place to fuel up for a day of hiking Mount Tamalpais or the Dipsea Trail. Go hearty with a chicken-fried steak and egg platter or opt for a more delicate pear-walnut omelet. With a farm scene painted on the wall and plaid tablecloths, the Dipsea has a country feel.

A partnership between celebrity chef Tyler Florence and rocker Sammy Hagar, **El Paseo** (17 Throckmorton Ave., 415/388-0741, www.elpaseomillvalley.com, Sun.-Thurs.

5:30pm-9pm, Fri. 5:30pm-10pm, Sat. 5pm-10pm, $19-83) serves up meaty entrées like veal chops and steak frites.

Bungalow 44 (44 E. Blithedale Ave., 415/381-2500, www.bungalow44.com, Mon.-Tues. 5pm-10pm, Wed.-Thurs. 5pm-10:30pm, Fri.-Sat. 5pm-11pm, Sun. 5pm-9:30pm, $15-30) cooks up salmon and coffee-crusted rib-eye on an old-fashioned wood-burning grill. They also offer vegetarian entrées like roasted stuffed peppers.

At **Molina Restaurant** (17 Madrona St., 415/383-4200, http://molinarestaurant.com, Mon.-Thurs. 5:30pm-10pm, Fri.-Sat. 5:30pm-11pm, Sun. 11am-2:30pm and 5:30pm-10pm, $21-41), Chef Todd Shoberg mans the wood oven and the turntable. Grab a seat at the chef's counter to survey the action or reserve a table in this intimate space. The menu is split into "Earlier" (appetizers) and "Later" (main courses). The latter includes half a game hen and a ribeye with a jalapeño chimichurri.

Information and Services

Stop into the **Mill Valley Chamber of Commerce** (85 Throckmorton Ave., 415/388-9700, www.millvalley.org, Tues.-Fri. 10am-2pm) on weekdays to learn more about Mill Valley's offerings.

Transportation

Mill Valley is easy to get to. Take U.S. 101 north from the city and over the Golden Gate Bridge, and then take the East Blithedale/Tiburon Boulevard exit. Turn left on East Blithedale and follow the road into downtown Mill Valley.

There is usually parking to be found in Mill Valley, but once here, it's best to leave your car as the downtown is small and everything is walkable.

★ MUIR WOODS NATIONAL MONUMENT

Established in 1908 and named for naturalist and author John Muir, **Muir Woods National Monument** (Panoramic Hwy., off Hwy. 1, 415/388-2596, www.nps.gov/muwo, daily 8am-7pm, adults $7, under age 15 free) comprises acres of staggeringly beautiful redwood forest nestled in Marin County. More than six miles of trails wind through the redwoods and adjacent Mount Tamalpais, crossing verdant creeks amid the lush forest. These are some of the most stunning—and accessible—redwoods in the Bay Area.

The visitors center is a great place to begin your exploration. The **Muir Woods Visitors**

Molina Restaurant

Center (1 Muir Woods Rd., daily 8am-close, closing hours vary) abuts the main parking area and marks the entrance to Muir Woods. In addition to maps, information, and advice about hiking, you'll also find a few amenities. Inside the park, slightly past the visitors center, is the **Muir Woods Trading Company Gift Shop and Cafe** (415/388-7059, www.muirwoodstradingcompany.com, daily 9am-close, closing hours vary) where you can purchase souvenirs and sustenance made from high-quality local ingredients.

Muir Woods is accessed via the long and winding Muir Woods Road. From U.S. 101, take the Stinson Beach/Highway 1 exit. On Highway 1, also named the Shoreline Highway, follow the road under the freeway and proceed until the road splits in a T-junction at the light. Turn left, continuing on Shoreline Highway for 2.5 miles. At the intersection with Panoramic Highway, make a sharp right turn and continue climbing uphill. At the junction of Panoramic Highway and Muir Woods Road, turn left and follow the road 1.5 twisty miles down to the Muir Woods parking lots on the right.

If you're visiting on a holiday or a summer weekend, get to the Muir Woods parking areas early—they fill fast, and afternoon hopefuls often cannot find a spot. Lighted signs on U.S. 101 will alert you to parking conditions at the main parking lot. To avoid the traffic hassle, there is a **Muir Woods Shuttle** (415/455-2000, http://goldengatetransit.org/services/muirwoods.php, summer Sat.-Sun., adults $2, children and seniors $1, children under 6 free) that leaves from various points in southern Marin County, including the Sausalito ferry terminal.

Hiking

Muir Woods boasts many lovely trails that crisscross the gorgeous redwood forest. First-time visitors should follow the wheelchair- and stroller-accessible **Main Trail Loop** (1 mile, easy). Leading from the visitors center on an easy and flat walk through the beautiful redwoods, this trail has an interpretive brochure (pick one up at the visitors center) that describes the flora and fauna, keyed to numbers along the trail. Hikers can continue the loop on the **Hillside Trail** for an elevated view of the valley.

One of the first side trails off the Main Trail, the **Ocean View Trail** (3.4 miles, moderate) soon appears to the left. Some advice: Either bring water, or pick up a bottle at the visitors center before starting up the trail. The trail climbs through the redwoods for 1.5 miles until its junction with **Lost Trail.** Turn right on Lost Trail and follow it downhill for 0.7 miles to **Fern Creek Trail.** Bear left onto Fern Creek Trail for a lush and verdant return to the Main Trail. Along the way you'll see the much-lauded Kent Tree, a 250-foot-tall Douglas fir.

Alternatively, continue on the Main Trail to where Fern Creek Trail starts and hike in the opposite direction to the junction with **Alice Eastwood Camp,** after a brief westward jog on Lost Trail. You can get a drink of water, use the restrooms, and even have a picnic in this developed area. Follow the **Camp Eastwood Trail** back to the starting point.

It's easier to avoid the crowds by following the Main Trail to its terminus with the **Bootjack Trail** (6.4 miles, moderate). The Bootjack Trail climbs uphill for 1.3 miles before its junction with the **TCC Trail.** Bear left for the TCC Trail and meander through the quiet Douglas firs. At 1.4 miles, the trail meets up with the **Stapleveldt Trail;** turn left again to follow this trail for 0.5 miles to **Ben Johnson Trail,** which continues downhill for one more mile to meet up with the Main Trail.

You may notice signs in this area for the **Dipsea Trail,** which goes from Mill Valley to Muir Beach. This is a strenuous, unshaded 7.1-mile hike, and the only way back is the way you came—but uphill.

Muir Beach

Few coves on the California coast can boast as much beauty as **Muir Beach** (just south of the town of Muir Beach, www.nps.gov/goga, daily sunrise-sunset). From the overlook above Highway 1 to the edge of the ocean beyond the dunes, Muir Beach is a haven for both wildlife and beachcombers. In the wintertime, beachgoers bundle up against the chill and walk the sands of the cove or along the many trails that lead from the beach. If you're lucky, you might find a Monterey pine tree filled with sleepy monarch butterflies, here to overwinter before making their long migration back north in the spring. Springtime brings rare rays of sunshine to Muir Cove, and as the air grows warmer in summer, the north end of the cove attracts another breed of beach life: nudists. If the clothing-optional California lifestyle makes you uncomfortable, stick to the south side, the brackish Redwood Creek lagoon, and the windswept picnic grounds.

Muir Beach is directly off Highway 1. The most direct route is to take U.S. 101 to the Stinson Beach/Highway 1 exit and follow Highway 1 (also called Shoreline Highway) for 6.5 miles to Pacific Way (look for the Pelican Inn). Turn left onto Pacific Way and continue straight to the Muir Beach parking lot. If arriving from Muir Woods, simply continue following Muir Woods Road down to the junction with Highway 1 and turn left onto Pacific Way.

ACCOMMODATIONS AND FOOD

One fine Marin lodging is **The Pelican Inn** (10 Pacific Way, Muir Beach, 415/383-6000, www.pelicaninn.com, $206-289). Inside the Tudor structure, the guest room decor continues the historic ambience, with big-beam construction, canopy beds, and historic portrait prints. The seven mostly small rooms each come with a private bath and full English-style breakfast, but no TVs or phones. (There is free Wi-Fi though.)

In addition to quaint bedchambers, you can also get hearty food at the **Pelican Inn** (Mon.-Fri. 11:30am-3pm and 5:30pm-9pm, Sat.-Sun. 8am-11am, 11:30am-3pm, and 5:30pm-9pm, $17-35). Dark wood and a long trestle table give the proper old English feeling

to the dimly lit dining room. The cuisine brings home the flavors of old England, with dishes like beef Wellington, shepherd's pie, and fish-and-chips. True fans of the British Isles will round off the meal with a pint of Guinness.

MOUNT TAMALPAIS STATE PARK

To see the whole Bay Area in a single day, go to **Mount Tamalpais State Park** (801 Panoramic Hwy., Mill Valley, 415/388-2070, www.parks.ca.gov, daily 7am-sunset, day-use parking $8). Known as Mount Tam, this park boasts stellar views of the San Francisco Bay Area—from Mount St. Helena in Napa down to San Francisco and across to the East Bay. The Pacific Ocean peeks from around the corner of the western peninsula, and on a clear day you can just make out the foothills of the Sierra Nevada to the east. This park is the Bay Area's backyard, with hiking, biking, and camping opportunities widely appreciated for both their beauty and easy access. Ample parking, interpretive walks, and friendly park rangers make a visit to Mount Tam a hit even for less outdoorsy travelers.

In addition to recreation, Mount Tam also provides the perfect setting for the arts. The **Mountain Theater** (E. Ridgecrest Blvd. at Pan Toll Rd., Mountain Play Association: 415/383-1100, www.mountainplay.org, May-June, ticket prices vary), also known as the Cushing Memorial Amphitheater, was built in the 1930s and still hosts plays amid its outdoor stone seating. Performances and dates vary; contact the Mountain Play Association for information and tickets. Plan to arrive early, as both parking and seating fill completely well before the show starts. The Mountain Theater also serves as the meeting place for the **Mount Tam Astronomy Program** (E. Ridgecrest Blvd. at Pan Toll Rd., 415/388-2070 or 415/455-5370, www.mttam.net). Held every Saturday April-October near the new and first quarter moon, the group hosts a talk by an astronomer that lasts about 45 minutes, followed by a tour of the night sky and star viewing through telescopes. Bring flashlights.

The **East Peak Visitors Center** (Sat.-Sun. 11am-4pm) at the top of Mount Tam contains a small museum and gift shop as well as a picnic area with tables and restrooms and a small refreshment stand. The on-site staff can assist with hiking tips or guided walks. The **Pantoll Ranger Station** (Panoramic Hwy. at Pantoll Rd., 415/388-2070, Fri.-Mon. 9am-5pm), which anchors the western and larger edge of the park, provides hikers with maps and camping information.

Enjoy the views without setting out on the trail at the **Bootjack Picnic Area** (Panoramic Hwy.), which has tables, grills, water, and restrooms. The small parking lot northeast of the Pantoll Ranger Station fills quickly and early in the day.

Hiking

Up on Mount Tam, you can try anything from a leisurely 30-minute interpretive stroll to a strenuous hike up and down one of the many deep ravines. Mount Tam's hiking areas are divided into three major sections: the East Peak, the Pantoll area, and the Rock Springs area. Each of these regions offers a number of beautiful trails, so you'll want to grab a map from the visitors center or online to get a sense of the mountain and its hikes.

For additional hikes, visit the Mount Tamalpais Interpretive Association website (www.mttam.net).

EAST PEAK

The charming interpretive **Verna Dunshee Trail** (0.75 mile, easy) offers a short, mostly flat walk along a wheelchair-accessible trail. The views are fabulous, and you can get a leaflet at the visitors center that describes many of the things you'll see along the trail. Turn this into a loop hike by continuing on Verna Dunshee counterclockwise; once back at the visitors center, make the climb up to **Gardner Lookout** for stellar views from the top of Mount Tam's East Peak (elev. 2,571 ft.).

PANTOLL

The Pantoll Ranger Station is ground zero for some of the best and most challenging hikes in the park. The **Old Mine Trail** (across Panoramic Hwy.) leads up to the Mountain Theater via the **Easy Grade Trail** (2 miles, easy-moderate). Eager hikers can continue on the **Rock Springs Trail** to West Point Inn and back via **Old Stage Road** for a more challenging 4.7 miles.

The **Steep Ravine Trail** (3.8 miles, moderate) descends through lush Webb Creek and gorgeous redwoods to meet with the Dipsea Trail. To return to the Pantoll parking area, turn left onto Dipsea Trail and climb the demanding steps back to the **Coastal Fire Road.** Turn left again, then right on the Old Mine Trail for an exhilarating 3.8-mile hike.

The **Dipsea Trail** (7.3 miles round-trip, strenuous) is part of the famous Dipsea Race (second Sun. in June), renowned for both its beauty and its challenging stairs. The trailhead begins in Muir Woods, near the parking lot, and leads through Mount Tam all the way to Stinson Beach. Hikers can pick up the Dipsea on the Old Mine Trail or at its intersection with the Steep Ravine Trail in Mount Tam, but a common loop is to take the **Matt Davis Trail** (across Panoramic Hwy. from the Pantoll parking area) west all the way to Stinson Beach and then return via the Dipsea Trail to Steep Ravine Trail. This is a long, challenging hike, especially on the way back, so bring water.

ROCK SPRINGS

Rock Springs is conveniently near the Mountain Theater, and a variety of trails radiate from this historic venue. Cross Ridgecrest Boulevard and take the **Mountain Theater Fire Trail** to Mountain Theater. Along the top row of the stone seats, admire the vistas while looking for **Rock Springs Trail** (it's a bit hidden). Once you find it, follow Rock Springs Trail all the way to the historic West Point Inn. The views here are stunning, and you'll see numerous cyclists flying downhill on Old Stage Road below. Cross this road to pick up Nora Trail, following it until it intersects with **Matt Davis Trail.** Turn right to reach the Bootjack day-use area. Follow the **Bootjack Trail** right (north) to return to the Mountain Theater for a 4.6-mile loop.

Visit waterfalls via the lovely **Cataract Trail** (3 miles, easy-moderate). From the trailhead, follow Cataract Trail for a short bit before heading right on **Bernstein Trail.** Shortly, turn left onto **Simmons Trail** and continue to Barth's Retreat, site of a former camp that is now a small picnic area with restrooms. Turn left on **Mickey O'Brien Trail** (a map can be helpful here), returning to an intersection with the Cataract Trail. It's worth the short excursion to follow Cataract Trail to the right through the Laurel Dell picnic area and up to Cataract Falls. Enjoy a picnic at Laurel Dell before returning to Cataract Trail to follow it down to the Rock Springs trailhead.

Cycling

To bike up to the peak of Mount Tam is a mark of local cyclists' strength and endurance. Rather than driving up to the East Peak or the Mountain Home Inn, sturdy cyclists pedal up the paved road to the East Peak. It's a long, hard ride, but for an experienced cyclist the challenge and the views make it more than worthwhile. Just take care: This road is open to cars, many of which may not realize that bikers frequent the area.

A hard but satisfying trip up the mountain begins at the Lagunitas Trailhead in Ross (15.8 miles, strenuous). From here you take the **Eldridge Grade Fire Road** all the way to East Peak. The scenery is as beautiful as the ride is challenging and technical. To make the trip into a loop, turn onto paved **Ridgecrest Boulevard** and follow it a little over four miles. On the right is the **Rock Springs Lagunitas Fire Road.** Take it all the way back to the trailhead. To reach the peak when you are already up on the mountain, consider parking at the Pantoll Ranger Station and taking **Old Stage Grade** north to either Middle Peak or East Peak (6 miles,

moderate). Make the ride into a longer loop by jumping on **Eldridge Grade** at East Peak, taking it to **Wheeler Trail,** where you will have to walk your bike a short distance and then turn right on **E-Koo Fire Road.** After a couple of miles it will intersect with **Old Railroad Grade** (stay right), which will then meet **Old Stage Grade.** Turn left and head down to the trailhead.

Accommodations

Reaching the **West Point Inn** (100 Old Railroad Grade Fire Rd., Mill Valley, 415/388-9955, www.westpointinn.com, Tues.-Sat., adults $50 pp, children $25 pp) requires hiking two miles on a dirt road to the entrance. The inn, which was built in 1904, has no electricity. It is lit by gaslights and warmed by fires in the large fireplaces in the downstairs lounge and parlor, where guests are encouraged to read, play games, and enjoy each other's company. There are seven rooms upstairs and five rustic cabins nearby. All guests must bring their own linens, flashlights, and food, which can be prepared in the communal kitchen. One Sunday a month during the summer, the inn hosts a **pancake breakfast** (9am-1pm, adults $10, children $5) that draws local hikers. The wait can be long, but it is a lot of fun.

At **Mountain Home Inn** (810 Panoramic Hwy., 415/381-9000, www.mtnhomeinn.com, $195-345), the innkeepers would prefer that you relax as much as possible. With 10 rooms, many with jetted tubs, wood-burning fireplaces, and private decks, it would be hard to exert yourself. Opt for a massage, slip downstairs for a complimentary breakfast, or dine on a three-course prix fixe dinner ($38) in the cozy and warmly lit dining room.

Camping

With spectacular views of the Pacific Ocean, it's no wonder that the rustic accommodations at ★ **Steep Ravine** (800/444-7275, www.reserveamerica.com, cabins $100, campsites $25) stay fully booked. On the steep ravine (the name is no exaggeration) there are seven primitive campsites and 10 cabins adjacent to a small cove. The cabins are considered rustic but each comes equipped with a small wood-stove, a table, a sleeping platform, and a grill; the campsites are also spare but each has a table, a fire pit, and a food locker. Restrooms and drinking water are nearby. To book either a cabin or a campsite, call at 8am six months before the date you intend to go.

If Steep Ravine is full or you want to camp within hiking distance of the top of the mountain, the **Pantoll Campground** (1393 Panoramic Hwy., 415/388-2070, http://mttam.net/activities/camping.html, $25) has 16 sites with drinking water, firewood, and restrooms nearby. Camping here operates on a first-come, first-served basis (paid for at the ranger station), so get here early. The sites are pleasantly removed from the parking lot, which means that once you have gone to the trouble of hauling in all your gear, you will enjoy the quiet of car-free camping.

Food

Is a gourmet meal at the end of a long hike your idea of the perfect end to the perfect day? If so, you'll be happy that the **Mountain Home Inn** (810 Panoramic Hwy., 415/381-9000, www.mtnhomeinn.com, Wed.-Sun.

11:30am-3pm and 5:30pm-8:30pm, Mon. 5:30pm-8:30pm, prix fixe dinner $38) opens its kitchen to the public. Enjoy a three-course prix fixe dinner of French-California cuisine while overlooking the surrounding mountains and mist-filled valleys. If you are spending the day in the Mount Tam area and don't want to pack a lunch, the Mountain Home Inn also offers grilled sandwiches and fresh salads. The **Wine Bar** (Mountain Home Inn, 810 Panoramic Hwy., 415/381-9000, www.mtnhomeinn.com, Wed.-Sun. 3:30pm-8pm, Mon. 3:30pm-7pm) is open between meals. Nibble on lighter fare such as a local cheese plate, ceviche, or paella while sipping fantastic local wine on the expansive deck.

Information and Services

For more information, contact the volunteer-run **Mount Tamalpais Interpretive Association** (415/258-2410, www.mttam.net). The ongoing California state budget crisis has left the Mount Tam visitors center and ranger station with limited hours, and both may be closed when you visit. The state park did manage to set up free Wi-Fi; if you arrive at the park and need information, you can access the Web just 150-200 feet from the ranger station.

the cabins at Steep Ravine in Mount Tamalpais State Park

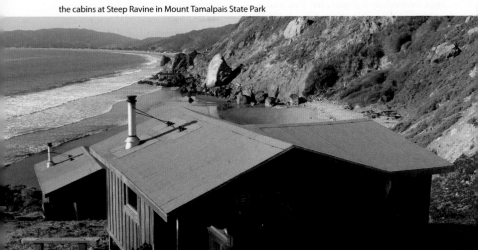

Transportation

Panoramic Highway is a long and winding two-lane road across the Mount Tamalpais area and extending all the way to Stinson Beach.

Once upon a time, well-heeled visitors could take a scenic train ride up to and across Mount Tam. Today, you'll probably want to drive up to one of the parking lots, from which you can explore the trails. Take Highway 1 to the Stinson Beach exit, then follow the fairly good signs up the mountain. Turn right at Panoramic Highway at the top of the hill. Follow the road for five winding miles until you reach the Pantoll Ranger Station. To get to the East Peak Visitors Center, take a right on Pantoll Road and then another right on East Ridgecrest Boulevard. To access the park from Stinson Beach, take a right on Panorama Highway at the T intersection with Highway 1 just south of town.

Bus access to the park is available via route 61 of the **West Marin Stagecoach** (415/226-0855, www.marintransit.org, daily, $2), which provides public transit from Stinson Beach or Mill Valley to Mount Tam, dropping and picking visitors up at the Pantoll Ranger Station.

STINSON BEACH

The primary attraction at **Stinson Beach** (415/868-1922, www.nps.gov/goga, daily 9am-close) is the tiny town's namesake: a broad 3.5-mile-long sandy stretch of coastline with weather that's unusually congenial. Although it's as plagued by fog as anywhere else in the Bay Area, on rare clear days Stinson Beach is the favorite destination for San Franciscans seeking some surf and sunshine.

Sports and Recreation

To get out on the water, swing by **Stinson Beach Surf and Kayak** (3605 Hwy. 1, 415/868-2739, www.stinsonbeachsurfand-kayak.com, Fri.-Sun. 10am-6pm, $20-50 per day). The owner, Bill, will set you up with a surfboard, kayak, boogie board, or stand-up paddleboard. Wetsuits, which you will certainly need, are available. He also offers surf lessons and is happy to give pointers to novices out on the lagoon about the general etiquette of paddling around wildlife. During the week the shop is "on call." This may require a bit of planning on your part if you are in Stinson Beach during the week. Call Bill (415/497-8260) and he'll be happy to help you out.

Accommodations

Given Stinson Beach's status as a resort town, you will find a few inns and motels in which to stay the night. The **Sandpiper Inn** (1 Marine Way, 415/868-1632, www.sandpiper-stinsonbeach.com, $145-300) has six rooms and four cabins, and you can choose between motel-style accommodations with comfortable queen beds, private baths, and gas fireplaces or the four individual redwood cabins, which offer additional privacy, bed space for families, and full kitchens.

Another nice spot is the **Stinson Beach Motel** (3416 Shoreline Hwy. 1, 415/868-1712, www.stinsonbeachmotel.com, $110-259). It features eight vintage-y beach bungalow-style rooms that sleep 2-4 guests each. Some rooms have substantial kitchenettes; all have private baths, garden views, flat-screen TVs, and blue decor. The motel is a great spot to bring the family for a beach vacation.

Food

A few small restaurants dot the town of Stinson Beach, most of which serve seafood. Among the best is the **Sand Dollar Restaurant** (3458 Hwy. 1, 415/868-0434, www.stinsonbeachrestaurant.com, Mon.-Fri. 11:30am-midnight, Sat.-Sun. 11am-midnight, $10-25). This so-called fish joint actually serves more land-based dishes than seafood, but perhaps the fact that the dining room is constructed out of three old barges makes the difference. In addition to lunch and dinner, the Sand Dollar serves a popular Sunday brunch.

Getting There

Stinson Beach is an unbelievably beautiful

place to get to. First, take the Stinson Beach exit off U.S. 101. Follow the Shoreline Highway (Hwy. 1) as it snakes up the hill past the turn-offs for Tennessee Valley, Muir Woods, and Mount Tamalpais State Park. The road will pass through Green Gulch, where produce is grown for the legendary Greens Restaurant in San Francisco; Muir Beach; and eventually along cliffs high above the Pacific. After about five miles, the highway descends into Stinson Beach. Most of the town is strung along the highway, and signs make it easy to navigate to the beach.

With only one lane in each direction and a couple of intersections with stop signs, traffic backups that stretch for miles are all too common, especially on summer weekends. Your best bet is to drive in on a weekday or in the evening when everyone else is leaving.

An alternative to driving is the route 61 bus from **West Marin Stagecoach** (415/226-0855, www.marintransit.org, daily, $2), which runs from Mill Valley into Stinson Beach.

BOLINAS

Situated alongside the Bolinas Lagoon under the wing of Point Reyes, the unincorporated community of Bolinas is one of the North Bay's most idyllic spots. And the town's reclusive residents want it to stay that way: They've been known to steal any road signs indicating how to get to their community from Highway 1. Bolinas is worth a stop for its beach, tide pools, old-timey saloon, and renowned art museum—if you can find it.

Bolinas Museum

The **Bolinas Museum** (48 Wharf Rd., 415/868-0330, www.bolinasmuseum.org, Fri. 1pm-5pm, Sat.-Sun. noon-5pm, free) has a rotating gallery that showcases the work of one coastal Marin artist for two months at a time. It also has a fine arts photography exhibit and a history gallery that illuminates the past of Bolinas and coastal Marin.

Agate Beach Park

Offshore of **Agate Beach Park** (end of Elm St., www.marincounty.org, daily dawn-dusk) is Duxbury Reef, one of the largest shale reefs in North America. Onshore is a coastline dotted with tide pools and bird habitats that are ripe for exploration by wildlife lovers.

Smiley's Schooner Saloon

Built back in 1851, **Smiley's Schooner Saloon** (41 Wharf Rd., 415/868-1311, http://smileyssaloon.com, Mon.-Fri. 11am-2am, Sat.-Sun. 10am-2am) has an Old West feel, a pool table, and live entertainment Thursdays-Saturdays. It's a good place to soak up the eccentric character of Bolinas.

Transportation

To find Bolinas, drive 4.5 miles north on Highway 1 and turn left onto Olema-Bolinas Road, which may be unmarked. Then drive into town. Once in town, street and beach parking can be a challenge, suggesting Bolinas's secret may be out. The town itself is easily and entertainingly walkable.

★ POINT REYES NATIONAL SEASHORE

A haven for wilderness buffs, the Point Reyes area boasts acres of unspoiled forest and beach country. Expect cool weather even in the summer, but enjoy the lustrous green foliage and spectacular scenery that result. **Point Reyes National Seashore** (1 Bear Valley Rd., 415/464-5100, www.nps.gov/pore, daily dawn-midnight) stretches for miles between Tomales Bay and the Pacific, north from Stinson Beach to the tip of the land at the end of the bay. Dedicated hikers can trek from the bay to the ocean, or from the beach to land's end. The protected lands shelter a range of wildlife. In the marshes and lagoons, a wide variety of birds—including three different species of pelicans—make their nests. Over a thousand elephant seals call these beaches home, while endangered Myrtle's silverspot butterflies can be found in the dunes and grasslands. The pine forests shade shy deer and larger elk.

Point Reyes National Seashore

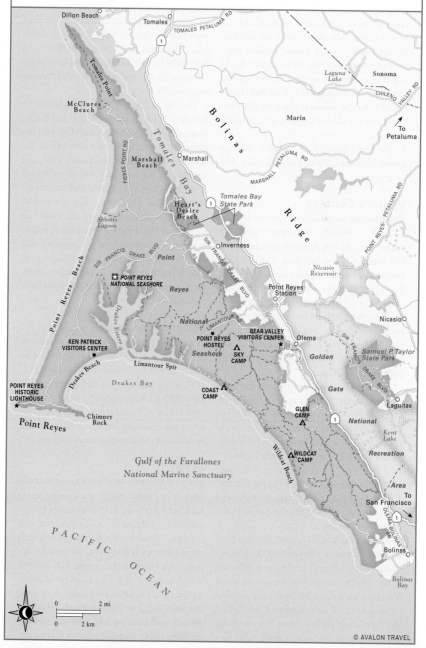

Dillon Beach

Tomales

TOMALES PETALUMA RD

1

Laguna
Lake

Sonoma

Marin

CHILENO VALLEY RD

To
Petaluma

McClures
Beach

Tomales Point

B o l i n a s

Tomales Bay

PIERCE POINT RD

Marshall
Beach

Marshall

MARSHALL PETALUMA RD

R i d g e

Heart's
Desire
Beach

1

Tomales Bay
State Park

POINT REYES- PETALUMA RD

Abbotts
Lagoon

SIR FRANCIS DRAKE BLVD

Inverness

SIR FRANCIS DRAKE BLVD

Point

Point Reyes Beach

✚ POINT REYES
NATIONAL SEASHORE

Reyes

Nicasio
Reservoir

Point Reyes
Station

Nicasio

National

LIMANTOUR RD

KEN PATRICK
VISITORS CENTER

Drakes Estero

POINT REYES
HOSTEL

Seashore

BEAR VALLEY
VISITORS CENTER
★

SKY
CAMP

Olema

SIR FRANCIS DRAKE BLVD

Samuel P. Taylor
State Park

Golden

Limantour Spit

Drakes Beach

POINT REYES
HISTORIC
LIGHTHOUSE
★

Point Reyes

Chimney
Rock

Drakes Bay

COAST
CAMP

GLEN
CAMP

Gate

1

National

Laguitas

Kent
Lake

Gulf of the Farallones
National Marine Sanctuary

Wildcat Beach

WILDCAT
CAMP

Recreation

Area
To
San Francisco

OLEMA-BOLINAS RD

1

P A C I F I C   O C E A N

Bolinas

Bolinas
Bay

0   2 mi

0   2 km

© AVALON TRAVEL

There are also a number of ranches and dairy farms that still operate inside the park. Grandfathered in at the time the park was created, these sustainable, generations-old family farms give added character and historical depth to Point Reyes. Another remnant of past times is the historic Point Reyes Lighthouse, which is on the cliffs of the Point Reyes Headlands, a point of land that is supposed to be the windiest place on the West Coast and the second-foggiest spot in North America.

The Point Reyes area includes the tiny towns of Olema, Point Reyes Station, and Inverness.

Visitors Centers

The **Bear Valley Visitors Center** (1 Bear Valley Rd., 415/464-5100, summer Mon.-Fri. 10am-5pm, Sat.-Sun. 9am-5pm, winter Mon.-Fri. 10am-4:30pm, Sat.-Sun. 9am-4:30pm) acts as the central visitors center for Point Reyes National Seashore. In addition to its maps, fliers, and interpretive exhibits, you can watch a short video introducing the Point Reyes region. You can also talk to the park rangers, either to ask advice or to obtain beach fire permits and backcountry camping permits.

Two other visitors centers are at different spots in the vast acreage of Point Reyes. The **Ken Patrick Visitors Center** (Drakes Beach, 415/669-1250, summer Sat.-Mon. 10am-4:30pm, winter hours vary) sits right on the beach in a building made of weathered redwood. Its small museum focuses on the maritime history of the region, and it acts as the host area for the annual Sand Sculpture event held on the beach every Labor Day Sunday.

Finally, the **Historic Lighthouse and Visitors Center** (415/669-1534, Thurs.-Mon. 10am-4:30pm) is the most difficult of the three to access. You must walk about 0.5 miles up a steep hill from the parking lot to get to this visitors center. You'll find the lighthouse right at your feet once you arrive.

Point Reyes Historic Lighthouse

The jagged, rocky shores of Point Reyes make for great sightseeing but incredibly dangerous maritime navigation. In 1870 the first lighthouse was constructed on the headlands. Its first-order Fresnel lens threw light far enough for ships to see and avoid the treacherous granite cliffs.

The **Point Reyes Historic Lighthouse** (415/669-1534, www.nps.gov/pore, Thurs.-Mon. 10am-4:30pm) still stands today on the point past the visitors center, accessed by descending a sometimes treacherous, cold, and windblown flight of over 300 stairs, which often closes to visitors during bad weather for safety reasons. It's worth a visit; the Fresnel lens and original machinery all remain in place, and the adjacent equipment building contains foghorns, air compressors, and other safety implements from decades past. Check the website for information about twice-monthly special events when the light is switched on.

Accommodations

One option for lodging in the area is to rent one of the vacation homes represented by **Point Reyes Vacation Rentals** (415/663-6113, http://pointreyesvacationrentals.com, $160-700). Choices include a studio cottage with views of Tomales Bay, a modern tree structure crowning Inverness Ridge, and a home surrounded by goats and chickens.

OLEMA

The **Point Reyes Seashore Lodge** (10021 Hwy. 1, 415/663-9000, www.pointreyes-seashorelodge.com, $155-370) offers budget and luxury lodging in its 22 rooms and two cottages. Attractive floral patterns mix with clean white walls and attractive wooden accents. All rooms have private baths, some with whirlpool tubs, and a couple of suites with special amenities are located away from the main lodge for extra privacy. Attractive gardens with winding brick pathways roll out to Olema Creek. The Farm House Restaurant,

Bar, and Deli adjoin the hotel, providing plenty of food and drink options.

Quiet **Olema Druid's Hall** (9870 Shoreline Hwy./Hwy. 1, 415/663-8727, www.olemadruids.com, $245-355) has only three rooms and one cottage. Housed in the 1885 meeting hall of the Druids Association, the inn has a distinct architectural charm, and the surrounding gardens are sculpted with lush flower beds, stands of mature cypresses and pines, and green lawns. Keep warm with the inn's radiant floor heating while wrapped in the 300-thread-count sheets. Each of the rooms is decorated in a style that melds with the Victorian building but is modern. Three of the four rooms have soaking tubs. There is a complimentary continental breakfast composed of local ingredients. Two-night minimum stays are required.

POINT REYES STATION

In the heart of Point Reyes Station is the **Point Reyes Station Inn** (11591 Hwy. 1, 415/663-9372, www.pointreyesstationinn.com, $125-225). The five-room inn is light and airy with turn-of-the-20th-century charm. The rooms are decorated in heavy antique furnishings that are lightened by the vaulted ceilings, large windows, and glass doors leading to private porches. All but one have fireplaces and private en suite baths. There is a communal hot tub in the garden, and the continental breakfast features eggs from the inn's own chickens and seasonal homegrown fruit.

Lingonberry Farm B&B (12430 Hwy. 1, 415/663-1826, www.lingonberryfarm.com, $125-225) is outfitted in bright, simple Swedish style. Each of the three rooms is distinctively decorated in blues, yellows, and crisp whites with trim farm-style furniture and minimalist artwork. All have private baths. Downstairs in the sunny dining area, guests are treated to a breakfast buffet with Swedish and American entrées.

The certified green ★ **Point Reyes Hostel** (1390 Limantour Spit Rd., 415/663-8811, www.norcalhostels.org/reyes, adult dorm beds $26-29, children dorm beds $13-14,

private rooms $87-130) is worth a stay for what's next door: Just off Limantour Road a few miles from the beach, the hostel is steps from fantastic hiking and lush natural scenery. Like most hostels, the dorm accommodations are spare but comfortable. Pick the affordable dorm rooms or a private room in one of two converted historic ranch buildings. These are very popular so try and book well in advance. The hostel also has a communal kitchen and a nice outdoor space on a brick patio.

At the west end of Sir Francis Drake Boulevard, near the historic Point Reyes Lighthouse, the **Drake Beach Café** (1 Drakes Beach, 415/669-1297, www.drakescafe.com, summer Thurs. noon-4pm, Fri.-Sun. 11am-5pm, Mon. noon-4pm, winter and spring Thurs. noon-4pm, Fri.-Sun. 11am-5pm) serves delicious food with an appropriate focus on the local, organic, and sustainable.

INVERNESS

Perhaps the most famous lodging around is ★ **Manka's Inverness Lodge** (30 Callendar Way, 415/669-1034, www.mankas.com, $275-850), with a woodsy charm that has made it a favorite of Bay Area weekenders. The lodge has four upstairs rooms decked out with deep reading chairs, plush beds with tree-limb posts, and antique fixtures. Four similar rooms are in the annex. Two of the four cabins are perched on Inverness Ridge to make the most of the views. All feature large sitting rooms with stone fireplaces. Some have private hot tubs or luxurious outdoor showers. Two more modern lodgings can be found a few miles from the main compound hanging over the edge of Tomales Bay: The Boat House is akin to a small, lushly appointed loft, with two baths and multiple sleeping spaces. The smaller Boatman's Quarters has lovely views of the bay, a private deck, and a fireplace. The celebrated dining room features a prix fixe multicourse dinner ($58).

In the center of the village of Inverness, **Ten Inverness Way** (10 Inverness Way, 415/669-1648, www.teninvernessway.com,

$160-190) is a 1904 craftsman building in which each of the five rooms—named for area hiking trails—is dressed in antiques and colorful quilts. Part of the charm are the coved ceilings, multi-paned windows, and built-in benches. Each room has a queen featherbed and a private bath. In the morning, enjoy coffee, a newspaper, and a full breakfast; evenings see complimentary wine and refreshments.

Motel Inverness (12718 Sir Francis Drake Blvd., 415/236-1967, www.motelinverness. com, $135-290) sits handsomely on the bay. Constructed of natural wood with lovely and fanciful flourishes, this is more like a classic lodge than a typical motel. There are rooms and suites with full kitchens, and all are decorated in light colors with minimal fuss. The parking lot abuts the entrance to each room, but the rooms open onto the breathtaking serenity of wetlands bordering the bay. Inside the main lodge is a grand lounge, where you can play pool on the antique pool table, read in front of the stone fireplace, or sip a glass of wine on the expansive deck.

Camping

While you would expect the Point Reyes area to abound in camping opportunities, finding a place to pitch a tent is a tall order. The only camping nearby is in the **Point Reyes National Seashore** (www.nps.gov/pore, 415/663-8054, reservations www.recreation. gov, $20), and all are hike-in sites that require reservations months in advance. All campsites have a pit toilet, a water faucet, a picnic table, a charcoal grill, and a food locker.

Sky Camp is the closest to the Bear Valley Visitors Center and is accessed via a trail on Limantour Road. The hike is a moderate 1.4 miles uphill, and the campground includes 11 individual sites and 1 group site. From its location at 1,025 feet elevation, you'll get great views of the Pacific Ocean and Drake's Bay (provided it's not foggy).

Near the end of Limantour Road before the beach is the trailhead for the aptly named **Coast Camp.** While not directly on the beach, the campground is in a quiet valley of coastal scrub and willow trees. It's just 200 yards from the beach. There are 12 individual campsites and 2 group sites. There are two routes to get here: one that is 1.8 miles uphill along the Laguna and Firelane Trails, and the longer 2.7-mile Coast Trail route, which is flat and considerably easier for carrying camping gear.

The other coastal campground is **Wildcat Camp.** It has five individual sites and three group sites. Like Coast Camp, it is set away from the beach on an open bluff-top meadow. From Bear Valley it is a 5.5-mile hike or an easier but longer 6.7-mile stroll on the Coast Trail.

The most secluded campground is **Glen Camp.** Hidden deep within a valley and protected from ocean winds, the campground is a healthy 4.6 miles from the Bear Valley Trailhead. There are 12 individual sites and no group sites, keeping this a quiet getaway.

Food
OLEMA

Attached to the Point Reyes Seashore Lodge, the **Farm House Restaurant and Bar** (10021 Hwy. 1, 415/663-1264, www.pointreyesseashore.com, Mon.-Thurs. 11:30am-9pm, Fri.-Sun. 11:30am-10pm, $12-32) is the oldest operating business in Olema. Diners can enjoy a pleasant range of fresh California cuisine in the elegant, bright dining room. There is an emphasis on seafood, as you would expect with so many great oyster farms and fishing waters nearby. There are pasta dishes, pork chops, steaks, and roast chicken. You can also get a burger or other hot sandwiches if you are looking for a lighter and cheaper meal. The bar menu features specialty cocktails, locally brewed beer, and oysters prepared half a dozen different ways.

POINT REYES STATION

If you're seeking a rarified organic California meal, you are in the right town. The **Station House Café** (11180 Hwy. 1, 415/663-1515, www.stationhousecafe.com, Thurs.-Mon. 8am-9pm, $10-17) is both casual and upscale.

Since 1974, it has been dedicated to serving food with ingredients that reflect the area's agrarian culture. The very reasonably priced California cuisine is top-notch, more comfort food than haute cuisine. The oyster stew is not to be missed. The dining room is open and unpretentious with large multi-paned windows letting in tons of light. On the left side of the restaurant is a full bar, where bartenders deftly mix cocktails and pour beer and glasses of wine. There is also an outside patio dripping with wisteria.

Osterina Stellina (11285 Hwy. 1, 415/663-9988, http://osteriastellina.com, daily 11:30am-9pm, $31-60) has brought white-tablecloth dining to Point Reyes Station. The Italian eatery has plenty of local items on the menu prepared in a rustic yet elegant Mediterranean fashion. There are thin-crust pizzas, robust pastas with seafood and organic vegetables, and hearty main dishes of pan-roasted pork loin and whole roasted local sole. Lunch is scaled down, but not by much. The wine list is a nice blend of Italian and California wines; nearly all are available by the glass.

For a drink (and a bit of local color), slip through the swinging doors of the **Old Western Saloon** (11201 Hwy. 1, 415/663-1661, daily 10am-2am). At this crusty old West Marin haunt you'll see ranchers yukking it up with park rangers, patrons young and old, longtime natives, and recent transplants. It's the place where everyone goes. Live music goes down on Friday and Saturday nights.

The Sir and Star (10000 Sir Francis Drake Blvd., 415/663-1034, www.sirandstar.com, Wed.-Sun. 5pm-9pm, $20) occupies the former Olema Inn and intrigues diners with a menu full of local references. Most nights, the menu is conveniently divided into three price categories: $10 appetizers, $12 appetizers, and $20 entrées. Dine on the bigger plates like short rib, quail, salmon, or kale with cheese in the candlelit dining area. On Saturday nights, the menu switches to a $75 chef's tasting menu.

For those traveling out of Point Reyes Station north along the bay, a stop at popular **Nick's Cove** (23240 Hwy. 1, 415/663-1033, www.nickscove.com, daily 11am-9pm, $14-29) may be in order. Overlooking the bay in an expansive weathered redwood building, Nick's Cove combines charm, relaxed atmosphere, and good-quality classic American food with a slightly modern twist. The menu accommodates all types of diners, from those who want a light nibble with their Bloody Mary to those eager for a high-end meal. They have an impressive selection of raw and cooked oyster platters. Out back is a long deck and a boathouse, perfect to explore with the little ones.

There is no better place to stock a picnic basket than the **Bovine Bakery** (11315 Hwy. 1, 415/663-9420, http://thebovinebakery.wordpress.com, Mon.-Fri. 6:30am-5pm, Sat.-Sun. 7am-5pm), where you can pick up a cup of coffee, loaves of bread, cookies, pizza, quiche, and salads.

Around the corner is **Cowgirl Creamery** (80 4th St., 415/663-9335, www.cowgirlcreamery.com, Wed.-Sun. 10am-6pm), which produces the best cheese in the Bay Area. All of their cheese is made on-site in the French brie style. Tours of the facility are available Friday mornings by appointment only. At the retail shop inside, pick up a stinky but oh-so-good round of Red Hawk, the milder Mount Tam and Pierce Point, or the subtle and seasonal St. Pat's. The store also sells other gourmet treats, from jams to crackers and even pasta and some sandwiches.

The **Tomales Bay Oyster Co.** (15479 Hwy. 1, 415/663-1242, http://tomalesbayoysters.com, Fri. noon-5pm, Sat.-Sun. 9am-5pm) is a low-key affair where you can buy a wide selection of oysters, clams, and mussels in an open-air market a few feet from where they are harvested. The smaller oysters tend to be sweeter, but the bigger, meatier ones better lend themselves to barbecuing at home. Note that you can no longer barbecue your oysters on-site due to county restrictions.

Dining around the Bay Area, you may have spotted oysters from **Hog Island Oyster Co.** (20215 Hwy. 1, 415/663-9218, www.hogislandoysters.com, daily 9am-5pm) on many upscale menus. Here they have an open-air stand where you can buy and barbecue oysters. Hog Island gets insanely busy on weekends as many Bay Area folks come to get their raw-oyster fix. Parking can be tricky, and unless you get here really early, you'll have to wait to get a grill and picnic table. To reserve a table and/or grill, visit the website.

INVERNESS

Vladimir's Czechoslovakian Restaurant (12785 Sir Francis Drake Blvd., 415/669-1021, Wed.-Sun. noon-9pm, Tues. 2pm-9pm, prix fixe dinner $27, prix fixe lunch $17, cash only) is a favorite of both locals and visitors. Enter the cool old dining room, complete with stuffed deer heads on the walls, and take a seat. The mugs of beer at this family-owned spot are generous, and the kitchen produces a prix fixe meal of serious Czech food: borscht, rabbit, duck, and all manner of delicious things. The bar menu offers Americanized items such as burgers and quesadillas. Vladimir's is very serious about its no-children policy, which makes it a perfect retreat for romantic couples. Also note that it is cash only.

The **Saltwater Oyster Depot** (12781 Sir Francis Drake Blvd., 415/669-1244, www.saltwateroysterdepot.com, Mon. and Thurs.-Fri. 5pm-9pm, Sat.-Sun. noon-9pm, $29-31) is an oyster bar, a wine shop, and a beloved restaurant. The restaurant serves plenty of oysters and wine along with some small plates and several entrées, mostly seafood. Both wine and beer are on tap.

Gather at the Market (Inverness Park Market, 12301 Sir Francis Drake Blvd., 415/663-1491, Thurs.-Sun. 5:30pm-9pm, $12-29) is an informal bistro that sets up in the Inverness Park Market four nights a week. The menu features just four or five small bites a night along with one meat-based entrée and one vegetarian entrée. Sunday nights feature fried chicken. Gather's chef Ed Vigil has also taken over the **Inverness Park Market Deli** (Mon. and Wed. 7am-8pm, Thurs.-Sat.

7am-8pm, Sun. 8am-8pm), which means killer breakfast sandwiches and Reuben sandwiches.

Information and Services

The Point Reyes area tends toward the remote and charmingly rural—there's not much out in the wilderness here. You can get gas only in Point Reyes Station. There are full-service grocery stores in Point Reyes Station (Palace Market) and in Inverness (the aptly named Inverness Store). For any other shopping needs, the biggest nearby towns are Novato and Petaluma. The **West Marin Chamber of Commerce** (Point Reyes Station, 415/663-9232, www.pointreyes.org, Fri.-Sun. 11am-4pm) can provide information on the region.

Cell phones do not work in most parts of Point Reyes National Seashore and the adjoining parklands. Check with your inn or hotel for information about Internet access. The closest hospital is **Novato Community Hospital** (180 Rowland Way, Novato, 415/209-1300, www.novatocommunity.org).

Transportation

Point Reyes is only about an hour north of San Francisco by car, but getting here can be quite a drive for newcomers. From the Golden Gate Bridge, take U.S. 101 north to just south of San Rafael. Take the Sir Francis Drake Boulevard exit toward San Anselmo. Follow Sir Francis Drake Boulevard west for 20 miles to the small town of Olema and Highway 1. At the intersection with Highway 1, turn right (north) to Point Reyes Station and the Bear Valley Visitors Center.

A slower but more scenic route follows Highway 1 into Point Reyes National Seashore and provides access to the trails near Bolinas in the southern portion of the park. From the Golden Gate Bridge, take U.S. 101 north to the Mill Valley/Stinson Beach exit. Follow the road under the freeway, and when the road splits at the stoplight, turn left onto Shoreline Highway (Hwy. 1). Follow Shoreline Highway—and do not turn right onto Panoramic Highway—for almost 30 miles through Stinson Beach and past Bolinas

Lagoon to the coast. From the lagoon, it's 11 miles north to Point Reyes Station. Expect twists, turns, and generally slow going as you approach Point Reyes.

East Bay

The East Bay is unique not only because of its ethnic and economic diversity but for the way its divergent groups come together, making it feel like a true melting pot. In addition to the world-class University of California, Berkeley, the Oakland Museum of California gives the museums across the bay a run for their money. Big music names are drawn to Berkeley's Greek Theater and Oakland's Fox Theatre, and nearly every old neighborhood has a classic movie house showing art house and foreign flicks, an erudite independent bookstore, and multiple cafés where you can hear patrons arguing over ideas big and small. Since the East Bay is farther from the Pacific, the region often receives sunny days when nearby San Francisco is socked in with fog.

BERKELEY

There's no place quite like Berkeley. The town has long been known for its progressive activism, with a youthful urban culture that revolves around the University of California, Berkeley. Yet well-heeled foodies also flock to town to sample some of the finest cuisine in Northern California.

University of California, Berkeley

Berkeley is a college town, and fittingly the **University of California, Berkeley** (www. berkeley.edu) offers the city's most interesting places to go and things to see. If your visit to the area includes your teenagers, think about taking a guided **campus tour** (510/642-5215, www.berkeley.edu, Mon.-Sat. 10am, Sun. 1pm, by reservation only, adults $3, children $2) to acquaint them with the university and all it has to offer. To get a great view of the campus from above, take an elevator ride up the **Campanile** (Mon.-Fri. 10am-3:45pm, Sat.

10am-4:45pm, Sun. 10am-1:30pm and 3pm-4:45pm, adults $3, seniors and ages 4-17 $2, under age 4 free), formally called Sather Tower. If you prefer, wander around campus on your own, discovering the halls where students live and learn; the newly renovated stadium, which is listed in the National Register of Historic Places; and architectural details such as Sather Gate and South Hall, built in 1873. Or stop in at the **Lawrence Hall of Science** (1 Centennial Dr., 510/642-5132, www.lawrencehallofscience.org, daily 10am-5pm, adults $12, seniors and students $9, ages 3-6 $6, under age 3 free) for a look at the latest exhibits and interactive displays.

Also on campus is the **University of California Botanical Garden** (200 Centennial Dr., 510/643-2755, http://botanicalgarden.berkeley.edu, daily 9am-5pm, adults $10, seniors $8, ages 13-17 $5, ages 5-12 $2, under age 5 free), an immense space with an astounding array of wild plants from around the world. Botany buffs love to spend hours in this place, studying and examining plants outdoors, in the greenhouses, and in the arid house (a habitat for plants requiring extremely hot and dry conditions). Others just come to amble through the peaceful plantings and perhaps stop to sniff a flower or two. See over 1,000 different kinds of sunflowers, nearly 2,500 types of cacti, thousands of native California plants, and hundreds of rare and endangered plants from around the world.

Entertainment and Events

There's a reasonable variety of evening entertainment to be had in Berkeley. The major regional theater is the **Berkeley Repertory Theatre** (2025 Addison St., 510/647-2949, www.berkeleyrep.org, Tues.-Sun., ticket

Berkeley and Oakland

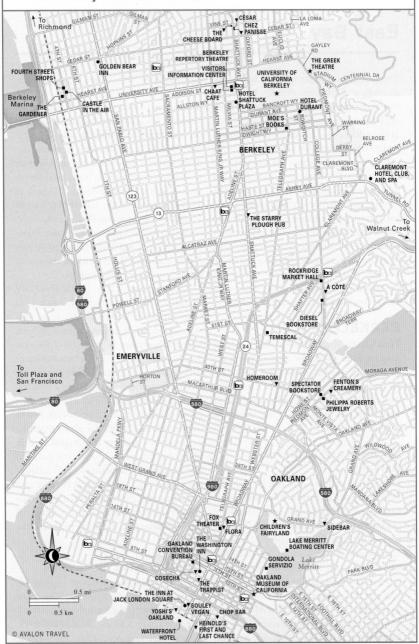

© AVALON TRAVEL

prices vary). Appropriate to its hometown, the Berkeley Rep puts on several unusual shows from world premieres of edgy new works to totally different takes on old favorites. Recent offerings have included a musical adaptation of the film *Amélie* and comic opera *Pirates of Penzance.*

Some of the best entertainment in Berkeley is at the live music venues. The **Starry Plough** (3101 Shattuck Ave., 510/841-2082, www.starryploughpub.com, Mon.-Fri. 4pm-2am, Sat.-Sun. 2pm-2am) is an Irish pub with a small stage setup. Fabulous Celtic rock groups, folk musicians, and indie bands play here almost every day of the week. Every Wednesday night is the famed Berkeley Poetry Slam—there's nothing like it. Hungry music and spoken-word fans can order a full meal from the kitchen, while the thirsty can quaff a pint or two of Guinness.

In Berkeley, the big-name acts come to the **Greek Theatre** (2001 Gayley Rd., 800/745-3000, www.apeconcerts.com). This outdoor amphitheater, constructed in the classic Greek style, sits on the UC Berkeley campus. Expect to see top-tier performers playing the Greek, including artists such as Bob Dylan, Death Cab for Cutie, and Willie Nelson, with a view of the bay in the background.

Shopping

Berkeley's citizens grow fierce at the very thought of big chain stores invading their precious downtown area. A few have succeeded, but you'll still find a variety of funky independent shops on **Telegraph Avenue** (between the UC campus and Parker Ave.). One of the best bookstores in the area is **Shakespeare & Co.** (2499 Telegraph Ave., 510/841-8916, http://shakespeareandcobooks.tumblr.com, Mon.-Thurs. 10am-8pm, Fri.-Sat. 10am-9pm, Sun. 11am-8pm). This new-and-used store definitely has an old-school vibe, complete with the dust and the semiorganized shelves and the musty smell. True bibliophiles can spend hours browsing for treasures.

Moe's Books (2476 Telegraph Ave., 510/849-2087, http://moesbooks.com, daily 10am-10pm) is another Berkeley institution. Also a new-and-used bookstore, Moe's has a more contemporary vibe, including an online retail presence, with lots of hip, up-to-date titles. Moe's also attracts literary talent to read and give talks for its regular active reading series. If you drop in on a random Thursday you may get to see Jonathan Lethem, Dave Eggers, or Lawrence Ferlinghetti.

The best Berkeley shopping is on the revitalized **4th Street** (www.fourthstreetshop.com) between Delaware Street and University Avenue. Scores of stores have set up shop and have created a slightly upscale retail district where national chains like Anthropologie, Apple, and Sur La Table mix with indie shops. **The Gardener** (1836 4th St., 510/548-4545, www.thegardener.com, Mon.-Sat. 10am-6pm, Sun. 11am-6pm) stocks inspired treasures for your home and garden, including beautifully crafted gardening tools, salad bowls made from unique and reclaimed wood, and luscious soaps. For a bit of whimsy, step into **Castle in the Air** (1805 4th St., 510/204-9801, www.castleintheair.biz, Mon.-Sat. 10am-6pm, Sun. 11am-6pm) for specialty pens, stationery, and notebooks as well as quirky gifts, cards, and art books.

Sports and Recreation
TILDEN REGIONAL PARK
Tilden Regional Park (Grizzly Peak Blvd., 888/327-2757, www.ebparks.org, daily 8:30am-5:30pm) covers the ridge directly above Berkeley. Within its more than 2,000 acres, the park has a celebrated botanical garden, the swimmable Lake Anza and its sandy beaches, an antique carousel, and miniature steam trains, perfect to thrill the little ones. But aside from the attractions, Tilden also offers scores of hiking and mountain biking trails that, except for the breathtaking views of the Bay Area, almost convince you that you are in absolute wilderness. Taking a trail map is advisable, as multiple trails crisscross one another, allowing for potential confusion.

For a simple stroll, consider taking the **Jewel Lake Nature Trail** (1 mile, easy), in the Nature Area of the park, generally a quiet area where no dogs are allowed. Park at the trailhead at the intersection of Central Park Drive and Canon Drive, near the Little Farm and Environmental Education Center. From the parking lot, the trail heads north along Wildcat Creek and out to Jewel Lake. You won't gain much elevation, and although there are exposed patches, the trail is mostly lush and leafy, surrounded by bay laurels, blackberries, and buckeye trees.

For a more rigorous climb, the **Wildcat Peak Loop** (3.5 miles, moderate) leaves from the same trailhead behind the Environmental Education Center. Take **Laurel Canyon Trail** through eucalypti and California bay laurels up through the canyon, which is a gentle grade most of the way. The trail then turns left toward the Rotary Peace Grove and on to Wildcat Peak (1,211 ft.). From the stony vista, you'll be able to see the Golden Gate Bridge, San Pablo Bay, and Mount Diablo, depending on which direction you're facing. To get back down the mountain, take **Wildcat Peak Trail** for about one mile until you hit **Jewel Lake Nature Trail.** Turn left, and it will take you back to the trailhead.

If you want to spend some time on the **Bay Area Ridge Trail** (3.5 miles, moderate), a pleasant loop starts at the Quarry Trailhead off Wildcat Canyon Road. Take **Wildcat Canyon Trail** to **Seaview Trail** and turn right. After some time, the trail changes names to **East Bay Skyline National Trail** and **Bay Area Ridge Trail.** At **Big Springs Trail,** take a right back down the mountain. You'll come to a parking lot, but the trail continues on the other side. After nearly one mile, take a left on **Quarry Trail;** it will take you back to the parking lot.

Tilden offers a great many roads and trails for cyclists. The paved roads snaking through the park (Wildcat Canyon Rd., Grizzly Peak Blvd., and South Park Dr.) twist and turn while gaining and losing enough elevation to keep any cyclist busy. As for mountain biking, many of the big trails are shared with hikers. The Bay Area Ridge, Meadows Canyon,

and Big Springs Trails are some of the most popular.

WILDCAT CANYON REGIONAL PARK

North of Tilden, the equally large **Wildcat Canyon Regional Park** (5755 McBryde Ave., Richmond, 510/544-3092, www.ebparks. org, daily sunrise-sunset) is filled with wide fire roads, all of which are open to cyclists. **Nimitz Way** is a paved trail along the ridgeline that is popular with cyclists young and old. **Harvey Canyon Trail** is a single-track trail also open to cyclists that descends from Nimitz Way down to Wildcat Creek. The only significant restriction for cyclists is that access via the south end of the park is only through the Tilden Nature Area, which allows limited bicycle access. The only route from the south starts at the Little Farm and Environmental Education Center. Bicycles are only permitted on Loop Road, which at Jewel Lake connects with Wildcat Creek Trail.

Wildcat Canyon has fewer trails than Tilden, but it is quieter, and the trails traverse a more challenging topography and allow for longer treks. A healthy loop (7 miles, moderate-strenuous) that allows you to see most of the park and some ridge-top views begins at the Alvarado Trailhead at the north end of the park. Start by taking **Wildcat Creek Trail** to **Harvey Canyon Trail,** which ascends sharply to the ridge. At the top you'll come to the paved **Nimitz Way.** After nearly one mile, continue straight (Nimitz Way veers slightly right) on **San Pablo Ridge Trail** until **Belgium Trail,** and turn left. This trail leads back down to the trailhead.

Accommodations

Offering great value for surprisingly low rates, the **Golden Bear Inn** (1620 San Pablo Ave., 510/525-6770, www.goldenbearinn.com, $100-120) has myriad small unique touches that make it special among budget motels. It's a family-friendly place where parents can rent an inexpensive guest room with two twin beds in a separate bedroom, providing privacy and relaxation for everyone. There is even a cottage that has two bedrooms, a living room, and a full kitchen. The cute rooms are nicely decorated and have TVs and wireless Internet access. Restaurants and attractions cluster nearby.

Lovely grounds are a highlight of the **Berkeley Brick Path Bed & Breakfast** (1805 Marin Ave., 510/524-4277, www.the-brickpath.com, $199-259). The garden is the pride of this inn, and you can stroll down the namesake brick path among the lush greenery and gorgeous flowers, take a seat out on the patio to enjoy your breakfast, or sip an afternoon glass of wine in the gazebo. Each of the three rooms has a unique style: one has a brick fireplace, another boasts a huge whirlpool tub, and the East-West Cottage has a full kitchen and private entrance.

The **Hotel Durant** (2600 Durant St., 510/845-8981, www.hoteldurant.com, $150-300) has it all: location, location, views, and location. Get a guest room on the upper floors to take in a view of Oakland, San Francisco, or the bay. All rooms have free Wi-Fi and coffeemakers. The hotel is within walking distance of the university, Telegraph Avenue, and the Elmwood shopping district.

You'll know you're in Berkeley upon entering the lobby of the ★ **Hotel Shattuck Plaza Berkeley** (2086 Allston Way, 510/845-7300, www.hotelshattuckplaza.com, $180-240): The marble floor is adorned with a peace sign. This boutique hotel is right in the heart of downtown and allows for good views of the city from its thick double-paned windows. The rooms in this historic 1910 hotel have modern features that include iPhone docking stations and flat-screen TVs. Guest can enjoy food and drink at the hotel's **FIVE Restaurant.**

The **Claremont Resort and Spa** (41 Tunnel Rd., 510/843-3000, www.fairmont.com, $300-500) was acquired by the Fairmont group in late 2015. Almost everything at this luxury hotel has been renovated, from the rooms and lobby to the expansive pool deck.

What hasn't changed are the stunning views of San Francisco Bay and the Golden Gate Bridge from the resort's enviable spot in the hills between Berkeley and Oakland.

Food
CASUAL DINING

A downscale ethnic enclave that is well worth a visit is the **Chaat Café** (1902 University Ave., 510/845-1431, www.chaatcafes.com, Sun.-Thurs. 11:30am-9pm, Fri.-Sat. 11:30am-9:30pm, $5-20), which offers spicy Indian cuisine for the right price. This Bay Area chain serves *chaat* (small plates and appetizers), of course, and you can also get a meaty curry, a tandoori dish, stuffed naan, and more. Although you'll find a few vegetarian specialties on the menu, this place sticks more to the meat-eating tradition.

Thin-crust wood-fired pizzas are all the rage among Bay Area foodies, but a trip to the north end of Berkeley to savor **Zachary's Chicago Style Pizza** (1853 Solano Ave., 510/525-5950, www.zacharys.com, Sun.-Thurs. 11am-9:30pm, Fri.-Sat. 11am-10:30pm, $10-20) is well worth the effort. Their deep-dish cornmeal-crust pies come with the standard Italian toppings (pepperoni, sausage, green peppers, mushrooms), or you can opt for more inventive offerings such as barbecue chicken and Mexican chorizo. All pizzas come slathered in tomato sauce to complete the authentic Chicago style. You can even get a thin-crust pizza. This small old-school pizzeria fills up quickly, especially on weekend nights. Luckily, if there is a long wait, you can put in your order when you put in your name. Your pizza might make it to your table as you sit down to eat.

A popular place for a pie is **The Cheese Board** (1504 Shattuck Ave., 510/549-3183, http://cheeseboardcollective.coop, Mon. 7am-1pm, Tues.-Fri. 7am-6pm, Sat. 8am-5pm). A cheese shop and bakery, The Cheese Board serves just one kind of pizza a day, utilizing unique ingredients like roasted corn, leeks, and limes.

FINE DINING

The city's very best fine-dining venue, and Alice Waters's baby, is ★ **Chez Panisse** (1517 Shattuck Ave., restaurant 510/548-5525, café 510/548-5049, www.chezpanisse.com, restaurant Mon.-Sat. seatings at 5:30pm and 8pm, café Mon.-Thurs. 11:30am-2:45pm and 5pm-10:30pm, Fri.-Sat. 11:30am-3pm and 5pm-11:30pm, restaurant prix fixe $75-125, café $10-30). Those wishing to dine in the restaurant at Chez Panisse should make their reservations early. You can make a dinner reservation up to one month in advance; the desk takes phone calls 9am-9:30pm Monday-Saturday and a $25 deposit is required. You'll get the chance to enjoy some of the best cuisine that's ever graced a plate in Berkeley or anywhere else. Waters and her successors create French-California dishes at the cutting edge of current trends.

Upstairs, the café offers food that's a bit more casual but just as good. It's much easier to get a reservation in the bustling, energetic café than the restaurant, and the casual atmosphere is less intimidating for diners who are new to California haute cuisine.

In north Berkeley, **César** (1515 Shattuck Ave., 510/883-0222, http://cesarberkeley.com, daily noon-midnight, $8-17) is a refreshingly modern tapas bar started by three Chez Panisse alumni. The menu is geared to small-plate Spanish cuisine, but many of the dishes, such as lamb chops with lentils and steak with caramelized red onions, plus the *bocadillos* (fresh Spanish-style sandwiches), could stand in for a modest entrée. The bright indoor-outdoor space also lends itself to enjoying one of the many Spanish and California wines or the classic and inventive collection of cocktails.

Information and Services

Newcomers to Berkeley can start at the **Visitors Information Center** (2030 Addison St., 510/549-7040, http://visitberkeley.com, Mon.-Fri. 9am-5pm). As a major metropolitan area, you'll find most services that you need in Berkeley. Be wary using ATMs, especially after dark.

For medical assistance, the **Alta Bates Summit Medical Center** (2450 Ashby Ave., 510/204-4444, www.altabatessummit.org) has a 24-hour emergency room.

OAKLAND

Oakland is the biggest city in the East Bay, and although its reputation hasn't always been perfect (and travelers should probably stay in the popular visitor areas), today a great deal of downtown urban renewal has made it a visitor-friendly place with plenty of attractions, accommodations, and good food.

Oakland Museum of California

The **Oakland Museum of California** (1000 Oak St., 510/318-8400, www.museumca.org, Wed.-Thurs. 11am-5pm, Fri. 11am-9pm, Sat.-Sun. 10am-6pm, adults $15, students and seniors $10, children ages 9-17 $6, children under 8 free, parking $1 per hour) has undergone a renovation that has launched it into the stratosphere of must-see museums. Its uniquely multidisciplinary approach tells California's story through art, history, and science. Within its modernist concrete walls are Thiebaud's and Diebenkorn's take on the urban California landscape, a rare and authentic Ohlone basket, home furnishings from elite homes of California's early days, and a casting of a mastodon. While it may seem that anything goes at the Oakland Museum, the one caveat is that its exhibits must reflect the character of California. The on-site Blue Oak café serves wine, espresso, salads, and sandwiches.

Chabot Space and Science Center

One of the most spectacular sights in the East Bay, **Chabot Space and Science Center** (10000 Skyline Blvd., 510/336-7300, www.chabotspace.org, summer Sun. and Tues.-Thurs. 10am-5pm, Fri.-Sat. 10am-10pm, fall-spring Sun. and Wed.-Thurs. 10am-5pm, Fri.-Sat. 10am-10pm, adults $18, students

The Trappist, a fine place for a beer

including a carousel, a roller coaster, and a train, to keep the excitement high.

Entertainment and Events

BARS

Oakland offers a range of drinking options, from dive bars to fancy establishments where "mixologists" create cocktails with small-batch liquors and homemade syrups. But no place in Oakland has been serving spirits or beers longer than **Heinold's First and Last Chance** (48 Webster St. in Jack London Square, 510/839-6761, http://heinolds.com, Fri.-Sat. noon-1am, Sun.-Thurs. noon-11pm). Surrounded by modern development, this small shack was constructed from the wood of a whaling ship in 1883 and still uses its original gaslights for illumination. It's where author Jack London wrote (and drank); it's referenced multiple times in his novel *John Barleycorn*. The floor and bar tilt at an unusual angle, a result of the 1906 earthquake.

Located downtown in a Victorian building dating to the 1870s, **The Trappist** (460 8th St., 510/238-2900, Sun.-Thurs. noon-midnight, Fri.-Sat. noon-1am) is the place for Belgian beer fans. The rotating menu features 25 beers on tap and 100 bottled beers.

Sidebar (542 Grand Ave., 510/452-9500, http://sidebar-oakland.com, Mon.-Thurs. 11:30am-10pm, Fri. 11:30am-10:30pm, Sat. 4pm-10:30pm) serves delicious throwback cocktails in a sleek bar and restaurant right on Lake Merritt.

LIVE MUSIC

You can find some good live music in Oakland. Perhaps the best-known venue is **Yoshi's** (510 Embarcadero W., 510/238-9200, www.yoshis.com, Mon.-Thurs. 5:30pm-9pm, Fri.-Sat. 5:30pm-10pm, Sun. 5pm-9pm, shows daily 8pm and 10pm). With a sushi restaurant in one room and the legendary jazz club next door, it's possible to enjoy the sushi without attending the concert, or vice versa. If you're a dinner patron, it's a very good idea to make reservations for the show and claim a seat before you sit down for your meal, as diners get

and seniors $15, children $14) makes science and space supercool. Up in the Oakland Hills, the Chabot complex includes observatories, a planetarium, a museum, and the Megadome theater, all open to the public. Create your own solar system in an interactive exhibit, ride a space shuttle in the Megadome, and check out Saturn's rings through some of the highest-quality telescopes on the West Coast. Grab a bite to eat and a cup of coffee at the on-site Celestial Café.

Oakland Zoo

For a day with creatures of the land, go to the **Oakland Zoo** (9777 Golf Links Rd., 510/632-9525, www.oaklandzoo.org, summer Mon.-Fri. 10am-4pm, Sat.-Sun. 10am-5pm, fall-spring daily 10am-4pm, adults $15.75, youths and seniors $11.75, under age 2 free), where you'll discover an astounding 660 different types of amphibians, mammals, reptiles, and birds living in humane and well-maintained enclosures around the lush and beautiful grounds. There are children's rides, priority seating. Performers at Yoshi's have included Otis Taylor and Kurt Elling.

The **Fox Theater** (1807 Telegraph Ave., 510/302-2250, www.thefoxoakland.com) books national touring bands in a historic theater. Originally opened in 1928 and closed for nearly 40 years, it was designed in the Moorish style. Recent acts in this relatively intimate venue have included Van Morrison and Joanna Newsom.

Shopping

The Temescal neighborhood of Oakland is a hotbed of eating and shopping. The **Temescal Alley** (http://temescalalleys.com) east of Telegraph Avenue at 49th Street has over a dozen locally owned shops. These include **Esqueleto** (482 A 49th St., 510/629-6216, http://shopesqueleto.com, Tues.-Sat. 11am-6pm, Sun. 11am-5pm), which sells jewelry by Lauren Wolf; the **Homestead Apothecary** (486 9th St., 510/495-6549, http://homesteadapothecary.com, Mon. noon-6pm, Tues.-Sun. 10am-5pm), which deals in herbs and tinctures; and **Mind's Eye Vintage** (486 49th St., 510/529-6519, www.mindseyevintage.com, Tues.-Sun. 11am-6pm), which carries secondhand clothing.

For local specialized shops with a neighborhood feel, head to **Rockridge** (College Ave. between Alcatraz Ave. and 51st St.). Foodies will want to explore epicurean **Rockridge Market Hall** (5655 College Ave., 510/250-6000, http://rockridgemarkethall.com, Mon.-Fri. 9am-8pm, Sat. 9am-7pm, Sun. 10am-7pm), where multiple gourmet shops share one roof. Inside the brick building, you'll find a coffee roaster, a bakery, a fresh pasta shop, a fish market, a butcher, wine, and flowers. Every store is known for its adherence to the "eat local" ethos and for its quality. Nearby, bookworms can get their fix at well-regarded and independent **Diesel Bookstore** (5433 College Ave., 510/653-9965, www.dieselbookstore.com, Mon.-Thurs. 10am-9pm, Fri.-Sat. 10am-10pm, Sun. 10am-6pm).

The **Piedmont Avenue District** is an old Oakland neighborhood with a historic movie theater and mom-and-pop stores. **Phillipa Roberts Jewelry** (4176 Piedmont Ave., 510/655-0656, www.philipparoberts.com, Mon.-Sat. 10am-6pm, Sun. 11am-5pm) is a charming jewelry and gift store owned and operated by a local jewelry maker. While she stocks an eclectic assortment of housewares and gifts, her handmade jewelry, made largely from silver and semiprecious stones in simple, elegant designs, are the real treat. **Spectator Books** (4163 Piedmont Ave., 510/653-7300, www.spectatorbooks.com, Sun.-Thurs. 11am-8pm, Fri. 11am-9pm, Sat. 11am-10pm) specializes in new, used, and rare books. The multiple rooms, stacked high with disheveled books, are a bibliophile's delight.

Hit up Oakland's **Grand Lake Farmers Market** (Splash Pad Park, Grand Ave. and Lake Park Ave., 415/472-6100, www.agriculturalinstitute.org, Sat. 9am-2pm) every Saturday for produce and great food stands.

Sports and Recreation

The jewel of Oakland is **Lake Merritt** (650 Bellevue Ave., 510/238-7275). Take a walk around the lake, play a few holes of golf, rent a kayak for a peaceful paddle, or even get in a set of tennis. For families, **Children's Fairyland** (699 Bellevue Ave., 510/452-2259, www.fairyland.org, summer Mon.-Fri. 10am-4pm, Sat.-Sun. 10am-5pm, spring-fall hours vary, $10, children under 1 year free) is a small amusement park that provides hours of entertainment and diversion on 10 acres at the edge of the lake.

If you're eager to get out on the water, the **Lake Merritt Boating Center** (568 Bellevue Ave., 510/238-2196, www2.oaklandnet.com, spring-fall Mon.-Fri. 11am-5pm, Sat.-Sun. 10:30am-5pm, summer Mon.-Fri. 10am-6pm, Sat.-Sun. 10:30am-6pm, $12-24 per hour, cash only) has everything from canoes to catamarans, kayaks, and sailboats. On the lake at Lakeside Park off Grand Avenue, it is run by the city, so the prices are fair; the only hitch is that it is cash only.

A unique way to experience Lake Merritt

is to book a private gondola tour through **Gondola Servizio** (1520 Lakeside Dr., 510/663-6603, http://gondolaservizio.com, $60-85). Feel like you are in Italy on one of the romantic 30- or 50-minute tours.

Oakland is home to several professional sports teams of varying reputations and records. The most consistent players are Major League Baseball's **Oakland A's** (510/638-4900, http://oakland.athletics.mlb.com). Part of the American League, the A's have seen their ups and downs, but they almost always put on a good show for their fans. The most notorious team in pro football, the **Oakland Raiders** (800/724-3377, www.raiders.com) calls the East Bay home. Be aware that the home side of the stadium can get rowdy and rough.

Nonstop action can always be found at a **Golden State Warriors** (888/479-4007, www.nba.com/warriors) game. In 2015, the NBA team won its first championship since 1975, inspiring a new generation of fans. Plans are developing to move the Warriors across the bay to San Francisco.

All three teams play at the **Oracle Arena and Coliseum** (7000 Coliseum Way, 510/569-2121, www.coliseum.com), a complex with both a covered basketball arena and an open-air stadium that hosts the A's and the Raiders. Though the vast majority of events and game-goers are perfectly safe, the Coliseum isn't in the best neighborhood, so pay attention as you walk out to your car.

Accommodations

In the thick of the Jack London Square District, the **Inn at Jack London Square** (233 Broadway, 510/452-4565, www.innatthesquare.com, $189-199) offers comfortable digs. In addition to its clean and modestly stylish decor, the hotel has complimentary Wi-Fi, local shuttle service, and room service. There is also an exercise room and an outdoor pool perfect for relaxing during Oakland's hot summer days. Best of all, the hotel is within easy walking distance of many of the popular eateries, entertainment venues, and other attractions around Oakland's revitalized waterfront.

Another option in the Jack London Square area is the ★ **Waterfront Hotel** (10 Washington St., 510/836-3800, www.jdvhotels.com, $129-369). The rooms are decorated with nifty nautical decor. All of the 145 units have flat-screen TVs, iPhone docking stations, fridges, and microwaves, while some have large private decks that offer views of the Oakland harbor, the island of Alameda, and San Francisco. The heated pool is perched right above the water. Another asset is a weekday shuttle service (7am-9am and 4pm-8:30pm) that runs guests to nearby locations. The hotel houses **Lungomare,** an Italian restaurant. This is an industrial area; the occasional boat horn sounds and trains rumble through periodically.

The Washington Inn (495 10th St., 510/452-1776, www.thewashingtoninn.com, $169-192) brings a hint of European elegance to Oakland. Rooms are done in clean lines, simple furnishings, and bright white linens with touches of brilliant color. This inn prides itself on pampering its guests, so take advantage of the extras. The inn's location in the heart of downtown makes it perfect for business and pleasure travelers alike.

Food

Uptown Oakland is having a foodie renaissance. One wildly popular Uptown eatery is **Flora** (1900 Telegraph Ave., 510/286-0100, www.floraoakland.com, Mon.-Thurs. 5:30pm-10pm, Fri. 11:30am-2:30pm and 5:30pm-11pm, Sat. 10am-2:30pm and 5:30pm-11pm, Sun. 10am-2:30pm, $15-35), which reinvents classic comfort food and cocktails in an art deco landmark dating back to 1931.

A vegan soul food joint? Believe it or not, it exists at **Souley Vegan** (301 Broadway St., 510/922-1615, http://souleyvegan.com, Tues.-Sat. 11am-10:30pm, Sun. 10am-3pm, $10). This popular spot serves southern classics like mustard greens and black-eyed peas, but also takes the down-home theme to the barbecued tofu and southern-fried tofu.

Cosecha means "harvest" in Spanish, and **Cosecha** (907 Washington St., 510/452-5900, www.cosechacafe.com, Mon.-Wed. 11am-3:30pm and 4:30pm-8:30pm, Thurs.-Fri. 11am-3:30pm and 5pm-9:30pm, Sat. 10:30am-3:30pm and 5pm-9:30pm, $7-14) features a Chez Panisse alum creating flavorful and fresh Mexican cuisine from a popular stand in downtown Oakland's Swan's Market. Lunch includes weekday blue-plate specials, tortas, quesadillas, and tacos including a crisp pork belly version. Dinner can feature braised pork in chile guajillo and grilled chicken marinated in achiote. Start with an order of the guacamole and salsa served with crispy, thick tortilla chips.

Homeroom (400 4th St., 510/597-0400, http://homeroom510.com, Sun.-Sat. 11am-10pm, $9-13) is meant to evoke your grade school days. This hipster favorite serves 10 varieties of mac and cheese including the popular "Gilroy Mac," where the classic is given new life from gouda, pecorino, and garlic. The decor includes a file cabinet and chalkboard wall. The menu suggests wine and beer pairings for each bowl of mac and cheese.

At the foot of the Oakland Hills, the Piedmont district's main draw is the delightfully retro **Fenton's Creamery** (4226 Piedmont Ave., 510/658-7000, www.fenton-screamery.com, Mon.-Thurs. 11am-11pm, Fri.-Sat. 9am-midnight, Sun. 9am-11pm, $10), which has been serving scoops since 1894. There are scores of flavors including Swiss milk chocolate, rum raisin, black walnut, and pomegranate, sold by the scoop, in classic waffle cones or made up into a sinful sundae. Or opt for a burger, grilled ham and cheese, or a Cobb salad. Fenton's also serves breakfast throughout the day.

Near Jack London Square, **Chop Bar** (247 4th St., 510/834-2467, www.oaklandchopbar.com, Mon.-Thurs. 7am-10pm, Fri. 7am-11pm, Sat. 9am-11pm, Sun. 9am-10pm, $12-23) serves breakfast, lunch, and dinner in a cozy, warmly lit space accented in recycled wood and old brass instruments. The food is simple but excellent with an emphasis on artisanal ingredients. The bar has local beer and wines on tap. Whether you decide to go for a plate of charcuterie with a glass of wine late in the afternoon, or for a sumptuous dinner of oxtail poutine or rabbit gallentine, Chop Bar won't disappoint.

In Rockridge is **À Côté** (5478 College Ave., 510/655-6469, www.acoterestaurant.com, Sun.-Thurs. 5:30pm-10pm, Fri.-Sat. 5:30pm-11pm, $8-24), which serves small-plate French,

Waterfront Hotel's pool deck

tacos at Cosecha

Basque, and Italian Mediterranean food. The quality and the price range imply that this is a fine-dining sort of a place, but the communal tables, outdoor patio, and generally relaxed atmosphere demonstrate that this is a place where everyone can be comfortable. There are an astounding 40 wines offered by the glass, perfect to pair with dishes including mussels in Pernod and a lobster mushroom flatbread. No meal here would be complete without an order of the *pommes frites*.

Information and Services
Start at the **Oakland Convention and Visitors Bureau** (463 11th St., 510/839-9000, http://visitoakland.org, Mon.-Fri. 9am-5pm, Sat.-Sun. 9:30am-4pm) to get good advice, maps, restaurant recommendations, and traffic tips.

It's a good idea to stick to the ATMs in well-lit, heavily trafficked areas. The same goes for gas stations and mini-marts.

For medical attention, head out to **Alameda Hospital** (2070 Clinton Ave.,

510/522-3700, www.alamedahospital.org), which has a 24-hour emergency room. In Oakland, **Alta Bates** (350 Hawthorne Ave., 510/655-4000, www.altabatessummit.org) has a campus that has a 24-hour emergency room.

TRANSPORTATION
Berkeley is north of Oakland along the east side of the San Francisco Bay. If you're driving from San Francisco into the East Bay, take the **Bay Bridge** (westbound toll $4-6). For Berkeley, turn north onto I-580/I-80. Oakland is accessed by via I-80 as well; I-580 borders Oakland to the north, while I-880 parallels I-80 downtown. Avoid driving I-80, I-880, or I-580 during the commuting hours (8am-10am and 4pm-7pm). Be warned that parking in Berkeley and Oakland can be a bona fide nightmare. If you're visiting for the day or for an evening show, consider taking the BART train to avoid the parking hassle.

BART (www.bart.gov, $1.75-5 one-way) is a major form of transit in and around the Bay Area. The Downtown Berkeley station is underneath Shattuck Avenue in the heart of Berkeley. Other Berkeley stations include North Berkeley, Ashby, and Rockridge. The 12th Street/Oakland City Center station is convenient to downtown Oakland, but there are also trains out to 19th Street and Lake Merritt. BART fares are based on distance (most East Bay destinations are $1.75-5 one-way); ticket machines accept cash and debit or credit cards.

Bus service in Oakland and Alameda is run by **AC Transit** (510/891-4706, www.ac-transit.org, adults $2.10, children and seniors $0.85). Transbay routes connect the East Bay and San Francisco (adults $4.20, children and seniors $2.10).

The **Oakland International Airport** (OAK, 1 Airport Dr., Oakland, 510/563-3300, www.flyoakland.com) sees less traffic than San Francisco's airport and has shorter security lines and fewer delays. Major airlines include Alaska, Delta, JetBlue, Southwest, and Spirit. From the Oakland airport, you can rent a car, catch a cab, or take the **AirBART**

Francisco, you can take BART from the airport across the bay to Berkeley.

San Jose

Sprawled across the south end of Silicon Valley, San Jose is home to companies like eBay, Cisco, Adobe, IBM, and many others, making it the beating heart of the high-tech industry. Once considered a cultural wasteland, San Jose has worked to change its image, supporting local art and attracting high-end restaurants.

SIGHTS

Rosicrucian Egyptian Museum

Perhaps San Jose's most unusual attraction is the imposing **Rosicrucian Egyptian Museum** (1660 Park Ave., 408/947-3635, www.egyptianmuseum.org, Wed.-Fri. 9am-5pm, Sat.-Sun. 10am-6pm, adults $9, students and seniors $7, children $5). The museum was opened by the Rosicrucian Order in 1928 and has a wonderful collection of ancient Egyptian artifacts, including several mummies. Local children and adults love the Rosicrucian's jewels, tomb artifacts, tools, and textiles. The complex also boasts a planetarium.

San Jose Museum of Art

The highly regarded **San Jose Museum of Art** (110 S. Market St., 408/271-6840, www.sjmusart.org, Tues.-Sun. 11am-5pm, also third Thurs. of the month 11am-8pm, adults $8, students and seniors $5, under age 6 free) is right downtown. Housed in a historic sandstone building, the beautiful, light-filled museum features modern and contemporary art. Its permanent collection focuses largely on West Coast artists, but major retrospectives of works by the likes of Andy Warhol, Robert Mapplethorpe, and Alexander Calder come through often. The museum store offers perhaps the best gift shopping in downtown San Jose. The café, with both an indoor lounge and outside sidewalk tables, is a great place to grab a quick bite.

Tech Museum of Innovation

The **Tech Museum of Innovation** (201 S. Market St., 408/294-8324, www.thetech.org, daily 10am-5pm, adults $12, seniors, students, and children $9) brings technology of all kinds to kids, families, and science lovers. The interactive displays at the Tech invite touching, allowing children to explore and learn about medical technology, computers, biology, chemistry, physics, and more using all their senses. Traveling exhibits also make the rounds here and help to flesh out the Tech's aging displays. Recently, these have included *Mythbusters: The Explosive Exhibition*. The IMAX theater (additional $4) shows films dedicated to science, learning, technology, and adventure.

Winchester Mystery House

For good old-fashioned haunted fun, stop in at the **Winchester Mystery House** (525 S. Winchester Blvd., 408/247-2101, www.winchestermysteryhouse.com, daily 9am-5pm, adults $5-40, seniors $5-37, children $5-30). The huge, bizarre mansion was built by famous eccentric Sarah Winchester. Kids love the doors that open onto brick walls, stairwells that go nowhere, and oddly shaped rooms, while adults enjoy the story of Sarah and the antiques displayed in many of the rooms. Sarah married into the gun-making Winchester family and became disturbed later in life by the destruction and death wrought by her husband's products. She designed the house to both facilitate communication with the spirits of the dead and to confound them and keep herself safe. Whether or not ghosts haunt the mansion is a matter of debate—visit and make up your own mind. Admission to the grounds is free, but to get a peek inside the house, you must be on one of the many tours. For an extra-spooky experience, take a Friday the 13th or Halloween flashlight tour (book early, as these tours fill up fast).

ENTERTAINMENT AND EVENTS

Live comedy is a popular Silicon Valley option. The **San Jose Improv** (62 S. 2nd St., 408/280-7475, http://sanjose.improv.com), in the historic San Jose Theatre, often hosts major-league headliners like Margaret Cho and Kevin Nealon while also granting stage time to local talent in showcases and contests.

SHOPPING

A variety of big shopping malls and an endless series of mini-malls fan out over San Jose's miles of terrain. The top place to shop is **Santana Row** (Stevens Creek Blvd. and Winchester Blvd., www.santanarow.com). This upscale outdoor center dazzles the eye with its array of chic chain and one-off boutiques, shops, and restaurants. Shops include Sur La Table, Anthropologie, Brooks Brothers, and many more.

SPORTS AND RECREATION

San Jose may be mocked by its cousins in San Francisco and the East Bay, but there are some great and different professional sports worth seeing. The big dog in the area is the **San Jose Sharks** (http://sharks.nhl.com) National Hockey League team. They haven't won a Stanley Cup yet, but everyone gets into the games at the downtown **SAP Center** (525 W. Santa Clara St.), making San Jose one of the league's loudest and liveliest places to watch a game.

ACCOMMODATIONS

The **Sainte Claire Hotel** (302 S. Market St., 408/295-2000, www.thesainteclaire.com, $199-499) offers big-city-style accommodations. Standard rooms are small but attractive,

with carved wooden furniture and rich linens and draperies. The suites are more luxurious. Amenities include a flat-screen TV with a DVD player, a CD and MP3 player, free Wi-Fi, plush robes, and turndown service upon request.

For a taste of true Silicon Valley luxury, stay at **The Fairmont San Jose** (170 S. Market St., 408/998-1900, www.fairmont. com, $159-450). With a day spa and limousine service, it's no surprise that the 731 rooms at the Fairmont are something special. Even the standard rooms have plenty of space, elegant fabrics and appointments, and a marble-clad private bath with a separate shower and bathtub. Of the Fairmont's two towers, the South Tower has the more luxurious rooms.

Consumer culture takes a turn for the absurd at the **Hotel Valencia Santana Row** (355 Santana Row, 408/551-0010, www.hotelvalencia-santanarow.com, $200-400). This top-tier hotel is right in the middle of the prestigious Santana Row shopping mall. Ultramodern elegance and amenities include a fitness center and outdoor pool. The lavish baths with upscale toiletries help to make the hotel experience pleasing to all the senses.

FOOD

Open seven days a week, **Gordon Biersch** (33 E. San Fernando St., 408/294-6785, www.gordonbiersch.com, Sun.-Wed. 11:30am-11pm, Thurs. 11:30am-11pm, Fri.-Sat. 11:30am-midnight, $12-28) is always busy, and the food and beer are tasty. Try the blackened ahi tacos or the Cajun pasta, but don't miss out on one of the handcrafted German-style beers brewed on-site. It has a lively happy hour, particularly if a local sports team is playing on the large overhead TVs in the bar.

Original Joe's (301 S. First St., 888/841-7030, http://originaljoes.com, Sun.-Thurs. 11am-11pm, Fri.-Sat. 11am-midnight, $11-46) has managed to survive downtown since 1956. This classic Italian does old-school classics including chicken piccata, top sirloin steaks, breaded veal cutlets, and calf's liver entrées. Another favorite is the classic Joe's omelet, made with hamburger meat, spinach, and eggs.

An unassuming French café near San Jose State University, **La Lune Sucree** (116 Paseo de San Antonio, 408/292-2070, Mon.-Sat. 8am-6pm, Sun. 8am-3pm, $7-20) is a small gem of an eatery. They do savory puffs, salads, and sandwiches including a standout breakfast version with hollandaise sauce. There's limited seating inside and out front.

INFORMATION AND SERVICES

Before you come to San Jose, visit www.san-jose.org to get all the information you need about the Silicon Valley region and its attractions. Once in town, stop in at the **San Jose Convention and Visitors Bureau** (408 Almaden Blvd., 408/295-9600) for maps, brochures, guidebooks, and local advice.

For medical attention, **Good Samaritan Hospital** (2425 Samaritan Dr., 408/559-2011, www.goodsamsj.org) has 24-hour emergency services.

TRANSPORTATION

Travelers heading straight for Silicon Valley should skip San Francisco International Airport and fly into **Mineta San Jose International Airport** (SJC, 1667-2077 Airport Blvd., 408/501-0979, www.flysanjose.com) if at all possible. It also has some of the best deals for flying into the Bay Area. This suburban commercial airport has shorter lines and less traffic congestion, and is convenient to downtown San Jose.

Amtrak (800/872-7245, www.amtrak.com) trains come into San Jose: the once-daily Seattle-Los Angeles *Coast Starlight* and the commuter *Capitol Corridor* to Sacramento

stop at the **San Jose-Diridon Station** (65 Cahill St.). See the Amtrak website for information about scheduling and fares.

San Jose-Diridon station is also a hub for **Caltrain** (800/660-4287, www.caltrain.com, $3-13), a commuter train that runs from Gilroy to San Francisco. If you'd like to spend a day or even two in San Francisco but base yourself in Silicon Valley, taking Caltrain is an excellent way to go.

At Diridon station you can also catch the **VTA Light Rail** (408/321-2300, www.vta.org, $2-6), a streetcar network that serves San Jose and other parts of Silicon Valley as far north as Mountain View.

The VTA also operates Silicon Valley **buses** (408/321-2300, www.vta.org, $2-4), which can get you almost anywhere you need to go if you're patient enough.

As with most of the Bay Area, it's best to avoid San Jose's freeways 7am-9:30am and 4pm-7:30pm Monday-Friday. Arterial U.S. 101 is a dank, dirty stretch of road that's convenient to much of the peninsula. I-280 is much prettier and less convenient, and it's definitely the easiest—but not the shortest—driving route north to San Francisco. Highway 17 is the fast, treacherous route over the hills from the coast and Santa Cruz; it turns into I-880 in the middle of San Jose and runs past the end of the bay and then north along the east side of the water all the way to Oakland. Highway 87, sometimes called the Guadalupe Parkway, can provide convenient access to downtown San Jose and the airport.

Parking in San Jose isn't anywhere near as bad as in San Francisco, but you should still be prepared to pay a premium for event parking and enclosed lots at the fancier hotels.

Coastside

Many Bay Area locals escape to the coast south of San Francisco for weekend vacations, enjoying the small-town atmosphere in Half Moon Bay and Pescadero along with the unspoiled beauty of the dozens of miles of undeveloped coastline. Peak seasons for major attractions include October's pumpkin season and winter, when elephant seals return to Año Nuevo.

MOSS BEACH

Midway down the coast between San Francisco and Half Moon Bay on Highway 1, Moss Beach is one of several residential towns that line the coast south of the imposing Devil's Slide. There is little here besides stunning scenery, a few small businesses, and the Fitzgerald Marine Reserve. North of Moss Beach is the lovely Montara, while south is the Half Moon Bay Airport, El Granada, Princeton, and then Half Moon Bay.

Fitzgerald Marine Reserve

For tide-pooling on the coast, the **Fitzgerald Marine Reserve** (200 Nevada Ave., 650/728-3584, http://fitzgeraldreserve.org, daily 8am-close) is the place to go. The 32-acre reserve, a marine protected area, is considered one of the most diverse intertidal zones in the Bay Area. On its rocky reefs you can hunt for sea anemones, starfish, eels, and crabs—there's even a small species of red octopus. The reserve is also home to egrets, herons, an endangered species of butterfly, and a slew of sea lions and harbor seals that enjoy sunning themselves on the rocks. Rangers are available to answer any questions and, if need be, to remind you of the strict tide pool etiquette. Persistent ocean spray and blankets of seaweed can keep the reefs slick, so wear shoes with good traction. For the best viewing, come at low tide and on weekdays, as this is a popular destination. For a more leisurely and drier experience, numerous trails crisscross the

windswept bluffs and go through sheltering groves of cypress and eucalyptus trees. There is a strict no-dog policy.

Montara State Beach

Just north of Moss Beach and the Marine Reserve is **Montara State Beach** (2nd St. and Hwy. 1, Montara, www.parks.ca.gov, 650/726-8819, daily 8am-sunset), one of the most beautiful beaches in this area. It is as popular with tide-poolers, surfers, and anglers as it is with picnickers and beachcombers. It is also dog-friendly, which is a big plus as many state beaches have restrictions on canines in the interest of preserving the endangered snowy plover. Thankfully, the beach also remains relatively uncrowded compared to many of the other beaches to the south; it has a tendency to get windy, and there is limited parking.

McNee Ranch State Park

For those who want sweeping views of the coast as well as a heart-pounding hike, **McNee Ranch** (Hwy. 1, across from Montara State Beach, 650/726-8819, www.parks.ca.gov, daily 8am-sunset) fits the bill. The big hike is eight miles up **Montara Mountain,** through dry California chaparral along a series of fire roads. The peak itself is 1,900 feet high (the parking lot is at 100 feet), and it is an arduous but worthwhile climb to the top. Although the trail is unmarked, there are maps at the information board just past the parking lot. Still, it's easy to wing it—just follow the roads uphill. From the top, you can see all the way across the Golden Gate and south past Half Moon Bay. The mountain is also home to the endemic Montara manzanita. There is no loop trail, so you must return down the mountain. But with the crisscrossing trails, you won't have to come back the same way. Free parking is in a small and poorly marked dirt lot directly across Highway 1 from Montara

Coastside

Pacifica
San Bruno
SAN FRANCISCO INTERNATIONAL AIRPORT
101
San Andreas Lake
McNee Ranch State Park
Montara State Beach
Pilarcitos Lake
280
Montara
POINT MONTARA LIGHTHOUSE HOSTEL
San Francisco Watershed Lands
Moss Beach
Pillar Point Harbor
Lower Crystal Springs Reservoir
FITZGERALD MARINE RESERVE
Half Moon Bay
Venice Beach
Dunes Beach
Francis Beach
92
Half Moon Bay
Burleigh H Murray Ranch
35
Half Moon Bay State Park
Purisima Creek Redwoods
PACIFIC OCEAN
Purisima Creek Redwoods OSP
1
TUNITAS CREEK RD
Tunitas Creek Ranch OSP
Toto Ranch
LA HONDA RD
Pomponio State Beach
San Gregorio
STAGE RD
Pescadero State Beach
Pescadero Marsh National Reserve
Pescadero
PESCADERO CREEK RD
1
CLOVERDALE ROAD
Cloverdale
PIGEON POINT LIGHTHOUSE ★

0   2 mi
0   2 km

© AVALON TRAVEL

State Beach. An easier option, also free, is to park at the beach and walk across the road to the trailhead. McNee Ranch is also a popular mountain biking area, and dogs are welcome on leash.

Hiking

The Devil's Slide was once a pesky section of Highway 1 between Montara and Pacifica known for its frequent landslides, car wrecks, and road closures. After years of construction, Highway 1 was moved east through a tunnel to avoid the section of coastline. The change has been a boon to local hikers, bicyclists, and equestrians who now have the paved and stunning 1.3-mile **Devil's Slide Trail** (650/363-4020, www.smcoparks.org, daily 8am-close) to recreate on. The former roadway is split into bicycle and pedestrian lanes. Along the way are observation scopes, interpretive plaques, and stellar coastal views. There are two small parking areas at the southern end of the trail. To reach them, drive north of Montara on CA-1. At the stoplight before the Tom Lantos Tunnels, take a left and then look for the two small parking areas.

Accommodations

For an old school bed-and-breakfast experience, spend a night at **The Goose and Turrets Bed and Breakfast** (835 George St., Montara, 650/728-5451, www.gooseandturretsbandb.com, $175-230). The Clipper Room is a unit decorated with model planes, flight charts, and propellers, while another room is dedicated to French cave paintings. Three rooms have gas fireplaces; all bathrooms have a heated towel rack. Learn about the building's past as Montara's former town hall and post office during afternoon tea with the innkeepers, who live upstairs. Mornings bring a four-course breakfast. This spot is best for guests who desire a quiet country stay.

For an indulgent hideaway, make a reservation at the **Seal Cove Inn** (221 Cypress Ave., Moss Beach, 800/995-9987, www.sealcoveinn. com, $300-400). Tucked away in the cypress and pine forest of Moss Beach, this highly

Distillery (140 Beach Way, Moss Beach, 650/728-5595, www.mossbeachdistillery. com, Mon.-Sat. noon-7:45pm, Sun. 11am-7:45pm, $15-38) for the ghost stories as for the hearty food and terrific ocean views. The restaurant operated as a speakeasy during Prohibition and was also frequented by mystery writer Dashiell Hammett. The restaurant offers something of a cross between traditional American food and California cuisine. Portions tend to be large, and service is friendly if occasionally slow. Folks who want to soak up the old-school atmosphere like to sit in the bar, while visitors who want to stare out over the ocean prefer the terrace, where plenty of blankets are on hand to ward off the Pacific chill.

Looking to pack a picnic lunch before you head out to the Fitzgerald Marine Reserve or Montara State Beach? Swing by **Gherkin's Sandwich Shop** (171 8th St., Montara, 650/728-2211, daily 9am-8pm, $10) for everything you can imagine between two slices of bread. You'll find oddities like breakfast frittata sandwiches and the Ooey Gooey, with peanut butter, Nutella, and marshmallows. There are also classics like BLTs, burgers, and pastrami and swiss cheese. Order from a variety of sides that include garlic fries and fried pickles, but beware: The sandwiches are huge and can easily be split between two people or saved for a later snack.

★ **La Costanera** (8150 Cabrillo Hwy., Montara, 650/728-1600, www.lacostanerarestaurant.com, Tues.-Sun. 5pm-9pm, $18-36), poised above Montara State Beach, is about more than just the view. Skillfully designed with grand sloping picture windows and sunken dining rooms, La Costanera is a sophisticated Peruvian restaurant and the only eatery on this part of the coast to earn a Michelin star two years in a row. There are a variety of ceviches to choose from as well as slow-cooked pork shoulder and lobster gnocchi, all accented in Peruvian sauces and spices. The bar menu offers hearty plates that could serve as a light dinner.

the entrance to The Goose and Turrets Bed and Breakfast

regarded 10-room B&B bills itself a "European sanctuary." Outside, the gabled roof, climbing ivy, and expansive gardens let guests know they have entered the inn's rarified world, as do the interior's warm colors, creamy soft linens, private decks, pre-breakfast coffee, and real wood-burning fireplaces.

The **Point Montara Lighthouse Hostel** (16th St. and Hwy. 1, Montara, 650/728-7177, www.norcalhostels.org, dorm $27-30, private room $73-79) offers even better views at a fraction of the price, albeit with a bit less luxury. Stay in the shared dorm rooms, each with 3-6 beds and either coed or gender-specific. Or spring for a private room. Either way, enjoy use of the shared kitchen, common areas with wood-burning fireplaces, the eclectic garden perched on the cliff, and the private cove beach. Other amenities include Wi-Fi, laundry facilities, an espresso bar, and complimentary linens.

Food

As many people come to the **Moss Beach**

Transportation

Moss Beach is 23 miles directly south of San Francisco on Highway 1 (Cabrillo Hwy.). From San Francisco, the easiest and most direct—not to mention scenic—route is to follow Highway 1 south all the way to Moss Beach.

Alternatively, if you are coming from I-280 on the peninsula, take Highway 92 west to Half Moon Bay and Highway 1. From Half Moon Bay, Moss Beach is only seven miles north on Highway 1.

HALF MOON BAY

The coastal city of Half Moon Bay is an agricultural town. The locals all know each other, even though the majority of residents commute "over the hill" to peninsula and Silicon Valley jobs. Strawberries, artichokes, and brussels sprouts are the biggest crops, along with flowers, pumpkins, and Christmas trees, making the coast the place to come for holiday festivities. Half Moon Bay enjoys a beautiful natural setting and earns significant income from tourism, especially during the world-famous Pumpkin Festival each October.

Some people know Half Moon Bay for Mavericks, a monster wave that can rise to 80 feet off nearby Pillar Point during the winter months. Mavericks is one of the world's most renowned surf spots and has been chronicled in the 2004 surf documentary *Riding Giants* and the 2012 feature film *Chasing Mavericks*. It is a treacherous wave known for its underwater rocks, great white shark danger, and cold waters.

Onshore from Mavericks is the Pillar Point Harbor and the neighboring town of **Princeton-by-the-Sea,** the other workhorse on the coast. Here, anglers haul in crab, salmon, and herring, and local businesses cater to their needs. This is the place to rent kayaks, go on a chartered fishing trip, and buy fresh fish, sometimes straight off the boat (especially during crab season).

Beaches

The beaches of Half Moon Bay draw visitors from over the hill and farther afield all year long. As with most of the North Pacific region, summer can be a chilly, foggy time on the beaches. For the best beach weather, plan your Half Moon Bay trip for September-October. **Half Moon Bay State Beach** (www.parks.ca.gov, parking $10 per day) actually encompasses three discrete beaches stretching four miles down the coast, each with its own access point and parking lot. **Francis Beach** (95 Kelly Ave.) has the most

La Costanera, near Montara State Beach

developed amenities, including a good-size campground with grassy areas to pitch tents and enjoy picnics, a visitors center, and indoor hot showers. **Venice Beach** (Venice Blvd., off Hwy. 1) offers outdoor showers and flush toilets. **Dunes Beach** (Young Ave., off Hwy. 1) is the southernmost major beach in the chain and the least developed.

Perhaps the most famous beach in the area is one that has no name. At the end of West Point Avenue in Princeton is the Pillar Point Marsh and a long stretch of beach that wraps around the edge of the point. This beach is the launchpad for surfers paddling out to tackle the infamous **Mavericks Break** (Pillar Point Marsh parking lot, past Pillar Point Harbor). Formed by unique underwater topography, the giant waves are the site of the legendary **Mavericks Surf Contest** (http://mavericks-surf.com). The competition is always held in winter, when the swells reach their peak, and scheduling left until the last minute to ensure that the waves are the biggest of the year. When perfect conditions present themselves, the best surfers in the world are given 48 hours' notice to make it to Mavericks to compete. Mavericks is not a beginner's break, especially in winter, and the giant breakers can be deadly. If you aren't positive you're up to the challenge, don't paddle out.

Entertainment and Events

Locals may complain that there is not a lot going on in Half Moon Bay, but the city boasts one of the best jazz venues and two of the biggest annual events in the Bay Area. Since it opened in 1964, the **Bach Dancing and Dynamite Society** (311 Mirada Rd., Half Moon Bay, 650/726-2020, www.bachddsoc. org) has been a hangout for bohemians and jazz aficionados, hosting the biggest names in jazz—Bill Evans, Dizzy Gillespie, Etta James, and Duke Ellington among them. Not only is the music fantastic, but the venue, the Douglas Beach House, can't be beat.

In contrast to the Bach's cool vibe, **Pacific Coast Dream Machines** (Half Moon Bay Airport, 9850 Hwy. 1, www.miramarevents.

com) is all muscle and revving engines. This two-day event includes a demolition derby, a flying motorcycle, World War II-era fighter planes, ultralight and antique biplanes, and automobiles from peddle cars to homemade kit cars. The event generally takes place on the last weekend in April, so plan accordingly; the traffic congestion is legendary.

The biggest annual event in this small agricultural town is the **Half Moon Bay Art & Pumpkin Festival** (www.miramarevents. com). Every October, nearly 250,000 people trek to Half Moon Bay to pay homage to the big orange squash. The festival includes live music, food, artists' booths, contests, activities for kids, an adults lounge area, and a parade. Perhaps the best-publicized event is the pumpkin weigh-off, which takes place before the festivities begin. Farmers bring their tremendous squash in on flatbed trucks from all over the country to determine which is the biggest of all. If anyone breaks the current world record, they'll take home an impressive $5,000.

Shopping

Strolling Main Street is another reason folks come to Half Moon Bay. A holdover from the town's agricultural roots is **Half Moon Bay Feed and Fuel** (331 Main St., 650/726-4814, http://halfmoonbay-feedandfuel.com, Mon.-Fri. 8:30am-6pm, Sat. 9am-5pm, Sun. 10am-4pm). Stopping by the Feed and Fuel is a fun little detour. There are often baby chicks and bunnies as well as quirky gift items that any Western fanatic or wannabe cowboy would love.

Step into a whole other world in **Abode** (417 Main St., 650/726-6060, www.abodehalfmoonbay.com, Mon.-Thurs. 10am-5pm, Fri.-Sat. 10am-6pm, Sun. 10am-5:30pm). Carefully crafted, Abode almost feels like a treatise on home decorating in which the goal is fluidity between the outside and the inside spaces. There are no bright plastic or enamel wares here, but instead furniture and home accents are all in an earthy palette and are largely made from glass, wood, and other natural materials and designed with artistic quality, craftsmanship, and utility.

Another Half Moon Bay treasure is **Toque Blanche** (604 Main St., 650/726-2898, www.mytoque.com, Mon.-Sat. 10am-6pm, Sun. 10am-5pm), perhaps the best kitchen store in the Bay Area. They have everything from coffeemakers to panini presses, cookie cutters to knives, dinner plates to linens. Some of the bonuses include free cooking demos, super-soft French dish towels, a wall full of different types of salt, and La Chamba Clay Cookware, a line of extremely versatile and attractive Colombian cooking pottery.

To see what Half Moon Bay does best, drop by the **Coastside Farmer's Market** (225 Cabrillo Hwy., 650/726-4895, www.coastside-farmersmarket.org, May-Dec. Sat. 9am-1pm). There is plenty of local meat, bread, produce, pottery, art, and even wool skeins, spun and dyed by hand. Local bands are always at the market, and there is plenty of street food. The **Half Moon Bay Coastal Flower Market** (Main St. and Kelly Ave., 650/712-9439, www.explorer1.com, third Sat. of the month, 9am-3pm) is even more of an institution, where local flower growers show off a multitude of blooms and houseplants that range from the domestic to the exotic.

Sports and Recreation

There are plenty of great trails around Half Moon Bay. Among the local favorites are those at **Purisima Creek Redwoods** (4.4 miles up Higgins Canyon Rd., 650/619-1200, www.openspace.org, daily dawn-half hour after sunset). There are a multitude of trails in this 4,412-acre preserve, and many ascend to Skyline Boulevard for an elevation gain of 1,700 feet. Take a leisurely stroll through the redwoods, complete with dripping ferns, flowering dogwood, and wood sorrel, along **Purisima Creek Trail** (3.9 miles, easy-strenuous) until it turns steep and eventually takes you to its literally breathtaking Skyline terminus. If you don't want to crest the ridge of the Santa Cruz Mountains, opt for **Harkins Ridge Trail** (6 miles, moderate), which rises

out of the canyon shortly past the trailhead. You'll hike through redwoods, then oaks and chaparral, and back again into firs, pines, and redwoods as you gain 800 feet in elevation over 2.5 miles. To make a loop, cut down Craig Britton Trail, which meets Purisima Creek Trail. To feel like you've conquered a mountain, make the climb to 2,102-foot **Bald Knob** (9.6 miles, strenuous). From **Purisima Creek Trail**, take **Borden Hatch Mill Trail** to **Bald Knob Trail,** where you will find a flat clearing among the dry madrones, live oaks, and chaparral. You will be rewarded with terrific coastal views.

Fortunately for mountain bikers, nearly all the trails in the preserve are open to cyclists. The trails are steep and knotted with rocks and tree roots, which makes for an exhausting, exhilarating, or terrifying ride, depending on your experience and attitude.

The most popular trail in Half Moon Bay is the **Coastside Trail** (650/726-8819, www.parks.ca.gov). Extending five miles from Miramar Beach to Poplar Beach, this flat, paved trail follows the coast and is filled with joggers, dog walkers, and bikes. There are a multitude of beach-access points along the way, and if you want to go downtown, jump off at Kelly Avenue and take it across Highway 1 to the heart of Half Moon Bay. Beyond the Poplar Beach parking lot, the trail crosses a wooden bridge and turns into a dirt trail. This area is known as the **Wavecrest Open Space** and goes all the way down to the Ritz-Carlton. It is much less traveled than the paved Coastside Trail and is a great place to spot herons, egrets, and gray whales off the coast during their spring migration. Parking is plentiful at Poplar Beach ($2 per hour), at the end of Poplar Street on the south end of town.

For a sedate ocean adventure, take a winter whale-watching cruise or a shallow-water rockfish fishing trip on the *Queen of Hearts* (Pillar Point Harbor, 510/581-2628, www.fishingboat.com, reservations strongly recommended, $80-98). Whale-watching trips (Jan.-Mar., $40) cost a bit less than fishing trips on the *Queen of Hearts*. Deep-sea fishing for albacore and salmon (if the season isn't canceled) makes for a more energetic day out on the Pacific, although motion-sickness medication is often recommended.

One of the coolest ways to see the coast is from the deck of a sea kayak or stand-up paddleboard. Many tours with the **Half Moon Bay Kayaking Company** (Pillar Point Harbor, 650/773-6101, www.hmbkayak.com, kayaks $25-60/hr., SUPs $25/hr., guided tours $75-150) require no previous kayaking experience. For an easy first paddle, try the Pillar Point tour, the full-moon tour, or the sunset paddle. If you're looking for a wilder ride, sign up for a kayak-surfing class—you'll learn how to catch waves safely in specially designed kayaks. The company also offers beginner through advanced classes in closed-deck kayaks. The harbor is also an ideal place to learn how to stand-up paddleboard.

Have you dreamed of riding a horse on a California beach with the sea breeze blowing through your hair? **Sea Horse Ranch** (1828 Hwy. 1, 650/726-9903, www.seahorseranch. org, daily 8am-close, $70-90) offers one-hour, 90-minute, and two-hour guided tours that take you along the cliffs and down onto the sands at Half Moon Bay's Poplar Beach.

Children over the age of seven are welcome, as are riders of all ability levels. Beginners can ask to have their horses led by a guide or can request to ride Tardy, an extremely laid-back horse known for his slow speed and gentle disposition.

Accommodations

Half Moon Bay offers several lovely bed-and-breakfasts along with one luxury resort hotel and a suites hotel right by the harbor, among other options.

A stunning property, the ★ **Ritz-Carlton Half Moon Bay** (1 Miramontes Point Rd., 650/712-7000, www.ritzcarlton.com, $600-4,000) resembles a Scottish castle transported to the California coast. Surrounding the luxury hotel are two emerald-green golf courses perched above the Pacific. The sprawling grounds are dotted with always-lit fire pits and chairs for taking in the marvelous ocean views. Out front is Half Moon Bay Coastside Trail, where you can hike for up to seven miles. Guests enjoy the finest of modern amenities: Bathrooms have marble floors and countertops, while many of the posh rooms overlook the sea. Another plus is the hotel's superb staff. The hotel also has a spa, restaurant, two fitness rooms, a pool, tennis courts,

Take a horseback tour with Sea Horse Ranch.

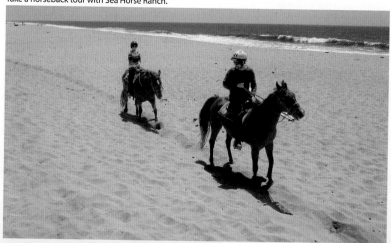

and a basketball court. Guests can also enjoy top-tier restaurant **Navio,** which has an extensive 54-page wine list.

The **Beach House at Half Moon Bay** (4100 N. Cabrillo Hwy., 650/712-0220 or 800/315-9366, www.beach-house.com, $210-465) is situated in an ideal location a few feet from Pillar Point Harbor and the popular Coastside Trail. All the rooms, which are multilevel lofts, have a private patio or balcony to take in the bobbing sailboats and the groaning foghorn. On fog-shrouded days, the Beach House has in-room wood-burning fireplaces and an outdoor hot tub and heated pool on the pool deck to warm up with.

Food

The quality of food in Half Moon Bay is superb. For seafood, go to ★ **Sam's Chowder House** (4210 N. Cabrillo Hwy., 650/712-0245, www.samschowderhouse.com, Mon.-Fri. 11:30am-9:30pm., Sat. 11am-9:30pm, Sun. 11am-9pm, $12-35), a fusion of an East Coast chowder and lobster shack with West Coast sensibilities and a view of the Pacific. The lobster clambake for two is a splurge, but it's an excellent introduction to Sam's seafood-heavy menu. Armed with a lobster cracker, bib, and wet nap, attempt to finish the starting bowl of clam chowder followed by a tasty mound that includes a whole lobster, clams, mussels, potatoes, and a spicy andouille sausage. Many other dinners opt for the buttery lobster roll. Owner Paul Shenkman, a veteran restaurateur once associated with nearby Pasta Moon and Cetrella, is a New Jersey native who takes seafood very seriously.

Open since 1987, **Pasta Moon** (315 Main St., 650/726-5125, www.pastamoon.com, Mon.-Thurs. 11:30am-2pm and 5:30pm-9pm, Fri. 11:30am-2:30pm and 5:30pm-9:30pm, Sat. noon-3pm and 5:30pm-9:30pm, Sun. noon-3pm and 5:30pm-9pm, $12-30) is the area's godmother of fine dining. Managing to be both casual and upscale at once, Pasta Moon serves updated Italian cuisine with an emphasis on fresh, light dishes. Their wood-fired pizzas are particularly good and affordable, as are any of the pasta dishes, made with house-made noodles. The rustic dining room, with a view of the woods and the creek, completes the experience, while the bar and new lounge offers a more casual and urbane evening out.

Cetrella (845 Main St., 650/726-4090, www.cetrella.com, Tues.-Thurs. and Sun. 5:30pm-9:30pm, Fri.-Sat. 5:30pm-10pm,

Beach House at Half Moon Bay

$10-36) bills itself as a Mediterranean bistro. In truth, the menu includes a range of Mediterranean-themed California cuisine, and the big-beam construction looks like something out of the redwood forests up north. The chef uses local, often organic ingredients to create stunning fare that varies by season. Look for Dungeness crab in winter and artichokes in the spring.

If you think good bread is the secret weapon of a great sandwich, come by the **Garden Deli Café** (356 Main St., 650/726-9507, www.sanbenitohouse.com, daily 10am-4:30pm, $7). In the historic San Benito House, the deli serves basic sandwiches like turkey, roast beef, and ham that stand out due to the slabs of tasty homemade bread that the ingredients lie between. Get your sandwich to go or eat it in the adjacent courtyard at multicolored picnic tables.

With its house-made brews and seafood-heavy menu, the ★ **Half Moon Bay Brewing Co.** (390 Capistrano Rd., 650/728-2739, Mon.-Thurs. 11am-9pm, Fri. 11am-close, Sat. 10am-close, $12-24) is a fine place to watch the sunset over Pillar Point Harbor. This landmark has a worn and comfy interior along with some outdoor seating for sunny days. The beers made on-site include five standard brews and five seasonal brews; the amber ale is the most popular. The golden-fried artichoke heart appetizer is a favorite, but the fish tacos are where the kitchen does its best work, especially the in-house smoked salmon version. They have live music on weekends.

Information and Services

Visit the **Half Moon Bay Chamber of Commerce** (235 Main St., 650/726-8380, www.halfmoonbaychamber.org, Mon.-Fri. 9am-5pm) in the red house just after you turn on Main Street from Highway 92. The chamber also doubles as a visitors center with maps, brochures, and a schedule of events.

Cell phones work fine in town, but coverage can be spotty up in the hills above town and out on the undeveloped coastline and beaches along Highway 1.

There is a 24-hour emergency room at the **Seton Coastside Hospital** (600 Marine Blvd., Moss Beach, 650/563-7100, www.seton-coastside.org). For less serious health services, the **Coastside Clinic** (Shoreline Station, Suite 100A, 225 S. Hwy. 1, Half Moon Bay, 650/573-3941, www.sanmateomedicalcenter.org) is just north of the intersection of Kelly Avenue and Highway 1.

Sam's Chowder House

Transportation

Half Moon Bay is on Highway 1 about 45 minutes south of San Francisco. From San Francisco, take I-280 south to Highway 92 west to Half Moon Bay and Highway 1. Or take the scenic route by following Highway 1 directly south from San Francisco all the way to Half Moon Bay.

Parking in downtown Half Moon Bay is usually a fairly easy proposition—except, of course, if you're in town for the Pumpkin Festival, when parking is a nightmare of epic proportions. Your best bet is to stay in town with your car safely stowed in a hotel parking lot before the festival.

PESCADERO

Pescadero is a tiny dot on the map south of Half Moon Bay and well north of Santa Cruz, with one main street, one side street, and several smallish farms. Despite its tiny size, many Bay Area denizens visit Pescadero for the twisty roads that challenge motorcyclists and bicyclists, fresh produce, the town's 19th-century buildings and, of course, the legendary Duarte's Tavern.

Pescadero State Beach

Pescadero State Beach (Hwy. 1, north of Pescadero Rd., 650/879-2170, www.parks. ca.gov, daily 8am-sunset, $8/vehicle) is the closest to town. It's a great spot to walk in the sand and stare out at the Pacific, but near-constant winds make it less than ideal for picnics or sunbathing. It does have some facilities, including public restrooms.

Bird lovers flock to **Pescadero Marsh Natural Preserve** (Hwy. 1, www.smcnha. org), on Highway 1 right across the highway from Pescadero State Beach. This protected wetland, part of Pescadero State Beach, is home to a variety of avian species, including blue herons, great and snowy egrets, and northern harriers. For the best birding, visit the marsh early in the morning or in late fall or early spring, when migration is in full swing. A footbridge erected in 2011 allows guests to visit the back of the marsh.

San Gregorio State Beach

North of Pescadero, **San Gregorio State Beach** (at the intersection of Hwy. 84 and Hwy. 1, 650/726-8819, www.parks.ca.gov, daily 8am-sunset, $8/vehicle) stretches farther than it seems. Once you're walking toward the ocean, the small-seeming cove stretches out beyond the cliffs that bound it to create a long stretch of beach. San Gregorio is a local favorite in the summer, despite the regular appearance of thick, chilly fog over the sand. Brave beachgoers can even swim and bodysurf here, although wearing a wetsuit is advisable. Picnic tables and restrooms cluster near the parking lot, although picnicking can be hampered by the wind.

San Gregorio General Store

San Gregorio is a tiny, picturesque town of rolling rangeland, neat patches of colorful crops, and century-old homes, including a one-room schoolhouse and an old brothel. Its beating heart is the **San Gregorio General Store** (Hwy. 84 and Stage Rd., 650/726-0565, www.sangregoriostore.com, Mon.-Thurs. 10:30am-6pm, Fri. 10:30am-7pm, Sat. 10am-7pm, Sun. 10am-6pm). Open since 1889, the San Gregorio General Store has an eclectic book section and a variety of cast-iron cookery, oil lamps, and raccoon traps. In the back of the store are coolers stocked with deli sandwiches made in the back kitchen. The real centerpiece is the bar, serving beer, wine, and a large selection of spirits to ranchers, farmers, and locals. On the weekends the store is packed with out-of-towners, and the live music keeps things moving. The deep picture windows out front make it a comfy place to pass the afternoon.

Pigeon Point Lighthouse

South of Pescadero is 115-foot-high **Pigeon Point Lighthouse** (210 Pigeon Point Rd. at Hwy. 1, 650/879-2120, www.parks.ca.gov, daily 8am-sunset), one of the tallest in the country. First lit in 1872, Pigeon Point is one of the most photographed lighthouses in the United States. Sadly, visitors will find the lighthouse itself in a state of disrepair, and recent earthquakes have made climbing to the top unsafe. Yet the monument stands, its hostel still shelters travelers, and visitors still marvel at the incomparable views from the point. During winter, look for migrating whales from the rocks beyond the tower.

Año Nuevo State Park

Año Nuevo State Park (Hwy. 1, south of Pescadero, 650/879-2025, reservations 800/444-4445, www.parks.ca.gov, daily 8:30am-sunset, $10 per car, guided tour $7) is world famous as the winter home and breeding ground of the once-endangered elephant seal. The reserve also has extensive dunes and marshland. The beaches and wilderness are open year-round. The elephant seals start showing up in December and stay to breed, birth pups, and loll on the beach until early March. Visitors are not allowed down to the elephant seal habitats on their own and must sign up for a guided walking tour. Book your tour at least a day or two in advance; the seals are popular with both locals and travelers.

Accommodations

Pescadero has a small but surprisingly good array of lodging options. If budget is a factor, try the **Pigeon Point Hostel** (210 Pigeon Point Rd., at Hwy. 1, 650/879-0633, http://norcalhostels.org/pigeon, dorm $25-28, private room $76-178). This Hostelling International hostel has simple but comfortable accommodations, both private and dorm-style. Amenities include three kitchens, free Wi-Fi, and beach access. But the best amenity of all is the cliff-top hot tub ($8 pp.).

At **Costanoa Lodge and Campground** (2001 Rossi Rd. at Hwy. 1, 650/879-1100, www.costanoa.com, campsite $30-65, rooms and cabins $209-379), you can pitch a tent in the campground or rent a whirlpool suite in the lodge. Other options include log-style cabins with shared baths, small tent cabins with shared baths, and private rooms. Costanoa's many nature programs educate visitors about the ecology of the San Mateo coast and the preservation efforts that are underway. A small general store offers s'mores fixings and souvenirs, while "comfort stations" provide outdoor fireplaces, private indoor-outdoor showers, baths with heated floors, and saunas that are open daily 24 hours to all guests.

For a little more luxury, the **Pescadero Creek Inn Bed & Breakfast** (393 Stage Rd., 888/307-1898, www.pescaderocreekinn.com, $165-240) is conveniently located in downtown Pescadero, an easy walk from Duarte's, the grocery stores, the local cemetery, and the creek. While the over 100-year-old house isn't completely soundproof, the rooms have high ceilings and are prettily appointed; amenities include down-feather bed tops. The owner serves a delectable breakfast each morning, and pours his homemade award-winning wines in the afternoon, along with cheese and fruit.

Camping

Most of the camping in Pescadero is inland, deep in the redwoods. **Butano State Park** (1500 Cloverdale Rd., 650/879-2040 or 800/444-7275, www.parks.ca.gov, $35) offers 21 drive-in and 18 walk-in campsites. While there are no showers, there are clean restrooms, fire pits, and drinking water. Perhaps the best amenity is the proximity to fantastic hiking in the park. There are quiet strolls through the canopy of redwoods or more athletic treks up dusty ridgelines. The most scenic is the Butano Fire Road that summits the ridge at an abandoned airstrip.

Farther inland, past the tiny town of Loma Mar, is **Memorial Park** (9500 Pescadero Creek Rd., 650/879-0238, www.co.sanmateo.ca.us, $30-40) and its 158 campsites. Each site accommodates as many as eight people, with a fire pit, picnic tables, and a metal locker to store food and sundries. There is also drinking water, baths with coin-operated showers, and a general store within the park that sells firewood, hot dog buns, ice cream, and soap. While there are fewer hiking trails than at Butano, Memorial boasts an amphitheater and swimming holes in Pescadero Creek.

Food

★ **Duarte's Tavern** (202 Stage Rd., 650/879-0464, www.duartestavern.com, daily 7am-8pm, $13-25) has been honored by the James Beard Foundation as "An American Classic," and once you walk through the doors you'll see why. The rambling building features sloping floors and age-darkened wooden walls. The food is good, the service friendly, and the coffee plentiful. And while almost everybody comes to Duarte's for a bowl of artichoke soup or a slice of olallieberry pie, it's really the atmosphere that's the biggest draw. Locals of all stripes—farmers, farmhands, ranchers, and park rangers—sit shoulder to shoulder with travelers sharing conversation and a bite to eat, particularly in the dimly lit bar but also in the dining room or at the old-fashioned lunch counter.

If Duarte's is too crowded, venture across the street to the **Pescadero Country Store** (251 Stage Rd., 650/879-0410, daily 9am-7pm, $11-18). This converted grocery store has a pizza counter serving wood-fired pies, a full-service deli, and a beer and wine bar decorated in a deep-blue nautical theme.

If you're heading to Pescadero from Half Moon Bay, stop at **Bob's Vegetable Stand** (Hwy. 1, 5 miles south of Half Moon Bay, 650/712-7740), which has a selection of local produce rivaling any grocery store. In Pescadero, **Harley Farms** (205 North St., 650/879-0480, www.harleyfarms.com, farm and shop hours summer daily 10am-5pm, winter Mon.-Thurs. 11am-3pm, Fri.-Sun. 10am-4pm, call for tour information) boasts of being the last working dairy on the San Mateo coast. Its locally famous goat cheese is sold in its farm store. During your stop, you can even assist in the cheese-making process, taking a tour that teaches you how to milk a goat and then create fresh artisanal cheese.

To round out your picnic, drop by **Arcangeli Grocery** (287 Stage Rd., 650/879-0147, www.normsmarket.com, daily 10am-6pm) across the street from Duarte's. All the breads are homemade and delicious, including the Italian artichoke herb bread and the garlic-herb sourdough loaf. The pastries—especially the raspberry twists—are also great.

Transportation

Pescadero is 17 miles south of Half Moon Bay. At Pescadero State Beach, Highway 1 intersects Pescadero Road. Turn east on Pescadero Road and drive two miles to the stop sign (the only one in town). Turn left onto Stage Road to find the main drag. Parking is free and generally easy to find on Stage Road or in the Duarte's parking lot. On weekends, you might need to park down the road a ways and walk a block or two.

Wine Country

Highlights

★ **Napa Valley Wine Train:** Who wants to be the designated driver when there's so much wine to drink? Enjoy local varietals and food on this train's trip from Napa to St. Helena and back (page 157).

★ **Oxbow Public Market:** This 40,000-square-foot space allows you to sample the valley's best wines, food, and produce (page 160).

★ **Grgich Hills Winery:** Home of the California chardonnay that won the Paris Tasting of 1976, Grgich Hills uses a biodynamic farming process to produce exquisite wines (page 171).

★ **Culinary Institute of America:** Inside buildings of ancient gray stonework, this culinary school comprises cooking classes and demonstrations, a museum, and an exemplary restaurant, all amid forested surroundings (page 175).

★ **Spas:** Submerge yourself in a bath of soothing warm mud. The quirky Napa County town of Calistoga has several spas that offer this treatment (page 181).

★ **Mission San Francisco Solano de Sonoma:** Sonoma is home to the last California mission to be built, now the centerpiece of Sonoma State Historic Park (page 186).

★ **The Russian River:** Swim, canoe, or simply float serenely downriver at this center of summer fun (page 201).

★ **A. Rafanelli:** The best Sonoma reds are produced at this small, unpretentious, and appointment-only winery. Pick up one of their stunning cabs (page 205).

15

Entering California's Wine Country is an unmistakable experience. From the crest of the last hill before you enter the valleys, sunlight paints golden streaks on endless rows of grapevines that stretch as far as the eye can see.

Trellises run along both sides of every road, tempting visitors to question the unpicked weeds beneath the vines, the rosebushes capping each row, and the strange, motionless fans standing guard high above. A heady aroma of earth and grapes permeates the area. Welcome to the Napa and Sonoma Valleys.

The area's beautiful grapevines are renowned worldwide for producing top-quality vintages and economical table wines. But foodies also know the area as a center for stellar cuisine. Yountville, a tiny, upscale town in the middle of Napa Valley, is the favorite haven of celebrity chef Thomas Keller. The food served at his French Laundry restaurant is legendary, as are the prices. Keller's influence helped to usher in a culinary renaissance, and today the lush flavors of local, sustainable produce are available throughout the region.

Sonoma Valley has long played second fiddle to Napa in terms of viticultural prestige, but the wines coming out of the area are second to none. The Russian River Valley wineries are often friendlier and less crowded than their Napa counterparts, while the wineries in the southern Carneros region are fewer and farther between. Each offers visitors a more personal experience than Napa and the chance to sample unique and amazing varietals. Sonoma County's craggy coastline and natural beauty also provide great recreation opportunities for visitors fonder of the outdoors than the grapes.

PLANNING YOUR TIME

Napa and Sonoma form the beating heart of California's Wine Country. Many visitors plan a weekend in Napa, with subsequent weekend trips to explore Sonoma and the Russian River. If you come during the summer or fall, you'll find a crush in almost every tasting room in the valley; even the smaller boutique labels do big business during the six-month high season (May-Oct.).

Previous: a Napa Valley vineyard; a few offerings from Grgich Hills Winery. **Above:** wine barrels in Sonoma.

Wine Country

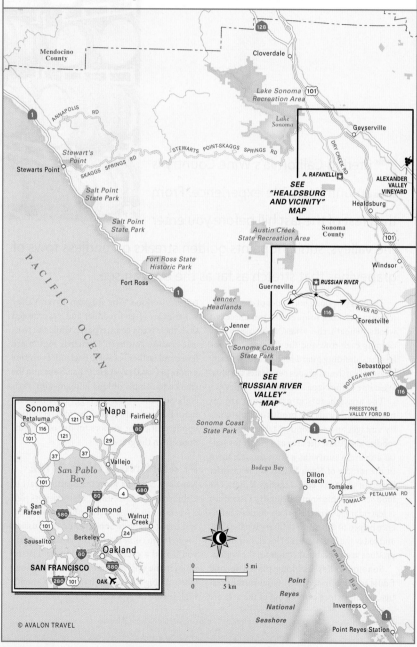

Mendocino
County

128

Cloverdale

Lake Sonoma
Recreation Area

101

ANNAPOLIS   RD

STEWARTS   POINT-SKAGGS   SPRINGS   RD

Stewart's
Point

Lake
Sonoma

Geyserville

DRY CREEK RD

Stewarts Point

SKAGGS   SPRINGS   RD

A. RAFANELLI

ALEXANDER
VALLEY
VINEYARD

Salt Point
State Park

**SEE
"HEALDSBURG
AND VICINITY"
MAP**

Healdsburg

Salt Point
State Park

Austin Creek
State Recreation Area

Sonoma
County

101

PACIFIC   OCEAN

Fort Ross State
Historic Park

Windsor

RUSSIAN RIVER

Guerneville

Fort Ross

1

Jenner
Headlands

116

RIVER RD

Forestville

Jenner

Sonoma Coast
State Park

**SEE
"RUSSIAN RIVER
VALLEY"
MAP**

Sebastopol

BODEGA HWY

116

FREESTONE
VALLEY FORD RD

Sonoma Coast
State Park

1

Sonoma   Napa

Petaluma

121   12

Fairfield

101

116

121

29

80

Bodega Bay

Dillon
Beach

37

37

Tomales

PETALUMA   RD

Vallejo

TOMALES

San Pablo
Bay

101

80

4

680

San
Rafael

580

Richmond

Walnut
Creek

Berkeley

24

Sausalito

Oakland

SAN FRANCISCO

880

280   101

OAK ✈

0   5 mi

0   5 km

Point
Reyes
National
Seashore

Tomales Bay

Inverness

1

Point Reyes Station

© AVALON TRAVEL

Be aware that Highway 29, which runs through the heart of Napa Valley, gets jammed up around St. Helena and can be very slow on weekends. U.S. 101 slows through Santa Rosa during the weekday rush-hour commutes and late in the day on sunny summer weekend afternoons. If you're not up for driving, downtown tasting rooms in the cities of Napa, Sonoma, and Santa Rosa are good alternatives to the slow trek up and down the wine roads.

Napa Valley

Napa Valley can feel like a wine theme park. Wineries cluster along Highway 29 and the Silverado Trail, each trying to outdo its neighbors to win the business of the thousands of weekend visitors. Tasting rooms are plentiful, tours sell out hours in advance, and special events draw hundreds of people. Then there's the food: As the wine industry in Napa exploded, top-tier chefs rose to the challenge, flocking to the area and opening amazing restaurants in the tiny towns that line the wine trails. Even if you don't love wine, a meal at one of the many high-end restaurants makes Napa worth a visit.

The region has weathered a couple of natural disasters in the last few years—a 2014 earthquake that damaged buildings in downtown Napa, a 2015 wildfire—but that has done nothing to tamp down the tourism industry in the popular valley.

NAPA

Napa Valley has a blue-collar heart: the city of Napa, many of whose 80,000 residents work in banking, construction, the medical industry, and other businesses that serve the rest of the valley. The Napa River snakes through the heart of downtown, tempering the hot summer weather and providing recreation as well as a healthy dose of natural beauty. It also gives the downtown a historic feel, particularly when among the many 19th-century buildings. The town boasts sparkling new structures with high-end clothiers and cutting-edge restaurants as well as the Oxbow Market—a one-of-a-kind culinary treat.

The Napa River runs through downtown Napa.

Napa Valley

Wildlake Ranch

SPAS
Calistoga

Angwin

Cedar Roughs ACEC

Lake Berryessa

Bothe-Napa Valley State Park

29

St. Helena

Lake Hennessey

128

CULINARY INSTITUTE OF AMERICA

FROG'S LEAP WINERY/MUMM

GRGICH HILLS WINERY

Sugarloaf Ridge State Park

Oakwood

Rutherford

OAKVILLE RD

Annadel State Park

Kenwood

TRINITY RD

MT VEEDER RD

Yountville

DOMAINE CHANDON

DRY CREEK RD

Glen Ellen

Jack London State Historic Park

12

REDWOOD RD

29

121

SEE "SONOMA VALLEY" MAP

MISSION SAN FRANCISCO SOLANO DE SONOMA
Sonoma

Napa

NAPA VALLEY WINE TRAIN
OXBOW PUBLIC MARKET

Skyline Wilderness Park

0   3 mi
0   3 km

116

12

121

CLINE CELLARS

12

© AVALON TRAVEL

Day Trips from San Francisco

The Napa Valley is less than 100 miles north of San Francisco, making it an ever-popular day-trip destination. If you plan to tour Wine Country as a day trip, choose one region to explore. Napa and Sonoma are closest to San Francisco, about one hour's drive. Traffic on the winding two-lane roads in these regions can easily become clogged with wine-tasting day-trippers, especially on weekends. To avoid the crowds, try to get an early start or visit on a weekday. Note that most wineries close by 4pm, and some are open only by appointment.

ONE DAY IN NAPA

In downtown Napa, get your bearings at the **Napa General Store** and sample some Napa vintages. Have lunch or just pick up some picnic supplies at **Oxbow Public Market** before hopping back on Highway 29. Drive north to Rutherford and enjoy a tasting at **Grgich Hills Winery,** which offers a relaxed Napa experience. Continue north on Highway 29 to St. Helena and the palatial estate of **Beringer Vineyards.** Many of Beringer's wines are only available here.

After a full day of wine-tasting, give your taste buds a rest with dinner at the **Culinary Institute of America,** where the country's top chefs are trained. The Greystone Restaurant is where that food is served; you can even watch as it's prepared in the open kitchen. From St. Helena, the drive back to San Francisco will take 1.5-2 hours.

Overnight: Spend the night at El Bonita Motel and spend a second day exploring Sonoma.

ONE DAY IN SONOMA

From Napa, Highway 121 winds west through the Carneros wine region. Stop off for a bit of bubbly at gorgeous **Domaine Carneros,** where the views and gardens are almost as impressive as the sparkling wines. From Highway 121, Highway 12 twists north into Sonoma. Stretch your legs in Sonoma Plaza and explore the charming downtown area. Stop in at the **Mission San Francisco Solano** in **Sonoma State Historic Park** for a bit of history, and then grab lunch at **The Girl and the Fig,** housed in the historic Sonoma Hotel.

After lunch it may be time for a massage at the **Garden Spa at MacArthur Place.** For more wine-tasting, take Highway 12 north to quaint Glen Ellen and stop in at the **Valley of the Moon,** where the landmark winery will enchant with its stone buildings and unusual sangiovese rosé.

From here, it's a 30-minute drive to downtown Santa Rosa, where you can catch U.S. 101 south to San Francisco, a little over an hour away. You may decide to grab a bite before you head back; if so, try **Jackson's Bar and Oven.**

Overnight: Spend the night at the **Gaige House Inn** in Glen Ellen or **The Sonoma Hotel** on the plaza in Sonoma.

Wineries

ROBERT SINSKEY VINEYARDS

Getting into the foodie act that's sweeping Wine Country, **Robert Sinskey Vineyards** (6320 Silverado Tr., 707/944-9090, www.robertsinskey.com, daily 10am-4:30pm by appointment only, $45-75) offers a menu of small bites alongside their list of current wines. The appointment-only tastings include a tour of the cave and cellar, and discussions about the art of winemaking. The more intensive Perfect Circle Tour is also more expensive. With or without the food, the red wines themselves are worth dropping in at this attractive stone-and-wood edifice.

STARMONT WINERY & VINEYARDS

Starmont Winery & Vineyards (1451 Stanly Ln., 707/252-8001, www.starmontwinery. com, daily 10am-5pm, $20-35) purveys moderately priced chardonnays and pinot noirs at an old ranch south of Napa. The tasting room is constructed of wood and concrete, and there's a fire pit outdoors. Break a light sweat on the daily Stanly Ranch Estate Hike & Barrel Tasting (11am, $65) that includes a short hike (0.75-1 mile) around the vineyards followed by a barrel tasting.

TRINITAS

Situated in a cool cave beneath a hilltop vineyard, the **Trinitas Tasting Room** (875 Bordeaux Way, 707/251-3012, www.trinitas-cellars.com, daily 11am-7pm, $20-30) functions as the on-site wine bar for the Meritage Resort. The bar is open to both hotel guests and passersby, offering tastings of Trinitas wines and bites of cheese, fruit, and tiny gourmet goodies. Seats at the bar make it easy to get comfortable and stay awhile—which quickly becomes desirable when you get your nose inside a glass. Trinitas wines do not tend toward down-market hotel freebies: These surprisingly balanced, well-crafted wines are more than worth your time, especially if you're serious about your vintages. Expect a small list featuring one or two whites, a rosé, and one or two red wines, all sold at shockingly low per-bottle prices, especially compared to other Napa wines of similar quality. Glasses of wine start at $6.

Sights

★ NAPA VALLEY WINE TRAIN

If trying to decide which wineries to visit, which restaurants are worth a stop, and how to avoid weekend traffic sounds exhausting, consider taking the **Napa Valley Wine Train** (1275 McKinstry St., 800/427-4124, www.winetrain.com, $124-264). The Wine Train offers a relaxing sightseeing experience aboard vintage train cars, where you can sit back and enjoy the food, wine, and views. The train runs from Napa to St. Helena and back, a 36-mile, three-hour round-trip tour. The least expensive option includes a barbecued lunch and a glass of wine. More amenities at higher prices include a gourmet three-course lunch or dinner, with the option of taking a winery tour along the way. Each package includes seating in a different historic railcar—you might lunch in the 1917 Pullman Car, or take an evening tour of Grgich Hills aboard the 1952 Vista Dome Car. Advance reservations are strongly suggested.

DI ROSA PRESERVE

At the unique **Di Rosa Preserve** (5200 Sonoma Hwy., 707/226-5991, www.dirosaart.org, Wed.-Sun. 10am-4pm, suggested

the stunning grounds of the Di Rosa Preserve

Know Your Grapes

California has a few distinctive and easy-to-find grapes that comprise the basics of winemaking in the state.

Chardonnay: Most of the white wine made and sold in California is chardonnay. The grapes grow best in a slightly cooler climate, which lends them well to the vineyards closer to the coast. Most chardonnay wines are made from nearly 100 percent chardonnay grapes. Chardonnay is typically fermented in steel tanks, then poured into steel or oak barrels to finish fermenting and to age just a little bit. California chardonnays taste smooth and buttery and a bit like fruit; they often take on the oak flavor of the barrels they sit in. Chardonnay doesn't keep, so most chards are sold the year after they're bottled, and consumed within a few months of purchase.

Sauvignon Blanc: This pale green grape is used to make both sauvignon blanc and fumé blanc wines in California. Sauvignon blanc grapes grow well in Napa, Sonoma, and warm parts of the state. The California sauvignon blanc wine goes well with salads, fish, vegetarian cuisine, and even spicy ethnic foods. Sauvignon blanc has such a light, fruity, and floral taste it almost seems to float away. The difference between a sauvignon blanc and a fumé blanc is in the winemaking more than the grapes. Fumé blanc wines have a strong odor and the taste of grapefruit. Fumés also pair well with fish dishes and spicy Asian cuisine.

Pinot Noir: Unlike the other red wine grapes, pinot noir grapes do best in a cool coastal climate with limited exposure to high heat. The Anderson Valley and the Monterey coastal growing regions specialize in pinot noir, though many Napa and Sonoma wineries buy grapes from the coast to make their own versions. California vintners make up single-varietal pinot noir wines that taste of cherries, strawberries, and smoke when they're great, and of mold and fish when they're not.

Zinfandel: A good California zinfandel is not what you think it is. For starters, it's not sweet and pale pink. A true zinfandel is a hearty, deep-red wine. These grapes grow best when tortured by their climate; a few grow near Napa, but most make their homes in Gold Country and the inland Central Coast. Zinfandel was one of the first grapes introduced in California. A few lucky vineyards have "Old Vines" that have been producing these grapes for nearly 100 years. A great zinfandel wine boasts the flavors and smells of blackberry jam and the dusky hues of venous blood. Zinfandel is good with beef, buffalo, and even venison.

Cabernet Sauvignon: If you spend any length of time in Napa or Sonoma, you'll hear the phrase "Cab is King." This always means cabernet sauvignon, a grape from the Bordeaux region of France that creates a deep, dark, strong red wine. The grapes that get intense summer heat make the best wine, which makes them a perfect fit in the scorching Napa Valley. In France, cabernet sauvignon grapes mix with several other varieties to create the famed bordeaux blends. In California, especially in Napa, winemakers use cabernet sauvignon on its own to brew some of the most intense single-grape wine in the world. A good dry cab might taste of leather, tobacco, and bing cherries. Harsh tannins can create a sandpapery feeling in the mouth and an unpleasant tree-bark flavor, making cabernet sauvignon difficult for newcomers to the wine world. Cabs age well, often hitting their peak of flavor and smoothness more than a decade after bottling.

donation $5, tours $12-15), you'll see the cutting edge of modern California art. With 217 acres, Di Rosa has ample room for three galleries, an outdoor sculpture meadow, and a lake. Take in the festival of color and creativity in the galleries and sculpture garden, or wander the undeveloped portion of the preserve to soak in the colors and shapes of nature.

SCIENTOPIA DISCOVERY CENTER

Show the kids some fun at the **Scientopia Discovery Center** (1785 B Tanen St., 707/259-1559, www.scientopiadiscoverycenter.com, Mon.-Tues. and Thurs.-Fri. 9am-3pm, Wed. 9am-5pm, Sun. 11am-5pm, adults free, children under 12 $8). The little ones will get a basic feel for scientific concepts by

Uptown Theatre

County Fairgrounds, 575 3rd St., www.bot-tlerocknapavalley.com, late May) brings an eclectic range of acts—among them Robert Plant, No Doubt, Outkast, The Cure, and Eric Church—to wine country.

Spas

Spa Terra (Meritage Resort and Spa, 875 Bordeaux Way, 707/251-3000, www.spa-terra.com, massages $65-195) is the jewel of the Meritage Resort's property. The interior, an artificial cave beneath a vineyard, seems like an odd choice for a luxury spa, but the gorgeous cavern rooms will make a believer of even the most discerning spa-goer. Begin your pampering with a warm greeting and a required tour of the public areas from your guide. Show up at least 30 minutes in advance of an appointment—you'll have the run of a tiled hot tub, steam room, and relaxation space both before and after your scheduled treatment. Grab a glass of lemon water, a cool moist cloth for your forehead, and warm out (it's not the least bit chilly in Spa Terra). The menu of treatments includes a full-body scrub using grape-seed extracts, couple's massages in two-person rooms, and an espresso-based facial.

Shopping

Downtown Napa strives to be a shopping destination, yet despite some redevelopment efforts, it's still not quite there. The north end of Main Street has some flashy buildings with equally flashy clothiers, but the place to go is the **Historic Napa Mill** (Main St., www.historicnapamill.com), one block down. Formerly the Hatt Warehouse, the mill has since been converted into a lovely shopping and dining center, decorated with rustic touches—weathered redwood, an abundance of trailing vines, and blooming planter boxes and hanging baskets. The historic Napa River Inn is here, as is the **Vintage Sweet Shoppe** (530 Main St., 707/224-2986, http://vintag-esweetshoppe.com, Mon.-Tues. 10am-10pm, Wed.-Sat. 8am-10pm, Sun. 10am-9pm), which specializes in chocolate but has enough treats

playing with pulleys, magnets, a smelling tube, and a shadow tunnel.

Live Music

Napa is home to two historic live music venues. Since its 2010 reopening, the **Uptown Theatre** (1350 3rd St., 707/259-0123, www.uptowntheatrenapa.com), which dates back to 1937, has become one of Wine Country's best music venues. The Uptown even lures Bay Area residents to Napa to see intimate performances by acts including Beck and Chris Botti, along with speakers and comedians like David Sedaris and Craig Ferguson.

The **Napa Valley Opera House** (1030 Main St., 707/226-7322, www.nvoh.org) has been around since 1880. It has hosted everyone from author Jack London to country music legend Willie Nelson. The Opera House also hosts other events, such as screenings for the **Napa Valley Film Festival** (http://napa-valleyfilmfest.org) in early November.

Napa has been hosting its own multiday music festival since 2013. **Bottlerock** (Napa to make anyone's teeth ache. In the same complex, the **Napa General Store** (540 Main St., 707/259-0762, www.napageneralstore.com, daily 8am-6pm) next door offers a bite to eat, a glass of wine, wine-related knickknacks, and other gifts. The store also sells local artwork, including leather crafts and fiber art, all of which has an arty, ecological bent.

With so much natural beauty in the Napa Valley, is it any wonder that there are so many artists living here? The **Napa Valley Art Association** (1520 Behrens St., 707/254-2085, www.nvart.org/gallery.html, Sun.-Thurs. 10am-6pm, Fri.-Sat. 10am-9pm) showcases some of the best. The gallery presents pen-and-ink drawings, watercolors, photography, glass jewelry, fiber art, and oil paintings. While there are plenty of lush portraits of vineyards, you'll also find some unusual subjects—jellyfish, abstract aerial photographs, or watery self-portraits. The association plans events that often pair wine-tasting with art shows; check the website before visiting.

★ OXBOW PUBLIC MARKET

Across the river from downtown Napa, **Oxbow Public Market** (610-644 1st St., 707/226-6529, www.oxbowpublicmarket. com, daily 9am-7pm) is a well-used piece of real estate. Next to the now-defunct COPIA museum, the Oxbow Public Market has once again breathed life into this "across the tracks" section of Napa. The market is a food lover's delight. Grab a cup of **Ritual Coffee** and browse through the epicurean wares or get lost in the myriad spices and seasonings at the **Whole Spice Company.** There is also a chocolatier, an olive oil company, and the venerable **Wine & Cheese Merchant,** where you can pick up some vino, cheese, and other treats for the road.

Sports and Recreation

Once you're on the trails of **Skyline Wilderness Park** (2201 Imola Ave., 707/252-0481, www.skylinepark.org, summer daily 8am-7pm, winter daily 8am-5pm, fall daily 8am-6pm, $5-6), you may forget you're even in Wine Country. Up at this park, no vineyards encroach on the natural chaparral landscape of Napa's high country. This park includes the Martha Walker Garden—a botanical garden planted with California and Napa native plants in honor of a legendary figure in the local horticultural community. The rest of this 850-acre park is given over to multiple community uses. You'll find campgrounds, hiking trails, horse and bicycle paths, a disc golf course, and more. Be aware that it gets hot here in the summertime, and not all the campgrounds and trails offer adequate shade to cool off. Even so, the natural beauty of this protected wilderness makes Skyline Park a favorite with both locals and travelers.

Since you're in a land of entertainment options, it seems only natural to enjoy a round of golf during your Wine Country vacation. At the par-72 **Napa Golf Course** (2295 Streblow Dr., 707/255-4333, www.playnapa.com, $30-39), golfers of all levels—even beginners—can enjoy a full 18 holes. More experienced players will enjoy (or curse) the plethora of water features and full-size trees on this course, known locally as a bargain.

Napa Valley Adventure Tours (Oxbow Public Market, 1147 1st St., 707/259-1833, www.napavalleyadventuretours.com, adults $50, children $25) offers 2.5-hour tours of the Napa River, through wetlands and alongside the historic downtown. Float along the river in a lovely small covered motor launch in cushy seats, enjoying the view out the massive wraparound windows. The trip takes you right into the heart of downtown Napa and back to the dock.

Rising in the morning sun over the valley in a brightly colored hot-air balloon is a unique experience. **Balloons Above the Valley** (3425 Solano Ave., 800/464-6824, www.balloonrides.com, $209-836) offer the full experience, including lodging packages that include transportation to the launch site and a champagne brunch after you touch down. On your trip, you'll float serenely over the vineyards of Napa Valley before a gentle descent at a predetermined spot. Make reservations in advance because trips can fill up quickly, especially during high season (May-Oct.). You must be an early riser too, since most balloon trips depart shortly after dawn. Note that booking online can save you as much as $30.

Accommodations
UNDER $150
The pretty, unassuming ★ **Wine Valley Lodge** (200 S. Coombs St., 707/224-7911, 800/696-7911, www.winevalleylodge.com, $119-250) welcomes guests with its redbrick and adobe-tile exterior. Inside, serene rooms feature unobtrusive art, pale yellow walls, and soothing pastel comforters. Rooms are a nice size; choose from a king bed, two queens, or a suite. The units encircle a heated pool deck and small picnic area. The Wine Valley Lodge also boasts a significant past: In the late 1950s and early 1960s, several movies were filmed in Napa, and various A-list stars, including Rock Hudson, Marilyn Monroe, and even Elvis stayed at the lodge during filming.

$150-250
Outside of town, the newly renovated **Napa Winery Inn** (1998 Trower Ave., 707/257-7220, www.napawineryinn.com, $179-349) is certainly one of the most affordable options. Standard amenities include complimentary Wi-Fi, and an outdoor pool sweetens the deal. Pricier rooms might boast a fridge, a wet bar, and a kitchenette. The inn also serves a complimentary breakfast.

At the **Chablis Inn** (3360 Solano Ave., 800/443-3490, www.chablisinn.com, $139-279), the rooms include all the usual amenities: a wet bar with a mini fridge, an in-room coffeemaker, a TV with cable, and more. Rooms are simply decorated, but the beds are comfortable, the carpets are dark (making it safe to drink just a little bit of red wine in your room), and the address is central to both the attractions of downtown Napa and the famous Highway 29 wine road. Dogs are welcome.

For a unique historic lodging experience, stay at the **Napa Inn** (1137 Warren St.,

800/435-1144, www.napainn.com, $219-389), which comprises two Victorian houses, both painted blue, in historic downtown Napa. You can walk from either to downtown shops and restaurants, and the Wine Train depot is a very short drive away. As bed-and-breakfasts go, the Napa Inn is a big one, with more than 10 rooms and suites. If you plan to travel with your pet, talk to the inn well in advance to get one of the two pet-friendly rooms. Elegant fabrics and lush modern textures moderate the floral and carved-wood decor of the Victorian era. The nicest rooms have corner whirlpool tubs and king beds. Breakfast at the Napa Inn is an event, with multiple courses served by candlelight.

OVER $250
The ★ **Napa River Inn** (500 Main St., 877/251-8500, www.napariverinn.com, $359-429) has one of the best locations in Napa—right inside the Historic Napa Mill. You can practically fall out of your guest room and hit the General Store, at least one restaurant, several galleries, and the candy store on the way down. Steps away from the center of Napa's bustling downtown, some rooms even afford a view of the Napa River. The interior of this luxury hotel is crammed with high-end antiques and reproductions. Choose from three styles of room decor: Historic Victorian rooms feature canopy beds, floral prints, cushy chairs, and slipper tubs; the nautical rooms, many of which face the river, resemble the inside of a yacht, with wood paneling, porthole-style mirrors, and rope-style accents; and the Wine Country rooms echo the natural wealth of the Napa Valley with floral linens, marble baths, and oak moldings.

The king of Napa lodging is the **Silverado** (1600 Atlas Peak Rd., 707/257-0200, www.silveradoresort.com, $379-529). You'll find the finest in modern amenities and decorations in your room (all guest suites at the Silverado have kitchens and dining rooms), including high-thread-count linens, complimentary Wi-Fi, and a private patio or deck overlooking the grounds. Pale colors with eye-popping jewel-toned accents speak of the best current designers. There's so much to do at the Silverado that you'll find it hard to pry yourself away from the grounds to go wine-tasting. Guests can choose from the immense spa with full fitness and salon services, two 18-hole golf courses, two pools, 17 tennis courts, 11 pools, and—believe it or not—more.

The Carneros Inn (4048 Sonoma Hwy., 707/299-4900, www.thecarnerosinn.com, $510-900) is an expansive and expensive cottage resort. The immense property, which backs onto countryside, has three restaurants, a spa, two pools, a fitness center, and even a small market. On arrival, follow the signs to the registration area and then keep driving to the lobby at the very top of the resort's hill. The unprepossessing (from the outside) cottages spread out in small clusters for acres, each group surrounding its own garden paths and water features. Inside, the cozy cottages sparkle with white linens, tile floors, and windows overlooking sizeable private backyards with decks and comfy chaises. Outdoors, there's a private patio and outdoor shower. But it's the baths that bring Carneros Inn clients back again and again.

The **Meritage Inn** (875 Bordeaux Way, 707/251-1900, www.themeritageresort.com, $200-575) is beside the small Napa Valley airport, convenient to businesspeople and travelers who want easy access to both the Napa Valley and Sonoma-Carneros wine regions. The grounds, common spaces, and rooms have the deep harvest colors and country-elegant style of Tuscany. The lush garden pool is the centerpiece of the property, which also includes a wine-tasting room, a fabulous spa, and a down-to-earth restaurant. The basic shape of the rooms remains true to the Meritage's motel roots, but the Tuscan-style decor and trimmings make a play for elegance, with comfortable beds, deep soaking tubs in the baths, and posh amenities. Expect a fridge stocked with free water, a coffeemaker, and a complimentary bottle of wine.

The prim white exterior of **Arbor Guest House** (1436 G St., 707/252-8144, www.arborguesthouse.com, $239-309) betrays little of the inn's lush Victorian decor. Rich fabric drapes the windows and beds, and polished antiques grace even the smallest corner, while soft lighting and flower-filled vases lend warm touches. There are only five rooms, each distinctively decorated; two offer gas fireplaces and two-person jetted tubs for a romantic stay. Guests are invited to a complimentary

Silverado

hot breakfast in the morning and wine and appetizers in the evening.

The newest boutique hotel in downtown, **Andaz Napa** (1450 1st St., 707/687-1234, www.andaz.hyatt.com, $289-700) has 141 modern rooms, all with hardwood floors and marble bathrooms. Upgrade to suites with soaking tubs and dual-sided glass fireplaces. Eat on-site at the **Andaz Farmers Table** or **Mercantile Social.** All guests get complimentary access to the nearby **Exertec Health & Fitness Center** (1500 1st St.).

Food
BARBECUE

Cheese and fruit pair well with wine, but the ★ **Bounty Hunter** (975 1st St., 707/226-3976, www.bountyhunterwinebar.com, Sun.-Thurs. 11am-10pm, Fri.-Sat. 11am-midnight, $13-35) proves that large slabs of barbecued meats complement local reds just as well. Start by selecting a glass or bottle from the 18-page list, a fine whiskey, or a craft beer. There are classic barbecue sandwiches (pulled pork, smoked brisket), but the truly hungry can go for the Smokin' BBQ Platter, three pounds of delicious barbecued meats piled high on a granite slab. It's served with a caddy containing three house-made sauces. The Bounty Hunter scores extra points for serving food until midnight on weekends.

CALIFORNIA CUISINE

The FARM (4048 Sonoma Hwy., 707/299-4880, www.farmatthecarnerosinn.com, daily 5:30pm-10pm, bar/pavilion 4pm-11pm, $32-49) at the Carneros Inn serves up the expected upscale California cuisine, complete with a chef's tasting menu ($110 pp) and big white plates topped with tiny, artistic piles of food. The food may be a touch pretentious, but it's cooked perfectly, and the chef has put imagination into the dishes. Expect unusual but deft flavor combinations, smaller portions appropriate to the number of courses, and just a touch of molecular gastronomy. The dining room feels comfortable, with cushy banquettes and padded chairs. Servers are

friendly and good at their jobs, and can help decipher anything on the menu. Do dress up a little—The FARM has a distinctly upscale vibe. For a more casual experience, ask about the bar menu, with a burger, flatbread, and even a grilled ham and cheese sandwich for considerably less.

Also at the Carneros Inn, the **Boon Fly Café** (4048 Sonoma Hwy., 707/299-4870, www.thecarnerosinn.com, daily 7am-9pm, $14-22) has classic breakfast dishes and almost down-to-earth salad and sandwich fare. If you're staying at the inn, skip the mediocre service of the café itself and order the Boon Fly menu via room service—the prices are the same in-cottage as in the diner. Eggs are cooked competently, salads are enormous, and the carefully designed down-home dining room is cute. The half-booth banquettes are comfortable to sit in, and lingering over coffee or tea is tolerated.

TORC (1140 Main St., 707/252-3292, www.torcnapa.com, Wed.-Mon. 5pm-9:30pm, $17-65) finds international flavors intermingling with American flair. That means items like deviled eggs might be sitting right next to Indian-style sweet potato fritters on the menu. Chef and owner Sean O'Toole has been in the restaurant world for over a decade, at places including San Francisco's Quince and Yountville's Bardessono. The airy, high-ceilinged interior is as unconfined as the globe-trotting menu.

CLASSIC AMERICAN

When Napa locals need a diner-style breakfast or lunch, they head to the **Butter Cream Bakery & Diner** (2297 Jefferson St., 707/255-6700, www.buttercreambakery.com, diner Mon.-Sat. 5:30am-3pm, Sun. 5:30am-2:30pm, bakery Mon.-Sat. 5:30am-6pm, Sun. 5:30am-4pm, $6-11). It's not in the ritzy part of downtown, but the brilliant pink-and-white-striped building is hard to miss. On the diner side, breakfast is served all day; choose between a small table in the fluorescent-lit linoleum dining room or a stool at the old-school counter. Service is indifferent, but you'll get decently cooked eggs, tasty sandwiches, reasonable portions, and best of all, reasonable prices. Over on the bakery side, mouthwatering turnovers, Danishes, and fruit rings make it easy to get a good breakfast on the go. Dessert pastries, cookies, and cakes tempt even dieters.

ITALIAN

The restaurant at the Meritage Inn, **Siena** (875 Bordeaux Way, 707/251-1950, www.themeritageresort.com, Mon.-Thurs. 6:30am-11am, 11:30am-2pm, and 5:30pm-9:30pm, Fri. 6:30am-11am, 11:30am-2pm, and 5:30pm-10pm, Sat. 7am-11am, 11:30am-2pm, and 5:30pm-10pm, Sun. 7am-2pm and 5:30pm-9:30pm, $15-42), doesn't serve typical Wine Country cuisine. The food is mostly Italian, much of it hot, hearty, and welcome after a long day of wine-tasting. Choose from fresh salads, pasta dishes, and big entrées, though if you've been in Napa for a while, you may not be able to resist a pizza or a cheeseburger. The waiter can even suggest the right wine or beer to accompany your burger. Desserts also tend toward the dense and filling—consider sharing one among your tablemates. The upholstered booths and dim lighting make a romantic dining experience possible, but the vibe in the dining room manages to stay low-key enough to make jeans-clad diners comfortable.

For simple Italian fare, go to **Azzurro** (1260 Main St., 707/255-5552, www.azzurropizzeria.com, Sun.-Thurs. 11:30am-9:30pm, Fri.-Sat. 11:30am-10pm, $14-17). Veterans of Tra Vigne in St. Helena, Michael and Christina Gyetvan opened Azzurro with the intention of bringing their style of Italian food to downtown Napa. A favorite with locals, this trattoria offers wood-fired pizzas in addition to hearty pasta dishes and big, rustic salads. The warm and modern interior welcomes diners with wood and stone tables and an open kitchen. Wines by the glass are affordable.

JAPANESE

Sake in Wine Country? Not a bad idea, particularly if it's paired with dinner at **Morimoto's** (610 Main St., 707/252-1600, www.morimotonapa.com, Sun.-Thurs. 11:30am-2:30pm and 5pm-10pm, Fri.-Sat. 11:30am-2:30pm and 5pm-11pm, entrées $22-70, tasting menu $120). Celebrity chef Masaharu Morimoto, who has appeared on the *Iron Chef* TV show, opened this esoteric and sleek Japanese eatery. The elegant interior features steel highlighted by bright yellow accents. The food includes traditional Japanese dishes, all with a unique and modern twist—*gyoza* with bacon cream and duck confit-fried rice are just some of the menu items. There are also a handful of non sequiturs like steak, lobster, and roasted fingerling potatoes. For a full idea of the chef's culinary vision, order the tasting menu.

MARKETS

For a bit of this and a bit of that, venture across the Napa River to the ★ **Oxbow Market** (610-644 1st St., 707/226-6529, www.oxbowpublicmarket.com, daily 9am-7pm). Inside this large, open space you can snack on oysters at the **Hog Island Oyster Co.** or blow your diet at **Kara's Cupcakes.** Hamburgers are just out the side door at **Gott's Roadside,** and around the corner is some of the best charcuterie around in delectable take-out sandwiches at the **Fatted Calf** or pizza by the slice at **The Model Bakery.** The bakery's bacon *levain,* made with hunks of bacon and bacon fat from next door, is irresistible.

Perhaps the most acclaimed of these options is the **Kitchen Door** (707/226-6529, www.kitchendoornapa.com, Mon. 11:30am-8pm, Tues.-Fri. 11:30am-9pm, Sat. 10am-9pm, Sun. 10am-8pm, $15-22). Unlike the market's loud and congested interior, the Kitchen Door has an air of calm. The white-tile wood oven, open seating, and large picture windows draw light in for an illuminating meal. Comfort food comes in all stripes, including some Armenian dishes, rice and noodle bowls, roast chickens, burgers, and sundaes.

Information and Services

The **Napa Valley Welcome Center** (600 Main St., 707/251-5895, 855/847-6272, www.

napavalley.org, daily 9am-5pm), in the middle of downtown Napa, has complimentary maps, guidebooks, and wine-tasting passes. Chat with a friendly local who can direct you to the favorite wineries and restaurants.

A privately run information outpost, the **Napa Tourist Information Center** (1331 1st St., 707/252-1000, www.napatouristinfo.com, Mon.-Weds. 10am-5pm, Thurs.-Sun. 10am-9pm) also has wine-tastings, olive oil tastings, a gift shop, and a limousine service.

Transportation

Napa, in all its bucolic beauty, does not have infrastructure designed for the number of visitors it receives. This is part of its charm—unless you spend your visit sitting in bumper-to-bumper traffic. The best way to experience the valley is to avoid the ever-popular autumn crush and summer weekend afternoons. November and early spring are beautiful seasons to see the valley. But if a summer Saturday spent wine-tasting is impossible to resist, hit the wineries early and stay off the roads from mid-afternoon to early evening. With great restaurants and seductive spas everywhere, you'll easily be able to pass the extra time.

CAR

Considering the number of people that go to Napa, it is not all that easy to get to. Most of the highways in this region are two lanes and frequently go by colloquial names. They are also susceptible to gridlocked traffic thanks to the numerous wine lovers and the occasional race at nearby Infineon Raceway.

Highway 29 is the central conduit that runs north into the valley from the city of Napa. It is also known as the Napa-Vallejo Highway between the two cities, and as the St. Helena Highway from Napa to Calistoga, where it becomes Foothill Boulevard. To reach Highway 29 from San Francisco, take U.S. 101 north across the Golden Gate Bridge to Novato. In Novato, take the exit for Highway 37 east to Napa. Highway 37 skirts the tip of San Pablo Bay and runs all the way to Vallejo.

From Vallejo, take Highway 29 (Sonoma Blvd.) north for seven miles until you reach downtown Napa. Highway 29 will take you as far north as Calistoga.

Connecting to **Highway 37** in Vallejo is especially easy if you're coming from the East Bay, Lake Tahoe, and Sacramento: Highway 37 intersects I-80 at the north end of Vallejo at the exit for Six Flags Discovery Kingdom.

Highway 128 connects the north end of Napa Valley near Rutherford with U.S. 101 in Geyserville. From Geyserville, follow this beautiful two-lane road south to Calistoga, where it joins Highway 29.

Coming from **Highway 121** in Sonoma, **Highway 12** east leads directly to Napa. Highway 121 then picks up again at West Imola Avenue and leads east to the **Silverado Trail,** an alternate route north-south in the Napa Valley.

BUS

To avoid the potential headache of driving in Napa, take the **VINE** bus (800/696-6443, http://nctpa.net, adults $1.60, children 6-18 $1.10, seniors $0.80), which provides public transportation around Napa Valley, including Napa, Yountville, Oakville, Rutherford, St. Helena, and Calistoga. If you don't want to drive at all, jump aboard the commuter VINE 29 Express, which runs all day Monday-Friday. The Express travels from the El Cerrito BART station in the East Bay and from the Vallejo Ferry Terminal into Napa Valley. Fares are cash-only and require exact change.

YOUNTVILLE

Named for George Calvert Yount, who planted the first vineyard in Napa Valley, Yountville is the quintessential wine-loving town. There are not even 3,000 residents, but the town has earned widespread fame for its epicurean spirit. You'll find a number of prestigious wineries and champagneries, but it is really restaurateur Thomas Keller who put this postage stamp-size town on the map. First came the French Laundry, then Bouchon and the Bouchon Bakery, and eventually Ad Hoc.

But it's not just a Keller company town; other notable eateries have opened up and keep pace with the big boy. Still, with so many fantastic dining options, you might wish there was more to do in Yountville to extend your stay in order to accommodate as many meals out as possible.

Wineries

DOMAINE CHANDON

One of the premier champagneries in Napa Valley, **Domaine Chandon** (1 California Dr., 888/242-6366, www.chandon.com, daily 10am-5pm, $20-25, tour and tasting $40) offers one of the best tours in Napa—it's a perfect introduction to the process of wine- and champagne-making. Walk out into the vineyards to look at the grapes, head down to the tank- and barrel-filled cellars to learn about the champagne-making process, and then proceed into the aging rooms to see the racked bottles, tilted and dusty, aging to the point of drinkability. Finally, you'll adjourn to the tasting room to sample the bubbly concoctions. Chandon also makes still wines, which you can also taste. Reservations are required for tours, and booking in advance is a good idea.

Domaine Chandon also boasts lovely gardens, a stream, and an immense estate. Visitors can walk the open paths among the vineyards and enjoy the delights of the tasting room.

HILL FAMILY ESTATE

Right on Washington Street in downtown Yountville, the **Hill Family Estate** (6512 Washington St., 707/944-9580, www.hillfamilyestate.com, daily 10am-6pm, $20) tasting room and antiques shop offers an elegant tasting and shopping experience. The most affordable item in the room is the tasting glass; you can get two-for-one tasting coupons if you first stop by the Yountville Visitors Center on the next block. Roam among the pricey French antiques as you sip, or stand at the bar to enjoy the company of the Hill family and a small selection of light, balanced red and white wines. The cabernet sauvignons are not made in the typical heavy-handed Napa style, so even tasters with delicate palates will find them drinkable. The Double Barrel Cab is sold in a box that the younger sons of the family have blasted with buckshot from their grandfather's double-barrel shotgun.

JESSUP CELLARS

In downtown Yountville, the tiny tasting room at **Jessup Cellars** (6740 Washington St., 707/944-8523, www.jessupcellars.com, daily 10am-6pm, $10-20) offers tastes of incredible boutique red wines that you'll have a hard time finding anyplace else. There are no tours here, no picnic grounds or fancy gardens, but you'll find lush, rich zinfandels and deep, smoky cabernets that are more than worth the sometimes-steep price tag. The tasting room boasts a cute little bar, a few shelves with items for purchase, and staff that love their jobs. If you chat them up, you may find yourself tasting rare Jessup vintages that are not on the usual list.

MA(I)SONRY NAPA VALLEY

Unique tasting room and art gallery **Ma(i)sonry Napa Valley** (6711 Washington St., 707/944-0889, www.maisonry.com, Sun.-Thurs. 10am-6pm, Fri.-Sat. 10am-7pm, $25-45) inhabits the old stone building that was once the Burgundy House. Step inside to taste rare Napa vintages at an antique wooden table topped with a chunk of mammoth bone or browse ultramodern leather and metal furniture paired with objets d'art, including an inlaid human skull. An ever-rotating collection of modern and antique decorative art has a distinctly industrial and macabre feel that you won't find anywhere else in the valley. You'll also get the chance to taste local wines made by Napa vintners who don't have their own tasting rooms. You'll have the undivided attention of your pourer, who will discuss the wines with you as you sip. Tasting selections are forever changing, so frequent visitors to the region can keep coming back to try something new.

Sights

The small **Napa Valley Museum** (55 Presidents Circle, 707/944-0500, www.napa-valleymuseum.org, Wed.-Sun. 11am-4pm, adults $7, seniors $3.50, children under 17 $2.50) is tucked behind Domaine Chandon on the other side of Highway 29 in Yountville. Here, you will find permanent exhibits about the land and people of Napa Valley. Learn about how the region's geological makeup contributes to winemaking, or take in the local art on display.

Spas

An easy walk from anywhere in downtown Yountville, the newly reimagined **Spa Villagio** (6481 Washington St., 707/948-5050, http://villagio.com, daily 7:30am-9pm, $135-250) has a beautiful space in which to pamper its patrons. You don't need to be a guest at the Villagio Inn to book a treatment at the spa, although you may want to try one of the five Spa Suites—private spaces where singles, couples, and friends can relax before, during, and after their treatments. Show up an hour early for your massage, facial, or treatment package—at the price you're paying for treatments, you'll want to take advantage of the saunas and hot tubs, relaxation rooms, and the other chichi amenities. The spa recommends making reservations for your treatment at least three weeks in advance, especially during the summer-fall high season.

Sports and Recreation

Biking is a popular way to see the vineyards, forests, and wineries of Napa, allowing visitors to get away from the highways and the endless traffic of the wine roads on two wheels. If you don't know the area, the best way to bike it is to take a tour. **Napa Valley Bike Tours** (6500 Washington St., 707/251-8687, www.napavalleybiketours.com, $99-374) offers standard and custom tours all over the area, from central Napa to Calistoga. You'll get a brand-name bike, a map, a helmet, and an orientation before beginning your trek. Then you'll be off on your chosen tour: a pedal through the vineyards, a half-day or full-day tour that includes both wine-tasting and meals, or a multiple-sport "adventure package" that includes kayaking or a balloon ride.

Accommodations

If you've come to Napa Valley to dine at the French Laundry or immerse yourself in the food scene, you'll want to stay in Yountville. Several inns are within stumbling distance of the French Laundry, which is convenient for gourmands who want to experience a range of wines with the meal.

$150-250

For a motel with a historic twist, book a room at the **Napa Valley Railway Inn** (6523 Washington St., 707/944-2000, www.napa-valleyrailwayinn.com, $200-225). The nine rooms are converted 100-year-old train cars tightly packed together, making a unique type of hotel. The rooms themselves are funky and narrow but carefully decorated in classic style with rich bedspreads. Stop by the Coffee Caboose to start your day with pastries and coffee.

A French-style inn, the **Maison Fleurie** (6529 Yount St., 800/788-0369, www.foursisters.com, $145-325) offers the best of small-inn style for a more reasonable rate. It is in a perfect location for walking to Bouchon, the Bouchon Bakery, and the many other amazing restaurants, boutiques, and tasting rooms in town. The 13 rooms in this "house of flowers" have an attractive but not overwhelming floral decorative theme. The more economical rooms are small but attractive. If you've got the budget to splurge, opt for a room in the Bakery Building, where you'll get a fireplace, a jetted spa tub, a king bed, and a private entrance. Enjoy a full breakfast each morning as well as an afternoon wine reception, fresh cookies, and use of the on-site pool and hot tub.

With a location next to Bouchon Bakery, you can wake up to mouthwatering smells at the cozy, five-room **Petit Logis Inn** (6527 Yount St., 877/944-2332, www.petitlogis.com,

$210-285). Each of the rooms has a fireplace, a jetted tub, and a fridge and is decorated in warm, creamy colors with an occasional wall mural. Low-key and unpretentious, the inn is best described as "the place to come to pretend you live in Yountville." Unlike many other inns, breakfast is not included but can be arranged for an additional charge at a nearby restaurant.

OVER $250

The **Napa Valley Lodge** (2230 Madison St., 707/944-2468, www.napavalleylodge.com, $380-875) is a stunner of a Mediterranean-style hotel with stucco walls and red tile roofs. Guests are steeped in the luxury that Yountville is known for: Book a spa treatment in your room or out beside the heated pool. Start each day with the complimentary champagne buffet breakfast, or order from the California cuisine room-service menu. Lodging options include the Parkside Terrace rooms, with king beds topped with European-style duvets; the Vineyard Courtyard Terrace rooms, with their own patios; and the luxurious King Junior Suite, with a fireplace, two-person soaking tub, and views of the courtyard.

At **The Cottages of Napa Valley** (1012 Darms Ln., 2 miles south of Yountville, 707/252-7810, www.napacottages.com, $395-575), you'll pay a princely sum to gain a home away from home in the heart of Wine Country. Each cottage has its own king bed, outdoor fireplace, kitchenette, and heated bathroom floor. Every morning the quiet staff drops off a basket of fresh pastries from Bouchon Bakery and a pot of great coffee to greet you upon waking up. Simple yet luxurious country-cottage furnishings feel welcoming and homey, and the staff can help you plan the ultimate Wine Country vacation. They also offer complimentary dinner shuttles into Yountville.

Enjoy the location and luxury of the **Vintage Inn** (6541 Washington St., 707/944-1112, www.vintageinn.com, $525-780), where rooms in the elegant hexagonal buildings feature soft sheets, jetted tubs, wood-burning fireplaces, and complimentary bottles of wine. The French country-meets-Wine Country decor extends to a private patio or deck overlooking the lush gardens. The dining room serves what might be the best complimentary hotel buffet breakfast in California, with buttery French pastries, fresh fruit, and made-to-order omelets. At 3pm, the staff sets out a free afternoon tea complete with finger sandwiches, homemade scones, and organic teas—plus wine, of course. As a sister property of the nearby Villagio, Vintage Inn guests get to use the Villagio's fitness center, tennis courts, and spa.

Food

The tiny town of Yountville boasts perhaps the biggest reputation for culinary excellence in California—a big deal when you consider the offerings of San Francisco and Los Angeles. The reason for this reputation starts and ends with restaurateur Thomas Keller's indisputably amazing ★ **French Laundry** (6640 Washington St., 707/944-2380, www. thomaskeller.com, Mon.-Thurs. 5:30pm-9pm, Fri.-Sun. 11am-1pm and 5:30pm-9pm, by reservation only, $295). Once you've obtained that all-important reservation, the fun begins. From the moment you walk in the door of the rambling Victorian, you're treated like royalty. You'll be led to your seat in one of the small dining rooms by one of the many immaculate black-and-white-clad staff. Even if you're new to this level of dining—and most people are—you'll be made to feel more than welcome. The menu, which changes often, offers two main selections: the regular nine-course tasting menu and the vegetarian nine-course tasting menu. Usually you'll see two options for the fish course and two options for the entrée. The waitstaff can help you identify anything you don't recognize or help make a decision. The sommelier is at your beck and call to assist with a wine list that weighs several pounds. From the start, servers ply you with extras—an *amuse-bouche* here, an extra middle

Reservations for the French Laundry

Most people familiar with the world of high-end food know that the best restaurant in all of California, and possibly all of the United States, is the French Laundry. Thomas Keller's culinary haven in tiny Yountville has earned the hallowed three-star rating from the Michelin Guide every year since 2006. The restaurant sits inside a charming vintage house; its kitchen garden grows right across the street where anyone can walk down the rows of vegetables and herbs.

Sounds like foodie paradise, right? There's just one problem: getting a table.

The difficulty in getting reservations to the French Laundry is almost as legendary as the French Laundry itself. Rather than expecting to dine at the French Laundry during a planned trip to the Wine Country, savvy travelers expect to plan their whole trip around whatever French Laundry reservation they manage to get.

The bare facts: The French Laundry takes reservations two months in advance. *Precisely* two months. The restaurant accepts reservations by phone, online, and via local concierges. Reservations are accepted for parties for between one and six individuals. Diners can choose between lunch and dinner seatings that offer the same menu. It's easier to get a table for lunch than it is for dinner. Lunch or dinner takes 2.5-4 hours to consume. Budget $500 *per person* for your meal if you plan to drink wine, and $300-350 if you don't. The meals are priced at $295 per person.

The French Laundry starts taking **phone reservations** at 10am daily. Between 9:30am and 9:45am, program their number on your speed-dial and begin calling. Continue calling again and again until you get an answer. If you get a continuous busy signal past noon, you'll probably need to try again the next day. And maybe the day after that.

Making **reservations online** works much the same way as on the phone, only it's harder. The French Laundry offers only two tables for each service (lunch and dinner) online per day. Go online at OpenTable (www.opentable.com) at about 8:30am and start trying to snag that table. If you're still trying at 9:30am, it's probably already gone.

So is it *really* worth all this rigmarole just to get into one lousy restaurant, then pay a sizeable part of a month's salary for a single meal? You have to decide for yourself. For many foodies, the gracious welcome at the door, the stunning service throughout the meal, and especially the food that can be found nowhere else are worth both the hassle and the price tag.

course there—and if you mention that someone else has something on their plate that you'd like to try, it appears in front of you as if by magic. Finally, the desserts come—in four separate courses. A meal can run up to 13 courses and take four hours.

If you can't access the French Laundry, try Thomas Keller's other Yountville option, **Bouchon** (6534 Washington St., 707/944-8037, www.thomaskeller.com, daily 11am-midnight, $19-59). Reservations are still strongly recommended, but you should be able to get one just a week in advance. Bouchon's atmosphere and food scream Parisian bistro. Order traditional favorites such as the *croque madame* or steak frites, or opt for a California-influenced specialty salad or entrée made with local, sustainable ingredients.

If you're just looking for a breakfast pastry or a sandwich, walk from Bouchon next door to the **Bouchon Bakery** (6528 Washington St., 707/944-2253, www.bouchonbakery.com, daily 7am-7pm). This ultra-high-end bakery supplies both Bouchon and the French Laundry with pastries and breads and operates a retail storefront. Locals and visitors flock to the bakery at breakfast and lunchtime, so expect a line.

The other big player in the Yountville restaurant scene is chef Richard Reddington's **Redd** (6480 Washington St., 707/944-2222, www.reddnapavalley.com, Mon.-Sat. 11:30am-2:30pm and 5:30pm-9:30pm, Sun. 11am-2:30pm and 5:30pm-9:30pm, $16-36). Reddington crafts Wine Country cuisine with shades of Asian, European, and Mexican influences. The menu might include items like sautéed skate or a steak with a bone marrow crust. Or explore with the five-course tasting menu ($85).

Situated in the V Market Place (formerly Vintage 1870), ★ **Bottega** (6525 Washington St., 707/945-1050, www.botteganapavalley.com, Tues.-Sun. 11:30am-3pm and 5pm-9:30pm, Mon. 5pm-9:30pm, $16-36) is the return to the kitchen for celebrity chef Michael Chiarello. The former host of *Easy Entertaining* on the Food Network has come back to Napa Valley and brought his flair for Italian cuisine. The exposed brick and bare ceiling beams of the dining room pair nicely with such classic dishes as *tagliarini* with veal and porcini *sugo,* duck served with duck liver mousse, and braised short ribs with spaetzle. The prices, particularly the wine list, are fairly reasonable for the area. While the menu changes with the seasons, try to finish your meal with the ricotta *zeppole*—Italian doughnuts fried to order and topped with praline cream.

Information and Services

Right in the thick of the epicurean madness, the **Yountville Chamber of Commerce** (6484 Washington St., 707/944-0904, http://yountville.com, daily 10am-5pm) also doubles as a visitors center. There are maps available along with always-helpful tips. Swing by to purchase two-for-one tasting coupons for Hill Family Estate, which is just down the street.

Head to Napa's **Queen of the Valley Hospital** (1000 Trancas St., 707/252-4411, www.thequeen.org) for medical emergencies.

Transportation

Yountville is on Highway 29, just nine miles north of Napa. Downtown Yountville is on the east side of Highway 29, and Washington Street is the main drag, connecting with Highway 29 at the south and north ends of town; to reach the heart of Yountville, exit on California Drive in the south and Madison Street in the north. The Yountville Cross Road will take you from the north end of town to the Silverado Trail.

To reach Yountville by bus, jump aboard the **VINE** (800/696-6443, 707/221-2800, www.ridethevine.com, adults $1.60, children $1.10), a commuter bus service that runs from the East Bay north through Calistoga.

Around town, consider taking the **Yountville Trolley** (707/944-1234, http://nctpa.net, Mon.-Sat. 10am-11pm, Sun. 10am-7pm, free). The trolley runs on a fixed track from Yountville Park along Washington Street to California Drive, conveniently near Domaine Chandon. It may also be useful for getting back to your hotel after imbibing too much.

RUTHERFORD AND OAKVILLE

Driving along on Highway 29, you might not even notice the tiny hamlets of Oakville and Rutherford. Neither town has much in the way of a commercial or residential district, and both have miniscule populations. Oakville earned a spot on the map in 1903 when the U.S. Department of Agriculture planted an experimental vineyard there. Since then, it has garnered distinction as a unique American Viticultural Area (AVA) known for its Bordeaux-style varietals. Oakville is also home to the outstanding Oakville Grocery, opened in 1881.

Rutherford was named for the 1,000 acres given to Thomas Rutherford by his father-in-law, George Yount. The area now has the distinction of growing some of the best cabernet grapes around. Yountville is also home to Grgich Hills, whose chardonnay crashed the Paris Wine Tasting of 1976. Like Oakville, Rutherford is also its own designated AVA.

Wineries
BEAULIEU VINEYARDS

Since 1900, **Beaulieu Vineyards** (1960 St. Helena Hwy., 800/373-5896, www.bvwines.com, daily 10am-5pm, $20) has been known for its cabernet sauvignon, even managing to survive Prohibition. Taste their wines in the Maestro Tasting Room or, even better, opt for their Historic Tour and Barrel Tasting ($35) that takes visitors to a section of the winery that was built in 1885. After touring the building, taste their famous cabernet sauvignon right out of a century-old redwood tank.

FROG'S LEAP WINERY

With so much outrageous winery architecture in the valley, **Frog's Leap Winery** (8815 Conn Creek Rd., Rutherford, 707/963-4704, www.frogsleap.com, daily 10am-4pm, $20-25) is an understated breath of fresh air. Its historic red barn and modest home and vineyard sit among gardens and vines. This big producer is just west of the Silverado Trail in the flats of Napa Valley; it has been a producer since 1981 and a leader in organic wine production and environmental stewardship. Tasting here is relaxing; sample a flight of four wines on the wrap-around porch or inside the vineyard house, accompanied by cheese, crackers, and jam. The highly recommended tour (Mon.-Fri. 10:30am and 2:30pm, $25) also provides a tasting of four wines, and each tasting is enjoyed somewhere different along the tour—the garden, the red barn, or in the vineyard, for example. Tours are by appointment only and last about one hour.

MINER FAMILY VINEYARDS

The estate tasting room at **Miner Family Vineyards** (7850 Silverado Trl., Oakville, 800/366-9463, www.minerwines.com, daily 11am-5pm, $25) provides Silverado Trail travelers with a typical taste of the Napa Valley. You'll need to climb a flight of stairs or take the elevator up to the oddly small tasting room that still manages to display an array of upscale souvenirs for sale. The winery mostly makes standard Napa Valley varietal wines such as chardonnay and cabernet sauvignon, with a viognier and a sangiovese thrown in. Most of the wines aren't bad, but they aren't remarkable either—certainly not as remarkable as the prices might indicate. If you've never tasted California wines before, Miner Family might make for a good baseline. If you're an experienced oenophile, give this one a pass.

OPUS ONE

Yup, that huge thing on the rise that looks like a missile silo really is a winery. **Opus One** (7900 Hwy. 29, Oakville, 800/292-6787, www.opusonewinery.com, daily 10am-4pm, reservations required, tasting $45, tours $75-125) boasts a reputation as one of the most prestigious, and definitely one of the most expensive, vintners in Napa. The echoing halls inside the facility add to the grandeur of the place, as does the price of a tasting: $45 for a three-ounce pour of a single wine. You're unlikely to find a bottle of Opus One for under $250. If you don't mind the price tag or just can't get enough of the Opus One experience, tours (appointment only) of the estate are also available.

★ GRGICH HILLS WINERY

At **Grgich Hills Winery** (1829 St. Helena Hwy., Rutherford, 707/963-2784, www.grgich.com, daily 9:30am-4:30pm, $20-50), active aging barrels crowd the main building and narrow the path to the tasting room's restrooms. If you're looking for a showy Napa Valley experience, this might not be the best place for you. What you will find at Grgich are some of the best wines in the valley and a biodynamic winemaking operation. Mike Grgich took his California chardonnay to the Paris Wine Tasting of 1976 and entered it in the white burgundy blind-tasting competition. After it won, French winemakers demanded that the contest be held again, and Grgich's chardonnay won a second time. That same year, Robert Mondavi's cabernet sauvignon also took top honors in its category at the same contest.

Visiting Grgich Hills, you'll find plenty of information about biodynamic farming, a process that takes organic practices to the next level. The best wines might be the legendary chardonnay—arguably the best chardonnay made in Napa or anywhere else. But don't ignore the reds, as Grgich offers lovely zinfandels and cabernets. And the Violetta, a dessert wine, is a special treat that's only made in years when the grape conditions are perfect. None of the Grgich wines are cheap, but it's more than worth it when you sip these rare, exquisite vintages.

MUMM

You may have already tasted the sparkling wines produced by **Mumm** (8445 Silverado Trl., Rutherford, 707/967-7700, http://mummnapa.com, daily 10am-6pm, $18-40). Even for genuine wine aficionados, it's worth spending an hour or two at Mumm Napa, a friendly and surprisingly down-to-earth winery among the estates on the Silverado Trail. Tastings happen at tables, with menus and service in restaurant fashion. The prices look very Napa Valley, but you'll get more wine and service for your money. Each pour is three ounces of wine—some of it high-end—and you get three pours per tasting. Nonalcoholic gourmet grape sodas or bottled water are complimentary. Dogs are allowed in the tasting room and get water, gourmet doggie bones, and plenty of petting from the tasting-room staff. Also, there's a 45- to 60-minute tour (daily 10am, 11am, 1pm, 3pm, $30) that ends in the photography gallery.

PEJU

Embodying the ultimate success of the Napa Valley, **Peju** (8466 St. Helena Hwy., Rutherford, 800/446-7358, www.peju.com, daily 10am-6pm, $25-40) is a family winery that has, through hard work, created great wines that have garnered the attention of international magazines and judging bodies. Today, visitors to Peju see gorgeous sycamore trees, hand-pruned by Tony Peju, running up the drive; a fabulous garden tended by Herta Peju; and solar panels on the roof of the elegant winery building. Inside you'll get tastes of an array of aromatic and award-winning red wines—from the lighter Bordeaux-varietal cabernet franc to the many vintages of classic California cabernet sauvignon. A few whites and perhaps a rosé or a port round out Peju's list.

INGLENOOK

Wine lovers come to enjoy the grand tasting room and museum at **Inglenook** (1991 St. Helena Hwy., Rutherford, 707/968-1161, www.inglenook.com, daily 11am-4pm, reservations required, tasting $45), formerly Rubicon and Niebaum-Coppola. Reservations are required for tastings in the large, elegant tasting room, where you'll find a generous bar area with plenty of staff to help you navigate the wine list. The winemakers take their job seriously, and the results can be spectacular. This estate winery also houses the small Centennial Museum, showcasing old Inglenook wines, zoetropes, and magic lanterns.

RUTHERFORD HILL

If you're planning in advance to visit **Rutherford Hill** (200 Rutherford Hill Rd., Rutherford, 707/963-1871, www.rutherford-hill.com, daily 10am-5pm, tasting $20-30), book a spot on the winery-and-cave tour. The winery is pretty standard for a Napa facility, but the caves impress even experienced wine lovers. Dug back into the hillside, Rutherford's caves provide a natural temperature-controlled space in which to age their array of wines, mostly hearty reds. (If you're looking for a place to hold a special dinner or midsize event, Rutherford rents out space in the caves.) Contrary to the myth perpetuated by the movie *Sideways,* Rutherford produces a fine merlot as well as rich cabernet sauvignons and other tasty varietals.

Accommodations

Perched above the valley and off the Silverado Trail, ★ **Auberge du Soleil** (180 Rutherford Hill Rd., St. Helena, 707/963-1211, www.aubergedusoleil.com, $725-5,200) is the ultimate in Wine Country luxury. The compound features multiple high-end wine-tasting and dining options in addition to a pool, a fitness room, a store, and well-kept gardens accented by modern art. The rooms are appointed with Italian sheets, private patios, fireplaces, and TVs in both the living room and the bath. The smallest guest room is 500 square feet, suites can top 1,400 square feet, and the Private Maison is 1,800 square feet. This is the place to stay if you have the cash to focus on the inn's amenities and have less interest in spending your time exploring the area.

Food

The historic ★ **Auberge du Soleil** (180 Rutherford Hill Rd., Rutherford, 800/348-5406, www.aubergedusoleil.com, daily 7am-11am, 11:30am-2:30pm, and 5:30pm-9:30pm, tasting menus $110-150) has an inn, but some visitors come just for the food—the charming Mediterranean-style dining room has drawn visitors from all over the world for decades. Sunny yellow tablecloths, a central fireplace, exposed wooden beams, and wall-to-wall picture windows welcome diners. Executive chef Robert Curry, a legend of the Napa Valley culinary scene, uses the finest local ingredients to create his own take on Mediterranean and California cuisine. Choose one item from each course list on the short but exquisite tasting menu to create a three-course or four-course dinner. If you ask, you can also dine à la carte from any of the courses. For Auberge du Soleil luxury without depleting your savings account, dine in the adjacent ★ **Bistro & Bar** (daily 11am-11pm, $12-38). Indoors is a bar and small dining area; outside is a deck with fine views of Napa Valley. Choose from braised short ribs, a charcuterie plate, a salad, a pizza, or the grilled Auberge burger; there's also a list of Napa Valley wines to enjoy while you soak up the view.

A long-standing Wine Country favorite is the **Rutherford Grill** (1180 Rutherford Rd., Rutherford, 707/963-1792, www.hillstone.com, Mon.-Thurs. 11:30am-9:30pm, Fri. 11:30am-10:30pm, Sat. 11am-10:30pm, Sun. 11am-9:30pm, $17-44), which is more casual than many of its Napa Valley peers. Some of the best seats in the house cluster outside the dining room on the wide deck; sheltered by a collection of umbrellas, guests enjoy the pretty gardens with their classic grill fare—cheeseburgers, salads with grilled items, bangers and mash, and a whole array of grilled meats—as well as an extensive and impressive wine list. Perhaps the best part: You can escape from the Rutherford Grill for well under $100 per person.

For a picnic lunch or just a few munchies for the road, stop by the **Oakville Grocery** (7856 St. Helena Hwy., Oakville, 707/944-8802, www.oakvillegrocery.com, Mon.-Thurs. 6:30am-5pm, Fri.-Sun. 6:30am-6pm) along Highway 29. A longtime Napa Valley institution, the Oakville Grocery has a reputation for stocking only the best food, wine, cheese, and other goodies. Browse the tightly packed shelves or order a hot lunch at the center counter; they serve slow-roasted beef and fried chicken sandwiches among other options. To find the building from the northbound highway, look for the large Coca-Cola sign painted on the south side of the building.

Transportation

Oakville is four miles north of Yountville on Highway 29; Rutherford is another two miles north. Both can be easy to miss because of their loose organization and rural character. The Silverado Trail runs parallel to Highway 29 along this stretch. To reach it from Oakville, take Oakville Road east; in Rutherford, take Rutherford Road (Hwy. 128) east.

ST. HELENA

There are few Northern California towns as picturesque and well-groomed as St. Helena. Bolstered by the lucrative wine industry, St. Helena has the glossy sheen of a reinvented old California farm town. It is filled with fine eateries and quaint, expensive shops housed in historic buildings and surrounded by block upon block by well-maintained craftsman homes. The Napa campus of the Culinary Institute of America is a major employer in the area, as is the St. Helena Hospital. Highway 29 runs north-south through the center of town, which can give you a quick peek at the sights, but it's not so nice when sitting in traffic on a sunny weekend.

Wineries

BERINGER VINEYARDS

The palatial stone estate buildings of **Beringer Vineyards** (2000 Main St., 707/257-5771, www.beringer.com, daily 10am-6pm, $25-60) belie the reasonably priced Beringer vintages available in supermarkets across the country. Inside, you'll find an array of wines for tasting, many of which are not readily available outside the tasting room. Outdoors, stroll in the beautiful estate gardens that stretch for acres on prime land next to Highway 29. Tours ($30-45) take you into the winemaking facilities and show off the highlights of the vast estate.

CORISON

A rarity among Napa Valley's large-scale producers, **Corison** (987 St. Helena Hwy., 707/963-0826, www.corison.com, daily 10am-5pm, by appointment, $55) is the genuine article—a tiny single-proprietor winery producing great wines in small quantities. Technically, Corison takes tasters by appointment only, but in truth they've never turned away a drop-in during regular business hours. After turning onto a short gravel driveway, you pass a vintage home to reach the small barn that serves as a tasting room. Open the huge white door and enter the tasting-, barrel-, and stockroom. A tiny bar offers tastings from the 3,000 cases the winery produces each year. Expect the attentive staff to talk in loving and knowledgeable terms about the delicious wines they're pouring. The signature tasting also includes a tour that allows for stops to sip aged cabernet sauvignon. Many of Corison's wines are only available for purchase here or via their wine club.

FLORA SPRINGS

This winery straddles the line between boutiques and big-deal Napa players. You'll find **Flora Springs** (677 S. St. Helena Hwy., 707/967-8032, www.florasprings.com, daily 10am-5pm, $20-55) on a few menus in upscale restaurants and here in the open, airy tasting room that sweeps in a half circle around the bar, with plenty of windows letting in the Napa sunlight. You'll taste a variety of reds and whites, but the cabernet sauvignons are the standouts here.

HEITZ

One of the oldest wineries in the valley, **Heitz** (436 St. Helena Hwy., 707/963-3542, www.heitzcellar.com, daily 11am-4:30pm, free) brings sincere elegance to the glitz and glamour of Napa. The high-ceilinged tasting room is dominated by a stone fireplace with comfy chairs. A low bar off to the right sets the stage for an array of Napa Valley cabernet sauvignons. To the happy surprise of many, Heitz's cabernets are well balanced and easy to drink, and though costly, they approach affordable by Napa standards. Most of the grapes used for these wines are grown right in the Napa Valley. In February, visitors can taste the current release of the Martha's Vineyard Cabernet—a vintage grown in the first wine-designated vineyard in the valley.

PRIDE MOUNTAIN VINEYARDS

Take advantage of some of Wine Country's scenic drives with a visit to **Pride Mountain Vineyards** (4026 Spring Mountain Rd., 707/963-4949, www.pridewines.com, daily 10:30am-3:45pm, reservations required, tour and tasting $25-75, tasting only $20-30), at the top of a scenic, winding road six miles from the turnoff on Highway 29. In addition to the wine, the views are the reward for the effort. Wine-tasting is by appointment only, so once you arrive you'll have the pourer's full attention. It's worth it to take the tour, as you'll see the vineyard and the caves and will be able to taste the wine straight out of the barrel. It's a great education in how wine matures with age.

ST. CLEMENT VINEYARDS

This winery is all about the cabs: While they produce one chardonnay for good measure, the rest of tasting menu at **St. Clement Vineyards** (2867 Hwy. 29, 707/265-5000, www.stclement.com, Thurs.-Mon. 11am-5pm, $35) features a flight of four different vintages of cabernet sauvignon. This translates into a fun introduction to the variety and qualities of the grape. But this is not the only reason to visit; St. Clement's elegant two-story Victorian farmhouse is perched on a hill above Highway 29 and is beautifully surrounded by sloping vineyards. The grounds are lush with English gardens and heavy-limbed oaks; in front, tables dot the split-level decks, affording both privacy and a splendid place for a picnic. The winery's deep-blue interior features more modern touches, such as the unique art deco chandeliers. The juxtaposition is unexpected, but it works.

V. SATTUI

A boutique winery that doesn't distribute to retailers, **V. Sattui** (1111 White Lane, 707/963-7774, www.vsattui.com, daily 9am-6pm, $15) won the Best Winery award at the California State Fair in 2006, 2007, and 2012—a mighty feat in a state filled with excellent vintners. V. Sattui produces a wide selection of varietals—everything from light-bodied whites to full-flavored cabernet sauvignons. The dessert madeira is particularly fine—if it's not on the tasting menu, ask your pourer at the bar if they've got a bottle open, and you might just get lucky.

The big tasting room on Highway 29 boasts three spacious bar areas, endless stacks and cases of wine out and ready for purchase, a separate register, and a full deli. The gardens surrounding the facility include a number of picnic tables, and Sattui is a popular lunchtime stop for all-day tasters. There's also a tower (Sat.-Sun. 11am-5pm, $20) open for weekend tastings. Even the big Sattui tasting room fills up on weekends in high season (May-Oct.).

Sights
★ CULINARY INSTITUTE OF AMERICA AT GREYSTONE

The premier institute for training professional chefs in the United States has only three campuses: one in upstate New York, one in Texas, and this one, the **Culinary**

Institute of America at Greystone (2555 Main St., 707/967-1100, www.ciachef.edu, restaurant Tues.-Sat. 11:30am-2pm and 5:30pm-8:30pm, café daily 10:30am-5pm, market daily 10:30am-6pm). The campus includes the Greystone Restaurant, the Bakery Café, the Spice Islands Marketplace, one-day cooking classes and demos, a food-history museum, and a stunning set of buildings nestled in the forests and vineyards near St. Helena on Highway 29. If Napa is the perfect place to introduce newcomers to the world of high-end food and wine, Greystone takes it to the intermediate and advanced levels. Serious foodies and cork dorks should sign up in advance to attend a cooking demo or seminar. Take a few minutes to marvel at the imposing gray-stone structures of the campus or opt for a 30-minute tour (daily 11:45am, 2:45pm, 5pm, $10) of the grounds.

Shopping

As you may be able to tell from the traffic in town, downtown St. Helena is hopping. Quaint and historic storefronts line Highway 29, housing galleries, clothiers, jewelers, kitchen stores, and, of course, wine shops, many of which offer wine-tasting. Over the years, olive trees have begun spreading across the landscape, which makes perfect sense—Napa Valley has an ideal Mediterranean climate for these trees. The resulting olive oil offers one more thing to taste.

Out of downtown St. Helena's hubbub, the **Napa Valley Olive Oil Manufacturing Co.** (835 Charter Oak Ave., 707/963-4173, daily 9am-5:30pm) is one of those treasures that travelers feel lucky to find. The tiny, funky old storefront is two blocks off Highway 29 and features a motley collection of plastic-covered picnic tables out front and a faded, hand-lettered sign on the door. Inside, take care not to trip over the uneven floor in the cramped, meandering rooms of the shop. You can't taste the oils and vinegars; you'll just have to go on faith that this Italian-owned and operated shop sells the best. The tiny store also has fabulous cheeses and fresh-baked breads, making it a great stop for picnic supplies. The shop bottles its products on-site.

Accommodations

The charming village of St. Helena is right on Highway 29, and its stop signs and traffic signals are often the cause of the endless Wine Country weekend traffic jams. But if you're staying here, you can avoid the worst of the traffic and enjoy the wooded central Napa Valley area.

For the best rates in St. Helena, the ★ **El Bonita Motel** (195 Main St./Hwy. 29, 800/541-3284, www.elbonita.com, $130-310) can't be beat. It is within walking distance of the historic downtown and has a 1950s motel charm. The low-slung 48-room hotel wraps about a patio shaded by oak trees, bordered by a clipped lawn, and filled with tables, chairs, and umbrellas. In the center is a pool, a hot tub, and a sauna, which all guests are encouraged to enjoy. The rooms may not match the indulgence of other Napa inns, but they are clean, comfortable, and pet-friendly, with refrigerators and microwave ovens; some even boast kitchenettes.

At the **Zinfandel Inn** (800 Zinfandel Ln., 707/963-3512, www.zinfandelinn.com, $300-500), you'll find yourself in a two-story English Tudor inn. Lavish stonework adorns the outside of this unique structure. Inside, you'll stay in one of three exquisitely decorated suite-like rooms. Each guest room boasts a unique design, complete with antique bedsteads and dressers, feather beds, fireplaces, and tiled whirlpool tubs. All guests enjoy a full breakfast every morning of their stay, plus the rich amenities characteristic of a Wine Country inn.

Food

A highlight of the St. Helena dining scene is the ★ **Wine Spectator Greystone Restaurant** (2555 Main St., 707/967-1010, http://ciachef.edu, Tues.-Sat. 11:30am-2pm and 5:30pm-8:30pm, $18-42), better known as "the restaurant at the CIA," where the world's top aspiring chefs practice their craft. It's easier to get a reservation here than at French Laundry and Bouchon; with several big dining rooms, the CIA can seat large numbers. From some tables, you can watch your food being prepared in the open kitchen. The ever-changing menu highlights the best of each season, and the wine list features the finest of Napa Valley's vintages; the student chefs plan menus with an eye to wine pairings. There's also a four-course prix fixe menu.

An imposing stone building draped in ivy and surrounded by grapevines is home to **Tra Vigne** (1050 Charter Oak Ave., 707/963-4444, www.travignerestaurant.com, Sun.-Thurs. 11am-9pm, Fri.-Sat. 11am-9:30pm, $16-32). When it opened, Tra Vigne helped bring a modern California culinary sensibility to Napa Valley. Today, it has been overshadowed by the profusion of high-end eateries and celebrity chefs, but its reputation for excellent Italian food is still intact. The warm dining room features white tablecloths, cream walls, plush leather booths, and wooden chairs. The food is equally comfortable, with crisply executed thin-crust pizzas, wood oven-roasted meats, and silky pasta dishes. The extensive wine list includes a number of Italian grappas.

Craving pizza or a low-key meal? **Pizzeria Tra Vigne** (1016 Main St., 707/967-9999, www.travignerestaurant.com, Sun.-Thurs. 11:30am-9pm, Fri.-Sat. 11:30am-9:30pm, $10-21), next door to Tra Vigne, is considerably more relaxed than its renowned sibling. Inside are long tables opposite the open kitchen, where a huge wood-fired oven sits center stage. The famous thin-crust Italian pizzas lure locals many weekend nights; you can also enjoy hearty plates of pasta or heavy Italian salads. Wash it all down with a pitcher of any number of beers on tap. There are also beers by the bottle in addition to a healthy selection of wine. If you're traveling with kids, Pizzeria Tra Vigne is a great place to stop and relax over a meal. There's even a pool table.

Tired of Wine Country fare? The **Himalayan Sherpa Kitchen** (1148 Main St., 707/963-4439, http://himalayansherpakitchen.com, daily 11:30am-9pm, $10-25) serves cuisine from the highest region in the world right in downtown St. Helena. With golden curries, tikka masala dishes, and samosas, the menu features the kinds of dishes you'd find in an Indian restaurant. The food here is superb, and like the rest of Napa, there is a selection of fine local wines to sip with your meal.

★ **Gott's Roadside** (933 Main St., 707/963-3486, http://gotts.com, summer daily 10am-10pm, winter daily 8am-9pm, $6-17) was once known as Taylor's Refresher, which explains the wooden sign on Highway 29. This classic roadside diner has been around since 1949, but the food has been updated with a modern local-organic sensibility; the burgers, fries, and milk shakes are made with quality ingredients. The Gott brothers, who took over the business in 1999, have added more California-eclectic comfort food like fish tacos, Chinese chicken salad, and wines by the glass. They have also earned three James Beard awards for bringing fast food up to the quality of well-respected sitdown restaurants.

Cook Tavern (1304 Main St., 707/963-8082, http://cooksthelena.com, Mon.-Thurs. 11:30am-10pm, Fri. 11:30am-midnight, Sat. 10am-midnight, Sun. 10am-10pm, $14-22) pairs wine, beer, and craft cocktails with small plates and "not so small" entrées. Some favorites include the duck confit tacos and the buttermilk fried chicken wings.

St. Helena has its own food truck with **Bruschetteria** (most days by Velo Vino, 709 Main St., Tues.-Sun. 11:30am-4pm, $5-19). The green truck focuses on grilled bread with toppings (heirloom tomatoes, seasonal mushrooms, smoked salmon). The porchetta is a favorite, with pork, herbs, onion, aioli, and parmesan.

Information and Services
Pick up maps, information, and discounted wine-tasting vouchers at the **St. Helena Welcome Center** (657 Main St., 707/963-4456, www.sthelena.com, Mon.-Fri. 9am-5pm, Sat. 10am-4pm, Sun. 11am-5pm).

Thankfully, there is parking in back; turn on Vidovich Lane just north of the visitors center.

The **St. Helena Hospital** (10 Woodland Rd., 707/963-6425, http://sthelenanowaiter.org) has a 24-hour emergency room for quick and reliable service.

Transportation
St. Helena is on Highway 29 in the middle of Napa Valley, eight miles south of Calistoga. To reach the Silverado Trail from St. Helena, take Zinfandel Lane or Pope Street east.

To avoid the headache of parking and driving around town, hop aboard **The VINE St. Helena Shuttle** (707/963-3007, www.ridethevine.com, Mon.-Thurs. 7:45am-6pm, Fri. 7:45am-11pm, Sat. 10am-11pm, Sun. noon-7pm, $1).

CALISTOGA
Despite their proximity, Calistoga and St. Helena couldn't be more different. While St. Helena leans toward the boutique side of the wine scene and often feels permanently congested, Calistoga has a more laid-back, almost mountain-town crunchiness to it. Far from the city of Napa, it is one of the most economically diverse towns in the valley, which is reflected in its restaurants, businesses, and hotels. Browse books, grab great barbecue, or sit at a sidewalk café to enjoy a cheap beer and even forget you are in Wine Country. It is also the land of great and affordable spas, where soaking is treated more as therapy than beauty treatment.

Calistoga gets its unique name from one of its early advocates, Samuel Brannan, who hoped to transform the mineral spring-rich region into a spa resort rivaling Saratoga Springs, New York. A drinker, Brannan once tried to proclaim the area the "Saratoga of California" but misspoke and said it would be the "Calistoga of Sarifornia."

Wineries
CASTELLO DI AMOROSA
When you first spy the ramshackle house and its sweetly tended garden near the entrance

to **Castello di Amorosa** (4045 Hwy. 29, 707/967-6272, www.castellodiamorosa.com, Mar.-Oct. daily 9:30am-6pm, Nov.-Feb. daily 9:30am-5pm, adults $25-35, children under 21 $15), you might imagine you are stopping in at one of those delightfully rustic north-valley wineries. You couldn't be more wrong. After passing through the gates and ascending a steep hill lined in vineyards and Italian cypress trees, you'll reach the castle at the top. The steep prices for tasting include access to the main floors of the castle. Tours, in addition to barrel-tasting, take visitors to the armory and torture chamber. Castello di Amorosa produces a number of varietals, such as pinot grigio and muscat, which are overshadowed by their environs. Children are permitted on the tour

CLOS PEGASE

Want some art to ponder while you sample wine? **Clos Pegase** (1060 Dunaweal Ln., 707/942-4981, www.clospegase.com, daily 10:30am-5pm, tasting $20-30) has over 100 artworks on its grounds, including sculptor Henry Moore's *Mother Earth* and a painting from Francis Bacon. The entrance is a work of art itself that was designed to resemble a Greek temple. In the tasting room, you can sample the winery's flagship cabernet sauvignon or their Hommage chardonnay. Clos Pegase also offers 1.5-hour winery tours (daily 11am, 1pm, 3pm, $75, reservations required 48 hours in advance) that go into winemaking, architecture, and art while including a visit inside the winery's caves. You can even bring a piece of art from Clos Pegase home with you; most of the wine labels feature an image of artwork that is displayed on the winery's grounds.

SCHRAMSBERG VINEYARDS

The oldest hillside vineyard in Napa that has been declared a historical landmark, **Schramsberg Vineyards** (1400 Schramsberg Rd., 707/942-4558, www.schramsberg.com, tours and tasting 9am-2:30pm, reservations required, $60) was

Castello di Amorosa

founded in 1862 and is considered to be one of the best producers of sparkling wine in California. Tastings include four wines, a tour of the 120-year-old caves, and an education in the art of making sparkling wines in the Champagne style. Schramsberg can be visited by appointment only and does not allow pets or children, no matter how small or quiet.

STERLING VINEYARDS

Sterling Vineyards (1111 Dunaweal Lane, 800/726-6136, www.sterlingvineyards.com, Mon.-Fri. 10:30am-4:30pm, Sat.-Sun. 10am-5pm, adults $29, children under 21 $15) is more appealing for first-timers than for serious wine aficionados. The jewel of the new "Disneyland with wine" culture of Napa, Sterling features a gondola ride and an obligatory tasting tour through the estate rather than a traditional tasting room experience. It's expensive, and the lines can be long on weekends in high season (May-Oct.).

The gondola ride up the mountain to the estate shows off Napa Valley at its best. Take advantage of the time to admire the stellar views of forested hills and endless vineyards. Once up at the estate, you'll be guided around by signs to each tasting venue. The wine isn't worth the effort or the high per-bottle price tag, but the estate has some charm, and the views from the deck match those from the gondola.

UP VALLEY VINTNERS

Up Valley Vintners (1371 Lincoln Ave., 707/942-1004, www.upvalleyvintners.com, Sun.-Thurs. noon-6pm, Fri.-Sat. noon-8pm, tasting $15) is a co-op of sorts where smaller winemakers can sell their wine and offer tastings directly to the public. The long and narrow shop features a dark wood bar that extends one-third the length of the room. Here you will find locals and travelers happily sitting on barstools, chatting with the pourer. Past the bar is a retail section where each winery has a profile and plenty of bottles for sale. There is a comfortable lounge area inside and a patio with a table and chairs outside. While all the wines featured come from veteran winemakers of the Calistoga AVA, a real standout is the Dyer cabernet blend. Made from grapes grown on a 2.2-acre vineyard on Diamond Mountain, the blends have a Bordeaux quality and a reputation for excellence, and they are difficult to come by.

Sights
OLD FAITHFUL GEYSER

No, you haven't accidentally driven east to Yellowstone. The Napa Valley has its own **Old Faithful Geyser** (1299 Tubbs Lane, 707/942-6463, www.oldfaithfulgeyser.com, May-Oct. daily 8:30am-8pm, Nov.-Apr daily 8:30am-7pm, adults $14, seniors $12, children 4-12 $8, under age 4 free). Unlike its more famous counterpart, this geothermal geyser is artificial. In the 19th and early 20th centuries, more than 100 wells were drilled into the geothermal springs of the Calistoga area, and many of these created geysers. Old Faithful is one of the few that wasn't eventually capped off, and it's the only one that erupts with clockwork

regularity. When you visit the geyser, expect no more than a 40-minute wait to see it erupt 60 feet or higher into the air. A grassy area surrounds the geyser, with benches and chairs scattered around to allow visitors an easy wait for the show. A bamboo garden surrounds the lawn (bamboo is one of the few plants that can tolerate the hot mineral water of this area). Also at Old Faithful you'll find an incongruous but cute petting zoo that houses several fainting goats, plus a few sheep and llamas. A coin-operated feeder lets visitors feed and pet the animals—perfect for children who may grow tired of waiting for the geyser to erupt. Note that the water in the pool from which the geyser erupts—as well as that from the geyser itself—is very hot. It's not safe to wade in the water or to stand too close when the geyser goes off. Keep an eye on small children.

PETRIFIED FOREST

The trees of the **Petrified Forest** (4100 Petrified Forest Rd., 707/942-6667, www.petrifiedforest.org, summer daily 10am-7pm, spring and fall daily 10am-6pm, winter daily 10am-5pm, adults $10, seniors and children age 12 to 17 $9, children 6-11 $5) no longer stand—technically this is an archaeological dig that uncovered a forest that existed more than three million years ago. A volcano that no longer exists erupted, blowing over the trees and covering them with ash. Over hundreds of thousands of years, the minerals in the ash traded places with the contents of the cells that made up the wood of the trees, petrifying them; now these long-dead trees are made of stone.

Follow your trail map along a 0.5-mile loop to visit the various excavated petrified trees and chunks of trees. You can touch some of the chunks of petrified wood, but most are protected by fences to preserve their pristine state. A number of petrified coast redwoods have been given names. All the trees fell in the same direction and still face that way, showing the direction the blast came from when the volcano erupted.

You can also take a 1.5-hour walk (daily

11am, 1pm, 3pm) with a naturalist over ash-fall to a view of Mount St. Helena. Inside the visitors center and gift shop, you'll find lots of rocks and minerals, books on geology, and a few rare shards of the petrified trees from this forest.

SHARPSTEEN MUSEUM OF CALISTOGA HISTORY

The **Sharpsteen Museum of Calistoga History** (1311 Washington St., 707/942-5911, www.sharpsteenmuseum.org, daily 11am-4pm, $3 donation) takes its name from its founder, Ben Sharpsteen, an Academy Award-winning animator for Disney who had a passion for dioramas. It was through his desire and funding that the immense, exquisitely detailed dioramas depicting the 1860s Calistoga hot springs resort and life in 19th-century Calistoga were built. The other major player in the museum, Sam Brannan, was the first pioneer in Calistoga to build a resort centered on the geothermal springs in the area. At the museum, you'll learn of Brannan's success and subsequent ruin in the resort business as well as his unsuccessful attempt to convert the Napa Valley to Mormonism. Other museum exhibits highlight daily life in 19th-century Napa, complete with artifacts and a nod to the Wappo people, the Native American first residents of this area.

PIONEER CEMETERY

If you're looking for your Napa ancestors or just enjoy historic graveyards, stop at the **Napa Valley Pioneer Cemetery** (Bothe-Napa Valley State Park, 3801 St. Helena Hwy. N., 707/942-4575, www.parks.ca.gov, $8), where you'll find the graves of many of Napa's earliest nonnative settlers and some of the more prominent early pioneer families. Paths between plots are kept clear, but many of the graves are overgrown with vines—some even have full-size oak trees growing through them. The area is covered by a dense canopy of forest foliage, making it a pleasantly cool place to visit on hot summer days. Explore up the hillside, where the paths get more overgrown and some of the tombstones are old wooden planks, their lettering worn away. If you're interested in genealogy, start at the front entrance of the cemetery, where a map and an alphabetical survey of the cemetery are posted. There's enough room at the front for one small car; otherwise, you have to park elsewhere and walk carefully along and across Highway 29 to the entrance.

Calistoga's Old Faithful Geyser

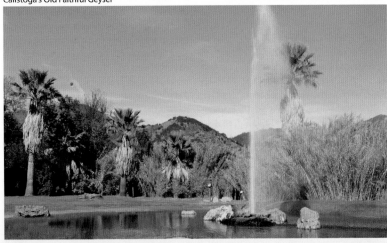

Bars

To get a local's perspective on Calistoga and the Wine Country, get a beer or a cocktail at **Susie's Bar** (1365 Lincoln Ave., 707/942-6710, Mon.-Fri. noon-2am, Sat.-Sun. 10am-2am). This dive bar is reached by a long alleyway that opens up into a high-ceilinged room with pool tables and brick walls.

On the other end of the spectrum is **Barolo** (1457 Lincoln Ave., 707/942-9900, www.baro-localistoga.com, daily 4pm-9:30pm), a wine and cocktail bar that bustles on weekend evenings. Take a seat at the marble bar or a table to have one last glass of wine or a cocktail after a day of relaxing in Calistoga. For those with an appetite, Barolo serves up tasty Italian food. The pizza, which has a cracker-thin crust, is recommended.

★ Spas

To experience a Napa County spa without draining your savings, set up an appointment at **Dr. Wilkinson's Hot Springs Resort** (1507 Lincoln Ave., 707/942-4102, www.drwilkinson.com, daily 8:30am-3:45pm, $89-200). Tucked into a 1950s motel building, this spa was opened by "Doc" Wilkinson in 1952. "The Works" treatment ($139-179) is a relaxing two-hour marathon that comprises submersion in a mud bath, a facial mask, a soak in a bubbling mineral whirlpool, a sauna steam, a blanket wrap, and a 30-minute full-body massage. The mud is a mix of sifted volcanic ash from the area and Canadian peat moss cut with local mineral water. It is quite simply a great deal. The spa also offers hour-long facials, hour-long massages, and a hot stone massage. The men and women's spa areas are separate. If you're a guest of the hotel, take a swim or a soak in one of the three mineral-water pools: There are two outdoor pools and one large spa inside.

At the **Calistoga Hot Springs Spa** (1006 Washington St., 707/942-6269, www.calistogaspa.com, Tues.-Thurs. 8:30am-4:30pm, Fri.-Mon. 8:30am-9pm, $45-252) you can indulge in a mud bath, a mineral bath, or other typical spa treatments. Also available to the public and guaranteed with a spa reservation is access to Calistoga Hot Springs's four outdoor mineral pools. The lap pool is the coolest at 80°F and is set up for serious swimmers. The 90°F wading pool with fountains offers fun and health benefits for the whole family. Another large soaking pool is set to 100°F and meant primarily for adults. Finally, the enormous octagonal 104°F jetted spa is under a

Soak in one of the pools at Dr. Wilkinson's Hot Springs Resort.

gazebo—the perfect location to relax and enjoy the serenity of spa country.

Two other lovely Calistoga spas, both of which offer full mud and mineral baths as well as spa services, are **Golden Haven** (1713 Lake St., 707/942-8000, www.golden-haven.com, daily 8am-11pm, massage treatments and mud baths $55-125) and **Indian Springs** (1712 Lincoln Ave., 707/942-4913, www.indianspringscalistoga.com, spa hours daily 9am-9pm, mud baths and massages $80-270). In operation since 1862, Indian Springs is the oldest continuously operating pool and spa facility in the state. It offers mud baths, facials, and a dip in an Olympic-sized mineral pool.

Sports and Recreation

Not every bit of open space in the Napa Valley is dedicated to grapes. There are several great state parks where you can indulge in the beauty of the valley and not just what it produces. **Bothe-Napa State Park** (3801 St. Helena Hwy., 707/942-4575, http://napa-valleystateparks.org, daily 8am-sunset, $8) is south of Calistoga on the west side of Highway 29. The park's 2,000-foot elevation provides fantastic views of the valley below and the craggy Mayacamas Mountains beyond, and the nearly 2,000 acres include oak woodlands, coastal redwoods, and occasional open grassland. There are a number of great hikes in the park. **Coyote Peak Trail** climbs to 1,170 feet and forms a 6.5-mile loop with **Upper Ritchey Canyon Trail,** providing great views and a backcountry feel. There is a public swimming pool, but you will have to check with park officials for its operating hours.

Robert Louis Stevenson State Park (Hwy. 29, seven miles north of Calistoga, 707/942-4575, www.parks.ca.gov, daily sunrise-sunset, free) is named for the author who spent his honeymoon in a tiny cabin here. The park offers fewer amenities than nearby Bothe-Napa State Park, but it does have a trail to the top of Mount St. Helena. The 11.2-mile round-trip hike is strenuous, especially when the trail rises above the lush canopy of bay,

Douglas fir, and madrone trees to exposed chaparral. All that huffing and puffing is rewarded at the 4,300-foot summit, where great views of the valley unfold. If it's a clear day, you may even see the San Francisco skyline to the south or Mount Shasta, 190 miles north. The park also has picnic tables for those simply looking for a lovely outdoor place to lunch.

Biking in Calistoga is a fun and scenic alternative to sitting in congested traffic, and it's a great way to get around any time of year. **Calistoga Bikeshop** (1318 Lincoln Ave., 707/942-9687, http://calistogabikeshop.com, daily 10am-6pm, bike rentals $39-165 per day) offers guided tours, self-guided tours, and bike rentals. With cruisers and touring bikes, mountain and road bikes, tandems, and trailers, this bike shop has everything you need to suit your travel plans. Ask at the shop for directions, maps, and suggestions—whether you're looking for a couple of hours in the vineyards or the most challenging mountain-bike tracks in the area.

Feel like a few rounds of golf? The **Mount St. Helena Golf Course** (2025 Grant St., 707/942-9966, www.mtsthelenagolfcourse.org, daily 7am-dusk, $21-42) is a charming and inexpensive par-34 nine-hole course; it's the perfect spot for younger or less experienced golfers. The course is flat and straight, with easier lines than many other courses. On the other hand, all those trees along the fairways and the small greens make it interesting for intermediate players.

If you care to take in Calistoga's dramatic scenery from the air, **Calistoga Balloons** (707/942-5758, www.calistogaballoons.com, $239-1,219) is the only company offering regular flights in the north end of Napa Valley. In addition to the vineyards, wineries, spas, and the charming town of Calistoga, you'll also see Mount St. Helena and the lush, forested hills surrounding this lovely area.

Accommodations

A plethora of places to stay cluster at the north end of Napa Valley, where you'll find most of the hotel-and-spa combos plus plenty of mineral-water pools and hot tubs for your pleasure. Calistoga also has some of the best lodging rates around.

UNDER $100
Mountain Home Ranch (3400 Mountain Home Ranch Rd., 707/942-6616, www.mountainhomeranch.com, $71-146) almost feels like summer camp. Set deep in the thickly forested mountains above Calistoga, it has an unpolished charm that's difficult to find elsewhere. Choose a guest room with a full bath, a rustic cabin, or a cottage with a full bath, a fireplace, and a kitchen. There are two pools, a lake, volleyball and tennis courts, table-tennis tables, a basketball hoop, and hiking trails. A menagerie of barnyard animals keeps animal-loving kids happy. This being Calistoga, there's also a mineral springs soaking tub. The main house serves breakfast, lunch (adults $17, children $12), and dinner (adults $22, children $16). Staying here is a relaxed, funky, and old-fashioned type of family vacation.

$100-150
The **Calistoga Inn** (1250 Lincoln Ave., 707/942-4101, www.calistogainn.com, $129-169) has been hosting visitors on and off since 1887. The 17 rooms all have shared bathrooms. There are no TVs, phones, or air-conditioning, but there is a restaurant and brewery downstairs for entertainment. A separate cottage ($189-239) with its own private bathroom is also available. All guests receive a complimentary continental breakfast.

$150-250
For a weekend of soaking, stay at ★ **Dr. Wilkinson's Hot Springs Resort** (1507 Lincoln Ave., 707/942-4102, www.drwilkinson.com, $195-310). The main attraction here are the three on-site mineral pools. Outdoors, there is an 80°F and 90°F pool, while indoors is a 103°F spa that is large enough to accommodate more than a dozen soakers. To spoil yourself even more, consider booking a treatment in the adjacent spa. The funky 1950s-era

resort has multiple lodgings to choose from. Motel rooms are decorated in brown, orange, and beige; bungalows include kitchens; and rooms in the restored Victorian do not lack for ruffles and floral patterns. Dr. Wilkinson's even has freshly laundered bathing suits on loan. While it's not fancy, the resort staff is friendly, and the pools are worth spending time in.

The old-school **Hideaway Cottages** (1412 Fair Way, 707/942-4108, www.hideawaycottages.com, $180-700) are 1940s-era bungalows primly decorated in cream with the occasional plaid bedspread. The cottages retain their original details, such as scalloped-edged kitchen cupboards, tile countertops, and charming built-in glass cabinets. Many of the cottages include sitting rooms, full kitchens, and outdoor seating; all are painted crisp white with country-blue trim. The lawns of the leafy grounds offer plenty of spots to lounge around the pool and hot tub. In the interest of quiet, no children under age 18 or pets are allowed.

With these rates, don't expect modern luxury at the **Golden Haven Hot Springs** (1713 Lake St., 707/942-8000, www.goldenhaven.com, $175-255). Still, the rooms are spacious and clean, and all come with complimentary use of the hotel's sundeck, hot tubs, and a swimming pool fed by Calistoga hot springs water. For a few extra dollars, they have rooms with full-size spas that can be filled with local mineral water. Golden Haven also has mud baths, massage services, facials, and body wraps for very reasonable prices. Keep your eyes peeled for online specials.

The **Roman Spa Hot Springs Resort** (1300 Washington St., 800/914-8957, www.romanspahotsprings.com, $169-650) in the heart of downtown Calistoga has it all: three mineral-water pools, each set at a different temperature (no children under age 4 are allowed in any pool, and the 105°F spa is adults-only), plus saunas to inspire guests to relax and refresh themselves with daily soaks and swims. Rooms run the gamut from inexpensive motel-style rooms with floral comforters to whirlpool rooms that include a private two-person mineral bath to kitchen suites (pots, pans, and dishes provided) that beckon families or groups who plan to stay awhile. The Roman Spa connects to the Calistoga Oasis, which offers an array of spa treatments, including the famous mud baths.

OVER $250

Mount View Hotel and Spa (1457 Lincoln Ave., 800/816-6877, www.mountviewhotel.com, $249-489) is perfectly located on Calistoga's main drag. Rooms, suites, and cottages are decorated with tasteful 19th-century antiques and soothing colors inspired by the vines and vintages of the local area. Rooms have either two twins, a queen, or a king bed, all feather beds with down comforters. An on-site spa offers facials, body wraps, steam showers, and scrubs. You can enjoy the outdoor pool and outdoor spa with mineral waters at your leisure.

For a more traditional bed-and-breakfast experience, don't miss **The Pink Mansion** (1415 Foothill Blvd., 800/238-7465, www.pinkmansion.com, $250-395): The 1875 mansion is painted bright pink, making it a local landmark. Each lush guest room features a

unique theme suitable to romance and wine. The more economical rooms have queen beds and pretty antique furnishings; the larger suites are spacious enough to dwarf their king beds, and you'll also find fireplaces, whirlpool tubs, and top-tier amenities. Enjoy the heated indoor pool and spa, a full breakfast each morning, and use of the various TVs and DVD players, plus a movie library, secreted around the house.

Food

Small, homey Calistoga offers a pleasing combination of high-end California cuisine and simple, delicious fare. If you need a break from rich, expensive food, a great place to stop for a meal is at the corner of Lincoln Street and Highway 29. ★ **Buster's Barbecue and Bakery** (1207 Foothill Blvd., 707/942-5605, http://busterssouthernbbq.com, Mon.-Sat. 10am-8pm, Sun. 10am-6pm, $8-27) brings unpretentious barbecue to Wine Country. You may find lines of mostly locals looking for a good, quick meal at this walk-up eatery at both lunch and dinner. The simple fare includes favorites like barbecue sauce-drenched tritip and pork loin sandwiches served on slabs of garlic toast. You'll also have your pick of

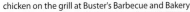

chicken on the grill at Buster's Barbecue and Bakery

traditional sides (baked beans, slaw, potato salad, corn bread) and Southern-style baked goods. The sweet-potato pie is a local favorite. Leave your fancy wine-tasting clothes at home; you might go through half a paper towel roll trying to clean up after having a Buster's barbecue sandwich.

Pacifico Mexican Restaurant (1237 Lincoln Ave., 707/942-4400, http://pacificomexicanrestaurant.com, Sun.-Thurs. 11am-9pm, Fri.-Sat. 11am-10pm, $8-12) serves great south-of-the-border fare in a relaxed, easygoing atmosphere. The restaurant, which includes a full bar, feels cool, dark, and cavernous. If the weather is nice, diners can take advantage of the outdoor seating along Cedar Street. Staff are very friendly and attentive, and the fajitas are especially good, as is the chile relleno. The chips are warm, crisp, and fresh, and the house-made salsa is exceptional.

With its high ceilings and stone fireplace decorated with a mounted elk head, **Brannan's Grill** (1374 Lincoln Ave., 707/942-2233, www.brannanscalistoga.com, Sun.-Thurs. 11:30am-9:30pm, Fri.-Sat. 11:30am-10pm, $15-55) feels like an upscale mountain lodge restaurant in Wine Country. It's popular on weekends, with diners waiting to settle into a comfortable booth for a meal that could include grilled quail, rack of lamb, seafood, or one of Brannan's tender steaks. Brannan's is also known for its fine cocktails. On some nights, live jazz bands contribute to the atmosphere.

Information and Services

For discounted wine-tasting vouchers, maps, or tips on the best mud bath, swing by the **Calistoga Visitors Center** (1133 Washington St., 707/942-6333, www.calistogavisitors.org, daily 9am-5pm), in the heart of downtown Calistoga.

The **Vermeil House Clinic** (913 Washington St., 707/942-6233, Mon.-Thurs. 9am-4:30pm, Fri. 9am-3pm) is affiliated with the St. Helena Hospital and treats nonemergency health concerns.

Transportation

Calistoga is eight miles north of St. Helena on Highway 29. In Calistoga, Highway 29 turns east, becoming Lincoln Avenue. To reach the northern end of the Silverado Trail, follow Lincoln Avenue east through town and turn right to intersect it.

Highway 128 also runs through Calistoga, connecting to U.S. 101 north near Healdsburg. To reach Calistoga from U.S. 101 in Santa Rosa, take the exit for Highway 12 east. Turn left on Farmers Lane, and then turn right on Sonoma Highway (Highway 12). Continue driving east on Highway 12 for 2.4 miles to Calistoga Road. Turn left on Calistoga Road and drive 7.1 miles. Calistoga Road intersects Porter Creek Road, becoming Petrified Forest Road for 4.4 miles. Petrified Forest Road intersects with Foothill Boulevard (Hwy. 128) in Calistoga. Turn right and follow Highway 128 south for one mile to Lincoln Avenue, Calistoga's main drag.

Sonoma Valley

The Sonoma and Carneros wine regions are in the southeast part of Sonoma Valley. The scenery features oak forests and vineyard-covered open spaces. The terminus of El Camino Real is in the small city of Sonoma, which includes the famed Sonoma Mission Inn, historic sites, and a charming town square with plenty of shopping and great places to grab a bite. Wineries cluster in this region, though not as many as in the Russian River Valley; the tasting rooms still have plenty of traffic, but the crowds can be less vicious than in the ultra-popular Napa and Dry Creek Valleys.

Carneros might be described as the "lost" area of Wine Country. The wineries are a bit more spread out than in the Napa and Russian

River Valleys, and fewer visitors cram into the tasting rooms. Some prestigious California names make their homes here, and some small boutique vintners quietly produce amazing varietals you won't find outside their tasting rooms.

SONOMA AND CARNEROS

Sonoma Wineries

RAVENSWOOD WINERY

Ravenswood Winery (18701 Gehricke Rd., 888/669-4679, 707/933-2332, www.ravenswood-wine.com, daily 10am-4:30pm, $18) prides itself on making "no wimpy wines." Although owned by a large conglomerate, Ravenswood wines are overseen by the original winemaker, Joel Peterson, who began making California zinfandel in 1976. Zinfandel remains the signature varietal under the Ravenswood label, and many of the prized zins come from individual vineyards in Sonoma County. Ravenswood sponsors a race car, hosts a bevy of summer barbecues, and strives to make tasters of all types feel at home in the winery. Tours and barrel tastings teach newcomers the process of winemaking, while "blend your own" seminars beckon to serious wine connoisseurs. Ravenswood wines are easy on the pocketbook, ranging $13-50 per bottle.

Carneros Wineries

DOMAINE CARNEROS

The Sonoma-Carneros region has perfect conditions for champagne-style grapes, and so the glorious Domaine Carneros (1240 Duhig Rd., Napa, 800/716-2788, www.domaine.com, daily 10am-5:30pm, $30-200) makes its estate home here. Visitors rarely fail to be impressed by the grand estate structure, where both the architecture and garden setting are styled like the great châteaux of France. Even more impressive are the finely crafted sparkling wines and a few pinot noirs the winery creates using grapes from the Carneros region. The Art of Sparkling Wine Tour (daily 11am, 1pm, 3pm, $40) is an excellent opportunity to sample

the best wines, tour the grounds, and see how bubbly is made. Domaine Carneros also offers a seated tasting, adding to the overall atmosphere of sophistication and indulgence. If you want to nibble on something while sipping, select from a cheese or charcuterie plate or a selection of caviar and smoked salmon.

GLORIA FERRER

For a taste of some of the upscale sparkling wines Sonoma can produce, take a long drive through immense estate vineyards to the tasting room at Gloria Ferrer (23555 Hwy. 121/Arnold Dr., Sonoma, 707/933-1917, www.gloriaferrer.com, daily 10am-4:45pm, flights $18-33, glasses $7-20). Ferrer also adheres to the popular format for sparkling wineries—there's no traditional tasting. Visitors order one or more full flutes of sparkling wine, then take a seat at an available table either inside the tasting room or out on the patio overlooking the Sonoma Valley. This style of tasting isn't cheap, but the wines here make the cost worth it for any serious sparkling-wine lover.

SCHUG CARNEROS ESTATE

You might recognize the labels at the Schug Carneros Estate (602 Bonneau Rd., Sonoma, 800/966-9365, www.schugwinery.com, daily 10am-5pm, $10). One of the Carneros region's elders, Walter Schug has made wine that has set the tone for California vintages for many years. The estate itself is worth a visit; the Tudor-esque barn sits on the valley floor in the middle of barns and fields of brilliant-yellow flowering mustard, with views of the surrounding mountains all around. Schug's hallmarks are chardonnays and pinot noirs, grapes that grow well in this cooler region, so try the latest releases of both.

Sights

★ MISSION SAN FRANCISCO SOLANO DE SONOMA

Mission San Francisco Solano de Sonoma (114 E. Spain St., 707/938-9560, www.sonomaparks.org, daily 10am-5pm, adults $3, children 6-17 $2) is the northernmost of the

Sonoma Valley

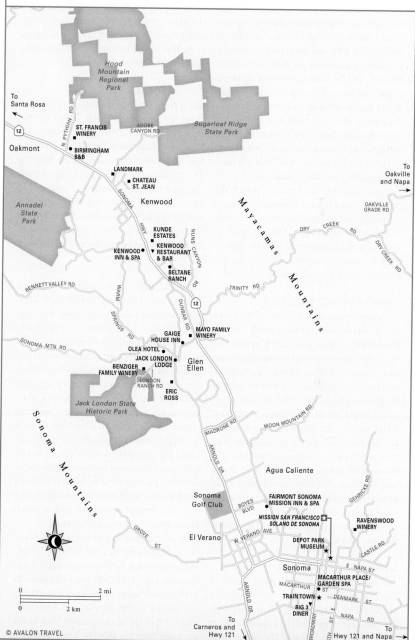

To Santa Rosa

Oakmont

12

Hood Mountain Regional Park

N PYTHIAN RD

ST. FRANCIS WINERY

ADOBE CANYON RD

BIRMINGHAM B&B

LANDMARK

CHATEAU ST. JEAN

Sugarloaf Ridge State Park

To Oakville and Napa

OAKVILLE GRADE RD

Kenwood

SONOMA HWY

Annadel State Park

KUNDE ESTATES

NUNS CANYON RD

DRY CREEK RD

DRY CREEK RD

KENWOOD INN & SPA

KENWOOD RESTAURANT & BAR

BELTANE RANCH

BENNETT VALLEY RD

TRINITY RD

Mayacamas Mountains

WARM SPRINGS RD

SONOMA MTN. RD

DUNBAR RD

12

GAIGE HOUSE INN

MAYO FAMILY WINERY

OLEA HOTEL

JACK LONDON LODGE

Glen Ellen

BENZIGER FAMILY WINERY

LONDON RANCH RD

ERIC ROSS

Jack London State Historic Park

Sonoma Mountains

MADRONE RD

MOON MOUNTAIN RD

ARNOLD DR

Agua Caliente

Sonoma Golf Club

BOYES BLVD

FAIRMONT SONOMA MISSION INN & SPA

GEHRICKE RD

MISSION SAN FRANCISCO SOLANO DE SONOMA

RAVENSWOOD WINERY

GROVE ST

W. VERANO AVE

El Verano

DEPOT PARK MUSEUM

CASTLE RD

Sonoma

MACARTHUR PLACE/ GARDEN SPA

MACARTHUR ST

E NAPA ST

ARNOLD DR

TRAIN TOWN

BIG 3 DINER

DENMARK ST

BROADWAY

5TH ST E

NAPA RD

0   2 mi

0   2 km

To Carneros and Hwy 121

To Hwy 121 and Napa

© AVALON TRAVEL

chain of Spanish missions in California. It is at the corner of the historic plaza in downtown Sonoma—a low, surprisingly unpretentious block of buildings without much in the way of decoration or crowds. The last mission established, in 1823, and one of the first restored as a historic landmark, in 1926, the Sonoma Mission isn't the prettiest or most elaborate of the 21 missions. But museum-style exhibits depict the life of the missionaries and Native Americans who lived here. Rest on benches by the fountain, observe a moment of silence at the Native American mortuary monument, or check out the cactus "wall" that has been growing here since the mission era.

California's state flag first came to be in the tiny rural mission town of Sonoma. To commemorate that historic beginning, the **Bear Flag Monument** (Sonoma Plaza, E. Spain St. and 1st St. E.) was erected. Visit the monument as you stroll the plaza or explore the various sites of the Sonoma State Historic Park.

CORNERSTONE GARDENS

For a break from all the history of Sonoma's main attractions, take a walk in the **Cornerstone Gardens** (23570 Arnold Dr., 707/933-3010, www.cornerstonegardens.com, daily 10am-5pm, free). This unique installation combines an art gallery with the work of the foremost landscape and garden designers in the world. Stroll these unusual gardens, which range from traditional plantings to postmodern multimedia installations, and then finish up your excursion with a crawl through the boutiques, upscale food shops, and wine bars that have recently sprung up around them. Daily wine-tastings and various snacks and nonalcoholic drinks provide welcome refreshment, especially on hot Sonoma summer afternoons.

DEPOT PARK MUSEUM

For more Sonoma history, make a stop at the **Depot Park Museum** (270 1st St. W., 707/938-1762, http://depotparkmuseum.org, Fri.-Sun. 1pm-4pm, free) right down the street from the plaza and around the corner from the mission. The museum hosts a small set of exhibits inside a reproduction of the historic Northwestern Pacific Railroad depot, hence the name. Inside are reconstructions of the active depot in the Rand Room, a showcase of the Bear Flag Rebellion, and exhibits on the life of the indigenous Miwok people.

TRAIN TOWN

Got a train enthusiast in the family? Take them to Sonoma's **Train Town** (20264 Broadway/Hwy. 12, www.traintown.com, June-Sept. daily 10am-5pm, Sept.-May Fri.-Sun. 10am-5pm, train rides $6.25). Ride the 15-inch scale train over four miles of track that goes through tunnels, over bridges, and into a miniature town complete with a petting zoo. Or opt for a spin on the roller coaster or the Ferris wheel, or a climb up the clock tower for a magnificent view of the park and beyond.

Spas

The most famous spa in the area is the **Willow Stream Spa** (100 Boyes Blvd., 877/289-7354, www.fairmont.com/sonoma, Mon.-Fri. 7am-7pm, Sat.-Sun. 7:30am-8pm, massages $169-289). A natural mineral hot spring beneath the Sonoma Mission Inn provides warm water for the indoor and outdoor pools and whirlpools that create the center of the spa's signature Bathing Ritual. Whether you choose a relaxing massage or a challenging yoga class, arrive at least an hour early to allow time for each step of the ritual. The spa offers an almost bewildering variety of massages, scrubs, wraps, facials, and even more rarified treatments designed to pamper even the most discerning spa-goer. The facilities are surrounded by the inn and a gourmet restaurant, both of which draw visitors from around the world.

At the **Garden Spa at MacArthur Place** (29 E. MacArthur St., 707/933-3193, www.macarthurplace.com/spa.php, daily 9am-8pm, massages $125-240), you won't just take in the serene beauty of the inn's lush garden; you will be healed, rejuvenated, and beautified. All of the spa's signature treatments are made from the flowers, herbs, and fruit found in the garden, distilled into such luscious effusions as pomegranate body polish, golden passionflower body wrap, peppermint foot soak, and the red-wine grape-seed bath. The spa also offers a mud-bath soak, a number of different massages, and facial and waxing treatments. Book treatments at least two weeks in advance, as space in this fragrant spa fills up fast.

Shopping

There's no more pleasant place to stroll, window shop, or browse for an extravagant trinket than in Sonoma. Around its leafy square are famous structures and state parks, little cafés and eateries, and yes, shops. Lots and lots of shops. Many are on the four main streets bordering the square, but most you will have to hunt for in the nooks and crannies inside the remodeled historic buildings and tiny retail alleyways on each block.

Despite the name, **Large Leather** (481 1st St. W., 707/938-1042, www.large-leather. com, daily 10am-7pm) is a pint-size store filled with purses, backpacks, belts, wallets, and bracelets. Anything you can think of that is or can be made out of leather can be found here. All items are handcrafted and designed by the owners, Paul Terwilliger and Jessica Zoutendijik.

A different kind of cooking store, **Bram** (493 1st St. W., 707/935-3717, www.bram-cookware.com, Thurs.-Mon. 10am-6pm, Tues. 10am-5pm) is devoted entirely to claypot cooking. Dark shelves are stocked with a beautiful selection of deep skillets, stew pots, rondeaux, open casseroles, tagines, rectangular bakers, brams, and roasters. Shoppers will be astounded by the range and diversity of the clay pots available. If you are at a loss for how to use such a beautiful pot, stacks of cookbooks fill the other side of the shop. The extremely knowledgeable staff are eager to share their experiences and preferences.

For handcrafted artistry with a bit more polish, stroll down to **Sonoma Silver Company** (491 1st St. W., 707/933-0999, www.sonomasilver.com, daily 11am-6pm), a

slender shop awash in silver rings, pendants, bracelets, and earrings. Multiple local jewelers sell and showcase their work here, but many of the shiny trinkets are made in-house by the company's resident jeweler of 20 years.

See other local artwork at the **Fairmont Gallery** (447 1st St. W., 707/996-2667, www. fairmontgallery.com, Thurs.-Sun. noon-5pm). Mostly concentrating in oil paintings and other classic brush-on-canvas fine art, the intimate space, set up in an old A-frame house, is a pleasant reprieve from other bustling shops.

Accommodations
$150-250

For a charming guest room at reasonable rates within the Sonoma town limits, stay at **Sonoma Creek Inn** (239 Boyes Blvd., 888/712-1289, www.sonomacreekinn.com, $145-225). The whimsical, colorful decor and unique art pieces brighten each guest room and each guest's stay. Amenities include cable TV, free wireless Internet access, and a fridge. Some rooms also have private garden patios. A few minutes from downtown Sonoma and convenient to the Carneros wineries, the inn is perfect for travelers who want to spend on wine and dining rather than a motel room.

Right on Sonoma Plaza in the heart of Sonoma, **Sonoma's Best Guest Cottages** (1190 E. Napa St., 707/933-0340, www.les-petitesmaisons.com, $199-399) offers four cute cottages for a homey stay in the Wine Country. Each cottage has its own style, but all have warm colors and comfy furniture to evoke the relaxation needed for a perfect vacation. All the cottages have fully equipped kitchens that allow you to cook your own fresh food after a visit to the fabulous Sonoma farmers markets. There's also a private patio with an outdoor fireplace and grill for spending some time outside.

In 1850 one of the first Spanish settlers in the Sonoma area built a home for his family on the town square, and for most of the last century, the **Swiss Hotel** (18 W. Spain St., 707/938-2884, www.swisshotelsonoma.

com, $150-240) in the structure has offered beds and meals to travelers. The five rooms are light, bright, and airy, with fresh paint and pretty floral comforters. Downstairs, enjoy a meal at the restaurant or have a drink at the historic bar, and then step outside to take a walk around the historic plaza.

For the price and the character, the **Sonoma Hotel** (110 W. Spain St., 800/468-6016, www.sonomahotel.com, $130-288) can't be beat. Built in 1880, the hotel is one of Sonoma's landmark buildings. The interior is decorated in the fashion of the era, with high wood wainscoting, cream-colored walls, polished antiques, and elegant light fixtures. The rooms, all with private baths (a rarity in historic digs), are similarly outfitted in trim Victorian fixtures, and many have sloped ceilings, creating a cozy and intimate atmosphere.

Not nearly as historic but conveniently located just a few blocks from the square is **El Pueblo Inn** (896 W. Napa St., 707/996-3651, www.elpuebloinn.com, $199-379). In true Spanish style, some rooms face a lush central courtyard. The grounds also have a pool and a hot tub that are open 24 hours. Some rooms boast walls of adobe bricks or lounge areas with fireplaces, but many are standard hotel accommodations—clean and modestly decorated. For the price and location, not to mention views of the garden, it's a good deal. The inn also offers a fitness room, complimentary breakfast, and an in-room safe. Another standout is the down comforters.

OVER $250

Neither historic nor centrally located, the **Fairmont Sonoma Mission Inn & Spa** (100 Boyes Blvd., 707/938-9000, www.fairmont.com/sonoma, $329-640) has another appeal: luxury. Of course, there is the spa, an 18-hole golf course, and the Michelin-starred restaurant, but the rooms themselves are enough. Your guest room is the kind of place you'll want to return to after a long day of sipping wine or soaking in a mud bath, decorated in smooth Provençal yellows with the occasional

brown or red thrown in and featuring four-poster beds with deep mattresses covered in down comforters. Some rooms have fireplaces, while others feature marble bathtubs; many overlook gardens.

Food
CALIFORNIA CUISINE

Hot spot **Harvest Moon Café** (487 1st St. W., 707/933-8160, http://harvestmooncafe-sonoma.com, Sun.-Mon. and Wed.-Thurs. 5:30pm-9pm, Fri.-Sat. 5:30pm-9:30pm, $19-32) has a beautiful outdoor patio and a seasonal, local-focused menu. The menu of this charmingly casual restaurant changes daily to take advantage of the best ingredients available. The owners previously worked at the Bay Area dining institutions Chez Panisse and BayWolf.

Need a hearty breakfast or brunch before you get going on a full day of wine-tasting? Stop in at the **Big 3 Diner** (18140 Hwy. 12, 707/939-2410, www.fairmont.com/sonoma, daily 7am-2pm, $11-25). The restaurant is part of the Fairmont Sonoma Mission Inn property, which explains both the high prices and the upscale cuisine. But it's good stuff—the kitchen uses high-quality, often organic and local ingredients to create its fancy benedicts and sandwiches. Even locals approve, coming in to be greeted by name by the friendly and efficient staff. If you're staying at the Sonoma Mission Inn, order room service from Big 3 or walk over to the large dining room, which is outfitted with wooden chairs and tables and maintains a pleasant, casual atmosphere.

COFFEE AND TEA

If you just need a cup of coffee and maybe a quick pastry, stop in at the **Barking Dog Coffee Roasters** (18133 Sonoma Hwy., 707/996-7446, www.barkingdogcoffee.com, Mon.-Fri. 6:30am-7pm, Sat.-Sun. 7am-7pm). Barking Dog is where locals go to get their morning mochas. Sip a latte or indulge in a scoop of Caffe Classico gelato or a smoothie, take a seat on a comfy old couch, and maybe even enjoy some live music.

FRENCH

A favorite with the local-sustainable-organic food crowd, ★ **The Girl and the Fig** (110 W. Spain St., 707/938-3634, www.thegirland-thefig.com, Fri.-Sat. 11:30am-11pm, Sun. 10am-10pm, Mon.-Thurs. 11:30am-10pm, $19-27) is right on Sonoma Plaza. The menu changes often to take advantage of the best local seasonal ingredients; for a special treat, order one of the amazing cheese plates or the three-course Bistro Plat du Jour. If you love the sauces and jams, look for The Girl and the Fig products on-site and at wineries and high-end food shops throughout Wine Country.

PORTUGUESE

Locals and travelers agree that traditional Portuguese eatery ★ **LaSalette** (452 1st St. E., 707/938-1927, www.lasalette-restaurant.com, Mon.-Thurs. 11:30am-2:30pm and 5pm-9pm, Sat.-Sun. 11:30am-9pm, $22-30) is the town favorite. It has a simple and charming atmosphere, with a wood-fired oven facing a curving bar. A large outdoor patio is the most popular seating area in summer, although the meandering tile-floored dining room offers plenty of appeal plus a bonus view of the open kitchen. The undisputed star of LaSalette is the food. The Portuguese menu features fresh fish and hearty meat dishes plus good meatless options. Simple yet delectable preparations let the principal ingredients shine. They're happy to accommodate special requests.

MARKETS

For travelers preparing most of their own meals, or if you're looking for gluten-free grains to take home, the **Fruit Basket** (24101 Arnold Dr., 707/938-4332, daily 8am-6pm) open-air market has a great selection. This isn't a local farm stand—much of the produce is emphatically not local, especially in the winter. But the array of dried beans and grains would put a San Francisco health-food store to shame, making it easy for people with celiac disease and those with food allergies to find great make-it-yourself food options. The Fruit Basket serves as a fully stocked market,

selling imported Italian and Mexican foods, dairy products, wines, and fresh fruits and vegetables. The only staple they don't stock is fresh meat. Prices are reasonable, and the market's location at the south end of the Sonoma-Carneros wine region is easy to access.

Information and Services

Before you begin your Sonoma and Carneros wine-tasting adventure, stop in at the 1st Street **Sonoma Valley Visitors Center** (453 1st St. E., 866/996-1090, www.sonomavalley.com, Mon.-Sat. 9am-5pm, Sun. 10am-5pm) or the Arnold Drive location (23570 Arnold Dr., 866/996-1090, daily 10am-4pm). Ask the volunteers for advice on which wineries to visit, and pick up some complimentary tasting passes.

The **Sonoma Valley Hospital** (347 Andrieux St., 707/935-5000, www.svh.com) has a full-service emergency room.

Transportation

The town of Sonoma is over the mountains west of the Napa Valley. The main route through the valley is Highway 12, also called the Sonoma Highway. To reach Sonoma from Napa, drive south on Highway 29 and turn west onto Highway 12/121. Turn north on Highway 12 to reach downtown Sonoma.

From the Bay Area, take U.S. 101 north to Highway 37 east. Highway 37 branches sharply north to become Highway 121, then Highway 116 as it winds into the city of Sonoma. Driving south on U.S. 101, turn onto Highway 12 south in Santa Rosa and take a scenic journey down into the Sonoma-Carneros wine region.

Parking in downtown Sonoma is easy in the off-season and tougher in the high season (May-Oct.). Expect to hunt for a spot during local events and be prepared to walk several blocks. Most wineries provide ample free parking on their grounds.

For your public transit needs, use the buses run by **Sonoma County Transit** (SCT, 707/576-7433, 800/345-7433, www.sctransit.

Raceway Traffic

Think you can safely ignore Sonoma Raceway's schedule because you don't give a darn about auto or bike racing? Not if you're wise in the ways of event traffic. The turnoff to **Sonoma Raceway** lies roughly at the intersection of Highways 37 and 121. These charming and scenic two-lane roads are great for motoring and sightseeing—unless, of course, you're stuck in bumper-to-bumper race traffic. The absolute worst time to try to drive either of these roads (particularly Hwy. 37 out of Sonoma) is when a major race event has finished. The wretched traffic jams, which truly are more stop than go, can last for hours as people try to exit the racetrack into the unprotected intersection. In the summer, the sweltering heat causes both engines and tempers to overheat, to no good end.

So what can you do?

· Check the race schedule (www.racesonoma.com), and avoid the roads in question for at least four hours after the scheduled or estimated end of a big race.

· Plot another route to your next destination, or stick around in Sonoma until well after the traffic is likely to have unsnarled. (Give it about six hours post-race.)

· Escape via Highway 12 east to Napa or west to Santa Rosa. From Santa Rosa, catch Highway 101 south to Marin or San Francisco or north toward the Russian River. If heading to Napa, pick up Highway 37 off of Highway 101 and then follow it south to Highway 80. Highway 80 will either take you south to the East Bay or east into Sacramento and beyond.

com, $1.25-3.65). Several routes serve the Sonoma Valley daily. Use SCT to get from Sonoma Valley to Santa Rosa, Guerneville, and other parts of the Russian River Valley as well.

Visitors can take a vineyard tour with **Sonoma Segway** (524 Broadway, 707/938-2080, www.sonomasegway.com, tours $129), which offers a 4.5-hour Segway tour that includes a visit to a local winery, a stop at a local food-based business, and a visit to historic Sonoma. The tour starts with a lesson on the Segway, and when you finish you'll get a complimentary bottle of wine if you're of age. If you'd prefer to explore the Sonoma streets and paths on your own, rent a Segway—rentals are available from two hours and up.

GLEN ELLEN

North of the town of Sonoma, the valley becomes more and more rural. The next hamlet on Highway 12 is Glen Ellen (population 784), which is surrounded by a couple of regional parks and Jack London State Historic Park, named for one of the town's famous residents (the other big name is Hunter S.

Thompson). Downtown Glen Ellen has not caught the Wine County bug of boutique shops, Michelin-starred restaurants, and over-the-top spas; instead, it still feels like a rural farm town with a few historic structures thrown in for character.

Wineries
MAYO FAMILY WINERY
Breaking from the chardonnay-cab-merlot juggernaut of Sonoma, the **Mayo Family Winery** (13101 Arnold Dr., at Hwy. 12, 707/938-9401, www.mayofamilywinery.com, daily 10:30am-6:30pm, tastings $8-12) produces an array of interesting Italian-style varietals. Here you might taste smoky rich Carignane or barbera, enjoy a fruity white viognier, or savor the chianti-based sangiovese. Mayo Family boasts a big presence in the region, with an on-site tasting room and, up north in Kenwood, the prized reserve tasting room (9200 Sonoma Hwy., Kenwood, daily 10:30am-6:30pm, reservations recommended, $40). At the reserve tasting room, your experience includes seven pours of Mayo's best wines, each paired with a small

bite of gourmet California cuisine created by chefs on-site.

VALLEY OF THE MOON

History mixes with the highest winemaking technology California has to offer at **Valley of the Moon** (777 Madrone Rd., 707/939-4510, www.valleyofthemoonwinery.com, daily 10am-5pm, $15-30), Since the Civil War era, this Sonoma institution has passed through many hands and produced hundreds of wines. The circa-1860s stone buildings house late-model stainless-steel fermentation tanks as well as classic oak barrels. In the tasting room is a small list of boutique wines, from an unusual sangiovese rosé to a classic California cabernet. Valley of the Moon takes pride in its awards, and you'll find that almost every wine you taste has its own list of medals. Check the website for a list of upcoming wine events that show off this great Sonoma landmark at its best.

Sports and Recreation
JACK LONDON STATE HISTORIC PARK

Literary travelers come to Sonoma not just for the fine food and abundant wine but for the chance to visit **Jack London State Historic Park** (2400 London Ranch Rd., 707/938-5216, www.jacklondonpark.com, daily 9:30am-5pm, $10). Famed author Jack London did in fact live and write at this spot in rural Sonoma County at the beginning of the 20th century. Docents offer tours of the park, which include talks on London's life and history. Explore the surviving buildings on London's prized Beauty Ranch or hike up Sonoma Mountain and check out the artificial lake and bathhouse. The pretty stone **House of Happy Walls** (daily 10am-5pm), a creation of London's wife, houses a small museum. There's no camping at Jack London State Historic Park, but you can bring a picnic to enjoy on the attractive grounds.

With its vineyards, open spaces, and state parks, the Sonoma Valley begs to be explored on horseback in homage to its pioneering

history. The **Triple Creek Horse Outfit** (707/887-8700, www.triplecreekhorseoutfit.com, $75-275) offers guided rides on the 1,850-acre Kunde Ranch.

SUGARLOAF RIDGE STATE PARK

Mossy waterfalls, hillside grasslands bordered by oaks, exposed rock outcroppings, and even Sonoma Creek's headwaters can be found at **Sugarloaf Ridge State Park** (2605 Adobe Canyon Rd., 707/833-5712, www.sugarloafpark.org, daily 6am-8pm, adults $8, seniors $7), just outside Kenwood. Despite its beauty, Sugarloaf is rarely visited, so if you're seeking solitude in nature, this may be your place. There are plenty of trails to suit your mood and hiking ability; meander down **Creekside Nature Trail** (1 mile, easy) or take **Canyon Trail** (1.6 miles, easy) to the waterfall, which descends 25 feet through mossy boulders beneath a canopy of redwoods. More athletic hikers can take **Vista Trail Loop** (4.1 miles, moderate-difficult) to the Indian Rock outcropping, which has a lovely view of the canyon below. To hike this trail, take Stern Trail to Bald Mountain Trail and turn right. Eventually, take another right on Vista Trail and cross the mountain, taking another right on Grey Pine Trail. Turn right again on Meadow Trail to return to the parking lot.

The crown jewel of the park, however, is Bald Mountain. Although only 2,729 feet high, the mountain sports views of nearly all of Wine Country as well as the Golden Gate and Sierra Nevada on clear days. The hike to the summit is not that challenging: **Bald Mountain Loop** (6.6 miles, moderate-difficult) begins at Stern Trail, and eventually you take a right turn onto Bald Mountain Trail and follow it to the top. To descend, turn right on Grey Pine Trail, and then make another right onto Meadow Trail.

While the lower part of the park has a lush, heavy canopy, the upper trails are quite exposed and can get hot in the summer and early fall. Bring sunscreen, a hat, plenty of water, and a map, as the trails can be confusing.

Sugarloaf is also home to the **Robert**

Ferguson Observatory (www.rfo.org), which has three telescopes to take in the night skies. From January to November, the observatory hosts monthly star parties. Check the website for upcoming star parties and night-sky classes.

Accommodations

With its wraparound porches and lush gardens, the **Beltane Ranch** (11775 Hwy. 12, 707/996-6501, www.beltaneranch. com, $215-305) looks like it belongs near Savannah, Georgia, rather than Sonoma. But this Valley of the Moon charmer sits in the middle of Wine Country, with five rooms and a detached cottage. After a good night's sleep in the pristine country-style rooms, guests enjoy a sumptuous breakfast in the dining room or on the porch overlooking the gardens and vineyards beyond. Guests are free to utilize the ranch's tennis court and walking trails.

For a bit of Asian-infused relaxation, stay at one of the best-reviewed inns in Wine Country: the ★ **Gaige House Inn** (13540 Arnold Dr., 800/935-0237, www.gaige.com, $275-595), which offers comfort and luxury built into the design of the rooms and common spaces. Special attention is paid to every detail, and each of the 23 rooms and suites resemble a spread in an interior-design magazine; suites have baths the size of bedrooms and their own tiny garden spaces. Outdoors is a pool and hot tub, while a breakfast buffet is laid out every morning.

Attached to the redbrick Jack London Saloon and Wolf House Restaurant, the **Jack London Lodge** (13740 Arnold Dr., 707/938-8510, www.jacklondonlodge.com, $130-195) anchors this part of downtown Glen Ellen. The 22-room lodge is modern, with a broad patio, a kidney-shaped pool, and groomed lawns. The inn's interior offers a more Victorian feel with dark wood furniture, rich floral linens, and low lighting, but the history of the building shines through. Vines draping the balcony are a nice touch, as is the hot tub and the creek running through the back of the property. They also rent the Warm Springs Cottage ($400-450), a three-bedroom rental in the woods that is minutes from the main lodge.

Food

At the **Glen Ellen Inn Restaurant** (13670 Arnold Dr., 707/996-6409, www.glenelleninn. com, Thurs.-Tues. 11:30am-9pm, Wed. 5pm-9pm, $14-26), French bistro cuisine meets California gastropub. You'll find this self-described oyster grill and martini bar's dining room inside a cute low building. In addition to the seafood-heavy gourmet menu, the Glen Ellen Inn boasts a full bar and a wine list worthy of its location.

The Fig Café (13690 Arnold Dr., 707/938-2130, www.thegirlandthefig.com, Mon.-Thurs. 5pm-9pm, Fri. 5pm-9:30pm, Sat. 10am-2:30pm and 5pm-9:30pm, Sun. 10am-2:30pm and 5pm-9pm, $13-24) serves the same excellent food as its namesake restaurant in Sonoma but slightly scaled down. The menu leans toward comfort food, with grilled sandwiches, thin-crust pizzas, and a laid-back wine bar. The warm interior and weekend brunch makes it a sure bet.

Information and Services

The small town of Glen Ellen does not have a visitors center, so stock up on maps and tips before you leave Sonoma. Some of the local inns and hotels can also provide some information.

Don't expect to find much in the way of wireless Internet access or reliable cell-phone reception.

Transportation

Glen Ellen is just off Highway 12, seven miles north of Sonoma. Arnold Drive is the main street through town, and it runs all the way south to Sonoma. To reach Glen Ellen from Santa Rosa, take Highway 12 east through Kenwood for 15.7 miles.

It is also possible to jump over to Glen Ellen from Highway 29 in Oakville. In Oakville, turn west onto Oakville Grade. After 3.2

miles, Oakville Grade becomes Dry Creek Road; the name changes again to Trinity Road in 2.8 miles. Keep to the right on Trinity Road, and in three miles you'll reach Sonoma Highway (Hwy. 12), where you turn left toward Glen Ellen.

Russian River Valley

The Russian River Valley may be the prettiest part of Wine Country. The Russian River runs through it, providing ample water for forests and meadows. There are wide, calm spots with sandy banks, while rafting, canoeing, and kayaking opportunities abound on the zippier stretches of the river. If you are visiting for the vino, the area called the Russian River Valley actually encompasses several prestigious American Viticultural Areas, including Dry Creek, Alexander Valley, and, of course, Russian River. Wineries are clustered along three main roads: the Gravenstein Highway (Hwy. 116), River Road, and U.S. 101.

A little to the west of the area's concentrated wine region, you'll reach the river in Guerneville, a noted gay and lesbian resort destination. Even if you're straight (but not narrow), you'll love the kitschy downtown, clothing-optional resorts, and general sense of friendliness and fun that permeates the area.

SANTA ROSA

Santa Rosa is the biggest city in Wine Country and the largest in the North Bay. As such, it is more preoccupied with big-city issues than with wine-tasting. This is a mixed-income area where many people work in building trades and other blue-collar professions. It is also ethnically diverse, with a large Latino population as well as strong Southeast Asian communities. Developed at the turn of the 20th century, the older neighborhoods are filled with charming Craftsman-style bungalows. Downtown boasts some historic buildings, but many did not survive the big earthquakes of 1906 and 1969. Santa Rosa's large size means that there are plenty of things to do with the kids, such as the Charles Shultz and Pacific Air Museums.

Sights
CHARLES M. SCHULZ MUSEUM

Schulz drew the world-famous *Peanuts* comic strip for almost 50 years, and from 1958 until his death in 2000 he lived in Sonoma County. The **Charles M. Schulz Museum** (2301 Hardies Lane, 707/579-4452, www.schulzmuseum.org, Memorial Day-Labor Day Mon.-Fri. 11am-5pm, Sat.-Sun. 10am-5pm, Labor Day-Memorial Day Mon. and Wed.-Fri. 11am-5pm, Sat.-Sun. 10am-5pm, adults $10, seniors and ages 4-18 $5, under age 3 free) honors Schulz and the *Peanuts* gang. Inside the 27,000-square-foot building, which looks like it comes from a four-inch comic strip, is an incredible wealth of multimedia art, original drawings, and changing exhibitions based on Schulz's work. The museum owns most of the original *Peanuts* strips, a large collection of Schulz's personal possessions, and an astonishing array of tribute artwork from other comic-strip artists. The grounds include attractive gardens, the Snoopy Labyrinth, and even the infamous Kite-eating Tree.

Schulz's influence is felt outside the museum property as well. Across the street, visitors can skate at **Snoopy's Home Ice**—Schulz was an avid hockey player. Throughout downtown Santa Rosa, especially in Historic Railroad Square, colorful sculptures depict members of the *Peanuts* gang.

LUTHER BURBANK HOME AND GARDENS

If you love plants and gardening, don't miss the **Luther Burbank Home and Gardens** (204 Santa Rosa Ave., 707/524-5445, www.lutherburbank.org, gardens year-round daily 8am-dusk, free, tours Apr.-Oct. Tues.-Sun. 10am-4pm, adults $7, children under 12

Russian River Valley

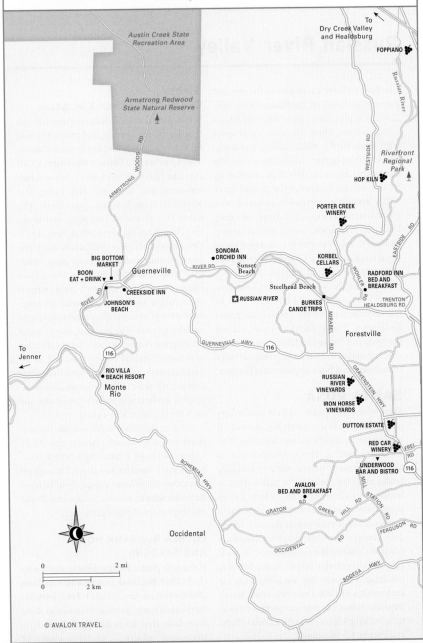

To Dry Creek Valley and Healdsburg

FOPPIANO

Austin Creek State Recreation Area

Armstrong Redwood State Natural Reserve

Russian River

Westside Rd

Riverfront Regional Park

HOP KILN

ARMSTRONG WOODS RD

PORTER CREEK WINERY

Eastside Rd

BIG BOTTOM MARKET

SONOMA ORCHID INN

KORBEL CELLARS

BOON EAT + DRINK

Guerneville

RIVER RD

Sunset Beach

WOHLER RD

RADFORD INN BED AND BREAKFAST

CREEKSIDE INN

Steelhead Beach

TRENTON HEALDSBURG RD

RIVER RD

JOHNSON'S BEACH

RUSSIAN RIVER

BURKES CANOE TRIPS

Forestville

MIRABEL RD

GUERNEVILLE HWY

116

To Jenner

116

RIO VILLA BEACH RESORT

Monte Rio

RUSSIAN RIVER VINEYARDS

GRAVENSTEIN HWY

IRON HORSE VINEYARDS

DUTTON ESTATE

RED CAR WINERY

FREI RD

UNDERWOOD BAR AND BISTRO

116

BOHEMIAN HWY

AVALON BED AND BREAKFAST

MILL STATION RD

GRATON RD

GREEN HILL RD

FERGUSON RD

Occidental

OCCIDENTAL RD

BODEGA HWY

0   2 mi

0   2 km

© AVALON TRAVEL

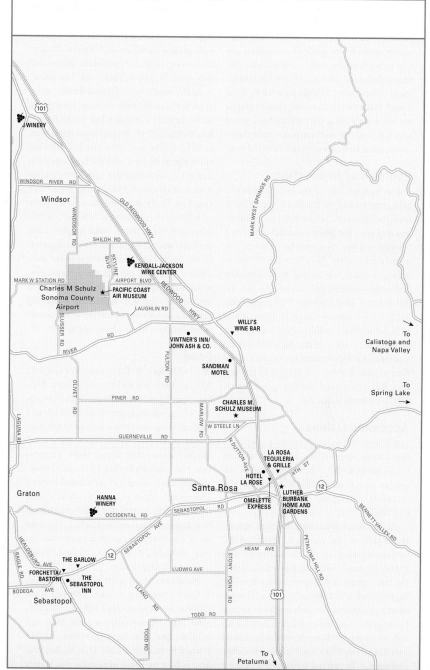

free). Using hybridization techniques, Luther Burbank created some of the most popular plants grown in California gardens and landscapes today. In the garden's more than one acre of horticulture, which also includes medicinal herbs and showy roses, glimpse the famous Shasta daisy, a hardy pure-white daisy hybrid that now blankets vast areas throughout the state. Check the website for a list of what's in bloom; something is sure to be showing its finest flowers every month of the year.

Sports and Recreation

Just as in Napa, one of the popular ways to get a great view of the Russian River Valley is from the basket of a hot-air balloon. Granted, you and your hangover must fall out of bed before dawn for this particular treat—so you might want to make this a first-day adventure before you start wine-tasting. **Wine Country Balloons** (meeting site Kal's Kaffe Mocha, 397 Aviation Blvd., 707/538-7359 or 800/759-5638, www.balloontours.com, daily, adults $225, seniors $215, children $195) can get you up in the air to start the day high above Wine Country. This big company maintains a whole fleet of balloons that can carry 2-16 passengers. Expect the total time to be 3-4 hours, with 1-1.5 hours in the air.

Accommodations

You'll find all the familiar chain motels in Santa Rosa. You'll also see a few charming inns and upper-tier hotels that show off the unique aspects of the city that serves as the transition from the Bay Area to true Northern California.

At the corner of Historic Railroad Square, **Hotel la Rose** (308 Wilson St., 800/527-6738, www.hotellarose.com, $129-285) exemplifies the luxury-hotel concept as it has evolved over the last century. The stone-clad main building rises high over Railroad Square, with more rooms available in the more modern carriage house just across the street. The hotel, with only 48 rooms, gives an attention to detail and a level of service that's missing in larger motels and hotels. The carriage house offers modern

decor and amenities, and each large room and suite feels light and bright. The main building possesses an older style of elegance, with antique furniture and floral wallpaper. Downstairs is on-site restaurant Bistro 1907 (Sun.-Wed. 7am-9pm, Thurs.-Sat. 7am-10pm).

At the north end of Santa Rosa, convenient to the major Russian River wine roads, is the upscale **Vintners Inn** (4350 Barnes Rd., 800/421-2584, http://vintnersinn.com, $275-620). The low, attractive red-tile-roof buildings of the inn and the fabulous John Ash & Co. restaurant are adjacent to a large stretch of vineyard. Every guest room has a king bed, fluffy down bedding, and a patio or balcony overlooking a cute garden-like courtyard. Many rooms boast fireplaces and spa tubs, and all feature luxurious appointments. Your stay includes access to the inn's outdoor whirlpool tub and the common den, which has a fireplace. The only downside to the Vintners Inn is its regrettable proximity to a local power station; just try to look in the other direction when admiring the view.

Food

★ **John Ash & Co.** (4350 Barnes Rd., 707/527-7687, www.vintnersinn.com, Fri.-Sat. 5pm-9pm, Sun.-Thurs. 5pm-8:30pm, $14-43) stands out as one of the best high-end California cuisine restaurants in the region. The large, elegant dining room, done up in Mediterranean style, is part of the Vintners Inn. The food, made with local and sustainable produce, shows off its natural flavors. The menu is short, making it easy to choose from the three courses that highlight seafood, beef, lamb, and seasonal specialties. The wine list is something special, with some amazing local vintages that are tough to find outside the Russian River Valley.

Need something a bit more casual? Get in line for breakfast, brunch, or lunch at the **Omelette Express** (112 4th St., 707/525-1690, http://omeletteexpress.com, Mon.-Fri. 6:30am-3pm, Sat.-Sun. 7am-4pm, $8-14). Owned by local character Don Taylor, who acts as host on some weekends, this spot is favored by locals. The very casual dining rooms are decorated with the front ends of classic cars, and the menu involves lots of omelets. Portions are huge and come with a side of toast made with homemade bread, so consider splitting one with a friend.

In downtown's Railroad Square area, **Jackson's Bar and Oven** (135 4th St., www.jacksonsbarandoven.com, Mon.-Thurs. 11:30am-10pm, Fri.-Sat. 11:30am-11pm, Sun. 11:30am-9pm, $14-22) is a popular spot for tasty cocktails, food, and, no surprise, wine. Dine on Jackson's small bites, salads, sandwiches, and entrées at the curved bar or at a table. Or, even better, order up one of their tasty wood-fired pizzas.

Information and Services
As a major city, Santa Rosa has plenty of medical services available. If you need help, try **Santa Rosa Memorial Hospital** (1165 Montgomery Ave., 707/525-5300, www.stjosephhealth.org), which has an emergency room.

Transportation
Santa Rosa is 50 miles north of San Francisco on U.S. 101. Be aware that traffic on this major corridor can get congested, particularly during the morning commute and 3pm-7pm Monday-Friday. It also slows on sunny summer afternoons when people go to cool themselves along the Russian River. Fortunately, the side roads that lead to various tasting rooms and recreation spots are seldom crowded.

From U.S. 101, take exit 489 toward downtown Santa Rosa to reach the historic district; downtown is east of the freeway. Wineries are on the west side of town and can be accessed by taking Highway 12 west, and also by the U.S. 101 exits for River Road and Guerneville.

Golden Gate Transit (415/455-2000, http://goldengatetransit.org, adults $12.50, children and seniors $6.25) runs buses between San Francisco and Santa Rosa on routes 72 and 74. These routes are geared toward commuters who work in San Francisco,

so the southbound buses run in the morning and those going north run in the afternoon.

Pilots can fly into regional **Charles M. Schultz-Sonoma County Airport** (STS, 2290 Airport Blvd., 707/565-7240, www.sonomacountyairport.org).

SEBASTOPOL
Low-key and a bit alternative, Sebastopol is undoubtedly the artistic heart of Sonoma County. The relatively modest digs, low cost of living, liberal politics, natural beauty, and small-town vibe have attracted artists that include heavyweights like Jerry Garcia and Les Claypool of Primus as well as independent painters, sculptors, and ceramists. Downtown Sebastopol contains a number of shops where local artists sell their works, along with bookstores, record stores, and the odd place selling tie-dyed T-shirts. The surrounding farmland was once devoted to orchards, particularly apples, but that has changed over the years; now grapes dominate the Gravensteins. Still, the few remaining orchards give fragrance and beauty to the already scenic country roads, especially during the spring bloom.

Wineries
DUTTON ESTATE
A small winery along the comparatively undiscovered Gravenstein Highway, **Dutton Estate** (8757 Green Valley Rd., 707/829-9463, http://sebastopolvineyards.com, daily 10am-4:30pm, tasting $10-15) is in the middle of its own vineyards (don't pick the grapes). Tasters enjoy plenty of personal attention from pourers, along with a small list of white and rosé wines, moving into the red pinots and syrahs that do so well in this area. Dutton's syrahs stand out among the offerings, which can include a few extra pours for those who seem genuinely interested in the wines.

MERRY EDWARDS WINERY
Merry Edwards was the first woman to earn a degree in enology (winemaking) from the prestigious University of California, Davis, program in 1993. After working as

a winemaker for numerous Sonoma vintners and developing her own pinot noir grape clone with the help of the facilities and staff at Davis, Merry finally opened her own winery. The **Merry Edwards Winery** (2959 Gravenstein Hwy., 707/823-7466 or 888/388-9050, www.merryedwards.com, daily 9:30am-4:30pm, free) offers tastings in its two glass-walled tasting rooms. Each member of the tasting staff works with one party of tasters at a time. You'll be led to a table with comfortable chairs set with four glasses ready for four different pinot noirs. There are four samples of the same varietal plus a bonus sauvignon blanc served at the end.

Accommodations

In Sebastopol, the best place to stay is the expensive but lovely **Avalon Bed and Breakfast** (11910 Graton Rd., 707/824-0880, www.avalonluxuryinn.com, $239-355). With only three rooms, it offers the ultimate in private and romantic accommodations. All rooms have king beds, hot tubs or access to the garden hot tub, fireplaces, air-conditioning, and many luxurious amenities. Because Avalon was purpose-built as a bed-and-breakfast, each guest room is actually a suite with a private entrance and there is plenty of space to spread out to enjoy a longer stay. Breakfast is a lovingly prepared organic feast with local produce.

Food

A great break from the endless fancy food is to find a nice ethnic restaurant. In Sebastopol, one of the best is the **Himalayan Tandoori and Curry House** (969 Gravenstein Hwy. S., 707/824-1800, Mon.-Sat. 11am-2pm and 5pm-9pm, $12-19), which serves up Indian food in the Himalayan style. You'll find vegetable curries and meat tandoori here, both properly spicy, as well as fresh naan, spicy rice pudding, and all sorts of treats. You'll even get a break from the endless river of wine, since there's plenty of beer on the drinks menu.

The **Underwood Bar and Bistro** (9113 Graton Rd., Graton, 707/823-7023, www.

underwoodgraton.com, Tues.-Sat. 11:30am-10pm, Sun. 5pm-10pm, $14-35) serves upscale cuisine in the tiny town of Graton. Plush red velvet and dark wood tables grace the Underwood's dining room, which is recommended by many locals as the best spot in this wine region to sit down to a serious dinner. With a heavy seafood focus, including raw oysters on the half shell, and top-quality meats and produce, Underwood does in fact exemplify Wine Country cuisine. A whole section of the menu is devoted to cheese. The wine list leans heavily toward small local vintners; ask your server for recommendations. The bar stays open late (10pm-11pm) on Friday-Saturday nights, serving a pared-down but satisfying late-night menu.

Calling the **Willow Wood** (9020 Graton Rd., Graton, 707/823-0233, www.willowwood-graton.com, Mon.-Sat. 8am-9pm, Sun. 9am-3pm, $10-25) a deli is somewhat misleading. Sure, they've got a counter, a take-out business, and well-trodden wooden floors. But really, Willow Wood is an upscale California-Italian restaurant for lunch, featuring souped-up versions of traditional deli sandwiches accompanied by pasta and pickled veggies. Diners sit on wooden benches to enjoy the large meals, which can also include giant salads and tureens of fresh soup. The open-faced egg salad hot sandwich with bacon and pesto is a favorite.

Information and Services

For maps of the area, souvenirs, newspapers, and wine-tasting coupons, swing by the **Sebastopol Chamber of Commerce Visitors Center** (265 S. Main St., 707/823-3032, www.sebastopol.org, Mon.-Fri. 10am-5pm, Sat. 10am-3pm).

The new **Sonoma West Medical Center** (501 Petaluma Ave., 707/823-8511, http://sonomawesthealth.org) has emergency medical care 24 hours a day.

Transportation

Sebastopol is west of Santa Rosa, accessed by Highways 116 and 12. The heart of downtown

Sebastopol is at the intersection of Sebastopol Avenue (Hwy. 12) and Main Street (Hwy. 116). Note that Sebastopol Avenue becomes the Bodega Highway once it hits downtown Sebastopol and extends all the way to, you guessed it, Bodega Bay.

To reach Sebastopol from U.S. 101, take either the exit for Highway 12 west in Santa Rosa or the exit for Highway 116 west at Cotati, eight miles south of Santa Rosa. Highway 116 is the most direct route to continue to the Russian River from Sebastopol.

GUERNEVILLE AND VICINITY

There are only a few wineries in the Guerneville area, but that's OK—people come here to float, canoe, or kayak the gorgeous Russian River that winds through town from Forestville all the way through Monte Rio to the Pacific Ocean at Jenner. In addition to its busy summertime tourist trade, Guerneville is also a very popular gay and lesbian resort area. The rainbow flag flies proudly here, and the friendly community welcomes all.

Wineries
RUSSIAN RIVER VINEYARDS

Ironically, **Russian River Vineyards** (5700 Gravenstein Hwy., Forestville, 707/887-3344, www.russianrivervineyards.com, daily 11am-5pm, $10) really isn't on the Russian River; it is in the coastal hills of nearby Forestville, which nurture the Sonoma Coast American Viticultural Area vineyards and wineries. The property doesn't look like a typical high-end winery, and the aging wooden buildings seem almost to be falling apart. (Don't worry, the tasting room has recently been shored up.) Sadly, the funky old Victorian house behind the tasting room isn't open for tours—it's part of the private production facility.

Despite the ramshackle look, the friendly staff create a classy, small-winery tasting experience. Russian River Vineyards' small list of red wines feature full-bodied, fruity pinot noirs and interesting varietals from the southern reaches of Europe. The charbono tastes

especially good. Enjoy lunch or dinner at **Corks** (Mon.-Fri. 11:30am-3:30pm and 5pm-8pm, Sat.-Sun. 10am-3pm and 5pm-8pm, $19-34), the on-site farm-to-table restaurant.

KORBEL CELLARS

Champagne grapes like cooler climates, so it makes sense that **Korbel Cellars** (13250 River Rd., Guerneville, 707/824-7000, www.korbel.com, daily 10am-4:30pm, tasting and tours free), the leading producer of California champagne-style sparkling wines, maintains a winery and tasting room on the Sonoma coast. The large, lush estate welcomes visitors with elaborate landscaping and attractive buildings, including a small area serving as a visitors center. Tours of the estate are offered daily (11am-3pm). Sample a wide variety of high-end California champagnes, plus a few boutique still wines. The facility also has a full-service gourmet deli (9am-4:30pm) and picnic grounds for tasters who want to stop for lunch. Korbel also sells (but does not sample) brandy on-site.

★ The Russian River

Guerneville and its surrounding forest are the center for fun on the river. In summer the water is usually warm and dotted with folks swimming, canoeing, or simply floating tubes serenely downriver amid forested riverbanks and under blue skies. **Burke's Canoe Trips** (8600 River Rd., Forestville, 707/887-1222, www.burkescanoetrips.com, Memorial Day-mid-Oct., $60) rents canoes and kayaks on the Russian River. The put-in is at Burke's beach in Forestville; paddlers then canoe downriver 10 miles to Guerneville, where a courtesy shuttle picks them up. Burke's also offers overnight campsites for tents, trailers, and RVs.

On the north bank, near the small enclave of Monte Rio, **Johnsons Beach & Resort** (16215 and 16217 1st St., 707/869-9022, www.johnsonsbeach.com, May-Oct. daily 10am-6pm, canoe or kayak rental $40/day) rents canoes, kayaks, pedal boats, and inner tubes for floating the river. There is a safe, kid-friendly section of the riverbank that is roped off for small children; parents and beachcombers can rent beach chairs and umbrellas for use on the small beach (mid-May-Sept. Sat.-Sun. 10am-6pm). The boathouse sells beer and snacks.

Fly fishers can cast their lines nearby off **Wohler Bridge** (9765 Wohler Rd., Forestville) and **Steelhead Beach** (9000 River Rd., Forestville).

Armstrong Redwoods

An easy five-minute drive from Guerneville on one mostly straight road, **Armstrong Redwoods State Natural Reserve** (17000 Armstrong Woods Rd., Guerneville, 707/869-2015, www.parks.ca.gov, daily 8am-60 minutes after sunset, $8 per vehicle, $7 senior rate) often gets overlooked, which makes it a bit less crowded than some of the most popular North Coast and Sierra redwood forests. But you can still take a fabulous hike—either a short stroll in the shade of the trees or a multiple-day backcountry adventure. The easiest walk ever to a big tree is the 0.1-mile stagger from the visitors center to the tallest tree in the park, named the Parson Jones Tree. If you saunter another 0.5 miles, you'll reach the Colonel Armstrong Tree, which grows next to the Armstrong Pack Station—your first stop if you're doing heavy-duty hiking. From the Pack Station, another 0.25 miles of moderate hiking leads to the Icicle Tree.

Right next to Armstrong is the **Austin Creek State Recreation Area** (17000 Armstrong Woods Rd., Guerneville, 707/869-2015, www.parks.ca.gov, daily 8am-60 minutes after sunset, $8 per vehicle, $7 senior rate). It's rough going on 2.5 miles of steep, narrow, treacherous dirt road to get to the main entrance and parking area; no vehicles over 20 feet long and no trailers of any kind are permitted. But once you're in, some great—and very difficult—hiking awaits you. The eponymous **Austin Creek Trail** (4.7 miles one-way) leads down from the sunbaked meadows into the cool forest fed by Austin Creek. To avoid monotony on this challenging route, create a loop by taking the turn onto **Gilliam Creek Trail** (4 miles one-way). This

way you get to see another of the park's cute little creeks as you walk back to the starting point.

Entertainment and Events

BARS

Guerneville wouldn't be a proper gay resort town without at least a couple of good gay bars that create proper nightlife for visitors and locals alike. The most visible and funky-looking of these is the **Rainbow Cattle Company** (16220 Main St., Guerneville, 707/869-0206, www.queersteer.com, daily 6am-2am). Mixing the vibes of a down-home country saloon with a happening San Francisco nightspot, the Rainbow has cold drinks and hot men with equal abandon. Think cocktails in Mason jars, wood paneling, and leather nights. This is just the kind of queer bar where you can bring your mom or your straight-but-not-narrow friends, and they'll have just as much fun as you will.

It may not look like much from the road, but the **Stumptown Brewery** (15045 River Rd., 707/869-0705, www.stumptown.com, Sun.-Thurs. 11am-midnight, Fri.-Sat. 11am-2am) is the place to hang out on the river. Inside this atypical dive bar is a pool table, Naugahyde barstools, and a worn wooden bar crowded with locals. Out back are the second bar and an outdoor deck with scattered tables overlooking the river. The brewery only makes a few of the beers sold on tap, but they are all great and perfect to enjoy by the pitcher. Stumptown also serves a menu of burgers and grilled sandwiches.

EVENTS

Held at Johnson's Beach in Guerneville, the **Russian River Jazz and Blues Festival** (www.russianriverfestivals.com, 707/869-1595, Sept., $55/day) is a two-day affair with jazz one day and blues the next. The main stage has some pretty big acts, including Buddy Guy, War, and Taj Mahal, but there is plenty of music to groove to throughout the festival grounds. In addition to live acts, food vendors showcase regional fare, local artists hawk their wares, and tents serve glass after glass of wine while sunburned devotees splash around in the river. Much more than just a music festival, this event is the last big bash of the summer season; it takes place at the end of September, just before the weather reliably turns cold. If you plan to stay both days, consider camping here. **Johnson's Beach** (707/869-2022) has designated campsites available on a first-come, first-served basis.

If you are in the area in mid-August, you may be able to get tickets for the Stumptown Brewery's annual **Russian River Beer Revival and BBQ Cook Off** (15045 River Rd., 707/869-0705, www.stumptown.com/revival, mid-Aug. Sat. noon-6pm). The event takes place along the river on a grassy field below the restaurant. Enjoy live music, beer tastings from 30 different breweries, and lots and lots of barbecue. Tickets generally go on sale in June and sell out quickly.

Accommodations

Because Guerneville is the major resort town for lovers of Russian River recreation, you'll find a few dozen bed-and-breakfasts and cabin resorts in town. Many of these spots are gay-friendly, some with clothing-optional hot tubs.

UNDER $150

The **Creekside Inn & Lodge** (16180 Neeley Rd., 800/776-6586, www.creeksideinn.com, $105-285) is right along the Russian River outside of downtown Guerneville. The river floods fairly regularly, hence the entire resort perches on stilts that provide pretty views as well as dry carpets. Cabins and cottages at the lodge run short on upscale amenities but long on woodsy kitsch. Every cabin has a full kitchen with a fridge, plenty of space, a comfortable bath, and some of the best complimentary coffee you'll ever get in a hotel room. Choose from economical studios, multiple-bedroom family units, and brand-new eco-cabins that were designed to have minimal impact on the local environment. The property is large and has a swimming pool, but it does not have good river frontage for swimmers. The owners can offer suggestions for local beaches and make appointments for wine-tasting at their favorite private local wineries.

$150-250

The ★ **Sonoma Orchid Inn** (12850 River Rd., Guerneville, 888/877-4466, www.sonomaorchidinn.com, pets welcome, $149-249) experience is made by its amazing owners. They've created beautiful rooms with elegant linens and furniture, plus just enough tchotchkes to keep things interesting. The best rooms have satellite TV with DVRs, DVD players, microwaves, and small fridges. On the economy end of the spectrum, the rooms are tiny but cute, with private baths and pretty decorations. The owners not only recommend restaurants and spas, they'll make reservations for you. They've got knowledge about the local wineries, hikes, river spots, and just about everything else in the region. The dog-friendly Orchid makes a perfect inn for visitors who've never been to the area.

On the road to Armstrong Redwoods, **Boon Hotel + Spa** (14711 Armstrong Woods Rd., Guerneville, 707/869-2721, www.boonhotels.com, $195-315) is the antithesis of Guerneville's woodsy funkiness. In almost a rebuff to its environs, Boon Hotel + Spa is minimal in the extreme, with white walls devoid of artwork, square armless couches, and beds vast enough to get lost in the fair-trade organic cotton sheets. The slate, chrome, and white palette are offset by bright slashes of red and orange. Many of the 14 rooms have freestanding cast-iron fireplaces, private patios, and fridges. True to its name, there is a pool and hot tub (both saltwater, for a little twist) and plenty of facial and massage options to work out the kinks. In the morning, wake up to a continental breakfast with a pressed pot of locally roasted coffee; in the evening, chill out with a cocktail by the pool. There are also three glamping tents ($139) to lightly rough it.

Riverfront balconies, a private beach, and beautifully landscaped grounds combine to make **Rio Villa Beach Resort** (20292 Hwy. 116, Monte Rio, 877/746-8455, www.riovilla.com, $195-315) an ideal Russian River getaway. With only 11 rooms—including some with kitchens—you're guaranteed both privacy with your companion and intimacy with the resort guests as well as the warm owners. A generous continental breakfast is available in the morning, and the Russian River is mere steps away.

OVER $250

The **Farmhouse Inn & Spa** (7871 River Rd., Forestville, 707/887-3300, www.farmhouse-inn.com, $545-1,195) is along River Road in the middle of prime wine-tasting country. The yellow-painted farmhouse is the inn's restaurant and contains the two rooms; most of the guest accommodations march up the gently sloped hillside in the form of a row of cottages. The cute little cabins have upscale decor, warm fireplaces, private baths, and precious little space. The most upscale rooms, with jetted tubs and private decks, are in a barn on the property. The pool area and restaurant aren't big either but make up what they lack in size with charm and an adorable outdoor fireplace area. A gourmet breakfast is available, but reservations are requested.

Food

River Inn Grill (16141 Main St., Guerneville, 707/869-0481, daily 7am-3pm, $7-15) is the first eatery you'll see when entering downtown Guerneville. In operation since 1946, this classic diner is the place for breakfast in Guerneville—the heavenly biscuits and gravy is a favorite.

A focal point of downtown Guerneville, **Main Street Station** (16280 Main St., 707/869-0501, www.mainststation.com, summer daily noon-11pm, winter Mon.-Thurs. 4pm-9:30pm, Fri.-Sun. noon-10:30pm, $14-25) offers a big menu filled with homey, casual grub. The mainstay is handmade pizza. Grab a quick slice for

lunch, or order a whole pie for dinner. In the evenings, locals and visitors order sandwiches and pizza, drink beer, and listen to live entertainment on the small stage. Live folk, jazz, blues, and even comedy happen every single night; this tiny venue gets crowded when a popular act comes to town. Consider making reservations in advance to ensure you'll get a seat.

Pat's Restaurant (16236 Main St., 707/869-9905, www.pats-restaurant.com, daily 6am-3pm, $10) is the kind of diner that travelers hope to find. It's homey, casual, and where locals come to sit at the counter for breakfast all day long. It doesn't look like much from the outside—a small storefront in the middle of downtown Guerneville—but when you peer in the plate-glass windows you'll notice quite a number of diners inside. Classic diner food is served fresh—the eggs are done perfectly, the hash browns are homemade, and the kitchen actually runs out of favorites like sausage gravy because it's made from scratch daily.

Light, airy, and open, tiny ★ **Boon Eat + Drink** (16248 Main St., Guerneville, 707/869-0780, www.eatatboon.com, Memorial Day-Oct. Mon.-Tues. and Thurs. 11am-3pm and 5pm-9pm, Wed. 5pm-9pm, Fri. 11am-3pm and 5pm-10pm, Sat. 10am-3pm and 5pm-10pm, Sun. 10am-3pm and 5pm-9pm, Oct.-Memorial Day Mon.-Tues. and Thurs. 11am-3pm and 5pm-9pm, Fri. 11am-3pm and 5pm-10pm, Sat. 10am-3pm and 5pm-10pm, Sun. 10am-3pm and 5pm-9pm, $12-24) lures diners to line up on the sidewalk in anticipation of local, organic, and sustainable cuisine served with simple elegance. Lunch usually consists of a simple menu of paninis, small plates, and the grass-fed Boon burger. For dinner, hearty main courses include a flat-iron steak with truffle fries. You really can't go wrong here—unless you can't get in.

Information and Services

Off the beaten wine path is the **Russian River Chamber of Commerce and Visitors Center** (16201 1st St., Guerneville,

707/869-9000, http://russianriver.com, daily 10am-5pm) in downtown Guerneville. Here you'll find staff that can give you serious local recommendations not only for wineries but also for river recreation, restaurants, and other less-traveled area attractions.

Transportation

Guerneville is on Highway 116, alternately named River Road. In downtown Guerneville, Highway 116 is briefly called Main Street. The most direct access is via U.S. 101 north of Santa Rosa; take the River Road/Guerneville exit and follow River Road west for 15 miles to downtown Guerneville.

Alternatively, a more scenic and often less crowded route is to take U.S. 101 to Highway 116 near Cotati, south of Santa Rosa. Named the Gravenstein Highway for its route through the apple orchards of Sebastopol, Highway 116 winds about 22 twisty miles through Sebastopol, Graton, and Forestville to emerge onto River Road in Guerneville.

Sonoma County Transit (707/576-7433, 800/345-7433, http://sctransit.com, adults $3.05, students $2.70, seniors $1.50) runs a Russian River Express bus, route 20, from downtown Santa Rosa to Guerneville.

HEALDSBURG

A different aspect of the Russian River from Guerneville is at Healdsburg, a small city of 11,000 that is so charming it's easy to forget that people live and work here. The plaza anchors downtown and the wide and slow Russian River, which creates the town's natural southern border. Boutiques, chic restaurants, and galleries dot the town, and fresh paint brightens the historic storefronts and planters lush with flowers and trailing vines. Healdsburg is also the nexus of three American Viticulture Areas (AVAs): the Russian River AVA, best known for producing pinot noir and chardonnay; Dry Creek AVA, famous for its zinfandel and sauvignon blanc; and the Alexander Valley AVA, which produces predominantly cabernet sauvignon and merlot.

Wineries

★ A. RAFANELLI

Tasting at **A. Rafanelli** (4685 W. Dry Creek Rd., 707/433-1385, www.arafanelliwinery.com, daily 10am-4pm, by appointment only) feels just about as different from the standard big-business high-end wineries of Wine Country as possible. Tastings are by appointment only. There's no marble-covered bar, no chic tasting room. The owner-winemaker will hand out glasses to your group, and you'll taste some of the best red wines produced anywhere in Sonoma County. In a region where the phrase "cab is king" comes up at almost every winery, Rafanelli's cabernet sauvignons are still special. If you can't taste at Rafanelli, look for their zins and cabs at local Sonoma restaurants. They don't sell to retail outlets, so a visit to the winery or a phone call to the vineyard are the only ways to get a bottle of A. Rafanelli into your collection.

ARMIDA

Come to the **Armida** (2201 Westside Rd., 707/433-2222, www.armida.com, daily 11am-5pm, $10) tasting room for the gorgeous scenery and the funky facilities, but stay for the wonderful wines. The driveway meanders up a Russian River hillside to a cluster of geodesic domes set among sustainable landscaping. Bring a picnic to enjoy on the big deck overlooking the duck pond and the valley beyond. Before you start eating, wander into the tasting room to check out some of the truly tasty Russian River red wines. You'll have your choice of smoky syrahs and jammy zinfandels. The flagship wine, Poizin, is well represented in the wines and logo-wear in the small gift shop that shares space with the tasting bar. Armida sells Poizin in a coffin-shaped box— ask nicely and they might open a bottle for you to taste (and even if they don't, it's still worth buying).

DRY CREEK VINEYARD

It seems odd that a winery named **Dry Creek Vineyard** (3770 Lambert Bridge Rd., 800/864-9463, 707/433-1000, www.

Healdsburg and Vicinity

© AVALON TRAVEL

drycreekvineyard.com, daily 10:30am-5pm, $10-15) should have sailboats on all its labels, but that's the signature icon on each bottle. This midsize winery focuses much effort within its own AVA (Dry Creek), producing many single-vineyard wines from grapes grown within a few miles of the estate. Other wines include grapes from the Russian River Valley AVA. Dry Creek prides itself on both its classic California varietals such as chardonnay, cabernet, and merlot, and on occasionally hopping out of that box and producing something unusual, like a musqué, a chenin blanc, or a Sauternes-style dessert wine. The

ivy-covered tasting room is styled after a French château.

FERRARI-CARANO

One of the best large wineries in Dry Creek Valley, **Ferrari-Carano** (8761 Dry Creek Rd., 707/433-6700, www.ferrari-carano.com, daily 10am-5pm, $10-25) provides great standard and reserve wines in an upscale tasting room and winery facility. Upstairs, visitors can taste from the extensive menu of large-production, moderately priced whites and reds and browse the larger-than-average gift shop for gourmet goodies, wine, kitchen gadgets, and Ferrari-Carano logowear. Downstairs, the elegant lounge area includes comfortable seating and a video describing the winemaking process, from grape to glass. Look down into the barrel storage areas, where wines age right before your eyes. Open the glass doors and enter the reserve tasting room, where (for an additional fee) you can taste the best of Ferrari-Carano's vintages—smaller runs that are mostly bold, assertive reds.

FOPPIANO

One of the oldest wineries in the Russian River Valley, **Foppiano** (12707 Old Redwood Hwy., 707/433-7272, www.foppiano.com, daily 11am-5pm, $5) dates from 1896. Today, Foppiano is still making a small list of premium red wines. Their signature wine is a legendary petite sirah, unusual for the area. They've also got a great sangiovese, a zin, a cab, and a merlot under the Foppiano label. A second label, Riverside, encompasses a few tasty but exceedingly inexpensive varietals that let drinkers on a budget enjoy Foppiano wines. Inside the farmhouse-style tasting room you can enjoy sips of the various vintages, and also ask for Susan's recipes; the hospitality director and fourth-generation member of the Foppiano family creates and adapts dishes to match the family wines.

FRANCIS FORD COPPOLA WINERY

The legendary director of iconic movies *Apocalypse Now* and *The Godfather* has his own winery in the Healdsburg area. Sure, the **Francis Ford Coppola Winery** (300 Via Archimedes, Geyserville, 707/857-1400, www.franciscoppolawinery.com, daily 11am-6pm, $12-25) allows you to taste its chardonnays and syrahs, but it also allows film buffs to tour the **Movie Gallery,** which is full of film memorabilia including Coppola's Academy Awards and Don Corleone's desk from *The Godfather*. In the summer months, two pools are open to entertain kids while their parents sip wine.

HOP KILN

Bringing truth in advertising to Sonoma, **Hop Kiln** (6050 Westside Rd., 707/433-6491, www.hopkilnwinery.com, daily 10am-5pm, $7) winery is housed in an old hop kiln. Earlier in its history, the Russian River Valley grew more beer-making ingredients than grapes, and this distinctively shaped hop kiln dried the valley's crop each year. Today, you'll find a gift shop inside the main kiln along with an extensive wine-tasting bar that includes typical Wine Country varietals. Hop Kiln also produces unique wines, such as their malbec, grenache, and award-winning pinot noir.

J WINERY

Unlike many wineries that cling to Old World traditions, **J Winery** (11447 Old Redwood Hwy., 888/594-6326, www.jwine.com, daily 11am-5pm, $20-75) loves the cutting edge of the California wine scene. J specializes in California-style sparkling wines. The tasting room is a triumph of modern design, and the tasting experience gives visitors a sample of the best that Wine Country has to offer. Make a reservation at the Bubble Room (Thurs.-Sun., reservations required), where, instead of the standard tasting bar and pouring staff, there are tables and waitstaff. Instead of the standard one-ounce pours, you'll enjoy wines specially paired with small bites of high-end California cuisine prepared in J's kitchens by their own team of gourmet chefs. You'll get the chance to taste the sparkly vintages as they are meant to be enjoyed—with an array of often spicy foods.

PORTER CREEK WINERY

Serious cork dorks recommend the tiny tasting room at **Porter Creek Winery** (8735 Westside Rd., 707/433-6321, www.portercreekvineyards.com, daily 10:30am-4:30pm, $15), which casual tasters might otherwise miss at a bend on a winding road. Turn onto the dirt driveway, pass the farm-style house (actually the owner's family home), and park in front of a small converted shed—the tasting room. This is old-school Sonoma wine tasting.

Porter Creek has been making its precious few cases of rich red wine each year for the last 30 years or so. You can occasionally find it at local restaurants, but if you like what you taste, buy it here at the winery. Porter Creek's wines are almost all reds, made from grapes grown organically within sight of the tasting room. You might even see the owner-winemaker walking through his vineyards with his family on a sunny afternoon in the off-season.

WHITE OAK

At **White Oak** (7505 Hwy. 128, 707/433-8429, www.whiteoakwinery.com, daily 10am-5pm, $5), you'll find a wonderful combination of whimsy and wine. This Spanish mission-inspired winery complex is surrounded by green gardens dotted with fun sculptures. Beyond the gardens, estate vineyards grow grapes for Old Vine Zinfandel and other fine wines. Go inside to taste some of the wines—the tasting list is small but prestigious. While white-wine drinkers enjoy the sauvignon blanc and chardonnay, big reds are the specialty of the house. Cabernet sauvignon and zinfandel lovers flock to White Oak for the fabulous regular releases and occasional special library selections. Tours at White Oak provide a look at wine tasting, describing and illustrating the various components that make up a wine's fragrance.

Sports and Recreation

Newcomers to bicycle touring in the area can choose among several reputable touring companies that will get them on two wheels and pointed in the right direction. **Wine Country Bikes** (61 Front St., 707/473-0610, www.winecountrybikes.com, tour $139 pp, bike rental $39-145 per day) is on the square in downtown Healdsburg. Its Classic Wine Tour starts at 10am and runs until 3:30pm. During your leisurely pedal through the Dry Creek region, you'll stop and taste wine, take walks in vineyards, and learn more about the history of wine in this small, proud AVA. A gourmet picnic lunch is included with the tour. Other tours are longer or more luxurious—check the

website for information about multiple-day bike-tour packages that include accommodations. For independent souls who prefer to carve their own routes, Wine Country Bikes also rents road bikes, tandem bikes, and hybrids that you can also take on moderately difficult park trails where biking is permitted.

To become part of the larger bicycling culture in the area, consider participating in the annual **Harvest Century Bicycle Tour** (Healdsburg Chamber of Commerce, 707/433-6935, www.healdsburg.com, July, $85). This event requires some degree of physical fitness, as riders register to ride 23, 37, or 60 miles. The roads are of moderate difficulty; while you'll find some inclines, experienced cyclists won't be so tortured as to preclude enjoying the rest of the day with great food, wine, and the companionship of plenty of like-minded souls.

Healdsburg also provides access to water sports on the Russian River. **Russian River Adventures** (20 Healdsburg Ave., 707/433-5599, http://russianriveradventures.com, adults $60, children $30) offers guided paddles down a secluded section of the river in stable, sturdy inflatable canoes. Dogs, children, and even infants are welcome. The trip usually lasts 4-5 hours, with little white water and lots of serene, shaded pools. They now provide half-day trips also.

Accommodations

Travelers planning to stay a night in Healdsburg will find that none of the boutique inns and hotels in town come cheap. If you take a room at the **Honor Mansion** (891 Grove St., 707/433-4277, www.honormansion.com, $340-615), you'll probably feel that you are getting your money's worth. Each of the 13 rooms and suites has been furnished and decorated with exquisite attention to even the smallest details. Whatever room you choose, you'll be overwhelmed with luxury and want to spend the day in the soft cocoon of your elegant, oversized feather bed. All rooms have private baths stocked with high-end toiletries, along with TVs, CD players, bathrobes, phones, air-conditioning, turndown service, and more. Naturally, all rooms come with a full gourmet breakfast each morning. The Honor Mansion also has a lap pool, a tennis court, a croquet lawn, a bocce pit, and outdoor professional massage service.

On the central town plaza, the **Hotel Healdsburg** (25 Matheson St., 800/889-7188, www.hotelhealdsburg.com, $499-1,100) is a local icon. The 56-room boutique hotel offers upscale amenities, including Frette towels and linens, smart TVs, soaking tubs and walk-in showers, and beautiful decor. Rooms have shining wooden floors and furniture, Tibetan throw rugs, and spotless white down comforters. All rooms include free Wi-Fi and a gourmet breakfast, among other amenities, and guests can enjoy the outdoor pool, fitness center, and full-service day spa.

Raford Inn Bed and Breakfast Inn (10630 Wohler Rd., 800/887-9503, www.rafordinn.com, $170-270) offers Healdsburg-level luxury at slightly less stratospheric prices than its nearby competitors. Each of the five rooms has air-conditioning, a CD player, and a private bath. Some have fireplaces, oversize showers, and other luxury amenities. All rooms have been decorated in attractive minimalist Victorian style that feels historic but doesn't overwhelm the modern guest. Every morning, the Raford serves up a hearty, organic country breakfast—the perfect start to a day of wine-tasting. They also do a nightly wine and cheese reception.

Food

In a sea of self-conscious chichi restaurants, the **Healdsburg Charcuterie** (335 Healdsburg Ave., 707/431-7213, http://charcuteriehealdsburg.com, Mon.-Thurs. 11:30am-3pm and 5pm-9pm, Fri. 11:30am-3pm and 5:30pm-9:30pm, Sat. noon-3:30pm and 5:30pm-9:30pm, Sun. noon-3:30pm and 5pm-9pm, $16-28) makes diners feel at home. With a cute but not annoying pig theme, local art on the walls, and a softly romantic atmosphere, the Charcuterie makes a great option for a romantic but not overwhelming dinner

out. The house-cured pork tenderloin sandwich is the specialty, but vegetarians certainly can find a tasty and well-prepared meal as well. The Charcuterie pours some lovely local vintages and offers wine flights.

The most famous restaurant in Healdsburg is probably **Dry Creek Kitchen** (317 Healdsburg Ave., 707/431-0330, http://drycreekkitchen.com, Sun.-Thurs. 5:30pm-9:30pm, Fri.-Sat. 5:30pm-10pm, $29-39), a chic Charlie Palmer dining room that takes the concept of California cuisine to the next level. Expect to see foam, froth, jus, and coulis splattered across the menu, which can range from upscale but recognizable to totally bizarre. Dry Creek Kitchen serves brunch and lunch on the weekend, offering its own unique take on eggs Benedict, sliders, and other standards. This is a great place to check out some Dry Creek AVA vintages.

For an independent cup of coffee in Healdsburg, head across the town square to **Flying Goat Coffee** (324 Center St., 707/433-3599, www.flyinggoatcoffee.com, daily 7am-7pm) or to their other downtown location (419 Center St., 707/433-8003, Mon.-Sat. 6am-noon). This attractive West Coast coffeehouse serves above-average lattes, defaults to "no whip" on the mochas, and doesn't make them too sweet either. The relaxed feel and pleasant seating area make it easy to stop and stay awhile.

Oakville Grocery (124 Matheson St., 707/433-3200, www.oakvillegrocery.com, Sun.-Mon. and Wed.-Thurs. 9am-5pm, Tues. and Fri.-Sat. 9am-7pm), like its cousin in the Napa Valley, sells high-end groceries and local gourmet products to well-heeled customers. It's a great place to pick up gifts for friends back home—they carry fine, expensive local olive oils, vinegars, soaps, and bath products. You can also get the goods for a proper picnic, with a great selection of cheeses, fresh local breads, an upscale deli counter, a redundant wine selection, and a few fine nonalcoholic beverages.

A funkier alternative to the Oakville Grocery is the **Jimtown Store** (6706 Hwy.

128, 707/433-1212, www.jimtown.com, Mon. and Wed.-Thurs. 7am-3pm, Fri. 7am-4pm, Sat. 7:30am-5pm, Sun. 7:30am-3pm), six miles out of town on a dusty country road. When owners Carrie Brown and her husband, the late John Werner, decided to leave New York City, they landed at this general store, in operation since 1895. The couple brought their gourmet sensibilities and turned the venue into a quirky update on an old-fashioned American country store, with house-made gourmet jams, jellies, and condiments; penny toys; housewares; and, best of all, hot lunches. The chalkboard menu presents a tasty assortment of smoked-brisket sandwiches, chili, and buttermilk coleslaw. The benches and picnic tables outside are a great place to unwrap your sandwich, or you can pick up one of their prepared box lunches to go.

Information and Services

Befitting such a desirable destination, the **Healdsburg Chamber of Commerce and Visitors Bureau** (217 Healdsburg Ave., 707/433-6935, www.healdsburg.com, summer Mon.-Fri. 10am-4pm, Sat.-Sun. 11am-3pm, winter Mon.-Fri. 10am-4pm, Sat.-Sun. 11am-2pm) is centrally located just off U.S. 101, just as you come into town on Healdsburg Avenue. The friendly staff is happy to load you up with maps, brochures, and helpful tips.

The **Healdsburg District Hospital** (1375 University Ave., 707/431-6500, http://healdsburgdistricthospital.org) has a 24-hour emergency room.

While cell-phone reception is reliable in town, don't expect service on Healdsburg's back roads. Getting online in Healdsburg is fairly easy. Most hotels and cafés offer access, and the plaza has free Wi-Fi service set up by the city.

Transportation

Healdsburg is an easy destination, as it is 14 miles north of Santa Rosa on U.S. 101. To reach downtown Healdsburg from U.S. 101, take exit 503, for Central Healdsburg. Healdsburg can also be accessed from Calistoga: Drive north of Calistoga on Highway 128 for 17.4 miles, and at Jimtown, Highway 128 intersects Alexander Valley Road. Continue straight on Alexander Valley Road as Highway 128 turns right, heading north to Geyserville. In 3.3 miles, turn left onto Healdsburg Avenue, which runs to downtown Healdsburg.

North Coast

Look for ★ to find recommended
sights, activities, dining, and lodging.

Highlights

★ **The Sea Ranch Chapel:** Embedded with seashells and sea urchins, this tiny place of worship and meditation is wholly unique (page 221).

★ **California Coastal National Monument Point Arena-Stornetta Unit:** Twelve miles of stunning coastline showcase sheer cliffs, giant tide pools, and several sea arches (page 225).

★ **Mendocino:** Spend an afternoon or a weekend wandering this arts-filled community and its headlands, which jut out into the Pacific (page 232).

★ **Avenue of the Giants:** The towering coast redwoods in Humboldt Redwoods State Park are a true must-see. Simply gaze at the silent giants or head to the nearby Eel River for a quick dip (page 258).

★ **Arcata Community Forest:** The first city-owned forest in California offers acres of trails winding through second-growth redwoods (page 277).

★ **Trinidad:** This tiny town perched above an idyllic bay is one of the most photogenic coastal communities in the state (page 282).

★ **Prairie Creek Redwoods State Park:** With big trees, impressive wildlife, a long, lonely beach, and one-of-a-kind Fern Canyon, this park is worth a stop (page 288).

★ **Battery Point Lighthouse:** This lighthouse on an island off Crescent City is only accessible at low tide. If you time it right, you can take

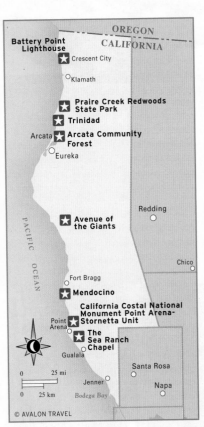

an insightful tour from the lighthouse keeper (page 294).

The rugged North Coast of California is spectacular, its wild beauty in many places unspoiled and almost desolate. The cliffs are forbidding, the beaches are rocky and windswept, and the surf thunders in with formidable authority.

This is not the California coast of surfer movies, though hardy souls do ride the chilly Pacific waves as far north as Crescent City.

From Bodega Bay, Highway 1 twists and turns north along hairpin curves that will take your breath away. The Sonoma and Mendocino Coasts offer lovely beaches and forests, top-notch cuisine, and a friendly, uncrowded wine region. Along the way, tiny coastal towns—Jenner, Gualala, Point Arena, Mendocino, Fort Bragg—dot the hills and valleys, beckoning travelers with bed-and-breakfasts, organic farms, and relaxing respites from the road. Between the towns are a wealth of coastal access areas to take in the striking meeting of land and sea. Inland, Mendocino's hidden wine region offers the rural and relaxed pace missing from that other famous wine district. Anderson Valley and Hopland can quench your thirst, whether it's for beer at the local microbrewery or wine at one of many tasting rooms.

Where Highway 1 merges with U.S. 101 is the famous Lost Coast, accessed only via steep, narrow roads or by backpacking the famous Lost Coast Trail. This is California at its wildest.

For most travelers, the North Coast means redwood country, and U.S. 101 marks the gateway to those redwoods. The famous, immense coastal sequoias loom along the highway south of the old logging town of Eureka and the hip college outpost of Arcata. A plethora of state and national parks lure travelers with numerous hiking trails, forested campgrounds, kitschy tourist traps, and some of the tallest and oldest trees on the continent; you can pitch a tent in Humboldt Redwoods State Park, cruise the Avenue of the Giants, and gaze in wonder at the primordial Founders Grove. Crescent City marks the northern terminus of the California Coast, a seaside town known for fishing, seafood—and for surviving a tsunami.

Previous: rock arches offshore of Point Arena; Avenue of the Giants. **Above:** Trinidad Memorial Lighthouse.

North Coast

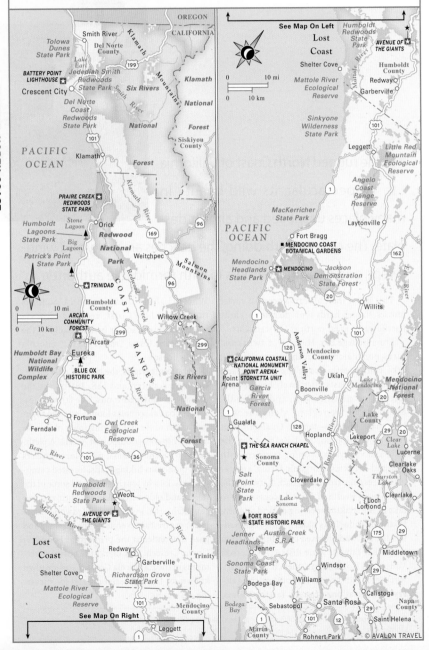

See Map On Left

See Map On Right

© AVALON TRAVEL

PLANNING YOUR TIME

If you're planning a road trip to explore the North Coast in depth and want to make stops in more than one destination, plan to spend a full week. Driving is the way to get from place to place, unless you're a hard-core backpacker. Highway 1 winds along the North Coast from Bodega Bay to above Fort Bragg, where it heads east to connect with U.S. 101 at its northern terminus near Leggett. U.S. 101 then heads inland through southern Humboldt County before heading back to the coast at Eureka. North of Eureka, U.S. 101 continues through Arcata, Trinidad, and Crescent City, along with the Redwood National and State Parks.

If you are heading to Mendocino or a section of the coast north of there, take U.S. 101, which is a great deal faster than Highway 1, and then take one of the connector roads from U.S. 101 to Highway 1. One of the best and most scenic connector roads is Highway 128, which heads west off U.S. 101 at Cloverdale and passes through the scenic Anderson Valley, with its many wineries, before joining Highway 1 just south of the town of Mendocino.

Driving times on Highway 1 tend to be longer on the North Coast due to the roadway's twists, turns, and many spectacular ocean vistas. On U.S. 101 north of Leggett, expect to share the road with logging vehicles. A lot of the roads off U.S. 101 or Highway 1 are worthwhile excursions, but expect mountainous terrain.

Many Bay Area residents consider Mendocino County ideal for a weekend getaway or romantic retreat. A weekend is about the perfect length of time to spend on the Mendocino Coast or in the Anderson Valley wine country. There are at least 3-4 days' worth of intriguing hikes to take in Redwood National and State Parks.

Along the Lost Coast, the most lodging and dining options can be found in Shelter Cove. If you want to explore the Lost Coast Trail, consider hiking it north to south, with the wind at your back. Spend the night in Ferndale or camp at the Mattole Recreation Site, where the trail begins, so that you can get an early start for the first day of backpacking.

If you're exploring the redwood parks, consider staying in the small towns of Arcata or Trinidad. The campgrounds at Patrick's Point State Park and Prairie Creek State Park are superb places to pitch a tent.

Summer on the North Coast has average daily temperatures in the mid-60s, which is comparable to the temps in Southern California during the winter. Expect rain on the North Coast from November to May. The chances of fog or rain are significantly lower in the fall, making it one of the best times to visit. Frequent visitors to the area know this, so many popular hotels book up quickly for fall weekends.

Sonoma Coast

One good way to begin your meanders up the coast is to take U.S. 101 out of San Francisco as far as Petaluma, and then head west toward Highway 1. This stretch of Highway 1 is also called the Shoreline Highway. As you travel toward the coast, you'll leave urban areas behind for a while, passing through some of the most pleasant villages in California.

BODEGA BAY

Bodega Bay is popular for its coastal views, whale-watching, and seafood—but it's most famous as the filming locale of Alfred Hitchcock's *The Birds*. The town sits on the eastern side of the harbor, while Bodega Head is a peninsula that shields the bay from the ocean. The tiny town with a population of just over 1,000 has kite shops, marinas, and

Sonoma Coast

© AVALON TRAVEL

unassuming seafood restaurants. The whole town shuts down around 7pm, even on summer evenings.

Whale-Watching

The best sight you could hope to see is a close-up view of Pacific gray whales migrating home to Alaska with their newborn calves. The whales head past the area January-May on their way from their summer home off Mexico. If you're lucky, you can see them from the shore. **Bodega Head,** a promontory just north of the bay, is a place to get close to the migration route. To get to this prime spot, travel north on Highway 1 about one mile past the visitors center and turn left onto Eastshore Road; make a right at the stop sign, and then drive three more miles to the parking lot. On

weekends from January to Mother's Day weekend, volunteers from **Stewards of the Coast and Redwoods** (707/869-9177, www.stewardsofthecoastandredwoods.org) are available to answer questions. Contact them for organized whale-watching tours or to learn more about their various educational programs.

Doran Regional Park

When you arrive in Bodega Bay, you'll see a sign pointing left for **Doran Regional Park** (201 Doran Beach Rd., 707/875-3540, http://parks.sonomacounty.ca.gov, daily 7am-sunset, day use $7 per vehicle). It is less than one mile down the road and worth the trip. It's a wide and level two-mile-long beach that has a small boardwalk. You can even swim at Doran Beach; although it's cold, it's protected from the open ocean waves, so it's much safer than most of the beaches along the coast.

Bodega Head

Bodega Bay looks like an open safety pin on maps; **Bodega Head** (3799 Westshore Rd., 707/875-3483, www.parks.ca.gov, free) is the thicker side, a knob that protects the bay from the open ocean. A part of Sonoma Coast State Park, it's the best place for a hike that gives you an overview of the area. The **Bodega Head Trail** (1.9 miles, 136-foot elevation change) showcases rock arches, sandy coves, and migrating gray whales before hitting the high point and winding back to views of Doran Beach, Bodega Bay, and Bodega Harbor.

Bodega Seafood, Art, and Wine Festival

This annual festival (16855 Bodega Hwy., Bodega, 707/824-8717, www.winecountryfestivals.com, Aug., adults $12-15, seniors $10-13, children aged 12-18 $8-11, children under 12 free) takes place the last weekend in August, combining all the best elements of the Bodega lifestyle with live music, wine-tastings, and special dinners. The proceeds benefit two worthy organizations: the Bodega Volunteer Fire Department and Stewards of the Coast and Redwoods.

Sonoma Coast State Park

Seventeen miles of coast are within **Sonoma Coast State Park** (707/875-3483, www.parks. ca.gov, day use $8 per vehicle). The park's boundaries extend from Bodega Head at the south up to the Vista Trailhead, four miles north of Jenner. As you drive up Highway 1, you'll see signs for various beaches. Although they're lovely places to walk, fish, and maybe sunbathe on the odd hot day, it is not advisable to swim here. If you go down to the water, bring your binoculars and camera. The cliffs, crags, inlets, whitecaps, mini-islands, and rock outcroppings are fascinating in any weather, and their looks change with the shifting tides and fog.

Sports and Recreation

With a usually calm bay and a protected harbor, Bodega Bay is a great place to try kayaking or stand-up paddleboarding on the North Coast. Stop into the **Bodega Bay Surf Shack** (Pelican Plaza, 1400 Hwy. 1, 707/875-3944, www.bodegabaysurf.com, Mon.-Fri. 10am-6pm, Sat.-Sun. 9am-7pm, kayaks $45/four hours, SUPs $40/four hours) to rent your SUP or kayak. Then set out in Bodega Bay, Salmon Creek, or the nearby lower portion of the Russian River. They also do private lessons

($165) and group lessons ($119). They also rent out surfboards ($17/day) and wetsuits ($17/day). Doran Beach has a usually unintimidating wave for beginners. Just north of town is Salmon Creek, a series of powerful and exposed beach breaks.

Long, rugged beaches with few people mean that the Sonoma Coast is a terrific place to go horseback riding. Just north of town at the 378-acre Chanslor Ranch, **Horse N Around Trail Rides** (2660 N. Hwy. 1, 707/875-3333, www.horsenaroundtrailrides.com, $40-250) has options including 30-minute wetlands trail rides and 1.5-hour beach rides. Choose between group rides and slightly pricier private rides.

Shopping

Gourmet au Bay (913 Hwy. 1, 707/875-9875, www.gourmetaubay.com, Sun.-Thurs. 11am-7pm, Fri.-Sat. 11am-8pm, $12/tasting) is a shop and tasting bar that offers the chance to taste wines from different vintners: some are major players in the Napa wine scene, and some are from wineries so small they don't have tasting rooms of their own. You might even get to taste the odd French or Australian wine when you "wine surf," tasting three wines poured and presented on a miniature

benches overlooking the water at Doran Regional Park

surfboard for you to carry out to the deck to admire the view of Bodega Harbor. Inside, peruse the gift shop, which includes some local artisanal foods plus plenty of handmade ceramics and pottery and an array of toys for wine lovers.

Accommodations

The ★ **Bodega Bay Lodge & Spa** (103 Hwy. 1, 707/875-3525 or 888/875-2250, www. bodegabaylodge.com, $279-669) is on a seven-acre property that sits high enough to take in the bay and harbor, Doran Beach, the bird-filled marshes, and Bodega Head in the distance. Most rooms have views of the water, while all the units in the seven separate buildings have their own private balconies or terraces. Warm up on a foggy day in the heated pool, sauna, and oversized infinity soaking tub. There's also a fitness center and spa in the same facility. Dine at the lodge's upscale **Duck Club Restaurant** (daily 7:30am-11am and 6pm-9pm, $20-36) and the more casual **Drake's Fireside Lounge** (daily 5pm-10pm, $6-17). It would be difficult to find a place more convenient than this.

For a B&B experience, head to the **Bay Hill Mansion** (3919 Bay Hill Rd., 877/468-1588, www.bayhillmansion.com, $269-354) on the north side of Bodega Bay. Be spoiled in one of just five rooms and wake up to a choice of breakfast options.

Sonoma Coast State Park (707/875-3483, www.parks.ca.gov, day use $8 per vehicle) encompasses several campgrounds along its 17-mile expanse. Both **Bodega Dunes Campground** (2485 Hwy. 1, www. reserveamerica.com, $35) and **Wright's Beach Campground** (7095 Hwy. 1, www. reserveamerica.com, $35-45) are developed, with hot showers and flush toilets. To get up-to-date information on closings or reopenings related to Sonoma Coast State Park, call the district office (707/865-2391) or stop in at the Salmon Creek Ranger Station a little farther north.

Food

The ★ **Fishetarian Fish Market** (599 Hwy. 1, 707/875-9092, www.fishetarianfishmarket.com, spring-summer Fri.-Sat. 11am-7pm, Sun.-Mon. and Thurs. 11am-6pm, fall Sun.-Mon. and Thurs. 11am-5pm, Fri.-Sat. 11am-6pm, $6-15) nails the Baja-style fish taco with rockfish, a cabbage slaw, and a zingy sauce. It's the best fish taco you'll have on the North Coast. They also do Point Reyes oysters and an award-winning clam chowder. Order at

the Bodega Bay Lodge & Spa

the counter above display cases of smoked salmon, oysters, and octopus salad, then dine casually inside or outside at one of the limited tables. Fishetarian has a few well-chosen craft beers on tap along with a fridge filled with bottled beers, sodas, and other cold beverages. Beware that this place closes early.

Another classic and unassuming seafood spot in Bodega Bay is the **Spud Point Crab Company** (1860 Westshore Rd., 707/875-9472, www.spudpointcrab.com, daily 9am-5pm, $7-11), right across the street from the boats that bring in its fresh seafood. There can be a line out the door on weekdays for the clam chowder and the crab sandwich. On crowded days, make a friend and share some space at one of the few picnic tables out front.

Right on the highway, **The Birds Café** (1407 Hwy. 1, 707/875-2900, Mon.-Thurs. 11:30am-7pm, Fri.-Sun. 11:30am-8pm, $10-20) is an easy pit stop when driving through Bodega Bay. Refuel on fried artichoke tacos, fish tacos, and shrimp tacos on a large deck with views of the harbor.

Bodega Bay Lodge's **Duck Club Restaurant** (103 Hwy. 1, 707/875-3525, www.bodegabaylodge.com, daily 7:30am-11am and 6pm-9pm, $20-36) offers a warm and elegant dining experience featuring hearty American entrées like steak, chicken, and local cod with seasonal vegetables. There's a fireside lounge overlooking the bay, and even some outdoor seating for warmer days.

One of the best restaurants in the area is **Terrapin Creek** (1580 Eastshore Dr., 707/875-2700, www.terrapincreekcafe.com, Thurs.-Mon. 4:30pm-9pm, $26-32), where they make creative use of the abundance of fresh seafood available and cook up tasty pasta, duck, and beef entrées.

Information and Services

The **Sonoma Coast Visitors Center** (850 Hwy. 1, 707/875-3866, Mon.-Sat. 9am-5pm, Sun. 10am-5pm) in Bodega Bay may look small, but it's chock-full of exactly what you came for: maps, brochures, lists, suggestions, trail guides, events schedules, and even live advice from a local expert.

Transportation

Bodega Bay is on Highway 1 north of Point Reyes National Seashore and west of Petaluma. From the Bay Area, it's a beautiful drive north, hugging the coast, but the cliffs and the road's twists and turns mean taking it slow. A faster way to get here is to take U.S. 101 to Petaluma, take the exit for East Washington Street, and follow Bodega Avenue to Valley Ford Road, cutting across to the coast. You'll hit Bodega Bay about two miles after you pass through Valley Ford. The latter route takes about 1.5 hours, with some of the route slow and winding.

JENNER

Jenner is on Highway 1 at the mouth of the Russian River. It's a beautiful spot for a quiet honeymoon or a paddle in a kayak. **Goat Rock State Beach** (Goat Rock Rd., 707/875-3483, www.parks.ca.gov, day use $8 per vehicle) is at the mouth of the Russian River inside Sonoma Coast State Park. A colony of harbor seals breed and frolic here, and you may also see gray whales, sea otters, elephant seals, and a variety of sea life. Pets are not allowed, and swimming is prohibited.

Accommodations and Food

Both the food and the views are memorable at ★ **River's End** (11048 Hwy. 1, 707/865-2484, www.ilovesunsets.com, summer daily noon-3:30pm and 5pm-9pm, winter Thurs.-Tues. noon-3:30pm and 5pm-8:30pm, $19-42). The restaurant is perched above the spot where the Russian River flows into the Pacific, and it's a beautiful sight to behold over, say, seafood or filet mignon. Prices are high, but if you get a window table at sunset, you may forget to think about them.

The **Jenner Inn and Cottages** (10400 Hwy. 1, 707/865-2377, www.jennerinn.com, $118-338) has a variety of quiet, beautifully furnished rooms that are mere steps from the river. Some rooms have hot tubs and private decks, and breakfast is included.

Fourteen miles north of Jenner proper is the large and luxurious **Timber Cove Inn** (21780 N. Hwy. 1, 707/847-3231 or 800/987-8319, www.timbercoveinn.com, $229-350), with a spacious bar and lounge, an oceanfront patio, rooms with spa tubs and fireplaces, and hiking trails nearby. You can't miss the inn from the road thanks to the 93-foot-tall obelisk rising above the building.

Information and Services

The small but friendly **Jenner Visitors Center** (10439 Hwy. 1, 707/865-9757, www.stewardsofthecoastandredwoods.org, daily 11am-3pm) is across the street from the Jenner Inn. The visitors center is staffed by volunteers, so hours can be unpredictable; call ahead to confirm.

Transportation

Jenner is on Highway 1, right along the ocean. There is no public transportation to get here, but it is a pretty drive from just about anywhere. The fastest route from San Francisco (about 1.75 hours) is to drive up U.S. 101 and make a left onto Washington Street in Petaluma. Washington Street becomes Bodega Avenue and then Valley Ford Road before you make a slight left onto Highway 1 and head north toward Jenner. From Sacramento (2.5 hours) or points in the East Bay, take I-80 west and then navigate to Petaluma, where you continue west to Highway 1.

NORTH OF JENNER

As you hug the shoreline north of Jenner, you'll soon pass through Fort Ross State Historic Park, Salt Point State Park, and Kruse Rhododendron State Reserve.

Fort Ross State Historic Park

There is no historic early American figure named Ross who settled here: "Ross" is short for "Russian," and this park commemorates the history of Russian settlement on the North Coast. In the 19th century Russians

came to the wilds of Alaska and worked with native Alaskans to develop a robust fur trade, harvesting seals, otters, sea lions, and land mammals for their pelts. The enterprise required sea travel as the hunters chased the animals as far as California. Eventually, a group of fur hunters and traders came ashore on what is now the Sonoma Coast and developed a fortified outpost that became known as **Fort Ross** (19005 Hwy. 1, Jenner, 707/847-3286, www.fortross.org, daily sunrise-sunset, compound and visitors center days and hours vary, parking $8). The area gradually became not only a thriving Russian American settlement but also a center for agriculture and shipbuilding and the site of California's first windmills. Learn more at the park's large visitors center, which provides a continuous film and a roomful of exhibits.

You can also walk into the reconstructed fort buildings and see how the settlers lived. (U.S. 101 was originally built through the middle of the fort area, but it was moved to make way for the historic park.) The only original building still standing is the captain's quarters—a large, luxurious house for that time and place. The other buildings, including the large bunkhouse, the chapel, and the two cannon-filled blockhouses, were rebuilt using much of the original lumber used by the Russians. Be aware that a serious visit to the whole fort and the beach beyond entails a level but long walk; wear comfortable shoes and bring a bottle of water.

Salt Point State Park

Stretching for miles along the Sonoma coastline, **Salt Point State Park** (25050 Hwy. 1, Jenner, 707/847-3221, www.parks.ca.gov, daily sunrise-sunset, day use $8 per vehicle) provides easy access from U.S. 101 to more than a dozen sandy state beaches. You don't have to visit the visitors center to enjoy this park and its many beaches—just follow the signs along the highway to the turnoffs and parking lots. If you're looking to scuba dive or free dive, head for **Gerstle Cove,** accessible from the visitors center just south of Salt Point proper. The cove was designated one of California's first underwater parks, and divers who can deal with the chilly water have a wonderful time exploring the diverse undersea wildlife.

Kruse Rhododendron State Reserve

For a genteel experience, head east off Highway 1 to the **Kruse Rhododendron State Reserve** (Hwy. 1 near milepost 43, 707/847-3221, www.parks.ca.gov, daily sunrise-sunset, free), where you can meander along the **China Gulf Trail** in the spring, admiring the profusion of pink rhododendron flowers blooming beneath the second-growth redwood forest. If you prefer a picnic, you'll find tables at many of the beaches—just be aware that the North Coast can be quite windy in the summer.

Stewart's Point

Stewart's Point is home to a post office, a small store, and a restaurant—and that's it. **Stewart's Point Store** (32000 S. Hwy. 1, 707/785-2406, www.stewartspoint.net, daily 6am-8pm, hours vary by season) sells groceries, wine, collectible dishes, hand-knitted hats, and Hostess Zingers. They've also got an on-site deli and a bakery. Upstairs, locally grown musicians perform in a historic dance hall for scheduled events.

Camping

Part of Fort Ross State Historic Park, the **Reef Campground** (19005 Hwy. 1, 707/847-3708, www.parks.ca.gov, Apr.-Nov., $35) has 21 first-come, first-served campsites within a small canyon winding down towards the coast. There are paths here to a couple of scenic coves. A little farther north, **Salt Point State Park** (2050 Hwy. 1, 800/444-7275, www.reserveamerica.com, $35) has scenic **Gerstle Cove Campground** on the west side of the highway and **Woodside Campground** on the eastern side.

THE SEA RANCH

The last 10 miles of the Sonoma Coast before entering Mendocino County are the property of The Sea Ranch, a private coastal community. In the late 1960s, developers purchased a former sheep ranch, planning to build homes that blended into the natural environment. Development was met with opposition from environmental and coastal access groups, which led to the formation of the California Coastal Commission, a state agency that oversees land use and coastal access on the state's coastline. The Sea Ranch was eventually built and the development included six points for public access to the ocean, including Gualala Point Regional Park.

Today, the community is known for its distinctive buildings with wood siding and shingles. One of its structures, Condominium 1, won the American Institute of Architects Gold Medal in 1991 and is now in the National Register of Historic Places. Those hard-won coastal access points make The Sea Ranch a good place to take a break from driving for a short beach stroll. Visitors who want to linger in this low-key community can spend the night at The Sea Ranch Lodge.

★ The Sea Ranch Chapel

Looking from the outside like a wooden stingray with a plume on top, **The Sea Ranch Chapel** (mile marker 55.66, Hwy. 1 at Bosun's Reach, www.thesearanchchapel.org, daily sunrise-sunset) is one of the smallest and most creatively designed places of worship that you'll ever see. Designed by architect James Hubble, this tiny building's beautiful interior has polished redwood benches, three stained glass windows, and a stone floor with an inserted mosaic, and there are local seashells and sea urchins embedded throughout the structure.

Annapolis Winery

You'll find a pleasant coastal climate and a small list of classic California wines at **Annapolis Winery** (26055 Soda Springs Rd., Annapolis, 707/886-5460, www.annapoliswinery.com, daily noon-5pm, free), a small family-owned winery seven miles east of Sea Ranch. You can usually taste pinot, cabernet, zinfandel, and port, depending on what they've made this year and what's in stock. Take a glass outside to enjoy the views from the estate vineyards out over the forested mountains.

Sports and Recreation

With its front nine holes perched above the Pacific, the **Sea Ranch Golf Links** (42000 Hwy. 1, 707/785-2468, www.searanchgolf. com, Mon.-Thurs. $55, Fri.-Sun. and holidays $65) are like the legendary golf courses at Pebble Beach except without the crowds. Designed by Robert Muir Graves, the course also allows you to putt past redwood trees.

Accommodations and Food

Situated on 52 acres of prime coastal real estate, ★ **Sea Ranch Lodge** (2.5 miles north of Stewart's Point on Hwy. 1, 707/785-2371, http://searanchlodge.com, $279-389) offers 19 rooms, all with simple 1960s throwback decor and ocean vistas that evoke paintings. Hiking trails on the grounds offer a self-guided wildflower walk and a short walk to Black Point Beach. Most rooms are equipped with gas fireplaces for those foggy days on the Sonoma Coast. The walls might be a bit thinner than more modern hotels, so earplugs are provided. Guests are also treated to a fine complimentary hot breakfast at the lodge's **Black Point Grill** (2.5 miles north of Stewart's Point on Hwy. 1, 707/785-2371, daily 7am-11am and 11:30am-9pm, $13-27). Black Point Grill is also open to the public, serving everything from burgers to local seafood in a dining area with large windows facing the sea.

The Sea Ranch Chapel

Mendocino Coast

The Mendocino Coast is a popular retreat for those who've been introduced to its specific charms. On weekends, Bay Area residents flock north to their favorite hideaways to enjoy windswept beaches, secret coves, and luscious cuisine. This area is ideal for deep-sea anglers, wine aficionados, and fans of luxury spas. Art is especially prominent in the culture; from the 1960s onward, aspiring artists have found supportive communities, sales opportunities, and homes in Mendocino County, and a number of small galleries display local artwork.

Be aware that the most popular inns fill up fast many weekends year-round. Fall-winter is the high season, with the Crab Festival, the Mushroom Festival, and various harvest and after-harvest wine celebrations. If you want to stay someplace specific on the Mendocino Coast, book your room at least a month in advance for weekday stays and six months or more in advance for major festival weekends.

GUALALA

With a population of 585, Gualala ("wa-LA-la") feels like a metropolis along the Highway 1 corridor in this region. While it's not the most charming coastal town, it does have some of the services other places lack.

Since 1961, the **Art in the Redwoods Festival** (46501 Gualala Rd., 707/884-1138, www.gualalaarts.org, mid-Aug., adults $6, under age 17 free) and its parent organization, Gualala Arts, have been going strong. This major event takes place over the course of a long weekend in mid-August and is run by the same people who bring you the Whale and Jazz Festival in Point Arena in April. Now featuring gallery exhibitions, special dinners, a champagne preview, bell ringers, a quilt raffle, and awards for the artists, this festival is a great reason to get the whole family to Gualala for some renewal and inspiration.

Accommodations

When it comes to food and lodging in Gualala, you're not going to hear so many of those Sonoma and Mendocino County adjectives (luxurious, elegant, pricey), but you will find choices.

For the budget-conscious, a good option is **The Surf Motel** (39170 Hwy. 1, 707/884-3571 or 888/451-7873, www.surfinngualala.com, $99-209). Only a few of the more expensive rooms have ocean views, but a full hot breakfast, flat-screen TVs with DVD players, and wireless Internet access are included for all guests.

The **Breakers Inn** (39300 Hwy. 1, 707/884-3200, www.breakersinn.com, $99-175) has 28 uniquely decorated rooms named after states and countries. All have decks, spas, and fireplaces.

The **Whale Watch Inn** (35100 Hwy. 1, 800/942-5342, www.whalewatchinn.com, $220-300) specializes in romance. Each of its 18 individually decorated, luxuriously appointed rooms has an ocean view and a wood-burning stove. Most also have whirlpool tubs. Every morning, a hot breakfast is delivered to your room. Explore the beach below via a staircase on the grounds.

Four miles north of Gualala, the **North Coast Country Inn** (34591 S. Hwy. 1, 707/884-4537, www.northcoastcountryinn.com, $190-245) was once part of a coastal sheep ranch. Six rooms are outfitted with antique furnishings and fireplaces; three also have kitchenettes. Mornings at the North Coast Country Inn begin with a hot breakfast buffet. An antique store and art gallery are also on the inn's grounds.

Camping

Two nearby parks provide good camping options. One is **Gualala River Redwood Park** (46001 Gualala Rd., 707/884-3533, www.gualalapark.com, May-Oct., day use $5 pp,

Mendocino Coast

restaurant Mon.-Fri. 11:30am-8pm or 9pm, Sat.-Sun. 8am-8pm or 9pm, bar 11:30am-10pm, $14-24) touts its "BBQ, brews and blues." It delivers. This casual barbecue-and-beer joint at the north end of town cooks its meats on a wood-burning, custom-built smoker for 4-12 hours, which results in tender, flavorful beef brisket, Memphis pulled pork, and St. Louis-style pork ribs.

Locals and visitors rave about the tacos at **Antonio's Tacos** (38820 S. Hwy. 1, 707/884-1789, Mon.-Sat. 8am-7pm, $2-12). Carne asada and carnitas are the favorite meat options here. Gussy up your tacos with toppings from the salsa bar.

The Gualala **farmers market** (47950 Center St., 707/884-3726, www.sonoma-county.com, late May-early Nov. Sat. 9:30am-12:30pm) is at the Gualala Community Center. **Surf** (39250 S. Hwy. 1, 707/884-4184, www.surfsuper.com, summer Sat.-Wed. 7:30am-8pm, Thurs.-Fri. 7:30am-9pm, winter daily 7:30am-8pm) is a supermarket that also sells flatbread pizzas and sandwiches.

Transportation
Gualala is 115 miles north of San Francisco on Highway 1, and 60 miles south of Fort Bragg. The **Mendocino Transit Authority** (800/696-4682, www.4mta.org) has a bus line that connects Gualala to Fort Bragg.

POINT ARENA
A small coastal town 1.5 miles south of its namesake point, Point Arena might be one of the North Coast's best secrets. The town's Main Street is Highway 1, which has a couple of bars, restaurants, markets, and the Arena Theater, which attracts all sorts of cultural events. One mile from the little downtown section is the scenic Point Arena Cove, which has a small fishing pier with rocky beaches on either side. The cove feels like the town's true center, a meeting place where fisherfolk constantly take in the conditions of the ocean. Just north of Point Arena Cove is the new California Coastal National Monument Point Arena-Stornetta

camping $42-49 for 2 people); the other is **Gualala Point Regional Park** (42401 Hwy. 1, 707/785-2377, www.sonoma-county.org, day use $7 per vehicle, camping $35), one mile south of the town of Gualala, technically in Sonoma County. Both places offer redwoods, the ocean, and the river.

Food
★ **Bones Roadhouse** (39080 Hwy. 1, 707/884-1188, www.bonesroadhouse.com,

Unit, a stunning park that is sure to make the area less of a secret.

Sights

POINT ARENA LIGHTHOUSE

Although its magnificent Fresnel lens no longer turns through the night, the **Point Arena Lighthouse** (45500 Lighthouse Rd., 707/882-2777 or 877/725-4448, www.pointarenalighthouse.com, summer daily 10am-4:30pm, winter daily 10am-3:30pm, adults $7.50, children $1) remains a Coast Guard light and fog station. But what makes this beacon special is its history. When the 1906 earthquake hit San Francisco, it jolted the land all the way up the coast, severely damaging the Point Arena Lighthouse. When the structure was rebuilt two years later, engineers devised an aboveground foundation that gives the lighthouse both its distinctive shape and additional structural stability.

The lighthouse's extensive interpretive museum, which is housed in the fog station beyond the gift shop, includes the lighthouse's Fresnel lens. Docent-led tours up 145 steep steps to the top of the lighthouse are well worth the trip, both for the views of the lighthouse from the top and for the fascinating story of its destruction and rebirth through the 1906 earthquake as told by the knowledgeable staff. Catch your breath by taking in the surrounding coastline from Manchester State Beach to the north to the new California Coastal National Monument Point Arena-Stornetta Unit to the south. For those who just can't get enough of the lighthouse during daylight hours, consider staying in one of the four former lighthouse keepers' homes (877/725-4448, www.pointarenalighthouse.com, $150-250, two-night minimum on weekends).

★ CALIFORNIA COASTAL NATIONAL MONUMENT POINT ARENA-STORNETTA UNIT

Until recently, the only way to get onto the California Coastal National Monument, a designation given to the rocks, reefs, and islands of California's shoreline, was via water. That changed in 2014 with the creation of **Point Arena-Stornetta Unit** of the **California Coastal National Monument** (North of Point Arena Cove to Manchester State Park, 707/468-4000, www.blm.gov, daily 30 minutes before sunrise-30 minutes after sunset), the first shoreline section of the parkland. The 1,655-acre park is like a greatest-hits compilation of the California coast: vertigo-inducing cliffs, far-ranging ocean views, sea arches, rocky points, and tide pools.

The area can be explored by eight miles of trails including a superb hike that starts from behind the Point Arena City Hall and continues 3.5 miles to Lighthouse Road. Walk another half mile on the road to visit the Point Arena Lighthouse. Parking is available at Point Arena City Hall and at the pullouts along Lighthouse Road.

B. BRYAN PRESERVE

Experience the animals of Africa in Point Arena at the **B. Bryan Preserve** (130 Riverside Dr., 707/882-2297, http://bbryanpreserve.com, Mar.-Sept. daily 9:30am-4pm, Nov.-Feb. daily 9:30am-3pm, adults $35, children 10 and under $20). Antelope, zebras, and giraffes wander around this 110-acre spread. Take a 1.5-hour tour of the preserve or opt to spend a night in one of three lodging options on-site ($165-235).

ARENA THEATER

If you prefer your entertainment on a screen but still like a little atmosphere, take in a show at the **Arena Theater** (214 Main St., 707/882-3456, www.arenatheater.org). This onetime vaudeville theater was also a movie palace when it opened in 1929. In the 1990s, the old theater got a facelift that returned it to its art deco glory. Today, you can see all kinds of films at the Arena, from recent box office toppers to new documentaries and unusual independent films. If a film isn't playing, you might find a live musical or theatrical show.

MANCHESTER STATE PARK

Seven miles north of the town of Point Arena, **Manchester State Park** (44500 Kinney Ln., Manchester, 707/937-5804, day use free) is a wild place perfect for a long, solitary beach walk. The 3.5-mile-long coast is littered with bleached white driftwood and logs that lie on the dark sand like giant bones amid crashing waves. Even the water offshore is protected as part of the 3,782-acre Point Arena State Marine Reserve. At the southwestern tip of the park is Arena Rock, a nautical hazard known for sinking at least six ships before the construction of the nearby Point Arena Lighthouse to the south.

Part of the 1,500 acres of onshore parkland was once a dairy ranch. Now, there's beach, dunes, a wetlands trail, and a campground. The drive-in campground (summer Fri.-Sun., $25, first come, first served) has 41 sites with basic amenities, including fire pits, picnic tables, and pit toilets. Some environmental campsites in the dunes are accessible via a one-mile hike. The sounds of crashing waves nearby will lull you to sleep.

SCHOONER GULCH STATE BEACH

The area around Point Arena is filled with coastal access points. A local favorite is

Schooner Gulch State Beach (intersection of Schooner Gulch Rd. and Hwy. 1, three miles south of Point Arena, 707/937-5804, www.parks.ca.gov). From a pullout north of Schooner Gulch Bridge, trails lead to two different beaches. The southern trail leads to **Schooner Gulch Beach,** a wide, sandy expanse with rocky headlands and a stream flowing into the sea. But the northern trail leads to a more memorable destination: **Bowling Ball Beach.** At low tide, the ocean recedes to reveal small spherical boulders lined up in rows. The end section of the trail is steep and has a rope to help your descent. Once on the beach, hike north about 0.25 mile to find the photo-worthy sight.

Entertainment and Events

With live music three times a week, **215 Main** (215 Main St., 707/882-3215, Sun.-Tues. 3pm-10pm, Wed.-Sat. 3pm-11pm) considers itself a venue for artists, with local art on the walls and offerings from poetry nights to pop-up dinners. The friendly staff pours California wines and craft beers. There is also have a small bar menu.

Despite the fact that local dive bar **Sign of the Whale** (194 Main St., 707/882-2259, Sun.-Thurs. 2pm-10pm, Fri.-Sat. 2pm-2am)

a cliffside trail at the Point Arena-Stornetta Unit of the California Coastal National Monument has only bottled beer and is cash only, it has a surprisingly sophisticated cocktail menu. Locals hold court at the long bar, but there's also a jukebox, arcade game, and two pool tables. Bar patrons can order food from the adjacent restaurant Pacific Plate.

The annual **Whale and Jazz Festival** (707/884-1138, www.gualalaarts.org/whale-jazz) takes place all around Mendocino County in April. Some of the nation's finest jazz performers play in a variety of venues, while the whales put on their own show out in the Pacific. Point Arena Lighthouse offers whale-watching from the shore each day, and the wineries and restaurants of the region provide refreshment and relaxation every evening of the festival weekend.

Accommodations

From 1901 to 1957, the ★ **Coast Guard House** (695 Arena Cove, 707/882-2442 or 800/524-9320, www.coastguardhouse.com, $185-295) was a working Coast Guard life-saving station. Now the main building, which used to house the enlisted men, hosts overnight guests, who enjoy nice views of Point Arena Cove. Four rooms are available, including a suite with two bedrooms. Two detached cottages offer more privacy. The friendly and informative innkeepers serve a hot breakfast in the main house every morning, while restaurants are just a short walk away.

Next door to the Coast Guard House is the **Wharf Master's Inn** (785 Iverson Ave., 707/882-3171 or 800/392-4031, www.wharf-masters.com, $109-499). Many rooms have a fireplace, a two-person spa, and a private deck. Twelve of the units have ocean views. The Wharf Master's House has a kitchen and can accommodate up to eight people.

Food

Arena Market & Café (183 Main St., 707/882-3663, www.arenaorganics.org, summer Mon.-Sat. 7am-7pm, Sun. 8am-6pm) is a co-op committed to local, sustainable, and organic food, and they do their best to compensate farmers fairly and keep money in the community. Stock up on staples at this medium-size grocery store or sit at one of the tables out front and enjoy a cup of homemade soup or coffee. They're one of the only places in town with Wi-Fi.

The **Uneda Eat Cafe** (206 Main St., 707/882-3800, www.unedaeat.com, Wed.-Sat. 5:30pm-8:30pm, $12-22) has preserved the sign of the former owner, an Italian butcher: The storefront still says "Uneda Meat Market."

coastline of Manchester State Park

Now a dine-in, take-out, and catering operation run by Jill and Rob Hunter, who previously owned the popular Pangaea Restaurant, the locavore menu offers international items like Indian-style cauliflower and clay-pot pork, though offerings change daily. The small, narrow restaurant is crowded on weekends when diners occupy the colorful tables and a small counter overlooking the kinetic kitchen.

Blue on the outside, pink on the inside, ★ Franny's Cup and Saucer (213 Main St., 707/882-2500, www.frannyscupandsaucer.com, Wed.-Sat. 8am-4pm, $2-6) is whimsical and welcoming. The owners, Franny and her mother, Barbara, do all their own baking and they even make truffles and other candies from scratch. More hearty fare at this beloved bakery includes mini-pizzas, croque monsieurs, and mind-blowing bacon slippers. It's take-out only, so stop in and pick up a picnic before you go to the lighthouse or one of the parks.

Slightly north of town is Rollerville Café (22900 S. Hwy. 1, 707/882-2077, www.rollervillecafe.com, summer Mon.-Thurs. 8am-2pm, Fri.-Sun. 8am-7:30pm, winter Sun.-Thurs. 8am-2pm, Fri.-Sat. 8am-6:30pm, lunch $8-10, dinner $20-24). Dinner may seem a little pricey, but lunch is available all day. Breakfast (order the crab cakes Benedict) is served until 11am. This is a small, homey place catering to guests at the adjacent timeshare resort as well as locals and travelers.

On the second floor of a two-story building, the Pier Chowder House & Tap Room (790 Port Rd., 707/882-3400, www.thepierchowderhouse.com, summer daily 11am-9pm, winter daily 11am-8pm, $18-25) has an outside deck perfect for taking in the sunset over Point Arena's scenic cove. The menu focuses on seafood. Go for the salmon or rock cod when in season; both are caught by local anglers. There is also a long bar with 31 beers on tap.

In the same building as the Pier Chowder House, Cove Coffee and Tackle (790 Port Rd., 707/882-2665, daily 7am-3pm, $6-10)

attracts locals with tasty items like "Nate's Special," an egg sandwich with pesto, cream cheese, sausage, onion, and swiss cheese. It's a perfect place to go for a morning coffee.

The weekly Mendocino County Farmers Market (214 Main St., 707/964-6718, www.mcfarm.org, Wed. 11am-2pm) is in the Point Arena Theater parking lot.

Information and Services

The Coast Community Library (225 Main St., 707/882-3114, www.coastcommunitylibrary.org, Mon. and Fri. noon-6pm, Tues. 10am-6pm, Wed. 10am-8pm, Thurs. noon-8pm, Sat. noon-3pm) is a hub of activity thanks to its central location—the impressive 1928 Point Arena Mercantile Company building—and its free Internet access.

Many places in Point Arena are cash-only. The Redwood Credit Union (280 Main St.) has an ATM right out front.

Transportation

Point Arena is 10 miles north of Gualala on Highway 1, and about 120 miles north of San Francisco.

The Mendocino Transit Authority (800/696-4682, www.4mta.org) runs the route 75 bus to connect Point Arena south to Gualala and north to Fort Bragg. The bus usually runs once a day, although schedules are subject to change; contact the transit authority for details.

ELK

The town of Elk used to be called Greenwood, after the family of Caleb Greenwood, who settled here in about 1850. Details of the story vary, but it is widely believed that Caleb was part of a mission to rescue survivors of the Donner Party after their rough winter near Truckee.

Greenwood State Beach

From the mid-19th century until the 1920s, the stretch of shore at Greenwood State Beach (Hwy. 1, 707/937-5804, www.parks.ca.gov, visitors center mid-Mar.-Nov.

Wed.-Sun. 10am-4pm) was a stop for large ships carrying timber to points of sale in San Francisco and sometimes even China. The visitors center displays photographs and exhibits about Elk's past in the lumber business. It also casts light on the Native American heritage of the area and the natural resources that are still abundant.

A short hike demonstrates what makes this area so special. From the parking lot, follow the trail down toward the ocean. You'll soon come to a fork; to the right is a picnic area. Follow the left fork to another picnic site and then, soon afterward, the beach. Turn left and walk about 0.25 mile to reach Greenwood Creek. Shortly past it is a cliff, at which point you have to turn around and walk back up the hill. Even in the short amount of time it takes to do this walk, you'll experience lush woods, sandy cliffs, and dramatic ocean overlooks. In winter, the walk can be dark and blustery and even more intriguing, although it's a pleasure in any season.

Greenwood State Beach is alongside the town of Elk, 10-15 miles north of Point Arena and about 17 miles south of Mendocino.

Accommodations and Food

Perched on a hillside over the stunning Greenwood State Beach cove, the ★ **Elk Cove Inn** (6300 S. Hwy. 1, 800/275-2967, www.elkcoveinn.com, $155-395) offers luxury accommodations, generous hospitality, and superb views of the nearby Pacific, studded with islands and a scattering of offshore rocks. Check-in comes with a complimentary cocktail or glass of wine and a welcome basket filled with wine, fruit, popcorn, and fresh-baked cookies. Choose from reasonably priced rooms in the main house, cozy cabins with an ocean view, or luxurious suites with jetted soaking tubs and private balconies or patios. A private staircase leads down to the beach below. There's also a full-service day spa with a sauna and aromatherapy steam shower. The innkeepers have thought of everything to make your stay top notch, from port wine and chocolates in the rooms to the big morning breakfast buffet of Southern comfort food with a glass of champagne.

Formerly the Griffin House Inn, the **Sacred Rock Resort** (5910 S. Hwy. 1, 707/877-3422, www.sacredrockresort.com, $138-260) has five cottages, three of which have private decks overlooking Elk Cove. Full breakfast can be delivered to your room, but there's also a lively dining room. Housed in a little blue cottage attached to the resort,

Bridget Dolan's Pub & Restaurant

Bridget Dolan's Pub & Restaurant (5910 S. Hwy. 1, 707/877-1820, www.griffinn.com, summer Thurs.-Mon. 4:30pm-9pm, winter Thurs.-Mon. 4:30pm-8pm, $9-16) is a terrific place to hole up with a draft beer on a rainy winter day or foggy summer afternoon. The tables are draped in white tablecloths and the small bar is lined with locals. The menu includes burgers, pizzas, and hearty pub fare like cottage pie.

With a perfect location in the center of town and across the street from the ocean, Queenie's Roadhouse Café (6061 Hwy. 1, 707/877-3285, http://queeniesroadhousecafe. com, Thurs.-Mon. 8am-3pm, $7-16) is the place to go for hot food and a friendly atmosphere. Expect to be full for a while after leaving this diner.

The Beacon Light by the Sea (7401 S. Hwy. 1, south of Elk, 707/877-3311, Fri.-Sat. 5pm-11pm) is the best bar in the area. Its colorful owner, R. D. Beacon, was born in Elk and has run the Beacon Light since 1971. He claims it's the only place you can get hard liquor for 14 miles in any direction. With 85 different brands of vodka, 20 whiskeys, and 15 tequilas, there's something for every sort of drinker. On clear days, the views stretch all the way to the Point Arena Lighthouse.

ALBION AND LITTLE RIVER

Tiny Albion is along Highway 1 almost 30 miles north of Point Arena and about 8 miles south of Mendocino. Little River is about five miles farther north, also on Highway 1. There is a state park and several plush places to stay.

Van Damme State Park

The centerpiece of Van Damme State Park (Hwy. 1, 3 miles south of Mendocino, 707/937-5804, www.parks.ca.gov, daily 8am-9pm, $8) is the Pygmy Forest, where you'll see a true biological rarity: Mature yet tiny cypress and pine trees perpetually stunted by a combination of always-wet ground and poor soil-nutrient conditions. To get there, drive along Airport Road to the trail parking lot (opposite the county airport) and follow the wheelchair-accessible loop trail (0.25 mile, easy). You can also get there by hiking along the Fern Canyon Trail (7 miles round-trip, difficult).

Kayak Mendocino (707/813-7117, www. kayakmendocino.com) launches four Sea Cave Nature Tours (9am, 11:30am, 2pm, and sunset, $60 pp) from Van Damme State Park. No previous experience is necessary; the expert guides provide all the equipment you need and teach you how to paddle your way through the sea caves and around the harbor seals.

Accommodations

There's no place quite like ★ The Andiron (6051 N. Hwy. 1, Little River, 707/937-1543, www.theandiron.com, $139-299). The one- and two-room cabins in a meadow above Highway 1 are filled with curiosities and kitsch. Every room is different. One has a unique camel-shaped bar, while another has a coin-operated vibrating bed. Most have vintage board games, View-Masters, and an eclectic library of books. Standard amenities include small wooden decks and small flat-screen TVs. A hot tub under the trees is available for guests. The fun-loving owners throw happy hour parties every weekend, including "Fondue Fridays," when they serve the melted cheese dish along with local beers and wines. The Andiron isn't fancy, but it's fun.

A longtime lodging destination, the ★ Heritage House Resort (5200 Hwy. 1, 707/202-9000, http://heritagehouseresort. com, $190-450) has been undergoing a massive, multiyear renovation. The property has a rich history that includes being the past hideout of bank robber "Baby Face" Nelson and being the setting of the 1978 film *Same Time, Next Year*. Perched on stunning cliffs pocked with coves, the numerous buildings spread across 37 acres. Though the resort itself is a work in progress, the rooms are top tier. Each is enhanced by private decks, rain showers, and wood-burning or gas fireplaces. The units are priced according to proximity to the water and quality of the view. Once completed, the resort will also have a full-service spa and restored garden.

The **Albion River Inn** (3790 N. Hwy. 1, 6 miles south of Mendocino, 707/937-1919 or 800/479-7944, www.albionriverinn.com, $195-355) is a gorgeous and serene setting for an away-from-it-all vacation. This cliffside inn is all about romance. A full breakfast is included in the room rates, but pets and smoking are not allowed, and there are no TVs.

The **Little River Inn** (7901 N. Hwy. 1, Little River, 707/937-5942 or 888/466-5683, www.littleriverinn.com, $130-375) appeals to coastal vacationers who like a little luxury. It has a nine-hole golf course and two lighted tennis courts, and all its recreation areas overlook the Pacific, which crashes on the shore just across the highway from the inn. The sprawling white Victorian house and barns hide the expansiveness of the grounds, which also have a great restaurant and a charming sea-themed bar. Relax even more at the in-house Spa at Little River Inn.

Stevenswood Spa Resort (8211 N. Hwy. 1, Little River, 800/421-2810, www.stevenswood.com, $269-499) is a modern facility with contemporary decor. A classy restaurant and a day spa help you feel relaxed and pampered, as does Van Damme State Park, which surrounds the resort on three sides. Book one of the outdoor in-ground hot tubs at the spa for a relaxing evening.

Camping

There's camping on the coast at **Van Damme State Park** (Hwy. 1, 707/937-5804, www.parks.ca.gov, reservations 800/444-7275, www.reserveamerica.com, $35), three miles south of Mendocino. The appealing campground offers picnic tables, fire rings, and food lockers, as well as restrooms and hot showers. The park's 1,831 acres include beaches as well as forest, so there's lots of natural beauty to enjoy. Reservations are strongly encouraged.

Food

★ **Ledford House Restaurant** (3000 N. Hwy. 1, Albion, 707/937-0282, www.ledfordhouse.com, Wed.-Sun. 5pm-close, $19-30) is beautiful even from a distance; you'll see it on the hill as you drive up Highway 1. With excellent food and nightly jazz performances, it's one of the true "special occasion" choices in the area. Try to reserve a table for sunset.

A fine restaurant with stunning coast views is the **5200 Restaurant & Lounge** (Heritage House Resort, 5200 N. Hwy. 1, 707/202-9000,

Heritage House Resort

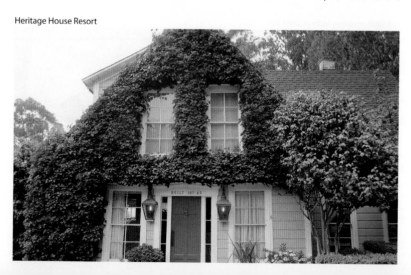

ext. 5200, http://heritagehouseresort.com, Mon.-Fri. 8am-10:30am and 5pm-9pm, Sat.-Sun. 8am-11am and 5pm-9pm, lounge daily 4pm-9pm, $12-33) at the Heritage House Resort. The restaurant has farm-to-fork cuisine for breakfast and dinner, while the lounge has a great happy hour (4pm-6pm) in a comfortable atmosphere that includes a fireplace, couches, and board games.

Starting the day at ★ **Circa '62** (7051 N. Hwy. 1, Little River, 707/937-5525, www.schoolhousecreek.com, Mon.-Fri. 8am-11am, Sat.-Sun. 8am-noon, $9-16) is highly recommended. Housed within a cozy blue-and-white former schoolhouse on the grounds of the Inn at Schoolhouse Creek, the building oozes charm, from its fireplace to its ocean-facing windows. Yet it's the glorious food that makes this place worthwhile. The creative, changing menu offers the likes of steak-and-egg tacos and a hash brown waffle drenched in sausage gravy.

Wild Fish (7750 N. Hwy. 1, 707/937-3055, www.wild-fish.com, Mon.-Thurs. 11:30am-2:30pm and 5pm-9pm, Fri.-Sat. 11:30am-2:30pm and 5pm-9:30pm, Sun. 5pm-9pm, $22-39) utilizes local assets, from organic produce to wild-caught seafood, on an ever-changing menu. The wild king salmon and petrale sole are caught right out of Fort Bragg's Noyo Harbor.

Tucked into a corner of a convenience store, the **Little River Market Grill & Gourmet Deli** (7746 N. Hwy. 1, Little River, 707/937-5133, market daily 8am-7pm, deli daily 8am-4pm, $8) is a local favorite. This better-than-average deli has a wide range of options, including burgers, pulled pork sandwiches, and fish tacos. Nice vegetarian options include the tasty pesto veggie and avocado sandwich. This is the place to grab a sandwich for a picnic on the coast.

★ **MENDOCINO**

Perched on a headland surrounded by the Pacific, Mendocino is one of the most picturesque towns on the California coast. Quaint bed-and-breakfasts, art colonies, and local sustainable dining add to its charm, making it a favorite for romantic weekend getaways.

Once a logging town, Mendocino was reborn as an artist community in the 1950s. One of its most striking buildings is the town's Masonic Hall, dating from 1866 and adorned with a redwood statue of Father Time on its roof. Many New Englanders settled in the region in its early years. With its old water towers and historic buildings, it resembles a New

the steak-and-egg tacos at Circa '62

Mendocino

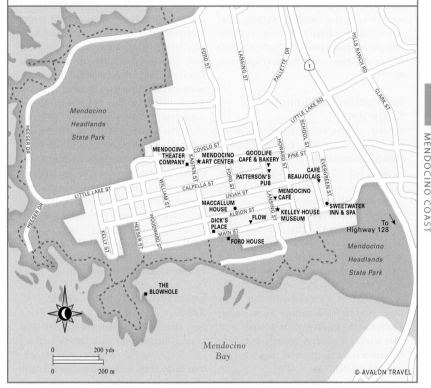

England fishing village—so much so that it played one in the long-running TV series *Murder, She Wrote*. It was also a stand-in for Monterey in the 1955 James Dean film *East of Eden*.

Mendocino Art Center

The town of Mendocino has long been an inspiration and a gathering place for artists of many varieties, and the **Mendocino Art Center** (45200 Little Lake St., 707/937-5818 or 800/653-3328, www.mendocinoartcenter. org, daily 10am-5pm, donation) gives these diverse artists a community, provides them with opportunities for teaching and learning, and displays contemporary works. Since 1959 the center has offered artist workshops and retreats. Today it has a flourishing schedule of

events and classes, five galleries, and a sculpture garden. You can even drop in and make some art of your own. Supervised open studios in ceramics, jewelry making, watercolor, sculpture, and drawing take place throughout the year (call for specific schedules, $12-15 per session).

Kelley House Museum

The mission of the lovely, stately **Kelley House Museum** (45007 Albion St., 707/937-5791, www.kelleyhousemuseum. org, Fri.-Mon. 11am-3pm, free) is to preserve the history of Mendocino for future generations. The permanent exhibits chronicle a notorious local shipwreck and the Native American population, while a collection of photos details the town in present times and

100 years ago. Ask about the town's water-rights issues for a great lesson in the untold history of the Mendocino Coast. On weekends, docents lead two-hour walking tours (11am, $10) that detail Mendocino's history. Self-guided audio tours ($10) are available when the museum or research office (1pm-4pm) is open.

Mendocino Headlands State Park

No trip to Mendocino is complete without a walk along the rugged coastline of **Mendocino Headlands State Park** (west of town, 707/937-5804, www.parks.ca.gov, daily sunrise-sunset). A series of trails along the seaside cliffs west of town offer views of the area's sea caves and coves. It's a favorite spot for painters and photographers hoping to capture the majesty of the coast. In winter, the park is a great vantage point for viewing migrating gray whales. In town, the **Historic Ford House** (735 Main St., 707/937-5397, www.mendoparks.org, daily 11am-4pm, free, donations encouraged) doubles as the Mendocino Headlands State Park Visitor Center. A favorite display in the center is a scale model of the town, constructed in 1890.

Point Cabrillo Light Station

Whether you're into scenery or history, nautical or otherwise, you won't want to miss a visit to the **Point Cabrillo Light Station Historic Park** (45300 Lighthouse Rd., 707/937-6122, www.pointcabrillo.org, daily 11am-4pm, $5), between Mendocino and Fort Bragg. This beautiful lighthouse has been functioning since the early 1900s. The light station was absorbed into the California State Parks system in 2002, and in 2009 it became a victim of state budget cuts and saw its services curtailed. The site is currently being managed by a volunteer organization, the Point Cabrillo Lightkeepers Association. Take a tour of the famous Fresnel lens, learn about the infamous *Frolic* shipwreck of 1850, and explore the tide-pool aquarium. For an overnight stay, rent the lightkeeper's house or two cottages on the grounds (800/262-7801, www.mendocino-vacations.com, $331-1,163).

Entertainment and Events
BARS

For a place to hunker down over a pint, head to cozy **Patterson's Pub** (10485 Lansing St., 707/937-4782, www.pattersonspub. com, daily 10am-midnight, restaurant daily

Mendocino

11am-11pm). This traditional Irish-style pub is in the former rectory of a 19th-century Catholic church. It nods to the 21st century with six plasma TVs that screen current sporting events. Order a simple, filling meal at the tables or at the bar, where you'll find 14 beers on tap, a full-fledged wine list, and liquor imported from around the world.

So where do the locals go for a drink in Mendocino? That would be **Dick's Place** (45080 Main St., 707/937-6010, daily 11:30am-2am), sometimes called Richard's by the Sea. Dick's is an old-school, cash-only bar, with a mounted buck head draped in Christmas lights as decor. Dick's is easy to find: Look for the only neon sign on Main Street, in the shape of a martini glass.

LIVE MUSIC

For live music on the Mendocino Coast, head to the **Caspar Inn** (14957 Caspar Rd., Caspar, 707/964-5565, http://casparinn.biz, Fri.-Sat. 7pm-2am, cover varies), about five miles north of Mendocino and six miles south of Fort Bragg. The Caspar offers a full bar and a roadhouse experience with live music on Friday and Saturday nights. Bands might play anything from Afrobeat to Americana.

THEATER

The **Mendocino Theater Company** (45200 Little Lake St., 707/937-4477, www.mendocinotheatre.org, shows Thurs.-Sat. 8pm, Sun. 2pm, adults $25, students $12) offers a genuine small-theater experience. All plays are staged in the 75-seat Helen Schoeni Theater for an intimate night of live drama or comedy. The small, old weathered building exudes just the right kind of charm to draw in lovers of quirky community theater. But this little theater company has big goals, and it tends to take on thought-provoking work by contemporary playwrights.

EVENTS

For two weekends every March, the Point Cabrillo Light Station is host to the annual **Whale Festival** (707/937-6123, www.pointcabrillo.org, Mar., $5), a chance to get expert guidance as you scan the sea for migrating gray whales headed north for the summer.

In July, musicians of all types descend on the temporarily warmish coast for the **Mendocino Music Festival** (707/937-2044, www.mendocinomusic.com, July, concert ticket prices vary). For 2.5 weeks, live performances are held at venues around the area. There's always chamber music, orchestral

Patterson's Pub

concerts, opera, jazz, and bluegrass, and there's usually world music, blues, singer-songwriters, and dance performances. A centerpiece of the festival is the famed big-band concert. In addition to 13 evenings of music, there are three series of daytime concerts: piano, jazz, and village chamber concerts. No series passes are available; all events require separate tickets.

If restaurants are the heart of the Mendocino food scene, festivals are its soul. **Taste of Mendocino** (888/636-3624, http://winecrab.com) comprises a couple of sub-festivals: **Mendocino Crab, Wine & Beer Days** takes place in January and offers a burst of crab-related events (prices vary); in November, the focus is on the wild mushroom season, and you can come to the **Beer, Wine & Mushroom Festival** for classes, tastings, and tours (prices vary) to learn to cook or just to eat. Check the website for a plethora of other special events.

Shopping

On the coast, the best place to browse is **Mendocino Village.** Not only are the galleries and boutiques welcoming and fun, the whole downtown area is beautiful. It seems that every shop in the Main Street area has its own garden, and each fills with a riotous cascade of flowers in the summer. Even if you hate to shop, make the trip down to the village just to literally smell the roses.

Panache (45120 Main St., 707/937-1234, www.thepanachegallery.com, daily 10:30am-5pm) displays and sells beautiful works of art in all sorts of media. You'll find paintings, jewelry, sculpture, and art glass. Much of the artistic focus is reminiscent of the sea crashing just outside the large multiroom gallery. The wooden furniture and boxes are a special treat: Handmade treasures using rare woods are combined and then sanded and polished to silky-smooth finishes.

If you love fine woodworking and hand-crafted furniture, you will not want to miss the **Highlight Gallery** (45094 Main St., 707/937-3132, www.thehighlightgallery.com,

daily 10am-5pm). Although the gallery has branched out in recent years to feature glass-work, ceramics, painting, and sculpture, its roots are in woodwork, which it maintains as a focus.

In the village, **The Gallery Bookshop** (Main St. and Kasten St., 707/937-2665, www.gallerybookshop.com, Sun.-Thurs. 9:30am-6pm, Fri.-Sat. 9:30am-9pm) is the place to go to pick up something to read. This large store has fiction from around the world along with the works of local authors. They host an array of literary events, too.

Sports and Recreation
HIKING

Some of the most popular hiking trails in coastal Mendocino wind through **Russian Gulch State Park** (Hwy. 1, 2 miles north of Mendocino, 707/937-5804, www.parks.ca.gov, $8). Russian Gulch has its own **Fern Canyon Trail** (3 miles round-trip), which winds into a second-growth redwood forest filled with lush green ferns. At the four-way junction, turn left to hike another 0.75 miles to the ever-popular waterfall. You're likely to be part of a crowd visiting the falls on summer weekends. Making a right at the four-way junction will take you on a three-mile loop, for a total hike of six miles that leads to the top of the attractive little waterfall. If you prefer the shore to the forest, hike west to take in the lovely wild headlands and see blowholes, grasses, and trawlers out seeking the day's catch. The biggest attraction is the **Devil's Punchbowl,** a collapsed sea cave 100 feet across and 60 feet deep. There's also a nice beach.

KAYAKING AND STAND-UP PADDLEBOARDING

Kayak and canoe trips are a popular summer activity on the Mendocino Coast. The shoreline is pocked with caves and coves that are ideal for kayaking or stand-up paddling. Some of the best can be accessed in the waters off Van Damme State Park. A short paddle to the north, there are some impressive sea caves that adventurous paddlers can pass through. **Kayak Mendocino** (707/813-7117, www.kayakmendocino.com, SUP rentals $25/two hours) has a bus parked down by the beach that rents kayaks and SUPs. From there, guides lead SUP and kayak sea cave tours (daily 9am, 11:30am, and 2pm, adults $60, children under 12 $40).

To explore the relatively sedate waters of the Big River estuary, consider renting an outrigger or even a sailing canoe from **Catch a Canoe & Bicycles Too** (44850 Comptche Ukiah Rd., 707/937-0273, www.catchacanoe.com, daily 9am-5 pm, boat and bike rentals adults $28 pp for 3 hours, children aged 6-17 $14 pp) at the Stanford Inn. The guided tours (June-Sept., $65 pp) include an estuary excursion with a naturalist and a ride on an outrigger that utilizes solar energy for power.

SURFING

Big River is a beach break surf spot just south of the town of Mendocino where the Big River flows into the ocean. It's a place you can check out from Highway 1, and on most days, all levels of surfers can try their hand at surfing the break. More experienced surfers should try **Smuggler's Cove,** in Mendocino Bay on the south side of Big River. It's a reef break that usually only works during winter swells.

DIVING

A good spot for abalone is **The Blowhole** (end of Main St.), a favorite summer lounging spot for locals. In the water, you'll find abalone and their empty shells; colorful, tiny nudibranchs; and occasionally, overly friendly seals. The kelp beds just offshore attract divers who don't fear cold water and want to check out the complex ecosystem. Check with the state Department of Fish and Game (916/445-0411, www.wildlife.ca.gov) for the rules about taking abalone, which is strictly regulated; most species are endangered and can't be harvested. Game wardens can explain the abalone season opening and closing dates, catch limits, licensing information, and the best spots to dive each year.

SPAS

Of all the reasons people choose to vacation on the Mendocino Coast, the main one seems to be plain old relaxation. The perfect way to do so is to seek out one of the many nearby spas. The **Sweetwater Spa & Inn** (44840 Main St., 800/300-4140, www.sweetwaterspa.com, Mon.-Fri. 1pm-9pm, Sat.-Sun. noon-9pm, $15-19/half-hour, $18-23/hour) rents indoor hot tubs by the half-hour and hour. They also have group tub and sauna rates ($10-12). Sweetwater offers a range of massage services ($90-154) at reasonable rates. The rustic buildings and garden setting complete the experience. Appointments are required for massage and private tubs, but walk-ins are welcome to use the communal tub and sauna.

For a massage in the comfort of your own accommodations, make an appointment for a foot rub, herbal facial, full-body massage, or acupuncture with **The Body Works** (707/357-5162, www.massagetime.biz, massages $80-250).

Accommodations
$150-250

The warm and welcoming ★ **Blackberry Inn** (44951 Larkin Rd., 707/937-5281 or 800/950-7806, www.mendocinomotel.com, $125-225) is in the hills beyond the center of Mendocino. The inn looks like a town from the Old West. Each of the 16 rooms has a different storefront outside, including the bank, the saloon, the barbershop, and the land-grant office. Each is charmingly decorated and beautifully maintained with plush, comfortable bedding cozied up with colonial-style quilts, along with the modern convenience of microwaves, fridges, and free wireless Internet. The manager-hosts are the nicest you'll find anywhere.

Sweetwater Inn and Spa (44840 Main St., 800/300-4140, www.sweetwaterspa.com, $125-300) harks back to the days when Mendocino was a colony of starving artists. A redwood water tower was converted into a guest room, joined by a motley connection of detached cottages that guarantee privacy.

Every guest room and cottage has its own style—you'll find a spiral staircase in one of the water towers, a hot tub on a redwood deck in the Garden Cottage, and fireplaces in many of the units. The eclectic decor makes each room different, and many return guests request their favorite room. Thick gardens surround the building complex and a path leads back to the Garden Spa. The location, just past downtown on Main Street, is perfect for dining, shopping, and art walks.

The luxurious **Glendeven Inn** (8205 N. Hwy. 1, 707/937-0083 or 800/822-4536, www.glendeven.com, $205-350) is situated in a historic farmhouse with ocean views. The hosts will help you settle in with complimentary wine and hors d'oeuvres in the late afternoon, and wake you in the morning with a three-course made-to-order breakfast, delivered to your room.

The 1882 **MacCallum House** (45020 Albion St., 800/609-0492, www.maccallumhouse.com, $159-279) is the king of luxury on the Mendocino Coast. The facility includes several properties in addition to the main building in Mendocino Village. Choose from private cottages ($199-279) with hot tubs, suites with jetted tubs, and rooms with opulent antique appointments.

The woodwork gleams and the service pleases. There's a two-night minimum on weekends, and a three-night minimum for most holidays. Room rates include a cooked-to-order breakfast.

The **Blue Door Inn** (10481 Howard St., 707/937-4892, www.bluedoorinn.com, $225-275) aims to spoil you. Five sleek, modern rooms come with flat-screen TVs and gas fireplaces. The two-course breakfast features homemade pastries and egg dishes.

OVER $250

Up and away from the beaches, sitting amid redwoods, the **Stanford Inn** (44850 Comptche Ukiah Rd., 0.5 mile east of Hwy. 1, 707/937-5615 or 800/331-8884, www.stanfordinn.com, $305-500) is an upscale forest lodge. The location is convenient to hiking and only a short drive from Mendocino Village and the coast. Rooms have beautiful, honey wood-paneled walls, pretty furniture, and fluffy down comforters. If you're traveling with a group, consider one of the elegant two-bedroom suites. Amenities include a wood-burning fireplace, Internet access, a pool, sauna and hot tub, and free use of mountain bikes. Gardens surrounding the resort are perfect for strolling after a

the front deck of the Brewery Gulch Inn

complimentary vegan breakfast at the on-site Ravens Restaurant.

A place of serenity just a mile south of the village, the ★ **Brewery Gulch Inn** (9401 Hwy. 1, 800/578-4454, www.brewerygulchinn.com, $325-495) provides a lot of amenities to guests staying in its 11 rooms, including a made-to-order hot breakfast and a light dinner buffet with wine. The rooms are modern and calming with plush carpets, feather beds, and gas fireplaces. All rooms have ocean views. Downstairs is a wonderful, roomy common area that has a steel fireplace. Relax with a newspaper, book, or magazine from the extensive collection. There's also a collection of over 500 DVDs that can be viewed in the comfort of your own room.

The beautifully restored 1909 **Point Cabrillo Head Lightkeeper's House** (45300 Lighthouse Rd., 707/937-5033, www.mendocinovacations.com, 2-night minimum, $331-1,163 for 2 nights) is a home-away-from-home. It's atop a cliff beside the Pacific, so you can watch for whales, dolphins, and seabirds without leaving the porch. Four bedrooms sleep eight people, with 4.5 baths and a very modern kitchen. Larger groups can also rent two of the cottages nearby.

Food
AMERICAN

Publications including the *Wall Street Journal* rave about **Trillium Café** (10390 Kasten St., 707/937-3200, Sun.-Thurs. 11:30am-2:30pm and 5:30pm-8:30pm, Fri.-Sat. 11:30am-2:30pm and 5:30pm-9pm, $22-36). The shellfish fettuccine is a favorite. Dine inside by the fireplace or out on the deck overlooking a garden where many of the restaurant's ingredients grow.

CAFÉS

The **Goodlife Café and Bakery** (10483 Lansing St., 707/937-0836, http://goodlifecafemendo.com, Mon.-Sat. 8am-5pm, Sun. 8am-4pm, $5-13) is a great place for a pick-me-up in the form of an espresso drink, a freshly made pastry, or a sandwich on delicious, pillowy focaccia. There are lots of gluten-free options as well. The busy café has seating inside and outside. The indoor counter seats have a view of busy Lansing Street.

One of the most appealing and dependable places to get a good meal any day of the week is the **Mendocino Café** (10451 Lansing St., 707/937-6141, www.mendocinocafe.com, daily 11am-4pm and 5pm-9pm, $14-32). The café has good, simple, well-prepared food, a small kids menu, a wine list, and a beer list. Enjoy a Thai burrito, fresh local rockfish, or a steak in the warm, well-lit dining room. Or sit outside: The café is in the gardens of Mendocino Village, and thanks to a heated patio, you can enjoy outdoor dining any time of day.

FARMERS MARKETS

Mendocino has a weekly **farmers market** (Howard St. and Main St., www.mcfarm.org, May-Oct. Fri. noon-2pm), where you can find seasonal produce, flowers, fish, wine, honey, and more.

FRENCH

★ **Café Beaujolais** (961 Ukiah St., 707/937-5614, www.cafebeaujolais.com, Mon.-Tues. 5:30pm-9pm, Wed.-Sun. 11:30am-2:30pm and 5:30pm-9pm, $23-38) is a standout French-California restaurant in an area dense with great upscale cuisine. This charming out-of-the-way spot is a few blocks from the center of Mendocino Village in an old vine-covered house. Despite the white tablecloths and crystal, the atmosphere is casual at lunch and only slightly more formal at dinner. The giant salads and delectable entrées are made with organic produce, humanely raised meats, and locally caught seafood. The portions are enormous, but come half-size by request. The waitstaff are friendly, helpful, and knowledgeable about the menu and wine list—and local attractions, for that matter. Reservations are available on the website.

VEGETARIAN

Vegetarians and carnivores alike rave about **Ravens Restaurant** (Stanford Inn, 44850

Comptche Ukiah Rd., 0.5 mile east of Hwy. 1, 707/937-5615 or 800/331-8884, www.ravensrestaurant.com, daily 8am-10:30am and 5:30pm-close, $12-27). Inside the lodge, which is surrounded by lush organic gardens, you'll find a big, open dining room. Many of the vegetarian and vegan dishes served use produce from the inn's own organic farm. At breakfast, enjoy delectable vegetarian (or vegan, with tofu) scrambles, omelets, and Florentines, complete with homemade bread and English muffins. At dinner, try one of the seasonal vegetarian entrées. The wine list reflects organic, biodynamic, and sustainable-practice wineries.

Information and Services

You can pick up a Mendocino County Map and a copy of *101 Things to Do in Mendocino County* (www.101things.com) at many local businesses.

Transportation

It's simplest to navigate to and within Mendocino with your own vehicle. From U.S. 101 near Cloverdale, take Highway 128 northwest for 60 miles. Highway 128 becomes Highway 1 on the coast; Mendocino is another 10 miles north. A slower, more scenic alternative is to take Highway 1 the whole way from San Francisco to Mendocino; this route takes at least 4.5 hours. Mendocino has a fairly compact downtown area, Mendocino Village, with a concentration of restaurants, shops, and inns just a few blocks from the beach.

The **Mendocino Transit Authority** (800/696-4682, http://mendocinotransit. org) operates a dozen bus routes that connect Mendocino and Fort Bragg with larger cities like Santa Rosa and Ukiah, where you can make connections to Amtrak, Greyhound, and airports for access to farther-away points.

FORT BRAGG

A former military outpost and the home to a major logging company, Fort Bragg is the Mendocino Coast's largest city. With chain fast-food joints and hotels lining Highway 1 as it passes through town, it doesn't have the immediate charm of its neighbor to the south. But it does offer some great restaurants, interesting downtown shops, and proximity to coastal landmarks, including Glass Beach and MacKerricher State Park.

Skunk Train

The California Western Railroad, popularly called the **Skunk Train** (depot at end of Laurel St., 707/964-6371, www.skunktrain. com, office 9am-3pm, adults $59, children $34), is perfect for rail buffs and traveling families. The restored steam locomotives pull trains from the coast at Fort Bragg 40 miles through the redwood forest to the town of Willits and back. Passengers see the majesty of the redwoods while experiencing a hint of life in Northern California before highways. The brightly painted trains appeal to children, and the historic aspects and scenery call to adults.

Board in either Fort Bragg or Willits, making a round-trip to return to your lodgings for the night. Another option is to take the Skunk Train to **Camp Noyo,** a former logging camp on the Noyo River where you can bed down in a campsite or a chalet ($100-200). Check the website for special events like a Halloween pumpkin patch excursion and a special Zombie Train.

The **Mendocino Coast Model Railroad and Navigation Company** (behind the Skunk Train Depot, end of Laurel St., www. mendorailhistory.org, daily 11am-2pm when Skunk Train runs, adults $5, children $3) is worth checking out. Within a shed in an operational train yard that recreates Fort Bragg's logging past in miniature. The large room is full of noise as model trains chug, bells ding, and lumber splashes into water. Try and spot the Bigfoot figurine within all of the action.

MacKerricher State Park

Three miles north of Fort Bragg, **MacKerricher State Park** (Hwy. 1, 707/964-9112, district office 707/937-5804, www.parks. ca.gov, daily sunrise-10pm, day use free) offers the small duck-filled Cleone Lake, six miles of sandy ocean beaches, four miles of cliffs and crags, and **camping** (reservations 800/444-7275, www.reserveamerica.com, $35). The main attraction is a gigantic, almost complete skeleton of a whale near the park entrance. Because there's no day-use fee, you can stop in to see the whale even if you don't have time to hang out at the park. If you're lucky, you can also spot live whales and harbor seals frolicking in the ocean. The coast can be rough here, so don't swim or wade unless it's what the locals call a "flat day"—no big waves and undertow. If the kids want to play in the water, take them to **Pudding Creek Beach** in the park, about 2.5 miles south of the campground, where they can play in the relatively sheltered area under the trestle bridge. Hikers will enjoy the **Ten Mile Beach Trail** (10 miles roundtrip), an old logging road that goes from Laguna Point to Ten Mile River.

Glass Beach

The most famous beach in the Mendocino area, **Glass Beach** (Elm St. and Glass Beach Dr.) is not a miracle of nature. This fascinating beach strewn with sea glass was once the city dump. As the ocean rose over the landfill, the heavy glass that had been dumped there

stayed put. Years of pounding surf polished and smoothed the broken edges. At the tideline, amber, green, and clear sea glass color the shore.

Beachcombers used to collect the smooth-coated shards of glass; now that the beach is under the management of MacKerricher State Park, it's against the rules to remove them. Unfortunately, there's less sea glass on the beach than there used to be, so visitors may be disappointed. The trail down to Glass Beach is short but steep and treacherous; don't wear sandals—good walking or hiking shoes and attention to safety are a must.

Triangle Tattoo Museum

The **Triangle Tattoo Museum** (356B N. Main St., 707/964-8814, www.triangletattoo.com, daily noon-6pm, free) displays the implements of tattooing and photos of their results. To enter, walk up a flight of narrow stairs and stare at the walls, which are completely covered with photos of tattoos. All forms of the art are represented, from those done by indigenous people to those done at carnivals and in prisons. In glass cases upstairs are all types of tattooing devices, some antique. More photos grace the walls of the warren of small rooms in a never-ending

Pudding Creek Beach in MacKerricher State Park

collage. The street-side rooms house a working tattoo parlor, where intrepid artists and their canvases work late into the evening.

Pacific Star Winery

The only winery on the Mendocino Coast, **Pacific Star Winery** (33000 N. Hwy. 1, 707/964-1155, www.pacificstarwinery.com, daily 11am-5pm, tasting free) makes the most of its location 12 miles north of Fort Bragg. Barrels of wine are left out in the salt air to age, incorporating a hint of the Pacific into each vintage. Friendly tasting-room staffers will tell you which of the winery cats most likes to be picked up. Wines are tasty and reasonably priced, and you can bring your own picnic to enjoy on the nearby bluff, which overlooks the ocean. They also have a less scenic tasting room in Fort Bragg (401 Main St., 707/962-9463, Thurs.-Mon. noon-5pm).

Mendocino Coast Botanical Gardens

Stretching 47 acres down to the sea, **Mendocino Coast Botanical Gardens** (18220 N. Hwy. 1, 707/964-4352, www.gardenbythesea.org, Mar.-Oct. daily 9am-5pm, Nov.-Feb. daily 9am-4pm, adults $14, seniors $10, ages 5-17 $5) offer miles of walking through careful plantings and wild landscapes. The star of the gardens is the rhododendron, with 125 species on the grounds. Children can pick up "Quail Trail: A Child's Guide" and enjoy an exploratory adventure.

Entertainment and Events

The **Gloriana Musical Theatre** (210 N. Corry St., 707/964-7469, www.gloriana.org) seeks to bring music and theater to young people, so they produce major musicals that appeal to kids, such as *Peter Pan*. On the other hand, *Into the Woods* and the *Rock 'N Roll Revue* appeal mostly to people past their second decade. Local performers star in the two major shows and numerous one-off performances that Gloriana puts on each year.

Art is a big deal on the Mendocino Coast. Accordingly, the area hosts a number of art events each year. **Art in the Gardens** (18220 N. Hwy. 1, Fort Bragg, www.gardenbythesea.org, Aug., $20 at the door, $15 in advance, children under 16 free) takes place each August at the Mendocino Coast Botanical Gardens, for which it is an annual fundraiser. The gardens are decked out with the finest local artwork, food, and wine, and there is music to entertain the crowds who come to eat, drink, view, and purchase art.

North Coast Brewery's Sequoia Room (444 N. Main St., 707/964-3400, www.northcoastbrewing.com) hosts jazz shows in a cabaret environment every Friday and Saturday night. The shows feature national touring acts or the local house band. Check the website for upcoming performances.

Shopping

Stop in at the **Glass Beach Museum and Gift Shop** (17801 N. Hwy. 1, 707/962-0590, www.glassbeachjewelry.com, daily 10am-5pm), a mile south of Fort Bragg. You can see a wide array of found treasures from over the years, hear stories from Captain Cass, a retired sailor and expert glass scavenger, and also buy sea glass set in pendants and rings.

Vintage clothing enthusiasts will love **If the Shoe Fits** (337 N. Franklin St., 707/964-2580, Mon.-Thurs. and Sat. 11am-5:30pm, Fri. 11am-6pm). Its eclectic collection of used clothing and accessories for men and women usually includes interesting pieces, well preserved and in good condition.

The place to go on the North Coast to feed your vacation reading habit is **The Bookstore and Vinyl Cafe** (353 Franklin St., 707/964-6559, Mon.-Sat. 10:30am-5pm, Sun. 11am-3pm), a small shop with a well-curated selection of new and used books likely to please discriminating readers. Music lovers can head upstairs where there is a selection of used records for sale.

Sports and Recreation
SPORTFISHING

The Mendocino Coast is an ideal location to watch whales do acrobatics, or to try to land the big one (salmon, halibut, rock cod, or tuna). During Dungeness crab season, you can even go out on a crab boat, learn to set pots, and catch your own delectable delicacy.

Many charters leave out of Noyo Harbor in Fort Bragg. The *Trek II* (Noyo Harbor, 707/964-4550, www.anchorcharterboats.com, fishing trips $80-275, 2-hour whale-watching $35) offers fishing trips and whale-watching jaunts (Dec.-May). They'll take you rockfishing in summer, crabbing in winter, and chasing after salmon and tuna in season.

The **Noyo Fishing Center** (32440 N. Harbor Dr., Noyo Harbor, 707/964-3000, www.fortbraggfishing.com, half-day fishing trips $100-250, 2-hour whale-watching excursion $35) can take you out salmon fishing or up off the Lost Coast for halibut fishing. They'll help you fish for cod and various deep-sea dwellers in season. The twice-daily trips are an intimate experience, with a maximum of six passengers.

HIKING
The hike to take in MacKerricher State Park (Hwy. 1, 707/964-9112, www.parks.ca.gov, visitors center daily 9am-3pm, day use free), three miles north of Fort Bragg, is the **Ten Mile Beach Trail** (10 miles roundtrip, moderate), starting at the Laguna Point Parking Area at the north end of Fort Bragg and running five miles up to the Ten Mile River. Most of this path is fairly level and paved. It's an easy walk, and you can turn around whenever you want. Street bikes and inline skates are also allowed on this trail. The trail is also known as Haul Road or the Coastal Trail.

HORSEBACK RIDING
What better way to enjoy the rugged cliffs, windy beaches, and quiet forests of the coast than on the back of a horse? **Ricochet Ridge Ranch** (24201 N. U.S. 101, 707/964-9669, www.horse-vacation.com) has 10-mile beach trail rides ($55) departing four times a day at 10am, noon, 2pm and 4pm. They also offer longer beach and trail rides, sunset beach rides, and full-fledged riding vacations by reservation.

SURFING
There are options for surfing in the Fort Bragg area. Just south of town is **Hare Creek** (southwest of the intersection of Hwy. 1 and Hwy. 20, north end of the Hare Creek Bridge), one of the region's most popular spots. North of town is **Virgin Creek** (1.5 miles north of Fort Bragg on Hwy. 1), another well-known break.

The **Lost Surf Shack** (319 N. Franklin St., 707/961-0889, www.surfmendo.com, daily 10am-6pm, surfboards $25/day, wetsuits $15/day) in downtown Fort Bragg rents surfboards and wetsuits to the surfing-inclined.

SPAS
The **Bamboo Garden Spa** (303 N. Main St., Suite C, 707/962-9396, www.bamboogardenspa.com, Mon.-Sat. 11am-7pm, massages $55-250) pampers its guests with a wide array of massage, skin, and beauty treatments. Get a 50-minute massage, or try the Balinese Soul Soother or the Vanilla Bean Sugar Scrub.

Accommodations
Stringent zoning laws about development and expansion of businesses in the coastal zone are the main reason you're not likely to find a lot of lodging bargains here; only a few chain hotels have managed to build in Fort Bragg.

UNDER $150
One budget option is the **Surf Motel** (1220 S. Main St., 707/964-5361, www.surfmotelfb.com, $95-275). The hotel provides a bike-washing station, a fish-cleaning station, an outdoor shower for divers, a garden to stroll through, and an area set aside for horseshoes and barbecues. Your spacious modern guest room comes with breakfast, free wireless Internet access, a microwave, a fridge, and a blow dryer. The two apartments have a kitchen and room for four people.

The stately **Grey Whale Inn** (615 N. Main St., 707/964-0640 or 800/382-7244, www.greywhaleinn.com, $135-190) was once a community hospital. The blocky crafts-man-style building was erected by the Union Lumber Company in 1915. Today, 13 spacious, simple rooms offer views of the water or the city. The lovely, individually decorated rooms feature a private bath and queen or king bed, perhaps covered by an old-fashioned quilt. The inn prides itself on simplicity and friend-liness, and its location in downtown Fort Bragg makes visitors feel at home walking to dinner or the beach. It also has a game room with a pool table and foosball.

$150-250

★ **Weller House** (524 Stewart St., 707/964-4415, www.wellerhouse.com, $150-320) is a picture-perfect B&B with elegant Victorian-style rooms, ocean views, and sumptuous home cooking. There are even a few secluded rooms in the old water tower. The manager, Vivien LaMothe, is a tango dancer, and the third floor of the main building—a gorgeous 1886 mansion listed in the National Register of Historic Places—is a ballroom. Tango danc-ers come from the Bay Area and beyond for monthly tango weekends and biannual tango festivals. Check the website for schedules, ce-lebrity dance teachers, and chamber music concerts. Weller House is one block west of

Main Street and an easy walk to good restau-rants and shopping.

The **Beachcomber Motel** (1111 N. Main St., 707/964-2402, www.thebeachcombermo-tel.com, $149-229) is just north of town right behind Pudding Creek Beach. It's one of the most pet-friendly motels along the coast. Not only are there pet-friendly rooms, but there is also a dog park and suites with doggie doors that open up to a fenced-in enclosure with a doghouse. The Beachcomber caters to hu-mans by having most of its rooms equipped with private balconies and decks to take in the bluffs and ocean. Some units even have hot tubs dominating the room. The motel also rents beach cruisers for use on the Coastal Trail at adjacent MacKerricher State Park. Next door, the ★ **Surf and Sand Lodge** (1131 N. Main St., 707/964-9383, www.surf-sandlodge.com, $149-255) is the slightly more upscale sister property of the Beachcomber. Most of the rooms in the six blue buildings have views of headlands and ocean. The trails, tide pools, crashing waves, and broad beaches of MacKerricher State Park are right out front. Every room has balconies or porches to take in the view. Opt for a room with a Jacuzzi spa tub to soak in hot water while looking out at the chilly Pacific.

Surf and Sand Lodge

Camping

MacKerricher State Park (Hwy. 1, 707/964-9112, www.parks.ca.gov, reservations 800/444-7275, www.reserveamerica.com, $35), three miles north of Fort Bragg, is also a fine place to spend a night or two as you explore the area. Reservations are recommended April 1-October 15, and they're site-specific. In the winter season, camping is available on a first-come, first-served basis. The park has 107 sites suitable for tents and RVs up to 35 feet in its wooded and pleasant West Pinewood and East Pinewood Campgrounds; there are also a group campground and walk-in hike-and-bike sites. Restrooms with flush toilets as well as hot showers are provided, and each campsite has a fire ring, picnic table, and food storage locker.

Food

It used to be that you had to go to the village of Mendocino for a restaurant meal, but lately Fort Bragg has developed a more-than-respectable culinary scene of its own. Many excellent restaurants are available within a few blocks of the town center and beach.

AMERICAN

Upstairs in an old Fort Bragg lumber building, the **Mendo Bistro** (301 N. Main St. No. J, 707/964-4974, http://mendobistro.com, daily 5pm-9pm, $16-35) has the sort of menu one might expect in a bigger city. One of the best parts of the menu is the "Choice" section, where you choose the style of meat, seafood, or vegetarian option and how it is cooked along with what sauce it is cooked in. The hormone- and antibiotic-free steaks are perfectly cooked and delicious. There is also a great deal of vegetarian offerings on the menu; the best is the polenta.

The **North Coast Brewing Company** (444 N. Main St., 707/964-3400, www.northcoastbrewing.com, summer Sun.-Thurs. 4pm-9:15pm, Fri.-Sat. 4pm-10:15pm, winter Sun.-Thurs. 4pm-8:15pm, Fri.-Sat. 4pm-9:15pm, taproom summer 2pm-10pm, Fri.-Sat. 2pm-11pm, winter Sun.-Thurs. 2pm-9pm, Fri.-Sat. 2pm-10pm, $15-33) opened in 1988, aiming at the then-nascent artisanal beer market. Today, they also serve seafood, steak, and creative salads, all washed down with a North Coast microbrew. Taste the magic in their Red Seal Ale, Old Rasputin Russian Imperial Stout, and Scrimshaw Pilsner. Sit at

North Coast Brewing Company

the cozy wooden bar in the taproom if you're just here for the beer.

The most popular burger in town is at **Jenny's Giant Burger** (940 N. Main St., 707/964-2235, http://jennysgiantburger.com, daily 10:30am-9pm, $4-7). This little place has a 1950s hamburger-stand feel. The burgers are fresh and antibiotic-free, with garden burger and veggie sandwich options. Jenny's followers are devoted, so it can get crowded, but there are a few outdoor tables, and you can always get your order to go.

BAKERIES AND CAFÉS

Despite the often drizzly, overcast weather, Mendocino Coast residents and visitors crave ice cream in the summer just like anyone else. **Cowlick's Ice Cream** (250 N. Main St., 707/962-9271, www.cowlicksicecream.com, daily 11am-9pm) serves delectable handmade ice cream in a variety of flavors. They even serve mushroom ice cream during the famous fall mushroom season. Get the perennial favorite flavors such as vanilla, chocolate, coffee, and strawberry or try a seasonal flavor (banana daiquiri, cinnamon, green tea). Ice cream from this local, family-owned chain is also sold at the Mendocino Coast Botanical Gardens (18220 N. Hwy. 1); at **Frankie's Ice Cream Parlor** (44951 Ukiah St., Mendocino, 707/937-2436, www.frankiesmendocino.com, daily 11am-9pm) in Mendocino Village; on the Skunk Train; and at **J. D. Redhouse** (212 S. Main St., Willits, 707/459-1214, daily 10am-6pm).

The **Headlands Coffeehouse** (120 E. Laurel St., 707/964-1987, www.headlandscoffeehouse.com, summer Mon.-Sat. 7am-10pm, Sun. 7am-7pm, winter Mon.-Sat. 7am-10pm, Sun. 7am-5pm) is unquestionably the place to go in Fort Bragg for a cup of joe. They have around 15 different self-serve roasts of coffee, as well as food ranging from breakfast burritos to paninis. There is free live music in the evenings and free Internet access. There are no electrical outlets available for customers, so you can only use your laptop as long as the battery lasts.

BREAKFAST

Egghead's (326 N. Main St., 707/964-5005, www.eggheadsrestaurant.com, daily 7am-2pm, $6-19) has been serving an enormous menu of breakfast, lunch, and brunch items to satisfy diners for more than 30 years. The menu includes every imaginable omelet combination, cinnamon raisin toast, burritos, Reuben sandwiches, and "flying-monkey potatoes," derived from the *Wizard of Oz* theme that runs through the place.

FARMERS MARKETS

Fort Bragg hosts a **farmers market** (Franklin St. between Laurel and Pine, www.mcfarm.org, May-Oct. Wed. 3pm-6pm, Nov.-Apr. inside Old Recreation Center Gym 3pm-5pm) that sells wild-caught seafood, free-range beef, and fresh-baked bread.

ITALIAN

Small and almost always packed, the ★ **Piaci Pub & Pizzeria** (120 W. Redwood Ave., 707/961-1133, www.piacipizza.com, Mon.-Thurs. 11am-9:30pm, Fri.-Sat. 11am-10pm, Sun. 4pm-9:30pm, $9-26) has an L-shaped bar and just a few tables, so you may have to share a table with some strangers. The 16 delicious pizzas range from traditional pepperoni to more creative combinations like pesto, Chevre, pears, prosciutto, and herbs. The Nonnie is a flavorful combination of prosciutto, grilled chicken, mozzarella, herbs, and a garlic sauce on a thin crust. Piaci's has an extensive list of brews, from Belgian-style beers to hearty ales, which make it a popular spot for locals wanting a post-work beer.

A relative newcomer, **Cucina Verona** (124 E. Laurel St., 707/964-6844, Mon.-Thurs. 8am-9pm, Fri.-Sat. 8am-9:30pm, Sun. 9am-9pm, $12-35) does northern Italian food with touches of Northern California. There's a gamut of menu items, from butternut squash lasagna to grilled local salmon. Complement your meal with a local wine or beer. Frequent live music in the dining room provides entertainment.

707/964-1300, Sun.-Thurs. 10am-10pm, Fri.-Sat. 10am-11pm, $6-13, cash only). They also have 18 beers on tap.

247

NORTH COAST
MENDOCINO COAST

THAI

Small and unassuming, but well worth a visit, **Nit's Café** (322 Main St., 707/964-7187, Tues.-Sat. 11am-2pm and 5pm-9pm, $14-26, cash only) specializes in Thai and Asian fusion. Noted for its beautiful presentations of both classic and creative dishes, Nit's gets rave reviews from nearly everyone who tries it. They have a special of the day and a fresh daily catch of the day.

Information and Services

The **Mendocino Coast Chamber of Commerce and Visitors Center** (217 S. Main St., 707/961-6300, www.mendocinocoast.com, Mon.-Fri. 10am-5pm) has unusually attentive and well-trained staff in addition to all the maps, brochures, and ideas you could possibly want. This operation also serves as the Mendocino County film office, which strongly encourages filmmaking in the area. Come in and get the inside story on where to see the filming locations of *Summer of '42,* in which the bluffs of Fort Bragg play the role of Long Island; *East of Eden; Karate Kid III; Humanoids from the Deep;* and many more.

The **Mendocino Coast District Hospital** (700 River Dr. at Cypress St., 707/961-1234, www.mcdh.org) has the nearest full-service emergency room.

Transportation

Fort Bragg is on Highway 1; driving from San Francisco takes about four hours. The road from any direction is narrow and full of curves, at least for an hour or two, so be prepared to make the scenic journey part of the fun. From Willits, take Highway 20 (Fort Bragg-Willits Rd.) west for 30 miles. If ever a road could be described as sun-dappled, this is it. The sun pops in and out among the redwood forest and makes you want to use all the pullouts to take photos. Keep in mind that there is no cell-phone service along this

pizza at Piaci Pub & Pizzeria

MEXICAN

Inside a Fort Bragg strip mall, **Los Gallitos** (130 S. Main St., 707/964-4519, Mon.-Sat. 11am-8pm, Sun. 10am-8pm, $7-16, cash only) doesn't look like much. But you know this is a better-than-average taqueria when the thick, fresh tortilla strips and superb salsa hit your table. Everything on the menu, from burritos to tostados, is what you'd expect, but the attention to little details like the grilled onions and beans on the very tasty carne asada torta make this place special.

SEAFOOD

With the small fishing and crabbing fleet of Fort Bragg's Noyo Harbor, it's natural that lots of seafood restaurants are clustered nearby. Head down to the harbor where any one of the several casual restaurants and fish markets offer the most authentic, freshest, and simplest preparations of salmon, mussels, and Dungeness crab in season. One spot known for its fish-and-chips is the **Sea Pal Cove Restaurant** (32390 N. Harbor Dr., road, so it is not a good place to run out of gas. Allow plenty of time—it takes longer than you'd expect to travel these 30 miles.

As one of the largest towns in the region, Fort Bragg has greater access to public transportation. The most enjoyable way to get here is to take the **Skunk Train** (707/964-6371, www.skunktrain.com) from Willits. The **Mendocino Transit Authority** (707/462-1422 or 800/696-4682, http://mendocinotransit.org) has a number of bus lines that pass through Fort Bragg, and it also offers **Dial-a-Ride Curb-to-Curb Service** (707/462-3881, Mon.-Fri. 7am-6pm, Sat. 10am-5pm, adults $6, seniors $3, children six and under $1.25). The most common way to get to and around Fort Bragg, however, is by car.

Westport

The next town north along Highway 1 is Westport, 16 miles north of Fort Bragg. It has its own patch of ocean, a few essential services, and one lodging gem. It's also the last settlement before the wild Lost Coast.

The motto at the ★ **Westport Hotel** (3892 Hwy. 1, 707/964-3688 or 877/964-3688, www.westporthotel.us, $150-225) is, "At last, you've found nowhere." The Westport Hotel is marvelous and private, perfect for a honeymoon spent in luxury and comfort. Each of the six rooms has one bed and a bath with fixtures that blend perfectly into the historic 1890 house. Some rooms have small private balconies overlooking the waves, and all guests have access to the redwood sauna. Fresh scones, fruit, and coffee are delivered to your room in the morning, and a full hot breakfast is served in the dining room.

The Old Abalone Pub is inside the Westport Hotel.

Inside the Westport Hotel is the **Old Abalone Pub** (3892 Hwy. 1, 707/964-3688 or 877/964-3688, www.westporthotel.us, Thurs.-Fri. 5pm-9pm, Sat. 3pm-9pm, Sun. 10am-2pm and 5pm-9pm, $10-25). Thanks to a large mirror over the bar, everyone in the dining room gets an ocean view.

Camping is available two miles north of Westport at **Westport-Union Landing State Beach** (Hwy. 1, 707/937-5804, www.parks.ca.gov, $25), with 86 first-come, first-served sites. There are no showers or other amenities—just the cliffs, the waves, the sunsets, and the views.

Mendocino Wine Country

Mendocino's interior valley might not be quite as glamorous as the coast, but it is home to history, art, and liquor. The Anderson Valley is the apex of Mendocino's wine region, although the tiny town of Hopland also has its share of tasting rooms. Ukiah, the county seat, is home to a number of microbreweries and a thriving agricultural industry. Up in determinedly funky Willits, a late-1960s art vibe thrives in the 21st century.

Unlike the chilly and windy coast, the interior valleys of Mendocino get hot in the summer. Bring shorts, a swimsuit, and an air-conditioned car if you plan to visit June-September.

ANDERSON VALLEY

The Anderson Valley wine trail, also known as Highway 128, begins in Boonville and continues northwest toward the coast, with most of the wineries clustered between Boonville and Navarro.

Wineries and Breweries

A big name in the Anderson Valley, **Scharffenberger Cellars** (8501 Hwy. 128, Philo, 707/895-2957, www.scharffenbergercellars.com, daily 11am-5pm, $3) makes wine in Mendocino. The tasting room is elegant and unusually child-friendly. It is decorated with the work of local artists.

A broad-ranging winery with a large estate vineyard and event center, **Navarro Vineyards** (5601 Hwy. 128, Philo, 707/895-3686 or 800/537-9463, www.navarrowine.com, summer daily 9am-6pm, winter daily 9am-5pm, free) offers a range of tasty wines as well as some interesting specialty products such as the nonalcoholic verjus.

In a valley full of great wineries, **Roederer Estate** (4501 Hwy. 128, 707/895-2288, www.roedererestate.com, daily 11am-5pm, $6) sparkles. Its sparkling wines are some of the best of the state. The large tasting room features a bar with sweeping views of the estate vineyards and huge cases filled with well-deserved awards. Pourers are knowledgeable, and you'll get to taste from magnum bottles—a rarity at any winery. Ask for a taste of Roederer's rarely seen still wines.

Handley Cellars (3151 Hwy. 128, Philo, 800/733-3151, www.handleycellars.com, summer daily 10am-6pm, winter daily 10am-5pm, free) offers a complimentary tasting of handcrafted wines you probably won't see in grocery stores. The intriguing Handley tasting room features folk art from around the world for sale. Books on wine are sold too, especially those that focus on women making and drinking wine.

A small operation, **Toulouse Vineyards** (8001 Hwy. 128, Philo, 707/895-2828, http://toulousevineyards.com, daily 11am-5pm) is the kind of winery where the winemaker's dog will greet you upon arrival. This boutique winery is known for its pinot noir. They also do a pinot gris and a gewürztraminer.

Anderson Valley Brewing Company (17700 Hwy. 253, Boonville, 707/895-2337, www.avbc.com, summer Sat.-Thurs. 11am-6pm, Fri. 11am-7pm, winter hours vary) serves up an array of microbrews that changes each season and year. The warehouse-size beer hall feels like a wine-tasting room, with a bar, tables, and a good-size gift shop. A beer garden out back is comfortable in spring and fall, and the disc golf course is popular with travelers and locals alike.

Accommodations

Lodging options in and around the Anderson Valley vary widely. In the valley proper you're likely to find funky hotels, cabins, and forest-shaded campgrounds.

The little, multi-building **Anderson Valley Inn** (8480 Hwy. 128, Philo, 707/895-3325, www.avinn.com, $95-180), between Boonville and Philo, makes the perfect spot

Mendocino Wine Country

from which to divide your time between the Anderson Valley and the Mendocino Coast. Six small rooms are done up in bright colors, homey bedspreads, and attractive appointments. A butterfly-filled garden invites guests to sit out on the porches. The two suites have full kitchens and are perfect for longer stays. The friendly owners welcome children and dogs in the suites and can offer hints about how best to explore the region. This inn often fills quickly on summer weekends, as it's one of the best values in the region. There's a two-night minimum on weekends April-November.

In the middle of Boonville, the quaint **Boonville Hotel** (14050 Hwy. 128, 707/895-2210, www.boonvillehotel.com, $145-395) has a rough, weathered exterior that contrasts with the 15 contemporary rooms, each of which is bright and airy with earth-tone furniture and mismatched decorations. Downstairs are spacious common areas and a huge garden. Amenities include a bookshop and a gift shop, a good-size bar, and a dining room. Book one of the rooms with a balcony, which comes with a hammock, or a guest room with an outdoor bathtub. Child- and pet-friendly rooms are available on request.

Camping

The campgrounds at **Indian Creek County Park** (Hwy. 128 at mile marker 23.48, 1 mile east of Philo, 707/463-4291, www.co.mendocino.ca.us, $25) are budget-friendly. Even better is **Hendy Woods State Park** (18599 Philo-Greenwood Rd., Philo, 8 miles northwest of Boonville, 707/895-3141, www.parks.ca.gov, campsites $40, cabins $55), which provides woodsy, shaded campsites along with four rustic cabins with wood-burning stoves.

Food

The only establishment serving liquor between Ukiah and Mendocino, **The Buckhorn** (14081 Hwy. 128, Boonville, 707/895-3224, Mon. and Wed.-Fri. 11am-9pm, Sat.-Sun. 10am-9pm, $11-32) also has over 40 local wines and 14 beers on tap, many from nearby Anderson Valley Brewing Company. They also do big portions of good food including burgers and hot sandwiches such as a worthwhile French dip.

A picnic makes a perfect lunch in the Anderson Valley, and farmers markets and farm stands can supply fresh local ingredients. The **Boonville Farmers Market** (14050 Hwy. 128, Boonville, www.mcfarm.org, May-Oct. Sat. 10am-12:30pm) draws a crowd, so be prepared to hunt for parking. For fresh fruit and vegetables every day, try **Gowan's Oak Tree Farm Stand** (6600 Hwy. 128, 2.5 miles north of Philo, 707/895-3353, www.gowansoaktree.com, June-Aug. 8am-7pm, Sept.-Oct. 8am-6pm, Nov.-May 8:30am-5:30pm). The stand belongs to the local Gowan's Oak Tree Farm and sells only in-season local produce and homemade products made with the same fruits and veggies.

For an elegant full-service dining experience, visit **Table 128** (14050 Hwy. 128, Boonville, 707/895-2210, www.boonvillehotel.com, by reservation only Apr.-Nov. Thurs.-Mon., Dec.-Mar. Fri.-Sun., $40-50), the restaurant at the Boonville Hotel. Table 128 is family-style and the menu is prix fixe. The food is so fresh and seasonal that the chef won't commit to a menu more than a week in advance, but you can sign up on the website to receive regular menus by email. Reservations are required and must be secured with a credit card for parties of five or more.

Transportation

You can see pretty much all of the Anderson Valley from the "wine road," Highway 128. You can get to Highway 128 from U.S. 101 either directly out of Hopland or from Ukiah on Highway 253. From Hopland, take Mountain House Road west for nine miles. Turn right onto Highway 128 and continue north for about 20 miles.

From Ukiah, take U.S. 101 south for three miles. Merge onto Highway 253 and head west for about 17 miles. When you reach Highway 128, turn right. The center of Boonville is less than one mile away.

Many of the major wine-country touring outfits that operate from San Francisco and the Napa Valley also offer trips in the Anderson Valley. **Mendo Wine Tours** (707/937-6700 or 888/805-8687, www.mendowinetours.com, group tours $175 pp, private tours for two $500-650) is a regional specialist that offers a Lincoln Town Car for small groups and an SUV limo for groups of up to 10.

HOPLAND

Hopland is inland on U.S. 101 about 15 miles south of Ukiah and 28 miles east of the Anderson Valley via Highway 253. The small farming town is on the upper section of the Russian River.

Solar Living Center

The **Solar Living Center** (13771 S. U.S. 101, 707/472-2450, http://solarliving.org, daily 10am-6pm) is a "12-acre sustainable living demonstration site," showing, among other things, what life might be like without petroleum. The center has exhibits on permaculture, an organic garden, and a demonstration of solar-powered water systems. Guided tours are available April through October

Boontling: The North Coast Dialect

Take your oddly broken English, throw in some old Scottish and Irish, add a pinch of Spanish and a dash of Pomo, then season with real names and allusions to taste. Speak among friends and family in an isolated community for a dozen years or more. The result: Boontling.

Boontling is a unique and almost dead language developed by the denizens of the then-remote town of Boonville in the Anderson Valley late in the 19th century. The beginnings of Boontling are obscured by time since all the originators of the language are "piked for dusties"—that is, in the cemetery. And many Boonters—speakers of Boontling—are intensely protective of the local lingo. But in the 1960s, Professor Charles C. Adams of Cal State Chico came to town to study the language. He gradually gained the trust of the locals, and was able to write a doctoral thesis, eventually published as a book titled *Boontling: An American Lingo*. The book documents the dialect's history and acts as a dictionary for the more than 1,000 Boontling terms on record.

So if you find yourself in Anderson Valley drinking "zeese" (coffee) or "aplenty bahl steinber horn" (a really great beer) and hear older folks speaking a language like none you've ever heard, you might just be listening to a rare and endangered conversation in Boontling.

(707-472-2450, Fri.-Sun. 11am and 3pm, $3/person, $5/family).

The **Real Goods** store (707/472-2403, daily 10am-6pm) on the property is also a draw for visitors, and the completely recycled restrooms are worth a look even if you don't need one. If your vehicle happens to run on biodiesel, you can fill your tank here.

Wineries

To get to the best wineries in Hopland, you don't even need to leave U.S. 101. The highway runs through the center of town, and almost all the tasting rooms are along it. For those who love wine but not crowds, the tiny wineries and tasting rooms in Hopland are the perfect place to relax, enjoy sipping each vintage, and really chat with the pourer, who just might be the winemaker and owner.

The star of this mini-region is **Brutocao Cellars** (13500 S. U.S. 101, 800/433-3689, www.brutocaocellars.com, daily 10am-5pm, free), whose vineyards surround the town. It created its tasting room and restaurant complex from a former high school. The wide, stone-tiled tasting room houses exceptional wines poured by knowledgeable staff. A sizeable gift shop offers gourmet goodies under the Brutocao label, and there are six regulation bocce ball courts to do some lawn bowling with your wine

sipping. There is a second tasting room in the Anderson Valley (7000 Hwy. 128, Philo, 800/661-2103, www.brutocaocellars.com, daily 10am-5pm, free).

Heading north out of town, the highway passes through acres of vineyards spreading out toward the forest in all directions. Many of these grapes belong to **Jeriko** (12141 Hewlett and Sturtevant Rd., 707/744-1140, www.jerikoestate.com, summer daily 10am-5pm, winter daily 11am-4pm, $10). Drive between the chardonnay and the pinot to get to the immense Napa-style tasting room. A glass wall exposes the barrel room, stacked high with aging wines.

Food

With the closing of the Hopland Inn, Hopland lost some of its best dining and one of its only places to stay. A casual place that most people enjoy is the **Bluebird Café & Catering Company** (13340 S. U.S. 101, 707/744-1633, Mon.-Thurs. 7am-2pm, Fri.-Sun. 7am-7pm, $17-20). They do wild game including bison burgers. Your best bet for a good night's sleep is to stay in Ukiah or Lakeport.

Another option is the **Hopland Tap House** (13551 S. Hwy. 101, 707/744-1255, http://hoplandtaphouse.com, Wed.-Mon. 11:30am-9pm, $9-13.50), which is within a historic brick building. There are eight craft beers on tap that go nicely with the small menu of burgers, hot dogs, paninis, and salads.

UKIAH

The largest city in Mendocino County, Ukiah is also the county seat. The low-key, historic downtown has worthwhile restaurants and shops. The surrounding area is home to organic wineries, the largest Buddhist monastery in the country, and historic mineral springs.

Sights

SAGELY CITY OF 10,000 BUDDHAS

There's plenty to interest the spiritually curious at the **Sagely City of 10,000 Buddhas** (4951 Bodhi Way, 707/462-0939, www.cttbusa.org, daily 8am-6pm). This active Buddhist college and monastery asks that guests wear modest clothing and keep their voices down out of respect for the nuns and monks who make their lives here. The showpiece is the temple, which really does contain 10,000 golden Buddha statues. An extensive gift- and bookshop provides slightly silly souvenirs as well as serious scholarly texts on Buddhism. For a treat, stop in for lunch at the **Jyun Kang Vegetarian Restaurant** (707/468-7966,

Wed.-Mon. 11:30am-3pm, $7) on the grounds, which is open to the public.

GRACE HUDSON MUSEUM AND SUN HOUSE

One of the few truly cultural offerings in Ukiah is the **Grace Hudson Museum** (431 S. Main St., 707/467-2836, www.gracehudson-museum.org, Wed.-Sat. 10am-4:30pm, Sun. noon-4:30pm, adults $4, seniors and students $3, family $10). This small set of galleries focuses on the life and work of the artist Grace Hudson and her husband, Dr. John Hudson. The life's work of this couple included the study of the Pomo people and other Native American groups. The museum's permanent collection includes many of Grace's paintings, a number of Pomo baskets, and the works of dozens of other California artists. The 1911 craftsman-style **Sun House** (docent tours available with museum ticket, Wed.-Sun. noon-3pm) adjacent to the main museum building, was the Hudsons' home, and docent-guided tours are available.

VICHY SPRINGS RESORT

Established in 1854, **Vichy Springs Resort** (2605 Vichy Springs Rd., 707/462-9515, www.vichysprings.com, daily 9am-dusk,

historic soaking tubs at Vichy Springs Resort

treatments $105-195 per hour, baths $50 per day) has been patronized by Mark Twain, Jack London, Ulysses S. Grant, Teddy Roosevelt, and California governor Jerry Brown. The hot springs, mineral-heavy and naturally carbonated, closely resemble the world-famous waters of their namesake at Vichy in France and spill into indoor and outdoor concrete tubs. Services include the baths, a hot pool, and an Olympic-size swimming pool as well as a day spa. The serene 700-acre property also has 12 miles of trails including one that goes to a waterfall.

Accommodations

There are plenty of lodgings in Ukiah, although they tend to be mostly standard chain motels. Out by the airport, the **Fairfield Inn** (1140 Airport Park Blvd., 707/463-3600, www. marriott.com, $179) is a good choice. With an elegant lobby, an indoor pool and spa, a small exercise room, and a generous complimentary continental breakfast, it has what you need to be comfortable. The rooms are what you'd expect of a decent midrange chain: floral bedspreads, durable nondescript carpet, and clean baths. There are also laundry facilities if you have been on the road for a while.

For a peaceful retreat, the best choice is ★ **Vichy Springs Resort** (2605 Vichy Springs Rd., 707/462-9515, www.vichysprings. com, $155-425). The rooms, in a genteel and rustic old inn and nearby cottages, are small but comfortable, with private baths, warm bedspreads, and cool breezes, and many have views of the mountains or creek. Two of the cottages date back to 1852. Use of all the pools and hiking trails on the 700-acre grounds in included in the rates, as is Internet access and a buffet breakfast. There are no TVs here.

Food

A local favorite, **Stan's Maple Restaurant** (295 S. State St., 707/462-5221, www.stans-maplecafe.com, daily 7am-2pm, $10) serves tasty and inexpensive breakfasts and lunches. Excellent service complements good, uncomplicated American-style food. Shockingly good coffee is a charming final touch at this lovely find.

For a cool, relaxing breather on a hot Ukiah day, stop in at one of the three locations of **Schat's Bakery Café** (113 W. Perkins St., 707/462-1670, Mon.-Fri. 5:30am-6pm, Sat. 5:30am-5pm, www.schats.com; 1255A Airport Park Blvd., 707/468-5850, Mon.-Fri. 7am-8pm, Sat. 7am-7pm, Sun. 8am-7pm; 1000 Hensley Creek Rd., 707/468-3145, Mon.-Thurs. 7am-8:15pm, Fri. 7am-3pm, $5-12). They'll make you a quick, filling sandwich on fresh-baked bread, and you can hang out as long as you want in the large, airy dining rooms.

Ellie's Mutt Hut & Vegetarian Café (732 S. State St., 707/468-5376, http://ellies-mutthutukiahca.com, Mon.-Sat. 6:30am-8pm, $8-15) has great vegetarian entrées and an impressive hot dog list. It's one of the best places in California for a mixed group of conscientious vegans and couldn't-care-less carnivores to have a good time together; Ellie's is one of the things that make Ukiah Ukiah. The atmosphere is hamburger-stand casual, and the food is mostly healthy.

Of the dining options in Ukiah, one of the very best is **Patrona** (130 W. Standley St., 707/462-9181, www.patronarestaurant. com, Sun.-Thurs. 11am-9pm, Fri.-Sat. 11am-11pm, $13-29), where especially innovative California cuisine is served in a bistro-casual atmosphere by attentive servers. The kitchen's attention to detail is impressive. The wine list features all sorts of Mendocino County vintages, plus a good range of European wines. Most wines are available by the bottle only, but the servers will cork an unfinished bottle so you can take it home to enjoy later.

The **Ritual Restaurant & Lounge** (102 S. State St., 707/468-5898, http://ukiahritual. com, Sun.-Thurs. 11am-9pm, Fri.-Sat. 11am-10pm, $11-28) has a wide menu that includes pizzas, sandwiches, salads, steak frites, and a chef's tasting menu, but it's their house-blended burgers on brioche buns that shine. There are 16 types of burgers and a build-your-own option. The Classic has bacon jam, white cheddar, and aioli. They also serve

Ukiah Brewing Co. beer, which is brewed on-site.

Information and Services

If you need assistance with local lodging, dining, or wine-tasting, try the visitors center at the **Ukiah Valley Conference Center** (200 S. School St., 707/463-6700). Since Ukiah is the county seat, you can find information here about both the city of Ukiah and Mendocino County.

The **Ukiah Valley Medical Center** (275 Hospital Dr., 707/462-3111, www.uvmc.org) has a 24-hour emergency room as part of its full-service facility.

Transportation

Ukiah is about 110 miles north of San Francisco (2 hours), a straight shot on U.S. 101. It's also about 60 miles north of Santa Rosa (1 hour) on U.S. 101. From Eureka (3 hours away), take U.S. 101 south for 157 miles. To get to Ukiah from Sacramento (under 3 hours), take I-5 north for 58 miles to exit 578 in Williams, and then get on Highway 20 west. After 79 miles, turn south on U.S. 101 to reach Ukiah in another 6.6 miles.

The **Mendocino Transit Authority** (800/696-4682, http://mendocinotransit.org) runs bus service throughout the county, with Ukiah as the hub; you can catch buses here and in Mendocino and Fort Bragg. Private pilots can land at **Ukiah Municipal Airport** (UKI, 1411 S. State St., 707/467-2817, www.cityofukiah.com).

The Redwood Coast

Of all the natural wonders California has to offer, the one that seems to inspire the purest and most unmitigated awe is the giant redwood. The coast redwood, *Sequoia sempervirens,* grows along the California coast from around Big Sur in the south and into southern Oregon in the north. Coast redwoods hold the records for the tallest trees ever recorded, and are among the world's oldest and all-around most massive living things. The two best places to experience extensive wild groves of these gargantuan treasures are Humboldt Redwoods State Park, in Humboldt County, and Redwood National and State Parks, near the north end of California around Eureka and Crescent City.

Most of the major park areas along the Redwood Coast can be accessed via U.S. 101 and U.S. 199. Follow the signs to the smaller roads that lead farther from civilization. To get to the redwood parks from the south, drive up U.S. 101 or the much slower but prettier Highway 1. The two roads merge at Leggett, north of Fort Bragg, and continue north as U.S. 101.

People camping in the parks usually pack in their own food and cook at their campsites. To restock, you can drive to Crescent City to find a market or to Eureka for a true supermarket.

LEGGETT

As Highway 1 heads inland toward Leggett, the ocean views are replaced with redwoods. This part of the road is curvy, winding, and sun-dappled. It's a beautiful drive, so take it slow.

At the junction of Highway 1 and U.S. 101, you'll enter Leggett, famed for the local attraction **Chandelier Drive-Thru Tree** (67402 Drive-Thru Tree Rd., 707/925-6464, www.drivethrutree.com, daily 8:30am-dusk, $5). The tree opening is about six feet wide and a little over six feet high. Kids will be thrilled. And of course, there's a gift shop.

The Peg House (69501 U.S. 101, 707/925-6444, http://thepeghouse.net), which was built with pegs instead of nails, gets raves for its burgers, tri-tip, and deli sandwiches. Sometimes there is live music.

The Redwood Coast

To Eureka

Ferndale
Fortuna

Bear River

★ AVENUE OF
THE GIANTS

Mattole River

Humboldt
Redwoods
State Park
Weott

King Range

Lost
Coast

101

Humboldt

Black Sands
Beach
Shelter Cove

Redway
Garberville

South Fork Eel River

Sinkyone
Wilderness
State Park

101

Richardson Grove
State Park
Leggett

To
Willits

0   5 mi
0   5 km

1

© AVALON TRAVEL

Shelter Cove, is accessible via a winding 23-mile road from Redway. (Shelter Cove is also the southern terminus of the Lost Coast Trail.) Both towns are good places to get a meal or fill your tank with gas before heading west to the coast or north to the redwoods.

As U.S. 101 continues north, logging trucks hauling massive slabs of lumber become more prevalent, and the roadsides are punctuated with dreadlocked hitchhikers trying to bum a ride.

Richardson Grove State Park

Even if your main destination is a redwood park farther north, save time for a stop at **Richardson Grove State Park** (1600 U.S. 101, 707/247-3318, www.parks.ca.gov, daily sunrise-sunset, $8), the first of the old-growth redwoods along U.S. 101. This park has special features all its own, like a tree you can walk through and the ninth-tallest coast redwood. The Eel River flows through the park, offering good fishing as well as camping, swimming, and hiking. The visitors center (May-Sept.) in the 1930s Richardson Grove Lodge has cool exhibits and a nature store. Richardson Grove State Park is seven miles south of Garberville.

Mateel Community Center

In Redway, the **Mateel Community Center** (59 Rusk Ln., Redway, 707/923-3368, www.mateel.org) brings music, theater, dance, comedy, film, and craft events to southern Humboldt. They also put on local annual events, including Reggae on the River, the Humboldt Hills Hoedown, and Hemp Fest. Check the website for a full list of upcoming events.

GARBERVILLE AND REDWAY

Garberville is the first real town in Humboldt County. Just three miles northwest is the slightly larger town of Redway, with just a few hundred more residents than Garberville. Known as the "Gateway to the Avenue of the Giants," the two towns can also be considered the gateway to the Lost Coast, since the biggest community along that remote coastline,

Accommodations

The area's best place to stay is the ★ **Benbow Inn** (445 Lake Benbow Dr., Garberville, 707/923-2124 or 800/355-3301, www.benbowinn.com, $190-400). A swank resort backing onto Lake Benbow, this inn has it all: a gourmet restaurant, a nine-hole golf course, an outdoor swimming pool, and a woodsy atmosphere that blends perfectly with the ancient redwood forest surrounding it. Rooms glow with dark polished woods and jewel-toned carpets. Wide king and comfy queen beds beckon guests tired after a long day of hiking in the redwoods or golfing beside the inn.

Several small motels offer reasonable rooms, and many have outdoor pools in which to cool off during the heat of summer. The best of these is the **Best Western Humboldt House Inn** (701 Redwood Dr., Garberville, 707/923-2771, www.bestwestern.com, $179-239). Rooms are clean and comfortable, the pool is sparkling and cool, the breakfast is hot, and the location is convenient to restaurants and shops in Garberville. Expect the usual comforts. Most rooms have two queen beds.

Camping

Richardson Grove State Park (1600 U.S. 101, 800/444-7275, www.parks.ca.gov, camping $35) has 169 campsites in three campground areas surrounded by redwoods and the Elk River.

You can park your RV year-round at the 112 sites of the posh **Benbow RV Park** (7000 Benbow Dr., Garberville, 707/923-2777 or 866/236-2697, www.benbowrv.com, campsites $41-73, cabins $190-200). Premium sites come with complimentary tea and scones at the nearby Benbow Inn.

Food

The restaurant at the ★ **Benbow Inn** (445 Lake Benbow Dr., Garberville, 707/923-2124 or 800/355-3301, www.benbowinn.com, daily 8am-3pm and 5pm-10pm, $19-45) matches the lodgings for superiority. It serves upscale California cuisine, with a vegan menu available on request, and features an extensive wine list with many regional wineries represented. The white-tablecloth dining room is exquisite, and the expansive outdoor patio overlooking the water is the perfect place to sit as the temperature cools on a summer evening.

An easy place to stop for a pick-me-up, **Flavors Coffeehouse** (767 Redwood Dr., Garberville, 707/923-7717, daily 7am-7pm, $9-11) refuels with a menu of caffeine drinks,

sandwiches, paninis, and salads. There's a build-your-own-grilled-cheese-sandwich option where you can add ingredients including bacon and roasted bell peppers. A good breakfast and lunch stop is the **Eel River Café** (801 Redwood Dr., 707/923-3783, Tues.-Sat. 6am-2pm, $6-12), a diner with black-and-white checkerboard floors and a long counter with red stools. Try the chicken-fried steak with biscuits and gravy. You can't miss the old-school sign towering above the establishment.

You can enjoy a taste of local Humboldt-roasted coffee in Redway at **Signature Coffee** (3455 Redwood Dr., Redway, 707/923-2661, www.signaturecoffeecompany.com, Mon.-Fri. 7am-5pm), which takes pride in its organic products and sustainable practices.

Enjoy a classic roadhouse experience at the **Riverwood Inn** (2828 Avenue of the Giants, Phillipsville, 707/943-3333, www.riverwoodinn.info, Mon.-Thurs. 2pm-midnight, Fri.-Sun. 11am-midnight), six miles north of Garberville. This classic tavern was one of the few buildings that survived the Eel River flood of 1964. The stage has hosted greats including John Lee Hooker and Norton Buffalo. It still has live music most Friday and Saturday nights. There's a grill on-site and five hotel rooms ($80-98) upstairs.

Ray's Food Place (875 Redwood Dr., 707/923-2279, www.gorays.com, daily 7am-10pm) is a supermarket in Garberville.

Information and Services

The **Garberville Redway Area Chamber of Commerce** (782 Redwood Dr., 800/923-2613, www.garberville.org, Mon.-Fri. 10am-3pm) is happy to help visitors get acquainted with the area.

The nearest hospital with an emergency room is **Redwood Memorial Hospital** (3300 Renner Dr., Fortuna, 707/725-3361, www.redwoodmemorial.org).

Transportation

Garberville is 65 miles south of Eureka and 200 miles north of San Francisco on U.S. 101. From Garberville, take Redwood Drive just three miles to Redway. The best way to get to Humboldt Redwoods State Park from either direction is via U.S. 101. You can also approach the center of the park from Mattole Road from the Lost Coast (Shelter Cove to Mattole). Road signs point to the Avenue of the Giants. Bicycles are not permitted on U.S. 101, but you can ride the Avenue of the Giants and Mattole Road.

The little towns of the Humboldt redwoods region can be short on necessary services such as gas stations. There is a **76 Gas Station** (790 Redwood Dr.) just feet off the highway.

The **Redwood County Transit** (707/443-0826, www.redwoodtransit.org) bus system offers limited service to Garberville from the north.

HUMBOLDT REDWOODS STATE PARK

Surprisingly, the largest stand of unlogged redwood trees isn't on the coast, and it isn't in the Sierra; it's here in Humboldt, bisected by U.S. 101. Come to this park to hike beneath 300-foot-plus old-growth trees that began their lives centuries before Europeans knew California existed. One highlight of the park is the 10,000-acre Rockefeller Forest, the largest contiguous old-growth redwood forest in the world. Start your visit at the **Humboldt Redwoods State Park Visitors Center** (707/946-2263, www.parks.ca.gov or www.humboldtredwoods.org, Apr.-Oct. daily 9am-5pm, Nov.-Mar. daily 10am-4pm), along the Avenue of the Giants (Hwy. 254) between the towns of Weott and Myers Flat. It's a nice visitors center, with plenty of information for anyone new to the region or looking for hiking or camping information. You can also enjoy the theater, interpretive museum, and gift shop. There is no entrance fee for Humboldt Redwoods State Park and no fee to use the visitors center; the only day-use fee in the park is for the Williams Grove Day Use Area ($8 per vehicle).

While it's more than worth your while to spend a weekend or more in the Humboldt redwoods, you can also enjoy yourself for a

redwood trees along the Avenue of the Giants

few hours just passing through. A drive along the Avenue of the Giants with a stop at the visitors center and a quick nature walk or picnic can give you a taste of the lovely southern end of the coastal redwoods region.

★ Avenue of the Giants

The most famous stretch of redwood trees is the **Avenue of the Giants** (www.avenue-ofthegiants.net), paralleling U.S. 101 and the Eel River for about 33 miles between Garberville and Fortuna; look for signs on U.S. 101. Visitors come from all over the world to drive this stretch of road and gaze in wonder at the sky-high old-growth redwoods along the way. Campgrounds and hiking trails sprout amid the trees off the road. It's easy to park your car at various points along the way and get out to walk among the giants or down to the nearby Eel River for a cool dip.

The Avenue's highest traffic volume is in July-August, when you can expect bumper-to-bumper stop-and-go traffic along the entire road. That's not necessarily a bad thing:

Going slow is the best way to see the sights. But if crowds aren't your thing, visit in spring or fall, or brave the rains of winter to gain a more secluded redwood experience.

To enhance your Avenue of the Giants drive, there's an eight-stop audio tour along the route. Pick up an audio tour card at the visitors center or on either side of the drive.

Hiking and Biking

Stop at the **Humboldt Redwoods State Park Visitors Center** (707/946-2263, www. parks.ca.gov or www.humboldtredwoods.org, Apr.-Oct. daily 9am-5pm, Nov.-Mar. daily 10am-4pm) to pick up a trail map showing the many hikes accessible on or near this road. Many are very short, so you can make a nice day of combined driving and walking without having to commit to one big trek.

Many visitors start with the **Founder's Grove Nature Loop Trail** (0.6 mile, easy), at mile marker 20.5 on the Avenue of the Giants. This sedate, flat nature trail gives walkers a taste of the big old-growth trees in the park. Sadly, the onetime tallest tree in the world, the Dyerville Giant, fell in 1991 at the age of about 1,600. But it's still doing its part in this astounding ecosystem, decomposing before your eyes on the forest floor and feeding new life in the forest.

Right at the visitors center, you can enjoy the **Gould Grove Nature Trail** (0.6 mile, easy), a wheelchair-accessible interpretive nature walk with helpful signs describing the denizens of the forest.

If you're looking for a longer walk in the woods, try the lovely **River Trail** (Mattole Rd., 1.1 miles west of Ave. of the Giants, 7 miles round-trip, moderate). It follows the South Fork Eel River, allowing access to yet another ecosystem. Check with the visitors center to be sure that the summer bridges have been installed before trying to hike this trail.

Hard-core hikers who like to go at it all day can get their exercise at Humboldt Redwoods State Park. Start at the **Grasshopper Multiuse Trailhead** (Mattole Rd., 5.1 miles west of Ave. of the Giants) to access the newer

Johnson Camp Trail (10.5 miles round-trip, difficult), which takes you to the abandoned cabins of railroad tie makers. Or pick another fork from the same trailhead to climb more than 3,000 feet to **Grasshopper Peak** (13.5 miles, difficult). From the peak, you can see 100 miles in any direction, overlooking the whole of the park and beyond.

You can bring your street bike to the park and ride the Avenue of the Giants or Mattole Road. A number of the trails around Humboldt Redwoods State Park are designated multiuse, which means that mountain bikers can make the rigorous climbs and then rip their way back down.

Swimming and Kayaking

The **Eel River**'s forks meander through the Humboldt redwoods, creating lots of great opportunities for cooling off on hot summer days. Check with the park's visitors center for this year's best swimming holes, but you can reliably find good spots at **Eagle Point,** near Hidden Valley Campground; **Gould Bar;** and **Garden Club of America Grove.** In addition to the usual precautions for river swimming, during August-September a poisonous (if ingested) blue-green algae can bloom late in the summer, making swimming in certain parts of the river hazardous.

Events

Humboldt Redwoods State Park is the site of a couple of the best marathons and half-marathons around. It offers flat courses, cool weather, and world-class scenery. If you're looking for an unintimidating place to try your first marathon, or if you need a fast time for a personal record or to qualify for Boston, this is an ideal choice. These events are also less crowded than the famous marathons, and you can camp right in the park where they begin. October has the **Humboldt Redwoods Marathon** (www.redwoodsmarathon.org, $55-65) with a related half-marathon ($50-60) and a 5K ($25). The **Avenue of the Giants Marathon** (www.theave.org, marathon $60, half-marathon $50, 10K $30) is held each May.

Camping

There are few lodging options close to the park. Fortunately, the camping at Humboldt Redwoods State Park (707/946-2263, www. reserveamerica.com, $35) is good, with three developed car-accessible campgrounds; there are also primitive backcountry campsites ($5). Each developed campground has its own entrance station, and reservations are strongly recommended, as the park is quite popular with weekend campers.

Burlington Campground (707/946-1811, year-round) is adjacent to the visitors center and is a convenient starting point for the marathons and other races that traverse the park in May and October. It's shaded and comfortable, engulfed in trees, and has ample restroom facilities and hot showers. **Albee Creek** (Mattole Rd., 5 miles west of Ave. of the Giants, 707/946-2472, mid-May-mid-Oct.) offers some redwood-shaded sites and others in open meadows, which can be nice in the summer if you want to get a little sun.

★ **Hidden Springs Campground** (Ave. of the Giants, 5 miles south of the visitors center, 707/943-3177, early May-Labor Day) is large and popular. Nearby a trail leads to a great Eel River swimming hole. Minimalist campers will enjoy the seclusion of hike-in trail camps at **Johnson Camp** and **Grasshopper Peak.**

Equestrians can also make use of the multiuse trails, and the **Cuneo Creek Horse Camp** (old homestead on Mattole Rd., 8 miles west of Ave. of the Giants, May-mid-Oct., 1 vehicle and 2 horses $35) provides a place for riders who want to spend more than just a day exploring the thousands of acres of forest and meadowland.

Information and Services

Get the best information at the **Humboldt Redwoods State Park Visitors Center** (707/946-2263, www.parks.ca.gov or www. humboldtredwoods.org, Apr.-Oct. daily 9am-5pm, Nov.-Mar. daily 10am-4pm).

Fill your gas tank in the nearby towns of Piercy, Garberville, Redway, Redcrest, Miranda, and Rio Dell. Markets to stock up on supplies are in Garberville, Redway, Miranda, Phillipsville, Redcrest, Myers Flat, Scotia, and Rio Dell.

The nearest hospital with an emergency room is **Redwood Memorial Hospital** (3300 Renner Dr., Fortuna, 707/725-3361, www.redwoodmemorial.org).

Transportation

Humboldt Redwoods State Park is 21 miles north of Garberville on U.S. 101. The Avenue of the Giants parallels U.S. 101 and there are several marked exits along the highway to reach the scenic redwood drive.

FERNDALE

Ferndale was built in the 19th century by Scandinavian immigrants who came to California to farm. Little has changed since the immigrants constructed their fanciful gingerbread Victorian homes and shops. Many cows still munch grass in the dairy pastures that surround the town.

The main sight in Ferndale is the town itself, which has been designated a historical landmark. Ferndale is all Victorian, all the time: Ask about the building you're in and you'll be told all about its specific architectural style, its construction date, and its original occupants. Main Street's shops, galleries, inns, and restaurants are all set into scrupulously maintained and restored late-19th-century buildings, and even the public restrooms are housed in a small Victorianesque structure.

Architecture buffs can spend hours just strolling around downtown. It's no surprise that Hollywood has discovered Ferndale as a picturesque setting for a movie: It has starred alongside Jim Carrey in *The Majestic* and Dustin Hoffman in *Outbreak*.

Sights

The **Ferndale History Museum** (515 Shaw St., 707/786-4466, www.ferndale-museum. org, June-Sept. Tues.-Sat. 11am-4pm, Sun.

1pm-4pm, Oct.-Dec. and Feb.-May Wed.-Sat. 11am-4pm, Sun. 1pm-4pm, $1) is a block off Main Street and tells the story of the town. Life-size dioramas depict period life in a Victorian home, and an array of antique artifacts brings history to life. Downstairs, the implements of rural coast history vividly display the reality that farmers and artisans faced in the preindustrial era.

To cruise farther back into the town's history, consider wandering out into the **Ferndale Cemetery** on Bluff Street. Well-tended tombstones and mausoleums wend up the hillside behind the town. Genealogists will love reading the scrupulously maintained epitaphs that tell the human history of the region.

Beaches

Ferndale locals love that they have their own beach just five miles outside of their quaint village. The **Centerville County Park and Beach** (five miles west of Ferndale on Centerville Rd., 707/445-7651, http://co.humboldt.ca.us, daily 5am-midnight, free) stretches for an impressive nine miles and is home to a winter congregation of tundra swans. You are able to drive your four-wheel-drive vehicle on the sand, ride a horse, or build a big beach bonfire at night here, which is unusual for beaches in California.

Entertainment and Events

Ferndale is a quiet town where the sidewalks roll up early. But for visitors who like to be out and about after 6pm, there are a few decent options. The **Ferndale Repertory Theater** (447 Main St., 707/786-5483 or 800/838-3006, www.ferndale-rep.org, $13-18), the oldest and largest of the North Coast's community theaters, puts on a number of shows each year. Some are wholesome and suitable for the whole family like *Annie,* while others, including *In the Next Room (Or the Vibrator Play),* feature more adult subject matter. Check the schedule for special events and performances.

If you want to get a beer or mixed drink in Ferndale, **The Palace** (353 Main St., 707/786-4165, daily 10am-2am) is the local bar with pool tables, shuffleboard, and a jukebox. Late into the night, you can fill the slots at the **Bear River Casino** (11 Bear Paws Way, Loleta, 707/733-9644, www.bearrivercasino.com, daily open 24 hours) in nearby Loleta.

Ferndale has hosted the **Humboldt County Fair** (1250 5th St., www.humboldt-countyfair.org, adults $8, seniors $6, children $5) each August since 1896. For 10 days people from all around the county come to celebrate at the old-fashioned fair, complete with livestock exhibits, horse racing, competitions, a carnival, musical entertainment each night, and a variety of shows for kids and adults on the fairground stages. If you're in the area, come join the fun.

Every Memorial Day weekend, moving sculptures race 42 miles in three days from Arcata's plaza to Ferndale's Main Street. It's the **Kinetic Grand Championship Sculpture Race** (www.kineticgrandchampionship.com), and it is the kind of event that only happens in Humboldt.

Shopping

A tour of Ferndale's Main Street shops makes for an idyllic morning stroll. The Victorian storefronts house antiques stores, jewelry shops, clothing boutiques, and art galleries. Ferndale is also a surprisingly good place to buy a hat.

The **Golden Gait Mercantile** (421 Main St., 707/786-4891, www.goldengaitmercantile.com, Mon.-Sat. 10am-5pm, Sun. noon-4pm) has it all: antiques, candies, gourmet foodstuffs, clothing, hats, souvenirs, and more. Antiques and collectibles tend to be small and reasonably priced.

Silva's Fine Jewelry (400 Ocean Ave., 707/786-4425 or 888/589-1011, www.silvas-jewelry.com, daily 8am-9pm), on the bottom floor of the Victorian Inn, is not a place for the faint of wallet. But the jewels, both contemporary and antique, are classically gorgeous.

The **Blacksmith Shop** (455 Main St., 707/786-4216, www.ferndaleblacksmith.com, daily 9:30am-5:30pm) displays a striking collection of useful art made by top blacksmiths and glassblowers from around the country. The array of jewelry, furniture, kitchen implements, fireplace tools, and metal things defies description.

Accommodations

In Ferndale, lodgings tend to be Victorian-style inns, mostly bed-and-breakfasts. Guests of the **Shaw House Inn** (703 Main St., 707/786-9958 or 800/557-7429, www.shawhouse.com, $125-275) must walk a block or two to get to the heart of downtown Ferndale, but the reward is a spacious garden on the inn's grounds. Huge shade trees and perfectly positioned garden benches make a lovely spot to sit and read a book, hold a quiet conversation, or just enjoy the serene beauty. The interior of the inn has eight rooms and three common parlor areas. A lush morning breakfast fortifies shoppers and adventurers alike.

The historic ★ **Victorian Inn** (400 Ocean Ave., 707/786-4949 or 888/589-1808, www.victorianvillageinn.com, $129-329) is an imposing structure at the corner of Ocean Avenue and Main Street that also houses Silva's Jewelry. The inn comprises 13 rooms, all decorated with antique furnishings, luxurious linens, and pretty knickknacks. For a special treat, rent the Ira Russ Suite, a spacious room with a tower alcove that takes in the town below. A full hot breakfast is served downstairs.

In a town full of history, the **Hotel Ivanhoe** (315 Main St., 707/786-9000, www.ivanhoe-hotel.com, $95-145) is the oldest extant hostelry. Plaques on the building's exterior describe its rich legacy. The four rooms are done in rich colors that evoke the Western-Victorian atmosphere of the original hotel.

An inexpensive non-inn lodging option in Ferndale is the **Redwood Suites** (332 Ocean Ave., 707/786-5000 or 888/589-1863, www.redwoodsuites.com, $110-145). Only a block off Main Street, the property has modern rooms that are simple but comfortable. Family suites with full kitchens are available, and the room rates are reasonable.

Food

Tucked into the bottom floor of the Victorian Inn, the **VI Restaurant & Tavern** (400 Ocean Ave., 707/786-4950, www.virestaurant.com, daily 11:30am-9pm, $12-36) feels like a spruced-up Western saloon. Perch yourself at the bar for casual options like fish-and-chips or sit down at a table for sophisticated dinner entrées like Portuguese paella or coldwater lobster. Sundays are prime rib nights, complete with piano music.

Locals come from as far away as Eureka to dine at the restaurant at the **Hotel Ivanhoe** (315 Main St., 707/786-9000, www.ivanhoe-hotel.com, Wed.-Sun. 5pm-9pm, Wed.-Sun. bar from 4pm, $11-32), where it's all about the hearty homemade Italian dishes and friendly personal service. A more casual Italian dining experience can be had down the street at the **Ferndale Pizza Co.** (607 Main St., 707/786-4345, Tues.-Thurs. 11:30am-9pm, Fri.-Sat. 11:30am-9:30pm, Sun. noon-9pm, $16-21).

For breakfast, stop in at the local favorite **Poppa Joe's** (409 Main St., 707/786-4180, Mon.-Fri. 6am-2pm, Sat.-Sun. 6am-noon, $5.50-9). The interior is dim and narrow, but the breakfast and lunch offerings are delicious.

If you need to grab some grub to go, **Valley Grocery** (339 Main St., 707/786-9515, daily 7am-10pm) stocks staples and also maintains a deli; it's a perfect last stop on the way out to a beach picnic. Don't forget to drop in at the heavenly candy store **Sweetness and Light** (554 Main St., 707/786-4403 or 800/547-8180, www.sweetnessandlight.com, Mon.-Sat. 10am-5pm, Sun. 11am-4pm).

Information and Services

If you need medical care, the **Redwood Memorial Hospital** (3300 Renner Dr., Fortuna, www.stjoehumboldt.org) is 10 miles away in Fortuna.

Transportation

Ferndale, like much of the nearby Lost Coast, is not directly accessible from U.S. 101; you must get off U.S. 101 at Fernbridge and then follow Highway 211 south to Ferndale. Mattole Road leads out of town south toward the Sinkyone Wilderness area, while Centerville Road heads out to the beach. Walking provides the best views and feel of the town.

The Lost Coast

The Lost Coast is one of California's last undeveloped coastlines. Encompassing northern Mendocino County and southern Humboldt County, this coast is "lost" because the rugged terrain makes it impractical—some might say impossible—to build a highway here. An arduous trek along its wilderness trails is worthwhile to soak up the raw beauty of its rugged beaches.

The King Range National Conservation Area encompasses the northern section of the Lost Coast. Here, King Peak rises over 4,000 feet from the sea in less than three miles. It's also home to the most popular version of the Lost Coast Trail: a 24-mile backpacking excursion along the region's wild beaches that begins at the mouth of the Mattole River and ends at Shelter Cove's Black Sand Beach.

Sinkyone Wilderness State Park makes up the southern section of the Lost Coast, which has its own Lost Coast Trail, heading slightly inland on its journey from Bear Harbor to Usal Beach. While the more popular King Range Lost Coast Trail traverses beaches right by the ocean, the 16-mile Sinkyone version is mostly along bluffs with less coastal access.

Situated between the two major sections of the King Range Conservation Area and Sinkyone Wilderness State Park is the small fishing community of Shelter Cove, which has a few restaurant and lodging options. It's also home to Black Sand Beach and the Cape Mendocino Lighthouse. The few other areas of the Lost Coast accessible by car include Usal Beach and Mattole Beach.

Reaching the Lost Coast involves short detours from U.S. 101. Shelter Cove can be reached by taking Briceland/Shelter Cove Road out of Redway, while Usal Beach is accessible from a dirt road that leaves Highway 1 three miles north of the town of Rockport. The Mattole Recreation Site is found by taking Lighthouse Road off Mattole Road.

MATTOLE ROAD

Mattole Road, a narrow, mostly paved two-lane road, affords views of remote ranchland, unspoiled forests, and a few short miles of barely accessible cliffs and beaches. It's one of the few paved, drivable routes that allows you to view the Lost Coast from your car (the other is Shelter Cove Road, farther south). In sunny weather, the vistas are spectacular. This road also serves as access to the even smaller tracks out to the trails and campgrounds of the Sinkyone Wilderness. The most common way to get to Mattole Road is from the Victorian village of Ferndale, where you take a right on Ocean Avenue and follow the signs towards the community of Petrolia.

MATTOLE BEACH

At the northern end of the Lost Coast, **Mattole Beach** (end of Lighthouse Rd., 707/825-2300, www.blm.gov) is a broad length of sand that's perfect for an easy contemplative stroll. It's also popular for picnicking and fishing. Mattole Beach is the northern entry point to the Lost Coast Trail, and the start of a shorter, six-mile round-trip day hike to the **Punta Gorda Lighthouse.** The lighthouse was built in 1911 after the coast and its rocks caused multiple shipwrecks. It was shut down in 1951 due to high maintenance costs.

There is a campground with 14 first-come, first-served campsites ($8) for those who want solitude or are preparing to hike the Lost Coast Trail.

To reach Mattole Beach from U.S. 101, take the Garberville, Honeydew, or Ferndale exits.

The Lost Coast

© AVALON TRAVEL

Mattole River down to Shelter Cove's Black Sand Beach. This is a once-in-a-lifetime experience that offers hiking alongside primal, mostly wild coastline, interrupted only by the abandoned Punta Gorda Lighthouse and numerous shipwrecks along the shore. Waterfalls feather the coastal bluffs, shorebirds fly above the crashing surf, sea lions congregate at the aptly named Sea Lion Gulch, and migrating whales surface along the horizon. On land, you might encounter deer and bears.

This is a strenuous hike, challenging even for experienced hikers. It demands both preparation and stamina. While scenic, the ocean along the trail is also cold, rough, and unforgiving. Use caution, as multiple people have been swept out to sea.

Planning Your Hike

You can hike the trail anytime between spring and fall. Spring is notable for blooming wildflowers. Summer is the most crowded. Fall is the least crowded, and often has the most pleasant weather. During winter, the trail can be impassable due to massive surf or flooding streams.

Allow three days and two nights to complete the trail, hiking around eight miles a day. Be prepared to walk on sand, cobblestones, and boulders. Plan on carrying in everything you'll need (tents, sleeping bags, equipment, food, and water). Carry it all (including any trash) back out to keep the area wild. There are creeks every 1.5-2 miles along the trail, but you need to purify the water before drinking it.

Most people begin the hike at the Mattole River and head south. This is so you are hiking with the wind at your back, rather than in your face. You'll need to park a vehicle at either end of the trail. Parking at the Mattole trailhead is free. There have been vehicle break-ins, so don't leave any valuables in your car. There's also the **Mattole Campground** (end of Lighthouse Rd., 707/825-2300, www.blm.gov, $8), with 14 first-come, first-served sites; this allows to camp near the trailhead the night before heading out.

Follow the signs to Petrolia on Mattole Road. Turn off Mattole Road onto Lighthouse Road, which is south of the Mattole River Bridge. Follow Lighthouse Road for five miles to the beach.

THE LOST COAST TRAIL

To fully experience one of the country's most remote and rugged coastal areas, backpackers head out on the **Lost Coast Trail.** This 24-mile beach hike stretches from the

Parking at Black Sand Beach, the southern end of the trail, is also free. The drive between the two trailheads is an hour and 45 minutes. To avoid a half-day of driving between the trailheads, contact **Lost Coast Shuttle** (707/986-7437, www.lostcoastshuttle.com, $200/two people, $25/each additional person), which will drive you from Shelter Cove's Black Sand Beach, where you can leave your car, to the start of the trailhead at Mattole Beach.

In addition to securing transportation, hikers also need a backcountry permit, but these are free as long as you're not an organized group or a commercial enterprise. They also double as fire permits. You can get a permit at a self-service box at one of the trailheads, at the **King Range office** (768 Shelter Cove Rd., 707/986-5400, Mon.-Fri. 8am-4:30pm) in Whitethorn or at the Bureau of Land Management **Arcata Field Office** (1695 Heindon Rd., 707/825-2300, www.blm.gov, Mon.-Fri. 7:45am-4:30pm).

Bear canisters are mandatory for storing food and scented items while on the trailRent bear canisters ($5) just a few miles from the Mattole Trailhead at the **Petrolia General Store** (40 Sherman Rd., Petrolia, 707/629-3455). They're also available in Shelter Cove at the **BLM Whitethorn Office** (768 Shelter Cove Rd., 707/986-5400, $5) or in Arcata at the **BLM Arcata Field Office** (1695 Heindon Rd., 707/825-2300, $5).

This is a wilderness hike, so there are few signs. You'll mostly just be hiking the beach except at a few spots. Two sections of the trail are impassable at high tide: The first is from Sea Lion Gulch to Randall Creek, and the second is from south of Big Flat down to Gitchell Creek. It's critical that you consult a tide chart and manage your time to make sure you pass through these areas of the trail during low tide.

There are no developed campgrounds or facilities along the trail, but dispersed camping is allowed at **Cooksie Creek, Randall Creek, Big Creek, Big Flat Creek, Buck Creek, Shipman Creek,** and **Gitchell Creek.**

Dogs are allowed on the trail as long as they are under voice control or on a leash. Dogs should be outfitted with booties so that their paws don't get scraped up by the rocks on the trail.

Before heading to the area, try to get your hands on a copy of Wilderness Press's **Lost Coast Map** (www.wildernesspress.com, $8). Check on trail conditions by visiting the **U.S. Department of the Interior** website (www.blm.gov) and searching "Lost Coast Trail." More information is also available at the **King Range Information Line** (707/825-2300).

SHELTER COVE

Get a taste of the Lost Coast in Shelter Cove, a fishing community with a scattering of restaurants and accommodations. A nine-hole golf course, a small airport, and 40 miles of paved roads and lots are remnants of a large planned community that failed to materialize. But the real highlight of Shelter Cove is its access to the shoreline.

Sights
BLACK SAND BEACH
One of the most beautiful and accessible features of the Lost Coast, the 3.5-mile **Black Sand Beach** (King Range National Conservation Area, www.blm.gov) is named for its unusually dark sand and stones, which contrast with the deep-blue ocean water and the towering King Range Mountains in the background. The main beach parking lot has interpretive panels about the region as well as bathrooms and a drinking fountain. It's just north of the town of Shelter Cove; to get there follow Shelter Cove Road and then take a right onto Beach Road, which dead-ends at Black Sand Beach. The long walk across the dark sands to either Horse Creek or Gitchell Creek is relatively easy. This beach also serves as the south end of the Lost Coast Trail.

CAPE MENDOCINO LIGHTHOUSE
At Mal Coombs Park in Shelter Cove, the 43-foot tower of the **Cape Mendocino**

Lighthouse (www.lighthousefriends. com, tours Memorial Day-Labor Day daily 10:30am-3:30pm) is quiet and dark. It began life on Cape Mendocino—a 400-foot cliff that marks the westernmost point of California—in 1868. In 1951 the tower was abandoned in favor of a light on a pole, and in 1999 the tower was moved to Shelter Cove, becoming a museum in 2000. When docents are available, you can take a tour of the lighthouse. The original first-order Fresnel lens is now on display in nearby Ferndale.

Sports and Recreation
HIKING
For another great hike, take the **King Crest Trail,** a mountain hike from the southern Saddle Mountain Trailhead to stunning King Peak and on to the North Slide Peak Trailhead. A good solid 10-mile one-day round-trip can be done from either trailhead. To reach Saddle Mountain Trailhead from Shelter Cove, drive up Shelter Cove Road and turn left onto King Peak Road. Bear left on Saddle Mountain Road and turn left on a spur road to the trailhead. Only high-clearance, four-wheel drive vehicles are recommended.

Also accessible from the Saddle Mountain Trailhead, **Buck Creek Trail** includes an infamous grade, descending more than 3,000 vertical feet on an old logging road to the beach.

An arduous but gorgeous loop trail, the eight-mile **Hidden Valley-Chinquapin-Lost Coast Loop Trail** can be done in one day, or in two days with a stop at water-accessible Nick's Camp. Access it by driving out of Shelter Cove and turning right onto Chemise Mountain Road. The trailhead will be less than a mile on your right.

The many other trails in the Kings Range National Conservation Area near Shelter Cove include **Rattlesnake Ridge, Kinsey Ridge, Spanish Ridge,** and **Lightning.** Before heading to the area, try to get your hands on a copy of Wilderness Press's Lost Coast Map (www.wildernesspress.com).

FISHING
The Lost Coast is a natural fishing haven. The harbor at Shelter Cove offers charter services for ocean fishing. Kevin Riley of **Outcast Sportfishing** (Shelter Cove, 707/223-0368, www.outcastsportfish.com, Apr.-Sept., $225 pp per day) can help plan a charter fishing trip chasing whatever is in season. The cost includes gear, tackle, and filleting and packaging your fish at the end of the day, but you must bring your own lunch. Another reputable charter service is **Shelter Cove Sport Fishing** (707/923-1668, www.codking.com, fishing trips $175-250 pp), offering excursions to hunt halibut, albacore, salmon, or rockfish.

If shellfish is your favorite, come to the Shelter Cove area to enjoy the Northern California abalone season. Ask locally for this year's best diving spots, and obtain a license: The state Department of Fish and Game (916/445-0411, www.wildlife.ca.gov) can explain the rules about taking abalone, which is strictly regulated.

SURFING
Big Flat is a legendary surf spot about eight miles north of Shelter Cove on the Lost Coast Trail. While the hike in is challenging, hardcore surfers will find it worth the effort. Local surfers are very protective of this break: Even a writer for *National Geographic Adventure* who wrote about the break refused to name it for fear of retaliation. He referred to it as "Ghost Point." Be careful: Big Flat is in the middle of nowhere, and help is a ways off.

Accommodations
Shelter Cove offers several nice motels for those who aren't up for roughing it in the wilderness overnight. **The Tides Inn of Shelter Cove** (59 Surf Point, 707/986-7900 or 888/998-4337, www.sheltercovetidesinn. com, $170-220) has standard rooms as well as luxurious suites. The suites come with fireplaces and full kitchens. All rooms face the sea, which is only steps from the inn. The Tides Inn is within walking distance of the airstrip, local shops, and restaurants.

The **Inn of the Lost Coast** (205 Wave Dr., 707/986-7521 or 888/570-9676, www.innofthelostcoast.com, $180-300) has an array of large, airy rooms and suites with stellar views to suit even luxurious tastes. While all rooms take in the coastline, the corner king bedrooms are the most popular. Ask about discounts for AOPA pilots and AARP members, as well as the AAA discount.

The **Cliff House at Shelter Cove** (141 Wave Dr., 707/986-7344, www.cliffhousesheltercove.com, $200) is perched atop the bluffs overlooking the black-sand beaches. Only two suites are available; they're perfect for a romantic vacation or family getaway. Each has a full kitchen, living room, bedroom, gas fireplace, and satellite TV.

Camping

For many, staying on the Lost Coast near Shelter Cove means camping in the wilderness near the trails. If you're planning to camp in the backcountry, you need a permit. Permits are free and can be obtained from self-service boxes at the trailheads, or by visiting the local office of the **Bureau of Land Management** (BLM, 768 Shelter Cove Rd., Whitethorn, 707/986-5400, www.ca.blm.gov). Bear canisters are mandatory; rent one ($5) with a major credit card at the **Petrolia General Store** (40 Sherman Rd., Petrolia, 707/629-3455).

If you prefer a developed campground in the area around Shelter Cove with amenities like restrooms, grills, fire rings, picnic tables, bear boxes, and potable water, there are a number of sites in the King Range National Conservation Area (no permit required). Campgrounds are open year-round. Reservations are not available but the odds of getting a site are pretty good, given the small number of people who come here, even in high season. Some of the larger BLM camping areas (707/986-5400, www.ca.blm.gov) in the King Range are **Wailaki** (Chemise Mountain Rd., 13 sites, $8), **Nadelos** (Chemise Mountain Rd., tents only, 8 sites, $8), **Tolkan** (King Peak Rd., 5 RV sites, 4 tent sites, $8), and **Horse Mountain** (King Peak Rd., 9 sites, no water, $5). Trailers and RVs (up to 24 feet) are allowed at most sites except Nadelos. If you are driving an RV, it's wise to check road conditions beforehand.

For more developed camping in Shelter Cove, the nearby **Shelter Cove RV Campground** (492 Machi Rd., Whitethorn, 707/986-7474, http://sheltercoverv.com, RVs $45, tents $35) is just feet away from the airport and has views of the ocean. They have a deli and store (grill daily 10am-5:30pm) onsite so you don't have to bring all your own food.

Food

For a delicious seafood meal, visit the glass-fronted A-frame **Chart Room** (210 Wave Dr., 707/986-9696, www.chartroom.cc, Mon.-Wed. 5pm-8:30pm, Sat. 5pm-9pm, $20-25). Seafood and hearty meat and pasta dishes are available along with vegetarian fare, sandwiches, and soups. The Chart Room also has beer, wine, and cocktails that you can drink on the deck. Check out the nautical and aeronautical gift shop.

The hearty menu at the **Cove Restaurant** (10 Seal Ct., 707/986-1197, www.sheltercove-oceanfrontinn.com, Thurs.-Sun. 5pm-9pm, $13-30), heavy on the seafood, is perfect after a hard day of hiking, fishing, or beachcombing, especially with the Cove's views of the coast.

The **Delgada Pizza and Bakery** (Inn of the Lost Coast, 205 Wave St., 707/986-7672, https://innofthelostcoast.com, daily 4pm-9pm, $9-30) is the place for pizza and pasta. The appropriately named Lost Coast Pizza is a favorite. There's bottled beer and wine to complement your meal. This is a small place with just one table inside and three tables outside. Next door, go for coffee, breakfast, or a sandwich at the **Fish Tank Espresso Gallery** (205 Wave Dr., 707/986-7850, Thurs.-Tues. 7am-2pm).

Information and Services

Don't expect much information or services in remote Shelter Cove. For an overview of the community, visit www.sheltercoveca.info and www.sheltercove-lostcoast.com.

There are no medical facilities in Shelter Cove, but emergency services are coordinated through the **Shelter Cove Fire Department** (9126 Shelter Cove Rd., Whitethorn, 707/986-7507, www.sheltercove-ca.gov). The nearest hospital with an emergency room is **Redwood Memorial Hospital** (3300 Renner Dr., Fortuna, 707/725-3361, www.stjoehumboldt.org).

Transportation

To reach Shelter Cove from U.S. 101 North, take the second Garberville exit. After exiting, look for the Shelter Cove signs and turn west on Briceland Road, which becomes Shelter Cove Road. Though it is just a 23-mile trip on Shelter Cove Road, it takes an hour because it's windy and goes down to one lane at one section.

Pilots can fly into the **Shelter Cove Airport** (707/986-7447, www.sheltercove-ca.gov) if weather conditions cooperate. There are live webcams on the airport's website to check the current weather.

SINKYONE WILDERNESS STATE PARK

Encompassing the southern section of the Lost Coast, the **Sinkyone Wilderness State Park** (707/986-7711, www.parks.ca.gov, daily sunrise-sunset) is a wild region of steep coastal mountains and surf-pounded beaches spotted with wildlife, including bears and elk. The Roosevelt elk had disappeared from the region until a herd from Prairie Creek State Park was reintroduced here. With their impressive antlers, the elk bulls usually weigh 700-1,100 pounds and can be quite a sight to see in the wild.

Though not as popular as the Lost Coast Trail connecting Black Sand Beach to the Mattole River up north, the Sinkyone Wilderness has a 16-mile **Lost Coast Trail** that starts at Bear Harbor, south of Needle Rock, and ends at Usal Beach. This trail, which takes backpackers 2-3 days, has more climbing than the more popular beach trail to the north. The rigorous hike is mostly on bluffs above the coastline. It passes through virgin redwood groves and mixed forest with beach access at **Wheeler Beach.**

Needle Rock

The most easily accessible spot in the northern Sinkyone is **Needle Rock,** the former site of a small settlement and the current location of a park visitors center. The area's namesake rock is nearby on a black-sand beach. Visitors can camp at three environmental campsites (first-come, first-served, $25), three miles from the visitors center, as well as at an old barn (first-come, first-served, $30) close to the visitors center. Camping is done by self-registration. To reach Needle Rock, head off U.S. 101 at the Garberville exit and take Redwood Road to Redway. Drive Briceland Road in Redway until it becomes Mendocino County Road 435. The road dead-ends into the state park. The last 3.5 miles are unpaved, steep, and narrow.

Needle Rock's visitors center was once a ranch house. Now it is staffed by a volunteer year-round. The visitors center has information on the region's history and various artifacts. You can also purchase maps and firewood here.

Usal Beach

At the southern tip of Sinkyone Wilderness State Park, **Usal Beach** is a remote, two-mile-long black-sand beach situated under cliffs bristling with massive trees. It's accessible to adventurous coastal explorers via a steep, unpaved six-mile dirt road that is not for the fainthearted or the squeamish. Passenger cars can make the drive until the winter rainy season, when four-wheel drive becomes necessary. To find it, drive about an hour north of Fort Bragg on Highway 1 and then turn left on an unmarked road at mile marker 90.88.

When you reach the beach, you can fish from shore or beachcomb the sandy expanse. Watch sea lions torpedo through the ocean and pelicans splash into the water looking for food. Facilities include 35 primitive drive-in campsites (first come, first served, $25) with picnic tables, fire pits, and pit toilets. The rangers come here to collect the camping fees on some days, but otherwise you self-register to camp. Be aware that although firearms are not allowed in the park, locals sometimes shoot guns at night here.

Eureka and Humboldt Bay

The town of Eureka began as a seaward access point to the remote gold mines of the Trinity area. Once settlers realized the value of the redwood trees, the town's logging industry was born.

Visitors can wander the town's five-block-long boardwalk on Humboldt Bay and the charming downtown shopping area, or enjoy the colorful murals and sculptures along the city streets. Outdoors enthusiasts can fish and hike, while history buffs can explore museums, Victorian mansions, and even a working Victorian-era lumber mill.

SIGHTS

For an introduction to Old Town Eureka, take a horse-drawn carriage tour of the historic district with the **Old Town Carriage Co.** (2nd St. and F St., 646/591-2058, $28-47). The carriage is usually downtown near the gazebo around the small square at 2nd and F Streets.

Blue Ox Millworks and Historic Park

Blue Ox Millworks and Historic Park (1 X St., 707/444-3437 or 800/248-4259, www. blueoxmill.com, self-guided tours Apr.-Nov. Mon.-Fri. 9am-5pm, Sat. 9am-4pm, Nov.-Apr. Mon.-Fri. 9am-5pm, adults $10, seniors $9, children ages 6-12 $5, children under 6 free, guided tour $12.50 pp) has a working lumber mill, an upscale wood and cabinetry shop, a blacksmith forge, an old-fashioned print shop, a shipbuilding yard, a rose garden, and a historic park. It also has the world's largest collection of human-powered woodworking tools made by the historic Barnes Equipment Company. Today, the rambling buildings are filled with purchased, donated, and rehabbed tools of all kinds. Workshops feature a glass-blowing kiln and a darkroom where students can learn nondigital photography methods, making their own photosensitive paper and developing black-and-white and sepia prints.

Visitors to the Blue Ox learn about the real lives and times of craftspeople of the late 1800s and early 1900s as they tour the facilities and examine the equipment. If you ask, you might be allowed to touch and even work a piece of wood of your own. Stop in at the gift shop—a converted lumberjack barracks—to check out the ceramics and woodwork the students have for sale.

Carson Mansion

Gables, turrets, cupolas, and pillars: the **Carson Mansion** (143 M St., www.ingomar.org, closed to the public) has all these architectural flourishes. The three-story, 18-room, elaborate Victorian mansion was built by William Carson in 1884 and 1885 after he struck it rich in the lumber business. Almost demolished in the 1940s, it was purchased and renovated by the Ingomar Club, which now uses it for private dinner parties. It's touted as one of the most photographed buildings in the country. The building and grounds are not open to the public.

Clarke Historical Museum

The privately owned **Clarke Historical Museum** (240 E St., 707/443-1947, www. clarkemuseum.org, Wed.-Sat. 11am-4pm, adults $3, families $5), housed in a regal old bank building, is dedicated to preserving the history of Eureka and the surrounding area. Changing exhibitions illuminate the Native American history of the area as well as the

Humboldt Bay

© AVALON TRAVEL

gold rush and logging eras. The Nealis Hall annex displays one of the best collections of Native American artifacts in the state.

Fort Humboldt State Historic Park

Established in 1853 to protect white settlers—particularly gold miners—from the local Native Americans, the original Fort Humboldt lasted only 17 years as a military installation. Today, **Fort Humboldt State**

Historic Park (3431 Fort Ave., 707/445-6567, www.parks.ca.gov, daily 8am-5pm) gives visitors a glimpse into the lives of 19th-century soldiers and loggers. In its early days, it was home to a young Ulysses S. Grant. The original fort hospital now serves as a museum. A sedate but fairly long walking tour takes you through recreations of historic fort buildings and then out to the logging display, where you'll find several "steam donkeys," a piece of equipment that revolutionized the logging industry, along with examples of the type and size of redwood trees loggers were cutting and removing from 19th-century forests. Spend a few minutes enjoying the tranquil historical garden, where master gardeners maintain the type of garden fort residents kept here 150 years ago. Come by on the third Saturday of the month from May to September to take a five-minute ride on a steam locomotive.

Humboldt Bay Tourism Center

The **Humboldt Bay Tourism Center** (205 G St., 707/672-3850, http://humboldtbay-tourismcenter.com, Tues.-Sun. noon-9pm) is no average visitors center with a forest of brochures. Rather, this essential tourist spot has hip 20- and 30-somethings pouring local craft beers and serving a menu of Humboldt delicacies including Humboldt Bay oysters. (Both the fresh, raw oysters and the oysters broiled and topped with local ingredients are exceptional.) There's a virtual visitors center in the back that has iPads loaded with local info along with a list of guided tours in the region. Tours include a historic walking tour of downtown Eureka and a special tour where participants get a tattoo and a beer.

Sequoia Park Zoo

The **Sequoia Park Zoo** (3414 W St., 707/441-4263, www.sequoiaparkzoo.net, summer daily 10am-5pm, winter Tues.-Sun. 10am-5pm, adults $8, seniors $7, children ages 3-12 $6) might seem small, but its mission is a big one: It seeks not only to entertain visitors but also to preserve local species and educate the public about their needs. The Secrets of the Forest exhibit recreates the ecology of a Northern California forest.

Humboldt Botanical Gardens

Staff and local volunteers have worked for years to create **Humboldt Botanical Gardens** (7707 Tompkins Hill Rd., 707/442-5139, www.hbgf.org, Apr.-Oct. Wed.-Sun. 10am-4pm, Nov.-Mar. Wed.-Sat. 10am-2pm, Sun. 11am-3pm, adults $8, seniors and children $5), a celebration of the ecosystems of Humboldt County. The 44-acre site includes native plants, ornamental plants, and plants that grow in riparian regions.

ENTERTAINMENT AND EVENTS
Bars

The biggest and most popular restaurant and bar in Eureka is the **Lost Coast Brewery & Café** (617 4th St., 707/445-4480, www.lost-coast.com, Sun.-Thurs. 11am-10pm, Fri.-Sat. 11am-11pm). The tall cream-and-green building is perched by itself on the main drag, easy to spot as you pass through town. The brewery draws crowds, especially on weekends, and makes popular microbrews including Great White and Downtown Brown, which are on tap. Try the tasty brewpub-style food and a few of the delicious beers.

As its name suggests, **The Local Beer Bar** (517 F St., 707/497-6320, www.thelocalbeerbar.com, Mon.-Thurs. 4pm-10pm, Fri.-Sat. 4pm-11pm, Sun. 2pm-8pm) is all about local beers. Chalkboard-painted skateboards announce the rotating 33 beers on tap, which always include Humboldt brews like Redwood Curtain and Mad River as well as rarities such as barrel-aged and sour beers. This great little beer hall has modern, creative touches like a bar made out of keg coolers, tabletops made from road signs, and local art decorating the walls.

In Opera Alley, **The Speakeasy** (411 Opera Alley, 707/444-2244, Sun.-Thurs. 4pm-11pm, Fri.-Sat. 4pm-2am) is the place to go in Eureka for tasty cocktails. This dark, narrow bar, which sometimes has live music, serves up Southern-style drinks, including a great mint julep.

One of the best dive bars on the North Coast, **The Shanty** (213 3rd St., 707/444-2053, daily noon-2am) impresses with friendly clientele, a superbly curated jukebox, and a lot of eclectic character. Hang out indoors and listen to the inspired mix of tunes from the jukebox, or the occasional live musicians. Head outdoors to play table tennis or pool or smoke a cigarette. The extended happy hour (Mon.-Fri. 4pm-7pm, Sat.-Sun. noon-4pm) offers top-shelf beers and liquors and rock-bottom prices.

The cool, worn-feeling Victorian space at **The Siren's Song Tavern** (325 2nd St., 707/442-8778, www.thesirenssongtavern.com, Mon.-Thurs. 3pm-10pm, Fri.-Sat. 3pm-11pm) hosts bands that perform on a rug in front of the window. Like the best Humboldt watering holes, Siren's Song has a superb craft beer list including 18 brews on tap.

Live Music

A restored theater in downtown Eureka, the **Arkley Center for the Performing Arts** (412 G St., 888/859-8797, www.arkleycenter.com) is the home of the Eureka Symphony and North Coast Dance. The elegant venue, which has chandeliers hanging from its ceilings, also hosts rock, country, and jazz acts. You can't miss the Arkley, with its striking mural of musicians and dancers on the back of the building.

Events

Music lovers flock to Eureka each year for a number of big music festivals. One of the biggest is the **Redwood Coast Jazz Festival** (various venues around town, 707/445-3378, www.redwoodcoastmusicfestivals.org, Mar., tickets $25-85). For four days in March, music lovers can enjoy every style of jazz imaginable, including Dixieland, zydeco, and big band. The festival also features dance lessons and contests.

Experience what Eureka was like during its logging heyday at the **Dolbeer Steam**

Donkey Days (Fort Humboldt State Historic Park, 3431 Fort Ave., 707/445-6567, www.parks.ca.gov, Apr.). This two-day event features working logging equipment, train rides, and logging skill competitions.

The **Kinetic Grand Championship** (Memorial Day weekend, http://kineticgrand-championship.com) is a pedal-powered moving sculpture race that originates in Arcata and ends in Ferndale. The second day of this arty event takes place on Eureka's waterfront.

SHOPPING

Eureka boasts the largest California antiques scene north of the Bay Area. In Old Town and downtown, seekers find treasures from the lumber baron era and Victorian delights, from tiny porcelain figurines to huge pieces of furniture. **Annex 39** (610 F St., 707/443-1323, Tues.-Sat. noon-5pm) specializes in vintage linens and laundry products and also has a great selection of art deco and midcentury modern pieces. **Heritage Antique & Coins** (521 4th St., 707/444-2908, Tues.-Sat. 10am-5pm) is a coin shop that also carries jewelry and Native American artifacts. Generalists will love rooting through the huge **Antiques and Goodies** (1128 3rd St., 707/442-0445, www.antiquesandgoodies.com, Wed.-Sat. 10am-5pm and by appointment) and **Old Town Antiques** (318 F St., 707/442-3235, Mon.-Sat. 10:30am-6pm).

For an afternoon of shopping in Eureka, head down toward the water to 2nd Street. Most of the buildings here are historic, and you might find an unassuming brass plaque describing the famous brothel that once inhabited what is now a toy store. Literature lovers have a nice selection of independent bookstores: **Eureka Books** (426 2nd St., 707/444-9593, www.eurekabooksellers.com, daily 10am-6pm) has a big airy room in which to browse a selection of new and used books. **Booklegger** (402 2nd St., at E St., 707/445-1344, Mon.-Sat. 10am-5:30pm, Sun. 11am-4pm), just down the street, is a small but well-organized new-and-used bookshop that specializes in antique books.

Galleries and gift shops abound, highlighting various aspects of California culture. **Many Hands Gallery** (438 2nd St., 707/445-0455, www.manyhandsgallery.net, Mon.-Sat. 10am-9pm) represents approximately 100 local artisans and also displays work from national and international artists cooperatives, fair-trade organizations, and commercial importers. The offerings are eclectic, representing many cultural, spiritual, and religious traditions from around the globe. Don't get the idea that this place is sanctimonious, though; you'll find plenty of humor and whimsy, and prices range from 10 cents to $10,000.

The Works (434 2nd St., 707/442-8121, www.theworkseureka.com, Mon.-Sat. 11am-7pm) has been providing Humboldt County music fans with vinyl records and CDs since 1971. There are lots of used CDs here to soundtrack a drive along the North Coast.

SPORTS AND RECREATION
Fishing

Eureka is a serious fishing destination. Oodles of both ocean- and river-fishing opportunities abound all over the region, and several fishing tournaments are held each year. Anywhere in California, you must have a valid state fishing license to fish in either the ocean or the rivers. Check with your charter service or guide to be sure they provide a day license with your trip. If they don't, you will have to get your own.

For deep-sea fishing, **Greenwater Fishing Adventures** (707/845-9588, www.eurekafishing.net, fishing trips $170-250, crabbing $75) heads out on the 36-foot *Shellback* to catch salmon, rockfish, halibut, tuna, and crab. **Full Throttle Sportfishing** (601 Startare Dr., 707/498-7473, www.fullthrottlesportfishing.com, $175-275) supplies all needed tackle and can take you out to fish for salmon, rockfish, tuna, or halibut. Trips last all day, and most leave at 6:30am. If you're launching your own boat, public launches are the **Samoa Boat Ramp** (New

Navy Base Rd., 707/445-7651, www.humboldtgov.org, daily 5am-midnight) and the **Fields Landing Boat Ramp** (Railroad Ave., 707/445-7651, www.humboldtgov.org, daily 5am-midnight).

Eureka also has good spots for pier fishing. In town, try the K Street Pier, the pier at the east end of Commercial Street, or the pier at the end of Del Norte Street. Farther north, the north jetty (Hwy. 255, across Samoa Bridge) also has a public pier open for fishing.

Bird-Watching

The national, state, and county parks lacing the Eureka area are ideal bird-watching havens. The **Humboldt Bay National Wildlife Refuge Complex** (1020 Ranch Rd., Loleta, 707/733-5406, www.fws.gov) encompasses several wildlife-refuge sites where visitors are welcome. At the Salmon Creek Unit, you'll find the **Richard J. Guadagno Headquarters and Visitors Center** (daily 8am-5pm), which is an excellent starting place for a number of wildlife walks. To get to the visitors center from U.S. 101, take the exit for Hookton heading north and turn left onto Eel River Drive. Take the first right onto Ranch Road, and you'll find the visitors center parking lot.

Hiking and Biking

Not only is there a vast system of trails in the state and national parks, the city of Eureka maintains a number of multiuse biking and hiking trails as well. Most familiar is the Old Town Boardwalk, part of the **Waterfront Trail** that comprises disconnected sections along Humboldt Bay. **Sequoia Park Trail** begins at the Sequoia Park Zoo and wends through redwood forests, past a duck pond, and through a meadow. This trail is paved and friendly for strollers and wheelchairs. The unpaved **Elk River Trail** (end of Hilfiker Ln.) stretches for one mile through wild meadows along the coast. **Cooper Gulch Trail** is a more sedate stroll than a strenuous hike, circling the Cooper Gulch park playing fields.

Kayaking, Rafting, and Stand-Up Paddleboarding

The water is cold, but getting out on it in a kayak can be exhilarating. If you're new to the sport or just want a guided tour of the area, guided paddles, lessons, rentals, and kayak-fishing trips are available through **Humboats Kayak Adventures** (Woodley Island Marina, 707/443-5157, www.humboats.com, canoe, kayak, and SUP rentals $30-110, tours $55-95). Guides lead a huge variety of tours, from serene paddles in the harbor suitable for children to a kayaking trip among the Avenue of the Giants redwoods.

River rafters and kayakers have great opportunities for rapids fun on the inland Klamath and Trinity Rivers. **Bigfoot Rafting Company** (Willow Creek, 530/629-2263, www.bigfootrafting.com, adults $89, children $79) leads half-day, full-day, and multiday trips on both rivers as well as on the Cal-Salmon and Smith Rivers. Experts can take inflatable kayaks down the Class IV rapids, and newcomers can find a gentle paddle with just enough white water to make things interesting.

Harbor Cruises

The Humboldt Bay Maritime Museum does narrated **Harbor Cruises** (end of C St., 707/445-1910, May-Sept., $140-200) on board a historic ferry dating back to 1910, where you'll learn about the city's waterfront attractions.

Drag Racing

For a down-home American experience, take in a car race at the **Samoa Drag Strip** (New Navy Base Rd., 707/845-5755, www.samoadragstrip.com, May-Sept., adults $10, children 12 and under free). The 0.25-mile track is out on the Samoa Peninsula. Special nights feature Harley motorcycles or diesel trucks.

ACCOMMODATIONS

With such a wealth of Victorian houses, Eureka is a natural location for classic bed-and-breakfast accommodations. Chain motels are also available in abundance, many of them quite cheap. But for a real taste of the town, try one of the charming inns.

Under $150

Originally built by one of the town's founders, **Abigail's Elegant Victorian Mansion** (1406 C St., 707/444-3144, www.eureka-california.com, $135-145) offers an authentic Victorian experience, having retained many of the large home's original fixtures. Each of the two rooms comes with its own story and an astonishing collection of antiques. They both have detached bathrooms. Guests can request a tour of Eureka in one of the inn's 1928 Fords. There are a couple of quirks here that may deter some visitors. First, there are no reservations. The rooms are on a first-come, first-served basis. Second, there is no breakfast service. Lastly, the owners only take cash. No credit cards are accepted.

If B&Bs aren't your style, get a room at the **Bayview Motel** (2844 Fairfield St., 707/442-1673 or 866/725-6813, www.bayviewmotel.com, $115-180). This hilltop motel has lovely views of Humboldt Bay from many of the rooms and the grounds. Rooms are spacious and decorated in elegant colors and fabrics. You'll find whirlpool suites, free Wi-Fi, cable

TV, wet bars, and coffeemakers. If you're traveling with the family, rent a double suite—two rooms with an adjoining door and separate baths. Although not in downtown Eureka, it's an easy drive from the Bayview for dinner, shopping, and strolling by the harbor.

$150-250

The ★ **Carter House Inns** (301 L St., 800/404-1390, www.carterhouse.com, $179-595) have a range of accommodations in a cluster of butter-yellow Victorian buildings near the Carson Mansion. The main building has 23 rooms and suites, a number of which have gas fireplaces and soaking tubs. Across the street, a reproduction of a Victorian mansion has six rooms, including a family suite with two bedrooms, while **The Bell Cottage** has three rooms and a full common kitchen. For a splurge, rent **The Carter Cottage,** which has two bathrooms, a deck with a fountain, a soaking tub, and a large den and kitchen area. All guests are treated to a hot breakfast and an afternoon wine and appetizer hour. Dine or snack in the inn's renowned Restaurant 301.

There's no place along the California coast quite like ★ **Oyster Beach** (865 B New Navy Base Rd., 707/834-6555, http://oysterbeach.

one of the unique accommodations at Oyster Beach

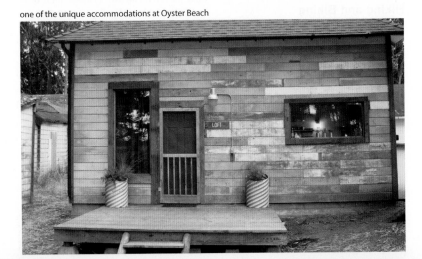

squarespace.com, $195-275), a set of refurbished buildings on the Samoa Peninsula. The 22-acre property has its own beach on Humboldt Bay and impressive eucalyptus groves. Oyster Beach has three units for rent: The Loft is hipster-rustic with reclaimed wood walls. There's also a kitchen and an adjacent water tower that has been transformed into a barbecue deck. The Mid-Century Waterfront is feet from the bay, while the adjacent Escape has a claw-foot tub on an enclosed porch. Future plans for the property include a renovation of the main house, which will yield a two-bedroom unit and a one-bedroom unit. Just eight minutes from downtown Eureka, Oyster Beach feels like it's a world away from anywhere.

FOOD
American

The ★ **Samoa Cookhouse** (511 Vance Rd., Samoa, 707/442-1659, www.samoacookhouse.net, summer daily 7am-9pm, winter daily 7am-8pm, $16) is a Eureka institution. Red-checked tablecloths cover long, rough tables to create the atmosphere of a logging-camp dining hall. All-you-can-eat meals are served family-style from huge serving platters. Diners sit on benches and pass the hearty fare down in turn. Think hunks of roast beef, mountains of mashed potatoes, and piles of cooked vegetables for lunch and dinner or a giant plate of eggs, hash browns, sausage, and toast for breakfast. This is the place to bring your biggest appetite. After dinner, browse the small Historic Logging Museum and gift shop.

Restaurant 301 (301 L St., 800/404-1390, www.carterhouse.com, daily 6pm-9pm, $22-29) at the Carter House Inns seems like a big-city spot. The chef creates an ever-changing menu of delectable delicacies, along with tasting menus. Menu options include exotic duck dishes, simple local seafood preparations, and items from the restaurant's on-site garden. For a treat, try the wine flights suggested with the menus. Restaurant 301 is known for its extensive wine list, with over 3,400 selections.

Visitors to Eureka might be surprised to find **Five Eleven** (511 2nd St., 707/268-3852, Mon.-Thurs. 5pm-9pm, Fri.-Sat. 5pm-9:30pm, Sun. 5pm-8pm, $10-35) in Old Town. There's a turquoise floor and jade lighting that gives the place a bold, metropolitan feel. The food changes frequently but the southern fried chicken and fresh oysters are staples. They also serve specialty craft cocktails, a few

a hearty breakfast at the Samoa Cookhouse

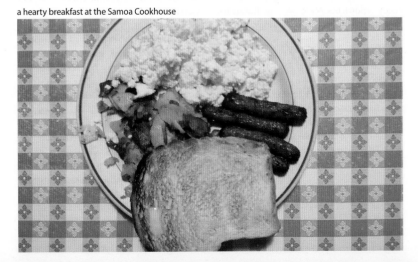

choice craft beers, and a wide variety of wines at their long stone bar.

The **Surfside Burger Shack** (445 5th St., 707/268-1295, Mon.-Sat. 11am-9pm, Sun. noon-7pm, $6-8) is nowhere near the ocean, but it does have surfing decor and darn good burgers made from grass-fed Humboldt cows. The classic cheeseburger hits the spot, but the shack also gets creative with the Surfside Sunrise, a burger topped with cheese, bacon, an egg, and maple syrup.

Bakeries and Cafés

Ramone's Bakery & Café (209 E St., 707/445-2923, Mon.-Fri. 7am-6pm, Sat. 8am-5pm, Sun. 8am-4pm) is a local North Coast chain, selling fresh from-scratch baked goods and candies. Enjoy a fresh cup of coffee roasted in-house and a Danish or a scone, indulge in an afternoon pastry, or even get a whole tart, cake, or loaf of fresh-baked bread to take out for an afternoon picnic.

Occupying a big space in Old Town Eureka, **Old Town Coffee & Chocolates** (211 F St., 707/445-8600, http://oldtowncoffeeeureka.com, Sun.-Mon. 7am-8pm, Tues.-Thurs. 7am-9pm, Fri.-Sat. 7am-10pm) does more than just caffeinate their customers. They also sell chocolate and fudge made on-site, as well as bagels, waffles, wraps, and grilled cheese sandwiches. Many evenings feature live music, open mics, or book readings.

Italian

Brick & Fire Bistro (1630 F St., 707/268-8959, www.brickandfirebistro.com, Wed.-Mon. 11:30am-2:30pm and 5pm-9pm, $14-22) updates Italian classics with a menu that includes fire-roasted polenta lasagna and pizzas with ingredients like locally smoked salmon and quail eggs. The wild mushroom cobbler appetizer is one of the most talked-about menu items.

INFORMATION AND SERVICES

The **Humboldt County Convention and Visitors Bureau** does not operate a public visitors center, but if you need something,

drop by the business office (322 1st St., Mon.-Fri. 9am-5pm) and they'll do their best to help you. The website (www.redwoods.info) is an ideal place to do research on the Redwood Coast region, and you can call the travel hotline (800/346-3482) for information.

The **Eureka Chamber of Commerce** (2112 Broadway, 707/442-3738, www.eureka-chamber.com, Mon.-Fri. 8:30am-5pm) runs a helpful facility, with plenty of literature about things to do in town and beyond.

You can pick up a Humboldt County map and a copy of *101 Things to Do in Humboldt County* (www.101things.com) at many local businesses.

The full-service **St. Joseph Hospital** (2700 Dolbeer St., 707/445-8121, www.stjosepheureka.org) has an emergency room and an urgent care center.

TRANSPORTATION

Eureka is on U.S. 101, easily accessed by car from north or south. From Crescent City, Eureka is less than an hour's drive south on U.S. 101.

Driving is the only option if you're not staying downtown. You can easily visit the 2nd Street shops and restaurants on foot. Parking downtown is metered or free on the streets, and not too difficult to find except on holiday or event weekends.

Bus service in and around Eureka is operated by the **Humboldt Transit Authority** (HTA, www.hta.org, adults $1.70, children and seniors $1.30). The HTA's **Eureka Transit System** (ETS, www.eurekatransit.org) runs within town limits, and the **Redwood Transit System** (RTS, www.redwoodtransit.org, adults $1.65-5.50, children and seniors $1.40-5) can take you around the area; it runs from Eureka north to Trinidad, south to Scotia, and east to Willow Creek.

Eureka has a small commercial airport, **Arcata-Eureka Airport** (ACV, 3561 Boeing Ave., McKinleyville, 707/839-5401, http://co.humboldt.ca.us/aviation), which serves the North Coast region with expensive but convenient flights on United Airlines.

Arcata

On the northern shore of barbell-shaped Humboldt Bay, Arcata has a distinctly different feel than its southern neighbor. The hippie daughter of blue-collar Eureka, Arcata is home to Humboldt State University. Students make up almost half of the city's population, and the town has become known for its liberal politics; at one point the city council was made up mostly of Green Party members. This progressive atmosphere feels a world away from most of the other small towns in the region.

With about half the population of Eureka, Arcata has a small-town feel. The heart of Arcata is the Arcata Plaza, a town park with a William McKinley statue, a couple of palm trees, and a grassy lawn. Here you'll almost always find folks hanging out, playing music, and smoking non-tobacco cigarettes. Circling the plaza are independent restaurants, bars, coffee shops, and stores selling items like shirts made out of hemp. (A local law limits chains and franchises downtown.)

Arcata has a lively arts and music scene along with a handful of restaurants that you might expect in a bigger city. It makes a great home base for exploring the wild North Coast.

SIGHTS
★ Arcata Community Forest
The first city-owned forest in California, the 2,134-acre **Arcata Community Forest** (east ends of 11th St., 14th St., and California St., 707/822-5951, www.cityofarcata.org, daily sunrise-sunset) has trails winding through second-growth redwoods, open for hiking, mountain biking, and horseback riding. Just east of the city's downtown and behind Humboldt State University, the forest is an ideal place to stroll between the silent giants, many of which are cloaked in moss, and take in stumps the size of compact cars and vibrant-green waist-high ferns. The park

also has a section with picnic tables and a playground. Visit the website to download a trail map.

Arcata Plaza
The undisputed center of town is **Arcata Plaza,** a large square with a grassy lawn. This downtown block was spared from development in 1850 when the Union Wharf and Plank Company laid out the city. In its early days, miners would camp in the plaza and some residents would allow their livestock to graze there. Now it has a statue of William McKinley in its center. The plaza hosts many events, from the Saturday farmers markets to the start of the annual Kinetic Grand Championship race.

Arcata Marsh and Wildlife Sanctuary
Believe it or not, one of Arcata's most popular places to take a hike is in a section of the town's wastewater treatment facility. The **Arcata Marsh Interpretive Center** (569 S. G St., 707/826-2359, www.cityofarcata.org, Mon. 1pm-5pm, Tues.-Sun. 9am-5pm) is an information station with a small museum that explains how the city transformed an industrial wasteland into a 307-acre wildlife sanctuary using Arcata's wastewater. Hike the sanctuary's five miles of hiking and biking paths, or try to spot some of the 270 bird species that now use the marsh as a migratory stop.

ENTERTAINMENT AND EVENTS
Bars
A strip of dive bars lines the edge of Arcata Plaza on 9th Street. The best of the bunch, **The Alibi** (744 9th St., 707/822-3731, www.thealibi.com, daily 8am-2am), dates back to the 1920s. The Alibi serves cheap, well-crafted cocktails with infused liquors, including a

wide range of Bloody Marys. It also has an extensive breakfast, lunch, and dinner menu with 28 specialty burgers and entrées from burger steaks to organic tofu cutlets. There are fewer college students in this bar than other places nearby.

A few feet away, **Everett's Club** (784 9th St., 707/822-2291, daily 10am-2am) is a place where you can drink with the locals while big-game heads mounted on the walls stare down at you. Out back is a small patio for the smoking crowd.

Humboldt Brews (856 10th St., 707/826-2739, www.humboldtbrews.com, daily noon-11pm except music nights when it stays open until 2am) serves 25 beers on tap, as well as food. This popular hangout also has a pool table and an adjacent room that serves as a concert space.

Richard's Goat Tavern & Tea Room (401 I St., 707/630-5000, http://richardsgoat.com, daily 3pm-2am) is an oasis of culture and cocktails blocks away from the plaza's dive bar scene. The liquors are house infused, and there's craft beer on tap. Relax on a couch or sidle up to the small bar. The bar also has its own tiny theater dubbed the Miniplex, where art house movies are screened and the occasional live act performs.

Live Music

Music legends play at Humboldt State University's **John Van Duzer Theatre** (1 Harpst St., 707/826-4411, www.humboldt.edu, check website for schedule). Acts including Elvis Costello, John Prine, Melissa Etheridge, The Growlers, and Jake Shimabukuro have all graced its stage. Up-and-coming acts visit campus as well, typically performing at **The Depot** (University Center, 1 Harpst St., 707/826-4411) and the **West Gym** (top of Union St.).

Humboldt Brews (856 10th St., 707/826-2739, www.humboldtbrews.com, daily noon-11pm; until 2am for performances) hosts midsized national jam bands, indie acts, and reggae outfits.

Funk bands and DJs fill up the dance floor at **Jambalaya** (915 H St., 707/822-4766, www.jambalayaarcata.com, Mon.-Fri. 9am-2am, Sat.-Sun. 10pm-2am), a few feet away from Arcata Plaza. The kitchen serves up New Orleans-style po'boys.

Cinema

Dating back to 1938, the art deco **Arcata Theatre Lounge** (1036 G St., 707/822-1220, www.arcatatheatre.com) screens movies, hosts concerts, and puts on events like Sci-Fi

Arcata Plaza

Pint and Pizza Night, where they show old science-fiction movies. You can even watch Monday Night Football on the big screen. The theater seats have been replaced by circular tables and chairs, and the full bar serves food as well as drinks, making it a perfect place for a night out.

A few blocks away, the 1914 **Minor Theatre** (1001 H St., 707/822-3456, www.catheatres.com) is one of the oldest still-operating movie theaters in the country, showing independent movies as well as Hollywood films.

Festivals and Events

Arcata Plaza is the starting line of the **Kinetic Grand Championship** (Memorial Day weekend, http://kineticgrandchampionship.com), a three-day, 42-mile race featuring human-powered art sculptures that continues on to Eureka and Ferndale.

Also in the plaza is June's annual **Arcata Main Street Oyster Festival** (707/822-4500, www.oysterfestival.net), which celebrates the local Kumamoto oyster with—you guessed it—oysters. This is the largest one-day event in Humboldt County. There's live music and flowing microbrewed beer to enjoy with the bivalves.

SPORTS AND RECREATION

Both the **Arcata Community Forest** (east ends of 11th St., 14th St. and California St., 707/822-5951, www.cityofarcata.org, daily sunrise-sunset) and the **Arcata Marsh and Wildlife Sanctuary** (569 S. G St., 707/826-2359, www.cityofarcata.org, Mon. 1pm-5pm, Tues.-Sun. 9am-5pm) have miles of hiking trails.

The famous 18-hole **Redwood Curtain Disc Golf Course** (accessible from Humboldt State University's Redwood Science Lab, though parking is only available in the lot after 5pm) winds its way through massive redwood trees. On the second hole, the tee is atop a 10-foot high redwood stump.

For local sports action, get a ticket to see the **Humboldt Crabs** (Arcata Ball Park, F St. and 9th St., 707/822-9990, http://humboldt-crabs.com), the oldest continually active collegiate summer baseball team in the country.

SHOPPING

There are shops around Arcata Plaza and along H Street, which has a number of unique stores. Head into **Pacific Paradise** (1087 H St., 707/822-7143, Mon.-Sat. 10am-7pm, Sun. 10:30am-6:30pm) to stock up on Humboldt

The Alibi

County essentials like golf discs, hoodies, tie-dyes, and smoking equipment.

Across the street, the **Tin Can Mailman Used & Rare Books Store** (1000 H St., 707/822-1307, www.tincanbooks.com, Mon.-Sat. 10am-7pm, Sun. 11am-6pm) crams together two floors full of used books. If you'd rather get the latest fiction or memoir, head over to **Northtown Books** (957 H St., 707/822-2834, www.northtownbooks.com, Mon.-Thurs. and Sat. 10am-7pm, Fri. 10am-9pm, Sun. noon-5pm). They also have an extensive magazine collection.

Solutions (858 G St., 707/822-6972, Mon.-Sat. 10am-5:30pm) is right on the plaza and is the place to pick up hemp clothing, organic bedding, and eco-goods.

A few blocks from the plaza, **Holly Yashi** (1300 9th St., 877/607-8361, www.hollyyashi. com, Mon.-Sat. 10am-6pm, Sun. noon-5pm) specializes in niobium jewelry. Niobium is a metal that gains streaks of color after being dipped in an electrically charged bath. Watch artists at work crafting the jewelry in the attached studio.

ACCOMMODATIONS

Downtown lodging options are surprisingly limited. The **Hotel Arcata** (708 9th St.,

707/826-0217, www.hotelarcata.com, $97-167) is nothing fancy, but it has a superb location right on the plaza. The rooms are small, but all the bathrooms have claw-foot tubs outfitted with showerheads. The hallways are decorated with framed historic photos of Arcata Plaza and other local landmarks. A stay includes complimentary Wi-Fi and continental breakfast. The bottom floor of the hotel is home to the popular Tomo Japanese Restaurant as well as a gift shop and beauty salon. Secure a free pass to the Arcata Community Pool from the front desk.

The **Lady Anne Bed and Breakfast** (902 14th St., 707/822-2797, http://ladyanne-inn.com, $115-220) has a little more character, with five rooms in an old Victorian built in 1888. All have private bathrooms and most include gas-burning woodstoves. A music room is decorated with all sorts of instruments including a piano, an accordion, and a bass guitar that guests are allowed to play. The Lady Anne serves a continental breakfast.

A few miles from the plaza, the **Best Western Arcata Inn** (4827 Valley West Blvd., 707/826-0313, http://bestwesterncalifornia.com, $107-139) is a well-regarded chain motel option in the area. The rooms have satellite TV and Wi-Fi, and there's an indoor/

Hotel Arcata

outdoor heated swimming pool and hot tub on the grounds. Fuel up with a complimentary breakfast.

FOOD

For a small city, Arcata has a lot of worthwhile dining options. Many of the restaurants are committed to using ingredients from local Humboldt farms and ranches.

American

Almost everything served up or sat on in **Luke's Joint** (887 H St., 707/826-0415, www. lukesjointarcata.com, daily 9am-8pm, $7-13) is made in Humboldt County. The produce hails from local farms and the furniture is made by local companies. Luckily, this small eatery has more to recommend it than its dedication to the local economy. Luke's serves big, tasty hot sandwiches, wraps, and salads for breakfast, lunch, and dinner. Review the section of the menu titled Sublime Swine, which has a series of smoked pork shoulder sandwiches and tacos.

French

★ **Renata's Creperie and Espresso** (1030 G St., 707/825-8783, Tues.-Thurs. and Sun. 8am-3pm, Fri.-Sat. 8am-3pm and 5pm-9pm, $4-12) is the best place to start the day. Their organic buckwheat crepes are artfully decorated with drizzled sauces and well-placed garnishes, and deliver on their promising looks with sweet and savory fillings. Expect a wait on weekends. Renata's is also open for dinner on Friday and Saturday nights.

Italian

Named for a region in central Italy, **Abruzzi** (780 7th St., 707/826-2345, www.abruzziarcata.com, Wed.-Sun. 5pm-9pm, $12-40) is the place to go for fine dining around the plaza. The menu includes free-range chicken dishes, seafood offerings, and classic pastas like Bolognese, primavera, and alfredo.

Japanese

A local institution for over 30 years, ★ **Tomo**

Japanese Restaurant (708 9th St., 707/822-1414, www.tomoarcata.com, Mon.-Sat. 11:30am-2pm and 4pm-9pm, Sun. 4pm-9pm, $10-22) serves sushi rolls and other entrées that are as eclectic as its hometown. Get a spicy tofu roll or a unique locally smoked albacore roll. Tomo has a list of sakes, and there's also a full bar.

Markets

Stop in **Wildberries Marketplace** (747 13th St., 707/822-0095, www.wildberries. com, daily 6am-midnight) to stock up for a picnic in the redwoods. Alongside the aisles of health foods, there's a café, juice bar, and coffee shop. Wildberries also hosts its own farmers market (www.humfarm.org, Tues. 3:30pm-6:30pm).

The Arcata Plaza also hosts a Saturday **farmers market** (www.humfarm.org, mid-Apr.-mid-Nov. Sat. 9am-2pm) that includes live music.

Mexican

Arcata locals swear by **Taqueria La Barca** (5201 Carlson Park Dr., 707/822-6669, Mon.-Fri. 10am-8pm, $7-11). People love the house-made horchata and chile rellenos, but the carnitas are the overall favorite.

Tapas

At **Crush** (11th St. and H St, 707/825-0390, http://crusharcata.com, Mon.-Fri. 3pm-10pm, Sat. 11am-10pm, Sun. 11am-8pm, $19-24), a special wine program pairs with the menu, which includes just a few entrées an evening along with a handful of appetizers, soups, and salads. One worthy app is the deviled duck egg of the day. This is a small space with just seven or so tables, so a reservation is a good idea.

INFORMATION AND SERVICES

Just north of downtown, the **Mad River Community Hospital** (3800 Janes Rd., 707/822-3621, http://madriverhospital.com) has an emergency room and urgent care department.

TRANSPORTATION

Arcata is eight miles north of Eureka on U.S. 101. Once there, it's easiest to just park your car and walk around the small city. If you grow weary of walking, the **Arcata & Mad River Transit System** (www.arcatatransit.org, adults $1.50, children and seniors $1.25) runs a fleet of red-and-yellow buses that travel all over Arcata.

Nearby McKinleyville has a small commercial airport, **Arcata-Eureka Airport** (ACV, 3561 Boeing Ave., McKinleyville, 707/839-5401, http://co.humboldt.ca.us/aviation) that serves the North Coast region. Fly in and out on United Airlines. Flights are expensive but convenient.

Trinidad Bay

With a population of just 360 people, Trinidad is one of the smallest incorporated cities in California; it's also one of the most beautiful. Perched on a bluff over boat-studded Trinidad Bay, Trinidad has a wealth of natural assets, including scenic headlands and wild beaches on either side of town. It also has a long history: The town was named by two Spanish Navy men who came to the area on Trinity Sunday in 1775. Right off U.S. 101, Trinidad is worth a visit, whether it's for a stop to stretch your legs or a tranquil weekend getaway.

★ TRINIDAD
Trinidad Memorial Lighthouse

Not an actual lighthouse but a replica of the one on nearby Trinidad Head, **Trinidad Memorial Lighthouse** (Trinity St. and Edwards St.) is the local photo opportunity. It was built by the Trinidad Civic Club in 1949. The small red-and-white building sits on a bluff above the bay where boats bob in the water. A marble slab and a series of plaques list names of people who have been lost at sea. To the left of the lighthouse is the old Trinidad fog bell.

Trinidad Head

A rocky promontory north of the bay, the 380-foot-high **Trinidad Head** (end of Edwards St.) affords great views of the area's beaches, bay, and town. A one-mile-long loop trail on the headlands goes under canopies of vegetation and then out to a series of clear spots with benches. A large stone cross on the west end of Trinidad Head marks where Spanish seamen initially erected a wooden cross. Below the cross is a small wooden deck where you can glimpse the top of the Trinidad Head Lighthouse. The squat lighthouse on a 175-foot-high cliff was activated in 1871. In 1914, the lighthouse made news when, according to the lighthouse keeper, a huge wave extinguished the light.

Trinidad State Beach

Below the bluffs of Trinidad Head, **Trinidad State Beach** (end of Edwards St., 707/677-3570, www.parks.ca.gov, daily sunrise-sunset, free) runs north for a mile to Elk Head. Spruce-tufted Pewetole Island and a scattering of scenic coastal islets lie offshore. The northern end has caves, an arch, and tide pools. It's a great place for a contemplative walk.

Humboldt State University Marine Laboratory

Students come to the **HSU Marine Laboratory** (570 Ewing St., 707/826-3671, www2.humboldt.edu/marinelab, Mon.-Fri. 9am-4:30pm, Sat.-Sun. 10am-5pm, tours by appointment only, self-guided tours $1, guided tours $2) to learn about the area's coastal critters. A tour of the lab includes looks at invertebrates from nearby intertidal zones, like sea cucumbers, tube worms, giant green anemones, and red octopi. Visitors can also sign up to explore the area's tide pools with a marine naturalist ($3).

SPORTS AND RECREATION

Kayaking and Whale-Watching

Protected Trinidad Bay is an ideal spot for a scenic sea-kayaking excursion. **Humboats Kayak Adventures** (707/443-5157, www.humboats.com, $90) runs guided whale-watching tours in the spring and early summer when gray whales migrate right through the protected harbor area.

Sportfishing

If you'd rather have the satisfaction of catching your own fresh seafood, head out to sea with one of two Trinidad-based fishing outfits. Fish for rockfish, salmon, or Dungeness crab with **Trinidad Bay Charters** (707/499-8878, www.trinidadbaycharters.net, $120). Trips leave daily at 6:15am and 12:15pm. **Patrick's Point Charters** (707/445-4106, www.patrickspointcharters.com, $120/half-day) leaves out of Trinidad Harbor for rockfish, salmon, and Dungeness crab.

Surfing

South of Trinidad are some of Humboldt County's best-known surf spots. **Moonstone Beach** (three miles south of Trinidad on Scenic Dr.) is a popular surf break where the

Little River pours into Trinidad Bay. Up the road a half a mile, **Camel Rock** (about 2.3 miles south of Trinidad on Scenic Dr.) has right breaks that peel inside of a distinct, double-humped offshore rock.

Need to rent a board and wetsuit? Visit **Salty's Supply Co.** (332 Main St., 707/677-0300, Mon.-Fri. 10am-5pm, Sat.-Sun. 8am-5pm, surfboards $30/day, wetsuits $30/day), which rents surf gear along with kayaks, bikes, books, and magazines (seriously!).

ACCOMMODATIONS

The only lodging in Trinidad proper is the **Trinidad Bay Bed and Breakfast** (560 Edward St., 707/677-0840, www.trinidadbay-bnb.com, $275-350), right across the street from the Trinidad Memorial Lighthouse. Each of the four rooms has a view of Trinidad Bay; two rooms have private entrances, and all have private bathrooms. A hot three-course breakfast is served every morning.

Between the main section of Trinidad and Patrick's Point State Park, **The Lost Whale Bed & Breakfast Inn** (3452 Patrick's Point Dr., 707/677-3425, http://lostwhaleinn.com, $275-325) has five rooms with great views of the Pacific and four with garden views. Two rooms have lofts to accommodate up to four

Trinidad State Beach

people. There's a private trail to the beach below, an oceanview hot tub, and a wood-burning sauna. A seven-course breakfast buffet is served every morning.

For those who want to rough it a bit, **The Emerald Forest** (753 Patrick's Point Dr., 707/677-3554, www.cabinsintheredwoods.com, $179-349) has a variety of rustic cabins for rent. The higher-end cabins have full kitchens and amenities like wood-burning stoves. RV and tent campsites are also available ($35-48), although the ones at nearby Patrick's Point State Park are more spacious.

FOOD

Stock up on delicious, locally smoked seafood at ★ **Katy's Smokehouse** (740 Edwards St., 707/677-0151, www.katyssmokehouse.com, daily 9am-6pm). There are smoked oysters and salmon jerky, but you can't go wrong with the smoked king salmon. It's not a sit-down restaurant, so you'll need to get your order to go. It's great to bring on a camping trip to the nearby parks—just don't leave it out, or you'll end up feeding it to the bears.

The friendly, spunky staff at the **Beachcomber Café** (363 Trinity St., 707/677-0106, http://trinidadbeachcomber.

blogspot.com, Mon.-Fri. 7am-4pm, Sat.-Sun. 8am-4pm) serve up coffee, cookies, paninis, and bagels. The café also has free Wi-Fi with a purchase.

The original café that was opened in the current spot of the **Seascape Restaurant** (1 Bay St., 707/677-3762, www.seascape-trinidad.com, summer daily 7am-9:30pm, winter daily 7am-8pm, $9-17) was blown away by a massive storm in 1959. While the Seascape might not blow you away, it has a great location on Trinidad Bay. It serves seafood sandwiches, burgers, and fish-and-chips, and something called a "Grilled Smokey" that's little more than salmon cream cheese spread between two toasted pieces of sourdough bread. Also of interest is a breakfast entrée of scrambled eggs topped with clam chowder.

Just north of Trinidad, the ★ **Larrupin Café** (1658 Patrick's Point Dr., 707/677-0230, www.larrupin.com, daily 5pm-9pm, $20-36) is probably the most loved restaurant in the area. They put their legendary mesquite barbecue sauce on everything from tofu kebabs to creole prawns. They are also known for their mustard dill and red sauces, which you can purchase to take home. Enjoy the heated patio from Father's Day through September.

Pick up some smoked salmon at Katy's Smokehouse.

INFORMATION AND SERVICES

To plan a trip to Trinidad, visit the **Official Trinidad Visitor Chamber of Commerce** website (www.trinidadcalif.com), which has lots of great information about the small community.

Trinidad is a small city, so don't expect too many services. Most major services can be found in nearby Arcata.

TRANSPORTATION

Trinidad is 15 miles north of Arcata on U.S. 101. Take exit 728 off the highway.

The **Redwood Transit System** (707/443-0826, www.redwoodtransit.org, adults $3, children and seniors $2.75) has buses that connect from Arcata and Eureka to Trinidad.

PATRICK'S POINT STATE PARK

Patrick's Point State Park (4150 Patrick's Point Dr., 707/677-3570, www.parks.ca.gov, daily sunrise-sunset, day use $8) is a rambling coastal park 25 miles north of Eureka, replete with beaches, historic landmarks, trails, and campgrounds. It's not the biggest of the many parks along the North Coast, but it is one of the best. The climate remains cool year-round, making it perfect for hiking and exploring, if not for ocean swimming. There's a native plant garden, a visitors center, and three campgrounds ($35), plus a recreated Yurok village. Because Patrick's Point is small in comparison to the other parks, it's easy to get around. Request a map at the gate and follow the signs along the tiny and often nameless park roads.

Sights

Prominent among the local landmarks is the place the park was named after: **Patrick's Point,** which offers panoramic Pacific views and can be reached by a brief hike from a convenient parking lot. Adjacent to Patrick's Point in a picturesque cove is **Wedding Rock,** a promontory sticking out into the ocean like an upturned thumb. People really do hike the narrow trail out to the rock to get married; you might even see a bride and groom stumbling hand-in-hand on their way back from the ceremony.

The most fascinating area in the park is **Sumeg Village,** a recreation of a native Yurok village based on an actual archaeological find east of here. Visitors can crawl through the perfectly round, hobbit-like hole-doors into semi-subterranean homes, meeting places, and storage buildings. Or check out the native plant garden, a collection of local plants the Yurok people used for food, basketry, and medicine. Today, the local Yurok people use Sumeg Village as a gathering place for education and celebrations, and they request that visitors tread lightly and do not disturb this tranquil area.

Those who want to dip a toe in the ocean rather than just gaze at it from afar will be glad to know that Patrick's Point has a number of accessible beaches. The steep trail leading down to **Agate Beach** deters few visitors. This wide stretch of coarse sand bordered by cliffs shot through with shining quartz veins is perfect for lounging, playing, and beach-combing. The semiprecious stones for which it is named really do appear here. The best time to find good agates is in the winter, after a storm.

Hiking

Only six miles of trails thread their way through Patrick's Point. Choose from the **Rim Trail** (four miles round-trip), which will take you along the cliffs for a view of the sea and, if you're lucky, a view of migrating whales. Tree lovers might prefer the **Octopus Tree Trail,** which provides a great view of an old-growth Sitka spruce grove.

Camping

The three campgrounds at Patrick's Point (information 707/677-3570, reservations 800/444-7275, www.reserveamerica.com, $35) have a total of 124 sites. It can be difficult to determine the difference between **Agate Beach, Abalone,** and **Penn Creek,** so get good directions from the park rangers when you arrive. Most campsites are pleasantly shaded by the groves of trees; all include a picnic table, fire pit, and food storage cupboard, and you'll find running water, restrooms, and showers nearby.

Information and Services

Get a map and information at the **Patrick's Point State Park Visitors Center**

(707/677-1945, summer daily 9am-5pm, winter usually daily 10am-4pm), immediately to the right when you get to the entry gate. Information about nature walks and campfire programs is posted on the bulletin board.

Transportation

Patrick's Point State Park is on the coast, 25 miles north of Eureka and 15 miles south of Orick on U.S. 101.

Redwood National and State Parks

The lands of Redwood National and State Parks (www.nps.gov/redw, day use and camping free) meander along the coast and include three state parks—Prairie Creek Redwoods, Del Norte Coast Redwoods, and Jedediah Smith. This complex of parkland encompasses most of California's northern redwood forests. The main landmass of Redwood National Park is just south of Prairie Creek State Park along U.S. 101, stretching east from the coast and the highway. To get to the park from the south, drive along Bald Hills Road.

REDWOOD NATIONAL PARK
Thomas H. Kuchel Visitors Center

If you're new to the Redwood National and State Parks, the **Thomas H. Kuchel Visitors Center** (U.S. 101, west of Orick, 707/465-7765, spring-fall daily 9am-5pm, winter daily 9am-4pm) is a large facility with a ranger station, clean restrooms, and a path to the shore. Get advice, maps, backcountry permits, and books. In the summer, rangers run patio talks and coast walks that provide a great introduction to the area for children and adults. Picnic at one of the tables outside the visitors center, or walk a short distance to Redwood Creek.

Trees of Mystery

Generations of kids have enjoyed spotting the gigantic wooden sculptures of Paul

Bunyan and his blue ox, Babe, from U.S. 101. The **Trees of Mystery** (15500 U.S. 101 N., 707/482-2251 or 800/638-3389, www.treesofmystery.net, June-Aug. daily 8am-7pm, Sept.-Oct. daily 8:30am-6:30pm, Nov.-May daily 9am-5pm, adults $15, seniors $11, ages 7-12 $8) doesn't disappoint as a great place to take a break from the road to let the family out for some good cheesy fun. Visitors can enjoy the original Mystery Hike, the SkyTrail gondola ride through the old-growth redwoods, and the palatial gift shop. Perhaps best of all, at the left end of the gift shop is a little-known gem: the Native American museum. A large collection of artifacts from both tribes across the country and those indigenous to the redwood forests grace several crowded galleries. The restrooms here are large and well maintained, which makes Trees of Mystery a nice rest stop.

Hiking

One of the easiest, most popular ways to get close to the trees is to walk the **Lady Bird Johnson Trail** (Bald Hills Rd., 1.4 miles, easy). This nearly level loop provides an intimate view of the redwood and fir forests that define this region. It's not far from the **Thomas H. Kuchel Visitors Center** (U.S. 101, west of Orick, 707/465-7765, summer daily 9am-5pm, winter daily 9am-4pm), and the staff there can direct you to the trailhead and provide a simple map. Another easy-access trail is **Trillium Falls** (Davison Rd. at

Tourist Traps

As you wend your way up U.S. 101 through the verdant forests filled with rare trees, you'll become aware of something besides parks and trails luring visitors to pull over and rest awhile. You'll know them by the collections of chainsaw carvings, the kitschy hand-painted signs, and the cheap, shiny toys out front. Whether you've found a Redwood Sculpture Emporium, a Drive-Thru Tree, or a Mystery Spot, hang on to your wallet when you stop at one of the Redwood Coast's tourist traps.

The granddaddy of all tourist traps—it's even an example of the concept in Wikipedia—is the **Trees of Mystery.** Trees of Mystery has it all: wood sculptures, a "mystery" visual-trickery trail, and a gondola ride. But most of all, it's got a gift shop the size of a supermarket selling souvenirs beyond your imagination (unless you've imagined varnished redwood slices painted with images of Jesus and the Virgin Mary).

The various Drive-Thru Trees are usually privately owned tourist traps, and you'll pay $10-20 to drive on a tiny one-way street through a large mutilated tree. The novelty of finding trees big enough to create drive-thru tunnels catches the attention of many out-of-state visitors. And families on long road trips often shell out for the drive-thru trees to sidetrack their kids for just five more minutes.

Finally, you can't miss the roadside redwood sculpture stands. They dot the sides of the highway, selling wooden animals lovingly sculpted by chainsaw artists. You'll also find T-shirts, coffee mugs, shot glasses, and dozens of other souvenirs. Little animal figurines made out of petrified moose and elk turds are a particular favorite with the children.

Elk Meadow, 2.8 miles, easy). You may not see elk or trillium flowers, but the redwood trees along this cool, dark trail are striking, and the small waterfall is a nice treasure in the woods. This little hike is lovely any time of year but best in spring, when the water volume over the falls is at its peak.

The **Lost Man Creek Trail** (east of Elk Meadow, 1 mile off U.S. 101, 0.5-22 miles, easy-difficult) has it all. The first 0.5 miles is perfect for wheelchair users and families with small children. But as the trail rolls along, the grades get steeper and more challenging. Customize the length of this out-and-back trail by turning around at any time. If you reach the Lost Man Creek picnic grounds, your total round-trip distance is 22 miles with more than 3,000 feet of elevation gain and several stream crossings.

Another fabulous long hike is the **Redwood Creek Trail** (Bald Hills Rd. spur off U.S. 101, difficult), which follows Redwood Creek for eight miles to the **Tall Trees Grove.** If you have someone willing to act as a shuttle driver, pick up the **Tall Trees Trail** and walk another 6 miles (a total of 14 miles) to

the **Dolason Prairie Trail,** which takes you back out to Bald Hills Road.

Camping

There are no designated campgrounds in Redwood National Park, but free backcountry camping is allowed; permits may be necessary in certain areas. The **Elam Camp** and the **44 Camp** are both hike-in primitive campgrounds along the Dolason Prairie Trail.

Contact the **Crescent City Information Center** (1111 2nd St., Crescent City, 707/465-7335, spring-fall daily 9am-5pm, winter daily 9am-4pm) if you're planning a backcountry camping trip. The center can help you determine whether you need a permit and issue one if you do.

Transportation

The Redwood National and State Parks line U.S. 101 from Prairie Creek Redwoods in the south all the way up to Jedediah Smith near Crescent City at the northern end. The Thomas H. Kuchel Visitors Center at the south end of the park is 40 miles north of Eureka on U.S. 101.

Redwood National and State Parks

★ PRAIRIE CREEK REDWOODS STATE PARK

In addition to the silent majesty of the redwoods, **Prairie Creek Redwoods State Park** (Newton B. Drury Dr., 25 miles south of Crescent City, 707/488-2039, campground 707/488-2171, www.parks.ca.gov, daily sunrise-sunset, day use $8) has miles of wild beach, roaming wildlife, and a popular hike through a one-of-a-kind fern-draped canyon. The 14,000 acres of Prairie Creek offer a sampler platter of the best natural elements of the North Coast.

For wildlife enthusiasts, one of the many reasons to visit Prairie Creek is a chance to view a herd of **Roosevelt elk.** This subspecies of elk can stand up to five feet high and can weigh close to 1,000 pounds. These big guys usually hang out at—where else?—the Elk Prairie, a stretch of open grassland along the highway. The best times to see the elk are early morning and around sunset. August to October is the elk mating season, when the calls of the bulls fill the air. The elk do roam all over the park, but there's a good chance you might see some in the prairie off the southern end of the Newton B. Drury Drive. The park asks that you stay in the viewing area and let the elk enjoy grazing in peace.

Prairie Creek Visitors Center

Just beyond the entrance off U.S. 101, the **Prairie Creek Visitors Center** (Newton B. Drury Dr., 707/488-2039, daily 9am-5pm) includes a small interpretive museum describing the history of the California redwood forests. A tiny bookshop adjoins the museum, well stocked with books describing the history, nature, and culture of the area. Many ranger-led programs originate at the visitors center, and permits are available for backcountry camping in the park.

Newton B. Drury Scenic Drive

A gorgeous scenic road through the redwoods, **Newton B. Drury Scenic Drive,** off U.S. 101 about five miles south of Klamath, features old-growth trees lining the roads, a close-up view of the redwood forest ecosystem, and a grove or trailhead every hundred yards or so. The turnoff is at the **Big Tree Wayside,** where you can walk up to the 304-foot-high **Big Tree.** Its life was almost cut short by a homesteader who wanted to cut it down to use the stump as a dance floor. Follow the short, five-minute loop trail near the Big Tree to see the other giants in the area.

Gold Bluffs Beach

Gold Bluffs Beach (Davison Rd., three miles north of Orick off U.S. 101) is truly wild. Lonely waves pound the shore, a spikey grove of Sitka spruce tops the nearby bluffs, and herds of Roosevelt elk frequently roam the wide, salt-and-pepper-colored beach. Prospectors found gold flakes here in 1850, giving the beach its name. But, unsurprisingly, the region was too remote and rugged to maintain a lucrative mining operation. Access Gold Bluffs Beach by taking Davison Road. No trailers are allowed on Davison Road.

Hiking

Perhaps the single most famous hiking trail along the redwood coast is **Fern Canyon** (Davison Rd., Prairie Creek Redwoods State Park), near Gold Bluffs Beach. This hike runs through a narrow canyon carved by Home Creek. Five-fingered ferns, sword ferns, and delicate lady ferns cascade down the steep canyon walls. Droplets from seeping water sources keep the plants alive. The unusual setting was used as a dramatic backdrop in the films *Return of the Jedi* and *Jurassic Park 2*.

To get to the trailhead, take U.S. 101 three miles north of the town of Orick and then, at the Prairie Creek visitors center, turn west onto Davison Road (no trailers allowed) and travel two more miles. This rough dirt road takes you through the campground and ends at the trailhead 1.5 miles later.

A short one-mile loop trail climbs out of the canyon, surrounded by the park's trees, their limbs sleeved in green mosses. Extend this hike into a longer loop (6.5 miles, moderate)

by starting at the same place; when the trail intersects with James Irvine Trail, bear right and follow that spur. Bear right again onto **Clintonia Trail** and walk through a redwood grove to Miners Ridge Trail. Bear right onto Miners Ridge, an old logging road, and follow it down to the ocean. Walk 1.5 miles along Gold Bluffs Beach to complete the loop.

Miners Ridge and **James Irvine Loop** (12 miles, moderate) covers some of the same ground but starts from the visitors center instead of the Fern Canyon trailhead, avoiding the rough dirt terrain of Davison Road. Start out on **James Irvine Trail** and bear right when you can, following the trail all the way until it joins Fern Canyon Trail. Turn left when you get to the coast and walk along Gold Bluffs Beach for 1.5 miles. Then make a left onto the Clintonia Trail and head back toward the visitors center.

If you're starting at the visitors center but don't want to do the entire 12-mile loop, you can cut this hike roughly in half. When you get to the Clintonia Trail on your way out to the coast, make a left instead of continuing on the James Irvine Trail. This will take you over to Miners Ridge, where you make another left to loop back to the starting point, for a total of about six miles. This is a pleasant hike with plenty of great trees; the drawback is that you don't get to see Fern Canyon.

If you're hiking the **California Coastal Trail** (www.californiacoastaltrail.info), you can do a leg here at Prairie Creek. The Coastal Trail runs along the park's northern coastline. Another way to get to the campground is via the **Ossagon Creek Trail** (north end of Newton B. Drury Dr., 2 miles round-trip, moderate). It's not long, but the steep grade makes it a tough haul in spots, and the stunning trees along the way make it worth the effort.

Camping

The **Elk Prairie Campground** (127011 Newton B. Drury Dr., Orick, campground 707/488-2039, reservations 800/444-7275, www.reserveamerica.com, reservations recommended Memorial Day-Labor Day, vehicles $35, hikers and cyclists $5) has 75 sites for tents or RVs and a full range of comfortable camping amenities. You can get a shower and purchase wood for your fire ring. Several campsites are wheelchair-accessible, so ask for one if you need it when you reserve your site. A big campfire area is north of the campground, an easy walk for campers interested in the evening programs put on by rangers and volunteers.

For a sand-camping experience, head out to **Gold Bluffs Beach Campground** (Davison Rd., 3 miles north of Orick, www. nps.gov/redw, no reservations, $35/regular sites, $20/environmental sites). There are 26 first-come, first-served sites for tents or RVs and 3 environmental sites. Amenities include flush toilets, water, solar showers, and wide ocean views. The surf can be quite dangerous here, so be extremely careful if you go in the water.

Backcountry camping is allowed in Prairie Creek, but only in two designated camping areas, Ossagon Creek and Miners Ridge (3 sites each, $5). Permits are available at the campground kiosk or the Prairie Creek visitors center (Newton B. Drury Dr., 707/488-2171, usually daily 9am-5pm).

Transportation

Prairie Creek Redwoods is 50 miles north of Eureka and 25 miles south of Crescent City on U.S. 101. Newton B. Drury Drive traverses the park and can be accessed from U.S. 101 north or south.

DEL NORTE COAST REDWOODS STATE PARK

South of Crescent City, **Del Norte Coast Redwoods State Park** (Mill Creek Campground Rd., off U.S. 101, 707/465-7335, www.parks.ca.gov, $8) encompasses a variety of ecosystems, including eight miles of wild coastline, second-growth redwood forest, and virgin old-growth forests. One of the largest in this system of parks, Del Norte is a great place to get lost in the backcountry with just your knapsack and your fishing rod, exploring the meandering branches of Mill Creek.

Hiking

Guided tours, nature trails, and wheelchair-accessible trails and campgrounds are all available at Del Norte. You'll want to dress in layers to hike as it can get down into the 40s even in summer. There are several rewarding yet gentle and short excursions that start and end in the Mill Creek Campground.

The **Trestle Loop Trail** (1 mile, easy) begins across from the campfire center in the campground. Notice the trestles and other artifacts along the way; the loop follows the route of a defunct railroad from the logging era. It's okay to eat the berries along this path—just keep in mind that bears and other animals like them as much as you do, so the more abundant the food, the more likely you'll have company. If you want more after this brief walk, take the nearby **Nature Loop Trail** (1 mile, easy), which begins near the campground entrance gate. This trail features interpretive signage to help you learn about the varieties of impressive trees you'll be passing.

These coastal parks are a cherished destination for serious hikers as well as sightseers, so it is possible to get a great workout along with the scenery. The northern section of the great **California Coastal Trail** (CCT, www. californiacoastaltrail.info) runs right through Del Norte Coast Redwoods State Park. The trail has been under development since 1972 and is ultimately envisioned as a 1,200-mile pathway along beaches and forests all the way from the Oregon border to the Mexican border. Not all of it will be completed for some time to come, but the parts available for use in Del Norte offer a great illustration of what the project is meant to be. The Coastal Trail is reasonably well marked; look for signs with the CCT logo.

The "last chance" section of the California Coastal Trail (Enderts Beach-Damnation Creek, 14 miles, strenuous) makes a challenging day hike. To reach the trailhead, turn west from U.S. 101 onto Enderts Beach Road in Del Norte, three miles south of Crescent City. Drive 2.3 miles to the end of the road, where the trail begins.

The trail follows the historic route of U.S. 101 south to Enderts Beach. You'll walk through fields of wildflowers and groves of trees twisted by the wind and saltwater. Eventually, the trail climbs about 900 feet to an overlook with a great view of Enderts Beach. At just over two miles, the trail enters Del Norte Coast Redwoods State Park, where it meanders through Anson Grove's redwood, fir, and Sitka spruce trees. At 4.5 miles, cross Damnation Creek on a footbridge, and at 6.1 miles, cross the Damnation Creek Trail. (For a longer hike, take the four-mile round-trip side excursion down to the beach and back.) After seven miles, a flight of steps leads up to milepost 15.6 on U.S. 101. At this point, you can turn around and return the way you came, making for a gloriously varied day hike of about 14 miles round-trip.

One alternative is to make this a point-to-point hike, either by dropping a car off at one end to get you back at the end of the day, or by having one group of hikers start at each end of the trail and exchange keys at a central meeting point.

If you've made arrangements for a lift back at the end of the day, continue on to the DeMartin section of the Coastal Trail. From here, descend through a lush grove of ferns and take a bridge over a tributary of Wilson Creek, enjoying views of the rocky coast far below. The wildflowers continue as you enter Redwood National Park and wander through the grasslands of DeMartin Prairie. The southern trailhead (where you pick up your vehicle if you're doing the trail one-way north-south) is at the Wilson Creek Picnic Area on the east side of U.S. 101 at the north end of DeMartin Bridge.

Camping

The **Mill Creek campground** (U.S. 101, 7 miles south of Crescent City, 800/444-7275, www.reserveamerica.com, May-Sept., vehicles $35, hikers and cyclists $5) is in an attractive setting along Mill Creek. There are 145 sites for RVs and tents, and facilities include restrooms and fire pits. Feel free to bring your camper to the Mill Creek campground; it has spots for RVs and a dump station on-site. Call in advance to reserve a spot and to be sure that your camper does not exceed the park's length limit. There are no designated backcountry campsites in Del Norte, and backcountry camping is not allowed.

Information and Services

Del Norte State Park has no visitors center, but you can get information from the **Crescent City Information Center** (1111 2nd St., Crescent City, 707/465-7335, spring-fall daily 9am-5pm, winter daily 9am-4pm). Minimal restroom facilities are available at the Del Norte campgrounds, and the park has an RV dump station but no RV hookups.

Transportation

Del Norte Coast Redwoods is seven miles south of Crescent City on U.S. 101. The park entrance is on Hamilton Road, east of U.S. 101.

JEDEDIAH SMITH REDWOODS STATE PARK

The best redwood grove in the old growth of **Jedediah Smith Redwoods State Park** (U.S. 199, 9 miles east of Crescent City, 707/465-7335, www.parks.ca.gov, daily sunrise-sunset, $8 per vehicle) is the **Stout Memorial Grove.** This bunch of coast redwoods is, as advertised, stout—although the grove was named for a person, not for the size of the trees. These old giants make humans feel small as they wander in the grove. These are some of the biggest and oldest trees on the North Coast and were somehow spared the loggers' saws. Another great thing about this grove is the lack of visitors, since its far-north latitude makes it harder to reach than some of the other big redwood groves in California.

Save the Redwoods

The stereotype of a tree-hugging conservationist usually brings to mind dirty, long-haired college students living on tarp-covered platforms and tying themselves to trees. Many visitors (and heck, residents) of California might imagine that it was a bunch of dreadlocked hippies and starving artists that saved the huge swaths of redwoods lining the North Coast region.

Nothing could be further from the truth. The California redwoods were saved by some very wealthy people.

In the early 20th century, rich and powerful white men poured their power, political connections, and, in some cases, millions of their own dollars into a group called the **Save the Redwoods League** (www.savetheredwoods.org). The three founders were a UC professor named John Merriam and fellow conservationists Madison Grant and Henry F. Osborn. After surveying the destruction of the forests surrounding brand-new U.S. 101 in 1917, the three men decided that something had to be done. And thus the League was born.

For the past century, the Save the Redwoods League has aggressively pursued the conservation of redwood forests in California. Using high-level political connections, the league successfully lobbied the U.S. government to create Redwood National Park and to expand the territory protected by Sequoia National Park. The league is also a major player at the state level, creating and expanding state parks all over the landscape.

So how did they get hold of all those groves? They bought them. Large donations, plus the resources of league members, have given the league the ability to buy thousands of acres of redwood forest and then donate them to various parks. They're still doing it to this very day, and in the 21st century the league has made several major purchases to expand Sequoia National Park, Redwood National Park, and several state parks.

Got some spare change? Make a gift to Save the Redwoods and help the group preserve and expand California's fabulous redwoods. Donate your life savings, and they might even name a grove after you! (No promises though.)

Visitors Centers

There are two visitors centers in Jedediah Smith, about five minutes apart. Both offer similar information and include materials about all of the nearby parks. One is the **Jedediah Smith Visitors Center** (U.S. 101, Hiouchi, 707/458-3496, summer daily noon-8pm) and the other is the **Hiouchi Information Center** (U.S. 199, Hiouchi, 707/458-3294, summer daily 9am-5pm, fall and spring hours vary).

Hiking

The trails running through the trees make for wonderfully cool and shady summer hiking. Many trails run along the river and the creeks, offering a variety of ecosystems and plenty of lush scenery to enjoy. Wherever you hike, stay on the established trails. By wandering into the forest, you can trample the delicate and shallow redwood root systems, unintentionally damaging the trees you're here to visit.

The **Simpson Reed Trail** (U.S. 199, 6 miles east of Crescent City, 1 mile, easy) takes you from U.S. 199 down to the banks of the Smith River.

To get a good view of the Smith River, hike the **Hiouchi Trail** (2 miles, moderate). From the Hiouchi Information Center and campgrounds on U.S. 199, cross the Summer Footbridge and then follow the river north. The Hiouchi Trail then meets the Hatton Loop Trail and leads away from the river and into the forest.

If you're looking for a longer and more aggressive trek, try the **Mill Creek Trail** (7.5 miles round-trip, difficult). A good place to start is at the Summer Footbridge. The trail then follows the creek down to the unpaved Howland Hill Road.

If it's redwoods you're looking for, take the

Boy Scout Tree Trail (5.2 miles, moderate). To get to the trailhead, you have to drive a rugged, unpaved road for a couple of miles, but there are plenty of impressive trees to enjoy. The trail is usually quiet, with few hikers, and the gargantuan forest will make you feel truly tiny. About three miles into the trail, you'll come to a fork. If you've got time, take both forks: first the left, which takes you to the small, mossy, and very green Fern Falls, and then the right, which takes you to the eponymous Boy Scout Tree, one of the impressively huge redwoods.

Boating and Swimming

You'll find two boat launches in the park: one at Society Hole and one adjacent to the Summer Footbridge; the latter is only open in winter. Down by the River Beach Trail, you'll find **River Beach** (immediately west of the Hiouchi Information Center), a popular spot for swimming in the river. Swimming is allowed throughout the park, but be very careful—rivers and creeks move unpredictably, and you might not notice deep holes until you're on them. Enjoy the cool water, but keep a close eye on children and others in your party to ensure a safe time.

Fishing

With the Smith River and numerous feeder creeks running through Jed Smith, it's not surprising that fishing is one of the most popular activities. Chilly winter fishing draws a surprising number of anglers to vie for king salmon up to 30 pounds and steelhead up to 20 pounds. Seasons for both species run October-February. In the summer, cast into the river to catch cutthroat trout.

Camping

The ★ **Jedediah Smith Campground** (U.S. 199, Hiouchi, 800/444-7275, www.reserveamerica.com, vehicles $35, hike-in or cycle-in primitive sites $5) is beautifully situated on the banks of Smith River, with most sites near the River Beach Trail (immediately west of the Hiouchi Information Center). There are 106 RV and tent sites. Facilities include plenty of restrooms, fire pits, and coin-operated showers. Reservations are advised, especially for summer and holiday weekends. The campground is open year-round, but reservations are accepted only Memorial Day-Labor Day. Jedediah Smith has no designated backcountry campsites, and camping outside the developed campgrounds is not allowed. If you're backpacking, check at one of the visitors centers for help in finding the nearest place to camp overnight.

Transportation

Jedediah Smith Redwoods State Park (U.S. 199, 9 miles east of Crescent City, 707/458-3018, www.parks.ca.gov, $8 per vehicle) is northeast of Crescent City along the Smith River, next door to the immense Smith River National Recreation Area (U.S. 199 west of Hiouchi). Get there by taking U.S. 199 nine miles east of Crescent City.

Crescent City

The northernmost city on the California coast perches on the bay that provides its name. Cool and windswept, Crescent City is a perfect place to put on a parka, stuff your hands deep into your pockets, and wander along a wide, beautiful beach. The small city also has a vibrant surf scene centered on South Beach, which frequently has good waves for longboarders.

Crescent City is also known for surviving tsunamis. In 1964, a tsunami caused by an Alaskan earthquake wiped out 29 city blocks and killed 11 people. It was the most severe tsunami on the U.S. West Coast in modern history. In 2011, the devastating earthquake in Japan resulted in a tsunami that laid waste to the city's harbor. The old rusted warning sirens on the tops of the city's utility poles still work; when they sound, there's a chance of massive waves coming to shore.

Due to the depressed logging and fishing economy, Crescent City's downtown has its fair share of shuttered businesses. But if you're looking for an inexpensive hotel room to use as a base to explore the nearby redwoods or the area's impressive beaches, a night or two in Crescent City will fit the bill.

SIGHTS
Point St. George

Wild, lonely, beautiful **Point St. George** (end of Washington Blvd., daily sunrise-sunset) epitomizes the glory of the North Coast of California. Walk out onto the cliffs to take in the deep blue sea, wild salt- and flower-scented air, and craggy cliffs and beaches. On a clear day, you can see all the way to Oregon. Short, steep trails lead across wild beach prairie land down to broad, flat, nearly deserted beaches. In spring-summer wildflowers bloom on the cliffs, and swallows nest in the cluster of buildings on the point. On rare and special clear days, you can almost make out the **St. George Reef Lighthouse** alone on its perch far out in the Pacific.

★ Battery Point Lighthouse

On an island just north of Crescent City Harbor, the **Battery Point Lighthouse** (end of A St., 707/464-3089, www.delnorte-history.org, Apr.-Sept. daily tides permitting 10am-4pm, Oct.-Mar. Sat.-Sun. tides permitting 10am-4pm, adults $3, children ages 8-15 $1) is only accessible at low tide, when a rocky spit littered with tide pools emerges, serving as a walkway for visitors. The 1856 lighthouse's current keepers reside on the island in one-month shifts; they also lead tours. You'll see a Fresnel lens and a working clock that was used by Battery Point's first lighthouse keeper. After viewing the two residential floors of the building, the docent leads any adventurous visitors up a metal ladder and through a small hole into the lantern room, where you'll be able to feel the heat of the still-working light just feet away. On a clear day, you'll also be able to see the pencil-like outline of the St. George Reef Lighthouse in the distance. St. George is situated on a small, wave-washed rock seven miles from shore, and its dangerous location resulted in the deaths of four keepers who worked there.

Ocean World

A great family respite is **Ocean World** (304 U.S. 101 S., 707/464-4900, www.oceanworldonline.com, summer daily 9am-8pm, winter daily 9am-5pm, adults $13, children ages 3-11 $8). Tours of the small sea park depart about every 15 minutes and last about 40 minutes. Featured attractions are the shark-petting tank, the 500,000-gallon aquarium, and the sea lion show. After the tour, take a stroll through the immense souvenir shop, which sells gifts of all sizes, shapes, and descriptions, many with nautical themes.

Del Norte County Historical Society Museum

The **Del Norte County Historical Society Museum** (577 H St., 707/464-3922, www.delnortehistory.org, daily 10am-4pm, free) provides an educational respite from the chilly sea breezes. The historical society maintains this small museum that features the local history of both the Native Americans who were once the only inhabitants of Del Norte County and the encroaching white settlers. Featured exhibits include the wreck of the *Brother Jonathan* at Point St. George, the story of the 1964 tsunami, and artifacts of the local Yurok and Tolowa people.

ENTERTAINMENT AND EVENTS

If you're looking for varied and rocking nightlife, Crescent City is not your town, but a few options exist for insomniacs. Most of the action after 9pm is at **Elk Valley Casino** (2500 Howland Hill Rd., 707/464-1020 or 888/574-2744, www.elkvalleycasino.com, daily 24 hours) at the eastern edge of town. Elk Valley is a bit more upscale than other local Native American casinos, with genuine aluminum-siding walls, poker and blackjack tables, a VIP card room, and a small nonsmoking slots area. The on-site restaurant is the **Full House Bar & Grill** (Sun.-Thurs. 7am-10pm, Fri.-Sat. 7am-11pm, $7-29); a late-night food menu (daily 7am-2am) is available from the bar.

The **Tsunami Lanes Bowling Center** (760 L St., 707/464-4323, www.tsunamilanes. com, Mon.-Fri. noon-10pm, Sat. noon-midnight, adults $3 per game, seniors and children $2) is a straight-up bowling alley, serving beer and greasy fries late into the evening.

Theater

The **Del Norte Association for Cultural Awareness** (Crescent Elk Auditorium, 994 G St., 707/464-1336, www.dnaca.net) hosts several live musical acts and other performances each year and provides a community arts calendar. Check this year's schedule for upcoming shows.

Cinema

If all else fails, take in a first-run movie at the **Crescent City Cinemas** (375 M St., 707/570-8438, www.catheatres.com). Or even better, take in a movie in an old-fashioned drive-in theater at the cash-only **Red's Crescent Drive-In Theatre** (four miles north of Crescent City, 2303 Elk Valley Cross Rd., 707/464-1813, $10/vehicle).

Events

For almost 50 years, the Yurok people have held a festival to honor a creature most precious to them: the mighty salmon. The **Klamath Salmon Festival** (Klamath Community Center, 190 Klamath Blvd., Klamath, www.yuroktribe.org) takes place in August each year and includes a parade, live music, games, and, of course, salmon dinners served all day.

Each August since the early 1980s, the **Crescent City Triathlon** (707/465-3995, www.crescentcitytriathlon.com, adults $55-65, children $20-25) has challenged participants of all ages. This triathlon is a 5K run, a 500-yard swim, and a 12-mile bike ride. There's also a duathlon, which involves a run, a bike ride, and then another run; there's also a triathlon for kids that varies in intensity by age group, making it possible for anyone ages 5-12 to join the fun.

SPORTS AND RECREATION

Beaches

The sands of Crescent City are a beachcomber's paradise. Wide, flat, sandy expanses invite strolling, running, and just sitting to contemplate the broad, crashing Pacific. **South Beach** (Hwy. 1 between Anchor Way and Sand Mine Rd.) is at the south end of town. Long, wide, and flat, it's perfect for a romantic stroll, as long as you're bundled up. The adventurous and chill-resistant can try surfing and boogie boarding. Farther south, **Crescent Beach** (Enderts Rd.) is two miles south of town. It's a wide, sandy beach. Down a half-mile dirt trail, **Enderts Beach**

(Enderts Rd.) is a superb beach nestled along the coast south of Crescent City. This pocket beach has a creek flowing into the ocean and an onshore rock arch.

It might look tempting on rare sunny days, but swimming from the beaches of Crescent City is not for the faint of heart. The water is icy cold, the shores are rocky, and as elsewhere in Northern California, undertow and rip currents can be dangerous. No lifeguards patrol these beaches, so you are on your own.

Bird-Watching

Birders flock to Crescent City because the diverse climates and habitats nourish a huge variety of avian residents. The parks and preserves have become destinations for enthusiasts looking for "lifers" hard to find anyplace else. Right in town, check out **Battery Point Lighthouse Park** and **Point St. George.** For a rare view of an Aleutian goose or a peregrine falcon, journey to **Tolowa Dunes State Park** (1375 Elk Valley Rd., 707/465-7335, www.parks.ca.gov, daily sunrise-sunset, free), specifically the shores of Lake Earl and Kellogg Beach. South of town, **Enderts Beach** is home to another large bird habitat.

Fishing

Anglers on the North Coast can choose between excellent deep-sea fishing and exciting river trips. The Pacific yields ling cod, snapper, and salmon, while the rivers are famous for chinook (king) salmon, steelhead, and cutthroat trout. The *Tally Ho II* (Crescent City Harbor, Citizen Dock R, Slip D29, 707/464-1236, http://tally-ho-sportfishing.com, May-Oct., half-day $120 pp) is available for a variety of deep-sea fishing trips.

River fishers have a wealth of guides to choose from. **Ken Cunningham Guide Service** (50 Hunter Creek, Klamath, 707/391-7144, www.salmonslayer.net, $200-250) will take you on a full-day fishing trip; the price includes bait, tackle, and the boat.

Hiking

The redwood forests that nearly meet the wide, sandy beaches make the Crescent City area a fabulous place to hike. The hikes at **Point St. George** aren't strenuous and provide stunning views of the coastline and surrounding landscape. **Tolowa Dunes State Park** (1375 Elk Valley Rd., 707/465-7335, www.parks.ca.gov, daily sunrise-sunset, free), north of Point St. George, offers miles of trails winding through forests, across beaches, and meandering along the shores of Lake Earl.

Horseback Riding

The rugged land surrounding Crescent City looks even prettier from the back of a horse. Casual riders can enjoy a guided riding adventure through redwoods or along the ocean with **Crescent Trail Rides** (2002 Moorehead Rd., 707/951-5407, www.crescenttrailrides.com, 1.5 hours $70, 3 hours $135). Under the same management, **Fort Dick Stable** (2002 Moorehead Rd., 707/951-5407, www.fort-dickstable.com) offers boarding and riding lessons.

A great place to ride is **Tolowa Dunes State Park** (1375 Elk Valley Rd., 707/465-7335, www.parks.ca.gov, daily sunrise-sunset, free), which maintains 20 miles of trails accessible to horses. Serious equestrians with their own mounts can ride in to a campsite with corrals at the north end of the park off Lower Lake Road.

Surfing

While Crescent City is a long way from the legendary Southern California surf scene, the northernmost coastal city in California has a collection of surf breaks. Pioneering big-wave surfer Greg Noll even lives in Crescent City. Just south of the harbor you'll find the most popular break in town, **South Beach** (Hwy. 1 between Anchor Way and Sand Mine Rd.), with peeling waves perfect for longboarders and beginners. It was once home to the Annual Noll Longboard Classic. North of town, **Point St. George** (end of Washington Blvd.) has a reef and point break that comes alive during winter. Run over to **South Beach Outfitters** (128 Anchor Way, 707/464-2963 or 877/330-7873, http://southbeachoutfitters.com, summer daily 10am-5pm, winter Wed.-Sun. 10am-5pm, board rental $25, wetsuit rental $15) to rent a board and wetsuit.

ACCOMMODATIONS

Lodgings in Crescent City are affordable even during the midsummer high season and can be surprisingly comfortable.

The aptly named **Curly Redwood Lodge** (701 U.S. 101 S., 707/464-2137, www.curlyredwoodlodge.com, $75-85) is constructed of a single rare curly redwood tree. You'll get to see the lovely color and grain of the tree in your large, simply decorated room. A 1950s feel pervades this friendly, unpretentious motel even though it offers free Wi-Fi. Some rooms even have antique TVs from the 1950s; others have flat screens. Right on U.S. 101, you can walk to South Beach or the Crescent City Harbor.

Few frills decorate the family-owned **Pacific Inn** (220 M. St., 707/464-9553 or 800/977-9553, $72-82), but the rooms are clean, inexpensive, and comfortable. Its central downtown location makes for easy access to restaurants, museums, and points of interest. Pets are permitted.

The **Lighthouse Inn** (681 U.S. 101 S., 707/464-3993 or 877/464-3993, www.lighthouse101.com, $89-125) has an elegant but whimsical lobby filled with dolphins and dollhouses to welcome guests, and the enthusiastic staff can help with restaurant recommendations and sights. Stylish appointments and bold colors grace each guest room. Corner suites with oversize whirlpool tubs make a perfect romantic retreat for couples at a reasonable nightly rate, while standard double rooms are downright cheap, given their comfort.

The **Anchor Beach Inn** (880 U.S. 101 S., 800/837-4116, www.anchorbeachinn.com, $89-185), at the south end of town, offers great access to South Beach, the harbor, and several good seafood restaurants. The ocean views also overlook a wide swath of asphalt RV park, but the rooms have attractive decor and are clean and well maintained; continental breakfast and Internet access are included.

The **Ocean View Inn** (270 U.S. 101 S., 707/465-1111, www.oceanviewinncrescentcity.com, $120-165) is next to Ocean World. The most deluxe rooms have both a Jacuzzi tub and a fireplace. Amenities include a continental breakfast and free Wi-Fi along with use of a self-service laundry and business room.

FOOD

Not surprisingly, seafood is standard fare in Crescent City, but family restaurants and one or two ethnic eateries add some appealing variety.

American

Enjoy an impressive variety of fresh and healthy food at **The Good Harvest Cafe** (575 U.S. 101 S., 707/465-6028, Mon.-Sat. 7:30am-9pm, Sun. 8am-8pm, $10-35). It serves the best breakfast in town, with vegetarian options like tofu rancheros and veggie frittata. Steak entrées are at the pricier end of the dinner menu, which also includes burgers, pasta, vegetarian entrées, and big salads. Kitschy Native American decorations abound inside and out.

Fishermans Restaurant (700 U.S. 101 S., 707/465-3474, summer daily 6am-9pm, winter daily 6am-8pm, $11-26) is a casual place to grab a bite. You can walk in wearing jeans and sandy sneakers. The diverse dinner menu includes fresh local seafood offerings. Breakfasts feature biscuits and gravy, pancakes, and thick, juicy bacon, all delicious—and big enough—to sustain you through a long day of hauling nets.

Coffee Shops and Markets

The **Java Hut** (437 U.S. 101 N., 707/465-4439, daily 5am-10pm, $5) is a drive-through and walk-up coffee stand that serves a wide array of coffee drinks. Beware of long lines of locals during the morning hours.

The small, family-owned, award-winning **Rumiano Cheese Co.** (511 9th St.,

707/465-1535 or 866/328-2433, www.rumi-anocheese.com, June-Dec. Mon.-Fri. 9am-5pm, Sat. 9am-3pm, Jan.-May Mon.-Fri. 9am-5pm) has been part of Crescent City since 1921. Come to the tasting room for the cheese and stay for, well, more cheese. The dry jack cheese is a particular favorite, though lots of varieties are available.

Crescent City runs a **farmers market** (Del Norte County Fairgrounds, 451 U.S. 101 N., 707/464-7441, www.delnorte.org, June-Oct. Sat. 9am-1pm). While the harvest season is more restricted here than points south, veggie lovers can still choose from an array of fresh local produce all summer long.

Sandwiches

The chef/owners behind **Vita Cucina** (1270 Front St., Ste. A, 707/464-1076, www.vi-tacucina.com, Mon.-Thurs. 7am-6pm, Fri. 7am-7pm, $4-15) worked in some intriguing restaurants (Napa's Auberge Soleil, Antarctica's McMurdo Station) before landing in Crescent City. They are upping the city's casual dining cred with bahn mi sandwiches and pulled pork. On Thursdays and Fridays, they do pizzas, calzones, and whole smoked chickens.

Seafood

Northwood's Restaurant (675 U.S. 101 S., 707/465-5656, daily 6am-9pm, $8-20) prides itself on serving the freshest fish available, and in Crescent City that can mean the fillet you're eating for dinner was caught that very morning by a local fishing boat. The varied menu also includes imported exotic fish plus a number of land-based entrées to appeal to every palate.

For better seafood still at a reasonable price, the best bet is **The Chart Room** (130 Anchor Way, 707/464-5993, www.chartroom-crescentcity.com, Wed.-Sat. 6:30am-8pm, Tues. 11am-8pm, $10-23). It's very casual, the food is excellent, and it's right on the ocean, so you can watch sea lions cavort on the pier while you eat. If anyone in your party is not a seafood lover, the lasagna is excellent.

Thai

A Thai restaurant in Crescent City? Believe it. The **Thai House** (105 N. St., 707/464-2427, Mon.-Thurs. and Sat 11am-8:30pm, Fri. 11am-9pm, Sun. noon-8pm, $10-15) does passable Thai food including curries and pad Thai.

INFORMATION AND SERVICES

The **Crescent City and Del Norte County Chamber of Commerce Visitors Center** (1001 Front St., 707/464-3174 or 800/343-8300, www.exploredelnorte.com, summer daily 9am-5pm, Labor Day-mid-Oct. Mon.-Sat. 10am-4pm, mid-Oct.-Memorial Day Tues.-Sat. 10am-4pm) is a good place to visit when you arrive. Knowledgeable staffers can advise you on "secret" local sights as well as the bigger attractions advertised in the myriad brochures lining the walls.

Also in town is the **Crescent City Information Center** (1111 2nd St., 707/465-7335, spring-fall daily 9am-5pm, winter daily 9am-4pm) run by Redwood National and State Parks. This friendly place has maps, souvenirs, and rangers who can chat about hiking, camping, and exploring the parks.

You can pick up a Del Norte County Map and a copy of *101 Things to Do in Del Norte/Southern Oregon* (www.101things.com) at the visitors center and many local businesses.

TRANSPORTATION

The main routes in and out of town are U.S. 101 and U.S. 199. Both are well maintained but are twisty in spots, so take care, especially at night. From San Francisco, the drive to Crescent City is about 350 miles (6.5 hours). It is 85 miles (under two hours) from Eureka north to Crescent City on U.S. 101. Traffic isn't a big issue in Crescent City, and parking is free and easy to find throughout town.

Jack McNamara Field (CEC, 5 miles northwest of town, 250 Dale Rupert Rd., 707/464-7288, http://flycrescentcity.com) is also called Del Norte County Airport and is the only airport in Crescent City. Alaska

Airlines and PenAir have two daily flights to Portland, Oregon.

Redwood Coast Transit (RCT, 707/464-6400, www.redwoodcoasttransit.org, adults $1, senior and disabled $0.75) handles bus travel in and around Crescent City. Make sure to have exact change handy. Four in-town routes and a coastal bus from Smith River to Arcata provide ample public-transit options for travelers without cars. Pick up a schedule at the visitors center (1001 Front St.) or local stores for current fares and times.

Monterey Bay

A half-moon-shaped indentation on California's Central Coast, Monterey Bay is the heart of the state's marine ecosystems. This wild and rugged coastline provides ample opportunities to enjoy and explore the largest marine sanctuary in the country. Dive into the pristine waters off Monterey to explore the bay's swaying kelp forests. Board a whale-watching boat to spot gray whales sounding outside the harbor. Or ride the waves at world-renowned surf breaks.

This area has become a favorite getaway for locals as much as visitors. It's easy to see why. Small cities and towns dot the coastline, each with its fair share of notable attractions. The Santa Cruz Boardwalk is a seaside amusement park that offers roller coasters and bumper cars alongside a family-friendly stretch of sand. The Monterey Bay Aquarium artfully presents close-up views of local sea creatures, from cuddly sea otters to sleek sharks and surreal glowing jellyfish. Historic Cannery Row, immortalized by John Steinbeck in his novel of the same name, now offers seaside dining and shopping. Victorian architecture, small-town charm, and butterfly migrations are the draws at Pacific Grove. Exclusive coastal community Pebble Beach offers luxurious amenities alongside some of the most-photographed coastal scenery in the state. Carmel-by-the-Sea, founded by artists, is an idyllic village gently descending to a white-sand beach. And inland Carmel Valley offers a sunny escape from encroaching seaside fog, as well as a burgeoning wine industry with enough tasting rooms to fill a long, relaxing afternoon.

PLANNING YOUR TIME

If you're coming to this part of the state for a weekend, pick an area and explore it in depth. Don't try to get everywhere in only two days. For a relaxed weekend without much travel, focus your trip on Santa Cruz or the Monterey Peninsula. If you've got more than a couple of days, start in either Santa Cruz or Monterey and work your way down or up the coast on Highway 1. In five days, you could easily hit major attractions including the Santa Cruz

02

Highlights

★ **Santa Cruz Beach Boardwalk:** With thrill rides, carnival games, and retro-cool live music, this is the best old-time boardwalk in the state (page 304).

★ **Surfing in Santa Cruz:** If there's anywhere in Northern California to don a wetsuit and go surfing, it's Santa Cruz. Breaks range from easy-rolling beginner waves at **Cowell's Beach** to more powerful breakers at **Steamer Lane** (page 313).

★ **Elkhorn Slough:** There's no better place to view the marine mammals of Monterey Bay than from a kayak in the Elkhorn Slough (page 319).

★ **Monterey Bay Aquarium:** This mammoth aquarium astonishes with a vast array of sea life and exhibits on the local ecosystem (page 323).

★ **Scuba Diving, Kayaking, and Stand-Up Paddleboarding:** Experience Monterey Bay's calm water and unique wildlife by getting into the water (page 328).

★ **17-Mile Drive:** This gorgeous scenic drive is worth the toll for an introduction to the region's coastal beauty (page 342).

★ **Carmel Beach:** A great place for a stroll, a surf, or a picnic, this is one of the finest beaches on Monterey Bay (page 344).

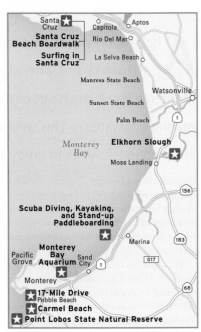

★ **Point Lobos State Natural Reserve:** The crown jewel of California's impressive state park system has pocket coves, tide pools, forests of Monterey cypress, and diverse marine and terrestrial wildlife (page 347).

Monterey Bay

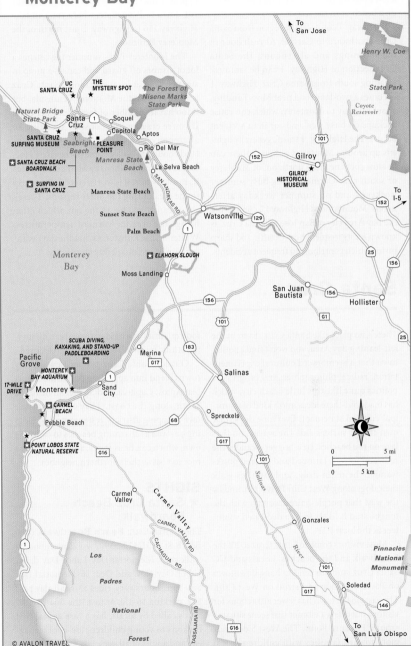

To San Jose

Henry W. Coe

State Park

Coyote
Reservoir

UC
SANTA CRUZ ★   THE
              MYSTERY SPOT ★

The Forest of
Nisene Marks
State Park

Natural Bridge
State Park
              Santa
              Cruz ★   ○ Soquel
SANTA CRUZ   ○ Capitola
SURFING MUSEUM ★   ○ Aptos
              Seabright   PLEASURE   ○ Rio Del Mar
              Beach   POINT
SANTA CRUZ BEACH   ○ La Selva Beach
BOARDWALK   Manresa State
                 Beach
SURFING IN
SANTA CRUZ   Manresa State Beach

              Sunset State Beach

              Palm Beach

101

152   Gilroy

GILROY
HISTORICAL
MUSEUM ★

To
I-5

152

Watsonville   129

25

156

Monterey
Bay   ELKHORN SLOUGH

Moss Landing ○

156

San Juan
Bautista   156

Hollister

101   G1

25

SCUBA DIVING,
KAYAKING, AND STAND-UP
PADDLEBOARDING
Pacific
Grove   Marina
MONTEREY   G17
BAY AQUARIUM
17-MILE
DRIVE   Monterey ★   Sand
                      City   Salinas

CARMEL
BEACH   68   Spreckels ○

Pebble Beach   G17

POINT LOBOS STATE
NATURAL RESERVE   G16   101

Carmel   Carmel Valley
Valley

CARMEL VALLEY RD

CACHAGUA RD

1

Los

Padres

National

Gonzales ○

Salinas

River

101

Pinnacles
National
Monument

Soledad ○   146

G17

TASSAJARA RD

G16

Forest

To
San Luis Obispo

0   5 mi
0   5 km

© AVALON TRAVEL

Boardwalk and Monterey Bay Aquarium, have a few great meals, and even find time to relax on a beach or in the woods.

Highway 1 connects the region from Santa Cruz southward to Carmel. At rush hour in the mornings and afternoons, the Santa Cruz section of Highway 1 can be jammed. Heading south from Santa Cruz, Highway 1 becomes a two-lane road near Moss Landing, about midway to Monterey, which can cause backups on busy weekends or if an accident occurs. The Highway 1 traffic generally lightens up around Monterey, although there can be slow spots heading north out of Monterey or south near Carmel during busy summer weekends and on summer weekday afternoons. Mountainous Highway 17, connecting the Bay Area city of San Jose to Santa Cruz, is known for its frequent heavy traffic and sharp turns, which contribute to frequent accidents.

If you're heading to Monterey and want to bypass Santa Cruz, consider taking Highway 101 down to Prunedale, where you can take Highway 156 to Highway 1 just north of the Monterey Peninsula.

The Monterey Bay's summer fog catches a lot of visitors off guard and causes a jump in sweater sales at local gift shops. Santa Cruz is warmer than the Monterey Peninsula, but it too has its number of foggy summer days. If you're craving sun, consider spending an afternoon out in Carmel Valley, which is inland enough to dodge some of the coast's fog. While summer is when the Monterey Bay sees its most visitors, it is worth considering a trip to the area during the other seasons. There's significantly less fog in the fall, which often brings the area its warmest temperatures. Winter brings rainstorms, but the days without rain offer remarkably clear skies.

Santa Cruz

There's no place like Santa Cruz. Even in the left-leaning Bay Area, you won't find another town that has embraced cultural experimentation, radical philosophies, and progressive politics quite like this little beach city, which has made out-there ideas into a kind of municipal cultural statement. Everyone does their own thing: surfers ride the waves, nudists laze on the beaches, tree-huggers wander the redwood forests, tattooed and pierced punks wander the main drag, and families walk their dogs along West Cliff Drive. Oh, and by the way, that purple-haired woman with the tongue stud is likely to be a dedicated volunteer at the local PTA.

Most visitors come to Santa Cruz to hit the Boardwalk and the beaches. Locals and UC Santa Cruz students tend to hang downtown on Pacific Avenue and stroll on West Cliff. The east side of town has fewer attractions for visitors, but offers a vibrant surf scene situated around Pleasure Point. The West Side tends more toward families with children. Local food qualifies as a hidden treasure, with myriad ethnic cuisines represented and enjoyed.

Outside Santa Cruz proper, several tiny towns blend into appealing beachside suburbia. Aptos, Capitola, and Soquel all lie to the south along the coast. They've all got their own shopping districts, restaurants, and lodgings, as well as charming beaches to call their own, which can be as foggy, as crowded, or as nice to visit as their northern neighbors.

SIGHTS
★ Santa Cruz Beach Boardwalk

The **Santa Cruz Beach Boardwalk** (400 Beach St., 831/423-5590, www.beachboardwalk.com, Memorial Day-Labor Day daily, Labor Day-Nov. and Dec. 26-Memorial Day Sat.-Sun., hours vary, rides $3-6, all-day pass $32, parking $6-15), or just "the Boardwalk" as it's called by locals, has a rare appeal that beckons to young children, too-cool teenagers, and adults of all ages.

Santa Cruz and Vicinity

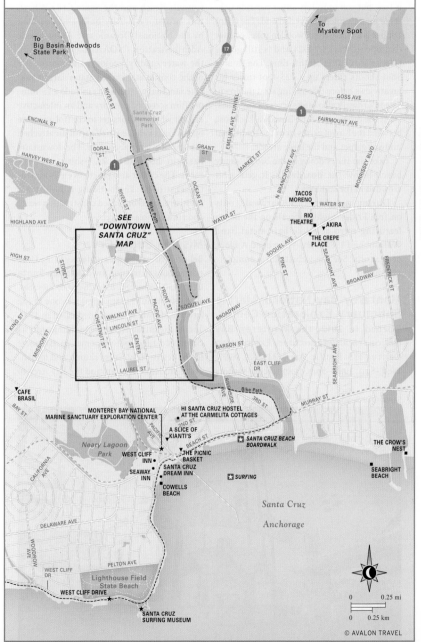

To Mystery Spot

To Big Basin Redwoods State Park

17

GOSS AVE

1

ENCINAL ST

FAIRMOUNT AVE

Santa Cruz Memorial Park

HARVEY WEST BLVD

CORAL ST

GRANT ST

EMELINE AVE TUNNEL

MARKET ST

N BRANCIFORTE AVE

MORRISSEY BLVD

1

RIVER ST

Bike Path

OCEAN ST

WATER ST

TACOS MORENO ▼

Water St

HIGHLAND AVE

RIO THEATRE

SOQUEL AVE

▼ AKIRA

THE CREPE PLACE

SEABRIGHT AVE

BROADWAY

FREDERICK ST

SEE "DOWNTOWN SANTA CRUZ" MAP

HIGH ST

STOREY ST

PINE ST

FRONT ST

PACIFIC AVE

SOQUEL AVE

KING ST

MISSION ST

CHESTNUT ST

WALNUT AVE

LINCOLN ST

CENTER ST

BROADWAY

BARSON ST

LAUREL ST

EAST CLIFF DR

SEABRIGHT AVE

RIVERSIDE AVE

3RD ST

Bike Path

MURRAY ST

▼ CAFE BRASIL

BAY ST

MONTEREY BAY NATIONAL MARINE SANCTUARY EXPLORATION CENTER

2ND ST

PACIFIC AVE

HI SANTA CRUZ HOSTEL AT THE CARMELITA COTTAGES

A SLICE OF KIANTI'S

BEACH ST

★ SANTA CRUZ BEACH BOARDWALK

THE CROW'S NEST ■

Neary Lagoon Park

WEST CLIFF INN ●

THE PICNIC BASKET ▼

SEAWAY INN ●

SANTA CRUZ DREAM INN ■

✚ SURFING

SEABRIGHT BEACH ■

CALIFORNIA AVE

COWELLS BEACH

DELAWARE AVE

Santa Cruz

Anchorage

WOODROW AVE

WEST CLIFF DR

PELTON AVE

Lighthouse Field State Beach

★ WEST CLIFF DRIVE

N

0   0.25 mi

0   0.25 km

★ SANTA CRUZ SURFING MUSEUM

© AVALON TRAVEL

The amusement park rambles along each side of the south end of the Boardwalk; entry is free, but you must buy either per-ride tickets or an unlimited-ride wristband. The Giant Dipper is an old-school wooden roller coaster that opened back in 1924 and is still giving riders a thrill after all this time. The Double Shot shoots riders up a 125-foot tower for great views before free-falling straight down. The Boardwalk also offers several kids' rides.

At the other end of the Boardwalk, choose between the lure of prizes from the traditional midway games and the large arcade.

Take the stairs down to the broad, sandy beach below the Boardwalk. It gets a bit crowded in the summer.

During summer, the Boardwalk puts on free Friday-night concerts on the beach featuring retro acts like hair metal band Warrant and 1980s New Wave band A Flock of Seagulls. See the website for a complete schedule.

Monterey Bay National Marine Sanctuary Exploration Center

Opened in 2012, the **Monterey Bay National Marine Sanctuary Exploration Center** (35 Pacific Ave., 831/421-9993, Wed.-Sun. 10am-5pm, free) teaches visitors about the protected waters off Santa Cruz and Monterey. Just across the street from Cowells Beach and the Santa Cruz Wharf, this two-story facility built and operated by the National Oceanic and Atmospheric Administration (NOAA) has exhibits on the water quality, geology, and marine life of the continental United States' largest marine sanctuary. Highlights include a 15-minute film screened upstairs and an interactive exhibit where visitors get to control a remote operational vehicle (ROV) with an attached camera in a large aquarium. The downstairs has a gift shop with books, T-shirts, and postcards. The center also practices environmental sensitivity: The building is built from mostly recycled or reused construction waste and runs on solar power.

Mission Santa Cruz

Believe it or not, weird and funky Santa Cruz started out as a mission town. **Mission Santa Cruz** (130 Emmet St., 831/426-5686, Tues.-Sat. 10am-4pm, Sun. 10am-2pm) was one of the later California missions, dedicated in 1791. Today, the attractive white building with its classic red-tiled roof welcomes parishioners to the active Holy Cross church and fourth-grade students from around the Bay Area to

Santa Cruz Beach Boardwalk

Downtown Santa Cruz

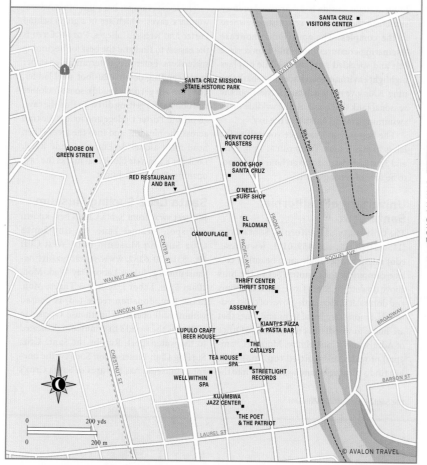

© AVALON TRAVEL

the historic museum areas of the old mission. In fact, the building is not the original complex built in the 18th century. Instead it's a replica that was built in the 1930s. Stop in at the Galeria, which houses the mission gift shop and a stunning collection of religious vestments—something you won't see in many other California missions.

Long Marine Laboratory

While the Monterey Bay Aquarium down the road in Monterey provides the best look into the nearby bay, the **Long Marine Laboratory** (100 Shaffer Rd., 831/459-3800, http://seymourcenter.ucsc.edu, Sept.-June Tues.-Sun. 10am-5pm, July-Aug. daily 10am-5pm, adults $8, seniors, students, and children $6) is worthwhile for people interested in sea creatures and marine issues. The large, attractive complex at the end of Delaware Avenue sits on the edge of the cliff overlooking the ocean—convenient for the research done primarily by students and faculty of UCSC. The **Seymour Marine Discovery Center** is the part of the lab that's open to the public. Outside the door is a blue whale skeleton that's lit up at night. Inside is a marine laboratory similar to those used by scientists elsewhere in the complex. The aquariums showcase fascinating creatures including monkeyface eels and speckled sand dabs, while displays highlight environmental issues like shark finning. Kids love the touch tanks; check out the seasonal tank that contains the wildlife that's swimming around outside in the bay.

The best way to introduce yourself to the lab is to take a tour. Tours run at 1pm, 2pm, and 3pm each day; sign up an hour in advance to be sure of getting a slot.

University of California, Santa Cruz

The **University of California, Santa Cruz** (1156 High St., 831/459-0111, www.ucsc.edu) might be the single most beautiful college campus in the country. Set in the hills above downtown Santa Cruz, the classrooms and dorms sit underneath groves of coast redwoods, among tangles of ferns and vines that are home to woodland creatures. The Office of Admissions (Cook House, Mon.-Fri. 9am-4pm) provides **self-guided tour maps.** Or just find a parking lot and wander out into the woods like the students do, looking for a perfect circle of trees to sit and meditate within.

The UCSC campus has some other natural wonders: caves, which are in a gulch behind Porter and Kresge Colleges. **Porter Cave** is the easiest to find and the best for beginning spelunkers. Enter the subterranean chamber by descending down a 20-foot steel ladder. The cave can get quite muddy, so wear clothes you don't mind getting dirty. To find the cave, go behind Porter College and follow the trail across the meadow and into the trees. Then head right alongside Empire Grade Road. Look for a concrete block that marks the cave opening. Bring a flashlight.

Santa Cruz Surfing Museum

Just feet away from Santa Cruz's best-known surf spot, Steamer Lane, the tiny **Santa Cruz Surfing Museum** (1701 West Cliff Dr., 831/420-6289, www.santacruzsurfingmuseum.org, July 4-Labor Day Wed.-Mon. 10am-5pm, Labor Day-July 3 Thurs.-Mon. noon-4pm, donation requested) is housed within a still-operating lighthouse. Opened in 1986, it is the world's first museum dedicated to the water sport. Run by the Santa Cruz Surfing Club Preservation Society, the one-room museum has pictures of Santa Cruz's

the Santa Cruz Surfing Museum

Surf City

There's a plaque outside the Santa Cruz Surfing Museum that explains how three Hawaiian princes introduced surfing to California in 1885. Apparently, they rode redwood planks from a nearby lumber mill on waves at the mouth of the San Lorenzo River in Santa Cruz.

While Santa Cruz's claim as being the birthplace of surfing on the mainland is not disputed, the popular surfing town calling itself "Surf City" has raised the hackles of Southern California's Huntington Beach, which also likes to have its tourist T-shirts adorned with "Surf City." In 2006, Huntington Beach was awarded exclusive use of the title "Surf City" by the U.S. Patent and Trademark Office and went after Santa Cruz beachwear stores that sold T-shirts with the words "Santa Cruz" and "Surf City."

Despite Huntington Beach's aggressive legal action, the residents of Santa Cruz might have the last laugh. In 2009, *Surfer Magazine* proclaimed that Santa Cruz is "The Real Surf City, USA" in a piece about the top 10 surf towns. To Huntington Beach's chagrin, it didn't even make the magazine's top 10 list.

surfing culture from the 1930s to the present. One haunting display on shark attacks includes a local surfboard with bite marks from a great white shark.

Wilder Ranch State Park

North of Santa Cruz's city limits, the land on both sides of Highway 1 suddenly gives way to farmland perched atop coastal terraces. The best place to get a feel for this mostly undeveloped stretch of coastline is to visit **Wilder Ranch State Park** (1401 Coast Rd., 831/423-9703, www.parks.ca.gov, daily 8am-sunset, $10/vehicle). The park allows visitors to step back in time and discover what it was like to live on a ranch over 100 years ago at its many living-history demonstrations. Other annual events include gardening demonstrations and the Old-Fashioned Independence Day Celebration. For those who would rather check out the park's natural beauty in the present, the 2.5-mile **Old Cove Landing Trail** is a flat, easy hike out to the coastline, which is pocked with sea caves and usually decorated with wildlife ranging from elegant cormorants to harbor seals lazing on the coastal shelves.

The east side of the park is very popular with mountain bikers for its beginner to intermediate climbs with coastal views. The **Wilder Ridge Loop** provides a good introduction to the park's trails along with its

coastal views. The **Enchanted Loop** traverses more technical terrain.

Wilder Ranch State Park is less than a 10-minute drive from downtown Santa Cruz. Just get on Mission Street, which doubles as CA-1 through town, and head north. It is less than three miles north of town.

The Forest of Nisene Marks State Park

Take a walk at **The Forest of Nisene Marks State Park** (four miles north of Aptos on Aptos Creek Rd., 831/763-7062, www.parks. ca.gov, daily sunrise-sunset, $8/vehicle), once the site of serious logging operations but now shaded by second-growth redwoods. Mountain bikers can ride up the fire road through the center of the park, while hikers can head out on more than 30 miles of hiking trails that take off from the roadway. One popular hike is the **Loma Prieta Grade Trail** (six miles round-trip), which follows an old railway bed up to the remnants of a lumber camp. Another point of interest within the park is the epicenter of the 1989 Loma Prieta earthquake, which interrupted the World Series and caused the collapse of a section of San Francisco's Bay Bridge.

The Mystery Spot

Santa Cruz has its own kitschy tourist trap: **The Mystery Spot** (465 Mystery Spot Rd.,

831/423-8897, www.mysteryspot.com, summer Mon.-Fri. 10am-6pm, Sat.-Sun. 9am-8pm, winter Mon.-Fri. 10am-4pm, Sat.-Sun. 10am-5pm, adults $6, children under 3 free, $5 parking). It's a tiny piece of land just outside of Santa Cruz where gravity fails. Balls can roll uphill and people can stand off the side of a wall. It may be an area of spatial distortion where the laws of physics don't apply . . . or it may be a collection of optical illusions. Regardless, it has a sweet gift shop that sells the near-iconic Mystery Spot bumper sticker and other necessities like thong underwear.

ENTERTAINMENT AND EVENTS
Bars and Clubs

Lovers of libations should grab a drink at **Red Restaurant & Bar** (200 Locust St., 831/425-1913, www.redsantacruz.com, daily 3pm-1:30am), upstairs in the historic Santa Cruz Hotel Building. Creative cocktails include signature creations like the Jean Grey, a mix of house-infused Earl Grey organic gin, lemon, and simple syrup. They also have a nice selection of 30 craft and Belgian beers on tap. With its dark wood paneling and burgundy barstools, Red feels like an old speakeasy. It also serves a comprehensive late-night menu until 1am for those who need some food to soak up their alcohol.

The Crepe Place (1134 Soquel Ave., 831/429-6994, http://thecrepeplace.com, Mon.-Thurs. 11am-midnight, Fri. 11am-1am, Sat.-Sun. 9am-midnight) has recently emerged as a hangout for the hipster crowd, who are drawn in by the high-profile indie rock acts and popular Bay Area bands that perform in its intimate front room. There is also outdoor seating and a comprehensive menu of creative crepes.

Beer fans should make their way to the **Lupulo Craft Beer House** (233 Cathcart St., 831/454-8306, www.lupulosc.com, Sun.-Thurs. 11:30am-10pm, Fri.-Sat. 11:30am-10:30pm). A small drinking establishment with a hip industrial feel, Lupulo has 16 rotating craft beers on tap and over 100 types of bottled beer to consume on premises or take to go. There is also a small-bites menu featuring tacos, salads, and sandwiches. This husband-and-wife-owned business also conducts brewing demos, tastings, and other beer-related events.

Set in an alley, **The Poet & The Patriot** (320 Cedar St., 831/426-8620, daily 1pm-2am) is a popular watering hole that was opened by a Santa Cruz politician and playwright. The bar has two main rooms including one where there is frequently live music and another one that has four regulation dartboards. Both rooms feature framed memorabilia on the walls and banners on the ceiling.

Live Music

The Catalyst (1011 Pacific Ave., 831/423-1338, www.catalystclub.com), right downtown on Pacific Avenue, hosts a variety of reggae, rap, and punk acts from Snoop Dogg to Agent Orange. Check the calendar when you buy tickets—some shows are 21 and over. The 800-person main concert hall is a standing-room-only space, while the balconies offer seating. The bar sits downstairs adjacent to the concert space. The vibe tends to be low-key, but it depends on the night and the event. The **Catalyst Atrium,** a smaller room in the same building, snags some superb national touring bands. Buy tickets online or by phone; purchasing in advance is recommended, especially for national acts.

The **Crow's Nest** (2218 East Cliff Dr., 831/476-4560, www.crowsnest-santacruz.com) is as a venue for all kinds of live musical acts. Rock, soul, reggae, and funk bands typically play Tuesday-Saturday. Sundays are live comedy evenings, and Tuesdays are reggae jam nights.

A former 1940s movie house, the **Rio Theatre** (1205 Soquel Ave., 831/423-8209, www.riotheatre.com) hosts everything from film festivals to performances by international touring acts like Ladysmith Black Mambazo and Built to Spill. Check the theater's website for a full list of upcoming events.

Bookshop Santa Cruz

Named one of the great jazz venues in the world by *Downbeat Magazine*, the **Kuumbwa Jazz Center** (320 Cedar St., 831/427-2227, http://kuumbwajazz.org) is a 200-seat treasure of a venue. It puts on 120 intimate concerts a year aided by a superb sound and lighting setup. Past performers have included Bobby Hutcherson, Pharaoh Saunders, Christian McBride, and David Grisman.

Comedy

For a good laugh in Santa Cruz, the **Crow's Nest** (2218 East Cliff Dr., 831/476-4560, www.crowsnest-santacruz.com) hosts a weekly **stand-up comedy show** (Sun. 9pm, $7). Because the show runs on Sunday nights, the Crow's Nest takes advantage of the opportunity to hire big-name comics who have been in San Francisco or San Jose for weekend engagements. This lets folks see headliners in a more casual setting for a fraction of the cost of the big-city clubs. The Crow's Nest, with its great views out over the Pacific, also has a full bar and restaurant.

Enjoy drinks and dinner while you get your giggle on.

Theater

When the long-running Shakespeare Santa Cruz went belly-up in 2013, the nonprofit **Santa Cruz Shakespeare** (The Sinsheimer-Stanley Festival Glen, UCSC Performing Arts Center, Meyer Dr., 831/460-6396, www.santa-cruzshakespeare.com, July-Aug., adults $40-52, seniors and military $36-48, children 18 and under $16, previews $20) was formed in 2014 so Bard lovers could still get their fix. Recent productions, presented in the Sinsheimer-Stanley Festival Glen, have included *Much Ado About Nothing, Macbeth,* and the Shakespeare-inspired *The Liar.*

SHOPPING

For a small city, Santa Cruz has a bustling downtown, centered on **Pacific Avenue,** which extends about nine blocks from Water Street to Laurel Street. At the northern end, shoppers peruse antiques, clothing, and kitchenware. In the middle, you can grab a cappuccino, a cocktail, or a bite to eat in one of the many independent eateries. At the (slightly seedy) south end, visitors can purchase body jewelry or tattoos. The sidewalks are often jammed with shoppers, street performers, panhandlers, and sightseers. It's a good idea to park in one of the structures a block or two off Pacific Avenue and walk from there.

Bookshop Santa Cruz (1520 Pacific Ave., 831/423-0900, www.bookshopsantacruz.com, Sun.-Thurs. 9am-10pm, Fri.-Sat. 9am-11pm) is a superb independent bookstore that hosts regular readings by literary heavy hitters like Jonathan Franzen and Daniel Handler.

Santa Cruz's Jack O'Neill is credited with making cold-water surfing possible with the invention of the wetsuit. His **O'Neill Surf Shop** (110 Cooper St., 831/469-4377, Sun.-Thurs. 10am-8pm, Fri.-Sat. 10am-9pm) specializes in surfboards, brand-name clothing, and, of course, wetsuits.

This town has plenty of secondhand clothing shops. One of the largest sits only a block off Pacific Avenue—the **Thrift Center Thrift Store** (504 Front St., 831/429-6975, Mon.-Sat. 9am-8pm, Sun. 10am-6pm). This big, somewhat dingy retail space offers a wide array of cheap secondhand clothes. You'll need to hunt a bit to find that one perfect vintage item, but isn't that the fun of thrift shopping?

Camouflage (1329 Pacific Ave., 831/423-7613, www.shopcamoflauge.com, Mon.-Thurs. 11am-8pm, Fri.-Sat. 11am-10pm, Sun. 11am-7pm) is an independent, family-owned and women-friendly adult store. The first room contains mostly lingerie and tame items. Walk through the narrow black-curtained passage and you'll find the *other* room, which is filled with grown-up toys designed to please women of every taste and proclivity.

Stop in to **Streetlight Records** (939 Pacific Ave., 831/421-9200, www.streetlight-records.com, Sun.-Mon. noon-8pm, Tues.-Thurs. 11am-9pm, Fri.-Sat. 11am-10pm) to pick up the latest music for your drive down the coast. With records and turntables making a serious comeback, Streetlight is also the place in Santa Cruz to find new and used vinyl.

SPORTS AND RECREATION
Beaches

At the tip of the West Side, **Natural Bridges State Park** (2531 West Cliff Dr., 831/423-4609, www.parks.ca.gov, daily 8am-sunset, $10) used to have three coastal arches right offshore. Even though there is only one arch remaining, this picturesque state park has a beach that doesn't stretch wide, but falls back deep, crossed by a creek that feeds into the sea. An inconsistent break makes surfing at Natural Bridges fun on occasion, while the near-constant winds that sweep the sands bring out windsurfers nearly every weekend. Hardy sun-worshippers brave the breezes, bringing out their beach blankets, umbrellas, and sunscreen on rare sunny days (usually in late spring and fall). Back from the beach, a wooded picnic area has tables and grills for small and larger parties. Even farther back, the park has a monarch butterfly preserve, where the migrating insects take over the eucalyptus grove during the fall and winter months. Rangers offer guided tours of the tide pools that range out to the west side of the beach. Access is by a scrambling short hike (0.25-0.5 mile) on the rocky cliffs. These odd little holes filled with sea life aren't like most tide pools—many are nearly perfectly round depressions in the sandstone cliffs worn away by harder stones as the tides move tirelessly back and forth. Just don't touch the residents of these pools, since human hands can hurt delicate tide pool creatures.

Cowell's Beach (350 West Cliff Dr.) is where lots of beginning surfers rode their first waves. This West Side beach sits right at a crook in the coastline that joins with underwater features to create a reliable small break that lures new surfers by the dozens.

At the south end of Santa Cruz, down by the harbor, beachgoers flock to **Seabright Beach** (East Cliff Dr. at Seabright Ave., 831/427-4868, www.santacruzstateparks.org, daily 6am-10pm, free) all summer long. This miles-long stretch of sand, protected by the cliffs from the worst of the winds, is a favorite retreat for sunbathers and loungers. While there's little in the way of snack bars, permanent volleyball courts, or facilities, you can still have a great time at Seabright. There is a lot of soft sand to lie in, plenty of room to play football or set up your own volleyball net, and, of course, easy access to the chilly Pacific Ocean. There's no surfing here—Seabright has a shore break that delights skim-boarders, but makes wave riding impossible.

Down in Capitola, one of the region's most popular sandy spots is **New Brighton State Beach** (1500 Park Ave., Capitola, 831/464-6330, www.parks.ca.gov, daily 8am-sunset, $10/vehicle). This forest-backed beach has everything: a strip of sand that's perfect for lounging and swimming, a forest-shaded campground for both tent and RV campers, hiking trails, and ranger-led nature programs. New Brighton can get crowded on sunny summer days, but it's nothing like the wall-to-wall people of the popular Southern California beaches. Call in advance to make camping reservations at this popular state park.

★ Surfing

The coastline of Santa Cruz has more than its share of great surf breaks. The water is cold, demanding full wetsuits year-round, and the shoreline is rough and rocky—nothing at all like the flat, sandy beaches of SoCal. But that doesn't deter the hordes of locals who ply the waves every day they can. The surfing culture pervades the town—if you walk the cliff, you'll likely pass the *To Honor Surfing* sculpture. Santa Cruz loves this statue, and it's often dressed up and always gets a costume for Halloween.

The best place for beginners is **Cowell's** (stairs at West Cliff Dr. and Cowell's Beach). The waves rarely get huge here, and they typically provide long, mellow rides, perfect for surfers just getting their balance. Because the Cowell's break is acknowledged as the newbie spot, the often-sizeable crowd tends to be polite to newcomers and visitors.

For more advanced surfers looking for smaller crowds in the water, **Manresa State Beach** (San Andreas Rd., Aptos, 831/761-1795, www.parks.ca.gov) is a nice beach break

south of Santa Cruz. Manresa is several minutes' drive toward Aptos. During summer, it's a great place to surf and then recline on the beach.

Visitors who know their surfing lore will want to surf the more famous spots along the Santa Cruz shore. **Pleasure Point** (between 32nd Ave. and 41st Ave.) encompasses a number of different breaks. You may have heard of The Hook (steps at 41st Ave.), a well-known experienced longboarder's paradise. But don't mistake The Hook for a beginner's break; the locals feel protective of the waves here and aren't always friendly towards inexperienced tourists. The break at 36th and East Cliff (steps at 36th Ave.) can be a better place to go on weekdays—on the weekends, the intense crowding makes catching your own wave a challenge. Up at 30th and East Cliff (steps at 36th Ave.), you'll find shortboarders catching larger, long peeling sets if there is a swell in the water.

The most famous break in all of Santa Cruz can also be the most hostile to newcomers. **Steamer Lane** (West Cliff Dr. between Cowell's and the Santa Cruz Surfing Museum) has a fiercely protective crew of locals. But if you're experienced and there's a swell coming

Natural Bridges State Park

in, Steamer Lane can have some of the best waves on the California coast.

Yes, you can learn to surf in Santa Cruz. Check out either **Club Ed Surf School and Camps** (831/464-0177, www.club-ed.com, beginner group lesson $90 pp, private lessons $120/hour) or the **Richard Schmidt School** (849 Almar Ave., 831/423-0928, www.richardschmidt.com, 2-hour class $90 pp, private lessons $100-150/hour) to sign up for lessons. Who knows, maybe one day the locals will mistake you for one of their own.

Stand-Up Paddleboarding

The latest water-sport craze has definitely hit Santa Cruz. Stand-up paddleboarders vie for waves with surfers at Pleasure Point and can also be found in the Santa Cruz waters with less wave action. **Covewater Paddle Surf** (726 Water St., 831/600-7230, www.covewatersup.com, 2-hour lesson $65) conducts beginner stand-up paddleboarding (SUP) classes in the relatively calm waters of the Santa Cruz Harbor. They also offer rent SUPs (Mon.-Fri. $30, Sat.-Sun. $35).

Hiking and Biking

To walk or bike where the locals do, just head out to **West Cliff Drive.** This winding street with a full-fledged sidewalk trail running its length on the ocean side is the town's favorite walking, dog walking, jogging, skating, scootering, and biking route. Start at Santa Cruz Municipal Wharf and go 2.75 miles to Natural Bridges State Park (the west end of West Cliff). You'll pass the *To Honor Surfing* statue along with flowering ice plant and views of the ocean studded with sea stacks. Bring your camera if you're strolling West Cliff on a clear day—you won't be able to resist taking photos of the sea, cliffs, and sunset. Watch for fellow path-users, as it can get crowded.

To rent a bike for cruising West Cliff Drive, head over to **Pacific Ave Cycles** (320-322 Pacific Ave., 831/471-2453, daily 10am-6pm, hourly bike rental $8-15, daily bike rental $25-45). The small shop with single- and multiple-speed bikes for rent is just a few blocks east of the start of West Cliff Drive.

Spas

It's hard to beat a hot-water soak after a day of surfing Santa Cruz's breaks or walking the city's vibrant downtown area. The **Tea House Spa** (112 Elm St., 831/426-9700, www.teahousespa.com, daily 11am-midnight, spa rooms $12-35/hour, massages $55-140) is a half-block off Pacific Avenue and offers

surfers at Steamer Lane

private hot tubs with views of a bamboo garden. It's not a fancy facility, but the tubs will warm you up and mellow you out.

The **Well Within Spa** (417 Cedar St., 831/458-9355, http://wellwithinspa.com, daily 11am-midnight, spa rooms and outdoor spas $15-44/hour, massages $45-115) has indoor spa rooms and outdoor spas and offers massages.

ACCOMMODATIONS
Under $150

The **Hostelling International Santa Cruz Hostel at the Carmelita Cottages** (321 Main St., 831/423-8304, www.hi-santa-cruz.org, dorm beds $31, private rooms $48-113) offers the area's only budget lodging. These historic cottages are just two blocks from the Santa Cruz Boardwalk. They're clean, cheap, friendly, and close to Cowell's Beach. The big, homey kitchen is open for guest use. There's a nice garden, an outdoor deck, free linens, laundry facilities, and a free Internet kiosk. The private rooms are a deal due to their size and cleanliness. The hostel is closed from 11am to 5pm daily, meaning there is no access to guest rooms or indoor common areas. Guests are allowed to leave their luggage inside or in outdoor lockers.

The hostel has a (basically unenforced) midnight curfew.

The ★ **Seaway Inn** (176 W. Cliff Dr., 831/471-9004, www.seawayinn.com, $139-288) offers a night's stay in a great location across from Cowell's Beach for a moderate price. The rooms are clean but not fancy, and the bathrooms are small. All rooms have a shared patio or deck with chairs. The 18 units in the main building have TVs with DVD players, microwaves, and mini-fridges. Family suites accommodate up to five adults. The complimentary breakfast boasts make-your-own waffles. The friendly staff also operate a nearby building that has five studio apartments, each with a full kitchen. Pets are welcome in all units with a $15 fee for the first night (and another $5 for each additional night).

$150-250

The ★ **West Cliff Inn** (174 W. Cliff Dr., 831/457-2200, www.westcliffinn.com, $210-350) is a gleaming white mansion topping the hill above Cowell's Beach and the Boardwalk. This three-story historic landmark was constructed back in 1877 and was the first of the bluff's Millionaires' Row residences. The nine rooms in the main house have stunning

The Seaway Inn is one of Santa Cruz's best overnight bargains.

white-marble bathrooms, some of which have oversized soaking tubs. The more moderately priced and pet-friendly Little Beach Bungalow is behind the main house. Fill up on a morning breakfast buffet and an afternoon wine and appetizer hour. The inn's veranda and second-floor balcony provide wonderful views.

The four-room **Adobe on Green Street** (103 Green St., 831/469-9866, www.adobeongreen.com, $169-219) offers lovely bed-and-breakfast accommodations within walking distance of downtown. A unifying decorative scheme runs through the rooms—a dark and minimalist Spanish mission style befitting Santa Cruz's history as a mission town. Each room has a queen bed, a private bath (two have whirlpool tubs), a small TV with a DVD player, and lots of other amenities. An expansive continental spread is set out in the dining room each morning 8am-10:30am. Expect yummy local pastries, organic and soy yogurts, hard-boiled eggs, coffee, and juice.

Escape the busy boardwalk and downtown areas for the **Ocean Echo Inn & Beach Cottages** (410 Johans Beach Dr., 831/462-4192, www.oceanecho.com, $155-385), a secluded gem on the East Side. The inn is just 53 footsteps (the innkeepers' count) down to a locals' pocket beach. The inn's water tower, chicken coop, and carriage house have all been converted into cozy cottages. There are 15 units, including the cottages and inn rooms. Eleven of the 15 have full kitchens. There are also multiple decks along with a Ping-Pong table and grills. A modest continental breakfast is put out in the morning.

Over $250

The ★ **Santa Cruz Dream Inn** (175 West Cliff Dr., 831/426-4330, www.dreaminnsantacruz.com, $349-556) is in an unbeatable location. Perched over Cowell's Beach and the Santa Cruz Wharf, the Dream Inn has 165 rooms, all with striking ocean views and either a private balcony or a shared common patio. The retro-chic rooms match perfectly with the vibrant colors of nearby Santa Cruz Boardwalk. On a sunny day, it would be difficult to leave the Dream Inn's sundeck, which is right on Cowell's Beach. Take in the action of surfers, stand-up paddleboarders, and volleyball players from the comforts of the deck's heated swimming pool or large hot tub. Or just relax on a couch or reclining chair while sipping a cocktail from the poolside bar.

FOOD
California Cuisine

The **Shadowbrook Restaurant** (1750 Wharf Rd., Capitola, 831/475-1511, www.shadowbrook-capitola.com, Mon.-Fri. 5pm-8:45pm, Sat. 4:30pm-9:45pm, Sun. 4:30pm-8:45pm, $22-34) is where to celebrate a special occasion. The adventure begins with a cable car ride down to the restaurant, which is perched on a steep slope above Soquel Creek. Entrées include a slow-roasted, bone-in pork prime rib, a one-pound surf-and-turf dish, and several vegetarian options. If you're staying within a three-mile radius of the restaurant, you can be shuttled to the restaurant in a 1950 Dodge (free, but tips are appreciated). Reserve a ride when you make your dinner reservations.

At **Assembly** (1108 Pacific Ave., 831/824-6100, http://assembleforfood.com, Wed.-Thurs. 11:30am-9:30pm, Fri. 11:30am-10:30pm, Sat. 10am-10:30pm, Sun. 10am-9:30pm, $11-19) the focus is on rustic Californian food. This might mean a burger, braised short rib tacos, or a chickpea bowl. Meals start off with tasty house-made bread and salted butter. Assembly also has an inspired beer menu and a wine list that highlights local products. Dine at a private table or at one of the large communal tables under chandeliers made of antlers.

Coffee and Bakeries

For a casual sandwich or pastry, head to **Kelly's French Bakery** (402 Ingalls St., 831/423-9059, www.kellysfrenchbakery.com, Sat.-Thurs. 7am-7pm, Fri. 7am-8pm, $10).

This popular bakery makes its home in an old industrial warehouse-style space, and its domed shape constructed out of corrugated metal looks like anything but a restaurant. It has both indoor and outdoor seating, and serves full breakfasts and luncheon sandwiches.

★ **Verve Coffee Roasters** (1540 Pacific Ave., 831/600-7784, www.vervecoffeeroasters.com, daily 6:30am-9pm) offers a hip, open space with lots of windows at the eastern edge of Pacific Avenue. After ordering your drink at the counter, grab a seat in this frequently crowded coffee shop. They also have locations on the East Side at 846 41st Avenue (831/475-7776, Mon.-Thurs. 6am-7:30pm, Fri. 6am-8:30pm, Sat. 7am-8:30pm, Sun. 7am-7:30pm) and 104 Bronson Street, Suite 19 (831/471-8469, daily 6am-5pm).

Italian

Right on bustling Pacific Avenue, **Kianti's Pizza & Pasta Bar** (1100 Pacific Ave., 831/469-4400, www.kiantis.com, Mon.-Fri. 11am-10pm, Sat.-Sun. 10am-10pm, $13-21) draws in crowds with individual and family-size servings of pastas, pizzas, and salads. Pizza toppings range from traditional Italian ingredients to more creative options (one pie is covered with seasoned beef, lettuce, tomato, avocado, and tortilla chips). People are also drawn in by Kianti's full bar and outdoor seating area right on Pacific Avenue. They also have a location near the Boardwalk called **A Slice of Kianti's** (46 Front St., 831/469-4421, summer daily 11am-7pm, winter Fri.-Sun. 11am-5pm).

Japanese

South of downtown, **Akira** (1222 Soquel Ave., 831/600-7093, http://akirasantacruz.com, daily 11am-11pm, $10-17) is a modern sushi bar with interesting creations. Some of the rolls here employ unconventional ingredients like skirt steak and spicy truffled shoestring yams. There are also more traditional rolls served up at the sushi bar or your table. Skateboard art decorates a portion of the

restaurant. Akira's happy hour (daily 4pm-6pm and 9:30pm-10:30pm) offers appetizers to go with your beer, sake, or wine.

Mexican

Santa Cruz has some great taquerias, but **Tacos Moreno** (1053 Water St., 831/429-6095, www.tacosmoreno.com, daily 11am-8pm, $6-11) may be the best, as evidenced by the locals lined up outside the nondescript eatery during lunch. Tacos Moreno serves just the basics: burritos, tacos, quesadillas, and beverages. The standout item is the al pastor burrito supreme with crispy barbecued pork, cheese, sour cream, and guacamole. They also have a second location near the Boardwalk (303 Beach St., 831/427-2200, daily 11am-8pm).

El Palomar (1336 Pacific Ave., 831/425-7575, http://elpalomarsantacruz.com, Mon.-Fri. 11am-3pm and 5pm-10pm, Sat.-Sun. 10am-3pm and 5pm-10pm, $13-27) is in the dining room of an old luxury hotel. Enjoy shrimp enchiladas or chicken mole while a roving mariachi band plays. Jose's Special Appetizer ($17) can be a light meal for two, though don't forget to try the tasty guacamole. Their informal taco bar is great for a quick bite and drink. El Palomar also has a happy hour (Mon.-Fri. 3pm-6pm).

Sandwiches

Just feet from the Santa Cruz Boardwalk is a casual eatery with a simple menu that utilizes locally sourced, tasty goodness: ★ **The Picnic Basket** (125 Beach St., 831/427-9946, http://thepicnicbasketsc.com, winter Thurs.-Mon. 7am-4pm, summer daily 7am-9pm, $3-9). Its attention to detail shines through even on a simple turkey, cheese, and avocado sandwich. Other options include breakfast items, salads, mac and cheese, and local beer and wine. Dine inside or out front, where you can take in the sounds of the bustling boardwalk.

South American

Cafe Brasil (1410 Mission St., 831/429-1855, www.cafebrasil.us, daily 8am-3pm, $6-11) serves up the Brazilian fare its name promises. Painted jungle green with bright yellow and blue trim, you can't miss this totally Santa Cruz breakfast and lunch joint. In the morning, the fare runs to omelets and Brazilian specialties, including a dish with two eggs topping a steak. Lunch includes pressed sandwiches, meat and tofu dishes, and Brazilian house specials.

INFORMATION AND SERVICES

While it can be fun to explore Santa Cruz just by using your innate sense of direction and eye for the bizarre, those who want a bit more structure to their travels can hit the **Santa Cruz County Visitors Center** (303 Water St., Ste. 100, 800/833-3494, www.santacruz. org, Mon.-Fri. 9am-noon and 1pm-4pm, Sat.-Sun. 11am-3pm) for maps, advice, and information. Or stop by the **Downtown Information Kiosk** (1130 Pacific Ave., K2, www.downtownsantacruz.com, May-Oct. Sun.-Thurs. 11am-6pm, Fri.-Sat. 11am-8pm, Nov.-April Sun.-Thurs. 11am-5pm, Fri.-Sat. 11am-7pm) on Pacific Avenue.

Medical treatment is available at **Dominican Hospital** (1555 Soquel Ave., 831/462-7700, www.dominicanhospital.org).

TRANSPORTATION

Visitors planning to drive or bike around Santa Cruz should get themselves a good map, either before they arrive or at the visitors center in town. Navigating the winding, occasionally broken-up streets of this oddly shaped town isn't for the faint of heart. Highway 1, which becomes Mission Street on the West Side, acts as the main artery through Santa Cruz and down to Capitola, Soquel, Aptos, and coastal points farther south. You'll find that Highway 1 at the interchange to Highway 17, and sometimes several miles to the south, is a parking lot most of the time. No, you probably haven't come upon a major accident or a special event. It's just like that all the time, and will be until the construction widening the highway is complete.

Car

If you're driving to Santa Cruz from Silicon Valley, you've got two choices of roads. Most drivers take fast, dangerous Highway 17. This narrow road doesn't have any switchbacks and is the main truck route "over the hill." Most locals take this 50-mile-per-hour corridor fast—probably faster than they should. Each year, several people die in accidents on

a sandwich from The Picnic Basket

Highway 17. So if you're new to the road, keep to the right and take it slow, no matter what the traffic to the left of you is doing. Check traffic reports before you head out; Highway 17 is known to be one of the worst commuting roads in all of the Bay Area, and the weekend beach traffic in the summer jams up fast in both directions.

For a more leisurely drive, opt for two-lane Highway 9. The tight curves and endless switchbacks will keep you at a reasonable speed; use the turnouts to let the locals pass, please. On Highway 9, your biggest obstacles tend to be groups of bicyclists and motorcyclists, both of whom adore the slopes and curves of this technical driving road. The good news is that you'll get an up-close-and-personal view of the gorgeously forested Santa Cruz Mountains, complete with views of the valley to the north and ocean vistas to the south.

Parking

Parking in Santa Cruz can be its own special sort of horror. Downtown, head straight for the parking structures one block off of Pacific Avenue on either side. They're much easier to deal with than trying to find street parking. The same goes for the beach and Boardwalk areas. At the Boardwalk, just pay the fee to park in the big parking lot adjacent to the attractions. You'll save an hour and a possible car break-in or theft trying to find street parking in the sketchy neighborhoods that surround the Boardwalk.

Bus

In town, the buses are run by the **Santa Cruz Metro** (831/425-8600 www.scmtd.com, adults $2 per ride, passes available). With routes running all around Santa Cruz County, you can probably find a way to get nearly anywhere you'd want to go on the Metro.

Moss Landing

At the halfway point of Monterey Bay, 25 miles south of Santa Cruz and 15 miles north of Monterey, Moss Landing is a picturesque, working fishing village—if you can ignore the rising smokestacks of the towering Moss Landing Power Plant. The main drag, Moss Landing Road, has a scattering of antique stores and art galleries, and Moss Landing Harbor is home to a fleet of fishing vessels. To the south of the harbor's mouth, Salinas River State Beach offers miles of wild, undeveloped shoreline. North of the inlet, Zmudowski State Beach is popular with local surfers during the winter months. Offshore, the Monterey Submarine Canyon is one of North America's largest submarine canyons. It's the reason that the Moss Landing Marine Laboratories and Monterey Bay Aquarium Research Institute have local addresses. The **Moss Landing Chamber of Commerce** website (www.mosslandingchamber.com) offers visitor information.

SIGHTS
★ Elkhorn Slough

Elkhorn Slough is the second-largest section of tidal salt marsh in California after San Francisco Bay. The estuary hosts an amazing amount of wildlife that includes marine mammals and over 340 bird species, which makes it one of the state's best birding spots. The best way to explore the slough is by kayak, where you can view rafts of lounging sea otters and a barking rookery of California sea lions from water level. In Moss Landing's North Harbor, which connects to the slough, **Monterey Bay Kayaks** (2390 Hwy. 1, 831/373-5357, www.montereybaykayaks.com, Mar.-late May daily 8:30am-6pm, late May-early Sept. daily 8:30am-7pm, early Sept.-Mar. daily 8:30am-5pm, guided tours $60-85, kayak rental $30-35/day, SUP rental $30/two hours) has kayak rentals as well as a range of guided tours from a 2.5-hour paddle up the slough to monthly full-moon tours. While paddling a kayak is the recommended way to view the slough, the **Elkhorn Slough Safari** (Moss Landing Harbor, Dock A, 831/633-5555, www.elkhorn-slough.com, adults $38, children $28, seniors $35) is a possibility for those who wish to take a 1.5- to 2-hour tour of the estuary by boat. Check the website for current tour times.

ENTERTAINMENT AND EVENTS
Bars
The **Moss Landing Inn** (7902 Hwy. 1, 831/633-9803, http://wenchilada.com, daily noon-close) is not a place to spend the night, but rather a dive bar where you can spend a few hours getting acquainted with the local characters. It's connected to The Whole Enchilada restaurant and offers live music on weekends.

Festivals and Events
On the last Sunday of July, Moss Landing is flooded with antiques enthusiasts for the annual **Moss Landing Antique Street Fair** (831/633-4501, www.mosslandingchamber.com). The giant outdoor antique market has over 200 booths selling collectibles, while other booths nearby serve local foods like fried fish and artichokes.

SHOPPING
Moss Landing it known for antique stores like the **Cottage By the Sea** (7981 E. Moss Landing Rd., 831/633-9909, Wed.-Mon. 11am-5pm) and **Hamlin Antiques** (8071 Moss Landing Rd., 831/633-3664, www.hauteenchilada.com, Thurs.-Tues. noon-5pm). It's also home to a growing arts community. Behind the Haute Enchilada Café, the **Haute Enchilada Gallery** (7902 Moss Landing Rd., 831/633-3743, www.hauteenchilada.com, daily 11am-5pm) has multiple rooms filled with sculptures, watercolors, woodworks, and ceramic items. Housed in the former post office, the aptly named **Old Post Office Gallery** (7981 Moss Landing Rd., 831/632-0488, Tues.-Sun. 11am-5pm) features visual arts including lots of landscape paintings.

Driftwood (8071-B Moss Landing Rd., 831/632-2800, www.driftwoodstore.com, Sun.-Thurs. noon-5pm, Fri.-Sat. 11am-6pm) bills itself as an "artisan gift boutique." Expect hipster-approved jewelry, home furnishings, and candles.

SPORTS AND RECREATION
Beaches
Just north of Moss Landing's harbor, **Moss Landing State Beach** (Jetty Rd., 831/649-2836, www.parks.ca.gov) and **Zmudowski State Beach** (20 miles north of Monterey on Hwy. 1, 831/649-2836, www.parks.ca.gov) stretch for miles. They're mostly enjoyed by locals who fish, surf, or ride horses on the beach. To get to the beaches from Highway 1, take Struve Road and turn onto Giberson Road.

Just south of Moss Landing is the **Salinas River State Beach** (Potrero Rd., 831/649-2836, www.parks.ca.gov), which doesn't get as many visitors as other area beaches. Expect some serenity among a few horseback riders or anglers.

Whale-Watching
For a glimpse of marine mammals in the wild, from gray whales to orcas, catch a ride with **Sanctuary Cruises** (7881 Sandholt Rd., 831/917-1042, www.sanctuarycruises.com, adults $50, children 12 and under $40). Running on biodiesel, the 43-foot ocean vessel *Sanctuary* takes passengers out daily for 4-5-hour cruises. **Blue Ocean Whale Watch** (7881 Sandholt Rd., 877/229-9142, www.blue-oceanwhalewatch.com, $50) also heads out into the bay for four-hour whale-watching expeditions.

Fishing
If you're interested in catching your own seafood, consider heading out with **Westwind Charter Sport Fishing & Excursions** (7881 Sandholt Rd., 831/392-7867, https://westwind-charter.com, $115 pp). Depending on what's in season, you can catch salmon, rock cod, halibut, or Dungeness crab.

ACCOMMODATIONS AND CAMPING

With its nautical decor, the ★ **Captain's Inn** (8122 Moss Landing Rd., 831/633-5550, www.captainsinn.com, $199-265) is the perfect place to spend an evening in the fishing village. The inn offers rooms in two buildings: a historic structure that was once the site of the Pacific Coast Steamship Company and the Boathouse, where every room has a superb view of the nearby tidal marsh. The Boathouse rooms are recommended for animal lovers and nautical enthusiasts. Wildlife-watchers might be able to catch a glimpse of marine mammals or birds in the nearby tidal marsh, while maritime fans will love the bed sets crafted out of boat parts. Wake up to a home-cooked breakfast that can be taken to-go.

Seeking solitude and miles of nearly empty coastline? The **Monterey Dunes Company** (407 Moss Landing Rd., 831/633-4883 or 800/553-8637, www.montereydunes.com, $345-690) rents 2-4-bedroom homes on the beach south of Moss Landing. Guests also have access to the development's tennis courts, swimming pool, saunas, and hot tub.

The **Moss Landing KOA Express** (7905 Sandholt Rd., 831/633-6800 or 800/562-3390, $68-75) has almost 50 RV sites right in the Moss Landing Harbor area.

FOOD

As a harbor town, Moss Landing is probably best known for its seafood restaurants. The most popular is ★ **Phil's Fish Market** (7600 Sandholt Rd., 831/633-2152, www.philsfishmarket.com, Sun.-Thurs. 10am-8pm, Fri.-Sat. 10am-9pm, $9-23), which is known for its cioppino—a hearty Italian American seafood stew that includes clams, mussels, fish, Dungeness crab, prawns, and scallops. A heaping bowl comes with salad and garlic bread. Another worthwhile order is the blackened sea scallops cooked with lemon butter and capers. This informal market/eatery has a bluegrass band playing on some nights.

The Whole Enchilada (7902 Hwy. 1, 831/633-3038, http://wenchilada.com, daily 11:30am-9pm, $10-24) does seafood with a Mexican slant. Dine on seafood enchiladas, Mexican-style cioppino, or chile relleno stuffed with crab, shrimp, and cheese in the brightly colored dining room or on the outdoor patio.

Part art gallery, part eatery, fanciful **Haute Enchilada Café & Galleries** (7902 Moss Landing Rd., 831/633-5843, www.hauteenchilada.com, Mon.-Thurs. 11am-9pm, Fri.-Sun. 9am-9pm, $17-26) is bursting with color. The menu includes items such as Peruvian empanadas and skirt steaks in Oaxacan black bean sauce.

Monterey

The best days in Monterey are picture-perfect: It's no wonder that so many artists have been inspired to paint this land- and seascape. The blue of the ocean calls you to wander the twisting coastline, taking in the boats, kayaks, and otters playing in the bay.

Monterey has roots as a fishing town. Native Americans were the first to ply the bay's waters, and fishing became an economic driver with the arrival of European settlers in the 19th century. Author John Steinbeck immortalized this unglamorous industry in his novel *Cannery Row*. Monterey's blue-collar past is still evident in its architecture, even though the cannery workers have been replaced by visiting tourists.

Monterey is the "big city" on the well-populated southern tip of the wide-mouthed bay. There are actually two main sections of Monterey: the old downtown area and "New Monterey," which includes Cannery Row and the Monterey Aquarium. The old downtown is situated around Alvarado Street and includes the historic adobes that make up Monterey

Cannery Row

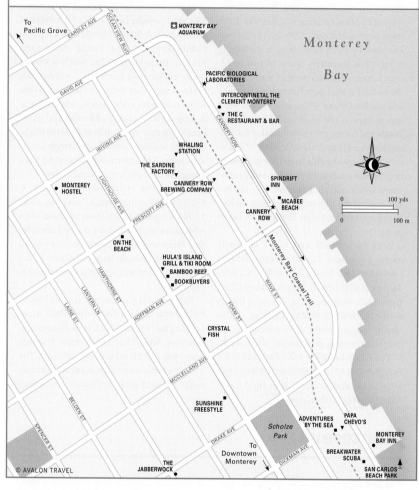

To Pacific Grove

EARDLEY AVE
OCEAN VIEW BLVD
DAVID AVE
IRVING AVE
LIGHTHOUSE AVE
PRESCOTT AVE
HAWTHORNE ST
LANTERN LN
LANE ST
BELDEN ST
SPENCER ST
HOFFMAN AVE
MCCLELLAND AVE
DRAKE AVE
DICKMAN AVE
FOAM ST
WAVE ST
CANNERY ROW

Monterey Bay

Monterey Bay Coastal Trail

MONTEREY BAY AQUARIUM

PACIFIC BIOLOGICAL LABORATORIES

INTERCONTINETAL THE CLEMENT MONTEREY

THE C RESTAURANT & BAR

WHALING STATION

THE SARDINE FACTORY

CANNERY ROW BREWING COMPANY

MONTEREY HOSTEL

SPINDRIFT INN

MCABEE BEACH

CANNERY ROW

ON THE BEACH

HULA'S ISLAND GRILL & TIKI ROOM

BAMBOO REEF

BOOKBUYERS

CRYSTAL FISH

SUNSHINE FREESTYLE

Scholze Park

To Downtown Monterey

ADVENTURES BY THE SEA

PAPA CHEVO'S

MONTEREY BAY INN

BREAKWATER SCUBA

SAN CARLOS BEACH PARK

THE JABBERWOCK

© AVALON TRAVEL

0   100 yds
0   100 m

State Historic Park. New Monterey bustles with tourists during the summer. The six blocks of Cannery Row retain much of the sardine-cannery look described in Steinbeck's novel, though the buildings have been spruced up a bit (and in some cases, completely rebuilt) since the 1940s. The canneries are long gone, and today Cannery Row is packed with businesses, including the must-see Monterey Bay Aquarium, seafood restaurants, shops, galleries, and wine-tasting rooms. The aquarium is constantly packed with visitors, especially on summer weekends. One way to get from one section to the other is to walk the Monterey Bay Coastal Recreation Trail, a paved path that runs right along a stretch of coastline.

SIGHTS
Cannery Row

Cannery Row (www.canneryrow.com) did once look and feel as John Steinbeck described it in his famed novel of the same name. In the

1930s and 1940s, fishing boats docked here and offloaded their catches straight into the huge, warehouse-like cannery buildings. Low-wage workers processed the fish and put it into cans, ready to ship across the country and around the world. But overfishing took its toll, and by the late 1950s Cannery Row was deserted; some buildings actually fell into the ocean.

A slow renaissance began in the 1960s, driven by new interest in preserving the historic integrity of the area, as well as a few savvy entrepreneurs who understood the value of beachfront property. Today, what was once a workingman's wharf is now an enclave of boutique hotels, big seafood restaurants, and souvenir stores selling T-shirts adorned with sea otters. Cannery Row is anchored at one end by the aquarium and runs for several blocks that include a beach; it then leads into the Monterey Harbor area.

★ Monterey Bay Aquarium

One of the first aquariums of its kind in the country, the **Monterey Bay Aquarium** (886 Cannery Row, 831/648-4800, www.montereybayaquarium.org, daily 9:30am-6pm, adults $40, students and seniors $35, children $25) is still unique in many ways. From the very beginning, the aquarium's mission has been conservation, and they're not shy about it. Many of the animals in the aquarium's tanks were rescued, and those that survive may eventually be returned to the wild. All the exhibits you'll see in this mammoth complex contain only local sea life.

The aquarium displays a dazzling array of species. When you come to visit, a good first step is to look up the feeding schedules for the tanks you're most interested in. The critters always put on the best show at feeding time, and it's smart to show up several minutes in advance of feeding to get a good spot near the glass. First-class exhibits include the Kelp Forest, which mimics the environment just outside; the Open Sea exhibit, with its deep-water tank that's home to giant bluefin tuna and hammerhead sharks; Wild About Otters, which gives an up-close view of rescued otters; and the Jellies Experience, which illuminates the delicate creatures.

The aquarium is a wildly popular weekend destination. Especially in the summer, the crowds can be forbidding. Weekdays can be less crushing (though you'll run into school groups during much of the year), and the off-season is almost always a better time to visit. Almost all exhibits at the aquarium are wheelchair-accessible.

Monterey Bay Aquarium

Downtown Monterey

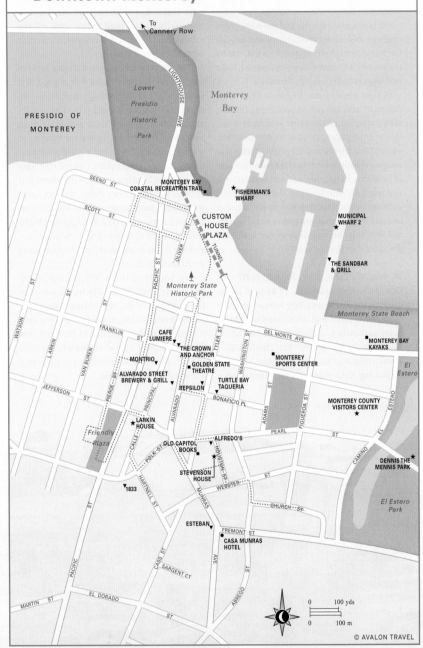

To Cannery Row

LIGHTHOUSE AVE

Monterey Bay

PRESIDIO OF MONTEREY

Lower Presidio Historic Park

SEENO ST

SCOTT ST

MONTEREY BAY COASTAL RECREATION TRAIL

★ FISHERMAN'S WHARF

CUSTOM HOUSE PLAZA

MUNICIPAL WHARF 2 ★

THE SANDBAR & GRILL ▼

Monterey State Historic Park

TUNNEL

OLIVER ST

PACIFIC ST

Monterey State Beach

WATSON ST

LARKIN ST

ST

FRANKLIN ST

VAN BUREN ST

DEL MONTE AVE

CAFE LUMIERE

THE CROWN AND ANCHOR

MONTEREY BAY KAYAKS ■

JEFFERSON ST

MONTRIO

ALVARADO STREET BREWERY & GRILL

REPSILON

GOLDEN STATE THEATRE

TURTLE BAY TAQUERIA

BONAFICIO PL

TYLER ST

WASHINGTON ST

MONTEREY SPORTS CENTER ■

El Estero

PIERCE ST

PRINCIPAL ST

ALVARADO ST

ADAMS ST

FIGUEROA ST

MONTEREY COUNTY VISITORS CENTER ★

EL ESTERO

CAMINO

★ LARKIN HOUSE

Friendly Plaza

CALLE PRINCIPAL

POLK ST

OLD CAPITOL BOOKS ■

ALFREDO'S

PEARL ST

ST

STEVENSON HOUSE

HOUSTON ST

DENNIS THE MENNIS PARK ★

HARTNELL ST

ST

MUNRAS AVE

WEBSTER ST

ST

El Estero Park

▼ 1833

CHURCH ST

ESTEBAN ▼

FREMONT ST

CASA MUNRAS HOTEL

CASS ST

PACIFIC ST

SARGENT CT

ABREGO ST

MARTIN ST

EL DORADO ST

0   100 yds
0   100 m

© AVALON TRAVEL

Steinbeck's Birthplace

John Ernst Steinbeck was born in Salinas, California, in 1902 and grew up in its tiny, isolated agricultural community. He somehow managed to escape life as a farmer, a sardine fisherman, or a fish canner, and ended up living the glamorous life of a writer for his too-short 66 years.

Steinbeck's experiences in the Salinas Valley farming community and in the fishing town of Monterey informed many of his novels. The best known of these is *Cannery Row,* but *Tortilla Flat* is also set in working-class Monterey (though no one knows exactly where the fictional "Tortilla Flat" neighborhood was supposed to be). The Pulitzer Prize-winning novel *The Grapes of Wrath* takes more of its inspiration from the Salinas Valley. Steinbeck used the valley as a model for farming in the Dust Bowl during the Great Depression.

Steinbeck was fascinated by the plight of workingmen and women; his novels and stories generally depict ordinary folks going through tough and terrible times. Steinbeck lived and worked through the Great Depression, thus it's not surprising that many of his stories do *not* feature happy Hollywood endings. Steinbeck was a realist in almost all of his novels, portraying the good, the bad, and the ugly of human life and society. His work gained almost immediate respect: In addition to his Pulitzer, Steinbeck also won the Nobel Prize for Literature in 1962. Almost every American high school student from the 1950s onward has read at least one of Steinbeck's novels or short stories; his body of work forms part of the enduring American literary canon.

As the birthplace of California's most illustrious literary son in the 20th century, Salinas became equally famous for spawning the author and inspiring his work. You'll find a variety of Steinbeck maps online (www.mtycounty.com) that offer self-guided tours of the regions made famous by his various novels. Poor Steinbeck's name is taken in vain all over now-commercial Cannery Row, where even the cheesy wax museum tries to draw customers in by claiming kinship with the legendary author. More serious scholars of Steinbeck prefer the **National Steinbeck Center** (1 Main St., Salinas, 831/796-3833, www.steinbeck.org, daily 10am-5pm, $11) and the **Steinbeck House** (132 Central Ave., Salinas, 831/424-2735, www.steinbeckhouse.com, summer tours 1pm-3pm), both in the still-agricultural town of Salinas. And if the museums aren't enough, plan to be in Monterey County in early August for the annual **Steinbeck Festival** (www.steinbeck. org), a big shindig put on by the Steinbeck Center that celebrates the great man's life and works in fine style.

Monterey State Historic Park

Monterey State Historic Park (831/649-7118, www.parks.ca.gov, gardens May-Sept. daily 9am-5pm, Oct.-Apr. daily 10am-4pm, free) pays homage to the long and colorful history of the city of Monterey. This busy port town acted as the capital of California when it was under Spanish rule, and then later when it became part of the United States. Today, this park provides a peek into Monterey as it was in the middle of the 19th century when it was a busy place filled with dockworkers, fishermen, bureaucrats, and soldiers. And yet it blends into the modern town of Monterey as well, and modern stores, galleries, and restaurants sit next to adobe structures dating from the 1800s.

It's tough to see everything in just one visit to Old Monterey. If you only get to one spot, make it the **Custom House** (20 Custom House Plaza, Fri.-Mon. and holidays 10am-4pm, adults $3, children under 12 free). Built in 1827, it's California State Historic Landmark No. 1 and the oldest government building still standing in the state. Spend some time wandering the adobe building, checking out the artifacts on display, or even just looking out the upstairs window towards the sea. Also on the plaza is the **Pacific House Museum** (Fri.-Mon. and holidays 10am-4pm, adults $3, children under 12 free). The first floor shows a range of Monterey's history from the Native Californians to the American Period, while the second floor has a plethora of Native American artifacts.

The other buildings that compose the park were built mostly with adobe and/or brick between 1834 and 1847. These include the **Casa del Oro** (210 Oliver St., 831/649-3364, Thurs.-Sun. 11am-3pm); the **Cooper-Molera Adobe** (525 Polk St.); the **First Brick House** (Fri.-Mon. and holidays 10am-4pm, free); the **Larkin House** (464 Calle Principal, tours Fri. and Sun. 12:30pm, Sat. noon, $5); the **Old Whaling Station** (not open to public); the **Sherman Quarters** (not open to public); and the **Stevenson House** (530 Houston St., Sat. 1pm-4pm, free), once a temporary residence of Robert Louis Stevenson.

A great introduction to the park is via a **guided tour** (meet at the Pacific House, Fri.-Mon. and holidays 10:30am, 12:30pm, and 2pm, $5). Approximately an hour long, the short walk begins at the Pacific House and includes the Custom House, the First Brick House, the Old Whaling Station with its whalebone sidewalk out front, and California's First Theatre. Visitors can also learn about the historic buildings by taking a cell phone tour, where a two-minute run-down on each building is accessible by dialing 831/998-9458 and entering the code listed outside the structure.

Fisherman's Wharf

Fisherman's Wharf (1 Old Fisherman's Wharf, www.montereywharf.com, daily, hours vary) resembles a smaller version of San Francisco's popular tourist attraction of the same name. Where tons of sardines were once shipped out of Monterey Harbor, you'll now find a collection of seafood restaurants, touristy gift shops, and whale-watching boats. (Most of the wharf's seafood restaurants offer free shots of their competing clam chowders to those walking by. It might be enough to stave off your hunger until the next meal.) To dive deeper into Monterey's fishing history, consider taking a **walking tour** (831/521-3394, www.montereywaterfrontcannery-rowtours.com, first Sat. of the month, 10am, adults $20, children 10-15 $15) of the wharf with local historian Tim Thomas. Tours start at the base of Old Fisherman's Wharf, by Harbor House Gifts.

The **Coast Guard Pier** is a 1,700-foot-long breakwater on the north end of the harbor. It is one of Monterey's best wildlife-viewing areas, and it's a guarantee that you'll be able to see some sea lions and harbor seals if you walk out on the structure.

Municipal Wharf II is on the eastern edge of the harbor. It still has working fishing

Monterey State Historic Park's Larkin House

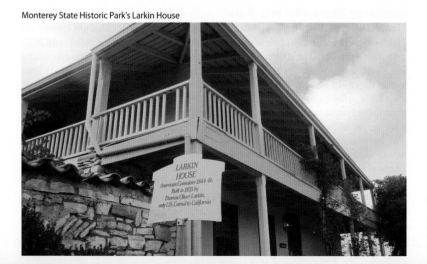

LARKIN
HOUSE
American Consulate 1844-46
Built in 1835 by
Thomas Oliver Larkin,
only U.S. Consul to California

operations along with a few wholesale fish companies, a couple of restaurants, an abalone farm underneath its deck, and fine views of the harbor and nearby Del Monte Beach.

Dennis the Menace Park

The brainchild of Hank Ketcham, the creator of the *Dennis the Menace* comic strip, **Dennis the Menace Park** (777 Pearl St., 831/646-3860, 10am-dusk daily) opened in 1956. Ketcham was heavily involved in the design process; he moved to the area after World War II, and lived here until his death in 2001. There's a nine-foot climbing wall, a suspension bridge, curvy slides, brightly colored jungle gyms, and a (fenced-in, nonworking) locomotive, as well as a bronze sculpture of the little menace near the entrance.

ENTERTAINMENT AND EVENTS
Live Music

Downtown Monterey's historic **Golden State Theatre** (417 Alvarado St., 831/649-1070, www.goldenstatetheatre.com) hosts live music, a speaker series, and dance, comedy, and theater productions. The theater dates back to 1926 and was designed to look like a Moorish castle. Performers in its ornate main room have included music legends like Patti Smith, Willie Nelson, and Darlene Love. The current owners also run the Fox Theatre in Redwood City.

Bars and Clubs

Descending down into **The Crown & Anchor** (150 W. Franklin St., 831/649-6496, www.crownandanchor.net, daily 11am-1:30am) feels a bit like entering a ship's hold. Along with the maritime theme, The Crown & Anchor serves up 20 international beers on tap. Sip indoors or on the popular outdoor patio. They also have good pub fare, including cottage pies and curries; the curry fries are a local favorite. Lively but not a pickup joint, The Crown & Anchor is a go-to place for locals, tourists, and even celebrities like Jon Hamm, who passed several nights here in 2014 during the filming of *Mad Men* in nearby Big Sur.

A good bet for a beer or cocktail is the **Cannery Row Brewing Company** (95 Prescott Ave., 831/643-2722, www.canneryrowbrewingcompany.com, Sun.-Thurs. 11:30am-midnight, Fri.-Sat. 11:30am-2am), just a block up from bustling Cannery Row. They pour 73 beers on tap, ranging from hefeweizens to barley wine. Sip your suds in the

Cannery Row Brewing Company

Sea Sanctuary

Monterey Bay is in a federally protected marine area known as the **Monterey Bay National Marine Sanctuary** (MBNMS). Designated a sanctuary in 1992, the protected waters stretch far past the confines of Monterey Bay to a northern boundary seven miles north of the Golden Gate Bridge and a southern boundary at Cambria in San Luis Obispo. The sanctuary was created for resource protection, education, public use, and research. The MBNMS is the reason so many marine research facilities including the Long Marine Laboratory, the Monterey Bay Marine Laboratory, and the Moss Landing Marine Laboratories dot the Monterey Bay shoreline.

Among the many marine treasures of the MBNMS is the Monterey Bay Submarine Canyon, which is right offshore of the fishing village of Moss Landing. The canyon is similar in size to the Grand Canyon and has a rim-to-floor depth of 5,577 feet. In 2009, the MBNMS expanded to include another fascinating underwater geographical feature: the Davidson Seamount. Located 80 miles southwest of Monterey, the undersea mountain rises an impressive 7,480 feet, yet its summit is still 4,101 feet below the ocean's surface.

large dining room, at the bar, or outside on the back deck by a fire pit. Expect good happy hour deals on food and beer 3pm-6pm. The occasional band or DJ performs in a little alcove facing the bar on some evenings.

A distinct stone building just a couple of blocks off Alvarado Street, **Alfredo's** (266 Pearl St., 831/375-0655, Sun.-Thurs. 10am-midnight, Fri.-Sat. 10am-2am, cash only) is a cozy dive bar for the downtown Monterey crowd. This comfortable drinking establishment has dim lighting, a gas fireplace, cheap drinks, and a good jukebox. It's a fine place for a drink if you actually want to hear what your companion is saying.

Festivals and Events

The Monterey region hosts numerous festivals and special events each year. Whether your pleasure is fine food or funky music, you'll probably be able to plan a trip around some sort of multiday festival.

In keeping with the Central Coast's obsession with food and wine, the annual **Monterey Wine Festival** (Custom House Plaza, 800/422-0251, www.montereywine.com, June) celebrates wine with a generous helping of food on the side. The wine festival is also incongruously home to the West Coast Chowder Competition. This festival is the perfect introduction to Monterey and Carmel wineries, many of which have not yet hit the "big time" in major wine magazines. It is set outdoors in Monterey's Custom House Plaza.

One of the biggest music festivals in California is the **Monterey Jazz Festival** (Monterey County Fairgrounds, 2004 Fairground Rd., 831/373-3366, www.montereyjazzfestival.org, Sept.). As the site of the longest-running jazz festival on earth, Monterey attracts 500 artists from around the world to play on the fest's eight stages. Held each September at the Monterey County Fairgrounds, this long weekend of amazing music can leave you happy for the whole year. Recent acts to grace the Monterey Jazz Festival's stages include Herbie Hancock, Booker T. Jones, and The Roots.

SPORTS AND RECREATION

Monterey Bay is the premier Northern California locale for a number of water sports, especially scuba diving.

★ Scuba Diving, Kayaking, and Stand-Up Paddleboarding

SCUBA DIVING

Any native Northern Californian knows that there's only one really great place in the region to get certified in scuba diving: Monterey Bay.

Even if you go to a dive school up in the Bay Area, they'll take you down to Monterey for your open-water dive. Accordingly, dozens of dive schools cluster in and around the city of Monterey.

A locals' favorite, **Bamboo Reef** (614 Lighthouse Ave., 831/372-1685, www.bambooreef.com, Mon.-Fri. 9am-6pm, Sat.-Sun. 7am-6pm) offers scuba lessons and rents equipment just a few blocks from popular dive spots, including Breakwater Cove. The aquamarine storefront on Lighthouse Avenue has been helping people get underwater since 1980.

Another of the many dive shop options is the **Aquarius Dive Shop** (2040 Del Monte Ave., 831/375-1933, www.aquariusdivers.com, Mon.-Fri. 9am-6pm, Sat.-Sun. 7am-6pm). Aquarius offers everything you need to go diving in Monterey Bay, including air and nitrox fills, equipment rental, certification courses, and help booking a trip on a local dive boat. Aquarius works with five boats to create great trips for divers of all interests and ability levels. Call 831/657-1020 for local dive conditions.

KAYAKING AND STAND-UP PADDLEBOARDING

Monterey's coastline is as scenic a spot as any to learn to stand-up paddleboard (SUP). Whether you want to try paddling for the first time or you're an expert who hasn't brought your own gear out to California, you'll find a local outfit ready and willing to hook you up.

The coast off Monterey is an ideal place for paddling. It is less exposed than other spots along the California coast. If the swells are big, duck into Monterey Harbor, where you can paddle past moored boats and harbor seal colonies. When the surf is manageable, the paddle from San Carlos Beach to the aquarium and back (1.16 miles round-trip) pretty much guarantees that you will see an otter or a harbor seal in the water near you. The Monterey Bay National Marine Sanctuary regulations require all paddlers to stay 150 feet from all sea otters, sea lions, and harbor seals.

Adventures by the Sea (299 Cannery Row, 831/372-1807, www.adventuresbythesea.com, summer daily 9am-8pm, winter daily 9am-6pm, kayak tours $60-85 pp, kayak rentals $30/day, SUP rentals $50/day) rents kayaks by the day to let you choose your own route around the magnificent Monterey Bay kelp forest. Adventures offers tours from Cannery Row. Your guide can tell you all about the wildlife you're seeing: harbor seals, sea otters, pelicans, gulls, and maybe even a whale in the winter. The tour lasts about 2.5 hours and the tandem sit-on-top kayaks make it a great experience for school-age children. They also run a tour of Stillwater Cove at Pebble Beach. Reservations are recommended for all tours, but during the summer the Cannery Row tour leaves regularly at 10am and 2pm, so you can stop by and see if there's a spot available. They have several other locations in Monterey (685 Cannery Row and 210 Alvarado St.).

Rent a kayak or SUP from **Monterey Bay Kayaks** (693 Del Monte Ave., 831/373-5357, www.montereybaykayaks.com, Mar.-late May 8:30am-6pm, late May-early Sept. daily 8:30am-7pm, early Sept.-Mar. daily 8:30am-5pm, kayak tours $55-150, kayak rentals $30-45 pp, SUP rentals $30/two hours) and paddle into the bay from the beach just south of the Municipal Wharf or paddle out with an experienced guide. The tours include kayak fishing, Sunday sunrise excursions, and a Point Lobos paddle. There's also a branch in Moss Landing on the Elkhorn Slough.

Fishing and Whale-Watching

Whales pass quite near the shores of Monterey year-round. While you can sometimes even see them from the beaches, any number of boats can take you out for a closer look at the great beasts as they travel along their own special routes north and south. The area hosts many humpbacks, blue whales, and gray whales, plus the occasional killer whale, minke whale, fin whale, and pod of dolphins. Bring your own binoculars for a better view, but the experienced boat captains will do all they can to get you as close as possible to the whales and dolphins. Most tours last 2-3 hours and leave from Fisherman's Wharf, which is easy to get to and has ample parking. If you prefer not to rise with the sun, pick a tour that leaves in the afternoon.

Monterey Bay Whale Watch (84 Fisherman's Wharf, 831/375-4658, www. montereybaywhalewatch.com, adults $40-145, children 4-12 $29-39, children 3 and under $15) leaves from an easy-to-find red building on Fisherman's Wharf and runs tours in every season. You must make a reservation in advance, even for regularly scheduled tours. Afternoon tours are available. **Princess Monterey Whale Watching** (96 Fisherman's Wharf, 831/372-2203, www.montereywhalewatching.com, $45 pp) prides itself on its knowledgeable guides/marine biologists and its comfortable, spacious cruising vessels. The *Princess Monterey* offers morning and afternoon tours, and you can buy tickets online or by phone.

Fast Raft Ocean Safaris (Monterey Harbor and Moss Landing Harbor, 800/979-3370, www.fastraft.com, $140/pp) offers an intimate way to see the Monterey coastline and the wildlife within Monterey Bay. The "fast raft" is a 33-foot-long inflatable boat with a rigid hull that accommodates just six

passengers. The outfit does whale-watching trips out of Moss Landing and coastal safaris that depart from Monterey and head south to Pebble Beach's Stillwater Cove and Point Lobos when the weather cooperates. It's worth noting that the fast raft does not have a restroom, and it doesn't allow passengers under 12 years old.

Randy's Fishing Trips (Fisherman's Wharf, 831/372-7400 or 800/251-7440, www. randysfishingtrips.com, $75-80) can take you out for salmon, halibut, albacore, mackerel, rock cod, flatfish, and even squid and Dungeness crab in season. They also lead whale-watching trips. The half-day trips can be scheduled for the morning or afternoon. You can bring your own food including a small cooler for your drinks. If you don't have a California fishing license, you can purchase a one-day license at the shop before your trip. While you can try to walk up to their bright teal shop at Fisherman's Wharf, it's best to get tickets for your trip in advance; either call or buy online from Randy's website. For another option in catching your own seafood, consider heading out with **Westwind Charter Sport Fishing & Excursions** (66 Fisherman's Wharf, 831/392-7867, www.westwindcharter.com, $140-150). Depending on what's in

the Monterey Bay Coastal Recreation Trail

season, you can catch salmon, rock cod, halibut, or albacore.

Hiking

If you want to explore Monterey's coastline without getting wet, head out on the **Monterey Bay Coastal Recreation Trail** (831/646-3866, www.monterey.org). The 18-mile paved path stretches from Pacific Grove in the south all the way to the north Monterey County town of Castroville. The most scenic section is from Monterey Harbor down to Pacific Grove's Lovers Point Park.

Jack's Peak County Park (25020 Jacks Peak Park Rd., 831/775-4895, www.co.monterey.ca.us, daily 10am-close, vehicles Mon.-Fri. $4, Sat.-Sun. and holidays $5) is home to the highest point on the Monterey Peninsula. Its 0.8-mile-long **Skyline Trail** passes through a rare Monterey pine forest and offers glimpses of fossils from the Miocene epoch before reaching the summit, which offers an overview of the whole peninsula.

Home to a U.S. Army post from 1917 to 1994, the dunes north of Monterey are now part of one of California's newest parks, **Fort Ord Dunes State Park** (831/649-2836, www.parks.ca.gov, 8am-30 minutes after sunset, free). Walk along a four-mile road past remnants of the military past or head down to the remote beach for a stroll. To reach Fort Ord Dunes State Park from Monterey, head north on Highway 1 and take the Lightfighter Drive exit. Turn left onto 2nd Avenue and then take another left on Divarty Street. Take a right on 1st Avenue and follow the signs to the park entrance at the 8th Street Bridge over Highway 1.

Golf

Yes, you can play golf outside of Pebble Beach! And it's often much cheaper to play here than to head for the hallowed courses of that gated community.

The **Monterey Pines Golf Course** (Fairground Rd. and Garden Rd., 831/656-2167, www.montereypeninsulagolf.com, Mon.-Fri. $18-34, Sat.-Sun. $20-37) might boost your confidence after a lousy day playing on Pebble Beach's challenging greens. The course is a beginner-friendly 18 holes next to the Monterey County Fairgrounds.

The Pebble Beach Company manages the **Del Monte Golf Course** (1300 Sylvan Rd., 831/373-2700, www.pebblebeach.com, $110). It opened as a nine-hole course way back in 1897 as a place for guests of the Hotel Del Monte to play. Now expanded to 18 holes, it claims to be the oldest continuously operating course west of the Mississippi.

Motor Sports

If you're feeling the need for speed, get lots of it at the **Mazda Raceway Laguna Seca** (1021 Monterey-Salinas Hwy., 831/242-8201, www.laguna-seca.com), one of the country's premier road-racing venues. Here you can see historic auto races, superbikes, speed festivals, and an array of Grand Prix events. The major racing season runs May-October. In addition to the big events, Laguna Seca hosts innumerable auto clubs and small sports car and stock car races. If you've always wanted to learn to drive or ride racecar-style, check the schedule to see if one of the track classes is happening during your visit. These often happen in the middle of the week, and are a near-daily event in the off-season.

Check the website for parking directions specific to the event you plan to attend—this is a big facility. You can camp here, and you'll find plenty of concessions during big races.

ACCOMMODATIONS
Under $150

The ★ **Monterey Hostel** (778 Hawthorne St., 831/649-0375, http://montereyhostel.org, dorm bed $32-37, private room $79-89, family room with five beds $99) offers inexpensive accommodations within walking distance of the major attractions of Monterey. This hostel has a men's dorm room, women's dorm room, private rooms, a five-person family room, and a coed dorm room with 16 beds. There's no laundry facility on-site, but there is a laundromat within walking distance. It's close to good restaurants, but there's a large, fully stocked kitchen if you want to save money. The hostel offers a free pancake breakfast. Linens are included with your bed, and there are comfy, casual common spaces with couches and musical instruments.

$150-250

Tucked into a residential street within New Monterey, the ★ **Jabberwock Inn** (598 Laine St., 831/372-4777, www.jabberwock-inn.com, $209-399) is named after a nonsense poem written by Lewis Carroll as part of his novel *Through the Looking Glass.* Despite its name, the amenities of this comfortable former convent turned eight-room bed-and-breakfast are no-nonsense. The common area includes a covered wraparound sun porch with views of Monterey Bay and two fireplaces. Breakfasts are tasty and filling, while the innkeepers are warm and knowledgeable. There are also perks including free parking and late-afternoon wine and appetizers along with evening milk and cookies. The B&B is just a short walk to Cannery Row, the aquarium, and Lighthouse Avenue. The lowest-priced room has a private detached bathroom down the hall, while the Borogrove Room has a long list of worthwhile features

like a large Jacuzzi tub, gas fireplace, and sitting area with a coastal view. There are no TVs or telephones here.

The ★ **Monterey Bay Inn** (242 Cannery Row, 831/373-6242 or 800/424-6242, www.montereybayinn.com, $249-449) is between San Carlos Beach and the start of Cannery Row. The boutique hotel's oceanfront rooms have private balconies that overlook Monterey Bay. The in-room binoculars are handy for spotting marine wildlife. The hotel's rooftop hot tub offers another vantage point to take in the action offshore. Enjoy a continental breakfast delivered to your room in the morning and tasty cookies in the evening.

The **Casa Munras Hotel & Spa** (700 Munras Ave., 831/375-2411, www.hotel-casamunras.com, $149-359) is named after a former residence that was built in the same spot back in 1824. A portion of one of the initial building's adobe walls can still be viewed within the modern hotel's Marbella Meeting Room. The 170 rooms of the Casa Munras, which are being renovated as this book goes to print, are upgraded but designed to have a decor and color scheme that nods to Monterey's old style. The comfortable but basic rooms provide a great base

the rooftop hot tub at Monterey Bay Inn

for exploring downtown Monterey's adobes. Amenities include a heated pool, a fitness center, and a complimentary DVD library. The hotel grounds also include the terrific tapas restaurant **Esteban Restaurant** (Casa Munras Hotel & Spa, 700 Munras Ave., 831/375-0176, Mon.-Thurs. 5pm-9pm, Fri.-Sat. 5pm-10:30pm, Sun. 5pm-9pm, $8-35) and a **spa** (831/372-1829, daily 9am-7pm).

Over $250

Luxury hotel **InterContinental The Clement Monterey** (750 Cannery Row, 831/375-4500, www.ictheclementmonterey. com, $250-850) has a can't-be-beat location just a splash away from the bay and feet from the aquarium. The hotel has 208 rooms and 12 luxury suites that are decorated with tasteful Asian elements including a bonsai tree, a book-sized Zen garden, and live orchids. Most of the marble-floored bathrooms have a separate soaking tub and walk-in shower. The oceanside rooms have views of the bay, while the units on the other side of Cannery Row all have fireplaces. There are a lot of amenities and features outside the comfortable rooms, including a fitness room, an outdoor whirlpool, **The Spa** (831/642-2075, daily 9am-7pm, massages $80-175), **The C Restaurant & Bar** (831/375-4800, daily 6:30am-10pm, $29-58), a sliver of an outdoor pool long enough to swim laps in, and an artsy jellyfish-inspired staircase connecting the first and second floors.

Hear the sounds of seals and the squawks of gulls at the ★ **Spindrift Inn** (652 Cannery Row, 831/646-8900, www.spindriftinn.com, $239-719), a boutique hotel towering above the golden sand and clear green waters of scenic McAbee Beach. This 45-room establishment has been called the country's most romantic hotel. Most of the hardwood-floored rooms have wood-burning fireplaces and full or half canopy beds. The very friendly staff serves up a wine and cheese reception every day (4:30pm-6pm) and delivers a complimentary continental breakfast to your room.

CAMPING

It's a little-known secret that there is a campground on the Monterey Peninsula. A mile up a hill from downtown Monterey, the 50-acre **Veterans Memorial Park** (Via Del Rey and Veterans Dr., 831/646-3865, www.monterey. org, $27/single vehicle, $32/two vehicles) has 40 first-come, first-served campsites with views of Monterey Bay.

FOOD

The organic and sustainable food movements have caught hold on the Central Coast. The Monterey Bay Seafood Watch program (www. montereybayaquarium.org) is the definitive resource for sustainable seafood, while the Salinas Valley inland hosts a number of organic farms.

American

Inside an old brick firehouse, ★ **Montrio** (414 Calle Principal, 831/648-8880, www. montrio.com, daily 4:30pm-close, $18-31) is an elegantly casual Monterey eatery. The ever-changing menu includes meat and seafood entrées, but Montrio is also an ideal place for a lighter dinner thanks to its nice small bites and appetizer offerings. One such dish is the Butchers Butter, delicious meat from the top of a rib eye cut. There's also a 40-ounce prime rib eye steak ($110) served family-style. Montrio mixologist Anthony Vitacca is well known around town for his creative cocktails that employ ingredients as far ranging as sea salt caramel and pickle juice. Dine inside under ceilings decorated with art that resembles clouds, or out front on the patio.

Restaurant 1833 (500 Hartnell St., 831/643-1833, www.restaurant1833.com, Sun.-Thurs. 5:30pm-10pm, Fri.-Sat. 5:30pm-1am, $18-50) is housed in one of Monterey's most historic buildings, a seven-room adobe built in 1833 that's now gussied up for a big-city crowd. At a white onyx bar, patrons can try interesting intoxicants, or lounge in the library for small bites by a roaring fire. Executive chef Jason Franey does approachable cuisine with a real love of details, like the tasty Hawaiian bread appetizer that is made in house (sometimes a matter of minutes before arriving at your table). The menu changes frequently but may include freshly made pastas and meat entrées like tender beef short ribs in a pool of polenta.

Coffee Shops

Connected to the Osio Cinemas, Monterey's art-house movie theater, **Café Lumiere** (365 Calle Principal, 831/920-2451, daily 7am-10pm) is where Monterey's old Sicilian anglers hang out in the morning while sipping coffee drinks and munching on pastries. There are a lot of tempting options behind the counter's glass case, but the café also offers made-to-order breakfast, lunch, and Sunday brunch dishes. In addition, the café has weekday lunch specials including a very popular giant bowl of pho (Vietnamese noodle soup) on Thursdays.

Markets

The primary farmers market in the county, the **Monterey Farmers Market** (Alvarado St. between Del Monte and Pearl, www.old-monterey.org, winter Tues. 4pm-7pm, summer Tues. 4pm-8pm) takes over downtown Monterey with fresh-produce vendors, restaurant stalls, jewelry booths, and live music every Tuesday afternoon.

Mexican

Brightly colored **Turtle Bay Taqueria** (431 Tyler St., 831/333-1500, www.turtlebay.tv, Mon.-Thurs. 11am-8:30pm, Fri.-Sat. 11am-9pm, Sun. 11:30am-8pm, $4-14) blares salsa music while serving up a healthy, seafood-heavy menu. This isn't a typical Mexican food joint: The hearty burrito wraps include items like calamari and locally caught sand dabs (when in season) over beans, rice, cabbage, and salsa. The sopa de lima, a Mexican-style chicken soup, hits the spot on cold days when Monterey is socked in with fog. They also have a Seaside location (1301 Fremont Blvd., 831/899-1010, Mon.-Sat. 11am-8pm).

Seafood

On weekends there is typically a line out the door at **Monterey's Fish House** (2114 Del Monte Ave., 831/373-4647, Mon.-Fri. 11:30am-2:30pm and 5pm-9:30pm, Sat.-Sun. 5pm-9:30pm, $11-30), one of the peninsula's most popular seafood restaurants. Once you get inside, expect attentive service and fresh seafood including snapper, albacore tuna, and calamari fished right out of the nearby bay. Nods to Monterey's Italian fishermen include Sicilian calamari and seafood pastas.

★ **The Sandbar & Grill** (Municipal Wharf II, 831/373-2918, www.sandbarandgrillmonterey.com, Mon.-Sat. 11am-9pm, Sun. 10:30am-9pm, $12-30) has the best fried calamari around: a plate of tender, flat pieces of squid golden-fried in a seasoned batter. They are also known for their fresh sand dabs and Dungeness crab sandwich with bacon. The restaurant hangs off the Municipal Wharf over Monterey Harbor, which means you might be able to catch a sea otter backstroking by as you dine.

For a South Pacific spin on seafood, head to ★ **Hula's Island Grill & Tiki Room** (622 Lighthouse Ave., 831/655-4852, www.hulastiki.com, Fri.-Sat. 11:30am-10pm, Sun. 4pm-9pm, Mon. 4pm-9:30pm, Tues.-Thurs. 11:30am-9:30pm, $12-23). With surfing movies playing on the TVs and tasty tiki drinks, Hula's is Monterey's most fun casual restaurant with tasty and sometimes imaginative food. In addition to fresh fish and a range of tacos, the menu has land-based fare like Jamaican jerk chicken. If you're on a budget, Hula's has long happy hours (Sun.-Mon. 4pm-6pm, Tues. all day, Wed.-Sat. 2pm-6pm) where you can score tiki drinks and pupus (appetizers) for just six bucks a pop.

Opened in 1968, **The Sardine Factory** (701 Wave St., 831/373-3775, Sun.-Thurs. 5pm-10:30pm, Fri.-Sat. 5pm-11pm, $26-59) is the area's iconic seafood and steak house. Its abalone bisque was served at one of President Ronald Reagan's inaugural dinners, and part of Clint Eastwood's directorial debut *Play*

Misty for Me was filmed in the restaurant. This place oozes old-school cool, from the piano player tickling the ivories by the bar to the stunning glass-domed conservatory. The menu has pastas, steaks, and wild abalone medallions.

Steak House

The **Whaling Station** (763 Wave St., 831/373-3778, Sun.-Thurs. 5pm-9pm, Fri.-Sat. 5pm-10:30pm, $24-58) has been a local institution since 1970. Before you order, waiters show off different cuts of meat on a tray and answer questions about the best qualities of each piece. Options include a New York steak, beef wellington, and red-wine braised beef short ribs. Non-beef items are also available, like rack of lamb, seafood, and pasta. Start with the decadent prime rib egg rolls or the lighter Caesar salad. The steamed broccoli comes with hollandaise sauce and the spinach sides come studded with chunks of bacon. The moderately priced bar menu offers a steak sandwich or a burger made with ground filet mignon.

Sushi

Fresh seafood and creative rolls make ★ **Crystal Fish** (514 Lighthouse Ave., 831/649-3474, Fri. 5pm-10pm, Sat. 1pm-10pm, Sun. 1pm-9:30pm, Mon.-Thurs. 5pm-9:30pm, entrees $14-27, rolls $4-13) the Monterey go-to for sushi. There's not a lot of ambience, but there are a lot of rolls, including fresh salmon, tuna, eel, octopus, and calamari, accentuated by sauces like creamy avocado, mango, wasabi, and miso. Unusual ingredients include lemon slices, asparagus, and eggplant.

INFORMATION AND SERVICES

A recommended first stop in Monterey is the **Monterey Visitors Center** (401 Camino El Estero, 888/221-1010, www.seemonterey.com, summer Mon.-Sat. 9am-6pm, Sun. 10am-5pm, winter Mon.-Sat. 9am-5pm, Sun. 10am-4pm). The two-room building has an impressive library of pamphlets. The main room has a staffed information desk and an interactive touch screen that visitors can utilize. The back room focuses on local lodging with maps and directories. There are phones that are set up to ring the front desks of area hotels, motels, and B&Bs to check availability and pricing.

For medical needs, the **Community Hospital of the Monterey Peninsula** (CHOMP, 23625 Holman Hwy., 831/624-5311

the giant beached boat outside of The Sardine Factory

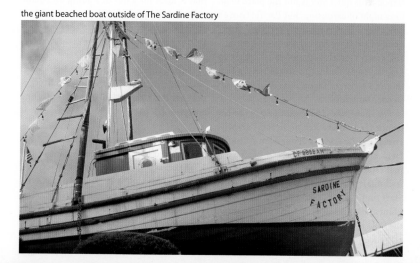

or 888/452-4667, www.chomp.org) provides emergency services to the area.

TRANSPORTATION

Most visitors drive into Monterey via scenic Highway 1. Inland, U.S. 101 allows access into Salinas from the north and south. From Salinas, Highway 68 travels west into Monterey.

For a more leisurely ride, Amtrak's *Coast Starlight* train (11 Station Place, Salinas, daily 8am-10pm) travels through Salinas.

The Greyhound bus station (19 W. Gabilan, Salinas, 831/424-4418, www.greyhound.com, daily 5am-11:30pm) offers service into Monterey from Salinas.

Once in Monterey, take advantage of the free WAVE bus (Waterfront Area Visitor Express, 831/899-2555, www.monterey. org, late May-late June daily 10am-7pm, late June-early Sept. Mon.-Fri. 10am-7pm, Sat.-Sun. and holidays 10am-8pm) that loops between downtown Monterey and the aquarium. Monterey-Salinas Transit (888/678-2871, www.mst.org, $1.25-2.50) has routes through Monterey.

Pacific Grove

Sandwiched between historic Monterey and exclusive Pebble Beach, and close to major attractions like the Monterey Bay Aquarium, Pacific Grove makes a fine base for exploring the peninsula. It's also worth a visit for its colorful turn-of-the-20th-century Victorian homes and its striking strand of coastline. The town has chosen "America's Last Hometown" as its nickname; it may make you nostalgic for small-town living. Founded in 1875 as a Methodist summer retreat, this quiet city is not the place to go for a night of carousing. But Pacific Grove's downtown is perfect for a relaxing afternoon of strolling among the yellow, purple, and green Victorian homes and cottages on Lighthouse Avenue. (It's worth noting that there's a different Lighthouse Avenue in adjacent Monterey.)

For those who don't want to pay the entrance fee to drive Pebble Beach's 17-Mile Drive, Pacific Grove's "Poor Man's 17-Mile Drive" winds around a piece of coastal real estate between Lover's Point Park and Asilomar Beach that's almost as striking. Start on Ocean View Boulevard by Lover's Point and continue onto Sunset Drive to get the full experience. In the springtime, flowering ice plant right along the road adds a riot of color to the landscape.

SIGHTS
Lover's Point Park

It is no surprise that the aptly named Lover's Point Park (Ocean View Blvd. and 17th St., 831/648-3100, www.ci.pg.ca.us) is one of the area's most popular wedding sites. A finger of land with a jumble of rocks at its northernmost point, Lover's Point offers expansive views of the interior section of the Monterey Bay.

The park also has a sheltered pocket beach that is ideal for a dip or wading on Pacific Grove's infrequent hot days. A kelp forest right offshore offers a superb spot for snorkelers to get a feel for Monterey Bay's impressive underwater ecosystem.

During summer there is an old-fashioned hamburger stand above the beach and a vendor that rents kayaks, bikes, and snorkeling equipment.

Point Pinos Lighthouse

Surrounded by a golf course, Point Pinos Lighthouse (80 Asilomar Ave. between Lighthouse Ave. and Del Monte Ave., 831/648-3176, www.pointpinoslighthouse. com, Thurs.-Mon. 1pm-4pm, adults $2, children $1) has the distinction of being the oldest continuously operating lighthouse on the West Coast. It was one of the first eight

Pacific Grove

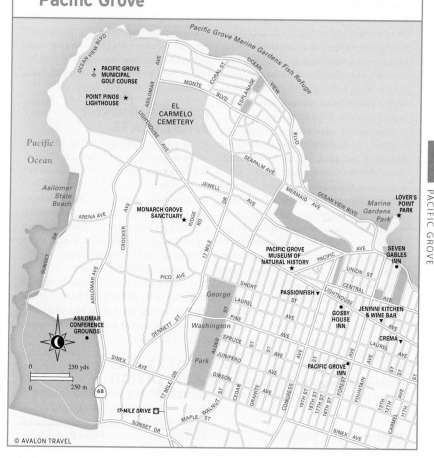

© AVALON TRAVEL

lighthouses built on the West Coast, starting operations in 1855. Point Pinos is also notable for the two female lighthouse keepers who served there during its long history. The light was automated in 1975, but it is still an active aid to local marine navigation. Lighthouse lovers and appreciators of the past will enjoy walking through the building's two floors and cellar.

Monarch Grove Sanctuary

Pacific Grove is also known as "Butterfly Town U.S.A." An impressive migration of monarch butterflies descends on the town each year. Tucked in a residential area, the small **Monarch Grove Sanctuary** (Ridge Rd. between Lighthouse Ave. and Short St., 831/648-5716, www.ci.pg.ca.us, free) offers stands of eucalyptus and pine trees that are cloaked with colorful insects during the migration period (October-February).

The best time to visit the sanctuary is in the early afternoon, when sunlight illuminates the butterflies on the trees and docents are around to answer your questions. Just don't get too close to any of our flying friends, because anyone who molests a butterfly will be slapped with a hefty $1,000 fine.

Asilomar State Beach

One of the Monterey Peninsula's most popular beaches, Asilomar State Beach (Sunset Dr., 831/646-6440, www.parks.ca.gov) draws beachgoers, walkers, and surfers. The beach itself is a narrow one-mile-long strip of coastline with a boardwalk trail on the dunes behind it. Keep walking on the trail to get to nearby Pebble Beach, an easy, cost-free way to get a taste of that exclusive community.

Right across Sunset Drive, visitors can explore the Asilomar Dunes Natural Preserve and the Asilomar Conference Grounds (800 Asilomar Ave., 831/372-8016, www.visitasilomar.com). The dunes preserve is 25 acres of restored sand dune ecosystem that can be accessed via a quarter-mile-long boardwalk. The conference grounds are shaded by Monterey pines and studded with arts and crafts-style structures designed by Hearst Castle architect Julia Morgan. Enjoy the facilities, including the Phoebe A. Hearst Social Hall, which has pool tables, a fireplace, and some comfy seats. Ranger-guided tours of the grounds are available by calling 831/646-6443. The one-hour tours focus on four aspects of the grounds: architecture, the dunes, the forest, and the coast.

To reach Asilomar, take the Route 68 West exit off Highway 1 and turn left onto Sunset Drive.

Pacific Grove Museum of Natural History

Nature enthusiasts visiting the area should stop into the Pacific Grove Museum of Natural History (165 Forest Ave., 831/648-5716, www.pgmuseum.org, Tues.-Sun. 10am-5pm, adults $9, children, students, and military $6), which will help them identify the animal and plant species they encounter while on the Monterey Peninsula. The museum feels of a past era, with its mounted and stuffed animals, but it does provide a fairly comprehensive overview of the region's biodiversity. One room is dedicated to our feathered friends and includes 300 mounted birds found around the county, including the gigantic California condor. Other rooms highlight large terrestrial mammals (mountain lions, bears) and whales. With this being Butterfly Town U.S.A., there's a space devoted to the monarch butterfly. Out front is a life-sized gray whale statue, while out back is a native plant garden that includes an impressive jade boulder that was found on the Big Sur coast.

ENTERTAINMENT AND EVENTS

If you want a wild night out on the town, you're not going to get it in Pacific Grove. But there are a couple of family-friendly annual events in "America's Last Hometown." Recalling another era, Pacific Grove's Good Old Days (831/373-3304, www.pacificgrove. org, Apr.) is a weekend of good clean fun every April that includes a parade, a quilt show, pony rides, and live entertainment.

For over 70 years, the kids of Pacific Grove have been getting dressed up like butterflies at the Butterfly Parade and Bazaar (www. pacificgrove.org, first Sat. of Oct.), which welcomes the wintering monarch butterflies to the area every fall.

SPORTS AND RECREATION
Scuba Diving and Snorkeling

Some of the best scuba diving and snorkeling spots on the Monterey Peninsula lie off Pacific Grove. Lover's Point Park (Ocean View Blvd. and 17th St., novice to advanced, 10-40 feet) has a protected cove and kelp forest right off its shores. The cove's protected sandy beach makes an easy entry point for scuba divers and snorkelers who want to explore the kelp forest. Just a few blocks away is Otter Cove (Ocean View Blvd. and Sea Palm Ave., novice to advanced, 10-60 feet) at the intersection of Ocean View Boulevard and Sea Palm Avenue. It's a dive spot that is best during days of calm seas. One of the highlights is an underwater pinnacle that rises from 50 feet to just 18 feet below the surface. Another notable site is the nearby Coral Street Cove (Coral St. and Ocean

View Blvd., advanced, 20-50 feet), which is known for its fish populations.

If you need equipment, visit **Bamboo Reef** (614 Lighthouse Ave., 831/372-1685, www. bambooreef.com, Mon.-Fri. 9am-6pm, Sat.-Sun. 7am-6pm), **Aquarius Dive Shop** (2040 Del Monte Ave., 831/375-1933, www.aquari-usdivers.com, Mon.-Fri. 9am-6pm, Sat.-Sun. 7am-6pm), or **Breakwater Scuba** (225 Cannery Row, 831/717-4546, http://breakwaterscuba.com, Mon.-Fri. 9am-6pm, Sat.-Sun. 7am-6pm) in nearby Monterey.

Surfing

During the summer and fall, clean swells produce fun waves at **Asilomar State Beach** (Sunset Dr., 831/646-6440, www.parks.ca.gov), making it one of the peninsula's most popular surf spots. Winter produces big, often dangerous swells, so stay out of the water during that time of the year. To get there, take the Route 68 West exit off Highway 1 and turn left onto Sunset Drive.

During big swells, **Lovers Point** (Ocean View Blvd. and 17th St.) turns into a nice left. There are some rocks in the lineup so it is probably best that first-timers go out with someone who knows the break.

Sunshine Freestyle (443 Lighthouse Ave., Monterey, 831/375-5015, http://sunshinefreestyle.com, Mon.-Sat. 10am-6pm, Sun. 11am-5pm, surfboard rental $30/day, wetsuit rental $15/day) and **On the Beach** (693 Lighthouse Ave., Monterey, 831/646-9283, http://onthebeachsurfshop.com, Sun.-Thurs. 10am-6pm, Fri.-Sat. 10am-7pm, surfboard rental $30/day, wetsuit rental $15/day) rent boards and wetsuits in nearby Monterey.

Golf

The **Pacific Grove Golf Links** (77 Asilomar Blvd., 831/648-5775, www.playpacificgrove.com, daily sunrise-sunset, Mon.-Thurs. $46, Fri.-Sun. and holidays $52) doesn't have the acclaim of the nearby Pebble Beach courses, but it's on a similarly gorgeous length of coastline just a few miles away.

ACCOMMODATIONS

Under $150

The ★ **Gosby House Inn** (643 Lighthouse Ave., 800/527-8828, www.gosbyhouseinn.com, $120-260) has been taking care of visitors since the 1880s. The white-and-yellow Queen Anne-style Victorian, which sits on downtown Pacific Grove's main street, is a welcome cross between a boutique hotel and B&B. Amenities include free Wi-Fi, flat-screen TVs in most rooms, and a complimentary breakfast. The photo- and antique-heavy main house has 22 rooms, some with gas fireplaces. The two deluxe rooms available in the adjacent Carriage House each have a balcony, a gas fireplace, a roomy bathroom, and a nice-sized soaking tub.

$150-250

Staying overnight at the ★ **Asilomar Conference Grounds** (804 Crocker Ave., 831/372-8016, www.visitasilomar.com, $190-335) can feel a bit like going back to summer camp. There are lots of common areas on the 107 acres including the Phoebe Apperson Hearst Social Hall, where visitors can relax by a roaring fire or play pool at one of two billiards tables. There is a real range of accommodations here, from historic rooms to family cottages to modern rooms with a view of nearby Asilomar Beach. The rooms with an ocean view and a fireplace are definitely recommended for those who don't mind spending a little more money. All the rooms here lack TVs and telephones, providing incentive to head outdoors. This frequently overlooked state park-owned lodging hosts a multitude of conferences, so expect to see corporate types with laminated conference badges walking through the forests of Monterey pine, Monterey cypress, and coast live oaks alongside the roaming herds of semi-wild deer.

★ **The Old St. Angela Inn** (321 Central Ave., 831/372-3246, www.oldstangelainn.com, $162-289) spoils with cozy accommodations, a friendly staff, and terrific food. The nine homey rooms have pine antiques, live plants, and comfortable beds. Downstairs are comfy common areas. Out back is a brick patio area with a fire pit and a waterfall fountain. One of the best features of The Old St. Angela Inn is its food. The afternoon teatime includes wine, a dessert, and an appetizer. The scrumptious breakfast includes yogurt, granola, muffins, and a hot sweet or savory item. All the food is made in-house. Pick up one of the inn's cookbooks when you check out.

Pacific Grove's Ocean View Boulevard has a handful of stunning Queen Anne Victorian buildings perched over the Pacific. One of the finest and most notable is the dark green and white **Green Gables Inn** (301 Ocean View Blvd., 831/375-2095 or 800/722-1774, www.greengablesinnpg.com, $155-295). The main building, which was built in 1888, has a downstairs common area offering ocean views. For Victorian-era enthusiasts, the main building is the place to stay, with a throwback feel and antique furnishings. Behind the main inn is the Carriage House, which has five spacious rooms all with a gas fireplace, a nice jetted tub, and ocean views. The inn also offers an afternoon wine and appetizer serving, a morning breakfast buffet, and a few bikes that can be borrowed for a spin on the nearby Monterey Bay Coastal Recreation Trail.

Crema offers gourmet comfort food.

Over $250

The most striking bed-and-breakfast on the coast of Pacific Grove, the **Seven Gables Inn** (555 Ocean View Blvd., 831/372-4341, www.sevengablesinn.com, $259-349) is perched just feet away from Lover's Point. Decorated with antique furniture and artwork, the Seven Gables Inn is for those who want to step back in time and experience ornate Victorian- and Edwardian-style lodging. Impressively, every single room has superb ocean views.

FOOD
American

Crema (481 Lighthouse Ave., 831/324-0347, http://cremapg.com, daily 7am-4pm, $7-15) is a gourmet comfort food restaurant housed in a multilevel building that feels like someone's house. Dine on oversized burgers or chicken

sandwiches beside a fireplace or a piano. They also offer a stout beer float (stout beer, ice cream, and espresso) and weekend pitchers of mimosas and sangria.

Breakfast

In the cavernous American Tin Cannery shopping mall, ★ **First Awakenings** (125 Oceanview Blvd., 831/372-1125, www.first-awakenings.net, Mon.-Fri. 7am-2pm, Sat.-Sun. 7am-2:30pm, $6-12) serves up oversized versions of classic breakfast fare including huevos rancheros, eggs Benedict, crepes, and omelets. Locals are fond of this place, frequently voting it the county's top breakfast spot. On sunny days, dine outside on the large patio while surrounded by the sounds of nearby Monterey Bay. With the aquarium just feet away, it's a great place to fuel up for a day of viewing the local sealife.

French

Fifi's Bistro Café (1188 Forest Ave., 831/372-5325, www.fifisbistrocafe.com, Mon.-Thurs.

11:30am-2:30pm and 5pm-8:30pm, Fri. 11:30am-2:30pm and 5pm-9pm, Sat. 5pm-9pm, Sun. 11am-2:30pm and 5pm-8:30pm, $18-31) celebrates French country cuisine in a space just east of downtown Pacific Grove. Inside, real flowers are placed on the tables, and wine bottles comprise a major part of the restaurant's decor. Do not miss Fifi's French onion soup, a thing of wonder served with a delectable melted cheese crust. The dinner menu includes set entrées, including goat cheese-stuffed chicken breast in a mushroom sauce, as well as dinner specials that change every few days. This is a place to spoil yourself with great food and wine. Fifi's sells their Old World and New World wines so that you can enjoy them in your hotel or at home.

Italian
★ **Il Vecchio** (110 Central Ave., 831/324-4282, Fri. noon-1:30pm and 5pm-9:30pm, Sat. 5pm-9:30pm, Sun. 5pm-9pm, Mon.-Thurs. noon-1:30pm and 5pm-9pm, $13-22) is a new Pacific Grove favorite, but the name Il Vecchio, meaning "the old," refers to traditional Italian fare like gnocchi with pesto. They make their pasta every day and offer traditional Italian takes on meats and seafood. Mondays are Piatti at Vecchio (5pm-9pm), where you can sample three popular dishes in smaller portions for $18. At the weekday Lunch for the Workers Special (Mon.-Fri. noon-1:30pm), diners get a salad and two pastas for just $9.

Mediterranean
The **Jeninni Kitchen & Wine Bar** (542 Lighthouse Ave., 831/920-2662, Thurs.-Tues. 4pm-close, $18-30) has elevated Pacific Grove's dining scene since opening in 2013. The menu changes frequently but the wagyu bullfighter's steak and the eggplant fries are favorites. Sit in the dining area in the front of the building or walk up a few stairs to the bar area to try small plates, wines, and craft beers.

Seafood
One of the Monterey Peninsula's most lauded seafood restaurants is ★ **Passionfish** (701 Lighthouse Ave., 831/655-3311, www.passionfish.net, Sun.-Thurs 5pm-9pm, Fri.-Sat. 5pm-10pm, $16-36), which is on a mission to spread the gospel about sustainable seafood. The top of their menu is adorned with a quote by Robert Redford about the importance of defending our natural resources, and every bill comes with a copy of the Monterey Bay Aquarium's Seafood Watch Guide. Passionfish does great food, especially creative and flavorful sustainable seafood. Their menu starts with a nice scallop appetizer and goes on to entrées that may include seared albacore tuna in a bacon sauce or basil-stuffed rainbow trout. They are also known for their extensive, moderately priced wine list. In addition to the very fine food and wine, the knowledgeable waitstaff here could teach a course on seafood, and the atmosphere is just right.

SHOPPING
A canning factory no more, the **American Tin Cannery** (125 Oceanview Blvd., 831/372-1442, www.americantincannery.com, daily 10am-6pm) is an indoor mall with discount outlets for national brands including Bass, Pendleton, and Nine West. Take a break from shopping at an indoor black light miniature golf course.

INFORMATION AND SERVICES
To pick up pamphlets on Pacific Grove's sights and lodging options, stop in at the **Pacific Grove Tourist Information Center** (100 Central Ave., 831/324-4668, www.pacificgrove.org, daily 10am-5pm).

For medical needs, the **Community Hospital of the Monterey Peninsula** (CHOMP, 23625 Holman Hwy., 831/624-5311 or 888/452-4667, www.chomp.org) provides emergency services to the area. It is actually closer to Pacific Grove than Monterey.

TRANSPORTATION
Most visitors drive into the area via scenic Highway 1. From Highway 1, take the Route 68 West exit to reach downtown Pacific Grove.

Pebble Beach

Between Pacific Grove and Carmel, the gated community of Pebble Beach lays claim to some of the Monterey Peninsula's best and highest-priced real estate. Pebble Beach is famous for the scenic 17-Mile Drive and its collection of high-end resorts, restaurants, spas, and golf courses, owned by the Pebble Beach Company, a partnership that includes golf legend Arnold Palmer and film legend Clint Eastwood. In February, Pebble Beach hosts the annual AT&T Pebble Beach National Pro-Am, a charity golf tournament that pairs professional golfers with celebrities.

SIGHTS
★ 17-Mile Drive

The best way to take in the stunning scenery of Pebble Beach is the 17-Mile Drive. But don't get too excited yet—long ago, the all-powerful Pebble Beach Corporation realized that the local scenery is also a precious commodity, and began charging a toll ($10/vehicle). The good news is that when you pay the fee at the gatehouse, you receive a map of the drive that describes the parks and sights that you will pass along the winding coastal road: the much-photographed Lone Cypress, the beaches of Spanish Bay, and Pebble Beach's golf course, resort, and housing complex. If you're in a hurry, you can get from one end of the 17-Mile Drive to the other in 20 minutes. But go slowly and stop often to enjoy the natural beauty of the area (and get your money's worth). There are plenty of turnouts to stop to take photos of the iconic cypress trees and stunning coastline. You can picnic at many of the beaches, most of which have basic restroom facilities and ample parking lots. The only food and gas to be had are at the Inn at Spanish Bay and the Lodge at Pebble Beach.

ENTERTAINMENT AND EVENTS

If you dream of watching Bill Murray or Kevin Costner play golf—and who doesn't?—plan a trip to Pebble Beach in February for the AT&T Pebble Beach National Pro-Am (831/649-1533, www.attpbgolf.com, Feb., event prices vary). This almost weeklong tournament pairing pro golfers with Hollywood celebrities is the biggest annual event in Pebble Beach and arguably the whole Monterey Peninsula.

SPORTS AND RECREATION
Biking

Traveling the 17-Mile Drive by bike means you don't have to pay the $10 vehicle admission fee. It's also a great bike route. Cyclists can enjoy the smells and sounds of the spectacular coastline in a way that car passengers just can't. Expect fairly flat terrain with lots of twists and turns, and a ride that runs...about 17 miles. Foggy conditions can make this ride a bit slick in the summer, but spring and fall weather are perfect for pedaling.

Bay Bikes (3600 The Barnyard Shopping Center, Carmel, 831/655-2453, www.baybikes.com, Sun.-Mon. 10am-5pm, Tues.-Fri. 10am-6pm, Sat. 9am-6pm, bike rentals $8-16/hr., $24-48/four hours) in Carmel is the closest place to rent a bike to tool around 17-Mile Drive. The options include cruisers, hybrid bikes, road bikes, and tandems.

Golf

There's no place for golfing quite like Pebble Beach. Golf has been a major pastime here since the late 19th century; today avid golfers come from around the world to tee off inside the gated community. Play courses trodden by the likes of Tiger Woods and Jack Nicklaus, pause a moment before you putt to take in the sight of the stunning Pacific Ocean, and pay $200 or more for a single round of golf.

One of the Pebble Beach Resort courses, the 18-hole, par-72 **Spyglass Hill** (1700 17-Mile Dr., 800/654-9300, www.pebblebeach.com, $395) gets its name from the Robert Louis Stevenson Novel *Treasure Island*. Don't be fooled—the holes on this beautiful course may be named for characters in an adventure novel, but that doesn't mean they're easy. Spyglass Hill boasts some of the most challenging play in this golf course-laden region. Expect a few bogeys, and tee off from the championship level at your own (ego's) risk.

Another favorite with the Pebble Beach crowd is the famed 18-hole, par-72 **Poppy Hills Golf Course** (3200 Lopez Rd., 831/622-8239, www.poppyhillsgolf.com, $210). Though it's not managed by the same company, Poppy Hills shares amenities with the other Pebble Beach golf courses. Expect the same level of care and devotion to the maintenance of the course and your experience as a player.

The **Pebble Beach Golf Links** (1700 17-Mile Dr., 800/877-0597, www.pebblebeach.com, $495) has been called nothing short of the nation's best golf course by *Golf Digest*. The high ranking might have something to do with the fact that some of the fairways are perched above the Pacific Ocean. The course will host its sixth men's U.S. Open championship in 2019 and is one of three courses utilized during the popular AT&T Pro-Am.

Less pricey to play than the Pebble Beach Golf Links course, **The Links at Spanish Bay** (2700 17-Mile Dr., 831/647-7495 or 800/877-0597, $155-270) is on some of Pebble Beach's native sand dune habitat. Due to the environmental sensitivity of the grounds, the course caps the amount of players and spectators on the greens.

Spas

Of course there's a spa in Pebble Beach, named **The Spa at Pebble Beach** (1518 Cypress Dr., 831/649-7615 or 800/877-0597, www.pebblebeach.com, daily 8:30am-7:30pm, massages $165-470). They have specialty massages for golfers before or after a day on the greens.

ACCOMMODATIONS AND FOOD

You need to drop some serious money to stay in Pebble Beach. Expect luxury amenities at **The Lodge at Pebble Beach** (1700 17-Mile Dr., 831/647-7500 or 800/654-9300, www.pebblebeach.com, $790-1,070), by the 18th hole of the Pebble Beach Golf Links. Most rooms and suites have wood-burning fireplaces as well as private patios or balconies. Some of the high-end rooms have their own spas. A stay also includes access to The Beach & Tennis Club, which has a heated outdoor pool, a whirlpool spa, and a tennis pavilion.

Like The Lodge at Pebble Beach, **The Inn at Spanish Bay** (2700 17-Mile Dr., 831/647-7500 or 800/654-9300, www.pebblebeach.com, $670-3,060) has rooms with fireplaces and decks or patios. There's also a fitness center and tennis pavilion on-site.

To experience the luxury of Pebble Beach without dropping your savings on a night's stay, consider having lunch, dinner, or a drink in the exclusive community and then head back to a less expensive lodging in nearby Pacific Grove or Monterey.

The Hawaiian fusion cuisine of celebrity chef Roy Yamaguchi takes center stage at **Roy's at Pebble Beach** (The Inn at Spanish Bay, 2700 17-Mile Dr., 831/647-7423, www.pebblebeach.com, daily 6:30am-10pm, $26-78). Island-inspired dishes include seafood and sushi, all with an Asian flair. Another option at The Inn at Spanish Bay is **Peppoli** (The Inn at Spanish Bay, 2700 17-Mile Dr., 831/647-7433, www.pebblebeach.com, daily 5:30pm-10pm, $20-100). Head here for a hearty Italian dinner of gnocchi with black truffle cream sauce or seared local halibut.

If you want to experience Pebble Beach in a low-key way, **The Tap Room** (The Lodge at Pebble Beach, 1700 17-Mile Dr., 831/625-8535, daily 11am-11:30pm, $17-52) is your place. This wood-walled bar serves burgers, bratwurst, Wagyu beef filet mignon, and fresh Maine lobster (the prime rib chili is also worth your time). The Tap Room has 14 beers on tap at an inflated price ($10.75), yet it will all be money well spent if you end up spending the afternoon drinking with Bill Murray, an occasional customer.

Golfers might not need to know much more than that **The Bench Restaurant** (The Lodge at Pebble Beach, 1700 17-Mile Dr., 800/654-9300, daily 10am-10pm, $18-31) overlooks the famed 18th hole of the Pebble Beach Golf Links. The chef employs wood-roasting and open-flame cooking techniques to create wood-fired brussels sprouts and grilled steaks.

Pebble Beach newcomer **Porter's in the Forest** (3200 Lopez Rd., 831/622-8240, http://poppyhillsgolf.com/porters, daily 6am-7pm, $13-25) is beside the Poppy Hills Golf Course.

It serves ingenious twists on typical clubhouse fare with items like a Korean Philly cheesesteak and short rib fries, braised ribs, and a muenster cheese au gratin over french fries. They serve breakfast, lunch, and a twilight menu.

GETTING THERE

There are several gates to get into Pebble Beach, including three in Pacific Grove and one in Carmel. Admission to Pebble Beach is $10 if you aren't staying here. You can get the fee waived if you are dining at a Pebble Beach restaurant. Just make a reservation and tell the guard at the entry gate that you have one.

Carmel-by-the-Sea

There are no addresses in Carmel-by-the-Sea (frequently referred to as simply Carmel). There are lots of trees and no street lights, and street signs are wooden posts with names written perpendicularly, to be read while walking along the sidewalk, rather than driving down the street. There's little to do at night. These are a few clues as to how this village facing the Pacific Ocean maintains its lost-in-time charm.

Formerly a Bohemian enclave where local poets George Sterling and Robinson Jeffers hung out with literary heavyweights, including Jack London and Mary Austin, Carmel-by-the-Sea is now a popular vacation spot for the moneyed, the artistic, and the romantic. People come to enjoy the small coastal town's almost European charm. They stroll its sidewalks, peering into the windows of upscale shops and art galleries that showcase the work of sculptors, plein air painters, and photographers. Between the galleries are some of the region's most revered restaurants. The main thoroughfare, Ocean Avenue, slopes down to Carmel Beach, one of the finest on the Monterey Peninsula.

The old-world charms of Carmel can make it a little confusing for drivers. Because

there are no addresses, locations are sometimes given via directions, for example: on 7th Avenue between San Carlos and Dolores Streets; or the northwest corner of Ocean Avenue. The town is compact, laid out on a plain grid system, so you're better off getting out of your car and walking anyway. Expect to share everything from Carmel's sidewalks to its restaurants with our canine friends. Carmel is very pro-pup.

SIGHTS
★ Carmel Beach

Found at the end of Carmel-by-the-Sea's Ocean Avenue, **Carmel Beach** (Ocean Ave., 831/624-4909, http://ci.carmel.ca.us/carmel, daily 6am-10pm) is one of the Monterey Bay region's best beaches. Under a bluff dotted with twisted, skeletal cypress trees, it's a long, white, sandy beach that borders a usually clear blue-green Pacific. In the distance to the south, Point Lobos juts out from the land like a pointing finger, while just north of the beach, the green-as-billiard-table-felt golf courses cloak the grounds of nearby Pebble Beach. Like most of Carmel, Carmel Beach is very dog friendly. On any given day, all sorts of canines fetch, sniff, and run on the white sand.

Carmel-by-the-Sea

17-MILE DRIVE

Pebble Beach
Golf Course

Carmel Way

1ST AVE

2ND AVE

2ND AVE

SANTA RITA ST

3RD AVE

3RD AVE

SANTA FE ST

N SAN ANTONIO AVE

2ND AVE

N CARMELO ST

N CAMINO REAL

PALOU AVE

LOPEZ AVE

CASANOVA ST

MONTE VERDE ST

LINCOLN ST

DOLORES ST

SAN CARLOS ST

MISSION ST

JUNIPERO ST

TORRES ST

4TH AVE

5TH AVE

CASANOVA ▼

CARMEL
VISITOR CENTER ■

KATY'S
PLACE ▼

STARLIGHT 65 ROOFTOP
TERRACE AT VESUVIO

CARMEL ART ■
ASSOCIATION

EM LE'S ▼

AKAONI ▼

BRUNO'S
MARKET ■

To
CA-1

LOBOS
LODGE ●

6TH AVE

OCEAN AVE

CARMEL VALLEY ▼
ROASTING COMPANY

CARMEL BAY
COMPANY
BICYCLETTE ▼

DAMETRA
CAFÉ

SALUMERIA LUCA ▼

TUCK BOX ▼

Carmel
Plaza

MOUNTAIN VIEW AVE

7TH AVE

7TH AVE

CYPRESS INN ●

Carmel Bay

THE FOREST
THEATER ■

8TH AVE

LA PLAYA
HOTEL ●

GOLDEN BOUGH
PLAHOUSE ■

SUNSET
CENTER ■

9TH AVE

SAN ANTONIO AVE

CAMINO REAL

CASANOVA ST

MONTE VERDE ST

LINCOLN ST

DOLORES ST

SAN CARLOS ST

MISSION ST

VIZCAINO AVE

CARMEL BEACH

10TH AVE

CARMELO ST

11TH AVE

SCENIC RD

12TH AVE

0   500 yds

0   500 m

13TH AVE

JUNIPERO ST

Mission

Trail

SCENIC RD

BAY VIEW AVE

SAN ANTONIO AVE

SANTA LUCIA AVE

14TH AVE

FRANCISCAN WAY

RIO RD

LASUEN DR

Park

OCEAN VIEW AVE

ISABELLA AVE

VALLEY VIEW AVE

CARMELO ST

15TH AVE

WALKER AVE

STEWART WAY

RIO AVE

16TH AVE

16TH AVE

MISSION RANCH
RESTAURANT AT MISSION
RANCH ●

CARMEL
MISSION ★

SCENIC RD

17TH AVE

Carmel River
State Beach

© AVALON TRAVEL

One of the best places to access the beach is at the west end of Ocean Avenue. There's a parking lot here, along with four beach volleyball courts, a wooden observation deck, and restrooms.

For surfers, Carmel Beach is one of the Monterey area's most consistent breaks. It's also the annual site of the Sunshine Freestyle Surfabout, the only surf contest in Monterey County.

Carmel Mission

San Carlos Borromeo de Carmelo Mission (3080 Rio Rd., 831/624-1271, www.carmelmission.org, daily 9:30am-7pm, adults $6.50, seniors $4, children $2), more commonly known as **Carmel Mission,** was Father Junípero Serra's favorite among his California mission churches. He lived, worked, and died here, and visitors can see a replica of his cell. A working Catholic parish remains part of the complex, so please be respectful when taking the self-guided tour. The rambling buildings and courtyard gardens show some wear, but enough restoration work has gone into the church and living quarters to make them attractive and eminently visitor friendly. The Carmel Mission has a small memorial museum in a building off the second courtyard, but don't make the mistake of thinking that this small and outdated space is the only historical display. In fact, the "museum" runs through many of the buildings, showing a small slice of the lives of the 18th- and 19th-century friars. The highlight of the complex is the church with its gilded altar front, its shrine to the Virgin Mary, the grave of Junípero Serra, and an ancillary chapel dedicated to his memory. Round out your visit by walking out into the gardens to admire the flowers and fountains and to read the grave markers in the small cemetery.

Tor House

Local poet Robinson Jeffers penned nature poems to the uncompromising beauty of Carmel Point and nearby Big Sur. He built this rugged-looking castle on the Carmel coast in 1919. He named it **Tor House** (26304 Ocean View Ave., 831/624-1813, www.torhouse.org, tours Fri.-Sat. 10am-3pm, adults $10, students $5) after its rocky setting, and he added the majestic Hawk Tower a year later.

The Tor House Foundation has volunteer docents that do tours of the property. Tours include a walk through the original home, which was hand built by Jeffers with giant stones. The poet once hosted luminaries

the white sand of Carmel Beach

like Ansel Adams, Charlie Chaplin, Edna St. Vincent Millay, and Dylan Thomas within the dining room, which offers fine views of Carmel Point and Point Lobos. The highlight of the tour is a visit to **Hawk Tower,** a four-story stone structure crowned with an open-air turret. Climb up a hidden staircase (not for the claustrophobic) or opt for the outside staircase to reach stunning views of Jeffers's property and the natural beauty that inspired his best work.

★ Point Lobos State Natural Reserve

Said to be the inspiration behind the setting of Robert Louis Stevenson's *Treasure Island*, **Point Lobos State Natural Reserve** (CA-1, three miles south of Carmel, 831/624-4909, www.parks.ca.gov and www.pointlobos. org, winter daily 8am-30 minutes after sunset, spring-fall daily 8am-7pm, $10/vehicle) is a wonderland of coves, hills, and jumbled rocks. The reserve's Cypress Grove Trail winds through a forest of antler-like Monterey cypress trees that are cloaked in striking red algae. Point Lobos also offers a lesson on the region's fishing history in the **Whaler's Cabin** (daily 9am-5pm, staff permitting), a small wooden structure that was

built by Chinese fishermen in the 1850s. Half of the reserve is underwater, open for scuba divers who want to explore the 70-foot-high kelp forests just offshore. The parking lots in Point Lobos tend to fill up on crowded weekends, but the reserve allows people to park on nearby Highway 1 and walk to the park during these times.

WINERIES

The town of Carmel has wine-tasting rooms in its downtown area. Visit the Carmel Chamber of Commerce website (www.carmelcalifornia.org) for a downloadable map of Carmel-by-the-Sea's tasting rooms.

At the wooden slab bar in the sleek **Caraccioli Cellars Tasting Room** (Dolores St. between Ocean and 7th Aves., 831/622-7722, www.caracciolicellars.com, Mon.-Thurs. 2pm-7pm, Fri.-Sat. 11am-10pm, Sun. 11am-7pm, $10-15), taste wines made from pinot noir and chardonnay grapes. They also pour a brut and a brut rosé.

The family-owned **De Tierra Vineyards Tasting Room** (Mission St. and 5th Ave., 831/622-9704, www.detierra.com, summer Tues.-Thurs. 2pm-8pm, Fri.-Sun. noon-8pm, winter Tues.-Thurs. 2pm-7pm, Fri.-Sun. noon-8pm, $10-15) has a rosé, syrah, merlot,

the scenic shoreline of Point Lobos State Natural Reserve

chardonnay, red blend, riesling, and a pinot noir. A chalkboard lists a cheese and chocolate plate menu.

Grammy Award-winning composer Alan Silvestri makes wines in Carmel Valley, and they can be sampled in the **Silvestri Tasting Room** (7th Ave. between Dolores and San Carlos Sts., 831/625-0111, www.silvestrivineyards.com, daily noon-7pm, $10-15).

Taste the wares at **Scheid Vineyards Carmel-by-the-Sea Tasting Room** (San Carlos St. and 9th Ave., 831/656-9463, www.scheidvineyards.com, Sun.-Thurs. noon-6pm, Fri.-Sat. noon-7pm, $10-20), a clean, friendly space. A large map behind the counter shows the locations of all the Scheid Vineyards.

ENTERTAINMENT AND EVENTS

The events and entertainment in Carmel tend to center around either art or food. This town loves its haute culture, so you won't find too many sports bars or generic movie theaters here. Instead, enjoy classical music, a wealth of live theater, and a glass of wine in the mild evenings.

Live Music

Classical music aficionados will appreciate the dulcet tones of the musicians who perform for **Chamber Music Monterey Bay** (831/625-2212, www.chambermusicmontereybay.org). This society brings talented ensembles and soloists in from around the world to perform on the lovely Central Coast. One night you might find a local string quartet, and on another night you'll get to see and hear a chamber ensemble. (String quartets definitely rule the small stage and intimate theater.) At its shows, all of which are performed at the **Sunset Cultural Center** (San Carlos St. at 9th Ave., 831/620-2048, www.sunsetcenter.org), Chamber Music Monterey Bay reserves up-front seats for children and their adult companions. The Sunset Cultural Center is a state-of-the-art performing center with over 700 seats that hosts a true range of events and artistic endeavors, including rock shows, dance recitals, classical music concerts, and theater performances. Recent performers have included LeAnn Rimes, Philip Glass, and Buddy Guy.

Bars and Clubs

Carmel's once nearly nonexistent nightlife gained a pulse with the opening of **Mundaka** (San Carlos St. and 7th Ave., 831/624-7400, Sun.-Wed. 5:30pm-9:30pm, Thurs.-Sat. 5:30pm-10pm), a Spanish-style tapas bar that attracts Carmel's younger crowd with live music and DJs. Many shirts have been ruined here by drinking wine from one of Mundaka's *porróns,* glass wine pitchers with a spout that allows you to pour wine into your mouth from above your head. Mundaka has proved so successful that the owners opened **Barmel** (San Carlos St. between Ocean Ave. and 7th Ave., 831/626-3400, daily 2:30pm-midnight) next door. Barmel has live music from Thursday to Saturday with a DJ following on weekend nights.

Theater

Despite its small size, Carmel has a handful of live theater groups. In a town that defines itself by its love of art, theater arts don't get left out. Don't hesitate to ask the locals what's playing where when you're in town.

The **Pacific Repertory Theater** (831/622-0100, www.pacrep.org, adults $15-39, seniors $15-28, students, teachers, and military $10-15, children $7.50) is the only professional theater company on the Monterey Peninsula. Its shows go up all over the region, most often in the **Golden Bough Playhouse** (Monte Verde St. and 8th Ave.), the company's home theater. Other regular venues include the **The Forest Theater** (Mountain View St. and Santa Rita St.) and the **Circle Theater** (Casanova St. between 8th and 9th Aves.) within the Golden Bough complex. The company puts on dramas, comedies, and musicals both new and classic. You might see a work of Shakespeare or a classic like *Fiddler on the Roof,* or maybe enjoy your favorite songs from *The Fantasticks,* or sing along to the newer tunes of *Hairspray!* Check the website for upcoming shows, and buy tickets online or over the phone to guarantee you'll get seats while you're in town.

Each fall, PacRep puts up the **Carmel Shakespeare Festival** (www.pacrep.org), a short showing of Shakespeare that's good enough to draw the notice of Bay Area theater snobs. Check the website for information on this year's shows and the venues.

Festivals and Events

In a town famed for art galleries, one of the biggest events of the year is the **Carmel Art Festival** (Devendorf Park at Mission St., www.carmelartfestival.org, May). This four-day event celebrates visual arts in all media with shows by internationally acclaimed artists at galleries, parks, and other venues all across town. This wonderful festival also sponsors here-and-now contests, including the prestigious plein air (outdoor painting) competition. It's a rare opportunity to witness the artists outdoors, engaging in their creative process as they use the Carmel scenery for inspiration. Round out the festival by bidding on paintings at the end-of-event auction. You can get a genuine bargain on original artwork while supporting both the artists and the festival. The Carmel Art Festival is a great place to bring your family—a wealth of children's activities help even the youngest festivalgoers become budding artists.

For a more classical experience, one of the most prestigious festivals in Northern California is the **Carmel Bach Festival** (831/624-1521, www.bachfestival.org, July). For 15 days each July, Carmel-by-the-Sea and its surrounding towns host dozens of classical concerts. Naturally the works of J. S. Bach are featured, but you can also hear renditions of Mozart, Vivaldi, Handel, and other heavyweights of Bach's era. Choose between big concerts in major venues or intimate performances in smaller spaces with only a small audience between you and the beautiful music. Concerts and recitals take place literally every day of the week—budget-conscious music lovers can just as easily enjoy the festival in the middle of the week as on the weekends.

The **Carmel International Film Festival** (831/624-1521, http://carmelfilmfest.com, Oct.) lures debut movies and Hollywood stars to Carmel and the adjacent communities in October. The 2015 lineup included critical favorites *Nightcrawler*, *Whiplash*, and *The Homesman*.

Barmel and Mundaka are next-door neighbors.

MONTEREY BAY
CARMEL-BY-THE-SEA

SHOPPING

It is easy to spend an afternoon poking into Carmel's many art galleries, browsing everything from the classical mythical sculptures at **Dawson Cole Fine Art** (Lincoln St. and 6th Ave., 800/972-5228, www.dawsoncolefineart.com, Mon.-Sat. 10am-6pm, Sun. 10am-5:30pm) to the playful paintings of a blue dog on display at **Rodrigue Studio Carmel** (Dolores St. between Ocean Ave. and 7th Ave., 831/626-4444, http://georgerodrigue.com, Mon.-Sat. 10am-6pm, Sun. noon-5pm). One of the best galleries in town is the **Weston Gallery** (6th Ave., 831/624-4453, www.westongallery.com, Tues.-Sun. 10:30am-5:30pm), which highlights the photographic work of 20th-century masters including Ansel Adams, Diane Arbus, Robert Mapplethorpe, and Edward Weston. A tiny art gallery owned by two local photographers, **Exposed** (Carmel Square, San Carlos St. and 7th Ave., 831/238-0127, http://galleryexposed.blogspot.com, Sat. 1pm-3pm or by appointment) is worth a peek.

When your head starts spinning from all the art, head to **Carmel Plaza** (Ocean Ave. and Mission St., 831/624-1385, www.carmelplaza.com, Mon.-Sat. 10am-6pm, Sun. 11am-5pm), which offers lots of ways to part with your money. This outdoor mall has luxury fashion shops like Tiffany & Co. as well as the hip clothing chain Anthropologie. But don't miss locally owned establishment **The Cheese Shop** (831/625-2272, www.thecheeseshopinc.com, Mon.-Sat. 10am-6pm, Sun. 11am-5:30pm), which sells delicacies like cave-aged gruyère cheese that you can pair with a local wine.

Worth a browse is the eclectic **Carmel Bay Company** (Ocean Ave. and Lincoln St., 831/624-3868, www.carmelbaycompany.com, daily 10am-5pm), which features copper armoires and a fascinating collection of vintage photographic prints.

For the environment lover in your life, pick up natural milk-based paint or books like *The Gorgeously Green Diet* at **Eco Carmel** (San Carlos St. and 7th Ave., 831/624-1222, www.ecocarmel.com, Mon.-Sat. 10am-6pm, Sun. 11am-5pm). If you carry your purchases out without a bag, you get a 25-cent token that you can donate to one of three rotating nonprofits.

SPORTS AND RECREATION
Surfing

Carmel Beach (Ocean Ave., 831/624-4909, daily 6am-10pm) has some of the area's most consistent beach breaks. Being a beach break, the sandbars shift, so the best spot on the beach frequently changes. The waves are usually at their finest from spring to late summer. The winds blow out a lot of area breaks in the spring, but Carmel Beach really comes alive during this time of year. In early summer, Carmel Beach is the venue for Monterey County's only annual surf contest, the **Sunshine Freestyle Surfabout** (831/375-5015, www.sunshinefreestyle.com). This is a great place to see the best surfers in the area in action and to experience a fun beach party, especially if it's sunny out.

Contact **Carmel Surf Lessons** (831/915-4065, www.carmelsurflessons.com) if you want to learn to surf at Carmel Beach. To rent a board, head to Monterey's **Sunshine Freestyle Surf & Sport** (443 Lighthouse Ave., Monterey, 831/375-5015, www.sunshinefreestyle.com, Mon.-Sat. 10am-6pm, Sun. 11am-5pm, surfboard rental $30/day, wetsuit rental $15/day) or **On the Beach** (693 Lighthouse Ave., Monterey, 831/646-9283, http://onthebeachsurfshop.com, Sun.-Thurs. 10am-6pm, Fri.-Sat. 10am-7pm, surfboard rental $30/day, wetsuit rental $15/day).

ACCOMMODATIONS
$150-250

Lobos Lodge (Monte Verde St. and Ocean Ave., 831/624-3874, www.loboslodge.com, $175-345) sits right in the midst of downtown Carmel-by-the-Sea, making it a perfect spot from which to dine, shop, and admire the endless array of art in this upscale town. Each of the 30 rooms and suites offers a gas fireplace, a sofa and table, a bed in an alcove, and enough space to stroll about and enjoy the quiet romantic setting. All but two of the rooms have a patio or balcony where you can enjoy the product of a local vineyard outside. In the morning, guests are treated to a continental breakfast and a newspaper.

In a neighborhood just a block from Carmel Beach, **Colonial Terrace Inn By The Sea** (San Antonio Ave. between 12th and 13th Aves., 831/624-2741, www.thecolonialterrace.com, $219-400) is the best place in the small town to fall asleep to the white noise of breaking waves. In addition to superb ocean views from the property, Colonial Terrace has a nice brick courtyard surrounded by blooming flowers.

Just two blocks from the beach, the ★ **Lamp Lighter Inn** (Ocean Ave. and Camino Real, 831/624-7372 or 888/375-0770, www.carmellamplighter.com, $185-450) has 11 rooms in five cottages with a comfortable, beachy decor. The cottages encircle a courtyard area that has two fire pits. Guests are treated to an afternoon wine and cheese reception and a morning continental breakfast that they can enjoy in the courtyard. This is a pet-friendly property; two of the units even have fenced-in backyards.

Coachman's Inn (San Carlos St. and 8th Ave., 831/624-6421, www.coachmansinn.com, $225-315) is a small downtown Carmel motel with 30 clean, well-appointed rooms. The rooms were recently refurbished with new carpeting and bedding, and they all include large flat screens, mini-fridges, microwaves, and Keurig coffeemakers. Some also have gas fireplaces and jetted spa tubs. A stay includes access to a hot tub, sauna, and exercise bike. The inn's staff delivers a light continental breakfast to your room.

Outside of downtown Carmel, **Mission Ranch** (26270 Dolores St., 831/624-6436, www.missionranchcarmel.com, $165-380) is a sprawling old ranch complex with views of sheep-filled pastures and Point Lobos in the distance. If you get a glimpse of Mission Ranch's owner, it might just make your day: It's none other than Hollywood icon and former Carmel-by-the-Sea mayor Clint Eastwood. On the grounds is a restaurant with a nightly sing-along piano bar that is popular with Carmel's silver-haired crowd.

Over $250

Touted by *Architectural Digest,* **Tradewinds Carmel** (Mission St. and 3rd Ave., 831/624-2776, www.tradewinds.com, $250-550) brings a touch of the Far East to California. Inspired by the initial proprietor's time spent in Japan, the 28 serene hotel rooms are decorated with Asian antiquities and live orchids. Outside, the grounds feature a water fountain that passes through bamboo shoots and horsetails along with a meditation garden, where an oversized Buddha head overlooks a trio of cascading pools. A stay comes with continental breakfast that includes French pastries and fruit.

The initial structure at ★ **La Playa Carmel** (Camino Real at 8th Ave., 831/293-6100 or 800/582-8900, www.laplayahotel.com, $219-479) was a mansion built for a member of the Ghirardelli family. Though La Playa underwent an extensive remodel in 2012, it still has many features from an earlier era, including the dark, wood-walled bar, stained glass windows, and a tiled staircase. Half of the 75 rooms at La Playa look out onto nearby Carmel Beach. The beach is only two blocks away, so you'll fall asleep to the sounds of the sea. Wander the grounds and stop by the library, the heated outdoor pool, and the courtyard with its oversized chessboard. The staff will treat you to an afternoon wine reception, a dessert of fresh-baked cookies, and a champagne breakfast with made-to-order omelets and waffles.

The landmark **Cypress Inn** (Lincoln St. and 7th Ave., 831/624-3871 or 800/443-7443, www.cypress-inn.com, $245-595) welcomes human and canine guests in a white, ornate Mediterranean-inspired building. This is one of the most pro-pup hotels in the state. They have dog cookies at the desk, water bowls are situated around the hotel, and they provide dog beds and dog towels by request. The rooms all come with complimentary cream sherry, fruit, and snacks for guests, while some also have fireplaces and/or jetted tubs. Human visitors are also treated to a breakfast that includes several hot items.

FOOD
American
Grasing's Coastal Cuisine (6th Ave. and Mission St., 831/624-6462, http://grasings. com, daily 11am-3pm and 5pm-9pm, $25-62) serves the creations of chef Kurt Grasing in a cute cottage atmosphere that is quintessential Carmel. Begin by flipping through the impressive 42-page wine list; cabernets, pinots, and burgundies are well represented. The dinner menu has a chophouse section featuring fine steaks from Nebraska. The other entrées include farm-raised Monterey Bay abalone and a tasty paella studded with prawns, clams, mussels, and spicy sausage. Waiters in vests and ties serve in the high-ceilinged dining room, while an outdoor patio can satisfy those bringing their dogs to dinner. Save room for the subtle but worthwhile apple-caramel bread pudding.

Breakfast
★ **Carmel Belle** (Doud Craft Studios, Ocean Ave. and San Carlos St., 831/624-1600, www. carmelbelle.com, Mon.-Tues. 8am-5pm, Wed.-Sun. 8am-9pm, $6-25) is a little eatery with big attention to detail. In the open section of an indoor mall, Carmel Belle serves up creative fare for breakfast and lunch, including an open-faced breakfast sandwich featuring a slab of toast topped with a poached egg, thick strips of bacon, a bed of arugula, and wedges of fresh avocado. Its slow-cooked Berkshire pork sandwich with red onion-currant chutney is a perfect example of what can happen when savory meets sweet. Dinner (Wed.-Sun. only) features a choice of two main items and three side items.

Chinese
For an authentic hole-in-the-wall locals' dining experience, seek out **Tommy's Wok** (San Carlos St. between Ocean Ave. and 7th Ave., 831/624-8518, Tues.-Sun. 11:30am-2:30pm and 4:30pm-9pm, $10-16). Dine in or take out items like moo shu pork. It's often crowded.

French
If the international feel of Carmel-by-the-Sea has put you in the mood for European food, have dinner at the quaint French eatery **La Bicyclette** (Dolores St. at 7th Ave.,

La Playa Carmel

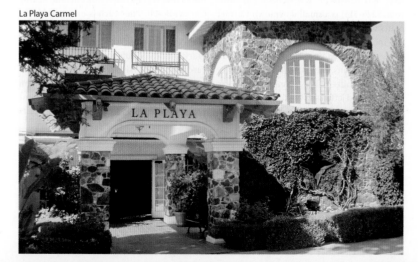

831/622-9899, www.labicycletterestaurant.com, daily 8am-11am, 11:30am-3:30pm, and 5pm-10pm, $14-28). The dinner menu changes nightly, but always includes wood-fired pizzas.

Mediterranean

While **Dametra Café** (Ocean Ave. at Lincoln St., 831/622-7766, www.dametracafe.com, daily 11am-11pm, $12-28) has a wide-ranging international menu that includes an all-American cheeseburger and Italian dishes like spaghetti alla Bolognese, it's best to go with the lively restaurant's signature Mediterranean food. The Greek chicken kebab entrée is a revelation, with two chicken and vegetable kebabs drizzled with a distinct aioli sauce, all served over yellow rice and with a Greek salad. The owner and his staff have been known to serenade evening diners.

Come into ★ **Yafa** (5th Ave. and Junipero St., 831/624-9232, www.yafarestaurant.com, daily 5pm-10pm, $14-30), and owner and manager Ben Khader and his father will make you feel utterly welcome in this popular one-room restaurant. The room occasionally erupts with singing, dancing, and clapping. The menu includes pasta (lamb ravioli, lobster ravioli) along with Mediterranean classics (Moroccan chicken, lamb kebabs).

Sushi

★ **Akaoni** (Mission St. and 6th Ave., 831/620-1516, Tues.-Sun. 5:30pm-8:30pm, $7-40) is a superb hole-in-the-wall sushi restaurant. The menu includes tempura-fried oysters, soft-shell crab rolls, and a unagi donburi (eel bowl). Look at the daily specials on the white board for the newest seafood including items flown in from Japan. For adventurous diners, the live Monterey spot prawn is the freshest seafood you'll ever eat.

Tapas

Affina (San Carlos St. and 6th Ave., 831/915/4756, Mon. 5:30pm-11pm, Tues.-Sun.

11:30am-4pm and 5:30pm-11pm, $17-45) has injected a dose of cool into Carmel's dining scene. The corner restaurant has a grand white piano and a popular wraparound bar. Old black-and-white movies are projected on a space above the piano for ambience. The menu may include fried chicken, pork shoulder, or baby octopus.

INFORMATION AND SERVICES

You'll find the **Carmel Visitors Center** (San Carlos St. between 5th and 6th Aves., 831/624-2522 or 800/550-4333, www.carmelcalifornia.org, daily 10am-5pm) right in the middle of downtown Carmel-by-the-Sea.

The nearest major medical center to Carmel-by-the-Sea and the Carmel Valley is in nearby Monterey: the **Community Hospital of the Monterey Peninsula** (23625 Holman Hwy., Monterey, 831/624-5311, www.chomp.org).

TRANSPORTATION

If you've made it to Monterey by car, getting to Carmel is a piece of cake. The quick and free way to get to Carmel from the north or the south is via Highway 1. From Highway 1, take Ocean Avenue into the middle of downtown Carmel. A more expensive but more beautiful route is via Pebble Beach's 17-Mile Drive.

As you read the addresses in Carmel-by-the-Sea and begin to explore the neighborhoods, you'll realize something interesting: There are no street addresses. (Some years ago Carmel residents voted not to enact door-to-door mail delivery, thus there is no need for numeric addresses on buildings.) So you'll need to pay close attention to the street names and the block you're on. Just to make things even more fun, street signs can be difficult to see in the mature foliage, and a dearth of streetlights can make them nearly impossible to find at night. Show up during the day to get the lay of the land before trying to navigate after dark.

Carmel Valley

When the Carmel coastline gets socked in with summer fog, locals flock inland to the reliably sunny Carmel Valley. But locals aren't the only people making their way to this corridor through the Santa Lucia Mountains: Carmel Valley is becoming known as a burgeoning but still unassuming wine region due to its tasty cabernet sauvignons, merlots, and other reds.

The landscape changes quickly as you leave the coast. You'll see the mountains rising above you, as well as farms, ranches, and orchards. Thirteen miles east of Highway 1 is the unincorporated Carmel Valley Village. In this small strip of businesses hugging Carmel Valley Road is a collection of wineries, tasting rooms, restaurants, and even an Old West saloon.

SIGHTS
Earthbound Farm

Today one of the largest purveyors of organic produce in the United States, Earthbound Farm began at **Earthbound Farm's Farm Stand** (7250 Carmel Valley Rd., 831/625-6219, www.ebfarm.com, Mon.-Sat. 8am-6:30pm, Sun. 9am-6pm). This 2.5-acre farm and roadside stand offers visitors easy access to the company's smallish facility in the Carmel Valley. Drive up to the farm stand and browse a variety of organic fruits, veggies, and flowers. Outdoors, ramble into the fields, checking out the chamomile labyrinth and the kids' garden (yes, your kids can look *and* touch). Select and harvest your own fresh herbs from the cut-your-own-herb garden, or leave the cooking to the experts and purchase delicious prepared organic dishes at the farm stand. If you're interested in a more in-depth guided tour of the farm, check the website for a schedule of walks, which will take you, a group, and an expert guide—perhaps a chef or famous local foodie—out into the fields for a look at what's growing and how to use it.

WINE-TASTING

The Carmel Valley's tiny size necessarily limits the number of vineyards and wineries that can set up shop there. But this small, charming wine region makes for a perfect wine-tasting day trip from Carmel, Monterey, or even Big Sur. Small crowds, light traffic, and meaningful tasting experiences categorize this area, which still has many family-owned wineries. You'll get personal attention and delicious wines, all in a gorgeous green setting.

One fun way to get around the Carmel Valley Village's wineries is to hitch a ride on the **Happy Trails Wagon Tour** (831/970-8198, Wed.-Sun. noon-4pm). Cowboy Pete pulls a 10-passenger wagon behind an antique tractor to wineries and restaurants in the immediate area.

In June, Carmel Valley Village shows off its local wines and locally produced art at the daylong **Carmel Valley Art & Wine Celebration** (831/659-4000, www.carmel-valleychamber.com, June, free).

The **Bernardus Winery** (5 W. Carmel Valley Rd., 831/298-8021 or 800/223-2533, www.bernardus.com/winery, daily 11am-5pm, tasting $12-20) sits on a vineyard estate that also hosts a luxurious lodge and gourmet restaurant. Bernardus creates a small list of wines. The grapes growing all around you go into the pride of the winery: the Bordeaux-style blended red Marinus Vineyard wine. Other varietals (chardonnay, pinot noir, and sauvignon blanc) come from cool coastal vineyards. If you're interested and lucky, you might also get to sip some small-batch vintages of single-vineyard wines that are available only in the tasting room.

On the other end of the spectrum, tiny **Parsonage Village Vineyard** (19 E. Carmel Valley Rd., 831/659-7322, www.parsonagew-ine.com, daily 11am-5pm, tasting $10) has a tasting room that sits in a little strip of shops, the space glowing with light that bounces off

Carmel Valley

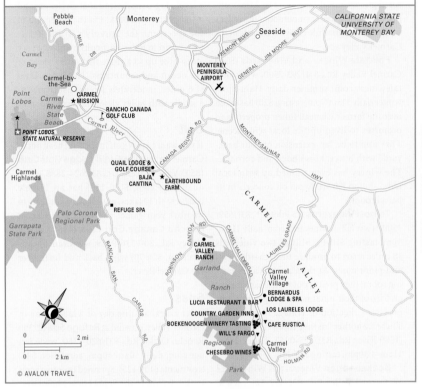

the copper of the bar. The space also is home to a display of quilts. At the bar, you'll taste wonderful syrahs, hearty cabernet sauvignons, and surprisingly deep and complex blends—the Snosrap (that's Parsons spelled backwards) table wine is inexpensive for the region and incredibly tasty. If you find a vintage you love at Parsonage, buy it then and there since they sell out of many of their wines every year.

Just a few feet away from Parsonage is the tasting room for **Chesebro Wines** (19 E. Carmel Valley Rd., Ste. D, 831/659-2125, www.chesebrowines.com, Thurs.-Fri. 1pm-5pm, Sat.-Sun. and holidays noon-5pm, tasting $10). A former Bernardus Winery employee, Mark Chesebro makes chardonnays, pinot noirs, grenache rosés, and vermentino, his

signature white wine. These wines are smart and affordable.

In the same strip of wineries, **Cima Collina** (19 E. Carmel Valley Rd., Ste. A, 831/620-0645, http://cimacollina.com, summer Sun.-Tues. noon-6pm, Wed.-Sat. noon-7pm, winter daily noon-6pm, tasting $5) has a tasting room that looks like a farmhouse with a front porch. Inside, enjoy pinot noir, chardonnay, sauvignon blanc, pinot blanc, and Cima Collina wines that are only available in the tasting room, like the Howlin' Good Red.

Another smaller, well-regarded Carmel winery is the **Heller Estate Organic Vineyards** (69 W. Carmel Valley Rd., 831/659-6220, www.hellerestate.com, daily 11am-5pm, tasting $11-15). Heller is a completely organic winery that uses natural methods, including predatory wasps, to get rid of vineyard insect pests rather than resorting to chemical-laden sprays. After visiting the tasting room, sit outdoors in Heller's sculpture garden while enjoying a bottle in the Carmel Valley sun.

Folktale Winery and Vineyards (8940 Carmel Valley Rd., 831/293-7500, www.folktalewinery.com, summer daily 11am-8pm, winter daily 11am-7pm, tasting $20) has taken over the former Chateau Julien property and promises to liven up the local wine scene. They aim to be "an extension of your backyard" with bocce, horseshoes, and cornhole. The winery has even teamed up with local radio station KRML to put on concerts in its barrel room.

Talbott Vineyards (25 Pilot Rd., 831/659-3500, www.talbottvineyards.com, daily 11am-5pm, tasting $10-15) utilizes two vineyards 18 miles apart to produce their chardonnays and pinot noirs. At the Carmel Valley tasting room, they pour six of their chardonnays and six of their pinot noirs alongside an impressive collection of vintage motorcycles. There's another tasting room near Salinas (1380 River Rd., 831/675-0942, Thurs.-Mon. 11am-4:30pm, tasting $10-15).

Boekenoogen Vineyard & Winery (24 W. Carmel Valley Rd., 831/659-4215, www.boekenoogenwines.com, daily 11am-5pm, tasting $8-10) was a cattle ranch before it became a winery. Their tasting room offers pinot noirs, chardonnays, and syrahs, as well as a garden patio for those sunny Carmel Valley afternoons.

SPORTS AND RECREATION
Hiking

The 4,462-acre **Garland Ranch Regional Park** (700 W. Carmel Valley Rd., 831/372-3196, www.mprpd.org, daily sunrise-sunset, free) allows hikers to take in all sorts of natural ecosystems from oak woodlands to redwood forests. With the park's elevation ranging 200-2,000 feet above sea level, it is also a great place to get a workout, and the park boasts the best **hiking trails** in Carmel Valley. The **Lupine Loop** (1.4 miles, easy) is a level, dog-friendly trail that circles around a flat part of the park. On the other end of the spectrum, the **Snively's Ridge Trail-Sky Loop** (6 miles, difficult) involves a very steep hike up to a ridge that offers views of the ocean and mountains. The **Mesa Trail** (1.6 miles, moderately strenuous) climbs to a saddle with valley views and a small pond.

Golf

If you want to play golf in the sun, head out to Carmel Valley. The **Quail Lodge Golf Club** (8505 Valley Greens Dr., 831/624-2888, www.quaillodge.com, $100-150) has an 18-hole course with 10 lakes, as well as an academy to improve your game. Two 18-hole courses at **Rancho Canada Golf Club** (4860 Carmel Valley Rd., 800/536-9459, www.ranchocanada.com, $20-70) wind back and forth over the Carmel River.

Spas

After an exhausting day of wine-tasting in Carmel Valley, unwind at **Refuge Spa** (27300 Rancho Carlos Rd., 831/620-7360, www.refuge.com, daily 10am-10pm, admission $44, treatments $109-125). Sprawled over two acres in the shadow of the Santa Lucia Mountains, this adult water park includes warm waterfalls tumbling into soaking pools and two kinds of cold plunge pools: one that is comparable to the body-shocking temperature of a mountain stream in the Sierra, and the other close to the chilling temp of the nearby Pacific Ocean. Don't miss the eucalyptus steam room, where a potent minty cloud of steam will purge all of your body's impurities.

ACCOMMODATIONS

For folks who come to Carmel Valley to taste wine, hike in the woods, and enjoy the less-expensive golf courses, **Country Garden Inns** (102 W. Carmel Valley Rd., 831/659-5361, www.countrygardeninns.com, $181-199) offers a perfect spot to rest and relax. Actually composed of two inns, the Acacia and the

Hidden Valley, Country Garden's small B&Bs offer violet and taupe French country-style charm in the rooms, as well as a pool, a self-serve breakfast bar, and strolling gardens. Rooms run from romantic king-bed studios up to big family suites; most sleep at least four people (with daybeds in the window nooks).

Hosting guests on and off since 1915, the former ranch at **Los Laureles Lodge** (313 W. Carmel Valley Rd., 831/659-2233, www.loslaureles.com, $130-285, three-bedroom house $650) can put you up in a room, a honeymoon cottage, or a three-bedroom house. Enjoy the property's restaurant, saloon, and, most of all, its swimming pool and adjacent pool bar.

There's plenty of space to absorb Carmel Valley's sunshine at the ★ **Blue Sky Lodge** (10 Flight Rd., 831/659-2256, www.blueskylodge.com, $119-413), whether on your unit's private patio or sundeck or in the lodge's courtyard, which has a pool, a lawn, a multi-person hot tub, table tennis, and lots of lounge chairs. The units have thick carpeting and are a bit dated, but in a charming, retro-chic way. Six of the rooms also have kitchens. Behind the pool is a comfy common room with a fireplace, an extensive library, a piano, a lot of houseplants, and a computer for guest use. The Blue Sky Lodge's location can't be beat—it is just a few hundred feet up from Carmel Valley Village and its many tasting rooms.

To spread out and relax, book a stay at the 500-acre ★ **Carmel Valley Ranch** (1 Old Ranch Rd., 831/625-9500, www.carmelvalleyranch.com, $400-600). The spacious suites range 650-1,200 square feet with fireplaces and decks to take in the valley views and wild turkeys. Carmel Valley Ranch has so many outdoor activities that it feels like an upscale summer camp. An activity calendar comes with your stay and includes everything from a beekeeping class to nightly s'mores roasting over an open fire. Don't miss the amazing pool deck with a saltwater swimming pool that's long enough for laps and an Infinity pool hot tub that overlooks some beautiful oak trees and the resort's vineyard.

FOOD

The **Lucia Restaurant & Bar** (Bernardus Lodge & Spa, 415 W. Carmel Valley Rd., 831/658-3400, www.bernarduslodge.com, daily 7am-11am, 11:30am-2:30pm, and 5pm-9pm, $21-62, chef's tasting menu $95) opened in 2015, taking the place of the Bernardus Lodge's Marinus and Wicket's Bistro. Led by revered local chef Cal Stamenov, Lucia truly utilizes the nearby land, using herbs from the garden out front and serving wines created from the adjacent vineyard. The menu starts with worthwhile items like a creamed spinach appetizer (once only a holiday menu option). Meat-centric dishes include brick-oven pizzas, Hudson Valley foie gras, prime beef, and a smoked duck stew. A favorite entrée is the grilled king salmon steak wrapped in pancetta with asparagus spears. It's one of the better pieces of fish around. Oenophiles and others should consider wine pairings, including the superb Bernardus Pisoni pinot noir and the Bernardus Ingrid's chardonnay. The knowledgeable and friendly staff will properly guide you.

The frequently sunny Carmel Valley is a great place to dine al fresco. With a large outdoor dining area, **Café Rustica** (10 Del Fino Pl., 831/659-4444, www.caferusticacarmel.com, Tues.-Sun. 11am-2:30pm and 5pm-9pm, $13-30) is known for its nightly fish specials and herb-roasted half chicken.

Sip a wide range of tasty, intoxicating margaritas on the large wooden deck at ★ **Baja Cantina** (7166 Carmel Valley Rd., 831/625-2252, www.carmelcantina.com, Mon.-Fri. 11:30am-11pm, Sat.-Sun. 11am-midnight, $13-20). Catch a sports game on one of the big-screen TVs and enjoy the car memorabilia covering the walls. The menu includes hearty Americanized Mexican cuisine, like rosemary chicken burritos and wild mushroom and spinach enchiladas. Even the nachos are worthwhile—they have so much baked cheese that they resemble a casserole.

★ **Will's Fargo** (16 W. Carmel Valley Rd., 831/659-2774, http://wfrestaurant.com, Sun.-Thurs. 4:30pm-9pm, Fri.-Sat. 4:30pm-10pm, $15-35) was a tea room, a roadhouse, and a restaurant called The Carousel before taking on its current incarnation in 1959. This place has a great Old West atmosphere. This unassuming steak house has an executive chef who has worked in Michelin-starred restaurants. The steaks (prime angus top sirloin, filet mignon, Kansas City, and porterhouse) are served a la carte. Choose from sides like quail, lobster tail, bacon, and vegetables.

INFORMATION AND SERVICES

Call or visit the website of the **Carmel Valley Chamber of Commerce** (831/659-4000, http://carmelvalleychamber.com) for basic information before arriving. Most services are available in nearby Carmel-by-the-Sea.

The nearest major medical center to Carmel Valley is in nearby Monterey: the **Community Hospital of Monterey** (23625 Holman Hwy, Monterey, 831/624-5311, www. chomp.org).

TRANSPORTATION

To get to Carmel Valley, take Highway 1 to Carmel Valley Road, which is a major intersection with a stoplight. Take Carmel Valley Road east for 13 miles to the Carmel Valley Village, where most of the area's restaurants and wineries are.

Big Sur and the Central Coast

Look for ★ to find recommended sights, activities, dining, and lodging.

Highlights

★ **Big Sur Coast Highway:** One of the most scenic drives in the world, Big Sur's Highway 1 passes redwood forests and crystal-clear streams and rivers while offering breathtaking, ever-present views of the coast (page 363).

★ **Point Sur Light Station:** Crowning a 361-foot-high rock towering above the sea, this lighthouse is arguably California's most stunning light station (page 365).

★ **Pfeiffer Beach:** With rock formations offshore and purple sand, Pfeiffer Beach is one of Big Sur's most picturesque spots (page 366).

★ **Hiking in Big Sur:** For the best way to take in Big Sur's beauty, take a hike in Andrew Molera State Park, with its coastal vistas and beach access, or Julia Pfeiffer Burns State Park, with its giant redwoods (page 368).

★ **Hearst Castle:** Newspaper magnate William Randolph Hearst's 56-bedroom manse is the closest thing that the United States has to a castle (page 384).

★ **Morro Rock:** The 576-foot-high "Gibraltar of the Pacific" is one of the great photo ops of the Central Coast (page 395).

★ **Montaña de Oro State Park:** This underrated natural treasure comprises 8,000 mostly undeveloped acres of coves, peaks, and canyons (page 396).

★ **Madonna Inn:** The rooms, restaurants, bars—and even the bathroom—are worth a look at this monument to kitsch (page 403).

Big Sur means a lot of different things. Is Big Sur a state park with a lot of redwoods? Is it a small city tucked in an undeveloped section of California? Is it a valley, a river, a scenic drive? Or is Big Sur really a state of mind?

Big Sur's 90 miles of rugged coastline begin just south of Carmel on the Monterey Peninsula, and stretch south all the way to San Simeon. Here, the mountains rise up suddenly, and drop just as dramatically into the sea. Highway 1 twists and turns like a two-lane snake, trying to keep up with the land-and seascape.

Big Sur is wild—a place where vertical cliffs drop straight into the ocean, redwood trees tickle the sky, and hiking trails lead to spouting waterfalls and secluded beaches. In fact, the miles and miles of hiking trails in this region outnumber the paved roads. With resorts like Ventana and Post Ranch, Big Sur offers retreats where visitors can experience this wild, indisputable natural beauty while pampering themselves with luxurious relaxation.

Continuing south, the road evens out and the coastline gets less extreme, becoming the host to a string of some of California's best beach towns, each with its own allure. San Simeon is home to one of California's biggest attractions: the magnificent Hearst Castle, a monument to the incredible wealth of newspaper magnate William Randolph Hearst. Just a few miles south, Cambria has a pleasant downtown and Moonstone Beach, where you can pick up pieces of the gemstone right off the sand. Cayucos is an old-fashioned beach town with its own strand of sand and a pier that dates back to the late 1800s. Morro Bay boasts an almost-600-foot domed rock formation that can be seen from the town's Embarcadero, which has a string of restaurants, hotels, and tourist shops. Just out of Morro Bay is one of the best coastal state parks in all of California: Montaña de Oro.

It's worth detouring a few miles inland to visit college town San Luis Obispo, with its vibrant weekly farmer's market, a California mission, and the kitschy but cool Madonna Inn, and nearby Paso Robles' thermal springs

Previous: horseback riders near Andrew Molera State Park; ocean vista near Bixby Bridge in Big Sur.
Above: Morro Bay.

Central Coast

Carmel
Salinas
68
Garrapata
State Park
1
Carmel Valley
Village
POINT SUR
LIGHT STATION   HIKING IN
BIG SUR
G17   101
Andrew
Molera SP
G16   Gonzales
BIG SUR COAST
HIGHWAY
Big Sur
PFEIFFER
BEACH
Soledad
MCWAY
FALLS
Los
Padres
National
Forest
John Little
SR
Greenfield
Ventana
Wilderness
Lopez Pt   Lucia
Limekiln
KIRK CREEK   SP
King City
PLASKETT   FORT
CREEK
Jade Cove
RA
HUNTER   0   5 mi
Cape
San Martin   TREEBONES
RESORT   0   5 km
LIGGET
1
Pacific
Ocean   Lake
HEARST   San
CASTLE   Antonio   101
Lake
San Simeon
Nacimiento   CAMP ROBERTS
San Simeon   MILITARY RES
State Park   Cambria
San Miguel
Harmony
Paso
Robles
1
46
Cayucos   Templeton
Morro Strand
State Beach   Atascadero
MORRO ROCK   Morro Bay   41
Morro Bay   41
State Park   Baywood Park
Point   Los Osos   101   229
Buchon   MONTAÑA DE ORO
STATE PARK   58
MADONNA
INN   San Luis Obispo
Avila Beach
Shell Beach   Los
Padres
Pismo Beach   National
Grover Beach   227   Forest
Oceano   Arroyo Grande
© AVALON TRAVEL

and up-and-coming wineries. Heading back to the coast again, Pismo Beach feels like a hip vacation spot—from 50 years ago.

PLANNING YOUR TIME

Summer is the busy season for Big Sur and the Central Coast. This is also when there can be frequent coastal fog. Away from the coast, the Big Sur Valley can offer some relief from the fog. Similarly, a trip inland to Paso Robles usually offers higher temperatures. In Big Sur and the Central Coast reservations are essential for hotels and campsites during the summer. The fall is the ideal time for a trip to the area, with warmer temperatures and fewer crowds.

Highway 1, the road into and out of Big Sur, is a twisting, sometimes-two-lane highway, with frequent construction and closures. Check the California Department of Transportation website (www.dot.ca.gov) for information about closures and possible delays. If you are driving slower than most traffic on Highway 1, pull over into a pullout and allow the traffic to pass. The roadway also connects the Central Coast towns south of Big Sur. Highway 1 passes right by San Simeon, Cambria, Cayucos, Morro Bay, San Luis Obispo, and Pismo Beach. Ample exit signs tell drivers when to turn off the highway. South of Cambria, Highway 46 over the hills connects Highway 1 to Paso Robles. Farther south, Highway 1 and U.S. 101 come together at San Luis Obispo. If you're heading to San Luis Obispo and aren't interested in a leisurely coastal drive, U.S. 101 will get you there quicker.

A lot of people drive through Big Sur in a day, taking Highway 1 from Carmel to San Simeon and pulling off at the road's many turnouts to take in the views. Outdoors enthusiasts who want to get off the highway and *really* experience Big Sur will need at least a couple of days. The Big Sur Valley (26 miles south of Carmel) is a good place to stay if you want both a great outdoors experience and amenities such as restaurants and lodging. The valley is also home to Pfeiffer Big Sur

State Park, which has over 200 campsites. The south coast of Big Sur toward San Simeon has significantly fewer amenities; there are a few campgrounds and the Treebones Resort. On the Central Coast south of Big Sur, pick a town as a base and plan to spend a few days exploring the area sights. In a weekend, you can visit Hearst Castle, hike Montaña de Oro, and get in some beach time.

A trip to Big Sur involves planning. It's a good idea to secure supplies and gas before entering Big Sur (at Carmel in the north or Cambria in the south). While Big Sur does have a few markets, you will pay higher prices for a smaller selection of goods. Definitely fill up your tank before heading into Big Sur. While there are a few gas stations on the 90-mile stretch of coastline, you will pay a premium for a gallon of gas. Gas stations in Big Sur have made headlines for having the most expensive gas in the nation.

The towns south of Big Sur have more infrastructure, with amenities including supermarkets, banks, and a range of lodging and restaurant options. You can also get gas here at prices more in line with the rest of the state.

Big Sur

Big Sur welcomes many types of visitors. Nature lovers come to camp and hike the pristine wilderness areas, to don thick wetsuits and surf often-deserted beaches, and even to hunt for jade in rocky coves. On the other hand, some of the wealthiest people from California and beyond visit to relax at unbelievably posh hotels and spas with dazzling views of the ocean. Whether you prefer a low-cost camping trip or a luxury resort, Big Sur offers its beauty and charm to all. Part of that charm is Big Sur's determination to remain peacefully apart from the Information Age (this means that your cell phones may not work in many parts of Big Sur).

SIGHTS
★ Big Sur Coast Highway

Even if you're not up to tackling the endless hiking trails and deep wilderness backcountry of Big Sur, you can still get a good sense of the glory of this region just by driving through it. The **Big Sur Coast Highway,** a 90-mile stretch of Highway 1, is quite simply one of the most picturesque roads in the country. A two-lane road, Highway 1 twists and turns with Big Sur's jagged coastline, running along precipitous cliffs and rocky beaches, through dense redwood forest, over historic bridges, and past innumerable parks. In the winter, you might spot migrating whales offshore spouting fountains of air and water, while spring finds yucca plants feathering the hillsides and wildflowers coloring the landscape. Construction on this stretch of road was completed in the 1930s, connecting Cambria to Carmel. Start out at either of these towns and spend a whole day making your way to the other end of the road. The road has plenty of wide turnouts set into picturesque cliffs to make it easy to stop to admire the glittering ocean and stunning wooded cliffs running right out to the water. Bring a camera on your trip along Highway 1—you'll find yourself wanting to take photos every mile for hours on end. Also be aware that there can be frequent highway delays due to road construction.

Bixby Bridge

You'll probably recognize the **Bixby Bridge** (CA-1, 5.5 miles south of Garrapata State Park) when you come upon it on Highway 1 in Big Sur. The picturesque, open-spandrel arched cement bridge is one of the most photographed bridges in the nation, and it has been used in countless car commercials over the years. The bridge was built in the early 1930s as part of the massive government works project that completed CA-1 through

Big Sur

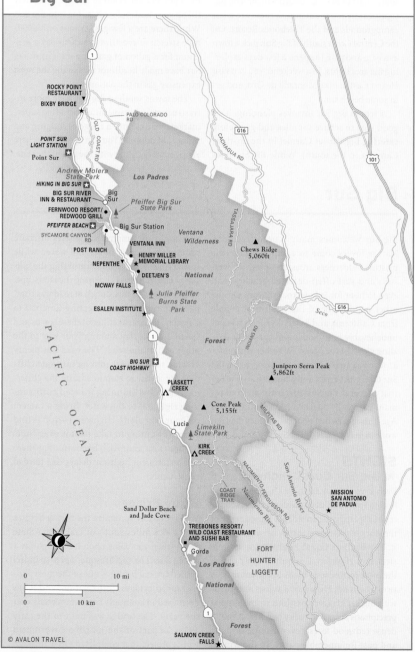

ROCKY POINT
RESTAURANT
BIXBY BRIDGE

PALO COLORADO
RD

*POINT SUR
LIGHT STATION*
Point Sur

*Andrew Molera
State Park*

Los Padres

HIKING IN BIG SUR
BIG SUR RIVER
INN & RESTAURANT
Big
Sur

*Pfeiffer Big Sur
State Park*

FERNWOOD RESORT/
REDWOOD GRILL
PFEIFFER BEACH
SYCAMORE CANYON
RD

Big Sur Station

*Ventana
Wilderness*

POST RANCH

VENTANA INN

HENRY MILLER
MEMORIAL LIBRARY

Chews Ridge
5,060ft

NEPENTHE

DEETJEN'S

National

MCWAY FALLS

*Julia Pfeiffer
Burns State
Park*

ESALEN INSTITUTE

Forest

BIG SUR
COAST HIGHWAY

Junipero Serra Peak
5,862ft

PLASKETT
CREEK

Cone Peak
5,155ft

Lucia

*Limekiln
State Park*

P A C I F I C

KIRK
CREEK

O C E A N

COAST
RIDGE
TRAIL

MISSION
SAN ANTONIO
DE PADUA

Sand Dollar Beach
and Jade Cove

TREEBONES RESORT/
WILD COAST RESTAURANT
AND SUSHI BAR

FORT
HUNTER
LIGGETT

Gorda

Los Padres

National

0   10 mi

0   10 km

Forest

SALMON CREEK
FALLS

OLD COAST RD

CACHAGUA RD

G16

101

TASSAJARA RD

INDIANS RD

Seco

G16

MILPITAS RD

NACIMIENTO-FERGUSSON RD

San Antonio River

Nacimiento River

© AVALON TRAVEL

the Big Sur area, finally connecting the north end of California to the south. Pull out north of the bridge to take photos or just look out at the attractive span and Bixby Creek flowing into the Pacific far below. Get another great view of the bridge by driving a few hundred feet down the dirt Old Coast Road, which is on the bridge's northeast side.

★ Point Sur Light Station

Sitting lonely and isolated out on its cliff, the **Point Sur Light Station** (CA-1, 6.7 miles south of Bixby Bridge, 831/625-4419, www. pointsur.org, Nov.-Mar. tours Wed. 1pm, Sat.-Sun. 10am, Apr.-June and Sept.-Oct. Wed. and Sat. 10am and 2pm, Sun. 10am, July-Aug. Wed. and Sat. 10am and 2pm, Thurs. 10am, Sun. 10am, adults $12, children $5) crowns the 361-foot-high volcanic rock Point Sur. It keeps watch over ships navigating near the rocky waters of Big Sur. It's the only complete 19th-century light station in California that you can visit, and even here access is severely limited. First lit in 1889, this now fully automated light station still provides navigational aid to ships off the coast; families stopped living and working in the tiny stone compound in 1974. But is the lighthouse truly uninhabited? Take one of the **moonlight tours** (call

for information) to learn about the haunted history of the light station buildings.

You can't make a reservation for a Point Sur tour, so you should just show up and park your car off CA-1 on the west side by the farm gate. Your guide will meet you there and lead you up the paved road 0.5 miles to the light station. Once there, you'll climb the stairs up to the light, explore the restored keepers' homes and service buildings, and walk out to the cliff edge. Expect to see a great variety of wildlife, from brilliant wildflowers in the spring to gray whales in the winter to flocks of pelicans flying in formation at any time of year. Dress in layers; it can be sunny and hot or foggy and cold, winter or summertime, and sometimes both on the same tour! Tours last three hours and require more than a mile of walking, with a bit of slope, and more than 100 stairs. If you need special assistance for your tour or have questions about accessibility, call 831/667-0528 as far in advance as possible of your visit to make arrangements.

Pfeiffer Big Sur State Park

The most developed park in Big Sur is **Pfeiffer Big Sur State Park** (CA-1, 26 miles south of Carmel, 831/667-2315, www.parks. ca.gov, day use 30 minutes before sunrise-30

Point Sur Light Station, atop Point Sur

minutes after sunset, $10/vehicle). It's home to a lodge, a restaurant and café, hiking trails, and lovely redwood-shaded campsites. This is one of the best parks in the area to see Big Sur's redwoods and a great place to dip into the cool Big Sur River.

Pfeiffer Big Sur has the tiny **Ernst Ewoldsen Memorial Nature Center,** which features taxidermy examples of local wildlife. It's open seasonally; call the park for days and hours. The historic **Homestead Cabin,** off the Big Sur Gorge Trail, was once the home of part of the Pfeiffer family, who were the first European immigrants to settle in Big Sur.

The **Nature Trail** (0.7 mile round-trip, no elevation gain, easy) leaves from Big Sur Lodge and provides an introduction to the park's natural assets. No bikes or horses are allowed on trails in this park, which makes it quite peaceful for hikers.

Big Sur Station

If you haven't yet stopped at one of the larger state parks in the area and hit the visitors center, pull in at **Big Sur Station** (Hwy. 1, 0.33 miles south of Pfeiffer Big Sur, 831/667-2315, Wed.-Sun. 9am-4pm). The ranger station offers maps and brochures for all the major parks and trails of Big Sur, plus a minimal bookshop. This is also where the trailhead for the popular backcountry **Pine Ridge Trail** is located. Get a free backcountry fire permit as well as pay for Pine Ridge Trailhead parking here.

★ Pfeiffer Beach

Big Sur has plenty of striking meetings of land and sea, but **Pfeiffer Beach** (end of Sycamore Canyon Rd., http://campone.com, daily 9am-8pm, $10/vehicle) is definitely one of the coastline's most picturesque spots. This frequently windswept beach has two looming rock formations right where the beach meets the surf, and both of these rocks have holes that look like doorways, allowing waves and sunlight to pass through. Occasionally, purple sand colors the beach; it is eroded manganese

garnet from the bluffs above. It can be incredibly windy here some days.

For newcomers, getting to Pfeiffer Beach is a bit tricky. It is at the end of the second paved right south of the Big Sur Station. Motorists (no motor homes) must then travel down a narrow, windy, two-mile road before reaching the entrance booth and the beach's parking lot. It's part of the adventure. This road gets very busy during the summer and on weekends. Plan a trip to Pfeiffer Beach when it's less busy. Otherwise, the two-mile drive might take a lot longer than expected.

Henry Miller Memorial Library

A number of authors have spent time in Big Sur, soaking in the remote wilderness and sea air to gather inspiration for their work. Henry Miller lived and wrote in Big Sur for 18 years, and his 1957 novel *Big Sur and the Oranges of Hieronymus Bosch* describes his time here. Today, the **Henry Miller Memorial Library** (48603 CA-1, between Nepenthe Restaurant and Deetjen's Big Sur Inn, 831/667-2574, www.henrymiller.org, daily 11am-6pm, free) celebrates the life and work of Miller and his brethren in this quirky community center, museum, coffee shop, and gathering place. What you won't find is a typical lending library or slicked-up museum. Instead, inside is a well-curated bookstore featuring the works of Miller as well as other authors like Jack Kerouac and Richard Brautigan, along with a crew of employees who are always worth striking up a conversation with. The controversial writer was a rabid table tennis player, so a table is available outside for those who'd like to play a game or work on their serve. The small redwood-shaded lawn hosts concerts and literary events. During summer, the library puts on an international short-film series every Thursday night. Check the library's website for a list of upcoming events.

McWay Falls

One of Big Sur's best postcard-perfect views can be attained at **Julia Pfeiffer Burns State Park** (CA-1, 37 miles south of Carmel,

831/667-2315, www.parks.ca.gov, day use 30 minutes before sunrise-30 minutes after sunset, $10/vehicle). To get to the stunning view of **McWay Falls,** take the **Overlook Trail** (0.6 mile round-trip) along a level wheelchair-accessible boardwalk. Stroll under CA-1, past the Pelton wheelhouse, and out to the observation deck. The 80-foot-high waterfall cascades year-round off a cliff and onto the beach of a remote cove, where the water wets the sand and trickles out into the sea. You'll look down on a pristine and empty stretch of sand—there's no way down to the cove that is even remotely safe.

Nacimiento-Fergusson Road

The only road that traverses Big Sur's Santa Lucia Mountains, the **Nacimiento-Fergusson Road** (four miles south of Lucia) offers spectacular coastal views to those who are willing to wind their way up this twisty, paved, 1.5-lane road. Simply drive a few miles up to get an eyeful of the expansive Pacific Ocean or to climb above Big Sur's summer fog. It also heads in and out of infrequent redwood forests on the way up. The road connects Highway 1 to U.S. 101, passing through Fort Hunter Liggett army base on its journey. The road is frequently closed during the winter months. Not recommended for those who get carsick.

Sand Dollar Beach

Sand Dollar Beach (9.2 miles south of Lucia, http://campone.com, daily sunrise-sunset, $10/vehicle) is one of Big Sur's biggest and best beaches. On Big Sur's south coast, this half-moon-shaped beach is tucked under cliffs that keep the wind down. Though frequently strewn with rocks, the beach is a great place to plop down for a picnic or an afternoon in the sun. From the beach, enjoy a striking view of Big Sur's south coast mountains including Cone Peak, rising like a jagged fang from a long ridgeline. A series of uncrowded beach breaks offer waves for surfers even during the flatter summer months. The area around the parking lot has picnic tables with raised grills, pit toilets, and a pay phone. If the parking lot is full, park on the dirt pullout to the south of the entrance.

Salmon Creek Falls

One of the best natural attractions in the southern portion of Big Sur is **Salmon Creek Falls** (CA-1, 8.8 miles south of Willow Creek). Flowing year-round, a pair of waterfalls pour down rocks over 100 feet high, their streams

Henry Miller Memorial Library

joining halfway down. To get a great perspective of the falls, take an easy 10-minute walk over a primitive trail littered with rocks fallen from the highway. The unmarked parking area is a pullout in the middle of a hairpin turn on Highway 1.

★ HIKING

The main reason to come to Big Sur is to get out of your vehicle and hike its beaches and forests. There are lots of hiking opportunities here from short walks under a canopy of redwood trees to multiday backpacking trips into Big Sur's wilderness interior.

Garrapata State Park

Garrapata State Park (Hwy. 1, 6.7 miles south of Rio Rd., 831/624-4909, www.parks.ca.gov, daily 8am-30 minutes after sunset) has most of the features that make Big Sur such a famed destination for outdoor enthusiasts: redwood trees, rocky headlands, pocket beaches, and ocean vistas from steep hills and mountains. Garrapata, which means "tick" in Spanish, includes **Garrapata Beach,** northern Big Sur's finest beach, and two miles of coastline. The two-mile round-trip **Soberanes Point Trail** to the west of the highway is a mild hike up and around the park's rocky headlands. Stroll along the beach, scramble up the cliffs for a better view of the ocean, or check out the seals, sea otters, and sea lions near Soberanes Point. In the wintertime, grab a pair of binoculars to look for migrating gray whales passing quite close to shore here.

For a more invigorating hike, connect the **Soberanes Canyon Trail** with the **Rocky Ridge Trail,** making a 4.5-mile loop. In Soberanes Canyon, you'll get a taste of a small redwood forest before climbing up to the outstanding coast views offered by 1,700-foot-high Rocky Ridge. In the spring months, the trail is littered with a profusion of wildflowers. A bench on the coastal side of Rocky Ridge offers a great place to catch your breath and take in the scenery. This is the same landscape that inspired nature poet

McWay Falls at Julia Pfeiffer Burns State Park

Robinson Jeffers to pen his popular poem, "The Place For No Story."

Expect little in the way of facilities here—you'll park in a wide spot on Highway 1, and if you're lucky you might find a pit toilet open for use.

Andrew Molera State Park

Andrew Molera State Park (CA-1, 3.1 miles south of Point Sur Light Station, 831/667-2315, www.parks.ca.gov, day use 30 minutes before sunrise-30 minutes after sunset, $10/vehicle) has several hiking trails that run down to the beach and up into the forest along the river. The beach is a one-mile walk down the easy, multiuse **Trail Camp Beach Trail** (two miles round-trip, no elevation gain, easy). From there, climb out to the headlands on the **Headlands Trail** (0.5 miles round-trip, 30-foot elevation gain, easy) for a beautiful view of the Big Sur River emptying into the sea. In the distance is Pico Blanco, one of the region's most distinct mountains, rising like a pyramid from behind a ridgeline.

If you prefer to get a better look at the river, take the flat, moderate **Bobcat Trail** (5.5 miles round-trip, negligible elevation gain, easy) and perhaps a few of its ancillary loops. You'll walk right along the riverbank, enjoying the local microhabitats.

For a longer and more difficult trek up the mountains and down to the beach, take the **Ridge Trail and Panorama Trail Loop** (eight miles round-trip, 1,000-foot elevation gain, moderate). This is one of the best coastal hikes in Big Sur. You'll start at the parking lot on the **Creamery Meadow Beach Trail,** then make a left onto the long and fairly steep **Ridge Trail** to get a sense of the local ecosystem. Then turn right onto the **Panorama Trail,** which has sweeping views of the coast, including Molera Point and Point Sur, as it runs down to the coastal scrublands. Take the small **Spring Trail** (0.2 miles round-trip, little elevation gain, easy) down a driftwood-littered gully to a scenic stretch of beach. Hike back out and take a left connecting to the **Bluffs Trail,** which takes you back to Creamery Meadow along the top of a marine terrace.

A fairly short but steep hike that is never crowded is the **East Molera Trail** (three miles round-trip, 1,300-foot elevation gain,

strenuous), which is on the east side of Highway 1. From the main parking lot, walk to the white barn and take the tunnel under the road that leads to the trail. The trail is a steep series of switchbacks that climb up to a saddle with coast views to the west and a glimpse of the imposing, pyramid-shaped Pico Blanco to the east.

At the park entrance, you'll find bathrooms but no drinkable water and no food concessions.

Pfeiffer Big Sur State Park

For a starter walk at **Pfeiffer Big Sur State Park** (CA-1, 2.7 miles south of Andrew Molera State Park, 831/667-2315, www.parks.ca.gov, 30 minutes before sunrise-30 minutes after sunset, $10/vehicle), take a short stroll on the Valley View Trail to **Pfeiffer Falls** (1.5 miles round-trip, 200-foot elevation gain, easy). The trail passes through a redwood forest, crosses a creek, and then heads up into the hills. The burnt redwoods you'll see are from the 2008 Basin Complex Fire, the third-largest wildfire in the state's history. Eventually, the trail reaches a T-intersection. A right turn heads into a redwood-shaded canyon and ends at a view of the 60-foot waterfall spilling down a rock face. The **Valley View Overlook** (1 mile

a rock formation on Garrapata Beach

from trailhead and 0.5 miles from Pfeiffer Falls) peers down the Big Sur Valley to Point Sur in the distance.

The **Buzzard's Roost Trail** (three miles round-trip, 750-foot elevation gain, moderate) explores the portion of the park on the west side of Highway 1. Climb from the river's edge through redwoods and oak trees on the way up to the summit of Pfeiffer Ridge, where you'll have a view of the coastline. Other coastal hikes such as Molera's Eight-Mile Loop have better vistas.

For a longer, more difficult, and interesting hike that leaves the park and goes into the adjoining Ventana Wilderness, start at the Homestead Cabin and head to the **Mount Manuel Trail** (10 miles round-trip, 3,150-foot elevation gain, strenuous). From the Y-intersection with the Oak Grove Trail, it's four miles of sturdy hiking up a steep grade to Mount Manuel, a 3,379-foot peak that looms high over the Big Sur Valley. On summer days, during the trail's initial climb, it's possible to hear swimmers in the Big Sur Gorge below. The tallest point has some rocks and a view of the ocean behind Pfeiffer Ridge. Bring lots of water for this hike.

Need to cool off after hiking? Scramble out to the undeveloped **Big Sur River Gorge**, where the river slows and creates pools that are great for swimming. Relax and enjoy the water, but don't try to dive here. The undeveloped trail to the gorge can be found at the eastern end of the campground.

Julia Pfeiffer Burns State Park

If you're up for a longer hike after taking in McWay Falls within **Julia Pfeiffer Burns State Park** (CA-1, 7.7 miles south of Henry Miller Memorial Library, 831/667-2315, www. parks.ca.gov, day use 30 minutes before sunrise-30 minutes after sunset, $10/vehicle), go back the other way to pick up the **Ewoldsen Trail** (4.5 miles round-trip, 1,500-foot elevation gain, moderate). This trek takes you through McWay Canyon, where you'll see the creek and surrounding lush greenery as you walk. Some of Big Sur's finest redwoods are here. Then you'll loop away from the water and climb up into the hills. One part of the trail is perched on a ridgeline where there is little vegetation growing on the steep hillside below. This is the site of a 1983 landslide that closed the highway below for a whole year. A quick detour can be made by taking the Overlook Trail, a short spur that goes to an open viewing area with a bench offering

a stunning beach off the Big Sur Coast Highway

a glimpse of the sea spread out to the horizon. Bring water, as this hike can take several hours.

To spend all day at Julia Pfeiffer Burns State Park, drive two miles north from the park entrance to the Partington Cove pullout and park along the side of the highway. On the east side of the highway, start out along the **Tanbark Trail** (6.4 miles round-trip, 1,900-foot elevation gain, strenuous). You'll head through redwood groves and up steep switchbacks to the top of the coastal ridge. Near the top is the Tin House, a dilapidated structure with a large concrete front porch still intact. Return back down the trail or take the fire road, which descends steeply to the highway. Utilizing the fire road creates a loop hike, though this also means hiking a mile on Highway 1 to get back to your vehicle.

The west side of the road is where you pick up the **Partington Cove Trail** (two miles round-trip, 200-foot elevation gain, easy) an underrated walk that goes to a striking, narrow coastal inlet. It begins as a steep dirt road and continues through a 60-foot-long tunnel blasted into the rock. The trail arrives at a cove where John Partington used to ship out the tanbark trees that he had harvested in the canyon above. There is a bench at the end of the trail offering views of the cove and the coastline to the south. To reach the trailhead from the north, drive nine miles south of Pfeiffer Big Sur State Park on Highway 1. Look for a big bend in the road to the east with dirt pullouts on either side. Park here and then begin your hike where the gated road departs from the west side.

The 1.2-mile **Waters Trail** (1.2 miles one-way, negligible elevation gain, easy) is the newest hiking option in Julia Pfeiffer Burns State Park. This worthy addition to the park connects the Tanbark Trail to the Ewoldsen Trail, traversing a piece of the park that was previously inaccessible. Begin either at the main park entrance—where you'll find the trailhead off the Ewoldsen Trail—or start from the Tanbark Trail. The path cuts across the hillside while offering postcard-worthy coastal views along most of its route. In the spring, this area is painted purple by fields of flowering lupine. Unless you use two cars, you will have to walk along the highway a short distance to return to your vehicle. This hike is worth all of the effort.

Jade Cove Recreation Area

It's easy to miss **Jade Cove Recreation Area** (Hwy. 1, two miles south of Sand

a hiker passing through the tunnel on Partington Cove Trail, Julia Pfeiffer Burns State Park

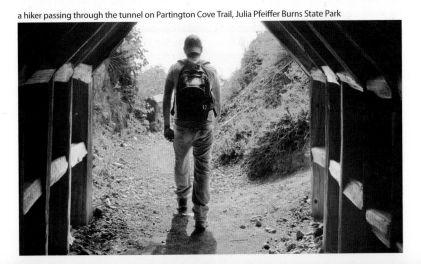

Dollar Beach) as you barrel down Highway 1 towards San Simeon. A road sign marks the area, but there's not much in the way of a formal parking lot or anything else to denote the treasures of this jagged, rough part of the Big Sur coastline. Park in the dirt/gravel strip off the road and head past the fence. It's fun to read the unusual signs along the narrow, beaten path that seems to lead to the edge of a cliff. The signs explain that you cannot bring in mining equipment, or take away rocks or minerals obtained from behind the high-tide line. If you're into aerial sports, you can hang glide off the cliffs here.

Once you get to the edge of the cliff, the short trail gets rough. It's only 0.25 mile, but it's almost straight down a rocky, slippery cliff. Don't try to climb down if you're not in reasonable physical condition, and even if you are, don't be afraid to use your hands to steady yourself. At the bottom, you'll find huge boulders and smaller rocks and very little sand. You may also see a small herd of locals dressed in wetsuits and scuba gear. But most of all, you'll find the most amazing minerals in the boulders and rocks. Reach out and touch a multi-ton boulder shot through with jade. Search the smaller rocks beneath your feet for chunks of sea-polished jade. If you're a hardcore rock nut, join the locals in scuba diving for jewelry-quality jade. As long as you find it in the water or below the high-tide line, it's legal for you to take whatever you find here. Be aware that there is also lots of serpentine here. Serpentine has a similar green color to jade but has no real value.

Jade Cove has no water, no restrooms, no visitors center, and no services of any kind.

SPORTS AND RECREATION
Horseback Riding

Take a guided horseback ride into the forests or out onto the beaches of Andrew Molera State Park with **Molera Horseback Tours** (831/625-5486, http://molerahorsebacktours. com, $48-84). Tours of 1-2.5 hours depart each day starting at 9am, 11am, 1pm, and 3:30pm.

Call ahead to guarantee your spot or to book a private guided ride. Each ride begins at the modest corral area, from which you'll ride along multiuse trails through forests or meadows, or aside the Big Sur River, and down to Molera Beach. There you'll guide your horse along the solid sands as you admire the beauty of the wild Pacific Ocean.

Molera Horseback Tours are suitable for children over age six and riders of all ability levels; you'll be matched to the right horse for you. All but one of the rides go down to the beach. Tours can be seasonal, so call ahead if you want to ride in the fall or winter.

Backpacking

If you long for the lonely peace of backcountry camping, the **Ventana Wilderness** (www. ventanawild.org) area is ideal for you. This area comprises the peaks of the Santa Lucia Mountains and the dense growth of the northern reaches of the Los Padres National Forest. It has 167,323 acres of steep V-shaped canyons and mountains that rise to over 5,000 feet. You'll find many trails beyond the popular day hikes of the state parks, especially as Big Sur stretches down to the south. One of the most popular hikes is the 10-mile-long climb on the **Pine Ridge Trail** (Big Sur Station, 0.25 miles south of Pfeiffer Big Sur State Park) to **Sykes Hot Springs,** a cluster of warm mineral pools at a backcountry camp situated on the Big Sur River. The trail leaves from the Big Sur Station, where you should secure a campfire permit and a parking pass before heading out. Farther south, the **Vicente Flat Trail** (4 miles south of Lucia on Hwy. 1, across from the Kirk Creek Campground, 10 miles round-trip) heads up towards Cone Peak, the jagged mountain rising in the distance, while gaining sweeping views of the coast. Do this one as a grueling up-and-back day hike to the Vincente Flat Camp or backpack it. Check the Ventana Wilderness Alliance website (www. ventanawild.org) in advance to find reports on the conditions of the trails you've decided to tackle, and stop in at Big Sur Station to get the latest news on the backcountry areas.

Fishing

No harbors offer deep-sea charters around Big Sur, but if your idea of the perfect outdoor vacation includes a rod and reel, the region offers your choice of shore or river fishing. Steelhead run up the Big Sur River to spawn each year, and a limited fishing season follows them up the river into **Pfeiffer Big Sur State Park** and other accessible areas. Check with Fernwood Resort (831/667-2422, www.fernwoodbigsur.com) and the other lodges around Highway 1 for the best spots this season.

The numerous creeks that feed into and out of the Big Sur River also play home to their fair share of fish. The California Department of Fish and Game (www.dfg.ca.gov) can give you specific locations for legal fishing, season information, and rules and regulations.

If you prefer the fish from the ocean, cast off several of the beaches for the rockfish that scurry about in the near-shore reefs. **Garrapata State Beach** has a good fishing area, as do the beaches at **Sand Dollar.**

Scuba Diving

There's not much for beginner divers in Big Sur. Expect cold water and an exposure to the ocean's swells and surges. Temperatures are in the mid-50s in the shallows, dipping into the 40s as you dive deeper down. Visibility is 20-30 feet, though rough conditions can diminish this significantly; the best season for clear water is September-November.

The biggest and most interesting dive locale here is **Julia Pfeiffer Burns State Park** (CA-1, 12 miles south of Pfeiffer Big Sur State Park, 831/667-2315, www.parks.ca.gov, daily sunrise-sunset). You'll need to acquire a special permit at Big Sur Station and prove your experience to dive at this protected underwater park. The park, along with the rest of the coast of Big Sur, is part of the Monterey Bay National Marine Sanctuary. You enter the water from the shore, which gives you the chance to check out all the ecosystems, beginning with the busy life of the beach sands before heading out to the rocky reefs and then into the lush green kelp forests.

Divers at access-hostile **Jade Cove** (CA-1, 0.7 miles south of Sand Dollar Beach) aren't usually interested in cute, colorful nudibranchs or even majestic gray whales. Jade Cove divers come to stalk the wily jade pebbles and rocks that cluster in this special spot. The semiprecious stone striates the coastline right here, and storms tear clumps of jade out of the cliffs and into the sea. Much of it settles just off the shore of the tiny cove, and divers hope to find jewelry-quality stones to sell for a huge profit.

If you're looking for a guided scuba dive of the Big Sur region, contact **Adventure Sports Unlimited** (303 Potrero St., Santa Cruz, 831/458-3648, www.asudoit.com).

Bird-Watching

Many visitors come to Big Sur just to see the birds. The Big Sur coast is home to innumerable species, from the tiniest bushtits up to grand pelicans and beyond. The most famous avian residents of this area are no doubt the rare and endangered California condors. Once upon a time, condors were all but extinct, with only a few left alive in captivity and conservationists struggling to help them breed. Today, more than 60 of these birds soar above the trails and beaches of Big Sur. You might even see one swooping down low over your car as you drive down CA-1!

The **Ventana Wildlife Society** (VWS, www.ventanaws.org) watches over many of the endangered and protected avian species in Big Sur. As part of their mission to raise awareness of the condors and many other birds, the VWS offers bird-watching expeditions. Check their website for schedules and prices.

Spas

The Spa at Ventana (48123 CA-1, 831/667-4222, www.ventanainn.com, daily 10am-7pm, massages $70-295) offers a large menu of spa treatments to both hotel guests and visitors. You'll love the serene atmosphere of the treatment and waiting areas. Greenery and weathered wood create a unique space

California Condors

With wings spanning 10 feet from tip to tip, the California condors soaring over the Big Sur coastline are some of the area's most impressive natural treasures. But, in 1987, there was only one bird left in the wild, and it was taken into captivity as part of a captive breeding program. The condors' population had plummeted due to their susceptibility to lead poisoning along with deaths caused by electric power lines, habitat loss, and their being shot by indiscriminate humans.

Today the reintroduction of the high-flying California condor, the largest flying bird in North America, to Big Sur and the Central Coast is truly one of conservation's greatest success stories. In 1997, the Monterey County-based nonprofit the Ventana Wildlife Society (VWS) began releasing the giant birds back into the wild. Currently, 70 wild condors soar above Big Sur and the surrounding area, and in 2006, a pair of condors were found nesting in the hollowed-out section of a redwood tree.

The species' recovery in the Big Sur area means that you might be able to spot a California condor flying overhead while visiting the rugged coastal region. Look for a tracking tag on the condor's wing to determine that you are actually looking at a California condor and not just a big turkey vulture. Or take a two-hour tour with the **Ventana Wildlife Society** (831/455-9514, tours the second Sun. of every month, $50/person), which uses radio telemetry to track the released birds. You can also visit the **VWS Discovery Center** (in Andrew Molera State Park, Hwy. 1, 22 miles south of Carmel, 831/624-1202, www.ventanaws.org, Memorial Day-Labor Day Sat.-Sun. 9am-4pm), where there's an exhibit that details the near extinction of the condor and the attempts to restore its population. For a once-in-a-lifetime condor viewing experience, opt for the **Condor Sanctuary Tour** (831/455-9514, May-Dec. by appointment, $1,000/up to four people), where the VWS executive director drives you up to a remote condor sanctuary in the Santa Lucia Mountains. Here the giant birds are in their element as they ride thermals in the sky overhead and perch on rocks and tree limbs like natural gargoyles. Lunch is included.

that helps to put you in a tranquil place, ready for your body to follow your mind into a state of relaxation. Indulge in a soothing massage, purifying body treatment, or rejuvenating or beautifying facial. Take your spa experience a step further in true Big Sur fashion with an astrological reading, essence portrait, or a jade stone massage. If you're a hotel guest, choose to have your spa treatment in the comfort of your own room or out on your private deck.

Just across the highway from the Ventana, the **Post Ranch Inn's Spa** (47900 CA-1, 831/667-2200, www.postranchinn.com, daily 9am-9pm, massages $160-400) is another ul-tra-high-end resort spa, only open to those who are spending the evening at the luxurious resort. Shaded by redwoods, the relaxing spa offers massages and facials along with more unique treatments including Big Sur jade stone therapy and craniosacral therapy.

ENTERTAINMENT AND EVENTS
Live Music

Over the last few years, Big Sur has become an unexpected hotbed of big concerts. More than just a place to down a beer and observe the local characters, **Fernwood Tavern** (47200 CA-1, 831/667-2422, www.fernwoodbigsur.com, Sun.-Thurs. 11am-11pm, Fri.-Sat. 11am-1am) also has live music. Most of the big-name acts swing through Big Sur in the summer and fall. Even when it isn't hosting nationally known touring bands, Fernwood has a wide range of regional acts on Saturday nights. You might hear country, folk, or even indie rock from the small stage. Most live music happens on weekends, especially Saturday nights, starting at 10pm.

Down the road, the **Henry Miller Memorial Library** (48603 CA-1, 831/667-2574, www.henrymiller.org) hosts concerts, book readings, and film screenings. Check the website for upcoming events.

The manager of the **Big Sur River Inn** (46480 CA-1, 831/667-2700, www.bigsurriverinn.com, concerts late April-early Oct. Sun. 1pm-5pm) jokes that they have been doing Sunday afternoon concerts on their back deck since "Jesus started riding a bicycle." The live music tradition here began in the 1960s with famed local act Jack Stock and the Abalone Stompers. Now it's mostly local jazz bands that play on the restaurant's sunny deck, while a barbecue is set up on the large green lawn. It's a great way to end a weekend.

Bars

The primary watering hole in Big Sur is **Fernwood Tavern** (47200 CA-1, 831/667-2422, www.fernwoodbigsur.com, Sun.-Thurs. noon-midnight, Fri.-Sat. noon-1am), a classic tavern with redwood timbers and a fireplace that warms the place up in the chilly months. It's also a great place to hear a band, especially on Saturday nights. Enjoy a beer or cocktail inside or out back on the deck under the redwoods. On any given summer evening Fernwood can be an intriguing mix of long-time locals, international tourists, and everyone in between.

The newest place to grab a beer in Big Sur is the **Big Sur Taphouse** (47250 CA-1, 831/667-2225, www.bigsurtaphouse.com, Mon.-Thurs. noon-10pm, Fri. noon-midnight, Sat. 10am-midnight, Sun. 10am-10pm). The Taphouse has 10 rotating beers on tap, with a heavy emphasis on West Coast microbrews. The cozy interior has wood tables, a gas fireplace, and board games. With two big-screen TVs, the Taphouse is also a good place to catch your favorite sports team in action. Out back is a large patio with picnic tables and plenty of sun. They also serve better-than-average bar food, including tacos and pork sliders.

The Maiden Publick House (Village Center Shops No. 2, 831/667-2355, daily noon-midnight), which is also just called The Pub, is in the Village Shops complex just a few feet north of the River Inn Restaurant. This is a

good stop for craft beer lovers, with 100 different brands of bottled beer and 16 rotating beers on tap. The only beer that ever stays on draft is Guinness. Settle in at the large wooden bar or the small outdoor patio.

The **Big Sur River Inn Restaurant** (46840 CA-1, 831/667-2700, www.bigsurriverinn.com, daily 8am-11am, 11:30am-4:30pm, and 5pm-9pm) is a fine place for a cocktail or beer any time of day. During the day, take your drink and plop down on a chair in the nearby Big Sur River. In the late afternoon and early evening, the intimate bar area gets a fun local crowd.

Festivals and Events

The **Big Sur International Marathon** (831/625-6226, www.bsim.org, contest fees $150-300, Apr.) is one of the most popular marathons in the world, due in no small part to the scenery. Begin at the Big Sur Station and then wind, climb, and descend again on the way to Carmel's Rio Road.

Throughout the summer, the **Henry Miller Memorial Library** (48603 CA-1, 831/667-2574, www.henrymiller.org, June-Aug.) hosts the **Big Sur International Short Film Screening Series,** where free films from all over the globe are shown on Thursday nights.

Each year, the Pacific Valley School hosts the fund-raising **Big Sur Jade Festival** (Pacific Valley School, 69325 CA-1, http://bigsurjadefest.com, Oct.). Come out to see the artists, craftspeople, jewelry makers, and rock hunters displaying their wares at this early-fall festival. The school is across CA-1 from Sand Dollar Beach. Munch snacks as you tap your feet to the live music. Check the website for the exact dates and information about this year's festival.

ACCOMMODATIONS
$100-150

You'll find a couple of small motels along CA-1 in the valley of Big Sur. One of the more popular of these is the **Fernwood Resort** (47200 CA-1, 831/667-2422, www.fernwoodbigsur.

com, motel rooms $135-180, cabins $215). The cluster of buildings includes a 12-room motel, a small convenience store, a restaurant, and a bar that is a gathering place for locals and a frequent host of live music. The motel units are on either side of the restaurant-bar-convenience store. The nicely priced units start at a simple queen bedroom and go up to a queen bedroom with a fireplace and a two-person hot tub on an outdoor back deck. Near the Big Sur River, the cabins have fully equipped kitchens and a refrigerator. The cabins are a good deal for groups of two to six people.

Your guest room at **Deetjen's Big Sur Inn** (48865 CA-1, 831/667-2378, www.deetjens. com, $100-270) will be unique, still decorated with the art and collectibles chosen and arranged by Grandpa Deetjen. The historic inn prides itself on its rustic construction, so expect thin, weathered walls, funky cabin construction, and no outdoor locks on the doors. Five rooms have shared baths, but you can request a room with private bath when you make reservations. Deetjen's prefers a serene environment, and so does not permit children under 12 (unless you rent both rooms of a two-room building). Deetjen's has no TVs or stereos, no phones in rooms, and no cell phone service.

To soak in Big Sur's solitude, the ★ **New Camaldoli Hermitage** (62475 CA-1, 0.5 mile south of Lucia, 831/667-2456, www.contemplation.com, $105-250) offers a quiet stay in the mountains above Lucia. The Hermitage is home to Roman Catholic monks who offer overnight accommodations for people of any or no religious denomination. The five private hermitages are basically trailers with porches that have stunning coast views. The trailers are decorated with religious iconography and outfitted with a bed, desk, bathroom, and kitchen with a gas stove. There are also nine private rooms with a half bath and garden. Male guests can stay overnight in a monk's cell within the monastic enclosure; there are also a few units outside the enclosure for groups of two guests. Head to the monastery's kitchen for meals, which are included in the

price. In addition to being a unique experience, staying at the Hermitage is one of the region's best deals. The accommodations can be rustic, but they are worth it if it's solitude you're after. Radios and musical instruments are not permitted.

$150-250

The best part about staying at the **Big Sur Lodge** (47225 CA-1, 800/424-4787, www. bigsurlodge.com, $229-394), inside Pfeiffer Big Sur State Park, is leaving your room and hitting the trail. The Big Sur Lodge evokes a classic woodsy vacation cabin. Set on a sunny knoll, the lodge has 62 units with the majority being two-bedroom options. Twelve units also have kitchenettes. The rooms could use an update, but all have a deck. There are no TVs here and Internet access is an extra fee, but all stays come with a pass to all of Big Sur's state parks, including Pfeiffer Big Sur State Park, Andrew Molera State Park, and Julia Pfeiffer Burns State Park. There are several amenities just a short walk down the hill from the rooms, including the **Big Sur Lodge Restaurant** (daily 8am-9:30pm), the **Deli & Café** (daily 8am-9:30pm), and the **Gift Shop & General Store** (Apr.-Oct. daily 8am-9pm, Nov.-Mar. daily 9am-7pm). Take advantage of the lodge's pool (Mar.-Oct. daily 9am-9pm) and watch for the semi-wild turkeys that roam the property.

The **Big Sur River Inn** (46480 CA-1, 831/667-2700 or 800/548-3610, www.bigsurriverinn.com, $200-350) has 14 rooms on the east side of Highway 1 and six suites on the west side of the road. The east-side rooms are cozy with knotty pine walls and small porches. The west-side suites each have two rooms, one with a king bed and the other with a trundle bed, which is good for families and small groups. The suites also have decks overlooking the Big Sur River. Also on site is a seasonally heated outdoor pool.

Filled with creative touches and thoughtful amenities, ★ **Glen Oaks Big Sur** (47080 CA-1, 831/667-2105, www.glenoaksbigsur. com, $225-550) offers the region's best lodging for the price. Its 16 units bring the motor lodge into the new millennium with heated stone bathroom floors, in-room yoga mats, spacious showers, and elegant gas fireplaces. Glen Oaks also has two cottages and eight cabins by the Big Sur River. The cabins are clean with a modern rustic feel and have kitchenettes along with outdoor fire pits. Guests have access to two on-site beaches situated on scenic sections of the Big Sur River.

Over $250

One of Big Sur's two luxury resorts, **Ventana Inn & Spa** (48123 CA-1, 831/667-2331, www. ventanainn.com, $1,000-1,200) is a place where the panoramic views begin on the way to the parking lot. Home-baked pastries, in-season fruit, and organic coffee can be delivered to your room in the morning or eaten in the restaurant. Don your plush spa robe and slippers and head for the Japanese bathhouses. Choose from two bathhouses, one at each end of the property. Both are clothing-optional and gender-segregated, and the upper house has glass and open-air windows that let you look out to the ocean. Two swimming pools offer a cool respite; the lower pool is clothing-optional, and the upper pool perches on a high spot for enthralling views. The rooms range from the "modest" standard rooms with king beds, tasteful exposed cedar walls and ceilings, and attractive green and earth-tone appointments, up through gorgeous suites to multibedroom houses. Take an evening stroll down to the **Restaurant at Ventana Inn** (831/667-4242, www.ventanainn.com, daily 11:30am-4pm and 6pm-9pm, tasting menu $75), the only spot on the property where you need to wear more than your robe and flip-flops. If you're headed to the **Spa at Ventana Inn** (831/667-4222, daily 10am-7pm) for a treatment, you can go comfy and casual. Ventana also has a car service for guests who want to dine at other Big Sur restaurants.

A night at ★ **Post Ranch Inn** (47900 CA-1, 888/524-4787 or 831/667-2200, www. postranchinn.com, $675-2,485), staring at the stars over the Pacific from one of the stainless steel hot soaking tubs, can temporarily cause all life's worries to ebb away. It's a singular experience to soak in the Infinity Jade Pool, an ocean-facing warm pool made from chunks of the green ornamental stone. Situated on a 1,200-foot-high ridgeline, all the rooms at this luxury resort have striking views of the ocean or the jagged peaks of the nearby Ventana Wilderness. The units blend in with the natural environment, including the seven tree houses, which are perched 10 feet off the ground. Each one has a king bed, an old-fashioned wood-burning fireplace, a spa tub, and a private deck. Take advantage of complimentary activities including yoga classes, nature hikes, garden tours, and stargazing. Breakfast includes made-to-order omelets and French toast as well as a spread of pastries, fruit, and yogurt served in the Sierra Mar Restaurant with its stellar ocean views.

CAMPING

To accommodate outdoors lovers, many of the parks and lodges in the area have overnight campgrounds. You'll find all types of camping here, from full-service, RV-accessible areas to environmental tent campsites to wilderness backpacking. Camp in a state park or out behind one of the small resort motels near a restaurant and a store and possibly the cool, refreshing Big Sur River.

In summer, especially on weekends, campers without reservations coming to Big Sur are frequently turned away from full campgrounds. A backup option is to try for one of the 12 first-come, first-served tent campsites at **Bottchers Gap** (Palo Colorado Rd., nine miles east of CA-1, 805/434-1996, http://campone.com, $15). There are few amenities and it can get hot up here, but at 2,100 feet, the camp has some good views of the Big Sur backcountry. Be aware that the longtime camp host here is a stickler for the rules.

Andrew Molera State Park (CA-1, 3.1 miles south of Point Sur Light Station, 831/667-2315, www.parks.ca.gov, $25) offers 24 walk-in, tent-only campsites 0.25-0.5 mile from the parking lot via a level,

Esalen: An Advanced California Experience

The **Esalen Institute** is known throughout California as the home of Esalen massage technique, a forerunner and cutting-edge player in ecological living, and a space to retreat from the world and build a new and better sense of self. Visitors journey from all over the state and beyond to sink into the haven that's sometimes called "The New Age Harvard."

One of the institute's biggest draws, the bathhouse, sits down a rocky path right on the edge of the cliffs overlooking the ocean. The bathhouse includes a motley collection of mineral-fed hot tubs with ocean views—choose the open-air Quiet Side or the indoor Silent Side, and then sink into the water and contemplate the Pacific Ocean's limitless expanse, meditate on a perfect sunset or arrangement of stars, or (on the Quiet Side) get to know your fellow bathers—who will be naked. Regardless of gender, marital status, or the presence of others, Esalen's bathhouse area is "clothing optional"; its philosophy puts the essence of nature above the sovereignty of humanity, and it encourages openness and sharing among its guests—to the point of chatting nude with total strangers in a smallish hot tub.

You'll also find a distinct lack of attendants to help you find your way around. Once you've parked and been given directions, it's up to you to find your way down to the cliffs. You'll have to find your own towel, ferret out a cubby for your clothes in the changing rooms, grab a shower, and then wander out to find your favorite of the hot tubs. Be sure you go all the way outside past the individual claw-foot tubs to the glorious shallow cement tubs that sit right out on the edge of the cliff with the surf crashing just below.

In addition to the nudity and new-age culture of Esalen, you'll learn that this isn't a day spa. You'll need to make an appointment for a massage (at $165 a pop), which grants you access to the hot tubs for an hour before and an hour after your 75-minute treatment session. If you just want to sit in the mineral water, you'll need to stay up late. Very late. Inexpensive ($20) open access to the Esalen tubs begins on a first-come, first-served basis at 1am and ends at 3am. Many locals consider the sleep deprivation well worth it to get the chance to enjoy the healing mineral waters and the stunning astronomical shows.

If you're not comfortable with your own nudity or that of others, you don't approve of the all-inclusive spiritual philosophy, or you find it impossible to lower your voice or stop talking for more than 10 minutes, Esalen is not for you. If you've never done anything like this before, think hard about how you'll really feel once you're in the changing area with its naked hippies wandering about. But if this description of a California experience sounds just fabulous to you, make your reservations now! **The Esalen Institute** (55000 Hwy. 1, 831/667-3000, www.esalen.org) accepts reservations by phone if necessary. Go to the website for more information.

well-maintained trail. You'll pitch your tent at a pretty meadow near the Big Sur River, in a site that includes a picnic table and a fire ring. No reservations are taken, so come early in summertime to get one of the prime spots under a tree. Look out for bobcats, foxes, deer, raccoons (stow your food securely!), and any number of birds. From the camping area, it's an easy one-mile hike to the beach.

The **Fernwood Resort** (47200 CA-1, 1.9 miles south of Andrew Molera State Park, 831/667-2422, www.fernwoodbigsur.com, tent site $55, campsite with electrical hookup $65, tent cabin $90, adventure tent $120) offers a range of options. There are 66 campsites around the Big Sur River, some with electrical hookups for RVs. Fernwood also has tent cabins with room for four in a double and two twins. You can pull your car right up to the back of your cabin. Bring your own linens or sleeping bags, pillows, and towels. Splitting the difference between camping and a motel room are the rustic Adventure Tents, canvas tents draped over a solid floor with fully made queen beds and electricity courtesy of an extension cord. All camping options have easy access to the river. Hot showers and restrooms are a short walk away.

The biggest and most developed campground in Big Sur is at ★ **Pfeiffer Big Sur State Park** (CA-1, 2.7 miles south of Andrew Molera State Park, 800/444-7275, www.parks. ca.gov, www.reserveamerica.com, standard campsite $35, riverside campsite $50), with more than 150 sites, each of which can handle two vehicles and eight people or an RV (maximum 32 feet, trailers maximum 27 feet, dump station on site). A grocery store and laundry facility operate within the campground, and plenty of flush toilets and hot showers are scattered throughout. In the evenings, walk down to the Campfire Center for entertaining and educational programs. Pfeiffer Big Sur fills up fast in the summer, especially on weekends. Reservations are recommended.

★ **Julia Pfeiffer Burns State Park** (CA-1, 7.7 miles south of Henry Miller Memorial Library, 831/667-2315 or 800/444-7275, www. parks.ca.gov, www.reserveamerica.com, $30) has two walk-in environmental campsites perched over the ocean behind McWay Falls. It's a 0.3-mile walk to these two sites, which have fire pits, picnic tables, and a shared pit toilet, but there is no running water. More importantly, they have some of the best views of the California coast that you can find in a developed state park campground. Fall asleep to the sound of waves crashing into the rocks below. Saddle Rock is the better of the two sites, but you can't go wrong with either. The sites book up far in advance, particularly in summer. Reservations can be made seven months in advance, but if you haven't planned that far ahead, there is an option on the Reserve America website that will alert you if there has been a cancellation. You will need to check in at Pfeiffer Big Sur State Park, which is 12 miles north on CA-1.

A popular U.S. Forest Service campground on the south coast of Big Sur, **Kirk Creek Campground** (CA-1, 1.7 miles south of Limekiln State Park, 805/434-1996, www. recreation.gov, $25) has a great location on a bluff above the ocean. Right across the highway is the trailhead for the Vicente Flat Trail and the scenic Nacimiento-Fergusson Road. The sites have picnic tables and campfire rings with grills, while the grounds have toilets and drinking water.

Plaskett Creek Campground (CA-1, seven miles south of Limekiln State Park, 805/434-1996, www.recreation.gov, $25) is right across the highway from Sand Dollar Beach. The sites are in a grassy area under

a yurt at Treebones Resort

Monterey pine and cypress trees. There are picnic tables and a campfire ring with a grill at every site, along with a flush toilet and drinking water in the campground.

For the ultimate high-end California green lodging-cum-camping experience, book a yurt (a circular structure made with a wood frame covered by cloth) at the **Treebones Resort** (71895 CA-1, 877/424-4787, www. treebonesresort.com, $225-355). The yurts at Treebones tend to be spacious and charming, with polished wood floors, queen beds, seating areas, and outdoor decks for lounging. They are really cool structures, but they are not soundproofed. There are also five walk-in campsites ($95-150 for two people, breakfast and use of the facilities included). For a truly different experience, camp in the human nest ($150), a bundle of wood off the ground outfitted with a futon mattress. A stay in any of the facilities includes a complimentary breakfast with make-your-own waffles. In the central lodge, you'll find nice hot showers and usually clean restroom facilities. There is also a heated pool with an ocean view and a hot tub on the grounds. Being away from any real town, Treebones has a couple of on-site dining options: the **Wild Coast Restaurant** (daily noon-2pm and 5:30pm-9pm, $25-36) and the **Oceanview Sushi Bar** (March-Dec. Wed.-Mon. 4:30pm-8pm, $8-19).

FOOD

As you traverse the famed Highway 1 through Big Sur, you'll quickly realize that a ready meal isn't something to take for granted. You'll see no In-N-Out Burgers, Starbucks, or Safeways lining the road here. Groceries feature in small markets attached to motels. Pick up supplies in Cambria or Carmel before you enter the area if you don't plan to leave again for a few days to avoid paying premiums at the mini-marts.

Casual Dining

The **Fernwood Bar & Grill** (47200 CA-1, 831/667-2129, www.fernwoodbigsur.com, daily 11am-9pm, $10-25) at Fernwood Resort looks and feels like a grill in the woods ought to. Even in the middle of the afternoon, the aging, wood-paneled interior is dimly lit and strewn with casual tables and chairs. Walk up to the counter to order tacos, burgers, or pizzas, then head to the bar to grab a soda or a beer.

One of Big Sur's most popular attractions is ★ **Nepenthe** (48510 CA-1, 831/667-2345, www.nepenthebigsur.com, 4th of July weekend-Labor Day daily 11:30am-4:30pm and 5pm-10:30pm, Labor Day-4th of July weekend daily 11:30am-4:30pm and 5pm-10pm, $15-44), a restaurant built on the site where Rita Hayworth and Orson Welles owned a cabin until 1947. The deck offers views on par with some of those you might attain on one of Big Sur's great hikes. Sit under multicolored umbrellas on long, bar-like tables with stunning south-facing views. Order a basket of fries with Nepenthe's signature Ambrosia dipping sauce and wash them down with a potent South Coast margarita. During dinner, there is glazed duck and an eight-ounce filet mignon, but the best bet is the restaurant's most popular item: the Ambrosia burger, a ground steak burger drenched in tasty Ambrosia sauce. When there's a line, consider dining at **Café Kevah** (weather permitting, President's Day Weekend-New Year's Day daily 9am-4pm, $9-16), an outdoor deck below the main restaurant that serves brunch, salads, and paninis.

The **Big Sur Bakery** (47540 CA-1, 831/667-0520, www.bigsurbakery.com, bakery daily from 8am, restaurant Mon. 9:30am-3:30pm, Tues.-Fri. 9:30am-3:30pm and 5:30pm-close, Sat.-Sun. 10:30am-2:30pm and 5:30pm-close, $18-32) might sound like a casual, walk-up eating establishment, and the bakery part of it is. Stop in beginning at 8am for a fresh-baked scone, a homemade jelly donut, or a flaky croissant sandwich. On the dining room side, an elegant surprise awaits diners. Make reservations or you might miss out on the creative wood-fired pizzas, wood-grilled meats, and seafood. At brunch, they serve their unique wood-fired bacon and three-egg breakfast pizza.

Easing into the day is easy at ★ **Deetjen's** (48865 CA-1, 831/667-2378, www.deetjens. com, Mon.-Fri. 8am-noon and 6pm-9pm, Sat.-Sun. 8am-12:30pm and 6pm-9pm, $10-32). The locals know Deetjen's for its breakfast, and it is an almost required experience for visitors to the area. Among fanciful knickknacks, framed photos of inn founder "Grandpa" Deetjen, and cabinets displaying fine china, diners can fill up on Deetjen's popular eggs Benedict dishes or the equally worthy Deetjen's dip, a turkey and avocado sandwich that comes with hollandaise dipping sauce. In the evening, things get darker and more romantic as entrées, including the spicy seafood paella and an oven-roasted rack of lamb, are served at your candlelit table.

If it's a warm afternoon, get a table on the sunny back deck of the **Big Sur River Inn Restaurant** (46840 CA-1, 831/667-2700, http://bigsurriverinn.com, daily 8am-11am, 11:30am-4:30pm, and 5pm-9pm, $12-32). On summer Sundays, bands perform on the crowded deck, and you can take your libation out back to one of the chairs situated right in the middle of the cool Big Sur River. If it's chillier out, warm up by the large stone fireplace and then eat in the wood-beamed main dining room. This restaurant serves sandwiches, burgers, and fish-and-chips for lunch along with steak, ribs, and seafood at dinner. For dessert, they still do the famous apple pie that put them on the map back in the 1930s. The bar is known for its popular spicy Bloody Mary cocktails. The cozy atmosphere, outdoor deck, and seats placed in the river make this a worthy stop for a meal.

Don't overlook the ★ **Ripplewood Café** (47047 CA-1, 831/667-2242, www.ripplewood-resort.com, daily 8am-2pm, $9-16) for breakfast or lunch. This unassuming spot may save the day on summer weekends when Deetjen's is flooded. Dine inside at the classic breakfast counter or on the outside brick patio among flowering plants. The breakfast menu includes pancakes, three-egg omelets, and a worthwhile chorizo and eggs. Order the grilled potato gratin with any breakfast dish; it may be the highlight of your meal. Ripplewood shifts to lunch at 11:30am, though it keeps a few breakfast items. Lunch offerings include sandwiches, Mexican food items, and salads.

The Big Sur Roadhouse (47080 CA-1, 831/667-2370, www.glenoaksbigsur.com, Wed.-Mon. 1pm-9pm, $19-32) is one of the best bets for affordable, creative California

the outdoor deck at Nepenthe

dining in Big Sur. The decor is homegrown modernism, with contemporary art hanging on the walls. The outdoor seating area has heating lamps and two fire pits. Chef Brendan Esons's seasonal menu and daily specials take advantage of the coastline's superb seafood and other local ingredients.

Treebones Resort's ★ **Oceanview Sushi Bar** (Treebones Resort, 71895 CA-1, 805/927-2390, Mar.-Dec. Wed.-Mon. 4:30pm-8pm, $8-19) offers an intimate place to eat artfully prepared sushi. Just 10 seats are available at a redwood sushi bar within a tent-like structure. The sushi chef helps to guide you through a menu that includes simple rolls, garden rolls, specialty rolls, and hearty rolls designed to resemble burritos. There are two beers on tap along with sake, Japanese beer, and California wine. The sushi bar is very popular and priority is given to Treebones's guests. They also allow groups to sit in the adjacent Wild Coast Restaurant while ordering from Oceanview's menu.

Fine Dining

You don't need to be a guest at the gorgeous Ventana to enjoy a fine gourmet dinner at **The Restaurant at Ventana** (48123 CA-1, 831/667-4242, www.ventanainn.com, daily 11:30am-4pm and 6pm-9pm, 4-course dinner tasting menu $75). The spacious dining room boasts a warm wood fire, an open kitchen, lodge-like wood beams, and comfortable banquettes with plenty of throw pillows to lounge against as you peruse the menu. Request a table outside to enjoy stunning views on the expansive patio. New chef Paul Corsentino has upped the quality of the menu, which at times has wild boar and Monterey sardine courses. Choose an à la carte main course entrée or go for the five-round prix fixe. Sit in the small bar area for a more casual dining and drinking experience. The Big Sur Burger ($19) is a unique burger with pickled toppings.

The **Sierra Mar** (47900 CA-1, 831/667-2800, www.postranchinn.com, daily 12:15pm-3pm and 5:30pm-9pm, lunch $55, dinner $125-175 pp) restaurant at the Post Ranch Inn offers a decadent four-course prix fixe dinner menu every night ($125) or a nine-course tasting menu ($175). There's also a less formal three-course lunch every day. With floor-to-ceiling glass windows overlooking the plunging ridgeline and the Pacific below, it's a good idea to schedule dinner during sunset. The daily menu rotates, but some courses have included farm-raised abalone in

Big Sur Bakery

brown butter and a succulent short rib and beef tenderloin duo.

Markets

With no supermarkets or chain mini-marts in the entire Big Sur region, the local markets do a booming business. Stock up on bread, lunchmeat, eggs, milk, marshmallows, and graham crackers at various local stores.

The best of the local markets is the ★ **Big Sur Deli** (47520 CA-1, 831/667-2225, www.bigsurdeli.com, daily 7am-8pm, $3.50-7). Very popular with the locals, the deli has large, made-to-order sandwiches, burritos, tamales, tacos, and pasta salads. If the line is long at the counter, opt for a premade sandwich for a quicker exit. They also have cold drinks, wine, beer, and some basic supplies. This is the best place to stock up for treats for a day hike or beach picnic.

River Inn Big Sur General Store (46840 CA-1, 831/667-2700, summer daily 7:30am-9pm, winter daily 7:30am-8pm, $7-10) has basic supplies, along with beer and a nice selection of California wines. Even better, it has a wonderful burrito bar and smoothie counter in the back. The burritos range from breakfast burritos to roasted veggie wraps and classic carnitas. These large burritos are some of Big Sur's best deals for the price. The freshly made fruit smoothies hit the spot after a long hike. There are also simple premade turkey and ham sandwiches in a nearby fridge for taking out on a hike or picnic.

INFORMATION AND SERVICES

There is no comprehensive visitors center in Big Sur, but the website for the **Big Sur Chamber of Commerce** (www.bigsurcalifornia.org) includes up-to-date information about hikes as well as links to lodging and restaurants. Pick up the *Big Sur Guide,* a publication of the Big Sur Chamber of Commerce that includes a map and guide to local businesses, or download one from the website.

Big Sur Station (CA-1, 0.33 mile south of Pfeiffer Big Sur State Park, 831/667-2315, daily 9am-4pm) is the closest thing to a visitors center. The staffed building offers maps and brochures for all the major parks and trails of Big Sur, plus a bookshop. This is also where the trailhead for the popular backcountry Pine Ridge Trail is located. Get a **free backcountry fire permit** as well as pay the $5 fee for the Pine Ridge Trailhead parking here.

Your **cell phone** may not work anywhere in Big Sur, but especially out in the undeveloped reaches of forest and on CA-1 away from the valley. The best places to get cell service are around Andrew Molera State Park and Point Sur, along with the large dirt pullout a quarter mile south of Big Sur Station on Highway 1. Likewise, GPS units may struggle in this region. It's best to have a map in your vehicle, or pick up a free *Big Sur Guide,* which has a general map of the region.

The **Big Sur Health Center** (46896 CA-1, Big Sur, 831/667-2580, http://bigsurhealthcenter.org, Mon.-Fri. 10am-1pm and 2pm-5pm) can take care of minor medical needs, and provides an ambulance service and limited emergency care. The nearest full-service hospital is the **Community Hospital of the Monterey Peninsula** (23625 Holman Hwy., Monterey, 831/624-5311 or 888/452-4667, www.chomp.org).

TRANSPORTATION

Big Sur is not a town but rather the name for the lightly developed coastline stretching from San Simeon to Carmel. It can only be reached via CA-1. The drive north from San Simeon into Big Sur is where the Pacific Coast Highway gets really interesting, twisting and turning along with the coastline. The largest concentration of businesses is within the Big Sur Valley, 61 miles north of San Simeon.

The drive from San Simeon to the Big Sur Valley usually takes around 1.5 hours, but it can be slow going, especially if you are behind an RV. You may want to stop every few miles to snap a photo of the stunning coastline. If traffic is backing up behind you, pull into a turnoff to let other cars pass; the local drivers can be impatient with tourist traffic. CA-1 can have one or both lanes closed at times, especially in the winter months when rockslides occur. Check the **Caltrans** website (www.dot.ca.gov) or the **Big Sur California Blog** (www.thebigsurblog.com) for current road conditions.

It is difficult to get around Big Sur without a car. However, **Monterey-Salinas Transit** (888/678-2871, www.mst.org, $3.50, Memorial Day-Labor Day daily, Labor Day-Memorial Day Sat.-Sun., check website for specific times) runs a bus route through Big Sur that stops at Nepenthe, Pfeiffer Big Sur State Park, the Big Sur River Inn, Andrew Molera State Park, Point Sur Light Station, and the Bixby Bridge as it heads to Carmel and Monterey.

Cambria and Vicinity

Cambria owes much of its prosperity to the immense tourist trap on the hill: Hearst Castle. About seven miles north in San Simeon, Hearst Castle, quite frankly, *is* San Simeon; the town grew up around it to support the overwhelming needs of its megalomaniacal owner and never-ending construction.

★ HEARST CASTLE

There's nothing else in California quite like **Hearst Castle** (Hwy. 1 and Hearst Castle Rd., 800/444-4445, www.hearstcastle.org, tours daily 8:20am-3:20pm). Newspaper magnate William Randolph Hearst conceived the idea of a grand mansion in the Mediterranean style on land his parents bought along the central California coast. His memories of camping on the hills above the Pacific led him to choose the spot where the castle now stands. He hired Julia Morgan, the first female civil engineering graduate from the University of California, Berkeley, to design and build the house for him. She did a brilliant job with every detail, despite the ever-changing wishes of her employer. By way of decoration, Hearst purchased hundreds of European and Renaissance antiquities, from tiny tchotchkes to whole gilded ceilings. Hearst also adored exotic animals, and he created one of the largest private zoos

Zebras roam the grounds of Hearst Castle.

in the nation on his thousands of Central Coast acres. Most of the zoo is gone now, but you can still see the occasional zebra grazing peacefully along Highway 1 south of the castle, heralding the exotic nature of Hearst Castle ahead.

The visitors center is a lavish affair with a gift shop, a restaurant, a café, a ticket booth, and a movie theater. Here you can see the much-touted film *Hearst Castle—Building the Dream,* which will give you an overview of the construction and history of the marvelous edifice, and of William Randolph Hearst's empire. (Only daytime tours offer free showings of the movie. During evening tours, a movie ticket is $6 for adults and $4 for children. To see the movie without going on a tour, tickets cost $10 for adults and $8 for children.) After buying your ticket, board the shuttle that takes you up the hill to your tour. No private cars are allowed on the roads up to the castle. There are several tours to choose from, each focusing on different spaces and aspects of the castle. Expect to walk for at least an hour on whichever tour you choose, and to climb up and down many stairs.

Even the most jaded traveler can't help but be amazed by the beauty and opulence that drips from every room in the house. Lovers of European art and antiques will want to stay forever. The **Grand Rooms Museum Tour** (45 minutes, 106 stairs, 0.6 miles, adults $25, children under the age of 12 $12) is recommended for first-time visitors. It begins in the castle's assembly room, which is draped in Flemish tapestries, before heading into the dining room, the billiard room, and the impressive movie theater, where you'll watch a few old Hearst newsreels. The guide then lets you loose to take in the swimming pools: the indoor pool, decorated in gold and blue, and the stunning outdoor Neptune Pool.

Buy tour tickets at least a few days in advance, and even farther ahead on summer weekends. Wheelchair-accessible Grand Rooms and Evening Tours are available for visitors with limited mobility. Strollers

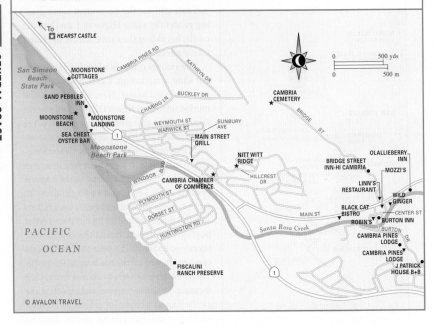

Cambria

are not permitted. The restrooms and food concessions are all in the visitors center. No food, drink, or chewing gum is allowed on any tour.

Historic San Simeon

The tiny town of San Simeon was founded primarily to support the construction efforts up the hill at Hearst Castle. The town dock provided a place for ships to unload tons of marble, piles of antiques, and dozens of workers. The general store and post office acted as a central gathering place for the community, and today you can still walk up its weathered wooden steps and make a purchase. Around the corner at the building's other door, buy a book of stamps or mail a letter at the tiny but operational post office.

The **William Randolph Hearst Memorial State Beach** (750 Hearst Castle Rd., San Simeon, 805/927-2020, www.parks. ca.gov, daily dawn-dusk) sits in San Simeon's cute little cove and encompasses what remains

of the old pier. Lie on the beach or have a picnic up on the lawn above the sand.

CAMBRIA

Once you're through with the castle tours, a few attractions in the lower elevations beckon as well. Cambria began as, and to a certain extent still is, an artists' colony. The windswept hills and sparkling ocean provide plenty of inspiration for painters, writers, sculptors, glassblowers, and more. The small beach town becomes surprisingly spacious when you start exploring it. Plenty of visitors come here to ply Moonstone Beach, peruse the charming downtown area, and just drink in the laid-back, art-town feel.

Sights
NITT WITT RIDGE

While William Randolph Hearst built one of the most expensive homes ever seen in California, local eccentric Arthur Harold Beal (aka Captain Nit Wit or Der Tinkerpaw) got busy building the cheapest "castle" he could. **Nitt Witt Ridge** (881 Hillcrest Dr., 805/927-2690, tours by appointment, $5) is the result of five decades of scavenging trash and using it as building supplies to create a multistory home like no other on the coast. The rambling structure is made of abalone shells, used car rims, and toilet seats, among other found materials. Features like the cobblestone archways reveal a true artist's touch. Make an appointment with owner Mike O'Malley to take a tour of the property; don't just drop in. O'Malley is a quirky spirit himself who relishes the chance to spread the gospel about this one-of-a-kind sight. It's weird, it's funky, and it's fun—an oddly iconic experience of the Central Coast.

To find Nitt Witt Ridge, drive on Cambria's Main Street toward Moonstone Beach and make a right onto Cornwall Street. Take the second right onto Hillcrest Avenue and look for the unique structure.

CAMBRIA CEMETERY

Artsy isn't a word that's usually associated with graveyards, but in Cambria it fits. The **Cambria Cemetery** (6005 Bridge St., 805/927-5158, www.cambriacemetery.com, daily 9am-4pm) reflects the artistic bent of the town's residents in its tombstone decor.

Unlike many cemeteries, at Cambria the family and friends of the deceased are allowed to place all manner of personal objects at their loved ones' graves. You'll see painted tombstones, beautiful panes of stained glass, unusual wind chimes, and many other unique expressions of love, devotion, and art as you wander the 12 wooded acres.

MOONSTONE BEACH

Known for its namesake shimmering stone, **Moonstone Beach** (Moonstone Beach Dr.) is a scenic, pebbly slice of coastline with craggy rocks offshore. Cambria's moonstones are bright, translucent pebbles that can be easiest to find at low tides and when the sun shines, highlighting their features. They are fairly easy to collect, especially after winter storms. The moonstones on Moonstone Beach are not gem quality, but they make a fun souvenir. Many Cambria boutiques and galleries carry moonstone jewelry.

Huts constructed from driftwood can be found on some sections of the beach, and there is plenty more than just moonstones on the shoreline. A wooden boardwalk runs along the top of the bluffs above the beach. From here, take in the scenery and watch moonstone collectors with buckets wander

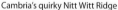
Cambria's quirky Nitt Witt Ridge

below in the tide line. Access is at Leffingwell Landing, Moonstone Beach Drive, and Santa Rosa Creek.

PIEDRAS BLANCAS LIGHT STATION

First illuminated in 1875, the **Piedras Blancas Light Station** (tours meet at the Piedras Blancas Motel, 1.5 miles north of the light station on Hwy. 1, 805/927-7361, www.piedrasblancas.gov, tours mid-June-Sept. Mon.-Sat. 9:45am, Sept.-mid-June Tues., Thurs., and Sat. 9:45am, adults $10, ages 6-17 $5, under age 5 free) and its adjacent grounds can be accessed on a two-hour tour. Piedras Blancas means "white rocks" in Spanish. In 1948 a nearby earthquake caused a crack in the lighthouse tower and the removal of its first-order Fresnel lens, which was replaced with an automatic aero beacon. Since 2001 the lighthouse has been run by the federal Bureau of Land Management.

PIEDRAS BLANCAS ELEPHANT SEAL ROOKERY

Stopping at the **Piedras Blancas Elephant Seal Rookery** (Hwy. 1, seven miles north of San Simeon, 805/924-1628, www.elephantseal.org, free) is like watching a nature documentary in real time. On this sliver of beach, up to 17,000 elephant seals rest, breed, give birth, or fight one another. The rookery is right along Highway 1; turn into the large gravel parking lot and follow the boardwalks north or south to viewing areas where informative plaques give background on the elephant seals. Volunteer docents are available to answer questions (daily 10am-4pm). The beaches themselves are off-limits to humans, since they're covered in the large marine mammals. But thanks to the wheelchair-accessible boardwalks built above the beach, visitors can get just a matter of feet away from the giant creatures. In the fall, most adult seals head out to sea, returning in early to mid-December. Most of the seal births occur between the end of December and the middle of February.

Nightlife

If touring Hearst Castle leaves you thirsty for a beer, Cambria has a few different options. **Mozzi's** (2262 Main St., 805/927-4767, http://mozzissaloon.com, Mon.-Fri. 1pm-midnight, Sat.-Sun. 11am-2am) is a classic old California saloon—there's been a bar on this site since 1866. Old artifacts like lanterns and farm equipment hang from the ceiling above the

elephant seals at the Piedras Blancas Elephant Seal Rookery

long redwood bar, jukebox, and pool tables in this historic watering hole. Save some money on "Two Dollar Tuesdays" when all well drinks and draft beers are just two bucks a pop.

Accommodations

Next to a church, the ★ **Bridge Street Inn-HI Cambria** (4314 Bridge St., 805/927-7653, http://bridgestreetinncambria.com, $32-95) used to be the pastor's house. Now it's a clean, cozy hostel with a dorm room and five private rooms. The kitchen has a collection of cast-iron kitchenware, and there's a volleyball court out front. There's no TV here, but they do offer Wi-Fi and an eclectic book library.

Many of the accommodations in Cambria sit along the small town's very own Hotel Row, aka Moonstone Beach Drive. One of these is the **Moonstone Landing** (6240 Moonstone Beach Dr., 805/927-0012, www.moonstone-landing.com, $225-330), which provides inexpensive partial-view rooms with the decor and amenities of a mid-tier chain motel, as well as oceanfront luxury rooms featuring porches with ocean views, soaking tubs, and gas fireplaces.

The Burton Inn (4022 Burton Dr., 805/927-5125, www.burtoninn.com, $150-350) offers apartment-sized accommodations, some decorated in an ornate English style and others with a casual beach feel. The tall-ceilinged family suites have multiple bedrooms that can sleep six while promoting both togetherness and privacy.

One of the cuter and more interesting options on Moonstone Beach Drive, **Moonstone Cottages** (6580 Moonstone Beach Dr., 805/927-1366, http://moonstone-cottages.com, $319-389) offers peace and luxury along the sea. Each of the three cottages includes a fireplace, a marble bath with a whirlpool tub, a flat-screen TV with a DVD player, Internet access, and a view of the ocean. Breakfast is delivered to your cottage each morning.

For a great selection of anything from economical standard rooms up to rustic cabins with king beds and a fireplace, pick the **Cambria Pines Lodge** (2905 Burton Dr., 805/927-4200 or 800/927-4200, www.cambriapineslodge.com, $165-365). All rooms have plenty of creature comforts, including TVs, private baths, and, in some cases, fireplaces. There's also a nice garden area with flowering plants, benches, and sculptures.

A favorite among the many inns of

Sand Pebbles Inn

Cambria, the **Olallieberry Inn** (2476 Main St., 805/927-3233, www.olallieberry.com, $150-225) is in a charming 19th-century Greek Revival home and adjacent cottage. Each of the nine rooms features its own quaint Victorian-inspired decor with comfortable beds and attractive appointments. A full daily breakfast, complete with olallieberry jam, rounds out the comfortable personal experience.

Her Castle Homestay Bed and Breakfast Inn (1978 Londonderry Ln., 805/924-1719, www.hercastle.cc, $130-170) is a bit different from your average B&B, with only two rooms available and lots of personal attention from the owners. When you make your reservations, ask about a half-day wine tour or dinner reservations. Her Castle can be the perfect hideaway for two couples traveling together who desire the privacy of "their own house."

A stone's throw from Moonstone Beach, the ★ **Sand Pebbles Inn** (6252 Moonstone Beach Dr., 805/927-5600, www.cambriainns. com, $159-279) is a gray two-story building where the clean, tastefully decorated rooms have comfortable beds, mini-fridges, and microwaves. The six rooms facing west have full ocean views, while the bottom three rooms

have patios. Expect amenities such as welcome cookies, a better-than-average continental breakfast, coffee and tea served in the lobby, and a lending library of DVDs.

Food

The best spot to fuel up for a Hearst Castle tour is easily **Sebastian's Store** (442 Slo San Simeon Rd., San Simeon, 805/927-3307, Wed.-Sun. 11am-4pm, $7-12). Housed alongside the Hearst Ranch Winery tasting room and the tiny San Simeon post office, this small eatery showcases tender, juicy beef from nearby Hearst Ranch in burgers, French dips, and unique creations like the Hot Beef Ortega Melt. This is a popular place, and the sandwiches take a few minutes to prepare, so don't stop in right before your scheduled Hearst Castle tour.

The ★ **Main Street Grill** (603 Main St., 805/927-3194, www.firestonegrill.com, June-Aug. daily 11am-9pm, Sept.-May daily 11am-8pm, $4-18) is a popular eatery housed in a cavernous building on the way into Cambria. The tri-tip steak sandwich—tri-tip drenched in barbecue sauce and placed on a French roll dipped in butter—is the favorite, even though the ABC burger, with avocado, bacon, and cheese

the amazing tri-tip sandwich at Main Street Grill

topping the meat, puts most burger joints to shame. The giant Cobb salad comes with lots of diced-up bacon and your choice of chicken or steak.

If the smell of the salt air on Moonstone Beach leaves you longing for a seafood dinner, head for the ★ **Sea Chest Oyster Bar** (6216 Moonstone Beach Dr., 805/927-4514, www.seachestrestaurant.com, daily 5:30pm-9pm, $20-30, cash only). The restaurant is in a wooden cottage with great ocean views. Framed photographs on the walls and books on bookshelves add to the homey feel of the place. No reservations are accepted, so expect a long line out the door at opening time, and prepare to get here early (or wait a long while) for one of the windowside tables. The wait is worth it. Sit at the bar to watch the cooks prepare the impressive dishes like halibut, salmon, and cioppino, which is served in the pot it was cooked in.

One of the most popular restaurants in Cambria is the **Black Cat Bistro** (1602 Main St., 805/927-1600, www.blackcatbistro.com, daily 5pm-9pm, $18-30), serving creative seafood, vegetarian, meat, and poultry entrées. The interior is homey, with a fireplace and wood floors. Reservations are recommended at this small spot.

Part of an expansive local family business, **Linn's Restaurant** (2277 Main St., 805/927-0371, www.linnsfruitbin.com, daily 8am-9pm, $14-32) serves tasty, unpretentious American favorites in a casual, family-friendly atmosphere. Think potpies, stroganoff, and pot roast. Save room for the olallieberry pie—or purchase a ready-to-bake pie, jam, or even vinegar to take home.

In otherwise high-priced Cambria, one of the best food bargains in town is **Wild Ginger** (2380 Main St., 805/927-1001, www.wildgingercambria.com, Mon.-Wed. and Fri.-Sat. 11am-2:30pm and 5pm-9pm, Sun. 5pm-9pm, $15). This tiny pan-Asian café serves delicious fresh food at its few tables, including Vietnamese caramelized prawns and eggplant curry. Wild Ginger also carries an array of take-out fare displayed in a glass case crammed into the back of the dining room. Come early for the best selection of dishes.

The eclectic menu at ★ **Robin's** (4095 Burton Dr., 805/927-5007, www.robinsrestaurant.com, Sun.-Thurs. 11am-9:30pm, Fri.-Sat. 11am-10pm, $16-26) has cuisine from around the world, including Thai green chicken, curries, and wild prawn enchiladas, as well as flatiron steak and the signature salmon

the Sea Chest Oyster Bar

bisque, all of which are done well. The menu also has vegetarian and gluten-free dishes. The historic building has a large dining room and a deck. Expect fine service from a staff that's proud of their product. Happy hour (Mon.-Fri. 3pm-5pm) has $5 small plates and $5 glasses of wine or cups of sangria.

Information and Services

The **Cambria Chamber of Commerce** (767 Main St., 805/927-3624, www.cambria-chamber.org, Mon.-Fri. 9am-5pm, Sat.-Sun. noon-4pm) is probably the best resource for information on the area. It also provides a free annual publication that lists many of the local stores, restaurants, and lodgings. Pick up a trail guide for additional hikes and walks—Cambria has great places to roam. The **Cambria Public Library** (1043 Main St., 805/927-4336, www.slolibrary.org, Tues.-Thurs. 9am-5pm, Fri. 9am-6pm, Sat. 11am-4pm) offers additional information and local history, including a map for a self-guided historical walking tour.

Cambria is served by three healthcare facilities: **Twin Cities Hospital** (1100 Las Tablas Rd., Templeton, 805/434-3500, www.twincitieshospital.com) in Templeton, 25 miles inland, and **Sierra Vista Regional Medical Center** (1010 Murray Ave., San Luis Obispo, 805/546-7600, www.sierravistaregional.com) and **French Hospital** (1911 Johnson Ave., San Luis Obispo, 805/543-5353, www.frenchmedicalcenter.org), both in San Luis Obispo, 37 miles south. Cambria and San Simeon are policed by the **San Luis Obispo Sheriff's Department** (805/781-4550, www.slosheriff.org). If you have an emergency, dial 911.

Transportation

Many Californians make a weekend getaway to Cambria from either Northern California or Southern California. You can drive the Pacific Coast Highway (Highway 1) right into Cambria—this is the prettiest but not the fastest way to get here. For a quicker route, take U.S. 101 to the Paso Robles area and then turn west onto Highway 46, which brings you right to the town of Cambria. If you use Cambria as a base to explore the Paso Robles wine area, or even for excursions to Morro Bay (15 miles), a car will be necessary. The only available taxi service is **Cambria Cab** (4363 Bridge St., 805/927-4357).

The regional bus system, the **RTA** (805/541-2228, www.slorta.org), connects San Luis Obispo, Morro Bay, Cayucos, Cambria, and San Simeon. Fares range $1.50-3.

If you prefer to travel by rail, take **Amtrak's Coast Starlight** (www.amtrak.com) to either the Paso Robles or the San Luis Obispo (SLO) stations, and make arrangements to rent a car (easiest from SLO) or get alternative transportation out to the coast.

CAYUCOS

Just 13 miles south of Cambria along Highway 1, Cayucos is one of California's best little beach towns. There are no real attractions here except for the small strip of a beach between open hillsides and the Pacific. But there are a good number of nice restaurants and places to stay, so it makes a pleasant, less touristy place to spend the night while visiting the area attractions, including Hearst Castle (which is just 30 miles north).

Cayucos is named after the indigenous Chumash people's word for kayak or canoe. One of the early proponents of the town was Captain James Cass, who with a business partner built the pier, along with a store and a warehouse, in the late 1800s. Today, the long narrow pier still stands, while the warehouse is the town's community center and home of the Cayucos Art Society Gallery.

Recreation

The major attraction in Cayucos is **Cayucos State Beach** (Cayucos Dr., 805/781-5930, www.parks.ca.gov, daily sunrise-sunset) and the pier, which was built in 1875 by Captain James Cass. The beach has volleyball courts, swing sets, and lifeguard stands, which are staffed during the summer months. The pier is lit at night for fishing. Cayucos is not known for consistent surf, but rideable waves can occur on the south side of the pier. This is a usually mellow beach-break spot good for beginners. The relatively calm waters off Cayucos Beach are a good place to try kayaking or stand-up paddleboarding.

Just a few feet from the beach, **Good Clean Fun** (136 Ocean Front Ln., 805/995-1993, http://goodcleanfunusa.com, daily 9am-6pm) rents out surfboards ($10/hour), wetsuits ($8/hour), body boards ($5/hour), stand-up paddleboards ($15/hour), and kayaks ($30-40/hour). They also have surf lessons, a surf camp, kayak tours, and kayak-fishing outings. Another place to pick up beach equipment is the **Cayucos Surf Company** (95 Cayucos Dr., 805/995-1000, www.cayucossurfcompany.com, winter daily 10am-6pm, summer daily 9am-6pm). They have wetsuits ($15/day), surfboards ($29/day), body boards ($20/day), and stand-up paddleboards ($40/day) for rent. They also offer private and group surfing lessons.

Nightlife

The **Old Cayucos Tavern** (130 N. Ocean Ave., 805/995-3209, www.oldcayucostavern.com, daily 10am-2am) is a classic Western saloon, with a poker room in the back and a bar up front. In the barroom, over 10 beers are available on tap, and topless cowgirl paintings adorn the walls. There are also two pool tables and a shuffleboard table for those who want to play games without the fear of losing their money in the card room. Western scenes decorate the walls and wooden barrels serve as tables. Live bands perform on weekends.

If you want to sample some local wines, the **Full Moon Wine Bar and Bistro** (10 N. Ocean Ave., Ste. 212, 805/995-0095, www.fullmoontastingroom.com, Thurs.-Sat. 4pm-10pm, Sun.-Mon. 2pm-7pm) has a large selection of wines from nearby Paso Robles, Monterey, and Santa Barbara as well as Europe. Full Moon serves soups, salads, dips, tapas, sandwiches, and desserts, all with an ocean view.

Shopping

Cayucos is known for its antiques. **Remember When** (152 N. Ocean Ave., 805/995-1232, daily 10am-5pm) is home to antiques and collectibles.

The **Lady Spencer Galleria and Distinctive Gifts** (148 N. Ocean Ave., 805/995-3771, www.ladyspencer.com, Mon.-Tues. and Thurs.-Sat. 10am-5pm, Sun. 10:30am-4pm) carries all sorts of unique items from barbed-wire earrings to soy candles and glass tableware.

In a red two-story building on Cayucos's main drag, **Brown Butter Cookie Company** (98 N. Ocean Ave., 805/995-2076, www.brownbuttercookies.com, daily 9am-6pm) bakes and sells original cookie creations, including their original brown butter sea salt cookie and more recent recipes such as coconut lime and cocoa mint. Witness the delectable creative process as it takes place right behind the counter.

Accommodations

★ **The Saltbox** (150 D St., 800/995-2322, www.thesaltbox.com, $150-220) makes a superb base for exploring the coast. The historic blue building, constructed by a ship's captain in the 1880s, is split into three units, each with fully equipped kitchens, private entrances, and a deck or patio. The ground-floor Captain's Quarters can accommodate 6-8 people with three bedrooms, two bathrooms, and an enclosed brick patio area. The Crow's Nest is an upstairs apartment with two bedrooms that can accommodate four people and has a nice view of the sea and the pier. The Carriage House is a small studio in the shade of the main house. The place is a bit dated, but that is outweighed by lots of character, a great location, and fair rates.

The **Cayucos Sunset Inn Bed and Breakfast** (95 S. Ocean Ave., 805/995-2500 or 877/805-1076, www.cayucossunsetinn.com, $189-349) has five two-room suites with private balconies, soaking tubs, and fireplaces. The innkeepers provide a full hot breakfast in the morning that is served in the dining room as well as milk and cookies delivered to your unit every evening.

The **Seaside Motel** (42 S. Ocean Ave., 805/995-3809 or 800/549-0900, www.seasidemotel.com, $110-180) has brightly colored and uniquely decorated rooms with names like "Birdhouse Bungalow" and "Sunflower Surprise." Some rooms have kitchenettes; all have flat-screen TVs and Internet access. Suites are available for larger groups. Guests have access to the on-site garden.

Food

Cayucos is a place for seafood, and there is probably nothing in town as revered as ★ **Rudell's Smokehouse** (101 D St., 805/995-5028, www.smokerjim.com, daily 11am-6pm, $4-11). Rudell's is nothing more than a little shack near the beach, but this place serves some of the tastiest fish tacos you'll ever eat, including salmon and albacore variations. The seafood is smoked, and the unexpected but welcome presence of chopped apples gives the fixings a sweet crunch. The seating options are limited to a few outdoor tables, so plan on taking your taco to the nearby beach.

Schooners Wharf (171 N. Ocean Ave., 805/995-3883, Sun.-Thurs. 11am-9pm, Fri.-Sat. 11am-10pm, $9-28) has a serious nautical theme going: It's a two-story compound of corrugated metal and wood decorated with marine flotsam and jetsam. The menu here is seafood-heavy, with a range of items from hearty cioppino to seared ahi. But the burgers, made with nearby Hearst Ranch beef, are also worthy of attention. Schooners is one of the only "late-night" spots in Cayucos.

At **Duckies Chowder House** (55 Cayucos Dr., 805/995-2245, www.duckieschowder.com, daily 11am-8pm, $6-13), you can get your chowder New England or Manhattan style and served in a cup, bowl, or bread bowl. Other seafood options are mostly fried; there are also salads and sandwiches on the menu. Pitchers of beer and the company of friends make it all go down easy.

Cayucos has its own **farmers market** (Cayucos Veterans Hall parking lot, 10 Cayucos Dr., 805/296-2056, summer Fri. 10am-12:30pm).

Information and Services

The website **Cayucos by the Sea** (www.cayucosbythesea.com) has information on everything from the town's history to its current lodging and restaurant options. Visit the brick-and-mortar location or the website of

The Saltbox

the **Cayucos Chamber of Commerce** (41 S. Ocean Ave., 805/995-8552, www.cayucos-chamber.com, winter Fri.-Sun. 11am-4pm, summer Fri.-Mon. 11am-4pm).

Morro Bay

The picturesque Central Coast fishing village of Morro Bay is dominated by Morro Rock, a 576-foot-high volcanic plug that looms over the harbor. In 1542, Juan Rodriguez Cabrillo, the first European explorer to navigate the California coast, named the landmark Morro Rock because he thought it resembled a moor's turban.

With a view of the rock, the small city's Embarcadero is a string of tourist shops, restaurants, and hotels strung along Morro Bay, a large estuary that includes the harbor, the Morro Bay State Marine Recreational Management Area, and the Morro Bay State Marine Reserve. Uphill from the water, more restaurants, bars, and stores are in Morro Bay's Olde Towne section.

With its natural attractions, including the stunning Montaña de Oro State Park just miles out of town, and with a nice waterfront

Getting There
Cayucos is right off Highway 1. It is 13 miles south of Cambria and 8 miles north of Morro Bay.

focus, Morro Bay is a worthy destination or detour for a short stay, even though a lot of the area's lodging books up during high-season weekends.

SIGHTS
★ Morro Rock
It would be difficult to come to the town of Morro Bay and not see **Morro Rock.** The 576-foot-high volcanic plug, which has been called the "Gibraltar of the Pacific," dominates the town's scenery, whether you are walking along the bayside Embarcadero or beachcombing on the sandy coastline just north of the prominent geologic feature. The rock was an island until the 1930s, when a road was built connecting it to the mainland. The area around the rock is accessible, but the rock itself is off-limits because it is home to a group of endangered peregrine falcons.

Morro Rock

Indeed, a multitude of birds always seem to be swirling around the rock they call home.

★ Montaña de Oro State Park

Montaña de Oro State Park (Pecho Rd., six miles south of Morro Bay, 805/528-0513, www.parks.ca.gov, daily 6am-10pm, free) is for those seeking a serious nature fix on the Central Coast. This sprawling 8,000-acre park with seven miles of coastline has coves, tide pools, sand dunes, and almost 50 miles of hiking trails. A great way to get a feel for the park's immense size is to hike up the two-mile **Valencia Peak Trail** (four miles round-trip). In springtime the sides of the trail are decorated with blooming wildflowers, and the 1,347-foot-high summit offers commanding views of Montaña de Oro's pocked coastline and Morro Rock jutting out in the distance. From this vantage point in spring, the park's sticky monkey flower, wild mustard, and California poppies dust the hillsides in gold. The hike is steep and exposed so make sure to bring plenty of water on warm days.

For a feel of the coast, park right in front of **Spooner's Cove** and walk out on its wide, coarse-grained beach. On the cove's north end, Islay Creek drains into the ocean. There's also a picturesque arch across the creek in the rock face on the north side. The **Spooner Ranch House Museum** informs visitors about early inhabitants of the park's land, the Spooner family. The small facility also has displays about the area's plants, mountain lions, and raptors.

Morro Bay State Park

Morro Bay State Park (Morro Bay State Park Rd., 805/772-7434, www.slostateparks.com, $8/vehicle) is not a typical state park. It has hiking trails, a campground, and recreational opportunities, but this park also has its own natural history museum, a golf course, and a marina. Just south of town, the park is situated on the shores of Morro Bay. One way to get a feel for the park is to hike the **Black Hill Trail** (three miles round-trip).

A unique aspect of Morro Bay State Park

is the **Morro Bay Museum of Natural History** (Morro Bay State Park Rd., 805/772-2694, www.ccnha.org, daily 10am-5pm, adults $3, under age 16 free). Small but informative, the museum has displays that explain the habitats of the Central Coast, and there are some interactive exhibits for kids. An observation deck hanging off the museum allows for a great view of Morro Bay. Beside the museum is a garden that shows how the area's original inhabitants, the Chumash people, utilized the region's plants.

Play a round of golf at the **Morro Bay State Park Golf Course** (201 State Park Rd., 805/772-1923, www.slocountyparks.com, Mon.-Fri. $40, Sat.-Sun. $49), or head out on the water in a kayak, a canoe, or a stand-up paddleboard rented from the **Kayak Shack** (10 State Park Rd., 805/772-8796, www.morrobaykayakshack.com, Sept.-June daily 9am-4pm, July-Aug. 9am-5pm, kayaks $12-16/hour, canoes $14/hour, stand-up paddleboards $12/hour).

Giant Chessboard

Morro Bay's most unusual sight is the 16-by-16-foot **Giant Chessboard** (Centennial Pkwy., 805/772-6278). The waist-high chess pieces used in the game weigh as much as 30 pounds. Four picnic tables adjoin the Giant Chessboard; each has a chessboard where the local chess fiends play. Reserve the board for a small fee (Mon.-Fri. 8am-5pm), or join the Morro Bay Chess Club when they play on Saturdays starting at noon.

ENTERTAINMENT AND EVENTS
Bars

Legends Bar (899 Main St., 805/772-2525, daily noon-2am) has a red pool table and a giant moose head poking out from behind the bar. Grab a drink and look at the historic photos covering the walls.

Down on the Embarcadero, **The Libertine Pub** (801 Embarcadero, 805/772-0700, www.thelibertinepub.com, Mon.-Wed. noon-11pm, Thurs.-Sun. noon-midnight) is the place for

Morro Bay

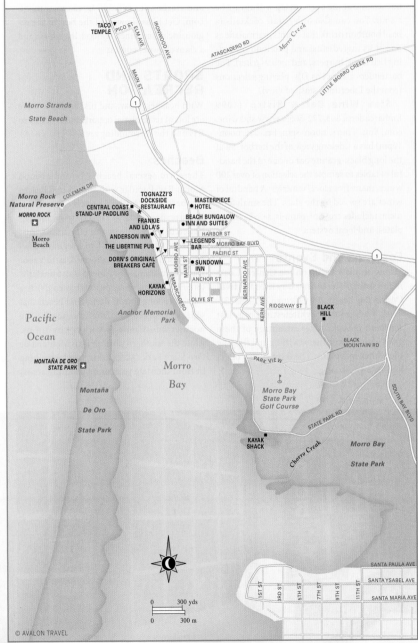

TACO TEMPLE
PICO ST
ELM AVE
IRONWOOD AVE
MAIN ST
ATASCADERO RD
Morro Creek
LITTLE MORRO CREEK RD

Morro Strands
State Beach

1

COLEMAN DR

Morro Rock
Natural Preserve

MORRO ROCK

Morro
Beach

TOGNAZZI'S DOCKSIDE RESTAURANT
CENTRAL COAST STAND-UP PADDLING
MASTERPIECE HOTEL
BEACH BUNGALOW INN AND SUITES
FRANKIE AND LOLA'S
HARBOR ST
ANDERSON INN
LEGENDS BAR
Morro Bay Blvd
THE LIBERTINE PUB
PACIFIC ST
MORRO AVE
MAIN ST
DORN'S ORIGINAL BREAKERS CAFÉ
SUNDOWN INN
BERNARDO AVE
ANCHOR ST
KAYAK HORIZONS
EMBARCADERO
OLIVE ST
KERN AVE
RIDGEWAY ST

1

BLACK HILL

Pacific

Ocean

Anchor Memorial
Park

BLACK MOUNTAIN RD

MONTAÑA DE ORO
STATE PARK

Morro

Bay

PARK VIEW

SOUTH BAY BLVD

Montaña

De Oro

State Park

Morro Bay
State Park
Golf Course

STATE PARK RD

KAYAK SHACK

Morro Bay

Chorro Creek

State Park

N

0   300 yds
0   300 m

SANTA PAULA AVE

1ST ST
3RD ST
5TH ST
7TH ST
9TH ST
11TH ST

SANTA YSABEL AVE

SANTA MARIA AVE

the discerning beer drinker, with 48 rotating craft beers on tap including some made in-house. One of the beers on tap will always be a sour. You can also order craft cocktails (a basil bourbon drink that counts marmalade as one of its ingredients) and pub food (including fish tacos, burgers, and *moules frites*). The bartenders also act as DJs, playing selections from the Libertine's stash of vinyl.

Stax Wine Bar & Bistro (1099 Embarcadero, 805/772-5055, www.staxwine. com, Sun.-Thurs. noon-8pm, Fri.-Sat. noon-10pm) has a sidelong view of the harbor. Sit at the long black-granite bar or one of the handful of tables to sample the selection of over 100 wines, many from local wineries. A handful of wines are served by the glass. The small food menu includes crostini, paninis, salads, cheese plates, and local oysters.

Festivals and Events
Strong winds kick up on the Central Coast in the spring. The **Morro Bay Kite Festival** (Morro Bay Beach, 200 Coleman Dr., 800/231-0592, www.morrobaykitefestival.org, last weekend in Apr.) takes advantage of these gales with pro kite fliers twirling and flipping their kites in the sky. The festival also offers kite-flying lessons.

For over 30 years, the **Morro Bay Harbor Festival** (Embarcadero between Marina St. and Harbor St., 800/366-6043, www.mbhf. com, Oct.) has showcased the best of the region, including wines, seafood, live music, and a clam chowder contest.

SPORTS AND RECREATION
With beaches, a bay, and hiking trails, there are lots of recreational opportunities in Morro Bay and the surrounding area.

Beaches
There are several beaches in and around Morro Bay. Popular with surfers and beach-combers, **Morro Rock Beach** (west end of Embarcadero, 805/772-6200, www.morro-bay.ca.us) lies within the city limits, just north of Morro Rock. Two lifeguard towers are staffed from Memorial Day to Labor Day (10am-6pm). The **Morro Bay Sandspit** (805/772-6200, www.morro-bay.ca.us) is a four-mile-long line of dunes and beach that separates Morro Bay from the ocean. The northernmost mile is within city limits, while the southern portion is in Montaña de Oro State Park. Access this area by walking in from the state park or by paddling across

The Libertine Pub

Nine Sisters

Among the distinctive features of San Luis Obispo County are the nine ancient volcanic peaks known as the Nine Sisters of the Morros. These extend from the prominent 576-foot **Morro Rock** of Morro Bay 14 miles south to the 775-foot **Islay Hill,** which is in the city of San Luis Obispo. The highest of the Nine Sisters is 1,559-foot **Bishop Peak,** the top portion of which is part of the 360-acre Bishop Peak Natural Reserve and a popular spot for hikers and rock climbers.

The Nine Sisters make for unique animal and plant habitats. Morro Rock is a nesting place for peregrine falcons, while **Hollister Peak** hosts a colony of black-shouldered kites.

Morro Harbor to the land south of the harbor mouth.

Just north of town is **Morro Strand State Beach** (two miles south of Cayucos, CA-1, 805/772-2560, www.parks.ca.gov). The three-mile strand of sand is popular with anglers, windsurfers, and kite fliers. **North Point** (Hwy. 1 at Toro Ln., 805/772-6200, www.morro-bay.ca.us) is a bluff-top city park with a stairway to the beach and great tide pools. From here, you can also walk north all the way to Cayucos or head south toward looming Morro Rock. The wetlands at **Cloisters Park** (San Jacinto St. and Coral St., 805/772-6200, www.morro-bay.ca.us) are home to fish and birds. This city park also offers access to the beach.

Boat Tours and Fishing

Sub Sea Tours (699 Embarcadero, No. 9, 805/772-9463, www.subseatours.com, adults $17, seniors and students $14, children $9) is like snorkeling without getting wet. The yellow 27-foot semisubmersible vessel has a cabin outfitted with windows below the water. The 45-minute tour takes you around the harbor is search of wildlife. Expect to see sea lions sunning on a floating dock and sea otters playing in the water. At a much-touted secret spot, fish congregate for feeding. You'll typically see smelt, appearing like silver splinters, but may also catch a glimpse of salmon, lingcod, perch, and sunfish. Kids love it. Sub Sea Tours also schedules **whale-watching excursions** (adults $45, seniors and students $40, under age 12 $35) to see California gray whales and humpback whales.

To cruise the bay with adult beverages, try **Lost Isle Adventure Tours** (845 Embarcadero, 805/771-9337, http://baycruisers.com, $10), which take place on a floating tiki bar. They also rent **electric boats** ($75/hour) that can accommodate up to eight people. **Chablis Cruises** (800/979-3370, http://chabliscruises.com) are held on a two-story riverboat with a rooftop deck. Options include a two-hour weekly champagne brunch excursion (Sat. 11am, adults $42, under age 12 $21) and two-hour harbor cruises ($20). **Virg's Landing** (1169 Market Ave., 805/772-1222, http://virgslanding.com, $49-89) sends four boats out for daily fishing trips, searching for rock cod, albacore, king salmon, and halibut. They also offer whale-watching excursions from December to April.

Surfing

Morro Rock Beach (west end of Embarcadero, 805/772-6200, www.morro-bay.ca.us) has a consistent beach break. It's a unique experience to be able to stare up at a giant rock while waiting for waves. **Wavelengths Surf Shop** (998 Embarcadero, 805/772-3904, daily 9:30am-6pm, board rental $20/day, wetsuit rental $10/day), on the Embarcadero on the way to the beach, rents boards and wetsuits, as does **TKD Surf Shop** (911 Main St., 805/772-2431, daily 10am-6pm, soft-top surfboard rental $10/day, wetsuit rental $10/day).

Kayaking and Stand-Up Paddleboarding

Paddling the protected, scenic waters of Morro Bay, whether you're in a kayak or on a stand-up paddleboard, is a great way to see wildlife up close. You might see otters lazily backstroking in the estuary or clouds of birds gliding just above the surface of the water.

Paddle over to the **Morro Bay Sandspit,** a finger of dunes in the northern section of Montaña de Oro State Park that separates the bay from the ocean. Then beach your vessel and climb over the dunes to the mostly isolated beach on the ocean side. Parts of the dunes are sometimes closed to protect the snowy plover. Away from the harbor area, the estuary can be very shallow; plan your paddling at high tide to avoid too much portaging.

Central Coast Stand-Up Paddling (1215 Embarcadero, 805/395-0410, www.central-coastsup.com, daily 9am-6pm) rents stand-up paddleboards and kayaks ($18/hour). They also offer a 2.5-hour Morro Bay Tour ($75 pp). **Kayak Horizons** (551 Embarcadero, 805/772-6444, www.kayakhorizons.com, daily 9am-5pm) rents kayaks ($12-18/hour) and paddleboards ($12/hour) and hosts a three-hour paddle around the estuary ($59). **Central Coast Outdoors** (805/528-1080, www.centralcoastoutdoors.com, kayak tours $55-110 pp) has a range of kayaking tours that depart from the **Morro Bay State Park Marina** (100 State Park Rd.). Options include short paddles, sunset paddles, full-moon paddles, half-day paddles, and a kayak trip to the sandspit for a dinner in the dunes. Visit their website for more information. In Morro Bay State Park, secure a canoe or kayak from **A Kayak Shack** (10 State Park Rd., 805/772-8796, www.morrobaykayakshack.com, Sept.-June daily 9am-4pm, July-Aug. 9am-5pm, kayaks $12-16/hour, canoes $14/hour, stand-up paddleboards $12/hour).

Hiking

Morro Bay State Park (Morro Bay State Park Rd., 805/772-2560, www.parks.ca.gov) has 13 miles of hiking trails. One of the most popular is the **Black Hill Trail** (3 miles round-trip, moderate), which begins from the campground road. This climb gains 600 vertical feet and passes through chaparral and eucalyptus on the way to 640-foot-high Black Hill,

part of the same system of volcanic plugs that produced nearby Morro Rock.

Montaña de Oro State Park (Pecho Rd., 7 miles south of Los Osos, 805/528-0513, www.parks.ca.gov) has almost 50 miles of hiking trails. Take in the park's coastline along the **Montaña de Oro Bluffs Trail** (4 miles round-trip, easy). The trailhead begins about 100 yards south of the visitors center and campground entrance and runs along a marine terrace to the park's southern boundary. On the way it passes **Corallina Cove,** where you may see harbor seals and sea otters. Starting at the parking area just south of the visitors center, the **Valencia Peak Trail** (4 miles round-trip, moderate) leads to its namesake 1,347-foot-high peak, which offers a nice view of the coastline spread out below. The **Hazard Peak Trail** (6 miles round-trip, moderate-strenuous) starts at Pecho Valley Road and climbs to the summit of 1,076-foot Hazard Peak, with unobstructed 360-degree views. The **Islay Canyon Trail** (6 miles round-trip, moderate) takes you through the park's inland creek beds and canyons. Starting at the bottom of Islay Creek Canyon, this wide dirt path is popular with birders because of the 25-40 different bird species that frequent the area. An abandoned barn makes a good marker to turn back toward the trailhead.

ACCOMMODATIONS
Under $150

The **Sundown Inn** (640 Main St., 805/772-3229 or 800/696-6928, http://sundowninn.com, $89-189) is a well-priced motel within walking distance of Morro Bay's downtown and waterfront areas. Rooms have fridges, microwaves, and coin-operated vibrating beds.

$150-250

The ★ **Masterpiece Hotel** (1206 Main St., 805/772-5633 or 800/527-6782, www.master-piecehotel.com, $189-249) is a great place to stay for art enthusiasts and lovers of quirky motels. Each guest room is decorated with framed prints from master painters, and the hallways also have prints of paintings by Henri Matisse, Vincent Van Gogh, and Norman Rockwell. There's also a large indoor spa pool decorated like a Roman bathhouse that further differentiates this motel from other cookie-cutter lodging options. Expect a deluxe breakfast in the morning and a wine and cheese serving in early evening.

Built in 1939, the bright ★ **Beach Bungalow Inn and Suites** (1050 Morro Ave., 805/772-9700, www.morrobaybeach-bungalow.com, $139-299) has been extensively renovated. The 12 clean, spacious, and modern rooms have hardwood floors, local art on the walls, and flat-screen TVs. Most of the rooms have gas fireplaces. Family suites accommodate four people, while king deluxe suites have full kitchens. Two bicycles are available for cruising around town. There's also a fire pit outside to enjoy the Central Coast evenings. In the morning, a hot breakfast is served to your room.

Over $250

The family-run **Anderson Inn** (897 Embarcadero, 805/772-3434, www.andersoninnmorrobay.com, $249-389) is an eight-room boutique hotel right on Morro Bay's busy Embarcadero. Three of the rooms are perched right over the estuary with stunning views of the nearby rock. Those premium rooms also include fireplaces and jetted tubs.

CAMPING

A couple of miles outside downtown Morro Bay, the **Morro Bay State Park Campground** (Morro Bay State Park Rd., 800/444-7275, www.parks.ca.gov, tents $35, RVs $50) has 140 campsites, many shaded by eucalyptus and pine trees; right across the street is the Morro Bay estuary. Six miles southwest of Morro Bay, **Montaña de Oro State Park** (Pecho Rd., six miles south of Morro Bay, 800/444-7275, www.parks.ca.gov, $25) has more primitive camping facilities. There are walk-in environmental campsites and a primitive campground behind the Spooner Ranch House that has pit toilets.

One mile north of Morro Rock, **Morro** **Strand State Beach** (Yerba Buena St. and CA-1, 800/444-7275, www.reserveamerica.com, $35) has over 80 sites within spitting distance of the beach.

FOOD
American

The giant parking lot outside **Carla's Country Kitchen** (213 Beach St., 805/772-9051, daily 6:30am-2pm, $6-12) attests to the popularity of this breakfast-and-lunch spot. With blue-and-white checkered tablecloths, Carla's serves heaping portions of breakfast classics, including scrambles and omelets, along with sandwiches and burgers. The Pooney scramble is a tasty mess of spinach, cheeses, eggs, bacon, and mushrooms. The biscuits can be on the dry side.

Breakfast

Frankie and Lola's (1154 Front St., 805/771-9306, www.frankieandlolas.com, daily 6:30am-2:30pm, $4-13) does breakfast right. Creative savory dishes include the fried green tomato Benedict topped with creole hollandaise sauce and tasty, colorful *chilaquiles* with red chorizo, avocado, and tomatillo salsa. Lunch focuses on salads and sandwiches with creations including an edamame flatbread and a tri-tip avocado sandwich.

Mexican

People worship the crab cake and fish tacos at **Taco Temple** (2680 N. Main St., 805/772-4965, Wed.-Mon. 11am-9pm, $5-22, cash only). Housed in a big multicolored building east of Highway 1, where colorful surfboards hang on the walls, this is not the standard taqueria. Their California take on classic Mexican dishes includes sweet potato enchiladas and tacos filled with soft-shell crab or calamari. The tacos are served like salads, with the meat and greens piled on tortillas. The chips and salsa are terrific.

Seafood

Seafood is the way to go when dining in the fishing village of Morro Bay. An unassuming fish house with views of the fishing boats and the bay, ★ **Tognazzini's Dockside Restaurant** (1245 Embarcadero, 805/772-8100, www.bonniemarietta.com, summer Sun.-Thurs. 11am-9pm, Fri.-Sat. 11am-10pm, winter Sun.-Thurs. 11am-8pm, Fri.-Sat. 11am-9pm, $18-27) has an extensive seafood menu as well as art depicting sultry mermaids hanging on the wall. Entrées include albacore kebabs and wild salmon in a unique tequila marinade. If you're an oyster lover, you simply can't go wrong with Dockside's barbecued oysters appetizer, which features the shellfish swimming in garlic butter studded with scallions. Behind the main restaurant is the **Dockside Too Fish Market** (summer daily 10am-8pm, winter Sun.-Thurs. 10am-6pm, Fri.-Sat. 10am-8pm), a local favorite with beer, seafood, and live music.

The upscale **Galley Seafood Bar & Grill** (899 Embarcadero, 805/772-7777, http://galleymorrobay.com, daily 11am-2:30pm and 5pm-close, $18-46) is popular for items like pan-seared scallops. The menu changes daily depending on the fresh catch.

INFORMATION AND SERVICES

The **Morro Bay Chamber of Commerce** (845 Embarcadero, Ste. D, 800/225-1633, www.morrobay.org) has a wonderful visitors center overlooking the bay at the end of a small boardwalk. It has a vast array of printed material you can take with you.

French Hospital Medical Center (1911 Johnson Ave., San Luis Obispo, 805/543-5353, www.frenchmedicalcenter.org) and **Sierra Vista Regional Medical Center** (1010 Murray Ave., San Luis Obispo, 805/546-7600, www.sierravistaregional.com) are the closest hospitals. Both are in San Luis Obispo, 13

miles from Morro Bay. If you have an emergency, dial 911. The local police are the **Morro Bay Police Department** (850 Morro Bay Blvd., 805/772-6225).

TRANSPORTATION

CA-1 cuts through Morro Bay. If you're traveling south from San Francisco, take U.S. 101 south to Atascadero, take Highway 41 west, and then head south on Highway 1. Exit at Main Street in Morro Bay. If you're traveling from Los Angeles, the best route is U.S. 101 north to San Luis Obispo, and then north on Highway 1 to Morro Bay; take the Morro Bay Boulevard exit into town.

Morro Bay is 30 miles south of Hearst Castle on CA-1. Simply look for the Main Street exit to get to downtown Morro Bay.

There is no direct bus service to Morro Bay, although **Greyhound** (805/238-1242, www.greyhound.com) travels along U.S. 101 and stops at 1460 Calle Joaquin Street in San Luis Obispo. From there you'll need to connect with **Regional Transit Authority** (805/781-4472, www.slorta.org, $1.50-3) buses to get to Morro Bay. There are various weekday and weekend routes.

The **Morro Bay Trolley** (595 Harbor Way, 805/772-2744, Memorial Day weekend-first weekend in Oct. Mon. 11am-5pm, Fri.-Sat. 11am-7pm, Sun. 11am-6pm, $1 per ride, children under 5 free) operates three routes. The **Waterfront Route** runs the length of the Embarcadero, including out to Morro Rock. The **Downtown Route** runs through the downtown (as in uptown) area all the way out to Morro Bay State Park. The **North Morro Bay Route** runs from uptown through the northern part of Morro Bay, north of the rock, along Highway 1. An all-day pass (not a bad idea if you plan on seeing a lot of sights) is $3.

San Luis Obispo

Eleven miles inland from the coast, San Luis Obispo (SLO) is a worthy home base for exploring nearby Montaña de Oro State Park and Morro Bay. Founded in 1772 by Junipero Serra, SLO is one of California's oldest communities. Despite this, the presence of the nearby California Polytechnic State University gives the small city a youthful, vibrant feel.

Higuera Street is a one-way, three-lane street lined with restaurants, clothing stores, and bars. A half-block away, restaurant decks are perched over the small San Luis Obispo Creek, a critical habitat for migrating steelhead.

In front of the Mission San Luis Obispo de Tolosa is a plaza overlooking the creek with grassy lawn sections, plenty of benches, and a fountain with sculptures of bears, a fish, and one of the area's first human residents.

SIGHTS
Mission San Luis Obispo de Tolosa

Founded by Junipero Serra way back in 1772, **Mission San Luis Obispo de Tolosa** (751 Palm St., 805/781-8220, www.missionsanluisobispo.org, summer daily 9am-5pm, winter daily 9am-4pm) was the fifth in the chain of 21 California missions. The church itself is narrow and long with exposed wooden beams on the ceiling. On the grounds, there is a small **museum** (805/543-6850, summer daily 9am-5pm, winter daily 9am-4pm, suggested donation $5) with artifacts from the Native Chumash people and exhibits on the mission and its missionaries. A nice garden and the Mission Plaza out front of the mission complex are pleasant places to spend the afternoon on a warm day.

★ Madonna Inn

A kitschy attraction worth seeing even if you aren't spending an evening there, the **Madonna Inn** (10 Madonna Rd., 805/543-3000, www.madonnainn.com) is a sprawling complex right off U.S. 101 that includes a café, a steak house, a bar, a dance floor, a wine cellar, and a collection of 110 themed rooms like "The Caveman," a unit with a solid-rock wall and a waterfall shower.

Madonna Inn

San Luis Obispo and Vicinity

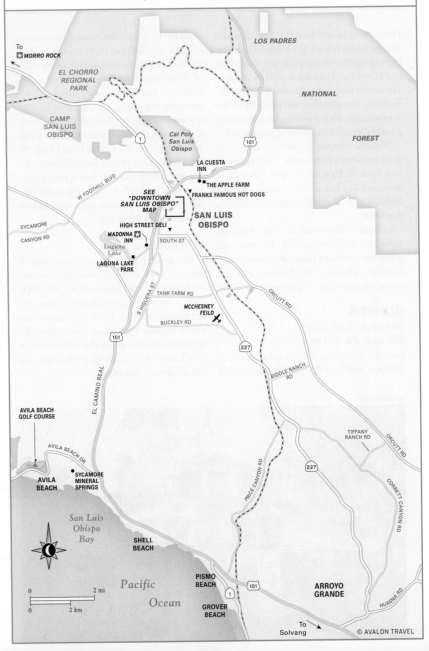

LOS PADRES

NATIONAL

FOREST

To MORRO ROCK

EL CHORRO REGIONAL PARK

CAMP SAN LUIS OBISPO

Cal Poly San Luis Obispo

LA CUESTA INN

THE APPLE FARM

FRANKS FAMOUS HOT DOGS

W FOOTHILL BLVD

SEE "DOWNTOWN SAN LUIS OBISPO" MAP

SAN LUIS OBISPO

SYCAMORE CANYON RD

HIGH STREET DELI

MADONNA INN

Laguna Lake

SOUTH ST

LAGUNA LAKE PARK

S HIGUERA ST

TANK FARM RD

ORCUTT RD

MCCHESNEY FEILD

BUCKLEY RD

EL CAMINO REAL

101

227

BIDDLE RANCH RD

AVILA BEACH GOLF COURSE

AVILA BEACH DR

AVILA BEACH

SYCAMORE MINERAL SPRINGS

TIFFANY RANCH RD

ORCUTT RD

227

PRICE CANYON RD

CORBETT CANYON RD

San Luis Obispo Bay

SHELL BEACH

Pacific Ocean

PISMO BEACH

1

GROVER BEACH

ARROYO GRANDE

HUASNA RD

0   2 mi
0   2 km

To Solvang

© AVALON TRAVEL

Downtown San Luis Obispo

PALMMILL ALY
MONTEREYPALM ALY
MILL ST
PALM ST
MORRO ST
OSOS ST
SANTA ROSA ST
KOBERL AT BLUE ▾
PALM THEATRE ■
COURT ST
CHORRO ST
★ SAN LUIS OBISPO CHAMBER OF COMMERCE VISITOR'S CENTER
FIRESTONE GRILL ▾
LCYC Cheng Park
MONTEREY ST
ROSE ALY
★ MISSION SAN LUIS OBISPO DE TOLOSA
BROAD ST
▾ LUNA RED
HIGUERA ST
GRANADA ● HOTEL & BISTRO
Mission
Plaza
CREEKSIDE BREWING COMPANY ▾
FROG & PEACH PUB ▾
BLACK ▾ SHEEP
MARSH ST
OSOS ST
NOVO ▾
★ MOTHER'S TAVERN ▾
BUBBLEGUM ALLEY ▾
GARDEN ALY
▾ BIG SKY CAFE
BROAD ST
GARDEN ST
PACIFIC ST
NIPOMO ST
PISMO ST
0   100 yds
0   100 m
© AVALON TRAVEL

Obviously, the rooms are for overnight guests, but there is still a lot to take in if you pull over for a peek. The **Copper Café & Pastry Shop** has copper-plated tables and a copper-plated circular bar, while the **Gold Rush Steak House** is a garish explosion of giant fake flowers and rose-colored furniture. It might remind you of a room in your grandmother or great aunt's home—on steroids.

Men have the unique pleasure of being able to use the famous rock waterfall urinal in the men's room.

Bubblegum Alley

Bubblegum Alley (Higuera St. between Broad and Garden) is a 70-foot-long alleyway whose walls are covered in pieces of already-chewed gum. The newly chewed chunks are bright green, red, yellow, and other such hues, while the older pieces have turned a darker color. Some people have called this oddity an "eyesore," while others have touted it as one of the city's "special attractions." Regardless, Bubblegum Alley, which is rumored to have possibly started as early as the late 1950s, is here to stay. Even after firemen blasted the alleyway with water hoses in 1985, another layer of gum appeared a little later.

SPORTS AND RECREATION

Just north of San Luis Obispo, the 1,546-foot high **Bishop Peak** (trailheads at the end of Highland Dr. and off Patricia Dr., 805/781-7300, www.slocity.org) is the city's natural treasure. A four-mile round-trip hike to the rocky crown of Bishop Peak offers commanding views of San Luis Obispo and the surrounding area. Named by Spanish missionaries who thought the mountain resembled a bishop's hat, Bishop Peak is the tallest of the morros or "Nine Sisters," a chain of nine volcanic peaks stretching from San Luis Obispo up to Morro Bay. In addition to the fine views, Bishop Peak teems with wildlife, especially birds that float on the mountain's thermals. You might see golden eagles, bald eagles, hawks, owls, vultures, or kestrels. The hour-long hike up passes through a forest, by Volkswagen Beetle-sized boulders and into a series of exposed switchbacks. (Bring water!) Just below the peak are a couple of benches, a dog-watering bowl, and a peak journal in a metal box where you can sign.

ENTERTAINMENT AND EVENTS
Bars and Clubs

Since San Luis Obispo is a college town, there are plenty of bars in the downtown area. A popular spot with the college students, **Mo/Tav** (725 Higuera St., 805/541-8733, www.motherstavern.com, daily 11am-1:30am) has two-for-one-drink nights, karaoke evenings, and weekend dance parties. Across the street is another popular drinking establishment called the **Frog & Peach Pub** (728 Higuera St., 805/595-3764, daily noon-2am). It has live music almost every night, along with a back deck where you can have a drink on a warmer evening.

The **Black Sheep Bar & Grill** (1117 Chorro St., 805/544-7433, www.blacksheepslo.

com, daily 11am-2am) has a cozy pub feel on uncrowded nights. This brick-walled, wood-floored tavern has a fireplace and a back patio. It also serves a burger basted in a Guinness beer reduction sauce.

Creekside Brewing Company (1040 Broad St., 805/439-4200, www.creeksidebrewing.com, daily 11am-1am) is a small brewpub that serves a menu of 5-6 house-made beers. Sip brews like their popular IPA on a deck hanging over the creek or in the cavernous downstairs bar.

Live Music

The **Performing Arts Center** (1 Grand Ave., 805/756-4849, www.pacslo.org), which is on the California Polytechnic State University campus, hosts live theater events, lectures, concerts, and comedy performances.

East of San Luis Obispo, the **Pozo Saloon** (90 West Pozo Rd., Pozo, 805/438-4225, www.pozosaloon.com) is a historic watering hole from 1858 that somehow pulls in acts like Willie Nelson, Dwight Yoakam, Snoop Dogg, and Wu Tang Clan to perform on its outdoor stage.

Cinema

The **Palm Theatre** (817 Palm St., 805/541-5161, www.thepalmtheatre.com) has the unique distinction of being the first solar-powered movie theater in the country. The Palm frequently screens independent, foreign, and art-house films. The **Fremont Theatre** (1035 Monterey St., 805/546-8600, www.themovieexperience.com) is an art deco movie house from 1942 that shows new films as well as classic movies.

Festivals and Events

The **San Luis Obispo Farmers Market** (Higuera St. between Osos and Nipomo Sts., 805/544-9570, www.slocountyfarmers.org, http://downtownslo.com, Thurs. 6:10pm-9pm) is a true phenomenon. One of the largest farmers markets in the state, this weekly gathering has the goods of 70 farmers and lots of live music.

Every March, the **San Luis Obispo International Film Festival** (817 Palm St. and 1035 Monterey St., 805/546-3456, http://slofilmfest.org) screens a range of films at the city's Palm Theatre and Fremont Theatre as well at other county spots including Paso Robles and Avila Beach. The five-day fest draws film folks like Josh Brolin and John Waters.

Festival Mozaic (various locations, 805/781-3009 or 877/881-8899, www.festivalmozaic.com, July and Nov.) has a winter concert series and a summer music festival. It features chamber music, orchestral performances, and educational events in venues including Mission San Luis Obispo de Tolosa and the Hearst Castle.

ACCOMMODATIONS
$100-150

A superb value, the ★ **Peach Tree Inn** (2001 Monterey St., 800/227-6396, http://peachtreeinn.com, $89-160) has nice rooms, a friendly staff, and a complimentary breakfast. The finest rooms at the Peach Tree are the Creekside Rooms, each with their own brick patio. Next to the lobby is a large common room with a back deck and rocking chairs for enjoying San Luis Obispo's frequently pleasant weather. The Peach Tree is on the Old SLO Trolley route and is an easy one-mile walk to San Luis Obispo's downtown.

Just across the street from the Peach Tree, the **La Cuesta Inn** (2074 Monterey St., 805/543-2777, www.lacuestainn.com, $139-249) has reasonably priced rooms right near U.S. 101. All rooms have microwaves and fridges. This privately owned hotel has a small heated pool and a hot tub. A deluxe continental breakfast is served; coffee and juice are available in the lobby at any hour.

Also in this cluster of accommodations is the **Apple Farm Inn** (2015 Monterey St., 805/544-2040 or 800/255-2040, www.applefarm.com, $129-269), which has more upscale rooms in the inn ($189-269) and less-expensive rooms in the surrounding Trellis Court ($129-189). The inn rooms are twice the size of the Trellis Court rooms and are decorated like traditional bed-and-breakfast offerings. But all the courtside rooms have gas fireplaces. On the grounds are a heated pool, soaking tub, and the Apple Farm Restaurant & Bakery.

$150-250

The ★ **Sycamore Mineral Springs Resort** (1215 Avila Beach Dr., 805/595-7302, www.sycamoresprings.com, $199-479) is on 100 acres in a tranquil canyon with mineral springs bubbling beneath it. The collection of accommodations here ranges from cozy rooms with a queen bed to a two-story guesthouse with three bedrooms and three bathrooms. Up on stilts, the Sycamore Mineral Springs Resort's West Meadows Suites include a living room with a gas fireplace and a bedroom with a four-poster king bed. The best feature of the suites are their back decks, which include large soaking tubs that can be filled with fresh mineral water from below at whatever temperature you desire.

Being 10 miles from San Luis Obispo, Sycamore Canyon might not be ideal if your plan is to maximize your time in the historic city's downtown. But if you want a rejuvenating stay in a nice natural setting, the mineral springs resort has plenty of amenities on its grounds, including a yoga dome, a labyrinth, a wellness center, a restaurant, some hillside hot tubs fed by sulfur mineral springs, and hiking options including the Bob Jones Trail, a paved walkway that goes two miles from the resort to the coastal community of Avila Beach.

If you ever wanted to know how it feels to spend the night in a cave or in a room inspired by the country of Portugal, you should plop down some money to spend a whole evening at the **Madonna Inn** (10 Madonna Rd., 805/543-3000, www.madonnainn.com, $199-469). An under-hyped asset on Madonna Inn's 2,200 acres is the pool deck, with a large heated pool, two hot tubs, a poolside bar, and a view of a man-made cascade tumbling down the hillside.

Over $250

The **Granada Hotel & Bistro** (1126 Morro St., www.granadahotelandbistro.com, $249-679) is a 17-room boutique hotel just a half block off Higuera Street. The 1920s-era hotel has been renovated and modernized, with exposed brick walls, steel-framed windows, and hardwood floors. Most rooms also have fireplaces. On the second floor is a comfortable indoor and outdoor lounge area. Attached to the hotel is the **Granada Bistro,** which serves Spanish-inspired cuisine from paella to squash-potato tacos.

FOOD

San Luis Obispo restaurants clearly take advantage of their location near farms and wineries. Even the higher-end establishments aren't that fancy due to the big college presence.

Being inside **Franks Famous Hot Dogs** (950 California Blvd., 805/541-3488, daily 6:30am-9pm, $2-5) feels a bit like you've traveled back to the 1950s. College students from nearby Cal Poly sit in the red-and-white booths snacking on Franks' daily handmade burgers, fries, or steamed hot dogs. Whether you get a chili cheese dog or a monster burger, the super-low prices recall another era. It's rumored that they have a great breakfast burrito as well.

Though it's in a neighborhood a few blocks from downtown, **High Street Deli** (350 High St., 805/541-4738, www.highstdeli.com, daily 9am-5:30pm, $6-8.50) is worth seeking out if you are a sandwich enthusiast. The "California Turkey" is a heated slab of tastiness with roasted turkey, an Ortega chile, slices of avocado, and more on toasted sourdough slices. They also sell Italian subs, hot pastramis, and meatloaf sandwiches. After ordering, hunker down on a stool at one of the barrel tables to eat these creations while they're still warm.

The ★ **Firestone Grill** (1001 Higuera St., 805/783-1001, www.firestonegrill.com, Sun.-Wed. 11am-10pm, Thurs.-Sat. 11am-11pm, $5-18) has a masterpiece in its tender and tasty tri-tip sandwich. Locals swear by it. Brought to you by the same folks behind Cambria's Main Street Grill, the Firestone Grill also serves pork ribs, burgers, and salads topped with tasty grilled meat. Enjoy the goods in a spacious indoor dining room with large TVs or in the outdoor seating plaza. Expect a line out the door.

On a nice day, **Novo** (726 Higuera St., 805/543-3986, www.novorestaurant.com, Mon.-Thurs. 11am-9pm, Fri.-Sat. 11am-1am, Sun. 10am-10pm, $16-32) has a collection of decks overlooking San Luis Obispo Creek for dining and drinking. Novo serves tapas including fresh shrimp avocado spring rolls, as well as full-on entrées like a daily fish special. International flavors creep into the menu on items like pork *carnitas sopes,* Thai curries, and a stir-fried noodle dish. They do a late-night limited menu from 10pm to 1am.

Another worthy place for dinner or lunch is the Rachael Ray-approved **Big Sky Café** (1121 Broad St., 805/545-5401, www.bigsky-cafe.com, Mon.-Thurs. 7am-9pm, Fri. 7am-10pm, Sat. 8am-10pm, Sun. 8am-9pm, $9-22). There are plenty of options for carnivores, but Blue Sky has some vegetarian entrées, including one that is a plate of local vegetables served in a variety of preparations.

Menu items at **Koberl at Blue** (998 Monterey St., 805/783-1135, www.epkoberl.com, restaurant daily 5pm-10pm, bar Sun.-Wed. 4pm-midnight, Thurs.-Sun. 4pm-2am, $23-48), like the tempura-fried oyster appetizer or the sautéed veal liver entrée, are designed to be paired with a glass of wine.

Luna Red (1023 Chorro St., 805/540-5243, www.lunaredslo.com, Mon.-Wed. 11am-10pm, Thurs.-Fri. 11am-midnight, Sat. 9am-midnight, Sun. 9am-10pm, $15-32) is in an enviable location between Mission Plaza and bustling Higuera Street. With ample outdoor patio seating, Luna Red serves what it calls "an amalgamation of world cuisines." This claim is supported with a menu that includes sashimi, ceviche, lamb kebabs, and a hummus platter.

INFORMATION AND SERVICES

Information about sights and lodging in San Luis Obispo County can be attained at the **San Luis Obispo Chamber of Commerce Visitor's Center** (895 Monterey St., 805/781-2777, www.slochamber.org, Sun.-Wed. 10am-5pm, Thurs.-Sat. 10am-7pm).

In case of emergencies, San Luis Obispo is home to two hospitals: **Sierra Vista Regional Medical Center** (1010 Murray Ave., 805/546-7600, www.sierravistaregional.com) and **French Hospital Medical Center** (1911 Johnson Ave., 805/543-5353, www.dignityhealth.org).

TRANSPORTATION

Both Highway 1 and U.S. 101 funnel into San Luis Obispo to the north. Coming from the south, take Highway 1/U.S. 101 into town.

There's also an **Amtrak** station in San Luis Obispo (1011 Railroad Ave., www.amtrak.com) where the *Coast Starlight* train stops.

Use **SLO Transit** (www.slocity.org, adults $1.25, seniors $0.60) to get around town.

Paso Robles

As an up-and-coming wine-growing region, Paso Robles has become a familiar destination and appellation for state residents as well as a popular side trip from nearby Cambria. Huge crowds do not descend on Paso every weekend as they do in the more popular wine regions, and you can still find room at the tasting bars, engage with knowledgeable tasting room staff, meet the occasional winemaker tending bar, and enjoy a friendly country atmosphere both in town and on the wine roads. For the best tasting experience, visit the Paso region over the weekend—many of the smaller tasting rooms are open only Thursday-Monday or even only Friday-Sunday. Most tasting fees are waived with a wine purchase.

WINERIES

The wine industry is growing by leaps and bounds in and all around Paso. The Paso Robles region now boasts more than 200 wineries, over 100 of which have tasting rooms open to the public. The hills outside of town are braided with rows of vines. For the purposes of this book, the sprawled landscape is divided into three easily navigable parts: Highway 46 West, Highway 46 East (which does not directly connect to Hwy. 46 West), and downtown Paso Robles.

Highway 46 West

The densest concentration of wineries cluster along Highway 46 West and the little roads that spring off that main thoroughfare. Many intrepid wine-tasters never make it past this short and easy-to-travel stretch, which locals refer to as the Westside.

Rotta Winery (250 Winery Rd., 805/237-0510, www.rottawinery.com, daily 10:30am-5:30pm, $5) has been making wine in the region since 1908. It is best known for its estate zinfandel and black monukka dessert wine, which is sweet but not cloying.

One of the best wineries in these parts is **Hunt Cellars** (2875 Oakdale Rd., 805/237-1600, www.huntcellars.com, daily 10am-5:30pm, tasting fee $5-10). Friendly and intensely knowledgeable staff members pour some of the best wines in Paso at this mid-sized, informal tasting room. You'll enter a building that looks more like a house than a winery, then choose the regular or reserve tasting. Check the chalkboard behind the bar for the day's specialty offerings. Almost all of the wines at Hunt are grown in the family-owned Destiny Vineyard. The specialty of the house is cabernet sauvignon, and Hunt makes some of the best in California. You'll also get to taste a few chardonnays, other red varietals, some red

Paso Robles Wineries

© AVALON TRAVEL

JUSTIN VINEYARDS

CYPRESS MOUNTAIN DR

GREEN VALLEY RD

SANTA ROSA CREEK RD

CHIMNEY ROCK RD

ADELAIDA CEMETERY

ADELAIDA RD

HALTER RANCH

VINEYARD DR

NACIMIENTO LAKE DR

Camp Roberts

OPOLO VINEYARDS

PEACHY CANYON RD

WILLOW CREEK RD

VINEYARD DR

HEARTHSTONE WINERY

JADA VINEYARDS

DENNER VINEYARDS

ADELAIDA RD

NIDEVER RD

CALCAREOUS VINEYARDS

SAN MARCOS RD

DONATI VINEYARD

FOUR VINES WINERY

OAKDALE RD

HUNT CELLARS

KILER CANYON RD

LIVE OAK RD

KIAMIE WINERY

VIHUELA WINERY

ARROYO ROBLES

PIANETTA WINERY'S

EDWARD SELLERS VINEYARDS

PEACHY CANYON RD

NACIMIENTO LAKE DR

ROTTA WINERY

WINERY RD

VINEYARD DR

LAS TABLAS RD

GREY WOLF

BETHEL RD

WINDWARD VINEYARD

HIGHWAY 46 WEST

LA BELLASERA HOTEL

Templeton

101

EL CAMINO REAL

46

46

ADELAIDE INN

EL CAMINO REAL

101

RIVER RD

MAIN ST

VINE ST

MCPHEE'S GRILL

TEMPLETON RD

WILD HORSE WINERY CT

WILD HORSE WINERY

HONEY OAK HOUSE

EL POMAR DR

LUPINE LN

NIBLICK RD

CIDER CREEK BAKERY

CHAROLAIS RD

GOLDEN HILL RD

PASO ROBLES

RIVER OAKS DR

RIVER OAKS HOT SPRINGS

RAVINE WATER PARK

ROBERT HALL WINERY

EBERLE WINERY

AIRPORT RD

WELLSONA RD

RIVER RD

NEAL SPRINGS RD

CRESSTON RD

LINNE RD

RIO SECO VINEYARD

VINA ROBLES

HUNTER RANCH GOLF COURSE/GRILL AT HUNTER RANCH

JARDINE RD

PLEASANT RD

SILVER HORSE WINERY

EL POMAR RD

CHAPARRAL RD

SCULPTERRA WINERY

PENMAN SPRINGS RD

LINNE RD

46

ESTRELLA RD

STILL WATERS VINEYARDS

EL POMAR DR

RODEO RD

UNION RD

BRANCH RD

BIANCHI WINERY

MILL RD

0   2 km

0   2 mi

N

blends, and the famed (and expensive) port and dessert wines.

If you favor small wineries that only produce tiny runs of wine, **Dark Star Cellars** (2985 Anderson Rd., 805/237-2389, www.darkstarcellars.com, Fri.-Sun. 10:30am-5pm, tasting fee $10) is perfect for you. Ask at the bar about the "synthetic gravity" that is so important to the slow fermentation process used at Dark Star. You'll taste about 10 vintages here—all red wines of the Bordeaux and Rhone tribe. Most visitors think that the best of the lot is the much-lauded Ricordati, a Bordeaux blend that wins international awards year after year. Perhaps the nicest surprise of all comes when you've picked your favorites; prices at Dark Star range up to about $35 a bottle, and many are under $30.

Highway 46 East

It's not as crowded as 46 West, but Highway 46 East has plenty of great wineries. You might even recognize one or two names out in the Eastside.

One of the biggest winemakers to maintain a tasting room in the Paso region is **Cellar 360 Paso Robles** (7000 Hwy. 46 E., 805/226-7133, www.meridianvineyards.com, Thurs.-Sun. 10am-5pm, $5) at Meridian Vineyards. You've no doubt seen these wines on many menus and countless supermarket shelves. They make all the classic California varietal vintages, with bestsellers in chardonnay and cabernet sauvignon. Check out the Limited Release list for, well, a bunch more of the same plus a few slightly less common wines like a gewürztraminer and a sangiovese. Meridian's deli and store provide a perfect place to gather up everything you need for the perfect wine picnic.

It might not be the biggest, but **Eberle Winery** (3810 Hwy. 46 E., 3.5 miles east of U.S. 101, 805/238-9607, www.eberlewinery.com, Apr.-Oct. daily 10am-6pm, Nov.-Mar. daily 10am-5pm, free) is one of the pioneers of the Paso wine region. Gary Eberle has been making wine here for more than 25 years, and winning a passel of gold medals over that time.

Get a spot on a cave tour while you're visiting, then head to the light-wood tasting room. The free cave tour is a great way to escape the heat on a hot summer's day. You'll learn about the winemaking process as you walk past barrels of wine stacked up like giant logs along the cave's walls. Despite the fun statuary and the great caves at Eberle, the star attraction here is the wine. The medium-sized list features mostly hearty, bold red wines such as cabernet sauvignon, barbera, zinfandel, and a few fabulous blends. A few whites find their way to the bar, such as the Paso favorite viognier and the lesser-known roussanne. Taste as many as you possibly can—and you'll be surprised at how many bottles you'll want to walk away with. With most vintages selling for $15-25, you might be able to afford a few extra.

Downtown Paso Robles

Many wineries have set up tasting rooms right in the middle of downtown Paso. Visit the Downtown Paso Robles Wineries website (www.downtownpasowine.com) for a map and information.

The Pianetta Winery's vineyards are 14 miles north of town, but the **Pianetta Winery Tasting Room** (829 13th St., 805/226-4005, www.pianettawinery.com, Sun.-Thurs. noon-6pm, Sat.-Sun. 11am-7pm, $10) is right in the heart of Paso Robles. Pianetta is known for its cabernet sauvignons.

The **LXV Wine Lounge** (1036 B Pine St., 805/296-1902, www.lxvwine.com, Thurs.-Mon. noon-7pm, $10) offers an exotic tasting experience. Recline on a daybed and take in local art while sipping wines inspired by the Kama Sutra. LXV also does a wine and spice pairing ($15) along with a food and wine option ($30, 24-hour advance reservation required).

Wine Festivals and Events

Consider coming to town during one of the several wine-oriented festivals held in and around Paso Robles. The biggest is the **Paso Robles Wine Festival** (www.pasowine.com, $55-125, May), which happens over the third weekend of May each year. The central event of the festival, the Grand Tasting, is held on Saturday in Paso's downtown city park. More than 80 wineries bring out their wares, making it fabulously easy to find your favorites and learn about some new vintners in the region. In addition to the central tasting, most Paso wineries keep their tasting room doors open, offering tours, special tastings, food pairings, lectures and tastings with winemakers, and more. Buy your tickets for the wine festival well in advance.

In the fall, the **Harvest Wine Tour Weekend** (www.pasowine.com, Oct.) celebrates the changing foliage of the grapevines and the frantic rush to bring in the grapes and start the juices fermenting. Nearly 100 wineries throughout Paso put on events during the third weekend of October. Check with your favorites to learn what's coming this year. You might want to sign up early for a cooking class, or just show up to join in on some messy but fun grape stomping. If you're lucky, you might even get to take a tour of a winemaking facility in full furor, and learn a bit about how your favorite vintages are made. As with the spring Wine Festival, it's a good idea to book your room and make your plans early for the Harvest Tour—the event has become quite popular with wine aficionados across the state and beyond.

Wine Tours

If you prefer not to do your own driving on your wine-tasting excursions (something to consider if everyone in your party enjoys wine), take one of the many available wine tours. **The Wine Wranglers** (866/238-6400, http://thewinewrangler.com, $109-122/full day depending on pick-up location) offers daily group tours, plus customized individual tours for a higher fee. Experienced guides will take you to some of the biggest and best wineries in the region. Group tour guests ride in the comfort of a small luxury bus; buses pick up tasters from Cambria, San Luis Obispo, Morro Bay, Pismo Beach, Paso Robles itself, and a number of other towns in the county.

A picnic lunch in one of the vineyards is included, as are all tasting fees at the wineries you visit. If you know the region, feel free to request a stop at your favorite winery.

To taste at your own pace, contact **The Wine Line** (805/610-8267, www.hoponthewineline.com, starts at $60), where a chauffeured van will drop you off and pick you up at your choice of 60 wineries.

SIGHTS

It's not the biggest or most diverse, but you'll have fun exploring the **Charles Paddock Zoo** (9305 Pismo Ave., Atascadero, 805/461-5080, www.charlespaddockzoo.org, Apr.-Oct. daily 10am-5pm, Nov.-Mar. daily 10am-4pm, adults $7, children $5, seniors $6). Plan an hour or two to make a leisurely tour that takes in the funky prehensile-tailed porcupines and the famous slender-tailed meerkats. Visit the aviary to enjoy the twitters and squawks of more than a dozen varieties of common and exotic birds. The zoo makes a fun destination if you've brought your kids to the largely adult playground that is Paso Robles.

A good spot for younger kids is the **Paso Robles Children's Museum at the Volunteer Firehouse** (623 13th St., 805/238-7432, www.pasokids.org, Sun. and Thurs.-Fri. 11am-4pm, Wed. and Sat. 10am-4pm, adults $7, children $6, seniors $5). As much a playground as a museum, the space offers themed interactive exhibits with a slight educational bent for toddlers and elementary school-aged children. Kids can draw, paint, climb, jump, play, and learn in one of the few spots in Paso Robles dedicated entirely to the younger set.

The **Paso Robles Pioneer Museum** (2010 Riverside Ave., 805/239-4556, www.pasoroblespioneermuseum.org, Thurs.-Sun. 1pm-4pm, free, donations welcome) celebrates the settlement of San Luis Obispo County. Exhibits have a distinctly Western Americana flavor and include some larger displays of carriages, farm equipment, and even an old one-room schoolhouse.

Nine miles north of downtown is **Mission San Miguel** (775 Mission St., San Miguel,

805/467-2131, www.missionsanmiguel.org, daily 10am-4:30pm, self-guided tours adults $3, children $2), which was founded in 1797. Mission San Miguel had an inauspicious beginning when one of its first friars was removed and sent back to Mexico after being found insane. That's just part of a rough-and-tumble history that includes possible poisonings, madness, and a documented mass murder. Today the grounds include a cemetery, a small museum with Native American and mission artifacts, and a series of rooms set up to depict what life at the mission was like during its heyday. The long and narrow church is known for its altar with a symbol meant to represent the "All-Seeing Eye of God." The church is also notable for being the only California mission with its original murals still intact.

ENTERTAINMENT

The **Firestone Taproom** (1400 Ramada Dr., 805/225-5911, www.firestonebeer.com, daily 11am-9pm) offers an airy, industrial bar where you can sample the Firestone Walker Brewing Company's beers, including the popular DBA British Pale Ale and taproom-only brews including a hoppy pilsner or a brown ale brewed with hemp seeds. Enjoy pub fare like burgers, pizzas, and steak ($12-24) at the U-shaped bar or adjacent dining area.

The **Pine Street Saloon** (1234 Pine St., 805/238-1114, www.pinestreetsaloon.com, Mon.-Fri. 11am-close, Sat.-Sun. 1pm-close), the town's dive bar, is in an old building that used to be a brothel. Take in live music or play pool in the wood-floored bar. Out back is a smoking area.

Vina Robles Amphitheatre (3800 Mill Rd., 805/286-3680, www.vinaroblesamphitheatre.com, May-Nov.) hosts performances by internationally known musical acts, including expected wine country performers like Tony Bennett and some edgier entertainment such as Marilyn Manson and Judas Priest. The 3,300-seat outdoor venue is on the grounds of a popular winery three miles east of downtown.

SPORTS AND RECREATION

Harris Stage Lines (5995 N. River Rd., 805/237-1860, www.harrisstagelines.com, $50 pp) doesn't offer the typical sedate trail rides. Instead of climbing up onto the back of a horse, you'll get into a refurbished historic coach or wagon and go for a ride like they did in the 19th century. Harris has a restored stagecoach, a chuck wagon, and even a couple of Hollywood-built Roman-style chariots. Call in advance to arrange the perfect outing for your party. If you're really into the historic vehicle scene, you can even book a private driving lesson. Riding lessons are also available.

Several minutes' drive from downtown Paso, the **River Oaks Hot Springs & Spa** (800 Clubhouse Dr., 805/238-4600, www.riveroakshotsprings.com, Tues.-Sun. 9am-9pm, $12-20/hour) sits on country club land over one of the local sulfur-heavy mineral springs. You'll smell the sulfur even as you drive up and walk from the parking lot to the spacious lobby. An attendant will show you the facilities and guide you to your room. A popular and reasonably priced option here is an hour of relaxation and healing in one of the private outdoor or indoor mineral spring spas. Use the faucets to set your own perfect temperature, and gaze out into the thick gardens that screen the spas from the adjacent golf course. For a more thoroughly relaxing experience, pick a massage or facial treatment to go with your hot tub (or alone, if you don't care for sulfur water). Check the website for package specials (many of which include wine served in the privacy of your hot tub room) and aesthetic treatment options.

Franklin Hot Springs (3015 Creston Rd., 805/712-5372, www.franklinhotsprings.com, Mon.-Thurs. 8am-10pm, Fri.-Sun. 8am-midnight, adults $7, children under 14, military, and seniors $5) is a locals' favorite soaking spot on a ramshackle farm just east of town. Past the rusting farm equipment and trailers, you can relax in a concrete pool with a natural bottom. The 97-degree water spills out of pipes at one end of the pool and into a lake at the other end.

ACCOMMODATIONS

Accommodations around Paso Robles tend toward upscale wine-themed B&Bs. While in downtown Paso Robles, there are a couple of unique hotels.

Under $150

A small family-owned and -operated motel, the ★ **Adelaide Inn** (1215 Ysabel Ave., 805/238-2770, www.adelaideinn.com, $112-209) offers nice details. The rooms are clean and modern with fridges and coffeemakers. The grounds have unexpected features that include a koi pond, a barbecue area, and a few miniature golf greens. The motel is 12 blocks from downtown in a strip of businesses by the U.S. 101 and Highway 46 East intersection.

$150-250

Even before Paso Robles was known for its wineries, the inland town was a destination for people who wanted to soak in its hot mineral waters. The **Paso Robles Inn** (1103 Spring St., 800/676-1713, http://pasoroblesinn.com, $169-305) taps into Paso's naturally occurring springs. Its deluxe spa rooms have a private mineral tub in the room or on its deck. Outside, there are gardens, a heated pool, and spa on the property, which dates back to 1891.

Over $250

Luxury and comfort can be found at the ★ **Hotel Cheval** (1021 Pine St., 805/226-9995, www.hotelcheval.com, $330-475), a 16-room boutique hotel just a half-block away from the city park. The generously sized rooms all have oversized showers, comfy California king beds and bathrooms with stone floors. Some rooms also have soaking tubs and gas fireplaces. All rooms face a sun-dappled courtyard with fireplaces. A complimentary continental breakfast is served in the Pony Club bar on the grounds.

Out in the wooded region between Paso and the coast, the **Chanticleer Vineyard Bed and Breakfast** (1250 Paint Horse Pl., 805/226-0600, www.chanticleervineyardbb.com, $255-285) offers relaxed vacationing. Each of the three rooms includes an iPod dock, organic spa toiletries, a fresh, seasonal breakfast, vineyard views, and access to the house stock of cute fuzzy animals.

The Canyon Villa (1455 Kiler Canyon Rd., 805/238-3362, www.thecanyonvilla.com, $275-325) is built in the Mediterranean style that suits this area so well. The decor of the four rooms continues the Italianate theme, while the oversized spa tubs, posh linens, private balconies, and gas fireplace create a feeling of lush comfort. Begin a day in wine country with a three-course breakfast.

The **Orchard Hill Farm Bed & Breakfast** (5415 Vineyard Dr., 805/239-9680, www.orchardhillbb.com, $305-329) has an English country feel. The attractive manor house offers luxurious rooms with top-tier amenities, a gourmet breakfast, balconies off each room, and attractive grounds for walking and lounging.

FOOD

To get back to the heavily Mexican influence of Paso's agricultural roots, grab a taco or two at **Papi's** (840 13th St., 805/239-3720, daily 11am-9pm, $10). Prices may be a bit higher than some taquerias in honor of Paso's new tourist status, but the casual atmosphere and tasty tortas make up for it.

It's not the fanciest place in Paso, but the food at **Panolivo** (1344 Park St, 805/239-3366, www.panolivo.com, daily 7:30am-8:30pm, $17-28) might be the tastiest truly traditional French cuisine in town. Panolivo serves breakfast, lunch, and dinner every day. The breakfast sandwich with cheese, ham, and a chives-and-parmesan egg omelet is a great way to start the day. For dinner, Panolivo serves a range of dishes from burgers to boeuf bourguignon.

Thomas Hill Organics Market Bistro & Wine Bar (1305 Park Ave., 805/226-5888, www.thomashillorganics.com, Mon.-Thurs 11am-3pm and 5pm-9pm, Fri.-Sat. 11am-3pm and 5pm-10pm, Sun. 10am-3pm and

5pm-9pm, $30-35) has a 10-acre farm just east of Paso Robles where they grow their produce. The menu changes weekly but you might find dinner items like pan-seared scallops with a noodle salad and jerk-marinated duck.

The town's culinary epicenter is ★ **Artisan** (843 12th St., 805/237-8084, www.artisanpasorobles.com, Mon.-Thurs. 11:30am-9pm, Fri. 11:30am-10pm, Sat. 10am-10pm, Sun. 10am-9pm, $28-34). The white tablecloths, bustling open kitchen, and numerous wine glasses hint at the fancy cuisine to come. Most of the ingredients at Artisan come from local sources including abalone from Cayucos and greens from Los Osos. The dinner entrees change seasonally.

INFORMATION AND SERVICES

The closest thing to a visitors center is the **Paso Robles Chamber of Commerce**

(1225 Park St., 805/238-0506, www.paso-robleschamber.com, Mon.-Fri. 8:30am-4:30pm, Sat. 10am-2pm). Pick up a guide to Paso Robles, or specific dining, lodging, and winery information.

For medical attention, the nearest hospital is **Twin Cities Community Hospital** (1100 La Tablas Rd., 805/434-3500, www.twincitieshospital.com) in nearby Templeton.

TRANSPORTATION

The two best ways to get to Paso Robles are by car and by train. Drivers can take U.S. 101 from the north or the south directly to town. Once in Paso Robles, take Highway 46 east or west for the main wine road.

On the rails, the **Amtrak** *Coast Starlight* (www.amtrak.com) stops right in Paso. Avoid driving altogether by taking the train into town, and then renting a limo or getting on with a wine tour.

Pismo Beach

Walking around Pismo Beach, it feels like you've stepped back in time to a Southern California beach town from 50 years ago. With its long, sandy beach studded with lifeguard stands and volleyball courts, the coastline in front of this community could be in Los Angeles County or Orange County. The main attraction—besides the surf and sand—is the 1,200-foot-long Pismo Pier. On either side of the pier, surfers ride peaky waves. Meanwhile, anglers dangle their fishing poles off the side, hoping to land a perch or smelt.

Formerly known as the "Clam Capital of the World," Pismo used to be the best place to gather the famous Pismo clam, an edible bivalve that can be found on sandy beaches from Half Moon Bay to Baja California. Because of over-farming and the fact that sea otters have been munching on lots of the tasty bivalves, the clam population is now so low that there is basically no clamming going on anymore in Pismo.

The town's one-way Pomeroy Avenue is like Main Street. It is lined with beachwear shops, candy stores, and fish-and-chips restaurants.

Getting to Pismo Beach is easy: Exit right off U.S. 101. While there may be no must-see attractions in Pismo, the town makes a good stopover between San Francisco and Los Angeles. It's close to Morro Bay, Hearst Castle, and Montaña de Oro State Park—and it's an ideal place to enjoy the simple pleasures of the beach.

SIGHTS
Pismo Pier

The first **Pismo Pier** (end of Pomeroy Ave.) was built for shipping back in 1881. Though that pier and another were destroyed by storms, the third version, built in 1985 and 1986, still stands today. Walking out on the pier is a great way to get an eyeful of the far-ranging Pismo Beach and the Oceano Dunes to the south. A small concession shack on the pier sells snacks and rents bodyboards and fishing rods.

Oceano Dunes

It's a rare treat to be able to actually drive on one of California's beaches. It is possible—as long as you have the right vehicle—at the **Oceano Dunes State Vehicular Recreation Area** (three miles south of Pismo Beach off Hwy. 1, 805/473-7220, www.parks.ca.gov, day use 6am-11pm, $5/day per vehicle). There are 3,600 acres of dunes, beach, wetlands, lakes, and riparian areas to explore by four-wheel drive, dune buggy, four-wheeler, or foot. In the 1930s and 1940s, the dunes were home to the "Dunites," a collective of mystics, nudists, writers, and artists who believed that the dunes were a center for creative energy. Be careful if you decide to drive on the beach without the proper vehicle: Getting your car stuck in the sand can make for a long afternoon. You can also rent ATVs for the dunes at **B. J.'s ATV Rentals** (197 Grand Ave., Grover Beach, 805/481-5411, www.bjsatvrentals.com, Mon.-Fri. 9am-6pm, Sat.-Sun. 8am-8pm, $45-300) and **Arnie's ATV Rentals** (311 Pier Ave., Oceano, 805/474-6060, http://pismoatvrentals.com, $60-243).

If you want to explore the dunes but you don't have the proper vehicle, the **Oceano Dunes Preserve Trail** (two or more miles round-trip) allows hikers to experience the region without fear of getting run over.

Pismo Beach Monarch Butterfly Grove

Sure, beachgoers and anglers flock to Pismo Beach, but the coastal community's most popular visitors are the thousands of monarch butterflies that take over a forest of eucalyptus and pine trees in the **Pismo Beach Monarch Butterfly Grove** (Hwy. 1 at the southernmost end of the City of Pismo Beach, 800/443-7778, www.monarchbutterfly.org) between November and February. During this time, docents and volunteers are on site to answer questions 10am-4pm.

Dinosaur Caves Park

Not your usual city park, **Dinosaur Caves Park** (corner of Cliff St. and Shell Beach Rd., 805/773-4657, www.pismobeach.org, daily sunrise-sunset, free) offers 11 acres of serious play for the wee ones, with concrete dolphins, an orca, and, best of all, a friendly-looking dinosaur and three cracked dinosaur eggs.

ENTERTAINMENT AND EVENTS

Harry's Night Club & Beach Bar (690 Cypress St., 805/773-1010, www.harryspismobeach.com, daily 10am-2am) has live bands every night of the week except for Thursday, which is karaoke night. Expect most of the acts to be classic rock cover bands. Harry's also has big-screen TVs for taking in sporting events and three pool tables for those who'd like to shoot a game or two.

The **Pismo Beach Clam Festival** (805/773-4382, www.pismoclamfestival.com, Oct.) honors the beach town's clamming past every fall with a clam chowder cook-off and a clam dig. The fest also highlights other aspects of Pismo with surf lessons, live music, and a wine walk.

In June, one of California's largest car shows takes over downtown Pismo and the pier during the **Classic at Pismo Beach Car Show** (909/890-0082, http://theclassicatpismobeach.com, June). Over 1,000 show vehicles are displayed at this free event.

SHOPPING

There is shopping to be done in Pismo Beach. To save money on some big-name clothing brands, head to the **Pismo Beach Premium Outlets** (333 Five Cities Dr., 805/773-4661, www.premiumoutlets.com, Mon.-Sat. 10am-9pm, Sun. 10am-7pm), where Levi's, Lane Bryant, PacSun, and others have outlet stores.

SPORTS AND RECREATION
Fishing

Anglers can try snagging a big one off the Pismo Pier. The pier is the most heavily fished and second-most productive pier on the Central Coast. If you didn't bring a rod, rent one from the small shack on the pier. No license is required for fishing off the pier.

If you'd rather head out into deeper waters, contact **Patriot Sportfishing** (805/595-7200, www.patriotsportfishing.com, adults $82/full day, children under 12 $60/full day) out of nearby Avila Beach. Their specialty is rock cod fishing.

Surfing

On either side of the Pismo Pier, waves consistently break for surfers. One of the best aspects of surfing the pier is that the surf is less susceptible to getting destroyed by the winds that wreck waves at other local breaks. Rent a board from **Pismo Beach Surf Shop** (470 Price St., 805/773-2089, www.pismobeach-surfshop.com, daily 9am-5pm, surfboard rentals $15/day).

Horseback Riding

Exploring the coastline just south of Pismo Beach by horseback is possible through the **Pacific Dunes RV Resort and Riding Stables** (1205 Silver Spur Pl., Oceano, 805/489-8100, http://pacificdunesranch.com, $50-75). Their rides (1-1.5 hours) go between dunes and out to the beach.

ACCOMMODATIONS

Pismo Beach's best lodging options are on bluffs north of the pier and the small downtown area.

Every room at the moderately priced **Kon Tiki Inn** (1621 Price St., 805/773-4833, www.kontikiinn.com, $188-228) has a sweeping view of the ocean as well as a patio or balcony. In front of the large hotel is a heated pool, hot tubs, and a staircase to the beach below. One perk of staying at the Kon Tiki is that guests get full use of the adjacent Pismo Beach Athletic Club, which offers Zumba classes and has an indoor lap pool.

The exteriors of the buildings at the **Cottage Inn By the Sea** (2351 Price St., 805/773-4617, www.cottage-inn.com,

$189-429) are meant to conjure images of the English countryside. All of the rooms have gas fireplaces, a fridge, and a microwave. The Cottage Inn also has a heated pool and hot tub. Past the small pool deck is a spot on the bluffs over the beach with chairs and tables set up. It's a perfect location to take in the sunset or the stars with the Pismo Pier in the distance. Before a day at the beach, enjoy the inn's deluxe continental breakfast.

For families or even couples who want to stretch out a bit, the ★ **Pismo Lighthouse Suites** (2411 Price St., 805/773-2411, www.pismolighthousesuites.com, $229-458) all have two rooms and two bathrooms, which is a rare hotel luxury. In addition, the suites have nautical decor, like lamps designed to resemble lighthouses and paintings of sea scenes, while the oceanfront suites each include a balcony or patio to take in the fine views of the Pacific or Pismo Beach. Kids will love the family play deck that has a small mini-golf course, Ping Pong tables, a badminton course, and a giant chess and checkers set. In addition, there's a heated pool, a spa, and beach access.

At the **Best Western Plus Shore Cliff Lodge** (2555 Price St., 805/773-4671, www.shorecliff.com, $229-489), every room has an ocean view and a patio or balcony. The Shore Cliff has a swimming pool and soaking tub. Out front of the building is a large, grassy bluff with a gazebo that offers views of Pismo Beach and Pismo Pier. The Shore Cliff also has seven pet-friendly rooms and a hot breakfast buffet.

Camping

Pismo State Beach has two campground options. The **Oceano Campground** (555 Pier Ave., Oceano, 800/444-7275, www.parks.ca.gov, tent sites $35, RVs $50) is ideal for birders. It is adjacent to a migratory bird habitat surrounding a lagoon. Also in the park is the **North Beach Campground** (Hwy. 1, Pismo Beach, 800/444-7275, www.parks.ca.gov, tent sites $35), which is close to the Pismo Beach Monarch Butterfly Grove.

FOOD
Italian

Guiseppe's Cucina Italiana (891 Price St., 805/773-2870, www.giuseppesrestaurant.com, Sun.-Thurs. 11:30am-10pm, Fri.-Sat. 11:30am-11pm, $12-32) began as the senior project of a Cal Poly student. Now, almost 25 years later, the restaurant is still highlighting the cuisine of the Pugilese region of Italy with pastas, meat dishes, and wood-fired pizzas, including one topped with clams.

Markets

Like most California coastal towns, Pismo Beach has its own weekly **farmers market** (Pismo Pier, 805/773-4382, www.pismochamber.com, Wed. 3pm-6pm). It's held on Wednesday afternoons.

In the community of Shell Beach, **DePalo & Sons** (2665 Shell Beach Rd., Shell Beach, 805/773-1589, daily 7am-10pm, $6-13) is a wonderful place to stock up on provisions or to grab a tasty sandwich for a picnic. There's a selection of gourmet goods and fine wine. The deli counter in the back of the building displays a variety of premade food including pesto artichoke chicken breasts and roasted garlic bulbs. Sandwiches include a Tuscan-roasted sirloin steak sandwich, an Avila crab sandwich, and a pancetta BLT with a slab of homemade mozzarella and pesto mayo.

Mexican

Sitting by the string of hotels on Price Street, the sleek, stylish ★ **Ventana Grill** (2575 Price St., 805/773-0000, http://ventanagrill.com, Mon.-Thurs. 11am-9pm, Fri.-Sat. 11am-10pm, Sun. 10am-9pm, $14-39) serves up tasty California-Mexican dishes with ocean views. Menu items include entrées like tequila lime chicken, Alaskan halibut ceviche, and crab-encrusted mahi mahi. Ventana also has some darn good margaritas in unique flavors like prickly pear and pineapple.

Away from the tourist strip in Shell Beach, **Zorro's Café & Cantina** (927 Shell Beach Rd., Shell Beach, 805/773-9676, daily 7:30am-9pm, $10-18) serves Mexican- and American-style breakfast, lunch, and dinners. Breakfast has unique offerings like chile relleno and eggs, while dinner has more typical items including fajitas and burritos.

Seafood

On most days a line snakes out of the brightly colored ★ **Splash Café** (197 Pomeroy Ave., 805/773-4653, www.splashcafe.com, summer daily 8am-9pm, winter Sun.-Thurs. 8am-8:30pm, Fri.-Sat. 8am-9pm, $5-10). People are willing to wait for a taste of the eatery's popular clam chowder. It's not health food, but the rich, buttery chowder (served in a cup, bowl, or bread bowl) utilizes three different types of clams and hits the spot on a chilly day or after spending some time in the nearby Pacific. They also serve fish tacos, burgers, and fried seafood.

For a more sophisticated menu and better views, dine at **Steamers of Pismo** (1601 Price St., 805/773-4711, www.steamerspismobeach.com, Mon.-Thurs. 11:30am-3pm and 4:30pm-9pm, Fri.-Sat. 11:30am-3pm and 4:30pm-10pm, Sun. 11:30am-3pm and 4pm-9pm, $16-33). The menu has deep-fried seafood-and-chips platters along with shrimp jambalaya and chorizo and clam linguine. Steamers's happy hour (Sun.-Thurs. 3pm-7pm, Fri.-Sat. 3pm-6pm) offers a sampler of steamed clams, a fish taco, and a cocktail for the price of a dinner entrée.

It's not a good idea to wear your best clothes to the **Cracked Crab** (751 Price St., 805/773-2722, www.crackedcrab.com, Sun.-Thurs. 11am-9pm, Fri.-Sat. 11am-10pm, $12-53). The signature dish is a bucket for two that features three kinds of shellfish steamed with Cajun sausage, red potatoes, and corn. You are given a mallet, a crab cracker, and a bib. If that sounds like too much work, order a seafood sandwich or another entrée like grilled albacore.

INFORMATION AND SERVICES

There's a **California Welcome Center Pismo Beach** (333 Five Cities Dr., Suite 100,

805/773-7924, www.visitcwc.com, Mon.-Sat. 10am-9pm, Sun. 10am-7pm) at the Pismo Premium Outlets. In the center of Pismo Beach, the **Pismo Beach Chamber of Commerce Visitor Information Center** (581 Dolliver St., 805/773-4382 or 800/443-7778, www.pismochamber.com, Mon.-Fri. 10am-5pm, Sat. 10am-2pm) has pamphlets, maps, and information. There are a few banks in Pismo Beach along with a **post office** (100 Crest Dr., 805/481-5971, www.usps.com, Mon.-Fri. 9am-5:30pm, Sat. 9am-2pm). The nearby **Arroyo Grande Community Hospital** (345 South Halcyon Rd., 805/489-4261, www.dignityhealth.org/arroyo-grande/) has services for emergencies.

Santa Barbara and Ventura

fine bases of operations to enjoy this region, though accommodations in the former can be quite pricey.

With U.S. 101 stringing Ventura, Santa Barbara, and the sections of the Gaviota Coast together, the region is easy to travel around in. For the most part, the City of Santa Barbara has ample signs directing you to its downtown and other sites, including the Santa Barbara Mission.

Those wanting to travel out to more remote places like Channel Islands National Park and remote sections of the Gaviota Coast, particularly Jalama Beach County Park, should add a few days to their stay in the region. Getting out to the Channel Islands involves getting a space on a boat or plane. In addition, boats travel to some islands only every few days. It is nice to secure a hotel in Ventura or Santa Barbara after a camping expedition on the islands to ease yourself back into civilization before heading on to your next destination.

Santa Barbara

It's been called the American Riviera, with weather, community, and sun-drenched beaches reminiscent of the Mediterranean coast. In truth, Santa Barbara is all California.

Nestled between the Pacific Ocean and the mountains, its copious sunshine, wide roads, sandy beaches, and challenging mountain trails inspire physical activity and healthy living. Along the waterfront, a paved path allows anyone on two feet, two wheels, or anything else that moves to enjoy the coastline alongside grassy areas with palm trees gently swaying in the breeze. At least five weekly area farmers markets make healthy produce abundant and accessible.

Santa Barbara is also where beach culture meets high culture. You'll find lots of museums, outdoor shopping areas, great restaurants, and four-star resorts. And a growing young wine region thrives. But the pace of life slows down enough to make it a favorite escape for Southern California locals as well. It's not surprising that many of these refugees from Los Angeles decide to stay and become Santa Barbara residents.

SIGHTS
★ State Street

Though **State Street** travels through different sections of Santa Barbara, the roadway that cuts through 12 blocks downtown is the heart of the city. Wide brick sidewalks on either side are shaded by palm trees and decorated with flowers, giving the city a tropical feel. Clothing stores, restaurants, and bars line the street along with popular attractions including the **Santa Barbara Museum of Art** and **The Granada Theatre.**

Santa Barbara Maritime Museum

It's only fitting that the **Santa Barbara Maritime Museum** (113 Harbor Way, Suite 190, 805/962-8404, www.sbmm.org, Thurs.-Tues. 10am-5pm, until 6pm Memorial Day-Labor Day, adults $8, students and seniors $5, children 6-12 $4, free for military personnel in uniform) sits right on the working harbor. It began as a government works project during the Depression. For more than 50 years, the station was used by the U.S. Navy as a training facility. After being sold back to the city of Santa Barbara in 1995, construction began on the museum, which opened in 2000. A dozen different exhibits, including ones on shipwrecks, commercial fishing, and surfing, show off the history of the California coast's relationship to the sea. The Munger Theater screens high-definition educational films each day. The Children's Area features hands-on exhibits that make learning about the sea lots of fun for younger visitors. Many other galleries tell the maritime history of California, beginning with the local Chumash

Santa Barbara and Ventura

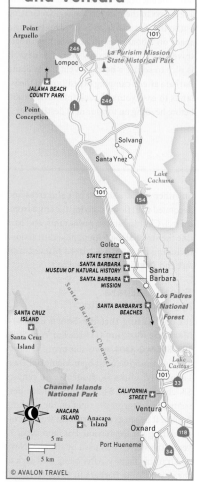

Native Americans, running through the whaling and fur-hunting eras and up through the modern oil drilling and commercial fishing industries. Learn a bit about sailing and yachting, safety on the Pacific, and how to help preserve the ocean's environment.

Stearns Wharf

Stretching out into the harbor for 2,250 feet, **Stearns Wharf** (intersection of State St.

and Cabrillo Blvd., www.stearnswharf.org, parking $2.50/hr, first 90 mins free with validation) was the longest deepwater pier between Los Angeles and San Francisco when it was constructed by John P. Stearns in 1872. Stearns Wharf has weathered many natural disasters, including a restaurant fire in 1973 that caused the closure of the wharf for almost nine years. A tourist favorite, the wooden wharf hosts candy stores, gift shops, and casual seafood eateries. It is also home to the **Ty Warner Sea Center** (211 Stearns Wharf, 805/962-2526, www.sbnature.org, daily 10am-5pm, adults $8, seniors and teens $7, children $5), which is operated by the Museum of Natural History.

★ Santa Barbara Museum of Natural History

Continuing the outdoors theme that pervades Santa Barbara, the **Santa Barbara Museum of Natural History** (2559 Puesta del Sol, 805/682-4711, www.sbnature.org, daily 10am-5pm, adults $12, seniors and teens $8, children $7) has exhibits to delight visitors of all ages. Inside are large galleries that display stories of the life and times of insects, mammals, birds, and dinosaurs. Of particular interest is a display showcasing the remains of a pygmy mammoth specimen that was found on the nearby Channel Islands. Learn a little about the human history of the Santa Barbara area at the Chumash exhibit. Head outdoors to circle the immense skeleton of a blue whale, and to hike the Mission Creek Nature Trail. If you're interested in the nature of worlds other than this one, go into the **Gladwin Planetarium** and wander the Astronomy Center exhibits. The planetarium hosts shows portraying the moon and stars, plus monthly Star Parties and special events throughout the year.

If you're more interested in the Earth's array of sealife, head down to Stearns Wharf and visit the **Ty Warner Sea Center** (211 Stearns Wharf, 805/962-2526, www.sbnature.org, daily 10am-5pm, multi-museum passes at either location, adults $8, seniors and teens $7, children $5), which is operated by the Museum of Natural History. Check out the tunnel through the 1,500-gallon tide pool tank, touch a sea cucumber, examine microscopic sea creatures, and get involved in the science of oceanography.

Santa Barbara Zoo

It's not the biggest zoo in the state, but the Santa Barbara Zoo (500 Ninos Dr., 805/962-5339, www.sbzoo.org, daily 10am-5pm, adults $15, children $10, seniors $12) is a cool little municipal zoo. It shelters its critters in enclosures that resemble those of the San Diego Zoo, including a multi-species habitat that mimics an African savannah with giraffes, tortoises, cranes, and meerkats all hanging out together. Granted, the pride of lions next door are corralled away from the giraffes, but you can get close to them and occasionally hear them roar. The Santa Barbara Zoo also takes pride in its local endangered species—the Channel Island foxes are indigenous to an area only 20 miles from the zoo. The "California Trail" exhibit shows off California condors, one of the rarest birds in the state and still an endangered species. As you slowly stroll along the paths, you'll also see giant anteaters, huge elephants, monkeys, and snow leopards. One of the best-named kids' exhibits ever, "Eeeww!" showcases reptiles, wonderfully slimy amphibians, and insects at children's eye level.

If you need a stroller or wheelchair, rent one just inside the entrance. Also close to the gate you'll find the Ridley-Tree House Restaurant, which offers plenty of outside tables and a walk-up arrangement that sells sandwiches and burgers. Also there's Mexican-inspired fare at The Wave. The gift shop offers cute souvenirs for both kids and adults.

Santa Barbara Botanic Gardens

The year-round sublime weather makes for a perfect spot to grow the gorgeous Santa Barbara Botanic Gardens (1212 Mission Canyon Rd., 805/682-4726, www.sbbg.org, Mar.-Oct. daily 9am-6pm, Nov.-Feb. daily 9am-5pm, adults $10, seniors and teens $8, children $6). The gardens focus solely on the indigenous plants of California, with plantings from the deserts, chaparral, arroyo, and more. The gardens spread out over many acres and cross several hiking trails. Check out the small stand of coast redwoods, the centerpiece of the park, which remains shaded and cool even when the sun beats down in the heat of summertime. Another proud garden shows off the beauty of native California lilacs. The mission of the gardens encompasses conservation of not only the California wilderness areas, but the water and soil in developed areas as well. Visit the Home Demonstration Garden for an example of beautiful landscaping using California natives that are suited to the climate and conditions, and thus need less irrigation and chemical fertilizers.

Guided tours are offered on Saturdays and Sundays at 11am and 2pm with your admission ticket—join the standard tour or call ahead to arrange a private tour. Take your own self-guided tour with a map and the advice of the docents. The shop offers books and garden-themed gifts, while the nursery sells native Californian plants. The garden does not include a restaurant or snack bar.

★ Santa Barbara Mission

It's easy to see why the Santa Barbara Mission (2201 Laguna St., 805/682-4713, http://santabarbaramission.org, daily 9am-5pm, self-guided tours adults $8, seniors $6, children $3, children 4 and under free, docent-guided tours Thurs.-Fri. 11am, Sat. 10:30am, adults $12, seniors and military $10, children $7) is referred to as the "Queen of the Missions." It is larger, more beautiful, and more impressive than many of the other missions. It is also second to none for its art displays and graceful architecture, all of which are complemented by the serene local climate and scenery. Unlike many of the California missions, the church at Santa Barbara remained in service after the secularization of the mission chain in the 19th century. When

Santa Barbara City

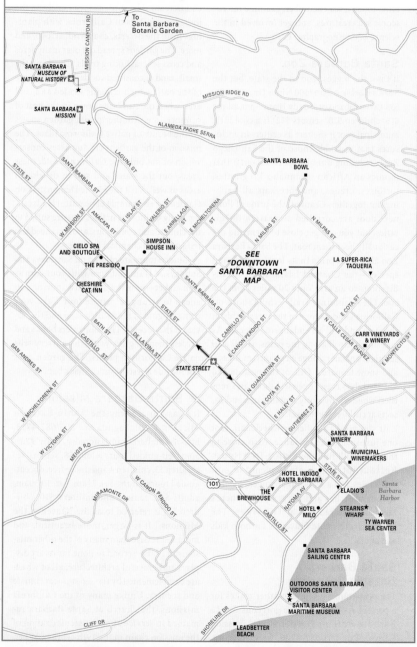

To
Santa Barbara
Botanic Garden

MISSION CANYON RD

SANTA BARBARA
MUSEUM OF
NATURAL HISTORY ★

MISSION RIDGE RD

SANTA BARBARA
MISSION ★

ALAMEDA PADRE SERRA

STATE ST

LAGUNA ST

SANTA BARBARA ST

SANTA BARBARA
BOWL

W MISSION ST

ANACAPA ST

E ISLAY ST

E VALERIO ST

E ARRELLAGA ST

E MICHELTORENA ST

N MILPAS ST

N MILPAS ST

CIELO SPA
AND BOUTIQUE

SIMPSON
HOUSE INN

SEE
"DOWNTOWN
SANTA BARBARA"
MAP

LA SUPER-RICA
TAQUERIA ▼

THE PRESIDIO ■

CHESHIRE
CAT INN

SANTA BARBARA ST

STATE ST

E CARRILLO ST

E CANON PERDIDO ST

N CALLE CESAR CHAVEZ

E COTA ST

CARR VINEYARDS
& WINERY ■

E MONTECITO ST

BATH ST

CASTILLO ST

DE LA VINA ST

SAN ANDRES ST

STATE STREET ★

N QUARANTINA ST

E COTA ST

E HALEY ST

E GUTIERREZ ST

W MICHELTORENA ST

W VICTORIA ST

MEIGS RD

W CANON PERDIDO ST

SANTA BARBARA
WINERY ●

MUNICIPAL
WINEMAKERS ■

MIRAMONTE DR

101

STATE ST

Santa
Barbara
Harbor

HOTEL INDIGO
SANTA BARBARA ●

THE
BREWHOUSE ▼

NATOMA AV

ELADIO'S ▼

CASTILLO ST

HOTEL
MILO ●

STEARNS ★
WHARF

TY WARNER
SEA CENTER ★

SANTA BARBARA
SAILING CENTER ■

SHORELINE DR

OUTDOORS SANTA BARBARA
VISITOR CENTER ★

SANTA BARBARA
MARITIME MUSEUM ★

CLIFF DR

LEADBETTER
BEACH ■

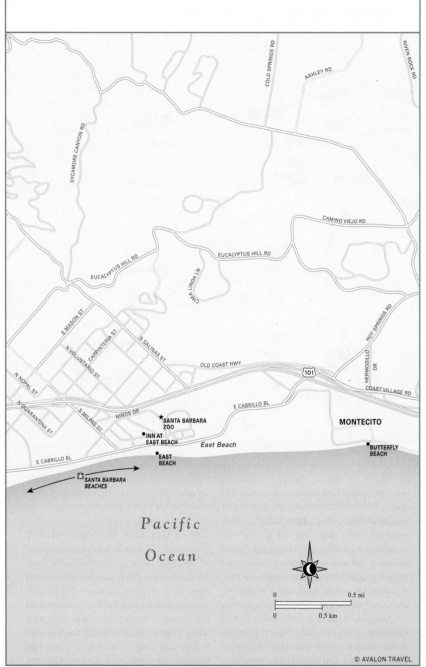

© AVALON TRAVEL

Downtown Santa Barbara

OPAL

ARLINGTON THEATRE

OLIO E LIMONE

BOUCHON

SOHO

TUPLEO JUNCTION CAFE

GRANADA THEATER

★ SANTA BARBARA COUNTY COURTHOUSE

★ SANTA BARBARA MUSEUM OF ART

LA ARCADA COURT

THE HUNGRY CAT

THE FRENCH PRESS

INN OF THE SPANISH GARDEN

ZAYTOON

SOJOURNER CAFE

LOBERO THEATER

CANARY HOTEL

STATE STREET

PASEO NUEVO SHOPING CENTER

CENTER STAGE THEATER

TONIC NIGHTCLUB

JOE'S CAFE

THE PALACE GRILL

NATURAL CAFE

THE JAMES JOYCE

LA REVE

E SOLA ST

E ANAPAMU ST

E FIGUEROA ST

OLIVE ST

STATE ST

CHAPALA ST

W ANAPAMU ST

W FIGUEROA ST

W CARRILLO ST

W CANON PERDIDO ST

CHAPALA ST

W ORTEGA ST

DE LA VINA ST

E CARRILLO ST

E CANON PERDIDO ST

LAGUNA ST

GARDEN ST

E DE LA GUERRA ST

E ORTEGA ST

E COTA ST

E HALEY ST

E GUTIERREZ ST

101

0   250 yds

0   250 m

© AVALON TRAVEL

you visit, you'll find the collection of buildings, artwork, and even the ruins of the water system in better shape than at many other missions in the state. The self-guided tour includes a walk through the mission's striking courtyard with its blooming flowers and towering palm trees and entrance to the mission museum, which has among other displays a photo of the church after an earthquake in 1925 toppled its towers and a collection of Chumash artifacts. The original purpose of the mission was to transform the native Chumash into Christians. The mission's cemetery is the final resting place of more than 4,000 of these Chumash people.

Santa Barbara Museum of Art

The two-floor **Santa Barbara Museum of Art** (1130 State St., 805/963-4364, www.sbma.net, Tues.-Wed. and Fri.-Sun. 11am-5pm, Thurs. 11am-8pm, adults $10, seniors, students with ID, and children $6) has an impressive art collection that would make some larger cities envious. Wander the spacious, well-curated museum and take in some paintings from the museum's collection of Monets, which is the largest collection of the French impressionist's paintings on the West Coast. Also the museum has ancient works like a bronze head of Alexander from Roman times and a collection of Asian artifacts including a 17th- or 18th-century Tibetan prayer wheel. There are interesting temporary exhibitions on display as well.

Santa Barbara County Courthouse

If only all government buildings could be as striking as the **Santa Barbara County Courthouse** (1100 Anacapa St., 805/962-6464, www.santabarbaracourthouse.org, Mon.-Fri. 8am-5pm, Sat.-Sun. 10am-4:30pm, free docent-led tours Mon.-Fri. 10:30am and 2pm, Sat.-Sun. 2pm). Constructed in 1929, the courthouse, which is actually four buildings comprising a whole city block, is one of the city's finest examples of Mediterranean-style architecture. The interior's high ceilings, tile floors, ornate chandeliers, and art-adorned walls give it the feel of a California mission. Visit El Mirador, the clock tower, where an open deck 85 feet off the ground provides great views of the towering Santa Ynez Mountains and the Pacific Ocean.

WINERIES

The wines of Santa Barbara County have been receiving favorable reviews and write-ups in the national media. The area is predominantly known for pinot noir and chardonnay, but with the diversity of microclimates, there are over 50 grape varietals planted here. This means you can find traditional varieties like cabernet sauvignon, merlot, sauvignon blanc, and syrah, but also sangiovese, dolcetto, viognier, cabernet franc, malbec, and others.

Santa Barbara

Not all wine-tasting is done surrounded by vineyards. On the **Urban Wine Trail** (www.urbanwinetrailsb.com) you can sample some of the county's best wines without even seeing a vine. Near Lower State Street, a block from the beach, it's possible to walk to six tasting rooms. Visiting others that are part of the trail will require a little driving. Recently passed legislation means that some, but not all, wineries can now offer wines by the glass in addition to wine-tasting, so if you sample something you like, purchase a glass to enjoy on the spot or a bottle to take with you.

Kalyra Winery (212 State St., 805/965-8606, www.kalyrawinery.com, Mon.-Fri. noon-7pm, Sat.-Sun. noon-8pm, $12-14) is famous for having been featured in the 2004 movie *Sideways*. This tasting room wasn't in the film, but you can still sample the California and Australian wines made by Mike Brown, an Aussie and an avid surfer. There's a tiki room setting here. Kalyra started out making sweet wines, and still offers quite a few, but has a broad portfolio.

Once you're done at Kalyra Winery, walk a block down Yanonali Street to **Santa Barbara Winery** (202 Anacapa St., 805/963-3633, www.sbwinery.com, Sun.-Thurs. 10am-6pm, Fri.-Sat. 10am-7pm, $10), the oldest winery in the county, started in 1962. The chardonnay is delightful and truly expresses a Santa Barbara character with its bright citrus notes. Other varieties include pinot noir, sangiovese, and sauvignon blanc. If you are looking to sample a diverse array of wines, this is your best stop. The tasting bar is just a few feet from the barrel room, and there's a good-size gift shop.

Municipal Winemakers (22 Anacapa St., 805/931-6864, www.municipalwinemakers.com, Sun.-Wed. 11am-7pm, Thurs.-Sat. 11am-11pm, $10) is in an unpretentious small space with an even smaller deck. Inside are rough wood ceilings and plain walls, with a four-top table and standing room at the bar. This is a weekend venture for owner Dave Potter, who will answer your questions and pour his wines. The offerings are Rhone-style wines, including grenache, syrah, and a sparkling shiraz.

Carr Winery (414 N. Salsipuedes St., 805/965-7985, www.carrwinery.com, Mon.-Sat. 11am-8pm, Sun. 11am-6pm, $10) focuses on small lots of syrah, grenache, cabernet franc, and pinot noir. The tasting room is in a World War II-era Quonset hut, with a bar up front and tables in the back. The wine bar features live music on Fridays and house wines on tap.

Santa Maria Valley

Detour to the Santa Maria Valley to sample wines in the region made famous by the movie *Sideways*. Running roughly parallel to U.S. 101, **Foxen Canyon Road** is a back road hugging the foothills, with multiple wineries along its route.

From the south, take the Alisos Canyon Road turnoff from U.S. 101, about 25 miles north of the Highway 1-U.S. 101 split. Take Alisos Canyon Road 6.5 miles and turn left onto Foxen Canyon Road. Foxen Winery is about 5.5 miles down the road. Foxen Canyon Road eventually turns into East Betteravia Road and connects back to U.S. 101.

From the north, take the East Betteravia Road exit from U.S. 101, and head east about three miles until it turns into Foxen Canyon Road. From this point, Tepusquet Road, where Kenneth Volk is located, is about 10 miles away.

Foxen Winery now has two tasting rooms: the solar-powered **Foxen** (7600 Foxen Canyon Rd., 805/937-4251, www.foxenvineyard.com, daily 11am-4pm, $10-20) and the rustic, shack-like **Foxen 7200** (7200 Foxen Canyon Rd., 805/937-4251, daily 11am-4pm, $10-20). The newer Foxen at the 7600 location is where you can sample burgundy, rhones and the underappreciated chenin blanc. Head to Foxen 7200 for Bordeaux or Tuscan varieties. Foxen's long-standing reputation goes back six generations, and its 10 acres are the only dry-farmed vineyard in the area, meaning that irrigation is not used.

Set in an old barn, **Rancho Sisquoc** (6600 Foxen Canyon Rd., 805/934-4332, www.ranchosisquoc.com, Mon.-Thurs. 10am-4pm, Fri.-Sun. 10am-5pm, $10) makes a beautiful spot for a picnic. The wood-sided tasting room is rustic but comfortable, and the surrounding setting—a vast field with low hills in the distance—is perfect for some quiet, wine-enhanced relaxation.

On clear days, the ocean can be seen from the hilltop **Presqu'ile Winery** (5391 Presquile Dr., Santa Maria, 805/937-8110, www.presquilewine.com, Apr.-Nov. Sun.-Thurs. 11am-5pm, Fri. 11am-6pm, Dec.-Mar. Fri.-Mon. 11am-5pm, Tues.-Thurs. by appointment, $15). Enjoy pinot noir, chardonnay, and sauvignon blanc with the wonderful views. They also have 1.5-hour winery tours (days open 11am and 2pm, $45) that include some time on their viewing deck and a tasting of pinots with artisan cheeses.

On a little road off Foxen Canyon Road, award-winning **Kenneth Volk Vineyards** (5230 Tepusquet Rd., 805/938-7896, www.volkwines.com, daily 10:30am-4:30pm, $10) offers all the strange wines you've never tried. In addition to the standard offerings like chardonnay, pinot noir, viognier, cabernet sauvignon, and merlot, Kenneth Volk is a champion of heirloom varieties: funky, wonderfully oddball wines like the Portuguese grape wine touriga and the jasmine-aroma white wine torrantes. You won't regret the long trek to get to the tranquil property along the Tepusquet Creek, surrounded by oak and sycamore trees.

At the southern end of Foxen Canyon is another cluster of wineries, not too far from Los Olivos. One of the oldest wineries in the county, **Zaca Mesa Winery** (6905 Foxen Canyon Rd., Los Olivos, 805/688-9339, www.zacamesa.com, Memorial Day-Labor Day Sun.-Thurs. 10am-4pm, Fri.-Sat. 10am-5pm, Labor Day-Memorial Day daily 10am-4pm, $10) is the kind of winery tasters love to discover. A midsize producer with a modest facility and tasting room, Zaca quietly makes some of the best Central Coast wines to be found anywhere in the region. The first vineyards on the property were planted in the early 1970s, long before anyone else saw Santa Barbara as a place with potential for great winemaking. In 1978, Zaca Mesa planted the first syrah in Santa Barbara County. Zaca makes many of the Rhone varietals that grow so well in the climate of the Central Coast, such as viognier, roussanne, and syrah. Classics lovers will enjoy the chardonnay, and adventurous types shouldn't skip the syrahs and the Z Cuvee. After or while imbibing, play a game of chess on the winery's life-size chessboard or take a stroll on their hiking trail.

ENTERTAINMENT AND EVENTS

A wealthy town with close ties to cosmopolitan Los Angeles, Santa Barbara offers visitors a wealth of live cultural displays, from a symphony and opera to a near-endless parade of festivals. The students of UCSB add a lively bit of zest to the town's after-dark scene.

Bars and Clubs

The proximity of UCSB to downtown Santa Barbara guarantees a livelier nighttime scene than you'll find elsewhere on the Central Coast. Check with the locals to discover the ever-changing hot spots. Bars cluster on State Street and beyond, and plenty of hip clubs dot the landscape here.

The best place to start an evening out on the town is at **Joe's Café** (536 State St., 805/966-4638, www.joescafesb.com, daily 7:30am-10pm). This steak house and bar is known for the stiffest drinks in town. Don't expect a fancy cocktail menu. Just go with the classics in this historic establishment with a throwback feel thanks to its checkered tablecloths, tin-paneled ceiling, and framed black-and-white photos of mostly old men adorning the walls.

Tonic (634 State St., 805/897-1800, www.tonicsb.com, Thurs.-Sat. 8pm-1:30am) has a hipster feel, complete with exposed brick walls and a long glass bar. Top-flight DJs spin a mostly hip-hop or house groove, with the occasional mash-up for variety. Tonic also hosts college nights and ladies nights. Two lounges provide a respite from the partiers at the main bar and on the dance floor. To cool down, go outside to the huge outdoor patio, which has its own funky octagonal bar.

In an upstairs suite, **Soho** (1221 State St., Suite 205, 805/962-7776, www.sohosb.com, Sun.-Wed. 6pm-11:30pm, Thurs. and Sat. 7pm-1:30am, Fri. 5pm-1:30am) has hosted big-time touring acts including Jimmy Cliff, Donovan, and Built to Spill. It has live music seven nights a week. With its brick walls, Soho is going for a sophisticated New York City-type of feel. Make reservations to have an organic dinner at the venue before taking in the evening's entertainment.

The James Joyce, on State Street

For a traditional Irish bar experience in downtown Santa Barbara, head to **The James Joyce** (513 State St., 805/962-2688, www.sb-jamesjoyce.com, daily noon-1:30am). Peanut shells litter the floor as locals sip Guinness at the bar or play competitive games of darts in the back room. The James Joyce has live entertainment six days a week including Irish music on Sundays.

The Brewhouse (229 W. Montecito St., 805/884-4664, www.sbbrewhouse.com, Sun.-Thurs. 11am-10pm, Fri.-Sat. 11am-10:30pm) feels like a neighborhood bar, but it distinguishes itself from other popular watering holes by brewing its own small batch beers and offering a comprehensive dining menu. The brews include the popular West Beach IPA along with the more adventurous habanero pilsner and apricot wheat. The food includes burgers, sandwiches, seafood, and a truly different filet mignon enchiladas plate where the items swim in soupy ancho-lime cream sauce. Live music takes place in one of the brewery's two rooms Wednesday through Saturday evenings.

Live Music

Founded in 1873, the **Lobero Theater** (33 E. Canon Perdido St., 805/963-0761, www.lobero.com) is the oldest continuously operating theater in the state. While it used to host entertainers like Tallulah Bankhead and Bela Lugosi, it now welcomes jazz acts like Pat Metheney and Diane Reeves along with indie rock darling Jenny Lewis and jam band Chris Robinson Brotherhood. The medium-size theater has only one level, and it's filled with cushy red-velvet seats—perfect for a music-filled night out on the town. Check the website for the shows coming up during your visit. Buy tickets online, by phone, or at the box office during your stay.

The **Santa Barbara Bowl** (1122 N. Milpas St., 805/962-7411, www.sbbowl.com) is a great place to take in a concert during the summer and fall. Built in 1936, the Santa Barbara Bowl is the largest outdoor amphitheater in the county. In the past it has hosted concerts by Neil Young, Florence & The Machine, and Death Cab for Cutie.

Classical Music

The **Santa Barbara Symphony** (Granada Theatre, 1214 State St., 805/898-9386, www.thesymphony.org) aspires to compete with its brethren in Los Angeles and San Francisco. The symphony orchestra puts up seasons that pay homage to the greatest composers the world has ever seen, plus the works of less-known but equally talented artists. Whether you prefer Mozart or Mahler, you can listen to it at the concert hall at the Granada Theatre. Every seat has a great view of the stage, and the acoustics were designed with music in mind, making for an overall great symphony experience.

Opera Santa Barbara (OSB, Granada Theatre, 1214 State St., 805/898-3890, www.operasb.com) has put up such classics as *Aida, Don Pasquale,* and *Madame Butterfly.* In fine tradition, OSB enjoys a focus on the classics and little-known works of the Italian masters. Operas are staged at the Granada Theatre.

Dance

The **Center Stage Theater** (751 Paseo Nuevo, 805/963-0408, www.centerstagetheater.org) puts on everything from plays with a formerly incarcerated cast to improv comedy performances. Center Stage focuses on dance, offering more ballet and modern dance performances than it does plays. A handful of local groups including the Lit Moon Theatre and Out of the Box Theater Company have made the Center Stage their home.

SHOPPING

If you're looking for a fairly standard shopping expedition in Santa Barbara, go to **State Street.** From end to end, this busy main drag hosts a near-unbelievable array of mall-style stores, plus a few independent boutiques for variety. You'll find lots of lovely women's apparel, plenty of housewares stores, and all the usual stuff you'd expect to find in a

Paseo Nuevo Shopping Center

Plaza as their canvas. The festival benefits the nonprofit Children's Creative Project.

Fiesta (various venues in Santa Barbara, 805/962-8101, www.oldspanishdays-fiesta. org, some events free), also known as Old Spanish Days, is Santa Barbara's biggest annual festival. Since 1924, it has paid tribute to the city's Spanish and Mexican heritage with parades, live music, horse shows, bull riding and the erection of public marketplaces known as mercados. During Fiesta, hotel rooms become near impossible to find, while those rare vacancies go for premium prices.

The 11-day **Santa Barbara International Film Festival** (various venues, 805/963-0023, http://sbiff.org) showcases over 200 films and includes 20 world premieres.

★ BEACHES

There's nothing easier than finding a beach in Santa Barbara. Just follow State Street to its end, and you'll be at the coastline.

East Beach

Named because it is east of Stearns Wharf, **East Beach** (1400 Cabrillo Blvd., www.santabarbaraca.gov, daily sunrise-10pm) is all soft sand and wide beach, with a dozen volleyball nets in the sand close to the zoo (if you look closely you can see the giraffes and lions). It has all the amenities a sun worshipper could hope for: a full beach house, a snack bar, a play area for children, and a path for biking and in-line skating. The beachfront has picnic facilities and a full-service restaurant at the East Beach Grill. The **Cabrillo Pavilion Bathhouse** (1119 East Cabrillo Blvd.), built in 1927, offers showers, lockers, a weight room, a single rentable beach wheelchair, and volleyball rental.

West Beach

On the west side of Stearns Wharf, **West Beach** (Cabrillo Blvd. and Chapala St., between Stearns Wharf and the harbor, daily sunrise-10pm) has 11 acres of picturesque sand for sunbathing, swimming, kayaking, windsurfing, and beach volleyball. There are

major urban shopping center. Also explore the **Paseo Nuevo Shopping Center** (651 Paseo Nuevo, 805/963-7147, www.paseonuevoshopping.com, Mon.-Fri. 10am-9pm, Sat. 10am-8pm, Sun. 11am-7pm), a series of pathways off State Street that has clothing stores, including Nordstrom and Macy's, along with chain eateries like Chipotle and California Pizza Kitchen.

Also right off State Street is **La Arcada Court** (1114 State St., 805/966-6634, www. laarcadasantabarbara.com), a collection of shops, restaurants, specialty stores, and art galleries. Along the tile-lined walkways, playful human-like sculptures appear in front of some of the shops.

FESTIVALS AND EVENTS

Inspired by a similar event in Grazie di Curtatone, Italy, the **I Madonnari Italian Street Painting Festival** (805/964-4710, ext. 4411, www.imadonnarifestival.com, late May, free) finds street painters using Mission also large palm trees, a wide walkway, and a bike path, making it a popular tourist spot. Outrigger canoes also launch from this beach.

Leadbetter Beach

Considered by many to be the best beach in Santa Barbara, **Leadbetter Beach** (Shoreline Dr. and Loma Alta Dr., daily sunrise-10pm) divides the area's south-facing beaches from the west-facing ones. It's a long, flat beach with a large grassy area. Sheer cliffs rise from the sand, and trees dot the point. The beach, which is also bounded by the harbor and the breakwater, is ideal for swimming because it's fairly protected, unlike the other flat beaches.

Many catamaran sailors and windsurfers launch from this beach, and you'll occasionally see surfers riding the waves. The grassy picnic areas have barbecue sites that can be reserved for more privacy, but otherwise there is a lot of room. The beach and the park can get packed during the many races and sporting events held here. There are restrooms, a small restaurant, and outdoor showers. Directly across the street is Santa Barbara City College. If you enter the stadium and walk up the many steps, you'll get some terrific views of the harbor, plus a workout.

Arroyo Burro Beach

To the north of town, **Arroyo Burro Beach** (Cliff Dr., 805/687-3714, www.sbparks.org, daily 8am-sunset), also known as Hendry's, is a favorite for locals and dog owners. To the right as you face the water, past Arroyo Burro Slough, dogs are allowed off-leash to dash across the packed sand and frolic and fetch out in the gentle surf. Arroyo Burro is rockier than the downtown beaches, making it less friendly to games and sunbathers. But the rocks and shells make for great beachcombing, and you might find a slightly smaller crowd on sunny weekend days. You'll find a snack bar, restrooms, outdoor showers, and a medium-size pay parking lot for your convenience. At peak times, when the parking lot is full, there's no other parking around.

Goleta Beach

At the base of the University of California, Santa Barbara campus, **Goleta Beach Park** (5986 Sandspit Rd., daily sunrise-10pm) is popular for its picnic tables, barbecue pits, horseshoes, multiple restrooms, and fishing opportunities. The grassy area is partially shaded by trees, and there's also a small jungle gym for the kids. The pier is popular for fishing, and the low breaks make it an easy entry for kayakers. You can also launch small boats from the pier on weekends, when a crane lowers boats into the water (there is no launch ramp directly into the water). On the mountain-facing side along the bike path are a few platforms for viewing birds in the slough behind the beach.

Butterfly Beach

Butterfly Beach (Channel Dr., across from the Four Seasons Hotel, Montecito, daily sunrise-10pm) is accessed by a handful of steps leading to the narrow beach. Many people come here hoping to catch a glimpse of a celebrity from nearby Montecito, but chances are that won't happen. Butterfly is the most west-facing beach in Santa Barbara, meaning that you can actually see the sun set over the Pacific here. To find it, take U.S. 101 to Olive Mill Road in Montecito (a few minutes south of Santa Barbara). At the stop sign, turn toward the ocean (away from the mountains) and follow it 0.25 miles along the coast; Butterfly Beach is on the left. The beach is packed most weekends and often weekdays too, and parking is limited. Park on either side of the street along the beach, or drive up Butterfly Road and park in the nearby neighborhoods. Bring your lunch, water, and sunscreen—there are no public facilities at this beach. Dogs roam freely here.

Carpinteria State Beach

Carpinteria State Beach (5361 6th St., Carpinteria, 805/968-1033, daily 7am-sunset, day use $10, camping $35-65) has designated itself the "world's safest beach." Whether that's true or not, this beautiful, wide, flat beach is definitely a favorite for locals and visitors alike. With plenty of campgrounds, picnic tables, outdoor showers, RV hook-ups, telephones, and a short walk to Linden Avenue's restaurants, shops, and grocery store, you'll have everything you need within walking distance. Parts of the campgrounds are tree-lined but right next to the train tracks; passing trains might wake up light sleepers. There is a great sense of community among the campers here.

SPORTS AND RECREATION

With the year-round balmy weather, it's nearly impossible to resist the temptation to get outside and do something energetic and fun in Santa Barbara. From golf to sea kaya-king, you've got plenty of options for recre-ation here.

Surfing

The trick to surfing Santa Barbara is to know that during the summer months the Channel Islands block the south swells that would otherwise hit the county. But, during fall and winter, the big north and northwest swells wrap around Point Conception and transform places like Rincon into legendary surf breaks.

Leadbetter Point (Shoreline Park, just north of the Santa Barbara Harbor) is a slow, mushy wave perfect for beginners and long-boarders. The locals are reasonably welcom-ing, and the small right break makes for easy and fun rides.

For a bit more of a challenge, paddle out to the barrels at **Sandspit** (Santa Barbara Harbor). The harbor's breakwater creates hol-low right breaks for adventurous surfers. Be careful though: Sandspit's backwash has been known to toss surfers onto the breakwater.

Known as the "Queen of the Coast," **Rincon** (U.S. 101 at Bates Rd. on the Ventura County/Santa Barbara County line) is con-sidered California's best right point break. If you catch a wave outside, there's a chance you can score a memorable-for-life 300-yard-long ride. You might also see three-time world champion and revered surfer Tom Curren in the lineup. But, if it's firing, you'll also most likely be sharing the break with lots of other surfers. The time to investigate Rincon is dur-ing the winter.

Looking for surfing lessons? Check out the **Santa Barbara Surf School** (805/708-9878, www.santabarbarasurfschool.com, surf les-sons $65-85, surf camp $395). The instructors have decades of surfing experience and pride themselves on being able to get beginners up and riding in a single lesson. They also offer five-day surf camps in the summer.

Kayaking and Stand-Up Paddleboarding

One of the best ways to see the Santa Barbara Harbor and Bay is under your own power in a kayak or stand-up paddleboard. A number of rental and touring companies offer lessons, guided paddles, and good advice for explor-ing the region. **Channel Islands Outfitters** (117B Harbor Way, 805/617-3425, www.chan-nelislandso.com, daily 7am-7pm, SUPs $30/hour, kayaks $15/hour) has everything you need to paddle the waters of Santa Barbara and Ventura. Rent a sea kayak or a stand-up paddleboard to take your own ride around the harbor or out into the bay. They also lead ad-venturous sea-kayak tours around the nearby Channel Islands.

The **Santa Barbara Sailing Center** (133 Harbor Way, 805/350-9090, www.sbsail.com, kayaks $10-15/hour, SUPs $15-30) also pro-vides kayak rentals and stand-up paddleboard rentals, as well as sea-kayaking tours.

Sailing

At the **Santa Barbara Sailing Center** (133 Harbor Way, 805/350-9090, www.sbsail.com, sailboat rental $295-745/day), learn to sail, charter a sailboat, or rent a powerboat. The sailing center also offers sailing excursions aboard the 50-foot *Jenny Lane* sailboat.

Fishing and Whale-Watching

Santa Barbara's prime location on the coast makes it a great spot for deep-sea fishing and whale-watching. With its proximity to the feeding grounds of the blue and humpback whales, Santa Barbara is one of the state's best places to spot the marine mammals.

If you're looking for a whale-watching expedition, birding expedition, or a dinner cruise, check out the **Condor Express** (301 W. Cabrillo Blvd., 805/882-0088, www.condorexpress.com, whale-watching trips adults $45-99, children $30-50). In the summertime, they can take you out to the Channel Islands to see the blue and humpback whales feed; in the winter, the captain sails into the path of migrating gray whales. The boat is an 88-foot vessel that can seat 68 people. Whale-watching cruises depart almost daily all year long; call to purchase tickets in advance.

If you want to go fishing, give **WaveWalker Charters** (Santa Barbara Harbor, Marine Gate 3, 805/964-2046, www.wavewalker.com) a call. This private six-passenger charter boat rents for $960 for a three-quarters day—expensive unless you bring five friends along to split the cost! Bait and all tackle are included with the charter, but a fishing license is not. Call for more information about what you can fish for when.

Golf

It might not get the most press of the many golf destinations in California, but with its year-round mild weather and resort atmosphere, Santa Barbara is a great place to play a few holes. There are six public courses within an hour of downtown Santa Barbara—everything from a popular municipal course to championship courses with views of the ocean from the greens.

It's still a golf course, but **Glen Annie** (405 Glen Annie Rd., 805/968-6400, www.glenanniegolf.com, $62-76, carts $13) has worked with Audubon International to create wildlife habitats on its land. Who knows what you might see when you're out walking the lush, green, 18-hole, par-72 course? Well, you'll definitely get great views of Santa Barbara, the ocean, and the Channel Islands on this hilly course. The Frog Bar & Grill, the on-site restaurant, draws any number of non-golfers up to Glen Annie for lunch. Set in a castle-like structure, the Frog serves California cuisine that is a far cry from most clubhouse fare. So come for the golf, but stay for the unusual and delicious fare.

If you're already interested in exploring Santa Barbara's wine country, consider reserving a tee time at **La Purisima Golf Course** (3455 Hwy. 246, Lompoc, 805/735-8395, www.lapurisimagolf.com, $30-84). This golf course, built in 1986, gets high praise for its design and difficulty level—even if you're an expert golfer, "La Piranha" will test your skills. The par-72 course is a 45-minute drive from downtown Santa Barbara, but many locals think it's worth the trip. In addition to the 18 holes, you can access the grass driving range, the short-game practice area, and the pro shop. A number of PGA and LPGA golf pros are on hand to help you improve your game.

The **Sandpiper** (7925 Hollister Ave., 805/968-1541, www.sandpipergolf.com, $145-165, cart $20) boasts some of the most amazing views you'll find in all of Santa Barbara. They're so great because they're right up close, and on several holes your ball is in danger of falling into the world's largest water trap (aka the Pacific Ocean). And hey, there's a great championship-rated 74.5, 18-hole, par-72 golf course out there on that picturesque beach too! Take advantage of the pro shop and on-site restaurant, but do be aware of the semiformal, denim-free dress code Sandpiper enforces. It's not cheap, but a long walk on the beach with a great golf game in the middle of it seems well worth it to an endless stream of golfers who rank Sandpiper as one of their favorite courses.

Spas

Folks who can afford to live in Santa Barbara tend to be able to afford many of the finer things in life, including massages, facials, and luxe skin treatments. You'll find a wide array of day spas and medical spas in town.

If you prefer a slightly more natural spa experience, book a treatment at **Le Reve** (21 W.

Solvang

Founded in 1911 as a Danish retreat, Solvang makes a fun side trip. It's ripe with Scandinavian heritage as well as a theme-park atmosphere not lacking in kitsch.

In the 1950s, far earlier than other themed communities, Solvang decided to promote itself via a focus on Danish architecture, food, and style, which still holds a certain charm more than 50 years later. You'll still hear the muted strains of Danish spoken on occasion, and you'll notice storks displayed above many of the stores in town as a traditional symbol of good luck.

Solvang draws nearly two million visitors each year. During peak summer season and holidays, people clog the brick sidewalks. Try to visit during off-season, when meandering the lovely shops can still be enjoyed. It's at its best in the fall and early spring when the hills are verdant green and the trees in town are beautiful.

a windmill in the Danish-inspired town of Solvang

The **Elverhøj Museum** (1624 Elverhoj Way, 805/686-1211, www.elverhoj.org, Wed.-Sun. 11am-4pm, $5 suggested donation) features exhibits of traditional folk art from Denmark, including paper-cutting and lace-making, wood clogs, and the rustic tools used to create them. It also offers a comprehensive history of the area with nostalgic photos of the early settlers.

The small **Hans Christian Andersen Museum** (1680 Mission Dr., 805/688-2052, www.solvangca.com, daily 10am-5pm, free) chronicles the author's life, work, and impact on literature. Displays include first editions of his books from the 1830s in Danish and English.

Contact the **Solvang Visitor Information Center** (1639 Copenhagen Dr., 805/688-6144, www.solvangusa.com, daily 9am-5pm) for more advice on a Solvang visit.

GETTING THERE

If you're heading from Santa Barbara north to Solvang, you have two choices. You can drive the back route, Highway 154, also known as the San Marcos Pass Road, and arrive in Solvang in about 30 minutes. This is a two-lane road, with only a few places to pass slower drivers, but it has some stunning views of the coast as you climb into the hills. You pass Cachuma Lake, then turn west on Highway 246 to Solvang. The other option is to take U.S. 101, which affords plenty of coastal driving before you head north into the Gaviota Pass to reach Solvang. This route is longer, about 45 minutes' drive time. Highway 246 is known as Mission Drive in the town, and it connects both to U.S. 101 and Highway 154, which connects to Santa Barbara in the south and U.S. 101 farther north.

Gutierrez, 805/564-2977, www.le-reve.com, daily 10am-7pm, massages $140-175). Using biodynamic skin care products and pure essential oils, Le Reve makes good on the advertising that bills it as an "aromatherapy spa." Choose from an original array of body treatments, massage, hand and foot pampering, facials, and various aesthetic treatments. If you're up for several hours of relaxation, check out the spa packages that combine facials with massage and body treatments.

Cielo Spa and Boutique (1725 State St., Ste. C, 805/687-8979, www.cielospasb.com, daily by appointment only, massages $110-165) prides itself on its warm, nurturing environment. Step inside and admire the scents and the soft lighting and the natural, New Agey decor. Contemplate the colorful live orchids, feel soothed by the flickering candlelight, and get lost in the tranquil atmosphere. The menu of services has an almost Northern Californian flare, with signature champagne treatments and a focus on organics and natural lotions and potions. Check into the luxury packages that combine massages, facials, and more for a full day in the spa.

ACCOMMODATIONS

If you want a posh beachside room in Santa Barbara, you'd better be prepared to pay for it. Actually, almost all of Santa Barbara's hotels charge a premium rate. On the other hand, there are a couple of charming and reasonably priced accommodations near downtown and other attractions.

Under $150

Even the hostels in Santa Barbara are upscale, but you'd be hard pressed to find a better room in a better location than at **The Wayfarer** (12 E. Montecito St., 805/845-1000, www.pacifica-hotels.com/thewayfarer, dorm beds $60-99, private rooms $220-399). In the city's arty Funk Zone, The Wayfarer has unhostel-like features including a heated outdoor pool and a sleek, contemporary decor. Save money by cooking in the communal kitchen and partaking in the morning continental breakfast.

$150-250

★ **Hotel Indigo Santa Barbara** (121 State St., 805/966-6586, www.ihg.com, $239-314) is part of an international boutique hotel chain. The Santa Barbara location offers sleek, compact rooms with hardwood floors and a European-style collapsible glass shower wall. Some rooms also have small outdoor patios. While the rooms are not spacious, they are artfully done, clean, and modern. The hallways are essentially art galleries, showcasing a rotating group of local artists. Upstairs is a vertical garden, two outdoor lounges, and a library with art-related books. The hotel is in a great location, one block from the beach and two blocks from Santa Barbara's downtown. It's also near the train station, so expect to hear a train roll by occasionally.

The Presidio (1620 State St., 805/963-1355, www.presidiosb.com, $139-269) has 16 clean, modern rooms at reasonable prices within walking distance of the downtown section of State Street. The second-floor rooms have vaulted ceilings, while every room has Wi-Fi and TVs with HBO. The staff here is friendly, and the small hotel has unique features including a sun deck and a fleet of beach cruisers for motel guests.

If you're in Santa Barbara to soak up the sun on the sandy beaches, book a room at the **Inn at East Beach** (1029 Orilla Del Mar,

Hotel Indigo Santa Barbara

commuters up from Los Angeles and the occasional Hollywood celeb, all of whom think La Super-Rica's got some of the best downhome Mexican cuisine in all of SoCal. This was Julia Child's favorite taco stand, and it's been reviewed by the *New York Times*.

Folks don't come for the ambience—it's a taqueria in what feels like a beach shack. You also need to adjust your concept of Mexican food; if you're looking for a fast-food burrito supreme with chips and salsa, you'll definitely be disappointed. (Actually, there's no burrito on the menu.) But if you're ready for the real deal, you've found it. The corn tortillas are made fresh for every order, the meat is slow cooked and seasoned to perfection, and the house special is a grilled pork-stuffed pasilla chile. Vegetarians can choose from a few delicious meat-free dishes including the rajas, a standout item of sautéed strips of pasilla peppers, sautéed onions, melted cheese, and herbs on a bed of two fresh corn tortillas.

Middle Eastern

For a Middle Eastern feast, go to **Zaytoon** (209 E. Canon Perdido St., 805/963-1293, www.zaytoon.com, Mon.-Thurs. noon-10pm, Fri.-Sat. noon-11pm, Sun. 5pm-10pm, $18-32). This restaurant and hookah bar appeals to a crowd that wants to enjoy an evening out with a group of friends, to share a hookah around the table, and to ogle talented belly dancers shimmying among the tables. While the interior dining room is attractive, with potted palms and gauzy fabric draped from the ceiling, it's not the best place to sit at Zaytoon. Instead, try to get a table out on the garden patio, a large, softly lit space almost completely enveloped by a living green jungle. It is out here that you can order up your own hookah. The menu has most standard Middle Eastern favorites, such as baba ghanoush, hummus, falafel, Greek salad, shawarma, and kebabs of many kinds.

Seafood

It takes something special to make Santa Barbara residents take notice of a seafood restaurant, and **Brophy Brothers** (119 Harbor Way, 805/966-4418, www.brophy-bros.com, daily 11am-10pm, $19-25) has it. Look for a small list of fresh fish done up California style with upscale preparations. The delectable menu goes heavy on locally caught seafood. At the clam bar, order some fresh steamed clams or oysters, a bowl of the house clam chowder, or a tasty seafood salad. With a prime location looking out over the masts of the sailboats in the harbor, it's no surprise that Brophy Brothers gets crowded at both lunch and dinnertime, especially on weekends in the summertime. There's also a location in Ventura Harbor.

Yes, they do mean *that* **Endless Summer** (113 Harbor Way, 805/564-4666, http://chuckswaterfrontgrill.com, daily 11:30am-9:30pm, $13-19). When they decided to create a new restaurant in the harbor area, the owners went to Bruce Johnson, a Santa Barbara resident and acknowledged creator of the "real" surfing movie genre, and asked him if he would mind having a restaurant named for his most famous film. Bruce thought it was a fine idea, and not only gave the project his blessing, he quickly became a regular in the dining room. Photos of Bruce, other famous surfers, and lots of surfing paraphernalia--including framed movie posters from *The Endless Summer* and *The Endless Summer II* films--deck the walls of this harborside bar and café. The drinks here are strong, and the menu nods towards burgers and seafood. The sesame-crusted ahi on a warm spinach salad rides the perfect wave of healthy and tasty. Service is friendly, and the atmosphere tends towards casual local hangout. Many patrons know each other and the staff, and the bar gets crowded as the evening wears on.

In downtown Santa Barbara, ★ **The Hungry Cat** (1134 Chapala St., 805/884-4701, www.thehungrycat.com, Tues.-Thurs. 3pm-10pm, Fri. 3pm-11pm, Sat. 11am-3pm and 5pm-11pm, Sun. 11am-3pm and 5pm-10pm, $17-32) is housed in a small but sleek modern space. This spot has the expected seafood options (ceviche, peel-and-eat shrimp) and more exotic offerings (sturgeon caviar, local sea urchin). One worthy menu item to enjoy in this popular corner restaurant is the house-made chorizo and clams with grilled bread. Sit at the bar for happy hour (Tues.-Fri. 3pm-6pm) to dine on a lobster roll or fried oysters while enjoying reduced-price cocktails and beers.

INFORMATION AND SERVICES

The **Santa Barbara Conference and Visitors Bureau** (1 Garden St., 805/965-3021, www.santabarbaraca.com, Feb.-Oct. Mon.-Sat. 9am-5pm, Sun. 10am-5pm, Nov.-Jan. Mon.-Sat. 9am-4pm, Sun. 10am-4pm) maintains an informative website and center. The **Outdoor Santa Barbara Visitors Center** (113 Harbor Way, Waterfront Center, 4th Fl., 805/456-8752, http://outdoorsb.sbmm.org, daily 11am-5pm) provides information about Channel Islands National Park, the Channel Islands National Marine Sanctuary, Los Padres National Forest, and the City of Santa Barbara.

The major hospital in town is **Santa Barbara Cottage Hospital** (400 W. Pueblo St., 805/682-7111, www.sbch.org), which includes a full-service emergency room.

TRANSPORTATION

To reach Santa Barbara by air, fly into the **Santa Barbara Municipal Airport** (500 Fowler Rd., 805/683-4011, www.

santabarbaraca.gov). A number of major commercial airlines fly into Santa Barbara, including United, Alaska/Horizon, U.S. Airways, and American Airlines.

A more beautiful and peaceful way to get to Santa Barbara is by train. The **Amtrak Coast Starlight** (www.amtrak.com) runs into town daily. It travels between Los Angeles and Seattle.

Santa Barbara is on U.S. 101, also known as the Pacific Coast Highway and El Camino Real in this neck of the woods. To head out to the Santa Ynez Valley and other local wine regions, take CA Highway 154 east. If staying in Santa Barbara proper, expect fairly standard city driving, complete with traffic jams during weekday business hours and on beach access roads on the weekends. Parking can be challenging, especially at the beach on sunny summer weekends. Expect to pay a premium for a good-to-mediocre spot, or to walk for several blocks. If possible, take the local public streetcar from the downtown area to the beach and leave your car elsewhere.

Santa Barbara has its own transit authority. The **MTD Santa Barbara** (805/963-3366, www.sbmtd.gov, regular fare: local service $1.75, waterfront service $0.50) runs both the local bus service and the Waterfront Shuttle and Downtown-Waterfront lines. Have exact change to pay your fare when boarding the bus or shuttle; if transferring buses, ask the driver for a free transfer pass.

The Gaviota Coast

In some ways, the Gaviota Coast is Southern California's last major stand against the encroachment of urbanization. It acts as a soothing balm to residents from Santa Barbara south to the sprawling metropolis of Los Angeles escaping civilization for a weekend in nature. This stretch of coastline (between Goleta's Coal Oil Point to Vandenberg Air Force Base's Point Arguello and beyond to remote Point Sal)

is unpopulated and only lightly touched by development.

It wasn't always this way. Before European settlers arrived, it was one of the most densely populated regions of native California. The Chumash lived here and harvested sustenance from the Santa Barbara Channel using canoes. Then the missionaries came and attempted major agricultural projects in now nearly unpopulated places including Jalama and Honda Canyon. After the mission system collapsed, the area was divided up by Mexican land grants before large ranches started popping up. Some large ranching operations, such as the Hollister Ranch, still exist today.

It's a great place for a day trip from Santa Barbara—it's only 20 miles to the first park, El Capitan State Beach—for a day of relaxing on a beach, hiking, surfing, or stand-up paddleboarding. Even though this is a rural stretch of coastline, the area's three state parks—El Capitan State Beach, Refugio State Beach, and Gaviota State Park—are typically crowded during the summer months. It's also a great place to camp for the night.

Pockets of the Gaviota Coast are protected by the presence of El Capitan State Beach, Refugio State Beach, Gaviota State Park, and the impressive Jalama Beach County Park. But there's still a push by local conservation groups, including the Gaviota Conservancy, to designate this area a National Shoreline.

EL CAPITAN STATE BEACH

Closest to Santa Barbara, **El Capitan State Beach** (10 Refugio Rd., Goleta, 805/986-1033, www.parks.ca.gov, daily dawn-dusk, $10) offers a narrow, rocky beach with tide pools and the largest campground of the three Gaviota Coast state parks.

On February 26, 1776, the Anza expedition camped in the region that would later become El Capitan State Beach. A day earlier, Father Pedro Font wrote in his journal: "the people of the expedition, some of whom have never seen the ocean, have much to admire."

There is still much to admire here: a nice but narrow strand of beach for sunbathing, surf fishing, a few infrequent waves offshore for surfers, and stands of sycamore and oak trees offering shade along El Capitán Creek. A stairway provides access from the bluffs to the beach area. Amenities include RV hookups, pay showers, restrooms, hiking and biking trails, a fabulous beach, a seasonal general store, and an outdoor arena. Many of the campsites offer an ocean view.

Camping

El Capitan State Beach (10 Refugio Beach Rd., Goleta, 800/444-7275, www.reserveamerica.com, $45) is the largest of the state park campgrounds on the Gaviota Coast. It has 123 campsites strung along multiple loops in the shade or sun depending on your preference—if you get here early enough. The sites offer a little more privacy than Refugio or Gaviota, and there is a walkway and stairs accessing the rocky beach below.

For the inexperienced camper, **El Capitan Canyon** (11560 Calle Real, 866/352-2729, www.elcapitancanyon.com, canvas safari tents $170, cabins $245-795) offers several ways to ease into the outdoors. On 300 acres of land that includes private hiking trails and a spa, El Capitan Canyon is also a place for more experienced outdoor enthusiasts to pamper themselves. The accommodations here—some are far from camping—begin with canvas safari tents and yurts that include beds and furniture but have no running water, even though there are bathhouses nearby. The cedar cabins are available in a range of options from a bunk cabin that is perfect for families to the property's priciest offering, the Safari Cabin, a two-bedroom suite with a loft and an ocean view. Most of the other cabins are like small wooden studio apartments complete with kitchenettes and, in some cases, deep soaking tubs. In front of each is a picnic table and fire pit for communing with nature.

On the grounds, the **Canyon Market** serves a nice selection of breakfast, lunch, and dinner options. They also will deliver barbecue kits to your cabin so you can prepare your meal on an open fire. These kits start at $50 for hamburgers, hot dogs, and veggie burgers, so expect more than Oscar Mayer wieners and Costco patties.

El Capitan Canyon's cabins appeal to couples seeking a restful, romantic retreat as well as families with children. Kids will love the heated pool and a short hike to an enclosure holding llamas and goats.

REFUGIO STATE BEACH

If Gaviota State Park is the region's hiking hot spot, **Refugio State Beach** (10 Refugio Beach Rd., Goleta, 805/968-1033, www.parks. ca.gov, $10) is the best place for a beach day on the Gaviota Coast. This thin but long finger of beach is lined with scenic palm trees. Here, brave children plunge into the chilly (but not cold) waters and scream while their parents look on, taking in the comforts of the frequent sun.

The land on which Refugio is based used to be a cattle ranch in the late 1700s called Nuestra Senora del Refugio. In 1798, Jose Maria Ortega took over the ranch and started to do a little smuggling on the side, trading with stocked foreign ships, which was forbidden by the ruling Spanish. These activities piqued the interest of the Monterey pirate Hippolyte de Bouchard, who traveled down hoping to score some of the smuggled goods in 1818. Even though Refugio's residents hid themselves and the loot, Bouchard took it upon himself to burn the ranch house and smuggling station before departing.

Now the only ominous presence offshore are the hazy oil rigs in the distance that look like ghostly pirate ships. As for Refugio, the waters are way less scary. This is a well-protected cove for sea kayaking or stand-up paddleboarding. There are also beginning and advanced kayak tours, which include kayak usage, provided by Refugio's park rangers.

Camping

Refugio State Beach (10 Refugio Beach Rd., Goleta, 800/444-7275, www.reserveamerica. com, $45) has 67 campsites to crash out at after a day at the nearby beach, which is just feet away from some sites. The sites are fairly close together, and in summer can feel a bit crowded, but this is still a scenic campground with plenty of trees providing shade.

GAVIOTA STATE PARK

Of the Gaviota Coast's three state parks, **Gaviota State Park** (10 Refugio Beach Rd., Goleta, 805/968-1033, www.parks.ca.gov, daily 7am-sunset, $10) is the place to head for hiking. The park has multiple trails leading into its 2,000 acres of oak woodland and chaparral backcountry. One of these is the 0.7-mile hike up to the **Gaviota Hot Springs.** If you get lost easily, this mostly unsigned trail is going to be a challenge. The trailhead is actually about 2.5 miles north of the state park's main entrance: From U.S. 101, take the exit for Highway 1 heading to Lompoc to reach it. Take an immediate right at the exit and then another right to an unmarked parking area. From there, it doesn't get any easier. Take the unmarked trail about a half a mile up and when the main trail veers left go straight on what looks like a spur trail. A few hundred yards up is a warm—not hot—pool behind a little dam and under a palm tree. It's a nice pool to relax in during the few times when it is not overrun.

More adventurous hikers can continue on the main path up to **Gaviota Peak,** a 2,458-foot peak that offers one of the best views of the Gaviota Coast. It's a strenuous three-mile hike one-way.

Besides the hiking trails, Gaviota State Park has a nice little beach area under the shadow of an 811-foot-high train trestle.

Camping

Gaviota State Park (10 Refugio Beach Rd., Goleta, 800/444-7275, www.reserveamerica. com, $45) has 39 campsites in a small loop by Gaviota Creek just 100 yards from the beach. Because there is little tree cover, these sites are mostly open to the elements, including the wind that roars through Gaviota Pass and the heat.

★ JALAMA BEACH COUNTY PARK

The western portion of Santa Barbara County around Point Conception is mile after mile of desolate beach, uncrowded waves, and

The UFOs of the Gaviota Coast

When spending a night camping at Jalama Beach County Park or another spot on the Gaviota Coast, you may look up and see a strange flying object overhead. Most likely it's not an alien craft searching for humans to probe, but an unmanned satellite or test missile launched from Vandenberg Air Force Base.

Encompassing over 99,000 acres of land on the elbow of the California coast by Point Conception, Vandenberg was initially an Army base called Camp Cooke. In 1965, the Air Force took over the sprawling base and began launching test missiles as a reaction to Russia's Sputnik launch in 1957. The base has the distinction of being the place where the first polar-orbiting satellite was sent into space in 1959.

Vandenberg was also designed to be the West Coast space shuttle launch and landing site. But the site's technical problems and the space program's decision to consolidate shuttle operations at Cape Canaveral in Florida caused the closure of the shuttle program at Vandenberg in 1989.

If you see a UFO in the sky while in the west section of Santa Barbara County, check out Vandenberg's website at www.vandenberg.af.mil to see if it's a missile being tested or a satellite being sent into space. If it's not listed, you have seen a true unidentified flying object.

---

mostly uninhabited coastal bluffs. The best way to experience a truly wild patch of the Gaviota Coast is to head out to **Jalama Beach County Park** (9999 Jalama Rd., Lompoc, front gate 805/736-3504, weather and information 805/736-6316, www.sbparks.org, day use $10). It is the only public beach between Gaviota State Beach and the beach at the tiny town of Surf, a stretch of more than 48 miles.

There have been some serious shipwrecks on this section of coast. In 1854, the steamship *Yankee Blade* hit some rocks and sank, killing 15 people. Later, in 1923, the largest peacetime loss of U.S. Navy ships occurred nearby at Honda Point when seven destroyers ran aground and 23 people perished.

As you wind around on the 14.5-mile-long Jalama Road towards the park, you'll know you are on the way to someplace special, at least if you are into out-of-the-way treasures. Despite its remote location, Jalama is a park with some unexpected amenities including a playground, a horseshoes pit, a basketball court, flush toilets, and the well-stocked **Jalama Beach Store and Grill.** The little store has almost all you could need, including canned goods, firewood, cold beer, cigars, and even DVD rentals. Meanwhile, the grill

serves breakfast, lunch, and dinner including their patented—seriously, the patent hangs by the pickup window—Jalama Burger, a tasty third-pounder that'll make burger fans drool.

While the park's facilities are impressive for its remote location, the coastline here is the draw. Surfers can ride waves right out front, while anglers cast off the beach for perch and rockfish. For the adventurous, from Jalama it's a six-mile beach hike to the east to Point Conception, one of California's best-known maritime landmarks. Check to make sure it's low tide before heading out.

Jalama draws families, surfers hoping to score uncrowded waves, anglers hoping to reel in a few fish, and beachgoers who like their beaches undeveloped.

Camping

Jalama Beach County Park (9999 Jalama Rd., Lompoc, 805/736-3504, www.sbparks.org, tent camping $30-45, RV camping with hookups $40-45) has 117 first-come, first-served campsites. There are 12 spots whose sites blend into the beach out front and a row of RV-friendly sites on a bluff with a view of the park below. The amenities here are surprisingly good, including clean bathrooms with flush toilets, fire pits, picnic tables, and an outdoor shower for washing off after any ocean recreation. Be aware that the spring and early summer winds in this area can be quite fierce.

The park also offers seven popular cabins for rent (805/686-5050, $170-220) for those who want to experience the region's beauty without roughing it.

Ventura

Ventura is short for San Buenaventura, which means the "city of good fortune." There is much that is good about Ventura, including its weather (daytime temperatures average 70 degrees), consistent waves for surfers, and a historic downtown that includes a restored mission.

Despite being so close to Los Angeles, Ventura has retained its seaside charm. Downtown Ventura is compact and easy to walk around; it is three blocks from the beach and still feels somehow unfettered by "progress," with buildings that date to the 1800s (a long time by California standards). In recent years, the city has encouraged the growth of an impressive arts scene and a thriving restaurant landscape. But it's still a bit scruffier than nearby Santa Barbara, with a sizeable homeless population for its relatively small size.

A few blocks from Main Street is Surfer's Point, a coastal area also known as "C Street." A ribbon of pavement by the ocean, the Omer Rains Bike Trail almost always hosts a collection of walkers, runners, and cyclists.

Farther away, the Ventura Harbor has a cluster of restaurants, bars, and hotels around the harbor, which is the gateway to the nearby Channel Islands National Park.

SIGHTS
Mission San Buenaventura
Referred to as the "mission by the sea," Mission San Buenaventura (211 E. Main St., 805/643-4318, www.sanbuenaventuramission.org, self-guided tours Sun.-Fri. 10am-5pm, Sat. 9am-5pm, adults $4, seniors $3, children $1) sits right on Ventura's Main Street and just blocks from the beach. The church is just one of six missions that was personally dedicated by Junipero Serra, the founder of California's mission system.

A seven-mile-long aqueduct was built to the mission to feed it water from the Ventura River. Because of its abundant water, Mission San Buenaventura became known for its lush orchards and gardens.

Not that living at this mission was without hardships. In 1812, a series of earthquakes and the resulting tsunami forced the mission's padres and the native people scrambling inland. Later, pirate Hippolyte de Bouchard's threat to pillage the mission again led to the mission's residents temporarily relocating.

Construction on the current-day mission began in earnest in 1792 after a fire burned the first church building. Today the mission is a peaceful remnant of California's past, with beautiful high ceilings and walls decorated with paintings of Jesus at various stations of the cross, the series of events before his crucifixion. A one-room museum on the grounds displays the church's original doors and a collection of native Chumash artifacts. Between the museum and the church is a scenic garden with a tile fountain, an old olive press, and a shrine.

★ California Street
California Street (end of Figueroa St. to end of California St.) or "C Street" hosted the world's first pro surfing event: 1965's Noseriding International. C Street extends 0.75 mile from Surfer's Point Park to the cove beside Ventura Pier, and its Ventura's recreation hub. Lines of white water streaming off the point entice surfers and stand-up paddleboarders, while longboarders catch waves that

Downtown Ventura

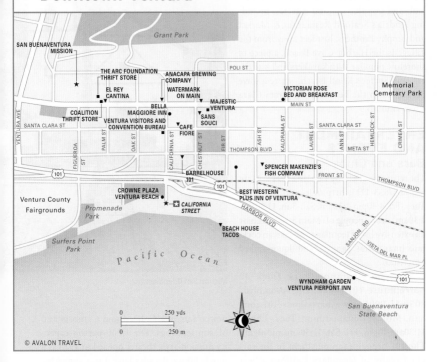

can continue for nearly a mile. The vibrant coastal scene includes the Promenade, which bustles with joggers and power walkers, and the popular Omer Rains Bike Trail. Facilities include an outdoor shower, bathrooms, and a picnic area. Parking can be challenging: There's a free lot that fills up quickly as well as a pay lot ($2 per day).

Olivas Adobe Historical Park

For a peek into California's 1800s rancho period, take a docent-led tour of **Olivas Adobe Historical Park** (4200 Olivas Park Rd., 805/658-4728, www.cityofventura.net/olivas-adobe, guided tours Sat.-Sun. 11am-4pm, adults $5, seniors and children $3), owned by the City of Ventura. Constructed in 1847, the main house on the 4,693-acre Rancho San Miguel was home to Raymundo Olivas, his wife Theodora, their 21 children, and their employees.

The 45-minute tour illuminates what life was like during the ranch period, from how the adobe walls were constructed to how bread was baked in outdoor baking ovens. Stops include a bedroom where the eight Olivas daughters somehow managed to live together and an impressive chapel on the second floor of the house. There are also some curiosities on display, including a desk made from an old piano, a wreath made of human hair, a Victorian-era mousetrap, and an upright barrel piano, a music box-like contraption that has figurines playing along to the music produced by a crank on the side of the machine.

Ventura Harbor Village

A collection of restaurants, art galleries, and shops has sprung up around the fairly large Ventura Harbor. The **Ventura Harbor Village** (1583 Spinnaker Dr., 805/642-8538, www.venturaharborvillage.com, gallery and shop daily 11am-6pm) hosts a comedy club and popular seafood eateries, including Andria's Seafood Restaurant & Market and Brophy Brothers. Just feet away from the village is the Harbor Cove Beach, a piece of shoreline popular with kayakers and kite fliers, and Surfer's Knoll Beach, where a wave breaks down the beach by the Santa Clara River's mouth.

ENTERTAINMENT AND EVENTS
Bars and Clubs

The retro sign at **El Rey Cantina** (294 E. Main St., 805/653-1111, http://elreycantina.com, Tues.-Fri. 4:30pm-1:30am, Sat.-Sun. 11:30am-1:30am) draws people off Main Street to enjoy an extensive list of tequilas and Mexican cocktails (margaritas, sangria, and liquor-spiked horchata).

True beer connoisseurs flock to **Barrelhouse 101** (545 E. Thompson Blvd., 805/643-0906, www.barrelhouse101.com, Sun.-Mon. 11:30am-10pm, Tues.-Thurs. 11:30am-10pm, Fri.-Sat. 11:30am-midnight). The 101 beers on tap put them in the rarefied realm of legendary California beer joints. Beers from California and Belgium are strongly represented but Oregon and the East Coast also make good showings. During happy hour (Mon. all day, Tues.-Fri. 4pm-7pm), draft beers are a dollar off.

By the end of the evening, a lot of people end up at dive bar **Sans Souci Cocktail Lounge** (21 S. Chestnut St., 805/643-4539, daily noon-2am), which stays open late. The small interior with red couches can get crowded; escape to the semi-covered courtyard out front before it fills up with smokers.

Live Music

The Majestic Ventura Theater (26 S. Chestnut St., 805/653-0721, www.venturatheater.net, box office Tues.-Fri. 11am-6pm) gets a variety of pretty big national acts, including music icons Alice Cooper and Snoop Dogg—yup, Snoop Dogg is an icon now—along with

Mission San Buenaventura

newer acts like Coheed and Cambria and Mason Jennings. The 1,200-person-capacity mission-style theater opened in 1928 as a movie house; decades later it was converted into a concert venue. The old chandeliers still hang in the auditorium, and other details of the 1920s decor remain.

Festivals and Events

In the summer, Ventura's art studios and other venues open their doors for a weekend during the **ArtWalk Ventura** (July, www.artwalkventura.org). Some places that participate include the Museum of Ventura County and the Ventura Visitors Center. Other participating venues include restaurants, salons, antiques shops, unique boutiques, and coffee shops—most any place with walls.

The **Ventura County Fair** (10 W. Harbor Blvd., 805/648-3376, www.venturacountyfair.org, July) goes down every summer within the Ventura County Fairgrounds, which is right by the city's main coastal recreation area. Expect the usual attractions: Ferris wheel, cotton candy, livestock exhibits. Live nightly entertainment often features 1980s acts like Chaka Khan and Huey Lewis and the News.

SHOPPING

For traditional shopping, visit the **Pacific View Mall** (at Mills and Main Sts., 805/642-5530, www.shoppacificview.com, daily 10am-9pm), with 140 stores such as Sears, Target, Old Navy, and many more. The two-story indoor mall offers Wi-Fi in the food court. Some of the restaurants are better than typical fast-food joints. There are several nail salons. It gets crowded on weekends, but it's pretty easy to get around midweek. Farther south are the **Camarillo Premium Outlets** (740 E. Ventura Blvd., off Los Posas Ave., Camarillo, 805/445-8520, www.premiumoutlets.com, Mon.-Sat. 10am-9pm, Sun. 10am-8pm, holiday hours vary). Actually in the town of Camarillo, east of Ventura's southern neighbor Oxnard, there are 160 outlet stores peddling reduced-price brand-name merchandise from Banana Republic and J. Crew.

Main Street in downtown Ventura is home to a surprising number of unique local and specialty stores and has managed to retain a sense of individuality. Thrift stores are popular downtown including **Coalition Thrift Store** (270 E. Main St., 805/643-4411, www.coalitionthriftstore.com, Mon.-Sat. 9am-6pm, Sun. 10am-5pm) and **The Arc Foundation of Ventura County Thrift Store** (265 E. Main St., 805/650-8611, Mon.-Sat. 9am-6pm, Sun. 10am-5pm).

BEACHES
San Buenaventura State Beach

San Buenaventura State Beach (San Pedro St. off U.S. 101, 805/968-1033, www.parks.ca.gov, daily dawn-dusk, $10) has an impressive two miles of beach, dune, and ocean. It also includes the 1,700-foot Ventura Pier, home to Eric Ericsson's Seafood Restaurant and Beach House Tacos. The historic pier was built way back in 1872. This is a safer place to swim than some area beaches, as it doesn't get

the breakers that roll into the nearby point. Cyclists can take advantage of trails connecting with other nearby beaches, and sports enthusiasts converge on the beach for occasional triathlons and volleyball tournaments. Facilities include a snack bar, an equipment rental shop, and an essential for the 21st-century beach bum—Wi-Fi (although to pick up the signal, you need to be within about 200 feet of the lifeguard tower).

Emma Wood State Beach

Bordering the estuary north of the Ventura River, **Emma Wood State Beach** (W. Main St. and Park Access Rd., 805/968-1033, www.parks.ca.gov, daily dawn-dusk, $10) includes the remnants of a World War II artillery site. There are no facilities, but a few minutes' walk leads to the campgrounds (one for RVs and one group camp; first come, first served in winter, reservations required spring-fall). At the far eastern side of the parking lot is a small path leading out to the beach that goes under the train tracks. To the right are views up the coast to Rincon. The beach itself has many rocks strewn about, some nearly the size of footballs. It is a great spot for windsurfing, as the winds come off Rincon Point just up from the mouth of the Ventura River to create ideal conditions. There's a 0.5-mile trail leading through the reeds and underbrush at the far end of the parking lot; although you can hear the surf and the highway, you can't see anything, and you'll feel like you're on safari until you reach the beach where the Ventura River ends.

Harbor Cove Beach

Families flock to **Harbor Cove Beach** (1900 Spinnaker Dr., http://venturaharbor.com, daily dawn-dusk), directly across from the Channel Islands Visitors Center at the end of Spinnaker Drive. The harbor's breakwaters provide children and less confident swimmers with relative safety from the ocean currents. The wind can kick up at times, but when it's calm it's practically perfect. There's plenty of free parking, lifeguards during peak seasons, restrooms, and foot showers. Food and other amenities can be found across the street at Ventura Harbor Village.

Faria Beach

Farther north, the Ventura County-run Faria Beach (4350 W. U.S. 101, at State Beach exit, 805/654-3951, www.ventura.org, daily 7am-sunset) is available for tent camping and has 15 RV hookups. The campground has a playground and horseshoe pits, barbecues, and shower facilities but is quite small. It's also very crowded with campers, trucks, and people during nice weather because of its proximity to the water. You might find you have more companions than you care for, but it's a long, flat beach, so you can spread out.

SPORTS AND RECREATION
Surfing

Ventura is definitely a surf town. The series of point breaks referred to as California Street, or "C Street" for short, is the best place for consistent right breaks. There are three distinct zones along this mile-long stretch of beach. At the point is the Pipe, with some pretty fast short breaks. Moving down the beach are the Stables, which continue with the right breaks, with an even, low shoulder, and then C Street, breaking both right and left. The waves get mushier and easier for beginners the closer you get to Ventura Pier. There is a pay parking lot right in front of the break across the street from the Ventura County Fairgrounds (10 W. Harbor Blvd.). South of downtown Ventura, Ventura Harbor has waves that refract off the harbor's jetties.

SURF CLASSES

Surfclass (805/200-8674, www.surfclass. com, $85) meets at various beaches around Ventura, depending on weather and swells. They teach everyone from novice landlubbers to rusty shredders. The two-hour class rates are quite reasonable, and they limit class size for individual attention. They will also teach you surf etiquette and lingo.

Ventura Surf School (461 W. Channel Islands Blvd., 805/218-1484, www.venturasurfschool.com, private two-hour lesson $125, two or more $80 pp, four or more $80 pp) can also teach you to surf, and they offer a weeklong surf camp and kids-only classes. Beginner lessons are at Mondos Beach.

SURF RENTALS

If you just need gear, swing by Seaward Surf and Sport (1082 S. Seaward Ave., 805/648-4742, www.seawardsurf.com, daily 9am-7pm, surfboard rental $15-25/two hours), which is the place to go to buy or rent most anything for the water (including bodyboards and wetsuits). It is half a block from the beach, so you can head straight to the water.

All sorts of gear, including longboards and boogie boards, are available at Beach Break Surf Shop (1557 Spinnaker Dr., Suite 108, 805/650-6641, www.beachbreaksurfshop.com, daily 10am-6pm, surfboard rentals $30-40). It's already at the harbor, so pick up your gear, cross the street, and hit the beach.

Whale-Watching

December-March is the ideal time to see Pacific gray whales pass through the channel off the coast of Ventura. Late June-late August is the narrow window for both blue and humpback whales as they feed offshore near the islands. Island Packers Cruises (1691 Spinnaker Dr., Suite 105B, 805/642-1393, www.islandpackers.com, $25-75) has operated whale-watching cruises for years and is the most experienced. It also runs harbor cruises with a variety of options, including dinner cruises and group charters. Most whale-watching trips last about three hours. Remember that whale watching is weather-dependent, so cancellations can occur.

Biking

The eight-mile-long, paved Omer Rains Trail heads along Ventura's beachfront from San Buenaventura State Beach past the Ventura Pier and Surfer's Point to Emma Wood State Beach. The Ventura River Trail

(Main St. and Peking St., www.ventura-usa. com) follows the Ventura River inland from Main Street just over six miles one-way, ending at Foster Park. From here it joins the Ojai Trail, a two-lane bike path that follows Highway 33 into Ojai (16 miles one-way). If you want to pedal it, Wheel Fun Rentals (850 Harbor Blvd., 805/765-5795, www. wheelfunrentals.com, daily 9am-sunset, bike rentals $10-40) rents out beach cruisers, surreys, mountain bikes, and low-riding chopper bikes.

ACCOMMODATIONS
Under $150

The ★ Bella Maggiore Inn (67 South California St., 805/652-0277, $75-180) has a great location a few blocks from the beach and just a block off Ventura's Main Street. Some of the rooms are no larger than a college dorm room but there is a lobby with couches, Italian chandeliers, a piano, and a fireplace. Even better is a courtyard with a fountain and dining area surrounded by vines. The moderate room prices include a tasty hot breakfast in the morning, with omelets, huevos rancheros, and French toast. Another asset of the Bella Maggiore is the free overnight parking behind the building. This place is not fancy, but it is very moderately priced considering its downtown location and full breakfast.

The Best Western Plus Inn of Ventura (708 E. Thompson Blvd., 805/643-3101, http:// bestwesterncalifornia.com, $109-169) doesn't look like much at first. But this two-story U-shaped motel complex has a few pleasant surprises. Ten rooms have partial ocean views (albeit close to the railroad tracks). The clean rooms are all stocked with refrigerators and microwaves, and there's a guest laundry room. The hot breakfast buffet includes eggs, breakfast meats, and make-your-own waffles. There's pool and small hot tub. A Jacuzzi suite is available for those who want to splurge. Across the street from grassy Plaza Park, and just a few blocks to downtown Ventura, it might be the best bang for your buck.

$150-250

If you are traveling to Channel Islands National Park out of Ventura Harbor, the ★ Four Points By Sheraton Ventura Harbor Resort (1050 Schooner Dr., 805/658-1212, www.fourpoints.com, $145-175) is a great place to lay your head before an early-morning boat ride or to relax after a few days camping on the islands. The rooms are clean and comfortable and have balconies and patios. With a gym, tennis court, pool, and basketball court, there is a wide array of recreational opportunities available at the resort. For folks who have hiked all over the Channel Islands, Four Points has a hot tub in a glass dome to ease your aching muscles.

A few hundred yards from the Ventura Pier and right by the beach, the Crowne Plaza Ventura Beach (450 East Harbor Blvd., 800/842-0800, www.cpventura.com, $139-389) has rooms with ocean-view balconies if you get a room on the fifth floor or higher. It also offers pet-friendly rooms for $75 more.

Also on the coast—specifically right back from San Buenaventura State Beach—The Pierpont Inn & Spa (550 Sanjon Rd., 805/643-6144, www.pierpontinn.com, $129-299) is situated on some nice manicured grounds with grassy areas and flowers. The historic property, which goes back to 1910, has rooms, suites, cottages, and a bungalow. In addition, there's a full-service spa on the grounds.

FOOD
American

With brick walls and beer-making vats behind the bar, the Anacapa Brewing Company (472 East Main St., 805/643-2337, http://anacapabrewing.com, Sun.-Wed. 11:30am-10pm, Thurs.-Sat. 11:30am-midnight, $14) looks like a brewpub should. Regulars sit at a long bar drinking the brewery's Pierpoint IPA, which goes down easy, while families eat burgers, salads, and pizzas at booths and tables. The menu also has a few unexpected entrées like the fried chicken-and-waffle plate.

VENTURA

Farmers Markets

Downtown Ventura County's Farmer's Market (Santa Clara St. and Palm St., www.vccfarmersmarkets.com, Sat. 8:30am-noon) has produce stands along with vendors selling tamales and pot stickers. If you miss that one, there's still the **Midtown Ventura Market** (front west parking lot at Pacific View Mall, 3301 E. Main St., www.vccfarmersmarkets.com, Wed. 9am-1pm) on Wednesdays.

Italian

Bolstered by a popular bar, **Café Fiore** (66 California St., 805/653-1266, www.fiorerestaurant.net, Mon.-Thurs. 11:30am-3pm and 5pm-10pm, Fri.-Sat. 11:30am-3pm and 5pm-11pm, Sun. 11:30am-3pm and 5pm-9pm, $16-32) is a hot spot for Ventura professionals grabbing a cocktail or meal after work. The food includes Italian favorites like cioppino and osso buco served in a sleek, high-ceilinged room decorated with furnishings that recall the interior of a Cost Plus World Market. Expect to wait awhile for service on crowded nights and during happy hour.

Mexican

In a prime spot on the Ventura Pier, ★ **Beach House Tacos** (668 Harbor Blvd.,

805/648-3177, Mon.-Fri. 11am-8:30pm, Sat.-Sun. 8:30am-8:30pm, $3-8) doesn't coast on its enviable location. Creative options include soy-ginger-lime cream sauce-soaked ahi and ground beef tacos with raisins. Beginners can try "The Combo," a lump of grilled meat (chicken, carne asada, or pork) topped with melted cheese, grilled pasilla chilies, zucchini, and carrots. Order at the counter and dine at an enclosed seating section on the pier. Expect long lines on summer weekends.

Seafood

Sleek **Lure Fish House** (60 California St., 805/567-4400, www.lurefishhouse.com, Sun.-Thurs. 11:30am-9pm, Fri.-Sat. 11:30am-10pm, $15-33) is already a local favorite for seafood downtown. The menu focuses on charbroiled seafood including fresh and sustainable wild local halibut, wild mahi-mahi, and other tasty morsels from the sea. They also do seafood pastas, cioppino, and live Maine lobster. You can also enjoy samples from the oyster bar or savor a cocktail.

Housed in a building that resembles a boat, ★ **Spencer Makenzie's Fish Company** (806 E. Thompson Blvd., 805/643-8226, www.smfishco.com, Sun.-Thurs. 11am-9pm,

tacos at Spencer Makenzie's Fish Company

Fri.-Sat. 10:30am-9pm, $5-13) is known for its giant fish tacos, a tasty fusion of Japanese and Mexican flavors. The sushi-grade fish is hand dipped in tempura batter and then fried. It's topped with the traditional Baja ingredients of white sauce, cabbage, and cilantro. Choose from the array of homegrown sauces along the counter to add splashes of sweet and heat.

INFORMATION AND SERVICES

The **Ventura Visitors Center** (101 California St., 800/333-2989, www.ventura-usa.com, summer Mon.-Sat. 9am-5pm, Sun. 10am-4pm, winter Mon.-Sat. 9am-4pm, Sun. 10am-4pm) occupies a big space in downtown Ventura and offers a lot of information, including a guided historical walking tour of the city.

Community Memorial Hospital (147 N. Brent St., 805/652-5011, www.cmhshealth.org) has the only emergency room in the area.

TRANSPORTATION

Ventura is 1.5 hours north of **LAX** (1 World Way, Los Angeles, 855/463-5252, www.lawa.org). To get to Ventura from LAX without a vehicle, contact the **Ventura County Airporter** (805/650-6600, www.venturashuttle.com, one-way $35, round-trip $65), a bus that goes back and forth between the places. The **Burbank Bob Hope Airport** (BUR, 2627 N. Hollywood Way, Burbank, 818/840-8840, http://bobhopeairport.com) is another option, just over an hour's drive from Ventura.

While Ventura's Greyhound station closed a few years back, **Amtrak** (Harbor Blvd. and Figueroa St., 800/872-7245, www.amtrak.com) still comes to town.

With a car, Ventura exits are right off U.S. 101. The city is 34 miles south of Santa Barbara on U.S. 101 and 65 miles north of Los Angeles on the highway.

Travel Ventura in a cab by calling **Gold Coast Cab** (805/444-6969, www.goldcoast-cab.com).

Channel Islands National Park

Channel Islands National Park sweeps visitors back in time to a past when coastal California was undeveloped. Only accessible by boat or plane, Channel Islands National Park is among 20 least crowded national parks due to its remote location. Those few who get to the four islands (San Miguel is currently closed to the public) are treated to uncrowded trails, isolated beaches, and an extensive marine sanctuary. It's a place to experience the state in its purest, most natural form. Kelp forests offshore sway in the ocean's surge as pumpkin-colored garibaldi (the California state fish) swim past rocks dotted with multicolored sea urchins. Onshore, rare species, including the island fox and the island scrub-jay, roam freely.

The islands have been federally protected for just over 30 years. Long before they were a national park they were ranchlands, and archaeological evidence suggests that the islands were inhabited as long as 12,000 years ago. Santa Cruz Island, in particular, was prime grazing land in the 1800s for cattle and sheep, which were safe from the predators found on the mainland. Santa Cruz was also home to a winery, the remnants of which are still visible.

The most traveled-to of the park's islands are **Anacapa,** a dramatic 5-mile spine jutting out from the sea, and **Santa Cruz Island,** California's largest island at 24 miles long and up to 6 miles wide. Sailing to the islands can take 3-4 hours, and motorboats make the trip even faster, yet exploring the islands isn't common. Santa Barbara is the smallest and southernmost of the islands. But Anacapa, Santa Cruz, and to a lesser degree Santa Rosa can be visited as day trips, although only Santa Cruz and Anacapa trips are available year-round.

There can be tough weather conditions, and it's often very windy since there's little shelter.

Inexpensive day trips allow visitors to explore, hike, kayak, snorkel, camp, and scuba dive at the islands. Multiday trips allow for extended camping excursions into the islands' interiors and for visiting several of the islands.

★ SANTA CRUZ ISLAND

Santa Cruz is the largest of the islands, and by far the most popular island to visit—in part because it most closely resembles the mainland and, frankly, because it is the most hospitable. There are more old buildings on this island than the others, and there is a day camp near Scorpion Bay where you can pitch a tent, store your food in metal lockers, and explore on foot. There are trees here, as well as old dried-out creeks and former grasslands that are often barren depending on the amount of winter rainfall. At the center of the island, the thick, dense vegetation feels almost prehistoric. This is also the only place in the world to see endemic species such as the Channel Islands fox and island scrub-jay, and large, beautiful ravens make their homes here.

The environmental organization The Nature Conservancy owns 76 percent of the scorpion-shaped Santa Cruz Island, while the National Park Service possesses and maintains the remaining 24 percent of the island. The two primary points of entry onto Santa Cruz are **Scorpion Anchorage** and **Prisoners Harbor.** The island has a range of hiking trails and snorkeling opportunities, along with two campgrounds and an abundance of amazing sea caves that can be explored by sea kayak.

Travel time from Ventura is 90 minutes, and travelers offload onto a short pier directly connected to shore, though shore landings from a skiff are possible depending on conditions.

Scorpion Ranch Complex

Believe it or not, Santa Cruz Island hosted an extensive ranching operation from the mid-1800s up until the 1980s. The **Scorpion Ranch Complex** gives park visitors a glimpse into this isolated way of life. The ranch area is home to various farming equipment and wooden ranch structures in various states of decay. The small visitors center has displays on threatened species, conservation, and the native Chumash people in one room and a model ranch kitchen in the other room.

Channel Islands National Park

Cavern Point

Cavern Point offers superb views of the ocean, the island's rugged coastline, and, on non-fog-shrouded days, the mainland. This cliff-top vista point is also a great place to spot migrating whales during the winter. Reached by a moderate two-mile loop trail, Cavern Point is a destination that even those spending just a few hours on the island can reach. At other points along the trail are fine views of Scorpion Anchorage and Anacapa Island in the distance. Hike the loop clockwise to avoid a steep climb.

Sports and Recreation

HIKING

A quick introduction to Santa Cruz's cliff-top coastal views and, on clear days, views to the mainland can be found on the moderate two-mile-long **Cavern Point Loop.** If you have more time, the more strenuous 7.5 mile round-trip **Smugglers Cove Trail** is an old ranch road that cuts across the island's eastern interior to arrive at a south-facing beach. Even if you don't find the elusive island scrub-jay on the 4.5-mile **Scorpion Canyon Loop,** you'll be treated to a hike up one of the island's unique canyons followed by a bunch of stunning coastal views.

KAYAKING

Santa Cruz Island is pocked with some of the world's most incredible and largest sea caves, and the best way to explore them is by kayak. Sea kayaking Santa Crux is no less than an amazing experience. The easiest way to find some sea caves is to paddle northwest (left) out of Scorpion Anchorage. Entering some of these cathedral-sized caves will take your breath away quicker than any artificially made architectural treasure. In some of the deeper caves, the ocean surge creates a deep, locomotive-like rumble. Meanwhile, almost all have starfish decorating their walls and a sublime green glow. Outside of the caves, sea lions and seals periscope their heads out of the water between mats of kelp.

Next door to Island Packers, the boat concession that gets most visitors to Santa Cruz and the other islands, is the **Channel Islands Kayak Center** (805/984-5995, www.cikayak.com, single kayaks $35, double kayaks $55, two-person tour with transportation $200), where you can rent kayaks for excursions or sign up for island cave tours or a history and wildlife tour. You must reserve a space for your kayak first through Island Packers.

Another option is to sign up for the multihour Caves and Coves Tour with **Channel Islands Outfitters** (805/899-4925, www.channelislandso.com, $140 pp). The knowledgeable guides will set you up onshore at Scorpion Anchorage and then take you on a tour of the area's caverns. This is a good option for first-timers to the island. Tours don't include transportation.

SNORKELING AND SCUBA DIVING

If you are taking Island Packers out to Santa Cruz Island, you can find some fine snorkeling and scuba diving right where the boat pulls in at Scorpion Harbor. Right east and west of the Scorpion Anchorage Pier are kelp beds that are terrific for snorkeling and scuba diving. For divers, there is the wreck of the **USS *Peacock*** 50 yards off Scorpion Rocks in 40 to 60 feet of water. The wreck is a fairly intact World War II minesweeper.

To dive the island's other spots, you'll have to have your own boat or be on a charter dive boat to access the sites. Diving trips need to be scheduled from Ventura Harbor. Options include the **Peace Dive Boat** (1691 Spinnaker Dr., G Dock, Ventura Harbor, 805/650-3483, www.peaceboat.com, $115-540 trips) and **Truth Aquatics** (301 W. Cabrillo Blvd., 805/962-1127, www.truthaquatics.com, $100-1,000).

Camping

The most popular campground on Santa Cruz Island is the **Scorpion Ranch Campground** (877/444-6777, www.recreation.gov, $15), a 0.5-1-mile walk in from where the boast drops you off at Scorpion Anchorage. The

The Channel Islands' Special Species

Where are you going to find the Santa Cruz Island scrub jay, the island fox, or the island night lizard? The answer is only in the Channel Islands.

Due to its remote location, the five islands of Channel Islands National Park have 23 endemic terrestrial animals and 11 land birds that are now island-only subspecies or races. These animals have evolved and changed from their counterparts on the mainland to adapt to the islands' unique natural habitat.

The island scrub jay has the smallest range of any North American bird species: the 96-square-mile Santa Cruz Island. It is a brighter blue, has a bigger bill, and is larger than its mainland counterpart. Meanwhile, the island fox is the largest of the Channel Islands' native mammals. But the animal is a third smaller than its relatives on the continent.

This doesn't mean that these special species are entirely safe even on the isolated Channel Islands. In the 20th century, habitat destruction, predation by feral cats, and a 1959 wildfire led to the extinction of an endemic subspecies of song sparrow on Santa Barbara Island.

Luckily, the island fox population has recovered since hitting a low of 100 animals on San Miguel, Santa Rosa, and Santa Cruz Islands in 1999. A captive breeding program has now stabilized the animal's numbers, and if you camp in Santa Cruz Island's Scorpion Ranch Campground, be prepared to hide your food from the clever canines.

lower campground has 22 sites in a euca-lyptus-shaded canyon, while the upper loop has three regular sites and six group sites in a meadow. The upper loop is a nice spot but it's twice as far to lug your camping gear. The campgrounds have a picnic table and food storage box at every site. There are also pit toilets and water available.

There's also camping out of Prisoners Harbor if you hike the strenuous 3.5 miles to the **Del Norte Backcountry Campsite** (877/444-6777, www.recreation.gov, $15). This remote spot in an oak grove at 700 feet elevation has picnic tables and a pit toilet.

★ ANACAPA ISLAND

From the sea, Anacapa Island looks like three long dashes on the horizon. Actually, Anacapa is three islets that are five miles long and a quarter-mile wide. Visitors are able to access East Anacapa, a desert-like island with steep cliffs that is home to the stunning Inspiration Point, the Anacapa Lighthouse, a two-mile trail system, a small visitors center, a campground, and Arch Rock, a 40-foot-high rock window in the waters just east of the island.

Anacapa is wilder and more barren than nearby Santa Cruz Island. There are no trees here, and the island's low vegetation resembles a landscape recovering from a forest fire. Though there is a ranger residence and a few buildings on Anacapa, it is still a difficult place to sustain an existence. On this isolated island with little resources, supplies are hauled up out of the steep Landing Cove. Electricity is provided by solar energy, while water has to come from the mainland and then be stored in the Water Tank Building, which has two 55,000-gallon redwood water tanks. Despite these challenges, Anacapa is a wonderful place to spend a day taking in the awesome views.

Inspiration Point

If you have seen a photo of the Channel Islands on a calendar or postcard, most likely that is the spectacular view from **Inspiration Point.** From this high vantage point on the west end of the island, Middle Anacapa Island and West Anacapa Island rise out of the ocean like a giant sea serpent's spine. Below, the healthy blue-green ocean is spotted with rust-colored kelp forests. Overhead and below, gulls soar and do aerial acrobatics. In the distance, the large mass of Santa Cruz Island bulges out from behind the other

Anacapa Islands. With a bench, Inspiration Point is a place to sit and soak in the view and the solitude of the Channel Islands. In a word, Inspiration Point is inspiring.

Sports and Recreation

With 130 sea caves and numerous arches on its small coastline, Anacapa is ripe for exploration by sea kayak. Access to the water is only available from East Anacapa's Landing Cove due to the islands' rugged cliffs. There is even a cave in East Anacapa's Landing Cove. This short cavern can be found on the rear wall of the cove. Another sea-kayaking adventure on East Anacapa is to paddle out to **Arch Rock,** the 40-foot-high rock arch in the waters just east of the islet. The arch is the official symbol of Channel Islands National Park.

On the north end of Anacapa west of Landing Cove is **Cathedral Cove.** This scenic section of coast has an arch known as **Cathedral Arch** as well as **Cathedral Cave,** which can be explored by kayak during higher tides. The cave has five entrances that lead into an impressive chamber.

To secure a kayak for Anacapa or a kayak tour of the waters around Anacapa Island, contact the **Channel Islands Kayak Center** (3600 S. Harbor Blvd., Suite 2-108, Ventura Harbor, 805/984-5995, www.cikayak.com, single kayaks $35, double kayaks $55) before heading out. You must first secure a space for your kayak by calling Island Packers (805/642-1393), the concession that takes people out to the island.

The **Channel Islands Kayak Center** offers sea cave tours of Anacapa Island. Out of Oxnard's harbor, **Blue Ocean Kayaking** (3600 Cabezone Circle, Oxnard, 805/204-0977, www.blueoceankayaking.com, $250 pp) specializes in kayaking tours of Anacapa Island. Their boat picks you up after kayaking so you get to see more of the island and never have to backtrack by previously seen areas.

There are only two hiking trails on Anacapa: the 1.5-mile round-trip **Inspiration Point Loop** and the 0.5-mile **Lighthouse Trail.** The easy, flat **Inspiration Point Loop**

(1.5 miles round-trip, easy, begins at visitor center) takes you around almost all of the island. On the way to the stunning Inspiration Point, the trail includes stops at Pinniped Point and Cathedral Cove, where you can view sea lions stacked like sandbags on pocket beaches hundreds of feet down.

Even shorter is the quick walk slightly uphill on the half-mile round-trip **Lighthouse Trail** (0.5 mile round-trip, easy, begins at visitor center). The trail doesn't go right up to the lighthouse, but it comes close enough for a great picture and view. After events including the 1853 wreck of the steamer *Winfield Scott*, a basic light consisting of a beacon on a metal tower was erected in 1912. A real light station with a 39-foot-high lighthouse tower housing a Fresnel lens was constructed in 1932. The Fresnel lens is on display in the nearby visitors center.

Camping

The **Anacapa Campground** (877/444-6777, www.recreation.gov, $15) is reachable by a 0.5-mile hike on East Anacapa that includes 154 stairs. This primitive camping area has seven sites with flat spots and picnic tables. There are also some regularly serviced pit toilets. Without the protection of trees like those at Santa Cruz Island's Scorpion Ranch, the Anacapa campsites are very exposed to the sun and the wind.

SANTA ROSA ISLAND

The second-largest island in Channel Islands National Park after Santa Cruz, the rugged, windy Santa Rosa Island is less visited than Anacapa and Santa Cruz. The 53,000-acre island has a mountainous spine inland that rises to 1,574 feet at Soledad Peak. The vistas from the tops of some of the plateaus are beautiful, with views of neighboring Santa Cruz Island and the mainland coastline in the distance. There are also some beautiful white-sand beaches as well as coastal lagoons and places that seem virtually untouched. It is also home to a rare subspecies of Torrey pine that is considered one of the rarest pines in the world.

On the island, the remains of a pygmy mammoth—just 4-6 feet tall!—were discovered in 1994. Santa Rosa also has protected archaeological sites from the native Chumash.

Travel time is about three hours by boat; you'll need to climb a 20-foot steel-rung ladder to reach flat land.

Sports and Recreation

Due to the frequent high winds, sea kayaking, snorkeling, diving, and swimming are only recommended for those with significant experience. But for those who want to explore dry land, Santa Rosa has a handful of trails for hikers who don't mind sweating. The strenuous 12-mile **East Point Trail** takes in the rare Torrey pine forest and some unrestricted beaches. The 13-mile **Lobo Canyon Trail** goes to a water-sculpted canyon that looks like it could be in the Southwest. There are also easier outings including exploring **Water Canyon Beach,** as long as it isn't too windy out.

Camping

Camping on Santa Rosa can be done at the **Water Canyon Campground** (877/444-6777, www.recreation.gov, $15), reached by a level 1.5-mile hike. There are 15 sites with picnic tables and pit toilets.

You can do backcountry camping (805/658-5711, free) right on the beach mid-August-December.

SANTA BARBARA ISLAND

The one-square-mile Santa Barbara Island is the smallest of the park's islands. It's little more than a small rock in the lonely Pacific, virtually impossible to see from the mainland. It's also the southernmost island. Santa Barbara is home to impressive seabird colonies, including one of the world's largest colonies of Xantus's murrelets. There is also a sea lion rookery on the island.

Secluded and lonely, Santa Barbara is a rare stop. Travel time is just over three hours; once here, you have to climb a steel-rung ladder

from a skiff, then laboriously trudge up a 0.25-mile set of steps to reach the top.

Sports and Recreation

The island has three hiking trails, including the moderate two-mile **Arch Point Trail,** the strenuous five-mile **Elephant Seal Cove Trail,** and a moderate four-mile hike to the **Sea Lion Rookery.**

One great way to explore Santa Barbara Island is by sea kayak. Paddling around the whole island is a six-mile trip. On the way, paddlers will be able to see a handful or arches and lots of sea lions. Access is only from Landing Cove.

Being the southernmost island, the waters off Santa Barbara Island are a little warmer for snorkeling. Though there is good visibility offshore, there have been sightings of great white sharks feeding on sea lions in the area. Access is only from Landing Cove.

Camping

The **Santa Barbara Island Campground** (877/444-6777, www.recreation.gov, $15) has 10 primitive sites with pit toilets and picnic tables that can be reached after a steep 0.5-mile hike.

INFORMATION

In preparation for a trip to the islands, visit the **Channel Islands National Park Visitors Center** (1901 Spinnaker Dr., 805/658-5730, www.nps.gov, daily 8:30am-5pm) in Ventura Harbor Village, where you'll find a bookstore, displays of marine life, exhibits, and a 25-minute introductory film on the islands.

GETTING THERE

The most popular way to get to Channel Islands National Park is by hopping onboard a boat run by **Island Packers Cruises** (1691 Spinnaker Dr., Suite 105B, Ventura Harbor, 805/642-1393, www.islandpackers.com). Even the boat ride out to the islands is an adventure, with porpoises frequently racing beside the boats. There's also a snack bar onboard selling what one crewmember called "college food," which is candy bars, beer, and salted snacks. The boat schedules change according to the seasons, so it's best to visit the website to find out what departing boat and returning boat times work best with your schedule. It's possible to have a full day on Anacapa Island or Santa Cruz Island by departing at 9am and returning at 4pm.

Trips to **Anacapa** (day trips adults $59, seniors $54, children ages 3-12 $41, overnight trips adults $79, seniors $74, children 3-12 $57), the closest island, take an average of 45 minutes.

The most common landing at **Santa Cruz** (May-Oct. daily, Nov.-Apr. Tues. and Fri.-Sun., day trips adults $59, seniors $54, children ages 3-12 $41, overnight trips adults $79, seniors $74, children 3-12 $57) is Scorpion Cove, with a crossing time of 90 minutes.

Santa Rosa trips (day trips adults $82, seniors $74, children ages 3-12 $65, overnight trips adults $114, seniors $104, children 3-12 $90) take 2.5-3 hours and include stops at Santa Cruz.

Santa Barbara is the southernmost island in the park. **Santa Barbara** trips (day trips adults $82, seniors $74, children ages 3-12 $65, overnight trips adults $114, seniors $104, children 3-12 $90) is traveled to infrequently and takes 2.5 to 3 hours.

If the high seas aren't your thing, go by air via **Channel Islands Aviation** (805/987-1301, www.flycia.com, starts at $1,100) to Santa Rosa Island.

Los Angeles and Orange County

Los Angeles is the California that the rest of the world envisions. It's true that palm trees line sunny boulevards and the Pacific Ocean starts to warm to a swimmable temperature here, and that traffic is always a mess. But celebrities don't crowd every sidewalk signing autographs, and movies aren't filming on every corner.

Instead, L.A. combines the glitz, crowds, and speed of the big city with an easier, friendlier feel in its suburbs. A soft haze often envelops the warm beaches, which draw lightly clad crowds vying to see and be seen while children play in the water. Power shoppers pound the pavement lining the ultra-urban city streets. Tourists can catch a premiere at the Chinese Theatre, try their feet on a surfboard at Huntington Beach, and view the prehistoric relics at the La Brea Tar Pits.

For visitors who want a deeper look into the Los Angeles Basin, excellent museums dot the landscape, as do theaters, comedy clubs, and live-music venues. L.A. boasts the best nightlife in California, with options that appeal to star-watchers, hard-core dancers, and cutting-edge music lovers alike.

Out in the suburbs of Orange County lies the single most recognizable tourist attraction in California: Disneyland. Even the most jaded native residents tend to soften at the bright colors, cheerful music, sweet smells, and sense of fun that permeate the House of Mouse.

PLANNING YOUR TIME

When you get into Los Angeles, you'll understand quickly that you'll need to pick and choose your itinerary. The vast urban sprawl is just too big to take in unless you've got several weeks in the area. Your best bet is to follow your own heart to whatever types of activities are your favorites. If you're a first-timer to the Los Angeles area, a great initial tour is a drive down Wilshire Boulevard from end to end, stopping to check out all the many and various sights along the 15-mile way.

If you're planning a trip to Disneyland with your family or a group of friends, stick with the Mouse as your main plan. Many people spend several days exploring the parks, never

Previous: Hollywood Boulevard; Santa Monica Pier. **Above:** TCL Chinese Theatre.

Look for ★ to find recommended
sights, activities, dining, and lodging.

Highlights

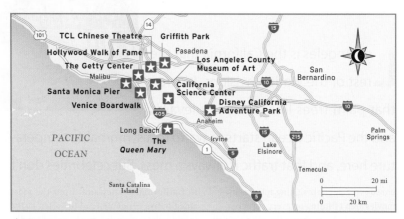

★ **California Science Center:** Learn about the daily life of an astronaut and then marvel at the space shuttle *Endeavour* at this museum (page 471).

★ **Griffith Park:** This large urban park in the Santa Monica Mountains is home to the iconic Hollywood sign and the Griffith Observatory (page 472).

★ **Hollywood Walk of Fame:** Walk all over your favorite stars—they're embedded in the ground beneath your feet (page 473).

★ **TCL Chinese Theatre:** Take in a movie premiere, step into the footprints of movie stars, or grab a photo op with one of the costumed superheroes hanging out in front of this Hollywood icon (page 475).

★ **Los Angeles County Museum of Art:** You can easily spend a full day taking in this diverse array of exhibits, showcasing art from the ancient to the ultramodern (page 477).

★ **The Getty Center:** The art collections alone would make this sprawling museum complex worth a visit. The soaring architecture, beautiful grounds, and remarkable views of the skyline make it a must. And except for paid parking, it's entirely free (page 479).

★ **Santa Monica Pier:** Ride the Scrambler, take in the view from the solar-powered Ferris wheel, or dine on a hot dog on a stick at this hundred-year-old amusement park by the sea (page 481).

★ **Venice Boardwalk:** It's hard not to be amused when walking down this paved coastal path in L.A.'s most free-spirited beach community, crowded with street performers, bodybuilders, and self-identified freaks (page 482).

★ **Disney California Adventure Park:** Tour a Disneyfied version of the Golden State at the newest theme park in the **Disneyland Resort,** which includes the Pixar-inspired Cars Land (page 521).

★ **The *Queen Mary:*** Take a tour or even stay the night on this huge art deco ocean liner that's rumored to be haunted (page 530).

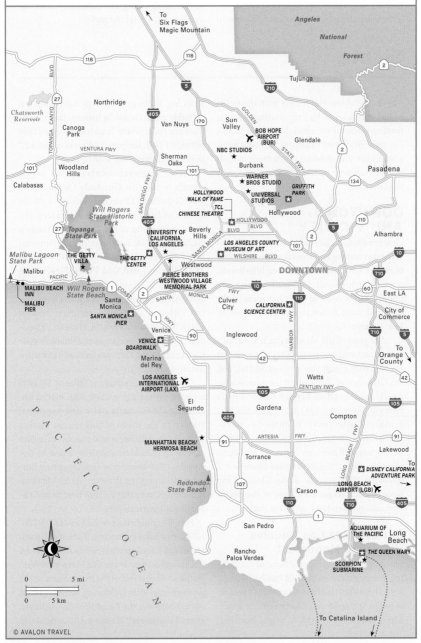

Greater Los Angeles

To Six Flags Magic Mountain

Angeles National Forest

Chatsworth Reservoir

Northridge

Canoga Park

Tujunga

Van Nuys

Sun Valley

BOB HOPE AIRPORT (BUR)

Glendale

NBC STUDIOS

Sherman Oaks

Burbank

Pasadena

Woodland Hills

WARNER BROS STUDIO

Calabasas

HOLLYWOOD WALK OF FAME

TCL CHINESE THEATRE

UNIVERSAL STUDIOS

GRIFFITH PARK

Will Rogers State Historic Park

UNIVERSITY OF CALIFORNIA, LOS ANGELES

HOLLYWOOD BLVD

Hollywood

Topanga State Park

Beverly Hills

LOS ANGELES COUNTY MUSEUM OF ART

Alhambra

Malibu Lagoon State Park

THE GETTY VILLA

THE GETTY CENTER

Westwood

WILSHIRE BLVD

DOWNTOWN

Malibu

PACIFIC

Will Rogers State Beach

PIERCE BROTHERS WESTWOOD VILLAGE MEMORIAL PARK

East LA

MALIBU BEACH INN

MALIBU PIER

Santa Monica

Culver City

City of Commerce

SANTA MONICA PIER

Venice

CALIFORNIA SCIENCE CENTER

To Orange County

VENICE BOARDWALK

Inglewood

Marina del Rey

Watts

LOS ANGELES INTERNATIONAL AIRPORT (LAX)

CENTURY FWY

El Segundo

Gardena

Compton

MANHATTAN BEACH/ HERMOSA BEACH

ARTESIA FWY

Lakewood

Torrance

Redondo State Beach

Carson

DISNEY CALIFORNIA ADVENTURE PARK

LONG BEACH AIRPORT (LGB)

PACIFIC OCEAN

San Pedro

AQUARIUM OF THE PACIFIC

Long Beach

Rancho Palos Verdes

THE QUEEN MARY

SCORPION SUBMARINE

0   5 mi

0   5 km

To Catalina Island

© AVALON TRAVEL

leaving the Anaheim area. Plenty of restaurants and hotels circle the theme park area, making staying and eating here a breeze.

Sun-worshippers and surfers will want to stick with the coastline. It's possible to drive from Malibu to San Juan Capistrano over a weekend, stopping at beachside towns for meals and to spend the night.

Sights

The only problem you'll have with the sights of Los Angeles and its surrounding towns is finding a way to see enough of them to satisfy you. You'll find museums, famed streets, ancient art, and modern production studios ready to welcome you throughout the sprawling cityscape.

DOWNTOWN AND VICINITY

Downtown L.A. has tall, glass-coated skyscrapers creating an urban skyline, and amid them are sports arenas, rich neighborhoods, poor neighborhoods, and endless shopping opportunities. Most of all, it has some of the best and most distinctive cultural icons in L.A. County.

After years of talk about revitalization, ambitious architectural projects such as architect Frank Gehry's Walt Disney Concert Hall and the Cathedral of Our Lady of the Angels have finally made good on hopes for Downtown's renewal. Koreatown is thriving in the 21st century. Little Tokyo is home to restaurants, shops, an Asian American theater, and the Japanese American National Museum. Neighboring Chinatown has spawned a booming gallery scene along Chung King Road. Even kids get a kick out of the museums and parkland of Exposition Park.

El Pueblo de Los Angeles Historical Monument

For a city that is famously berated for lacking a sense of its own past, El Pueblo de Los Angeles Historical Monument (Olvera St. between Spring St. and Alameda St., 213/485-6855, tours 213/628-1274, http://elpueblo.

lacity.org, visitors center daily 9am-4pm) is a veritable crash course in history. Just a short distance from where Spanish colonists first settled in 1781, the park's 44 acres contain 27 buildings dating from 1818 to 1926.

Facing a central courtyard, the oldest church in the city, Our Lady Queen of the Angels Catholic Church, still hosts a steady stream of baptisms and other services. On the southern end of the courtyard stands a cluster of historic buildings, the most prominent being Pico House, a hotel built in 1869-1870. The restored Old Plaza Firehouse (Tues.-Sun. 10am-3pm), which dates to 1884, exhibits firefighting memorabilia from the late 19th and early 20th centuries. And on Main Street, Sepulveda House (Tues.-Sun. 10am-3pm) serves as the Pueblo's visitors center and features period furniture dating to 1887.

Off the central square is Olvera Street, an open-air market packed with mariachis, clothing shops, crafts stalls, and taquerias. Hidden in the midst of this tourist market is the Avila Adobe, a squat adobe structure said to be the oldest standing house in Los Angeles. The home now functions as a museum detailing the lifestyle of the Mexican ranchero culture that thrived here before the Mexican-American War.

Free 50-minute docent-led tours (213/628-1274, www.lasangelitas.org, Tues.-Sat. 10am, 11am, and noon) start at the Las Angelitas del Pueblo office, next to the Old Plaza Firehouse on the southeast end of the Plaza. Some of the best times to visit are during festive annual celebrations like the Blessing of the Animals, around Easter, and, of course, Cinco de Mayo.

Downtown Los Angeles

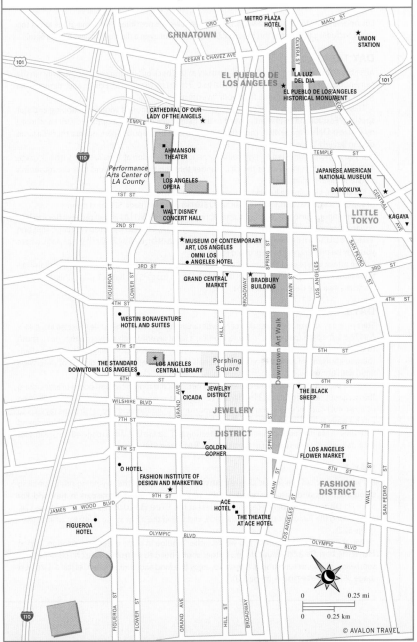

CHINATOWN

METRO PLAZA
HOTEL

ORO ST

MACY ST

★ UNION
STATION

CESAR E CHAVEZ AVE

101

101

EL PUEBLO DE
LOS ANGELES

LA LUZ
DEL DIA

★ EL PUEBLO DE LOS ANGELES
HISTORICAL MONUMENT

CATHEDRAL OF OUR
LADY OF THE ANGELS ★

TEMPLE ST

TEMPLE ST

■ AHMANSON
THEATER

Performance
Arts Center of
LA County

■ LOS ANGELES
OPERA

JAPANESE AMERICAN
NATIONAL MUSEUM

DAIKOKUYA ▼

1ST ST

■ WALT DISNEY
CONCERT HALL

2ND ST

LITTLE
TOKYO

KAGAYA ▼

CENTRAL AVE

SAN PEDRO ST

★ MUSEUM OF CONTEMPORARY
ART, LOS ANGELES

● OMNI LOS
ANGELES HOTEL

3RD ST

3RD ST

GRAND CENTRAL
MARKET

BRADBURY
BUILDING

LOS ANGELES ST

MAIN ST

FIGUEROA ST

FLOWER ST

4TH ST

SPRING ST

BROADWAY

4TH ST

● WESTIN BONAVENTURE
HOTEL AND SUITES

HILL ST

Downtown Art Walk

5TH ST

5TH ST

THE STANDARD
DOWNTOWN LOS ANGELES ●

★ LOS ANGELES
CENTRAL LIBRARY

Pershing
Square

6TH ST

6TH ST

WILSHIRE BLVD

GRAND AVE

■ JEWELRY
DISTRICT
CICADA

THE BLACK
SHEEP ▼

JEWELERY

7TH ST

7TH ST

DISTRICT

SPRING ST

8TH ST

▼ GOLDEN
GOPHER

LOS ANGELES
FLOWER MARKET ■

8TH ST

● O HOTEL

FASHION INSTITUTE OF
DESIGN AND MARKETING ★

MAIN ST

FASHION
DISTRICT

WALL ST

SAN PEDRO ST

JAMES M WOOD BLVD

9TH ST

ACE ●
HOTEL

▼ THE THEATRE
AT ACE HOTEL

LOS ANGELES ST

● FIGUEROA
HOTEL

OLYMPIC BLVD

OLYMPIC BLVD

0   0.25 mi

0   0.25 km

FIGUEROA ST

FLOWER ST

GRAND AVE

HILL ST

BROADWAY

110

© AVALON TRAVEL

Los Angeles Weekend

Los Angeles is notoriously sprawling, but in a few days, it's possible to hit some of the area's top spots, including the best of the beaches, Disneyland, and even a dash of Hollywood glamour.

DAY 1

After breakfast, drive to **Hollywood Boulevard.** Check out the movie-star handprints in the cement outside of the historic **TCL Chinese Theatre** (page 475). Poster and memorabilia shops abound, so pick up a still from your favorite movie.

Then it's off to Beverly Hills for a light lunch and an afternoon of window-shopping and star spotting. Fashionistas will want to head to the glamorous designer shopping district anchored by **Rodeo Drive** (page 492). You'll find signs to a number of public parking lots; there's a large one on Beverly Drive.

If you're more interested in high culture, spend the afternoon at **The Getty Center** (page 479). Take in dizzying views of the city, wander through the gardens, and tour the museum's outstanding art collections.

For dinner, sample the luxurious slices at **Pizzeria Mozza** (page 511) on Highland Avenue, or some luscious pasta at sister restaurant **Osteria Mozza** (page 511) next door.

After dinner, cruise the nightlife scene along the **Sunset Strip,** where revelers flock to legendary music clubs like the **Whisky a Go Go** (page 487), **The Roxy Theatre** (page 488), and **The Troubadour** (page 488). Or just head to the **Rainbow Bar & Grill** (page 485), where you may be drinking next to a grizzled rocker.

If an attack of late-night munchies strikes, cap off your night with another local tradition—an after-hours hot dog at **Pink's Famous Hot Dogs** (page 511). Rain or shine, this venerable stand draws a line deep into the night.

DAY 2

Start your day with orange pancakes or huevos rancheros and European-style espresso at **Cora's Coffee Shoppe** (page 514) in Santa Monica, a local favorite with a lovely patio. Head south to the **Venice Canals** (page 482) for an after-breakfast stroll. Originally built as a Venetian-themed amusement park, this network of canals is now a quiet residential district of waterways lined with bungalows.

Pack a picnic lunch, hop in the car, and head north for dazzling views and ocean breezes along the gorgeous **Pacific Coast Highway.** The highway connects Santa Monica with Malibu and its beautiful beaches, giving you plenty of opportunity to hit the sand and catch some rays. Try to catch a wave at **Malibu Surfrider Beach** (page 495). If you've had your fill of sunshine, spend your time in Malibu touring the small art collection at **The Getty Villa** (page 483) instead. End your day with seaside seafood at **Neptune's Net** (page 514).

DAY 3

Let your inner child run free at **Disneyland** (page 519). Spend the day riding rides, rambling through crowds, and watching parades at the most lovingly crafted theme park in the world. For a full on Disney-rific experience, enjoy a meal at the **Blue Bayou Restaurant** (page 524) overlooking the Pirates of the Caribbean ride, and spend the night at the **Disneyland Hotel** (page 522).

Skip the Disney attractions if you would rather indulge in some outdoor recreation. Surf at **Huntington Beach** (page 546) or, farther south, head to **Laguna Beach** (page 549) for snorkeling, diving, or sunbathing. Afterward, enjoy fine food and drink at **Carmelita's Kitchen** (page 551) or **Watermarc** (page 551).

Cathedral of Our Lady of the Angels

Standing on a hillside next to the Hollywood Freeway (U.S. 101), the colossal concrete **Cathedral of Our Lady of the Angels** (555 W. Temple St., 213/680-5200, www.ola-cathedral.org, Mon.-Fri. 6:30am-6pm, Sat. 9am-6pm, Sun. 7am-6pm, open later for special events, free tours Mon.-Fri. 1pm, parking $4-18) is the first Roman Catholic cathedral to be built in the United States in 25 years and the third-largest cathedral in the world. Since its 2002 opening, it has attracted millions of visitors for free guided tours and such events as Christmas and Chinese New Year.

Every aspect of Spanish architect Rafael Moneo's design is monumental: the 25-ton bronze doors, 27,000 square feet of clerestory windows of translucent alabaster, and the 156-foot-high campanile topped with a 25-foot-tall cross.

The building's sleek design suggests a more forward-looking posture for the Catholic Church. The cathedral is proving to be a monument not just for the more than four million Catholics in L.A. County; with events like music recitals, wine-tastings, and art exhibitions, it welcomes the city as a whole.

Union Station

When **Union Station** (800 N. Alameda St., Amtrak 800/872-7245, www.amtrak.com, daily 24 hours) opened in 1939, 1.5 million people supposedly passed through its doors in the first three days, all wanting to witness what is now considered one of the last of the nation's great rail stations. Architects John and Donald Parkinson's design is an elegant mixture of Spanish mission and modern styles, incorporating vaulted arches, marble floors, and a 135-foot clock tower. It was a fitting monument to the soaring aspirations of a burgeoning Los Angeles.

During the 1940s, Union Station thrived as a hub for both civilian and military traffic, and in the following decades its stucco facade became a familiar backdrop in scores of classic films.

Today, as the hub for the city's commuter rail network, it houses L.A.'s first modern subway line, which runs from Union Station to the Mid-Wilshire and Hollywood districts.

MOCA

The **Museum of Contemporary Art, Los Angeles** (250 S. Grand Ave., 213/626-6222, www.moca.org, Mon. and Fri. 11am-5pm, Thurs. 11am-8pm, Sat.-Sun. 11am-6pm, adults $12, students and seniors $7, under age 12 free) is better known to its friends as MOCA. Here you'll see an array of artwork created between 1940 and yesterday afternoon. Highlights of the permanent collections include pop art and abstract expressionism from Europe and the United States. Temporary exhibits have displayed the work of Andy Warhol and British artist turned Oscar-winning filmmaker Steve McQueen. MOCA has two other locations: The **Geffen Contemporary at MOCA** (152 N. Central Ave., www.moca.org, Mon. and Fri. 11am-5pm, Thurs. 11am-8pm, Sat.-Sun. 11am-6pm, adults $12, students and seniors $7, under age 12 free) and the **MOCA Pacific Design Center** (8687 Melrose Ave., West Hollywood, Tues.-Fri. 11am-5pm, Sat.-Sun. 11am-6pm, free). Enjoy free admission to the Grand Avenue facility and the Geffen Contemporary Thursdays 5pm-8pm.

Downtown Art Walk

The dramatic sculptures and fountains adorning two blocks on Hope Street (300-500 Hope St.) include Alexander Calder's enormous *Four Arches* (1974) beside the Bank of America Plaza and Nancy Graves's whimsical *Sequi* (1986) near the Wells Fargo Center. A free, self-guided, public **Downtown Art Walk** (213/617-4929, http://downtownartwalk.org, hours vary by gallery but usually noon-10pm) on the second Thursday evening of each month centers predominantly on the galleries bounded by Spring, Main, 2nd, and 9th Streets, but it spreads out to the Calder and Graves pieces on Hope Street.

Los Angeles Central Library

Bringing studious quiet to the bustle of Downtown, the **Central Library** (630 W. 5th St., 213/228-7000, www.lapl.org, Mon.-Thurs. 10am-8pm, Fri.-Sat. 10am-5:30pm, Sun. 1pm-5pm) is the third-largest public library in the United States. The exterior's Egyptian influence owes much to the discovery of King Tut's tomb in 1922, the year the library was designed. Enter at Flower Street to visit the Maguire Gardens.

Bradbury Building

One of several historic L.A. structures featured in the movies *Chinatown* (1974), *Blade Runner* (1982), and *The Artist* (2011), the 1893 **Bradbury Building** (304 S. Broadway, lobby daily 9am-5pm) is an office building that wows filmmakers with its light-filled Victorian court that includes wrought-iron staircases, marble stairs, and open-cage elevators. On Saturday mornings, the 2.5-hour docent-led Historic Downtown Walking Tour (213/623-2489, www.laconservancy.org, Sat. 10am, reservations required, adults $10, under age 13 $5), run by the Los Angeles Conservancy, take visitors through Downtown to sights including the Bradbury Building.

Japanese American National Museum

The **Japanese American National Museum** (100 N. Central Ave., 213/625-0414, www.janm.org, Tues.-Wed. and Fri.-Sun. 11am-5pm, Thurs. noon-8pm, adults $9, students and seniors $5, under age 5 free) focuses on the experiences of Japanese people coming to and living in the United States. Japanese immigrants came by the thousands to California, one of the easiest and most pleasant places in the United States to get to from Japan. From the beginning they had a hard time of it, facing unending prejudice, exclusion, fear, and outright hatred. Despite this, the immigrants persisted, even after the horrific treatment of the Japanese American population by the U.S. government during World War II. Today, sushi bars are almost as common as diners in urban centers, and whole nurseries are devoted to bonsai gardening. But the influence of Japanese culture reaches far beyond these everyday reminders; it has become integral to the unique mix of California culture. This museum shows the Japanese American experience in vivid detail, with photos and artifacts telling much of the story. Subjects of temporary exhibitions have included origami and Japanese tattoos.

Fashion Institute of Design and Marketing

Is your all-time favorite TV show *Project Runway*? Then L.A. has the perfect museum for you. The **Fashion Institute of Design and Marketing Museum and Galleries** (FIDM, 919 S. Grand Ave., Suite 250, 213/623-5821, http://fidmmuseum.org, Tues.-Sat. 10am-5pm, free) are open to the public, giving costume buffs and clotheshorses a window into high fashion. Each winter around award season, the museum shows off a collection of costumes from the previous year's movies, highlighting the film honored with the Oscar for Best Costume Design. Through the rest of the year, FIDM pulls exhibits from its collection of more than 10,000 costumes and textiles. Parking is available in the underground garage for a fee. When you enter the building, tell the folks at the security desk that you're headed for the museum.

Also housed in the FIDM building is the **Annette Green Perfume Museum** (Mon.-Sat. 10am-5pm, free). This is the world's first museum dedicated to scent and the role of perfume in society.

Natural History Museum of Los Angeles County

If you'd like your kids to have some fun with an educational purpose, take them to the **Natural History Museum of Los Angeles County** (900 Exposition Blvd., 213/763-3466, www.nhm.org, daily 9:30am-5pm, adults $12, students and seniors $9, teens $9, children $5, parking $10 cash only). This huge museum features many amazing galleries; some are transformed into examples of mammal habitats, while others display artifacts of various peoples indigenous to the Western Hemisphere. The Discovery Center welcomes children with a wide array of live animals and insects, plus hands-on displays that let kids learn by touching as well as looking. Dinosaur lovers can spend a whole day examining the museum's collection of fossils and models, which includes a trio of different-age *T. rex* specimens. Visit the megamouth shark as you walk through; it's the second specimen of the species ever recorded. Rock nuts flock to the Natural History Museum to see the fabulous gem and mineral display, complete with gold and a vault filled with rare precious stones. If you're interested in the natural history and culture of California, spend some time in the Lando Hall of California History.

The Natural History Museum sits within the larger Exposition Park complex. The **Natural History Museum Grill** (daily 10am-4pm) is the museum café. All exhibits are accessible for both wheelchairs and strollers, but ask at the ticket booths if you need special assistance to tour the museum. Admission is free on the first Tuesday of the month. The surrounding neighborhood can be rough, so don't plan to explore the area on foot.

★ California Science Center

The **California Science Center** (700 Exposition Park Dr., 323/724-3623, www.californiasciencecenter.org, daily 10am-5pm, admission free, parking $10) focuses on the notable achievements and gathered knowledge of humankind. There are many interactive exhibits here including one that lets visitors "lift" a giant truck off the ground. The Ecosystems section showcases 11 different natural environments, including a living kelp forest and a polar ice wall. Other galleries are dedicated to air and space technology, life as we know it, and human creativity.

One major reason people come to the California Science Center is to view the last of NASA's space shuttles, the *Endeavour.* Before seeing the impressive space vehicle, visit the Endeavour Exhibit that includes a toilet from the shuttle along with amusing anecdotes about dining in microgravity. The 132-foot-long shuttle hangs on display in a pavilion and will be eventually displayed in its launch position. To see the shuttle exhibit, reserve a timed entry by calling (213/744-2019) or by going online (www.californiasciencecenter.org).

California Science Center

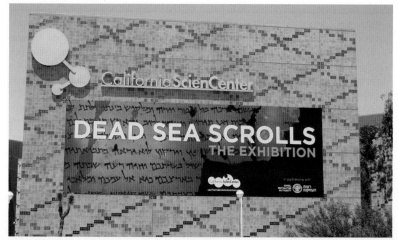

Many people also come to the California Science Center for the **IMAX theater** (213/744-2019, daily, adults $8.25, seniors, teens, and students $6, children $5), which shows educational films on its tremendous seven-story screen. Your IMAX tickets also get you onto the rideable attractions of the Science Court.

The parking lot only takes cash, so have a $10 bill handy.

LOS FELIZ AND SILVER LAKE

East of Hollywood and northwest of Downtown, Los Feliz, doggedly pronounced by most locals as "loss FEEL-is," is home to an eclectic mix of retired professionals, Armenian immigrants, and movie-industry hipsters lured by the bohemian vibe, midcentury modern architecture, and proximity to Griffith Park. Despite recent gentrification, this enclave and its neighbor to the southeast, Silver Lake, have so far managed to retain their unique, laid-back flavor.

★ Griffith Park

Griffith Park (Los Feliz Blvd., Zoo Dr., or Griffith Park Blvd., 323/913-4688, www. laparks.org, daily 5am-10:30pm, free) is the country's largest municipal park with an urban wilderness area. It has an endless array of attractions and amenities to suit every style of visitor. If you love the night skies, visit the **Griffith Observatory** (2800 E. Observatory Rd., 213/473-0800, www.griffithobservatory. org, Tues.-Fri. noon-10pm, Sat.-Sun. 10am-10pm, free), where free telescopes are available and experienced demonstrators help visitors gaze at the stars—the ones in the sky, that is. Or take in a film about the earth or sky in the aluminum-domed **Samuel Oschin Planetarium** (in Griffith Observatory, visit www.griffithobservatory.org for showtimes, $3-7).

Golfers can choose among two 18-hole courses, one 9-hole course, and a 9-hole, par-3 course on the parklands. A swimming pool cools visitors in the summer. You'll find a baseball field, basketball and tennis courts, children's playgrounds, and endless miles of hiking and horseback riding trails threading their way far into the backcountry of the park.

If you prefer a more structured park experience, try the **L.A. Zoo and Botanical Gardens** (5333 Zoo Dr., 323/644-4200, www.lazoo.org, daily 10am-5pm, adults $19, seniors $16, children $14, parking free), where you can view elephants, rhinos, and gorillas. If the weather is poor (yes, it does rain in L.A.), step inside **The Autry National Center of the American West** (4700 Western Heritage Way, 323/667-2000, www.theautry.org, Tues.-Fri. 10am-4pm, Sat.-Sun. 10am-5pm, adults $10, students and seniors $6, children $4), which showcases artifacts of the American West.

Kids love riding the trains of the operating miniature railroad at both the **Travel Town Railroad** (5200 Zoo Dr., 323/662-9678, www.griffithparktrainrides.com, winter Mon.-Fri. 10am-3:15pm, Sat.-Sun. 10am-4:15pm, summer Mon.-Fri. 10am-3:15pm, Sat.-Sun. 10am-4:45pm, $2.75), which runs the perimeter of the **Travel Town Museum** (5200 Zoo Dr., 323/662-5874, http://travel-town.org, summer Mon.-Fri. 10am-5pm, Sat.-Sun. 10am-6pm, winter Mon.-Fri. 10am-4pm, Sat.-Sun. 10am-6pm), and the **Griffith Park & Southern Railroad** (4730 Crystal Springs Rd., www.griffithparktrain-rides.com, winter Mon.-Fri. 10am-4:15pm, Sat.-Sun. 10am-4:30pm, summer Mon.-Fri. 10am-4:45pm, Sat.-Sun. 10am-5pm, adults $2.75, seniors $2.25), which takes riders on a one-mile track.

Griffith Park has played host to many production companies over the years, with its land and buildings providing backdrops for many major films. Scenes from *Rebel Without a Cause* were filmed here, as were parts of the first two *Back to the Future* movies. Its use is appropriate to the park's rich history. Much of the land that now makes up the 4,210-acre park was donated by miner and philanthropist Griffith J. Griffith (really). It has changed much over the years, but remains one of Los Angeles's great prizes.

The **Hollywood Sign** sits on Mount Lee, which is part of the park and indelibly part of the mystique of Hollywood. A strenuous five-mile hike will lead you to an overlook just above and behind the sign. To get there, drive to the top of Beachwood Drive, park, and follow the Hollyridge Trail. The Griffith Observatory is a great place to snap a photo of the Hollywood sign (and it offers a free parking lot).

Hollyhock House

Hollyhock House (4800 Hollywood Blvd., 323/913-4031, www.barnsdall.org, self-guided tours Thurs.-Sun. 11am-3pm, adults $7, seniors and students $3, children under 12 free) was the first L.A. home designed by Frank Lloyd Wright. Finished in 1923, it was built for Aline Barnsdall, a patron of the arts, and is in what is now **Barnsdall Art Park.** Hollyhocks, Barnsdall's favorite flower, are an elemental theme in the decor. There are also private 45-minute docent-led tours (Tues.-Wed. 10am, 11am, $70) that can accommodate up to 10 people.

HOLLYWOOD

You won't find blocks of movie studios in Hollywood, and few stars walk its streets except on premiere evenings. It's an odd irony that what the world perceives to be the epicenter of the film industry has little left of that industry beyond its tourist destinations. The only "real" movie businesses remaining are the blockbuster premieres at the major movie theaters here. Most of the other destinations range from the oversold to the downright kitschy. But still, if you've ever had a soft spot for Hollywood glamour or American camp, come and check out the crowds and bustle of downtown Tinseltown (and be aware that no local would *ever* call it that). Hollywood is also famous for its street corners. While the most stuff sits at Hollywood and Highland, the best-known corner is certainly Hollywood and Vine.

★ Hollywood Walk of Fame

One of the most recognizable facets of Hollywood is its star-studded **Walk of Fame** (Hollywood Blvd. from La Brea Ave. to Vine St., 323/469-8311, www.walkoffame.com). This area, portrayed in countless movies, contains more than 2,500 five-pointed stars honoring both real people and fictional characters that have contributed significantly to the entertainment industry and the Hollywood legend. Each pink star is set in a charcoal-colored square and has its honoree's name in bronze. The walk was dedicated in November 1960. At each of the four corners of Hollywood and Vine, check out the four moons that honor the three Apollo 11 astronauts: Neil Armstrong, Michael Collins, and Edwin E. "Buzz" Aldrin Jr. Also look for your favorite nonhuman characters: Kermit the Frog, Mickey Mouse, and Bugs Bunny.

You don't need to pay to get into anything, just get out on the sidewalk and start to stroll; the complete walk is about 3.5 miles. If you desperately need to find a specific star, check out the Walk of Fame website (www.walkoffame.com).

Hollywood Wax Museum

It immortalizes your favorite stars, all right. If you want to see the Hollywood heavyweights all dressed up in costume and completely unable to run away, visit the **Hollywood Wax Museum** (6767 Hollywood Blvd., 323/462-5991, www.hollywoodwaxmuseum.com, daily 10am-midnight, adults $17, seniors $15, children $10). You can't miss it, since the brilliant sign lights up a good chunk of Hollywood Boulevard, especially at night. Inside, you'll see everyone from Charlie Chaplin to Angelina Jolie. You can even get a glimpse of stars on the red carpet at an awards show-style set. The Hollywood Wax Museum first opened to amazed crowds in February 1965. To this day, it remains inexplicably popular with visitors and locals alike. Save a dollar by purchasing a ticket online.

If you need yet another cotton-candy

Hollywood

THE ABBEY FOOD AND BAR

SUNSET STRIP

West Hollywood

THE GRIDDLE CAFE

THE PIKEY

FORMOSA CAFE

PINK'S FAMOUS HOT DOGS

OSTERIA MOZZA

RIPLEY'S BELIEVE IT OR NOT

TCL CHINESE THEATRE

HOLLYWOOD WAX MUSEUM

EGYPTIAN THEATER

BOSSA NOVA

Hollywood

PARAMOUNT STUDIOS

HOLLYWOOD FOREVER CEMETERY

KARMA LOUNGE

JUMBO'S CLOWN ROOM

HOLLYWOOD HOTEL

Barnsdall Park

HOLLYWOOD WALK OF FAME

HOLLYWOOD BOWL

Runyon Canyon Park

MULHOLLAND DRIVE

Laurel Canyon Park

UNIVERSAL STUDIOS HOLLYWOOD

Universal City

Lake Hollywood

Mt Lee

Forest Lawn Memorial Park-Hollywood Hills

GRIFFITH OBSERVATORY

GRIFFITH PARK

Mt Hollywood

Los Feliz

Silver Lake

Echo Park Lake

AVALON TRAVEL

Glendale

Burbank

0   0.5 mi

0   0.5 km

Film Festivals

Home of Hollywood and many of the world's most famous movie stars, Los Angeles is an ideal place to go to the movies. It's even better when you can attend a film festival.

There seems to be an endless array of film festivals in the Los Angeles area. Cofounded by actor Danny Glover, the **Pan African Film and Arts Festival** (310/337-4737, www.paff.org) takes place in February and highlights the works of people of African descent from all over the world.

Movies including Pixar's *Brave* have debuted at the **Los Angeles Film Festival** (866/345-6337, www.lafilmfest.com). The LAFF happens in June and includes the screening of 100 films.

Outfest (213/480-7088, www.outfest.org) is the oldest continuous film festival in Los Angeles, and it highlights LBGT-oriented movies in July.

The **Downtown Film Festival L.A.** (www.dffla.com), which also goes down in July, is for filmgoers who enjoy under-the-radar indie cinema.

The nonprofit American Film Institute plays some of the biggest pictures of the year at its November **AFI Fest** (866/234-3378, www.afi.com). Come to see what are sure to be some of the year's most talked-about movies.

The **Sundance Next Fest** (www.sundance.org/next) is a new and worthy entry to the L.A. film festival scene. This unique summer fest in August includes movie premieres and concerts by musical acts.

museum experience, right across the street is the **Ripley's Believe It or Not Odditorium** (6780 Hollywood Blvd., 323/466-6335, www.ripleyattractions.com, daily 10am-midnight, adults $15, children $9). You'll find everything from duct tape art to a real shrunken head. Save two dollars by grabbing tickets off their website.

★ TCL Chinese Theatre

You can't miss the **TCL Chinese Theatre** (6925 Hollywood Blvd., 323/461-3331, www.tclchinesetheatres.com) on Hollywood Boulevard. With its elaborate 90-foot-tall Chinese temple gateway and unending crowd of visitors, the Chinese Theatre may be the most visited and recognizable movie theater in the world. Along with the throngs of tourists out front, there are usually elaborately costumed movie characters from Captain Jack Sparrow to Spiderman shaking hands with fans and posing for pictures (for a fee). Inside the courtyard you'll find handprints and footprints of legendary Hollywood stars. Stop and admire the Chinese artifacts in the courtyard; most were imported from China by special permit in the 1920s. The theater was built by Sid Grauman and opened in all its splendor on May 18, 1927, with the premiere of *The King of Kings*.

The studios hold premieres at the Chinese Theatre all the time. Check the website for showtimes and ticket information. The Chinese Theatre has only one screen but seats over 1,000 people per showing. Daily 20-minute tours (323/463-9576 or tours@chinesetheatres.com for tickets, adults $13.50, seniors $11.50, children $6.50) are available with a reservation. While you're welcome to crowd the sidewalk to try to catch a glimpse of the stars at a premiere, most are private events.

Egyptian Theater

Built under the auspices of the legendary Sid Grauman, the **Egyptian Theater** (6712 Hollywood Blvd., 323/466-3456, www.americancinematheque.com, adults $11, students and seniors $9) was the first of the grandiose movie houses in Hollywood proper and a follower of those in Downtown Los Angeles. King Tut's tomb had been discovered in 1922, and the glorified Egyptian styling of the theater followed the trend for all things Egyptian that came after. The first movie to premiere at the Egyptian was *Robin Hood*, in 1922, followed nine months later by the premiere of *The Ten Commandments.*

Today, get tickets to an array of old-time films, film festivals, and double features, or take a morning tour to get a glimpse at the history of this magnificent old theater. Expect to pay $5-20 for parking in one of the nearby lots.

Hollywood Forever Cemetery

The final resting place of such Hollywood legends as Rudolph Valentino, Marion Davies, Douglas Fairbanks, and Johnny Ramone, the **Hollywood Forever Cemetery** (6000 Santa Monica Blvd., 323/469-1181, www.hollywoodforever.com, daily 8am-5pm) has received a dramatic makeover and now offers live funeral webcasts. During the summer, the cemetery screens films and holds concerts by national touring acts on its Fairbanks Lawn and in its Masonic Lodge. Visit the website for a list of upcoming events.

Paramount Studios

Paramount Studios (5515 Melrose Ave., 323/956-1777, www.paramountstudiotour. com, tours $55-178) is the only major movie studio still operating in Hollywood proper. The wrought-iron gates that greet visitors were erected to deter adoring Rudolph Valentino fans in the 1920s. Tours ranging 2 to 4.5 hours are available. Visit the website or call the studio for tour information.

Mulholland Drive

As you drive north out of central Hollywood into the residential part of the neighborhood, you will find folks on street corners hawking maps of stars' homes on **Mulholland Drive** (entrance west of U.S. 101 via Barham Blvd. exit) and its surrounding neighborhoods. Whether you choose to pay up to $10 for a photocopied sheet of dubious information is up to you. What's certain is that you can drive the famed road yourself. Whether you care about movie-star homes or not, the view itself is worth the trip. You won't see the facade of Britney Spears's multimillion-dollar hideaway facing the street, but a few homes do face the road. If you can see them, they probably don't belong to movie stars, who guard their privacy from the endless intrusion of paparazzi and fans.

Universal Studios Hollywood

The longtime Hollywood-centric alternative to Disneyland is the **Universal Studios Hollywood** (100 Universal City Plaza, Los Angeles, 800/864-8377, www.universalstudios.com, hours vary, adults $95, ages 3 to 9 $87, parking $16-22) theme park. (Save up to $10 by getting tickets online.) Kids adore this park, which puts them right into the action of their favorite movies. Flee the carnivorous dinosaurs of *Jurassic Park,* take a rafting adventure on the pseudo-set of *Waterworld,* quiver in terror of an ancient curse in *Revenge of the Mummy,* or race around in the new *Fast & Furious* ride. You can also experience the shape-shifting Transformers in a ride based on the movies and the Hasbro toy.

If you're more interested in how the movies are made, take the Studio Tour with a recorded Jimmy Fallon as host. Get tickets to be part of the studio audience of TV shows currently taping at the Audiences Unlimited Ticket Booth. Serious movie buffs can get a VIP pass for $329; a six-hour tour takes you onto working sound stages and into the current prop warehouse.

Enjoy a meal, store your heavier things in a locker, and browse a near-infinite number of souvenirs at Universal Studios. If you need a little help getting around, rent a wheelchair or stroller; most rides and shows are wheelchair-accessible. Ask at the ticket booth for more information on accessibility and assistance.

LA BREA, FAIRFAX, AND MIRACLE MILE

This midtown district can seem a bit of a mishmash, lacking an overarching identity of its own. And yet the area's streets are among the best known and most heavily trafficked in Los Angeles.

Lined with fabric emporiums, antiques dealers, and contemporary furniture design shops, Beverly Boulevard and La Brea Avenue north of Wilshire Boulevard are increasingly trendy haunts for interior decorators. Along bustling and pedestrian-friendly Fairfax Avenue, kosher bakeries and signs in Hebrew announce the presence of the neighborhood's sizable Jewish population. Around the corner on 3rd Street, the Farmers Market is one of L.A.'s historic gathering places. And farther south, Wilshire Boulevard is home to some of the city's many museums, including the Los Angeles County Museum of Art.

La Brea Tar Pits and Museum

Even if you've never been within 1,000 miles of California before, you've probably heard of the **La Brea Tar Pits** and the wonders found within them. While crude fences once protected tour groups from the stinky pits, paved paths now lead around the most accessible pits, and others (mostly those that are in active excavation) are accessible by guided tour only. Nothing can stop the smell of the tar, or the slow bubbling of the shallow miasma of water that covers the tar.

If what interests you most are the fossilized contents of the tar pits, head for the beautiful **La Brea Tar Pits Museum** (5801 Wilshire Blvd., 213/763-3499, www.tarpits.org, daily 9:30am-5pm, adults $12, students and seniors $9, children $5, parking $10). The museum contains the bones of many of the untold thousands of animals that became trapped in the sticky tar and met their fate there. The museum's reasonably small size and easy-to-understand interpretive signs make it great for kids and good for a shorter stop for grown-ups. You'll see some amazing skeletal remains, including sloths the size of Clydesdale horses. Genuine mammoths died and were fossilized in the tar pits, as were the tiniest of mice and about a zillion dire wolves. For a closer look at how the fossils were buried, get tickets to one of the **Excavator Tours** (Mon.-Fri. 11am and 3pm, Sat.-Sun. noon, 1pm, 2pm, and 3pm, free with museum ticket), which are available on the museum's website. Another way to fire up your imagination about the giant creatures now encased in tar is to take in the 3-D film *Titans of the Ice Age* ($4 extra with museum admission).

★ Los Angeles County Museum of Art

Travelers who desperately need a break from the endless shiny and mindless entertainments of L.A. can find respite and solace in the **Los Angeles County Museum of Art**

La Brea Tar Pits Museum

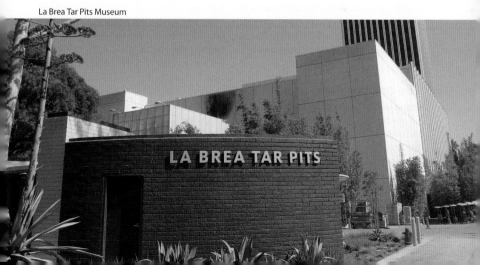

(5905 Wilshire Blvd., 323/857-6000, www. lacma.org, Mon.-Tues. and Thurs. 11am-5pm, Fri. 11am-8pm, Sat.-Sun. 10am-7pm, adults $15, seniors and students with ID $10, under age 17 free), the largest art museum in the western United States. Better known to its friends as LACMA, this museum complex prides itself on a diverse array of collections and exhibitions of art from around the world, from ancient to modern. With nine full-size buildings filled with galleries, don't expect to get through the whole thing in an hour, or even a full day. Specialties of LACMA include Japanese art and artifacts in the beautifully designed Pavilion for Japanese Art and the costumes and textiles of the Doris Stein Research Center. Several galleries of LACMA West are dedicated to art and craft for children. Perhaps best of all, some of the world's most prestigious traveling exhibitions come to LACMA. The 120,000 pieces at LACMA include works by Andy Warhol, David Hockney, and Roy Lichtenstein.

You'll do a lot of walking from gallery to gallery and building to building at LACMA. The layout resembles a Southern California shopping mall, with lots of space to take in the warm weather between buildings. Inquire at one of the two welcome centers for wheelchairs. The complex is equipped with four dining options, including the acclaimed farm-to-table restaurant Ray's, an ATM, and a gift and bookshop. And finally, if you're in need of some fine rental artwork, LACMA can hook you up.

The Original Farmers Market

Begun in 1934 as a tailgate co-op for a handful of fruit farmers, **The Original Farmers Market** (6333 W. 3rd St., 323/933-9211 or 866/993-9211, www.farmersmarketla.com, Mon.-Fri. 9am-9pm, Sat. 9am-8pm, Sun. 10am-7pm) quickly became an institution for Angelenos who flocked here to buy produce, flowers, and candy, or just to cool their cars and have a chat.

The market was built by entrepreneurs Roger Dahlhjelm and Fred Beck, who leased

Levitated Mass by artist Michael Heizer at the Los Angeles County Museum of Art

the land at 3rd Street and Fairfax Avenue from oil tycoon Arthur Fremont Gilmore; it quickly grew beyond its initial wooden produce stalls into a bustling arcade. A whitewashed clock tower went up in 1941, signaling the market's growing importance as an ersatz village square for local residents. During the 1940s and 1950s, the tables at Magee's and Du-Par's were crowded with regulars, and over the years the site has hosted circus acts, parades, petting zoos, and Gilmore's "Gas-a-teria," reputedly the world's first self-service gas station.

Today, the market remains a favorite locale for people-watching and, along with the adjacent shopping center, The Grove, now has over 30 restaurants and 50 shops hawking everything from hot sauce to stickers. Gourmands will find fresh fruit, chocolate truffles, sushi, gumbo, Mexican cuisine, and a plethora of other foods. There are even annual events, such as a vintage auto show in early June, free summer concerts every Friday, and a fall festival.

BEVERLY HILLS AND WEST HOLLYWOOD

Although the truly wealthy live above Hollywood on Mulholland Drive, in Bel Air, or on the beach at Malibu, there's still plenty of money floating around Beverly Hills. Some of the world's best and most expensive shops line its streets. You'll also find plenty of high-end culture in this area, which bleeds into West L.A.

Sunset Strip

The **Sunset Strip** really is part of Sunset Boulevard—specifically the part that runs 1.5 miles through West Hollywood from the edge of Hollywood to the Beverly Hills city limits. The Strip exemplifies all that's grandiose and tacky about the L.A. entertainment industry. Few other places, even in California, boast about the number and glaring overstatement of their billboards. You'll also find many of the Strip's legendary rock clubs, such as **The Roxy** and the **Whisky a Go Go** and the infamous after-hours hangout **The Rainbow Bar & Grill.** Decades worth of up-and-coming rock acts first made their names on the Strip and lived at the "Riot Hyatt."

At night, especially on weekends, no one's alone on the Strip. Don't plan to drive quickly or park on the street after dark; the crowds get big, complete with celebrity-hounds hoping for a glimpse of their favorite star out for a night on the town.

WESTWOOD

Designed around the campus of UCLA and the Westwood Village commercial district, this community situated between Santa Monica and Beverly Hills won national recognition in the 1930s as a model of innovative suburban planning. And while the nondescript offices and apartment blocks have since encroached on the area, recent slow-growth initiatives have preserved the heart of Westwood as one of L.A.'s most pleasant neighborhoods.

University of California, Los Angeles

From its original quad of 10 buildings, the campus of the **University of California, Los Angeles** (UCLA, bounded by Hilgard Ave., Sunset Blvd., Le Conte Ave., and Gayley Ave., tours 310/825-8764, www.ucla.edu) has become the largest in the University of California system, with more than 400 buildings set on and around 419 beautifully kept acres; it has a student population of nearly 40,000. Today its facilities include one of the top medical centers in the country, a library of more than eight million volumes, and renowned performance venues, including Royce Hall and Schoenberg Hall.

Running from the south edge of the UCLA campus along Westwood Boulevard toward Wilshire Boulevard, the Westwood Village shopping district caters to a lively mix of students and local residents with a clutch of bookstores, record shops, and cafés. The district also boasts the highest density of movie theaters in the country, with a number of restored landmarks.

★ The Getty Center

On a hilltop above the mansions of Brentwood and the 405 freeway, **The Getty Center** (1200 Sepulveda Blvd., 310/440-7300, www.getty.edu, summer Tues.-Thurs. and Sun. 10am-5:30pm, Fri.-Sat. 10am-9pm, winter Tues.-Fri. and Sun. 10am-5:30pm, Sat. 10am-9pm, admission free, parking $15) is a famed institution of art and culture. Donated by the family of J. Paul Getty to the people of Los Angeles, this museum features European art, sculpture, manuscripts, and European and American photos. The magnificent works are set in fabulous modern buildings with soaring architecture, and you're guaranteed to find something beautiful to catch your eye and feed your imagination. The spacious galleries have comfy sofas to let you sit back and take in the paintings and drawings. There are frequent temporary exhibitions on diverse subjects. Take a stroll outdoors to admire the sculpture collections on the lawns as well as the exterior architecture.

On a clear day, the views from the Getty, which sweep from Downtown L.A. clear west to the Pacific, are remarkable. But the museum pavilions themselves are also stunning. Richard Meier's striking design is multi-textured, with exterior grids of metal and unfinished Italian travertine marble, similar to that used by the Romans to build the Colosseum. The blockish buildings have fountains, glass windows several stories high, and an open plan that permits intimate vistas of the city below. There is also a central garden to stroll through and a cactus garden perched on a south-facing promontory with a view of the city below.

Pierce Brothers Westwood Village Memorial Park

Not known as well as L.A.'s Hollywood Forever Cemetery or Forest Lawn, the **Pierce Brothers Westwood Village Memorial Park** (1218 Glendon Ave., 310/474-1579, www. dignitymemorial.com, daily 8am-sunset) is the final resting place of some of the world's most popular entertainers and musicians. Under the shadows of the towering high-rises of Wilshire Boulevard, this small cemetery is the home of Marilyn Monroe's crypt, which is frequently decorated with lipstick marks from her enduring legion of fans. Westwood Village Memorial Park is home to other entertainment icons, including Rat Packer Dean Martin, author Truman Capote, eclectic musician Frank Zappa, and the stars of *The Odd Couple,* Walter Matthau and Jack Lemmon.

SANTA MONICA, VENICE, AND MALIBU

For many people around the world, when they think of L.A., what they're really picturing are the beach communities skirting the coastline. Some of the most famous and most expensive real estate in the world sits on this stretch of sand. The focal points are Malibu to the north, Santa Monica, and Venice to the south.

The "town" of Malibu stretches for more than 20 miles, hugging the beach the whole way. A few huge homes perch precariously on the mountains rising up over the coastline, also part of Malibu. Many beach-loving superstars make their homes here, and the price of a beach house can easily exceed $20 million.

A few more liberal and social stars prefer to purchase from among the closely packed dwellings of Venice Beach. A bastion of true California liberal-mindedness and the home

the cactus garden at The Getty Center

Santa Monica and Venice

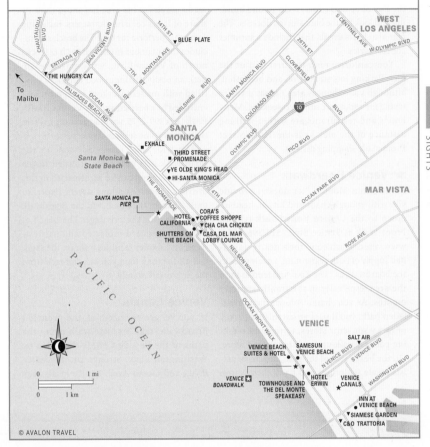

© AVALON TRAVEL

of several famous landmarks, Venice might be the perfect (if expensive) place to take a movie-style L.A. beach vacation.

With its fun-but-not-fancy pier, its inexpensive off-beach motels, and a huge variety of delicious and inexpensive dining options, Santa Monica is a great choice for a family vacation.

★ Santa Monica Pier

For the ultimate in SoCal beach kitsch, you can't miss the **Santa Monica Pier** (Ocean Ave. at Colorado Ave., 310/458-8901, www. santamonicapier.org, hours vary). As you

walk the rather long stretch of concrete out over the water, you'll see an amazing array of carnival-style food stands, an arcade, a small amusement park, a trapeze school, and restaurants leading out to the fishing area at the tip of the pier. There's even an aquarium under the pier! The main attraction is **Pacific Park** (310/260-8744, www.pacpark.com, hours vary, $3-5 per ride, all-ride pass $15-27, parking $6-12). This park features a roller coaster, a Scrambler, and the world's first solar-powered Ferris wheel. Several rides are geared for the younger set, and a 20-game midway provides fun for all ages.

Hour-long **tours** (Sat.-Sun. 11am and noon, free) are available on weekends. Meet at the Pier Shop at the Merry-Go-Round building and look for the blue-shirted docents. The pier also hosts events that include a summer concert series.

You can drive onto the first half of the pier. Parking lots sit both on and beneath it, although your chances aren't great if you're trying for a spot on a summer weekend. Many hotels and restaurants are within walking distance of the pier, as is the Third Street Promenade shopping district.

★ Venice Boardwalk

If the Santa Monica Pier doesn't provide you with enough chaos and kitsch, head on down to the **Venice Boardwalk** (Ocean Front Walk at Venice Blvd., 310/396-6764, www.venicebeach.com) for a nearly unlimited supply of both year-round. Locals refer to the Boardwalk as "The Zoo" and tend to shun the area, especially in the frantic summer months. As you shamble down the tourist-laden path, you'll pass an astonishing array of tacky souvenir stores, tattoo and piercing parlors, walk-up food stands, and more. On the beach side of the path, dozens of artists create sculptures and hawk their wares.

Watch sculptors create amazing works of art out of sand, or purchase a piece of locally made jewelry. This area has more than its share of L.A.'s colorful characters, including some that perform for tips. The beach side includes the infamous **Muscle Beach** (2 blocks north of Venice Blvd., www.musclebeach.net), an easily distinguished chunk of sand filled with modern workout equipment and encircled by a barrier, and the **Venice Skate Park** (310/399-2775, www.laparks.org), where skaters get some serious air.

The wide, flat beach adjacent to the Boardwalk gets incredibly crowded in the summer. Parking can be nightmarish in this district of car-free walking streets. Expect to park far from the beach and the Boardwalk and to pay for the privilege. The beach at Venice is lifeguard-protected and has restroom and shower facilities built on the sand. Get all the junk food you can stomach from the Boardwalk stands.

Venice Canals

If you've grown tired of the frenzied Boardwalk, take a sedate walk along the paths of the **Venice Canals** (bounded by Washington Blvd., Strongs Dr., S. Venice Blvd., and Ocean Ave.). Venice locals seek

Santa Monica Pier

fountain at The Getty Villa

Will Rogers State Historic Park (1501 Will Rogers Park Rd., Pacific Palisades, 310/454-8212, www.parks.ca.gov, grounds daily 8am-sunset, tours Thurs.-Fri. on the hour 11am-3pm, Sat.-Sun. on the hour 10am-4pm, admission free, parking $11-12). This 186-acre ranch with its sprawling 31-room house was the home and retreat of Will Rogers and his family. Rogers's widow, Betty, donated the property to the state on her death in 1944. Today, you can tour the large home and check out some of the facilities of the active working ranch that still exist on the property. Or take a walk around the regulation-size polo field that was Will's joy. If you share Will's love of horses, visit the stables to take a lesson or go out for a ride out on the local range. Travelers who prefer their own two feet can take a three-mile hike to Inspiration Point or a longer trek on the Backbone Trail out into the Santa Monica Mountains.

Malibu Pier
There are few "sights" along the long, thin stretch of sand that is Malibu besides sand and surf. One of those worth checking out is the **Malibu Pier** (23000 Pacific Coast Hwy., 888/310-7437). The pier gets busy in the summer and lonely in the winter, though the die-hard surfers plying the adjacent three-point break stick around year-round. A few pier anglers also brave the so-called chilly weather of the Malibu off-season, but you'll feel a sense of some solitude when you walk out across the planks. Some attractions out on the pier include interpretive signs describing the history of Malibu, sport fishing and whale-watching charters, restaurants, and food stands. In the near future, a surf museum is scheduled to open on the structure. If you'd prefer to ride the waves yourself, rent surf and boogie boards as well as other beach toys on the pier.

out the canals when they want to take a stroll or walk their dogs (Venice is a very dog-oriented town) and enjoy the serenity and peace of the quiet waterways. The home gardens and city-maintained landscaping add a lush layer of greenery to the narrow canals. Taking these paths gets you deep into the neighborhood and close to the impressive 20th-century Southern California architecture of Venice. Many of the people who own homes on the canals launch small boats and put on an annual boat parade for the holidays. As you wander this area, marvel at the history of the canals, modeled after those in this beach town's European namesake city and admire the tenacity with which the city saved these last few from the landfill that removed their brethren from the landscape.

Will Rogers State Historic Park
Did you grow up loving the films and culture of the early Hollywood western? If so, one of the best sights in Santa Monica for you is

The Getty Villa
Even driving up to **The Getty Villa** (17985 Pacific Coast Hwy., Pacific Palisades, 310/440-7300, www.getty.edu, summer Wed.-Fri. and Sun.-Mon. 10am-5pm, Sat. 10am-9pm, winter

Wed.-Mon. 10am-5pm, reservations required, admission free, parking $15) on its Roman-inspired stone driveway will send your mind back to ancient times. The two-floor villa is modeled after a Roman country house that was buried by the AD 79 eruption of Mount Vesuvius. The villa's architecture and surrounding gardens replicate the type of world the 1,200 works of art inside were produced in. The museum features amazingly intact statues and jewelry from the ancient Greeks, Romans, and Etruscans. Stare at the larger-than-life "Marbury Hall Zeus" from around AD 100 or a Greek sculpture of the same god that was submerged in the sea, causing it to look like coral. Tickets are free, but you have to reserve them in advance if you want to enjoy this exclusive, intimate, and dazzling experience.

PASADENA

Pasadena is the elder statesman of Los Angeles neighborhoods and towns. Once a resort-like haven for the very wealthy, Pasadena gently decayed, then was recreated as a charming upper-middle-class residential town. Dotted throughout Pasadena you can still see fabulous examples of the craftsman architecture that was prevalent throughout Southern California in the early 20th century. This older city also lays claim to one of the best-known and most-attended parades (and ensuing college football games) in the United States, the Rose Parade on New Year's Day.

The Huntington

Some of the most beautiful botanical gardens in the world grow in Pasadena. **The Huntington** (1151 Oxford Rd., San Marino, 626/405-2100, www.huntington. org, Memorial Day-Labor Day Wed.-Mon. 10:30am-4:30pm, Labor Day-Memorial Day Wed.-Fri. and Mon. noon-4:30pm, Sat.-Sun. 10:30am-4:30pm, adults $23-25, seniors and students $19-21, children free) also includes an amazing library filled with rare and ancient books and manuscripts. Literary travelers and locals come to the Huntington to view and worship the Gutenberg Bible and a

manuscript of *The Canterbury Tales.* Art lovers come to view works by Van der Weyden, Gainsborough, Hopper, and more. And everyone comes to explore the 120 acres of gardens, the most popular part of the complex.

More than a dozen different gardens beckon, including the Desert Garden, the Japanese Garden, and the Rose Garden. Admission to the center includes a docent-led garden tour. Check the website for a look at what will be in bloom when you're in town.

Some of the best museum café food in the state can be had at the **Rose Garden Tea Room and Café** (Tea Room reservations 626/683-8131, no reservations needed for café, Mon. and Wed.-Fri. noon-4:30pm, Sat.-Sun. 10:45am-4:30pm, adults $31, ages 4-8 $15, ages 2-3 $7.50). You can get a scrumptious buffet-style high tea when the museum is open. For a more traditional snack or light lunch, the walk-up café offers salads, sandwiches, and hot soups.

The Gamble House

Where Northern California prides itself on its Victorian architecture, major construction didn't get underway quite as fast in the southern part of the state. Here many of the wealthy residents, such as the Gambles (of Procter & Gamble), built homes in the early 20th century. **The Gamble House** (4 Westmoreland Pl., 626/793-3334, www.gamblehouse.org, Thurs.-Sun. noon-4pm, Tues. 11:30am-1:30pm, adults $15, seniors and students $12.50, under age 12 free) was designed and decorated by legendary SoCal architects Greene and Greene in the American craftsman or American arts and crafts style. The only way to get inside is to take a tour (schedules vary by season). To buy tickets, go to the side of the main mansion and into the garage, built in the same style as the house, that now acts as a bookstore and ticket office.

Inside the house, you'll be led from room to room as the docent describes the construction and decor in detail. The craftsman aesthetic attempted to answer the overly ornate and precious Victorian style with long, clean lines and botanical motifs. The Greenes took this philosophy to heart in the construction of the Gamble House—you'll learn how they created this masterpiece as you view each unique room. You'll also hear some of their stories, even that of the house's possible haunting by Aunt Julia.

Norton Simon Museum

Believe it or not, much of the nearly two millennia of art displayed at the **Norton Simon Museum** (411 W. Colorado Blvd., 626/449-6840, www.nortonsimon.org, Wed.-Thurs. and Mon. noon-5pm, Fri.-Sun. 11am-8pm, adults $12, seniors $9, students and children free) were once part of a private collection. Wealthy industrialist Norton Simon collected the thousands of works of art over 30 years. He particularly loved the European Renaissance, the works of South and Southeast Asia, and 20th-century sculpture. Several of his most famous Auguste Rodin sculptures decorate the walkway up to the main entrance to the museum. Visit the lovely modern building housing large, airy galleries to study the beautiful works of fine art. Head outside to walk through the sculpture gardens in the courtyards behind the building. Purchase books and reproductions in the museum store or grab a bite to eat at the simple, walk-up Garden Café.

Rose Bowl Stadium

The **Rose Bowl Stadium** (1001 Rose Bowl Dr., 626/577-3101, www.rosebowlstadium.com, office Mon.-Fri. 8:30am-5:30pm), true to its name, is the home to the famed granddaddy of the bowl games and to the UCLA college football team. Built in 1922, this huge elliptical bowl at first had an open side. It was closed only a few years later, and now seats almost (but not quite) 100,000 people—perfect for the five Super Bowls it has hosted as well as the flea markets and the long slate of college games. In addition to the endless vista of seats, you'll find plenty of restrooms and concessions scattered throughout the stadium—far more than the average college football team's home turf.

You can visit the Rose Bowl anytime, although you might need a ticket during an event, and you'll definitely need to plan in advance to attend the Rose Bowl game. Check the online calendar to find a fun event to attend for the best sense of this National Historic Landmark.

Entertainment and Events

NIGHTLIFE
Bars

Whatever your taste in bars, whether it tends toward hipster dives, old-school watering holes, or beautiful lounges, L.A. will be able to offer its version.

Hit **The Rainbow Bar & Grill** (9015 W. Sunset Blvd., 310/278-4232, www.rainbow-barandgrill.com, daily 11am-2pm) to see an amazing myriad of rock-and-roll memorabilia and get a taste of music history. A group of musicians known as the "Hollywood Vampires," which included Alice Cooper, Keith Moon, John Lennon, Ringo Starr, Harry Nilsson, and Micky Dolenz, congregated here in the 1970s. Today, rockers still drop in after playing shows in the neighborhood. You never know who you'll bump into as you weave your way through the main dining room and outdoor patio to get your next drink. The crowds trickle in as the sun goes down; by the time the shows let out at the nearby Roxy and Whisky a Go Go, your chances of finding a booth diminish significantly. The back rooms also open up late, for dancing, drinking, and smoking. To the surprise of some diners, the hallowed haven also serves a tasty cheeseburger, available until 2am.

The Golden Gopher (417 W. 8th St., 213/614-8001, http://213nightlife.com/

goldengopher, daily 5pm-2am), jump-started the Downtown nightlife scene. It may not be as hip as it once was, but it's still a great place to enjoy a drink, with a smoking patio and a liquor store on the premises for bottles to go. Featured in films like *L.A. Confidential,* the historic **Formosa Café** (7156 Santa Monica Blvd., 323/850-9050, Mon.-Fri. 4pm-2am, Sat.-Sun. 6pm-2am) is a West Hollywood landmark that has changed little since 1925. Chinese decor embellishes the dimly lit main bar, and two large patios pack in young hipsters.

There are few dive bars that will entertain as well as **Jumbo's Clown Room** (5153 Hollywood Blvd., 323/666-1187, http://jumbos.com, daily 4pm-2am), which has a blood-red interior, a circus theme, and a low stage where burlesque dancers impress with acrobatic moves. The dancers gyrate to Tom Waits, Iggy Pop, and David Bowie while being reflected on the mirrored ceiling above. It's no surprise that David Lynch was inspired to write a section of his film *Blue Velvet* after a visit here.

In the Sunset Tower Hotel, **The Tower Bar** (8358 Sunset Blvd., 323/654-7100, Sun.-Thurs. 6pm-11pm, Fri.-Sat. 6pm-11:30pm) offers a glimpse of old Hollywood. Mobster Bugsy Siegel once had an apartment here. Today, it has walnut-paneled walls, a fireplace, and dim lighting so that celebrities can keep their cool.

Across from the Chateau Marmont, **The Den on Sunset** (8226 W. Sunset Blvd., 323/656-0336, www.thedenonsunset.com, Mon.-Fri. 5pm-2am, Sat. 3pm-2am, Sun. noon-2am) has an outside fire pit, while inside there is a collection of board games including Rock 'Em, Sock 'Em Robots. Some nights have DJs and karaoke.

With beautiful ocean views, glittering mosaics, marble floors, and romantic piano music, **Casa del Mar Lobby Lounge** (1910 Ocean Way, Santa Monica, 310/581-5533, www.hotelcasadelmar.com, Sun.-Thurs. 10:30am-midnight, Fri.-Sat. 10:30am-1:30am) is a dramatic real-life sand castle on Santa Monica State Beach and offers perhaps the most elegant cocktail experience in the city.

Also in Santa Monica, **Ye Olde King's Head** (116 Santa Monica Blvd., Santa Monica, 310/451-1402, www.yeoldekingshead.com, daily 10am-2am) is a totally different experience. Stretching down a long half block, Ye Olde King's Head is a British pub, restaurant, and gift shop. Crowded on most nights, the pub is home to dart games and a wide range of imbibing patrons visiting from far and near.

While in Venice Beach, skip the loud tourist bars and head to the **Townhouse and the Del Monte Speakeasy** (52 Windward Ave., Venice Beach, 310/392-4040, www.townhousevenice.com, Mon.-Fri. 5pm-2am, Sat.-Sun. noon-2am). Upstairs, enjoy the candlelit tables and pool table of the oldest bar in Venice. Downstairs, the speakeasy is a cellar space that hosts jazz bands, DJs, comedians, and burlesque troupes.

The Lost Knight (1538 W. Sunset Blvd., 213/278-0408, http://thelostknight.snack.ws, Mon.-Thurs. 5pm-close, Fri.-Sat. 5pm-2am, Sun. noon-10pm) is a spacious British pub in Echo Park with different themed sections. Choose the Train Car, with separated booths, or the Taproom, with high-top tables and sporting events projected on movie screens. They serve classic pub grub including sausage rolls, shepherd's pie, and fish-and-chips with plenty of sauces. Upstairs is the **otheroom** (Mon.-Sat. 7pm-close, Sun. 4pm-10pm), another bar that has a nice outdoor patio.

Echo Park's beer lovers flock to the **Sunset Beer Company** (1498 W. Sunset Blvd., 213/481-2337, www.sunsetbeercompany.com, store Mon.-Thurs. noon-11pm, Fri.-Sat. noon-midnight, Sun. noon-10pm, bar Mon.-Thurs. 4pm-11pm, Fri.-Sat. 1pm-midnight, Sun. 1pm-10pm), part well-stocked craft beer store and part intimate beer bar. They have the latest brews from California to Iceland and beyond. Sip your suds outside on a smoker's patio or inside with board games and books.

The Thirsty Crow (2939 W. Sunset Blvd., 323/661-6007, www.thirstycrowbar.com, Mon.-Fri. 5pm-2am, Sat.-Sun. 2pm-2am) is a neighborhood bar in hip Silver Lake. The focus is on whiskey, with 100 different kinds, including over 60 small-batch bourbons. Stop by happy hour (Mon.-Fri. 5pm-8pm, Sat.-Sun. 2pm-8pm) to get a low-priced, finely crafted Old Fashioned, Manhattan, or Moscow Mule. It's the setting of the Father John Misty song "Nothing Good Ever Happens at the Goddamn Thirsty Crow."

Clubs

Want to know which of the many dance and nightclubs in the L.A. area is the hottest or hippest or most popular with the stars? You'll need to ask the locals or read the alternative weekly papers when you arrive, since these things change almost weekly. Clubs in L.A. get crowded on weekend nights and bouncers take joy in allowing only the chicest hipsters into the sacred spaces beyond the doors. Being young and beautiful helps, of course, as does being dressed in the latest designer fashions.

For those in the know, **Karma Lounge** (3954 Beverly Blvd., 213/375-7141, http://karmaloungela.com, Tues.-Thurs. 5pm-midnight, Fri.-Sat. 5pm-2am) is a worthy stop for drinks or dancing. Karma frequently hosts DJs spinning everything from industrial to Latin along with burlesque shows. They also serve small plates if you need some fuel.

Dance to world-famous DJs under pulsating lights, falling confetti, or floating bubbles at **Create** (6021 Hollywood Blvd., 323/463-3331, http://sbe.com, Fri.-Sat. 10pm-4am). You may catch Kaskade or Afrojack on the turntables at this weekend-only dance club.

The **Three Clubs Cocktail Lounge** (1123 Vine St., Hollywood, 323/462-6441, www.threeclubs.com, daily 5pm-2am) acts both as a locals' watering hole and a reasonably priced nightclub catering mostly to the collegiate set. Expect to find the dance floor of the rear club crowded and sweaty, with modern dance mixes blaring out over the crush of writhing bodies. Two bars serve up drinks to the masses, and drinks are cheaper than in the hotter spots. Three Clubs has no decent parking, so you may have to walk several blocks

along Hollywood Boulevard long after dark. Bring friends along for safety.

Gay and Lesbian

An alternative to glammed-up West Hollywood gay bars, **Akbar** (4356 Sunset Blvd., Silver Lake, 323/665-6810, www.akbarsilverlake.com, daily 4pm-2am) pulls in a gay-friendly crowd with its cozy Moroccan-themed decor, neighborhood vibe, and friendly, unpretentious bartenders.

Sleek, glamorous, and candlelit, **The Abbey Food and Bar** (692 N. Robertson Blvd., West Hollywood, 310/590-7440, http://sbe.com, Mon.-Thurs. 11am-2am, Fri. 10am-2am, Sat.-Sun. 9am-2am) is a popular bar with a great outdoor patio and pillow-strewn private cabanas, all of which are usually jampacked. Savvy bartenders mix 22 different specialty martinis in flavors that include chocolate banana and Creamsicle.

Every Thursday night, **Avalon Hollywood** (1735 Vine St., Hollywood, 323/462-8900, http://avalonhollywood.com, Thurs. 9:30pm-3am, Fri. 9:30pm-5am, Sat. 9:30pm-8am) hosts **TigerHeat,** which is said to be the West Coast's largest gay event. Lady GaGa, Britney Spears, and Elton John have made appearances in the club, which is a renovated theater that the Beatles performed their first West Coast show in.

Live Music

The clubs in the West Hollywood district, particularly those on the Sunset Strip, incubated some of the biggest rock acts of all time long before anybody knew who they were. The **Whisky a Go Go** (8901 Sunset Blvd., West Hollywood, 310/652-4202, www.whiskyagogo.com, cover from $10) has helped to launch the careers of The Doors, Mötley Crüe, and Guns N' Roses. Truth be told, the Whisky doesn't draw many big-name acts anymore, even though go-go dancers still gyrate on either side of the stage at times. Most nights you'll get a lineup of new bands, sometimes including as many as seven in one evening. The Whisky also hosts cover bands that pay homage to the elders that once played here, such as Led Zeppelin and The Doors.

Almost next door to the Whisky you'll find **The Roxy Theatre** (9009 Sunset Blvd., West Hollywood, 310/278-9457, www.theroxy.com, ticket prices vary), which has done a better job of staying relevant. The Roxy opened in 1973 with Neil Young performing. Today, you'll find icons like Dave Davies of The Kinks or new acts like the Savages gracing the stage. The big black-box theater has an open dance floor, comfy-ish booths, and bare-bones food service during shows. Street parking is nearly nonexistent, and nearby lots will cost $5-15 or more, so think about taking public transit or a cab. Many music acts have recorded live albums at The Roxy, including Patti Smith, Bob Marley, and Social Distortion.

It's not on the Strip, but **The Troubadour** (9081 Santa Monica Blvd., West Hollywood, 310/276-1158, www.troubadour.com, ticket prices vary) is just as big and bad as its brethren. Over its more than 50 years, Bob Dylan jammed, totally unknown comic Steve Martin sang, Tom Waits was discovered, Billy Joel opened for somebody else, Metallica headlined for the first time, and countless A-list bands have recorded songs in and even about The Troubadour. Buy tickets online. If you've decided on a whim to hit tonight's show, you can buy tickets at the on-site box office on the day of the show only.

With less history under its belt, **The Echo and Echoplex** (1822 W. Sunset Blvd., Echo Park, 213/413-8200, www.attheecho.com) hosts a lot of up-and-coming indie acts, along with the occasional big act (Jamie xx) and some impressive coups, including a performance by the Rolling Stones in 2013.

Another relative newcomer, **The Theatre at Ace Hotel** (929 Broadway, 213/623-3233, www.acehotel.com) has already hosted big acts like Coldplay. The restored 1,600-seat movie theater from the 1920s features more than just rock shows; it also puts on lectures, film festivals, and dance productions.

Comedy

Not far behind the live music scene, L.A.'s live comedy scene is second only to Manhattan's as a way to see the brightest current stars and the most impressive new talent. More than a dozen major live comedy clubs make their home in the smog belt. Pick your favorite, sit back, and laugh (or groan) the night away.

In the former Ciro's Nightclub on the Strip, **The Comedy Store** (8433 Sunset Blvd., West Hollywood, 323/650-6268, www.thecomedystore.com, age 21 and older, $15-20) is owned by 1980s comedian Pauly Shore's mother, Mitzi. With three separate rooms, you'll find a show going on at The Store every night of the week; most start at 9pm or later. Check the website's calendar for early and late shows. In all three rooms you'll often find a showcase featuring more than a dozen stand-up comics all performing one after another, and leaving space for possible celebrity drop-ins. Local sketch and improv groups also have regular gigs at The Store. Once upon a time, legendary comics got their start here. Imagine being among the first to see Yakov Smirnoff, Steve Martin, or Whoopi Goldberg perform. You can buy tickets online for bigger shows, and at the door for shows that don't sell out and The Belly Room.

Current comedy greats including Will Ferrell, Kristen Wiig, Lisa Kudrow, and Will Forte are alumni of **The Groundlings Theatre and School** (7307 Melrose Ave., 323/934-4747, www.groundlings.com, prices vary). Get tickets to take in some sketch comedy by up-and-coming talents or enroll in the improv comedy school.

For a true grassroots comedy experience, watch comedians in hostess Marissa's backyard every second Saturday of the month at underground favorite **Brew Haha** (4221 Normal Ave., www.brewhahacomedy.com, free). For such an unorthodox venue, the talent level is high, featuring comedians from *MADtv* and *Drunk History*.

THE ARTS
Theater

Even with all the hoopla over film in L.A., there's still plenty of room for live theatrical entertainment in and around Tinseltown.

In addition to the Academy Awards, the **Dolby Theatre** (6801 Hollywood Blvd., 323/308-6300, www.dolbytheatre.com, box office Mon.-Sat. 10am-5pm, Sun. 10am-4pm) hosts various live performances, from ballet to shows from music legends like Bob Dylan. Of course, all shows utilize the theater's state-of-the-art Dolby sound system. Half-hour **tours** (on the half-hour daily 10:30am-4pm, adults $19, seniors and children $15) that include a view of an Oscar statuette are available daily.

The **Ahmanson Theater** (135 N. Grand Ave., 213/628-2772, www.centertheatregroup.org, box office Tues.-Sun. noon-6pm and 2 hours before performances, ticket prices vary) specializes in big Broadway-style productions. You might see a grandiose musical, a heart-wrenching drama, or a gut-busting comedy. Expect to find the titles of classic shows alongside new hits on the schedule. With hundreds of seats (all of them expensive), there's usually enough room to provide entertainment, even for last-minute visitors.

The intimate **Kirk Douglas Theatre** (9820 Washington Blvd., Culver City, 213/628-2772, www.centertheatregroup.org) hosts world premieres and edgy productions like David Mamet's *Race* and Samuel Beckett's *Endgame.*

Well-known television actors, including Jason Alexander and Neil Patrick Harris, frequently act in the productions at the **Geffen Playhouse** (10886 Le Conte Ave., 310/208-5454, http://geffenplayhouse.com, ticket prices vary). Some shows developed here move on to Broadway.

Classical Music

Although L.A. is better known for its rock than its classical music offerings, you can still find plenty of high-culture concerts as well. The **Los Angeles Opera** (135 N. Grand Ave., 213/972-8001, www.laopera.org, box office Tues.-Sat. 10am-6pm, prices vary) has only existed since 1986 but has grown to become one of the largest opera companies in the United States, gaining national recognition. The dazzling performances are held in the Dorothy Chandler Pavilion at the Music Center of Los Angeles County. Grammy-winning singer Placido Domingo has been the opera's general director since 2003.

Better known to its friends as the L.A. Phil, the **Los Angeles Philharmonic** (111 S. Grand Ave., 323/850-2000 or 800/745-3000, www.laphil.com, prices vary) performs primarily at the **Walt Disney Concert Hall** (111 S. Grand Ave.). Concerts can range from classics by famed composers like Tchaikovsky, Bach, and Beethoven to the world music of Asha Bhosle or jazz by Herbie Hancock. Guest performers are often the modern virtuosos of classical music.

With its art deco band shell set against canyon chaparral, the **Hollywood Bowl** (2301 N. Highland Ave., 323/850-2000 or 800/745-3000, www.hollywoodbowl.com, box office Tues.-Sun. noon-6pm) has long been a romantic setting for outdoor summer concerts by the L.A. Philharmonic and other artists. It also hosts some rock and pop acts.

The **Los Angeles Doctors Symphony** (310/476-5512, http://ladso.org, prices vary) has been performing regularly since its inception in 1953. Many, though not all, of the musicians are members of the medical profession. They play everything from Mozart to Schubert.

Cinema

Movie premieres are a big deal in L.A. for obvious reasons. Crowds throng the streets outside of the **Chinese Theatre** and the **Egyptian,** where the stars tromp down the red carpets.

The current favorite movie house for star sightings is the **ArcLight Hollywood Cinema** (6360 W. Sunset Blvd., Hollywood, 323/464-1478, www.arclightcinemas.com). Perhaps this is due to the ArcLight's 21-and-older-only screenings of major blockbuster movies, which allow patrons to purchase beer and wine at the café and bring their drinks into the theater with them. But most of all, the ArcLight complex offers the best visual and sound technologies, all-reserved seating, and the updated geodesic Cinerama Dome theater. Make reservations in advance (buy tickets online or at the theater). The ArcLight also shows a few art-house flicks and even the occasional retrospective. Ask for parking validation for a discount on the adjacent parking structure. You'll pay above even the usual high L.A. movie theater rates to see a film here.

For eclectic films and movie-related events that will not be at your local multiplex, seek out **The Cinefamily at the Silent Movie Theatre** (611 N. Fairfax Ave., 323/655-2510, www.cinefamily.org). The nonprofit Cinefamily presents screenings of eclectic gems, midnight movies, and under-the-radar films. They also frequently host Q&As with directors and actors.

Acclaimed filmmaker and movie enthusiast Quentin Tarantino owns and programs the slate of 35-millimeter films at the **New Beverly Cinema** (7165 Beverly Blvd., 323/938-4038, www.thenewbev.com). The movies screened here reflect Tarantino's sensibilities and include spaghetti westerns, horror films, classics, and selections from the filmmaker's personal collection. They are shown as double features, midnight movies, and children's matinees.

FESTIVALS AND EVENTS
Pasadena Tournament of Roses Parade

The **Pasadena Tournament of Roses Parade** (Pasadena, 626/449-4100, www.tournamentofroses.com, New Year's Day) is one of the nation's most popular New Year's Day events. Watched by millions on TV, the parade with its flower-covered floats has been

occurring since 1890. The accompanying Rose Bowl is the oldest of the college football bowl games.

Los Angeles Marathon

The **Los Angeles Marathon** (213/542-3000, www.lamarathon.com, Feb.) offers a unique opportunity: a chance to run through the city without having to worry about traffic. The course begins at Dodger Stadium and skirts the Hollywood Hills on the way to the finish line at Santa Monica Pier.

Fiesta Broadway

Fiesta Broadway (S. Broadway and W. 1st St., 310/914-0015, http://fiestabroadway.la, Apr.) is the largest Cinco de Mayo celebration in the world. Enjoy the fun, food, music, and culture along with the occasional appearance of a Mexican pop superstar.

L.A. Pride Festival

Overshadowed by celebrations in San Francisco and San Diego, the **L.A. Pride Festival** (West Hollywood, 323/969-8302, http://lapride.org, June) draws 400,000 celebrants to West Hollywood. There's a multiblock parade along with lots of music and art events. The 2015 entertainment lineup included Wilson Phillips, Tinashe, and Kesha.

July 4th Fireworks Spectacular at the Hollywood Bowl

Summer nights in Los Angeles are for getting outdoors, and the annual **July 4th Fireworks Spectacular** (Hollywood Bowl, 2301 N. Highland Ave., 323/850-2000, www.hollywoodbowl.com, July 4) offers a good reason to do so, with a popular Independence Day celebration featuring fireworks and musical acts. Previous performers have included big-time acts like The Beatles, Black Sabbath, and Cher.

Shopping

If it exists anywhere on earth, you can probably buy it somewhere in L.A. Different areas and towns have their own unique shopping feel, so decide what kind of retail experience you want and then pick the right spot to find it.

DOWNTOWN AND VICINITY
Flower District

If you have even the slightest love of plants and flowers, don't miss the world-famous **L.A. Flower District** (700 block of Wall St., 213/622-1966, www.laflowerdistrict. com, Mon. and Wed. 8am-noon, Tues. 6am-11am, Thurs. 6am-noon, Fri. 8am-2pm, Sat. 6am-2pm, admission $1-2). Sometimes called "America's Flower Market," this vast sea of color and beauty is a triumph of American multicultural entrepreneurial spirit. The first flower cultivators in Los Angeles were Japanese Americans, and today many growers are of Hispanic descent, perhaps especially fitting for an industry that creates products in all colors of the rainbow. When you visit this vast sea of beauty, you'll find a fun cacophony of different languages being spoken as floral retailers vie for the best products available on any given day.

One caution: While the flower market itself is safe for visitors, the area to the south is not. Don't wander the neighborhood on foot.

Jewelry District

If you're looking for the bleeding edge of style, you can't do much better than the Los Angeles **Jewelry District** (bounded by 5th St., 8th St., Broadway, and Olive St.). With more than 3,000 wholesalers, even the most avid lover of sparkly stones and glittering gold will get his or her fill. You can shop in reasonable peace here, and even in some confidence that you won't get ripped off as long as you do some preliminary research. The district's website provides information on vendor ratings and a map to help you get around more easily. From wholesale dealers of unset gems to professional gem setters who'll create a beautiful piece from the stones you've bought, you can find just about anything. Be careful if you're a woman alone, especially after dark, as this isn't the safest part of L.A.

Chung King Road

A mix of modern art galleries and fun, touristy gift shops line the 900 block of **Chung King Road,** a one-block stretch of Chinatown. Interior decorators often browse the eclectic selection. It can be quiet during the day, but it comes alive during art opening evenings. Visit http://chungkingroad.wordpress.com/galleries/ for a list of galleries.

LOS FELIZ AND SILVER LAKE

The shopping options in Los Feliz and Silver Lake reflect the neighborhoods' penchant for variety, with everything from secondhand resale stores to sophisticated boutiques.

Artsy, hip boutiques, cafés, and restaurants line **Sunset Junction** (Sunset Blvd. from Santa Monica Blvd. to Maltman Ave.), a colorful stretch of Sunset Boulevard concentrated around where Sunset meets Santa Monica Boulevard (or, rather, where Santa Monica Boulevard ends). Weekend mornings bring floods of neighborhood locals down from the hills. This strip is also home to the **Silver Lake Certified Farmers Market** (323/661-7771, Tues. 2pm-7:30pm, Sat. 9am-1pm).

The fiercely independent **Skylight Books** (1818 N. Vermont Ave., 323/660-1175, www. skylightbooks.com, daily 10am-10pm) in Los Feliz features alternative literature, literary fiction, Los Angeles-themed books, and an extensive film section. They host frequent author events and sell signed books. They have an arts annex a couple of doors down with art books and magazines.

HOLLYWOOD

At the center of the efforts to revitalize Hollywood, next to the Chinese Theatre and connected to the Dolby Theatre, **Hollywood and Highland Center** (6801 Hollywood Blvd., 323/467-6412 or 323/817-0200, www.hollywoodandhighland.com, Mon.-Sat. 10am-10pm, Sun. 10am-7pm, parking $2-13) flaunts outlandish architecture that's modeled after the set of the 1916 film *Intolerance*. Stroll amid the over 70 retail stores and 25 eateries that surround the open-air Babylon Court. Save yourself stress and park in the center's lot ($2 for up to two hours with validation).

Encompassing an entire city block and two floors, **Amoeba Music** (6400 Sunset Blvd., 323/245-6400, www.amoeba.com, Mon.-Sat. 10:30am-11pm, Sun. 11am-10pm) is the world's largest independent music store. There are smaller Amoeba Music stores in the San Francisco Bay Area, but this is the place in L.A. to find that rare record or used CD. Amoeba also hosts free performances by acts of all sizes, which have included the Flaming Lips and Elvis Costello in the past.

LA BREA, FAIRFAX, AND MIRACLE MILE

The stretch of charming and eclectic shops on **West 3rd Street** between Fairfax Avenue and La Cienega Boulevard encompasses one-of-a-kind clothing boutiques, home stores, and bath-and-body shops. At one end you'll find the Farmer's Market and The Grove shopping center; at the other, the Beverly Center.

Among the various home and clothing stores on West 3rd Street, you'll find **Traveler's Bookcase** (8375 W. 3rd St., 323/655-0575, www.travelbooks.com, Mon. 11am-7pm, Tues.-Sat. 10am-7pm, Sun. noon-6pm). Both armchair travelers and true globetrotters browse the extensive selection of guidebooks at this comfortable and friendly bookstore. Travel-oriented literature rounds out the stock.

BEVERLY HILLS AND WEST HOLLYWOOD

The hottest stars and other big spenders come to the three-block stretch of luxury stores at **Rodeo Drive** (www.rodeodrive-bh.com) to purchase the best and most expensive goods the world has to offer. Among the upscale retailers are **Chanel** (400 N. Rodeo Dr., Beverly Hills, 310/278-5500, www.chanel.

Skylight Books, Los Feliz

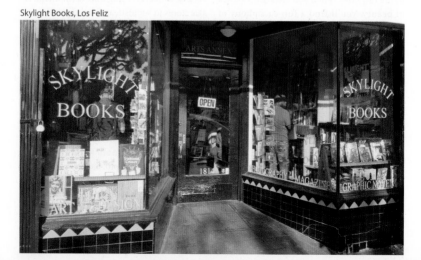

On the strip of Sunset Boulevard famous for nightlife, indie bookstore **Book Soup** (8818 Sunset Blvd., 310/659-3110, www.booksoup.com, Mon.-Sat. 9am-10pm, Sun. 9am-7pm) crams every nook and cranny of its space, but the film section is particularly strong. Check out the schedule of high-profile readings, or pick up a signed edition.

SANTA MONICA, VENICE, AND MALIBU

Shopping down by the beaches can be as much fun as anyplace else in the L.A. area. Santa Monica offers the best bet for an entertaining retail experience, since Venice Beach and Malibu tend more toward strip malls.

Looking for the place where middle-class locals come to shop in the L.A. area? Head for the **Third Street Promenade** (3rd St., Santa Monica, 310/393-8355, www.downtownsm.com). Much of 3rd Street in Santa Monica is closed to auto traffic to make it easier to walk along the Promenade. This long, vertical outdoor mall features all your favorite chain stores for clothing, shoes, jewelry, housewares, computers, and just about anything else. People ply the Promenade day and night, seven days a week.

PASADENA

Once a quaint downtown area serving a small but wealthy community, **Old Town Pasadena** (Colorado Blvd., 626/356-9725, www.oldpasadena.org) today is essentially a street-based shopping mall, with upscale chain stores inhabiting classic art deco and midcentury modern buildings.

Off the main strip along Colorado Boulevard, one block down Raymond Avenue, is **Distant Lands** (20 S. Raymond Ave., 626/449-3220 or 800/310-3220, www.distantlands.com, Mon.-Thurs. 10:30am-8pm, Fri.-Sat. 10:30am-9pm, Sun. 11am-6pm), a one-stop shop for travelers that has guidebooks, maps, travel accessories, clothing, and luggage. Even if you're not planning a special trip, the store's ambience is conducive to armchair travel.

Hollywood and Highland Center

com, Mon.-Sat. 10am-6pm, Sun. noon-5pm), **Tiffany's** (210 N. Rodeo Dr., Beverly Hills, 310/273-8880, www.tiffany.com, Mon.-Sat. 10am-7pm, Sun. 11am-5pm), and **Frette** (445 N. Rodeo Dr., Beverly Hills, 310/273-8540, www.frette.com, Mon.-Sat. 10am-6pm, Sun. noon-5pm). The Rodeo Drive Walk of Style salutes fashion and entertainment icons with sidewalk plaques.

Melrose Avenue (between San Vicente Blvd. and La Brea Ave.) is really two shopping districts. High-end fashion and design showrooms dominate the western end, near La Cienega Boulevard; head east past Fairfax Avenue for tattoo parlors and used clothing.

For vintage castoffs, check out **Decades** (8214 Melrose Ave., 323/655-1960, www.decadesinc.com, Mon.-Sat. 11am-6pm, Sun. noon-5pm), while **Ron Robinson at Fred Segal** (8118 Melrose Ave., 323/651-1935, www.ronrobinson.com, Mon.-Sat. 10am-7pm, Sun. noon-6pm) is a deluxe department store that has everything from the ridiculously trendy to the severely tasteful.

Sports and Recreation

You'll find an endless array of ways to get outside and have fun in the L.A. area. Among the most popular recreation options are those that get you out onto the beach or into the Pacific Ocean.

BEACHES

Southern California has a seemingly endless stretch of public beaches. Unlike their Northern California counterparts, most of these have lots of visitor amenities, such as snack bars, boardwalks, showers, beach toy rental shacks, surf schools, and permanent sports courts. Those listed here are just a drop in the bucket; beaches stretch in a nearly unbroken line from one end of the county to the other.

Not all L.A. beaches are created equal. With few exceptions, you won't always find clean, clear water to swim in, since pollution is a major issue on the L.A. coast. Also keep in mind that Los Angeles County is not a tropical zone. The water does warm up in the summer, and it's not in the icy 50s, as in the northern reaches of the state, but expect to cool off significantly when you dive into the surf. If you plan to be out in the water for an extended period, get a wetsuit to prevent chills that can turn into hypothermia.

Leo Carrillo State Park

Just 28 miles north of Santa Monica on the Pacific Coast Highway, **Leo Carrillo State Park** (35000 West Pacific Coast Hwy., 310/457-8143, www.parks.ca.gov, daily 8am-10pm, $12/vehicle) feels like a Central Coast beach even though it is right outside the Los Angeles city limits. Explore the park's natural coastal features, including tide pools and caves. A point break offshore draws surfers when the right swell hits. Dogs are also allowed on a beach at the northern end of the park.

Zuma Beach

David Hasselhoff fan alert: **Zuma Beach** (30000 Pacific Coast Hwy. in Malibu, 19 miles north of Santa Monica, surf report 310/457-9701, http://beaches.lacounty.gov, daily sunrise-sunset, parking $3-12.50) is where a lot

Leo Carrillo State Park

of the TV show *Baywatch* was filmed. This popular surf and boogie-boarding break, complete with a nice big stretch of clean white sand, fills up fast on summer weekends but isn't as crowded on weekdays. Grab a spot on the west side of the Pacific Coast Highway (CA-1) for free parking, or pay for one of the more than 2,000 spots in the beach parking lot. Zuma has all the amenities you need for a full day out at the beach, from restrooms and showers to a kid-friendly snack bar and a beachside boardwalk.

Water lovers can ride the waves or just take a swim in the cool and (unusual for the L.A. area) crystal-clear Pacific waters. Zuma has lifeguards during daylight hours, and for landlubbers, it's got beach volleyball courts set up and a playground for the kids. Perhaps best of all, this beach doesn't fill up with litter-happy visitors; it's actually a locals' favorite for weekend R&R.

Malibu Beach

Amid the sea of mansions fronting the beach, **Malibu Lagoon State Beach** (23200 Pacific Coast Hwy., 310/457-8143, www.parks.ca.gov, daily 8am-sunset, $12/vehicle) and its ancillary **Malibu Surfrider Beach,** which was the epicenter of the 1960s surf culture, offer public access to the great northern L.A. location. Running alongside the **Malibu Pier** (23000 Pacific Coast Hwy.), this pretty stretch of sugar-like sand offers a wealth of activities as well as pure California relaxation. This beach offers a number of unusual attractions, including both the **Adamson House** (23200 Pacific Coast Hwy., 310/456-8432, www.adamsonhouse.org, Fri.-Sat. 11am-3pm, adults $7, ages 6-16 $2, under age 5 free) and the adjoining **Malibu Lagoon Museum.** Take a guided tour that goes through the museum and out to the wetlands, butterfly trees, tide pools, and flower gardens. Malibu Creek runs into the ocean here. At the intersection that leads to the museum, you can also drive down to the main parking lot. It's likely to fill up fast in the summer, so get here early for a spot.

Surfers work the break here year-round.

It is one of the most popular point breaks in California. If a beach party is more your style, rent beach toys at the pier and stake your spot on the sand.

Will Rogers State Beach

If you're a film buff and a beach bum, head to **Will Rogers State Beach** (17000 Pacific Coast Hwy., Pacific Palisades, 310/305-9503, http://beaches.co.la.ca.us, daily 6am-10pm, parking $4-15), yet another fabulous full-service L.A. beach where movies have been filmed. You'll love the nearly two miles of sandy beach, which are easy to get to from the parking lot and studded with volleyball courts, playground equipment, restrooms, and picnic tables. The bike path running along the land side of the sand runs for 22 miles or so south. Out in the water, swim, skin-dive, or surf. A mild right point break offers a good learning ground for beginners. Lifeguards protect the shores during the day in summer, and the locals think their lifeguards are some of the best looking in the county. Pollution can be a problem at Will Rogers due to storm drains emptying into the ocean.

Bring cash to pay for parking, but be happy that with more than 1,750 spots, you'll probably find one that's legal and reasonably secure.

Santa Monica State Beach

Santa Monica State Beach (Pacific Coast Hwy., 310/458-8300, www.smgov.net, parking from $7) lines the water-side edge of town. For 3.5 miles, the fine sand gets raked daily beneath the sun that shines over the beach more than 300 days each year. Enjoy the warm sunshine, take a dip in the endless waves, stroll along the boardwalk, or look for dolphins frolicking in the surf. The best people-watching runs south of the pier area and on toward Venice Beach. For more elbow room, head north of the pier to the less populated end of the beach.

Due to its location right in town, you'll find a near-endless array of services at the beach. On the pier and just across from the beach, get snacks and meals, rent surf and boogie boards, hit the arcade, and go shopping. Parking varies, depending on which part of the beach you head for. The north end has spotty parking, the pier area can get really crowded but has more options, and the south probably has the best bet for a good spot.

SURFING

The northern section of Los Angeles has some of the region's best surf breaks including County Line, which is on the L.A.-Ventura county line, and Zuma, a series of beach breaks along the beach of the same name. But L.A.'s premier surf spot is Malibu, one of the world's most famous waves. This is where the 1960s surf culture took hold thanks to legends like Miki Dora, an iconic Malibu-based surfer. It's also the setting of the 1978 cult surf film *Big Wednesday*. Malibu is known for its crowds, but if you are able to score one of those long peeling rights off the cobblestone point, all in the world will be all right. The southern section of L.A. County's coastline offers places to surf, but not with the same quality as the breaks up around Malibu.

If you've left your board at home, run to the **Malibu Surf Shack** (22935 Pacific Coast Hwy., 310/456-8508, www.malibusurfshack. com, daily 10am-6pm, surfboards $20/hour, $25-35/day, wetsuits $10-15) to rent a board. It's walking distance to the break.

Surf Lessons

If you've never surfed before, sign up for a lesson or two with a reputable surf school. Most schools can get you standing up on your longboard on the first lesson. One of these, **Learn to Surf LA** (641 Westminster Ave., Suite 5, Venice, 310/663-2479, www. learntosurfla.com, $75-120), has lessons on the beach near the Santa Monica Pier (near lifeguard tower No. 18), Manhattan Beach's 45th Street Lifeguard Tower, and Venice Beach's Navy Street Lifeguard Tower. Take a private or semiprivate lesson, or join a regularly scheduled group. Each lesson lasts almost two hours and includes all equipment (you'll get a full wetsuit in addition to a board), shore

instruction and practice, and plenty of time in the water. No, the brightly colored foam longboards you'll learn on aren't the coolest or most stylish, but they're perfect for new surfers looking for a stable ride on smaller waves. Learn to Surf LA offers lessons for both kids and adults, and this can be a great activity for the whole family to tackle together. Intermediate and advanced surfers can also find great fun with this school, which has advanced instructors capable of helping you improve your skills.

STAND-UP PADDLEBOARDING

There has been friction between stand-up paddleboarders and surfers at breaks including Malibu. Still, if you want to try out the latest water sports craze, contact **Poseidon Stand-Up Paddle Surfing** (1654 Ocean Ave., Santa Monica, 310/694-8428, www.poseidonstandup.com, 1.5-hour lesson $120-140) for rentals or lessons in Santa Monica, Marina del Rey, and Malibu.

HANG GLIDING

Pick the kind of ground you want to soar over in L.A.: the ocean or the inland mountains and valleys. If you prefer to see the water slipping past beneath you, head for **Dockweiler State Beach Training Park** (12661 Vista del Mar, El Segundo, 818/367-2430, Wed.-Sun. noon-sunset). For a higher-altitude adventure, head to the San Fernando Valley and up to **Sylmar Flight Park** (12584 Gridley St., Sylmar, 818/362-9978, http://shga.com, daily 8am-dusk). For a good school and rental facility, call **Windsports Hang Gliding** (12623 Gridley St., Sylmar, 818/367-2430 or 800/644-8988, http://windsports.com, reservations office Tues.-Fri. 10am-6pm, $85-229). Go tandem with an instructor at Sylmar Flight Park or get bold and try a solo ride, which starts at an altitude of five feet out on the beach at Dockweiler. Windsports provides all the equipment and training you need, so all you have to bring are a good pair of athletic shoes, a bottle of water, and, of course, a camera.

SPAS

Inside the Westin Bonaventure Hotel in Downtown L.A., enjoy some good pampering at the **Bonaventure Club and Spa** (404 S. Figueroa St., 213/629-0900, www.bonaventureclub.com, daily 11am-11pm, massages $75-198). With a focus on beauty as well as health and relaxation, the Bonaventure Club features a number of heavy-duty facials as well as dermabrasion and collagen treatments. You'll also find a full nail and waxing salon along with an array of massages and body scrubs. The Bonaventure isn't the most upscale spa around, but you'll get decent service. The locker rooms, sauna, and other facilities are clean, and the spa is open later than most to accommodate busy travelers. Book in advance if you want a specific treatment at a specific time of day, but you're likely to find a same-day appointment if you aren't too picky about exactly which treatment you want.

For a taste of Beverly Hills luxury, try **Thibiant Beverly Hills** (449 N. Canon Dr., 310/278-7565, www.thibiantbeverlyhills.com, Mon.-Sat. 8am-7pm, massages $90-170), where you can blast yourself clean with a deluge shower, and then have your body slathered with mud, milk, seaweed, or papaya.

Over in Santa Monica, **Exhale** (Fairmont Miramar Hotel and Bungalows, 101 Wilshire Blvd., 310/319-3193, www.exhalespa.com, Mon., Wed., and Fri. 6:30am-9pm, Tues. and Thurs. 6am-9pm, Sat. 8am-9pm, Sun. 8:30am-8pm, massages $95-200) explores the mind-body connection with fusion yoga classes, massage, and acupuncture.

SPECTATOR SPORTS

After two decades of not having a National Football League team, there's a chance that Los Angeles could have two. In 2016, the St. Louis Rams moved to Los Angeles to become the **Los Angeles Rams.** They will play their home games at the **Los Angeles Memorial Coliseum** (3939 S. Figueroa St., 213/747-7111, www.lacoliseum.com) until a new stadium is completed in Inglewood by 2019. Though the San Diego Chargers also have the opportunity to move to Los Angeles, they are staying in their current city at least through the 2016-17 season.

The **L.A. Kings** (213/742-7100 or 888/546-4752, http://kings.nhl.com, ticket prices vary) are no joke now after winning the Stanley Cup in 2012 and 2014. They play lightning-fast NHL ice hockey in Downtown L.A. at the **Staples Center** (1111 S. Figueroa St., 213/742-7100, www.staplescenter.com).

Both the individual players and the **Los Angeles Lakers** (310/426-6031 or 866/381-8924, www.nba.com/lakers, ticket prices vary) organization as a whole have well and truly earned their places as legends of the National Basketball Association. They play at the Staples Center (1111 S. Figueroa St., 213/742-7100, www.staplescenter.com) along with the often overlooked L.A. Clippers (213/742-7530, www.nba.com/clippers), who are now rising in stature since Steve Ballmer bought the organization in 2014.

Major League Baseball takes advantage of the perfect climate in L.A. to host some of the most beautiful outdoor summer games anywhere in the country. The **Los Angeles Dodgers** (1000 Elysian Park Ave., Los Angeles, 866/363-4377, http://los-angeles.dodgers.mlb.com, ticket prices vary) make their home in this hospitable climate, playing often and well throughout the long baseball season. Just one thing: Don't refer to **Dodger Stadium** (1000 Elysian Park Ave.) as "Chavez Ravine" unless you really mean it. That old field designation has become a derogatory term used primarily by San Francisco Giants fans.

Accommodations

From the cheapest roach-ridden shack motels to the most chichi Beverly Hills hotel, Los Angeles has an endless variety of lodgings to suit every taste and budget.

DOWNTOWN AND VICINITY

If you want to stay overnight in Downtown L.A., plan to pay for the privilege. Most hostelries are high-rise towers catering more to businesspeople than the leisure set. Still, if you need a room near the heart of L.A. for less than a month's mortgage, you can find one if you look hard enough. Once you get into the Jewelry District and farther south toward the Flower Market, the neighborhood goes from high-end to sketchy to downright terrifying. If you need a truly cheap room, avoid these areas and head instead to the San Fernando Valley.

Under $150

You won't miss the sign for the **Metro Plaza Hotel** (711 N. Main St., 213/680-0200, http:// metroplazahoteldowntownla.com, $119-189). The low-rise hotel with its white facade and big, oddly constructed front marquee sits near Union Station, convenient for rail travelers and public-transit riders. Inside, you'll find your room looks like a dated, cheaply decorated motel room. The options range from studio rooms to suites with kitchenettes. A complimentary continental breakfast comes with your room, and the Metro Plaza has an on-site fitness center. Stay here for the location (parking is just $4 a night), central to transportation to all the major L.A. attractions, and the lower-than-average price for the region.

$150-250

With its red-tiled floor, painted furniture, and lushly landscaped poolside bar, the **Figueroa Hotel** (939 S. Figueroa St., 213/627-8971 or 800/421-9092, www.figueroahotel.com, $160-200) is a Spanish-Moroccan oasis in the heart of downtown. The rooms look like they could have been in the movie *Casablanca,* though they have TVs outfitted with cable stations. There's also a fitness center (daily 5am-11pm).

Can you imagine staying at a cute B&B only a mile from the towering skyscrapers of Downtown Los Angeles? The **Inn at 657** (657 and 663 W. 23rd St., 213/741-2200, www.patsysinn657.com, $149-249) is two side-by-side buildings with one-bedroom guest accommodations and two-bedroom suites, each individually decorated. You'll find a comfortable antique bed in a room scattered with lovely fabrics and pretty antiques. Each morning, you'll head downstairs to the long, dark table set with fine china for a full breakfast complete with fruit, hot food, great coffee, and fresh juice. The inn has a massage therapist on retainer, a nail salon they love just down the street, Wi-Fi, and laundry service. You're within easy distance of the Staples Center, the Downtown shopping areas, and the rest of the attractions of Los Angeles.

The **O Hotel** (819 S. Flower St., 213/623-9904 or 855/782-9286, www.ohotelgroup.com, $139-400), formerly known as The Orchid Hotel, is an upscale property that takes the modern urban-chic hotel concept and does it L.A.-style. True to its original name, orchids are a major theme of this hotel, and you'll find plants in the common areas. A boutique establishment, the O has only 67 rooms. The nicest suites are spacious with a bedroom, living room, and two baths. You'll find tapas, fish, burgers, and poultry at the on-site restaurant, plus a full bar. The health spa offers both fitness facilities and massage along with other spa services. Guests can also use the Gold's Gym just a block and a half away. Perhaps best of all for travelers who come to L.A. for its retail possibilities, you won't need the services of the 24-hour concierge desk to find the Macy's Plaza center just across the street from the hotel.

The ★ **Ace Hotel** (929 Broadway, 213/623-3233, www.acehotel.com/losangeles, $200-500) is one of the hippest places to stay in Downtown. Enjoy an evening's entertainment without venturing off the hotel's grounds: The property's 1,600-seat theater hosts the Sundance Next Fest and music performances by acts from Marilyn Manson to Philip Glass and Yo La Tengo. DJs spin poolside at the rooftop bar on the 14th floor, with the downtown skyline as a backdrop. Downstairs, dine at the trendy **L.A. Chapter** (213/235-9660, daily 7am-3:30pm and 5:30pm-11pm, $17-32). The modern and minimalist rooms, converted from the former offices of the United Artists film studio, feel like arty studio apartments, with concrete ceilings and exposed concrete floors. Some rooms have private terraces; all have Internet radios. There's a fitness center (daily 24 hours) if you need to counteract all the partying.

Over $250

For a taste of true L.A. style, get a room at the **Omni Los Angeles at California Plaza** (251 S. Olive St., 213/617-3300, www.omnihotels. com, $276-542). From the grand exterior to the elegant lobby and on up to your room, the stylish decor, lovely accents, and plush amenities will make you feel rich, if only for one night. Business travelers can request a room complete with a fax machine and copier, while families can enjoy suites with adjoining rooms specially decorated for children. On-site meals are available at the **Noé Restaurant** (213/356-4100, Sun.-Thurs. 5pm-10pm, Fri.-Sat. 5pm-11pm, $26-45) and the **Grand Café** (213/617-3300, ext. 4155, Mon.-Fri. 6:30am-3pm, Sat.-Sun. 7am-3pm, $9-24). Take a swim in the lap pool, work out in the fitness room, or relax at the spa.

Hipster hotelier André Balazs, of the Chateau Marmont and the Mercer, has transformed the former home of Superior Oil into **The Standard** (550 S. Flower St., 213/892-8080, www.standardhotels.com, $260-1,500), a mecca for the see-and-be-seen crowd. From its upside-down sign to the minimal aesthetic in the rooms, the hotel gives off an ironic-chic vibe. If you're sharing a room, be aware that the shower is only separated from the rest of the room by clear glass. On-site amenities include a gym, a barbershop, and a restaurant open 24-7. The rooftop bar, seen in the 2005 film *Kiss Kiss, Bang Bang*, features spectacular views of the L.A. cityscape.

If you're yearning to stay someplace with a movie history, book a room at the **Westin Bonaventure Hotel and Suites** (404 S. Figueroa St., 213/624-1000, www.starwoodhotels.com, $379-2,500). The climactic scene of the Clint Eastwood thriller *In the Line of Fire* was filmed in one of the unusual elevators in the glass-enclosed, four-leaf-clover-shaped high-rise building. This hotel complex has every single thing you'd ever need: shops, restaurants, a day spa, a concierge, and plenty of nice rooms. You'll find your room comfortable and convenient, complete with fancy beds and clean, spacious baths. Views range from innocuous street scenes to panoramic cityscapes. The most fun restaurant and lounge to visit at the Bonaventure is without doubt the **Bona Vista Lounge** (213/612-4743, daily 5pm-1am), which slowly rotates through 360 degrees at the top of the building.

HOLLYWOOD

If you're star-struck, a serious partier, or a rock music aficionado, you'll want to stay the night within staggering distance of the hottest clubs or the hippest music venues. You might find yourself sleeping in the same room where Axl Rose once vomited or David Lee Roth broke all the furniture.

Under $150

Reputed to be one of the best hostels in the state, the **USA Hostels—Hollywood** (1624 Schrader Blvd., 323/462-3777 or 800/524-6783 or 323/462-3777, www.usahostels.com, dorm $42-52, private room $125-130) still offers the same great prices you'll find at seedier, more bare-bones hostels. OK, so the exterior doesn't look like much. But in this case, it's what's inside that counts. Choose between dorm rooms and private rooms, but even the larger dorm rooms have baths attached, which is a nice convenience that's unusual in the hostel world. (You'll also find several common baths in the hallways, helping to diminish the morning shower rush.) The daily all-you-can-make pancake breakfast is included with your room, along with all the coffee or tea you can drink. Add that to the $7 barbecue nights on Monday, Wednesday, and Friday, and you've got a great start on seriously diminished food costs for this trip. This smaller hostel also goes a long way to fostering a sense of community among its visitors, offering a standard array of area walking tours and a beach shuttle, plus free comedy nights. There's also free Wi-Fi and complimentary Internet kiosks.

$150-250

The ★ **Magic Castle Hotel** (7025 Franklin Ave., 323/851-0800, www.magiccastlehotel.com, $190-370) is named for the world-renowned magic club next door. It boasts the best customer service of any L.A.-area hostelry. Sparkling light rooms with cushy white comforters and spare, clean decor offer a haven of tranquility. A courtyard pool invites lounging day and night. All suites have their own kitchens, and guests enjoy unlimited free snacks (sodas, candy, salted goodies). Enjoy the little luxurious touches, such as high-end coffee, baked goods in the free continental breakfast, plushy robes, and nightly turndown service. The most notable perks are tickets to the exclusive **Magic Castle** (7001 Franklin Ave., Hollywood, 323/851-3313, www.magiccastle.com), although there is a door charge.

The ★ **Hollywood Hills Hotel** (1999 N. Sycamore Ave., check-in at the Magic Castle Hotel, 7025 Franklin Ave., at the base of the hill, 323/874-5089 or 800/741-4915, www.hollywoodhillshotel.com, $160-175) is a bastion of old Hollywood. The Magic Castle Hotel rents out just 11 studios and suites. The rest are residential units where folks like Richard Pryor and Pernell Roberts once lived. Though the rooms are dated, the view from the units take in a good portion of the Los Angeles Basin; the Hollywood sign can be seen in the hills to the east. Many of the rooms feature balconies. The decor includes Chinese styling and attractive greenery. You'll find a cool Chinese pagoda from the 1600s, a prettily landscaped swimming pool, and a grand California-Asian restaurant, **Yamashiro** (323/466-5125, www.yamashirorestaurant.com, Sun.-Thurs. 5:30pm-9:30pm, Fri. 5:30pm-10:30pm, Sat. 5pm-10:30pm, valet

the wonderful pool at the Hollywood Hills Hotel

parking $9), where a scene from Quentin Tarantino's *Kill Bill* was filmed. Check in at the nearby Magic Castle Hotel, and in the morning partake in that property's continental breakfast. A stay here also includes a ticket to the Magic Castle.

The **Hollywood Celebrity Hotel** (1775 Orchid Ave., 323/850-6464 or 800/222-7017, www.hotelcelebrity.com, $169-229) is a nice budget motel that aspires to Hollywood's famed luxury. Rooms have TVs with HBO and mini-fridges for leftovers, while some have kitchens as well. Amenities include free wired high-speed Internet and a valet laundry service. In the morning, come down to the lobby for a complimentary continental breakfast, and in the evenings take advantage of otherwise hard-to-come-by passes to the nearby **Magic Castle** (7001 Franklin Ave., Hollywood, 323/851-3313, www.magiccastle. com). Leave your car in the gated, off-street parking lot for just $10 per night, which is a deal.

For a nice-priced room in the Hollywood vicinity, stay at the **Hollywood Orchid Suites** (1753 Orchid Ave., 323/874-9678 or 800/537-3052, www.orchidsuites.com, $169-419). The Orchid's location couldn't be better; it's in the Hollywood and Highland Center,

right behind the Chinese Theatre, next door to the Dolby Theatre, and around the corner from Hollywood Boulevard and the Walk of Fame. If you're a film lover or star seeker on a budget, it's tough to do better than this, especially with the inexpensive parking and proximity to public transit. Rooms are actually suites, with plenty of space and an eye toward sleeping your large family or several friends all in the same suite. All suites but the juniors have full kitchens. Don't expect tons of luxury in the furnishings or the decor; it all looks like last decade's motel stuff, although you'll get a coffeemaker, free Wi-Fi, and other better-than-average perks. The rectangular pool offers cooling refreshment in the summer, perfect after a long day of stalking Brad or Britney.

The ★ **Hollywood Hotel** (1160 N. Vermont St., 800/800-9733 or 323/315-1800, www.hollywoodhotel.net, $209-309) is in East Hollywood, near the action. Close to Los Feliz and Griffith Park, the 130 rooms surprise with a handful of unexpected amenities including a complimentary hot breakfast with made-to-order omelets, a sauna, an on-site laundry room, and its own comedy club (Thurs.-Sat.) with nationally known comedians. Other pluses include a sunny pool area and a large

the back entrance of the Hollywood Hotel

gated parking lot. Live like Hollywood royalty for a night by staying in one of the hotel's Jacuzzi suites, which have a large bar and the namesake tub in the room. Ongoing renovations will include opening a rooftop common area with views of downtown Los Angeles in the distance.

BEVERLY HILLS AND WEST HOLLYWOOD

If you want to dive headfirst into the lap of luxury, stay in Beverly Hills. Choose wisely and save up your pennies, and you may get to see how the 1 percent lives. West Hollywood, which serves as L.A.'s gay mecca, offers a wider range of accommodations, including budget options, chain motels, and unique upscale hotels.

$150-250

Comfortable and quiet, the ★ **Élan Hotel** (8435 Beverly Blvd., 323/658-6663, www.elanhotel.com, $189-259) has a great location where Beverly Hills and West Hollywood meet. With its friendly staff, this unassuming hotel makes a fine base for exploring Hollywood attractions and the Sunset Strip. The understated rooms are decorated with soothing abstract art. All have mini-fridges, coffee makers, flat-screen TVs, and iPod docking stations; many rooms have small balconies or porches for a breath of fresh air. Wine and cheese is served every evening and a complimentary continental breakfast is served every morning.

The **Hotel Beverly Terrace** (469 N. Doheny Dr., Beverly Hills, 310/274-8141 or 800/842-6401, www.hotelbeverlyterrace.com, $209-349) is a rare affordable alternative. This spruced-up, retro-cool motor hotel enjoys a great spot on the border of Beverly Hills and West Hollywood. Enjoy one of the 39 recently renovated rooms and lounge in the sun in the garden courtyard or on the rooftop sundeck. In the morning, enjoy a complimentary continental breakfast. The on-site **Trattoria Amici** (310/858-0271) can satisfy your Italian food cravings.

The **Le Montrose Suite Hotel** (900 Hammond St., West Hollywood, 310/855-1115 or 800/776-0666, www.lemontrose.com, $209-399) will give you a taste of the kind of luxury celebrities expect in their accommodations, especially in trendy, gay-friendly West Hollywood. The atmosphere and decor are almost desperately modern, but you'll find lots of plush comfort among the primary colors and plain geometric shapes in your room. A high-end entertainment system sees to your every audio-visual and gaming need, and a gas fireplace provides just the right romantic atmosphere for an evening indoors. Outside your upscale suite, take a dip in the rooftop saltwater swimming pool and whirlpool, play a set on the tennis courts, or get in a good workout inside the fitness center. Hotel guests alone can enjoy the gourmet delicacies of the private dining room or order from 24-hour room service.

Over $250

The Mosaic Hotel (125 Spalding Dr., Beverly Hills, 310/278-0303 or 800/463-4466, www.mosaichotel.com, $415-769) offers a laid-back, urban vibe in both its chill common areas and its comfortable guest accommodations. Rooms are furnished in contemporary fabrics, with soothing light colors blending into attractive wall art and fluffy white down comforters. Mattresses are topped with feather beds, and the baths sparkle and soothe with Frette towels and Bvlgari bath products. If you've got the cash to spring for a suite, you'll be treated to something that feels like your own elegant apartment, with a living room with 42-inch plasma TV, a sofa, and an armchair. Downstairs, a hip bar and small dining room offer top-shelf cocktails and tasty California cuisine. Friendly, helpful staff will serve you tidbits in the bar and can help with any travel or room needs.

The most famous of all the grand hotels of Beverly Hills, the **Beverly Wilshire** (9500 Wilshire Blvd., Beverly Hills, 310/275-5200, www.fourseasons.com, $800-5,000) is now a Four Seasons property. But never fear: The multimillion-dollar renovation didn't scour away all the classic charm of this historic hotel. Nor did it lower the price of the privilege of sleeping inside these hallowed walls. Even the plainest rooms feature exquisite appointments such as 55-inch plasma TVs, elegant linens, and attractive artwork. The presidential suite resembles a European palace, complete with Corinthian columns. With an in-house spa, a dining room, room service, and every other service you could want, folks who can afford it consider a stay at the Beverly Wilshire worth the expense.

In West Hollywood, the **Sunset Tower Hotel** (8358 Sunset Blvd., West Hollywood, 323/654-7100, www.sunsettowerhotel.com, $285-2,500) might look familiar to recent visitors to Disney California Adventure Park. Indeed, its architecture inspired the "Tower of Terror" ride at the amusement park. But there's no terror in the Sunset Tower today. Instead, you'll find a gorgeous art deco exterior and a fully renovated modern interior. Guest accommodations range from smallish standard queen rooms with smooth linens and attractive appointments up to luxurious suites with panoramic views and limestone baths. All rooms include flat-screen TVs, 24-hour room service, and free Wi-Fi.

With architecture like a French castle, **Chateau Marmont** (8221 Sunset Blvd., West Hollywood, 323/656-1010 or 800/242-8328, www.chateaumarmont.com, $550-5,000) looks out on the city from its perch above the Sunset Strip. It has long attracted the in crowd, from Garbo to Leo. It is also where writers from F. Scott Fitzgerald to Hunter S. Thompson have holed up to produce work. The design is eccentric and eclectic, from vintage 1940s suites to Bauhaus bungalows. The hotel was front and center in Sofia Coppola's 2010 film *Somewhere*.

In a section of the Miracle Mile near Hollywood, the **Hotel Wilshire** (6317 Wilshire Blvd., 323/852-6000, www.hotelwilshire.com, $275-500) is close to both cultural attractions like the Los Angeles County Museum of Art and shopping possibilities including Rodeo Drive and The Grove. Upon entering the sleek, modern lobby, you'll know you are in good hands. All of the rooms follow through with down duvets and iPod docking stations. Take in the abundant L.A. sun from within the rooftop pool or while dining at **The Roof on Wilshire** (323/852-6002), a restaurant and bar run by celebrity chef Eric Greenspan.

WESTWOOD
Over $250

A few fancy hotels rise along Westwood's Wilshire Boulevard. Close to attractions including the Getty Museum and UCLA, the **Hotel Palomar Los Angeles-Beverly Hills** (10740 Wilshire Blvd., 310/475-8711, www.hotelpalomar-lawestwood.com, $250-500) is a great place to lay your head if you don't mind throwing down some money. (Actually, you might be able to score a deal at the hotel on weekends, because weekdays the Palomar is filled with business travelers.) In this boutique luxury hotel, the red-glowing elevator and red accents in the rooms are inspired by the lipstick of nearby Hollywood starlets. The hotel's spa suites feature luxurious soaking tubs along with striking views of the sprawling city laid out below. The Hotel Palomar is also just a half mile from the restaurants, bars, and stores of Westwood Village.

SANTA MONICA, VENICE, AND MALIBU

The best place to stay in Los Angeles is down by the beach. It's ironic that you can camp in a park for $25 in exclusive Malibu or pay over $1,000 for a resort room in "working-class" Santa Monica. But whether you choose either of those or a spot in Venice Beach, you'll get some of the best atmosphere in town.

Under $150

For a bed indoors for cheap, your options near the beach run to youth hostels. The huge **HI-Santa Monica** (1436 2nd St., Santa Monica, 310/393-9913, www.hilosangeles.org, dorm beds $49-65, private rooms $140) offers 260 beds in a building constructed specifically to house the hostel. You'll be right in the thick of downtown Santa Monica in a good neighborhood, within walking distance of the Santa Monica Pier, the Third Street Promenade, the beach, and good restaurants. This ritzy hostel offers tons of amenities for the price, including a computer room, a TV room, a movie room, excursions, wheelchair access, sheets included with the bed price, and even a complimentary continental breakfast every morning. The local public transit system runs right outside the door.

The **Samesun Venice Beach** (25 Windward Ave., Venice, 310/399-7649 or 888/718-8287, www.venicebeachcotel.com, dorm beds $39-45, private rooms $110-175) provides inexpensive lodging steps from the sand in the midst of Venice Beach. Serviceable options for budget travelers run from dorm beds with shared baths to private rooms. Amenities include linens, pillows, and a full kitchen facility, although this is the kind of place that you really want to use just for sleep—which can be a challenge, since some of the rooms are right above a loud bar. All guests must show a valid passport upon checking in, even if they are U.S. citizens.

$150-250

The reasonably priced and fantastically fun **Custom Hotel** (8639 Lincoln Blvd., 310/645-0400, www.jdvhotels.com, $179-220) is south of Venice near LAX. The in-room Wi-Fi is free, as are the views of the city. You'll find the staff incredibly friendly and helpful, ready to help with anything from valet parking to dinner reservations. Fear not if you're seeking food and drink and would rather not leave the hotel: Custom Hotel has six social lounges, each with its own concept, including the VIP lounge-inspired LAX Lounge; the Transonic gaming lounge; the Axis Annex art gallery; and the Duty Free vending machine room. There are places throughout the hotel to relax while gathering with others to share ideas. Want a little more? Try out **DECK 33 Bar Restaurant** (310/258-5706), featuring Pacific

Rim-influenced cuisine and overlooking the sundeck and pool. Less unique but crucial, the Custom offers complimentary shuttle buses to nearby LAX.

The **Venice Beach Suites & Hotel** (1305 Ocean Front Walk, 310/396-4559 or 888/877-7602, www.venicebeachsuites.com, $209-329) is a surprisingly lovely and affordable little Venice hotel. It sits right on the beach, but it's far enough from the Boardwalk to acquire a touch of peace and quiet. Stroll over to Washington Boulevard to grab a meal or a cup of coffee, or just wander out of the lobby and straight onto the beach. Inside, the rooms and suites all have mini-kitchens so you can cook for yourself, which is perfect for budget-conscious travelers and folks staying in Venice for several days. The decor is cuter than that of an average motel; you might find exposed brick walls and polished hardwood floors stocked with rattan furniture and appealing accessories. Two common-area balconies and a rooftop deck let guests take in the beach scene.

For a charming hotel experience only a block from the ever-energetic Boardwalk, stay at the **Inn at Venice Beach** (327 Washington Blvd., 310/821-2557 or 800/828-0688, www.innatvenicebeach.com, $299-369). The attractive orange-and-brown exterior, complete with a lovely bricked interior courtyard-cum-café, makes all guests feel welcome. Inside, you might be surprised by the brightly colored modern furniture and decor. Common spaces are done in a blocky postmodern style, while the rooms pop with brilliant yellows and vibrant accents. The two-story boutique hotel offers 45 rooms, and its location on Washington Boulevard makes it a perfect base from which to enjoy the best restaurants of Venice. Start each day with a complimentary continental breakfast, either in the dining room or outside in the Courtyard Café. There's complimentary Wi-Fi throughout.

There's always a trade-off for moderate rates in a high-priced area. At **The M Malibu** (22541 Pacific Coast Highway, Malibu, 310/456-6169, www.themmotel.com, $159-259), you get a basic room with thin walls.

But your room might have a partial ocean view and you can walk to Malibu businesses, including restaurants. This small motel with just 18 rooms has units with wood floors, TVs with HBO, and balconies. Ask for a room on the second or third floor; those are the ones with a view of the ocean.

Over $250

There's probably no hotel in Venice Beach that is a better reflection of the edgy beach town's attitude than ★ **Hotel Erwin** (1697 Pacific Ave., 800/786-7789, www.hotelerwin.com, $280-700). Situated just feet from the Venice Boardwalk and Muscle Beach, Hotel Erwin has graffiti art adorning the outside wall by its entrance and in some of its rooms. The rooms all have balconies and playful decor including lamps resembling the barbells used by the weightlifters at nearby Muscle Beach. Sitting atop the hotel is **High,** a rooftop bar that allows you to take in all the action of the bustling boardwalk while sipping a cocktail. The staff is laid-back, genial, and accommodating. Parking is a nightmare in Venice Beach during the summer, but a stay at the Erwin includes complimentary valet parking, a major plus.

Yes, you really can stay at the **Hotel California** (1670 Ocean Ave., Santa Monica, 310/393-2363 or 866/571-0000, www.hotelca. com/losangeles, $309-369). Appropriately decorated with classic longboards and electric guitars, this midrange hotel sits a short block from the beach and next to the Santa Monica Pier. You'll be in the perfect spot to enjoy all the best of Santa Monica without ever having to get into a car or worry about finding parking. Inside the hotel, you'll find hardwood floors and matching bedsteads, calming pale-yellow walls, and white comforters and linens. Choose between a classic room and a suite with a jetted tub. Outside, enjoy the lush greenery of the oddly named Spanish Courtyard, which looks more like something from the tropics than from Europe. Other perks include free Wi-Fi and a mini-fridge.

One of the best-known resort hotels at the beach in L.A. has long been **Shutters on the Beach** (1 Pico Blvd., Santa Monica, 310/458-0030, www.shuttersonthebeach. com, $695-1,140). Make no mistake: You'll pay handsomely for the privilege of laying your head on one of Shutters' hallowed pillows. On the other hand, the gorgeous, airy rooms will make you feel like you're home, or at least staying at the home you'd have if you could hire a famous designer to decorate for you. Even the most modest rooms have not only the comfortable beds, white linens, plasma TVs, and oversize bathtubs of a luxury hotel, but also a comfortable clutter of pretty ornaments on tables and shelves. Head down to the famed lobby for a drink and a people-watching session. Get a reservation for the elegant **One Pico** (310/587-1717) or grab a more casual sandwich or salad at beachside **Coast** (310/587-1717).

The impressive multilevel resort edifice sits right on the beach, so there's no need to find a premium parking spot to enjoy a day in the sand. Book a massage at the **ONE Spa** (310/587-1712). Art lovers can spend hours just wandering the halls of the hotel, examining the works of many famous modern photographers and painters.

PASADENA

Pasadena lodgings run to the old standard national chains plus a few funky 1950s-era motor lodges and the occasional upscale B&B. If you're planning to stay in Pasadena over the New Year, book early: The town fills up for the legendary Rose Parade. If your aim is to get yourself a room from which you can watch the Rose Parade, book earlier still: Such places are at a premium during parade season.

Under $150

The top pick of the quaint motor inns is the **Saga Motor Hotel** (1633 E. Colorado Blvd., 626/795-0431 or 800/793-7242, www.the-sagamotorhotel.com, $80-135). Outside it's all 1950s, including the structure of the low buildings. The ambience extends to the door of your room, which includes a doorknob and an actual metal key to open it with. But inside your room, the decor gets a lot more contemporary. The big space has either a king or two double beds, clean (if worn) carpeting and linens, and a nice bath with a surprisingly good bathtub and nice hot showers. Location-wise, the Saga is right on the Rose Parade route on broad Colorado Boulevard, but it's not right downtown or in Old Town. Sadly, the service is spotty at best, but few people expect concierges at motor hotels.

Of the main chain motels, the best inexpensive one might be the **Comfort Inn** (2462 E. Colorado Blvd., 626/405-0811, www.comfortinn.com, $120). You'll find comfortable amenities in pleasant standard motel rooms, along with a good set of views of the Rose Parade. Expect room prices to skyrocket for the parade.

$150-250

Once upon a time, Pasadena was the resort haven of wealthy East Coasters. To revisit this wealthy past, stay at **The Bissell House Bed & Breakfast** (201 Orange Grove Ave., 626/441-3535 or 800/441-3530, www.bissellhouse.com, $199-350) on "Millionaire's Row." The tall mint-green Victorian, surrounded by the deeper green of lush mature landscaping, opens its doors to well-heeled travelers who want a luxurious place to stay while they're in the L.A. area. It is named for one of its residents, Anna Bissell McCay, heiress to the original Bissell vacuum-cleaner fortune. Each of the five rooms and two suites has a unique decorating scheme, yet they share a European floral theme that binds the inn together into a coherent whole. Rooms have comfy beds, a luxurious bath (most have claw-foot tubs), and lots of wonderful amenities, and the property has a swimming pool with a hot tub and lots of lovely plants scattered about. Your room rate includes a full breakfast each morning, served at the long table in the downstairs dining room.

Food

Whatever kind of food you prefer, from fresh sushi to Armenian, you can probably find it in a cool little hole-in-the-wall somewhere in L.A. Local recommendations often make for the best dining experiences, but even just walking down the right street can yield a tasty meal.

DOWNTOWN AND VICINITY

Sure, you can find plenty of bland, tourist-friendly restaurants serving American and Americanized food in the Downtown area—but why would you, when one of Downtown L.A.'s greatest strengths is its ethnic diversity and the great range of cuisine that goes along with it? An endless array of fabulous holes-in-the-wall awaits you. Getting local recommendations is the best way to find the current hot spots, or choose from among this tiny sampling of what's available.

Classic American

Get a good pastrami sandwich at **Langer's Delicatessen and Restaurant** (704 S. Alvarado St., 213/483-8050, www.langersdeli.com, Mon.-Sat. 8am-4pm, $12-25). Operating continuously since 1947, the house specialty at Langer's is a hot pastrami sandwich that some say is the best in the world (yes, that includes New York City). Whether you're willing to go that far or not, Langer's serves both hot and cold dishes in the traditional Jewish deli style to satisfy any appetite level or specific craving. Granted, it's still California, so you can get fresh avocado on your tongue sandwich if you really want to. You'll also find a vast breakfast menu and plenty of desserts (noodle kugel, anyone?). Take a look at the photos on the walls; the family you'll see has run this deli since it opened in the postwar era. You can also order in advance and pick up your meal curbside.

Gastropubs

Worth seeking out, **The Black Sheep** (126 E. 6th St., 213/689-5022, Sun. and Tues.-Thurs. 6pm-midnight, Fri.-Sat. 6pm-1am, $4-8) has a small menu that focuses on sausages, house-blended beef burgers, creative tater tots, and Asian-influenced pub food like *bánh-mì* sliders. Enjoy this new-school pub food with one of the eatery's fine microbrews. This small space has booths and tables lit by candlelight, and an outdoor seating section (expect a constant parade of panhandlers if you sit outside).

As its name makes clear, **Beer Belly** (532 S. Western Ave., 213/387-2337, www.beerbellyla.com, Mon.-Tues. 5pm-11pm, Wed.-Thurs. 5pm-midnight, Fri. 5pm-1am, Sat. noon-1am, Sun. noon-11pm, $9-21) in Koreatown is not the place for people who are watching their weight. Start with the popular duck fat fries and then order a California craft beer for fortification as you try to take down the quadruple-decker grilled cheese sandwich with smoked bacon and maple syrup. Finish the meal with a deep-fried Pop-Tart—and vow to eat nothing but salads for the rest of the week.

Greek

Originally a Greek import company in the 1960s, the **Papa Cristos Taverna** (2771 W. Pico Blvd., 323/737-2970, www.papacristos.com, Tues. 9:30am-3pm, Wed.-Sat. 9:30am-8pm, Sun. 9am-4pm, $9-22) restaurant opened in the 1990s. The import shop still supplies the local Greek community with hard-to-come-by delicacies, which also become ingredients in the cuisine at the Taverna. Dishes are traditionally Greek, from the salads to the kebabs to the baba ghanoush. After you're finished with your meal, wander the aisles of the store to pick up a few unusual Greek delicacies to take with you.

Italian

It seems odd to name a high-end restaurant after a decidedly low-end bug, but that's what the owners of **Cicada Restaurant** (617 S. Olive St., 213/488-9488, www.cicadarestaurant.com, Wed.-Sat. 5:30pm-9pm, $24-42) did. Set in the 1920s Oviatt building, decorated in high French art deco style, the beautiful restaurant glitters with some of its original Lalique glass panels—check out the elevator doors. The palatial dining room features huge round tables for large parties and balcony seating for intimate duos. The immense space lets Cicada place its tables farther apart than in most restaurants, giving diners a sense of privacy and romance. The cuisine fuses Italian concepts with California ingredients, techniques, and presentations. Expect a varied seasonal menu of inventive dishes, including pastas and meats. Save room for dessert.

Bestia (2121 7th Pl., 213/514-5724, www.bestiala.com, Sun.-Thurs. 5pm-11pm, Fri.-Sat. 5pm-midnight, $16-140) is drawing adventurous diners and drinkers to the Arts District for its Italian food and raved-about cocktails. The drink menu includes a white Negroni and an old-fashioned made with salami-infused bourbon. Food ranges from pizza to a whopping 39-ounce rib eye for $140 (though most entrées are closer to $20). The space is appropriately industrial for its Arts District location and includes an outdoor patio.

Japanese

For a serious authentic Japanese cuisine experience, visit ★ **Kagaya** (418 E. 2nd St., 213/617-1016, Tues.-Sat. 6pm-10:30pm, Sun. 6pm-10pm, $47-128). Even L.A. denizens who've eaten at shabu-shabu places in Japan come back to Kagaya again and again. They make reservations in advance, because the dining room is small and the quality of the food makes it popular even on weeknights. The term *shabu-shabu* refers to paper-thin slices of beef and vegetable that you dip and swish into a pot of boiling *daishi* (broth), then dunk in *ponzu* or other house-made sauces before eating. The shabu-shabu is but one course in the meal you'll get at Kagaya, since all meals include several appetizers (varieties change daily), shabu-shabu with beef and seafood, udon noodles, and dessert. Pay a premium for Wagyu beef if you choose, but the king crab legs (in season) are part of the regular price of dinner. Even the regular beef isn't cheap, but the quality makes it worth the price. Sit at the counter if you want to watch all your food be prepared before your eyes.

There are lots of ramen places in Little Tokyo, but busy, noisy **Daikokuya** (327 E. 1st St., 213/626-1680, www.daikoku-ten. com, Mon.-Thurs. 11am-midnight, Fri.-Sat. 11am-1am, Sun. 11am-11pm, $8-17) is among the best, hailed by no less an authority than Pulitzer Prize-winning food writer Jonathan Gold. The steaming bowls of hearty pork broth and noodles satisfy even the brawniest appetite.

Korean

It's only fitting that a city with such a large Korean population has plenty of good Korean restaurants. One of these is **Chunju Han-il Kwan** (3450 W. 6th St., 213/480-1799, Mon.-Sat. 11am-11pm, Sun. 11am-10pm, $10-30), a casual restaurant in a strip mall with gas burners on the tables that caters primarily to the Korean expat community. You may not find English menus, but you will find helpful wait staff that can guide you through the process of ordering. If your server says a dish is spicy, she means it, but that doesn't mean you won't love it anyway. The menu is eclectic: You can get a hot dog, octopus, fish soup, Korean stew (thickened with American cheese), kimchi, and much more.

Markets

In operation since 1917, the **Grand Central Market** (317 S. Broadway, 213/624-2378, www.grandcentralmarket.com, Sun.-Wed. 8am-6pm, Thurs.-Sat. 8am-9pm) houses dozens of food vendors. Most sell hot prepared foods, but you'll also find stalls selling spices and Latino pantry goods. Enjoy a burger from Belcampo Meat Co., carne asada from Tacos Tumbras a Tomas, some Thai barbecued chicken from Sticky Rice, or an egg sandwich from the provocatively named Eggslut.

Mexican

La Luz del Dia (1 W. Olvera St., 213/628-7495, www.luzdeldia.com, Mon. 11am-3:30pm, Tues.-Thurs. 10am-8pm, Fri.-Sat. 10am-9pm, Sun. 8:30am-9pm, $7-10) has been dishing up simple, spicy Mexican food in a cafeteria-like setting since 1959. Order a combination plate with delicious homemade corn tortillas and watch the Olvera Street tourists go by.

LOS FELIZ, SILVER LAKE, AND ECHO PARK
Coffee and Tea

The baristas at **Intelligentsia** (3922 Sunset Blvd., 323/663-6173, www.intelligentsiacoffee.com, Sun.-Wed. 6am-8pm, Thurs.-Sat. 6am-11pm) are true artisans, pulling shots and steaming milk with cultish reverence. Many of the beans are direct-trade and shade-grown. Linger on the lovely patio, paved with gorgeous blue tiles imported from Nicaragua. It's a favorite of celebrities, so if you think that's Drew Barrymore getting a coffee, it probably is.

Contemporary

French fries in origami bags. Toasters on every table. Dishes with names like Bearded Mr. Frenchy and farm-to-table dinners named after sitcoms. Everything plays into the love-it-or-leave-it hip factor at **Fred 62** (1850 N. Vermont Ave., 323/667-0062, www. fred62.com, daily 24 hours, $7-15), where the booths feel like old Chevy backseats and everyone's a garage-band star. The hip eatery hosts many celebrities and was featured in a recent Prince video.

French

The ★ **Taix French Restaurant** (1911 W. Sunset Blvd., 213/484-1265, http://taix-french.com, Mon.-Thurs. 11:30am-10pm, Fri. 11:30am-11pm, Sat. noon-11pm, Sun. noon-10pm, $13-34) in Echo Park has been serving superb French cuisine in a dimly lit old-world setting since 1927. The menu includes nightly dishes like roast chicken and frog legs Provençal as well as recurring

Follow That Food Truck!

Some of Los Angeles's most interesting and tasty food is not coming from upscale restaurants with tables draped in white linens; a lot of the city's best culinary creations are being served out of food trucks. Gourmet chefs can follow their dreams with little overhead, and the result is some of the L.A. food scene's most blogged-about bites. There is even an **LA Street Food Fest** (Rose Bowl, 1001 Rose Bowl Dr., http://lastreetfoodfest.com, July, general $60, VIP $90) held annually at the Rose Bowl due to the rise of this foodie phenomenon. Websites including **Find LA Food Trucks** (www.findlafoodtrucks.com) and **Roaming Hunger** (http://roaminghunger.com) have sprung up to help you find some of your roving favorites.

One of the early food truck favorites that is still going strong is **Kogi BBQ** (twitter @kogibbq, http://kogibbq.com). Kogi serves a hybrid of Mexican and Korean food with items that include kimchi quesadillas and short-rib tacos.

The owner of **The Grilled Cheese Truck** (twitter @grlldcheesetruk, www.thegrilledcheese-truck.com) was inspired to start a truck selling grilled cheeses after he entered the Annual Grilled Cheese Invitational at the Rose Bowl and realized how many people loved this basic sandwich. His famous item is the cheesy mac and rib, which has barbecued pork tucked into the grilled cheese.

The **Green Truck** (twitter @GreenTruck, 310/204-0477, http://greentruckonthego.com) rolls around L.A. on veggie-oil fuel, and the kitchen is solar powered. The menu is full of healthy organic items including a vegan burger and a kale bowl, but they also have a grass-fed chipotle cheeseburger to sate carnivores.

weekly soups and entrées. Enjoy live music or comedy during your dinner at the on-site **321 Lounge.**

Mediterranean

Los Angeles is a hotbed of hybrid culture and cuisine, so why not have a small, city-based chain that does Mediterranean street food, craft beer, and sangria in a hip, casual atmosphere? ★ **Spitz** (1725 Hillhurst Ave., 323/522-3309, www.eatatspitz.com, Sun.-Thurs. 11am-10pm, Wed.-Thurs. 11am-11pm, Fri.-Sat. 11am-midnight, $8.50-12) in Los Feliz wraps lots of flavor and texture into its doner kebabs including the favorite Street Cart Doner, a tight and tasty roll of meat, fried lavash chips, chopped veggies, garlic aioli, and tzatziki. They also have locations in Little Tokyo (371 E. 2nd St., 213/613-0101, Sun.-Wed. 11am-10pm, Thurs. 11am-11pm, Fri.-Sat. 11am-midnight), Eagle Rock (2506 Colorado Blvd., 323/257-5600, daily 11am-10pm), and Studio City (3737 Cahuenga Blvd., 818/755-0400, Mon.-Thurs. and Sun. 11am-10pm, Fri.-Sat. 11am-11pm).

Mexican

Not every taco stand wins awards from the James Beard Foundation. **Yuca's** (2056 Hillhurst Ave., 323/662-1214, www.yucasla.com, Mon.-Sat. 11am-6pm, $6-12) received the honor in 2005, but that only confirmed what Los Feliz locals have known for decades: This shack serves truly memorable (and cheap) tacos and burritos. Vegetarians beware: Even the beans are made with pork fat. They have expanded into Hollywood with a new location (4666 Hollywood Blvd., 323/661-0523, Mon.-Sat. 8am-9pm, Sun. 10am-4pm).

In the nearby enclave of Eagle Rock, the ★ **Cacao Mexicatessan** (1576 Colorado Blvd., 323/478-2791, www.cacaodeli.com, Tues.-Thurs. 11am-9pm, Fri.-Sat. 8:30am-10pm, Sun. 8:30am-8pm, $4-23) is definitely worth the short trip a few miles east. Frequently praised by the *LA Weekly*, this specialty deli/taqueria/wine bar has a unique menu that includes the beloved duck confit tacos, fig mole poblano, and cochinta pibil (spicy, juicy shredded pork). Expect to wait awhile in line to order and then at a table or the bar for your food. Consider one of the superb aqua frescas, a craft beer, or a wine cocktail as your hunger grows. Don't worry; it's worth the wait.

Pizza

Two Boots (1818 W. Sunset Blvd., 213/413-2668, http://la.twoboots.com, Mon.-Wed. 4pm-midnight, Thurs. noon-2am, Fri.-Sat. noon-2:30am, Sun. noon-midnight, $5-20) dishes out pizza slices and pies late into the night. It's a perfect place to stop in for a casual bite before or after seeing a show at the nearby Echo. One favorite is the Night Tripper, with sun-dried tomatoes, roasted garlic, and jalapeño pesto on a whole-wheat crust. Two Boots has outposts in other hipster-heavy spots like New York City, Baltimore, and Nashville.

Thai

Routinely topping critics' lists of the best Thai restaurants in Los Angeles, elegant **Jitlada** (5233 W. Sunset Blvd., 323/667-9809, www.jitladala.com, Tues.-Sun. 11am-3pm and 5pm-10:30pm, $10-30) specializes in the cuisine of southern Thailand, which is rarely seen on U.S. menus. *LA Weekly* food writer Jonathan Gold once proclaimed that Jitlada offered "the spiciest food you can eat in Los Angeles at the moment."

Vegan

Run by a true Renaissance woman—who is a spoken word poet, filmmaker, and chef—**Sage** (1700 W. Sunset Blvd., 213/989-1718, www.sageveganbistro.com, Mon.-Fri. 11am-11pm, Sat.-Sun. 9am-4pm and 5pm-11pm, $12-15) keeps Echo Park's hipsters healthy with organic, plant-based cuisine. Order tempura-battered avocado tacos, housemade veggie burgers, flavorful veggie bowls, or butternut squash ravioli at the counter and then wait for your order at a table. Food this healthy means you can justify a scoop of gelato after your meal. There are also locations in Culver City (4130 Sepulveda Blvd., 424/228-5835, Mon.-Fri. 11am-11pm, Sat.-Sun. 9am-11pm) and Pasadena (319 S. Arroyo Parkway, 877/985-5463, Mon.-Sat. 11am-10pm, Sun. 11am-8pm).

HOLLYWOOD

Hollywood's got just as many tasty treats tucked away in strip malls as other areas of Los Angeles. If you want to rub elbows with rock stars, you're likely to find yourself at a big, slightly raunchy bar and grill. For a chance at glimpsing stars of the silver screen, look for upscale California cuisine or perhaps a high-end sushi bar. If all you need is tasty

a wrap at Spitz

sustenance, you can choose from a range of restaurants.

Brazilian

Need food really, really, *really* late? **Bossa Nova** (7181 W. Sunset Blvd., 323/436-7999, www.bossanovafood.com, Sun.-Wed. 11am-3:30am, Thurs.-Sat. 11am-4am, $10-20) can hook you up. A big menu of inexpensive entrées can satisfy any appetite from lunch to way past dinnertime at Bossa. Some of the dishes bear the spicy flavors of the owners' home country of Brazil, but you'll also find a ton of pastas, plenty of salads, and classic Italian-American build-your-own pizzas. Check out the desserts for some South American specialties if you need sweets after a long night out at the clubs. Not near the Sunset Strip? Bossa Nova has two other L.A. locations: one at 685 North Robertson Boulevard (310/657-5070, Mon.-Thurs. 11am-11:30pm, Fri.-Sat. 11am-3:30am, Sun. 11am-midnight) and one in West L.A. at 10982 West Pico Boulevard (310/441-0404, Sun.-Thurs. 11am-1am, Fri.-Sat. 11am-3:30am). If you've made it back to your hotel room and aren't inclined to leave again, Bossa delivers.

Breakfast

If you're a flapjack fan, a trip to Hollywood should include a breakfast at ★ **The Griddle Café** (7916 Sunset Blvd., 323/874-0377, www.thegriddlecafe.com, Mon.-Fri. 7am-4pm, Sat.-Sun. 8am-4pm, $11-30). This hectic, loud breakfast joint serves up creations like a red velvet pancake and a pancake with brown sugar-baked bananas in a buttermilk batter. For those who prefer savory to sweet, the Griddle has delicious breakfast tacos and a Cobb omelet with all the fixings of a Cobb salad except the lettuce. With the Director's Guild of America building next door, The Griddle Café is also a place where you may spot a celebrity.

Classic American

On the casual end of the spectrum, **Pink's Famous Hot Dogs** (709 N. La Brea Ave., 323/931-4223, www.pinkshollywood.com, Sun.-Thurs. 9:30am-2am, Fri.-Sat. 9:30am-3am, $3.50-7) is hot dog heaven. Frankophiles line up at this roadside stand (lit up like a Las Vegas show club into the wee hours of the morning) for variations on a sausage in a bun that range from the basic chili dog to the more elaborate Martha Stewart Dog. It has been at the same location since 1939.

Gastropub

A playful California take on British pub food, **The Pikey** (7617 Sunset Blvd., 323/850-5400, www.thepikeyla.com, Mon.-Fri. 11:45am-2am, Sat.-Sun. 11am-2am, $15-32) has a sense of humor. One of their cocktails is named the Divine Brown for the prostitute that actor Hugh Grant was caught with on this same city block back in 1995. The dinner menu is divided into small plates and large plates. The buttery burger with cheddar and Worcestershire aioli is a highlight. It can get loud and crowded at dinnertime. Happy hour (daily 4pm-7pm) offers well cocktails at half price.

Italian

The warm but clamorous dining room at **Pizzeria Mozza** (641 N. Highland Ave., 323/297-0101, www.pizzeriamozza.com, daily noon-midnight, $11-29) has been packed since chef Nancy Silverton, founder of La Brea Bakery, opened the doors in 2006. The wood-fired oven turns out rustic, blistered pizzas with luxurious toppings. Reservations are tough to get, but bar seats are available for walk-ins.

Just as smashingly popular (and as raucous) as Pizzeria Mozza is the chef's Italian restaurant next door, **Osteria Mozza** (6602 Melrose Ave., 323/297-0100, www.osteriamozza.com, Mon.-Fri. 5:30pm-11pm, Sat. 5pm-11pm, Sun. 5pm-10pm, $19-38). Serving more than just pizza, the Osteria offers a fuller menu of luscious pastas and adventurous meat dishes. Check out the "mozzarella bar menu," an assortment of appetizer-size dishes featuring *bufala, burrata,* and ricotta.

LA BREA, FAIRFAX, AND MIRACLE MILE

California Cuisine

Pairing meat and potatoes with a retro-clubby dining room, **Jar** (8225 Beverly Blvd., 323/655-6566, www.thejar.com, Mon.-Thurs. 5:30pm-9:30pm, Fri.-Sat. 5:30pm-11pm, Sun. 10am-2pm and 5:30pm-10pm, $21-49) puts a Southern California spin on the traditional steak house. Meats and grilled fishes are served à la carte with your choice of sauce, and the side orders serve two. Jar is also known for its Sunday brunch; try the lobster Benedict. On Sundays, order a burger for $15 from the bar, while Monday nights feature lobster.

Deli

Midnight snackers unhinge their jaws on the hulking corned beef sandwiches at **Canter's Deli** (419 N. Fairfax Ave., 323/651-2030, www.cantersdeli.com, daily 24 hours, $12-18), in the heart of the Jewish Fairfax district. They also do burgers, deli melts, triple-decker sandwiches, and hearty dinner entrées. This venerable 24-hour deli also boasts its share of star sightings, so watch for noshing rock stars in the wee hours of the morning.

Lunch doesn't get much better than the high-end bounty in the deli cases at **Joan's on Third** (8350 W. 3rd St., 323/655-2285, www.joansonthird.com, Mon.-Sat. 8am-8pm, Sun. 8am-7pm, $10-15). Mix and match fine sandwiches, roasted vegetables, and artisanal cheeses. There are also sidewalk tables, and a breakfast kitchen serving organic eggs and French toast.

New American

With items including crispy pig head, veal brains, and bone marrow, **Animal** (435 N. Fairfax Ave., 323/782-9225, Sun.-Thurs. 6pm-11pm, Fri.-Sat. 6pm-midnight, $18-47) is a hot restaurant for foodies. They serve adventurous dishes like a foie gras take on the Hawaiian dish loco moco with a quail egg, Spam, and hamburger. The Hamachi tostada is frequently raved about.

BEVERLY HILLS AND WEST HOLLYWOOD

Between Beverly Hills and West L.A. you'll find an eclectic choice of restaurants. Unsurprisingly, Beverly Hills tends toward high-end eateries serving European and haute California cuisine. On the other hand, West L.A. boasts a wide array of international restaurants. You'll have to try a few to pick your favorites, since every local has their own take on the area's best eats.

Burgers

Here's a win for the little guy. **Irv's Burgers** (7998 Santa Monica Blvd., 323/650-2456, Mon.-Fri. 7:30am-8pm, Sat. 8am-7pm, $3-7) lost its lease in 2014 on its unassuming shack that it had occupied since 1950. In its earlier days, everyone from Jimi Hendrix to Shelly Winters was known to dine here. Luckily, the family that owns Irv's found a new spot, so folks can still enjoy their tasty burgers and hand-cut french fries.

Brazilian

There's nothing like a good steak dinner, Brazilian style. At **Fogo de Chao** (133 N. La Cienega Blvd., Beverly Hills, 310/289-7755, www.fogodechao.com, Mon.-Thurs. 11:30am-2pm and 5pm-10pm, Fri. 11:30am-2pm and 5pm-10:30pm, Sat. 4:30pm-10:30pm, Sun. 11:30am-2pm and 4pm-9:30pm, lunch $15-34, dinner $25-50), be prepared for an interactive dining experience. The meat is slow roasted, then skewered and cut right onto your plate by ever-moving servers. Use the red-and-green token on your table; if you don't turn it over to the red side occasionally, you will be continuously bombarded with the 15 different kinds of meat the restaurant offers. The fixed-price meal includes endless trips to the salad bar, fresh-cut veggies, and traditional Brazilian side dishes (fried bananas are a starch, not a dessert). The extensive wine list includes plenty of both California and European vintages, plus a wider-than-average selection of ports and dessert wines.

Coffee and Tea

A grand afternoon tea in stately Beverly Hills just seems like the right thing to do at least once. Get some of the best tea in L.A. at **The Living Room in The Peninsula Hotel** (9882 Santa Monica Blvd., Beverly Hills, 310/975-2736, www.peninsula.com, seatings daily noon, 2:30pm, and 5pm, $18-45). The Peninsula has three restaurants, but for tea head to the elegant Living Room and grab a comfy chair near the fireplace. Sit back and enjoy the delicate harp music while admiring the elegant and tasteful furnishings in this upscale space. If you skipped lunch or plan to miss dinner, go with the heartier Royal Tea or Imperial Tea. Lighter eaters prefer the Full Tea or the Light Tea. All come with tea sandwiches, scones, pastries, and, of course, a pot of tea. The loose-leaf teas are Peninsula originals; many are flavored. For an extra fee, add a glass of champagne to complete your high tea experience. Dress is business casual. Don't show up in jeans, flip-flops, or a T-shirt.

Italian

If you're looking for upscale Italian cuisine in a classy environment, enjoy lunch or dinner at **Il Pastaio Restaurant** (400 N. Canon Dr., Beverly Hills, 310/205-5444, www.giacominodrago.com, Mon.-Thurs. 11:30am-11pm, Fri.-Sat. 11:30am-midnight, Sun. 11:30am-10pm, $17-35). The bright dining room offers a sunny luncheon experience, and the white tablecloths and shiny glassware lend an elegance to dinner, served reasonably late into the evening even on weekdays. Boasting a large menu for a high-end restaurant, Il Pastaio offers a wide variety of salads, risotto, and pasta dishes as well as some overpriced antipasti and a smaller list of entrées. Preparations and dishes evoke authentic Italy, so you might see osso buco or fettuccine Bolognese on the menu. Go for broke with the six-course chef's tasting menu ($65). The blue-painted bar offers a tasteful selection of California and Italian vintages, and serious wine lovers will be pleased to see the Italian selections broken out by region.

Seafood

With a roof that resembles a giant ray gliding through the sea, **Connie and Ted's** (8171 Santa Monica Blvd., 323/848-2722, www.connieandteds.com, Mon.-Tues. 4pm-10pm, Wed.-Sat. 11:30am-11pm, Sun. 11:30am-10pm, $12-44) brings the fruit of the sea to West Hollywood. The menu is inspired by New England clam shacks, oyster bars, and fish houses and includes a raw bar of oysters and clams. A West Coast influence creeps in on items like the smoked albacore starter, lobster rolls, and a Mexican shrimp dish.

Tapas

★ **AOC** (8700 W. 3rd St., 310/859-9859, www.aocwinebar.com, Mon. 11:30am-10pm, Tues.-Fri. 11:30am-11pm, Sat. 10am-11pm, Sun. 10am-10pm, $14-88) is wildly popular with Angelenos for three reasons: breakfast, lunch, and dinner. Breakfast is served until 3pm and includes fried chicken and cornmeal waffles along with house-made corned beef hash as another option. Lunch features focaccia sandwiches, salads, and plate lunches. At dinner, go small (fig and prosciutto flatbread) or very big (a whole roasted chicken or whole grilled fish). Sample from an acclaimed wine list and creative cocktails (including *LA Weekly*'s choice for the alcoholic drink of the year).

SANTA MONICA, VENICE, AND MALIBU

Yes, there's lots of junky beach food to be found in Santa Monica and Venice Beach, but there are also amazing gems hiding in these towns.

Caribbean

How can you not love a restaurant called **Cha Cha Chicken** (1906 Ocean Ave., Santa Monica, 310/581-1684, www.chachachicken.com, Mon.-Fri. 11am-10pm, Sat.-Sun. 10am-10pm, $7-12)? It looks just like it sounds—a slightly decrepit but brightly painted shack only a short walk from the Santa Monica Pier and the Third Street Promenade. You can't miss it even if you're driving quickly down

Ocean Avenue. The best place to get a table is definitely the palm tree-strewn patio area outdoors. It's the perfect atmosphere to enjoy the wonderful and inexpensive Caribbean dishes that come from the fragrant kitchen. The jerk dishes bring a tangy sweetness to the table, while the *ropa vieja* heats up the plate, and the funky enchiladas put a whole new spin on a Mexican classic. Salads, sandwiches, and wraps are popular with lighter eaters and the lunch crowd. Quaff an imported Jamaican soda or a seasonal *agua fresca* with your meal, since Cha Cha Chicken doesn't have a liquor license.

Contemporary

Cora's Coffee Shoppe (1802 Ocean Ave., Santa Monica, 310/451-9562, www. corascoffee.com, Tues.-Sat. 7am-10pm, Sun.-Mon. 7am-3pm, dinner $14) doesn't look like much: It's a tiny building with a smallish, old-fashioned diner sign. But don't be fooled by the unpretentious exterior. The small, exquisite restaurant inside is a locals' secret hiding in plain sight, serving breakfast, lunch, and dinner to diners who are more than willing to pack into the miniscule spaces, including the two tiny marble-topped tables and miniature marble counter inside, and a small patio area screened by latticework and venerable bougainvillea vines. The chefs use high-end and sometimes organic ingredients to create typical breakfast and lunch dishes with a touch of the unexpected. The dinner menu includes short rib tacos and all kinds of burgers (including turkey and veggie).

An unpretentious eatery is **Blue Plate** (1415 Montana Ave., Santa Monica, 310/260-8877, www.blueplatesantamonica.com, daily 8am-9pm, $9-20). This sleek diner with a clean blue-and-white decor serves the basics: salads, sandwiches, and wraps. While the cuisine includes a mac and cheese pancake, Blue Plate's tasty menu items are usually healthy. There is also an expanded menu for dinner that includes tacos, seafood, and steak. The dining room is small and loud; you may be inches away from another table.

Italian

The ★ **C&O Trattoria** (31 Washington Blvd., Marina del Rey, 310/823-9491, www.cotrattoria.com, Sun.-Thurs. 11:30am-10pm, Fri.-Sat. 11:30am-11pm, $13-23) manages to live up to its hype and then some. Sit outside in the big outdoor dining room, enjoying the mild weather and the soft pastel frescoes on the exterior walls surrounding the courtyard. C&O is known for its self-described gargantuan portions, which are best-shared family-style among a group of diners. Start off with the addictive little garlic rolls. Your attentive but not overzealous server can help you choose from the creative pasta list; the rigatoni al forno is a standout. While C&O has a nice wine list, it's worth trying out the house chianti, where you get to serve yourself on an honor system.

Seafood

Situated on the Malibu coastline adjacent to the County Line surf break, ★ **Neptune's Net** (42505 Pacific Coast Hwy., Malibu, 310/457-3095, www.neptunesnet.com, summer Mon.-Thurs. 10:30am-8pm, Fri. 10:30am-9pm, Sat.-Sun. 10am-8:30pm, winter Mon.-Thurs. 10:30am-7pm, Fri. 10:30am-8pm, Sat.-Sun. 10am-7pm, $11-30) catches all kinds of seafood to serve to hungry diners. You'll often find sandy and salt-encrusted local surfers satisfying their enormous appetites after hours out on the waves or bikers downing a beer after a ride on the twisting highway. One of the Net's most satisfying options is the shrimp tacos: crispy fried shrimp on tortillas topped with a pineapple salsa. The large menu includes a seemingly endless variety of other combinations, à la carte options, and side dishes.

Serious seafood lovers should make time for **The Hungry Cat** (100 W. Channel Rd., Santa Monica, 310/459-3337, http://thehungrycat.com, Mon.-Thurs. 5pm-10pm, Fri. 5pm-11pm, Sat. 11am-3pm and 5:30pm-11pm, Sun. 11am-3pm and 5pm-10pm, $11-30). Start with something from the raw bar and move on to a dinner entrée of local white sea bass or a lamb-and-clams dish. Seafood is also the star at weekend brunch, with dishes like soft-shell crab BLT, lobster frittata, and crab-cake Benedict. On Monday, all raw bar oysters are half price. There's a second location in Hollywood (1535 N. Vine St., 323/462-2155, http://thehungrycat.com, Mon.-Wed. noon-10pm, Thurs.-Fri. noon-11pm, Sat. 11am-11pm, Sun. 11am-10pm).

Salt Air (1616 Abbot Kinney Blvd., Venice Beach, 310/396-9333, www.saltairvenice.com, Sun. 10am-3pm and 5pm-10pm, Mon.-Tues. 11:30am-2:30pm and 5pm-10pm, Wed.-Fri. 11:30am-2:30pm and 5pm-11pm, Sat. 10am-3pm and 5pm-11pm, $16-36) is a seafood restaurant with a busy bar. Everyone gets a plate of tasty corn fritters stuffed with cheddar cheese and a dollop of molasses butter to start. The raw bar has oysters from both coasts, while the dinner menu highlights seafood, including slow-cooked cod, grilled trout, and olive oil-poached salmon.

Thai

If your tastes run to the exotically spicy and romantic, walk across Pacific Avenue from Venice Beach into Marina Del Rey and to the Siamese Garden (301 Washington Blvd., Marina Del Rey, 310/821-0098, Mon.-Fri. 11am-3pm and 5pm-10pm, Sat. 5pm-9pm, Sun. 5pm-10pm, $10-30). A favorite of local couples looking for a romantic evening out, Siamese Garden boasts outdoor tables set in a lantern-lit garden, complete with glimpses of the Venice canals through the foliage and fencing. In the kitchen, Siamese Garden prides itself on creating delightful dishes with only the freshest and best produce and ingredients available. The wide menu offers all of your favorite Thai classics, such as coconut soup, pad thai, and a rainbow of curries. Mint, lemongrass, peanut sauce, basil, and hot chilies crowd the menu with their strong and distinct flavors. Vegetarians have a great selection of tasty dishes, while carnivores can enjoy plenty of good beef, poultry, and seafood. For dessert, try one of the fun sticky rice and fruit dishes. To accompany your meal, get a rich Thai iced tea or a light Thai beer.

PASADENA
Afghan

For a delicious and upscale dining experience, have lunch or dinner at Azeen's Afghani Restaurant (110 E. Union St., 626/683-3310, www.azeensafghanirestaurant.com, Mon.-Fri. 11am-2pm and 5:30pm-9:30pm, Sat.-Sun. 5:30pm-9:30pm, $14-22). Inside you'll find white tablecloths, black furniture, and unusual paintings. On the menu, the offerings take you into another world—one largely mysterious to Westerners. Trade routes, invasions, religion, ethnicity, and lots and lots of sand all contribute to the way Afghanistan and its cuisine have evolved. Vegetarians, be aware that while you will find some limited options, Afghan food tends heavily toward meat. Kebabs of all kinds are a regional specialty, and the country's proximity to India brings with it a love for truly spicy (and incredibly flavorful) dishes. At Azeen's, you can get kebabs, spicy lamb dishes, dumplings, and traditional desserts.

Asian

If you're just dying for Thai or Vietnamese food, one of the better spots in Pasadena is Daisy Mint (1218 E. Colorado Blvd., 626/792-2999, www.daisymint.com, daily 11am-3pm and 5pm-9pm, $8-21). The tiny green dining room's exposed brick and original artwork speak of SoCal, while the menu items tend to come from Southeast Asia and beyond. You'll find the aforementioned Thai and Vietnamese, plus Korean and uniquely Californian Asian-fusion dishes here. Some of the fun special touches of the house include a variety of steamed rice that you can choose to accompany your meal, and a large selection of unusual and fragrant teas. Pick whatever you think will go best with your satay, curry, seafood, or soup. Reservations are recommended on weekend evenings.

Barbecue

If you're looking for some down-home Southern food, head straight for Big Mama's Rib Shack (1453 N. Lake Ave., 626/797-1792, www.bigmamaspasadena.com, Tues.-Thurs.

LOS ANGELES
FOOD

11:30am-9pm, Fri.-Sat. 11:30am-10pm, Sun. noon-8pm, $7-25). While Big Mama never brewed up the sauce at this Pasadena kitchen, she was a Southern restaurateur who made her way from Georgia across the country to California over her long life. Today, her legacy lives on in the big ol' menu at Big Mama's, which boasts traditional Southern cuisine plus a number of creole and Cajun dishes that speak to a strong New Orleans influence. Whether your poison is a po'boy or good gumbo, get it in hearty portions at Big Mama's. Fish lovers will find oysters and catfish, but strict vegetarians will find their dining options limited. And Big Mama's isn't a diet-friendly establishment since few salads balance out the weight of the fried chicken, smothered ribs, and velvet cake.

California Cuisine

For an upscale meal without having to fight the crowds on the West Side or Downtown, check out **Bistro 45** (45 S. Mentor Ave., 626/795-2478, www.bistro45.com, Tues.-Thurs. 5pm-9pm, Fri.-Sat. 5pm-10pm, Sun. 5pm-8:30pm, $20-40). This nationally lauded restaurant has beautiful dining rooms: one light and bright with hardwood floors and peach walls with beautiful glass lantern

fixtures, and one semi-outdoor space done in gray-blues with distinctive woven chairs and classic French prints. The cuisine is grounded in the French tradition but includes a hearty twist of California in the preparation. Menus change seasonally (or more often), and offer lots of fresh seafood as well as high-end meat and veggie-based dishes. The wine list shifts seasonally to complement the food, and Bistro 45 boasts a full bar with a list of signature martini-esque cocktails.

Greek

For a quick and reasonably healthy lunch in downtown Pasadena, try **Pita! Pita!** (927 E. Colorado Blvd., Suite 101, 626/356-3099, www.pitapitapasadena.net, Mon.-Fri. 10am-2pm, $5-10). This walk-up Greek place offers tasty meals with lots of fresh veggies that fill you up without emptying your wallet in the process. If you eat in, find your own seat on the uncovered tables in the narrow dining room with its worn tile floor. Fill up your own cup with soda or water while you wait for your pita wrap or falafel and hummus plate. If you're in a hurry, order your food to go. The pita wrap sandwiches are big and a bit juicy, but properly wrapped, they can be reasonably sidewalk-friendly.

Information and Services

TOURS

If you don't feel up to driving around Los Angeles on your own (and no one will blame you if you don't), dozens of tour operators would love to do the driving for you and let you sit back and enjoy the sights and sounds of Southern California. Choose between driving tours, walking tours, and even helicopter tours that take you up to get a bird's-eye view of the city, beaches, and the wide Pacific Ocean.

Walking Tours

In among the dozens of cheesy "walking tour" operators who will charge you to walk you over

the stars on Hollywood Boulevard (which you can do yourself for free), one organization can give you a better, more in-depth look into the true history of the Los Angeles area. The **Los Angeles Conservancy** (213/623-2489, www. laconservancy.org, adults $10, children $5) offers eight walking tours that explore the city's architectural history in depth. Pick a style-themed tour, such as Art Deco or Modern Skyline, or a specific street, area, or major structure, such as Union Station, the Broadway Theaters, or the Biltmore Hotel. Self-guided tours are also available on the conservancy's website, including one on eclectic Venice

Beach architecture and another on sites featured in the 2009 film *(500) Days of Summer*.

Bus Tours

For bus tours, you can't beat the weight of history provided by **Starline Tours** (800/959-3131, www.starlinetours.com, adults $40-220, children $32-212), which has been in the business of showing L.A. and Hollywood to visitors since 1935. Take a tour of Movie Stars Homes (which actually covers many famous star-studded spots around the region), Hollywood, or celebrity hotspots, on a tour tied in with celebrity gossip juggernaut TMZ. Starline can pick you up at almost any hotel in L.A. Your tour vehicle will be either an air-conditioned minibus, a full-size bus, or a topless "Fun Bus" with a second open-air deck that lets visitors breathe the native smog of L.A. unhindered. "Hop-On, Hop-Off" Tours also allow passengers to jump on and off at various sights and attractions as they please. Expect your tour to last 2-6 hours, depending on which route you choose. Once you're on board, sit back, relax, and enjoy the sights and stories of Los Angeles.

INFORMATION
Visitor Information

The **Los Angeles Convention and Visitors Bureau** (www.discoverlosangeles.com) maintains several visitors centers. The **Hollywood and Highland Visitors Center** (6801 Hollywood Blvd., 323/467-6412, Mon.-Sat. 9am-10pm, Sun. 10am-7pm) is adjacent to a Metro station and includes a self-serve kiosk where you can purchase discount tickets to area attractions. There are additional self-serve centers at the Los Angeles Convention Center, the Port of Los Angeles (Berth 93), and the California Science Center.

Medical Services

The greater L.A. area offers some of the best medical care options in the world. People come from all over to get novel treatments and plastic surgery in the hospitals frequented by the stars. If you need immediate assistance, **Los Angeles County+USC Medical Center** (1200 N. State St., emergency 911, 323/409-1000, www.ladhs.org) can fix you up no matter what's wrong with you.

Transportation

AIR

L.A. is one of the most commercial airport-dense metropolitan areas in the country. Wherever you're coming from and whichever part of L.A. you're headed for, you can get there by air. **Los Angeles International Airport** (LAX, 1 World Way, Los Angeles, 855/463-5252, www.lawa.org), known as LAX, has the most flights to and from the most destinations of any area airport. LAX is also the most crowded of the L.A. airports, with the longest security and check-in lines. If you can find a way around flying into LAX, do so. One option is to fly into other airports in the area, including **Bob Hope Airport** (BUR, 2627 N. Hollywood Way, Burbank, 818/840-8840, www.burbankairport.com) and the

Long Beach Airport (4100 Donald Douglas Dr., Long Beach, 562/570-2600, www.lgb.org). It may be a slightly longer drive to your final destination, but it can be well worth it. If you must use LAX, arrive a minimum of two hours ahead of your domestic flight time for your flight out, and consider three hours on busy holidays.

TRAIN AND BUS

Amtrak (800/872-7245, www.amtrak.com) has an active rail hub in Los Angeles. Most trains come in to **Union Station** (800 N. Alameda St., 213/683-6729), which has been owned by the Los Angeles Metropolitan Transportation Authority (MTA, www.metro.net) since 2011. From Union Station, you can get to the Bay Area, Redding, and eventually Seattle on the *Coast Starlight* train, or take the *Pacific Surfliner* down the coast to San Diego. The *San Joaquin* runs out to Sacramento via the Bay Area. To get to and from L.A. from the east, the *Southwest Chief* comes in from Chicago, Kansas City, and Albuquerque. The famed *Sunset Limited* runs from Jacksonville, Florida, to New Orleans, El Paso, and then Los Angeles.

From Union Station, which also acts as a Metro hub, take Metro Rail to various parts of Los Angeles. Against fairly significant odds in the region that invented car culture, Los Angeles has created a functional and useful public transit system. The **Metro** (www. metro.net, cash fare $1.75, day pass $7) runs both the subway Metro Rail system and a network of buses throughout the L.A. metropolitan area. Pay on board a bus if you have exact change. Otherwise, purchase a ticket or a day pass from the ticket vending machines at all Metro Rail Stations.

Some buses run 24 hours. The Metro Rail lines start running as early as 4:30am and don't stop until as late as 1:30am. See the website (www.metro.net) for route maps, timetables, and fare details.

CAR

Los Angeles is crisscrossed with freeways, providing numerous yet congested access points into the city. From the north and south, I-5 provides the most direct access to downtown L.A. From I-5, U.S. 101 south leads directly into Hollywood; from here, Santa Monica Boulevard can take you west to Beverly Hills. Connecting from I-5 to I-210 will take you east to Pasadena. The best way to reach Santa Monica, Venice, and Malibu is via Highway 1, also known as the Pacific Coast Highway. I-10 can get you there from the east, but it will be a long, tedious, and trafficked drive.

Think you're up to the challenge of driving the world-infamous L.A. freeway system? Consider carefully. It's not as much fun as you might think. Traffic can be awful all the time. (If you believe you'll miss the jam on I-405 just because it's 8pm, you're flat wrong. I-405 often stays jammed up.) Local drivers accustomed to the conditions don't bother being polite, so expect to be cut off constantly and to deal with drivers paying attention to everything in the world but the road. And finally, if you're planning to use the traffic reports or local advice, there's a catch: Most road signs use numbers. But locals, including the radio traffic reporters, use names. There's no visible name-to-number translation on most maps, and just to make things even more fun, the names change (sometimes into one another) depending on where you are. Public transit is an increasingly viable and definitely preferable alternative.

Parking

Parking in Los Angeles can be as much of a bear as driving. And it can cost you quite a lot of money. You will find parking lots and structures included with many hotel rooms—L.A. is actually better than San Francisco about that. But parking on the street can be difficult or impossible, parking lots in sketchy areas (like the Flower and Jewelry Districts) can be dangerous, and parking structures at popular attractions can be expensive.

Taxis

Taxis aren't cheap, but they're quick, easy, and numerous. And in some cases, when you add up gas and parking fees, you'll find that the cab ride isn't that much more expensive than driving yourself.

To call a cab, try **Yellow Cab** (424/222-2222, www.layellowcab.com, L.A., LAX, Beverly Hills, Hollywood) and **City Cab** (888/248-9222, www.lacitycab.com, San Fernando Valley, Hollywood, and LAX), which now has a small fleet of green, environmentally friendly vehicles. Or check out www.taxicabsla.org for a complete list of providers and phone numbers.

Another idea is to try ride-sharing apps like **Uber** (www.uber.com) or **Lyft** (www.lyft. com); check the websites for coverage areas.

Disneyland Resort

The "Happiest Place on Earth" lures millions of visitors of all ages each year with promises of fun and fantasy. During high seasons, waves of humanity flow through **Disneyland Resort** (1313 N. Harbor Blvd., Anaheim, 714/781-4623, http://disneyland. disney.go.com, daily 9am-midnight, ticket prices vary, one-day over age 9 $99, ages 3-9 $93, one-day Hopper Ticket for entry to both parks over age 9 $150, ages 3-9 $144), moving slowly from land to land and ride to ride. The park is well set up to handle the often-immense crowds. Everything from foot-traffic control to ample restrooms makes even a Christmastime trip to Disneyland a happy time for the whole family. Despite the undeniable cheese factor, even the most cynical and jaded resident Californians can't quite keep their cantankerous scowls once they're ensconced inside Uncle Walt's dream. It really *is* a happy place.

Disney's rides, put together by the park's "Imagineers," are better than those at any other amusement park in the state—perhaps better than any in the world. The technology of the rides isn't more advanced than other parks, but it's the attention to detail that makes a Disneyland ride experience so enthralling. Even the spaces where you stand in line match the theme of the ride you're waiting for, from the archaeological relics of Indiana Jones to the tombstones of the Haunted Mansion. If you've got several days in the park, try them all, but if you don't, pick from the best of the best in each land.

Of course, Disney is going to capitalize on their purchase of Lucasfilm and the Star Wars franchise with a large expansion of the park that will feature a 14-acre themed Star Wars land (actual name to be announced). The park already has a few Star Wars-related attractions up and running, including the 3-D flight simulator ride **Star Tours,** with more to items to be added through 2017. One hotly anticipated new addition is a Millennium Falcon spaceship ride.

ORIENTATION

The Disneyland Resort is a massive kingdom that stretches from **Harbor Boulevard** on the east to **Walnut Street** on the west and from **Ball Road** to the north to **Katella Avenue** to the south. It includes two amusement parks, three hotels, and an outdoor shopping and entertainment complex. The Disneyland-affiliated hotels (Disneyland Hotel, Paradise Pier Hotel, and Disney's Grand Californian) all cluster on the western side of the complex, between Walnut Street and **Disneyland Drive (West St.).** The area between Disneyland Drive and Harbor Boulevard is shared by **Disneyland** in the northern section and **Disney California Adventure Park** in the southern section, with **Downtown Disney** between them in the central-west section. There is no admission fee for Downtown Disney. You can reach the amusement park entrances via Downtown Disney (although visitors going to Disneyland or Disney California Adventure Park should park in the paid lots, rather than the Downtown Disney self-park lot, which is only free for the first three hours) or from the walk-in entrance (for those taking public transportation or being dropped off) on Harbor Boulevard. There are also trams from the parking lot to the entrance.

DISNEYLAND

Your first stop inside the park should be one of the information kiosks near the front entrance gates. Get a map, a schedule of the day's events, and the inside scoop on what's going on in the park during your visit.

New Orleans Square

In New Orleans Square, the unquestioned favorite ride for the 21st century is the revamped

Pirates of the Caribbean. If you haven't visited Disneyland in a few years, you'll notice some major changes to this old favorite. Beginning in the dim swamp overlooked by the Blue Bayou Restaurant, the ride's classic scenes inside have been revamped to tie in more closely to the movies. Look for Captain Jack Sparrow to pop up among your other favorite disreputable characters engaged in all sorts of debauchery. Lines for Pirates can get long, so grab a Fastpass if you don't want to wait. Pirates is suitable for younger children as well as teens and adults.

For a taste of truly classic Disney, line up in the graveyard for a tour of the **Haunted Mansion.** Next to Pirates, this ride hasn't changed much in the last 40 years. It hasn't needed to. The sedate motion makes the Haunted Mansion suitable for younger children, but beware: The ghosties and ghoulies that amuse adults can be intense for kids.

Adventureland

Adventureland sits next to the New Orleans Square area. **Indiana Jones Adventure** is arguably one of the best rides in all of Disneyland, and the details make it stunning. As you stand in the line, check out the signs, equipment, and artifacts in mock-dusty tunnels winding toward the ride. The ride itself, in a roller-coaster style variant of an all-terrain vehicle, jostles and jolts you through a landscape that Indy himself might dash through, with booby traps and villains in pursuit. This one isn't the best for tiny tots, but the big kids love it, and everyone might want a Fastpass for the endlessly popular attraction.

On the other end of the spectrum, you'll either love the **Enchanted Tiki Room** or hate it. Pseudo-Polynesian entertainment is provided by animatronic birds. Even the smallest children love the bright colors and cheerful songs, though some adults can't quite take the cheesiness.

Frontierland

Take a ride on a Wild West train on the **Big**

Thunder Mountain Railroad. This older roller coaster whisks passengers away on a brief but fun thrill ride through a "dangerous, decrepit" mountain's mineshafts. As you stand in line, read the names of the locomotives as the trains come rushing by.

Fantasyland

The favorite of many Disneyland visitors, Fantasyland rides tend to cater to the younger set. For many Disneyphiles, **"it's a small world"** is the ultimate expression of Uncle Walt's dream. Toddlers adore this ride, which introduces their favorite Disney characters and the famous (some would say infamous) song. You can almost feel the fairy dust sprinkling down on you as you tour this magical miniature kingdom. (Warning: If cutesiness makes you gag, you might want to skip this one.)

Older kids might prefer the crazy fun of **Mr. Toad's Wild Ride.** Even though it's not really a roller coaster, this ride makes for big fun for children and adults alike. What's cool about Mr. Toad's is the wacky scenery you'll get to see along the ride, from a sedate library to the gates of hell.

If it's a faster thrill you're seeking, head for one of the most recognizable landmarks at Disneyland. The **Matterhorn Bobsleds** roller coaster looks like a miniature version of its namesake in the Swiss Alps. Inside, you board a sled-style coaster car and plunge down the mountain on a twisted track that takes you past rivers, glaciers, and the Abominable Snowman.

Tomorrowland

The best thrill ride of the main park sits inside a space-age building. **Space Mountain** is a fast roller coaster that whizzes through the dark. All you'll see are the stars overhead. You will hear your screams and those of your fellow passengers as your "spaceship" swerves and plunges along unseen tracks. Despite its age, Space Mountain remains one of the more popular rides in the park. Get a Fastpass to avoid long lines.

Here at Disney, We Have a Few Rules

Think that anything goes at the Happiest Place on Earth? Think again. Uncle Walt had distinct ideas about what his dream theme park would look like, and that vision extended to the dress and manners of his guests. When the park opened in 1955, among the many other restrictions, no man sporting facial hair was allowed into Disneyland. The rules on dress and coiffure have relaxed a bit since the opening, but you still need to mind your manners when you enter the park.

- Adults may not wear costumes of any kind except on Halloween.

- No shirt, no shoes, no Disneyland.

- No smoking.

- Guests under 14 must be accompanied by a guest older than 14 at all times.

- All bags are subject to screening.

- If you must use the F word, do it quietly. If staff catches you cussing or cursing in a way that disturbs others, you can be asked to desist or leave.

- The happiest of happiness is strictly prohibited inside Disneyland. If you're caught having sex on park grounds, not only will you be thrown out, you'll be banned from Disneyland for life (at least that's the rumor).

- Ditto for any illicit substances.

★ DISNEY CALIFORNIA ADVENTURE PARK

Disney California Adventure Park (http://disneyland.disney.go.com, daily 8am-10pm, ticket prices vary, one-day over age 9 $99, ages 3-9 $93, one-day Hopper Ticket for entry to both parks over age 9 $150, ages 3-9 $144) celebrates much of what makes California special. If Disney is your only stop on this trip but you'd like to get a sense of the state as a whole, this park can give you a little taste. (For my money, though, you'd do better to spend some time exploring California in all its real, non-Disneyfied glory.)

Like Disneyland proper, Disney California Adventure Park is divided into themed areas. Rides tend toward the thrills of other major amusement parks but include the great Disney touches that make the Mouse special.

You'll find two information booths just inside the main park entrance, one off to the left as you walk through the turnstile and one at the opening to Sunshine Plaza.

Hollywood Land

Celebrating SoCal's famed film industry, the back lot holds the ultimate thrill ride inside: **The Twilight Zone Tower of Terror.** Enter the creepy "old hotel," go through the "service area," and take your place inside an elevator straight out of your worst nightmares. This ride aims for teens and adults rather than little kids, and it's not a good one for folks who fear heights or don't do well with free-fall rides.

Less extreme but also fun, **Monsters, Inc. Mike & Sully to the Rescue!** invites guests into the action of the movie of the same name. You'll help the heroes as they chase the intrepid Boo. This ride jostles you around but is suitable for smaller kids as well as bigger ones.

A Bug's Land

Want to live like a bug? Get a sample of the world of tiny insects on **It's Tough to Be a Bug!** This big-group, 3-D, multisensory ride offers fun for little kids and adults alike. You'll fly through the air, scuttle through the grass, and get a good idea of what life is like on six little legs. Beware: When they say this ride engages *all your senses,* they mean it.

For the littlest adventurers, **Flik's Fun Fair** offers almost half a dozen rides geared toward toddlers and little children. They can ride pint-size hot-air balloons known as Flik's Flyers, climb aboard a bug-themed train, or run around under a gigantic faucet to cool down after hours of hot fun.

Paradise Pier

Paradise Pier mimics the Santa Monica Pier and other waterfront attractions like it, with thrill rides and an old-fashioned midway. Most of the extreme rides cluster in the Paradise Pier area. It seems reasonable that along with everything else, Disney does the best roller coasters in the business. They prove it with **California Screamin'**, a high-tech roller coaster designed after the classic wooden coasters of carnivals past. This extra-long ride includes drops, twists, a full loop, and plenty of time and screaming fun. California Screamin' has a four-foot height requirement and is just as popular with nostalgic adults as with kids. **Toy Story Midway Mania!** magnifies the midway mayhem as passengers of all ages take aim at targets in a 4-D ride inspired by Disney-Pixar's *Toy Story.*

Condor Flats

Want a bird's-eye view of California? Get on board **Soarin' Over California.** This combination ride and show puts you and dozens of other guests on the world's biggest "glider" and sets you off over the hills and valleys of California. You'll feel the wind in your hair as you see the vineyards, mountains, and beaches of this diverse state.

Grizzly Peak

Get Disney's version of a wilderness experience at Grizzly Peak. Enjoy a white-water raft ride through a landscape inspired by the Sierra Nevada foothills on the **Grizzly River Run.** Kids can earn badges in tracking

and wolf howling on the **Redwood Creek Challenge Trail.**

Cars Land

This section of the park is inspired by the hit 2006 film *Cars.* Float on larger-than-life tires on the **Luigi's Flying Tires** ride or be serenaded by Mater as you ride in a tractor on **Mater's Junkyard Jamboree.** The **Radiator Springs Racers** finds six-person vehicles passing locations and characters from *Cars* before culminating in a real-life race with a car of other park visitors.

Parades and Shows

Watch your favorite Pixar characters come to life in the **Pixar Play Parade.** Other regular shows are **Disney Junior—Live on Stage!** and **Disney's Aladdin—A Musical Spectacular.** Both of these shows hark back to favorite children's activities and movies. Your kids can sing along with favorite songs and characters while you take a load off your feet and relax for a while. Check your park guide and *Time Guide* for more information about these and other live shows.

DOWNTOWN DISNEY

You don't need an admission ticket to take a stroll through the shops of the Downtown Disney District. In addition to the mammoth World of Disney Store, you'll find Ridemakerz, a Build-a-Bear workshop, and a Lego Imagination Center. For adults, the House of Blues Store, Sephora, and the Sunglass Icon boutique beckon. You can also have a bite to eat or take in some jazz or a new-release movie.

ACCOMMODATIONS

The best way to get fully Disneyfied is to stay at one of the park's hotels. Several sit just beside or across the street from the park.

Disney Hotels

For the most iconic Disney resort experience, you must stay at the **Disneyland Hotel** (1150 Magic Way, Anaheim, 714/778-6600, http://

disneyland.disney.go.com, $460-1,016). This nearly 1,000-room high-rise monument to brand-specific family entertainment has everything a vacationing Brady-esque bunch could want: themed swimming pools, themed play areas, and even character-themed rooms that allow the kids to fully immerse themselves in the Mouse experience. Adults and families on a budget can also get rooms with either a king or two queen beds and more traditional motel fabrics and appointments. The monorail stops inside the hotel, offering guests the easiest way into the park proper without having to deal with parking or even walking.

It's easy to find the **Paradise Pier Hotel** (1717 S. Disneyland Dr., Anaheim, 714/999-0990, http://disneyland.disney.go.com, $344-952); it's that high-rise thing just outside Disney California Adventure Park. This hotel boasts what passes for affordable lodgings within walking distance of the parks. Rooms are cute, colorful, and clean; many have two doubles or queens to accommodate families or couples traveling together on a tighter budget. You'll find a (possibly refreshing) lack of Mickeys in the standard guest accommodations at the Paradise, which has the feel of a beach resort motel. After a day of wandering the park, relax by the rooftop pool.

Disney's Grand Californian Hotel and Spa (1600 S. Disneyland Dr., Anaheim, 714/635-2300, http://disneyland.disney.go.com, $547-1,216) is inside Disney California Adventure Park, attempting to mimic the famous Ahwahnee Lodge in Yosemite. While it doesn't quite succeed (much of what makes the Ahwahnee so great is its views), the big-beam construction and soaring common spaces do feel reminiscent of a great luxury lodge. The hotel is surrounded by gardens and has restaurants, a day spa, and shops attached on the ground floors; it can also get you right out into Downtown Disney and thence to the parks proper. Rooms here offer more luxury than the other Disney resorts, with dark woods and faux-craftsman detailing creating an attractive atmosphere.

Get anything from a standard room that sleeps two up to spacious family suites with bunk beds that can easily handle six people. As with all Disney resorts, you can purchase tickets and a meal plan along with your hotel room (in fact, if you book via the website, they'll try to force you to do it that way).

Outside the Parks

The massive park complex is ringed with motels, both popular chains and more interesting independents. **The Anabella** (1030 W. Katella Ave., Anaheim, 714/905-1050 or 800/863-4888, www.anabellahotel.com, $170-215) offers a touch of class along with a three-block walk to the parks. The elegant marble-clad lobby seems like it belongs closer to Downtown L.A. than Downtown Disney. Rooms are furnished with an eye toward modern, stylish decor (occasionally at the expense of practicality). Adults looking for an overnight escape from the endless parade of kid-oriented entertainment and attractions will find a welcome respite at the Anabella. A decent restaurant, two pools, a whirlpool tub, and a fitness center are on-site. You can get limited room service at the Anabella, and you can leave your car in their parking lot to avoid the expense of parking at Disneyland.

Also in walking distance is the **Desert Palms Hotel & Suites** (631 W. Katella Ave., 888/788-0466, www.desertpalmshotel.com, $175-415). Its spacious and elegant lobby welcomes visitors, the pool and spa provide fun for children and adults alike, and the many amenities make travelers comfortable. Regular rooms have one king or two queens, a TV, a phone, Internet access, and not a ton of room to walk around after all your luggage is crowded in with the furniture. Guests with more discretionary income can choose from a number of suites, some designed to delight children and others aimed at couples on a romantic getaway. There are even condo-style accommodations with kitchens.

Away from the Disneyland complex and surrounding area, the accommodations in Orange County run to chain motels with little character or distinctiveness, but the good news is that you can find a decent room for a reasonable price.

The **Hyatt Regency Orange County** (11999 Harbor Blvd., Garden Grove, 714/750-1234, http://orangecounty.hyatt.com, $199-289) in Garden Grove is about 1.5 miles (10 minutes' drive on Harbor Blvd.) south of the park. The attractive rooms are decorated in the latest style inside a tall glass-fronted tower. White linens emphasize the cleanliness of beds and baths, while bright yellows and deep blues provide classy artistic touches. In the sun-drenched atrium, enjoy a cocktail or sit back and read a good book in the attractive atmosphere. Grab a chaise longue by the pool or take a refreshing dip. The family-friendly suites have separate bedrooms with bunk beds and fun decor geared toward younger guests.

FOOD
Disneyland

One of the few things the Mouse doesn't do too well is haute cuisine. For a truly good or healthy meal, get a hand stamp and go outside the park. But if you're stuck inside and you absolutely need sustenance, you can get it. The best areas of the park to grab a bite are Main Street, New Orleans, and Frontierland, but you can find at least a snack almost anywhere in the park.

For a sit-down restaurant meal inside the park, make reservations in advance for a table at the **Blue Bayou Restaurant** (New Orleans Square, 714/781-3463, $30-50 pp). The best part about this restaurant is its setting in the dimly lit swamp overlooking the Pirates of the Caribbean ride. Appropriately, the Bayou has a reputation for being haunted. The Cajun-ish cuisine matches the junglelike setting, although if you're looking for authenticity, you'd do better to look elsewhere. You will get large portions, and tasty sweet desserts make a fine finish to your meal. Watch your silverware, though; the alleged ghosts in this restaurant like to mess around with diners' tableware.

If you need to grab a quicker bite, *don't* do it at the French Market restaurant in the New Orleans area. It sells what appears to be day-old (or more) food from the Bayou that has been sitting under heat lamps for a good long time.

Disney California Adventure Park

If you need a snack break in Disney California Adventure Park, you'll find most of the food clustered in the Golden State area. For a Mexican feast, try **Cocina Cucamonga Mexican Grill** (under $15 pp). For more traditional American fare, enjoy the food at the **Pacific Wharf Cafe** (under $15 pp) or the **Taste Pilots' Grill** (under $15 pp).

Unlike Disneyland proper, in Disney California Adventure Park, responsible adults can quaff their thirst with a variety of alcoholic beverages. If you're just dying for a cold beer, get one at **Bayside Brews.** Or, if you love the endless variety of high-quality wines produced in the Golden State, head for the **Mendocino Terrace,** where you can learn the basics of wine creation and production. Have a glass and a pseudo-Italian meal at the sit-down **Wine Country Trattoria at the Golden Vine Winery** (714/781-3463, $15-36).

Downtown Disney

Downtown Disney is outside the amusement parks and offers additional dining options. National chains like **House of Blues** (1530 S. Disneyland Dr., Anaheim, 714/778-2583, www.houseofblues.com, daily 11am-1am, $15-30) and **Rainforest Café** (1515 S. Disneyland Dr., Anaheim, 714/772-0413, www.rainforestcafe.com, Sun.-Thurs. 8am-11pm, Fri.-Sat. 8am-midnight, $11-18) serve typical menu staples like sandwiches, burgers, pasta, and steak and seafood entrées, with House of Blues putting a Southern spin on these items and adding live-music shows, while kid-friendly Rainforest Café puts on tropical touches like coconut and mango. **ESPN Zone** (1545 Disneyland Dr., Anaheim, 714/300-3776, www.espnzone.com, Sun.-Thurs. 11am-11pm,

Fri.-Sat. 11am-midnight, $11-26) has similar offerings; due to numerous closures across the country, the Downtown Disney spot is now just one of two locations of this "sports bar on steroids" concept restaurant. The other is in Los Angeles (1011 S. Figueroa St., 213/765-7070).

There are also more individual restaurants, but even these feel a little like chains. The most distinctive of them, **Ralph Brennan's Jazz Kitchen** (1590 S. Disneyland Dr., Anaheim, 714/776-5200, www.rbjazzkitchen. com, Sun.-Thurs. 11am-10pm, Fri.-Sat. 11am-11pm, $24-39), is meant to replicate the experience of eating in New Orleans's French Quarter. The Cajun menu hits all the staples, including jambalaya, beignets, and various blackened meats and seafood.

The Patina Restaurant Group runs **Catal Restaurant** (1580 Disneyland Dr., Anaheim, 714/774-4442, www.patinagroup.com, daily 8am-11am and 5pm-10pm, $19-41), with Mediterranean fare; **Naples Ristorante** (1550 Disneyland Dr., Anaheim, 714/776-6200, www.patinagroup.com, daily 8am-10pm, $15-46) for Italian food; and **Tortilla Jo's** (1510 Disneyland Dr., Anaheim, 714/535-5000, www.patinagroup.com, Sun.-Thurs. 11am-10pm, Fri.-Sat. 11am-11pm, $15-21) for Mexican food.

Finally, **La Brea Bakery** (1556 Disneyland Dr., Anaheim, 714/490-0233, www.labreabakery.com, Sun.-Thurs. 8am-9pm, Fri.-Sat. 8am-2pm, $10-28) is the Disney outpost of an L.A. favorite. This bakery, founded by Nancy Silverton of the highly touted Campanile restaurant in L.A., supplies numerous markets and restaurants with crusty European-style loaves. The morning scones, sandwiches, and fancy cookies are superb.

Outside the Parks

The surrounding city of Anaheim is the second-largest metropolis in Orange County, so it has a wide range of dining options. **Reunion Kitchen & Drink** (5775 E. Santa Ana Canyon Rd., 714/283-1062, www.reunionkitchen.net, Mon.-Thurs. 11am-10pm,

Fri. 11am-11pm, Sat. 8am-11pm, Sun. 8am-10pm, $13-36) puts a modern spin on comfort food like barbecue-glazed meatloaf, turkey potpie, and chicken and biscuits. Cocktails, wine, and beer are also available, with a serious focus on local brews. Save room for the warm butter-cake dessert.

The Ranch Restaurant (1025 E. Ball Rd., 714/817-4200, daily 5pm-10pm, $26-115) takes western food and style upscale. People raved about the "Cowboy Rib Eye," a 36- to 40-ounce bone-in chop. The menu also hits on seafood, short ribs, and smoked free-range chicken. Live country acts play at the adjacent **Ranch Saloon** (Thurs.-Sat. 5:30pm-2am, Sun. 4pm-10pm, $13-39).

Cortina's Italian Market (2175 W. Orange Ave., 714/535-1948, http://cortinasitalianfood.com, Mon.-Thurs. 11am-8pm, Fri.-Sat. 11am-9pm, $5-15) has been serving pizzas, sandwiches, and pastas since 1963.

PRACTICALITIES
Tickets

There are as many varied ticket prices and plans as there are themes in the park. A single-day theme park ticket will run adults $95-119, ages 3-9 $89-113. A variety of other combinations and passes are available online (http://disneyland.disney.go.com).

To buy tickets, go to one of the many kiosks in the central gathering spot that serves as the main entrance to both Disneyland and Disney California Adventure Park. Bring your credit card, since a day at Disney is not cheap. After you've got tickets in hand (or if you've bought them online ahead of time), proceed to the turnstiles for the main park. You'll see the Disneyland Railroad terminal and the large grassy hill with the flowers planted to resemble Mickey's famous face. Pass through, and head under the railroad trestle to get to Main Street and the park center. You can exit and reenter the park on the days your tickets are valid for.

The already expensive regular one-day Disneyland ticket doesn't include Disney California Adventure Park. If you're interested in checking out Disney California Adventure Park as well as Disneyland, your best bet is to buy a **Park Hopper pass** (additional $40), which lets you move back and forth between the two parks at will for a slight discount. If you're planning to spend several days touring the Houses of Mouse, buy multiday passes in advance online to save a few more bucks per day. It'll help you feel better about the cash you'll spend on junk food, giant silly hats, stuffed animals, and an endless array of Disney apparel.

Fastpasses are free with park admission and might seem like magic after a while. The newest and most popular rides offer Fastpass kiosks near the entrances. Feed your ticket into one of the machines and it will spit out both your ticket and a Fastpass with your specified time to take the ride. Come back during your window and enter the always-much-shorter Fastpass line, designated by a sign at the entrance. If you're with a crowd, be sure you all get your Fastpasses at the same time, so you all get the same time window to ride. It's possible to claim three Fastpasses at a time. Once you've used up your initial allotment, you can visit a Fastpass kiosk to reload.

Information and Services

Each park has information booths near the park entrance. On the website for **Visit Anaheim** (http://visitanaheim.org), you can plan a trip to the area in advance by looking at the upcoming events and suggested itineraries or by downloading the travel guide.

If you need to stow your bags or hit the restroom before plunging into the fray, banks of lockers and restrooms sit in the main entrance area.

If mobility is a problem, consider renting a **stroller, wheelchair,** or **scooter.** Ask for directions to the rental counter when you enter the park.

Disneyland offers its own minor medical facilities, which can dispense first aid for scrapes, cuts, and mild heat exhaustion. They can also call an ambulance if something nastier has occurred. The **West Anaheim**

Medical Center (3033 W. Orange Ave., Anaheim, 714/827-3000, www.westanaheimmedctr.com) is a full-service hospital with an emergency room.

Getting There

The nearest airport to Disneyland, serving all of Orange County, is **John Wayne Airport** (SNA, 18601 Airport Way, Santa Ana, 949/252-5200, www.ocair.com). It's much easier to fly into and out of John Wayne than LAX, though it can be more expensive. John Wayne's terminal has plenty of rental car agencies, and many shuttle services that can get you where you need to go—especially to the House of Mouse.

If you have to fly into LAX for scheduling or budget reasons, catch a shuttle straight from the airport to your Disneyland hotel. Among the many companies offering and arranging such transportation, the one with the best name is **MouseSavers** (www.mousesavers.com). Working with various shuttle and van companies, MouseSavers can get you a ride in a van or a bus from LAX or John Wayne to your destination at or near Disneyland.

Disneyland is on Disneyland Drive in Anaheim and is most accessible from I-5 south where it crosses Ball Road (stay in the left three lanes for parking). The parking lot (1313 S. Disneyland Dr.) costs $17 for a car or motorcycle, $22 for an oversize vehicle such as a motor home or tractor without the trailer, and $27 for buses and tractor-trailer rigs.

If you're coming to the park from elsewhere in Southern California, consider leaving the car (avoiding the parking fees) and taking public transit instead. **Anaheim Resort Transit** (ART, 1280 Anaheim Blvd., Anaheim, 714/563-5287, www.rideart.org) can take you to and from the Amtrak station and all around central Anaheim for $4 per day. Buy passes via the website or at conveniently located kiosks.

Getting Around

Disney California Adventure Park sits across the main Disney entry plaza from

Disneyland. Enter from the main parking lots, from Downtown Disney, or hop over from Disneyland. Need a tram for the long-distance walk in or out of the park? The **Lion King Tram Route** can get you to and from the main parking areas. The **Mickey & Friends Tram Route** takes you toward Downtown Disney and the resort hotels.

INLAND ORANGE COUNTY

The lure of inland O.C., a primarily residential area, tends to be dominated by the Mouse. But if you just have to get away from the overwhelming cutesy happiness for a while, a few other entertaining attractions lurk in the shadows.

Knott's Berry Farm

Believe it or not, other amusement parks make their home in Orange County. For a taste of history along with some ultramodern thrill rides and plenty of cooling waterslides, head for **Knott's Berry Farm** (8039 Beach Blvd., Buena Park, 714/220-5200, www.knotts.com, park hours vary, adults $38, seniors and children $34, parking $15). This park's unusual name stems from its agricultural past. The fertile land beneath the roller coasters really was a berry farm decades ago. The Knott family grew strawberries, raspberries, boysenberries, and more here, and then made the fruits of their labors into preserves. Knott's jams retain their popularity in supermarkets across the country to this day.

Today, instead of berry vines you'll find twisting tracks at this thrill-oriented park. From the tall landmark GhostRider wooden coaster to the 30-story vertical drop ride to the screaming Silver Bullet suspended coaster, even the most hard-core ride lover will get excited by Knott's. For the younger crowd, Camp Snoopy offers an array of pint-sized rides and attractions, plus Snoopy and all the characters they love from the Peanuts comics and TV shows.

In the heat of the summer, many park visitors adjourn from the coasters to **Knott's**

Soak City (Memorial Day-Labor Day daily, May-Sept. weekends, adults $28-34, seniors and children $24, parking $15-20). The full-sized water park has 22 rides, a kid pool and water playground, and plenty of space to spread out and enjoy the O.C. sunshine after cooling off on the waterslides. Score significant savings on admission tickets at both the amusement park and water park by purchasing tickets online.

Discovery Science Center

If you'd like your kids to spend at least one day in the O.C. doing something educational, take them to the **Discovery Science Center** (2500 N. Main St., Santa Ana, 714/542-2823, www.discoverycube.org, daily 9am-6pm, adults $18, seniors $15, children $13, parking $5). The star attraction, the interactive DinoQuest, lets kids get inside the lost world of dinosaurs—way inside! You can also take a quick nap on a bed of nails, create your own clouds and tornadoes, and experience the buffeting of a hurricane inside a wind tunnel. The Discovery Science Center combines interactive play with scientific learning to create a fun day.

Accommodations

Away from the Disney resorts, the accommodations in inland Orange County run to chain motels. The good news is that you can find a decent room for a reasonable price almost everywhere you go in the O.C. The less-good news is that you won't find much of anything in the way of character or distinction in any of them.

The **Days Inn Buena Park/Knotts Berry Farm** (7121 Beach Blvd., Buena Park, 714/670-9000, www.daysinn.com, $150-200) used to be a Red Roof Inn. The latest incarnation offers a clean bed and bathroom near Knott's and Disney. Amenities include a heated pool and a spa, free Wi-Fi, and a fitness center. Medium-sized motel rooms feature a standard motel setup with a variety of bed configurations, dark carpets, and floral bedspreads.

At the **Best Western Orange County**

Alternatives to the Mouse

The longtime Hollywood-centric alternative to Disneyland is the **Universal Studios Hollywood** (100 Universal City Plaza, Los Angeles, 800/864-8377, www.universalstudios.com, hours vary, adults $85-95, children under 48 inches tall $72, parking $10-15) theme park. Kids adore this park, which puts them right into the action of their favorite movies. Flee the carnivorous dinosaurs of *Jurassic Park,* take a rafting adventure on the pseudo-set of *Waterworld,* or quiver in terror of an ancient curse in *Revenge of the Mummy.* One of the newest major attractions recreates the racing world of *Fast and Furious;* or experience the shape-shifting Transformers in a new ride based on the movies and the Hasbro toy. If you're the parent rather than the child, you may find some of the effects on the rides pretty cheesy. On the other hand, you may be thrown back to your childhood with memories of your favorite TV shows and movies.

If you're more interested in how the movies are made than the rides made from them, take the Studio Tour. You'll get an extreme close-up of the sets of major blockbuster films like *War of the Worlds.* The King Kong set (along with the famed New York set and a number of others) was destroyed in an accidental fire in 2008, but replaced in July 2010 with King Kong: 360 3-D. Better yet, get tickets to be part of the studio audience of TV shows currently taping at the Audiences Unlimited Ticket Booth. If you're a serious movie buff, consider getting a VIP pass—you'll get a six-hour tour that takes you onto working sound stages, into the current prop warehouse, and through a variety of working build shops that service films and programs currently filming.

It's possible to enjoy a meal and buy a near-infinite number of souvenirs at Universal Studios. If you need a little help getting yourself or your child around, rent a wheelchair or stroller. Pretty much every ride and show is wheelchair-accessible—ask at the ticket booth for more information about how to get around easily or if you need assisted-listening devices and TTD phones. Heavier items can be stored in a locker.

For yet another amusement park adventure, hit **Six Flags Magic Mountain** (Magic Mountain Parkway, Valencia, 661/255-4100, www.sixflags.com, hours vary, adults $73, children $48). This park provides good fun for the whole family—even the snarky teenagers who hate almost everything. Magic Mountain has long been the extreme alternative to the Mouse, offering a wide array of thrill rides. You'll need a strong stomach to deal with the g-forces of the major-league roller coasters and the death-defying drops including the new Lex Luthor: Drop of Doom, where you plummet 400 feet at speeds up to 85 mph. For the younger set, plenty of rides offer a less intense but equally fun amusement-park experience. Both littler and bigger kids enjoy interacting with the classic Warner Brothers characters, especially in Bugs Bunny World, and a kids' show features Bugs, Donald, and others. Other than that, Magic Mountain has little in the way of staged entertainment—this park is all about the rides. The park is divided into areas, just like most other major theme parks—get a map at the entrance to help you maneuver around and pick your favorite rides.

You'll find services, souvenirs, and snacks galore throughout the park. The food offerings run to burgers, pizza, and international fast food. The highest concentration of snack shacks sits in the Colossus County Fair area; others are evenly distributed throughout the other areas. You can also buy tchotchkes in any area, but most of the shopping centers around Cyclone Bay. All major services can be found at the park, including many ATM machines, a first-aid station, ample restrooms, and disability assistance. The Guest Relations office at Six Flags Plaza can help you with just about anything you need.

Airport (2700 Hotel Terrace, Santa Ana, 714/432-8888, www.bestwestern-oc.com, $100-170) you'll find everything you expect of the popular national chain, including floral and wine-colored decor in your comfortable room, a pool and hot tub, and a free shuttle to and from John Wayne Airport. Down in the lobby, you'll find a complimentary "cook-to-serve" breakfast each morning (that is, prepackaged heat-and-eat items plus cold cereals, bagels, and coffee).

In Garden Grove, stay at the **Hyatt**

Regency Orange County (11999 Harbor Blvd., Garden Grove, 714/750-1234, http://orangecounty.hyatt.com, $170-395). The attractive rooms are decorated in the latest style inside a tall, glass-fronted tower. White linens emphasize the cleanliness of beds and bathrooms, while bright yellows and deep blues provide classy artistic touches. In the sun-drenched atrium, enjoy a cocktail or sit back and read a good book in the attractive atmosphere. Grab a chaise lounge by one of the two pools or take a refreshing dip. Or grab a beer at the on-site OC Brewhouse. If you're bringing your family, consider renting one of the "family-friendly suites" that have separate bedrooms with bunk beds and fun decor geared toward younger guests.

If your major destination is Knott's Berry Farm, consider staying at the Knott's Berry Farm Resort Hotel (7675 Crescent Ave., Buena Park, 714/995-1111, www.knotts.com, $155-222). This high-rise resort includes all the extras and amenities you'd expect from a corporate hotel. Lounge by the pool and spa, work out at the fitness center, and have dinner in one of the on-site restaurants, the Amber Waves dining room. Get a drink at the Sports Bar after a long day out at the park or seeing the sights of O.C. Your comfortable room will greet you each night; choose one queen, two queens, or a king bed. Also, for kids, there are Snoopy-themed rooms available. Check the Internet for a variety of specials and discount rates.

Food

Want to keep the kids—and yourself—entertained during dinner? Check out one of the dinner-and-a-show restaurants, both near Disney and Knott's Berry Farm in Buena Park. At the famous Medieval Times (7662 Beach Blvd., Buena Park, 866/543-9637, www.medievaltimes.com, adults $62, children 12 and under $37), you'll enter a castle-shaped building, take your seat, and watch as gallant knights battle for the title of First Knight. You'll see live jousts (there's a big courtyard in this restaurant!),

swordfights, and ladies in gowns parading for your pleasure. Your meal, served on a pewter-styled plate, provides hearty if not particularly healthy or high-quality sustenance. Vegetarian and kids' meal options are available upon request.

If you prefer pirates to knights, the O.C. can hook you up. Practically next door to the castle, buckle your swash at the Pirate's Dinner Adventure (7600 Beach Blvd., 714/690-1497, www.piratesdinneradventure.com, adults $62, children 3-11 $37). Combining dinner theater, the current pirate craze, and a touch of Cirque du Soleil, everyone in your family will find something to watch at dinner with the pirates. Even if the cheesy acting and the swordfights don't do it for you, the aerobatics that form an integral part of this show can be great fun to marvel at. A four-course meal includes both chicken and meat (or fish), plus salad and dessert. It's not the best food, but hopefully you'll be too busy enjoying the show to care. Check for special holiday shows in season.

If you're looking for a bite to eat sans pirates and knights, Casa De Soto Restaurant (8562 Garden Grove Blvd., Garden Grove, 714/530-4200, www.casadesoto.com, daily 11:30am-9pm, $10) offers standard Mexican fare in three festive rooms.

Thasos Greek Island Grill (3940 S. Bristol St., Santa Ana, 714/708-3000, www.thasos.com, Sun.-Thurs. 11am-9pm, Fri. 11am-9:30pm, Sat. 11am-10pm, $10) serves Mediterranean specialties including souvlaki, gyros, and moussaka.

Information and Services

Visit Anaheim (Anaheim Convention Center, 800 W. Katella Ave., http://visitanaheim.org), formerly the Anaheim/Orange County Visitor & Convention Bureau, has a usually unmanned kiosk in the Anaheim Convention Center where guests can pick up a travel guide and menus for area restaurants.

The West Anaheim Medical Center (3033 W. Orange Ave., Anaheim, 714/827-3000, www.westanaheimmedctr.com) is a full-service hospital with an emergency room.

South Bay and Long Beach

The South Bay is a name given to the cities along the southern end of Los Angeles County's Santa Monica Bay. The South Bay's beach cities include Manhattan Beach, Hermosa Beach, and Redondo Beach, which are all known for their abundant sand and sun along with their beach volleyball scene, gourmet dining, shopping opportunities, nightlife, small beach-city appeal, and The Strand, a concrete jogging and biking path connecting all of the communities with Santa Monica to the north and Palos Verdes to the south.

Long Beach is a large city (the seventh largest in California) and major shipping port south of the beach cities. It has several worthy attractions befitting its size including the historic and possibly haunted ocean liner The *Queen Mary* and the Aquarium of the Pacific. Long Beach Harbor is also one of the best places to catch a boat ride out to Catalina Island, about 22 miles from shore.

SIGHTS
★ The *Queen Mary*

The major visitor attraction of Long Beach is **The** *Queen Mary* (1126 Queens Hwy., Long Beach, 877/342-0738, www.queenmary.com, daily 10am-6pm, adults $31, children $19, parking $15), one of the most famous ships ever to ply the high seas. This great ship, once a magnificent pleasure-cruise liner, now sits at permanent anchor in Long Beach Harbor. The *Queen Mary* acts as a **hotel** (877/342-0742, $99-389), a museum, and an entertainment center with several restaurants and bars. Book a stateroom and stay aboard, come for dinner, or just buy a regular ticket and take a self-guided tour. The museum exhibits describe the history of the ship, which took its maiden voyage in 1936, with special emphasis on its tour of duty as a troop transport during World War II. Explore many of the decks, including the bow, the engine

room (which still boasts much of its massive machinery), the art gallery, and the gazebo on the stern deck.

It's not just the extensive museum and the attractive hotel that make the *Queen Mary* well known today. The ship is also one of the most famously haunted places in California. Over its decades of service, a number of people lost their lives aboard the *Queen Mary*. Rumors say several of these unfortunate souls have remained on the ship since their tragic deaths. If you're most interested in the ghost stories of the *Queen Mary*, book a spot on the **Paranormal Ship Walk** (877/342-0738, Sun.-Thurs. 8pm-10pm, $39), which takes you to the hottest haunted spots, or **Dining with the Spirits** (Fri.-Sat. 7pm, includes three course dinner, $129), a combination dinner and two-hour haunted tour, or **Paranormal Investigation** (Fri.-Sat. 11pm, Sun. 10pm, $75), for serious ghost hunters. During the day, the 35-minute **Ghosts and Legends Tour** (Mon.-Thurs. 11am-6pm, Fri.-Sat. 11am-9pm, prices vary) includes a haunted experience complete with smoke machines and flashing lights.

The **Queen Mary Passport** (adults $27, children 4-11 $17.50) includes a self-guided audio tour, a look at the vessel's historic exhibits, a viewing of a film showing in the 4-D Theater, and admission to the Ghosts and Legends Tour. The **First Class Passport** (adults $34, children 4-11 $24.50) includes all of the *Queen Mary* Passport attractions along with a ticket to your choice of the Glory Days Historical Tour or the Haunted Encounters Tour.

The *Queen Mary* offers a large paid parking lot near the ship's berth. You'll walk from the parking area up to a square with a ticket booth and several shops and a snack bar. Purchase your general-admission ticket to get on board the ship. It's also a good idea to buy any guided tour tickets at this point. Night tours can fill up in advance, so call ahead to reserve a spot.

Scorpion Submarine

Berthed right next to the luxurious *Queen Mary* is a much smaller and more lethal boat, the **Scorpion Submarine** (877/342-0752, www.queenmary.com, daily 10am-5pm, adults $14, children $12). This Russian sub helped the Soviet Union spy on the United States for more than 20 years during the Cold War. Admission includes the opportunity to explore the innards of the undersea vessel by squeezing through the tiny spaces, mimicking how the Soviet submariners lived and worked during the sub's secret mission.

Aquarium of the Pacific

The **Aquarium of the Pacific** (100 Aquarium Way, 562/590-3100, www.aquariumofpacific.org, daily 9am-6pm, adults $29, seniors $26, children $15) hosts animals and plant life native to the Pacific Ocean, from the local residents of SoCal's sea up to the northern Pacific and down to the tropics. Overall, there are 11,000 ocean animals representing 500 species on view. While the big modern building isn't much to look at from the outside, it's what's inside that's beautiful. Kids and adults all love the unusual feel of the sea stars, urchins, and rays in the touch-friendly tanks. More exciting, you can dip your fingers into the Shark Lagoon and pet a few of the more than 150 sharks that live here. If you prefer tamer and more colorful denizens of the air, spend time in the loud Lorikeet Forest.

Roundhouse Aquarium

Far smaller than the Aquarium of the Pacific, the **Roundhouse Aquarium** (Manhattan Beach Pier, 310/379-8117, www.roundhouseaquarium.org, Memorial Day-Labor Day Mon.-Fri. 2pm-8pm, Sat.-Sun. 9am-8pm, Labor Day-Memorial Day Mon.-Fri. 2pm-5pm, Sat.-Sun. 9am-sunset, $2/person, $5/family) is a two-story facility on the end of the Manhattan Beach Pier. View seahorses, eels, and sharks in tanks or touch a starfish.

BEACHES
Manhattan Beach

Manhattan Beach (The Strand, 310/305-9503, http://beaches.lacounty.gov) is about 12 miles south of Santa Monica. The route along surface streets, with some stretches of coastside driving, will take about 30 minutes. The beach is centered on the fishing pier that is essentially an extension of Manhattan Beach Boulevard beyond The Strand, a popular paved path.

Hermosa Beach

Hermosa Beach (Hermosa Beach Blvd. at 33rd St., 310/305-9503, http://beaches.lacounty.gov) lies about two miles south of Manhattan Beach. Administered by Los Angeles County Beaches and Harbors, both Hermosa and Manhattan Beaches offer volleyball nets, pristine sand, and wave breaks that surfers love. A paved path is packed with bikers, runners, and in-line skaters.

Redondo State Beach

Sitting next to the Redondo Beach Pier, **Redondo State Beach** (400-1700 Esplanade, 310/305-9503, surf report 310/399-8471, http://beaches.lacounty.gov, usually daily sunrise-sunset, parking $5-12 depending on beach and season) gets really crowded in the summer, so if rubbing elbows with your fellow sun worshippers doesn't work for you, Redondo isn't your best bet. On the other hand, the lack of surfers makes swimming a prime activity here, complete with lifeguards during daytime. You'll also find the usual volleyball and other beach games, the bike path (which is lit at night), and the restaurants of the pier. The beach features restrooms and showers, and a large multilevel pay parking structure at the pier offers ample space to stow your car for the day.

ENTERTAINMENT AND EVENTS
Live Music

Hermosa Beach's **The Lighthouse Café** (30 Pier Ave., 310/376-9833, Mon.-Fri. 6pm-2am,

Sat.-Sun. 11am-2am) used to be one of the premier jazz venues on the West Coast, where big cats like Chet Baker, Miles Davis, and Max Roach would perform. These days, the Lighthouse's music calendar has widened to include country, reggae, and Latin music acts, though they still have jazz on Wednesday nights and jazz brunches on the weekend.

With its blood-red interior, **Alex's Bar** (2913 E. Anaheim St., Long Beach, 562/434-8292, Mon.-Sat. 5pm-2am, Sun. 3pm-2am) was where the HBO series *True Blood* shot scenes of its vampire nightclub Fangtasia. In real life, it's a classic punk-rock bar that has hosted performances by The Offspring, Jello Biafra, Black Flag, and the Foxboro Hot Tubs, a Green Day side project.

Bars and Clubs

You could catch acts by some of the world's biggest comedians in the coastal town of Hermosa Beach. **The Comedy & Magic Club** (1018 Hermosa Ave., Hermosa Beach, 310/372-1193, http://comedyandmagicclub.com, performances Tues.-Fri. 8pm, Sat. 7pm and 9:15pm, Sun. 7pm, two-item minimum) hosts a set of comedy every Sunday night by Jay Leno. The small venue, which holds just 250 people, also has had big-time comedians including Jerry Seinfeld, Ray Romano, and Bob Saget onstage to do their bits. The small club doubles as a comedy museum with memorabilia including Seinfeld's puffy shirt and Kevin James's uniform from his show *King of Queens.*

The Deck (1272 The Strand, Hermosa Beach, 310/921-8226, Mon.-Thurs. 11am-11pm, Fri.-Sat. 10am-2pm, Sun. 10am-11pm) has resurfaced in the site of the former Hermosa Beach bar The Poop Deck. The new version has seven beers on draft, wine, and a pool table.

Manhattan Beach's **Ercoles** (1101 Manhattan Ave., Manhattan Beach, 310/372-1997, daily 10am-2am) is one of the oldest bars in the Los Angeles area, but it also has another claim to fame: the dive bar with the best burger. Visit this cash-only establishment on Wednesdays when the burgers are two for the price of one if you purchase two drinks.

The Stache Bar (941 E. 4th St., Long Beach, 562/606-2529, daily 2pm-2am) does classic cocktails including an old-fashioned, a Manhattan, and a Dark and Stormy, but what sets them apart is that their mixers and ginger beer are house-made daily. This is one of the main reasons that people love their Moscow Mules.

The Federal Bar (102 Pine Ave., Long Beach, 562/435-2000, Mon.-Tues. 11:30am-10pm, Wed.-Thurs. 11:30am-midnight, Fri. 11:30am-2am, Sat. 10:30am-2am, Sun. 10:30am-10pm) is an upscale watering hole and gastropub in an old bank building. Downstairs is The Federal Underground, a speakeasy and concert venue.

Festivals and Events

Fiesta Hermosa (Hermosa Beach, 310/376-0951, http://fiestahermosa.net, Memorial Day weekend and Labor Day weekend) is billed as the largest arts and crafts festival in Southern California. In addition to shopping opportunities, there's live music, food, wine, beer, and a children's carnival. It takes place at both the beginning and the end of summer.

Long Beach is a big city that has its fair share of big annual events. One of these is the **Toyota Grand Prix of Long Beach** (Long Beach Convention & Entertainment Center, 300 E. Ocean Blvd., Long Beach, 888/827-7333 or 562/981-2600, www.gplb.com, Apr., adult daily tickets $30-83), which has seven racing events including a sports car race, an IndyCar race, and a pro/celebrity race.

Celebrate the Big Easy during the three-day **Long Beach Bayou Festival** (Rainbow Lagoon Park, E. Shoreline Dr., Long Beach, 562/912-4451, www.longbeachbayou.com, June, adults $25-30, seniors and students $20-30) with music, dancing, and lots of food—including a crawfish-eating contest.

The third-largest pride fest and parade in the country, **Long Beach Pride** (Shoreline Dr., Long Beach, 562/987-9191, http://longbeachpride.com, May, $20) celebrates the

LBGT lifestyle with a parade and lots of entertainment. Jennifer Hudson, Queen Latifah, and Patti LaBelle have performed in previous years.

ACCOMMODATIONS
Manhattan Beach

For a cute near-the-sand motel in Manhattan Beach, stay at the **Sea View Inn at the Beach** (3400 Highland Ave., 310/545-1504, www.theseaviewinn.com, $175-375). Only two blocks from the beach, this is a great place to hole up if you're in town for some surfing, volleyball, or sunbathing along the shore. (You'll avoid the traditional summer beach parking nightmare by leaving your car at the motel.) Just grab a boogie board and some beach chairs from the lobby and head out. Inside, room appointments are prettier and more coordinated than those of most moderate motels. Rooms are done in light blues and whites, with matching prints on the walls and possibly even a live plant to add a homelike touch. The complex of blocky, midcentury modern buildings has its own small swimming pool as well, set in a small, plant-strewn courtyard. Just around the corner, you'll find an array of restaurants, shops, bars, and clubs.

Live in luxury just blocks from the beach at the **Shade Hotel** (1221 N. Valley Dr., 310/546-4995, $389-469). Each of the 38 units at this boutique hotel have spa tubs and Keurig coffeemakers. Take a break from the sea by enjoying the rooftop pool and bar. Mornings begin with a complimentary breakfast buffet followed by yoga on the rooftop on Mondays and Saturdays.

Hermosa Beach

For a full beach experience, stay at the ★ **Beach House at Hermosa Beach** (1300 The Strand, 310/374-3001 or 888/895-4559, www.beach-house.com, $289-669). Right on The Strand, a paved coastal path popular with bikers and runners, every room at the Beach House has a patio or deck to take in all the nearby beach action. The "Loft Suite" has a cushy king bed with Frette sheets, a big bath with a separate tub and shower, two TVs, a stereo, a range, and a gas fireplace. The casual, upscale decor makes visitors feel at home, but you'll probably want to spend more time out on the porch or balcony on sunny days. Guests get a free continental breakfast, the use of the outdoor spa, and access to the on-site gym. If you prefer an outdoor workout, enjoy The Strand for a walk, run, or bike ride.

Long Beach

★ **The Varden** (335 Pacific Ave., 562/432-8950, www.thevardenhotel.com, $139-179) offers the type of tiny, clean, and modern rooms you'd expect to find in Europe. If you don't mind your bathroom being a foot or two from your bed, the sleek little rooms in this hotel, which dates back to 1929, are a great deal. The oldest operating hotel in Long Beach, The Varden is named after an eccentric circus performer named Dolly Varden, who is rumored to have hoarded jewels on the premises. The staff is very friendly and helpful, and coffee, ice, and fresh fruit are available to guests 24 hours a day. It's also one block from Pine Street, which is lined with restaurants and bars.

Looking for something completely different? At **Dockside Boat and Bed** (Dock 5A, Rainbow Harbor, 562/436-3111 or 800/436-2574, www.boatandbed.com, $175-350, overnight parking $24, unless you get the $10 discount parking pass from Dockside), you won't get a regular old hotel room, you'll get one of four yachts. The yachts run 38-54 feet and can sleep four or more people each ($25 pp after the first 2). Amenities include TVs with DVD players, stereos, kitchen facilities, wet bars, and ample seating. The boats are within walking distance from the harbor's restaurants and the aquarium. Don't expect to take your floating accommodations out for a spin; these yachts are permanent residents of Rainbow Harbor.

FOOD
Manhattan Beach

Have you come to Los Angeles to seek genuine

home-style Mexican food? Find it at **Sion's Mexican Restaurant** (235 N. Sepulveda Blvd., 310/372-4504, Sun.-Mon. 8am-2pm, Tues.-Sat. 8am-9pm, $6-14). Expect nothing fancy, but everything fresh—from tacos to salsa—in this utterly casual and family-owned hole-in-the-wall.

Who says there's no fine dining in beach towns? Michelin-starred chef David LeFevre owns and runs **Manhattan Beach Post** (1142 Manhattan Ave., 310/545-5405, Mon.-Thurs. 5pm-10pm, Fri. 11:30am-10:30pm, Sat. 10am-10:30pm, Sun. 10am-10pm, $13-39), which has a menu that can include a Thai marinated shrimp ceviche and a barbecued Moroccan lamb belly. The general manager curates an alcohol list of just five beers on tap, 10 cocktails, and 30 wines by the glass, though there are more wines on the bottle list. Enjoy Manhattan Beach Post's attention to detail in a space furnished with reclaimed wood and communal tables.

Hermosa Beach

★ **Hot's Kitchen** (844 Hermosa Ave., 310/318-2939, www.hotskitchen.com, Sun.-Wed. 11am-9pm, Thurs.-Sat. 11am-10pm, $4.50) has a taco menu you have to see to believe. The over 50 tacos offered include wildly inventive takes on the taco like a shrimp tempura with unagi sauce number and a duck confit offering with grits, braised greens, and a maple glaze. Sure, most Southern California taquerias serve tacos at half the price of those at Hot's Kitchen, but almost every single taco served in this hip reclaimed-wood restaurant—with a great beer selection, I might add—is a singular culinary creation.

Redondo Beach

The **Green Temple Vegetarian Restaurant** (1700 S. Catalina Ave., 310/944-4525, www.greentemple.net, Tues.-Thurs. 11am-4pm and 5pm-9pm, Fri.-Sat. 11am-4pm and 5pm-10pm, Sun. 9am-4pm and 5pm-9pm, $9-13) strives for Southern California Zen in both its cuisine and its dining room.

The vegetarian menu includes a broccoli pine nut casserole and a shepherd's pie made with crumbled veggie burger instead of ground beef.

Long Beach

Combining elegance, fine Continental-California cuisine, and great ghost stories, **Sir Winston's Restaurant and Lounge** (1126 Queens Hwy., 562/499-1657, www.queenmary.com, Tues.-Sun. 5:30pm-10pm, $34-85) floats gently on board the *Queen Mary*. For the most beautiful dining experience, request a window table and make reservations for sunset. Dress in your finest; Sir Winston's requests that diners adhere to their semiformal dress code.

A locals' favorite down where the shops and cafés cluster, **Natraj Cuisine of India** (5262 E. 2nd St., 562/930-0930, www.natrajlongbeach.com, Mon.-Thurs. 11am-2:30pm and 5pm-10pm, Fri. 11am-2:30pm and 5pm-11pm, Sat. 11am-11pm, Sun. 11am-9:30pm, $13-20) offers good food for reasonable prices. Come by for the all-you-can-eat lunch buffet Monday-Saturday to sample a variety of properly spiced meat and vegetarian dishes created in classic Indian tradition.

Beachwood BBQ & Brewing (210 E. 3rd St., 562/436-4020, www.beachwoodbbq.com, Tues.-Sun. 11:30am-9:30pm, bar Tues.-Sun. 11:30am-midnight, $9-28) brings the South to SoCal. They do things the North Carolina way, with a pulled pork sandwich with a vinegar barbecue-sauce base. Other items include baby back ribs, wild boar meatloaf, and shrimp and grits. All pair well with the 22 craft beers on tap.

INFORMATION AND SERVICES

For information, maps, brochures, and advice about Long Beach and the surrounding areas, visit the **Long Beach Convention and Visitors Bureau** (301 E. Ocean Blvd., Suite 1900, 562/436-3645 or 800/452-7829, www.visitlongbeach.com, Mon.-Fri. 8am-5pm).

For medical attention, visit the emergency

room at the **Long Beach Memorial Medical Center** (2801 Atlantic Ave., Long Beach, 562/933-2000, www.memorialcare.org).

GETTING THERE

While you can get to the coast easily enough from LAX, the **Long Beach International Airport** (LGB, 4100 Donald Douglas Dr., 562/570-2600, www.lgb.org) is both closer to Long Beach and less crowded than LAX.

I-710, which runs north-south, is known as the Long Beach Freeway. Along the coast, the Pacific Coast Highway (Hwy. 1) can get you from one beach town to the next.

Parking in Long Beach and the other beach towns is just as bad as parking anywhere else in L.A. Prepare to pay for the privilege of stuffing your car someplace for the day. Beach parking on summer weekends is the worst, but on weekdays and in the off-season you can occasionally find a decent space down near the beach for reasonable rates.

Catalina Island

For a slice of Greece in Southern California, take a ferry or a helicopter out to Catalina Island (Catalina Island Chamber of Commerce, 310/510-1520, www.catalina-chamber.com). You can see Catalina from the shore of Long Beach on a clear day, but for a better view, you've got to get onto the island. The port town of Avalon welcomes visitors with plenty of European-inspired hotels, restaurants, and shops. But the main draw of Catalina lies outside the walls of its buildings. With its Mediterranean summer climate, Catalina draws hikers, horseback riders, and ecotourists. Most of all, it beckons to water lovers of all kinds, from scuba divers and snorkelers to kayakers and anglers.

The climate on Catalina tends toward the temperate, with beautiful, warm, sunny summer days that make getting out into the ocean a pleasure. Even in the winter, you'll find pleasantly warmish days and cool nights. But every once in a while, when the Santa Ana winds come billowing down from the mainland, life in Avalon harbor gets exciting. Storms and winds can whip up the seas, which then come crashing up onto and over the beaches and walkways of Avalon. When you see the yellow sandbags, be aware that the locals are serious. Even on a nonflooding morning, the Pacific can completely engulf the harborside beaches, hit the retaining walls, and spray dozens of feet into the air.

If you're lucky enough to be around, take a walk down toward the waterside and enjoy the show.

SIGHTS
The Casino Theatre and Ballroom

No, it's not that kind of casino. **The Casino Theatre and Ballroom** (1 Casino Way, 310/510-7428, www.visitcatalinaisland.com) at Avalon harks back to the older Italian meaning of the word, "a gathering place." The round, white art deco building, which opened in 1929, acts as a community gathering place and home for all sorts of different activities, including the Catalina Island Jazz Festival. The Avalon Theatre, home to a Page organ, is on the main level and plays first-run movies. Check out the murals by John Gabriel Beckman, of Grauman's Chinese Theatre fame, inside the theatre.

Wrigley Memorial and Botanical Garden

Upcountry, the coolest place to visit may be the **Wrigley Memorial and Botanical Garden** (Avalon Canyon Rd., 1.5 miles west of town, 310/510-2897, www.catalinaconservancy.org, daily 8am-5pm, adults $7, seniors and veterans with ID $5, ages 5-12 and students with ID $3, under age 5 and active military and their families free), operated by the

Catalina Island Conservancy. Stroll through serene gardens planted with flowers, trees, and shrubs that are native to California. Just don't eat the wild tomatoes—they're incredibly poisonous. Also, don't bother with the Catalina cherries. They're not deadly, but they don't taste very good.

At the center of the garden you can't miss the Wrigley Memorial, a 130-foot-tall edifice dedicated to the memory of chewing-gum magnate William Wrigley, Jr., who adored Catalina and used his sticky fortune to make many improvements to it. Most notably, he funded the building of the Avalon Casino. The monument is made and decorated with mostly local materials: the crushed stone on the facade, the blue flagstones, the red roof tiles, and the decorative ceramic tiles.

For a more thorough look at the history, culture, and diverse natural abundance of Catalina, visit the **Nature Center at Avalon Canyon** (1202 Avalon Canyon Rd., 310/510-0954, www.catalinaconservancy.org, summer daily 10am-4pm, winter Fri.-Wed. 10am-4pm, free) just down the road from the botanical garden.

Catalina Island Museum

Another take on the history of Catalina is displayed at the **Catalina Island Museum** (The Casino, 1 Casino Way, Avalon, 310/510-2414, www.catalinamuseum.org, daily 10am-5pm, adults $6, seniors $4, children under 15 free). On the ground floor of the landmark Casino, this small museum makes for a great 15-30-minute culture stop in the middle of a beach vacation. Learn about William Wrigley Jr.'s development of the island and the World War II history of Catalina in revolving exhibits. You'll find a good-size collection of Native American artifacts. Purchase reproductions of tiles, photos, and more in the museum store, and check the website for museum activities geared to kids and adults.

SPORTS AND RECREATION

Outdoor recreation is the main reason most people venture across the channel to Catalina. Whether on land or in the water, you'll likely find activities that are right for you.

Scuba and Snorkeling

If you want to get out into the water on your own, you'll find plenty of places to kick off from shore. The most popular spot is the **Avalon Underwater Park** (Casino Point). This protected area at the north end of town

The Casino Theatre and Ballroom

has buoys and markers to help you find your way around the reefs and keep safe. Not only will you see the famous bright-orange garibaldi fish, you'll get the opportunity to meet gobies, jellyfish, anemones, spiny lobsters, and plenty of other sealife. Out at the deeper edge of the park, nearly half a dozen wrecked ships await your examination. Snorkeling and scuba tour groups come here, as do locals and visitors who rent equipment from local shops and shacks or bring their own. Expect big crowds on summer weekends.

If you prefer to take a guided tour, a number of companies offer snorkeling, scuba, kayaking, and combinations of those at locations all around the island. **Catalina Snorkel & Scuba** (310/510-8558, www.catalinasnorkel-scuba.com, tours $49-199) is right on Lover's Cove a short walk from the ferry terminal and offers guided snorkel tours of the Lover's Cove Marine Reserve; all equipment is included with the fees. This clear-water preserve sits just southeast of the boat terminal and includes a life-filled kelp forest. If you're a certified scuba diver, book a two-hour guided tour of Avalon Underwater Park. If you want to become a scuba diver, Catalina Snorkel & Scuba offers certification classes as well as intro tours that give you a taste of the world underwater. Catalina Snorkel & Scuba also offers equipment rental for snorkelers and divers who want to take off on their own.

Another company to try is **Snorkel Catalina** (107 Pebbly Beach Rd., Avalon, 562/547-4185 or 877/218-9156, www.snorkel-ingcatalina.com, tours $49-52). This company specializes in deeper-water excursions farther away from shore, taking guests out on a custom pontoon boat all year long. If your purpose in coming to Catalina is to see dolphins and sea lions, Snorkel Catalina can make it happen for you. Standard tours run 1-2 hours and let you check out the prettiest fish, sleekest seals, and friendliest dolphins around the island.

If it's hard-core scuba you're interested in, take a walk out to **Catalina Divers Supply** (800/353-0330, www.catalinadiverssupply.

com, daily 8am-5pm). The little green shack out toward the end of the pier offers everything from certification and referral classes to guided shore dives to charter trips on the 46-foot *Scuba Cat*. You'll see things that just aren't visible from the surface with a snorkel. The company highly recommends making reservations for any of their tours and trips.

Kayaking

Kayaking is one of the most popular ways to see otherwise unreachable parts of Catalina. Rent a kayak, or if you're not confident in your own navigation abilities, take a tour with a reputable company. **Descanso Beach Ocean Sports/Catalina Island Kayak & Snorkel** (310/510-1226, www.kayakcatali-naisland.com, $40-60 half-day-full-day) offers several kayak tours to different parts of the island. You don't need previous river- or sea-kayaking experience to take these tours, since the double sit-on-top kayaks make the trip easy and safe even for total beginners and small kids. But if you are a rescue-certified sea kayaker, the folks at Descanso Beach also have an array of lean, sleek, enclosed ocean kayaks for advanced paddlers. This company offers regular year-round trips to Frog Rock (2 hours), Fox Canyon (3 hours, includes a nature walk), and Willow Cove (half-day excursion with snorkeling and hiking). All trips start at Descanso Beach Club, north of Avalon and the Casino.

Another kayak tour provider, **Wet Spot Rentals** (off Pebbly Beach Rd. across the bay from the Casino, 310/510-2229, www.catali-nakayaks.com, $45-85 half-day-full-day) specializes in a full-day land and sea tour that includes both kayaking and an auto tour into the Catalina backcountry. After a van trip and nature tour at the airport on top of the hill, you'll travel down to the less-traveled windward side of the island. You'll get a rare opportunity to kayak on the other side of the island from Avalon, exploring the coves and cliffs around Little Harbor. A brief portage and hike takes you to a waterfall. This fabulous, nearly whole-island tour takes all day, and lunch, water, and all equipment, including sit-on-top beginner kayaks, are provided. Wet Spot also offers several shorter kayak expeditions; they're a great operator if you want to combine kayaking with snorkeling the reefs of the leeward (Avalon) side of the island.

These operators also rent kayaks to individuals (you'll have to prove yourself capable to rent an enclosed sea kayak). They also have an array of snorkel equipment, and you can take a kayak out for some fabulous fish-watching and even skin diving.

Swimming

In the summer, the waters of Catalina can reach more than 70°F—perfect for taking a long, lazy swim in the salty waters of the Pacific. Bring your family out to any one of the charming beaches in the sunny coves for a lazy day on the beach and in the water. The most crowded spots will be at the Avalon Underwater Park, the harbor, and other coves near Avalon. For a more deserted beach, try the windward side of the island; just be aware that it may be, well, windy. Keep a close eye on your children and even adult friends wherever you swim. Catalina's beaches, like most of the California coastline, are subject to dangerous rip currents.

Wildlife-Watching

If you're not keen on swimming in the ocean, but you want a peek at the famous Catalina garibaldi (a bright-orange fish), take a semi-submersible or glass-bottomed boat tour. The **Undersea Tour** (310/510-8687 or 800/626-7489, www.visitcatalinaisland.com, daily 11am, noon, 1pm, 2pm, and 3pm, adults $32, seniors and children $25) takes you a few feet underwater for 45 minutes in a comfy cabin to watch the abundant array of aquatic life around Avalon. For a special (and budget-conscious) treat, book a nighttime Undersea Tour to check out a whole different variety of sea species. Every seat on the boat has a great view of the water, and kids love the colorful fish and mysterious bat rays that glide gracefully by.

In the summer, take another boat trip out at night to see one of the legends of Catalina. A **Flying Fish Boat Trip** (310/510-8687 or 800/626-1496, www.visitcatalinaisland.com, adults $28, seniors $26, children $22) lights up the air just over the waterline, making visible the famous Catalina flying fish as they leap out, putting on a unique show.

Biking

Even most of the locals on Catalina eschew cars in favor of smaller, lighter forms of transportation. A great way to get around and beyond Avalon is on a bicycle. Bring your own aboard the ferries that travel to and from the harbor. If you don't have one, rent a bicycle right on the island at **Brown's Bikes** (underneath Holly Hill House, 100 yards from the ferry dock, 310/510-0986, www.catalinabiking.com, daily 9am-5pm, $8-18 per hour, $20-45 per day). If you're looking for a simple, one-speed cruiser to putter around downtown Avalon and down to the beach, you can get one for $8 per hour or $20 per day. With no gas to buy, it's the ultimate in affordable transportation. Brown's also has 6- and 21-speeds, tandems, an array of mountain bikes, and electric bicycles. You'll also get a map of the bikeable roads and trails in Avalon and around the island.

Mountain bikers, this island's for you: An array of trails from easy to steep and difficult take you up into the hills, providing views and thrills galore. Street bikers will find that Avalon is bike-friendly; the road that runs along the shore on either side of the town is paved, mostly level, and zoned for bicycles. If you've got the legs for it, obtain a permit from the Catalina Conservancy to ride farther afield. Call or email Brown's Bikes for more information on biking outside Avalon.

Golf

As most of Catalina Island is devoted to wildlife preservation, you won't find a wealth of golf courses here. But if you just can't abide the notion of going for a trip without exercising your clubs, get yourself a tee time at the 9-hole

Catalina Island Golf Course (1 Country Club Dr., Avalon, 310/510-0530, www.visit-catalinaisland.com, daily 7am-6pm, $36-70), which has 9- or 18-hole rounds, discounts for seniors, and higher rates on weekends. You'll be walking on greens built in 1892, used for the Bobby Jones Invitational Tournament from the 1930s through the 1950s, and more recently played on by up-and-coming SoCal junior players such as Craig Stadler and Tiger Woods as they built their skills. Heck, even if you don't play, it's worth walking the course on a sunny day just to enjoy the unbelievable views out to the Casino, the town of Avalon, and the clutch of sailboats bobbing in the harbor. The full-service pro shop provides rental equipment and golf carts as well as a set of **tennis courts** you can rent by the hour.

If your taste in golf runs a little less serious, head for **Golf Gardens** (10 Island Plaza, 310/510-1200, www.balboapavilion.com, hours vary, adults $7, children $4), a miniature golf course one block inland from the fountain just past the Discovery Tours Plaza and across the street from the City Library. This is a great break for kids tired of sightseeing and ecotouring. This cute 18-hole course has a tropical feel, complete with palm trees and good putting challenges.

Spas

You've got a surprising number of massage and spa options right in and around Avalon. If you prefer your massage in the privacy of your hotel room or condo, call **Catalina Sea Spa** (310/510-8920, www.catalinamassage-bymichelle.net, massage $85-150), formerly known as Massage by Michelle. The therapists love to work with couples looking for a relaxing day or evening of romance, and they are trained in a variety of massage techniques and spa therapies, including heated stones and Thai massage. Book a simple Swedish massage or a full spa package with facials, body scrubs, and massages for one or two people. Check the website for a full list of available treatments. Book in advance to get the date and time you want. Studio sessions are also available.

Whether you're looking for a divine romantic experience with your sweetie or a solo day of spa-induced respite from your busy life, you'll find it at **The Spa at Catalina** (888 Country Club Rd., Avalon, 310/510-9255, www.catalinaspa.com, massages $55-169). This full-service day spa offers all sorts of massage and treatment packages, from a simple half-hour of bodywork up to nearly three hours of head-to-toe bliss. The spa has dual rooms (many complete with private baths for two) to serve couples or pairs of friends who want to enjoy their treatments together. Choose from the many packages that focus on facials and scalp treatments using lavender, peppermint, and other delicious essential oils. You can also breathe deep and detox with a body wrap or heated stone massage. The spa sits in Falls Canyon outside downtown Avalon; ask about getting a free shuttle from your hotel to the spa at the Best Western Canyon Hotel when you book your treatments. It's best to make reservations at least a couple of days in advance; even in winter, same-day appointment availability is rare.

Decide for yourself whether the treatments you receive in downtown Avalon live up to the name **A Touch of Heaven** (205 Crescent Ave., 310/510-1633, www.atouchofheavenday-spa.com, daily 9am-5pm, $45-240) at the back of the Metropole Market Place. This day spa echoes the European flavor of the town surrounding it; you'll find an extensive menu of Euro-style facials, from the intense relaxation of a LaStone Facial to the aesthetically focused glycolic-lactic acid peel and facial. Also look for a few unusual treatments, including raindrop therapy and ear candling, as well as practitioners of both Eastern and Western massage modalities. The spa also offers massage for children, and well-behaved young people are welcome to enjoy the treatments here.

Tours

One of the main forms of entertainment on the island is touring. Take a bus tour, a Jeep tour, a glass-bottomed boat tour, and more. The Catalina Island Conservancy offers **Jeep**

Eco-Tours (310/510-2595, www.catalinaconservancy.org, up to 6 people $549 chartered half-day, $889 chartered full-day, non-chartered two-hour tour $70 pp, non-chartered three-hour tour $109 pp) out in the wilds of Catalina. You can go much farther on these tours than you can by yourself—out into the wilderness to see the bison, the wild horses, plant species unique to the island, and more. Bring your camera, both for close-ups and for views out toward the sea. On the full-day trips, you'll get lunch, drinks, and snacks, while on the half-day trip you'll get snacks and drinks.

For a sedate view of Catalina's more settled areas as well as it's road-viewable wilderness, try an **Inland Motor Tour** (800/626-7489, www.visitcatalinaisland.com, year-round daily, adults $79, seniors and children $76). This 3.5-hour tour aboard a restored 1950s cruising bus takes you away from the coastline and into the island's interior via old stagecoach routes. Along the way you'll see Middle Ranch, the magnificent Arabian horses and Old West mementos of El Rancho Escondido, and the Airport in the Sky Nature Center. A shorter version of this tour is the **Skyline Drive** (310/510-8687 or 800/626-1496, daily year-round, adults $49, seniors and children $45), a two-hour trip that takes you up from Avalon to the Airport in the Sky Nature Center along a route cluttered with spectacular vistas of island and ocean.

If you want a guided walking tour of Avalon, try **Catalina Adventure Tours** (877/510-2888, www.catalinaadventuretours.com, adults $22, seniors $18, children $14) for a 90-minute look at Avalon's attractions, history, and architecture. And for the more independent-minded visitor, try **GPS Walking Tours** (310/510-8687, www.visitcatalinaisland.com, $15 per device). Each device can guide 4-6 people, an ideal money saver for families.

The newest way to see the island is by zipping down its hillsides. The **Catalina Zip Line Eco Tour** (800/626-1496, www.visitcatalinaisland.com, Mon.-Fri. 9am-4pm, Sat.-Sun. 7am-6pm, $109-125) is a two-hour tour by zip line that drops from 440 feet to 60 feet above sea level.

ACCOMMODATIONS

You'll find plenty of charming inns and hotels on Catalina; most sit in or near Avalon. You can also camp on Catalina, and ecotourists often prefer to immerse themselves in the natural world of the island by sleeping and eating outdoors.

Under $150

The **Hotel Atwater** (125 Sumner Ave., 800/322-3434, www.visitcatalinaisland.com, spring-fall, $140-390) has bright, cheerful rooms for reasonable rates. Take in the history of a budget hotel that's been hosting guests since the 1920s. Clean, light-colored economy rooms provide the best value for your buck, while the more upscale suites cost more and offer prettier decor and better amenities. Whichever type of room you book, you'll have a TV, air-conditioning, and more. You'll find storage for your diving gear and bikes, and a rinse-off area outside for divers, snorkelers, and swimmers. The Atwater usually closes each winter; call ahead to confirm availability.

For inexpensive indoor accommodations, your best bet is the **Hermosa Hotel & Cottages** (131 Metropole St., 310/510-1010 or 877/453-1313, www.hermosahotel.com, $115-175). This simple budget hotel has rooms that now have their own bathrooms. (Be aware of a two-night minimum for stays involving a Saturday night in the high season.) The cottages have private baths, and some have kitchens and TVs. "Family units" can sleep up to nine in the main building and have kitchens—perfect for larger families or groups of friends traveling together on a budget. The 100-plus-year-old building sits only about a block from the harbor beaches and a short walk from the Casino, shops, and restaurants.

$150-250

Want to stay right on the waterfront? Book a room at the bright yellow **Hotel Mac Rae**

(409 Crescent Ave., 310/510-0246 or 800/698-2266, www.hotelmacrae.com, $160-260). This bit of Catalina history has been in the Mac Rae family for four generations, and they've been running the hostelry since 1920. The Mediterranean flavor of Avalon follows you into the rooms and common spaces of the Mac Rae. Relax with a drink in the bright brick courtyard. Choose one of the premium rooms that looks right out into the harbor, or a more economical courtyard-view room. Grab a complimentary continental breakfast downstairs, and either eat in the courtyard or take your coffee and your pastries back to your pretty Côte d'Azur-styled room for more privacy. Catching the afternoon ferry but want to enjoy one last morning in the warm Catalina water? The Mac Rae has luggage storage and even a public shower for use after you check out.

For a European hotel experience in Avalon, stay at the **Hotel Metropole** (205 Crescent Ave., 310/510-1884, www.hotel-metropole.com, $230-1,100). The comfortably cluttered and warmly decorated rooms feel like home almost immediately. You'll find gas fireplaces in some rooms and oversize two-person whirlpool bathtubs in a few pretty tiled baths. The beds feel great after a long day of ocean swimming or the ferry ride over from Long Beach. The little extras are nice too, from the nightly turndown service to the L'Occitane toiletries. You can also use the Wi-Fi service in your room. The Metropole is built in a modern style with a pretty gray paint job. On the roof you'll find a whirlpool tub with glass walls enclosing its deck, letting you look out over the rooftops into the harbor. The lower-end rooms don't have much in the way of ocean views, so for a window on the water, you have to pay premium rates for an oceanfront room or suites ($500-800). You can walk half a block down the street to the ocean. For extra pampering, make an appointment at the day spa on the bottom floor of the hotel appropriately named A Touch of Heaven (205 Crescent Ave., 310/510-1633, www.atouchofheavendayspa.com, daily 9am-8pm, $40-240). Just outside

by the back elevator, start a shopping jaunt in the little Metropole center, where you can grab a cup of coffee, or walk down Crescent Avenue for a meal.

The **Villa Portofino** (111 Crescent Ave., 310/510-0555 or 888/510-0555, www.hotel-villaportofino.com, rooms $125-550) offers Mediterranean elegance on the Avalon waterfront. The bright-white exterior with red tile roofs invites you inside this 34-room boutique hotel. Rooms range from small standards up through immense, lush, individually named suites with fireplaces, soaking tubs, and richly colored furnishings. Amenities include a complimentary continental breakfast, free Wi-Fi, free beach chairs and towels, and an on-site restaurant, Ristorante Villa Portofino (101 Crescent Ave., 310/510-2009, www.ristorantevillaportofino.com, $15-36). The Portofino's location is perfect—right on the main drag running along the harborside beach. There's also a rooftop sundeck with chairs and a great view of the harbor.

Over $250

A striking, clean, white-and-yellow building just feet from one of Avalon's most popular beaches, the **Pavilion Hotel** (513 Crescent Ave., 877/778-8322, www.visitcatalinaisland.com, $300-800) boasts a nice private patio very close to downtown's action. The rooms are clean and modern but not luxury caliber, though there is a nice courtyard with a tropical garden and fire pit to hang out in.

CAMPING

Camping is the best way to get away from Avalon and stay on other parts of the island. It's also a great way to get to know the precious Catalina wilderness in an up-close-and-personal way. Check the island's visitors website (www.visitcatalinaisland.com) for a list and descriptions of all the major campgrounds around the island. Read the regulations, which are more stringent than at some other camping areas and are strictly enforced. Permits are required for all campsites. Also check out the equipment rentals; if you don't want to bring your own tent and gear, rent it at the Two Harbors campground (310/510-8368).

You have a choice of more than half a dozen campgrounds, some on the coast and some up the mountains in the interior. One of the largest and most developed campgrounds sits just outside the tiny town of **Two Harbors** (310/510-8368, www.visitcatalinaisland.com, adults $21, children $12, tent cabins $50). Book online to avoid the $25 "administration fee" for reservations phoned in. Go to the website and see a photo gallery of the campgrounds and check out a map of the campsites before you make a reservation. Bring your own tent and equipment, rent it, or book one of the tent cabins at this site. The tent cabins come with cots and mattresses, sunshades, and a camp stove and lantern in addition to the usual barbecue grill, fire ring, and picnic table. All campers have access to showers, restroom facilities, and lockers to keep valuables safe while you're out exploring the area.

If you're looking to camp on the beach, check out the **Little Harbor** (310/510-8368, www.visitcatalinaisland.com, summer adults $18, children $9, winter adults $16, children $8, tent cabins $50) campground. Seven miles from the town of Little Harbor, the sandy campsites make a perfect place to sleep if your aim is snorkeling, kayaking (Wet Spot Rentals, 310/510-2229), and playing away from all the casual island visitors. You'll find potable water, showers, and toilets here. The best way to get to the Little Harbor campground is to take the Safari Bus, so book seats and space for your gear when you book your campsite.

Perhaps the coolest way to stay on Catalina is to bring or rent a kayak and paddle into one of the **boat-in campsites** (310/510-8368, www.campingcatalinaisland.com, adults $12-16, children $6-8). These 11 primitive campsites can't be accessed by land at all—you must bring and moor your own boat. You'll get a wholly natural experience at any of these beautiful remote locations, with no running water, showers, toilet facilities, or shade structures. Whatever you want and need, you must pack into your boat with you. A ranger checks each campsite daily, so you're not completely cut off from the outside world. However, take precautions such as bringing a two-way radio and an above-average first-aid kit just in case an emergency crops up.

FOOD

To be honest, the culinary presence on Catalina isn't much to write home about. While there's certainly no lack of restaurants in Avalon, the statewide trend toward delicious cuisine at both the high and low ends hasn't made it across the channel to the island yet. You might consider getting a room or a condo with a kitchen and cooking a few of your own meals to save a bit of cash while you're here. Still, a traveler has to go out to eat sometimes. Here are a few places to try.

Classic American

All the locals recommend that tourists try **Steve's Steakhouse** (417 Crescent Ave., 310/510-0333, www.stevessteakhouse.com, daily 11:30am-2pm and 5pm-11pm, $16-37). Steve's offers a wide array of classic steak house fare with plenty of seafood options thrown in as a nod to the water lapping the harbor beach just outside. The burgers also hit the spot after a day of hiking and swimming. Generous portions of meat or fish are accompanied by traditional steak house sides, and the desserts up the ante with some tasty sweetness (the mud pie's not half bad).

El Galleon (411 Crescent Ave., 310/510-1188, www.catalinahotspots.com, Sun.-Fri. 11am-9pm, Sat. 11am-midnight, $18-50) is probably a better place to get a drink than have dinner. El Galleon's decor is a busy, improbable mix of maritime items and Mardi Gras paraphernalia. The large menu speaks to hearty American diners with lots of aged steaks, chicken dishes, and fresh fish. Lighter eaters can peruse the selection of salads, soups, and seafood appetizers. For a major feast, take a look at the prix fixe menu, which, when available, offers a hearty four-course dinner (about $70 pp). The dessert menu offers a few unusual treats, plus a wide array of sweet and strong coffee drinks to round off your evening. Better yet, order one of El Galleon's 18-ounce cocktails or one of their German beers on tap and watch the bar's nightly karaoke, which kicks off at 9pm.

A more refined dining experience can be had at the **Avalon Grille** (423 Crescent Ave., 310/510-7494, www.visitcatalinaisland.com, daily 11:30am-4pm and 5pm-10pm, $25-45). There are the typical seafood and meat offerings along with some surprises including an entrée of grilled wild boar pork chops and buffalo ribs. Eat them inside under twirling ceiling fans or in tables under a canopy beside the restaurant.

Coffee

Most coffee shops in Avalon don't offer Wi-Fi. The **Café Metropole** (113 Metropole, 310/510-9095, www.cafemetropole.com, daily 11am-3pm) has Internet availability with a purchase of a coffee or one of its daily iced teas. The café also serves up an inviting selection of sandwiches and vegetarian fare.

Italian

The **Ristorante Villa Portofino** (101 Crescent Ave., 310/510-2009, www.ristorante-villaportofino.com, daily 5pm-close, $15-36), attached to the Villa Portofino hotel, serves tasty pasta and protein dishes with a distinct Italian flair—and you'll get a fabulous harbor view with your cannelloni or calamari. In homage to the locale, the menu here runs to seafood, with some classic and a few inventive preparations. The pastas bring homey comfort food to Catalina, and the hot appetizer menu is well worth a look. For dessert, the Ristorante offers a goodly selection of Italian favorites, such as cannoli and *panna cotta*. In the summer, see if you can get a table on the patio to enjoy the balmy island breezes—you'll feel almost as though you're really on the Mediterranean coast of Italy.

Mexican

Looking for an unpretentious taco? Get one at the **Catalina Cantina** (313 Crescent Ave.,

310/510-0100, daily 11am-9:30pm, $10-25) or its fast-food walk-up neighbor, the **Topless Taco.** Serving a mix of American diner fare (think burgers and fries, wings, and fish-and-chips) and Americanized Mexican staples (burritos, fajitas, combo plates), the Catalina Cantina offers tasty food for decent prices. Better still, if you come in the evening, cool off with one of the Cantina's buckets o' liquor. Rum punch, margaritas, something called the Blue Shark, and more come in either normal human-size glasses or in a 24-ounce bowl that they really hope you'll share with friends.

Seafood

Part locals' bar and part no-frills seafood restaurant, ★ **The Lobster Trap** (128 Catalina St., 310/510-8585, www.catalinalobstertrap.com, daily 11am-late, $12-30) serves up stuffed lobster, lobster salad, and lobster tacos. (It is strange though that the local lobster costs more than the imported Maine and Atlantic lobster on the menu.) Plastic lobsters and plastic fish decorate the wall, and some diners can eat their seafood, pasta, poultry, or steak on a raised platform that looks like a boat.

INFORMATION AND SERVICES

If you are camping in a remote location, talk to the rangers at the Two Harbors station before leaving to learn how best to contact them or the police in an emergency. Bring a two-way radio, since cell signals may be unreliable or nonexistent.

For medical assistance, go to the **Catalina Island Medical Center** (100 Falls Canyon Rd., 310/510-0700, www.catalinaislandmedicalcenter.org).

TRANSPORTATION

There are two ways to get to Catalina: by boat and by air.

Boat

Most folks take the ferry over from the mainland coast. The **Catalina Express**

(800/481-3470, www.catalinaexpress.com, round-trip adults $75, seniors $68, ages 2-11 $59, under age 2 $5, bikes and surfboards $7) serves as the major carrier, with multiple departures every day, even in the off-season. During the summer high season, you can choose to leave from Long Beach, San Pedro, or Dana Point. Most ferries dock at Avalon, but you can arrange to travel directly to Two Harbors from San Pedro if you prefer. Bring your bike, your luggage, and your camping gear aboard for a comfortable hour-long ride on one of eight ferries. Bars on both levels offer snacks and drinks, and TVs help make the cruise go by a little faster. On the way it's worth looking out the window, however: You might spot seals or sea lions, different varieties of pelicans, or even a pod of dolphins playing in the swells. Catalina Express also offers plenty of return cruises to the mainland each day.

An alternate ferry service, the **Catalina Flyer** (Balboa Pavilion, 400 Main St., Newport Beach, 800/831-7744, www.catalinainfo.com, round-trip adults $70, seniors $68, ages 3-12 $59, under age 2 $5, parking $15-25) offers one trip out and one trip back each day. The Flyer operates primarily March-November.

Air

You can also get to Catalina by air. There is a helicopter pad just northwest of Avalon harbor. **Island Express Helicopter Service** (1175 Queens Hwy. S., Long Beach, 800/228-2566, www.islandexpress.com, Sun.-Tues. 7:30am-6:30pm, Wed.-Sat. 7:30am-9pm, round-trip $250-300 pp) can fly you from Long Beach or San Pedro to Catalina in about 15 minutes. You can get a cab into town from the helipad. Island Express also offers aerial tours of the island and various travel packages. Or if you prefer to fly your own small plane to Catalina, the **Airport in the Sky** (310/510-2495, www.catalina.com, mid-Mar.-mid-Oct. 8am-7pm, mid-Oct.-mid-Mar. 8am-5pm) offers general aviators a 3,250-foot runway, $10 parking, a $25 landing fee, and $15 overnight fee—there is no gas, though, so fuel up for a round-trip before you head out. The Catalina Island Conservancy's **Wildlands Express/ Airport Shuttle** (310/510-0143, adults $26, ages 5-11 $21, under age 5 free) is one way to make it the 10 miles or so from the airport to Avalon and back again. Reservations are required, so call ahead.

Car

On Catalina, cars just aren't the fashionable way to get around. Even the locals tend to eschew full cars since they aren't practical in the tiny town of Avalon. Instead, locals and visitors in the know prefer to drive golf carts. Walk from the ferry dock down toward town, and you'll see any number of rental services, complete with herds of carts out and ready for use. The cost runs $80-120 per hour for a 4-6 passenger cart with a $40-60 deposit. A couple of easy-to-find companies include **Island Rentals** (125 Pebbly Beach Rd., 310/510-1456) underneath the Holly Hill House near the ferry dock and **Cartopia** (615 Crescent Ave., 310/510-2493).

Grab a taxi if you need to get somewhere in a hurry, especially with your luggage. Taxis hover near the ferry dock when the ferries are due in each day, and it's customary to share your ride with as many people as can fit into the car (which is often a minivan). To get a cab back to the ferry or the helipad when it's time to leave, call **Catalina Transportation Services** (310/510-0025, www.catalinatransportationservices.com, rates vary) for a taxi, shuttle, charter, or trolley. It takes only about 10 minutes for a taxi to get to just about anywhere in town.

Bus

Public transit on Catalina includes the **Safari Bus** (310/510-2800, adults $16-57, children $13-42, depending on destination), which runs from Avalon to Two Harbors each day. The bus stops at the southeast corner of Island Plaza in Avalon. You can buy tickets at Visitors Services and the Discovery Tours booth on the Pleasure Pier. The **Avalon Trolley** (310/510-0025 or 310/510-0342, mid-June-mid-Sept.

daily, mid-Sept.-mid-June Sat.-Sun., holidays, and cruise ship days, $2/one way, $7/day pass) runs in and around Avalon, hitting most of the major sightseeing and outdoor adventuring spots near town. With two lines that converge inland, you can get where you need to go for a reasonable fare without having to hoof it. The trolley runs approximately every 30-40 minutes, with the entire route taking about an hour.

Orange County Coast

The Orange County coast begins north of Huntington Beach and stretches south across a collection of sunny, scenic beaches until ending at San Clemente. Along the way, Newport Beach, Laguna Beach, and Dana Point provide surf, sun, and sand galore.

Huntington Beach is Surf City USA, a beach town with a vibrant culture. The annual Vans U.S. Open of Surfing, the largest surf contest in the world, happens every summer.

Newport Beach boasts one of the largest recreational harbors in the world, making it a destination for those who want to head out fishing, sailing, paddling, or boating. Its Balboa Peninsula has been entertaining families since 1936 with its Balboa Fun Zone and its popular Ferris wheel.

Just south of Newport Beach, Laguna Beach has several attributes that make it worth visiting including a long-running arts scene, some of SoCal's most revered restaurants, and superb ocean visibility for scuba divers, snorkelers, and paddleboarders.

Dana Point and San Clemente have long played prominent roles in surf culture, just like Huntington Beach to the north. Both southern Orange County beach towns are home to many surfboard manufacturers and surf publications. Dana Point is also known for its large constructed harbor with towering bluffs above, while San Clemente is close to Trestles, one of SoCal's most revered surf spots. Three miles inland, San Juan Capistrano is known for the Mission San Juan Capistrano, which has long influenced the character of the Orange County city.

HUNTINGTON BEACH

This Orange County beach town is known for its longtime association with surfing and surf culture beginning when Hawaiian legend Duke Kahanamoku first rode waves here back in 1922. Surfers still ride the surf on either side of the Huntington Beach Pier, a large concrete pier that offers fine views of the beach scene on both sides. Across the Pacific Coast Highway, Huntington Beach's Main Street is full of restaurants, bars, and shops including lots of surf shops.

Sights

The small **International Surfing Museum** (411 Olive St., 714/960-3483, www.surfingmuseum.org, Wed.-Fri. and Sun. noon-5pm, Sat. noon-7pm, Tues. noon-8pm, donations appreciated) celebrates the surf-obsessed with some worthy artifacts including Duke Kahanamoku's board, Dick Dale's guitar, and the camera used to film the 1966 surf film *The Endless Summer*. The museum also puts on surf music concerts in its parking lot and in nearby Pier Plaza.

Beaches

Huntington City Beach (Pacific Coast Hwy. from Beach Blvd. to Seapoint St., beach headquarters 103 Pacific Coast Hwy., 714/536-5281, www.huntingtonbeachca.gov, beach daily 5am-10pm, office Mon.-Fri. 8am-5pm) runs the length of the south end of town, petering out toward the oil industry facilities at the north end. This famous beach hosts major sporting events such as the U.S. Open of Surfing and the X Games. But even the average beachgoer can enjoy all sorts of activities

Orange County Coast

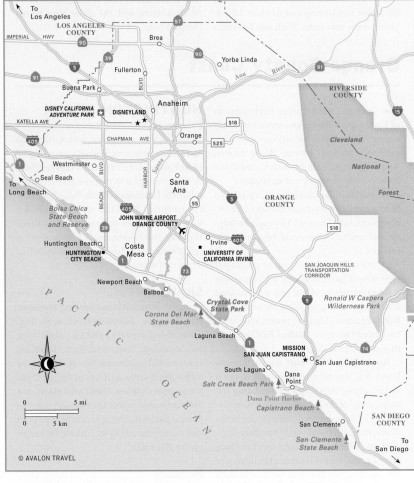

To
Los Angeles

LOS ANGELES
COUNTY

IMPERIAL HWY

90

57

Brea

Yorba Linda

90

5

39

Fullerton

Buena Park

91

FULLERTON BLVD

Anaheim

91

RIVERSIDE
COUNTY

15

DISNEY CALIFORNIA
ADVENTURE PARK ★ DISNEYLAND
★ ★

KATELLA AVE

405

CHAPMAN AVE

Orange

S18

S25

Cleveland

405

Westminster

Seal Beach

To
Long Beach

Bolsa Chica
State Beach
and Reserve

Huntington Beach

HUNTINGTON
CITY BEACH

1

39

405

BEACH BLVD

HARBOR BLVD

Santa
Ana

Santa Ana River

National

Forest

55

5

JOHN WAYNE AIRPORT
ORANGE COUNTY

ORANGE
COUNTY

S18

Costa
Mesa

73

Irvine

405

UNIVERSITY OF
CALIFORNIA IRVINE

SAN JOAQUIN HILLS
TRANSPORTATION
CORRIDOR

Newport Beach

Balboa

5

Ronald W Caspers
Wilderness Park

P A C I F I C

Crystal Cove
State Park

Corona Del Mar
State Beach

Laguna Beach

1

MISSION
SAN JUAN CAPISTRANO
★ San Juan Capistrano

74

South Laguna

Dana
Point

Salt Creek Beach Park

O C E A N

Dana Point Harbor
Capistrano Beach

SAN DIEGO
COUNTY

San Clemente

San Clemente
State Beach

To
San Diego

0   5 mi
0   5 km

© AVALON TRAVEL

on a daily basis. There's a cement walkway for biking, in-line skating, jogging, and walking. On the sand, get up a game of Frisbee or take advantage of the beach volleyball courts. Out in the water, catch a wave on either side of the pier or make use of prevailing winds for a thrilling kite-surfing run. Nonriders can boogie-board, bodysurf, and skim-board closer to the shore. Anglers and strolling couples prefer the Huntington Beach Pier. There's a dog-friendly section at the north end of the beach where dogs can be let off-leash. You may even see an occasional surfer riding tandem with a four-legged friend.

There are plenty of services and amenities, including lifeguard stations (in high season), restrooms and outdoor showers at regular intervals, concession stands, and even wetsuit and surfboard rentals.

Surfing

With all this talk of Huntington Beach's surf

culture, it's time to hit the waves. There are popular breaks on either side of the pier. Hope that the Santa Ana winds are blowing, because they can cause epic conditions. If you need a board, head across the PCH to **Jack's Surf Shop** (101 Main St., 714/536-4516, daily 8am-10pm, surfboard rentals $10-15/hour, wetsuit $5/hour).

Nightlife

Johnny's Saloon (17428 Beach Blvd., 714/848-0676, daily 1pm-2am) calls itself a rock-and-roll whiskey bar. With over 100 craft whiskeys and punk rock paraphernalia on the walls, who is to argue with them?

Events

The **Duck-A-Thon** (Huntington Beach Pier, 714/500-0382, www.duckathon.org, May) is a race from ocean to shore featuring competing bathtub rubber ducks. This charity event benefits the Huntington Beach Community Clinic.

The largest surfing contest in the world, the **U.S. Open of Surfing** (Huntington Beach Pier, Main St. and Pacific Coast Hwy., www.vansusopenofsurfing.com, July-Aug.) is a weeklong surfing competition that provides a way for surfers to qualify for the pro surfing world tour. It draws lots of spectators on the beach to witness the action in the water.

Accommodations

The 17-room **Sun 'N Sands Motel** (1102 Pacific Coast Hwy., 714/536-2543, www.sunnsands.com, $169-269) is a tiny place (17 rooms) where you can expect standard motel-room decor in your king or double-queen room, plus an adequate private bath, a TV with movie channels, and Wi-Fi access. But the main attraction is across the treacherous Pacific Coast Highway: long, sweet Huntington Beach. Be careful crossing the highway to get to the sand. Find a traffic light and a crosswalk rather than risking life and limb for the minor convenience of jaywalking.

For something more upscale, book a room at the **Shorebreak Hotel** (500 Pacific Coast Hwy., 714/861-4470, www.jdvhotels.com, $350-890). Some rooms have private balconies looking out over the beach and pier. Everyone can enjoy the hotel's on-site restaurant, fitness center, and courtyard with fire pits.

Food

The Black Trumpet Bistro (18344 Beach Blvd., 714/842-1122, www.theblacktrumpetbistro.com, Tues.-Sat. 4pm-10pm, $12-23) is not named for a mushroom but rather for the jazz greats that lend their names to the entrees. Here, Duke is a Cornish game hen entrée, while Louis is a Greek spaghetti dish. Paintings of jazz legends also adorn the walls. The owner wants to represent Mediterranean cuisine from tapas to more substantial entrees. His endeavor caused The Black Trumpet to be proclaimed one of Huntington Beach's best restaurants by the *OC Weekly*.

For a quick bite to eat, stop off at the **Bodhi Tree Vegetarian Cafe** (501 Main St., Suite E, 714/969-9500, www.bodhitreehb.com, Wed.-Mon. 11am-10pm, $6-10) for vegetarian soups, salads, and sandwiches. **Sugar Shack Café** (213 Main St., 714/536-0355, www.hbsugarshack.com, Mon.-Tues. 6am-2pm, Wed. 6am-8pm, Thurs.-Fri. 6am-2pm, Sat.-Sun. 6am-3pm, $7-10) is a great place for breakfast, serving breakfast burritos and omelets.

Information and Services

For injuries (surf-related and otherwise), head to the **Huntington Beach Hospital** (17772 Beach Blvd., 714/843-5000, www.hb-hospital.org).

Information on the city and other Orange County locales can be found at the **Huntington Beach Marketing and Visitors Bureau** (301 Main St., Suite 208, 714/969-3492 or 800/729-6232, www.surfcityusa.com, Mon.-Fri. 9am-5pm), which also has a visitors information kiosk (Pacific Coast Hwy. and Main St., times vary according to season).

NEWPORT BEACH

Newport Beach has a peninsula of sand protecting its bay studded with residential islands from the ocean. The presence of the bay caused for the city to be named "Newport." The beach has "The Wedge," a wave that quickly reaches impressive heights right before it crashes on the sand, while Balboa Island is the place to take a ride on the long-running Balboa Fun Zone Ferris wheel.

Sights

Since 1936, the **Balboa Fun Zone** (600 E. Bay Ave., www.thebalboafunzone.com, daily 11am-10pm) has been entertaining families with its shops, restaurants, arcade, boat rentals, rides, and Ferris wheel that has views of the harbor and sea.

Beaches

Most of the activity in **Newport Beach** (www.visitnewportbeach.com) centers around Newport Pier (McFadden Pl.) and Main Street on the Balboa Peninsula. This 10-mile stretch of sand is popular for fishing, swimming, surfing, and other ocean activities. On the east end of Balboa Peninsula, **The Wedge** is the world's most famous bodysurfing spot. On south swells, the wave jacks up off the adjacent rock jetty and creates monsters up to 30 feet high that break almost right on the beach. Beginners should stay out of the water and enjoy the spectacle from the sand.

Nightlife

The **Goat Hill Tavern** (1830 Newport Blvd., Costa Mesa, 949/548-8428, www.goathill-tavern.com, Mon.-Thurs. 1pm-2am, Fri. noon-2am, Sat.-Sun. 11am-2am) is a legendary dive with an impressive 141 beers on tap. The beers are all available as pitchers that you can drink under broken bikes, license plates, and photos hanging off the bar's walls and ceiling. An outside patio is available for smokers.

Also in Costa Mesa, **Casa** (820 W. 19th St., Costa Mesa, 949/877-4011, http://casa-costamesa.com, Wed.-Sun. 8pm-2am) is a speakeasy known for its cocktails and live entertainment (jazz, blues, DJ music). Make a reservation to this intimate bar on their website, at which time you'll receive a password.

Accommodations

With both luxury and comfort in abundance, **The Island Hotel Newport Beach** (690 Newport Center Dr., 866/554-4620, www.the-islandhotel.com, $200-400) offers perhaps the ultimate O.C. experience. It's a high-rise situated in a giant shopping mall a few minutes' drive from the beach. The tropical-themed rooms have all the best amenities: cushy beds with white linens, attractive private baths, big TVs, and views of the mall (and if you're lucky, of the ocean beyond it).

Food

For something French, colorful **Pescadou Bistro** (3325 Newport Blvd., 949/675-6990, www.pescadoubistro.com, Tues.-Sun. 5:30pm-9pm, $21-36) fits the bill. Meanwhile, **Eat Chow** (211 62nd St., 949/423-7080, www.eatchownow.com, Mon.-Thurs. 8am-9pm, Fri. 8am-10pm, Sat. 7am-10pm, Sun. 7am-9pm, $9-18) is a local favorite with items like breakfast *carnitas* tacos and shredded redeye burritos.

Expect a line outside **Cappy's Café & Cantina** (5930 W. Coast Hwy., 949/646-4202, Mon.-Fri. 6am-3pm, Sat.-Sun. 6am-4pm, $10-20), a low-slung building that has served breakfast and lunch since 1957. Cappy's serves expand-your-waistband items including a 20-ounce porterhouse steak and eggs and a knockwurst and eggs dish. Enjoy the fare while mellowing out in a beachy atmosphere with plenty of colorful murals.

Information and Services

If you need medical care while you're visiting the beach, **Hoag Hospital** (1 Hoag Dr., Newport Beach, 949/764-4624, www.hoag-hospital.org) can probably fix whatever's broken.

LAGUNA BEACH

Between Los Angeles and San Diego, Laguna Beach stands apart from other Orange County beach communities with its long-running arts scene, touted fine-dining restaurants, tide pool-pocked coastline jammed between sandy beaches, and clear ocean water that beckons snorkelers and divers underwater. It doesn't fully bleed into the rest of Orange County's sprawl due to its abundant parkland, steep hills, and lack of highways except for the Pacific Coast Highway.

The coastal resort community has been a tourist destination since the late 1880s. It also drew painters, filmmakers, photographers, and writers to its scenic coastline, causing the foundation of the Laguna Beach Art Association in 1918.

While it may be known now to some as the former setting of the vapid reality TV show of the same name, Laguna Beach was an edgy, countercultural community in the late 1960s and early 1970s. At that time, it was home to LSD guru Timothy Leary and the Brotherhood of Eternal Love, which was also known as the "Hippie mafia."

Sights

Laguna Beach has long been known for its artists and their arts, beginning back in the 1920s when the Laguna Beach Art Association started showcasing their works in a cottage. These days, the **Laguna Art Museum** (307 Cliff Dr., 949/494-8971, http://lagunaartmuseum.org, Mon.-Tues. and Fri.-Sun. 11am-5pm, Thurs. 11am-9pm, adults $7, seniors and students $5) highlights California-related art in a larger, more modern structure right off the Pacific Coast Highway. The over 3,500 works in the collection here include pieces by marine subject painter W. A. Coulter, romantic landscape artist Edwin Deakin, pop art icon Andy Warhol, and punk-rock artist Raymond Pettibon. Take a free, docent-led tour of the current highlights Tuesdays, Thursdays, and Saturdays at 11am.

Laguna Beach has a lot more undeveloped space than other Orange County communities, and **Crystal Cove State Park** (8471 N. Coast Hwy., 949/494-3539, www.crystalcovestatepark.org, daily 6am-sunset, $15/vehicle) just north of town has 3.2 miles of lightly developed coastline with sandy coves and tide pools. The reason it isn't totally undeveloped is due to the presence of the 46 historic cottages constructed in the late 1930s on or beside the beach. (These structures can still be rented for overnight stays.) Offshore is the Crystal Cove Underwater Park, which has several snorkeling and diving sites. The park also includes a 2,400-acre inland section with unpaved roads and trails that are open to hikers, bikers, and horseback riders.

Beaches

In Laguna, **Heisler Park** and **Main Beach Park** (Pacific Coast Hwy., www.lagunabeachinfo.com) offer protected waterways, with tide pools and plenty of water-based playground equipment. The two parks are connected, so you can walk from one to the other. Both display works of local art in the form of benches and sculptures. Hang out on a bench, pick a spot on the sand to lounge, or take a swim in the cool Pacific. If you're into scuba diving, there are several reefs right off the beach. You'll find all the facilities and amenities you need at Heisler and Main Beach Parks, including picnic tables, lawns, and restrooms. Use the charcoal grills provided rather than bringing your own. Park on the street if you find a spot, but the meters get checked all the time, so feed them well.

Sports and Recreation

With its abundant parkland and rocky coastline pocked with sandy beaches, Laguna Beach is one of Orange County's best bets for recreating. The waters offshore have SoCal's best snorkeling and scuba sites. Within Heisler Park, **Diver's Cove** (Cliff Dr. between Beverly Street and Myrtle Street) is a well-protected cove ideal for beginning divers and snorkelers. On the reefs, you might see lobsters, eels, rays, octopi, and garibaldi. Another popular diving and snorkeling spot in the park is **Shaw's Cove** (Fairview St. and Cliff Dr.). Both ends of the beach are worthy sites, but the north end is known for an underwater arch. **Laguna Sea Sports** (925 N. Coast Hwy., 949/494-6965, www.beachcitiesscuba.com, Mon.-Thurs. 10am-6pm, Fri. 10am-7pm, Sat. 6am-7pm, Sun. 6am-5pm, snorkeling gear $20/day, scuba gear $65-90/day, dive tour of Shaw's Cove $75 plus equipment) rents scuba and snorkel gear. They also do a local guided dive at Shaw's Cove.

Many of the hills and mountains around Laguna Beach are undeveloped and crisscrossed with mountain biking trails. El Moro Canyon in **Crystal Cove State Park** (8471 N. Coast Hwy., 949/494-3539, www.crystalcovestatepark.org, daily 6am-sunset, $15/vehicle) offers beginner biking trails, while the expert Top of the World Trail quickly plummets 800 feet. Talk to **Laguna Beach Cyclery** (240 Thalia Street, 949/494-1522, www.lagunabeachcyclery.com, Tues.-Fri. 9am-7pm, Sat. 9am-6pm, Sun. 10am-5pm, mountain bike rentals $45-95/day) for more information or to rent a mountain bike.

Laguna Beach is not as well known for its waves as other Orange County beach communities, but there is surfing and skim boarding to be had at Thalia Street Beach. **Thalia Surf Shop** (915 S. Coast Hwy., 949/497-3292, http://thaliasurf.com, daily 9am-9pm, surfboards $20/day, wetsuits $15/day) is just a block from the break.

Nightlife

The **Marine Room Tavern** (214 Ocean Ave., 949/494-3027, www.marineroomtavern.com, Mon.-Fri. 3pm-2am, Sat.-Sun. 10am-2am) has live music most nights. Some evenings they have up to three bands performing. In addition to taking in music, you can also shoot a game of pool in the brick-walled establishment.

Known to some as "The Dirty Bird," **The Sandpiper** (1183 S. Coast Hwy., 949/494-4694, daily 1pm-2am) is Laguna Beach's dive bar. The Dirty Bird has live music every single night of the year.

Events

Laguna Beach's **Pageant of the Masters** (650 Laguna Canyon Rd., 800/487-3378, www.foapom.com, July-Aug., $15-17) is a truly trippy event where live actors do life-sized recreations of famous artworks in an outdoor amphitheater. The live art is accompanied by an orchestra and narration.

Accommodations

Perched on a bluff over Laguna Beach's Main Beach, ★ **The Inn at Laguna Beach** (211 N. Pacific Coast Hwy., 800/544-4479, $289-1,074) is the ideal place to stay for an upscale beach vacation. The inn really takes advantage of its location, with half of its rooms facing the ocean and a majority of those having balconies to take in the salt air and sound of the sea. Hit up the inn's beach valet for complimentary beach umbrellas, chairs, and towels. After time on Main Beach, retire to the inn's brick pool deck with its pool and hot tub or head up to the rooftop terrace and warm up by the fire pit. The rooms have upscale beach décor and binoculars to take in passing marine life. The friendly staff also serves wine in the afternoon and cookies at night.

Run by the same folks behind The Inn at Laguna Beach, the ★ **Laguna Beach House** (475 N. Pacific Coast Hwy., 800/297-0007, www.thelagunabeachhouse.com, $299-559) is the casual, surf culture-obsessed sibling to the other upscale beach property. This motel is geared towards wave riders and surf-culture aficionados, with killer decor (including a surfboard shaped by the owner) in every room and a daily surf report written up on a chalkboard in the lobby. The Beach House rides the wave even further with killer surf-photo coffee books in each of its 36 rooms. The U-shaped structure surrounds a pool deck with pool, hot tub, and fire pit. Before hitting the waves, enjoy a complimentary breakfast parfait and coffee put out in the lobby.

North of downtown Laguna Beach, the **Crystal Cove Beach Cottages** (35 Crystal Cove, 949/376-6200, www.crystalcovebeachcottages.org, reservations www.

reserveamerica.com, dorm $42-83, cabins $162-249) give anyone the opportunity to experience life right on the Southern California sand. Some of the cabins are individual rentals that you can have all to yourself. The other dorm cottages offer by-the-room accommodations for solo travelers (linens included; room doors lock). Four cottages have been restored with disabled guests in mind. Maid service is minimal, with towels changed every four days and trash taken out daily. None of the cottages have TVs or any type of digital entertainment. And all the cottages include a common refrigerator and microwave, but no full kitchen, so plan to eat out, perhaps at the adjacent **Beachcomber Cafe** (15 Crystal Cove, 949/376-6900, www.thebeachcomber-cafe.com, daily 7am-9:30pm, $18-37), where items like breakfast *chilaquiles* and crab-stuffed salmon are served.

Food

★ **Carmelita's Kitchen De Mexico** (217 Broadway, 949/715-7829, www.carmelitaskdm.com, Mon.-Fri. 11am-10pm, Sat. 9am-10pm, Sun. 9am-9pm, $14-28) is a popular local favorite serving upscale Mexican cuisine. The open kitchen puts out terrific entrees including *tampiquena* (marinated skirt steak)

and a seafood trio platter with a lobster enchilada, shrimp taco, and a crab relleno. They also do some twists on the classic margarita with cilantro-cucumber and strawberry-jalapeno versions.

There are few fine-dining restaurants that admit that they specialize in small plates, when they also have entrees like seafood paella and filet mignon. But ★ **Watermarc** (448 S. Coast Hwy., 949/376-6272, http://watermarcrestaurant.com, Mon.-Fri. 11am-10pm, Sat. 8am-11pm, Sun. 8am-10pm, small plates $7-14, entrees $24-34), run by executive chef Marc Cohen, focuses on its "grazing plates," from filet mignon potpie to smoked bacon-wrapped dates. The two-story restaurant in downtown Laguna Beach also has exceptional cocktails. This is a great place to snack and sip. Happy hour (daily 4pm-6pm) offers burgers at half price, while all drinks and appetizers are two dollars off.

For a casual meal, visit **The Stand** (238 Thalia St., 949/494-8101, daily 7am-8pm, $7-11), a shack that has lovingly served up vegan food for over 40 years. Carnivores may cringe at menu items including a gourmet sprout sandwich and a bean pate salad, but they'll probably feel healthier just by being around all the happy and fit clientele. Order at the

The Inn at Laguna Beach perches over Main Beach.

window and dine on the small outdoor porch or take your meal a couple of blocks to the beach.

Also in Laguna Beach, **Eva's Caribbean Kitchen** (31732 S. Coast Hwy., 949/499-6311, www.evascaribbeankitchen.com, Tues.-Thurs. and Sun. 5pm-9pm, Fri.-Sat. 5pm-10pm, $19-36) serves up classic island cuisine from conch fritter appetizers to jerk chicken entrées. The impressive seven-page rum list is worthwhile reading.

At **Sapphire Laguna** (1200 S. Coast Hwy., 949/715-9888, www.sapphirellc.com, Mon.-Thurs. 11am-10:30pm, Fri.-Sat. 10am-11pm, $24-37), chef Azmin Ghahreman knows no national boundaries. His international seasonal cuisine might include a Greek octopus salad, Moroccan couscous, a half *jidori* chicken, or Hawaiian-style steamed mahi-mahi.

Information and Services

Pick up pamphlets and ask questions about Laguna Beach to the friendly staff at the **Visit Laguna Beach Visitors Center** (381 Forest Ave., 949/497-9229 or 800/877-1115, www.visitlagunabeach.com, daily 10am-5pm) in the Laguna Wine, Coffee, and Specialty Foods Store. They also have a touch-screen interactive kiosk if you'd rather gather information on your own.

For medical emergencies, the **Mission Hospital** (31872 Coast Hwy., 949/499-1311, www.mission4health.com) in Laguna Beach has an emergency department that is usually available anytime day or night.

DANA POINT, SAN CLEMENTE, AND SAN JUAN CAPISTRANO

Dana Point, San Clemente, and San Juan Capistrano are the southernmost cities of Orange County, sitting just above the San Diego County line and the sprawling Camp Pendleton Marine Corps Base. Dana Point is notable for its large harbor at the foot of scenic coastal bluffs. Like many other coastal communities, San Clemente is a surf town, though it differentiates itself with Spanish colonial architecture. Three miles inland, San Juan Capistrano is a city designed to resemble its popular mission.

Sights

One of the most famous and beloved of all the California missions is **Mission San Juan Capistrano** (26801 Ortega Hwy., 949/234-1300, www.missionsjc.com, daily 9am-5pm, adults $9, seniors $8, ages 4-11 $6, under age 3 free). The mission and the lovely little town of San Juan Capistrano hosts flocks of swallows, which return every year at about the same time in the spring to townwide fanfare and celebration. These celebrations began during the mission's heyday in the 18th century, and may have been started by Native Americans centuries before that. (Swallows are extremely loyal to their nesting grounds.) The swallow is a major theme in the town, which nestles in a tiny valley only minutes from the sea.

Today, the mission has a beautiful new Catholic church on-site, extensive gardens and grounds, and an audio tour of the museum, which was created from the old mission church and buildings. In late fall and early spring, monarch butterflies flutter about in the flower gardens and out by the fountain in the courtyard. Inside the original church, artifacts from the early time of the mission tell the story of its rise and fall. This was the only mission church where Father Junípero Serra, founder of the chain of missions in California, presided over Sunday services. The complex includes adequate restrooms for visitors, plus plenty of garden and courtyard benches for rest, relaxation, and quiet meditation and reflection.

When you exit the mission into the charming town of San Juan Capistrano, turn the corner to find yourself on the town's main street, which positively drips Spanish colonial history. Each old adobe building boasts a brass plaque describing its history and use over the years.

Beaches

At the southern tip of the O.C., Dana Point has a harbor (34551 Puerto Pl., 949/923-2280, www.ocparks.com) that has become a recreation marina that draws locals and visitors from all around. It also has several beaches nearby. One of the prettiest is **Capistrano Beach** (35005 Beach Rd., 949/923-2280 or 949/923-2283, www.ocparks.com, daily 6am-10pm, parking $1-2 per hour). Relax on the soft sand or paddle out and catch a wave. Paths make biking, in-line skating, and walking popular pastimes, while others prefer a rousing game of volleyball out on the sand. You'll find a metered parking lot adjacent to the beach, plus showers and restrooms available.

Also in Dana Point, **Doheny State Beach** (25300 Dana Point Harbor Dr., 949/496-6172, www.parks.ca.gov, daily 6am-10pm, $15) is popular with surfers and anglers. The northern end of Doheny has a lawn along with volleyball courts, while the southern side has a popular campground with 121 campsites.

Visit **Salt Creek Beach** (33333 S. Pacific Coast Hwy., 949/923-2280, www.ocparks.com, daily 5am-midnight, parking $1 per hour) for a renowned surf break and a great place to spend a day in the sun. There's a grassy area above the beach in case you don't want to get sandy.

Surfing and Stand-Up Paddleboarding

Salt Creek Beach (33333 S. Pacific Coast Hwy., 949/923-2280, www.ocparks.com) is known for its point break that produces peeling lefts and its feisty shore break.

Though the construction of the Dana Point Harbor in 1966 destroyed one of Southern California's most famous surf spots, it has created a placid area ideal for stand-up paddleboarding (SUP). To experience the phenomenon firsthand, rent an SUP from the **Dana Point Jet Ski and Kayak Center** (34671 Puerto Pl., 949/661-4947, Mon.-Fri. 10am-6pm, Sat.-Sun. 9am-6pm, SUP rental $15 per hour, $65 per day), which is right on the harbor by Doheny State Beach.

One of California's most revered surf spots is in San Clemente, just south of Dana Point. It is called **Trestles,** and it is a series of world-class breaks that includes Uppers and Lowers. On any given day, Trestles is home to some of Southern California's finest surfers, who rip the waves apart. The breaks are also where a pro surf contest is held every year. Trestles is a 20-minute walk from the San Onofre State Beach parking lot, under I-5 and over a train track.

Accommodations

Travelers looking to escape the endless crowds of the Newport-Huntington Beach scene have options farther south on the O.C. coast. The **Blue Lantern Inn** (34343 St. of the Blue Lantern, Dana Point, 800/950-1236, www.bluelanterninn.com, $200-600) crowns the bluffs over the Dana Point Harbor. This attractive contemporary inn offers beachfront elegance, from the exterior to the downstairs restaurant to the rooms. Each of the 29 rooms boasts soothing colors, charming appointments, and lush amenities, including a spa tub in every bath, gas fireplaces, and honest-to-goodness free drinks in the mini-fridge. Seventeen of the rooms feature patios or balconies with impressive views of the harbor and the Pacific. The inn also offers complimentary bike usage, a hot breakfast, and an afternoon wine-and-appetizers spread.

Stay in a historic and stunning Spanish colonial villa at the **Beachcomber Inn** (533 Avenida Victoria, San Clemente, 949/492-5457, $270-405). The 10 standard villas and two deluxe villas all come with porches, full kitchens, and full views of the ocean, the beach, and the pier.

Food

In San Clemente, **South of Nick's** (110 N. El Camino Real, San Clemente, 949/481-4545, http://thenickco.com, Sun.-Thurs. 11am-10pm, Fri.-Sat. 11am-11pm, $10-38) offers a menu with an upscale Mexican twist. The seafood and meat entrées come with creative sauces like a tomatillo Serrano sauce and a poblano cream sauce. The fresh-made guacamole and chips may be the best you'll ever have. The bar keeps up with the kitchen's creativity by serving up regular margaritas as well as coconut and cucumber versions.

Worth the trip inland, **The Ramos House** (31752 Los Rios St., San Juan Capistrano, 949/443-1342, www.ramoshouse.com, daily 8:30am-3pm, $16-20) is in a building that dates back to 1881. The Ramos House is known for their soju Bloody Mary that comes with a Scotch quail egg and a crab claw. They also do a smoked bacon scramble, a crab hash, and a buttermilk biscuit with apple butter.

Information and Services

Unfortunate emergencies in the San Clemente area can be dealt with at **Saddleback Memorial Hospital** (654 Camino De Los Mares, San Clemente, 949/496-1122).

GETTING THERE

John Wayne Airport (SNA, 18601 Airport Way, Santa Ana, 949/252-5200, www.ocair. com) is the closest airport to the main beaches of the Orange County coast. It's much easier to fly into and out of John Wayne than LAX, though it can be more expensive. John Wayne's terminal has plenty of rental car agencies.

The Orange County Transportation Authority (OCTA, 550 S. Main St., Orange, 714/560-6282, www.octa.net, $1.50 fare, $4 day pass) runs buses along the O.C. coast. The appropriately numbered Route 1 bus runs right along the Pacific Coast Highway (Hwy. 1) from Long Beach down to San Clemente and back. Other routes can get you to and from inland O.C. destinations, including Anaheim. Regular bus fares are payable in cash on the bus with exact change. You can also buy a day pass from the bus driver.

The one true highway on the O.C. coast is the Pacific Coast Highway, often called "the PCH" for short and officially designated Highway 1. You can get to the PCH from I-405 near Seal Beach, or catch I-710 to Long Beach and then drive south from there. From Disneyland, take I-5 to Highway 55, which takes you into Newport Beach. If you stay on I-5 going south, you'll eventually find yourself in San Juan Capistrano.

Parking along the beaches of the O.C. on a sunny summer day has been compared to one of Dante's circles of hell. You're far better off staying near the beach and walking out to your perfect spot in the sand. Other options include public transit and pay parking.

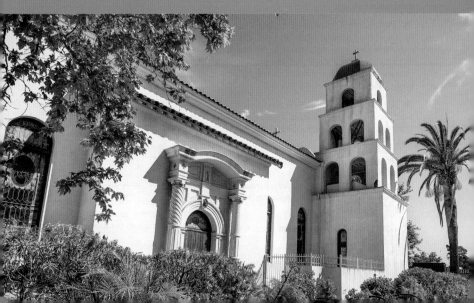

San Diego

Look for ★ to find recommended sights, activities, dining, and lodging.

Highlights

★ **Gaslamp Quarter:** This former red-light district is now the hub of San Diego's downtown, filled with restaurants, bars, and shops (page 560).

★ **USS *Midway*:** This aircraft carrier, once the largest ship in the world, served during the Cold War, Vietnam, and Desert Storm. Docents, many of them veterans, vividly recall what life was like on board (page 562).

★ **San Diego Zoo:** The most popular tourist attraction in Balboa Park is home to all sorts of animals, including giant pandas (page 562).

★ **Old Town San Diego State Historic Park:** Wander back into the 1800s when San Diego was the state's first town in this park enlivened with music, vendors, and people in period dress (page 567).

★ **Hotel del Coronado:** You don't have to stay at the luxurious Hotel del Coronado to enjoy this San Diego landmark. The Del has a historical museum, shopping center, a range of restaurants, and a relaxing beach right out front (page 570).

★ **La Jolla Cove and Scripps Park:** Snorkel or scuba dive offshore, kayak through sea caves, or just relax on the sand at this scenic spot (page 573).

★ **Torrey Pines State Reserve:** Take a break from San Diego's beaches at this reserve, which has impressive eroded cliffs, panoramic coast views, and the world's rarest pine trees (page 574).

★ **California Surf Museum:** Up in North

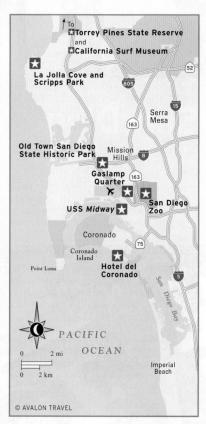

County, this museum offers homage to the pioneers of the coastal sport with exhibits and regularly occurring summer events (page 575).

San Diego is the ideal destination for anyone whose idea of the perfect California vacation is a day (or a week, or a month) lying on a white sand beach, sipping cocktails and looking out over the Pacific Ocean. Resort hotels and

restaurants perch along the seaside, beckoning visitors to what is often thought to be the friendliest big city in California.

Even though San Diego's physical area seems small compared to other parts of California, it can't be beat for density of things to see. From a world-famous zoo to dozens of museums to the thick layer of military and mission history, San Diego offers education, enlightenment, and fun to visitors with all different interests.

Animal lovers flock to the San Diego Zoo and Sea World, while water spirits dive into the Pacific Ocean to catch a wave or examine a variety of sealife in its natural habitat. Travelers who want a little more of the trappings of city life will enjoy the bar and club scene, as well as a thriving theater community.

Across the bay, the long, blue Coronado Bridge connects San Diegans to Coronado, an island-like enclave that beckons beach bums and film aficionados alike to the grandly

historic (and reputedly haunted) Hotel del Coronado, where the Marilyn Monroe picture *Some Like It Hot* was filmed.

North of San Diego proper, the towns of La Jolla, Del Mar, Encinitas, and Oceanside offer a more relaxed pace for exploring. Snorkel the azure water of La Jolla Cove or vie for a piece of that pristine sand with the beach crowd. Splurge some of that vacation cash on a horse race at the Del Mar Racetrack, or have an up-close-and-personal interaction with the exotic animals at the San Diego Zoo Safari Park.

PLANNING YOUR TIME

Compared to other parts of California, San Diego's major attractions sit relatively close together, and it's easy to get from one place to another in a reasonable amount of time. San Diego County has arguably the best beaches in the state. If your travel goals are focused on sand and surf, consider staying in Mission Bay or Point Loma, or farther afield in the

Previous: a beach in San Diego's North County; Mission San Diego del Alcala. **Above:** brown pelicans in La Jolla.

San Diego

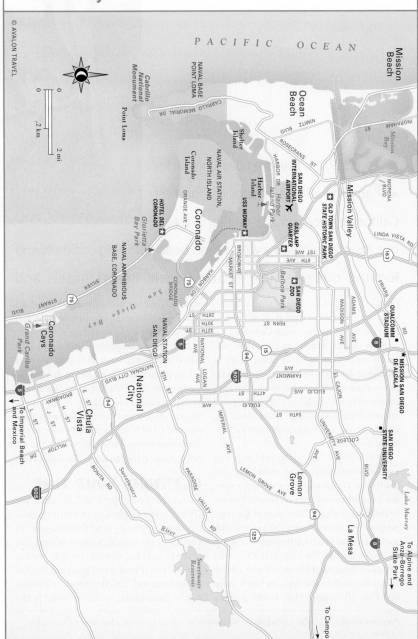

SAN DIEGO

PACIFIC OCEAN

Mission Beach

Ocean Beach

Mission Bay

Cabrillo National Monument

Point Loma

NAVAL BASE POINT LOMA

CABRILLO MEMORIAL DR

Shelter Island

Coronado Island

NAVAL AIR STATION, NORTH ISLAND

Harbor Island

SAN DIEGO INTERNATIONAL AIRPORT

Harbor Island Park

USS MIDWAY

GASLAMP QUARTER

OLD TOWN SAN DIEGO STATE HISTORIC PARK

Mission Valley

LINDA VISTA RD

163

HOTEL DEL CORONADO

Coronado

ORANGE AVE

Glorietta Bay Park

NAVAL AMPHIBIOUS BASE, CORONADO

San Diego Bay

Coronado Cays

Grand Caribe Park

SILVER STRAND BLVD

75

HARBOR DR

CORONADO BRIDGE

75

BROADWAY

MARKET ST

1ST AVE

6TH AVE

Balboa Park

SAN DIEGO ZOO

ADAMS AVE

MADISON AVE

FRIARS RD

QUALCOMM STADIUM

8

MISSION SAN DIEGO DE ALCALA

MORENA / BLVD

NIMITZ BLVD

ROSECRANS ST

INGRAHAM ST

NAVAL STATION, SAN DIEGO

5

National City

Chula Vista

NATIONAL CITY BLVD

E ST

L ST

J ST

H ST

HILLTOP DR

BONITA RD

Sweetwater River

5

To Imperial Beach and Mexico

605

54

BROADWAY

28TH ST

30TH ST

32TH ST

NATIONAL AVE

8TH ST

LOGAN AVE

FERN ST

94

15

605

47TH ST

54TH ST

IMPERIAL AVE

PARADISE VALLEY RD

LEMON GROVE AVE

Lemon Grove

FAIRMONT AVE

EUCLID AVE

EL CAJON BLVD

UNIVERSITY AVE

COLLEGE AVE

SAN DIEGO STATE UNIVERSITY

Lake Murray

La Mesa

94

125

8

To Alpine and Anza-Borrego State Park

Sweetwater Reservoir

To Campo

0   2 km
0   2 mi

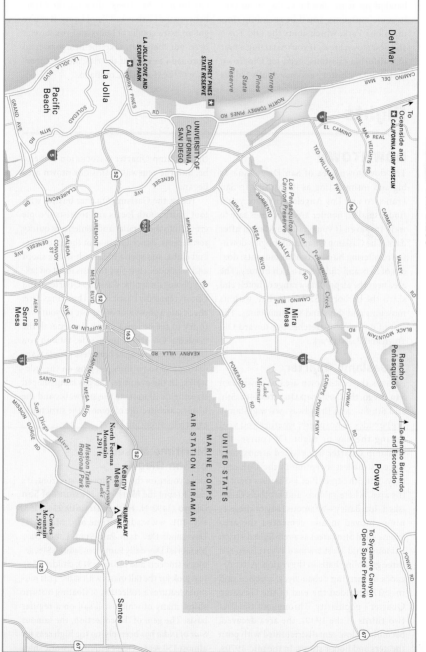

North County coastal area. On the other hand, if you're in town to see the zoo or take in some museums, you'll be spending time in Balboa Park, which abuts the Old Town and downtown areas. If you're starting a tour of California missions, head for Old Town first. Military history and navy buffs will be content to spend their whole trip within the city limits of San Diego, dividing their time between the Harbor and Point Loma. If you've got an extra couple of hours and you haven't been out there yet, take the bridge over to Coronado to gawk at the ridiculous exuberance of the Hotel del Coronado.

Sights

DOWNTOWN

The downtown area of San Diego isn't as big and intimidating as its cousins in San Francisco and Los Angeles. Instead, you'll find a smaller, homier area that feels safe to walk in—even if you're a lone woman after dark. The Gaslamp Quarter highlights downtown, offering hundreds of restaurants, dozens of bars and clubs, and a rich history. The area near the airport has a range of hotels and skirts the harbor of San Diego Bay, with its museums and ships and ship-museums. The rest of downtown stretches out toward Old Town and Balboa Park.

★ Gaslamp Quarter

Perhaps the best-known area of downtown San Diego, the **Gaslamp Quarter** (4th, 5th, and 6th Sts. and Broadway, www.gaslamp. org) exudes atmosphere, whether you visit during the day or night. Of course, the Gaslamp Quarter has exuded atmosphere since its earliest inception in the 19th century. The 5th Street Pier led sailors right to the area, where saloons and brothels flourished. Ida Bailey—a famous lady of the evening—moved in and cemented the area (then called Stingaree) as a red-light district. Famous Wild West lawman Wyatt Earp ran three gambling halls in the region. After decades of thriving debauchery, a police raid in 1912 heralded the end of the Gaslamp Quarter's popularity. Throughout the first two-thirds of the 1900s, the area decayed, becoming a low-rent district filled with porn theaters and liquor stores. In the mid-1970s,

the Gaslamp Quarter Association came to be, and the renewal of this downtown area began.

Today, the Gaslamp Quarter bustles with foot traffic, both locals and tourists. People crowd into the popular and sometimes quirky restaurants, dance like mad at the many bars and clubs, and spend their cash in the shops and boutiques. (But only tourists insist on taking photos under the Gaslamp Quarter sign.) Ghosts reputedly haunt several buildings here; check into a ghost tour or explore on your own to try to see or feel a spook. In general, the Gaslamp Quarter is quite safe, though you will see a scattering of homeless people wandering and sometimes sleeping on the sidewalks. In the evenings, the gas lamp-shaped streetlights illuminate the sidewalks and the historic architecture of some of the structures, especially along 5th Street.

Maritime Museum of San Diego

Once you're on the downtown waterfront, it's easy to spot the **Maritime Museum of San Diego** (1492 N. Harbor Dr., 619/234-9153, ext. 101, www.sdmaritime.org, Memorial Day-Labor Day daily 9am-9pm, Labor Day-Memorial Day daily 9am-8pm, adults $16, seniors, students and military $13, children $8): Just look for the tall masts with sails. This museum features a collection of floating historic ships, many of which still sail on a regular basis. The gem of the collection, the famous *Star of India* has been plying the high seas for almost 150 years. Other genuine historic ships

Downtown San Diego

© AVALON TRAVEL

include the *Medea,* the *Berkeley,* and a Soviet submarine. Another ship that makes regular passenger cruises is the *Californian*—the state's Official Tall Ship. (Yes, California has such a thing!)

Come any day to tour the various ships at dock—on board you'll find a wealth of exhibits depicting the maritime history of San Diego, war at sea in centuries past, the story of the ship you're on, and more. This museum makes a perfect outing for anyone who loves naval history, sailing, ships in general, or even just being out on the water. The museum recommends that you make reservations in advance for their historic ship cruises.

★ USS *Midway*

Once the largest ship in the world, the **USS *Midway*** (910 N. Harbor Dr., 619/544-9600, www.midway.org, daily 10am-5pm, last admission 4pm, adults $20, seniors $17, students $15, children and retired military $10) is now docked along San Diego's Navy Pier. This carrier, which dates to the period just after World War II, served as an active part of the U.S. Navy through Desert Storm in 1991. You'll get to roam throughout the ship, checking out everything from the enlisted mess to the dreaded brig as you climb narrow metal steps from deck to deck. Up top, the flight deck includes military planes and helicopters including the F-14 Tomcat, the costar of the 1980s movie *Top Gun.* One of the best parts of a trip to the *Midway* is the opportunity to talk to the docents, many of whom are veterans who served aboard the ship during the Cold War, Vietnam, or Desert Storm. Consider taking one of the docent-guided tours if you're interested in the realities of life aboard an aircraft carrier. The self-guided audio tour also makes a good introduction to the ship. After, check out the flight simulators, linger near the exciting aircraft, or head to the café and gift shop at the stern. Parts of the ship are wheelchair accessible and there are restrooms on board. Save a couple dollars by purchasing tickets online.

BALBOA PARK, HILLCREST, AND NORTH PARK

The Balboa Park you see today was created for the 1915 Panama-California World Exposition. The Spanish Revival architecture is set amid immense, almost tropical greenery and welcomes visitors with a wealth of museums, halls, exhibitions, gardens, and open spaces. Stop at the **Balboa Park Visitors Center** (1549 El Prado, 619/239-0512, www. balboapark.org, grounds daily 24 hours) for a park map and to plan your visit—there won't be time to see it all!

Hillcrest, immediately northwest of the park, was once a genteel residential area. Today, a touch of shabbiness has met with hip urban renewal to create a mixed neighborhood that still shelters many older residents while providing entertainment and energy to a younger crowd. Hillcrest beckons to the San Diego gay community as well, with clubs and bars creating a hip queer nightlife scene.

★ San Diego Zoo

The jewel of San Diego's vast interconnected wildlife park system, the **San Diego Zoo** (2920 Zoo Dr., 619/231-1515, http://zoo.sandiegozoo.org, summer daily 9am-9pm, rest of the year daily 9am-5pm, adults $48, children $38) lives up to its reputation and then some. The 100-acre zoo actually doubles as the state's largest botanical garden. The zoo grows lovely plants from around the globe that serve as shelter, hiding places, and food for the hundreds of exotic animals that inhabit state-of-the-art enclosures. You'll see perennial zoo favorites including elephants, lions, and polar bears, and you'll also meet a host of other famous and exotic species, such as meerkats, one-foot-tall deer, pythons, and parrots. Other exhibits include two mountain lions and a rare Amur leopard. For the comfort of the human visitors, ample restrooms, benches, concessions, and gift shops are scattered throughout the zoo.

To get the best zoo experience possible, stroll its meandering paved walkways,

San Diego Weekend

While you might not see everything in San Diego within a couple of days, you can see some of the city's best sights and even have a little time to kick back at the beach.

DAY 1

Fortify yourself for a full day of sightseeing at the Hillcrest neighborhood's **Hash House A Go Go** (page 605), where the portions are enormous and tasty. Then head out into nearby **Balboa Park** (page 562), a sprawling urban park with everything from an art museum to a cactus garden. Visit the world famous **San Diego Zoo** (page 562), home to lots of exotic animals including giant pandas.

From Balboa Park, drive out to Point Loma. This peninsula has the **Cabrillo National Monument** (page 568), which marks where the Spanish explorer first landed on the West Coast, and the **Old Point Loma Lighthouse** (page 569), one of the oldest lighthouses in the state.

For sunset, drive up to the top of the 822-foot-high **Mount Soledad** (page 571), which offers 360-degree views of the city. While there, take in the sobering veterans' memorial.

Treat yourself to dinner at the elegant **Grant Grill** (page 602) in the **US Grant Hotel** (page 593) or wander a few blocks to **Currant** (page 603) for drinks and snacks. If you still have energy, head out into the surrounding **Gaslamp Quarter** (page 560) for a post-dinner cocktail. If you are adventurous, try to find your way into the **Vin de Syrah Spirit & Wine Parlor** (page 578).

DAY 2

Start the morning right with a tasty French American breakfast in downtown's **Café Chloe** (page 603). Take a few minutes to sip your coffee and read some of the restaurant's magazines or watch people pass by on the sidewalk heading to work.

Get in your car and head out to **La Jolla Cove** (page 573). Snorkel in the offshore marine reserve and then soak up some of Southern California's famous sun on the cove's small, scenic beach.

Dry out by going out to the island-like Coronado for a sunset cocktail at the historic **Hotel del Coronado** (page 570). When hunger strikes, beeline to the **Blue Water Seafood Market & Grill** (page 604), north of downtown, for fish tacos. End the evening with a trip to Old Town for a night tour of the **Whaley House** (page 567), considered to be the most haunted house in America.

stopping whenever and wherever you feel a need to watch the birds and beasts as they sleep, eat, and play. Some of the paths can be steep—if you're visiting with kids or folks who have trouble walking, keep that in mind when you plan. The map provided by the zoo can help with good walking routes for your party's endurance levels. If you can't do it all, pick the paths that take you to your primary points of interest—be those pandas, birds, or big kitty-cats. For another great way to enhance your experience, pick up one or more of the fliers that describe the park's extensive flora in detail.

Plant lovers love playing Spot the Acacia as they enjoy the animals.

If walking the whole zoo just isn't for you, consider one of the bus rides. The Guided Bus Tour takes you to many of the highlights of the zoo, letting dozens of animals show off for you as you snap photos from the coveted upper deck of the two-story bus. Friendly and knowledgeable docents drive the buses and describe each of the animals and their habitats as you pass. If you just want to get from one section of the zoo to another, jump on an Express Bus. For a special treat, take the Skyfari from the front of the park to the

Balboa Park

rear, where the polar bears play in their pond. You'll get a lovely view of the whole of Balboa Park out to the sea as you traverse the length of the zoo in less than 10 minutes.

San Diego Museum of Art

The **San Diego Museum of Art** (1450 El Prado, 619/232-7931, www.sdmart.org, summer Sun. noon-5pm, Mon.-Tues., Thurs., and Sat. 10am-5pm, Fri. 10am-8pm, fall-spring Sun. noon-5pm, Mon.-Tues. and Thurs.-Sat. 10am-5pm, Sun. noon-5pm, adults $12, seniors and military $9, students $8, children $4.50) is a highlight, even among the

15 incredible museums of Balboa Park. The collections and exhibitions at the Museum of Art range from old masters to Asian art to modern American painting and sculpture. From photography to painting in unusual media to modern sculpture, you'll see many media as you stroll through the galleries admiring the art of several centuries. For a deeper experience, take one of docent tours that run a few times each day. Check the website for the latest special exhibitions and upcoming fun museum events including the ongoing Culture & Cocktails that features art, DJs, and drinks.

San Diego Museum of Man

Rather than focusing solely on the arts and achievements of humankind, the **San Diego Museum of Man** (1350 El Prado, 619/239-2001, www.museumofman.org, daily 10am-4:30pm, adults $12.50, seniors $10, students $8, children $5) hones in on humans themselves. In the Egyptian collection, you'll find mummified humans and the possessions they planned to take with them to the next world, while in the Maya exhibit you'll see reproductions and relics of Central American daily life. The museum also features exhibits on the daily life and times of the Kumeyaay, the native people of the San Diego region. Further exhibits describe the process of human evolution and physiology. A tour through these galleries teaches kids and adults alike about their own history, growth, development, and lifestyles. For an added $10, take a tour of the seven-story California Tower to gain fabulous views of the city. The museum website highlights special events and traveling exhibitions on everything from the history of craft brewing to instruments of torture.

Palm Canyon

For a peaceful break from the endless educational opportunities of Balboa Park, take a walk through **Palm Canyon** (1549 El Prado, daily 24 hours, free). The canyon offers visitors an intense look at various varieties of that ubiquitous California icon: the palm tree. With 58 species of palms creating a cool, shady space, the canyon is a perfect place to slow down and enjoy a break on a hot summer day. The Mexican fan palms at the center of the garden have lived here almost 100 years. The groomed paths connect the canyon to the Old Cactus Garden; the Alcazar Garden also sits adjacent to the palms, and a tram stop nearby makes access a breeze.

Japanese Friendship Garden

Cultural centers form an important element of Balboa Park. The **Japanese Friendship Garden** (2125 Park Blvd., 619/232-2721, www.niwa.org, summer Mon.-Fri. 10am-6:30pm, Sat.-Sun. 10am-4:30pm, fall-spring daily 10am-4:30pm with last entrance at 3:30pm, adults $8, senior, students, and military $7, children under 6 free) began as a teahouse during the 1915-1916 Panama-California Exposition, and grew over the years to include many elements of a traditional Japanese formal garden. Enjoy the tranquility of the Zen garden, koi pond, and wisteria arbor, or take tea and noodle soup at the **Tea Pavilion**

flamingos at the San Diego Zoo

(2215 Pan American Way, 619/231-0048, www.cohnrestaurants.com/teapavilion, Mon. 10:30am-8pm, Tues.-Thurs. 10:30am-7pm, Fri.-Sun. 10:30am-5pm, $3-7). This is the perfect place to enjoy a quiet walk hand-in-hand with your sweetie. For variety, the garden displays temporary exhibitions that mesh with the Japanese cultural traditions exemplified here. Check the website for one-day classes in Japanese arts, usually held on weekends.

Botanical Building

To experience flora indoors, visit the striking **Botanical Building** (1549 El Prado, 619/239-0512, www.balboapark.org, Fri.-Wed. 10am-4pm, free). Inside the lattice structure are 2,100 plants including ferns and orchids. Of special interest is a carnivorous plant bog with pitcher plants and Venus flytraps and a "touch and smell garden" with fragrant lemon mint and chocolate.

Other Museums and Gardens

Balboa Park is filled with a number of other worthy museums, and meandering paths lead to even more botanical areas and gardens. It's impossible to see everything in one day, but a repeat visit could include the **San Diego Air and Space Museum** (2001 Pan American Plaza, 619/234-8291, www.aerospacemuseum. org, adults $18, seniors, students, and military $15, children 3-11 $9) for a history of human flight; the **Reuben H. Fleet Science Center** (1875 El Prado, 619/238-1233, www.rhfleet. org, summer Sun.-Thurs. 10am-6pm, Fri.-Sat. 10am-7pm, fall-spring Mon.-Thurs. 10am-5pm, Fri.-Sun. 10am-6pm, adults $20, seniors $18, children 3-12 $17), where young ones can explore the interactive science exhibits and everyone can view films in an IMAX dome theater; and the **Natural History Museum** (1788 El Prado, 619/232-3821, www.sdnhm. org, daily 10am-5pm, adults $19, seniors $17, student, military, and children 7-17 $14, children 3-6 $11), which houses a vast collection of fossils and other artifacts presenting San Diego's geologic history.

OLD TOWN

San Diego is the oldest European-settled "town" in California. The Old Town area encompasses the first Spanish settlements of what would eventually become California, 19th-century homes and businesses, parks, and modern shops and restaurants. Old Town is the perfect place to get started on a historic tour of California, a ghost-hunting visit to San Diego, or a good sightseeing trip.

the allegedly haunted Whaley House

Whaley House

Billed as the most haunted house in all of the United States, the **Whaley House** (2476 San Diego Ave., 619/297-7511, www.whaley-house.org, Memorial Day-Labor Day daily 10am-9:30pm, Labor Day-Memorial Day Sun.-Tues. 10am-4:30pm, Thurs.-Sat. 10am-9:30pm adults daytime $8, seniors and children daytime $6, adults evening $13, seniors and children evening $8) was built by Thomas Whaley in 1856. Over the century it was inhabited, many members of the Whaley family lived and died inside the brick-constructed Greek Revival mansion. Before Whaley built the house on the corner of San Diego Avenue and Harney Street, the spot was used for at least one recorded public hanging.

Reportedly, the haunting of the Whaley House began almost as soon as the Whaleys first moved in. Thomas Whaley believed that the specter of a criminal hanged on the land was the source of loud, ominous footfalls that rattled the floorboards of his new home late at night. More recently, children and adults have seen male shades, female spirits, and even the vision of a spaniel dog that matches the description of Thomas Whaley's family pet. If you love a good ghost story, consider coming to visit at night, or call ahead to book one of the 90-minute **Ghost-Hunting Tours** (select evenings 10:30pm-midnight, $50).

Self-guided tours are enhanced by the wandering docents, who can answer questions about the artifacts inside the house as well as the house itself.

★ Old Town San Diego State Historic Park

The **Old Town San Diego State Historic Park** (corner of San Diego Ave. and Twigg St., 619/220-5422, www.parks.ca.gov, daily 10am-5pm, free) makes a great place to start exploring the history of California's first town. The park hosts many events over the course of each year. The visitors center sits in the **Robinson Rose House,** first built in 1853 as a family home and set of offices by attorney James Robinson. Another major home,

the **McCoy House** was built in 1869, and now serves as the park's interpretive center. Each room details different eras in San Diego history with displays, interpretive plaques, and recreated scenes. Move on to the early 19th-century Mexican pueblos, including La Casa de Machado y Stewart; this adobe structure contains many artifacts that would have been part of the daily life of San Diego citizens in 1821-1872. Enjoy period music, pet the burros, and observe the park staff engaging in activities folks might have done 150 years ago. If you're more into the afterlife of the residents of Old San Diego, visit the El Campo Santo Cemetery—the oldest cemetery in the city. The park also includes a number of known haunted sites, including the Robinson-Rose House, Casa de Bandini, and La Casa de Estudillo. There are even shops and restaurants within the park at **Fiesta de Reyes** (2754 Calhoun St., 619/297-3100, http://fiestadereyes.com, Mon.-Thurs. 10am-10pm, Fri.-Sat. 10am-11pm, Sun. 9am-10pm). In the center of the colorful courtyard is **Casa de Reyes** (2754 Calhoun St., 619/220-5040, http://fiestadereyes.com, Mon.-Thurs. 10am-10pm, Fri.-Sat. 10am-11pm, Sun. 9am-10pm, $10-19), recommended for its potent margaritas, strolling mariachis, and terrific atmosphere—but not its food.

Presidio Park

One of the early Mexican settlements in San Diego was a military installation, now **Presidio Park** (2811 Jackson St., 619/525-8213, www.sandiego.gov). Inside the park, the **Junípero Serra Museum** (2727 Presidio Dr., 619/297-3258, www.sandiegohistory.org, Sat.-Sun. 10am-5pm, adults $6, seniors and students $4, children $3) sits on the spot where Father Junipero Serra and Captain Gaspar de Portola established the Presidio fort. Its collections include housewares, artifacts, and a cannon; the exhibits span from the Mexican occupation through the early California period of San Diego through 1929. If you prefer nature with your history, take a stroll along the more than two miles of trails winding through the acres of gardens and wild areas of the park. Palm Canyon features lawns surrounded by stately old palm trees. The Arbor has a more formal garden feel, complete with pillars and flowers. It's hard to believe as you wander the charming parkland that you're on the site of a former military base.

Mission San Diego del Alcala

The first mission erected in California was **Mission San Diego del Alcala** (10818 San Diego Mission Rd., 619/281-8449, www.missionsandiego.com, daily 9am-4:30pm). It was blessed by Father Junipero Serra in 1769, making it the first Christian church in California. Ironically, it was also the poorest mission for most of its heyday. Native Americans raided and burned it, the harsh soil resisted cultivation, and eventually Mexican independence from Spain rendered the church a secular building. Time and renovation came to the mission, and it was reestablished as a sacred space. It still operates as an active Catholic church today; if you visit, please respect the mission as a house of worship even as you appreciate its significance as a museum. The church you see is actually the fifth church built on this site, erected and fortified against California's infamous earthquakes. One of the bells in the tower is original (dating to 1801). Inside, you'll see evidence of the life of the Franciscan monks who operated the mission until 1834, and of the native Kumeyaay people who lived here before the Europeans came and whose lives were changed forever by their arrival.

POINT LOMA

Point Loma is at once one of the most beautiful and one of the most important pieces of land in the San Diego region. From the tip of the point, you can see everywhere, from the Cuyamaca Mountains to the land and seas of Mexico, and down into the safe harbor of San Diego Bay. This fabulous view also meant Point Loma was a perfect place to build defenses for the harbor and the settlements beyond. Accordingly, Point Loma has served

more than 200 years as a military installation. From owl limpets to soldiers' graves, there are innumerable unique items to see in the area.

Fort Rosecrans Military Reserve

San Diego has historically hosted an extensive military presence, regardless of whose rule the land fell under. Even today, a large U.S. Navy installation remains here, guarding the Pacific shores. Fort Rosecrans began as a Spanish presidio that was fortified against imminent British threat in the late 1700s. Then called Fort Guijarro, it lasted as an active Spanish military base only 40 years, after which it began to decay. After the creation of California as a state, the U.S. government refurbished the fort to protect the San Diego harbor once more. It was rechristened Fort Rosecrans, and parts of it are still used to this day for Army Reserve activities.

Today, when you visit the parklands of Cabrillo National Monument, you can see remnants of old buildings belonging to the fort, many used during the two World Wars. But the highlight of any visit to the site is the **Fort Rosecrans National Cemetery** (1880 Cabrillo Memorial Dr., 619/553-2084, www.cem.va.gov, Mon.-Fri. 8am-4:30pm, Sat.-Sun. 9:30am-5pm). In addition to the haunting rows of stark white tombstones marching in dressed line across green lawns, you'll find graves here from combatants who fought wars of the California Republic. Wander the grounds to view graves old and recent, as well as monuments to fallen soldiers from little-known battles and near-forgotten tragedies such as the 1905 boiler explosion on the USS *Bennington*.

Cabrillo National Monument

Cabrillo National Monument (1800 Cabrillo Memorial Dr., 619/557-5450, www.nps.gov, daily 9am-5pm, $5/vehicle, $3 bike-in, $3/walk-in) celebrates the initial encounter of San Diego Bay by Spanish explorer Juan Rodriguez Cabrillo in the mid-16th century. This was the first landing of the

Spanish—indeed of any Europeans—on the West Coast of North America. Today, a large statue of Cabrillo stands within the monument lands, overlooking the San Diego Bay. At the visitors center, learn more about the history of Cabrillo's life and explorations.

The wildlife and the scenery are other great reasons to visit the national monument. Views from the high places here are second to none. Turning around, you can see the harbor, the San Diego cityscape, the Pacific Ocean, and all the way south to Mexico. Bring your camera! For a micro-view of San Diego's seas, check the tide tables and head down to the tide pools on the west side of Point Loma. Here you'll find myriad sealife waiting for discovery. Just be sure that you and your children look with your eyes, not your fingers—many tide pool creatures can be injured or even killed by a mere touch from a human.

The parkland of Cabrillo offers hiking trails through the southern coastal scrub ecosystem so precious and unique to this part of the state. Enjoy the wildlife and lovely plants, and come in spring for the best profusion of wildflowers.

Old Point Loma Lighthouse

Among the oldest lighthouses in California,

the **Old Point Loma Lighthouse** (1800 Cabrillo Memorial Dr., 619/557-5450, www. nps.gov, daily 9am-5pm) began its watch over San Diego Bay in 1855. Unfortunately, the light was often dimmed by pernicious fog, and a new lighthouse went into operation in a better location in 1891. Luckily for visitors today, the old lighthouse remained unmolested. Come in to peruse the exhibits and imagine what life was like on the site back in the 1880s. You'll see the restoration of the lighthouse by the National Park Service to its original mid-19th-century glory. Perhaps the most interesting stories you'll hear during your visit are of the lighthouse keepers and their families. Several descendants of the original keepers have provided family stories to round out the human history of the lighthouse. Stop in the old assistant keeper's house for information on all the lighthouses of the Point Loma area. Old Point Loma Lighthouse is part of the Cabrillo National Monument (and covered in its admission fee), perfectly located for a day spent exploring the early history of California's statehood.

Sunset Cliffs Natural Park

Sunset Cliffs Natural Park (west of Sunset Cliffs Blvd. between Adair and Ladera Sts.,

Sunset Cliffs Natural Park

619/525-8213, www.sandiego.gov and www. famosaslough.org/sc.htm) is a 68-acre parcel with 1.5 miles of shoreline on the western flank of Point Loma, one of San Diego's best coastal areas. The steep coastal bluffs showcase panoramic views and sometimes passing California gray whales, while the sandy coves and rocky reefs below lure surfers, tidepoolers, and sunbathers. A mile-long trail crowning the bluff heads from Osprey Point south to eroded sandstone badlands.

CORONADO
★ Hotel del Coronado

When it opened in 1888, the **Hotel del Coronado** (1500 Orange Ave., 800/468-3533, www.hoteldel.com) was the largest hotel resort in the world. Since then, it has hosted a parade of presidents and movie stars. The Del, as it's called by some, has also had its influence on popular culture. It's where author L. Frank Baum wrote some of *The Wonderful Wizard of Oz,* while the Stephen King story *1408,* which later became a film, was partially inspired by a supposed haunting in the hotel. But the Del might be best known as the setting of the 1959 comedy *Some Like It Hot,* which starred Marilyn Monroe, Tony Curtis, and Jack Lemmon.

Today, even though it's not the largest resort in the world, the Del's stately red-shingle-roofed buildings still sprawl over a couple of blocks. Even if you are not staying over at the hotel, it's worth a visit to imagine the glamour of days gone by. You can also wander around the resort's historic buildings, go shopping in its shops, dine in its restaurants, grab a drink in one of its bars, or just sit on the beach out front.

MISSION BAY

Mission Bay offers serene waters untroubled by the sometimes-pounding Pacific surf. It's a perfect place to center your family vacation, take in the natural wonders of Mission Bay Park, or head for the colorful fun of Sea World. The Mission Bay area also has three beach communities that feel far removed

Hotel del Coronado

from the tall buildings of downtown. While the main attractions here are the wide expanses of beach, these towns are worth a visit for people who love little beach communities. The farthest south of these is **Ocean Beach,** which was flooded with hippies during the 1960s. Centered on Newport Avenue, which is lined with cigar-shaped palm trees, Ocean Beach seems to have retained a bit of its countercultural feel.

On the north side of the San Diego River estuary is **Mission Beach.** The community is still home to Belmont Park, a beachfront amusement park.

Between La Jolla and Mission Beach is **Pacific Beach.** During summer days, the three-mile-long boardwalk and beach are filled with sunbathers, runners, and surfers. On Pacific Beach's Crystal Pier are a hotel and a bait shop.

Mission Bay Park

The lands of **Mission Bay Park** (Mission Blvd., 619/276-8200, www.sandiego.gov) are not a natural wonder. The over 4,000 acres include the largest artificially made aquatic park in the country. The popular recreation area was once a tidal marsh—the primary outlet of the San Diego River. In the 1940s, the marsh was dredged and the beaches and land formations you see today were created. Among them are 19 miles of charming sandy beach perfect for sunbathing, sand castle making, beach volleyball, and more—and 14 miles of bike paths. Half of the designated parkland is actually off the shore, in the abundant calm waterways. Swim in one of the eight designated, lifeguard-protected areas throughout the park, or take a deeper dive out into the channel to kite surf or water-ski. In the non-swimming, non-skiing areas, string out a line and go fishing. The park has several areas that have become significant wildlife preserves. Go birding at Perez Cove, Telecote Creek, Fiesta Island, or a number of other spots throughout the park.

SeaWorld San Diego

SeaWorld San Diego (500 SeaWorld Dr., 800/257-4268, www.seaworld.com, hours vary, $50-59) is open for business despite taking a PR beating from the 2013 documentary *Blackfish,* which raised controversy about the park's captive killer whales. For those interested in visiting, SeaWorld is navigable in half a day, even when taking the time to include some rides and shows. Kids love meeting Shamu and his brothers and sisters in the killer whale pool just inside the park entrance. Also in SeaWorld you'll meet sharks, endangered sea turtles, dolphins, and other denizens of the deep. On hot days, the river ride and splashdown roller coaster cool off overheated park visitors. Plenty of food concessions (including a coffee stand) revive weary families, getting them ready for more animal shows and action-packed rides. If you want to have breakfast or dinner with Shamu at the restaurant looking out into the killer whale tank, advance reservations are recommended.

While SeaWorld offers great fun for small children, the laboriously cute decor, roller-coaster-style rides, and trained animal acts can get a bit tiresome for more sophisticated or outdoor-oriented adult travelers. The food in the park also caters to the younger set, and tends to be higher on fat content than quality. Frankly, better adult-oriented wild animal experiences are available in the San Diego area at both the zoo and the Safari Park. But, if you go, buy your tickets online to save some significant money.

Belmont Park

Belmont Park (3146 Mission Blvd., 858/228-9317, www.belmontpark.com, rides $3-6, unlimited ride wristband for people over 48 inches $29, unlimited ride wristband for people under 48 inches $18, hours vary seasonally) is a Mission Beach amusement park that was initially built in the 1920s. The only remnant of the original park is the **Giant Dipper** rollercoaster and the **Mission Beach Plunge,** a pool that is now part of the **WaveHouse Beach Club** (3125 Ocean Front Walk, 858/228-9283, www.wavehouseathleticclub.com, wave machines daily 11:30am-7:30pm, restaurant daily 11am-sunset, wave-riding fee $40-500/hour). There's also a vertical plunge, bumper cars, and a carousel.

LA JOLLA

North of San Diego, La Jolla (which means "The Jewel") is a well-to-do neighborhood filled with high-end boutiques, exemplary restaurants, and a coastline awash in scenic beauty.

Mt. Soledad Veterans Memorial

A great way to get a grip on the layout of San Diego is to drive to the top of 822-foot-high Mount Soledad and take in its amazing, 360-degree panoramic view of the city. The land is part of the **Mt. Soledad Veterans Memorial** (6905 La Jolla Scenic Dr., 858/459-2314, www.soledadmemorial.com, daily 7am-10pm), where six walls at the peak have 3,300 granite plaques honoring

La Jolla

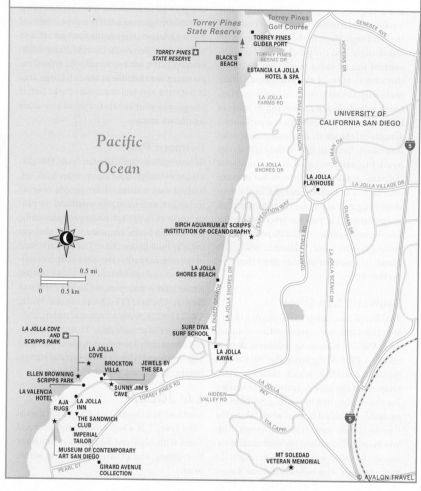

U.S. veterans from the Revolutionary War up to the recent Iraq War. The highest point of the small mountain above the walls and plaques is a large concrete cross that caused a national controversy in 2011 about religious symbols being displayed on government land. Whatever your view on that issue is, your view of San Diego will be superb and can include the city's downtown, Scripps Pier, and on clear days, the Coronado Islands off the coast of Baja California.

Sunny Jim's Cave

Of the seven sea caves in the La Jolla cliffs, **Sunny Jim's Cave** (1325 Coast Blvd., 858/459-0746, www.cavestore.com, Mon.-Fri. 10am-5pm, Sat.-Sun. 10am-5:30pm, adults $5, children 16 and under $3) is unique. You don't need a kayak or scuba gear to get down into this cave; an artificially made tunnel created 100 years ago lets visitors into the cavern via a reliable land route. You'll purchase admission at the weathered, shingle-fronted Cave Store, then climb carefully down the 145 steps to the cavern proper. You'll see a sizeable sea cave of sandstone, carved over the millennia by the Pacific into the cliffside. Look from inside the cave out towards the ocean—an interesting and eerie view.

But how did the tunnel get built? Gustav Schultz, a retiree and painter, hired laborers to hand-dig the tunnel in 1903 as a tourist attraction. L. Frank Baum, the author of *The Wonderful Wizard of Oz,* named the cave "Sunny Jim's" after a cartoon breakfast cereal mascot. Schultz painted local landscapes in the Cave Store until his death in 1912.

★ La Jolla Cove and Ellen Browning Scripps Park

One of the most photographed beaches in the state, La Jolla Cove (1100 Coast Rd.) differs from other San Diego beaches. The small cove sits sandwiched between two sandstone cliffs, and the coarse sand feels more like the rough pebbles of the northern part of the state than the silky-soft stretches of the south. There's also a cave at the west end of the beach that delights children. Visitors snap pictures of the picturesque scenery, swim in the warm water, and trek up to Ellen Browning Scripps Park (Coast Blvd., www.sandiego.

gov, 4am-8pm) for a picnic or a game of soccer on the manicured lawn. La Jolla Cove is famous for its sparkling clear water, and at low tide scuba divers and snorkelers enjoy the local marine life in the offshore La Jolla Underwater Park Ecological Reserve, which is full of silver sardines and bright orange garibaldi navigating between swaying kelp. You may even catch a glimpse of a leopard shark. Lifeguards stay on duty year-round from 9am until sunset during the high season and from 10am in wintertime. Up at Scripps Park, landlubbers enjoy walking on the boardwalk along the cliffs overlooking the vast Pacific, playing on the lawns, and admiring the oddly grown trees scattered around providing shade. The park has restrooms and showers. Parking for either the beach or the park can be tough, especially in the summer. Consider parking in a pay lot downtown and hoofing it down to the beach.

Birch Aquarium at Scripps

The Birch Aquarium at Scripps (2300 Expedition Way, 858/534-3474, http://aquarium.ucsd.edu, daily 9am-5pm, adults $17, seniors $13, college students $12, children 13-17 $14, children 3-12 $12.50) is run by the University of California, San Diego. Both

a busy summer day at La Jolla Cove

children and adults love the Scripps Institute's research and displays in this state-of-the-art aquarium complex. The tour starts with an opportunity to view sealife from oceans the world over in the Hall of Fishes. This area includes coral reef displays from Mexico and the Caribbean, as well as a kelp forest similar to the ones right off the La Jolla coast. The sea horse display highlights the unique fish, while the more somber climate change exhibit includes a fictional weather forecast from 2050.

Museum of Contemporary Art San Diego–La Jolla

The **MCASD La Jolla** (700 Prospect St., 858/454-3541, www.mcasd.org, Thurs.-Tues. 11am-5pm, general admission $10, seniors and students $5, free for those 25 and under) is one of two MCASD campuses in the area. (The other is in downtown San Diego.) At the La Jolla site, perfectly located on Prospect Street for easy access, you'll see works of art in all media, created from 1950 to the present. MCASD takes particular pride in its collections of pop and minimalist art from the 1960s and 1970s, as well as a selection of pieces from artists working in the San Diego and Tijuana areas. Step outside to view the site-specific installations of the **Edwards**

Sculpture Garden. If you love the new, unique, and misunderstood arts of the modern era, the MCASD La Jolla is a must-see. And if all that art makes you hungry, stop at the museum café for a quick bite.

★ Torrey Pines State Reserve

Most outdoor recreation opportunities in San Diego center on the city's fine beaches, but the **Torrey Pines State Reserve** (12600 N. Torrey Pines Rd., 858/755-2063, www.torreypine.org, daily 7:15am-sunset, $10-15/vehicle) has beaches along with miles of hiking trails, maritime chaparral, a lagoon popular with migrating birds, and sculpted bluffs. The stars of the reserve are its Torrey pines, the rarest species of pine tree in the world, only found here and on the Channel Islands. Just 10,000 of the trees exist in their native habitat.

The best way to experience the 2,000-acre reserve is to head out on one of its trails. The paths are not long (just 1.75 miles at the most) but offer an introduction to this dramatic collision of desert and coastal habitats. Before or after your hike, stop by the **Visitor Center** (summer daily 9am-6pm, winter daily 10am-4pm) in the adobe Torrey Pines Lodge to learn more about this unique ecosystem.

Torrey Pines State Reserve is one of just 16

Torrey Pines State Reserve

state reserves in California. There are stricter regulations in place to preserve its natural features. No dogs are allowed anywhere and no food or drink (except water) is allowed in the reserve above the beach.

NORTH COUNTY

As you drive north up the Pacific Coast Highway from downtown San Diego, you begin to see where all the legends about California beaches and surfing came from. The sun shines down over desert plants, pale sands, little surf towns, the mountains to the east, and the glittering blue sea to the west. If you want a movie-style California beach vacation, you can't do better than a weekend in Encinitas, Del Mar, Carlsbad, or Oceanside. At the same time, the north end of San Diego County offers some great sights and activities, from the Safari Park to Mission San Luis Rey.

★ California Surf Museum

It's impossible to think of California without at some point thinking of surfing or the state's surf culture. And at the legendary **California Surf Museum** (312 Pier View Way, Oceanside, 760/721-6876, www.surfmuseum.org, Fri.-Wed. 10am-4pm, Thurs. 10am-8pm, adults $5, students, military, and seniors $3, children under 12 free), you can admire, appreciate, and learn about the ancient sport and art of surfing. While surfing's origins may be in the South Pacific islands, the unusual sport began to catch on at the warm beaches of Southern California, catching on big once surf movies began to appear in theaters. From the silly Frankie Avalon and bongo drum fluff pieces to the semi-documentary *Endless Summer,* surf movies inspired thousands of boys and young men to get out and try to catch a wave. With the novel *Gidget* and subsequent movies, what had been an almost all-male endeavor caught on with girls, too. Surfing became a part of the California version of the 1960s and 1970s hippie movement—earning the respect of the young and the animosity of the older generation. Today, there's no such thing as an "average" surfer. You might find a

10-year-old out tearing it up and a 70-year-old hanging ten, both at the same break.

At the small but interesting Surf Museum, you'll see and pay homage to all that has gone into the California surf scene over its many decades. One exhibit on the history of board shaping shows the progression of the surfboard from the wooden Hawaiian models to the lightweight foam boards used today. Among the boards showcased is world champion surfer Andy Iron's thruster, which is a modern surfboard with three fins. Also on display in another exhibit is the sharkbitten board of Bethany Hamilton, a pro surfer who lost her left arm in 2003 after being attacked by a shark while surfing.

San Diego Zoo Safari Park

The San Diego Zoo doesn't keep too many large animals in the confines of its limited site. To see and experience the life and times of giraffes, lions, elephants, and other natives of spacious grasslands in Africa and Asia, visit the wildly popular **San Diego Zoo Safari Park** (15500 San Pasqual Valley Rd., Escondido, 619/231-1515, www.sdzsafaripark.org, daily 9am-4pm or later, adults $48, children $38, parking $10), formerly known as the Wild Animal Park. Deliberately set well away from the center of urban San Diego, this huge park gives a variety of animals the space they crave to live more naturally. You could spend days in the Safari Park and not see all the diverse species that live here. Walking trails offer miles of adventure through different areas of the park, such as Condor Ridge, Lion Camp, Gorilla Forest, and the African Plains. If you're not up for a day of hard-core hiking, consider paying extra for one of the "Safari" tours that take guests out into different areas of the park in colorful vehicles. On Safaris, docents tell their groups about the wildlife (both animal and vegetable) as they come upon it. Experience the thrill of seeing a cheetah run full-speed, the simple pleasure of the grazers enjoying an afternoon munching grasses and leaves, or the vista of the full park from the air by zip line or from the ground by

Temecula Wine-Tasting

Wine? In Southern California? Yes, indeed! It's not Napa or Sonoma, but if you want to sample all the wine the state has to offer, don't miss out on the terrific vintages available in SoCal.

The major wine-producing region is the Temecula Valley. An hour north of San Diego, off I-15, this small, hot valley hosts 35 wineries. Most tasting rooms cluster along Rancho California Road, but it's also worth exploring farther into the valley for hidden gems. The **Temecula Valley Winegrowers Association** (951/699-3626, www.temeculawines.org) offers a tasting map.

With vineyards first planted in 1974, **Hart Family Winery** (41300 Avenida Biona, 951/676-6300, www.hartfamilywinery.com, daily 9am-5pm, $12-15) produces only 5,000 cases of wine each year. Low production allows for intense attention to detail and quality in every single bottle. Despite the small total case number, you can try a number of varietals. Try the fruity white viognier, the stunning syrah, and less famous varietals like grenache rose and tempranillo.

Built on an 11-acre estate in the style of a French chateau, **Churon Winery** (33233 Rancho California Rd., 951/694-9070, www.innatchuronwinery.com, Sun.-Fri. 10am-4:30pm, Sat. 10am-5pm, $10) also operates as a high-end inn—you can enjoy the wines all night long. Their list encompasses many French-styled reds and classic California whites plus a few select dessert sweets (including sherry).

Elegant **Falkner Winery** (40620 Calle Contento, 951/676-8231, www.falknerwinery.com, daily 10am-5pm, $10-15) takes particular pride in producing different wines than the average California vintner. Try the wonderful blended reds, made in the traditions of Tuscany and Bordeaux. For wine drinkers who like a little sweet with their savory, Falkner offers a number of not-quite-dry wines that are *not* as syrupy as a standard dessert wine. Enjoy a Mediterranean lunch at the on-site restaurant, Pinnacles, and tour the winery on weekends.

From the colorful frescoes decorating the tasting room to the posh GrapeSeed Spa, **South Coast Winery & Resort** (34843 Rancho California Rd., 951/587-9463, www.wineresort.com, daily 10am-6pm, $15-20) caters to luxury-loving travelers. Book a private villa or reserve a table at the Tuscan-style Vineyard Rose restaurant. Try wines from four different South Coast labels, from the splashy and moderately priced Elevation wines to the elegant Carter Estate Reserve vintages. The inclusive $40 winery tour concludes with a private wine-and-cheese tasting.

A large extended family owns and runs most every aspect of the **Wilson Creek Winery & Vineyards** (35960 Rancho California Rd., 951/699-9463, www.wilsoncreekwinery.com, daily 10am-5pm, $15-20). One of the Wilson mainstays is Almond Champagne, a true special-occasion beverage. Other sweet wines might include muscat canelli, cream sherry, and chocolate port. More traditional wine lovers will enjoy the hefty cabernet, zinfandel, and petit sirah. If jazz is your vice, check the website for the annual calendar of concerts.

A tiny family operation, **Palumbo Family Vineyards & Winery** (40150 Barksdale Circle, 951/676-7900, www.palumbofamilyvineyards.com, daily 11am-5pm, $15) takes pride in growing every grape that goes into each bottle. With 13 acres of vineyards, the winery produces 2,500 cases of wine each year. A season's release might include five wines—mostly reds with a token viognier or other hot-weather white for variety. Nicholas Palumbo is a chef as well as winemaker, and has been known to entertain private parties.

electric trike. If you can't get your fill of the animals in a day, book a tent overlooking a plain inhabited by rhinos, giraffes, and antelopes with the Roar & Snore package.

The San Diego Zoo Safari Park caters both to families and to adults without children seeking a more grown-up experience. Check your map for the location of playgrounds and family-themed attractions. On the website, find out which tours and dates are best for an adults-only day at the park. Ample food, restrooms, and concessions cluster around the entrance area, but services get thinner as you get farther out into the park.

Mission San Luis Rey

Sometimes referred to as the "King of the Missions," **Mission San Luis Rey** (4050 Mission Ave., Oceanside, 760/757-3651, www.sanluisrey.org, self-guided tours Mon.-Fri. 9:30am-5pm, Sat.-Sun. 10am-5pm, adults $5, seniors and children 6-16 $4) certainly is the biggest of the California missions. It is also one of the most lavishly restored. Visit the stately formal gardens, complete with manicured lawns, roses, antique sculptures, and ruins of structural elements of the mission buildings. Or take a tour of the museum and church, both of which relate the history of Mission San Luis Rey through interpretive panels and many artifacts. Special **Behind the Scenes Tours** (reservations 760/757-3651, ext. 115, times and prices vary) occur once a week. In front of the mission, a unique experience awaits as you explore the ruins of the Lavanderia. This large open space contains the remains of the area where Native Americans washed their clothes and themselves outside of the mission grounds. Take the stairs down to find the remains of the gargoyles that once sprayed water for laundry. The cemetery is one of the largest and best maintained in the mission system, with memorials dating from the earliest days of this 1798-founded Franciscan church.

San Diego Botanic Garden

Plant and garden lovers come from around the world to visit the **San Diego Botanic Garden** (230 Quail Gardens Dr., Encinitas, 760/436-3036, www.sdbgarden.org, daily 9am-5pm, adults $14, seniors, students, and military $10, children 3-12 $8), formerly called Quail Botanical Gardens. The 30-plus-acre spread is home to sub-gardens highlighting rare plant species from almost every continent. No visit is complete without viewing the famous Bamboo Garden and the Undersea Succulent Garden. The Rainforest Garden has its own waterfall, and the Subtropical Fruit Garden boasts plump offerings that grow no elsewhere in California.

A coffee cart offers minimal refreshments, or bring your own picnic to enjoy in the designated picnic areas on the grounds. Restrooms hide delicately among the plants, and the visitors center and gift shop sit at the center of the gardens. Knowing that kids often get bored when presented with endless plants, the grounds host the West Coast's largest interactive children's garden.

LEGOLAND

Kids have long built castles and spaceships from Lego bricks. Now let your little builders see Legos on a grand scale at **LEGOLAND** (1 Legoland Dr., Carlsbad, 760/918-5346, http://california.legoland.com, hours vary, adults $91-115, children $85-109). Peer at dinosaurs built from Lego bricks on Coastersaurus, a roller coaster that reaches the relatively benign speed of 21 miles per hour. The main attraction is Miniland, which has reproductions of seven places in the country (including San Francisco and New York City) made with Lego bricks. Don't worry; there are plenty of shops here to purchase the latest Lego toys.

TOURS

If you've only got a limited time in the San Diego area and want to see as much as possible, consider taking a tour. Several fun, unique tours show off different sides of the city, some you may not have explored before. For instance, to see the city from the bay, consider a harbor tour. **Flagship Cruises & Events** (990 N. Harbor Dr., 800/442-7847, www.flagshipsd.com, adults $24-29, seniors and military $22-27, children $12-14.50) offers one-hour tours of the north and south ends of the bay, and a two-hour tour that covers the bay in full. You'll see some of the most famous San Diego sights from a new perspective: the Maritime Museum ships, the USS *Midway*, the Coronado Bay Bridge, and Fort Rosecrans. This excursion company also provides regular dinner and brunch cruises; reservations are recommended.

Hitch a ride on the **Old Town Trolley Tours** (888/910-8687, www.trolleytours.com, adults $35-39, children 4-12 $17-19, children three and under free) for travel and entertainment. This fleet of orange and green trolley-like buses hits San Diego's major sights including Balboa Park, the Hotel del Coronado, and Old Town San Diego.

For a unique look at San Diego Bay, add a **Seal Tour** (800/868-7482, www.sealtours.com, adults $35-39, children 4-12 $17.10-19) to your Old Town Trolley ticket. You'll get a ride on a strange-looking amphibious contraption that will take you from the road around the harbor out into the harbor itself to look at the city from the water.

To take your own tour of San Diego with just a little bit of help, book a cute talking **Go Car** (2100 Kettner Blvd., 800/914-6227, www.gocartours.com, daily 8am-7pm, $56/hour). In your Go Car, you'll be directed through town by a talking GPS navigation unit that also knows stories about the sights of San Diego. With a Go Car, you can take a standard tour or program your own routes through the area.

Looking for something fun and a little spooky? Take the **Haunted San Diego Ghost Tour** (619/255-6170, www.hauntedsandiegotours.com, daily 7pm and 9pm, $35). This two-hour combination bus and walking tour includes stops at haunted sites in the Gaslamp Quarter, downtown, and Old Town. Highlights include a historic cemetery and the notorious Whaley House. For the best experience, take the 9pm tour to experience the haunted places in darkness.

Entertainment and Events

NIGHTLIFE
Bars and Clubs

The Gaslamp Quarter is the hottest part of downtown San Diego for the young and energetic nighttime crowd. Consider just walking around 4th Street and seeing what bar or club suits you for the evening.

Getting into the ultrahip **Vin de Syrah Spirit & Wine Parlor** (901 5th Ave., 619/234-4166, www.syrahwineparlor.com, Tues.-Wed. and Sun. 4pm-midnight, Thurs.-Sat. 4pm-2am) is an adventure. Go down a graffiti-covered staircase to a subterranean area with an unmarked, vegetation-covered door. That's the entrance. Sip creative cocktails or wine—there's a whole page of French wines offered here—while taking in the bar's eclectic decor that includes wine vines, lots of mirrors, and umbrellas hanging from the ceiling.

Formerly The Bitter End, **The Tipsy Crow** (770 5th St., 619/338-9300, http://thetipsy-crow.com, Mon.-Thurs. 3pm-2am, Fri.-Sat. noon-2am, Sun. 9am-2am) offers three different bar experiences in a building that dates back to 1874. "The Nest" is a place to lounge while sipping drinks including The Tipsy Crow's signature cocktail the "Salty Dog," which is simply freshly squeezed grapefruit juice and vodka in a glass with a salted rim. Or drink craft beers in "The Main" at the large room's 40-foot mahogany bar. If you seek entertainment, head downstairs to "The Underground," where there is frequent live entertainment including bands and comedians.

One of the more refreshingly unassuming bars in the Gaslamp Quarter is **Patrick's Gaslamp Pub** (428 F St., 619/233-3077, http://patricksgaslamppub.com, Mon.-Fri. 10am-2am, Sat.-Sun. 9am-2am). The bartenders are friendly, the vibe is low-key, and there's a small stage where blues, soul, and rock bands perform every night of the week. Patrick's has been serving drinks and fun since the 1930s.

A locals' favorite, **Hamilton's Tavern** (1521 30th Ave., 619/238-5460, http://hamiltonstavern.com, Mon.-Fri. 3pm-2am, Sat.-Sun. 1pm-2am, $10) is in a neighborhood near Balboa Park. Like a dive bar with impeccable tastes, the tavern serves a range of 28 craft beers on tap and a surprisingly creative bar food menu with items including chicken wings in a mole sauce, house-made sausages,

San Diego Brewery Tour

Sometime over the last few years, San Diego became a craft brewery capital, with over 40 brewery locations having opened around the county. These newcomers join longtime legacy brewers Stone Brewing Co., Ballast Point, AleSmith Brewing Company, Green Flash Brewing Company, and many more. Local breweries are primarily known for creating potent and flavorful India pale ales and double India pale ales, but with so many breweries there are plenty of suds to suit your taste.

The website of the **San Diego Brewers Guild** (www.sandiegobrewersguild.org) is a good place to visit to plan your brewery visits. It has a map of the area's breweries and a list of upcoming events.

Behemoth **Stone Brewing Co.** (1999 Citracada Pkwy., Escondido, 760/294-7866, daily 11am-11pm) is the largest brewery in Southern California. The North County location is the site of the actual brewery, and there you can embark on **tours** (Mon.-Fri. noon, 2pm, 4pm, 6pm, Sat.-Sun. noon-6pm on the hour, adults $3, nondrinkers and children $1) that include a beer tasting at the end. Or just post up in the World Bistro and Gardens and order their very popular Stone Pale Ale and food.

Another heavyweight brewery and local favorite is **Port Brewing Co.** (http://portbrewing. com), an outfit that sprang out of a local pizza parlor in 1992. Sip on suds like the Wipeout IPA while enjoying pizza at one of their five San Diego County locations including one in **Ocean Beach** (1956 Bacon St., 619/224-4700, www.pizzaport.com, Mon.-Thurs. 11am-10pm, Fri.-Sat. 11am-midnight, Sun. 11am-11pm).

For a break from IPAs, head over to the hip North Park neighborhood to visit the family- and dog-friendly **Mike Hess Brewery** (3812 Grim Ave., 619/255-7136, www.mikehessbrewing. com, Sun.-Thurs. noon-10pm, Fri.-Sat. noon-midnight). The most popular beer here is their Grazias Vienna Cream Ale. The space has an unassuming warehouse feel ideal for an afternoon or evening of sipping. They also have a **tasting room** (7955 Silverton Ave., Ste. 1201, 619/786-4377, Wed.-Sun. 1pm-8pm) in Miramar.

The **Modern Times North Park Flavordome** (3000 Upas St., 619/269-5222, http:// moderntimesbeer.com, Sun.-Thurs. noon-10pm, Fri.-Sat. noon-midnight) has fanciful decor befitting their creative brews. Modern Times focuses on complex session beers along with hybrid brews. Test their Blazing World, a hoppy amber, in a space where the bar is constructed out of old VHS cassettes and lampshades hang from the ceiling. They also have the **Point Lomaland Fermentorium** (3725 Greenwood St., 619/546-9694, Sun.-Thurs. noon-10pm, Fri.-Sat. noon-midnight, tours Sat. 1pm, Wed. 3:30pm) where they brew their beer and have 16 varieties on tap.

and a grilled cheese with brie, honey, apples, and walnuts.

Enjoy a fine whiskey at **Seven Grand** (3054 University Ave., 619/269-8820, http:// sevengrandbars.com, Mon.-Sat. 5pm-2am, Sun. 8pm-2am). In the hip North Park neighborhood, Seven Grand has a 15-page menu devoted to whiskey, though they also have craft beers on tap and cocktails. Many of the libations are based around whiskey, from their old fashioned made with Old Grand-Dad to their mint julep created with Woodford Reserve.

Gay and Lesbian

With a young, hip scene and a significant gay presence, nightlife in Hillcrest is happening most every night of the week.

The Brass Rail (3796 5th Ave., 619/298-2233, www.thebrassrailsd.com, Mon. and Thurs. 9pm-2am, Fri.-Sat. 2pm-2am, Sun. 10am-2am) is one of San Diego's oldest gay venues. Offerings include drag shows, DJs, and happy hours.

Urban Mo's (308 University Ave., 619/491-0400, www.urbanmos.com, daily 9am-2am) describes itself as a "hetero-friendly gay restaurant." It has everything from line dancing nights to all-you-can-eat spaghetti nights with show tunes as a soundtrack.

Live Music

San Diego enjoys its music, and you'll find plenty of opportunities to hear live classical, jazz, rock, and more throughout town. You'll have no trouble finding everything from tiny dive bars with mini-stages up to huge multiday music festivals. Whether you prefer mellow jazz, danceable blues, or hard-hitting rock, odds are it's playing live. The **San Diego Reader** (www.sandiegoreader.com) and the **San Diego CityBeat** (www.sdcitybeat.com) have comprehensive guides to upcoming concerts by local and touring bands.

Since 1989, **The Casbah** (2501 Kettner Blvd., 619/232-4355, www.casbahmusic.com, most nights 8:30pm-2am) has been snagging some of the biggest national touring acts in indie rock, punk, and metal. The bands play in a small, dimly lit room to crowds of just 200 people, which means that it is a great place to see a rowdy rock show. Kill time before the music starts with the vintage arcade games by the back bar or in a narrow smoker's alley.

The music venue chain **House of Blues** (1055 5th Ave., 619/299-2583, www.houseofblues.com) has shows by national touring acts of all types. The revered San Diego music venue The Casbah even books some performances here.

Though it's a half hour north of San Diego proper, Solana Beach's **Belly Up Tavern** (143 S. Cedros Ave., Solana Beach, 858/481-8140, www.bellyup.com, hours vary) regularly scores legends including Willie Nelson, Toots & the Maytals, and Buddy Guy to perform for just 600 lucky folks. They also have up-and-comers and indie favorites.

The Observatory North Park (2891 University Ave., 619/239-8836, http://observatorysd.com) is a restored 1930s theater that brings big indie acts including Morrissey, Miguel, and Future Islands to perform in the North Park area. No alcoholic drinks can be brought in, though you can enjoy a preshow libation at the adjacent West Coast Tavern.

The Soda Bar (3615 El Cajon, 619/255-7224, www.sodabarmusic.com) gets smaller national touring acts and local bands in a dive

bar atmosphere seven nights a week. There's also 20 craft beers on tap to complement the music.

If you're in Point Loma for the evening, head to Humphreys for live music any time of year. **Humphreys Backstage Live** (2241 Shelter Island Blvd., 619/224-3577, www.humphreysbackstagelive.com) offers a lounge-style venue with live music or DJs spinning danceable tunes or playing charming smooth jazz to drink and converse by. Check the website for this month's schedule. If you're around in the summer season, buy tickets in advance for the local favorite concert series, **Humphreys Concerts by the Bay** (www.humphreysconcerts.com). National acts come out to play against the backdrop of the marinas of Shelter Island as the sun sets over San Diego Bay. The outdoor venue takes advantage of the evening climate, so you can bask in the warm air under the stars as you listen to the tunes of your favorite rock band or folk singer.

Comedy

A Greek restaurant by day, **The Comedy Palace** (8878 Clairemont Mesa Blvd., 858/492-9000, www.thecomedypalace.com) serves up comedy most nights of the week. The weekend comics have frequently appeared on TV. Aspiring comics can test their acts on Tuesday open-mic nights.

CASINO GAMBLING

It may surprise some that San Diego has 11 casinos, most located 30-45 minutes from downtown in the eastern section of the county or inland North County. Many (but not all) are run by Native American tribes.

A few miles east of San Diego, two casinos offer a good time. **Club Sycuan** (5485 Casino Way, El Cajon, 800/279-2826, www.sycuan.com) sits in the suburb of El Cajon. This casino and resort offers fun for all comers, with a hotel, several restaurants (including a buffet), a golf course, tennis courts, and gaming floors. At Club Sycuan, you'll find thousands of slot machines, plus an array of table games including blackjack, pai gow poker, mini-baccarat, roulette, and craps. You can also enjoy the tension of the Bingo Palace and the smoke-free atmosphere of the Poker Room. Vegas-style stage acts entertain weary gamers and golfers in the evening. There's also a complimentary shuttle to Club Sycuan from different parts of San Diego.

Nope, that's not a Back East boarding school. That big, classically styled building east of La Jolla is actually the **Barona Valley Ranch Resort and Casino** (1932 Wildcat Canyon Rd., Lakeside, 619/443-2300, www. barona.com). This upscale resort brings a touch of class to the Las Vegas-style casino. Stay in the large, posh hotel (that's the big building), eat dinner at the steak house or the buffet and grab lunch at the noodle house, pamper yourself in the day spa or out at the pool, or play around at the Barona Creek Golf Club. Finally, hit the casino for plenty of up-to-date loose slots plus 70 table games, including craps, roulette, cash baccarat, and much more. Hang out in the poker room, or play the ponies at the off-track betting parlor.

While no casinos grace the North County coastline, if you're vacationing in Del Mar or Encinitas, gaming possibilities lurk only a few miles east. You'll find an outpost of the ever-popular **Harrah's** (777 Harrah's Southern California Way, Valley Center, 760/751-3100, www.harrahsrincon.com) chain off Highway 76 northeast of Oceanside. The typical Harrah's tower rises high over the tiny town of Valley Center, offering over 600 hotel rooms, eight different eateries (including an oyster bar, a buffet, and a coffeehouse), and a full-service spa. The gaming rooms offer hundreds of slots, a poker room, and plenty of table games, including craps, roulette, and blackjack. To cool off in the heat of summer, rent a cabana or pull up a chaise lounge at the gorgeous two-tiered pool.

Yet another large, blocky, luxurious casino, the **Pala Casino Resort and Spa** (11154 Hwy. 76, Pala, 877/946-7252, www.palacasino.com) dominates the landscape on hot, dry Highway 76 east of Oceanside. The dining options are especially fine here: there's a casual Asian meal at Noodles; all-you-can-eat at Choices, The Buffet; or elegance at The Oak Room. Entertainment also comes big at the Pala, with two large theaters (one indoor, one outdoor), a lounge, and an event center. In the casino proper, you'll find the largest array of new slot machines in the area, plus more than 80 table games. A high-limit room offers fun for high rollers, and a smoke-free room provides relief for sensitive noses who still want to play.

THE ARTS
Theater

Live theater lives well in San Diego. Most every area and district has at least a theater or two, and several big houses garner national acclaim for world-class productions. If you're in San Diego for more than one night, it will be worth your while to take in a show at the Old Globe, the La Jolla Playhouse, or one of the innumerable repertory theaters.

The **Old Globe** (Copley Plaza, Balboa Park, 619/234-5623, www.oldglobe.org, box office Tues.-Sun. noon-6pm or end of show), one of the most famous theater complexes in California, sits in the middle of Balboa Park. Originally constructed to produce abbreviated Shakespeare plays for the 1935 California Pacific International Exposition, the magnificent Old Globe was remodeled to permanence in 1937. It has been producing a full season ever since, growing to add two auxiliary theaters: the Sheryl and Harvey White Theatre and the Lowell Davis Festival Stage. The Old Globe, restored to its original magnificence after a fire in 1978, seats almost 600 people, and has produced world premieres of plays such as *Into the Woods* and *The Full Monty* that go on to become Broadway spectaculars and worldwide hits. If you can get a ticket to something new at the Old Globe, you may see history being made. Today the Globe puts on 15 plays and musicals a year.

The Old Globe theaters are reminiscent of the complex at the legendary Oregon Shakespeare Festival. The huge outdoor Lowell Davis facility can seat almost 700 spectators and puts up shows during the summer and fall festival season. The smaller Cassius Carter Stage presents theater in the round, in an intimate black-box-style setting. See the website for a list of the shows playing at each theater, as well as for ticket sales and seating charts. At the Jacobs Music Center complex, enjoy a snack and a drink at Lady Carolyn's Pub or browse for souvenirs at the gift shop.

For a night of high-budget, fabulous Broadway theater or an adventurous off-center world premiere, check out a show at the **La Jolla Playhouse** (2910 La Jolla Village Dr., 858/550-1010, www.lajollaplayhouse.com, box office show-day hours Mon. noon-6pm, Tues.-Wed. noon-7:30pm, Thurs.-Sat. noon-8pm, Sun. noon-7pm, non-show-day hours Mon.-Sat. noon-6pm). This top-tier theater company produces big musicals, small experimental plays, historical dramas, and everything in between. Check the website for this year's main season schedule. They usually have a handful of world premieres every season, whether it's musicals, dramas, or musical comedies. The playhouse actually encompasses a building complex with three separate theaters. Look for originality in sets and costuming, as well as top-notch acting.

For a charming night out on the North County coast, grab a seat at the **North Coast Repertory Theater** (987 Lomas Santa Fe Dr., Solana Beach, 858/481-1055, http://northcoastrep.org, box office non-performance days daily noon-4pm, performance days noon-curtain). The North Coast Rep produces about eight shows each year, including musicals, dramas, comedies, and family favorites. With ticket prices at around $20 per show, a laid-back evening of good repertory theater isn't hard to obtain. The theater at Lomas Santa Fe Plaza is conveniently near I-5 and the Del Mar Racetrack, for easy access after a day's sightseeing.

Classical Music

The **Spreckels Organ Society** (619/702-8138, http://spreckelsorgan.org) provide a unique, free live music experience that all visitors and locals can enjoy. Every week of the year for almost a century, the Spreckels Organ has serenaded the Spreckels Organ Pavilion of Balboa Park (Pan American Rd. E.) with beautiful music. Concerts happen on Sundays 2pm-3pm, and on Monday nights at 7:30pm in the summertime. Come out, take a seat on a park bench, and relax as the music washes over you.

If you love opera, get tickets to the **San Diego Opera** (box office 619/533-7000, www.sdopera.com, Mon.-Fri. 8:30am-4:30pm) during your visit. Originally created to produce San Francisco Opera productions in the 1950s, the San Diego Opera quickly grew into an independent production company to rival even its famed neighbor to the north. In addition to the regular season filled with original productions of famous operas, you'll find the San Diego Opera hosting international stars at special concerts and presenting a variety of musicals to the San Diego community. The productions take place at the **Balboa Theatre** (868 4th Ave.), the **Jacobs Music Center** (750 B St.), and the **San Diego Civic Theatre** (1100 3rd Ave.).

Cinema

You'll find plenty of first-run multiplexes scattered throughout the San Diego area. But if you're looking for a fun vintage moviegoing experience, try the **Ken Cinema** (4061 Adams Ave., 619/283-3227, www.landmarktheatres.com). Built in 1912, this single-screen theater now specializes in running independent and foreign films and restored classics. Happily, the seats are not the same vintage as the rest of the theater—new, comfortable theater chairs were installed in 2004. There's no parking lot, so you'll have to try your luck on the street with the locals who come to the Ken regularly to see something other than the standard new Hollywood fare.

The best deal in town is the throwback **South Bay Drive-In Theatre** (2170 Coronado Ave., 619/423-2727, www.southbaydrivein.com, adults $9, children 5-9 $1), where you can catch a double feature of the latest movies for just $9 a person. You also get to view them from the comforts of your own car. In 2013 they updated to a modern digital projection system.

FESTIVALS AND EVENTS

Summer is event season in San Diego. If you're visiting between June and October, you can hardly help tripping over some fun congregation of folks. Check the web or the tourist bureau for tickets to your favorite events and for information about what's going on in the area during your visit.

Adams Avenue Street Fair

San Diego's massive annual music festival Street Scene called it quits after its 2009 installment. But the smaller **Adams Avenue Street Fair** (http://adamsaveonline.com, Sept.) is just as much fun. For those who need a music fix, 100 acts perform on eight stages. There are also carnival rides, vendors, and booths at this long-running street fair, one of the largest in California.

LGBT Pride Parade and Festival

There's nothing sexier than loving yourself. To celebrate being yourself, each year San Diego hosts its own **San Diego LBGT Pride** (619/297-7683, www.sdpride.org, July). Smaller than the mammoth festival in San Francisco, San Diego Pride is still one of the city's biggest annual celebrations. The weekend is packed with events and attractions, from a 10K run to a Ferris wheel. No matter who you are or what you're into, there's something for you here. You'll find almost a dozen stages, each offering a different style of music from hip-hop to acoustic to Latino to lavender. One of the biggest events is the Saturday Pride Parade featuring creative floats, music, and wildly celebratory people. If you love baseball and queer life, plan ahead and purchase tickets to the Padres Pride event called "Out in the Park."

The parade and festival take place in Balboa Park, spilling out to the Hillcrest neighborhood especially in the evening, and out to Petco Park for the Padres baseball event. Check the website for information about park-and-ride services, parking, bicycle parking, public transit, and more. Purchase tickets in advance, or at the festival. There's no smoking at the festival. If you need wheelchair assistance, contact the festival organizers in advance.

San Diego Bay Fair

For an event that's unique to San Diego and totally noisy, you can't beat the **San Diego Bay Fair** (760/789-8870, www.sandiegobayfair.org, Sept.), formerly known as the Thunderboat Regatta. For one weekend each September, Mission Bay revs up and gets loud, hosting a supercharged powerboat-racing event. See drag boat racing, Formula One, cracker box inboards, and much more. Stands are set up on beaches around the bay to allow the most people the best views of the races—buy your tickets in advance to get a good seat. The excitement at this event is contagious, and the tension is real. Bring earplugs and extra money for parking if you want a space anywhere near the bay. (Alternately, check the website and the local resorts for deals on hotel rooms within walking distance of race-viewing areas.) Kids of all ages are welcome.

San Diego County Fair

The **San Diego County Fair** (2260 Jimmy Durante Blvd., Del Mar, 858/755-1161, www.sdfair.com, June-July) runs for several weeks every summer and boasts of being one of the very best in the state. It's held at the famed Del Mar County Fairgrounds, which were purposely built for this celebration of San Diego agriculture.

Shopping

Shopping in San Diego runs primarily to malls and shopping centers that offer a good, if selective, experience. Downtown, wander the Gaslamp Quarter for San Diego-grown clothing or hit the immense Horton Plaza for stores you know. Old Town is fun for unique Mexican souvenirs and is a short jump from Mission Valley where the mall is king. Farther north, La Jolla provides a more relaxed, upscale experience.

DOWNTOWN
Gaslamp Quarter

As you stroll the streets of the Gaslamp Quarter you'll find many stores are local chains, like the **San Diego Trading Company** (376 5th Ave., 619/232-1674, www. sandiegotradingcompany.com, Mon.-Thurs. 9am-9:30pm, Fri.-Sat. 9am-10pm, Sun. 10am-7pm) or surfing/resort wear purveyors such as **Quiksilver Boardriders Club** (402 5th Ave., 619/234-3125, www.quiksilver.com, Sun.-Thurs. 10am-8pm, Fri.-Sat. 10am-9pm).

In casual California, it makes sense to find several stores devoted to the sale of jeans. **G-Star** (470 5th Ave., 619/238-7088, www.g-star.com, Mon.-Sat. 11am-8pm, Sun. 11am-7pm) offers fun, eclectic men's and women's wear made mostly from denim. Their motto is "luxury denim for the streets." You'll find familiar jeans, jackets, and accessories inside the chain **Lucky Brand Jeans** (621 5th Ave., 619/230-9260, www.luckybrandjeans.com, Mon.-Sat. 10am-10pm, Sun. 11am-9pm).

Specialty items of obvious types are available at **Urban Lighting** (301 4th Ave., 619/232-6064, www.urbanlighting.net, Mon.-Fri. 9am-5pm, Sat. 10am-4pm) and **Fourth Avenue Rug Gallery** (827 4th Ave., 619/234-8700, www.armanfinerugs.com, Mon.-Sat. 11am-8pm).

Westfield Horton Plaza

Looking for a big mall that gathers all your favorite shops into one place? Visit **Westfield Horton Plaza** (324 Horton Plaza, 619/239-8180, www.westfield.com, Mon.-Fri. 10am-9pm, Sat. 10am-8pm, Sun. 11am-6pm). With all the standard Westfield mall amenities, including day spas, salons, and plenty of food options, you'll feel right at home here.

Many of your favorite midrange to upscale chain boutiques make a home at Horton Plaza. Shop at Gap, Bebe, Guess, and Victoria's Secret, among others. Horton Plaza also offers an immense array of jewelry shops, accessory stores, and leather boutiques. For shoes, you'll find everything from Vans to Foot Locker.

OLD TOWN
Bazaar del Mundo

A perfect way to experience shopping in Mexico without making the trek down to Tijuana is to visit Old Town's famed **Bazaar del Mundo** (4133 Taylor St., 619/296-3161, Sun.-Mon. 10am-5:30pm, Tues.-Sat. 10am-9pm). Easily accessed from I-5 and I-8, this cheerful and colorful shopping center brings the best of Mexico across the border. From the familiar figures in the **Laurel Burch Gallerita** to the unusual and often elegant imports of **Artes de Mexico,** you'll find perfect gifts for everyone on your list (and for yourself, of course). When you come down to the bazaar, come hungry: Some of the best and most visitor-friendly Mexican food is served here.

Fashion Valley

Another big urban mall, **Fashion Valley** (7007 Friars Rd., 619/688-9113, www.simon.com, Mon.-Sat. 10am-9pm, Sun. 11am-7pm) has plenty of the shopping experience you desire. A bit higher-end than Horton Plaza, Fashion Valley focuses more on the home and offers some designer boutiques.

Appropriately, fashions for men, women, and children of all ages abound at Fashion

Valley. Kids can grow up here, going from Gymboree to GapKids and on up to The Limited. Gentlemen have a number of options for all parts of life, from the casual times at J. Crew to more formal situations at Gucci.

Not surprisingly, women have the most clothing options here at the mall. The mature crowd prefers Ann Taylor, while the teens and twentysomething shoppers flock to Abercrombie & Fitch, Anthropologie, and Forever 21.

LA JOLLA

Shopping in La Jolla feels a little like a spending spree in the sophisticated areas of Los Angeles. This upscale suburb prides itself on its walking-and-shopping, much of which is centered on Prospect Street. Shoppers should veer off onto the side streets, which hide some true gems.

Prospect La Jolla

Big-name and upscale chain stores rent space on Prospect, as do locally owned one-of-a-kind boutiques. Look for monochromatic women's wear at **White House/Black Market** (7927 Girard Ave., 858/459-2565, www.whitehouseblackmarket.com, Mon.-Sat.

10am-8pm, Sun. 10am-6pm), or a matching men's tuxedo at **Imperial Tailor and Formal Wear** (7744 Fay Ave., 858/459-8891, Mon.-Fri. 9:30am-4:30pm, Sat. 10:30am-1pm). Dozens more apparel stores, from the casual to the highest of high-end, cluster in this section of La Jolla.

Naturally, only the funkiest or fanciest jewels will complement the lovely clothing sold in La Jolla. There are plenty of jewelry stores to browse, offering everything from reasonably priced costume jewelry all the way up to designer diamonds. For local fine jewelry, visit **Jewels by the Sea** (1237 Prospect St. B, 858/459-5166, www.jewelsbythesea.biz, Mon. and Wed.-Sat. noon-6pm, Sun. 1pm-6pm).

Elegant antiques stores cluster in La Jolla, beckoning wealthy patrons to furnish and decorate their homes with the beautiful artifacts of the past. Pick up a great new piece for your collection at shops such as **AJA Rugs** (955 Prospect St. E, 858/523-9570, http://ajadesign.com, Mon.-Sat. 10am-6pm, Sun. noon-5pm) or the **Girard Avenue Collection** (7505 Girard Ave., 858/459-7765, http://girardavenuecollection.com, daily 10:30am-5:30pm).

Sports and Recreation

San Diego has more than its share of sunny days year-round, so get outside! With dozens of miles of beaches, zoos, parks, trails, and endless opportunities for recreation, even the most dedicated couch potatoes can find something great to do under the famed California sun.

BEACHES

If you come to San Diego, you must go to the beach. It's an imperative. From Encinitas and Del Mar down almost to the Mexican border, the California coast shows off its best. The San Diego beaches all seem to be 100 yards wide, perfectly flat, entirely composed of pale, soft,

sugar sand, and run as far in either direction as the eye can see. A few rocks appear in spots, but they're few and far between (especially in comparison to the rugged northern coastline). Bring your towel, umbrella, sunscreen, swimsuit, and surfboard. And if it's a weekend in the summertime, come early in the morning to stake a prime spot in the sand.

For a list of beaches maintained by the City of San Diego, check out www.sandiego.gov.

Ocean Beach

Small for a San Diego beach, **Ocean Beach** (1950 Abbot St., Ocean Beach, daily 24 hours) is a one-mile stretch of sand broken up by several rock jetties. It beckons locals and visitors alike with its lifeguard-protected waters, multiuse areas, and famous Dog Beach. On Dog Beach, at the north end of Ocean Beach, dogs are allowed off-leash all day, every day. (Please clean up after your dog!) Farther south, you'll find designated areas for fishing, surfing, and swimming. Check with the lifeguards to figure out which is which. Be aware that rip currents can be strong at Ocean Beach, and take care when you're out in the water. At the south end of the beach, take a walk out on the Ocean Beach Municipal Pier; some people even bring a pole to spend some quiet time fishing from the structure.

If you need a restroom or showers, head for the main lifeguard station at Abbot Street, which has both. Lifeguards stay on duty from 9am until dusk daily. Amazingly ample parking can be found at three lots that range from the south to the north end of the beach. (The smallest lot is the one by the lifeguard station; go north or south for better parking opportunities.)

Black's Beach

Locals' favorite **Black's Beach** (north of downtown La Jolla and south of Torrey Pines State Beach) has found fame as a surf break. A deepwater canyon offshore acts as a wave magnet, pulling in any swell from a westerly direction. But pause a second before grabbing your board and clambering down the 300-foot cliffs: Black's doubles as a well-known nude beach.

The main difficulty with Black's Beach is getting here. As an unofficial beach without a permanent lifeguard station, you won't find any parking lots; you'll have to do the best you can on the street. No well-built or easily climbed stairways lead down to Black's, so either scramble down the cliff paths, or take your chances with the tides and enter from an adjacent beach to the north or south. Finally, lifeguards are stationed here in the summer months only and the waters are unregulated, so be extremely careful of your fellow surfers and swimmers.

Coronado Main Beach

The can't-miss Hotel del Coronado marks the **Coronado Main Beach** (Ocean Blvd.). Anyone can walk through the outdoor common areas of the Del to get out to this charming sandy beach. This beach is not a surfing beach, but rather a place to relax. Yet another fabulous sun-drenched chunk of coastline, the Coronado Main Beach gets ultra-crowded in the summertime, so come early if you want a prime spot of your own. Do pay attention to the signs and flags— a nasty breakwater of large boulders hides under the water just in front of the Del at high tide. Also take a look at the odd-shaped dunes; from the air, they spell out "Coronado."

Del Mar City Beach

Running along the length of downtown Del Mar, **Del Mar City Beach** (15th St. and Coast Blvd. to the Rivermouth) is touted as one of the best beaches in an area, famous for its welcoming sands. With the exception of easy parking, this huge strip of coastline has it all. The soft sand invites sunbathers, who can spend all day soaking up rays. The ocean beckons, the cool Pacific making a perfect counterpoint to hot San Diego summer days. A decent surf break near the center of City Beach beckons to new and experienced wave riders alike. (You can even take surf lessons here.) Dogs are allowed on a section of the beach north of 29th Street. Lifeguards protect the shores, complete with the towers that mark all guarded San Diego County beaches. Pay attention to the colored flags on the beach: Blue means swimming is okay, and a red flag means the water in front is a surfing area.

Once you find a place on the street to park (bring quarters for the meters), getting onto the beach is easy. The area is flat and simple to access, and in some places boardwalks and paths make beach access even simpler. Just off the beach, the **Powerhouse Community Center** (1658 Coast Blvd.) offers restrooms, restaurants, and a stage.

SURFING AND STAND-UP PADDLEBOARDING

With its endless sunshine and magnificent breaks, San Diego offers some of the best surfing in California. The temperate water (averaging 65-70°F in the summer) allows surfing year-round down here, although wetsuits can be a good idea in winter. San Diego is also an ideal place to learn how to stand-up paddleboard (SUP), if for no other reason than if you fall off the board the water is warmer than it is in the rest of California! The calm waters of Mission Bay are ideal for beginners, while the waves at La Jolla Shores are usually not too big for those who want to try riding a wave on a SUP.

Surf Breaks

San Diego boasts plenty of classic Southern California surfing. In La Jolla, **Black's Beach** is the best beach break in the county. But access to the spot involves hiking down the twisting path of a 300-foot-high cliff face. **Del Mar City Beach** (15th St. and Coast Blvd. to the Rivermouth, Del Mar), in addition to being a great sandy spot to hang out, offers fine beginning and intermediate waves. There's also a reef that produces waves at 15th Street. **Mission Beach** boasts year-round waves as well as lifeguards, restroom facilities, and about a zillion tourists and sun worshippers in the summertime. If you're serious about surfing, check out **Windansea Beach** (6800 Neptune Pl.), which has a heavy shore break and a rockier coastline with a reef that produces one of the region's most revered waves. You will find dense crowds of fellow surfers, so this isn't the best spot for beginners to try out their boards. On the other hand, the small, consistent waves at **La Jolla Shores** (8200 Camino del Oro, La Jolla), also called Scripps, bore the hard-core masters, but are perfect for novice surfers. Just stick within the lifeguard-designated surfing areas to avoid the swimmers and scuba divers sharing the water here. North of Del Mar, **Cardiff Reef** is a great spot for longboarding, while **Swami's** is a legendary right point break in Encinitas in front of a gold-domed temple.

Surf Lessons and Rentals

Never ridden a wave before? Check out one of San Diego's many surf schools. You'll go to a small-wave beach, learn the basics on dry land, and then paddle out for the first time. Most schools promise to get you up and riding (if only for a few seconds) the very first time. Or if you've come to Southern California specifically to surf, check with the schools about multiday, all-inclusive (lodging too!) "surf camps" that get you surfing all day, every day. Most of the surf schools rent and sell boards, leashes, wetsuits, and board-care equipment—everything you need for your first surf setup—and repair and replacement equipment if you're an expert.

Competitive surfer Rick Gehris started **Surfari** (3740 Mission Blvd., 858/337-3287, www.surfarisurfschool.com, $55 group lesson, $85 private lesson, start times 9am, 11am, 1pm, 3pm), which operates at Mission Beach. Each 2.5-hour lesson includes land instruction, interactive in-the-water instruction, and an hour afterward on your own to play. Regular group lessons happen almost every day of the year.

The **San Diego Surfing Academy** (800/447-7873, 760/230-1471, www.sandiegosurfingacademy.com, $200/group lesson, $150/three-hour private lesson) runs year-round at the Oceanside Harbor. You must make an appointment to take lessons with the SDSA, but the quality of instruction makes it worth the bother. All equipment is included in the fee. With two-hour group classes and by-the-hour private lessons, this safety-oriented school makes certain you'll know what you're doing out there in the surf. Relive the moment you stand up for the first time again and again with a complimentary GoPro video of your accomplishment.

The first women-centered surf school in the world, **Surf Diva** (2160 Avenida de la Playa, La Jolla, 858/454-8273, www.surfdiva. com, $85/hour private lessons, $150/two-day clinic, $355/weeklong clinic) creates an estrogen-friendly, supportive atmosphere for girls ages five and up to learn the ins and outs of the waves at La Jolla Shores. They are branching out with SUP rentals and lessons, as well as classes for the whole family (including males!). Book a private lesson, or take a 2-5-day clinic to get serious about the sport. Lessons at Surf Diva make a fun and creative kickoff for a bachelorette party.

Stand-Up Paddleboarding Lessons

Learn on land before stand-up paddleboarding into the water with a two-hour beginner course at **Mission Bay Aquatic Center** (1001 Santa Clara Pl., 858/488-1000, www.mbaquaticcenter.com, $49). They also take paddlers out on moonlight tours ($50) and for yoga sessions ($35) with the boards taking the place of yoga mats.

Up the coast, **Paddle Planet** (996 N. Coast Hwy., Leucadia, 760/602-9767, www.paddle-planet.net, $58-138) conducts SUP instruction at North County beaches including Cardiff State Beach, San Elijo State Beach, Ponto State Beach, and the South Carlsbad Campground. Lessons range from beginning paddling to ocean paddling and ocean paddle surfing.

BOATING

The calm waters of Mission Bay and San Diego Bay make great fun of all forms of boating, from paddleboating to waterskiing to sailing. Kayaking is a special local favorite pastime, especially for would-be explorers of the famous La Jolla Caves. If you plan to exit the bays for the open ocean, be sure you're either competent to navigate a watercraft on the open sea, or have somebody with you who can do it. Watch the weather reports, and pay attention to local experts.

Powerboating and Waterskiing

On the calm waters of the two bays, you can water-ski and wakeboard, dash around on a Jet Ski, or just cruise offshore in a speedboat. **Seaforth Boat Rentals** (888/834-2628, www.seaforthboatrentals.com, $40-900) has four locations: in Mission Bay (1641 Quivira Rd.), downtown San Diego (Marriott Hotel and Marina, 333 W. Harbor Dr., Gate 1), Harbor Island (955 Harbor Island Dr., Suite 130), and Coronado (1715 Strand Way). If you're planning to cruise, rent one of the large speedboats, which range up to over 50 feet and have plenty of room for passengers, coolers, and snacks. If you've got an athletic crew with you, reserve a ski boat. For a more motorcycle-like on-the-water experience, pick up a modern, powerful Jet Ski that rides 2-3 people.

Another multi-boat rental outfit with several locations in and around San Diego is **Action Sport Rentals** (619/241-4794, www.actionsportrentals.com, $85-185). Rent yourself a three-seater Jet Ski or 6-12-passenger speedboat and tool around the bays. For a bigger party, Action offers 13-passenger power pontoon boats. If you want to water-ski or wakeboard but don't have anyone to drive the boat, reserve some time with Action's professional driver. You'll get rides on whatever type of toy (wakeboard, skis, kneeboard, tube) you want behind their competitive-class ski boat.

Sailing

Whether you want a quiet putter around the bay or an exhilarating adventure on the open ocean, you can get just the sailing experience you want in San Diego. **Seaforth Boat Rentals** (888/834-2628, www.seaforthboatrentals.com, $45-350) offers 16- to 54-foot rental sailboats. You can also book a sailing lesson, or even hire a captain to take care of the practicalities while you and your party enjoy a glass of wine and a meal or snack on the water.

Kayaking

With so many calm, protected bays, plus an array of exciting sea caves, it's no wonder that San Diego boasts some of the best sea kayaking in the state. Whether you've got your own boat or you plan to rent or take a tour, the most popular spots to paddle are the La Jolla Caves, part of the larger **La Jolla Cove**

Ecological Reserve (1100 Coast Blvd., www. sandiego.gov). **La Jolla Kayak** (2199 Avenida de la Playa, 858/459-1114, www.lajollakayak. com, single kayaks start at $45, double kayaks start at $59, tours $59-109) rents kayaks and does a two-hour tour of the caves and underwater park of La Jolla.

SNORKELING AND SCUBA DIVING

The reefs and wrecks off San Diego offer amazing sights, clear waters, and brightly colored sea life—whether you take a guided tour or go off on your own.

A great place to enjoy a calm snorkel with your family is the **La Jolla Cove.** Make a reservation with a professional outfit such as **Scuba San Diego, Inc.** (619/260-1880, www. scubasandiego.com, $75) to take a guided tour of the La Jolla Cove Ecological Reserve. They also offer an exciting night dive; a Scuba Adventure trip for new divers who are not yet certified; and a dive trip to Wreck Alley, where eight shipwrecks rest on the ocean floor, including an almost-400-foot-long destroyer. Or bring your own (or rent some) equipment and kick offshore on your own (with at least one friend, of course).

FISHING

Any number of charter companies offer half- to full-day deep-sea fishing trips for everything from rock cod to yellowfin tuna and mahi-mahi, depending on the season. Most companies include both Mexico and California fishing licenses with your charter as needed, as well as rental or included tackle and fish cleaning and filleting services. The tuna season (for fishing well offshore for large tuna) runs from early summer through the fall most years.

Leaving right out of the San Diego harbor, **H&M Landing** (2803 Emerson St., 619/222-1144, www.hmlanding.com, half-day adults $48, seniors, military, and children $40, tackle rental $12-20) offers half-day, three-quarter-day, overnight, and multiday trips year-round. Shorter trips ply the Point Loma

kelp beds, while longer trips can head out to the Coronado Islands or farther into the open water.

Seaforth Sportfishing (1717 Quivira Rd., 619/224-3383, www.seaforthlanding. com, half-day adults $45, seniors, military, and children $38, tackle rental $14) offers half-day through multiday trips to fish for most of the major sport species in the San Diego area. You can even catch a barracuda! Seaforth's half-day trips, offered year-round, last five hours (morning or afternoon), allow the catching of more than half a dozen types of fish, and are perfect for families with children or new anglers. Three-quarter-day trips really last all day (eight hours) and can range down as far as the Coronado Islands in Mexico. The Overnight Mexico and Multi-Day Tuna trips are best for more experienced fishers who don't suffer from too much seasickness, and are looking to reel in a bigger catch. On any Seaforth trip, expect a full galley with snacks, meals, and beverage service.

Point Loma Sportfishing (1403 Scott St., 619/223-1627, www.pointlomasportfishing.com, adults half-day $45, seniors, children, and military $38, tackle extra) offers 18 boats and an extensive list of fishing options. With Point Loma, hard-core anglers can book a two-week cruise that ranges more than 1,000 miles from San Diego, going after enormous deepwater tuna and other major-league sport fish. On the other hand, several of Point Loma's boats offer sedate, family- and beginner-friendly half-day (6 hours) and three-quarter-day (8-10 hours) trips for rockfish, sea bass, barracuda, and yellowtail near the San Diego and northern Mexico coastlines. Private charter boats are available for parties of 5-25.

For small groups looking to fish together, **Action Sport Rentals** (2580 Ingraham St., 619/226-2929, www.danalanding.com) at Dana Landing maintains a fleet of six-passenger fishing boats that can handle half-day to two-day fishing trips. Action Sport Rentals offers bay-safe skiffs, tackle, and bait year-round. You'll also find a launch here if you've brought your own boat.

MARINE ANIMAL TOURS

If you prefer to catch marine life with your camera rather than a hook and line, consider taking a whale-watching cruise out from the San Diego coastline. Most of the sportfishing outfits also offer whale-watching trips and charters in season (winter through mid-spring). **Hornblower Cruises** (1066 N. Harbor Dr., 619/686-8700, www.hornblower. com, harbor cruises $24-29) offers six bay cruises daily. Choose the one- or two-hour version; both include narration about the landmarks and animals. They also do blue whale-watching tours from late June to early September. Hornblower offers one of the most comfortable, tourist-friendly sea experiences, with a snack bar, indoor decks with panel windows for good viewing, and a yacht highly rated for its stability.

AIR SPORTS

With a strong military history and endlessly fabulous weather, it's no wonder that aviation-based sports are a big deal in San Diego.

Flying and Skydiving

Yes, you really can go to "war" during your otherwise tranquil vacation in San Diego. **Barnstorming Adventures** (Montgomery Field Airport, 3750 John J. Montgomery Dr., Ste. D, 800/359-2939, www.barnstorming. com, $199-459 per person, depending on type of flight) offers the rare opportunity to fly an air-combat mission in a light plane designed for dogfighting. For a more peaceful aviation experience, book a scenic flight for one or two people in an old-fashioned biplane.

If you prefer jumping out of planes to riding in them, head up north to **Skydive Elsinore** (20701 Cereal St., Lake Elsinore, 877/359-2939, www.skydiveelsinore.com, $189). This full-service skydiving school and outfitter can take you on a great jump, regardless of your experience level. Beginners can take a tandem jump after a brief introductory lesson, or go more intensive with a full-fledged skydiving course culminating with a solo jump. If you're a more experienced jumper, take a look at the website for your diving options.

Gliding

For perhaps the most unusual views of northern San Diego County, go **Sky Sailing** (31930 Hwy. 79, Warner Springs, 760/782-0404, www.skysailing.com, daily 9am-sunset, rides $145-250). In a silent glider or "sail plane," you'll catch thermal updrafts, see Palomar Mountain and Warner Springs Ranch, and feel the wonder of birdlike flight. If you're interested in sightseeing, make a weekday reservation or just drop by on the weekend for a flight flown by an FAA-certified pilot. If it's actually flying a glider yourself that lights your fire, book a lesson or rent a glider of your own. (Hand-controlled gliders are available for pilots with special needs.) And if you've got a strong stomach and great faith in your ability to survive, ask about the Super Spectacular Rides.

If you prefer the notion of gliding off a sea cliff into the air above the Pacific Ocean, your destination is the **Torrey Pines Glider Port** (2800 Torrey Pines Scenic Dr., La Jolla, 858/452-9858, www.flytorrey.com, $175/paragliding, $225/hang gliding). Book a tandem flight on either a hang glider or a paraglider with only 20 minutes of preflight instruction. The specialty of the house is paragliding, and you can sign up for lessons and get certified to paraglide all on your own. Save $10 by paying in cash.

Jetpack Flight

Ever wanted to take flight like Superman? Fly over the bay propelled by a state-of-the-art jetpack at **Jetpack America** (Mission Bay Sports Center, 1010 Santa Clara Pl., 888/553-6471, www.jetpackamerica.com, daily 10am-5pm, $97-699). They offer everything from 10-minute tandem flights to pricey Rockstar and Superhero jetpack experiences.

GOLF

With fabulous sunny weather year-round, San Diego and its surrounding countryside are a golfer's dream. Wherever you go, you'll find a course or two awaiting you, from easy nine-holers up to U.S. Open hosts. If you're new to the area, consider calling **Showtime Golf** (866/661-2334, www.showtimegolf.com). This golf service provider can get you advance or last-minute tee times, book you into local tournaments, and answer all your questions about the vast range of golfing options in the San Diego area.

If you know anything about golf in San Diego and La Jolla, you know that the One True Golf Course here is **Torrey Pines** (11480 N. Torrey Pines Rd., La Jolla, 858/452-3226, www.torreypinesgolfcourse.com, 18 holes $183). Home of the 2008 U.S. Open, the Torrey Pines Golf Course has two championship 18-hole courses on coastal cliffs with views of the ocean. Plan to book well in advance for a tee time at this gorgeous course.

DISC GOLF

San Diego can lay claim to one of the oldest disc golf courses in the world with the **Morley Field Disc Golf Course** (3090 Pershing Dr., 619/692-3607, www.morleyfield.com, daily sunrise-sunset, Mon.-Fri. $3, Sat.-Sun. $4), established back in the early years of the Carter presidency. The course might be considered posh to some disc golfers with its greens fees, maintained grounds, and pro shop that rents discs.

HIKING

In addition to walks on the beach, the **Torrey Pines State Reserve** (12600 North Torrey Pines Rd., 858/755-2063, www.torreypine.org, daily 7:15am-sunset, $10-15) offers some beautiful wilderness trails. Look for *Pinus torreyana*—the rarest species of pine tree in the United States. The shortest walk is the **High Point Trail,** only 100 yards up to views of the whole reserve, from the ocean to the lagoon to the forest and back. For an easy, under-one-hour walk, take the **Guy Fleming Trail** for a level 0.66 miles through forest, wildflower patches, and views of the ocean. A slightly longer excursion, the **Razor Point Trail** (one mile round-trip) descends down a sandy path to a blufftop lookout with a fine view of waves rolling onto the coast below. For a longer walk, leave the visitors center by the road, then take the **North Fork Trail** west to the **Broken Hill Trail,** which will bring you right down to the beach stairway and a great view of Flat Rock.

SPECTATOR SPORTS
San Diego Chargers

Are you ready for some football, without the snow, sleet, or freezing rain of the Northeast's outdoor stadiums? Then grab tickets to **Qualcomm Stadium** (9449 Friars Rd., 619/641-3100, www.sandiego.gov) in the Mission Valley neighborhood. The **San Diego Chargers** (www.chargers.com) play in the AFC West. If you're driving in, plan to arrive at the parking lot at least two hours early since the lot often fills up and even closes an hour before kickoff. Also, try to avoid going in or out via I-15, which is the most congested route to the stadium. A better way to get here might be the Mission Trolley System (MTS), which has special-event bus service to the stadium, as well as regular stops at Qualcomm on the Blue and Green trolley lines. The North County Transit District (NCTD) system also provides express bus service to all home games.

Once you've made it into the stadium, you'll find ample food, drink, restrooms, souvenirs, ID bracelets for your kids, and first aid and other services throughout. Alcohol sales are limited and end at the close of the third quarter. For a more posh NFL experience, check whether tickets are available at the club level, which has squishier seats and a waitstaff.

At the time this book was going to print, the Chargers were going to stay put in San Diego for the 2016-17 season with the hope that they could get a new stadium built there. If the new project doesn't move forward, the Chargers have the option to move to Los Angeles, where they would share a new field in Inglewood with the Los Angeles Rams. The Chargers have until early 2017 to decide if they want to move to L.A.

San Diego Padres

While you're in San Diego, why not take yourself and your family out to a baseball game? The **San Diego Padres** (http://sandiego.padres.mlb.com) play throughout the regular season (and hopefully into the World Series) at **Petco Park** (100 Park Blvd., 619/795-5000) in downtown San Diego. Few rainouts mar the Padres' home season, and in addition to the game, you can view Balboa Park, the cityscape, and San Diego Bay from the lovely and spacious modern stadium. Sit back with a brew or a soda, enjoy the extra legroom, and bask in the perfect spring baseball weather of San Diego.

Petco Park is well situated for fans that prefer to avoid the inevitable parking nightmares and take public transit in to the game. The MTS trolleys and buses have multiple stops within a block or two of the ballpark, and the Coaster rail line offers extra trains on game nights for fans coming in from the North County towns. If you're staying in the Gaslamp Quarter, consider just walking over to the stadium from your lodgings. If you must drive, prepare to pay $8-15 for downtown lot parking and $20 for a slot right by the park.

Del Mar Racetrack and Fairgrounds

In horse-racing season, you'll find significant crowds descending on the tiny town of Del Mar and the famous **Del Mar Fairgrounds** (2260 Jimmy Durante Blvd., Del Mar, 858/755-1161, www.delmarfairgrounds.com), where some of the finest thoroughbreds ever to grace a track have raced to victory. The track was built in the late 1930s, with Bing Crosby supplying both funds and fame to create the glorious equestrian facilities that continue to delight race and horse fans to this day. The structures at the fairgrounds are built in the style of various California missions, and careful attention to detail has created possibly the most beautiful permanent indoor-outdoor exhibition facilities in the state.

Races usually run July-early September. Wagering rules can be found at the track or on the fairgrounds website, as can information about the off-season telecast racing series. Show up on some Friday and Saturday afternoons to enjoy the **Del Mar Summer Concert Series,** where you can see acts like Weezer and Paul Oakenfold.

If you prefer a different style of equestrian event, come to Del Mar a little bit earlier in the year for the **Del Mar National Horse Show** (858/792-4288, www.delmarnational.com). This event lasts three weeks each spring, with a full week each devoted to Western events, dressage, and hunter/jumper activities. Book your room and buy tickets in advance, as this is one of the most popular horse shows in the western United States each year.

Any number of other events take place at the fairgrounds every month of the year. Check the website for a calendar of upcoming events, plus ticket information. Ample pay parking surrounds the fairgrounds, or if you're taking the train, grab a free shuttle from the Coaster straight to the racetrack.

Accommodations

DOWNTOWN

Acres of hotels cluster throughout downtown San Diego. Whether you need a budget hostel or want a high-end luxury resort, you'll find it. Many mid-tier and upscale chains offer bed and board downtown—all you have to do is walk around to find the Sheraton, Hilton, or Holiday Inn. For a more interesting lodging experience, look to the smaller chains and the independents.

Under $100

Looking for budget accommodations in the heart of San Diego? For a start, call the **HI-San Diego** (521 Market St., 800/909-4776, www.sandiegohostels.org, dorm beds $30-58, private rooms $85-175). Get just about anywhere from this almost-elegant youth hostel right in the middle of the Gaslamp. (Bring your HI card for lower rates.) Inside, you'll find private and double rooms, as well as dorm rooms that sleep 4-10 people in single beds. The amenities include all standard hostel fare: coin-op laundry, an open kitchen, a common room with a TV, and a courtyard area. Plan to bring or buy a lock for the lockers provided in the dorm rooms. The hostel's packed events calendar includes free walking tours of Balboa Park and the downtown area. Between the food and nightlife of the Gaslamp and the endless stream of interesting people and activities, the HI-San Diego is the perfect resting place for young people visiting San Diego.

Looking for a Mediterranean-style student hotel for a whole week? Try the **Hotel Occidental** (410 Elm St., 619/232-1336, www.hoteloccidental-sandiego.com, $190-320/week), where the minimum stay is for seven nights. Only a block and a half from the entrance to Balboa Park, don't expect tons of in-room luxury here—smaller rooms share baths, and even some of the larger rooms have only a half-bath, with shower facilities down the hall. Decor feels European (in the Ikea sense when it comes to furniture), with lots of clean lines and plain linens and small, ingeniously used spaces. Hotel-wide amenities include free Wi-Fi and private kitchenettes that let you keep some of your own food rather than depending on restaurants for every meal.

$150-250

With enough rooms for a medium-sized motel, but the feel of a small inn, **La Pensione Hotel** (606 W. Date St., 800/232-4683, www.lapensionehotel.com, $170-180) prides itself on offering the best value in the best location in downtown San Diego. The exterior blends the look of a Mediterranean home with the Spanish colonial revival style of Southern California. A standard room has one queen-sized bed, unusual photographic wall art, and a clean bathroom. Work out in the fitness center (daily 24 hours), and wake up to complimentary coffee and a pastry at the on-site Caffe Italia. The hotel is in Little Italy, within easy walking distance of great restaurants and cafés, and only blocks from the Gaslamp Quarter. The staff can help you with taxis and public transit, making it possible to avoid driving.

La Pensione does not have as many off-street parking spots as they do rooms, so parking is first come, first served during the high season. And if you're bringing your kids, be aware that trundle beds and such are not available, and the hotel requests that only two people stay in any one room.

Over $250

If you want to stay in *the* classic San Diego hotel and you've got the money to do it, book a room at the ★ **US Grant Hotel** (326 Broadway, 619/232-3121, www.starwoodhotels.com, $280-500). Built in 1910, the US Grant has anchored the Gaslamp Quarter for 100 years. Inside, you'll be showered with luxury, from the elegant lobby to the in-house spa to the gorgeous rooms (which include luxurious showers). Even the standard rooms have plush linens, nine-foot ceilings, original artwork, and the many amenities that mark the US Grant worth the cost of admission. You've got all the restaurant options of the Gaslamp within staggering distance, or stay in the hotel and dine at the upscale California-style Grant Grill. Whether your interests are surfing or golfing, the concierges can help you with arrangements for activities around the city.

★ **The Sofia Hotel** (150 W. Broadway, 800/678-8946, www.historichotels.org, $200-400) is an imposing gothic revival-style building in downtown San Diego, with metal fire escapes plunging down its front like giant zippers. The comfortable rooms feel classic with their mahogany-stained furniture and armchairs with ottomans, but they also have contemporary amenities including TVs with HBO. The hotel also puts on complimentary yoga classes every morning and guided walking tours on weekends. Or head out on one of the hotel's complimentary bikes to explore on your own. Another plus is the on-site **Currant Restaurant** (619/702-6309, www.currantrestaurant.com, Mon.-Fri. 7am-10am, 11:30am-2:30pm, and 5pm-10pm, Sat.-Sun. 9am-2:30pm and 5pm-10pm, $15-33), which does great food and drink.

For a fun hotel stay downtown, hit the exclusive **W Hotel San Diego** (421 W. B St., 619/398-3100, www.starwoodhotels.com, $190-500). This swanky, ultramodern hotel has the perfect location—convenient to the airport, walking distance to the harbor, and a short jaunt to the fabulous restaurants in the Gaslamp Quarter. Upper-level rooms offer views of city and the bay. Rooms feature cushy beds with featherbeds and down comforters, and are done in an almost-industrial, urban-chic style that echoes the grander decor of the entrance, lobby, and bars. Despite the hard lines and cool blue-and-silver color scheme, touches of whimsy abound. (Take a moment to read the labels on your toiletries—it's worth the time.) But best of all, the service here is exceptional, even in this tourist-friendly region. Just call down, and anything you want will be at your doorstep, probably in about 15 minutes. You'll find every amenity you could dream of, from room service to first-aid kits to Wi-Fi to condoms—but beware, none of these are complimentary. For a fun night out without the hassle of a car or a cab, head up to The

The Sofia Hotel

Rooftop Bar, the W's bar with a cool bonfire sculpture that mimics a SoCal beach scene.

For a great view of downtown and the bay beyond, book a room on one of the top floors at ★ **Hotel Palomar San Diego** (1047 S. 5th Ave., 619/515-3000 or 888/288-6601, www. hotelpalomar-sandiego.com, $250-900). With lots of windows, these elegant, modern rooms also have wood floors and stone washbasins in the bathroom. On site is a heated rooftop swimming pool, spa, and the Saltbox, a "gastro-lounge" serving creative plates and tasty cocktails. The friendly staff at the Hotel Palomar host a daily wine tasting 5pm-6pm and allow guests to borrow surfboards and bikes.

BALBOA PARK AND HILLCREST

Lodgings right by the park aren't plentiful. For a better selection, check out downtown and Old Town, which are within easy public transit and driving distance of the wonders of Balboa Park and the fun of Hillcrest.

$100-150

Stay just a block and a half from a row of Hillcrest restaurants with an evening at the **Hillcrest House Bed and Breakfast** (3845 Front St., 619/990-2441, www.hillcresthouse-bandb.com, $149-189). The five rooms are named for San Diego attractions, with the Zoo room featuring animal prints. A stay includes a continental breakfast, 24-hour beverages, and use of a leash to walk the B&B's Yorkshire terrier. Another big plus is the free off-street parking.

OLD TOWN

You'll find a massive cluster of national chain motels in Old Town, so this is a great place to land if you need a place to stay on short notice. However, if you want something a little less generic but still reasonably priced, Old Town can hook you up with that too.

$100-150

The **Kings Inn** (1333 Hotel Circle S., 619/297-2231, www.kingsinnsandiego.com, $99-300) offers spacious, nonsmoking motel rooms at affordable prices. Rooms are done in florals with jewel-colored carpets and light walls, with either one king or two queen beds. Outside, take a dip in the cute apostrophe-shaped pool or accompanying spa. The location is convenient to sightseeing and transportation, and attached are two family restaurants that provide room service to the motel. The Amigo Spot serves authentic Mexican cuisine, and the Waffle Spot has (surprise) waffles, as well as Mexican and American egg breakfast dishes and a kids' menu.

For thrift, exterior charm, and location, location, location, you can't beat the **Old Town Inn** (4444 Pacific Hwy., 619/260-8024, www. oldtown-inn.com, $99-209). Built to resemble a rancho with a low profile and narrow columns, this motel sits across the street from the Old Town Transit Center, so you can catch a bus or trolley and get virtually anywhere in San Diego County from here. The white-painted, red-tile-roofed exterior of the motel gives way to plain motel rooms inside, with muted pastels, dark carpets, and floral bedspreads. If you plan to cook your own meals, go for a deluxe room, which includes a two-burner stove, refrigerator, and microwave. Grab a DVD or two from the inn's library and watch a flick in your room. This family-friendly motel has a heated pool, free parking, and a free daily continental breakfast.

$150-250

For a cheerful modern stay in San Diego that feels almost like home, stay in the **Sommerset Suites Hotel** (606 Washington St., 800/962-9665, www.sommersetsuites. com, $189-350). Light, bright bedrooms offer a touch of class in this 80-unit, all-suite, nonsmoking motel, and each room offers a full kitchen. Enjoy free Wi-Fi in your room or down by the pool, where you can take a refreshing dip on a hot day or a hot spa soak on a cool evening. Technically the Sommerset is in the Uptown neighborhood adjacent to Old

Town, but it's easy to reach the shopping and dining establishments in Old Town, or all the major attractions in San Diego.

POINT LOMA

While your kids will love the proximity to SeaWorld, you'll love the almost European stylings of the classic oceanside resorts on Point Loma and Shelter Island. You're still within easy driving range of all major San Diego attractions, but without the crowds and the downtown feel. If you own your own boat and plan to bring it to San Diego, consider one of the resorts on Shelter Island—most have private marinas that rent slips.

Under $100

For the cheapest accommodations near the beach, book a bed or a family room in the ★ HI-San Diego, Point Loma Hostel (3790 Udall St., 619/223-800/909-4776, www.sandiegohostels.org, dorm beds $31-33, private rooms $76-156). A short drive or a longish two-mile-walk from famous Ocean Beach, this charming bright-red hostel sits in the midst of a residential area of Point Loma. The proprietors encourage bicycling exploration of San Diego by providing ample bike racks for secure storage. Or if you prefer, the bus stop is only a block away from the hostel, making it easy to get to the zoo, Old Town, the beaches, or wherever else you want to go. Inside, you'll find 4-10-bed dorms and private or family rooms that include linens, Internet access, and storage lockers. Cook in the common kitchen and eat in the living room or play Ping-Pong out on the courtyard or clean some clothes in the laundry. The owners love to see families as well as budget-minded singles here at the hostel, and this is a great place to stay for a truly inexpensive family beach vacation.

For folks who want a budget bed with more privacy than a hostel can afford, the family-owned **Dolphin Motel** (2912 Garrison St., 619/758-1404 or 866/353-7897, www.dolphin-motel.com, $60-155) offers comfortable rooms at reasonable rates in two modest white buildings with blue trim. The white walls match the pristine white bedspreads, daring you to find fault with the cleanliness at this budget motel. While the rooms aren't huge, you'll get a comfortable bed, TV with basic cable, air-conditioning, free Wi-Fi, and a fridge for the duration of your stay. Best of all, you're only a short walk from the sea, and the fishing, kayaking, and other water sports of San Diego are easily accessible (some only across the street). Enjoy a complimentary pastry and a morning

Dolphin Motel

cup of coffee out in the attractive little courtyard. Or get your own food and sit out on the balcony, enjoying the calm air of Point Loma. The motel is right across from the sportfishing landing.

Another budget option in Point Loma is **The Pearl Hotel** (1410 Rosecrans St., 619/226-6100, www.thepearlsd.com, $110-250), a hip and lively boutique hotel with a happening social scene. The 33 rooms here horseshoe around a saltwater pool that's home to "Dive-In" movie nights on Wednesdays. The decor here is meant to evoke a cool 1960s vibe. Guests also get complimentary use of the property's bikes. The hotel is home to **EAT at The Pearl** (619/226-6100, Mon.-Sat. 6pm-10pm, $16-21), a popular restaurant.

$150-250

A Shelter Island charmer, **The Bay Club Hotel and Marina** (2131 Shelter Island Dr., 800/672-0800, www.bayclubhotel.com, $209-239) provides bay and harbor views, comfortable rooms, and charming amenities. Outside your room, you'll find a funky geometric swimming pool with matching spa, a fitness center, and a brown-and-white bar and grill with a 1950s-style tropical resort feel. Stop at the desk before heading out into town to grab discount passes to various attractions.

The exterior of the **Kona Kai Resort** (1551 Shelter Island Dr., 619/221-8000 or 800/566-2524, www.resortkonakai.com, $189-389) evokes the legendary Hotel del Coronado—but on this property you'll find a sense of peace and tranquility that feels more like a Hawaiian resort out away from the city. With a fitness center, a pool, and a full-service spa, you won't lack for pampering and amenities as you bask in the Shelter Island sunshine. Inside, your room will fulfill all your oceanside vacation ideals with soft neutral tones on the walls, and colorful and green accents creating a tropical paradise. Befitting a tropical resort, the Kona Kai has its own private beach by the marina. If you plan to take a seagoing adventure, moor your personal or rental boat at the private marina (slips up to 200 feet),

or head over to SeaWorld or downtown for landlubber activities. Even if you get seasick, it might be worth a stroll down to the marina to check out the mega-yacht docking area and get a glimpse at how the other 1 percent live.

Over $250

Consider staying across the bay from downtown San Diego, on Shelter Island at **Humphreys Half Moon Inn & Suites** (2303 Shelter Island Dr., 800/542-7400, www.halfmooninn.com, $320-450). This resort property looks out over the bay towards the city skyline. It has its own private marina and a lush tropical garden (heavy on the palm trees, of course). Your large, home-styled room might look out into the greenery or over the great blue bay. If you're in the mood for luxury, add an "enhancement," such as champagne and strawberries or an in-room massage, to your room reservation. If you're feeling lazy, spend a day by the pool, enjoying fruity rum drinks from the poolside bar. On the other hand, energetic travelers can take a boat out onto the water, head into town to check out the attractions, or take a bike ride around Shelter Island. Come evening, dine at the on-site gourmet restaurant, then dance the night away to live music at the hotel's own club. In the summertime, get tickets to one of the famed outdoor concerts held on the resort property.

CORONADO

While the Hotel del Coronado dominates the Coronado scenery and certainly makes for a fun place to stay, the island town also offers an array of other accommodations. You can find a good place to lay your head for a reasonable rate here, or go over the top at the Del or one of the other big beach resorts.

Under $150

For an inexpensive stay on Coronado Island, visit the **El Rancho Motel Coronado** (370 Orange Ave., 619/435-2251, www.elranchocoronado.com, $99-150). A few blocks from the Del, the beaches, and the downtown area of Coronado, the El Rancho lets you enjoy the high life without the high prices. Each unit of the El Rancho has its own air-conditioning, TV, fridge, and microwave, plus a comfortable bed and a pleasant tiled bathroom. You'll feel right at home in the small lodge-like motel with its white exterior and mostly matching interior. Ask the innkeeper (who lives on-site at the motel) about the best food, shopping, and good beach spots on the island.

$150-250

If you can't quite afford a stay at the Del this time, the next best thing might be the **Glorietta Bay Inn** (1630 Glorietta Blvd., 619/435-3101, www.gloriettabayinn.com, $219-700). Literally across the street from the Del, the stately white mansion was the dream home of John D. Spreckels, who in the latter half of the 19th century owned the Del and most of the rest of San Diego in the bargain. Today, the lovely structure oozes charm, even as the less-glamorous motel buildings behind it offer spacious budget accommodations. For a premium, book a room inside the mansion proper; each of these is uniquely decorated and includes upscale services and amenities. The "Inn Rooms" behind the mansion are spacious, with adequate amenities and cheerful tropical-resort decor. If you're bringing your family for several days of beach time, the Inn Suites offer a full kitchen and a living room as well as one or two bedrooms, making them an ideal base of operations. No matter which building you stay in, a free continental breakfast is served each morning in the mansion's breakfast room. Grab a pastry and your coffee and enjoy exploring the mansion common rooms, which boast photos commemorating the history of the house and the Spreckels family. Then jog across the street to gape at the Del or just pass through onto Coronado Beach. After that, grab some complimentary beach amenities and head to the sand.

At **Villa Capri By the Sea** (1417 Orange Ave., 800/231-3954, www.villacapribythesea. com, $199) you get all the benefits of staying right at the hot center of Coronado (that is, near the Del), without the costs or the ghosts. Bring your whole family or several friends— the suites sleep up to six people, and include a full kitchen with all pots and pans necessary for cooking great meals. Yet you can still walk across the street to enjoy the restaurants and shops of the Del, and to get out onto Coronado Beach. Inside, the living rooms are dimly lit but comfortable, the kitchens are light and homey, and the bright bedrooms look perfect for a sunny beach vacation. On the hottest days, you'll appreciate your own oasis of air-conditioning, cable TV, and Wi-Fi after hours out on the sand playing with on-loan beach toys. Check the website for special Internet rates. There's a three- to four-day minimum during the summer.

Over $250

★ **Hotel del Coronado** (1500 Orange Ave., 800/468-3533, www.hoteldel.com, $400-2,200) dominates the landscape of Coronado Island. Even in Southern California, the Del, as it's called by its friends and neighbors, wins a prize for grandiosity. The white-painted, red-roofed mammoth sprawls for acres from the beach to the road, taking up a couple of blocks all its own. Inside, the Del is at once a historical museum, shopping mall, food court, and, oh yeah, a hotel. Famously haunted, the Del offers almost 700 rooms, plus another 70-plus individual cottages at Beach Village. Your best bet to catch a ghost in action is to book a room in the Victorian Building. For a more modern hotel experience, stay in the Ocean Towers or California Cabanas. Room sizes and decor vary, from smaller Victorian-decorated rooms to expansive resort-themed suites; pick what you (and your budget) like best. If you want a view, be aware that ocean-facing rooms cost extra.

The best thing about staying at the Del is that you almost never have to leave. You can fall out of the hotel onto Coronado Beach, grabbing a spot early on this oft-crowded strip of sand in the summertime. In the winter, the hotel puts up an improbable ice rink out on the "back porch." Pick from among several restaurants (or room service) for meals, and even shop for a new bikini in the downstairs of the main building.

MISSION BAY

The perfect location to find a room if you're traveling to SeaWorld or want something with easy access to the water, Mission Bay offers plenty of inexpensive chain and independent motels. If you're looking for luxury, you can also check in to one of the upscale resorts along the beach.

$150-250

Almost-affordable rates seem a surprise at oceanside **The Dana on Mission Bay** (1710 W. Mission Bay Dr., 800/445-3339, www.the-dana.com, $160-430). It's so close to SeaWorld that you can walk to the park, and it has its own private marina for serious sea lovers. Pick from two blocks of rooms: The Marina Cove section offers less-expensive rooms without views of the ocean; you might look over the garden or the pool. Inside, Marina Cove rooms are fairly small, with brightly colored, tropical-themed decor. The Waters Edge premium rooms have wonderful views out over the Pacific and a subtler, elegant design scheme. Rent a personal watercraft or a boat directly from The Dana and take a spin on Mission Bay. Or stay on the 10-acre resort property and splash in one of the two large swimming pools.

Mission Bay Motel (4221 Mission Blvd., 866/649-5828, www.missionbaymotel.com, $149-199) offers clean, comfortable accommodations at the right price near the beach and Mission Bay Aquatic Park. This cheerful, white-and-blue-painted, low-built motor hotel has small, white-painted and pastel-decorated rooms, and makes a perfect base from which to enjoy the many sights and sun-drenched beaches of San Diego. Choose from rock-bottom-priced singles (which actually sleep two people) up to multi-bed rooms with kitchenettes that can accommodate the whole family. The residential Pacific Beach neighborhood offers affordable local restaurants, a beach a

block away, and car or public transit access to the rest of the San Diego area.

San Diego is littered with gorgeous high-end resort hotels, and the Mission Bay area is no exception. One of the nicest of these is the **Catamaran Resort** (3999 Mission Blvd., 800/422-8386, www.catamaranresort.com, $229-600). Garden rooms and studios, which have one or two beds, stylish decor, and top-tier amenities (plus full kitchens in the studios), can have surprisingly reasonable rates. The premier rooms—bayfront rooms and suites—have grand views of the ocean, some with direct access right down to the Catamaran's beach. A great reason to stay at the Catamaran, the private beach runs to a private pier with a water-sports rental facility that can hook you up whether you prefer high-powered, wind-powered, or human-powered watercraft. (Windsurfing is a favored activity on Mission Bay.) For younger guests, the Catamaran Kids Club keeps children occupied and happy while their parents enjoy the sea, the spa, or the private comforts of their hotel room. Also on-site you'll find the Oceano Coastal Kitchen with its sushi bar and live jellyfish tank.

Sleep over the ocean at the **Crystal Pier Hotel** (4500 Ocean Blvd., 800/748-5894, www.crystalpier.com, $215-525). These cottages and suites are perched right on Pacific Beach's Crystal Pier above the crashing surf. Each place has a fully equipped kitchenette and private deck over the beach. A guaranteed parking space helps to seal the deal.

Over $250

If your reason for coming to San Diego is to loll about on the beach sipping fruity cocktails, the **Bahia Resort** (998 W. Mission Bay Dr., 800/576-4229, www.bahiahotel.com, $289-569) is the perfect place to drop your suitcase and change into your swimsuit. Stumble out of your room onto a strip of Mission Bay's sun-warmed sugar sand. If you prefer your water a bit more contained, the charming Moroccan decor surrounding the large pool and tremendous (30-person) spa is for you. For the ultimate in splendid relaxation, order from the café and waiters will deliver right to you at poolside. Inside, the understated rooms are done in a variety of styles. Enjoy the comfort of the plush beds, the overstuffed furniture, and the homey touches prevalent especially in the larger apartment-like suites. The hotel restaurant, Café Bahia, offers tasty traditional breakfast, lunch, and dinner with just a touch of Middle Eastern flavor. For a treat, eat outdoors.

LA JOLLA

If you want to stay in ritzy La Jolla, be prepared to bust out your credit card. This uptown burg doesn't come cheap. While a few motels offer decent rooms for under $200, you'll find the best locations and rooms well over that price point. If you simply must stay in La Jolla on a budget, a few major chain motels lurk around near downtown.

$100-150

One of the few pleasant lower-budget La Jolla accommodations is the **Sands of La Jolla** (5417 La Jolla Blvd., 800/643-0530, www.sandsoflajolla.com, $99-189). It's not in the center of the action, which helps the price point stay a little bit lower, but you can still use a car to reach the beaches, the La Jolla Cove, and the top attractions in San Diego proper. Inside, you'll find pleasant motel rooms furnished with light woods and sunny yellow wall and window treatments. Deluxe rooms and suites offer full kitchenettes, and all rooms have refrigerators, microwaves, and toaster ovens to help you save money by buying some of your own food from the store rather than eating at a pricey restaurant. This nice little motel also offers family-friendly, multi-bed rooms and suites for great beach vacations.

$150-250

Perfectly located and reasonably priced (for La Jolla), the **La Jolla Inn** (1110 Prospect St., 888/855-7829, www.lajollainn.com, $169-199) sits comfortably between the main shopping drag and the sloping sidewalk that leads down to the beach. The brick facade with dark blue awnings stands out in an area of wood and adobe-style construction. Inside, you'll think you've found a boutique hotel on the Mediterranean, with small, bright rooms that feature natural wood furniture and colorful homemade quilts. Upper rooms also offer the best art ever: a view out over the Pacific. Be sure to take advantage of the paid underground parking (two blocks away), as this area gets crowded in high season.

Over $250

In La Jolla, upscale accommodations abound. One of the most charming is the ★ **Estancia La Jolla Hotel and Spa** (9700 Torrey Pines Rd., 858/550-1000, www.estancialajolla.com, $250-500). Built on a historic Mexican rancho, the traditional arrangement of buildings and courtyards gleam with restoration and vitality. (When driving in, look for the resort name on a standard cross-street sign.) Palm trees and succulents grace the landscape. Inside, spacious rooms in neutral tones are accented with bright oranges, yellows, and greens. Beds offer an extra-comfy night's sleep, made even better by a visit to the spa or a day spent lounging under a cabana by the vast swimming pool, sipping drinks from the poolside bar. The hotel offers many of the amenities of a full-scale resort, including a restaurant and wine bar. As you stroll the groomed paths through the endless gardens dotted with native plants, you'll also find the main lobby and the main sitting room, complete with huge stone fireplace and all the help you need from friendly concierges at the desk.

The candy-colored **La Valencia Hotel** (1132 Prospect St., 858/454-0771, www.lavalencia.com, $285-3,500) has it all: ocean views, high-end restaurants, sumptuous rooms, and a great downtown location. Rooms, suites, and villas are decorated tastefully in earth tones with splashes of bright color. Living plants provide both oxygen and a homey sense of elegance both in the rooms and throughout the resort. Downstairs, take advantage of the state-of-the-art workout room, then cool off in the large sparkling blue pool. Walk to the cliffside boardwalk or down to the beach from the La Valencia, and enjoy the shopping and restaurants of Prospect Street.

The Lodge at Torrey Pines (11480 N. Torrey Pines Rd., 858/453-4420, www. lodgetorreypines.com, $350-600) offers luxury, service, amenities, and access to the amazing Torrey Pines Golf Course. You'll be struck by the classic Southern California craftsman architecture—the exterior of the lodge is a work of art in itself. The craftsman elegance continues into the rooms, with designer fabrics, tasteful appointments, gorgeous marble bathrooms, and views of the golf course and ocean. If you plan to play golf, check the golf packages and arrange your tee time through the hotel. Non-golfers have a number of great recreation options too. Book an appointment at the full-service spa, rent one of the charming cabanas down at the beach, or take a guided hike at the state reserve. If traveling with family, there are numerous kids' activities and amenities available at the resort.

NORTH COUNTY

If your one major purpose in coming to the San Diego area is to lounge on a white-sand beach, consider booking a stay north of the city proper. Some of the best beaches cluster in the North County area. Accordingly, you'll find everything from modest motels to fancy resorts available in the area.

Under $150

For a good, modest motel that's clean and reasonably close to the beach and everything else, stay at the **Moonlight Beach Motel** (233 Second St., Encinitas, 800/323-1259, www.moonlightbeachmotel.com, $130-175). Cheerful budget motel rooms greet guests with floral bedspreads and light-painted walls. Most rooms have a kitchenette, complete with refrigerator and microwave, making it easy to store and chill beach drinks

and snacks in your room. Rooms are clean enough to feel comfortable sleeping in, but not so fancy that you'll be horrified if a little bit of sand makes it onto the carpet. The motel sits near both U.S. 101 and I-5, making it a perfect base from which to get anywhere in the San Diego area. The motel is only a few blocks from Moonlight Beach, where you can surf, play a game of volleyball, or just relax into the sand for a day. (On a busy summer weekend day, walk from the motel to the beach to avoid the parking nightmare down closer to the sand.)

$150-250

Built in the charming Spanish colonial revival style, **Les Artistes** (944 Camino Del Mar, Del Mar, 858/755-4646, www.lesartistesinn.com, $200-450) offers something different from the standard chain-motel experience. Each room is named for and decorated in the style of a particular artist or style, from the French countryside of Monet to the peace of Zen. Despite its unique and fun decor, this is a budget motel; the rooms are small and you won't be able to trip over your doorsill and fall into the ocean. But the beach and downtown Del Mar with its restaurants and shops are only a few blocks away. And you can bring your family (several rooms have multiple beds), including your beloved pet, to Les Artistes and receive a warm welcome. Don't bring your cigarettes, however, as Les Artistes is entirely nonsmoking.

If you want a beach house of your own rather than a motel room that's part of a huge block, book a daily or weekly bungalow or suite at the **Wave Crest Resort** (1400 Ocean Ave., Del Mar, 858/755-0100, www.wavecrest-resort.com, $210-495). Here you'll get a studio or a one-bedroom or two-bedroom private unit. These are condo-style accommodations, so you'll get nice furnishings but no daily maid service. Even if you go for a more economical garden-facing unit, you'll enjoy the view of the meticulous landscaping that makes the whole complex lovely. For a modest extra fee, your unit will face the near-enough-to-touch

Pacific Ocean. Take a quick walk to Seagrove Park and down to the beach beyond. Perhaps the only downside, which can also be an upside, is the resort's proximity to the rail line and the highways. They provide both easy transportation and noise.

Over $250

For a classic luxury-resort experience complete with a golf course, multiple swimming pools, ocean views, and almost every service you can dream up, stay at the **Four Seasons Aviara** (7100 Four Seasons Point, Carlsbad, 760/603-6800, www.fourseasons.com, $352-525). You'll find everything in your room exactly as you'd expect from a Four Seasons hotel, from the L'Occitane toiletries to the specially made comfy beds to the tasteful tropical decor. Downstairs, the lobby and common areas shine with marble floors and columns. Indulge at the various independently owned shops, including a wonderful little jewelry store that specializes in unique colored gems, many of which are mined in San Diego County. The concierge and desk staff is as friendly and helpful as possible at all times—get whatever you want whenever you want, pretty much.

On the Four Seasons property you can play 18 holes of golf and a set of tennis, splash with the kids in the family swimming pool, or get serious in the adults-only pool. Round out your day with a treatment from the hotel spa. In the evening, dine at one of the three on-site restaurants. If you've come with your family, get the kids involved in a number of activities tailored for the younger set, and escape and enjoy some of the more adult aspects of the resort.

For another tip-top resort experience, book a room at the newly reopened **L'Auberge Del Mar** (1540 Camino Del Mar, Del Mar, 800/245-9757, www.laubergedelmar.com, $400-4,100). Enjoy the elegant rooms, posh spa, upscale dining, and superior amenities, all with glorious views overlooking the ocean. Enjoy floating around in the leisure pool or getting a workout in the lap pool. For guaranteed access to the tennis courts, book a court and a time in advance.

Food

San Diego doesn't have the celebrated culinary culture of San Francisco or the Wine Country, but you can still get a good meal in this town. Due to San Diego's proximity to the border and the ocean, you'll easily find delicious Mexican food and fresh seafood. In places like the Gaslamp Quarter, Hillcrest, and La Jolla, it's easy to find great food just by wandering down the main drag and reading menus as you go.

DOWNTOWN AND GASLAMP QUARTER

Downtown San Diego offers an astonishing array of dining choices, from comfortable American fare to wonderful French café food and a surprisingly diverse Italian option, and on to upscale California cuisine.

California Cuisine

A local legend, the ★ **Grant Grill** (326 Broadway, 619/744-2077, www.grantgrill.com, Mon.-Fri. 6:30am-11am, 11:30am-2:30pm, and 5:30pm-10pm, Sat.-Sun. 6:30am-2:30pm and 5:30pm-10pm, $28-52) has been serving upscale cuisine since 1951. The wonderful ambience of the posh dining room makes even the most casual of diners feel wealthy and "part of the crowd." The Grant Grill, part of the US Grant hotel, serves breakfast, lunch, and dinner every day, and offers a full-service lounge with live music and a lobby where you can enjoy top-end aperitifs and digestifs. At lunch and dinner, you'll find the fanciest of California-style cuisine on the menu like a beef filet with bone marrow or a dry-aged rib eye. While the Grant Grill is clearly aware

Currant

French

★ **Café Chloe** (721 9th Ave., 619/232-3242, www.cafechloe.com, Mon.-Thurs. 8am-10pm, Fri. 8am-10:30pm, Sat. 8:30am-10:30pm, Sun. 8:30am-9:30pm, $21-32) transports diners and coffee sippers to a Parisian café. While Chloe's intimate café feel and attentive service should be noted, it's the food here that truly stands out. Brunch is served all day, every day and is a tasty way to begin the day while sipping coffee. Later on, the dinner menu changes according to what's freshest in the meat and vegetable departments and could include entrées like duck confit or salmon and morels. While dining, stare at the passersby from one of the café's sidewalk seats or flip through a magazine from the restaurant's magazine rack.

★ **Currant** (140 W. Broadway, 619/702-6309, www.currantrestaurant.com, Mon.-Fri. 7am-10am, 11:30am-2:30pm, and 5pm-10pm, Sat.-Sun. 9am-2:30pm and 5pm-10pm, $15-28) is an eclectic French American eatery on the ground floor of the Sofia Hotel. Within the tile-floored dining room or at the oval bar, start the morning with their house-made beignets with a range of dipping sauces including a lavender-orange-scented honey and chocolate Chambord. Later in the day, the playful "Popcorn of the Moment" appetizer is based on what the chef feels like creating that day. Past versions have included feta with chorizo and bacon with blue cheese. Dinner includes a burger with Irish white cheddar and pistachio-crusted halibut. There's also a good bar here with a daily happy hour (4pm-7pm) and Wine Wednesdays, where bottles of wine are half price.

Italian

Looking for some comfortable, warm Italian food without high prices or pretenses? Go where the locals go: **Filippi's Pizza Grotto** (1747 India St., 619/232-5094, www.realcheesepizza.com, Tues.-Thurs. 11am-10:30pm, Fri.-Sat. 11am-11:30pm, Sun.-Mon. 11am-10pm, $10-15). Walk through the tempting Italian market and into the dimly lit restaurant at the rear of the building. Enjoy the

SAN DIEGO FOOD

of current culinary trends, it also honors its storied past. It still serves the mock turtle soup that was a hit during its early days and a superbly smooth Manhattan made with old-fashioned bitters that are blended and aged in oak for 100 days. To soak up the ambience of the Grant without spending as much money, post up in the **Lounge** (daily 2:30pm-close), where you can gnaw on bar food accompanied by fine cocktails.

With its borderline gaudy decor (including a giant silver candelabra at the bar), you may think that **Allure Restaurant** (825 4th Ave., 619/236-0800 or 619/236-0801, http://allurerestaurantsd.com, Sun.-Thurs. noon-10pm, Fri.-Sat. noon-11pm, $25-38) is a better place for club-hopping than getting a good meal. But executive chef Melissa Magallan will surprise diners right out of the gates with a complimentary off-menu amuse bouche and on through a menu that includes a bone marrow appetizer and short rib entrée. Large parties can dine upstairs at a long table that takes up the better part of its upper-level dining area.

classic atmosphere, complete with red-and-white checkered tablecloths. Order a pizza, some lasagna, or a giant meatball sandwich. Pastas come with classic and uncomplicated marinara and the pizza might be the best in all of San Diego. Best of all, Filippi's serves late into the evening—until almost midnight on weekends. You'll definitely have to jostle with the local crowd for a seat on Friday and Saturday nights. Filippi's has locations in other parts of San Diego County, but the original is this one.

Mexican

Enter the giant wooden doors of **La Puerta** (560 4th Ave., 619/696-3466, www.lapuertasd.com, Mon.-Fri. 11am-2am, Sat.-Sun. 10am-2am, $9-14) for a unique take on Mexican food and cantina cuisine. The dark and cool interior is dimly lit with orange lightbulbs hanging overhead and candles. La Puerta doesn't do typical Mexican fare, as evidenced by a menu that includes carnitas pancakes and the popular surf-and-turf tacos stuffed with steak and shrimp along with grilled vegetables. The terrific guacamole darts ahead of other area versions due to its Serrano peppers and crumbled panela cheese. If you have a thirst for tequila, the bar will slake it with over 100 varieties and their margaritas made with freshly squeezed lime juice.

Steak and Seafood

A couple miles north of San Diego's downtown, the Mission Hills neighborhood has one popular locals' eatery worth seeking out if you want some great seafood. The ★ **Blue Water Seafood Market & Grill** (3667 India St., 619/497-0914, http://bluewaterseafoodsandiego.com, Mon.-Thurs. 11am-9pm, Fri. 11am-10pm, Sat. 11:30am-10pm, Sun. 11:30am-9pm, $4-25) has a simple concept done really well. First, you pick what fresh seafood you want. Then you choose what kind of marinade you'd like it cooked in. Finally, you select it as a sandwich, salad, plate, or taco. Or opt for the cioppino, a lobster taco, or a tuna melt. Expect

La Puerta

to wait in a long line out the door if you come during busy hours.

Looking for a rich slab of beef after a long day playing outside? Head for the **Greystone Steakhouse** (658 5th Ave., 619/232-0225, www.greystonesteakhouse.com, Sun.-Thurs. 4pm-11pm, Fri.-Sat. 4pm-midnight, $28-52) in the heart of the Gaslamp Quarter. This upscale eatery makes a great start to a night out on the town with your sweetie. The white tablecloths light up the dim interior, where the dining area surrounds a staircase leading down into the belly of the restaurant. Or if you prefer, get a table on the small patio out front to people-watch as the Gaslamp heats up with the evening crowd. The menu includes all your favorite steak-house standards—great cuts of beef, lobster and tuna, and an array of yummy sides. You'll also find some interesting California-style entrées and appetizers. Portions are big, so consider splitting an entrée with your dinner partner so you can both enjoy an appetizer and some dessert. The wine list focuses on California wines and includes a good selection of local vintages, and the full bar offers predinner cosmos and martinis. The service can be a bit slow during the dinner hours, but it's friendly and helpful.

BALBOA PARK, HILLCREST, AND NORTH PARK

The fun and funky Hillcrest neighborhood offers an array of dining options, from ethnic to upscale to down-home. To pick your own favorite, wander up and down India Street and read the menus in the windows. Most every restaurant on India wins local approval. Adjacent to Hillcrest, North Park is a neighborhood stuffed with breweries and trendy eateries.

American

If you're looking for a hearty breakfast or a unique American dinner, the local Hillcrest favorite hangout is **Hash House A Go Go** (3628 5th Ave., 619/298-4646, www.hashhouseagogo.com, Mon. 7:30am-2:30pm, Tues.-Thurs. 7:30am-2pm and 5:30pm-9pm, Fri. 7:30am-2pm and 5:30pm-9:30pm, Sat. 7:30am-2:30pm and 5:30pm-9:30pm, Sun. 7:30am-2:30pm and 5:30pm-9pm, breakfast and lunch $8-17, dinner $15-39). The Hash House puts its own spin on casual American food, including an array of fresh local ingredients that take the oversized dishes up a notch. You'll dine in a modern atmosphere with industrial-urban decor, complete with brushed-metal tabletops. For breakfast, the obvious choice is of course hash, which is served in a skillet, though you've got dozens of other options including French toast that's as thick as a phone book. Lunch and dinner feature especially wonderful salads, plus plenty of great entrées from duck mac and cheese to burgers stuffed with mashed potatoes, bacon, and cheddar cheese. You won't go hungry here.

If you want a quiet dinner, try the **Crest Café** (425 Robinson Ave., 619/295-2510, www.crestcafe.net, daily 7am-midnight, $8-16). This colorful, cheerful diner welcomes a more sedate crowd with a bright dining room and three wonderful meals per day. In among the traditional diner fare, you'll find a few upscale dishes, such as lemon-ricotta pancakes and orange marmalade-stuffed French toast. You'll also see a wide array of Mexican-inspired entrées, alongside diner dishes that have been reworked with an eye towards modern health-consciousness. Dinner includes comfort-food favorites like turkey meatloaf and chicken potpie. Open till midnight, the Crest is the perfect place to stop and grab a late-night snack after (or during) a night out in Hillcrest.

If you're in Balboa Park, chances are you're visiting the museums or the zoo. At the zoo, grab a bite at **Albert's Restaurant** (Gorilla Tropics at the San Diego Zoo, 619/685-3200, www.sandiegozoo.org, Mon.-Sat. 11am-8:30pm, Sun. 10am-8:30pm, $11-29). This sit-down eatery serves lunch year-round and dinner during the summer nights when the zoo stays open late. Sit indoors to escape the heat, or out on the patio to enjoy the view of the gardens surrounding the animal enclosures. Relax with a drink at the bar, order a simple salad or sandwich, or enjoy a hearty steak dinner.

A modest palace dedicated to all things pork, ★ **Carnitas' Snack Shack** (2632 University Ave., 619/294-7675, http://carnitassnackshack.com, daily noon-midnight, $8-10) can be found by looking for the pig atop its roof or the line spilling down the sidewalk in front of this small eatery. The menu changes daily and is written up on a chalkboard, but needless to say the fare is pig-heavy. The Triple Threat Pork Sandwich includes pork schnitzel, pulled pork, and bacon, while the juicy carnitas tacos are about the best you'll find anywhere. There is a small shaded place to eat on the side of the building, but if there's a long line, it might be better to get your food to go. And don't forget to double up on your cholesterol medication.

Coffee and Tea

Round out your Balboa Park experience with a cup of tea and a meal at the **Tea Pavilion**

(2215 Pan American Plaza, 619/231-0048, www.balboapark.org, Mon. 10:30am-8pm, Tues. 10:30am-7pm, Wed.-Sun. 10:30am-5pm, $6-8). As advertised, the specialty of the house is tea. You'll find a great cuppa, whether you favor herbal, green, or black teas. You can also get a bowl of noodles, some sushi, or a quick snack. To take some of the Japanese experience home with you, wander into the market section to peruse the unusual imported food and drink.

If all that tromping around the park has tired you out, perk up with a drink from **Daniel's Coffee Cart** (1549 El Prado, www. balboapark.org, Tues.-Sun. 8am-5:30pm). You'll find all your favorite espresso drinks, along with plain ol' coffee, tea, and pastries.

A favorite Hillcrest coffee shop is **Gelato Vero Caffe** (3753 India St., 619/295-9269, Mon.-Thurs. 6am-midnight, Fri. 6am-1am, Sat. 7am-1am, Sun. 7am-midnight, $10), which serves the workday-morning caffeine-jonesing crowd *and* the late-night dessert and coffee hounds. The gelato is all made in-house, and the owners and fans assert that you won't find any better this side of Italy. The small café has little seating in the main room; if you want to sit down and enjoy your coffee or gelato and there doesn't seem to be room,

hit the stairway off to the side of the café to find the upper deck and inside cottage seating.

Gastropub

It seems like every block of North Park has its own brewery, and **Waypoint Public** (3794 30th St., 619/255-8778, Mon.-Tues. 4pm-10pm, Wed.-Thurs. 11am-10pm, Fri. 11am-1am, Sat. 10am-1am, Sun. 10am-10pm, $12-19) capitalizes on this phenomenon with a menu that zooms in on food paired with craft beer. Brisket, grilled cheese, and mussels with pork belly are ideal counterparts to IPAs and lagers. The brews include 30 on tap and over 100 in bottled form. They even have a breakfast beer menu. Hipster crowds enjoy the fare in a space with reclaimed wood and decorated with old kitchenware.

Mexican

Tacos go well with beer, so stop by **Tacos Perla** (3000 Upas St., Ste. 105, 619/795-0700, Sun.-Thurs. 11:30am-10pm, Fri.-Sat. 11:30am-midnight, $4-5), conveniently close to the Modern Times Brewery's Flavordome. Within the small interior, traditional tacos (carne asada, adobada) and less traditional offerings (grilled octopus, smoked albacore) are served on freshly made corn tortillas. Spice them up

Carnitas' Snack Shack

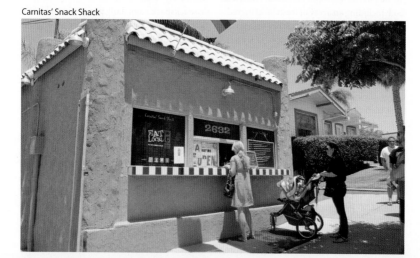

with the six salsas that you serve yourself from mason jars in a wooden box. The adventurous can opt for grilled crickets atop their taco.

OLD TOWN

Old Town is more about the history, shopping, and sights than it is about dining. Most locals head downtown for a meal. But if you really want to eat here, Mexican food is your best bet.

In Old Town's little corner of Mexico, Bazaar del Mundo, you'll find some great south-of-the-border eats in a variety of styles and price ranges. Join the party at **Casa Guadalajara** (4105 Taylor St., 619/295-5111, www.casaguadalajara.com, Mon.-Thurs. 11am-10pm, Fri. 11am-11pm, Sat. 8am-11pm, Sun. 8am-10pm, happy hour Mon.-Fri. 4pm-7pm, $10-33). From the moment you see the low, whitewashed, adobe-style building with the red-tiled roof, you'll start to feel the Mexican atmosphere. Inside, enjoy the music of strolling mariachis as you sip a margarita and dine on excellent regional Mexican cuisine. The seafood-heavy menu features Mexican classics as well as the chef's unique creations. Check out the daily specials.

POINT LOMA

Out on Point Loma, the food is all about the fish—not a surprise, considering that this spit of land juts out into the water, surrounded on three sides by bay and ocean. Whatever style you like your fish cooked (or uncooked) in, Point Loma can serve it to you.

Japanese

In the world of high-end seafood, the Japanese are famed for creating some of the best dishes on Earth. For some amazing sushi, go to **Umi Sushi** (2806 Shelter Island Dr., 619/226-1135, www.umisushisandiego.com, Mon.-Sat. 11:30am-2pm and 5pm-9pm, Sun. 5pm-9pm, $4-16). If you love your rolls, choose from among the three dozen on the menu, plus plenty of nigiri, sashimi, specialty platters, and "sushi boats." For folks who love Japanese food but quail at the thought of raw fish, Umi

offers hot entrées, noodle dishes, salads, and more. Sit up at the sushi bar to see your food put together, or pick a table in the classically Japanese-styled dining room.

Mediterranean

Weary of fish and looking for a respite from the endless seafood of Point Loma? Grab a bite of something completely different at the **Fairouz Cafe and Gallery** (3166 Midway Dr., 619/225-0308, www.fairouzcafegallery-sandiego.com, Sun.-Thurs. 11am-9pm, Fri.-Sat. 11am-10pm, $15-20). The bright, cheerful dining room features the original artwork of Al Nashashibi, a painter with roots in Jerusalem. (Yes, you can purchase works you see while dining; inquire with your server.) As for the food, you'll find meat and vegetarian entrées in the Middle Eastern tradition, with lots of lamb and chicken, plus several Greek specialties, such as stuffed grape leaves. At lunchtime, look to the appetizers and salads for lighter fare.

Steak and Seafood

For the best of the land out by the sea, visit ★ **Island Prime** (880 Harbor Island Dr., 619/298-6802, www.cohnrestaurants.com, Sun.-Thurs. 5pm-10pm, Fri.-Sat. 5pm-11pm, $27-54). This huge house of steak and fish seats more than 600 on a busy evening. Ask in advance for a window seat or a table out on the deck overlooking the harbor and the San Diego skyline. On the deck, you might find yourself by one of the fires, feeling as though you were dining at your own private beach house (well, except for the crowd, of course). The simple decor makes use of the wooden architectural features of the building. If you're boating on the San Diego waters, dock-and-dine at the neighboring Sunroad Marina. The menu boasts shellfish, finned fish, and plenty of hearty meats in a classic steak house-meets-California style. Start (or finish) your meal with a martini or another fabulous cocktail.

For a lighter meal, head for the **C Level Cocktail Lounge** (Sun.-Thurs. 11am-10pm, Fri.-Sat. 11am-11pm, $10-38). In addition to

Dinner Cruises

An unforgettable way to dine in this coastal community is to take a dinner cruise in the calm waters of San Diego Bay. While you shouldn't expect the food on these cruises to be the best for the price, the atmosphere and scenery make up for any culinary deficiencies. Be forewarned that the drinks tend to be a bit weak as well; if you love a strong cocktail, plan to hit one of the many downtown bars before or after your cruise.

The juggernaut of the dinner- and event-cruise industry in California, **Hornblower** (1066 N. Harbor Dr., 619/686-8700, www.hornblower.com, daily boarding 6:30pm, dinner $79, brunch $63) offers a popular three-hour dinner cruise every night. Pick up a glass of complimentary champagne as you walk down the gangplank and onto the yacht. Enjoy your three-course dinner (or more, if you pay extra) as the sun drops below the horizon. Take a constitutional on the deck and then return for dessert, or make for the entertainment deck and dance the evening away as the yacht slowly makes its way around the bay. If you prefer a daytime cruise, book passage for a Sunday champagne brunch.

Flagship Cruises & Events (1050 N. Harbor Dr., 800/442-7847, www.flagshipsd.com, dinner adults $70-105, children $41-51, brunch adults $65, children $38) also offers nightly dinner cruises and Sunday champagne brunches out on the bay. Flagship Cruises & Events offers a fun cruise and a tasty meal. Reserve your place at the table a few days in advance for Friday and Saturday nights and for Sunday brunches in summertime.

the high-octane libations, the lounge serves a light dinner menu—that really isn't all that light. Whichever venue you choose, you'll find a pleasant trend towards local and organic ingredients in Prime's dishes.

One of the best things about dining in San Diego is the opportunity to enjoy a fabulous meal while looking out over the harbor or the ocean. That's just what you'll get at **Humphreys Restaurant** (2241 Shelter Island Blvd., 619/224-3577, www.humphreys-bythebay.com, Mon.-Thurs. 6:30am-9pm, Fri. 6:30am-10pm, Sat. 7am-10pm, Sun. 7am-9pm, $14-29). The white tablecloths on the candlelit tables look right out over the Humphreys Marina and off toward the San Diego skyline. This hotel-based restaurant serves three meals a day, plus brunch on Sundays. On the dinner menu, seafood reigns, though various land-based entrées get their due as well. Or combine the two for an extravagant meal that makes for the best of everything. At lunchtime, upscale sandwiches and salads make the most of lighter midday standards. Whichever you choose, lunch or dinner, don't miss the awesome seafood soups. The breakfast menu includes all the standard egg-based

standards, fresh fruits, and pastries, plus a few scrumptious surprises. Sunday brunches are buffet-style, with plenty of made- and carved-to-order specialties.

If what you really want is the freshest slab of fish to be found on Point Loma, eat at the aptly named **Point Loma Seafoods** (2805 Emerson St., 619/223-1109, www.pointlomaseafoods.com, Mon.-Sat. 9am-8pm, Sun. 10am-8pm, $5-14). Much of the fish sold here, either as a hot meal to eat right here or chilled in paper and ready to cook, comes straight off the fishing boats in the harbor. Shellfish, including local spiny lobster, is fresh, top quality, and sold only in season—making Point Loma Seafood the perfect place for a seafood lunch. Hot food and sandwiches come with slaw and fries. The cold foods include seafood salads plus a small array of sushi and sashimi. The atmosphere is the antithesis of upscale, which make it perfect for many visitors looking for reasonable prices and truly great fish.

CORONADO

To find your own food in Coronado, stroll down Orange Avenue. While you'll definitely encounter your fellow tourists here, you'll also find a large number of restaurants in a bunch of different styles and ethnicities that are worth trying out.

American

If you're a night owl looking for nourishment after hours, you'll find it at the **Night & Day Café** (847 Orange Ave., 619/435-9976, www.thenightanddaycafe.net, Mon. 6am-10pm, Tues. 6am-midnight, Wed. and Sun. 6am-1am, Thurs. 6am-2am, Fri.-Sat. 24 hours, $7-15). This small, hole-in-the-wall diner will make you feel right at home. You'll find a wide range of pancakes, omelets, burgers, and lots of Mexican food from huevos rancheros to churros. Tacos are just $2 from 2pm to 10pm every day.

French

With the opulence of the Del overseeing the town, a night out for French cuisine seems appropriate here. You'll do well at **Chez Loma French Bistro** (1132 Loma Ave., 619/435-0661, www.chezloma.com, Mon.-Wed. 5pm-8:30pm, Thurs.-Fri. 5pm-9pm, Sat. 9:30am-2pm and 5pm-9pm, Sun. 9:30am-2pm and 5pm-8:30pm, $26-37). Walk to this charming restaurant that's in the historic Carez Hizar House, a white-frame building that houses warm, red dining rooms. The cuisine tends toward the classic French brasserie style, with the occasional hint of California color in some of the dishes. The wine list is worth a visit all on its own; it's not immense, but it shows off the best of California and France, including a large selection of flights (samples of three different wines all in one type). The food and the ambience have caught the attention of local foodies, and Chez Loma has been highly praised and presented with a number of regional restaurant awards.

Thai

If your preference is hot and casual, eat at **Swaddee Thai Restaurant** (1001 C St., 619/435-8110, Mon.-Sat. 11am-3pm and 5pm-10pm, Sun. 5pm-10pm, $13-25). Off the main tourist drag, Swadee's tasty Thai cuisine

appeals to locals, and is something of a hidden gem. They have typical Thai fare like Pad Thai as well as tasty green and red curry dishes.

MISSION BAY

Locals and visitors alike flock to Mission Bay for a day's entertainment. As the sun sets, the need for food kicks in. Along Mission Bay, you'll find an array of ethnic eats to please any palate.

Burgers

Regularly proclaimed one of the best burger joints in the country, **Hodad's** (5010 Newport Ave., Ocean Beach, 619/224-4623, www.hodadies.com, daily 11am-10pm, $5-10) has been serving burgers in San Diego's Ocean Beach neighborhood since 1969. Today a line still snakes out the door at mealtimes as people attempt to get inside the license plate-decorated shack to munch down delicious burgers, including the worth-the-wait single bacon cheeseburger with its perfectly crispy bacon. You can also find their burgers at Petco Park during Padres games and at their downtown location (945 Broadway, 619/234-6323, Sun.-Thurs. 11am-9pm, Fri.-Sat. 11am-10pm).

Seafood

At the boastfully named **World Famous** (711 Pacific Beach Dr., 858/272-3100, daily 7am-midnight, $10-55) in Pacific Beach you can enjoy breakfast, lunch, or dinner with a view. Fish, purchased fresh daily, is the specialty of the house here, and preparations range from classic American to a variety of ethnic stylings that might be called "fusion" if this were San Francisco. Grab a drink at the bar and take a seat either indoors in the Vegas-inspired dining room or outdoors on the seaside patio. The wine list features some of the best-known California vintners.

LA JOLLA

For a good selection of food in La Jolla, stroll or drive down Prospect Street. You'll find an array of high-class California cuisine, plus coffee shops and more casual dining options.

California Cuisine

★ **George's at the Cove** (1250 Prospect St., 858/454-4244, www.georgesatthecove. com, daily 11am-3:45pm and 5pm-9:45pm) is a La Jolla institution. The complex actually includes three separate restaurants. The favorite, **Ocean Terrace** (daily lunch and dinner, $16-39) offers casual outdoor seating on the roof of the building year-round, with unpretentious and delicious cuisine. Enjoy seafood as you look out over La Jolla Cove, or choose a simple salad or sandwich for a lighter meal. Downstairs, you'll find the ultra-urban **California Modern** (daily dinner, $28-36). The industrial design of the dining room precedes the chic, if sometimes a bit overwrought, dishes you'll find on the menu here. Windows offer views of the Cove, while cushioned seats make diners along the wall comfortable as they settle in for a multicourse dinner. Diners can opt for the four-course tasting menu ($75) as well. Finally, if you're really looking for a cocktail out on the balcony, **George's Bar** (daily lunch and dinner, $16-39) has just what you're seeking. Order from the Ocean Terrace menu, or just sip your drinks as you enjoy the warm evening air.

Sandwiches

Not everywhere to eat in La Jolla is fancy. **The Sandwich Club** (7825 Fay St., Ste. C, 858/456-7548, Mon.-Fri. 7am-2:45, Sat. 10:30am-2pm, $5-9) is a throwback breakfast and lunch joint in the Merrill Lynch Building. The sandwiches are named after old-school icons Joe Namath, Charlie Chaplin, and Cassius Clay (the birth name of Muhammad Ali), while the Shamoo is a tuna salad sandwich. Caricatures decorate the walls of this unassuming shop that frequently wins readers polls for its fare.

Seafood

Looking for good seafood and a fabulous view to go with it? Have a meal at **Brockton Villa** (1235 Coast Blvd., 858/454-7393, www.brocktonvilla.com, daily 8am-9pm, $14-32), which is open for breakfast, lunch, and dinner. Here you can enjoy classic American dishes with a California twist, plus plenty of fish, of course. The casual atmosphere of this beach bungalow blends perfectly with the sugar-sand beaches of the San Diego area. Wooden tables, funky mismatched chairs, and the bright white paint inside evoke a sense of the casual resort atmosphere of historic La Jolla. For fun, read the menu for information on the quirky history of the bungalow, which dates from the late 1800s.

NORTH COUNTY

Each town ranging up the Pacific Coast Highway to Del Mar and Carlsbad has a main drag filled with restaurants. You'll find ethnic enclaves, homey diners, and more.

California Cuisine

Looking for elegant yet casual beach-town dining? Try the famed **Arterra** (11966 El Camino Real, Del Mar, 858/369-6032, www. arterrarestaurant.com, Mon.-Fri. 6:30am-10:30am, 11:30am-2pm, and 5:30pm-10pm, Sat. 7am-11am and 5:30pm-10pm, Sun. 7am-11am, $17-28). Improbably located inside the San Diego Marriott Del Mar, Arterra offers anything but standard chain hotel fare. Start with a drink and perhaps a seafood appetizer in the modern, comfortable outdoor lounge. Once you're seated for dinner inside the plush, red-splashed dining room, you'll find great service and top cuisine created from the freshest local and organic ingredients around. The tasting menus (with or without wine pairing) are a popular option, letting you sample the greatest variety of dishes. Get adventurous and try something new, since there's plenty of cutting-edge cuisine on the menu. And don't forget the wine; the list includes many boutique California charmers that pair wonderfully with the cuisine. If your preference is for uncooked fish, go for something from the surprisingly good sushi bar.

Italian

On the almost Mediterranean-feeling north coast of San Diego County, sunny Italian food

Juanita's Taco Shop in Encinitas

Resort Dr., Carlsbad, 760/603-3773, www.vi-vace-restaurant.com, Mon.-Sat. 6pm-9:30pm, $46-76). A perfect restaurant for a romantic night out, Vivace offers contemporary Italian cuisine in several courses. Attentive, knowledgeable servers can help you with both the menu and the wine list, which provides great menu-matching selections from California, Italy, and other wine regions of Europe. As you sip your wine, admire the elegant tropical-themed decor throughout the several interconnected dining spaces. (Look down; the floor is gorgeous!) Plan at least an hour and a half so that you can enjoy the whole dining experience, right through dessert and coffee.

Mexican

A favorite of local surfers after a day in the waves, ★ **Juanita's Taco Shop** (290 N. Coast Hwy., Encinitas, 760/943-9612, Sun.-Thurs 7am-midnight, Fri.-Sat. 7am-3am, $5) doesn't look like much from the outside. Under metal bars, the windows of this small taqueria are plastered with surf stickers, while inside, an ocean mural covers the walls and ceiling of the small dining area. But here it's the tasty Mexican food that counts. You can't go wrong with the juicy carnitas burrito. It might be the best meal that you've had for under $5 on your whole trip.

Sandwiches

Started by a German immigrant in 1967, **Tip Top Meats** (6118 Paseo Del Norte, Carlsbad, 760/438-2620, www.tiptopmeats.com, daily 6am-8pm, $5-15) is a butcher shop, specialty market, deli, and restaurant. Tip Top makes its own sausages and does hefty dinners including stuffed pork chops and veal cordon bleu. Despite this, it might be best known for the Big John Breakfast, consisting of three eggs, home fries, and all of the breakfast meats you can eat.

somehow seems appropriate. Some of the best is served just off the beach in Encinitas at **Via Italia Trattoria** (569 S. Pacific Coast Hwy., Encinitas, 760/479-9757, www.viaitaliapizzeria.com, daily noon-10pm, $12-30). This Italian-owned and -operated casual restaurant feels like a real trattoria on the coast of Italy. Get a budget-friendly yet fabulously delicious thin-crust pizza, a dish of steaming pasta with your choice of traditional sauce, or an upscale seafood entrée. The food is fresh, cooked just right, and delectable. Whatever you order from the large menu, you'll enjoy eating it in the casual dining room. Or if you just want a quick drink and an appetizer, take a seat at the bar.

For haute cuisine with an Italian flair, make the drive out to the Four Seasons Aviara and have dinner at **Vivace** (7100 Aviara

Information and Services

INFORMATION
Tourist Information

For information on Old Town, head for the **Old Town San Diego Chamber of Commerce & Visitor Center** (2415 San Diego Ave., No. 104, 619/291-4903, www.oldsandiego.org, daily 11am-6pm). In La Jolla, make use of the **La Jolla Visitor Center** (1162 Prospect St., 858/454-5718, www.lajollabythesea.com, summer daily 10am-6pm, winter daily 10am-5pm). To get a feel for the town before you arrive, check out the SDCVB website at www.sandiego.org. Friendly folks can answer emails and phone calls about most anything pertaining to San Diego County.

Medical Services

With UC San Diego in town, the number of major medical centers in and around San Diego is higher than the average. If you must get sick on vacation, San Diego isn't the worst place to do it. In town, the **UCSD Medical Center-Hillcrest** (200 West Arbor Dr., 619/543-6222, http://health.ucsd.edu)

offers emergency and clinic services, as does **Scripps Mercy Hospital** (4077 5th Ave., 619/294-8111, www.scripps.org). The **Kaiser Permanente Medical Center** (4647 Zion Ave., 619/528-5000) includes a full-service, 24-hour emergency room. La Jolla also has a heavy load of hospitals, with **Scripps Green Hospital** (10666 N. Torrey Pines Rd., 858/554-9100, www.scripps.org) and **Scripps Memorial Hospital** (9888 Genesee Ave., 858/626-4123, www.scripps.org).

In the North County area, the only trauma center is within the **Palomar Medical Center** (2185 Citracado Pkwy., 442/281-5000, www.palomarhealth.org) in Escondido. Get regular hospital services at the **Scripps Memorial Hospital** (354 Santa Fe Dr., 760/633-6501, www.scripps.org) in Encinitas.

Most of the beaches in San Diego County maintain a lifeguard presence in the summertime, and many have lifeguards patrolling in the winter as well. Look for the light blue towers on the beach to find the nearest available lifeguards, or for permanent buildings bearing a large red cross.

Transportation

If you're coming to San Diego from Los Angeles, you'll be relieved by the easing of traffic. If you're coming from anyplace else, you may be horrified by the packed highways. In the grand scheme of California transit, San Diego isn't the worst place to try to get around. The highway network makes some sense, there's almost adequate in-town public transit, and the rail and air travel centers bustle with activity.

If you prefer human-powered transportation, San Diego's fabulous weather, generally safe streets, and miles of mostly along-the-coast paths make bicycling and walking

eminently possible as your major mode of transportation.

GETTING THERE
Air

The major-league **San Diego International Airport** (3665 N. Harbor Dr., 619/400-2404, www.san.org), aka Lindbergh Field, is stuffed right along San Diego Bay, convenient to downtown, Coronado, and almost every major San Diego attraction. Short-term parking sits adjacent to the terminals and costs $1 per hour on average. Long-term lots surround the airport; check the airport website for specifics. A 60-minute maximum, free "cell phone lot" lets drivers wait for incoming passengers without having to drive endlessly around the airport.

If you're flying a light plane in, the most convenient general-aviation airports to downtown San Diego are Brown Field (8,000-foot runway) and Montgomery Field (4,600-foot runway). Eight additional general-aviation airports are scattered throughout the county. For information, check www.miramarairshow.com.

Train

To get to San Diego by train from the north or the east, find your way aboard the **Amtrak Pacific Surfliner** (www.amtrak.com), a train that runs a dozen times a day from Paso Robles along the Pacific Coast down to San Diego. Boarding is easy from most major California destinations in the area, including San Luis Obispo, Santa Barbara, Los Angeles, and Anaheim. Check into transfers from the *Coast Starlight* and the *Capitol Corridor* routes as well. Amtrak services the **Santa Fe station** (1050 Kettner Blvd.) and the **Old Town Transit Center** (4005 Taylor St.).

For a reliable local commuter train, jump on board **The Coaster** (760/966-6500, www.gonctd.com/coaster, Mon.-Sat., adults $4-5.50 one-way, senior and people with disabilities $2-2.75 one-way, children under 6 free). The Coaster runs from Oceanside into downtown San Diego and back a dozen times a day Monday-Friday, with six trains running Saturdays, plus special-event and holiday service. Purchase tickets from the vending machines in every train station. In the North County, NCTD Coaster Connecter bus routes can connect to the train station. In San Diego proper, catch the trolley or the bus from either the Old Town Transit Center or the Santa Fe station.

Car

Most visitors drive into San Diego via the heavily traveled I-5 from the north or south. I-805 runs parallel to I-5 at La Jolla and leads south into Mission Valley. To drive between the North County and San Diego, take I-15, which runs north-south farther inland. Avoid rush hour, as the backup on I-15 can become extensive after Poway. Both I-805 and I-15 cross I-8, which runs east-west through Mission Valley. The smaller yet surprisingly pretty Route 163 runs north-south from I-5 in Balboa Park north to I-15 in Miramar.

GETTING AROUND
Car

This is Southern California. Most people drive here whether they need to or not. Happily, this is *not* the Los Angeles Basin, so traffic sometimes relaxes into a bearable state.

Parking is the hardest at the beaches in the summertime. Everyone else in the state seems to be trying to find a parking spot close to the sand between June and September. If you possibly can, find another way to get from your accommodations to the beach, be it bicycle, public transit, or your own two feet. If you must drive, check out the parking situation ahead of time (most beaches' websites offer parking information) and plan ahead. Bring cash for pay parking, come early in the morning, and be prepared to walk up to a mile from your parking spot down to the beach itself.

In the various downtown areas, you'll find fairly average city parking issues. Happily, San Diego's major attractions and event venues tend to be accompanied by large parking structures. Just be prepared to pay a premium if you're doing something popular.

Bus and Trolley

In downtown San Diego, Coronado, and La Jolla, the **MTS** (www.sdmts.com, bus ticket $1-5, trolley ticket $1.25-6) operates both an extensive bus system and trolley routes. The North County is served by the North County Transit District, or NCTD. If you plan to make serious use of the trolleys and buses, use the vending machines at trolley stations to get a day pass—a regular day pass is a bargain at $5, and two-, three-, and four-day passes can save you even more money. Day passes work on NCTD Breeze buses as well as most MTS routes.

See the website for more information about schedules, routes, and fares for both the MTS and NCTD services. If you plan to pay your fare for buses or trolleys on board, have exact change available. The vending machines are more forgiving, as many take $1 and $5 bills and make change.

If you don't have a car with you, or just want to avoid driving for a while, hop onto the **Old Town Trolley** (866/754-0966, www.trolleytours.com, adults $35-39, children $17-19) for a great look at the highlights of San Diego without the headaches of parking and traffic.

The trolley can take you in a loop through downtown (including the Gaslamp Quarter), Old Town, out over the bridge to the Del on Coronado, and around the harbor. Get on and off the trolley at any time to visit a museum, go shopping, or grab a bite to eat. Another trolley will appear to take you on your way. As long as you stay on board, the driver will narrate, pointing out the sights as you pass them, and make stops at the biggest and most important. While the Old Town Trolley is way too expensive to use in place of public transportation, it's a great way to get out and see the highlights of the city in a day. Check the website for discounted online tickets.

Background

The Landscape

GEOGRAPHY

California's geographic profile is as diverse as its population. At nearly 159,000 square miles, California is the third-largest state in the United States, stretching 770 miles from the Oregon state line to the Mexican border. California includes the **Sierra Nevada** mountain range, numerous national parks and monuments, coast and giant redwoods, volcanoes, and the tallest mountain in the continental United States, **Mount Whitney,** at 14,505 feet. In addition, two major tectonic plates—the north-moving Pacific and south-moving North American Plate—give California a reputation for shaking things up a bit.

Mountain Ranges

The California coast is characterized by craggy cliffs, rocky beaches, and enormous coast redwoods *(Sequoia sempervirens)* that reach heights up to 380 feet. The coast is bounded by the aptly named Coast Range, ruggedly steep mountains formed 30 million years ago when part of the Pacific Plate jammed, folded, and compressed to form the Coast Range and Transverse Range. In addition to the Coast Range, there are two other significant high-elevation regions in the state. In the north, the Cascade Mountains evolved through volcanic activity 10 million years ago when the Juan de Fuca Plate, earth's smallest tectonic plate and caught between the North American and Pacific Plates, collided with the North American Plate and was forced under the larger plate. Magma from the melting plate raised a series of mountains, including California's two active volcanoes—Mount Lassen and Mount Shasta. Mount Lassen (10,462 feet) last blew its top

in 1915; today, the surrounding park offers a glimpse into the earth's formation. Majestic Mount Shasta, along I-5 north of Redding, has not erupted in quite some time. At 14,179 feet, Mount Shasta's extreme height creates its own weather system.

To the east is the Sierra Nevada, stretching 400 miles north-south and forming the eastern spine of the state. Its peaks and valleys include Mount Whitney, Lake Tahoe, Yosemite, and the giant sequoias *(Sequoiadendron giganteum)* in Sequoia and Kings Canyon National Parks. The Sierra Nevada formed 60 million years ago when magma seeped up between the Pacific and North American Plates. It created a massive pool of granite that slowly cooled to form a batholith, a massive dome-shaped formation of intrusive igneous rock. For the past 12 million years the formation has been pushing upward.

Earthquakes and Faults

Earthquakes occur when the tectonic plates that compose the earth's crust shift along faults, the boundaries between the plates—and California's seat on the Pacific Ring of Fire is well established. The North American Plate and Pacific Plate came together about 150 million years ago, causing the compression and folding of the earth's crust that ultimately created the Sierra Nevada; meanwhile, the area west of the Sierra eroded and filled with sediment, forming the Central Valley. About 30 million years ago a ridge of the Pacific Plate became jammed and caused the folding and compression that formed the Coast and Transverse Ranges. More importantly, the contact caused the Pacific Plate to change direction and move northward, forming the San Andreas Fault. This infamous strike-slip fault, where two tectonic plates move horizontally—the North American Plate moving mostly southward and the Pacific Plate moving mostly northward—runs from along the North Coast, down near San Francisco, and then east of Los Angeles before branching off into Mexico and the Pacific Ocean.

The plates frequently catch as they move past each other, storing energy and causing tension to build. When the plates jolt past one another, they release this energy in the form of an earthquake. Earthquakes along numerous faults happen daily, a total of 10,000-37,000 times each year. Most register less than magnitude 3 and go unnoticed by Californians used to the shake, rattle, and roll. However, there have been several significant earthquakes in California history. The **1906 San Francisco earthquake** had a magnitude of 7.7-8.3 and involved the "rupturing" of the northern 300 miles of the San Andreas Fault from San Juan Bautista to Cape Mendocino. The **1989 Loma Prieta earthquake,** with an epicenter near Loma Prieta Peak in the Santa Cruz Mountains, was small by comparison at magnitude 6.9 and with only 25 miles of ruptured fault. California's stringent building codes, developed in the wake of deadly and destructive earthquakes, include an extensive seismic retrofit program that has brought older buildings, overpasses, bridges, and other structures up to stringent standards.

CLIMATE

Vast in size and varied in geography, California also has a vastly varied climate, from boiling heat in the Central Valley to subarctic temperatures at mountain summits.

Along the North Coast, the weather stays fairly constant: chilly, windy, and foggy. Summer days rarely reach 80°F, and winter rainstorms can pound the area. San Francisco shares its cool and foggy climate with temperatures in the 50s and 60s well into summer. South on the peninsula or across the Bay in Marin County and the East Bay,

the temperature may rise 20-30°F, and the fog often makes way for sun. North of San Francisco, the Wine Country is graced with milder weather and warm summers, perfect for growing grapes.

The Central Coast is a bit warmer than the San Francisco Bay Area, but still, expect cool temperatures and fog in summer. A chilly wind accompanies the rain in the winter, often closing mountain roads and highways, including Highway 1.

From the Los Angeles Basin down to San Diego and up the coast to Santa Barbara, temperatures are mild all year long. Expect fog on the beaches during the summer, cool days in the wintertime, and hotter temperatures in the inland valleys and at Disneyland. For the best summertime beach weather in the state, head for San Diego.

ENVIRONMENTAL ISSUES

Californians face several major environmental issues. The state battles drought, and water for crops, farms, and human consumption is always in short supply. Conservation measures can include limiting development and urban sprawl, restricting water usage, and designating set periods for personal and recreational use, such as watering lawns.

Water pollution is also an issue. Most tap water is safe to drink, but swimming in California's plentiful bays, lakes, and rivers as well as the Pacific Ocean requires more caution. Pollution may cause *E. coli* outbreaks at beaches, affecting wildlife and beachgoers alike. Fishing is no longer permitted in San Francisco Bay due to high mercury levels in the Bay's fish.

Many of the state's grand oak trees have succumbed to sudden oak death, a disease that spreads through spores to eventually kill live oaks, black oaks, and tan oaks. To control its spread, travelers are advised to clean all camping equipment thoroughly and to buy and burn local firewood rather than importing it from elsewhere.

Plants and Animals

PLANTS
Redwoods

A visit to California's famous redwoods should be on every traveler's list. The **coast redwood** *(Sequoia sempervirens)* grows along the North Coast as far south as Big Sur. Coast redwoods are characterized by their towering height, flaky red bark, and moist understory. Among the tallest trees on earth, they are also some of the oldest, with some individuals almost 2,000 years old. Coast redwoods occupy a narrow strip of coastal California, growing less than 50 miles inland to collect moisture from the ocean and fog. Their tannin-rich bark is crucial to their ability to survive wildfires and regenerate afterward. The best places to marvel at the giants are within the Redwood National and State Parks, Muir Woods, and Big Basin State Park.

The **giant sequoia** *(Sequoiadendron giganteum)* grows farther inland in a 260-mile belt at 3,000-8,900 feet elevation in the Sierra Nevada mountain range. Giant sequoias are the largest trees by volume on earth; they can grow to heights of 280 feet with a diameter up to 26 feet and can live for thousands of years. Giant sequoias share the ruddy bark of the coast sequoia as well as its fire-resistant qualities. The best places to see giant sequoias up close are at Sequoia and Kings Canyon National Parks, Calaveras Big Trees, and the Mariposa Grove at Yosemite National Park.

Oaks

California is home to many native oaks. The most common are the **valley oak, black oak, live oak,** and **coastal live oak.** The deciduous valley oak *(Quercus lobata)* commonly grows on slopes, valleys, and wooded foothills in the Central Valley. The black oak, also deciduous, grows throughout the foothills of the Coast Range and Sierra Nevada; it is unfortunately one of the victims of sudden oak death. The live oak habitat is in the Central Valley, while the coastal live oak occupies the Coast Range. The acorns of all these oaks were an important food supply for California's Native American population and continue to be an important food source for wildlife.

Wildflowers

California's state flower is the **California poppy** *(Eschscholzia californica).* The pretty little perennial grows just about everywhere, even on the sides of the busiest highways. The flowers of most California poppies are bright orange, but they also appear occasionally in white, cream, and an even deeper red-orange.

ANIMALS
Mountain Lions

Mountain lions *(Felis concolor)* are an example of powerful and potentially deadly beauty. Their solitary territorial hunting habits make them elusive, but human contact has increased as more homes are built in mountain lion habitat throughout California. Many parks in or near mountain lion territory post signs with warnings and advice: Do not run if you come across a mountain lion; instead make noise and raise and wave your arms so that you look bigger. The California Fish and Game Department (www.dfg.ca.gov) offers a downloadable brochure with other tips.

Black Bears

Don't take the name **black bear** *(Ursus americanus)* too literally. The black bear can actually have brown and even cinnamon-colored fur, sometimes with a white patch on the chest. The black bear is pretty common throughout North America, including in the forests of Northern California south to Sonoma County, the Sierra Nevada, and the Transverse Range. They are also frequently spotted on the North Coast's Lost Coast Trail. While the black bear can appear cuddly from a distance, distance is exactly what should separate bears and humans—at least 25 feet or more. These are wild animals; do not attempt to feed or approach them, and never come between a mama bear and her cubs. Bears can run up to 30 mph, and they can definitely outrun you. Campers should use bear-proof food lockers at campgrounds or a bear canister in the backcountry; never keep food or any scented products (toothpaste, energy bars, hair products) in a tent or in view inside a car. Bears can be crafty and destructive—some have broken into cars and shredded the interiors looking for food. Bears are mostly nocturnal but can be seen out during the day, and they do not always hibernate in winter.

Whales

The massive, majestic **gray whale** (Eschrichtius robustus) was once endangered, but its numbers have rebounded with international protection. The gray whale measures about 40 feet long and has mottled shades of gray with black fins; its habitat is inshore ocean waters, so there is a chance to get a glimpse of them from headlands up and down the coast. Gray whales generally migrate south along the coast November-January, and closer to shore February-June when they migrate northward. Mendocino County is a perfect place to watch the water for a glimpse of whales breaching.

Perhaps a more recognizable behemoth is the **humpback whale** (Megaptera novaeangliae). At 45-55 feet long, the humpback is the only large whale to breach regularly; it then rolls and crashes back into the water, providing one of the best shows in nature. The whale also rolls from side to side on the surface, slapping its long flippers. Humpbacks generally stay a little farther from shore, so it may be necessary to take a whale-watching cruise to catch a glimpse of them, but their 20-foot spouts can help landlubbers spot them from shore. Look for humpbacks April-early December off the coast near Big Sur, particularly at Julia Pfeiffer Burns State Park.

The **blue whale** (Balaenoptera musculus) is the largest animal on earth. At 70-90 feet long, the blue whale even exceeds dinosaurs in size. With a blue-gray top and a yellowish bottom, the blue whale has a heart the size of a small car, along with two blowholes; alas, it does not breach. They can be seen June-November off the California coast, especially at Monterey and north of Point Reyes.

California Sea Lions

Watching a beach full of **California sea lions** (Zalophus californianus) sunning themselves and noisily honking away can be a pleasure. Sea lions are migratory, so they come and go at will, especially in the fall when they head to the Channel Islands for breeding. If you have a serious hankering to see California sea lions, try Pier 39 near Fisherman's Wharf or on the coast at Seal Rocks, both in San Francisco.

Sea Otters

Much higher on the cuteness scale is the **sea otter** (Enhydra lutris), which can be spotted just offshore in shallow kelp beds. Once near extinction, the endearing, playful sea otter has survived; now there are more than 2,000 in California waters. It can be a bit mesmerizing to witness a sea otter roll on its back in the water and use a rock to break open mollusks for lunch. Sea otter habitat runs mainly from Monterey Bay to Big Sur, but they have also been spotted in the waters near Mendocino.

Birds

California has a wide range of habitat with accessible food and water that makes it perfect for hundreds of bird species to nest, raise their young, or just stop over and rest during long migrations. Nearly 600 species have been spotted in California, so it may be just the place for a bird-watcher's vacation.

Among the most regal of California's bird species are raptors. The **red-tailed hawk** (Buteo jamaicensis) is found throughout California and is frequently sighted perched in trees along the North Coast highway, in the Central Valley, and even in urban areas such as San Francisco. The red-tailed hawk features a light underbelly with a dark band and a distinctive red tail that gives the bird its name.

Although not as common as it once was, **Swainson's hawk** *(Buteo swainsoni)* has been an indicator species in California's environment. The Swainson's hawk population has declined due to loss of habitat and excessive pesticide use in agricultural lands in the Central Valley; its main diet consists of the locusts and grasshoppers that feed on these crops, passing the contaminants on to the birds. These hawks are smaller than the red-tailed hawk, with dark brown coloring and some white underparts either on the chest or under the tail.

With wings spanning 10 feet from tip to tip, the **California condor** *(Gymnogyps californianus)* is the largest flying bird in North America. In the recent past, the condors' population had plummeted due to its susceptibility to lead poisoning, along with deaths caused by electric power lines, habitat loss, and gunshots from indiscriminate humans. In 1987, there was only one California condor left in the wild; it was taken into captivity as part of a breeding program. In 1997, the Monterey County-based nonprofit the Ventana Wildlife Society (VWS) began releasing the giant birds back into the wild. Currently, 70 wild condors soar above California's Central Coast. The species' recovery is one of conservation's great success stories.

Reptiles

Several varieties of **rattlesnakes** are indigenous to the state. The northern Pacific rattler makes its home in Northern California, while more than half a dozen different rattlesnake varieties live in Southern California, including the western diamondback and the Mojave rattlesnake.

If you spot California's most infamous native reptile, keep your distance. All rattlesnakes are venomous, although death by snakebite is extremely rare in California. Most parks with known rattlesnake populations post signs alerting hikers to their presence; hikers should stay on marked trails and avoid tromping off into meadows or brush. Pay attention when hiking, especially when negotiating rocks and woodpiles, and never put a foot or a hand down in a spot you can't see first. Wear long pants and heavy hiking boots for protection from snakes as well as insects, other critters, and unfriendly plants you might encounter.

Butterflies

California's vast population of wildflowers attracts an array of gorgeous butterflies. The **monarch butterfly** *(Danaus plexippus)* is emblematic of the state. These large orange-and-black butterflies have a migratory pattern that's reminiscent of birds. Starting in August, they begin migrating south to cluster in groves of eucalyptus trees. As they crowd together and close up their wings to hibernate, their dull outer wing color camouflages them as clumps of dried leaves, thus protecting them from predators. In spring, the butterflies begin to wake up, fluttering lazily in the groves for a while before flying north to seek out milkweed on which to lay their eggs. Pacific Grove, Santa Cruz, and Pismo Beach are great places to visit these California "butterfly trees."

History

THE FIRST RESIDENTS

The diverse ecology of California allowed Native Americans to adapt to the land in various ways. Communities settled from the border of present-day Oregon south through the mountain ranges and valleys, along the coast, into the Sierra Nevada, and in the arid lands that stretch into Mexico. These groups include the Maidu, Miwok, Yurok, and Pomo. More than 100 Native American languages were spoken in California, and each language had several dialects, all of which were identified with geographic areas. There are about two dozen distinct Native American groups in the Del Norte-Humboldt-Mendocino area alone. The following is an overview of the groups most commonly encountered when traveling around the state.

Yurok

The Yurok people are the largest Native American population in California, and they continue to live along the Klamath River and the Humboldt County coast near Redwood National Park, north of Eureka and south of Crescent City. Spanish explorers arriving in 1775 were the Yurok's first contact with Europeans. Fur traders and trappers from the Hudson's Bay Company arrived around 1827, but it wasn't until gold miners arrived in 1850 that the Yurok faced disease and destruction that diminished their population by 75 percent. Researchers put the 1770 population at 2,500-3,100, which dropped to 669-700 by 1910. Today, there are more than 5,000 Yurok living in California and about 6,000 in the United States overall.

Pomo

The name for the Pomo people and their language first meant "those who live at the red earth hole," possibly referring to the magnesite the tribe used for its red beads or the reddish earth and clay mined in the area. It was also once the name of a village near the present-day community of Pomo in Potter Valley. The Pomo territory was large, bounded by the Pacific Ocean to the west and extending inland to Clear Lake in Lake County. Today, the territory includes present-day Santa Rosa and much of the Sonoma County wine country.

In 1800 there were 10,000-18,000 Pomo living in approximately 70 communities that spoke seven Pomo languages. But as the Pomo interacted and traded with the Russians at Fort Ross, added pressure came from the Spanish missionaries and American settlers pressing in from the south and east. European encroachment may have been the reason Pomo villages became more centralized and why many Pomo retreated to remote areas to band together in defense.

The Pomo suffered not only from lifestyle changes and loss of territory but from diseases for which they had no immunity. Missionaries, traders, and settlers brought with them measles, smallpox, and other diseases that devastated indigenous populations. In 1850 miners began settling in the Russian River Valley, and the Lake Sonoma Valley was homesteaded. As a result, the U.S. government forced the Pomo off their land and onto reservations. Historians believe there were 3,500-5,000 Pomo in 1851, but only 777-1,200 by 1910. There were nearly 5,000 Pomo by the early 1990s.

Miwok

Before contact with white settlers in 1769, the Miwok people lived in small bands in separate parts of California. The Plains and Sierra Miwok lived on the Sacramento-San Joaquin Delta, in parts of the San Joaquin and Sacramento Valleys, and the foothills and western slopes of the Sierra Nevada. The Coast Miwok—including the Bodega Bay Miwok and the Marin Miwok—lived in what is now Marin and southern Sonoma Counties.

Lake Miwok people were found in the Clear Lake Basin of Lake County. The Bay Miwok were in present-day Contra Costa County. Miwok domesticated dogs and grew tobacco but otherwise depended on hunting, fishing, and gathering for food. Miwok in the Sierra exploited the California black oak for acorns, and it is believed that they cultivated the tree in parts of what is now Yosemite National Park.

Like so many indigenous people in California, the Miwok suffered after explorers, missionaries, miners, and settlers arrived. Historians estimate there were at least 11,000 Miwok in 1770, but in all four regions there were only about 671 Miwok in 1910 and 491 in 1930. Today, there are about 3,500 Miwok.

Ohlone

The Ohlone people once occupied what is now San Francisco, Berkeley, Oakland, Silicon Valley, Santa Cruz, Monterey, and the lower Salinas Valley. The Ohlone (a Miwok word meaning "western people") lived in permanent villages, only moving temporarily to gather seasonal foods such as acorns and berries. The Ohlone formed an association of about 50 different communities with an average of 200 members each. The villages interacted through trade, marriages, and ceremonies. Basket weaving, ceremonial dancing, piercings and tattoos, and general ornamentation indicated status within the community and were all part of Ohlone life. Like other Native Americans in the region, the Ohlone depended on hunting, fishing, gathering, and agrarian skills such as burning off old growth each year to get a better yield from seeds.

The Ohlone culture remained fairly stable until the first Spanish missionaries arrived to spread Christianity and to expand Spanish territorial claims. Spanish explorer Sebastián Vizcaíno reached present-day Monterey in December 1602, and the Rumsen group of Ohlone were the first they encountered. Father Junípero Serra's missionaries built seven missions on Ohlone land, and most of the Ohlone people were brought to the missions to live

and work. For the next 60 years, the Ohlone suffered, as did most indigenous people at the missions. Along with the culture shock of subjugation came the diseases for which they had no immunity—measles, smallpox, syphilis, and others. It wasn't until 1834 that the California missions were abolished and the Mexican government redistributed the mission land holdings.

The Ohlone lost the vast majority of their population between 1780 and 1850 because of disease, social upheaval from European incursion, and low birth rates. Estimates are that there were 7,000-26,000 Ohlone when Spanish soldiers and missionaries arrived, and about 3,000 in 1800 and 864-1,000 by 1852. There are 1,500-2,000 Ohlone people today.

Yokuts

The Yokut people have inhabited the Central Valley for at least 8,000 years; they may even have been the first people to settle here. The Yokuts lived in the San Joaquin Valley from the Sacramento-San Joaquin River Delta south to Bakersfield and east to the Sierra foothills. Sequoia and Kings Canyon National Parks are included in this area, as are the cities of Fresno and Modesto. Like other Native Americans, the Yokuts developed water transportation, harvesting abundant tule reeds to work them into canoes.

Spanish explorers entered the valley in 1772 and found 63 different Yokut groups scattered up and down the Central Valley. Many of the Yokuts were taken to the various missions, where they suffered from European subjugation and diseases. Later, as miners entered the region, the Yokut people were forced from their lands. There may have been as many as 4,500 Yokuts when the Spaniards arrived, but the last full-blooded member of the Southern Yokuts is said to have died in 1960. Yokut descendants today live on the Tule River Reservation near Porterville and at the Santa Rosa Rancheria near Lemoore.

Paiute

The Paiute people are grouped by their

language—despite location, political connection, or even genetic similarity. For the Northern Paiutes and the Southern Paiutes, that language is the Numic branch of the Uto-Aztecan family of Native American languages. The Northern Paiutes live in the Great Basin; the Southern Paiutes lived in the Mojave Desert on the edge of present-day Death Valley National Park. Between the Northern Paiutes and the Southern Paiutes are the Mono Lake Northern Paiutes and the Owens Valley Paiutes.

The Northern Paiute lifestyle was well adapted to the harsh environment of the Great Basin. Each band occupied a territory usually centered around a lake or other water source that also provided fish and waterfowl. Food drives to capture rabbits and pronghorn were communal and often involved nearby bands. Piñon nuts were gathered and stored for winter, and grass seeds and roots were part of the diet. Because of their remoteness, the Northern Paiutes may have completely avoided the hardships of the mission period. Their first contact with European Americans may have occurred in 1820, but sustained contact did not happen until the 1840s; several violent confrontations over land and other conflicts occurred in this period. In the end, smallpox did more to decimate the Northern Paiutes than warfare. The Northern Paiutes established colonies that were joined by Shoshone and Washoe people and eventually received recognition by the federal government.

The Southern Paiutes were not as fortunate as the Northern Paiutes. The first contact with Europeans came in 1776, when the priests Silvestre Vélez de Escalante and Francisco Atanasio Domínguez met them while seeking an overland route to the California missions. The Southern Paiutes suffered slave raids by the Navajo and Ute before Europeans arrived, and the raids increased afterward. In 1851, Mormon settlers arrived and occupied local water sources, and the slave raids ended. Settlers and their agrarian practices such as cattle herding drove away game and limited the Southern Paiutes' ability to gather food, disrupting their traditional lifestyle.

Chumash

The Chumash lived on land from Malibu up to Paso Robles, but they also traveled out to the northern Channel Islands. Before the Mission Period, they had over 20,000 people living in 150 independent villages scattered along the coast.

The Chumash were a maritime culture that built large wooden canoes called tomols, which they used to fish and travel among their coastal enclaves. They are also known for their cave paintings in places like Santa Barbara's Painted Cave State Historic Park.

During the Mission Period, five missions were built in Chumash territory. Shortly after the foundation of these missions, European diseases wiped out a large number of the Chumash. By 1831, there were fewer than 3,000 Chumash on this section of the California coast. Today there is a band of Chumash living on a reservation in Santa Barbara's Santa Ynez Valley.

EXPLORATION

Juan Rodríguez Cabrillo, a Portuguese explorer and adventurer, was commissioned in 1542 by the Viceroy of New Spain (Mexico) to sail into what is now San Diego Bay. He continued north as far as Point Reyes before heading to Catalina Island in late November 1542 to winter and make repairs to his ship. On Christmas Eve, Cabrillo tripped, splintering his shin, and the injury developed gangrene. He died on January 3, 1543, and is buried on Catalina. The rest of his party arrived in Barra de Navidad on April 14, 1543. Having found no wealth, advanced Native American civilization or agriculture, or Northwest Passage, Portuguese interest in exploring California lapsed for more than 200 years.

English explorer **Francis Drake** claimed a chunk of the Northern California coast in 1579. It is thought that Drake landed somewhere along Point Reyes to make extensive repairs to his only surviving ship, *The Golden*

Hind. Drakes Bay, just east of Point Reyes, is marked as the spot of his landing, but the actual location is disputed. Drake eventually left California and completed the second recorded circumnavigation of the world (Ferdinand Magellan's was the first).

THE MISSION PERIOD

In the mid-1700s, Spain pushed for colonization of Alta California, rushing to occupy North America before the British beat them to it. The effort was overly ambitious and underfunded, but missionaries started to sweep into present-day California.

The priest **Junípero Serra** is credited with influencing the early development of California. A Franciscan monk, Serra played an active role in bringing Christianity and European diseases to Native American people from San Diego north to Sonoma County. The Franciscan order built a string of missions; each was intended to act as a self-sufficient parish that grew its own food, maintained its own buildings, and took care of its own people. However, mission structures were limited by a lack of suitable building materials and skilled labor. Later, the forced labor of Native Americans was used to cut and haul timbers and to make adobe bricks. By the time the missions were operating, they claimed about 15 percent of the land in California, or about one million acres per mission.

Spanish soldiers used subjugation to control indigenous people, pulling them from their villages and lands to the missions. Presidios (royal forts) were built near some of the missions to establish land claims, intimidate indigenous people, and carry out the overall goal of finding wealth in the New World. The presidios also housed the Spanish soldiers that accompanied the missionaries. The cities of San Francisco, Santa Barbara, San Jose, and later Santa Cruz grew from the establishment of these missions and the presidios.

In 1821, Mexico gained independence from Spain along with control of Alta California and the missions. The Franciscans resisted giving up the land and free labor, and Native Americans continued to be treated as slaves. From 1824 to 1834 the Mexican government handed out 51 land grants to colonists for land that had belonged to Native Americans and was held by nearby missions. From 1834 to 1836 the Mexican government revoked the power of the Franciscans to use Native American labor and began to redistribute the vast mission land holdings.

In the 20th century, interest in the history of the missions was rekindled, and funds were invested to restore many of the churches and complexes. Today, many of the missions have been restored as Catholic parishes, with visitors centers and museum displays of varying levels of quality and polish. Some have been restored as state parks.

THE BEAR FLAG REVOLT

Mexico gained independence in 1821, claiming the Spanish lands that would become California and the U.S. Southwest. Hostilities between U.S. and Mexican troops began in April 1846 when a number of U.S. Army troops in the future state of Texas were attacked and killed. The first major battle of the Mexican-American War was fought the following month, and Congress responded with a declaration of war.

Rumors of possible Mexican military action against newly arrived settlers in California led a group of 30 settlers to seize the small Sonoma garrison in 1846. The uprising became known as the Bear Flag Revolt after a hastily designed flag depicting a grizzly bear and a five-point star was raised over Sonoma as the revolutionaries declared independence from Mexico. John A. Sutter, who had received a land grant near present-day Sacramento, and his men joined and supplied the revolt.

Captain John C. Frémont, who was leading a U.S. Army Corps of Topographical Engineers Exploratory Force, returned to Northern California when he received word that war with Mexico was imminent and that a revolt had occurred. The Bear Flag Revolt was short-lived; Frémont took over the rebellion and replaced the Bear Flag with the U.S. flag. Without orders and without knowing about the declaration of war, Frémont went on to the San Francisco Presidio to spike, or disable, the canons there. More U.S. ships, marines, and sailors arrived and took control of California ports up and down the coast. Frémont's forces grew into the California Battalion, whose members were used mainly to garrison and keep order in the rapidly surrendering towns.

THE GOLD RUSH

James Marshall was a carpenter employed by **John Sutter** to build a sawmill in Coloma near Placerville. Marshall made a glittery discovery on January 24, 1848, in a nearby stream: gold. Soon news spread to Sacramento and San Francisco that chunks of gold were on the riverbeds for the taking, and the Gold Rush was on. Thousands of people streamed into Northern California seeking gold. After panning streams and water-blasting hillsides for gold, the famous hard-rock mines of California began construction. Although panning continued, by the 1860s most of the rough men had taken jobs working in the dangerous mines. The most productive region was a swath of land nearly 200 miles long, roughly from El Dorado south to Mariposa, known as the Mother Lode or Gold Country. Mining towns such as Sonora, Volcano, Placerville, Sutter's Creek, and Nevada City swelled to huge proportions, only to shrink back into obscurity as the mines eventually closed one by one. Today, Highway 49 winds from one historic Gold Rush town to the next, and gold mining has mostly given way to tourism.

As American and European men came to California to seek their fortunes in gold, a few wives and children joined them, but the number of families in the average mining town was small.

Another major group of immigrants came to California from China—not to mine but to labor and serve the white miners. Most were forced to pass through the wretched immigration facilities on Angel Island in the middle of San Francisco Bay before being allowed onto the mainland; others were summarily shipped back to China. San Francisco's Chinatown became a hub for the immigrants, a place where their language was spoken and their culture understood. Thousands headed east into the Sierra foothills, becoming low-level laborers in the industry surrounding the mines or workers on the railroads continuously being built to connect Gold Country to the rest of the country.

The dramatic population boom caused by the Gold Rush ensured that California would be on the fast track to admission into the United States, bypassing the territorial phase. California became a state in 1850—it had gone from a Mexican province to the 31st U.S. state in little more than four years.

THE RAILROADS

California's population swelled to more than 250,000 within three years of the Gold Rush. To avoid the grueling cross-country trip, Eastern industrialists pushed for a railroad to open the West. While politicians argued, **Theodore D. Judah** got to work. Judah came to California from New York at the bidding of the promoters of the Sacramento Valley Railroad. The route linked the Embarcadero along the Sacramento River to Folsom, the jumping-off point to the goldfields. When the Sacramento Valley Railroad project ended in 1856, Judah became a passionate advocate for a transcontinental railroad. He lobbied in Washington D.C. and in 1861 convinced a group of merchants—men who would become known as the Big Four—to incorporate the Central Pacific Railroad in Sacramento.

The Big Four were **Leland Stanford, Charles Crocker, Collis Huntington,** and **Mark Hopkins,** and they were instrumental in developing the state railroad system between 1861 and 1900. Stanford operated a general store for miners before becoming an American tycoon, industrialist, politician, and the founder of Stanford University. Crocker founded a small independent iron forge, invested in the railroad venture, and eventually gained a controlling interest in Wells Fargo Bank before buying the rest of the bank for his son. Huntington was a Sacramento merchant who later went on to build other railroads. Hopkins was another Sacramento merchant who formed a partnership with Huntington before joining him in investing in the transcontinental railroad.

In mid-1862 President Abraham Lincoln signed the Pacific Railroad Act, giving the Central Pacific Railroad the go-ahead to build the railroad east from Sacramento and the Union Pacific Railroad to build west from Omaha. The government used land grants and government loans to fund the project. Workers for the two companies met May 10, 1869, at Promontory Summit, Utah, to complete the nation's first transcontinental railroad with a ceremonial golden spike.

THE GREAT DEPRESSION

The stock market crash of 1929 led to the Great Depression. Many property owners lost their farms and homes, and unemployment in California hit 28 percent in 1932; by 1935, about 20 percent of all Californians were on public relief.

The Great Depression transformed the nation. Beyond the economic agony was an optimism that moved people to migrate to California. Settling primarily in the Central Valley, these Midwest transplants preserved their ways and retained identities separate from other Californians. The Midwest migrant plight was captured in **John Steinbeck**'s 1939 novel *The Grapes of Wrath*. Steinbeck, a Salinas native, gathered information by viewing firsthand the deplorable living and labor conditions under which Okie families existed. The novel was widely read and was turned into a movie in 1940. Government agencies banned the book from public schools, and libraries and large landowners campaigned to have it banned elsewhere. That effort lost steam, however, when Steinbeck won the 1940 Pulitzer Prize.

Even during the worst economic depression in U.S. history, Californians continued to build and move forward. The San Francisco-Oakland Bay Bridge was completed in 1936 and the Golden Gate Bridge in 1937, connecting the land around San Francisco Bay and putting people to work. The 1939 Golden Gate International Exposition on Treasure Island in San Francisco Bay helped show the Great Depression the door.

WORLD WAR II

During World War II, San Francisco became home to the Liberty ships, a fleet of like-design ships built quickly to help supply the war effort. Some Liberty ships, known as the Mothball Fleet, are now tied together farther up Carquinez Strait and can be seen while driving south on I-680 near one of the state's first capitals, Benicia.

Unfortunately, California was also home to a deplorable chapter in the war—the internment camps for Japanese people and Japanese Americans. In reaction to the attack on Pearl Harbor, President Franklin Roosevelt signed Executive Order 9066 in 1942, creating "military exclusion zones" for people of Japanese ancestry. Approximately 110,000 Japanese Americans were uprooted and sent to relocation camps in desolate areas such as Manzanar, in the dry basin of the eastern Sierra; Tulelake, in the remote northeast corner of the state; and as far away as North Dakota and Oklahoma.

In San Francisco, the immigration station on Angel Island became a deportation center in addition to interning Japanese prisoners of war. Today, examples of their carved inscriptions on the prison walls remain as part of the museum in the old barracks building.

THE 1960S

Few places in the country felt the impact of the radical changes of the 1960s more than California. It's arguable that the peace and free-love movements began here, probably on the campus of the indomitable **University of California, Berkeley.** Certainly Berkeley helped to shape and foster the culture of hippies, peaceniks, and radical politics. The college campus was the home of the Black Panthers, anti-Vietnam War sit-ins, and numerous protests for many progressive causes.

If Berkeley was the de facto home of 1960s political movements, then San Francisco was the base of its social and cultural phenomena. Free concerts in Golden Gate Park and the growing fame of the hippie community taking over a neighborhood called Haight-Ashbury drew young people from across the country. Many found themselves living on Haight Street for months and experimenting with the mind-altering chemicals emblematic of the era. The music scene became the stuff of legend. The Grateful Dead—one of the most famous and longest-lasting of the 1960s rock bands—hailed from the Bay Area.

THE DOT-COM ERA

The spectacular growth of the electronics industry started in Silicon Valley, south of San Francisco. Many firms settled in the area of Palo Alto, Santa Clara, Sunnyvale, and San Jose, producing innovations such as personal computers, video games, and networking systems at an incredible pace. All these firms were based in the Santa Clara Valley, dubbed Silicon Valley after the material used to produce integrated circuits. Hewlett-Packard and Varian Associates were among the early

companies that grew here. Even today, the tenant list is impressive: Facebook, YouTube, LinkedIn, Adobe Systems, Apple, Cisco Systems, Intel, Oracle Corporation, SanDisk, and Symantec.

The demand for skilled technical professionals was so great in the high-tech industry that firms had difficulty filling openings and began lobbying to have visa restrictions eased so they could recruit professionals from abroad. Later, however, the dot-com financial bubble that formed in the mid-1990s burst, and tech-industry stock values plummeted in April 2000; many tech companies went into bankruptcy or were sold for a fraction of their worth, and jobs evaporated overnight. Within a few years, it seemed that many of the coveted high-tech jobs were "off-shored" (sent to India for 10 percent of the U.S. labor cost) or "on-shored" by recruiting among newcomers from China and India.

The nation's electronics industry has bounced back and Silicon Valley continues to be the technological hub of the state. Among metropolitan areas, Silicon Valley has the highest concentration of tech workers, with nearly 286 out of every 1,000 private-sector jobs. And the money is good too—the San Jose-Sunnyvale-Santa Clara metropolitan area has the most millionaires and billionaires per capita in the United States.

Government and Economy

GOVERNMENT

California is often viewed as a place where liberalism has run amok. It's true that California is home to what many consider liberal views: political protests and free speech, legalized medical marijuana use, environmental activism, and gay and lesbian rights. These beliefs are not incorporated as a whole throughout the state, however. Major metropolitan areas, such as San Francisco, and areas along the coast have become havens for artists,

musicians, and those seeking alternatives to mainstream America. Populations in the Central Valley and the Sierra Nevada foothills often show more conservative leanings at the polls.

California is overwhelmingly Democratic, but when it comes to politics, not everything is predictable. In 2008 California voters approved Proposition 8, which outlawed same-sex marriage equality, by 52.2 percent to 47.8 percent; voters in some counties approved the ban by more than 75 percent. A ballot measure to legalize marijuana use was defeated that same year. Yet Californians also voted for Barack Obama as president the same year by a definitive majority, 61 percent to 37 percent. Obama took the state again in the 2012 election with 53 percent of the vote.

ECONOMY

California boasts the eighth-largest economy in the world, although the ongoing global economic downturn may put a dent in that ranking in the years to come. Still, California's contribution to the United States outpaces even its immense size and population; it continues to be the country's number-one economy.

California's number-one economic sector is farming. The Central Valley's agricultural juggernaut supplies the world with crops that include grapefruit, grass-fed beef, rice, corn, and tomatoes. Sweet strawberries and spiky artichokes grow in abundance in the cooler Central Coast region. As the fog gets colder and drippier in Marin, ranchers take advantage of the naturally growing grasses to feed herds of cattle. Agriculture, including fruit, vegetables, nuts, dairy, and wine production, help make California the world's fifth-largest supplier of food and agriculture commodities.

Today, organic farms and ranches are proliferating across the state. In addition to the giant factory farms prevalent in the Central Valley, you'll also see an increasing number of small farms and ranches growing crops using organic, sustainable, and even biodynamic practices. Most of these farmers sell directly to consumers by way of farmers markets and farm stands—almost every town or county in California has a weekly farmers market in the summer, and many last year-round.

And then there's the wine. It seems like every square inch of free agricultural land has a grapevine growing on it. The vineyards that were once seen primarily in Napa and Sonoma can now be found on the slopes of the Sierra foothills, on the northern Mendocino coast, and in Carmel Valley and Paso Robles. It's actually the wine industry that's leading the charge beyond mere organic and into biodynamic growing practices—using sheep to graze and maintain vineyards weeds, providing natural fertilizer, harvesting grapes, and pruning vines.

Essentials

Transportation

FLYING INTO SAN FRANCISCO

San Francisco's major airport is **San Francisco International Airport** (SFO, U.S. 101, San Mateo, 800/435-9736, 650/821-8211, www.flysfo.com), located approximately 13 miles south of the City. Plan to arrive at the airport up to three hours before your flight leaves. Airport lines, especially on weekends and holidays, are notoriously long, and planes can be grounded due to fog.

To avoid the SFO crowds, consider booking a flight into one of the Bay Area's less-crowded airports. **Oakland International Airport** (OAK, 1 Airport Dr., Oakland, 510/563-3300, http://oaklandairport.com) serves the East Bay with access to San Francisco via the Bay Bridge and commuter trains. **San Jose International Airport** (SJC, Airport Blvd., San Jose, 408/392-3600, www.flysanjose.com) is south of San Francisco in the heart of Silicon Valley. These airports are quite a bit smaller than SFO, but service is brisk from many U.S. destinations.

Several public and private transportation options can get you into San Francisco. **Bay Area Rapid Transit** (BART, www.bart.gov, one-way ticket to any downtown station $8.65) connects directly with SFO's international terminal, providing a simple and relatively fast (under one hour) trip to downtown San Francisco. The BART station is an easy walk or a free shuttle ride from any point in the airport. **Caltrain** (800/660-4287, www.caltrain.com, tickets $3.25-13.25) is a good option if you are staying farther south on the peninsula. To access Caltrain from the airport, you must first take BART to the Millbrae stop, where the two lines meet. This station is designed for folks jumping from one line to the other. Caltrain tickets range in price depending on your destination.

Shuttle vans are another cost-effective option for door-to-door service, although these make several stops along the way. From the airport to downtown San Francisco, the average one-way fare is $17-25 per person. Shuttle vans congregate on the second level of SFO above the baggage claim area for domestic flights, and on the third level for international flights. Advance reservations guarantee a seat, but these aren't required and don't necessarily speed the process. Some companies to try include **Quake City Shuttle** (415/255-4899, www.quakecityshuttle.com) and **SuperShuttle** (800/258-3826, www.supershuttle.com).

For **taxis,** the average fare to downtown San Francisco is around $40. Or use a smartphone app to hitch a ride with **Uber** (www.uber.com, airport to downtown $27-85) or **Lyft** (www.lyft.com, airport to downtown $28-41).

FLYING INTO LOS ANGELES

The greater Los Angeles area is thick with airports. **Los Angeles International Airport** (LAX, 1 World Way, 855/463-5252, www.lawa.org) serves the greater Los Angeles area, and is located about 10 miles south of the city of Santa Monica. If you're coming in from another country or from across the continent, you're likely to find your flight coming into this endlessly crowded hub. If you're flying home from LAX, plan plenty of time to get through security and the check-in lines—up to three hours for a domestic flight on a holiday weekend.

To miss the major crowds, consider flying

---

into one of the many suburban airports. **John Wayne Airport** (SNA, 18601 Airport Way, Santa Ana, 949/252-5200, www.ocair.com) serves Disneyland perfectly, and the **Long Beach Airport** (LGB, 4100 Donald Douglas Dr., Long Beach, 562/570-2600, www.lgb. org) is convenient to the beaches. **Ontario Airport** (ONT, 1923 E. Avion Dr., Ontario, 909/937-2700, www.lawa.org) is farther out but a good option for travelers planning to divide their time between Los Angeles, Palm Springs, and the deserts.

In Los Angeles, free shuttle buses provide service to the Los Angeles County Metropolitan Transportation Authority **Metro Rail** (323/466-3876, www.metro.net), accessible at the Green Line Aviation Station. Metro Rail trains connect Long Beach, Hollywood, North Hollywood, Downtown Los Angeles, and Pasadena. Passengers should wait under the blue "LAX Shuttle Airline Connection" signs outside the lower-level terminals and board the "G" shuttle. Passengers may also take the "C" shuttle to the **Metro Bus Center** (323/466-3876, www.metro.net), which connects to buses that serve the entire L.A. area. Information about bus service is provided via telephones on the Information Display Board inside each terminal.

Shuttle services are also available if you want to share a ride. **Prime Time Shuttle** (800/733-8267, www.primetimeshuttle.com) and **SuperShuttle** (800/258-3826, www.supershuttle.com) are authorized to serve the entire Los Angeles area out of LAX. These vans can be found on the lower arrivals deck in front of each terminal, under the orange "Shared Ride Vans" signs.

Taxis can be found on the lower arrivals level islands in front of each terminal, below the yellow "Taxi" signs. Only licensed taxis are allowed into the airport; they have standard rates of about $40 to downtown and $30 to West Los Angeles. Or opt for utilizing ride-sharing services **Uber** (www.uber.com) and **Lyft** (www.lyft.com), which can cost $27-155 to get downtown from LAX. Look for signs reading "Ride Service Pick Up."

REGIONAL AIRPORTS

Domestic flights can be an economical and faster option when traversing between major cities within the state. San Francisco International Airport (SFO, www.flysfo. com), Oakland International Airport (OAK, http://oaklandairport.com), and San Jose International Airport (SJC, www.flysanjose. com) connect with several smaller regional airports. These include the **Monterey Regional Airport** (MRY, www.montereyairport.com), the **Santa Barbara Airport** (SBA, www.santabarbaraca.gov), the **San Luis Obispo County Regional Airport** (SLO, www.sloairport.com), and the **Arcata-Eureka Airport** (ACV, http://co.humboldt. ca.us). **Southwest Airlines** (www.southwest. com) provides affordable flights among the larger airports, while **United Airlines** (www. united.com) has regular flights to regional airports. Geared toward commuters, flights are generally frequent but a bit pricy.

TRAIN

Several long-distance **Amtrak** (www.amtrak.com) trains rumble through California daily. There are eight train routes that serve the region: The *California Zephyr* runs from Chicago and Denver to Emeryville; the *Coast Starlight* travels down the West Coast from Seattle and Portland as far as Los Angeles; the *Pacific Surfliner* will get you to the Central Coast. There is no train depot in San Francisco; the closest station is in Emeryville in the East Bay. Fortunately, comfortable coach buses ferry travelers to and from the Emeryville Amtrak station, with many stops in downtown San Francisco.

CAR

California is great for road trips. Scenic coastal routes such as Highway 1 and U.S. 101 are often destinations in themselves. **Highway 1,** also known as the Pacific Coast Highway, follows the North Coast from Leggett to San Luis Obispo on the Central Coast and points south. Running parallel and intertwining with Highway 1 for much of its length, **U.S. 101** stretches north-south from Crescent City on the North Coast through the Central Coast, meeting Highway 1 in San Luis Obispo.

Road closures are not uncommon in winter. Highway 1 along the coast can shut down due to flooding or landslides. I-5 through the Central Valley can either close or be subject to hazardous driving conditions resulting from tule fog, which can reduce visibility to only a few feet.

Traffic jams, accidents, mudslides, fires, and snow can affect highways and interstates at any time. Before heading out on your adventure, check road conditions online at the **California Department of Transportation** (Caltrans, www.dot.ca.gov).

Common-sense maintenance consciousness is required on the road. If the car gets hot or overheats, stop for a while to cool it off. Never open the radiator cap if the engine is steaming. After it has sat, squeeze the top radiator hose to see if there's any pressure in it; if there isn't, it's safe to open. Never pour water into a hot radiator—you could crack your block. If you start to smell rubber, your tires are overheating, and that's a good way to have a blowout. Stop and let them cool off. In winter in the high country, a can of silicone lubricant such as WD-40 will unfreeze door locks, dry off humid wiring, and keep your hinges in shape.

Car and RV Rental

Most car-rental companies are located at each of the major California airports. To reserve a car in advance, contact **Budget Rent A Car** (U.S. tel. 800/218-7992, outside U.S. tel. 800/472-3325, www.budget.com), **Dollar Rent A Car** (800/800-5252, www.dollar.com), **Enterprise** (855/266-9289, www.enterprise.com), or **Hertz** (U.S. and Canada tel. 800/654-3131, outside U.S. tel. 800/654-3001, www.hertz.com).

To rent a car, drivers in California must be at least 21 years of age and have a valid driver's license. California law also requires that all vehicles carry liability insurance. You can purchase insurance with your rental car, but it generally costs an additional $10 per day, which can add up quickly. Most private auto insurance will also cover rental cars. Before buying rental insurance, check your car insurance policy to see if rental-car coverage is included.

The average cost of a rental car is $40 per day or $210 per week; however, rates vary greatly based on the time of year and distance traveled. Weekend and summer rentals cost significantly more. Generally, it is more expensive to rent from car rental agencies at an airport. To avoid excessive rates, first plan travel to areas where a car is not required, then rent a car from an agency branch in town to further explore more rural areas. Rental agencies occasionally allow vehicle drop-off at a different location from where it was picked up for an additional fee.

Another option is to rent an RV. You won't have to worry about camping or lodging options, and many facilities, particularly farther north, accommodate RVs. However, RVs are difficult to maneuver and park, limiting your access to metropolitan areas. They are also expensive, both in terms of gas and the rental rates. Rates during the summer average $1,300 per week and $570 for three days, the standard minimal rental. **Cruise America** (800/671-8042, www.cruiseamerica.com) has branches in San Francisco, San Jose, San Mateo, San Luis Obispo, Los Angeles, Costa Mesa, Oceanside, and San Diego. **El Monte RV** (888/337-2214, www.elmonterv.com) operates out of San Francisco, Santa Cruz, Los Angeles, Newport Beach, and San Diego among other places.

Another way to get around is with **Jucy Rentals** (800/650-4180, www.jucyrentals.com), rental minivans with pop-up tops. The colorful vehicles are smaller and easier to manage than large RVs, but still come equipped with a fridge, a gas cooker, a sink, a DVD player, and two double beds. Rental locations are in San Francisco and Los Angeles.

BUS

A very affordable way to get around California is on **Greyhound** (800/231-2222, www.greyhound.com). The San Francisco Station (200 Folsom St., 415/495-1569) is a hub for Greyhound bus lines. They also have stations all along the coast from Crescent City down to San Diego. Greyhound routes generally follow the major highways, traveling U.S. 101. Most counties and municipalities have bus service with routes to outlying areas.

Visas and Officialdom

PASSPORTS AND VISAS

If you are visiting from another country, you must have a valid passport and a visa to enter the United States. If you hold a current passport from one of the following countries, you may qualify for the Visa Waiver Program: Andorra, Australia, Austria, Belgium, Brunei, Chile, Czech Republic, Denmark, Estonia, Finland, France, Germany, Greece, Hungary, Iceland, Ireland, Italy, Japan, Latvia, Liechtenstein, Lithuania, Luxembourg, Malta, Monaco, the Netherlands, New Zealand, Norway, Portugal, San Marino, Singapore, Slovakia, Slovenia, South Korea, Spain, Sweden, Switzerland, Taiwan, and the United Kingdom. To qualify, you must apply online with the Electronic System for Travel Authorization and hold a return plane or cruise ticket to your country of origin dated less than 90 days from your date of entry. Holders of Canadian passports don't need visas or visa waivers.

In most other countries, the local U.S. embassy should be able to provide a tourist visa. The average fee for a visa is US$160. While a visa may be processed as quickly as 24 hours on request, plan at least a couple of weeks, as there can be unexpected delays, particularly during the busy summer season (June-Aug.).

EMBASSIES

San Francisco and Los Angeles are home to embassies and consulates from many countries around the globe. If you should lose your passport or find yourself in some other trouble while visiting California, contact your country's offices for assistance. To find an embassy, check online at www.state.gov, which lists the websites for all foreign embassies in the United States. A representative will be able to direct you to the nearest embassy or consulate.

CUSTOMS

Before you enter the United States from another country by sea or by air, you'll be required to fill out a customs form. Check with the U.S. embassy in your country or the **Customs and Border Protection website** (www.cbp.gov) for an updated list of items you must declare.

If you require medication administered by injection, you must pack your syringes in a checked bag; syringes are not permitted in carry-ons coming into the United States.

Also, pack documentation describing your need for any narcotic medications you've brought with you. Failure to produce documentation for narcotics on request can result in severe penalties in the United States.

If you're driving into California along I-5 or another major highway, prepare to stop at Agricultural Inspection Stations a few miles inside the state line. You don't need to present a passport, a visa, or even a driver's license; instead, you must be prepared to present all your fruits and vegetables. California's largest economic sector is agriculture, and a number of the major crops grown here are sensitive to pests and diseases. In an effort to prevent known pests from entering the state and endangering crops, travelers are asked to identify all produce they're carrying in from other states or from Mexico. If you've got produce, especially homegrown or from a farm stand, it could be infected by a known problem pest or disease. Expect it to be confiscated on the spot.

You'll also be asked about fruits and veggies on your U.S. Customs form, which you'll be asked to fill out on the airplane or ship before you reach the United States.

Travel Tips

CONDUCT AND CUSTOMS

The legal **drinking age** in California is 21. Expect to have your ID checked if you look under age 30, especially in bars and clubs, but also in restaurants and wineries. Most California bars and clubs close at 2am; you'll find the occasional after-hours nightspot in San Francisco.

Smoking has been banned in many places throughout California. Don't expect to find a smoking section in any restaurant or an ashtray in any bar. Smoking is illegal in all bars and clubs, but your new favorite watering hole might have an outdoor patio where smokers can huddle. Taking the ban one step further, many hotels, motels, and inns throughout California are strictly nonsmoking, and you'll be subject to fees of hundreds of dollars if your room smells of smoke when you leave.

There's no smoking in any public building, and even some of the state parks don't allow cigarettes. There's often good reason for this; the fire danger in California is extreme in the summer, and one carelessly thrown butt can cause a genuine catastrophe.

ACCESS FOR TRAVELERS WITH DISABILITIES

Most California attractions, hotels, and restaurants are accessible for travelers with disabilities. State law requires that public transportation must accommodate the special needs of travelers with disabilities and that public spaces and businesses have adequate restroom facilities and equal access.

This includes national parks and historic structures, many of which have been refitted with ramps and wider doors. Many hiking trails are also accessible to wheelchairs, and most campgrounds designate specific campsites that meet the Americans with Disabilities Act standards. The state of California also provides a free telephone TDD-to-voice relay service; just dial 711.

If you are traveling with a disability, there are many resources to help you plan your trip. **Access Northern California** (http://accessnca.org) is a nonprofit organization that offers general travel tips, including recommendations on accommodations, parks and trails, transportation, and travel equipment. **Access-Able** (http://access-able.com) is another travel resource, as is **Gimp-on-the-Go** (www.gimponthego.com). The message board on the **American Foundation for the Blind** (www.afb.org) website is a good forum to discuss travel strategies for the visually impaired. For a comprehensive guide to wheelchair-accessible beaches, rivers, and shorelines from Santa Cruz to Marin County, including the East Bay and Wine Country, contact the **California Coastal Conservancy** (510/286-1015, www.scc.ca.gov), which publishes a free and downloadable guide. **Wheelchair Getaways** in San Francisco (800/638-1912, www.wheelchairgetaways.com, $95-110 per day) and Los Angeles (800/638-1912) rents wheelchair-accessible vans and offer pickup and drop-off service from airports ($100-300). Likewise, **Avis Access** (800/669-9585, www.avis.com) rents cars, scooters, and other products to make traveling with a disability easier; click on the "Services" link on their website.

TRAVELING WITH CHILDREN

Many spots in California are ideal destinations for families with children of all ages. Amusement parks, interactive museums, zoos, parks, beaches, and playgrounds all make for family-friendly fun. On the other hand, there are a few spots in the Golden State that beckon more to adults than to children. Frankly, there aren't many family activities in Wine Country. This adult playground is all about alcoholic beverages and high-end dining. Similarly, the North Coast's focus on original art and romantic B&Bs brings out couples looking for weekend getaways rather than families. In fact, before you book a room at a B&B that you expect to share with your kids, check to be sure that the inn can accommodate extra people in the guest rooms and whether they allow guests under age 16.

WOMEN TRAVELING ALONE

California is a pretty friendly place for women traveling alone. Most of the major outdoor attractions are incredibly safe, and even many of the urban areas boast pleasant neighborhoods that welcome lone female travelers. But you'll need to take some basic precautions and pay attention to your surroundings, just as you would in any unfamiliar place. Carry your car keys in your hand when walking out to your car. Don't sit in your parked car in a lonely parking lot at night; just get in, turn on the engine, and drive away. When you're walking down a city street, be alert and keep an eye on your surroundings and on anyone who might be following you. In rural areas, don't go tromping into unlit wooded areas or out into grassy fields alone at night without a flashlight; many of California's critters are nocturnal. Of course, this caution applies to men as well; mountain lions and rattlesnakes don't tend to discriminate.

SENIOR TRAVELERS

California makes an ideal destination for older or retired folks looking to relax and have a great time. You'll find senior discounts nearly every place you go, including restaurants, golf courses, major attractions, and even some hotels, although the minimum age can range 50-65. Just ask, and be prepared to produce ID if you look young or are requesting a senior discount. You can often get additional discounts on rental cars, hotels, and tour packages as a member of **AARP** (888/687-2277, www.aarp.org). If you're not a member, its website can also offer helpful travel tips and advice. **Elderhostel** (800/454-5768, www.roadscholar.org) is another great resource for senior travelers. Dedicated to providing educational opportunities for older travelers, Elderhostel provides package trips to beautiful and interesting destinations. Called "Educational Adventures," these trips are generally 3-9 days long and emphasize history, natural history, art, music, or a combination thereof.

GAY AND LESBIAN TRAVELERS

California is known for its thriving gay and lesbian communities. In fact, the Golden State is a golden place for gay travel—especially in the bigger cities and even in some of the smaller towns around the state. As with much of the country, the farther you venture into rural and agricultural regions, the less likely you are to experience the liberal acceptance the state is known for. The **International Gay and Lesbian Travel Association** (www.iglta.org) has a directory of gay- and lesbian-friendly tour operators, accommodations, and destinations.

San Francisco has the biggest and arguably best **Gay Pride Festival** (www.sfpride.org) in the nation, usually held on Market Street on the last weekend in June. Meanwhile, San Diego has a large celebration called **San Diego LBGT Pride** (https://sdpride.org) in July. Year-round, San Francisco's Castro District offers fun of all kinds, from theater to clubs to shopping, mostly targeted at gay men but with a few places sprinkled in for lesbians. If the Castro is your primary destination, you can even find a place to stay in the middle of the action.

West Hollywood in Los Angeles has its own upscale gay culture. Just like the rest of L.A.'s clubs, the gay clubs are havens of the see-and-be-seen crowd.

Santa Cruz on the Central Coast is a quirky town known for its lesbian-friendly culture. A relaxed vibe informs everything from underground clubs to unofficial nude beaches to live-action role-playing games in the middle of downtown. Even the lingerie and adult toy shops tend to be woman-owned and operated.

Health and Safety

MEDICAL SERVICES

For an emergency anywhere in California, **dial 911.** Inside hotels and resorts, check your emergency number as soon as you get to your guest room. In urban and suburban areas, full-service hospitals and medical centers abound, but in more remote regions, help can be more than an hour away.

If you're planning a **backcountry expedition,** follow all rules and guidelines for obtaining **wilderness permits** and for self-registration at trailheads. These are for your safety, letting the rangers know roughly where you plan to be and when to expect you back. National and state park visitors centers can advise in more detail on any health or wilderness alerts in the area. It is also advisable to let someone outside your party know your route and expected date of return.

Being out in the elements can present its own set of challenges. Despite California's relatively mild climate, **heat exhaustion** and **heat stroke** can affect anyone during the hot summer months, particularly during a long, strenuous hike in the sun. Common symptoms include nausea, lightheadedness, headache, or muscle cramps. **Dehydration** and loss of electrolytes are the common causes of heat exhaustion. If you or anyone in your group develops any of these symptoms, get out of the sun immediately, stop all physical activity, and drink plenty of water. Heat exhaustion can be severe, and if untreated can lead to heat stroke, in which the body's core temperature reaches 105°F. Fainting, seizures, confusion, and rapid heartbeat and breathing can indicate the situation has moved beyond heat exhaustion. If you suspect this, call 911 immediately.

Similar precautions hold true for **hypothermia,** which is caused by prolonged exposure to cold water or weather. For many in California, this can happen on a hike or backpacking trip without sufficient rain gear, or by staying too long in the ocean or another cold body of water without a wetsuit. Symptoms include shivering, weak pulse, drowsiness, confusion, slurred speech, or stumbling. To treat hypothermia, immediately remove the wet clothing, cover the person with blankets, and feed him or her hot liquids. If symptoms don't improve, call 911.

WILDERNESS SAFETY

Many places are still wild in California, making it important to take precautions with regard to wildlife. While California no longer has any grizzly bears, **black bears** thrive and are often seen in the mountains foraging for food in the spring, summer, and fall. Black bears certainly don't have the size or reputation of grizzlies, but there is good reason to exercise caution. Never get between a bear and her cub, and if a bear sees you, identify yourself as human by waving your hands above your head, speaking in a calm voice, and backing away slowly. If a bear charges, do not run. One of the best precautions against an unwanted bear encounter is to keep a clean camp; store all food in airtight, bear-proof containers; and strictly follow any guidelines given by the park or rangers.

Even more common than bears are **mountain lions,** which can be found in the Coast Range as well in as grasslands and forests. Because of their solitary nature, it is unlikely you will see one, even on long trips in the backcountry. Still, there are a couple things to remember. If you come across a kill, probably a large partly eaten deer, leave immediately. And if you see a mountain lion and it sees you, identify yourself as human, making your body appear as big as possible, just as with a bear. And remember: Never run. As with any cat, large or small, running triggers its hunting instincts. If a mountain lion should attack, fight back; cats don't like to get hurt.

The other treacherous critter in the backcountry is the **rattlesnake.** They can be found in summer in generally hot and dry areas from the coast to the Sierra Nevada. When hiking in this type of terrain—many parks will indicate if rattlesnakes are a problem in the area—keep your eyes on the ground and an ear out for the telltale rattle. Snakes like to warn you to keep away. The only time this is not the case is with baby rattlesnakes that have not yet developed their rattles. Unfortunately, they have developed their fangs and venom, which is particularly potent. Should you get bitten, remain calm and seek immediate medical help.

Mosquitoes can be found throughout the state. At higher elevations they can be worse, prompting many hikers and backpackers to don head nets and apply potent repellents, usually DEET. The high season for mosquitoes is late spring-early summer.

Ticks live in many of the forests and grasslands throughout the state, except at higher elevations. Tick season generally runs late fall-early summer. If you are hiking through brushy areas, wear pants and long-sleeve shirts. Ticks like to crawl to warm, moist places (armpits are a favorite) on their host. If a tick is engorged, it can be difficult to remove. There are two main types of ticks found in California: dog ticks and deer ticks. Dog ticks are larger, brown, and have a gold spot on their backs, while deer ticks are small, tear-shaped, and black. Deer ticks are known to carry Lyme disease. While Lyme disease is relatively rare in California—there are more cases in the northernmost part of the state—it is very serious. If you get bitten by a deer tick and the bite leaves a red ring, seek medical attention. Lyme disease can be successfully treated with early rounds of antibiotics.

There is only one major variety of plant in California that can cause an adverse reaction in humans if you touch the leaves or stems: **poison oak,** a common shrub that inhabits forests throughout the state. Poison oak has a characteristic three-leaf configuration, with scalloped leaves that are shiny green in the spring and then turn yellow, orange, and red in late summer-fall. In fall, the leaves drop, leaving a cluster of innocuous-looking branches. The oil in poison oak is present year-round in both the leaves and branches. Your best protection is to wear long sleeves and long pants when hiking, no matter how hot it is. A product called Tecnu is available at most California drugstores—slather it on before you go hiking to protect yourself from poison oak. If your skin comes into contact with poison oak, expect a nasty rash known for its itchiness and irritation. Poison oak is also extremely transferable, so avoid touching your eyes, face, or other parts of your body to prevent spreading the rash. Calamine lotion can help, and in extreme cases a doctor can administer cortisone to help decrease the inflammation.

CRIME AND SAFETY PRECAUTIONS

The outdoors are not the only place that harbors danger. In both rural and urban areas, theft can be a problem. When parking at a trailhead or in a park or at a beach, don't leave any valuables in the car. If you must, place them out of sight, either in a locked glove box or in the trunk. The same holds true for urban areas. Furthermore, avoid keeping your wallet, camera, and other expensive items, including lots of cash, easily accessible in backpacks; keep them within your sight at all times. Certain urban neighborhoods are best avoided at night. If you find yourself in these areas after dark, consider taking a cab to avoid walking blocks and blocks to get to your car or to wait for public transportation. In case of a theft or any other emergency, call 911.

Information and Services

MONEY

California businesses use the U.S. dollar ($). Most businesses also accept the major credit cards Visa, MasterCard, Discover, and American Express. ATM and debit cards work at many stores and restaurants, and ATMs are available throughout the region. In more remote areas, such as the North Coast, some business may only accept cash, so don't depend entirely on your plastic.

You can exchange currency at any international airport in the state. Currency-exchange points also crop up in downtown San Francisco and at some of the major business hotels in urban areas.

California is not a particularly expensive place to travel, but keeping an eye on your budget is still important. San Francisco and the Wine Country are the priciest regions for visitors, especially with the amount of high-quality food and luxury accommodations. Advance reservations for hotels and marquee restaurants in these areas are recommended.

Banks

As with anywhere, traveling with a huge amount of cash is not recommended, which may make frequent trips to the bank necessary. Fortunately, most destinations have at least one major bank. Usually Bank of America or Wells Fargo can be found on the main drags through towns. Banking hours tend to be Monday-Friday 8am-5pm, Saturday 9am-noon. Never count on a bank being open on Sundays or on federal holidays. If you need cash when the banks are closed, there is generally a 24-hour ATM available. Furthermore, many cash-only businesses have an on-site ATM for those who don't have enough cash

ready in their wallets. The unfortunate downside to this convenience is a fee of $2-4 per transaction. This also applies to ATMs at banks at which you don't have an account.

Tax

Sales tax in California varies by city and county, but the average rate is around 7.5 percent. All goods are taxable with the exception of food not eaten on the premises. For example, your bill at a restaurant will include tax, but your bill at a grocery store will not. The hotel tax is another unexpected added expense to traveling in California. Most cities have enacted a tax on hotel rooms largely to make up for budget shortfalls. As you would expect, these taxes are higher in areas more popular with visitors. In Wine County you can expect to add an additional 12-14 percent onto your hotel bill, while in San Francisco the tax tops 15 percent. Some areas like Eureka have a lower hotel tax of 10 percent.

Tipping

Tipping is expected and appreciated, and a 15-20 percent tip for restaurants is about the norm. When ordering in bars, tip the bartender or waitstaff $1 per drink. For taxis, plan to tip 15-20 percent of the fare, or simply round up the cost to the nearest dollar. Cafés and coffee shops often have tip jars out. There is no consensus on what is appropriate when purchasing a $3 beverage. Often $0.50 is enough, depending on the quality and service.

COMMUNICATIONS AND MEDIA

With the exception of rural and wilderness areas, California is fairly well connected.

Cell-phone reception is good except in places far from any large town. Likewise, you can find Internet access just about anywhere. The bigger cities are well wired, but even in small towns you can log on either at a library or in a café with a computer in the back. Be prepared to pay a per-minute usage fee or purchase a drink.

The main newspapers in California are the *San Francisco Chronicle* (www.sfgate.com) and the *Los Angeles Times* (www.latimes.com). Of course, there are other regional papers that may offer some international news in addition to the local color. As for radio, there are some news stations on the FM dial, and in most regions you can count on finding a National Public Radio (NPR, www.npr.org) affiliate. While they will all offer some NPR news coverage, some will be more geared toward music and local concerns.

Because of California's size both geographically and in terms of population, you will have to contend with multiple area codes—the numbers that prefix the seven-digit phone number—throughout the state. The 800 or 866 area codes are toll-free numbers. Any time you are dialing out of the area, you must dial a 1 plus the area code followed by the seven-digit number.

To mail a letter, find a blue post office box, which are found on the main streets of any town. Postage rates vary by destination. You can purchase stamps at the local post office, where you can also mail packages. Stamps can also be bought at some ATMs and online at www.usps.com, which can also give you the location and hours of the nearest post office. Post offices are generally open Monday-Friday, with limited hours on Saturday. They are always closed on Sunday and federal holidays.

MAPS AND VISITOR INFORMATION

When visiting California, you might be tempted to stop in at one of several Golden State Welcome Centers scattered throughout the state. In all honesty, these visitors centers aren't that great. If you're in an area that doesn't have its own visitors center, the State Welcome Center might be a useful place to pick up maps and brochures; check www.visitcwc.com to find a local Welcome Center wherever you're visiting. Otherwise, stick with local, regional, and national park visitors centers, which tend to be staffed by volunteers or rangers who feel a real passion for their locale.

If you are looking for maps, almost all gas stations and drugstores sell maps both of the place you're in and of the whole state. **California State Automobile Association** (CSAA, https://calstate.aaa.com) offers free maps to auto club members.

Many local and regional visitors centers also offer maps, but you'll need to pay a few dollars for the bigger and better ones. But if all you need is a wine-tasting map in a known wine region, you can probably get one for free along with a few tasting coupons at the nearest regional visitors center. Basic national park maps come with your admission payment. State park maps can be free or cost a few dollars at the visitors centers.

The state's **California Travel and Tourism Commission** (877/225-4367, www.visitcalifornia.com) also provides helpful and free tips, information, and downloadable maps and guides.

California is in the Pacific time zone (PST and PDT) and observes daylight saving time March-November.

Internet Resources

It should come as no surprise that the California travel industry leads the way in the use of the Internet as a marketing, communications, and sales tool. The overwhelming majority of destinations have their own websites—even tiny towns in the middle of nowhere proudly tout their attractions on the Web.

California Department of Transportation
www.dot.ca.gov/hq/roadinfo/
statemap.htm
Check here for state map and highway information before planning a coastal road trip.

Visit California
www.visitcalifornia.com
Before your trip, visit the official tourism site of the state of California.

California Outdoor
and Recreational Information
www.caoutdoors.com
This recreation-focused website includes links to maps, local newspapers, festivals, and events as well as a wide variety of recreational activities throughout the state.

California State Parks
www.parks.ca.gov
The official website lists hours, accessibility, activities, camping areas, fees, and more information for all parks in the state system.

SFGate
www.sfgate.com
This website affiliated with the *San Francisco Chronicle* offers information on activities, festivals, and events in the city by the bay.

SF Weekly
www.sfweekly.com
This website for one of the city's weekly alternative papers has a strong arts and entertainment emphasis.

WineCountry
www.winecountry.com
This tourism website offers information on all of California's wine regions, including Napa, Sonoma, Mendocino, Carmel Valley, Paso Robles, Santa Barbara, and Temecula.

LATourist
www.latourist.com
This informative tourist website is dedicated to the City of Angels.

Los Angeles Times
www.latimes.com
This daily newspaper for Los Angeles covers Southern California and the world.

L.A. Weekly
www.laweekly.com
One of the best alternative weeklies out there, the *L.A. Weekly* has superb arts, music, and food coverage.

Los Angeles Convention
and Visitors Bureau
www.discoverlosangeles.com
It's the official website of the Los Angeles Convention and Visitors Bureau.

Disneyland
http://disneyland.disney.go.com
Find information on all things Disney here.

Index

North Point: 399
Norton Simon Museum: 485

O

Oakland: 128-134
Oakland A's: 131
Oakland International Airport: 133, 630
Oakland Museum of California: 128
Oakland Raiders: 131
Oakland Zoo: 129
oak trees: 618
Ocean Beach (San Diego): 27, 28, 570, 585-586
Ocean Beach (San Francisco): 21, 73-74
Oceanside: 13
Ocean World: 294
Old Faithful Geyser: 179
Old Plaza Firehouse: 466
Old Point Loma Lighthouse: 569
Old Town (San Diego): 566-568, 584-585, 595-596, 607
Old Whaling Station: 326
Olema: 118-119, 120
Olivas Adobe Historical Park: 449
Olvera Street: 466
Ontario Airport: 631
opera: 66-67, 159, 432, 489, 582
Oracle Arena and Coliseum: 131
Orange County: 11, 545-554
Original Farmers Market (L.A.): 478
Otter Cove: 338
Outdoor Exploratorium: 51-52
Oxbow Public Market: 160

PQ

Pacific Beach: 570
Pacific Coast Highway: 11, 13, 14, 15, 16, 468
Pacific Grove: 336-341
Pacific Grove Museum of Natural History: 338
Pacific Heights: 51-52, 60, 62-63, 66, 71, 83-85, 93
Pacific House Museum: 325
Pacific Park: 481
Pacific Star Winery: 242
Pala Casino Resort and Spa: 581
Palace of Fine Arts: 51
Palm Canyon: 565
Palumbo Family Vineyards & Winery: 576
Paramount Studios: 476
parking: Los Angeles 518; San Francisco 98; Santa Cruz 319
Parsonage Village Vineyard: 354-355
Pasadena: 484-485, 493, 505-506, 515-516
Paso Robles: 409-415
Paso Robles Children's Museum: 412
Paso Robles Pioneer Museum: 412
passports: 633

Patrick's Point State Park: 285-286
Pebble Beach: 18, 342-344
Pescadero: 146-148
Pescadero Marsh Natural Preserve: 146
Pescadero State Beach: 146
pet-friendly places: 28
Petrified Forest: 179-180
Pfeiffer Beach: 17, 25, 30, 366
Pfeiffer Big Sur State Park: 17, 365-366, 369-370, 373, 379
Pfeiffer Falls: 369
Pianetta Winery: 411
Piedras Blancas Elephant Seal Rookery: 15, 388
Piedras Blancas Light Station: 388
Pierce Brothers Westwood Village Memorial Park: 480
Pier 39: 15, 45-46
Pigeon Point Lighthouse: 146-147
Pismo Beach: 25, 415-419
Pismo Beach Monarch Butterfly Grove: 416
Pismo Pier: 415-416
planning tips: 10-31; see also specific place
Pleasure Point: 313
Point Arena: 224-228
Point Arena Lighthouse: 225
Point Arena-Stornetta Unit: 20, 225
Point Bonita Lighthouse: 101
Point Cabrillo Light Station: 234
Point Lobos State Natural Preserve: 17, 347
Point Loma: 568-570, 596-597, 607-608
Point Pinos Lighthouse: 336-337
Point Reyes Historic Lighthouse: 118
Point Reyes National Seashore: 15, 116-123
Point Reyes Station: 119, 120-122
Point St. George: 294, 296
Point Sur Light Station: 365
poison oak: 637
pollution: 617
Porter Cave: 308
Porter Creek Winery: 207-208
Prairie Creek Redwoods State Park: 20, 288-290
Precita Eyes Mural Arts: 54
Presidio: 52, 75, 76
Presidio Park: 567-568
Presqu'ile Winery: 430
Princeton-by-the-Sea: 140
Pudding Creek Beach: 241
Punta Gorda Lighthouse: 263-264
Purisima Creek Redwoods: 142
Pygmy Forest: 230
Queen Mary: 13, 530-531

R

rafting: 273
railroads: 625-626
Rancho Sisquoc: 430

List of Maps

Photo Credits

Acknowledgments

One of the real pleasures of doing this edition and the last edition of *Moon Coastal California* has been reconnecting with friends on the road, including John Jayasinge, Marcos Ortega, Alex Theodoropulos, Scott Plymale, Jason Williams, Erin Williams, Geoff Latham, Julie Latham, Bruce Moore, and Minja Moore. Thank you all for your hospitality!

This book wouldn't be possible without the longtime support of family and friends. I don't know how I missed shouting out my brother Allen and my sister-in-law Macon in previous acknowledgments, so I'll do it here. As always, thanks to my parents John and Ronnie Thornton for all of their love and support. In addition, thanks and love to Sarah Kenoyer for changing my bandages in my time of need.

Of course, a big, hearty thanks to everyone at Avalon Travel, including Leah Gordon, Grace Fujimoto, Kevin McLain, Elizabeth Hollis Hansen, Darren Alessi, and Albert Angulo, for all of their crucial work on this book and others.

This book is dedicated to the loving memory of Greg Gilmour, who introduced me to the California coast many years ago. I'll never forget my first evening on the Central Coast standing with you on the cliffs as we sipped 22-ounce beers and listened to waves break in the fog at Steamer Lane. I miss and love you buddy!

Also Available

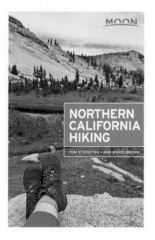

MAP SYMBOLS

▦ Expressway	○ City/Town	✈ Airport	⚑ Golf Course	
▦ Primary Road	◉ State Capital	✈ Airfield	℗ Parking Area	
▦ Secondary Road	◉ National Capital	▲ Mountain	⬟ Archaeological Site	
▦ Unpaved Road	★ Point of Interest	✚ Unique Natural Feature	⬚ Church	
─── Feature Trail	• Accommodation		⬛ Gas Station	
----- Other Trail	▼ Restaurant/Bar	🦢 Waterfall	◠◡ Glacier	
⋯⋯ Ferry	■ Other Location	⚑ Park	▦ Mangrove	
▦ Pedestrian Walkway		⬛ Trailhead	▦ Reef	
▦ Stairs	⛺ Campground	⛷ Skiing Area	▦ Swamp	

CONVERSION TABLES

°C = (°F − 32) / 1.8
°F = (°C × 1.8) + 32
1 inch = 2.54 centimeters (cm)
1 foot = 0.304 meters (m)
1 yard = 0.914 meters
1 mile = 1.6093 kilometers (km)
1 km = 0.6214 miles
1 fathom = 1.8288 m
1 chain = 20.1168 m
1 furlong = 201.168 m
1 acre = 0.4047 hectares
1 sq km = 100 hectares
1 sq mile = 2.59 square km
1 ounce = 28.35 grams
1 pound = 0.4536 kilograms
1 short ton = 0.90718 metric ton
1 short ton = 2,000 pounds
1 long ton = 1.016 metric tons
1 long ton = 2,240 pounds
1 metric ton = 1,000 kilograms
1 quart = 0.94635 liters
1 US gallon = 3.7854 liters
1 Imperial gallon = 4.5459 liters
1 nautical mile = 1.852 km

MOON COASTAL CALIFORNIA
Avalon Travel
An inprint of Perseus Books
A division of Hachette Book Group
1700 Fourth Street
Berkeley, CA 94710, USA
www.moon.com

Editor: Leah Gordon
Series Manager: Kathryn Ettinger
Copy Editor: Brett Keener
Graphics Coordinator: Darren Alessi
Production Coordinator: Darren Alessi
Cover Design: Faceout Studios, Charles Brock
Moon Logo: Tim McGrath
Map Editor: Albert Angulo
Cartographers: Albert Angulo, Brian Shotwell
Indexer: Deana Shields

ISBN-13: 978-1-63121-325-0
ISSN: 1531-1325

Printing History
1st Edition — 2000
5th Edition — July 2016
5 4 3 2 1

Text © 2016 by Stuart Thornton & Avalon Travel.
Maps © 2016 by Avalon Travel.
All rights reserved.

Some photos and illustrations are used by
permission and are the property of the original
copyright owners.

Front cover photo: Refugio State Beach at Sunset,
Santa Barbara © Kip Evans / Alamy Stock Photo
Back cover photo: California redwoods © Mtilghma |
Dreamstime.com

Printed in China by RR Donnelley.

KEEPING CURRENT

If you have a favorite gem you'd like to see included in the next edition, or
see anything that needs updating, clarification, or correction, please drop
us a line. Send your comments via email to feedback@moon.com, or use the
address above.